Hoover's Handbook of Private Companies

2000

BUSINESS PRESS

Austin, Texas

1- 2000

338.4
H

ADM - 4710

Hoover's Handbook of Private Companies 2000 is intended to provide readers with accurate and authoritative information about the enterprises covered in it. Hoover's asked all companies and organizations profiled to provide information for the book. Many did so; some did not. The information contained herein is as accurate as we could reasonably make it. In many cases we have relied on third-party material that we believe to be trustworthy, but were unable to independently verify. We do not warrant that the book is absolutely accurate or without error. Readers should not rely on any information contained herein in instances where such reliance might cause loss or damage. The publisher, the editors, and their data suppliers specifically disclaim all warranties, including the implied warranties of merchantability and fitness for a specific purpose. This book is sold with the understanding that neither the publisher, the editors, nor any content contributors are engaged in providing investment, financial, accounting, legal, or other professional advice.

The financial data in this book are from the companies profiled or from trade sources deemed to be reliable. Hoover's, Inc., is solely responsible for the presentation of all data.

Many of the names of products and services mentioned in this book are the trademarks or service marks of the companies manufacturing or selling them and are subject to protection under US law. Space has not permitted us to indicate which names are subject to such protection, and readers are advised to consult with the owners of such marks regarding their use. Hoover's is a trademark of Hoover's, Inc.

BUSINESS PRESS

10 9 8 7 6 5 4 3 2 1

Publishers Cataloging-in-Publication Data

Hoover's Handbook of Private Companies 2000

   Includes indexes.

   1. Business enterprises — Directories. 2. Corporations — Directories.

HF3010 338.7

Hoover's Company Information is also available on America Online, Bloomberg Financial Network, Dialog, Dow Jones Interactive, EBSCO, LEXIS-NEXIS, Reuters NewMedia, and on the Internet at Hoover's Online (www.hoovers.com), Alta Vista (www.altavista.com), CBS MarketWatch (cbs.marketwatch.com), GO.com (www.go.com), MSN MoneyCentral (moneycentral.com), The New York Times (www.nytimes.com), dowjones.com (www.dowjones.com), The Washington Post (www.washingtonpost.com), Yahoo! (www.yahoo.com), and others.

   A catalog of Hoover's products is available on the World Wide Web at www.hoovers.com.

   ISBN 1-57311-058-2

   ISSN 1073-6433

Cover design is by Shawn Harrington. Electronic prepress and printing were done by Quebecor Printing (USA) Corp. in Fairfield, Pennsylvania. Text paper is 60# Postmark White.

US AND WORLD DIRECT SALES
Hoover's, Inc.
1033 La Posada Drive, Suite 250
Austin, TX 78752
Phone: 512-374-4500
Fax: 512-374-4501
e-mail: orders@hoovers.com

EUROPE
William Snyder Publishing Associates
5 Five Mile Drive
Oxford OX2 8HT
England
Phone & fax: +44-186-551-3186
e-mail: williamsnyder@compuserve.com

HOOVER'S, INC.

Founder: Gary Hoover
Chairman, President, and CEO: Patrick J. Spain
EVP and COO: Carl G. Shepherd

DATABASE EDITORIAL
Managing Editor: Nancy Regent
Managing Editor, Hoover's Business Press: George Sutton
Senior Editor, Books & Editorial Projects: Ruth McClendon Linton
Senior Editors: Chris Barton, Gene Bisbee, Travis Brown, Tom Dowe, Valerie Pearcy, Amy Silverman
Senior Contributing Editors: Paul Mitchell, Barbara M. Spain
Information Resources Manager: Toni Loftin
Director, Financial Information and MasterList: Dennis Sutton
Associate Editors: Sally Alt, Jodi Berls, Larry Bills, Rachel Brush, Bobby Duncan, Jennifer Furl, Carrie Geis, Allan Gill, Joe Grey, Melanie Hall, Jennifer Hinger, Mary Mickle, John Mitchell, Jim Moore, Vanita Trippe, David Woodruff
Writers: Joy Aiken, Linnea Anderson, Alexander Blunt, Angela Boeckman, Amanda Bowman, Joe Bramhall, James Bryant, Troy Bryant, Robert Carranza, Jason Cella, Jason Cother, David Crosby, Kevin Dodds, Stewart Eisenhart, Max Farr, Kevin Furr, Dan Gattuso, Paul Geary, David Hamerly, Stuart Hampton, Jeanette Herman, Guy Holland, John Katzman, John MacAyeal, Nancy McBride, Nell Newton, Sheri Olander, Lynett Oliver, Rob Reynolds, Patrice Sarath, Joe Simonetta, Mike Sims, Randy Williams
Financial Editors: Adi Anand, Shaun McDonald, Bill Ramsey
Quality Control Editor, MasterList: John Willis
Senior Editor, MasterList: Yvonne Cullinan
Associate Editor, MasterList: April Karli
Editorial Training Coordinator: Diane Lee
Training Evangelist: Holly Hans Jackson
Copyeditors: Regan Brown, Theresa Hackley, Kristi Kingston, Kerry O'Brien, Christina Vallery, Emily Weida
Assistant Editors: Rebecca Bycott, Margaret Claughton, Jim Harris, Callie Henning, Kathleen Kelly, Matt Saucedo, Ashley Schrump
Senior Production Specialist: Cecilia Martinez VanGundy
Production Specialists: JoAnn Estrada, Kristin Jackson-Isbell
Editorial Assistants: Danny Cummings, Michaela Drapes, Lesley Epperson, Delia Garza, Daniel Johnson, Pei Lee, Josh Lower, David Porter, Tranea Prosser, David Ramirez, Kcevin Rob, Sara Taylor, Shannon Timmerman, Jennifer Westrom, Bryan Zilar
Documents Coordinator: Carla Baker
Information Resources Assistant: Vanh Phoummisane
Library Assistants: Litto Paul Bacas, Melissa Chinn, Lisa Putnam
Intern: Daniel Croll

WEB EDITORIAL
Senior Editor: David King
Business Travel Editor: Kate Ewing
Industry Editor: Sarah Hallman
IPO Central Editor: Wei San Hui
Money Editor: Kenan Pollack
Professions Editor: Clemon Goodin
News Editors: Natasha Rosofsky, Amy Young
Directory Editors: Tara Fatemi, Kerrie Green, Karin Marie
Online Editorial Assistant: Christian Ethridge

HOOVER'S, INC. MISSION STATEMENT

1. To produce business information products and services of the highest quality, accuracy, and readability.

2. To make that information available whenever, wherever, and however our customers want it through mass distribution at affordable prices.

3. To continually expand our range of products and services and our markets for those products and services.

4. To reward our employees, suppliers, and shareholders based on their contributions to the success of our enterprise.

5. To hold to the highest ethical business standards, erring on the side of generosity when in doubt.

Abbreviations

AFL-CIO – American Federation of Labor and Congress of Industrial Organizations
AMA – American Medical Association
AMEX – American Stock Exchange
ARM – adjustable-rate mortgage
ATM – asynchronous transfer mode
ATM – automated teller machine
CAD/CAM – computer-aided design/computer-aided manufacturing
CASE – computer-aided software engineering
CD-ROM – compact disc – read-only memory
CEO – chief executive officer
CFO – chief financial officer
CISC – complex instruction set computer
CMOS – complementary metal oxide semiconductor
COO – chief operating officer
DAT – digital audiotape
DoD – Department of Defense
DOE – Department of Energy
DOS – disc operating system
DOT – Department of Transportation
DRAM – dynamic random access memory
DVD – digital versatile disk/digital videodisk
EPA – Environmental Protection Agency
EPROM – erasable programmable read-only memory
EPS – earnings per share
ESOP – employee stock ownership plan
EU – European Union
EVP – executive vice president
FCC – Federal Communications Commission
FDA – Food and Drug Administration
FDIC – Federal Deposit Insurance Corporation
FTC – Federal Trade Commission
FTP – file transfer protocol
GATT – General Agreement on Tariffs and Trade
GDP – gross domestic product
GUI – graphical user interface
HMO – health maintenance organization
HR – human resources
HTML – hypertext markup language
ICC – Interstate Commerce Commission
IPO – initial public offering
IRS – Internal Revenue Service
ISDN – integrated services digital network
kWh – kilowatt-hour
LAN – local area network

LBO – leveraged buyout
LCD – liquid crystal display
LNG – liquefied natural gas
LP – limited partnership
Ltd. – limited
mips – millions of instructions per second
MW – megawatt
NAFTA – North American Free Trade Agreement
NASA – National Aeronautics and Space Administration
Nasdaq – National Association of Securities Dealers Automated Quotations
NATO – North Atlantic Treaty Organization
NYSE – New York Stock Exchange
OCR – optical character recognition
OECD – Organization for Economic Cooperation and Development
OEM – original equipment manufacturer
OPEC – Organization of Petroleum Exporting Countries
OS – operating system
OSHA – Occupational Safety and Health Administration
OTC – over-the-counter
PBX – private branch exchange
PCMCIA – Personal Computer Memory Card International Association
P/E – price-to-earnings ratio
RAM – random access memory
R&D – research and development
RBOC – regional Bell operating company
REIT – real estate investment trust
RISC – reduced instruction set computer
ROA – return on assets
ROE – return on equity
ROI – return on investment
ROM – read-only memory
S&L – savings and loan
SEC – Securities and Exchange Commission
SEVP – senior executive vice president
SIC – Standard Industrial Classification
SPARC – scalable processor architecture
SVP – senior vice president
VAR – value-added reseller
VAT – value-added tax
VC – vice chairman
VP – vice president
WAN – wide area network
WWW – World Wide Web

Contents

Companies Profiled

Companies Profiled

ABOUT *HOOVER'S HANDBOOK OF PRIVATE COMPANIES 2000*

In today's IPO-crazed climate, many formerly private companies have made the leap to the public arena, trading their inside information for the right to sell stock in their company. Yet, the full disclosure required by the SEC makes many companies forgo the appeal of a ticker symbol in order to keep their private information private. Publishing current, relevant information on these often secretive companies is, therefore, a constant challenge.

In this fifth edition of *Hoover's Handbook of Private Companies*, we have risen to that challenge, compiling the hard-to-find facts on 770 privately held enterprises. This book contains two-page, in-depth profiles on 250 of these companies, the largest and most influential along with several smaller but equally interesting ones as well. In addition, we provide basic information, including officers, sales, and top competitors for 520 other key private enterprises with revenues of $650 million or more. We believe no other guide to private companies provides the comprehensive information contained in *Hoover's Handbook of Private Companies 2000*.

Hoover's Handbook of Private Companies is one of a four-title series that is available as an indexed set. The other three titles are *Hoover's Handbook of American Business* (two volumes), *Hoover's Handbook of Emerging Companies*, and *Hoover's Handbook of World Business*.

In addition to the 2,350 companies featured in our handbooks, coverage of nearly 50,000 business enterprises is available in electronic format on our World Wide Web site, Hoover's Online: The Business Network (www.hoovers.com). Our goal is to provide one site that addresses all the needs of business professionals. Hoover's has partnered with other prestigious business information and service providers to bring you all the right business information, services, and links in one place, including information on the hot IPO market. Additionally,

Hoover's Company Information is available on more than 25 other sites on the Internet, including The Wall Street Journal, The New York Times, and online services Reuters, GO.com, and America Online.

We believe anyone who buys from, sells to, invests in, lends to, competes with, interviews with, or works for a company should know about that enterprise. Taken together, this book and the other Hoover's products and resources represent the most complete source of basic corporate information readily available to the general public.

This book consists of five sections:

1. Using the Profiles describes the contents of our profiles and explains the ways in which we gather and compile our data.

2. A List-Lover's Compendium contains lists of the largest private companies. The lists are based on the information in our profiles, or compiled from well-known sources.

3. The profiles make up the largest and most important part of the book — 250 profiles of major private enterprises are arranged alphabetically.

4. Following the profiles are capsule summaries of 520 key private companies (including summaries for companies with in-depth profiles in the book). The page number of the full profile is listed on the capsule page for quick reference.

5. Three indexes complete the book. The companies are indexed by industry group and headquarters location, and there is a main index of all the brand names, companies, and people mentioned in the profiles in the book.

As always, we hope you find our books useful. We invite your comments by phone (512-374-4500), fax (512-374-4501), mail (1033 La Posada Drive, Suite 250, Austin, TX 78752), or e-mail (comments@hoovers.com).

The Editors
Austin, Texas
February 2000

USING THE PROFILES

COMPANIES PROFILED

The 770 enterprises profiled in this book include the largest and most influential private enterprises in America. Among them are:

- private companies, from the giants (Cargill and Koch) to the colorful and prominent (King Ranch and Skidmore, Owings & Merrill)
- mutuals and cooperative organizations owned by their customers (Prudential Insurance, Ace Hardware, Ocean Spray Cranberries)
- not-for-profits (American Red Cross, Kaiser Foundation Health Plan, Smithsonian Institution)
- joint ventures (Caltex Corporation, Dow Corning)
- partnerships (Baker & McKenzie, Kohlberg Kravis Roberts & Co.)
- universities (Columbia, Harvard, University of California)
- government-owned corporations (US Postal Service, New York City's Metropolitan Transportation Authority)
- and a selection of other enterprises (National Basketball Association, AFL-CIO, Texas Lottery Commission).

ORGANIZATION

The profiles are presented in alphabetical order. We have shown the full legal name of the enterprise at the top of the page, unless it is too long, in which case you will find it above the address in the Where section of the profile. If a company name is also a person's name, such as Edward J. DeBartolo or Mary Kay, it will be alphabetized under the first name; if the company name starts with initials, for example, L.L. Bean or S.C. Johnson, look for it under the combined initials (in the above examples, LL and SC, respectively). All company names (past and present) used in the profiles are indexed in the main index in the book. Basic financial data are listed under the heading Historical Financials & Employees.

The annual financial information contained in the profiles is as current as possible through fiscal year-ends as late as December 1999. We have included certain nonfinancial developments, such as officer changes, through January 2000.

OVERVIEW

In the first section of the profile, we have tried to give a thumbnail description of the company and what it does. The description will usually include information on the company's strategy, reputation, and ownership. We recommend that you read this section first.

HISTORY

This extended section reflects our belief that every enterprise is the sum of its history, and that you have to know where you came from in order to know where you are going. While some companies have limited historical awareness and were unable to help us much and other companies are just plain boring, we think the vast majority of the enterprises in this book have colorful backgrounds. We have tried to focus on the people who made the enterprises what they are today. We have found these histories to be full of twists and ironies; they make for fascinating reading.

OFFICERS

Here we list the names of the people who run the company, insofar as space allows.

While companies are free to structure their management titles any way they please, most modern corporations follow standard practices. The chief officer, the person on whose desk the buck stops, is usually called the chief executive officer (CEO). Often, he or she is also the chairman of the board.

As corporate management has become more complex, it is common for the CEO to have a right-hand person who oversees the day-to-day operations of the company, allowing the CEO plenty of time to focus on strategy and long-term issues. This right-hand person is usually designated the chief operating officer (COO) and is often the president of the company. In other cases one person is both chairman and president.

A multitude of other titles exists, including chief financial officer (CFO), chief administrative officer, and vice chairman (VC). We have always tried to include the CFO, the chief legal officer, and the chief human resources or personnel officer (HR). The Officers section also includes the name of the company's auditing (accounting) firm, where available.

The people named in the profiles are also included in the main index.

LOCATIONS

Here we include the company's headquarters, street address, telephone and fax numbers, and Web site, as available. The back of the book includes an index of companies by headquarters location.

In some cases we have also included information on the geographical distribution of the company's business, including sales and profit data. Note that these profit numbers, like those in the Products/Operations section below, are usually operating or pretax profits rather than net profits. Operating profits are generally those before financing costs (interest income and payments) and before taxes, which are considered costs attributable to the whole company rather than to one division or part of the world. For this reason the net income figures (in the Historical Financials & Employees section) are usually much lower, since they are after interest and taxes. Pretax profits are after interest but before taxes.

PRODUCTS/OPERATIONS

This section lists as many of the company's products, services, brand names, divisions, subsidiaries, and joint ventures as we could fit. We have tried to include all its major lines and all familiar brand names. The nature of this section varies by company and amount of information available. If the company publishes sales and profit information by type of business, we have included it. The brand, division, and subsidiary names are listed in the main index in the book.

COMPETITORS

In this section we have listed companies that compete with the profiled company. This feature is included as a quick way to locate similar companies and compare them. The universe of key competitors includes all public companies and all private companies with sales in excess of

$500 million. In a few instances we have identified smaller private companies as key competitors.

HISTORICAL FINANCIALS & EMPLOYEES

Here we have tried to present as much data about each enterprise's financial performance as we could compile. Many private companies don't readily give out information about themselves, but we have tried to provide annual sales and employment figures (although in some cases they are estimates). The following information is generally present.

A 10-year table, with relevant annualized compound growth rates, covering:

- **Sales** — fiscal year sales (year-end assets for most financial companies)
- **Net Income** (where available) — fiscal year net income (before accounting changes)
- **Income as a Percent of Sales** (where available) — fiscal year net income as a percent of sales (as a percent of assets for most financial firms)
- **Employees** — fiscal year-end or average number of employees

The information on the number of employees is intended to aid the reader interested in knowing whether a company has a long-term trend of increasing or decreasing employment. As far as we know, we are the only company that publishes this information in print form.

The year at the top of each column in the Historical Financials & Employees section is the year in which the company's fiscal year actually ends. Thus a company with a September 30, 1999, year-end is shown as 1999. Generally, for private companies, we have graphed net income or, where that is unavailable, sales.

Key year-end statistics are included in this section for insurance companies and companies required to file reports with the SEC. They generally show the financial strength of the enterprise, including:

- Debt ratio (total debt as a percent of combined total debt and shareholders' equity)
- Return on equity (net income divided by the average of beginning and ending common shareholders' equity)

- Cash, marketable securities, and short-term investments on hand
- Current ratio (ratio of current assets to current liabilities)
- Total long-term debt (including capital lease obligations)

In the case of companies that do not publicly disclose financial information, we have gathered estimates of sales and other statistics from numerous sources. For certain enterprises (e.g., American Red Cross, International Brotherhood of Teamsters), membership or contributions are shown rather than sales.

KEY PRIVATE COMPANIES

Each of the 520 shorter capsule summaries contains the company's name, headquarters address, phone and fax numbers, and Web address (where available); the names of the chief executive officer (CEO), chief financial officer (CFO), and chief human resources officer (HR); the company's fiscal year-end; the most recent annual sales figure available; the sales change over the prior year; and the number of employees. It also includes an overview of the company's operations and ownership and a list of key competitors. Since some entities (associations, lotteries, universities) do not compete against one another in the traditional sense, for them we have omitted the list of key competitors.

Hoover's Handbook of Private Companies

A LIST-LOVER'S COMPENDIUM

The 300 Largest Companies by Sales in
Hoover's Handbook of Private Companies 2000

Rank	Company	Sales ($ mil.)	Rank	Company	Sales ($ mil.)
1	Blue Cross and Blue Shield	94,700	51	ARAMARK Corporation	6,718
2	United States Postal Service	60,072	52	Cenex Harvest States Cooperatives	6,435
3	Cargill, Incorporated	50,000	53	Ascension Health	6,400
4	TIAA-CREF	45,899	54	JM Family Enterprises, Inc.	6,200
5	Koch Industries, Inc.	35,000	55	Alliant Foodservice Inc.	6,100
6	State Farm	27,706	56	C&S Wholesale Grocers Inc.	6,050
7	CalPERS	27,514	57	The Marmon Group, Inc.	6,032
8	Prudential	27,087	58	Amway Corporation	6,000
9	MetLife	27,077	59	Levi Strauss & Co.	6,000
10	Nationwide Insurance Enterprise	25,301	60	Penske Corporation	6,000
11	Equilon Enterprises LLC	22,246	61	Anthem Insurance Companies, Inc.	5,878
12	Marathon Ashland Petroleum	19,339	62	Catholic Healthcare Network	5,851
13	New York Life Insurance	18,350	63	MTA	5,707
14	IGA, INC.	18,000	64	Motiva Enterprises LLC	5,371
15	Caltex Corporation	17,174	65	Cox Enterprises, Inc.	5,355
16	Andersen Worldwide	16,300	66	The University of Texas System	5,244
17	Kaiser Foundation	15,500	67	Huntsman Corporation	5,200
18	PricewaterhouseCoopers	15,300	68	Land O'Lakes, Inc.	5,174
19	Mars, Inc.	15,000	69	Catholic Health Initiatives	5,000
20	John Hancock	13,653	70	DHL Worldwide Express	5,000
21	NASA	13,500	71	MacAndrews & Forbes	4,900
22	Northwestern Mutual	13,479	72	SAIC	4,740
23	University of California	13,074	73	Enterprise Rent-A-Car	4,730
24	Bechtel Group, Inc.	12,645	74	NUMMI	4,699
25	Ernst & Young International	12,510	75	State University of New York	4,564
26	KPMG International	12,200	76	Catholic Healthcare West	4,400
27	Publix Super Markets, Inc.	12,067	77	Equistar Chemicals, LP	4,363
28	MassMutual	11,728	78	Giant Eagle Inc.	4,360
29	Carlson Wagonlit Travel	11,000	79	TruServ Corporation	4,328
30	Liberty Mutual	10,964	80	S.C. Johnson & Son, Inc.	4,200
31	Farmland Industries, Inc.	10,709	81	New York City Health and Hospitals Corporation	4,131
32	Deloitte Touche Tohmatsu	10,600	82	Clark USA, Inc.	4,043
33	ContiGroup Companies, Inc.	10,500	83	Menard, Inc.	4,000
34	Federal Reserve Bank (NY)	10,482	84	Topco Associates Inc.	4,000
35	The ASCII Group, Inc.	9,200	85	GenAmerica Corporation	3,914
36	Guardian Life	8,499	86	Hallmark Cards, Inc.	3,900
37	Blue Cross (Michigan)	8,432	87	American Family Insurance Group	3,888
38	Meijer, Inc.	8,300	88	Advance Publications, Inc.	3,859
39	Health Care Service Corporation	7,819	89	New York State Lottery	3,831
40	Carlson Companies, Inc.	7,800	90	Catholic Health East	3,800
41	The Principal Financial Group	7,697	91	Graybar Electric Company, Inc.	3,744
42	USAA	7,687	92	Pathmark Stores, Inc.	3,655
43	Highmark Inc.	7,544	93	Montgomery Ward Holding Corp.	3,634
44	H. E. Butt Grocery Company	7,500	94	United Way of America	3,580
45	AmeriServe Food Distribution, Inc.	7,421	95	Hy-Vee, Inc.	3,500
46	Dairy Farmers of America	7,325	96	Rosenbluth International	3,500
47	The Trump Organization	6,900	97	Wakefern Food Corporation	3,500
48	Army & Air Force Exchange	6,783	98	The Mutual of Omaha Companies	3,487
49	FMR Corp.	6,770	99	Phoenix Home Life	3,464
50	Tennessee Valley Authority	6,729	100	Peter Kiewit Sons', Inc.	3,403

Source: Hoover's, Inc., Database, January 2000

Rank	Company	Sales ($ mil.)	Rank	Company	Sales ($ mil.)
101	Hyatt Corporation	3,400	151	Southern Wine & Spirits	2,450
102	Massachusetts State Lottery	3,382	152	Wegmans Food Markets, Inc.	2,450
103	The Kemper Insurance Companies	3,327	153	A-Mark Financial Corporation	2,446
104	WorldTravel Partners	3,300	154	University of Illinois	2,446
105	Empire Blue Cross Blue Shield	3,277	155	Delta Dental Plan of California	2,440
106	National Football League	3,271	156	Partners HealthCare System, Inc.	2,434
107	Los Angeles County Dept. of Health	3,257	157	Hendrick Automotive Group	2,434
108	Pension Benefit Guaranty	3,250	158	The American Red Cross	2,421
109	Associated Wholesale Grocers Inc.	3,180	159	Kohler Co.	2,400
110	Major League Baseball	3,174	160	Neuman Distributors, Inc.	2,400
111	Texas Lottery Commission	3,156	161	Peabody Group	2,387
112	YMCA of the USA	3,137	162	The Martin-Brower Company	2,380
113	Ace Hardware Corporation	3,120	163	The Hearst Corporation	2,375
114	Asbury Automotive Group	3,100	164	Mayo Foundation	2,370
115	Milliken & Company Inc.	3,100	165	The Port Authority of NY & NJ	2,361
116	Subway	3,100	166	Keystone Foods Corp.	2,342
117	Aid Association for Lutherans	3,061	167	Bonneville Power Administration	2,313
118	Raley's Inc.	3,000	168	California State Lottery	2,294
119	National Amusements Inc.	2,918	169	Amtrak	2,285
120	Sutter Health	2,881	170	Brown Automotive Group Ltd.	2,200
121	The University of Michigan	2,881	171	Gilbane, Inc.	2,200
122	Schwan's Sales Enterprises, Inc.	2,875	172	Guardian Industries Corp.	2,200
123	The University of Pennsylvania	2,823	173	Maritz Inc.	2,200
124	Pacific Mutual Holding Company	2,809	174	Sisters of Mercy	2,169
125	AAA	2,800	175	North Shore-Long Island Jewish Health System	2,165
126	Visa International	2,800			
127	The Lefrak Organization	2,750	176	Intermountain Health Care	2,156
128	J.R. Simplot Company	2,730	177	Ohio Lottery Commission	2,140
129	Schneider National	2,711	178	Florida Lottery	2,131
130	Sisters of Providence	2,709	179	NRT Incorporated	2,121
			180	Transammonia, Inc.	2,104
131	Rosenthal Group	2,700			
132	Spartan Stores, Inc.	2,672	181	Black & Veatch	2,100
133	Harvard Pilgrim Health Care, Inc.	2,670	182	Sisters of Charity	2,100
134	Ag Processing Inc	2,615	183	Belk, Inc.	2,091
135	The California State University	2,612	184	Salvation Army USA	2,078
			185	TAP Holdings Inc.	2,063
136	Los Angeles Water and Power	2,588			
137	VT Inc.	2,587	186	Goodman Holding Co.	2,055
138	Randall's Food Markets, Inc.	2,585	187	Jitney-Jungle Stores of America	2,054
139	Roundy's, Inc.	2,579	188	University of Minnesota	2,051
140	Dow Corning Corporation	2,568	189	Blue Cross Massachusetts	2,041
			190	University System of Maryland	2,033
141	International Data Group	2,560			
142	The University of Wisconsin	2,543	191	Schnuck Markets, Inc.	2,010
143	Mercy Health Services	2,534	192	LifeStyle Furnishings	2,007
144	Perdue Farms Incorporated	2,515	193	Ingram Industries Inc.	2,000
145	Allina Health System	2,500	194	Jordan Motors Inc.	2,000
			195	MBM Corporation	2,000
146	Gulf States Toyota, Inc.	2,500			
147	McKinsey & Company	2,500	196	Metromedia Company	2,000
148	Renco Group Inc.	2,500	197	NASCAR	2,000
149	Core-Mark International, Inc.	2,476	198	Pilot Corporation	2,000
150	Carpet Co-op Association	2,450	199	Quexco Incorporated	2,000
			200	Consolidated Electrical	1,950

The 300 Largest Companies by Sales in
Hoover's Handbook of Private Companies 2000 (continued)

Rank	Company	Sales ($ mil.)	Rank	Company	Sales ($ mil.)
201	The Ohio State University	1,923	251	J. F. Shea Co., Inc.	1,621
202	Do it Best Corp.	1,900	252	Trammell Crow Residential	1,617
203	Global Petroleum Corp.	1,900	253	BDO International B.V.	1,610
204	Cornell University	1,899	254	Booz, Allen & Hamilton Inc.	1,600
205	Unified Western Grocers	1,894	255	California Dairies Inc.	1,600
206	Holman Enterprises Inc.	1,870	256	Central National-Gottesman Inc.	1,600
207	Stater Bros. Holdings Inc.	1,830	257	GeoLogistics Corporation	1,600
208	Catholic Healthcare Partners	1,821	258	Golden State Foods Corporation	1,600
209	H.T. Hackney Company	1,818	259	Parsons Corporation	1,600
210	Gulf Oil, L.P.	1,808	260	Tufts Associated Health Plans, Inc.	1,600
211	QuikTrip Corporation	1,804	261	Alex Lee Inc.	1,588
212	Alcoa Fujikura Ltd.	1,800	262	Illinois Department of the Lottery	1,577
213	Kinko's, Inc.	1,800	263	DFS Group Limited	1,574
214	Penske Truck Leasing	1,800	264	Detroit Medical Center	1,573
215	UniGroup, Inc.	1,800	265	Packaging Corporation of America	1,571
216	The Texas A&M University System	1,792	266	Roll International Corporation	1,570
217	The Pennsylvania State University	1,789	267	Health Insurance New York	1,568
218	Harvard University	1,788	268	Flying J Inc.	1,562
219	The City University of New York	1,784	269	BJC Health System	1,561
220	New York University	1,771	270	Stanford University	1,558
221	Gold Kist Inc.	1,766	271	Leprino Foods Company	1,550
222	Morse Operations, Inc.	1,762	272	NovaCare Employee Services, Inc.	1,545
223	University of Washington	1,748	273	Indiana University	1,541
224	Adventist Health	1,740	274	Salt River Project	1,537
225	Big Flower Holdings, Inc.	1,740	275	The Structure Tone Organization	1,520
226	Emory University	1,739	276	Haworth Inc.	1,510
227	Georgia Lottery Corporation	1,735	277	The University of Chicago	1,507
228	The Scoular Company	1,729	278	Goodwill Industries	1,507
229	Sammons Enterprises, Inc.	1,725	279	Grant Thornton International	1,506
230	The Golub Corporation	1,720	280	The University of Alabama System	1,505
231	Michigan Lottery	1,703	281	American Retail Group, Inc.	1,500
232	Demoulas Super Markets Inc.	1,700	282	Bloomberg L.P.	1,500
233	Eby-Brown Co.	1,700	283	Clark Enterprises, Inc.	1,500
234	Gordon Food Service Inc.	1,700	284	E. & J. Gallo Winery	1,500
235	Holiday Companies	1,700	285	Harbour Group	1,500
236	Lumbermens Merchandising	1,700	286	Holy Cross Health	1,500
237	Northwestern Healthcare	1,700	287	JELD-WEN, inc.	1,500
238	Shurfine International, Inc.	1,700	288	J. M. Huber Corporation	1,500
239	Navy Exchange System	1,696	289	Nikken Global Inc.	1,500
240	Lutheran Brotherhood	1,693	290	ON Semiconductor, L.L.C.	1,500
241	Puerto Rico Electric	1,688	291	Purity Wholesale Grocers Inc.	1,500
242	The Pennsylvania Lottery	1,682	292	RaceTrac Petroleum, Inc.	1,500
243	AgriBank, FCB	1,681	293	Simpson Investment Co.	1,500
244	The Johns Hopkins University	1,664	294	Tracinda Corporation	1,500
245	Johns Hopkins Health	1,661	295	UJC of North America	1,500
246	Brookshire Grocery Company	1,650	296	Wilbur-Ellis Company	1,500
247	Duke University	1,634	297	Sentry Insurance	1,497
248	Minnesota Mutual	1,633	298	University of Missouri System	1,487
249	New Jersey State Lottery	1,630	299	Agway Inc.	1,484
250	84 Lumber Company	1,625	300	Power Authority (New York)	1,484

The 300 Largest Companies by Employees in
Hoover's Handbook of Private Companies 2000

Rank	Company	Number of Employees	Rank	Company	Number of Employees
1	United States Postal Service	792,041	51	Nationwide Insurance Enterprise	32,815
2	PricewaterhouseCoopers	155,000	52	Mayo Foundation	32,531
3	ARAMARK Corporation	152,000	53	University of Minnesota	30,708
4	Blue Cross and Blue Shield	150,000	54	Bechtel Group, Inc.	30,000
5	Carlson Companies, Inc.	147,000	55	Chick-fil-A Inc.	30,000
6	Andersen Worldwide	135,000	56	Levi Strauss & Co.	30,000
7	Publix Super Markets, Inc.	117,000	57	LifeStyle Furnishings	30,000
8	National Amusements Inc.	116,700	58	Marathon Ashland Petroleum	30,000
9	KPMG International	102,000	59	Mars, Inc.	30,000
10	Kaiser Foundation	100,000	60	YMCA of the USA	30,000
11	University of California	99,890	61	The Ohio State University	29,502
12	Ernst & Young International	97,800	62	Catholic Healthcare Partners	29,000
13	IGA, INC.	92,000	63	University System of Maryland	28,115
14	Deloitte Touche Tohmatsu	90,000	64	The City University of New York	28,000
15	Little Caesar Enterprises, Inc.	90,000	65	FMR Corp.	28,000
16	Meijer, Inc.	86,200	66	Penske Corporation	28,000
17	Cargill, Incorporated	84,000	67	North Shore-Long Island	
18	Hyatt Corporation	80,000		Jewish Health System	27,000
19	The University of Texas System	77,112	68	Pathmark Stores, Inc.	26,700
20	State Farm	76,257	69	Mercy Health Services	26,436
			70	University of Illinois	26,148
21	Ascension Health	67,000	71	Sisters of Mercy	26,000
22	State University of New York	65,000	72	BJC Health System	25,853
23	Metromedia Company	63,000	73	Giant Eagle Inc.	25,600
24	DHL Worldwide Express	60,486	74	The University of Wisconsin	25,500
25	Goodwill Industries	60,000	75	Asplundh Tree Expert Co.	25,000
26	MTA	57,551	76	Delaware North Companies Inc.	25,000
27	Cox Enterprises, Inc.	55,500	77	Kinko's, Inc.	25,000
28	NovaCare Employee Services	54,784	78	Wegmans Food Markets, Inc.	25,000
29	Army & Air Force Exchange	54,000	79	Advance Holding Corporation	24,976
30	Prudential	50,000	80	Advance Publications, Inc.	24,000
31	Montgomery Ward	49,000	81	Amtrak	24,000
32	Catholic Health East	45,000	82	Intermountain Health Care	23,000
33	H. E. Butt Grocery Company	45,000	83	The Johns Hopkins University	23,000
34	Hy-Vee, Inc.	42,900	84	RTM Restaurant Group	23,000
35	MetLife	42,300	85	Sisters of Providence	23,000
36	Enterprise Rent-A-Car	40,000	86	Texas A&M University System	23,000
37	Salvation Army USA	39,883	87	The University of Michigan	23,000
38	The California State University	39,000	88	University of Florida	22,500
39	EPIX Holdings Corporation	38,300	89	Belk, Inc.	22,000
40	Catholic Healthcare West	38,000	90	Life Care Centers of America	22,000
41	AAA	37,000	91	The Trump Organization	22,000
42	Liberty Mutual	37,000	92	Los Angeles County Dept. of Health	21,694
43	SAIC	35,200	93	Allina Health System	21,200
44	CARQUEST Corp.	35,000	94	Advocate Health Care	21,000
45	The Marmon Group, Inc.	35,000	95	ClubCorp, Inc.	21,000
46	RGIS Inventory Specialists	35,000	96	MedStar Health	21,000
47	Sutter Health	35,000	97	The Johns Hopkins Health	20,987
48	University of Washington	34,757	98	Hallmark Cards, Inc.	20,945
49	New York City Health		99	Perdue Farms Incorporated	20,500
	and Hospitals Corporation	33,403	100	SSM Health Care System Inc.	20,500
50	The Freeman Companies	33,296			

Source: Hoover's, Inc., Database, January 2000

The 300 Largest Companies by Employees in
Hoover's Handbook of Private Companies 2000 (continued)

Rank	Company	Number of Employees	Rank	Company	Number of Employees
101	Grant Thornton International	20,160	151	Domino's Pizza, Inc.	14,200
102	USAA	20,120	152	Penske Truck Leasing	14,200
103	Carlson Wagonlit Travel	20,100	153	ContiGroup Companies, Inc.	14,000
104	Bon Secours Health System, Inc.	20,000	154	Equilon Enterprises LLC	14,000
105	Duke University	20,000	155	Long John Silver's Restaurants	14,000
106	NASA	19,559	156	ON Semiconductor, L.L.C.	14,000
107	MacAndrews & Forbes Holdings	19,500	157	Vanderbilt University	13,993
108	Partners HealthCare System, Inc.	19,407	158	Tennessee Valley Authority	13,818
109	Viasystems Group, Inc.	19,350	159	The Hearst Corporation	13,555
110	Holy Cross Health System	19,135	160	OhioHealth	13,400
111	Louisiana State University	19,030	161	CareGroup, Inc.	13,362
112	The University of Pennsylvania	18,331	162	Inova Health System	13,000
113	The Golub Corporation	18,000	163	New York Life Insurance	13,000
114	Kohler Co.	18,000	164	The University of Kentucky	13,000
115	Farmland Industries, Inc.	17,700	165	New York University	12,937
116	Randall's Food Markets, Inc.	17,650	166	Baylor Health Care System	12,900
117	BDO International B.V.	17,500	167	The University of Chicago	12,869
118	Gold Kist Inc.	17,500	168	Stater Bros. Holdings Inc.	12,700
119	Adventist Health	17,129	169	AMSTED Industries	12,600
120	The University of Iowa	17,129	170	University of Rochester	12,568
121	Henry Ford Health System	17,000	171	UCSF Stanford Health Care	12,500
122	Jitney-Jungle Stores of America	17,000	172	Demoulas Super Markets Inc.	12,350
123	Schneider National	17,000	173	Alliant Foodservice Inc.	12,000
124	University of Southern California	17,000	174	Community Health Systems	12,000
125	The Principal Financial Group	16,837	175	Highmark Inc.	12,000
126	Day & Zimmermann, Inc.	16,500	176	International Data Group	12,000
127	Detroit Medical Center	16,500	177	J.R. Simplot Company	12,000
128	Peter Kiewit Sons', Inc.	16,200	178	Memorial Hermann	12,000
129	DynCorp	16,000	179	Novant Health, Inc.	12,000
130	Investors Management Corp.	16,000	180	Regal Cinemas, Inc.	12,000
131	Koch Industries, Inc.	16,000	181	Wawa Inc.	12,000
132	The Lefrak Organization	16,000	182	Cornell University	11,873
133	Milliken & Company Inc.	16,000	183	Franciscan Health Partnership	11,807
134	Navy Exchange System	16,000	184	Anthem Insurance Companies	11,504
135	Northwestern Healthcare	16,000	185	Mashantucket Pequot Gaming Enterprise Inc.	11,500
136	Schnuck Markets, Inc.	16,000			
137	Sisters of Charity	16,000	186	Provena Health	11,500
138	The Jones Financial Companies	15,795	187	George Washington University	11,272
139	Carondelet Health System	15,500	188	Hobby Lobby Stores, Inc.	11,000
140	Emory University	15,491	189	JELD-WEN, inc.	11,000
141	University of Alabama System	15,468	190	Parsons Corporation	11,000
142	Columbia University	15,300	191	Quad/Graphics, Inc.	11,000
143	Allegheny Health, Education and Research Foundation	15,000	192	Taylor Corporation	11,000
144	American Retail Group, Inc.	15,000	193	Tri Valley Growers	11,000
145	Guardian Industries Corp.	15,000	194	White Castle System, Inc.	11,000
			195	William Beaumont Hospital	11,000
146	Raley's Inc.	15,000	196	Hewitt Associates LLC	10,930
147	Renco Group Inc.	15,000	197	Brookshire Grocery Company	10,700
148	Texas Health Resources	15,000	198	JMB Realty Corporation	10,700
149	University of Tennessee	14,967	199	Variety Wholesalers, Inc.	10,500
150	Health Midwest	14,700	200	University of Massachusetts	10,296

The 300 Largest Companies by Employees in
Hoover's Handbook of Private Companies 2000 (continued)

Rank	Company	Number of Employees	Rank	Company	Number of Employees
201	University of Virginia	10,294	251	Duchossois Industries, Inc.	8,000
202	Puerto Rico Electric	10,194	252	Fiesta Mart Inc.	8,000
203	General Parts, Inc.	10,150	253	Follett Corporation	8,000
204	Amway Corporation	10,000	254	Ilitch Ventures, Inc.	8,000
205	Big Flower Holdings, Inc.	10,000	255	Knowledge Universe, Inc.	8,000
206	Harbour Group	10,000	256	Methodist Healthcare	8,000
207	Haworth Inc.	10,000	257	Minyard Food Stores Inc.	8,000
208	Huntsman Corporation	10,000	258	John Hancock	7,959
209	McKinsey & Company	10,000	259	Montefiore Medical Center	7,935
210	Platinum Equity Holdings	10,000	260	Caltex Corporation	7,900
211	Samaritan Health System	10,000	261	Graybar Electric Company, Inc.	7,900
212	Sisters of Charity	10,000	262	MaaMutual	7,885
213	Turner Industries, Ltd.	10,000	263	Peabody Group	7,800
214	United Artists Theatre Circuit	10,000	264	Boston University	7,760
215	United Way of America	10,000	265	Cushman & Wakefield Inc.	7,700
216	The Vanguard Group, Inc.	10,000	266	Packaging Corporation of America	7,700
217	Yale University	10,000	267	Parsons Brinckerhoff, Inc.	7,700
218	TravelCenters of America, Inc.	9,800	268	The MacManus Group	7,619
219	Group Health Co-op of Puget Sound	9,602	269	Bashas' Inc.	7,600
220	University of Pittsburgh	9,600	270	Goodman Holding Co.	7,500
221	Stanford University	9,535	271	H. B. Zachry Company	7,500
222	S.C. Johnson & Son, Inc.	9,500	272	Incarnate Word Health System	7,500
223	Wake Forest University Baptist	9,400	273	MTS, Incorporated	7,500
224	Beaulieu Of America, LLC	9,347	274	R. B. Pamplin Corporation	7,500
225	Steiner Corporation	9,100	275	Roll International Corporation	7,500
226	The Leo Group, Inc.	9,029	276	Timex Corporation	7,500
227	Black & Veatch	9,000	277	Rush System for Health	7,250
228	Booz, Allen & Hamilton Inc.	9,000	278	Agway Inc.	7,200
229	Dow Corning Corporation	9,000	279	Baptist Health Systems	7,200
230	Flying J Inc.	9,000	280	The Port Authority of NY & NJ	7,200
231	The Kemper Insurance Companies	9,000	281	Save Mart Supermarkets	7,200
232	MediaNews Group, Inc.	8,997	282	Alex Lee Inc.	7,154
233	J. Crew Group Inc.	8,900	283	The Mutual of Omaha Companies	7,111
234	Holiday Retirement Corp.	8,750	284	Jordan Industries, Inc.	7,092
235	Lane Industries, Inc.	8,650	285	Battelle Memorial Institute	7,060
236	BE&K Inc.	8,617	286	Big Y Foods Inc.	7,000
237	UIS, Inc.	8,614	287	CH2M Hill Companies, Ltd.	7,000
238	Carilion Health System	8,500	288	Foster Poultry Farms	7,000
239	Contran Corporation	8,500	289	Freedom Communications, Inc.	7,000
240	DFS Group Limited	8,500	290	The Longaberger Company	7,000
241	MIT	8,500	291	Menard, Inc.	7,000
242	ScrippsHealth	8,400	292	Pilot Corporation	7,000
243	Specialty Foods Corporation	8,300	293	Quexco Incorporated	7,000
244	Watkins Associated Industries	8,300	294	W. L. Gore and Associates, Inc.	7,000
245	Los Angeles Water and Power	8,290	295	Journal Communications Inc.	6,968
246	Sentara Health System	8,190	296	American Family Insurance Group	6,940
247	Sweetheart Cup Company	8,050	297	AECOM Technology Corporation	6,900
248	Washington University	8,017	298	Baker & McKenzie	6,900
249	AmeriServe Food Distribution	8,000	299	Cumberland Farms, Inc.	6,900
250	Dillingham Construction	8,000	300	Schottenstein Stores Corporation	6,820

The *Inc.* 500 Fastest-Growing Private Companies in America

Rank	Company	1994–98 Sales Growth Increase (%)	1998 Sales ($ thou.)
1	Roth Staffing	20,332	73,761
2	Tedesco Steakhouse	16,804	46,825
3	Techstaff	16,693	36,945
4	Gaiam	13,352	30,805
5	CyberTech Systems	12,748	51,904
6	Jules and Associates	12,500	58,844
7	Creative Technology	11,742	86,564
8	Info Technologies	8,491	20,104
9	SafeNet Consulting	7,718	16,106
10	Computech Resources	7,075	14,350
11	Abacus Software Group	6,827	14,269
12	Computer Hardware Maintenance	6,592	15,926
13	Efficient Machine Tool Sales	6,537	14,534
14	Inforte	6,226	13,917
15	Access Cash International	6,197	43,513
16	QSS Group	6,164	25,306
17	VoCall Communications	6,132	46,742
18	Systems Group	6,029	18,202
19	PRISM	5,889	12,517
20	Cypress Food Distributors	5,870	17,312
21	ATP Oil & Gas	5,073	21,777
22	Think Tank Systems	4,999	10,350
23	Aegis Mortgage Acceleration	4,718	33,777
24	Phoenix Transportation Services	4,636	11,556
25	NovaSoft Information Technology	4,630	14,000
26	Priority Call Management	4,269	30,936
27	Omicron Systems	4,255	13,195
28	Custom Computer Systems	4,236	10,624
29	Computer Enterprises	4,180	28,591
30	Gorell Enterprises	4,115	15,805
31	Construct Two Group	4,112	20,471
32	Twin Hills Collectables	4,088	8,878
33	Ingear	4,054	53,131
34	UTStarcom	3,985	165,165
35	MetaSolv Software	3,963	42,576
36	Prism Mortgage	3,907	90,842
37	Jamba Juice	3,864	39,839
38	SHK Foods	3,830	9,197
39	Corex Technologies	3,801	15,020
40	RE/COM Group	3,762	18,694
41	HealthLink	3,757	9,874
42	Triple Point Technology	3,667	9,002
43	Surefoot	3,601	8,549
44	Heritage Communities	3,552	39,809
45	Frontier Systems	3,485	12,582
46	Al Signal Research	3,446	12,554
47	Doral Dental USA	3,410	65,038
48	Hubbard Health Care	3,350	31,534
49	Dataforce	3,263	8,643
50	Intuitive Manufacturing Systems	3,239	7,312
51	TAMCo	3,204	44,509
52	Creative Financial Staffing	3,165	25,596
53	Advanced Integration Technology	3,162	23,913
54	iQuest Solutions	3,146	7,303
55	CFC Refimax	3,097	9,430

Source: *Inc.* 500; 1999

The *Inc.* 500 Fastest-Growing Private Companies in America (continued)

Rank	Company	1994–98 Sales Growth Increase (%)	1998 Sales ($ thou.)
56	Wasatch Energy	3,091	31,177
57	Vitrex	3,080	11,733
58	ISI	3,054	28,635
59	ByteWorks	3,037	24,346
60	Paramount Computer	2,984	6,723
61	Forte Consulting Group	2,982	11,926
62	Pacific Industrial Development	2,954	12,583
63	CyberWarehouse Computer Outlet Ceneter	2,870	9,445
64	BSI Consulting	2,865	9,281
65	Techniki Informatica	2,825	28,222
66	InterAccess	2,786	10,218
67	Logicare	2,779	414,604
68	FeelGood Catalog	2,754	6,421
69	New West Products	2,698	15,136
70	Hyland Software	2,624	8,146
71	Riester-Robb	2,621	19,268
72	Unitel	2,616	14,995
73	Heartland Mortgage/Heartland Home Finance	2,612	29,533
74	Panacea Consulting	2,603	7,486
75	TelStrat	2,562	15,785
76	IntelliNet	2,562	8,411
77	Catapult Systems	2,466	7,825
78	U.S. Energy Services	2,367	14,432
79	SOS Temporary Services	2,344	10,143
80	Monitronics International	2,343	25,793
81	Datamatics Consultants	2,323	17,881
82	Atlantic Corporate Interiors	2,267	8,498
83	EBC Computers	2,246	13,488
84	World One Technologies	2,239	16,632
85	CodeSoft International	2,213	9,829
86	RAM Sports	2,192	4,607
87	MediHealth Outsourcing	2,176	5,031
88	Destia Communications	2,173	193,737
89	Twin Rivers Foods	2,170	55,337
90	Knitting Factory	2,134	6,010
91	Ea Consulting	2,112	11,193
92	Shupe Consulting	2,105	20,064
93	Jasc Software	2,092	16,943
94	Triton Systems	2,086	70,749
95	Thermagon	2,047	7,881
96	WAN Technologies	2,039	7,552
97	NewTek	2,018	8,685
98	Lockwood Sign Group	2,013	10,056
99	System Design Group	2,007	4,678
100	iBASEt	2,001	18,570
101	Staffing Technologies	1,999	7,369
102	Capital Technologies Integration	1,954	6,141
103	Upper Valley Utilities	1,943	8,785
104	Cavanaugh Promotions	1,935	4,600
105	McNeil Technologies	1,899	13,255
106	American Recruitment	1,893	5,242
107	U.S. Marketing & Promotions Agency	1,879	43,911
108	Vixel	1,876	39,445
109	Spencer Reed Group	1,872	49,711
110	Comnet International	1,872	7,354

The *Inc.* 500 Fastest-Growing Private Companies in America (continued)

Rank	Company	1994–98 Sales Growth Increase (%)	1998 Sales ($ thou.)
111	Inotech	1,865	14,326
112	IVP Pharmaceutical Care	1,860	28,775
113	Infosys Networks	1,860	5,586
114	Global Consultants	1,842	15,708
115	Vistronix	1,834	10,886
116	Aquascape Designs	1,831	8,168
117	MACI	1,826	11,904
118	RS Information Systems	1,824	12,621
119	iGo	1,818	12,945
120	Digital Optics	1,810	4,240
121	East Coast Concrete	1,810	14,915
122	360	1,787	5,320
123	Xtras	1,767	12,192
124	Meridian Technology Group	1,747	6,114
125	Energy Savings	1,741	30,154
126	Epic Solutions	1,740	5,042
127	Fresh Samantha	1,740	15,692
128	Lenel Systems International	1,740	11,240
129	Market Scan Information Systems	1,738	27,978
130	Research Triangle Consultants	1,734	4,714
131	Professional Cutlery Direct	1,710	4,850
132	Capella University	1,707	4,844
133	Western Pacific Housing	1,705	423,313
134	Lynk Systems	1,683	87,526
135	Symvionics	1,678	22,103
136	Witness Systems	1,676	13,122
137	Compri Consulting	1,673	3,759
138	Platinum Capital Group	1,649	23,373
139	Thixomat	1,631	8,015
140	Record Technologies	1,630	3,478
141	Analytical Computer Services	1,629	26,795
142	MS Rental Services	1,627	36,694
143	HighMark	1,623	6,184
144	Helga Designs	1,619	4,522
145	In Person Payments	1,604	3,477
146	Accord Human Resources	1,603	123,265
147	NexCycle	1,602	101,518
148	PC Club	1,594	80,054
149	Hamilton Anderson Associates	1,590	4,293
150	Direct Partners	1,585	19,008
151	Neuristics	1,542	4,089
152	Research Data Design	1,540	4,214
153	Bloomfield Computer Systems	1,536	126,947
154	Direct Lease	1,535	4,626
155	Peripheral Vision InfoSystems	1,528	38,207
156	GWI Software	1,524	5,164
157	Unified Technologies	1,517	22,917
158	DeMarini Sports	1,503	14,444
159	Account Resource	1,500	3,681
160	Tushaus Computer Services	1,498	10,960
161	Global Dynamics International	1,496	4,628
162	Chesapeake Sciences	1,492	21,492
163	Cyber Dialogue	1,483	3,626
164	Triad Management Systems	1,483	14,592
165	Optimum Solutions	1,474	3,919

The *Inc.* 500 Fastest-Growing Private Companies in America (continued)

Rank	Company	1994–98 Sales Growth Increase (%)	1998 Sales ($ thou.)
166	Tactics	1,463	33,564
167	Reliacom	1,458	3,304
168	Sanvision Technology	1,447	4,147
169	ArrayComm	1,441	13,347
170	Albin Engineering Services	1,427	8,583
171	Orion Construction	1,427	67,950
172	Health Decisions	1,410	8,941
173	CourtLink	1,408	4,449
174	Informatics	1,401	19,418
175	MedSpan	1,397	56,605
176	Schumacher Group of Delaware	1,374	24,011
177	Digital Connections	1,371	14,844
178	T.R. Hughes	1,365	18,823
179	InstallShield Software	1,360	28,585
180	Inline	1,355	3,069
181	Petroleum Services of Florida	1,352	46,828
182	Async Technologies	1,351	6,078
183	Essex Builders Group	1,349	64,510
184	Alpha Computer Services	1,349	3,521
185	Pioneer Mortgage	1,349	8,808
186	Clif Bar	1,345	29,167
187	Edgewise Media Services	1,337	5,922
188	Amanda Gray	1,330	7,908
189	Diversified Communications Group	1,327	4,508
190	Lighthouse Medical Management	1,323	4,440
191	Oakley Tank Lines	1,321	6,054
192	Computer Consultants of America	1,320	15,319
193	3-G International	1,319	8,304
194	Sys-Con Publications	1,307	3,897
195	Innovision Technologies	1,297	4,400
196	SoftSol Resources	1,294	10,103
197	Telecommunications Analysis Group	1,293	18,195
198	T.R. White	1,292	26,622
199	Ryder-Bush Staffing	1,291	3,075
200	Net2000 Communications	1,285	9,419
201	Advanced Concepts	1,282	7,558
202	CTES	1,275	3,176
203	Pensar Tuscon	1,274	3,489
204	Indus	1,272	11,377
205	Security Leasing Partners	1,266	12,469
206	Prime Response	1,257	17,036
207	Workforce	1,248	8,261
208	Allied Group	1,244	58,315
209	Accent Marketing Services	1,241	29,480
210	AnciCare PPO	1,236	11,006
211	SensAble Technologies	1,233	3,025
212	ProTrans International	1,230	28,559
213	ASK Data Communications	1,221	10,755
214	Search Connection	1,220	6,163
215	CTX	1,216	9,370
216	DataLogic	1,216	2,658
217	TCG	1,208	8,124
218	Johnsson Group	1,207	3,608
219	Marina Mortgage	1,207	18,756
220	Total Scope	1,205	2,792

The *Inc.* 500 Fastest-Growing Private Companies in America (continued)

Rank	Company	1994–98 Sales Growth Increase (%)	1998 Sales ($ thou.)
221	Sytel	1,200	50,667
222	Mainline Information Systems	1,199	81,022
223	ASAP Messenger	1,190	2,863
224	Caelum Research	1,185	17,042
225	Crystal Group	1,184	20,898
226	STG	1,184	34,132
227	Aspen Conusulting	1,184	19,010
228	Wall Street Services	1,180	11,290
229	Card Capture Services	1,172	40,313
230	QA1 Precision Products	1,168	11,819
231	PC Age	1,161	3,808
232	Vector Strategic Resources	1,161	11,699
233	Nova Development	1,159	11,154
234	ISSI Consulting Group	1,157	12,679
235	Cue Data Services	1,157	14,375
236	Tecmark Services	1,153	3,709
237	Diversified Computer Consultants	1,150	11,585
238	Lilly Software Associates	1,146	35,304
239	Commtech	1,144	19,734
240	Dansko	1,142	16,345
241	Akili Systems Group	1,139	15,191
242	BDS	1,139	22,870
243	Electronic Manufacturing Services	1,139	185,185
244	Air One Transport Group	1,135	14,590
245	T2 Systems	1,135	2,482
246	Thompson Brooks	1,134	10,374
247	Pac-Van Leasing & Sales	1,133	14,737
248	Mathews	1,133	17,793
249	2 Places at 1 Time	1,127	2,810
250	Solutions Consulting	1,111	54,519
251	Staffing Solutions Group	1,110	3,086
252	Capital Information Systems	1,107	13,157
253	Nationwide Communications	1,102	21,744
254	Cytronics Technology	1,092	28,799
255	IntelliNet Technologies	1,086	2,775
256	Clarkston-Potomac Group	1,085	29,947
257	Advanced Systems Design	1,082	9,021
258	Best Computer Consultants	1,081	8,867
259	Franklin American Mortgage	1,080	7,280
260	Versatile Systems	1,079	6,318
261	Telecom Technologies	1,072	2,040
262	CenterPoint Solutions	1,071	2,400
263	Spinecare	1,068	4,530
264	Hi Tech Consultants	1,066	19,365
265	VW International	1,063	7,000
266	Taylor Group	1,061	10,232
267	Roundhouse	1,061	15,741
268	Relocation Management Resources	1,060	6,301
269	Petrolsoft	1,056	5,204
270	GEMCo	1,055	19,897
271	Integral Care Provider	1,055	3,996
272	CSA	1,050	16,325
273	Speedcom Technologies	1,041	16,414
274	Iriscan	1,040	3,546
275	Office Solutions	1,040	8,207

The *Inc.* 500 Fastest-Growing Private Companies in America (continued)

Rank	Company	1994–98 Sales Growth Increase (%)	1998 Sales ($ thou.)
276	Plitt	1,040	21,085
277	People Solutions	1,037	3,934
278	Cambridge Search	1,036	2,420
279	Elucidex	1,034	2,233
280	Axxis	1,027	17,995
281	Miramar Systems	1,025	8,390
282	Network Management Services	1,020	10,122
283	R Systems	1,016	30,264
284	Deva Systems Group	1,016	2,556
285	CTSinc.net	1,009	60,605
286	Enterprise Development Services	1,003	2,240
287	CommerceQuest	1,003	31,598
288	Bay Home & Window	999	3,132
289	AC Technologies	988	4,983
290	Tensor Information Systems	987	9,197
291	Modernica	983	6,239
292	Qualified Resources	983	7,806
293	CoreTech Consulting Group	979	41,726
294	Advanced Technology Systems	977	14,476
295	Simutronics	975	5,096
296	ACS International Resources	974	2,900
297	CEG Construction	973	13,633
298	LAN Tamers	973	2,145
299	Midland Data-Electric Installation	969	8,310
300	TX CC	967	28,619
301	Dlt Solutions	966	60,219
302	Image Process Design	964	14,433
303	Union Payroll Agency	963	10,149
304	Megasoft Consultants	962	12,834
305	Syscom	958	33,314
306	Concorde Flooring Systems	958	12,595
307	New Age Electronics	956	433,193
308	Carsan Engineering	953	2,305
309	DataPath Systems	946	12,497
310	Breakaway Solutions	945	10,018
311	Advanced Systems Applications & Products	943	20,891
312	Wyndham Mills International	940	4,088
313	Alpha Data	935	5,216
314	Mid-American Specialties	932	4,035
315	Advantage Credit International	931	3,899
316	Landmark Financial Services	930	11,933
317	Newton & Associates	928	4,388
318	DB Basics	927	13,829
319	Perry, Pyron & McCown Consultants	925	3,782
320	Brew Ha Ha	924	3,686
321	Smart Staffing	922	2,054
322	High Technology Solutions	921	32,141
323	Quick Solutions	920	17,906
324	Reliable Software Technologies	916	4,520
325	Zephyr Environmental	912	2,682
326	Linksys	909	65,581
327	Network One	908	22,186
328	Terra-Kleen	905	2,080
329	P&R Environmental Industries	903	8,553
330	PB	900	17,956

The *Inc.* 500 Fastest-Growing Private Companies in America (continued)

Rank	Company	1994–98 Sales Growth Increase (%)	1998 Sales ($ thou.)
331	Adastra Systems	900	5,059
332	August Technology	894	5,787
333	JBA Consulting	878	3,686
334	Lowestrate.com	876	3,075
335	Property & Portfolio Research	875	4,057
336	Bass & Associates	871	8,090
337	ITS	868	8,816
338	Progressive Medical	864	9,107
339	OnLine Staffing	862	8,431
340	Synygy	858	8,104
341	Hartex Property Group	858	85,091
342	Prime Systems	857	3,131
343	Sierra Lobo	856	2,314
344	Kinoo	855	2,970
345	Applied Control Engineering	850	4,505
346	Rapidigm	843	195,716
347	Employee Benefit Administrators	842	3,496
348	Washington Square Associates	841	2,719
349	Micromarketing	840	2,895
350	Wakefield Pharmaceuticals	839	5,963
351	Vision Solutions	838	19,332
352	Cambria Environmental Technology	837	4,086
353	InfoMaker	837	1,958
354	PSCI	833	10,043
355	APB Energy	827	12,485
356	Ipswitch	824	9,934
357	Versicom Communications	820	2,024
358	Jones Business Systems	820	67,075
359	Restaurants on the Run	819	5,204
360	Johnson & Michaels	819	2,720
361	Analytical Graphics	818	14,863
362	Avico	816	3,159
363	Loan Administration Network	815	6,586
364	M & H Enterprises	814	2,898
365	Big River Brewery	813	27,423
366	United States Information Systems	813	36,831
367	Securities Service Network	813	54,228
368	Advanced Financial Solutions	811	23,917
369	Right Stuf International	808	2,153
370	Progressive Support Services	808	5,966
371	Force 3	808	78,480
372	Rockford Construction	807	110,881
373	North Highland	807	10,851
374	Time Save Transportation	805	2,318
375	IT Solutions	801	18,246
376	Black Oak Computer Services	801	16,413
377	Solutech	796	14,304
378	FaxWatch Strategic Information Services	796	2,195
379	Before You Move	793	5,843
380	David Gomez & Associates	790	4,459
381	TriNet VCO	790	398,663
382	ThoughtWorks	789	13,040
383	Software Architects	789	3,210
384	PayMaxx	789	4,800
385	PWR Systems	788	8,768

The *Inc.* 500 Fastest-Growing Private Companies in America (continued)

Rank	Company	1994–98 Sales Growth Increase (%)	1998 Sales ($ thou.)
386	AOS	780	12,050
387	CHills Tobacco	779	2,304
388	DataProfit	778	26,381
389	Configuration Management	776	7,359
390	Hamel Group	775	9,707
391	Jupiter Communications	770	14,802
392	Factual Data	769	3,397
393	Lifecodes	767	22,781
394	Employment Trends	766	11,020
395	CB Technologies	765	8,173
396	WPL Laboratories	765	2,395
397	Springbok Technologies	764	1,935
398	International Postal Consultants	764	25,812
399	Personnel Services	761	12,245
400	Inside Source	760	13,050
401	Total Containment of New York	758	1,827
402	BlackHawk Information Services	755	4,036
403	Product Data Integration Technologies	752	5,562
404	Logical Choice Technologies	748	12,892
405	Trogan Notebook Computer	747	17,618
406	Citipost	747	20,723
407	BCI	746	6,489
408	Goldmine Software	744	24,561
409	PIRI	743	36,862
410	BL Cos.	743	15,820
411	T.H. Properties	740	51,755
412	Tech Express	738	5,176
413	Precision Heliparts	735	3,641
414	GammaGraphX	728	5,357
415	BMS	726	2,717
416	Managed Business Solutions	725	7,998
417	Reliant General Insurance Services	722	17,215
418	CCAi	721	50,505
419	Ideal Financial Services	720	5,273
420	Synergy Investment	718	2,717
421	Cecchetti Sebastiani Cellar	715	6,949
422	Windows on Washington	714	1,725
423	Westwinds Wholesale Doors	710	1,968
424	Internet Research Group	705	2,085
425	Binary Tree	704	5,697
426	Optive	703	132,984
427	Kiosk Information Systems	701	4,502
428	Matrix Resources	699	127,272
429	Innovative Technology Solutions	699	3,006
430	SimStar Digital Media	695	2,927
431	Gardenside	694	3,429
432	Strategic Partners International	692	1,592
433	FitzGerald Communications	690	8,907
434	WorkRite Ergonomics	689	13,515
435	Drake Associates	688	2,190
436	Plus Group	687	51,470
437	Navigator Systems	686	4,034
438	Sky Helicopters	686	2,302
439	Signal	685	145,860
440	Persistence Software	684	10,159

The *Inc.* 500 Fastest-Growing Private Companies in America (continued)

Rank	Company	1994–98 Sales Growth Increase (%)	1998 Sales ($ thou.)
441	Ascent Solutions	682	8,078
442	Business Integrators	681	11,364
443	Parrett Trucking	680	9,230
444	Sensitech	680	9,467
445	Black Cat Computer Wholesale	675	7,354
446	McKibben Communications	674	3,459
447	Quality Research	671	22,432
448	DeJarnette Research Systems	669	3,100
449	Joseph Graves Associates	669	3,090
450	Intelliware Systems	669	9,568
451	Respond	667	12,060
452	Spectrum Communications Cabling Services	666	5,579
453	Contractor Management Group	665	38,600
454	American Audio-Visual Center	664	5,760
455	ProLaw Software	662	4,459
456	International Business	660	14,985
457	Edge Software Services	660	6,077
458	Stratford Financial Services	659	2,468
459	Snack Factory	656	4,889
460	Chesapeake Computer Consultants	652	12,470
461	TeleSales	650	3,360
462	Extol	649	4,421
463	Advanced Modular Power Systems	644	6,915
464	Give Something Back	641	12,237
465	J & B Software	639	20,575
466	Hard Drives Northwest	637	25,443
467	Artemis Alliance	637	3,060
468	Soldering Technology International	635	6,854
469	ATX Forms	634	3,569
470	E-Tek Dynamics	633	106,924
471	Transaction Information Systems	632	84,820
472	SMArts	630	2,816
473	Computer Science & Technology	628	7,393
474	Setpoint Engineered Systems	627	4,683
475	BP Microsystems	625	20,571
476	Spartan	623	8,167
477	Focus2	623	2,233
478	Sonic Air Systems	620	6,618
479	Tape Resources	620	5,637
480	Collection Co. of America	620	12,711
481	MicroMass Communications	619	3,422
482	Quality Imaging Products	618	4,756
483	Cardiac Fitness/Main Medical	617	8,605
484	Lone Star Direct	613	1,854
485	VIA	611	6,884
486	Central Pharmacy Services	610	31,331
487	Bath Concepts and Supplies	610	1,442
488	Abdon Callais Offshore	610	10,994
489	Edifice	607	62,880
490	Stout Risius Ross	605	3,957
491	Rainbow Analysis Systems Group	604	1,726
492	Peeper's Sunglasses/Binoculars.com	604	1,472
493	Born Information Services Group	603	92,258
494	Apexx Technology	603	3,808
495	Tangent Software Consulting	599	5,250
496	Management Decisions	598	19,042
497	Dove Data Products	597	7,678
498	Soma Group	596	2,081
499	AccuData America	595	16,385
500	GreenPages	595	84,624

The *Forbes* 500 Largest Private Companies in the US

Rank	Company	Revenues ($ mil.)	Rank	Company	Revenues ($ mil.)
1	Cargill	50,000	51	A-Mark Financial	2,446
2	Koch Industries	33,050	52	Wegmans Food Markets	2,440
3	PricewaterhouseCoopers	17,300	53	Neuman Distributors	2,400
4	Andersen Worldwide	16,200	54	Peabody Group	2,387
5	Mars	15,600	55	Martin-Brower	2,375
6	Bechtel Group	12,600	56	Keystone Foods	2,342
7	Ernst & Young	12,500	57	Kohler	2,300
8	KPMG	12,200	58	Gilbane	2,295
9	Publix Super Markets	12,067	59	Hearst	2,200
10	Deloitte Touche Tohmatsu	10,800	60	Penske Truck Leasing	2,199
11	Conti Group Cos	10,500	61	Black & Veatch	2,147
12	Holberg Industries	9,279	62	Connell	2,100
13	Meijer	8,300	63	Guardian Industries	2,100
14	Huntsman	8,000	64	Belk Stores Services	2,091
15	H.E. Butt Grocery	7,500	65	Jitney Jungle Stores of America	2,054
16	Fidelity Investments	6,776	66	Goodman Manufacturing	2,050
17	Aramark	6,450	67	Core-Mark International	2,010
18	JM Family Enterprises	6,200	68	LifeStyle Furnishings International	2,002
19	Alliant Foodservice	6,100	69	Andersen Corp.	2,000
20	C&S Wholesale Grocers	6,050	70	Capital Group of Companies	2,000
21	Marmon Group	6,032	71	Gordon Food Service	2,000
22	Levi Strauss & Co	6,000	72	H Group Holding	2,000
23	Science Applications Intl	4,740	73	Schnuck Markets	2,000
24	Enterprise Rent-A-Car	4,730	74	Ingram Industries	1,992
25	Giant Eagle	4,350	75	Eby-Brown	1,950
26	S.C. Johnson & Son	4,200	76	Sammons Enterprises	1,930
27	Menard	4,000	77	Stater Bros Markets	1,850
28	Clark USA	3,981	78	JELD-WEN	1,825
29	Hallmark Cards	3,900	79	HT Hackney	1,818
30	Graybar Electric	3,732	80	Gulf Oil LP	1,808
31	Pathmark Stores	3,655	81	UniGroup	1,808
32	Hy-Vee	3,500	82	QuikTrip	1,804
33	Peter Kiewit Sons'	3,403	83	Bloomberg LP	1,800
34	Cox Enterprises	3,378	84	DeMoulas Super Markets	1,782
35	Milliken & Co	3,100	85	Carlson Companies	1,735
36	Advance Publications	3,075	86	Scoular	1,729
37	Amway	3,000	87	Holiday Companies	1,725
38	Schwan's Sales Enterprises	3,000	88	Golub	1,700
39	JR Simplot	2,730	89	JF Shea Co.	1,700
40	Schneider National	2,711	90	Golden State Foods	1,650
41	Gulf States Toyota	2,700	91	ON Semiconductor	1,636
42	Consolidated Electrical Distributors	2,600	92	Brookshire Grocery	1,625
43	Raley's	2,600	93	84 Lumber	1,625
44	Southern Wine & Spirits	2,600	94	BDO International	1,610
45	International Data Group	2,560	95	Booz, Allen & Hamilton	1,600
46	Perdue Farms	2,515	96	Central National-Gottesman	1,600
47	MBM	2,500	97	Grant Thornton	1,600
48	McKinsey & Co	2,500	98	Leprino Foods	1,600
49	Renco Group	2,500	99	Parsons Corp	1,600
50	Venture Industries	2,500	100	Quality King Distributors	1,600

Source: *Forbes;* December 13, 1999

The *Forbes* 500 Largest Private Companies in the US (continued)

Rank	Company	Revenues ($ mil.)	Rank	Company	Revenues ($ mil.)
101	Alex Lee	1,588	151	Ebsco Industries	1,200
102	Packaging Corp of America	1,571	152	IMG	1,200
103	Flying J	1,562	153	Life Care Centers of America	1,200
104	Haworth	1,540	154	S&P Co	1,200
105	JM Huber	1,536	155	Sierra Pacific Industries	1,200
106	Metromedia	1,525	156	Sinclair Oil	1,200
107	Clark Enterprises	1,500	157	Tang Industries	1,200
108	Day & Zimmermann	1,500	158	Taylor	1,200
109	Purity Wholesale Grocers	1,500	159	DiGiorgio	1,197
110	Structure Tone	1,500	160	Dillingham Construction	1,189
111	Comark	1,478	161	Domino's Pizza	1,177
112	Schottenstein Stores	1,475	162	DPR Construction	1,175
113	Bridge	1,470	163	Packerland Packing	1,174
114	Save Mart Supermarkets	1,452	164	Asplundh Tree Expert	1,172
115	WL Gore & Associates	1,450	165	Beaulieu of America Group	1,169
116	Edward Jones	1,450	166	Hensel Phelps Construction	1,165
117	Republic Technologies Intl	1,450	167	ABC Supply	1,162
118	AG Spanos Companies	1,440	168	Sheetz	1,161
119	Borden	1,400	169	Schreiber Foods	1,155
120	Clark Retail Enterprises	1,400	170	Wawa	1,147
121	Quad/Graphics	1,400	171	Riverwood International	1,136
122	Rich Products	1,400	172	Cumberland Farms	1,135
123	Simpson Investment	1,400	173	SF Holdings Group	1,130
124	Southwire	1,400	174	Ingram Entertainment	1,125
125	RaceTrac Petroleum	1,395	175	Mary Kay	1,125
126	Transammonia	1,386	176	Crowley Maritime	1,114
127	Maritz	1,378	177	Baker & Taylor	1,112
128	Grocers Supply	1,375	178	Connell Limited Partnership	1,110
129	Services Group of America	1,375	179	Kinray	1,110
130	Amsted Industries	1,370	180	Jordan Industries	1,106
131	Fry's Electronics	1,360	181	CC Industries	1,100
132	E&J Gallo Winery	1,350	182	Dart Container	1,100
133	Ty	1,350	183	Heico Companies LLC	1,100
134	DHL Airways	1,348	184	Kingston Technology	1,100
135	Whiting-Turner Contracting	1,340	185	Wilbur-Ellis	1,100
136	Pilot	1,312	186	Young's Market	1,090
137	Berwind Group	1,300	187	GAF	1,088
138	Delaware North Companies	1,300	188	Shamrock Foods	1,081
139	Dade Behring	1,285	189	Hewitt Associates	1,075
140	National Distributing	1,275	190	Nesco	1,075
141	Duchossois Industries	1,265	191	Dunavant Enterprises	1,065
142	General Parts	1,248	192	TravelCenters of America	1,061
143	Follett	1,240	193	Bashas'	1,050
144	DynCorp	1,234	194	GSC Enterprises	1,050
145	Micro Electronics	1,230	195	Minyard Food Stores	1,050
146	Towers Perrin	1,230	196	Express Services	1,040
147	Quality Stores	1,225	197	Huber Hunt & Nichols	1,039
148	Advance Holding	1,221	198	L.L. Bean	1,033
149	Builders FirstSource	1,220	199	Flint Ink	1,030
150	United Defense LP	1,218	200	Lanoga	1,027

The *Forbes* 500 Largest Private Companies in the US (continued)

Rank	Company	Revenues ($ mil.)	Rank	Company	Revenues ($ mil.)
201	MTS	1,026	251	Dunn Industries	871
202	Outboard Marine	1,026	252	SAS Institute	871
203	Swagelok	1,025	253	Swifty Serve	867
204	Royster-Clark	1,020	254	TAC Worldwide Cos.	863
205	UIS	1,020	255	MacManus Group	860
206	MediaNews Group	1,010	256	Walsh Group	860
207	Big Y Foods	1,007	257	PMC Global	859
208	Tishman Realty & Construction	1,005	258	Wherehouse Entertainment	858
209	Honickman Affiliates	1,000	259	Community Health Systems	855
210	SC Johnson Commercial Markets	1,000	260	Gould Paper	855
211	Foster Farms	995	261	McKee Foods	855
212	Aecom Technology	990	262	ICC Industries	850
213	Coca-Cola Bottling Co of Chicago	975	263	McCarthy	850
214	North Pacific Group	970	264	Roseburg Forest Products	850
215	Crown Equipment	968	265	Printpack	846
216	North American Van Lines	967	266	RB Pamplin	844
217	BE&K	960	267	Manufacturers' Services	838
218	American Bottling	955	268	Stevedoring Services of America	835
219	Menasha	952	269	GS Industries	832
220	Bose	950	270	Barnes & Noble College Bookstores	830
221	Knoll	949	271	Vitality Beverages	825
222	Parsons Brinckerhoff	945	272	Wirtz	825
223	Hartz Group	940	273	J. Crew Group	824
224	WinCo Foods	940	274	Barton Malow	820
225	ViewSonic	939	275	M. Fabrikant & Sons	820
226	Leo Burnett	934	276	Fiesta Mart	820
227	Parkdale Mills	934	277	OmniSource	820
228	Motor Coach Industries Intl	932	278	Sunbelt Beverage	820
229	Discount Tire	931	279	Hale-Halsell	815
230	O'Neal Steel	930	280	Big V Supermarkets	814
231	CH2M Hill Companies	927	281	Dot Foods	814
232	Carpenter	925	282	Austin Industries	808
233	Rooney Brothers	925	283	Gantrade	800
234	Club Corporation International	918	284	Ilitch Ventures	800
235	Earle M Jorgensen	916	285	Inductotherm Industries	800
236	Boscov's Department Stores	915	286	Knowledge Universe	800
237	Watkins Associated Industries	915	287	Mark III Industries	800
238	Glazer's Wholesale Distributors	910	288	Newark Group	800
239	MA Mortenson	904	289	Red Apple Group	800
240	Swinerton	902	290	Sanford C Bernstein & Co	800
241	Battelle Memorial Institute	901	291	Variety Wholesalers	800
242	Opus Group of Companies	900	292	Parsons & Whittemore	790
243	Spear Leeds & Kellogg LLC	900	293	Conair	787
244	Sealy	891	294	Ben E Keith	787
245	Skadden, Arps, Slate, Meagher & Flom	890	295	Ormet	780
246	Arctic Slope Regional	888	296	Grove Worldwide	775
247	Avondale	881	297	Sutherland Lumber	775
248	Chemcentral	880	298	K-VA-T Food Stores	773
249	Safelite Glass	876	299	DeBruce Grain	772
250	Baker & McKenzie	875	300	Horsehead Industries	770

The *Forbes* 500 Largest Private Companies in the US (continued)

Rank	Company	Revenues ($ mil.)	Rank	Company	Revenues ($ mil.)
301	Pella	770	351	Holiday Retirement	675
302	WWF Paper	768	352	Walbridge, Aldinger	675
303	Iasis Healthcare	765	353	Turner Industries	673
304	Watson Wyatt Worldwide	761	354	Tutor-Saliba	673
305	Medline Industries	756	355	Koppers Industries	671
306	Genuardi's Family Markets	754	356	Brookshire Brothers Ltd	670
307	Topa Equities	754	357	Cameron & Barkley	670
308	Hunt Consolidated/Hunt Oil	750	358	HB Zachry	670
309	Inserra Supermarkets	750	359	El Camino Resources	668
310	Les Schwab Tire Centers	745	360	Hobby Lobby Creative Centers	665
311	Washington Cos	744	361	Modern Continental Cos	665
312	Shapell Industries	743	362	RTM Restaurant Group	664
313	Golden Rule Financial	742	363	Steiner	655
314	Specialty Foods	742	364	Ashley Furniture Industries	650
315	Simplex Time Recorder	736	365	Columbia Forest Products	650
316	Freedom Communications	735	366	Feld Entertainment	650
317	HomeLife	735	367	Green Bay Packaging	650
318	Drummond	734	368	Landmark Communicaitons	650
319	Favorite Brands International	733	369	Ritz Camera Centers	650
320	FreshPoint	732	370	International Wire Group	646
321	Journal Communications	732	371	Maxxim Medical	645
322	McJunkin	731	372	American Commercial Lines	639
323	ASI	730	373	ACF Industries	638
324	Boston Consulting Group	730	374	American Golf	638
325	National Textiles LLC	727	375	Grede Foundries	633
326	CenTra	725	376	Soave Enterprises	630
327	Roll International	725	377	Leiner Health Products Group	627
328	Sherwood Food Distributors	725	378	Darby Group Companies	625
329	American Century Investments	720	379	Joan Fabrics	625
330	Marnell Corrao Associates	718	380	Peerless Importers	625
331	Great Lakes Cheese	717	381	TTC Illinois	625
332	Deseret Management	715	382	Genman Holdings	619
333	Icon Health & Fitness	710	383	Lifetouch	612
334	King Kullen Grocery	710	384	Concentra Managed Care	611
335	MTD Products	710	385	Arthur D Little	610
336	Regal Cinemas	707	386	TRT Holdings	610
337	Borden Foods Holdings	706	387	AFC Enterprises	609
338	Bartlett and Co.	705	388	David Weekley Homes	608
339	Charmer Industries	705	389	Builder Marts of America	607
340	Rooms to Go	705	390	LDI	605
341	Goya Foods	700	391	Dawn Food Products	603
342	Longaberger	700	392	RAB Holdings	602
343	Platinum Equity Holdings	700	393	Simmons	601
344	Sarcom	700	394	Celotex	600
345	Georgia Crown Distributing	697	395	Empire Beef	600
346	Everett Smith Group	695	396	Forever Living Products Intl	600
347	S Abraham & Sons	693	397	Meridian Automotive Systems	600
348	Pepper Cos	690	398	Quality Distribution	600
349	Doane Pet Care Enterprises	687	399	Rosen's Diversified	600
350	Bozzuto's	685	400	Russell Stover Candies	600

The *Forbes* 500 Largest Private Companies in the US (continued)

Rank	Company	Revenues ($ mil.)	Rank	Company	Revenues ($ mil.)
401	BancTec	598	451	Marathon Cheese	540
402	Alberici	595	452	Morris Communications	540
403	Marc Glassman	595	453	PC Richard & Son	540
404	Oxford Automotive	592	454	Weitz	540
405	Houchens Industries	590	455	Clark Material Handling	539
406	Ingersoll International	590	456	Oxbow	535
407	Kraus-Anderson	590	457	TIC-The Industrial Company	534
408	McWane	590	458	Corning Consumer Products	533
409	Murphy Family Farms	590	459	Intersil	533
410	Warren Equities	587	460	Hardin Construction Group	531
411	Perry H Koplik & Sons	582	461	Bain & Co.	530
412	Cook Group	580	462	Findlay Industries	530
413	Pacific Coast Building Products	580	463	Jones, Day, Reavis & Pogue	530
414	Utility Trailer Manufacturing	580	464	Ukrop's Super Markets	530
415	JC Bradford	578	465	Wells' Dairy	530
416	Guide	575	466	Hoffman	527
417	HBE	575	467	Harold Levinson Associates	526
418	HomePlace of America	575	468	E-Z Mart Stores	525
419	Cinemark USA	571	469	Hampton Affiliates	525
420	Gilman Investment	570	470	Ris Paper	525
421	Henkels & McCoy	570	471	Rocco	525
422	Brasfield & Gorrie	566	472	Scotty's	525
423	Copps	565	473	Sundt Companies	525
424	Rudolph & Sletten	565	474	F Dohmen	524
425	Moyer Packing	562	475	Bradco Supply	523
426	Carter Jones Cos	560	476	Dynatech	523
427	Fairchild Aerospace	556	477	Fellowes Manufacturing	523
428	Pitman	556	478	Unicco Service	522
429	Suffolk Construction	556	479	Haggen	521
430	Beck Group	555	480	American Color Graphics	520
431	Fareway Stores	555	481	Federal Data	520
432	Goss Graphic Systems	555	482	Pacific Holding	520
433	LDM Technologies	553	483	Estes Express Lines	519
434	National Wine & Spirits	553	484	Atlas World Group	512
435	Dick Corp.	552	485	FNC Holdings	512
436	American Cast Iron Pipe	550	486	American Foods Group	510
437	Bellco Health	550	487	Atrium Companies	510
438	Chef America	550	488	Montgomery Watson	510
439	Formica	550	489	Hudson Group	508
440	Greenwood Mills	550	490	CIC International Ltd	505
441	Johnson Brothers Wholesale Liquor	550	491	Danner Companies	505
442	Kiel Brothers Oil Co	550	492	Rodale	505
443	Krueger International	550	493	Koch Enterprises	504
444	McNaughton-McKay Electric	550	494	Latham & Watkins	502
445	United Supermarkets	550	495	Spalding Holdings	501
446	Team Health	548	496	Academy	500
447	Webcor Builders	548	497	Elkay Manufacturing	500
448	Jockey International	545	498	Flint Industries	500
449	Sauder Woodworking	545	499	Charles Levy	500
450	Ampacet	540	500	State Industries	500

Top 25 US Foundations

Rank	Name	State	Assets ($ mil.)
1	Lilly Endowment Inc.	Indiana	15,780.3
2	The Ford Foundation	New York	9,654.9
3	The David and Lucile Packard Foundation	California	9,527.9
4	J. Paul Getty Trust	California	8,002.9
5	The Robert Wood Johnson Foundation	New Jersey	6,734.9
6	W. K. Kellogg Foundation	Michigan	5,549.2
7	The Pew Charitable Trusts	Pennsylvania	4,734.2
8	John D. and Catherine T. MacArthur Foundation	Illinois	4,030.1
9	Robert W. Woodruff Foundation, Inc.	Georgia	3,677.1
10	The Andrew W. Mellon Foundation	New York	3,431.5
11	The Annenberg Foundation	Pennsylvania	3,349.1
12	The Rockefeller Foundation	New York	3,094.7
13	The Starr Foundation	New York	2,541.6
14	Charles Stewart Mott Foundation	Michigan	2,346.5
15	The Duke Endowment	North Carolina	2,108.0
16	The Kresge Foundation	Michigan	2,103.0
17	The McKnight Foundation	Minnesota	1,890.0
18	The Harry and Jeanette Weinberg Foundation, Inc.	Maryland	1,845.1
19	The William and Flora Hewlett Foundation	California	1,766.6
20	The California Endowment	California	1,759.5
21	The New York Company Trust	New York	1,759.0
22	Ewing Marion Kauffman Foundation	Missouri	1,650.0
23	The Annie E. Casey Foundation	Maryland	1,569.1
24	Robert R. McCormick Tribune Foundation	Illinois	1,555.1
25	Richard King Mellon Foundation	Pennsylvania	1,531.3

Source: The Foundation Center; fdncenter.org; December 20, 1999

Top 10 Mutual Companies

Rank	Mutual	Revenues ($ mil.)
1	State Farm Mutual Auto Ins Co	27,201
2	Metropolitan Life Ins Co	21,215
3	Prudential Ins Co of America	19,146
4	Northwestern Mutual Life Ins Co	12,360
5	New York Life Ins Co	9,839
6	Massachusetts Mutual Life Ins	7,548
7	Nationwide Mutual Ins Co	6,600
8	Guardian Life Ins Co of America	6,598
9	Principal Life Ins Co	6,556
10	Liberty Mutual Ins Co	5,573

Source: *Forbes;* December 13, 1999

Top 10 Cooperatives

Rank	Cooperative	Revenues ($ mil.)
1	Farmland Industries	8,775
2	Cenex Harvest States	7,959
3	Dairy Farmers of America	7,325
4	Land O'Lakes	5,174
5	Wakefern Food	5,159
6	TruServ	4,328
7	Topco Associates	4,000
8	Associated Wholesale Grocers	3,180
9	Ace Hardware	3,120
10	Ag Processing	2,615

Source: *Forbes;* December 13, 1999

Top 25 Universities

Rank	School
1	California Institute of Technology
2	Harvard University
3	Massachusetts Institute of Technology
4	Princeton University
4	Yale University
6	Stanford University
7	Duke University
7	Johns Hopkins University
7	University of Pennsylvania
10	Columbia University
11	Cornell University
11	Dartmouth College
13	University of Chicago
14	Brown University
14	Northwestern University
14	Rice University
17	Washington University in St. Louis
18	Emory University
19	University of Notre Dame
20	University of California — Berkeley
20	Vanderbilt University
22	University of Virginia
23	Carnegie Mellon University
23	Georgetown University
25	University of California — Los Angeles
25	University of Michigan — Ann Arbor

Ranked by composite score, including such factors as graduation and retention rates, faculty resources, and student/faculty ratio.

Source: *U.S. News and World Report;* August 30, 1999

Top 25 Public Universities

Rank	School
1	University of California — Berkeley
2	University of Virginia
3	University of California — Los Angeles
3	University of Michigan — Ann Arbor
5	University of North Carolina — Chapel Hill
6	College of William and Mary
7	University of California — San Diego
8	University of Illinois — Urbana-Champaign
8	University of Wisconsin — Madison
10	Georgia Institute of Technology
10	Pennsylvania State University
12	University of California — Davis
13	University of California — Santa Barbara
13	University of Texas — Austin
13	University of Washington
16	University of California — Irvine
16	University of Florida
18	Purdue University — West Lafayette
18	Texas A&M University — College Station
18	University of Minnesota — Twin Cities
21	University of Iowa
22	Miami University — Oxford
22	Rutgers — New Brunswick
22	SUNY — Binghamton
22	University of Delaware
22	University of Georgia
22	University of Maryland — College Park

Ranked by composite score, including such factors as graduation and retention rates, faculty resources, and student/faculty ratio.

Source: *U.S. News and World Report;* August 30, 1999

Top 10 Health Care Systems by Net Patient Revenues

Rank	System	Revenues ($ mil.)
1	U. S. Department of Veterans Affairs	20,027.1
2	Columbia/HCA Healthcare Corp.	18,681.0
3	Tenet Healthcare Corp.	8,821.0
4	Catholic Health Initiatives	4,587.3
5	New York City Health and Hospitals Corp.	3,834.5
6	Daughters of Charity National Health System	3,767.4
7	Catholic Healthcare West	3,301.3
8	New York Presbyterian Healthcare Network	3,238.0
9	Sisters of Mercy Health System-St. Louis	2,169.2
10	North Shore-Long Island Jewish Health System	2,164.9

Source: *Modern Healthcare;* May 24, 1999

American Lawyer's Top 25 US Law Firms

Rank	Firm	Number of Lawyers	Gross Revenues ($ mil.)
1	Skadden, Arps, Slate, Meagher & Flom	1,187	890.0
2	Baker & McKenzie	2,330	784.0
3	Jones, Day, Reavis & Pogue	1,164	530.0
4	Latham & Watkins	832	502.0
5	Davis Polk & Wardwell	464	435.0
6	Sullivan & Cromwell	454	426.5
7	Shearman & Sterling	683	425.5
8	Sidley & Austin	783	421.0
9	Mayer, Brown & Platt	765	400.0
10	Weil, Gotshal & Manges	640	399.5
11	Morgan, Lewis & Bockius	907	397.0
12	McDermott, Will & Emery	752	389.5
13	Simpson Thacher & Bartlett	490	386.0
14	Gibson, Dunn & Crutcher	603	374.0
15	Cleary, Gottlieb, Steen & Hamilton	492	366.0
16	White & Case	742	351.5
17	Cravath, Swaine & Moore	334	334.0
18	O'Melveny & Myers	635	328.0
19	Kirkland & Ellis	542	310.0
20	Akin, Gump, Strauss, Hauer & Feld	741	301.0
21	Fulbright & Jaworski	641	282.5
22	Vinson & Elkins	561	281.5
23	LeBoeuf, Lamb, Greene & MacRae	674	280.0
24	Foley & Lardner	693	277.0
25	Morrison & Foerster	614	274.0

Source: *American Lawyer;* July 6, 1999

Top 7 Accounting Firms

Rank	Company	Employees	Revenues ($ mil.)
1	PricewaterhouseCoopers	150,000	17,300
2	Andersen Worldwide	140,000	16,200
3	Ernst & Young	97,800	12,500
4	KPMG	102,000	12,200
5	Deloitte Touche Tohmatsu	97,500	10,800
6	BDO International	17,500	1,610
7	Grant Thornton	21,400	1,600

Source: *Forbes;* December 13, 1999

Hoover's Handbook of Private Companies

THE COMPANIES PROFILED

84 LUMBER COMPANY

OVERVIEW

84 = 2x4s. Based in Eighty Four, Pennsylvania, 84 Lumber sells lumber and do-it-yourself (DIY) kits for kitchens, garages, decks, and even entire homes through about 390 stores. The stores (or lumberyards, depending on your view) are located mostly in the eastern US, the Southeast, and the Midwest. The outlets adhere to the company's unwritten motto, "no frills, no fringes, and no heat" (most 84 Lumber outlets have no heating or air conditioning).

The company is re-emphasizing its spartan business plan. Founded to serve professionals, 84 Lumber expanded its product offering to attract more DIY consumers. It has since re-shifted its focus to professional builders, which account for about three-fourths of sales. The rest of sales are in the DIY and commercial building segments. While the contractor market is less profitable and more cyclic than the DIY segment, it has the advantage of being less crowded with heavy competitors such as The Home Depot. 84 Lumber plans to open some 50 stores a year until 2002.

President Maggie Hardy Magerko, daughter of CEO and founder Joseph Hardy Sr., owns 80% of the company.

HISTORY

In 1956 Joseph Hardy Sr. opened the first 84 Lumber store in Eighty Four, Pennsylvania, a town near Pittsburgh. (The town was named to honor the year Grover Cleveland was elected president.) Hardy epitomized the bare-bones approach, keeping a tight rein on his company (he once ordered the office staff to weed the company headquarters lawn), paying cash for new building sites (he was known to lowball landowners by dressing like a simple country hick), and driving to work in an old car.

The strategy was successful, and for the next two decades 84 Lumber prospered, growing steadily to more than 350 stores in the early 1980s under Hardy's reign. But the 1980s brought trouble, not only for 84 Lumber but also within the Hardy family. Paul Hardy, the second-eldest son, left the company after continued sparring with Hardy Sr. Another son, Joe Hardy Jr., seemed to be his father's handpicked successor: He had worked for 84 Lumber since 1967, rising to the level of COO. However, Joe Jr. and Joe Sr. clashed and under pressure from his father, Joe Jr. angrily resigned in 1988 and went on to run a real estate development company outside Pittsburgh.

Joe Sr. also underwent a transformation during this time, opening his once-tight purse strings to buy himself an honorary English title — lord of the manor of Henley-in-Arden — for about $170,000. He also spent $10 million to amass an art collection, and in 1987 he paid $3.1 million to purchase a retreat in southwestern Pennsylvania, the Nemacolin Woodlands. He placed the renovation of the resort (at the cost of some $100 million) in the hands of his daughter Maggie, who was in her early twenties at the time.

While Hardy was transforming, so was 84 Lumber. The company started moving away from its traditional approach in an attempt to gain a piece of the budding yuppie market. This approach, along with an ill-timed expansion, led to a loss of customers and falling profits. Earnings fell from $52 million in 1987 to $22 million in 1989.

84 Lumber started to right itself in 1991. Hardy transferred stock to Maggie, his heir apparent. While running luxury resort Nemacolin Woodlands, Maggie strove to emulate her father's business style, including obscenity-laced staff meetings. 84 Lumber shut stores and returned to its basic operating scheme as a low-cost provider of lumber in small towns. The company also added do-it-yourself (DIY) building kits for kitchens and baths that year, and it expanded that DIY concept a year later in 1992, with home building kits (land not included).

Under new president Maggie, 84 Lumber's sales topped the $1 billion mark in 1993 and the company refocused on its professional contractor customers. The company first shipped its building materials internationally in 1996 (to New Zealand) and added customers in Australia, China, Korea, and Switzerland in the late 1990s.

In 1997 84 Lumber opened Maggie's Building Solutions Showroom, a 7,500-sq.-ft. remodeling center featuring upscale home products. By 1997 84 Lumber was the US's largest dealer of building supplies to professional contractors.

In a further effort to attract contractors' business, 84 Lumber introduced a builder financing program in 1999 and began converting some of its stores to an 84 Plus store format, in which its traditional lumberyard setup is matched with a 10,000-sq.-ft. hardware store. The company opened a 17,000-sq.-ft Maggie's Building Solutions Showroom in 1999.

CEO: Joseph A. Hardy Sr.
President: Maggie Hardy Magerko
COO: Bill Myrick
CFO: Dan Wallach
VP Operations: Frank Cicero
VP Purchasing: Jason Burnett
VP Marketing: Rick Campbell
VP Human Resources: Mark Mollico

LOCATIONS

HQ: Rte. 519, Eighty Four, PA 15384
Phone: 724-228-8820   **Fax:** 724-228-4145
Web site: http://www.84lumber.com

84 Lumber operates stores in 30 states and sells its products in Australia, China, New Zealand, South Korea, and Switzerland.

1998 Store Locations

Alabama	Michigan
Arizona	Mississippi
California	Missouri
Colorado	New Jersey
Connecticut	New Mexico
Delaware	New York
Florida	North Carolina
Georgia	Ohio
Illinois	Pennsylvania
Indiana	South Carolina
Kansas	Tennessee
Kentucky	Texas
Louisiana	Virginia
Maryland	West Virginia
Massachusetts	Wyoming

PRODUCTS/OPERATIONS

Selected Products

Doors	Garages
Drywall	Houses
Flooring	Kitchens
Insulation	Playsets
Lumber	Roofing
Construction	Room additions
Engineered	Siding
Treated	Skylights
Paneling	Trim
Plywood	Trusses
Pole barns	Ventilation
Project kits	Vinyl siding
Barns (pole and storage)	Windows
Decks	

COMPETITORS

Ace Hardware
Building Materials Holding
Carolina Holdings
Contractors' Warehouse
Home Depot
Lowe's
Menard
Payless Cashways
Sutherland Lumber
TruServ
Wickes

HISTORICAL FINANCIALS & EMPLOYEES

Private FYE: December	Annual Growth	1989	1990	1991	1992	1993	1994	1995	1996	1997	1998
Sales ($ mil.)	10.4%	—	—	—	898	1,060	1,275	1,275	1,590	1,600	1,625
Employees	5.5%	—	—	—	3,200	3,500	3,500	3,500	4,500	4,815	4,400

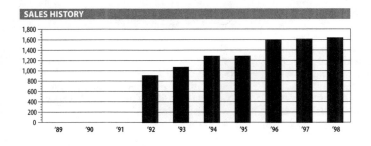

SALES HISTORY

AARP

AARP: It's not just for retired people anymore. The Washington, DC-based association is the nation's largest organization for the improvement of life for older Americans with about 33 million members, 40% of whom still work. Anyone 50 years or older can be a member ($8 annual dues) and receive services from or contribute to the not-for-profit organization's four main areas of activity: information and education, community service, advocacy, and member services. AARP disseminates information in a variety of formats (a Web site, forums, radio and TV spots, *Modern Maturity* magazine) and pursues educational and research efforts through the AARP Andrus Foundation, the Research Information Center, and the Public Policy Institute.

AARP may not be the most exclusive club around, but it is one of the most powerful. One of the largest lobbying groups in the US, the organization spends more than $40 million a year on lobbying and related activities. AARP, which has about 4,000 chapters across the US, is attempting to transform itself as baby boomers age and become eligible for membership. The organization is adapting to its changing demographics by issuing different editions of *Modern Maturity* for age-specific groups and offering seminars geared toward younger members.

AARP members are eligible for services including savings on health, life, and auto insurance; prescription drugs; mutual funds; and credit cards. Retired educators who join the National Retired Teachers Association (a division of AARP) can receive both AARP services and other benefits designed specifically for them.

Ethel Andrus, a retired Los Angeles high school principal who founded the National Retired Teachers Association (NRTA) in 1947, founded the American Association of Retired Persons (AARP) in 1958 with the help of Leonard Davis, a New York insurance salesman who had helped her find an underwriter for the NRTA. The new organization's goal: to "enhance the quality of life" for older Americans and "improve the image of aging."

Andrus offered members the same low rates for health and accident insurance provided to NRTA members. She also started publishing AARP's bimonthly magazine, *Modern Maturity*, in 1958. The organization's first local chapter opened in Youngstown, Arizona, in 1960. Still an insurance man, Davis formed Colonial Penn Insurance in 1963 to take over the AARP account. Andrus led the AARP and its increasingly powerful lobby for the elderly until her death in 1967.

With criticism of Colonial Penn mounting in the 1970s (critics charged the organization was little more than a front for the insurance company), Prudential won AARP's insurance business in 1979. The NRTA merged with AARP in 1982, and the following year it lowered the membership eligibility age from 55 to 50. The organization continued to expand its offerings, adding an auto club and financial products such as mutual funds and expanded insurance policies. The organization also started a federal credit union for members in 1988, but despite rosy projections, it ceased operations two years later.

AARP forked over $135 million to the IRS in 1993 as part of a settlement regarding the tax status of profits from some of its activities, but the dispute remained unresolved. AARP switched insurance providers again in 1996 (New York Life) and started offering discounted legal services. Also that year, AARP said it would let HMOs offer managed-care services to members. After drawing objections from government officials and HMOs for the plan's potential violation of Medicare anti-kickback laws, AARP devised a payment plan in 1997 based on the estimated numbers of potential AARP members in an HMO's market area.

AARP's image was bruised in 1998 when Dale Van Atta wrote a scathing account of the organization, *Trust Betrayed: Inside the AARP.* The book accused the organization of operating out of lavish accommodations, being a vehicle for businesses to hawk their wares, and concealing a drop in membership. AARP said the book was riddled with factual errors and unsubstantiated claims. Also in 1998, recognizing that nearly a third of its members were working, the organization dropped the American Association of Retired Persons moniker and began to refer to itself by the AARP abbreviation.

To end the long-running dispute with the IRS, in 1999 AARP reached a settlement over its alleged profit-making enterprises by creating a new taxable subsidiary called AARP Services.

Chairman: Allan W. Tull
VC: John G. Lione
President: Joseph S. Perkins
President-elect: Esther Canja
CFO: Jocelyn Davis
Executive Director: Horace Deets
Chief of Staff: Cheryl Cooper
Associate Executive Director Operations:
Richard Henry
Associate Executive Director Field Operations:
Tom Nelson
Director Audit and Advisory Services:
Mary Ann Riesenberg
Chief Information Officer: Vida Durant
Secretary and Treasurer: Kenneth Huff Sr.
Director Administration and Membership Operations:
Jim Laney
Director Advocacy and Management: Kevin Donnellan
Director Communications: Jim Holland
Director Human Resources: J. Robert Carr
Director Legislation and Public Policy: John Rother
Director Program Development: Anne Harvey
Director Publications: Martha Ramsey
General Counsel: Joan Wise
Auditors: Arthur Andersen LLP

HQ: 601 E St. NW, Washington, DC 20049
Phone: 202-434-2277   **Fax:** 202-434-2525
Web site: http://www.aarp.org

1998 Sales

	$ mil.	% of total
Membership dues	137.1	29
Administrative allowance	107.7	23
Programs & royalties	90.5	19
Investment income	71.7	15
Publication advertising	63.6	13
Other	0.9	1
Total	**471.5**	**100**

Selected Community Service Programs
AARP 55 ALIVE/Mature Driving
AARP Connections for Independent Living
AARP Grief and Loss Programs
AARP Tax-Aide
AARP Telemarketing Fraud Campaign
AARP VOTE: Voter Education Campaign
Independent Living: How to Help

Selected Member Benefits

Discount programs	AARP Health Care
Airlines	Options
America Online	AARP Homeowners
Auto rentals	Insurance from The
CompuServe	Hartford
Cruise lines	AARP Legal Services
Flowers	Network
Hotels, motels,	AARP Life Insurance
and resorts	from New York Life
MSN Internet	AARP Mobile Home
Prodigy Internet	Insurance from
Sightseeing	Foremost
Services	AARP Motoring Plan
AARP Auto Insurance	from Amoco
from The Hartford	AARP Pharmacy Service
AARP Credit Card from	from Retired Persons
First USA Bank	Services

Selected Publications
AARP Bulletin
Modern Maturity

NCSC
The Seniors Coalition
United Seniors Association

Association FYE: December	Annual Growth	1989	1990	1991	1992	1993	1994	1995	1996	1997	1998
Sales ($ mil.)	5.5%	291	296	297	305	369	469	506	475	529	471
Employees	3.0%	1,532	1,593	1,635	1,718	1,793	1,752	1,800	1,850	1,900	2,000

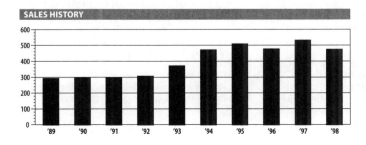

SALES HISTORY

ACE HARDWARE CORPORATION

OVERVIEW

Luckily, Ace has John Madden up its sleeve. Despite the growth of warehouse-style competitors, Ace Hardware has remained a household name, thanks to ads featuring the well-known football commentator (an appropriate choice considering the company primarily targets men). The Oak Brook, Illinois-based company is the US's #2 hardware cooperative, behind TruServ (operator of True Value and several other hardware chains). Ace dealer-owners operate about 5,100 Ace Hardware stores throughout the US

and in more than 60 other countries. The company provides a number of member services, including advertising, insurance, purchasing incentives, and training.

Ace buys in bulk and distributes products, such as electrical and plumbing supplies, power tools, garden equipment, and housewares, to its members through about 20 warehouses nationwide. It also makes its own brand of paint and offer thousands of other Ace-brand products. Ace dealers own the company and receive dividends from Ace's profits.

HISTORY

A group of Chicago-area hardware dealers — Frank Burke, Richard Hesse, E. Gunnard Lindquist, and Oscar Fisher — decided in 1924 to pool their hardware buying and promotional costs. In 1928 the group incorporated as Ace Stores. Hesse became president the following year, retaining that position for the next 44 years. The company also opened its first warehouse in 1929, and by 1933 it had 38 dealers. That year Ace held its first convention so dealers could review and purchase merchandise.

The organization had 133 dealers in seven states by 1949. In 1953 Ace began to allow dealers to buy stock in the company through the Ace Perpetuation Plan. During the 1960s Ace expanded into the South and West, and by 1969 it had opened distribution centers in Georgia and California — its first such facilities outside Chicago.

By the early 1970s the do-it-yourself market began to surge as inflation pushed up plumber and electrician fees. As the market grew, large home center chains gobbled up market share from independent dealers such as those franchised through Ace. In response, Ace and its dealers became a part of a growing trend in the hardware industry — cooperatives.

Hesse sold the company to its dealers in 1973 for $6 million (less than half its book value), and the following year Ace began operating as a cooperative. Hesse stepped down in 1973 and Arthur Krausman became head of the co-op. In 1976 the dealers took full control when the company's first Board of Dealer-Directors was elected.

Two years later the co-op signed up a number of dealers in the eastern US. By 1979 it had dealers in all 50 states. Ace implemented an aggressive building program the following year to add more distribution centers to serve its growing network of dealers.

The co-op opened a paint plant in Matteson, Illinois, in 1984 and began making its own paint. By 1985 Ace had reached $1 billion in sales and had initiated its Store of the Future Program, allowing dealers to borrow up to $200,000 to upgrade their stores and conduct market analyses. Football commentator John Madden began representing the firm in 1988.

A year later the co-op began to test ACENET, a computer network that allowed Ace dealers to check inventory, send and receive e-mail, make special purchase requests, and keep up with prices on commodity items such as lumber. Also in 1989 it began an annual Lumber & Building Materials convention.

In 1990 Ace established an International Division to handle its overseas stores (it had been exporting products since 1975). EVP and COO David Hodnik was named president in 1995. That year the co-op added a net of 67 stores, including a three-store chain in Russia, and it added an additional 60 stores in 1996. (Since then growth has been stagnant.) Expanding further internationally, Ace signed a five-year joint-supply agreement in 1996 with Canadian lumber and hardware retailer Beaver Lumber. Hodnik added CEO to his title in 1996.

Ace fell further behind its old rival, True Value, in 1997 when SERVISTAR and True Value merged to form TruServ, a hardware giant that operated more than 10,000 outlets at the completion of the merger.

Late in 1997 Ace launched an expansion program in Canada. (The co-op already operated distribution centers in Ontario and Calgary.) In 1999 Ace merged its lumber and building materials division with Builder Marts of America to form a dealer-owned buying group to supply about 2,700 retailers.

Chairman: Howard J. Jung, age 51
President and CEO: David F. Hodnik, age 51,
$600,000 pay
EVP Retail: William A. Loftus, age 60
SVP International and Technology:
Paul M. Ingevaldson, age 53
SVP Wholesale: Rita D. Kahle, age 42
VP Sales and Marketing: Michael C. Bodzewski, age 48
VP and Controller: Lori L. Bossmann, age 38
VP Merchandise: Ray A. Griffith, age 45
VP, General Counsel, and Secretary: David W. League,
age 59
VP Retail Support: David F. Myer, age 53
VP Human Resources: Fred J. Neer, age 59
VP Information Technology: Donald L. Schuman, age 60
Auditors: KPMG LLP

LOCATIONS

HQ: 2200 Kensington Ct., Oak Brook, IL 60523
Phone: 630-990-6600   **Fax:** 630-990-6838
Web site: http://www.acehardware.com

Ace Hardware wholesales products to dealers with retail
operations in the US and more than 60 other countries.

1998 Sales

	$ mil.	% of total
US	2,904	93
Other countries	216	7
Total	**3,120**	**100**

PRODUCTS/OPERATIONS

1998 Sales

	% of total
Paint, cleaning & related supplies	20
Plumbing & heating supplies	15
Hand & power tools	14
Electrical supplies	13
Garden, rural equipment & related supplies	13
General hardware	12
Sundries	7
Housewares & appliances	6
Total	**100**

Selected Services

Mail/office
  Bridal registry
  Care mail
  Fax service
  Film processing
  Photocopies
  Utility payments
Repair Work
  Bikes
  Chainsaws
  Lamps
  Power equipment and
    tools
  Screens and windows
  Vacuums
  VCRs

Specialty Services
  Delivery
  Hunting/fishing licenses
  Key cutting and lock
    servicing
  Pipe cutting and
    threading
  Rentals
  Trophies/engraving
Miscellaneous
  Gift certificates
  Live bait
  Pool water and soil
    testing

Subsidiaries

Ace Corporate Stores (operations of company-owned
  stores)
Ace Hardware Canada (hardware wholesaler in Canada)
Ace Insurance Agency (dealer insurance program)
A.H.C. Store Development Corp. (operations of
  company-owned stores)
Loss Prevention Services (security training and loss
  prevention services for dealers)

COMPETITORS

84 Lumber
Akzo Nobel
Benjamin Moore
Building Materials
  Holding
Carolina Holdings
Costco Companies
D.I.Y. Home Warehouse
Do it Best
Grossman's
Home Depot
HomeBase
ICI Americas
Kmart
Lanoga
Lowe's

McCoy
Menard
Montgomery Ward
Payless Cashways
Pergament Home
Reno-Depot
Rona
Sears
Sherwin-Williams
Sutherland Lumber
TruServ
United Hardware
  Distributing Co.
Wal-Mart
Wickes

HISTORICAL FINANCIALS & EMPLOYEES

Cooperative FYE: December	Annual Growth	1989	1990	1991	1992	1993	1994	1995	1996	1997	1998
Sales ($ mil.)	8.1%	1,546	1,625	1,704	1,871	2,018	2,326	2,436	2,742	2,907	3,120
Net income ($ mil.)	6.2%	51	60	59	61	57	65	64	72	76	88
Income as % of sales	—		3.3%	3.7%	3.5%	3.2%	2.8%	2.8%	2.6%	2.6%	2.6%	2.8%
Employees	5.5%	2,875	2,931	3,110	3,256	3,405	3,664	3,917	4,352	4,685	4,672

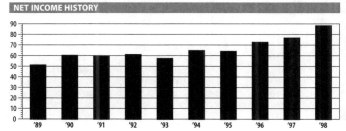

NET INCOME HISTORY

1998 FISCAL YEAR-END

Debt ratio: 30.6%
Return on equity: 34.7%
Cash ($ mil.): 54
Current ratio: 1.32
Long-term debt ($ mil.): 115

ADVANCE PUBLICATIONS, INC.

OVERVIEW

Advance Publications is always moving forward. The Staten Island, New York-based publishing conglomerate is launching a major offensive to claim control of Internet real estate with specialized Web sites (The Yuckiest Site on the Internet) and online versions of its newspapers. It also owns AdOne Classified Network (online classified ad site) with four other media companies, and it is a partner in Time Warner's Road Runner high-speed Internet access service.

But Advance has not retreated from words in print. Its high-profile Condé Nast Publications division is the ultimate source for lifestyle and fashion magazines *Glamour, Vogue* and *GQ*. It also offers more thoughtful fare such as *The New Yorker, Wired,* and *Vanity Fair.* Its 1999 acquisition of Disney's Fairchild Publications

unit (*W, Women's Wear Daily*) gave Condé Nast control of virtually the entire fashion publishing industry.

On the home front, the company owns small and midsized newspapers in 22 cities, including the *Times-Picayune* (New Orleans) and *The Plain Dealer* (Cleveland). It also publishes about 40 local business weeklies through its American City Business Journals unit, and it owns Parade Publications, purveyor of Sunday newspaper supplements *Parade* and the teen-focused *react.* Other interests include cable TV operations and a minority stake in Discovery Communications.

Advance Publications, secretive to the extreme, is controlled by CEO Samuel "Si" Newhouse Jr. and his brother, president Donald Newhouse.

HISTORY

Solomon Neuhaus (later Samuel I. Newhouse) got started in the newspaper business after dropping out of school at age 13. He went to work for a lawyer who had taken possession of the *Bayonne Times* in New Jersey as payment for a debt. The 16-year-old Newhouse was put in charge of the failing newspaper in 1911 and turned it around. In 1922 he bought his own newspaper, the *Staten Island Advance,* and used the profits to buy other papers in the New York area. By the 1950s he owned local papers in New York, New Jersey, and other middle markets and had expanded into Alabama.

In 1959 Newhouse bought magazine publisher Condé Nast as an anniversary gift for his wife. He joked that she had asked for a fashion magazine, so he bought her *Vogue.* Newhouse continued building his newspaper empire and expanded into cable television.

Newhouse died in 1979, leaving his sons Si and Donald as trustees of the company's voting stock. Although they reported inheritance taxes of $48.7 million, the IRS sought more. When the case — the largest until then — was decided in 1990, the IRS lost.

Meanwhile, the company continued to expand. The sons bought book publishing giant Random House from RCA in 1980. Si also built up the magazine business, resurrecting the Roaring Twenties standard *Vanity Fair* in 1983 and adding other titles under the Condé Nast banner, including *The New Yorker* in 1985.

During this period, Advance focused less on costs and more on creating prestigious products. Despite a recession and falling ad revenues, editorial decisions became severed from

financial considerations until the 1990s. As profits evaporated at some magazines, management shuffling became common. In 1993 Condé Nast added Knapp Publications (*Architectural Digest, Bon Appetit*) to its stable, but discontinued *House & Garden* (the magazine was revived in 1996). *New Yorker* president Steven Florio became president of Condé Nast in 1994 and helped most Condé Nast titles become profitable again in 1995.

Advance bought American City Business Journals in 1995. Two years later it began exploring links with the Discovery Channel, of which it owns about 25%. It also announced plans to debut new publications *Sports for Women* and *Businesses to Watch* (which profiles companies that advertise in *Vanity Fair*). The company sold the increasingly unprofitable Random House in 1998 for between $1.2 billion and $1.6 billion. That year also saw the purchase of Wired Ventures' trademark Internet magazine, *Wired.* Revered *New Yorker* editor Tina Brown, a former *Vanity Fair* editor credited with jazzing up the magazine's content and increasing its circulation by 200,000, left the company in 1998; staff writer and Pulitzer Prize winner David Remnick was named as Brown's replacement.

In 1999 Advance joined Donrey Media Group, E.W. Scripps, Hearst Corporation, and MediaNews Group to purchase the online classified advertising network AdOne and created strategic partnerships with Web sites such as Proteam.com and WeddingChannel.com. It also bought Walt Disney's magazine publishing unit, Fairchild Publications, for $650 million.

**Chairman and CEO; Chairman, Condé Nast
Publications:** Samuel I. Newhouse Jr.
President: Donald E. Newhouse
Chairman, American City Business Journals: Ray Shaw
Chairman, Condé Nast International:
Jonathan Newhouse
President and CEO, Condé Nast Publications:
Steven T. Florio
President and CEO, Fairchild Publications:
Mary Berner
President, Advance Internet: Steven Newhouse
**President, Condé Nast Asia-Pacific; Chairman,
Interculture Communications Ltd. (Taiwan):**
Didier Guerin
Publisher, Staten Island Advance: Richard Diamond
EVP and CFO, Condé Nast Publications:
Eric C. Anderson
Comptroller, Staten Island Advance: Arthur Silverstein

HQ: 950 Fingerboard Rd., Staten Island, NY 10305
Phone: 718-981-1234   **Fax:** 718-981-1456
Web site: http://www.advance.net

Selected Operations

American City Business
  Journals Inc. (39 weekly
  business newspapers)
Condé Nast Publications
  Allure
  Architectural Digest
  Bon Appetit
  Bride's
  Conde Nast Traveler
  Details
  Glamour
  Gourmet
  GQ
  House & Garden
  Jane
  Los Angeles Magazine
  Mademoiselle
  The New Yorker
  Self

  Vanity Fair
  Vogue
  W
  Wired
  Women's Sports
    & Fitness
  Women's Wear Daily
Newhouse Broadcasting
  Cable television
  Discovery
  Communications
  (24%, cable TV
  channel)
Newhouse Newspapers
  (small to midsized
  papers in 22 cities)
Parade Publications
  Parade
  react

Selected Newspapers
The Birmingham News (AL)
The Plain Dealer (Cleveland)
The Times-Picayune (New Orleans)

American Express
Cablevision Systems
Comcast
Crain Communications
Dow Jones
E. W. Scripps
Gannett
Hachette Filipacchi
Hearst
Knight Ridder
McClatchy Company
McGraw-Hill
Meredith

New York Times
News Corp.
PRIMEDIA
Pearson
Reader's Digest
Salon
Time Warner
Times Mirror
Tribune
Viacom
Walt Disney
Washington Post

Private FYE: December	Annual Growth	1989	1990	1991	1992	1993	1994	1995	1996	1997	1998
Sales ($ mil.)	2.7%	3,040	3,095	4,287	4,416	4,690	4,855	5,349	4,250	3,669	3,859
Employees	2.6%	19,000	19,500	19,000	19,000	19,000	19,000	24,000	24,000	24,000	24,000

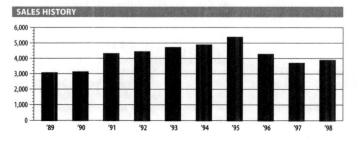

SALES HISTORY

AFL-CIO

OVERVIEW

Talk about spending a long time in labor: The American Federation of Labor and Congress of Industrial Organizations (AFL-CIO) has been at it for more than a century. Based in Washington, DC, the AFL-CIO is an umbrella organization for 68 autonomous unions representing 13 million workers — ranging from actors and airline pilots to teachers and Teamsters — and works to improve wages and working conditions. Union members generally receive about 32% higher pay and more benefits than do nonmembers.

The organization's membership has been decreasing because of the decline in manufacturing jobs and the increased use of temporary workers and automation. However, the AFL-CIO is reviving under the leadership of John Sweeney, primarily because of his aggressive emphasis on recruiting in newer service and white-collar industries, as well as enlisting women, minorities, and younger workers. It also is restructuring for the first time in almost 45 years; the plan calls for consolidating some of the AFL-CIO's 600 local labor councils and giving the national office greater power to set the agenda for the more autonomous state affiliates.

HISTORY

The American Federation of Labor (AFL) was formed in 1886 in Columbus, Ohio, by the merger of six craft unions and a renegade craft section of the Marxist-oriented Knights of Labor. Samuel Gompers, a New York cigar factory worker who headed the AFL until his death in 1924, initiated the AFL's pragmatic focus: to work within, not overthrow, the economic system to increase wages, shorten hours, improve working conditions, and abolish child labor.

Gompers' successes incensed employers, whose arsenal, supported by the US courts and public opinion, included injunctions, government-backed police forces to crush strikes, and the Sherman Anti-Trust Act (used to assail union monopoly powers).

WWI's production needs boosted AFL membership to 4 million by 1919. Labor clashes with management were widespread in the 1920s amid the fear of Bolsheviks. As part of open-shop drives, employers replaced strikers with southern African-Americans and Mexican workers.

The Great Depression brought more supportive public and pro-labor laws, including the National Industrial Recovery Act (NIRA, 1933), which allowed union organizing and collective bargaining. After NIRA was declared unconstitutional, the Wagner Act (1936) restated many of NIRA's provisions and established the legal basis for unions.

Union power split in 1935 when AFL coal miner John L. Lewis began organizing unskilled mass production workers. Lewis and his allies, expelled from the AFL, formed the Congress of Industrial Organizations (CIO, 1938) and enjoyed success in unionizing the auto, steel, textile, and other industries. By 1946 the AFL and CIO had 9 million and 5 million members, respectively.

Amid postwar concern over rising prices, communist infiltration, and union corruption, Congress passed the Taft-Hartley Act in 1947 (which outlawed closed shops). The new climate of hostility led the AFL (headed by plumber George Meany) and the CIO (headed by autoworker Walter Reuther) to merge in 1955. The AFL-CIO soon expelled the Teamsters and other unions on charges of corruption. (The Teamsters reaffiliated in 1987.)

AFL-CIO membership jumped after President Kennedy gave federal employees the right to unionize (1962); state, county, and municipal workers soon followed.

Union membership, which peaked in the mid-1940s with more than a third of the US labor force, was particularly hurt by a jump in imported goods in the 1970s and automation's triumph over manual labor in the 1980s. Legislation supported by the AFL-CIO included a law requiring 60 days' notice for plant closings (1988) and the Family Leave Act (1993). But labor lost its battle against NAFTA, which it feared would export jobs to Mexico.

In 1995 John Sweeney, former head of the Service Employees International Union, became president of the AFL-CIO in its first contested election. Under Sweeney the union spent $35 million in advertising in 1996 to draw attention to issues. After years with little focus on organizing, in 1997 the AFL-CIO launched a massive campaign to organize construction, hospital, and hotel workers in Las Vegas, and committed a third of its budget to recruiting and reorganizing. It supported the Teamsters' successful strike against UPS in 1997, and in 1998 threw its weight behind the Air Line Pilots Association's walk-out on Northwest Airlines. It approved a restructuring plan in 1999.

President: John J. Sweeney, age 65
EVP: Linda Chavez-Thompson, age 55
Secretary and Treasurer: Richard L. Trumka, age 50
VP; President, American Federation of State, County, and Municipal Employees: Gerald W. McEntee
VP; President, American Federation of Teachers: Sandra Feldman
VP; President, International Association of Machinists and Aerospace Workers: R. Thomas Buffenbarger
VP; President, International Brotherhood of Electrical Workers: John J. Barry
VP; President, International Brotherhood of Teamsters: James P. Hoffa
VP; President Sheet Metal Wokers Union: Mike Sullivan
VP; President, U.A.W.: Stephen P. Yokich
VP; President, United Food and Commercial Workers International Union: Douglas H. Dority
Director Corporate Affairs: Ron Blackwell
Director Education: Bill Fletcher
Director International Affairs: Barbara Shailor
Director Human Resources: Carl Garland
Director Legislative: Peggy Taylor
General Counsel: Jonathan Hiatt

LOCATIONS

HQ: 815 16th St. NW, Washington, DC 20006
Phone: 202-637-5000   **Fax:** 202-637-5058
Web site: http://www.aflcio.org

PRODUCTS/OPERATIONS

Selected Departments

Civil rights	Political education
Corporate affairs	Public affairs
Education	Public policy
Human rights	Working women
International affairs	Workplace safety
Legislation	and health
Organization and	
field services	

Selected Trades and Workers Represented

Acting	Hotel employees
Airline pilots	Industrial trades
Athletics	Maritime trades
Broadcasting	Metal trades
Building trades	Mining
Education	Music
Electrical trades	Newspaper trades
Engineering	Office employees
Farm workers	Oil/chemical/atomic
Firefighters	workers
Flight attendants	Police
Food trades	Postal employees
Garment workers	Restaurant employees
Government workers	Transportation trades
Hospital and	Utility workers
health care employees	Writers

AG PROCESSING INC

OVERVIEW

Ag Processing (AGP) could be called Soys "R" Us. The Omaha, Nebraska-based cooperative, one of the largest soybean refiners in the US, processes more than 15,000 acres of soybeans every day. AGP coaxes oil, flour, grits, meal, hulls, and other products out of soybeans and helps turn these products into livestock feeds and food ingredients, including meat extenders for ground beef. Valuable by-products include lecithin, bio-fuels, and the base for vitamin E production. The co-op's grain operations — AGP Grain and AGP Grain Cooperative — have the capacity to store more than 50 million bushels of grain, while its Consolidated Nutrition joint venture with Archer Daniels Midland is the #4 commercial feed manufacturer in the US.

Member-owned, AGP includes more than 300 local co-ops and 12 regional co-ops representing some 300,000 farmers. Members come from 16 states in the US and Canada; most are in Iowa, Kansas, Minnesota, Missouri, Nebraska, and South Dakota. Internationally, AGP is involved in feed manufacturing through joint ventures in Hungary and Venezuela.

To capitalize on new EPA emission limits and mandates, the co-op is lobbying hard to increase retail demand for ethanol, which it produces from corn. Additionally, AGP is promoting methyl ester, a by-product of soy oil refining, for use as a clean fuel and fuel additive, agricultural spray, and non-toxic solvent to replace petroleum-based products.

HISTORY

Seeking strength in numbers, Ag Processing (AGP) was formed in 1983 when agricultural cooperatives Land O' Lakes and Farmland Industries merged their money-losing soybean operations into similarly struggling Boone Valley Cooperative.

Separately, AGP's six soybean mills had been unable to compete successfully against each other and larger corporations. The entire industry had been hampered by the Soviet grain embargoes imposed by the US in 1973 and 1979, and US government policies had contributed to increased competition from heavily subsidized soy producers in Argentina and Brazil. Soy exports from the US had fallen dramatically, leading to a production capacity surplus.

Collectively, AGP was able to attract a stronger management staff than its predecessors had; it hired 21-year Archer Daniels Midland (ADM) veteran James Lindsay as CEO and general manager. With operations scattered over four states, AGP placed its headquarters in Omaha, Nebraska — chosen for its central location and close proximity to the co-op's main bank.

In its first two years, AGP cut employee rolls by 20% and scaled back production, thus trimming costs and squeezing higher prices for finished products. A turnaround came quickly, and in 1985 members received a dividend from the co-op's $8 million pretax profit. That year AGP purchased two Iowa plants from AGRI Industries.

AGP dismantled two plants in 1987. By the next year the co-op witnessed an increase in domestic demand and had resumed selling to the Soviet Union. It generated additional sales by further processing soybean oil into food-grade products such as hydrogenated oil and lecithin.

With an eye on diversification and value-added products, by 1991 AGP had expanded to eight soybean plants and two vegetable oil refineries; it also acquired the feed and grain business of International Multifoods that year through an 80%-owned joint venture with ADM. The acquisition included 29 feed plants in the US and Canada, 26 retail centers, 18 grain elevators, and the brands Supersweet and Masterfeeds. In 1994 AGP formed feed manufacturer Consolidated Nutrition, a 50-50 joint-venture with ADM.

Consolidated Nutrition introduced a Swine Operations program in 1996. The program quickly grew through the development of PORK PACT, a partnership program to serve pork producers. The next year AGP's grain division sold nine grain elevators in Ohio and Indiana to Cargill. That year the co-op gained control of Venezuelan feed manufacturer Proagro.

By 1998 passage of the Freedom to Farm Act and growing demand had spurred soybean planting. The co-op in 1998 opened an additional processing plant in Emmetsburg, Iowa; began construction on another one in Hastings, Nebraska; and broke ground for a new soy oil refining plant in Eagle Grove, Iowa. AGP sold off its pet food operations in 1998 to Windy Hill, which was then acquired by Doane Pet Care Enterprises. To strengthen its brand, in 1998 Consolidated Nutrition combined two of its Master Mix and Supersweet feed brands into the Consolidated Nutrition label.

Chairman: Denis E. Leiting
CEO and General Manager: James W. Lindsay
SVP Corporate Relations: Larry Burkett
SVP Human Resources: Gordon V. Dorff
SVP Food Group: George L. Hoover
SVP Transportation: Terry J. Voss
Group VP Finance, CFO, and Assistant Secretary:
Kenneth S. Grubbe
Group VP Food, Industrial, Pet Foods: Joseph L. Meyer
Group VP Soybean/Corn Operations, Transportation:
Anthony L. Porter
Group VP Grain: Martin P. Reagan
VP Government Relations: John B. Campbell
VP Technical Operations: Richard P. Copeland
VP Hedging: Daryl D. Dahl
VP Administration: William K. Hahn
VP Pet Foods: Farouk G. Horani
VP Grain: Michael J. Knobbe
VP Soybean/Corn Operations: Gary L. Olsen
VP Research and Technology: Wayne L. Stockland
VP and Corporate Controller: Tim E. Witty
General Counsel and Assistant Secretary:
Frederick D. Thompson

HQ: 12700 W. Dodge Rd., Omaha, NE 68103
Phone: 402-496-7809   **Fax:** 402-498-5548
Web site: http://www.agp.com

Selected Products
Bio-diesel
Commercial feeds
Deodorizer distillate (tocopherols)
Ethanol
Industrial products
Lecithin
Soybean meal
Soybean oil

Selected Brands
Consolidated Nutrition (feeds, US)
Masterfeeds (feeds, Canada)
SOYGOLD (bio-diesel, solvents, fuel additives)
Tindle Mills (feeds)

Selected Subsidiaries
Ag Environmental Products (soybean methyl ester
products)
AGP Grain Cooperative
AGP Grain, Ltd.
Consolidated Nutrition (50%, commercial feed)

ADM
Agribrands
International, Inc.
Agway
Andersons
Cargill
ConAgra
ContiGroup
Corn Products International
Farmland Industries
High Plains
JR Simplot
MFA
Riceland Foods
Southern States
Tate & Lyle

HISTORICAL FINANCIALS & EMPLOYEES

Cooperative FYE: August	Annual Growth	1989	1990	1991	1992	1993	1994	1995	1996	1997	1998
Sales ($ mil.)	17.1%	—	—	865	1,127	1,219	1,377	2,132	2,765	2,948	2,615
Employees	(8.6%)	—	—	—	—	—	—	—	3,050	3,000	2,550

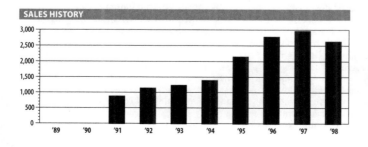

SALES HISTORY

Ag Processing Inc

AGWAY INC.

OVERVIEW

Feed, seed, and fuel are the Ag-ways. De-Witt, New York-based Agway, a farmers' cooperative with about 80,000 member-owners, provides supplies and services for farmers, and, increasingly, non-farm consumers in 12 northeastern states.

Agway Agricultural Products operates plants making feeds, fertilizers, and other farm-related products. The Country Products Group processes and sells fresh produce, edible beans, sunflower seeds, flour, and vegetable seeds from growers. These two divisions account for nearly half of Agway's total revenues (but less than 15% of income). Agway Retail Services operates about 500 Agway

stores in suburban and rural areas of the Northeast, selling yard and garden supplies, pet food and supplies, and farm-related products. Agway also offers insurance and finances leases for buildings and equipment.

Deregulation is helping fuel Agway's more profitable energy business, which accounts for about one-third of sales. Agway Energy Products sells and services oil, gas heating, and air-conditioning equipment, and it sells heating oil, propane, and diesel fuel to farms, residences, and small businesses. It also has started marketing natural gas and electricity in states where that is permitted.

HISTORY

Agway was formed in 1964 by the merger of three large northeastern agricultural cooperatives: Eastern States Farmers Exchange, founded in 1918; Cooperative Grange League Federation Exchange, founded in 1920; and Pennsylvania Farm Bureau Cooperative Association, founded in 1934. The combined sales of the three co-ops at the time of the merger was $375 million.

About the time of the merger, Agway indirectly acquired voting control of Curtice Burns Foods through a co-op that a group of Agway's members owned. Curtice Burns quickly became a fast-growing food products business, one that bought most of its raw materials from Agway members and focused almost exclusively on regionally popular niche products. Between 1971 and 1981 the subsidiary acquired at least eight other food companies, including Nalley's Fine Foods, National Brands Beverage, and National Oats. Excited by the success of Curtice Burns, Agway purchased a leading dairy processor, H.P. Hood, in 1980.

In the early 1990s plain-talking chairman Ralph Heffner, owner of a large farm in Pennsylvania, set his sights on re-engineering Agway. He had listened to the grim forecasts from industry pundits: More than 20,000 northeastern farms had closed down since 1990, and 17,000 more closures were expected by 1995. Slimming down and stockpiling cash were two of his early goals. More than 400 employees took early retirement in 1992, persuaded by an attractive retirement package. Agway Energy Products, the energy group, was trimmed considerably: Eight fuel distribution businesses were sold, and the group turned its focus from low-margin commercial accounts to higher-profit homeowner accounts. Agway's

retail stores underwent renovation, getting wider aisles and brighter lighting. Perhaps most significant, Agway separated its retail arm from its agricultural services and wholesale farm supply business, forming a single-margin system by removing retail as the middleman and creating a virtually direct pipeline between farmer and supplier.

Also in 1992 Agway took a $75 million hit related to restructuring costs. That year the co-op launched its "Customer Driven: 1995" plan, a two-pronged program designed to prepare it for the 21st century. It aimed to secure a strong financial standing for the organization and to provide efficient delivery of products and services.

The co-op's biggest move in this direction was its 1993 decision to sell the two food operations that had been providing almost 50% of overall revenues: H.P. Hood (on which it had blamed a revenues slide in 1991 and 1992) and Curtice Burns. In 1994 Agway sold its share of Curtice Burns (which had sales of $829 million that year) to Pro-Fac Cooperative. In 1995 it sold its H.P. Hood dairy food processing business to Catamount Dairy Holdings, and in 1996 it sold its lawn care business, Pro-Lawn, to leading turf care products company LESCO.

Taking advantage of deregulation of energy markets, in 1997 the firm began offering natural gas to customers, and later that year it began a pilot program supplying electricity to farmers in New York. Diversifying its money-losing retail operations, in 1998 Agway opened a new store format, Cultivations, aimed primarily at women interested in gardening and home decor.

Chairman: Gary K. Van Slyke, age 56
VC: Andrew J. Gilbert
President and CEO: Donald P. Cardarelli, age 43, $478,276 pay
SVP, General Counsel and Secretary: David M. Hayes, age 55
SVP, Public Affairs: Stephen H. Hoefer, age 44
SVP, Finance & Control: Peter J. O'Neill, age 52
SVP, Administration Services; President, Agway Insurance Group: Gerald R. Seeber, age 52
VP and Chief Information Officer: William L. Parker, age 52
VP and Chief Investment Officer: G. Leslie Smith, age 56
VP, Membership: Robert D. Sears, age 58
President, Telmark: Daniel J. Edinger, age 48, $199,710 pay
President, Agriculture & Retail Group: Robert A. Fischer Jr., age 51, $316,442 pay
President, Agway Energy Products: Michael R. Hopsicker, age 34, $218,087 pay
President, Country Products Group: Dennis J. LaHood, age 53, $252,639 pay
Treasurer: Karen A. Johnson
Corporate Controller: John F. Feeney, age 38
Director, Human Resources: Richard Opdyke
Auditors: PricewaterhouseCoopers LLP

LOCATIONS

HQ: 333 Butternut Dr., DeWitt, NY 13214
Phone: 315-449-6436   **Fax:** 315-449-6253
Web site: http://www.agway.com

PRODUCTS/OPERATIONS

1999 Sales

	$ mil.	% of total
Product sales	1,386	93
Leasing	70	5
Insurance	28	2
Total	**1,484**	**100**

Major Operating Units

Agriculture
Agway Agricultural Products (animal feeds, fertilizers, crop protectants, and farm supplies)
Country Products Group (selected vegetables, pastry flour, paper bags, pet food, and seeds)

Energy
Agway Energy Products (heating oil, propane, natural gas, and motor vehicle fuel; heating and air-conditioning equipment; electricity in certain markets)

Retail
Agway Retail Services (about 180 company-owned stores and more than 300 franchised stores selling farm-related products, yard and garden products, and pet food and supplies)

Leasing
Telmark Inc. (lease financing for buildings, equipment, and vehicles)

Insurance
Agway Insurance Co. (property, auto, and liability insurance)

COMPETITORS

ADM	Home Depot
Ag Processing	Niagara Mohawk
AgriBioTech	Pioneer Hi-Bred
AmeriGas Partners	Purina Mills
CF Industries	Quality Stores
CH Energy Group, Inc.	RGS Energy Group
Cargill	Savia
ConAgra	Smith & Hawken
ContiGroup	Southern States
DEKALB Genetics	Universal Corporation
Energy East	Wal-Mart
Farmland Industries	Wilbur-Ellis

HISTORICAL FINANCIALS & EMPLOYEES

Cooperative FYE: June	Annual Growth	1990	1991	1992	1993	1994	1995	1996	1997	1998	1999
Sales ($ mil.)	(3.2%)	1,985	1,971	1,801	1,720	1,695	1,592	1,663	1,671	1,563	1,484
Net income ($ mil.)	(15.4%)	8	(6)	(59)	20	(3)	(16)	13	11	13	2
Income as % of sales	—	0.4%	—	—	1.1%	—	—	0.8%	0.6%	0.8%	0.1%
Employees	(1.2%)	8,000	8,000	8,400	6,600	7,900	9,000	7,500	7,100	7,000	7,200

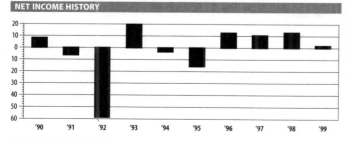

NET INCOME HISTORY

1999 FISCAL YEAR-END

Debt ratio: 58.4%
Return on equity: 0.9%
Cash ($ mil.): 0
Current ratio: 1.11
Long-term debt ($ mil.): 279

ALLIANT FOODSERVICE INC.

OVERVIEW

An orderly wheeled that tray of meatloaf and carrots into your hospital room, but Alliant Foodservice probably wheeled it into the hospital first. Deerfield, Illinois-based Alliant is the US's largest food service distributor to hospitals. It serves other customers in the health care industry through its Dietary Products unit, and it's also a leading broadline distributor to hotels, restaurants, and other non-retail outlets.

Alliant distributes fresh produce, frozen and refrigerated foods, seafood, meats, other grocery products, cleaning supplies, and equipment. Formerly a division of Philip Morris' Kraft Foods, Alliant is the exclusive distributor of more than 700 Kraft-brand food service products, including Miracle Whip, Velveeta, and Philadelphia Brand cream cheese. The company also distributes more than 6,000 of its own private-label products, including Esplendido Mexican food products and Luzzatti Italian food products.

For years Alliant has been leading an acquisition conga line, and that continues as the company adds regions and nets hefty contracts. However, its five-year agreement for exclusive distribution of Kraft-brand products will be up for renewal in 2000, and it's unclear if it will be extended.

Investment firm Clayton, Dubilier & Rice owns Alliant.

HISTORY

Cheese kingpin Kraft got into the food service business around 1950, but it wasn't until 1976 that the company created a distribution unit, Kraft Foodservice, to sell large volumes of its products (Miracle Whip, Parkay, Philadelphia Brand cream cheese) to institutional users.

Led by Dean Nelson, the unit expanded rapidly in the mid-1980s, though it fell short in its 1984 effort to buy #2 food service distributor CFS Continental. Internal growth as well as acquisitions of leading regional food service distributors took Kraft Foodservice's sales from $686 million in 1983 to about $1.85 billion by the end of 1986.

Kraft Foodservice's many deals — a dozen or so in 1986 alone — coincided with the growth of national restaurant chains that needed consistent product distribution, and they expanded the company's product offerings well beyond those that bore the Kraft name. By 1988 Kraft Foodservice was the nation's second-largest food service distributor, behind SYSCO. Still, it controlled only a tiny percentage of the highly fragmented market.

That year parent company Kraft was acquired by cigarette maker Philip Morris, which also owned General Foods (Jell-O, Maxwell House, Oscar Mayer). Philip Morris combined the two food businesses into one subsidiary called Kraft General Foods, and Kraft Foodservice became part of the KGF Commercial Products division.

Acquisitions began to slow, although by the end of 1989, Kraft Foodservice had $3.2 billion in sales and covered 97% of the US. The company made inroads into the health care industry that year through a marketing alliance with medical products supplier Baxter International.

In 1995 Philip Morris sold low-margin Kraft Foodservice to investment firm Clayton, Dubilier & Rice for $700 million. The deal gave the new company exclusive rights to distribute the line of Kraft institutional products (which accounted for $650 million of its sales) for five years. As part of the agreement, the company rechristened itself Alliant Foodservice within the year.

The company reorganized along geographic lines, and it teamed with Fresh America to distribute fresh produce. Alliant further developed its health care business in 1996 by acquiring Dietary Products, the sales and marketing joint venture it had created with Baxter, and by winning a five-year, $3.75 billion contract from Premier Inc., an alliance representing 1,800 hospitals.

To deepen its regional reach, the company resumed doing the acquisition cha-cha. Alliant bought City Meat and Provisions (Tucson, Arizona) in 1996, and in 1997 it acquired Atlantic Food Services (Baltimore/Washington, DC) and four other distributors serving Atlanta, Detroit, northern Ohio, and northern New York. It bought K-B Foods (Omaha, Nebraska) in 1998.

Alliant introduced its own private-label products in 1997, which involved converting thousands of items to the Alliant brand. The company won big contracts the next year from hotel firms Promus (later bought by Hilton) and Starwood. In 1999, after 33 years with Alliant, CEO James Miller retired and was replaced by former Inland Steel and Compaq Computer executive Earl Mason.

Chairman: James W. Rogers
President and CEO: Earl L. Mason
EVP, General Counsel, and Secretary: Cathy Anderson
EVP National Accounts Solutions: Douglas J. Cassidy
SVP and Chief Information Officer: Barbara Moss
SVP Marketing and Category Management:
  Jeffrey Posner
SVP and CFO: Joan E. Ryan
VP Operations: James M. Beck
VP and Corporate Controller: Raymond J. Roman
VP and Treasurer: Andrew B. Szafran
VP Corporate Initiatives: M. Robert Weidner III
Manager Human Resources: Paula Raybould
Division President West: John Baldi
Division President Southeast: Tommy Dail
Division President Central: Bruce Horner
Division President Northeast: Gregory Nickele
Market President for Metropolitan New York,
  Philadelphia, and Tri-State Area:
  Victor R. Harshberger
Market President for Albany Area: Michael J. Mulhern
Market President for Denver & Rocky Mountain Area:
  Mark A. Robertson
President, Southwest Division: Gregory Schaffner

LOCATIONS

HQ: 1 Parkway North, Deerfield, IL 60015
Phone: 847-405-8500   **Fax:** 847-405-8980
Web site: http://www.alliantboston.com

PRODUCTS/OPERATIONS

Selected Products
Cleaning supplies
Disposables
Food service equipment
Grocery products
Meats
Poultry
Produce
Refrigerated and frozen foods
Seafood
Tabletop items

Selected Exclusive-Brand Products
Beyond (oils and shortenings)
Distinct (food bases, condiments, oils, and vinegar)
Esplendido (Mexican food)
Glenview Farms (dairy products)
Home Taste (frozen and canned entrees)
Kraft Brands
  Mayonnaise
  Miracle Whip salad dressing
  Philadelphia Brand cream cheese
  Prepared salad dressings
  Velveeta pasteurized process cheese spread
Luzzatti (Italian food)
Monogram (nonfood items)
Natural Resource (fresh produce)
OPTIMA (oils and shortenings)
Quali-Bake (oils and shortenings)
Quali-Fry (oils and shortenings)
Royal Select (coffees and teas)
Thirster (juices and fruit drinks)

COMPETITORS

AmeriServe
Ben E. Keith
Gordon Food Service
International Multifoods
MBM
Performance Food
SYSCO
Sara Lee
Services Group
U.S. Foodservice

HISTORICAL FINANCIALS & EMPLOYEES

Private FYE: December	Annual Growth	1989	1990	1991	1992	1993	1994	1995	1996	1997	1998
Sales ($ mil.)	9.9%	—	—	—	—	3,800	4,100	4,230	4,500	5,200	6,100
Employees	8.1%	—	—	—	—	—	8,800	9,400	9,700	11,500	12,000

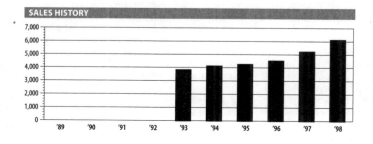

SALES HISTORY

AMERICAN CANCER SOCIETY, INC.

OVERVIEW

Fighting one of the deadliest of diseases, the American Cancer Society (ACS) has more than 3,400 local units nationwide. The Atlanta-based organization is staffed by professionals as well as 2 million volunteers. It is the largest source of private cancer research funds in the US, providing about $90 million a year — more than $2 billion since its inception. Recipients of the society's funding include 29 Nobel Prize laureates. Patient services include moral support; transportation; assistance in obtaining hairpieces, swimwear, and prostheses; and camps for children who have or have had cancer.

The ACS has generated considerable income by marketing its name for antismoking nicotine patches and orange juice, and is contemplating even more lucrative deals. Programs account for about 71% of expenses; 29% goes to administration and fund-raising. In 1999 the organization reported a decrease in cancer deaths from 1990-1996 — the most recent figures available — and attributed it primarily to a decrease in tobacco use.

HISTORY

Concerned over the lack of progress in detecting and treating cancer, a group of 10 physicians and five laymen met in New York City in 1913 to form the American Society for the Control of Cancer (ASCC). Because public discussion of cancer was taboo, the group struggled with how to educate people without raising unnecessary fears. Some physicians even preferred keeping knowledge of the disease from the public. In the 1920s the ASCC began sponsoring cancer clinics and collecting statistics on the disease. By 1923 some states reported improvements in early diagnosis and treatment. In 1937 the ASCC started its first nationwide public education program, with the help of volunteers known as the Women's Field Army. President Franklin Roosevelt named April National Cancer Control Month, a practice since followed by every president.

By 1944 some cancer rates were rising but the word "cancer" still couldn't be mentioned on radio. Mary Lasker, the wife of prominent advertising executive Albert Lasker, was instrumental in getting information about cancer broadcast. At her insistence, in 1945 the newly renamed American Cancer Society began donating at least 25% of its budget to research. The society raised $4 million in its first major national fund-raising campaign in 1945.

The link between smoking and lung cancer became known after a study in the early 1950s of nearly 200,000 subjects (society volunteers) by ACS medical director Charles Cameron. That information became part of the Surgeon General's Report of 1964. In 1973 an ACS branch in Minnesota held the first Great American Smokeout to encourage people to quit smoking.

The ACS backed the 1971 congressional bill that inaugurated the War on Cancer. The society was attacked in the 1970s for emphasizing cures rather than prevention because, critics claimed, research would reveal environmental causes from industrial products made by companies with connections to ACS directors. In the 1970s and 1980s, the ACS backed tougher restrictions on tobacco and, in response to earlier criticism, directed research toward prevention as well as treatment. The society played a major role in the 1989 airline smoking ban.

The first of several genetic breakthroughs came in the 1990s when ACS grantees isolated genes believed to be responsible for triggering various types of cancer. In 1995 the ACS publicly accused the tobacco industry of infiltrating its offices in the 1970s and using its papers to aid in the early marketing of low-tar cigarettes.

In 1996 the ACS announced that new data showed a drop in the US cancer death rate for the first time ever. The ACS entered agreements with SmithKline Beecham (NicoDerm antismoking patches) and the Florida Department of Citrus in 1996 to allow the use of the American Cancer Society name in marketing — generating about $4 million for the ACS.

The proposed $369 billion settlement between the attorneys general of 40 states and the tobacco industry was big news in 1997. The ACS had wanted more concessions, such as a $2-per-pack tax increase, more power for industry regulation by the FDA, and underage use rate-reduction targets for smokeless tobacco products as stringent as those for cigarettes.

In 1998 the ACS launched a $5 million national advertising campaign to combat what it sees as "misleading" information spread by the tobacco industry. The ACS argued in Supreme Court in 1999 to help the FDA gain control over cigarette production and distribution.

LOCATIONS

HQ: 1599 Clifton Rd. NE, Atlanta, GA 30329
Phone: 404-320-3333   **Fax:** 404-329-5787
Web site: http://www.cancer.org

PRODUCTS/OPERATIONS

Selected Patient Services Programs

Breast Cancer Awareness and Solutions Network
Candlelighters Childhood Cancer Family Alliance
(information and support for children with cancer
and their families)
Children's Camps (for children and teens with cancer;
some for siblings)
Community Connection: Resources, Information, &
Guidance Group support programs
Home Care (assistance in obtaining medical equipment
or supplies)
Hope Lodge (housing assistance)
I Can Cope (education and support classes on
living with cancer)
Laryngectomy Rehabilitation
Look Good ... Feel Better (cosmetics and beauty
techniques for women experiencing side effects
of cancer treatment)
Man To Man Prostate Cancer Support
Ostomy Rehabilitation
Pamphlets and brochures for cancer patients
and their families
Reach to Recovery (support for women with breast
cancer and their families)
Road to Recovery (transportation services)
We Can Weekend (weekend retreat for adult cancer
patients and their families)

Selected Professional Training Programs

Cancer Control Career Development Awards for
Primary Care Physicians
Physician Training Awards in Preventive Medicine
Professorships of Clinical Oncology
Professorships of Oncology Nursing
Scholarships in Cancer Nursing
Training Grants in Clinical Oncology Social Work

Selected Public Education Programs and Publications

Changing the Course (public school curricula)
5 A Day Power Play! (nutritional curriculum for fourth
through sixth grade)
Great American Smokeout
(national stop-smoking-for-a-day event)
Great American SmokeScream (national event for
middle school and high school students to scream
their protests against tobacco use)
Making Strides Against Breast Cancer (fund-raiser)
Relay for Life (fund-raiser)

HISTORICAL FINANCIALS & EMPLOYEES

Not-for-profit FYE: August	Annual Growth	1989	1990	1991	1992	1993	1994	1995	1996	1997	1998
Sales ($ mil.)	7.3%	358	366	336	358	388	392	420	458	602	677
Employees	(0.5%)	—	—	—	4,650	4,200	4,100	4,656	4,500	4,418	4,500

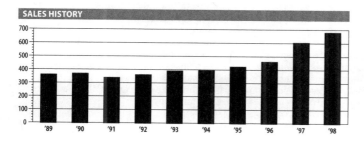

SALES HISTORY

AMERICAN FAMILY INSURANCE

OVERVIEW

American Family Insurance Group can protect you at home, at work, and on the drive in between. The Madison, Wisconsin-based mutual insurance company specializes in commercial and personal property/casualty insurance, life insurance, health insurance, investment products, and retirement planning products. American Family sells homeowners policies and individual accident and health policies, mainly to its auto customers. It offers whole and universal life policies and annuities for small-business owners. Other lines include consumer finance (home equity and other personal loans, which it sells through its agents) and health plans. American Family also offers specialized business coverage for apartment owners and garages, restaurants, and other institutions. Its auto insurance coverage includes motorcycles, snowmobiles, and boats.

American Family has around 3,750 agents operating in the Midwest and in Arizona, Colorado, and Oregon.

HISTORY

In 1927 Herman Wittwer founded Farmers Mutual Automobile Insurance Co. to provide auto insurance to Wisconsin farmers. This market was growing in the 1920s as farms became mechanized. Wittwer was not the first to realize that the low density of auto traffic in rural areas reduced the potential for accidents; State Farm had been founded to serve the same markets in neighboring Illinois in 1922. Wittwer also noted that the severity of rural Wisconsin winters often made cars unusable for a good part of the year, further reducing risk.

Farmers Mutual grew despite the Depression and WWII, spreading to Minnesota (1933); Missouri (1939); Nebraska and the Dakotas (1940); and Indiana, Iowa, and Kansas (1943). The war years were generous to insurance companies, as rising incomes made people wealthy enough to insure their cars, but rationing programs limited their use. The postwar suburban boom also helped auto insurers as cars became a necessity rather than a luxury.

Growing prosperity for single-earner households in the 1950s helped increase the demand for life insurance. In 1958 Farmers Mutual formed American Family Life Insurance Co. The company was able to write $1.6 million in insurance on its first day in the life insurance business. During that decade Farmers Mutual moved into Illinois.

The 1960s were a period of growth and change for the company. To capture more auto insurance, it founded American Standard Insurance Co. to write nonstandard auto insurance. The firm also began consumer finance operations for insurance customers and noncustomers alike, departing from standard industry practice by selling through agents rather than offices. In 1963, in recognition of its growing diversification, Farmers Mutual changed its name to American Family Mutual Insurance.

The firm was preoccupied during the 1970s and 1980s with strengthening its infrastructure and adding new regional offices. The company also continued developing its business, moving into Arizona and later forming American Family Brokerage, to fill in gaps in its own coverage by obtaining insurance for clients through other insurers.

During this period American Family suffered cultural pains. It moved beyond its traditional rural clientele and into the urban unknown as it sought to increase its market share in Milwaukee. In 1981 community groups questioned whether the company was adequately serving racially mixed neighborhoods. In 1988 the US Justice Department began investigating allegations that the firm engaged in redlining (offering inferior or no service for minority neighborhoods); a class-action suit based on similar claims was filed in 1990. The suit went all the way to the Supreme Court, which ruled that the Fair Housing Act does apply to insurance sales.

The company had begun rectifying its practices even before the case was decided. Nevertheless, when American Family settled the case in 1995, it agreed to mend its ways and to pay a $14.5 million settlement plus about $2 million in court costs. Part of the settlement was to compensate people who had suffered from the company's discrimination. But most of the money went to fund community programs begun in 1996 to promote home ownership among minorities. In 1997 American Family came under fire from a lawsuit claiming that the company falsely promised to shrink premiums as policies earned dividends and from two dissident agents' civil complaints of wrongful termination. The company settled the latter case the following year.

Chairman and CEO: Dale F. Mathwich
President and COO: Harvey R. Pierce
EVP Administration: James R. Klokner
EVP Corporate Legal and Secretary: James F. Eldridge
EVP Finance and Treasurer: Paul L. King
EVP Sales: Daniel R. DeSalvo
VP and Controller: J. Brent Johnson
VP Actuarial: Bradley J. Gleason
VP Claims: Darnell Moore
VP Corporate Research: Nancy M. Johnson
VP Human Resources: Vicki L. Chvala
VP Information Services: David R. Anderson
VP Investments: Thomas S. King
VP Marketing: Alan E. Meyer
VP Office Administration: Richard J. Haas
VP Sales, Great Lakes Region: David N. Krueger
VP Sales, Midland Region: Russell W. Lemons
VP Sales, Mountain Region: Don D. Alfermann
VP Sales, Valley Region: Ralph E. Kaye
VP Underwriting Services: Alan F. Hunter
Auditors: PricewaterhouseCoopers LLP

LOCATIONS

HQ: American Family Insurance Group,
6000 American Pkwy., Madison, WI 53783
Phone: 608-249-2111 **Fax:** 608-243-4921
Web site: http://www.amfam.com

PRODUCTS/OPERATIONS

1998 Assets

	$ mil.	% of total
Cash & equivalents	1	—
Bonds	4,963	55
Stocks	2,001	22
Mortgage loans	124	1
Real estate	183	2
Receivables	623	7
Other assets	1,052	13
Total	**8,949**	**100**

1998 Sales

	$ mil.	% of total
Property/casualty	3,220	83
Life	275	7
Net investments	335	9
Other	58	1
Total	**3,888**	**100**

Selected Services

Commercial and personal property/casualty insurance
Financial services (consumer loans and auto leasing)
Health insurance (short-term and Medicare supplement)
Life insurance (universal, term, and whole life; annuities)

COMPETITORS

20th Century	Lincoln National
AIG	Loews
Allstate	Mutual of Omaha
American Financial	Nationwide Insurance
American General	Ohio Casualty
Berkshire Hathaway	Old Republic
CIGNA	Progressive Corporation
CNA Financial	Prudential
Chubb	SAFECO
Cincinnati Financial	St. Paul Companies
Citigroup	State Farm
General Re	The Hartford
Kemper Insurance	USAA
Liberty Mutual	

HISTORICAL FINANCIALS & EMPLOYEES

Mutual company FYE: December	Annual Growth	1989	1990	1991	1992	1993	1994	1995	1996	1997	1998
Assets ($ mil.)	11.5%	3,351	3,672	4,228	4,698	5,228	5,706	6,256	6,836	8,348	8,949
Net income ($ mil.)	—	—	(13)	68	144	159	163	218	55	252	40
Income as % of assets	—	—	—	1.6%	3.1%	3.0%	2.9%	3.5%	0.8%	3.0%	0.4%
Employees	1.7%	5,971	6,330	6,371	6,436	6,373	6,365	6,411	6,506	6,800	6,940

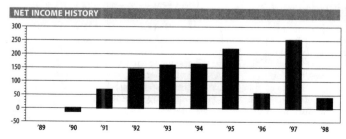

NET INCOME HISTORY

1998 FISCAL YEAR-END
Equity as % of assets: 36.0%
Return on assets: 0.4%
Return on equity: 1.3%
Long-term debt ($ mil.): —
Sales ($ mil.): 3,888

THE AMERICAN RED CROSS

OVERVIEW

When it comes to disaster, the American Red Cross is the master. The American Red Cross is a member of the International Red Cross and Red Crescent Movement, a not-for-profit organization committed to helping those in need. Based in Washington, DC, the American Red Cross is chartered by Congress to provide relief services, but it isn't a government agency. It has more than 1.3 million volunteers — about 40 for every paid staffer.

Aside from providing relief to victims of more than 60,000 natural and man-made disasters nationwide each year, the American Red Cross teaches CPR and AIDS awareness courses, provides counseling and emergency message transmission for US military personnel, and is guardian of the nation's largest blood, plasma, and tissue banks.

HISTORY

The Red Cross traces its start to a trip made in 1859 by Jean-Henri Dunant, a Swiss businessman. Dunant was traveling in northern Italy when he saw the aftermath of the Battle of Solferino — 40,000 dead or wounded troops, left without help. He published a pamphlet three years later calling for the formation of international volunteer societies to aid wounded soldiers.

In 1863 a five-member committee (including Dunant) formed the International Committee of the Red Cross in Geneva. Delegates of 16 countries attended the first conference, which resulted in the formation of national Red Cross societies across Europe. A red cross on a white background (the reverse of the Swiss flag) was chosen as the organization's symbol; the Red Crescent symbol was added in 1876 by Muslim relief workers during the Russo-Turkish War. In 1864 the group's principles were codified into international law — initially signed by 12 nations — through the Geneva Convention.

Clara Barton, famous for her aid to soldiers during the US Civil War, learned about the Red Cross when she assisted with relief efforts during the Franco-Prussian War (1870-71). After the war, Barton returned home and persuaded Congress to support the Geneva Convention. In 1881 she and some friends founded the American Association of the Red Cross, with the first chapter in Dansville, New York. The US signed the Geneva Convention in 1882.

Barton soon expanded the Red Cross' mission to include aiding victims of natural disasters. The group received a congressional charter in 1905, making it responsible for providing assistance to the US military and disaster relief in the US and overseas.

Membership soared during WWI as the number of chapters jumped from 107 to 3,864 and volunteers from the US and other nations served with the armed forces in Europe. After the war, the American Red Cross helped

refugees in Europe, recruited thousands of nurses to improve the health and hygiene of rural Americans, and provided food and shelter to millions during the Depression.

The Red Cross established its first blood center, in New York's Presbyterian Hospital, in 1941. During WWII the American Red Cross again mobilized massive relief efforts. At home, volunteers taught nutrition courses, served in hospitals, and collected blood.

In 1956 the Red Cross began research to increase the safety of its blood supply. It also continued to provide assistance during natural disasters, as well as during the Korean and Vietnam Wars and other US military conflicts.

During the 1980s the Red Cross was criticized for moving too slowly to improve testing of its blood supply for the HIV virus. Elizabeth Dole, named the organization's president in 1991, reorganized the blood collection program. (Dole took a leave of absence in 1996 to help her husband, Bob Dole, in his unsuccessful bid for the US presidency.)

In 1996 *Money* magazine reported that the Red Cross spent more than 91 cents of every dollar on programs, the best ratio of any major charity. The next year HemaCare settled a blood-product-pricing lawsuit against the Red Cross without disclosing terms, and Ellis & Associates challenged the organization's hold on lifeguard training (certifying about 32,000 guards versus 185,000 for the Red Cross).

In 1998 the organization ran up against its costliest year ever, spending more than $162 million to fight some 240 disasters across the US. The next year Dole resigned from the Red Cross and followed in her husband's footsteps by making her own bid for the US presidency in 2000. Dole was succeeded by Dr. Bernadine Healy, a former dean of the Ohio State University College of Medicine and the first physician to head the association.

Chairman: Norman R. Augustine
President and CEO: Bernadine P. Healy, age 54
COO: E. Matthew Branam
CFO and VP Finance: John D. Campbell
SVP Biomedical Services: Jimmy D. Ross
SVP Chapter Services: Donald W. Jones
SVP Corporate Services: Jennifer Dunlap
VP Disaster Services: John Clizbe
VP Human Resources: Nancy Breseke
Chief Diversity Officer: Anthony J. Polk
Chief Information Officer: Tom Woteki
Corporate Secretary: Marianne Eby
National Co-Chair of Volunteers: Bernie Ceilley
National Co-Chair of Volunteers: Linda Ceilley
General Counsel: Richard L. Dashefsky

LOCATIONS

HQ: 430 17th St. NW, Washington, DC 20006
Phone: 703-737-8300   **Fax:** 703-248-4256
Web site: http://www.redcross.org

PRODUCTS/OPERATIONS

1999 Sales

	$ mil.	% of total
Products & services	1,433	59
Contributions	817	34
Other	171	7
Total	**2,421**	**100**

Selected Activities

Armed Forces Emergency Services
Counseling
Emergency assistance
Veterans assistance

Biomedical Services
Blood
Dental programs
Plasma operations
Research and development
Stem cell
Tissue

Disaster Services
Disaster mitigation
Emergency assistance
Long-term assistance
Mass care

Health and Safety Education
Babysitting courses
CPR courses
First aid courses
HIV/AIDS education
Nurse assistant training

COMPETITORS

America's Blood Centers
Daxor
Ellis & Associates
HemaCare
SeraCare
Tissue Banks

HISTORICAL FINANCIALS & EMPLOYEES

Not-for-profit FYE: June	Annual Growth	1990	1991	1992	1993	1994	1995	1996	1997	1998	1999
Sales ($ mil.)	5.7%	1,466	1,410	1,568	1,796	1,740	1,724	1,814	1,940	2,080	2,421
Employees	2.6%	—	25,000	25,000	25,000	32,169	31,000	30,021	29,850	30,000	—

SALES HISTORY

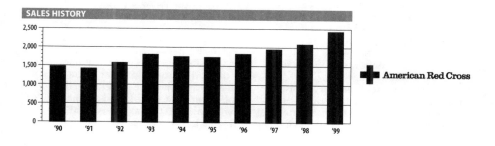

American Red Cross

AMERICAN STOCK EXCHANGE, INC.

OVERVIEW

After years as the perennial odd man out in the US securities markets game, the American Stock Exchange (AMEX) has joined forces with Nasdaq, the electronic stock market arm of the National Association of Securities Dealers (NASD) in hopes of presenting a united front against the New York Stock Exchange (NYSE) in the competition for stock listings.

AMEX is a unit of The Nasdaq-Amex Market Group, an NASD subsidiary. The New York-based AMEX lists small and midsized companies, derivatives, foreign issues, ADRs (American depositary receipts), ADSs (American depositary shares), and options. The number of companies listed on AMEX — about 800 — has remained fairly static in the past two decades, while listings on the NYSE and Nasdaq soared. AMEX had spent heavily on technology, advertising, and promotion but remained a market in search of stocks.

In addition to reducing trading costs, the Nasdaq-AMEX combination was intended both to facilitate technical upgrades for the struggling floor-based exchange (NASD pledged $110 million for the cause) and also to give investors a choice between the AMEX's auction trading and Nasdaq's dealer system.

HISTORY

For 128 years after the 1792 formation of what is now known as the NYSE, a gypsy crew of traders continued to deal in stocks on the streets of New York City. The trade was risky, as both the traders and their stocks were unfettered by listing or dealing standards, and pricing and volume reporting was impossible.

In 1911 some of these traders formed the New York Curb Market Association to set trading rules. Ten years later it moved indoors at its current location as the New York Curb Market (later the New York Curb Exchange). The move indoors allowed it to begin reporting trades. "The Curb" grew in the 1920s.

Renamed the American Stock Exchange in 1953, it suffered scandals over price manipulation and the trading of unregistered stocks during the 1950s. AMEX was always less an old-boys preserve than the NYSE, and the exchange appointed its first woman governor, Mary Roebling, in 1958. Though it soon granted women regular membership, women did not trade on the floor until 1977.

In the 1960s the exchange began to automate, offering computerized telephone quotations and, later, computerized ticker, clearing, and surveillance systems. In 1972 AMEX joined with the NYSE to form Securities Industry Automation Corporation. That year NYSE and AMEX had nearly equal listings. But then Nasdaq, a new electronic marketplace without a trading floor, began grabbing listings, particularly of high-tech companies that would ordinarily have gone to AMEX. AMEX's market share began a decade-long decline.

In response, the exchange added Treasury instruments, options, and derivatives and sought foreign listings and alliances. After the 1987 stock crash, AMEX raised margin limits and established circuit-breaker procedures to control price declines.

Having fallen to a distant third place in the securities market, AMEX sought new blood, appointing Wall Street outsider and former congressman James Jones as chairman in 1989. But his tenure was marked by dissension. Jones was named ambassador to Mexico by President Clinton in 1993, and the chairmanship remained open for nearly a year.

AMEX continued to seek niche markets. It formed the Emerging Companies Market (ECM), a micro-cap market. But inadequate vetting of listees resulted in embarrassment when it was found that officers of several companies had had previous problems with the SEC. Despite the ECM's tendency to attract risky, even shady, ventures, AMEX proposed creating an index of even smaller companies.

During the 1990s AMEX upgraded its technical systems, becoming the first exchange to feature an electronic system of recording trades with wireless, handheld terminals.

Richard Syron, a former president of the Boston Federal Reserve Bank, came aboard as chairman and CEO in 1994. He upgraded AMEX's image, shuttered the ECM in 1995, and increased promotional efforts. The exchange began a restructuring the next year to reduce costs and further emphasize customer service.

In 1997 AMEX lost one of its biggest listings, New York Times Co., to the NYSE. AMEX and the NASD began discussing their proposed combination that year, and the deal was completed in 1998. Shortly thereafter the Philadelphia Stock Exchange agreed to join the new entity, but those plans fizzled by 1999. In 1999, Syron announced plans to leave AMEX to join Thermo Electron Corp.

Chairman and CEO: Salvatore F. Sodono, age 43
VC: Anthony J. Boglioli
SEVP Administration and Operations: Mark D. Fichtel
EVP and Chief Information Officer: Gregor S. Bailar
EVP Derivative Securities: Joseph B. Stefanelli
EVP Marketing: Ronald D. Corwin
EVP Member Firm Regulation: Stephen L. Lister
EVP: Richard G. Ketchum
EVP: Mary L. Shapiro
SVP Capital Markets: Richard A. Mikaliunas
SVP Corporate Relations and Library: Lois A. Schmidt
SVP Derivatives Marketing and Research:
  Michael T. Bickford
SVP Derivative Securities: Lawrence Larkin
SVP Finance and CFO: Paul R. Shackford
VP Listing Qualification: Michael S. Emen
SVP Market Operations and Trading Floor Systems:
  Ralph R. Rafaniello
SVP Member Liaison: Steven Lesser
SVP New Product Planning: Gary L. Gastineau
Director Human Resources: Suzanne Johnson
Auditors: KPMG LLP

LOCATIONS

HQ: 86 Trinity Place, New York, NY 10006
Phone: 212-306-1000   **Fax:** 212-306-1218
Web site: http://www.amex.com

PRODUCTS/OPERATIONS

1997 Sales

	$ mil.	% of total
Trading fees	81	41
Market data fees	78	39
Listing fees	16	8
Member dues & fees	14	7
Other	9	5
Total	**198**	**100**

Selected Products and Services
Equities trading
Equity options
Flexible exchange options (FLEX)
Index options
Long-term Equity Anticipation Securities (LEAPS)
Standard & Poor's Depositary Receipts (SPDRs)

Selected Companies Listed

Equity Issues	Options
Echo Bay Mines	American Express
Gaylord Container	Apple Computer
Greyhound Lines	Chase Manhattan
Hanover Direct	Digital Equipment
Hasbro	Intel
Media General	Philip Morris
TWA	Walt Disney
Viacom	

COMPETITORS

CBOE
NYSE
Reuters

HISTORICAL FINANCIALS & EMPLOYEES

Subsidiary FYE: December	Annual Growth	1988	1989	1990	1991	1992	1993	1994	1995	1996	1997
Sales ($ mil.)	7.5%	103	110	107	101	114	131	144	153	170	198
Net income ($ mil.)	18.0%	3	4	0	(1)	1	7	8	5	6.5	13.3
Income as % of sales	—	2.9%	3.6%	—	(1.0%)	0.9%	5.3%	5.6%	3.3%	3.8%	6.7%
Employees	(5.7%)	—	—	—	—	—	850	708	690	676	—

The American Stock Exchange was acquired by the National Association of Securities Dealers, Inc. in 1998.

NET INCOME HISTORY

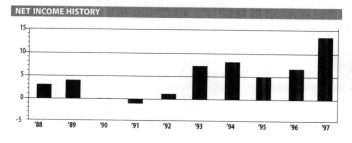

AMERISERVE FOOD DISTRIBUTION

OVERVIEW

The American way of dining — out — serves AmeriServe well. The #2 food service distributor in the US (far behind SYSCO), Addison, Texas-based AmeriServe Food Distribution serves about 36,000 fast-food and casual dining restaurants coast to coast. It supplies restaurant chains with most of their needs: food (dairy products, meat, poultry, seafood, canned goods, produce), beverages, cleaning supplies, paper products, and equipment.

AmeriServe's biggest customers are restaurants operated or franchised by Burger King, TRICON Global Restaurants (KFC, Pizza Hut, Taco Bell), and Darden Restaurants (Red Lobster, Olive Garden). It also serves Arby's, Dairy Queen, Applebee's, and Chick-fil-A, among other restaurants.

To borrow a term from non-customer McDonald's, AmeriServe has been supersizing itself. It more than doubled in size with its 1997 purchase of PepsiCo's PFS food distribution operations, which served the TRICON restaurants in the US, Canada, and Mexico. AmeriServe's sales surged again with its 1998 purchase of rival distributor ProSource. While still digesting PFS and ProSource, the company is continuing to seek tasty acquisitions.

Holberg Industries owns 93% of AmeriServe. The other 7% is owned by Norwegian consumer goods company Orkla, which also owns 34% of Holberg. John Holten owns the rest of Holberg, whose other major holding is parking-lot management firm APCOA/Standard Parking.

HISTORY

AmeriServe Food Distribution's ingredients began coming together in 1986 when John Holten and Gunnar Klintberg formed Holberg Inc. to acquire and manage companies in the food service distribution industry. That year, in partnership with Norway's Nora Industrier (now part of Orkla), Holberg bought NEBCO Distribution of Omaha, a Nebraska concession company that had been formed in 1946.

Holberg formed Holberg Industries in 1989. In 1990 Holberg Industries created NEBCO EVANS Distribution with its acquisition of Evans Brothers, a Wisconsin-based regional distributor that had begun roasting nuts around 1940. Additional acquisitions in the early 1990s included regional operators L.L. Distribution Systems and Condon Supply, both of Minnesota.

In 1996, when NEBCO EVANS had sales of $400 million, it bought AmeriServ, a wholesale distributor that had also been formed by buying small distributors. Dallas investment banker John Lewis had led a group of Texas investors in buying Sonneveldt (Michigan) in 1988 and Interstate Distributors (Georgia) the next year; he merged the two and incorporated the company in 1989 as AmeriServ Food Co.

By the end of 1991, AmeriServ had added four more companies — Alpha Distributors (Wisconsin), First Choice Food Distributors (Texas), Harry H. Post Co. (50%, Colorado), and Food Service Systems (Missouri). The company filed for an IPO several times over the years but never went public, partly because of investor concerns over its heavy dependence on one customer — hamburger chain Wendy's.

With NEBCO EVANS' purchases of AmeriServ and the remaining 50% of the Harry H.

Post Co., it became NEBCO-AmeriServ, a company with sales of $1.4 billion. Early in 1997 it dropped the "NEBCO," and consolidated all of its companies under the name AmeriServe Food Distribution.

That year the company was awarded a $325 million contract to service more than 2,500 Arby's restaurants. But the Arby's deal was small potatoes next to AmeriServe's mid-1997 acquisition of PFS, PepsiCo's food service unit, which primarily supplied PepsiCo's fast-food chains. (To focus on its beverage and snack businesses, later that year PepsiCo spun off its KFC, Pizza Hut, and Taco Bell restaurants, forming TRICON Global Restaurants.)

The $830 million PFS purchase more than doubled AmeriServe's size and made it one of the nation's largest food distributors to restaurant chains. Besides adding more than 15,000 PFS restaurant customers, the buy expanded the firm into the Northeast and the West Coast, and it boosted 1997 sales to $3.4 billion.

AmeriServe had barely burped when it acquired ProSource in 1998 for $320 million, which added casual dining restaurant chains T.G.I. Friday's and Red Lobster to its customer base; that deal bumped up the company's sales by about $4 billion. However, later that year, Wendy's yanked $600 million worth of sales from AmeriServe and handed them to top rival SYSCO.

To reduce costs and boost its cash reserves, in late 1999 AmeriServe announced that it would cut 1,500 jobs, or about 15% of its workforce, and raise at least $110 million through asset sales and inventory reductions.

Chairman and CEO: John V. Holten, age 42
VC and EVP: Raymond E. Marshall, age 49, $823,977 pay
VC: David R. Parker, age 55
EVP and COO: Dick Lane, age 51, $533,730 pay
EVP and CFO: Diana Moog, $534,312 pay
SVP, General Counsel, and Secretary: Kevin J. Rogan, age 47
VP Planning: Nancy M. Bittner, age 35
VP Human Resources: Bonnie MacEslin
VP, Treasurer, and Assistant Secretary: Paul A. Garcia de Quevedo, age 45
VP: A. Peter Ostberg
VP Investor Relations and Chief Accounting Officer: Stanley J. Szlauderbach, age 50
VP and Controller: Ginette Wooldridge, age 41
President, ProSource: Robert S. Donaldson
President, Purchasing & Logistics: John D. Gainor
Acting Chief Information Officer: Bruce Graham, age 36

LOCATIONS

HQ: Ameriserve Food Distribution, Inc.,
   15305 Dallas Pkwy., Addison, TX 75001
Phone: 972-364-2000   **Fax:** 972-364-2235
Web site: http://www.ameriserve.com

PRODUCTS/OPERATIONS

1998 Sales

	% of total
Burger King	25
Taco Bell	17
Pizza Hut	16
KFC	7
Red Lobster	7
Arby's	4
Other	24
Total	**100**

Selected Customers

Applebee's	Olive Garden
Arby's	Pizza Hut
Burger King	Red Lobster
Chick-fil-A	Sonic
Chili's	Subway
Dairy Queen	Taco Bell
KFC	TCBY
Lone Star Steakhouse	T.G.I. Friday's
Long John Silver's	

COMPETITORS

Alliant Foodservice	McLane
Ben E. Keith	Performance Food
Golden State Foods	SYSCO
Gordon Food Service	Sara Lee
Keystone Foods	Services Group
MBM	U.S. Foodservice
Martin-Brower	

HISTORICAL FINANCIALS & EMPLOYEES

Subsidiary FYE: December	Annual Growth	1989	1990	1991	1992	1993	1994	1995	1996	1997	1998
Sales ($ mil.)	71.3%	—	—	—	294	328	359	400	1,281	3,446	7,421
Net income ($ mil.)	—	—	—	—	0	0	0	1	3	(74)	(147)
Income as % of sales	—	—	—	—	0.0%	0.1%	0.0%	0.1%	0.2%	—	—
Employees	37.2%	—	—	—	1,200	1,150	1,250	1,500	5,100	5,000	8,000

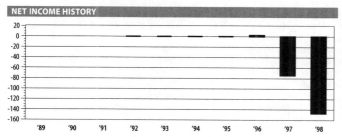

NET INCOME HISTORY

1998 FISCAL YEAR-END
Debt ratio: 99.9%
Return on equity: —
Cash ($ mil.): 5
Current ratio: 0.62
Long-term debt ($ mil.): 903

AMWAY CORPORATION

OVERVIEW

They did it . . . Amway. The DeVos and Van Andel families' direct-sales firm has grown into a global enterprise, distributing home and personal care products in more than 80 countries and territories. The Ada, Michigan-based company includes about 50 affiliates and two majority-owned sister companies: Amway Japan (Japan is Amway's top market) and Amway Asia Pacific. About 70% of the firm's sales come from outside North America.

The world's largest direct-sales company, Amway sells what it calls "soap and hope." The "soap" is its line of more than 450 personal care, nutrition, home, and commercial products such as ARTISTRY cosmetics and NUTRILITE vitamins. Like rivals Herbalife and Mary Kay, Amway uses an army of distributors to sell products and bring in new sales recruits; to these 3 million (mostly part-time) distributors, it offers "hope," in part through giant rallies akin to fundamentalist Christian revivals.

Amway, a major Republican Party donor, is owned by billionaire founders Richard DeVos and Jay Van Andel and their families. A policy board composed of DeVos and Van Andel and four children from each family governs the firm.

The company's new venture, Quixtar, is a departure from its history of selling face-to-face. The venture sells Amway's household brands online without using the Amway name.

HISTORY

After serving in the Army Air Corps in WWII, high school pals Richard DeVos and Jay Van Andel tried several moneymaking projects. In the late 1940s they became distributors for NUTRILITE, a California vitamin company that had pioneered network sales (in which distributors receive commissions on sales made by the people they recruit). In 1958, when NUTRILITE's leadership was failing, DeVos and Van Andel decided to develop their own product line. They founded the American Way Association (later shortened to Amway) in 1959. Van Andel oversaw Amway's nuts and bolts while DeVos provided the motivational spark.

Amway's first product was a multipurpose solution called L.O.C. (Liquid Organic Cleaner). The firm then began making laundry detergent, other household cleaners, and personal grooming products. In 1963 Amway was in Canada. By 1964 the company's sales had reached $10 million. Administration and sales support could barely keep up with the growth of the distributor network: 70 building projects, including factories and warehouses, were begun between 1960 and 1978. The "American Way" soon caught on in Australia and Europe.

In the early 1970s Amway bought NUTRILITE (1972) and expanded to Asia (Hong Kong, 1974). In 1977 the company bought the Mutual Broadcasting System (radio stations in Chicago and New York City; sold 1985). Two years later an FTC ruling exonerated Amway of charges that it was a pyramid scheme, saying that because distributors receive commissions only on actual sales of their recruit network — and Amway buys back excess inventory — the business was legitimate. In 1982 Amway was charged with defrauding the Canadian government of $22 million in import duties. It pleaded guilty and paid $50 million.

Following several suits alleging abusive sales practices, in 1984 Amway brought in William Nicholson (a former assistant to President Gerald Ford) to help it reorganize; he beefed up training and added new products and services, including MCI long-distance service and a car discount program. In 1991 rival Procter & Gamble (P&G) won a $75,000 judgment against Amway distributors for spreading rumors linking P&G with Satanism. Nicholson stepped down as COO in 1992.

The company formed a $29 million joint venture in 1992 to build a plant in China. The next year, to finance its China strategy, it spun off 13.4% of Hong Kong-based subsidiary Amway Asia Pacific. Amway Japan also went public in 1993. That year DeVos retired as president and was replaced by his son Dick. In 1995 Van Andel retired, handing the chairmanship to his son Steve. P&G charged in 1996 that Amway distributors had used the company's AMVOX voice-mail system for continued rumormongering.

The next year Amway formed alliances with Rubbermaid to sell its products overseas and with Waterford Crystal to sell vases in North America. China banned direct selling in 1998; revised rules allowed Amway to sell its products there by having distributors act as sales representatives rather than buy the products and resell them. P&G lawsuits against Amway continued, and Amway filed a similar lawsuit against P&G in 1998. Amway teamed up with Columbia Energy Group in 1998 to begin selling gas to households.

In 1999 Amway began selling items online under the name Quixtar.

Chairman and Co-CEO; Chairman, Amway Asia/Pacific:
Steve Van Andel, age 43
President and Co-CEO; Chairman, Amway Japan:
Richard M. DeVos Jr., age 43
SVP, CFO, and Treasurer: Lawrence Call
SVP New Business Ventures: David Brenner
SVP Operations: Al Koop
SVP Europe and Americas: Dave Van Andel
SVP Global Distributor Relations, Amway Asia/Pacific:
Doug DeVos
SVP and General Counsel, Amway and Amway Asia/Pacific: Craig Meurlin
VP Human Resources: Pamela Linton
VP Catalog and Communications: Nan Van Andel

LOCATIONS

HQ: 7575 Fulton St. East, Ada, MI 49355
Phone: 616-787-6000   **Fax:** 616-787-6177
Web site: http://www.amway.com

Amway has manufacturing facilities in the US, China, and South Korea and farming operations in the US, Mexico, and Brazil. It sells its products worldwide.

PRODUCTS/OPERATIONS

Selected Products

Cosmetics
ARTISTRY Cosmetics
ARTISTRY Skin Care

Home Care
Dish Drops dishwashing liquid
Household cleaners
L.O.C. multipurpose cleaner
SA8 laundry detergent

Home Tech (Living)
Queen cookware
Water treatment

Nutrition and Wellness
Active 8 Beverages
Modern Magic Meals foods
NUTRILITE multivitamins and dietary supplements
Positrim Weight Control System
Snack Sense snacks

Personal Care
Body washes and soaps
Children's care
Glister/Spreedent toothpaste
Hair care
Lotion

Other
Franklin Covey Day Planner
Oneida flatware
Rubbermaid food storage
Waterford Crystal stemware
Wedgwood Home dinnerware
WiltonArmetale serveware

Selected Services
Auto leasing
Columbia Energy natural gas
Home mortgage
MCI WorldCom long distance

COMPETITORS

Avon	Johnson & Johnson
Brown-Forman	Kao
Clorox	L'Oréal
Colgate-Palmolive	MacAndrews & Forbes
Daiei	Mary Kay
Dial	Newell Rubbermaid
Esteé Lauder	Nu Skin
Fingerhut	Procter & Gamble
GNC	S.C. Johnson
Gillette	Shaklee
Henkel	Tupperware
Herbalife	Unilever

HISTORICAL FINANCIALS & EMPLOYEES

Private FYE: August	Annual Growth	1990	1991	1992	1993	1994	1995	1996	1997	1998	1999
Sales ($ mil.)	14.0%	1,842	2,550	3,069	3,465	4,309	4,958	5,352	6,000	5,700	6,000
Employees	3.2%	7,500	9,500	10,000	11,000	12,500	13,000	13,000	13,000	14,000	10,000

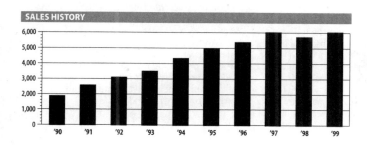

SALES HISTORY

ANDERSEN CORPORATION

OVERVIEW

A room with a view always suits Andersen, one of the world's largest manufacturers of wooden windows and patio doors. Based in Bayport, Minnesota, Andersen produces 15 styles of windows, and it has products that come in more than 50,000 dimensions. The company sells its products through independent distributors in Argentina, Brazil, Canada, Ireland, Israel, Japan, Kuwait, Mexico, Panama, Portugal, South Korea, Spain, the UK, and the US.

The company's targets include residential builders, contractors, professional remodelers, and homeowners. Known for its benefits and incentive programs, the company compensates employees well; its nonunion employees own stock and receive in the profits as well. Members of the Andersen family continue to be major shareholders.

HISTORY

Danish immigrant Hans Andersen and his two sons, Fred and Herbert, founded Anderson in 1903. Andersen's first words in English, "All together, boys," became the company motto. Andersen arrived in Portland, Maine, in 1870 and worked as a lumber dealer and manufacturer. In the 1880s he purchased a sawmill in St. Cloud, Minnesota, and later managed one in Hudson, Wisconsin. When the Hudson mill owners asked him to let workers go during the off season, Andersen refused and then resigned. He subsequently launched his own lumber operations — Andersen Lumber Company — and hired some of the men who were laid off. He started a second lumberyard, in Afton, Minnesota, in 1904. Andersen and his sons revolutionized the window industry in the early 1900s by introducing a standardized window frame with interchangeable parts. Buoyed by success, the Andersens sold their lumberyards in 1908 to focus on the window-frame business. (Andersen purchased lumberyards again in 1916 before exiting the lumberyard business for good in the 1930s.)

Thrifty Hans launched the company's first (and the US's third) profit-sharing plan shortly before his death in 1914. Herbert became VP, secretary, treasurer, and factory manager, and Fred became president. Herbert died in 1921 (at age 36), but Fred proved to be a versatile and capable replacement. Among his accomplishments, Fred came up with the tag line "Only the rich can afford poor windows."

In 1929 the company changed its name to Andersen Frame Corporation. In the following decade Andersen introduced a number of innovations, including Master Frame (a frame with a locked sill joint, 1930); a casement window, the industry's first complete factory-made window unit (1932); and a basement window (1934). The company adopted its current name in 1937.

Andersen introduced a new concept, the gliding window, in the early 1940s. It also launched a consumer ad campaign, the Home Planners Scrap Book, in 1943. During the 1950s Andersen created new products, including the Flexivent awning window (featuring welded insulating glass), which served as an alternative to traditional storm windows. In the 1960s the company launched a gliding door and the Perma-Shield system. This system featured easy-to-maintain vinyl cladding to protect wood frames from weathering. By 1978 Perma-Shield products accounted for three-quarters of sales. Fred, who had run the company as president until 1960 (when he handed over control to Andersen veteran Earl Swanson) and subsequently held the positions of chairman and chairman emeritus, died in 1979 at age 92.

Between 1984 and 1994 the company increased its sales threefold by introducing additional customized and state-of-the-art products, including patio doors. In 1995 it launched Andersen-Renewal, a retail window-replacement business now in nine US locations.

In 1997 Andersen acquired former long-term strategic partner Aspen Research, a company engaged in materials testing, research, and product development. Among their jointly developed products is Fibrex, a composite material used in replacement windows. Also in 1997 the company moved its international division office from Bayport, Minnesota, to the Minnesota World Trade Center in St. Paul to help boost its export drive.

Company veteran Donald Garofalo succeeded Andersen's president and CEO Jerold Wulf, who retired after a 39-year career in 1998. The same year, Andersen represented the industry in the federal government's ENERGY STAR program, aimed at producing energy-efficient windows. Andersen reinforced its presence in the door industry in 1999 when it acquired millwork distributor Morgan Products.

Chairperson: Sarah J. Andersen
President and CEO: Donald Garofalo
EVP: Charles W. Schmid
SVP Corporate Business Services and CFO:
   Michael O. Johnson
SVP Corporate Operation Services: W. Patrick Riley
VP Technology and Business Development:
   Kurt E. Heikkila
Treasurer and Controller: Keith Olsen
Manager Human Resources: Jan Grose

LOCATIONS

HQ: 100 4th Ave. North, Bayport, MN 55003
Phone: 651-439-5150   **Fax:** 651-430-5107
Web site: http://www.andersencorp.com

PRODUCTS/OPERATIONS

Selected Products
Patio doors
Windows
   Awning
   Casement
   Double-hung
   Gliding
   Roof
   Skylight
   Specialty

COMPETITORS

Anglian Group	Royal Group Technologies
JELD-WEN	Sierra Pacific Industries
Overhead Door	Thermal Industries
Pella	Weru

HISTORICAL FINANCIALS & EMPLOYEES

Private FYE: December	Annual Growth	1989	1990	1991	1992	1993	1994	1995	1996	1997	1998
Estimated sales ($ mil.)	6.5%	—	—	900	1,000	1,000	1,100	1,200	1,250	1,300	1,400
Employees	0.0%	—	—	—	—	—	3,700	3,700	3,700	3,700	3,700

SALES HISTORY

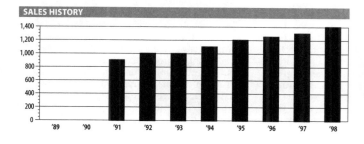

ANDERSEN WORLDWIDE

OVERVIEW

The battle Andersen Worldwide faces with the other Big Five accounting/consulting firms is nothing compared to what's going on within its own ranks. The Chicago-based partnership — #2 after PricewaterhouseCoopers — operates in nearly 80 countries and has correspondent relationships with other accounting firms in nearly 50 more.

The Arthur Andersen accounting unit's tradition of intensive training and discipline bordering on regimentation has earned its professionals the sobriquet "Arthur Androids." Andersen Consulting, which provides application management, business processing, and information technology services, has a much more relaxed culture.

When Arthur Andersen's traditional auditing services business became vulnerable to price competition and client mobility, it began offering internal audit and tax process oversight and outsourcing services, which provide steadier income. It also moved into human resources, international trade, and risk and legal consulting. This brought Arthur Andersen into direct competition with Andersen Consulting, which brings in about 54% of sales. The consultants, unwilling to share their wealth with the accountants, are trying to dismantle Andersen Worldwide. The accountants, who subsidized the consulting operations for years, want the firm to remain unified.

HISTORY

Arthur Andersen worked in Price Waterhouse's Chicago office in 1907. After becoming Illinois' youngest CPA, he began teaching accounting at Northwestern University in 1908, at age 23 and later became head of the accounting department there. In 1913 he joined with Clarence DeLany to form Andersen, DeLany & Company.

The establishment of both the Federal Reserve System and the federal income tax that year increased the demand for accounting services. In 1915 the firm opened a Milwaukee office. After DeLany's departure in 1918, the firm became Arthur Andersen & Co.

The company grew rapidly in the 1920s and began performing financial investigations, which formed the basis for its management consulting practice. When Samuel Insull's utility empire collapsed in 1932, Andersen was appointed the bankruptcy trustee during the refinancing. The firm opened additional offices in Boston and Houston in 1937 and in Atlanta and Minneapolis in 1940.

Andersen dominated the firm until his death in 1947. His successor was Leonard Spacek, who presided over the firm until 1963; during his tenure Arthur Andersen opened 18 US offices and began its international expansion with the establishment of a Mexico City office, followed by 25 more in other countries. The firm entered the consulting business in 1954.

Arthur Andersen was an innovator in its field. The firm's Center for Professional Education (Andersen University) was opened in the early 1970s in St. Charles, Illinois, and the firm provided the industry's first worldwide annual report in 1973.

The firm's consulting arm was growing too; by 1988 it was the world's largest consulting business, with consulting fees accounting for 40% of total sales. Tension between consultants and auditors built until 1989, when Arthur Andersen and Andersen Consulting were established.

In the 1990s Arthur Andersen was drawn into several lawsuits alleging that it should have detected the financial misdeeds that caused several S&Ls to fail; these issues were settled in 1993. In response to changes in the auditing business, and under pressure to limit the number of partners sharing the profits, in 1995 the firm changed its career tracks to lengthen the partnership track and to provide a nonpartnership path.

The rift between the audit and consulting sides widened in 1997 when managing partner and CEO Lawrence Weinbach announced his retirement. Neither side was able to elect a successor and the board appointed accounting partner W. Robert Grafton as CEO. Soon thereafter, Andersen Consulting's partners voted to break away.

In 1998 a migration of workers between the units brought rumors that the split was at hand. Instead, the dispute dragged on into 1999 and went into arbitration. In a surprise move just as the process was entering its testimony stage, George Shaheen, who had presided over Andersen Consulting's explosive growth and had been a major hawk on the breakup issue, resigned to join an online grocery company, Webvan. The same year, Andersen Consulting said it would form a $1 billion venture capital fund to invest in e-commerce companies.

Managing Partner and CEO: W. Robert Grafton
Managing Partner Finance and Administration:
James R. Kackley
Worldwide Managing Partner, Arthur Andersen:
Jim Wadia
Managing Partner and CEO, Andersen Consulting:
Joe W. Forehand, age 51
Managing Partner and CFO, Arthur Andersen:
Clement W. Eibl
**Managing Partner and Chief Information Officer,
Arthur Andersen:** Eric C. Dean
**Managing Partner and General Counsel, Arthur
Andersen:** Daniel D. Beckel
**Managing Partner Assurance and Business Advisory,
Arthur Andersen:** Michael L. Bennett
**Managing Partner Business Consulting, Arthur
Andersen:** Charles H. Ketteman
**Managing Partner Global Corporate Finance, Arthur
Andersen:** Martin E. Thorp
**Managing Partner Global Risk Management, Arthur
Andersen:** Robert G. Kutsenda
Managing Partner Global 1000, Arthur Andersen:
James D. Edwards
**Managing Partner Human Resources and Partner
Matters, Arthur Andersen:** Peter Pesce
**Managing Partner Strategy and Planning, Arthur
Andersen:** Richard E.S. Boulton
**Managing Partner Tax, Legal, and Business Advisory,
Arthur Andersen:** Alberto E. Terol
**Managing Partner Worldwide Communications and
Integrated Marketing, Arthur Andersen:**
Matthew P. Gonring
Area Managing Partner, Asia/Pacific, Arthur Andersen:
Terry E. Hatchett
**Area Managing Partner, Europe, Middle East, India,
and Africa, Arthur Andersen:** Xavier de Sarrau
**Area Managing Partner, Latin America, Arthur
Andersen:** Jose Luis Vazquez
**Country Managing Partner, United States, Arthur
Andersen:** Steve M. Samek

HQ: 33 W. Monroe St., Chicago, IL 60603
Phone: 312-580-0033   **Fax:** 312-507-6748
Web site: http://www.arthurandersen.com

1998 Sales

	$ mil.	% of total
Consulting	9,000	55
Accounting	7,300	45
Total	**16,300**	**100**

Operating Units

Andersen Consulting
Application management (software applications for
  clients)
Business process outsourcing
Design, Build, Run (creation, delivery, and operation of
  integrated, enterprise-wide applications)
Information technology outsourcing

Arthur Andersen
Assurance and Business Advisory Services
  Assurance and Process Assessment Services
  Business Ethics Services
  Business Risk Consulting Services and Assurance
  Contract Audit Services
  Contract Finance and Accounting services
Business Consulting
Economic and Financial Consulting
Tax, Legal, and Business Advisory Services

American Management
Arthur D. Little
BDO International
Bain & Company
Booz, Allen
Boston Consulting
Computer Sciences
Deloitte Touche Tohmatsu
EDS
Ernst & Young
Grant Thornton
  International
IBM
KPMG
MCI WorldCom
Marsh & McLennan
McKinsey & Company
Perot Systems
Policy Management
  Systems
PricewaterhouseCoopers
Towers Perrin

Partnership FYE: August	Annual Growth	1990	1991	1992	1993	1994	1995	1996	1997	1998	1999
Sales ($ mil.)	16.4%	4,160	4,948	5,577	6,017	6,738	8,134	9,499	11,300	13,900	16,300
Employees	10.1%	56,801	59,797	62,134	66,478	72,722	82,121	91,572	104,933	123,791	135,000

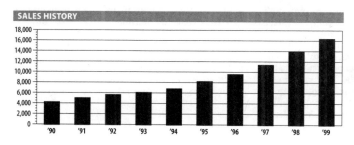

SALES HISTORY

ANDERSEN WORLDWIDE

ANTHEM INSURANCE COMPANIES

OVERVIEW

Anthem Insurance Companies is finding out what B. B. King already knows: Getting the blues ain't easy. Indianapolis-based Anthem is a mutual health care management company that licenses the Blue Cross and Blue Shield name, providing health insurance to more than 5 million customers in Connecticut, New Hampshire, Indiana, Kentucky, and Ohio. Subsidiaries administer Medicare and military health insurance programs.

Selling noncore health care operations has made the company leaner, meaner, and more focused on the Blues, which it is looking to expand left and right. State regulators and public watchdog groups are fighting Anthem's proposed acquisition of Blue Cross and Blue Shield operations in Rhode Island, Maine, and Colorado, despite the Blues' eagerness to be acquired. Critics say Anthem's for-profit status would jeopardize health care for the poor, a traditional market for the Blues.

HISTORY

Anthem's earliest predecessor, prepaid hospital plan Blue Cross of Indiana, was founded in 1944. Unlike other Blues, Blue Cross of Indiana never received tax advantages or mandated discounts, so it competed as a private insurer. Within two years it had 100,000 members; by 1970 there were nearly 2 million.

Blue Shield of Indiana, another Anthem precursor, also grew rapidly after its 1946 formation as a mutual insurance company to cover doctors' services. The two organizations shared expenses and jointly managed the state's Medicare and Medicaid programs.

The 1970s and early 1980s were difficult as Indiana's economy stagnated and health insurance competition increased. In 1982 the joint operation restructured, adding new management and service policies to improve its performance.

Following the 1982 merger of the national Blue Cross and Blue Shield organizations, the Indiana Blues merged in 1985 as Associated Insurance Companies. The next year the company moved outside Indiana and began diversifying to help insulate itself from such industry changes as the shift to managed care. That year the company was renamed Associated Group to reflect its broader focus.

By 1990 Associated Group had more than 25 operating units with nationwide offerings, including health insurance, HMO services, life insurance, insurance brokerage, financial services, and insurance software and services.

The group grew throughout the mid-1990s, buying health insurer Southeastern Mutual Insurance (including Kentucky Blue Cross and Blue Shield) in 1992, diversified insurer Federal Kemper (a Kemper Corporation subsidiary) in 1993, and Seattle-based property/casualty brokerage Pettit-Morry in 1994. That year it entered the health care delivery market with the creation of American Health Network, which accepts patients from the group's managed care competitors.

In 1995 the company merged with Ohio Blues licensee Community Mutual and took the Anthem name. Merger-related charges caused a loss that year.

Anthem bounced back the next year thanks to cost-cutting and customers switching to its more profitable managed care plans. Anthem divested its individual life insurance and annuity business and its Anthem Financial subsidiaries. Its 1996 deal to buy Blue Cross and Blue Shield of New Jersey fell apart in 1997 because of New Jersey Blue's charitable status. Anthem did manage to buy Blue Cross and Blue Shield of Connecticut that year.

Anthem in 1997 sold four property/casualty insurance subsidiaries to Vesta Insurance Group. It bought the remainder of its Acordia property/casualty unit (workers' compensation), then sold Acordia's brokerage operations. That year Anthem was involved in court battles regarding the Blue mergers in Kentucky, as well as in Connecticut, where litigants feared a rise in their premiums. Expenses related to merging Blues organizations contributed to a loss that year.

Anthem shed the rest of its noncore operations in 1998, selling subsidiary Anthem Health and Life Insurance Company to Canadian insurer Great-West Life Assurance. Anthem's 1999 bid for the parent of Blue Cross and Blue Shield of Colorado (countered by an offer from WellPoint Health Networks) is still pending. Anthem's proposed purchase of Blue Cross and Blue Shield of Maine and merger with the Blues in Rhode Island have stalled because of outcries similar to those that dogged earlier pairings.

In 1999 the company agreed to settle lawsuits related to its 1997 merger with Blue Cross and Blue Shield of Connecticut by financing public health foundations. Anthem also bought the Blues plan in New Hampshire that year.

Chairman, President, and CEO: L. Ben Lytle
President and COO; Acting President, Anthem Blue Cross and Blue Shield of Connecticut: Larry C. Glasscock
EVP and CFO: Michael L. Smith
EVP and Chief Legal and Administrative Officer: David R. Frick
SVP Human Resources: Robert C. Heird
VP and Chief Actuary: Cynthia S. Miller
VP and Chief Information Officer: Jane Niederberger
VP and Chief Investment Officer: Michael C. Koetters
VP and Corporate Secretary: Nancy L. Purcell
VP and Treasurer: George D. Martin
VP Finance and Controller: Robert Schneider
President, AdminaStar: Barbara J. Gagel
President, Anthem Blue Cross and Blue Shield, Midwest Operations: Keith R. Faller
President, Anthem Life: John J. Gainor
President, Anthem Prescription Management: James Lang
Auditors: Ernst & Young LLP

LOCATIONS

HQ: Anthem Insurance Companies, Inc.,
120 Monument Circle, Indianapolis, IN 46204
Phone: 317-488-6000   **Fax:** 317-488-6028
Web site: http://www.anthem-inc.com

PRODUCTS/OPERATIONS

1998 Assets

	$ mil.	% of total
Cash & equivalents	218	5
Bonds	2,230	51
Stocks	454	10
Other securities	29	1
Receivables	668	15
Other assets	781	18
Total	**4,380**	**100**

1998 Sales

	$ mil.	% of total
Premiums	4,946	84
Administrative fees	554	9
Net realized gains on investments	156	3
Net investment income	148	3
Other income	74	1
Total	**5,878**	**100**

Selected Operations

AdminaStar (Medicare contracting)
Anthem Alliance (military health insurance)
Anthem Blue Cross and Blue Shield - Connecticut
Anthem Blue Cross and Blue Shield Midwest (Indiana, Kentucky, and Ohio)
Anthem Blue Cross and Blue Shield (New Hampshire)
Anthem Health and Life Insurance Company of New York

COMPETITORS

Aetna
CIGNA
Coventry Health Care
Highmark
Kaiser Foundation
Maxicare Health Plans
Oxford Health Plans
UnitedHealth Group
WellPoint Health Networks

HISTORICAL FINANCIALS & EMPLOYEES

Mutual company FYE: December	Annual Growth	1989	1990	1991	1992	1993	1994	1995	1996	1997	1998
Sales ($ mil.)	0.7%	—	—	—	—	—	5,722	6,038	6,270	6,299	5,878
Net income ($ mil.)	19.4%	—	—	—	—	71	72	(98)	64	(159)	172
Income as % of sales	—	—	—	—	—	—	1.3%	—	1.0%	—	2.9%
Employees	(2.6%)	—	—	—	—	—	12,800	16,290	17,061	14,974	11,504

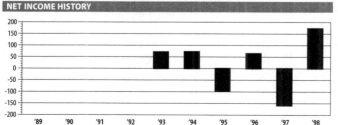

NET INCOME HISTORY

1998 FISCAL YEAR-END

Debt ratio: 15.1%
Return on equity: 10.7%
Cash ($ mil.): 121.3
Current ratio: —
Long-term debt ($ mil.): 302

Anthem

ARAMARK CORPORATION

OVERVIEW

"Take me out to the ball game, take me out to the crowd. Buy me some peanuts and . . . " Sushi? It's a big seller at some ballparks where ARAMARK has the refreshment concession. The world's third-largest food service provider, the Philadelphia-based firm is a major concessionaire for sports and other recreational facilities and national parks. It also provides food, building maintenance, and housekeeping services for schools, businesses, hospitals, and prisons. Food and support operations make up more than 65% of sales.

In addition to its food business, ARAMARK is the US's second-largest uniform rental company (behind Cintas). It provides uniform services

primarily to public employees and the public safety, hospitality, and health care industries. Through its Children's World Learning Centers, ARAMARK provides before- and after-school and employee on-site childcare services. The company transferred its magazine distribution business to a joint venture project in which it retains a minority interest.

Chairman and CEO Joseph Neubauer owns about 25% of the privately held firm. Altogether, employees own more than 93% of the company. About 150 ARAMARK employees are "paper millionaires" thanks to the company's stock ownership program.

HISTORY

In 1959 Davidson Automatic Merchandising, owned by Davre Davidson of California, merged with a Chicago vending machine company owned by William Fishman. The two men had become friends through their individual roles as vending machine suppliers to local Douglas Aircraft factories during WWII. Davidson became chairman and CEO, and Fishman became president of the new enterprise, Automatic Retailers of America (ARA).

ARA serviced mainly candy, beverage, and cigarette machines and by 1961 was the US's leading vending machine company, with operations in 38 states. The firm moved into food vending in the early 1960s and served clients such as Southern Pacific Rail. Between 1959 and 1963 it acquired 150 food service businesses, including Slater Systems in 1961, making ARA a leader in the operation of cafeterias at colleges, hospitals, and work sites. ARA went into the food service business despite slimmer profit margins because food servicing was less capital-intensive and more responsive to price changes than vending machines. The company (which changed its name to ARA Services in 1966) grew so rapidly in this period that the FTC stepped in; ARA agreed to restrict future food vending acquisitions.

ARA began providing food services to the Olympics at the 1968 Mexico City games and has been present at most subsequent Olympics. (Atlanta in 1996 was its tenth.) Also that year it began to diversify into other service businesses, such as publication distribution, and in 1970 it expanded into janitorial and maintenance services by buying Ground Services (airline cleaning and loading services; sold in 1990). A foray into residential care for the elderly — National Living Centers, now Living Centers of America

— began in 1973 (and ended in fiscal 1993 with the sale of the last of its stock). This acquisition also led to ARA's entry into emergency room staffing services (sold 1997). The company expanded into childcare (National Child Care Centers) in 1980.

CFO Joseph Neubauer became CEO in 1983 and chairman a year later. Shortly after, to avoid a hostile takeover, he led a $1.2 billion LBO of ARA. Since then the company has been repurchasing shares from other investors (investment banks and employee benefit plans).

After the buyout, the company began refining its core operations. It acquired Szabo (correctional food services) in 1986, Children's World Learning Centers in 1987, and Coordinated Health Services (medical billing services) in 1993. ARA sold its airport ground-handling service in 1990.

ARA became ARAMARK in 1994 as part of an effort to raise its profile with its ultimate clients, the public. But all has not been rosy — the company's concession operations suffered when baseball and hockey players went on strike in 1994 and 1995.

Acquisitions in 1996 included Gall's, North America's #1 supplier of public safety equipment. In 1997 ARAMARK cooked more than 3,000 pounds of barbecue for baseball fans during opening day of Atlanta's new Turner Field. That year it announced a plan, contingent on stockholder approval, to become 100% employee-owned.

In 1998 ARAMARK entered into a joint venture with privately held Anderson News Company, exchanging its magazine distribution operations for a minority stake in the new business.

Chairman and CEO: Joseph Neubauer, age 57,
$948,000 pay
VC: James Ksansnak
President and COO: William Leonard, age 50,
$500,000 pay
EVP and CFO: L. Frederick Sutherland, age 46,
$364,000 pay
EVP, Secretary and General Counsel: Martin Spector
EVP: Charles E. Kiernan, age 53
EVP Human Resources and Public Affairs:
Brian G. Mulvaney, age 42
SVP and Treasurer: Barbara A. Austell, age 45
VP, Chief Accounting Officer, and Controller:
Alan J. Griffith, age 44
VP: Dean E. Hill, age 47
VP: John P. Kallelis, age 60
Director Audit and Controls: Michael R. Murphy, age 41
Assistant Secretary and Associate General Counsel:
Donald S. Morton, age 50
Assistant Treasurer: Richard M. Thon, age 43
Auditors: Arthur Andersen LLP

HQ: Aramark Tower, 1101 Market St.,
Philadelphia, PA 19107
Phone: 215-238-3000   **Fax:** 215-238-3333
Web site: http://www.aramark.com

ARAMARK has operations in Belgium, Canada, the
Czech Republic, Germany, Hungary, Japan, Mexico,
South Korea, Spain, the UK, and the US.

1999 Sales & Operating Income

	Sales		Operating Income	
	$ mil.	% of total	$ mil.	% of total
Food, leisure & support services	4,968	74	254	63
Uniform services	1,350	20	111	28
Educational resources	400	6	35	9
Adjustments	—	—	(25)	—
Total	**6,718**	**100**	**375**	**100**

Major Operations

Food and Support Services Group
Business services (dining, meeting, janitorial)
Campus services (grounds, custodial)
Correctional services (food, commissary)
Facility services (housekeeping, groundskeeping)
Health care support services (patient transportation,
groundskeeping, food & nutrition)
Refreshment services
School support services (facility and food management)
Sports and entertainment services

Educational Resources Group
Children's World Learning Centers
Daybridge Child Development Centers
Medallion School Partnerships
Meritor Academy (private school system)

Uniform and Career Apparel Group
ARAMARK Uniform Services
Crest Uniform Co. (hospitality and health care uniforms)
E.T. Wright (direct marketer of hard-to-find shoe sizes)
Gall's, Inc. (direct marketer of police, medical,
fire/rescue equipment, public employee uniforms)
WearGuard (direct marketer of work clothes)

Alex Lee	KinderCare
Angelica	La Petite Academy
Cintas	Levy Restaurants
Compass Group	Ogden
Delaware North	Sara Lee
Fine Host	ServiceMaster
G&K Services	Sodexho Marriott Services
Host Marriott Services	UniFirst
ISS	Viad
International Multifoods	

Private FYE: September	Annual Growth	1990	1991	1992	1993	1994	1995	1996	1997	1998	1999
Sales ($ mil.)	4.3%	4,596	4,774	4,865	4,891	5,162	5,601	6,122	6,310	6,377	6,718
Net income ($ mil.)	12.5%	52	64	67	77	86	94	110	146	129	150
Income as % of sales	—	1.1%	1.3%	1.4%	1.6%	1.7%	1.7%	1.8%	2.3%	2.0%	2.2%
Employees	(1.8%)	134,000	135,000	124,000	131,000	133,000	140,000	150,000	150,000	150,000	152,000

Debt ratio: 92.7%
Return on equity: 314.5%
Cash ($ mil.): 28
Current ratio: 1.13
Long-term debt ($ mil.): 1,610

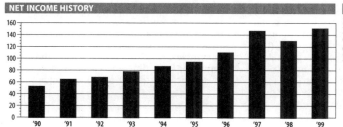

ARMY AND AIR FORCE EXCHANGE

OVERVIEW

Armies of shoppers — armed with wallets instead of weapons — march through the doors of the Army and Air Force Exchange Service (AAFES). The Dallas-based AAFES runs more than 10,000 facilities at Post Exchanges (PXs) and Base Exchanges (BXs) on Army and Air Force bases, respectively, around the world. Its operations include military clothing stores, food outlets, movie theaters, gas stations, catalog services, and beauty shops. AAFES facilities serve soldiers, airmen, guardsmen, reservists, retirees, and their family members.

AAFES is a government agency under the Department of Defense (DoD). It receives no funding from the DoD but pays neither taxes nor rent for US government property. More than 70% of AAFES' profits go into a Morale, Welfare, and Recreation fund for amenities such as libraries and youth centers. Other profits are used to renovate or build stores. Although AAFES is headed by military personnel, its staff consists mainly of military family members and other civilians.

HISTORY

During the American Revolution, peddlers known as sutlers followed the Army, selling items such as soap, razors, and tobacco. The practice lasted until after the Civil War, when post traders replaced sutlers. This system was replaced in 1889 when the War Department authorized canteens at military bases.

The first US military exchanges were established in 1895, creating a system to supply military personnel with personal items on US Army bases around the world. The exchanges were run independently, with each division creating a Post Exchange (PX) to serve its unit. The post commander would assign an officer to run the PX (usually along with other duties) and would decide how profits were spent.

In 1941 the Army Exchange Service was created, and the system was reorganized. A five-member advisory committee made up of civilian merchandisers was created to provide recommendations for the reorganization. The restructuring made the system more like a chain store business. The independent PXs were bought by the War Department from the individual military organizations that ran them. Civilian personnel were brought in to staff the PXs, and a brigadier general was named to head an executive staff made up of Army officers and civilians that provided centralized control of the system. The Army also created a special school to train officers to run the PXs.

Sales at the PXs skyrocketed during WWII; a catalog business was added so soldiers could order gifts to send home to their families. The Department of the Air Force was established in 1947, and the exchange system organization was renamed the Army and Air Force Exchange Service (AAFES) the next year.

In 1960 the government allowed the overseas exchanges to provide more luxury items in an effort to keep soldiers from buying foreign-made goods. By the time the military had been cranked up again for the Vietnam War, big-ticket items such as TVs, cameras, and tape recorders were among the exchanges' best-sellers. In 1967 AAFES moved its headquarters from New York City to Dallas.

By 1991 the exchanges were open to the National Guard and the Reserve; AAFES' customer base had grown to 14 million. When the military began downsizing during the 1990s, AAFES reorganized to streamline its operations. When Texas' Carswell Air Force Base closed in 1993, AAFES began a pilot program to keep its stores open for military retirees living in the area; this program was later expanded to other bases after their closures.

AAFES stores sold more than $12 million of pornographic materials in 1995. The House of Representatives passed the Military Honor and Decency Act the next year prohibiting the sale of pornography on US military property, including AAFES stores; this ban was struck down as unconstitutional in 1997. That year AAFES was approved as a provider of medical equipment covered by federal CHAMPUS/TRICARE insurance. It also created a Web site to offer online shopping in 1997.

In 1998 the Supreme Court upheld the 1996 porn ban; the Pentagon banned the sale of more than 150 sexually explicit magazines (such as *Penthouse*), while a military board permitted the continued sale of certain publications (including *Playboy*). Maj. Gen. Barry Bates took over as AAFES head in 1998. To better battle other retailers, in 1998 AAFES announced its stores would offer best-price guarantees, matching prices of local stores and refunding price differences if customers found lower prices within 30 days of buying products.

Chairman of the Board: Lt. Gen. John W. Handy, USAF
Commander and CEO: Maj. Gen. Barry D. Bates, USA
Vice Commander: Brig. Gen. Rodney Wood, USAF
COO: W. Michael Beverly
CFO: Terry B. Corley
SVP Sales Directorate: Steve Fair
SVP Human Resources Directorate: James K. Winters
General Counsel: Col. Alfred L. Faustino, USA
Auditors: Ernst & Young LLP

LOCATIONS

HQ: Army and Air Force Exchange Service,
3911 S. Walton Walker Blvd., Dallas, TX 75236
Phone: 214-312-2011   **Fax:** 214-312-3000
Web site: http://www.aafes.com

The Army and Air Force Exchange Service has operations in all 50 US states and in 25 countries and overseas areas.

PRODUCTS/OPERATIONS

Selected Operations
Barber and beauty shops
Bookstores
Catalog services
Class Six package stores
Concessions
Florists
Food facilities (mobile units, snack bars, name-brand fast-food franchises, and concession operations)
Gas stations and auto repair
Laundry and dry cleaning
Military clothing stores
Movie theaters
Retail stores
Vending centers
Video rentals

COMPETITORS

7-Eleven	Kmart
Barnes & Noble	Kroger
Best Buy	METRO AG
Blockbuster	May
Circuit City	Montgomery Ward
Costco Companies	Regis
Dayton Hudson	Sears
Dillard's	Service Merchandise
Federated	Venator Group
Home Depot	Wal-Mart
J. C. Penney	Walgreen

HISTORICAL FINANCIALS & EMPLOYEES

Government-owned FYE: January	Annual Growth	1990	1991	1992	1993	1994	1995	1996	1997	1998	1999
Sales ($ mil.)	0.9%	6,255	6,868	6,908	6,763	7,276	6,746	6,710	6,874	6,620	6,783
Net income ($ mil.)	0.4%	332	316	297	301	315	269	228	348	337	343
Income as % of sales	—	5.3%	4.6%	4.3%	4.5%	4.3%	4.0%	3.4%	5.1%	5.1%	5.1%
Employees	(4.7%)	—	79,609	75,584	72,562	60,000	58,556	56,495	57,583	53,946	54,000

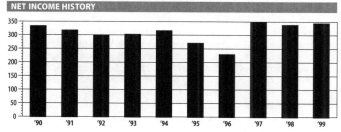

NET INCOME HISTORY

1999 FISCAL YEAR-END
Debt ratio: 4.5%
Return on equity: 12.8
Cash ($ mil.): 174
Current ratio: 2.16
Long-term debt ($ mil.): 129

ARTHUR D. LITTLE, INC.

OVERVIEW

While it's not nearly as big as some of its competitors, there's nothing small about Arthur D. Little (ADL). From its base in Cambridge, Massachusetts, ADL's staff of more than 3,500 provides consulting services to *FORTUNE* 100 corporations, governments, and emerging companies. One of the world's oldest consultancies, ADL operates more than 50 offices and laboratories in more than 30 countries around the globe. Its strong point is technology and product development, helping clients refine their manufacturing, research, and systems operations, and developing products for in-house

commercialization. ADL's management consulting unit concerns itself with organization, project management, and strategy, while its environmental, health, and safety consulting services run the gamut of industrial and government needs in those areas.

ADL also offers a graduate program in management through its Arthur D. Little School of Management. ADL's international operations have grown dramatically over the past decade and account for more than 60% of revenue. Arthur D. Little is an employee-owned company.

HISTORY

Former Massachusetts Institute of Technology chemistry student Arthur D. Little and chemist Roger Griffin opened their Boston office of Griffin & Little, Chemical Engineers in 1886, a time when chemists and their science were held in low regard. The firm developed a reputation for expertise in papermaking, then tragedy struck — Griffin was killed in a laboratory accident in 1893. Little persevered and picked up William Walker as a partner in 1900, and the firm was renamed Little & Walker. Walker left for a teaching post at MIT five years later, and the firm was permanently renamed Arthur D. Little, Inc. (ADL) in 1909.

Throughout the years leading up to WWII, ADL was instrumental in a number of new developments, including an odor classification system (to aid in the development of consumer products such as food and cosmetics), glass fibers (the basis for Fiberglas), and a sea-to-fresh water converter. Little died in 1935, but ADL continued to thrive after WWII and played a significant role in the industrialization of Puerto Rico by developing a technical-economic plan for the island in 1946.

In the meantime, Arthur Little's nephew, Royal Little (who is credited with creating the modern conglomerate and served on ADL's board of directors), devised a scheme to buy back the 55% of the company that MIT had come to own through a trust that Royal controlled. He created the Memorial Drive Trust in 1953, a profit-sharing trust for the company's employees, and transferred the shares into it.

The 1950s brought on a new concept at ADL called operations research (business operations analysis), and John Magee (who eventually would become CEO) was brought on board to help run the department. The company picked up several new and prominent industrial

clients. In the 1960s ADL helped develop the Sabre reservations system with IBM for American Airlines. The company started its management education program, then in 1969 ADL took 30% of the company public.

The world economy slowed drastically in the 1970s, and ADL was no exception. Other consulting firms had moved into ADL's technical territory, but ADL resisted moving into management consulting. And while the rest of the consulting industry charged into business reengineering (in response to the economic upheavals of the 1970s), ADL poked along with small contracts.

By the mid-1980s ADL had become a takeover target (which it successfully resisted), its laboratories were sliding into obsolescence, and it was losing its best and brightest because of low pay. Magee brought in Charles LaMantia, an ADL alum then working for Koch Industries, as CEO. The employee trust bought the outstanding shares of the company in 1988, taking it private again. LaMantia pruned the firm to its current organization, spun off noncore operations, and moved ADL more solidly into strategic consulting.

Results started improving in the 1990s, and LaMantia expanded the company again by increasing its international presence. ADL consulted in the privatization of British Rail in 1995. LaMantia became chairman in 1998. ADL acquired Contactica, an international telecommunications consultant the next year. After leading the company on its international expansion drive, LaMantia announced his retirement in 1999 and was replaced as chairman by Gerhard Schulmeyer (chairman and CEO of Siemens USA) and as CEO by Lorenzo Lamadrid.

Chairman: Gerhard Schulmeyer
President and CEO: Lorenzo C. Lamadrid
EVP Finance and Development: Mark A. Brodsky
EVP Operations: Ashok S. Kalelkar
SVP Human Resources: Michael Eisenbud
Chairman and CEO, Cambridge Consultants Limited: Howard W. Biddle
VP and Managing Director, North America Environmental, Health, and Safety Consulting: Robert N. Lambe
VP and Managing Director, North America Public Sector: Paul Brenner
Managing Director, Japan: Glen S. Fukushima
Managing Director, Latin America: George Kastner
Managing Director, North America Management Consulting: Ladd Greeno
Managing Director, North America Technology and Product Development: John Collins

LOCATIONS

HQ: 25 Acorn Park, Cambridge, MA 02140
Phone: 617-498-5000   **Fax:** 617-498-7200
Web site: http://www.arthurdlittle.com

1998 Offices

	No.
Europe	21
North America	14
Asia/Pacific	8
Latin America	6
Middle East	2
Total	**51**

PRODUCTS/OPERATIONS

Selected Subsidiaries and Affiliates
Arthur D. Little Enterprises (commercialization of company and client technologies)
Arthur D. Little School of Management
Cambridge Consultants Limited (European technology center, UK)
Contactica (international telecommunication consulting)
Epyx (fuel processors)
Innovation Associates (training programs)
Strategic Food Solutions (joint venture with the Netherlands Organization for Applied Scientific Research)

COMPETITORS

Andersen Consulting
Bain & Company
Booz, Allen
Boston Consulting
CH2M Hill
Cap Gemini
Deloitte Touche Tohmatsu
Ernst & Young
KPMG
McKinsey & Company
PricewaterhouseCoopers
Towers Perrin

HISTORICAL FINANCIALS & EMPLOYEES

Private FYE: December	Annual Growth	1989	1990	1991	1992	1993	1994	1995	1996	1997	1998
Sales ($ mil.)	8.8%	—	—	—	367	385	433	514	574	589	608
Employees	7.2%	—	—	—	2,300	2,400	2,600	3,039	3,200	3,300	3,500

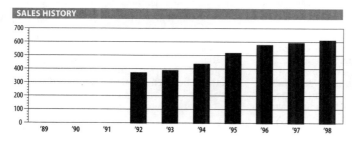

SALES HISTORY

Arthur D Little

ASCENSION HEALTH

Ascension Health rises to the occasion. Formed by the merger of the Daughters of Charity National Health System and the Sisters of St. Joseph Health System in 1999, the St. Louis-based company is a network of about 80 hospitals, residential centers, and other healthcare facilities. Located in 15 states and Washington, DC, Ascension is the largest Catholic health care system by sales, ahead of Denver-based Catholic Health Initiatives (which has more hospitals), and is also the largest not-for-profit healthcare provider. Following words of guidance from the order's co-founder, St. Vincent de Paul, the system serves "the poor sick bodily, ministering to them in all their needs, and spiritually also so that they will live and die well."

Nuns from the Daughters of Charity and the Sisters of St. Joseph orders who sponsor Ascension sit on the network's governing board, which is led by non-clergy CEO Don Brennan. In the past, Ascension predecessor DCNHS stirred up controversy when it proposed merging with non-Catholic hospitals, since Catholic doctrine forbids abortion, most forms of birth control, and artificial means of conception; the merger with Sisters of St. Joseph put those concerns to rest.

In this age of low-cost health care, Ascension realizes the need for fiscal health. In addition to selling money-losing hospitals, Ascension has reorganized its facilities by geographic regions with each region headed by a VP who controls costs and speeds decision making. The system derives about 60% of its income from investments, prompting Wall Street to label the nuns the "Daughters of Currency" (a sobriquet they frown upon).

The Daughters of Charity order was formed in France in 1633 when St. Vincent de Paul recruited a rich widow (St. Louise de Marillac) to care for the sick on battlefields and in their homes.

Elizabeth Ann Seton, the first American saint (canonized 1974), brought the order to the US. Seton earned the title of Mother in 1809 and that year started the Sisters of Charity. The Sisters adopted the vows of the Daughters of Charity and added service to them in 1812.

The Sisters officially became part of the Daughters of Charity in 1850. The Daughters cared for soldiers during the Civil War and even trained Florence Nightingale. The Daughters pioneered exclusive provider arrangements (much like today's managed care contracts) with railroads, lumber camps, and the like in the late 1800s. During the next 100 years, the order furthered its mission of caring for the sick and the poor. To support their efforts, the nuns founded hospitals (44 by 1911), schools, and other charity centers.

In 1969 the charity association formed a health care services cooperative, which became the Daughters of Charity National Health System (DCNHS).

DCNHS operated as two regional institutions (one based in Maryland, the other in Missouri) until 1986, when the systems merged. The first task was to balance their holy mission with the need to make money. With competition from managed care companies increasing, DCNHS responded in the late 1980s by cutting staff and diversifying into nursing homes and retirement centers.

The Daughters of Charity's western unit combined its six hospitals in California with Mullikin Centers (a physician-owned medical group) in 1993 to form one of the largest health care associations in the state.

DCNHS expanded its network in 1995 by merging its hospitals with and becoming a co-sponsor of San Francisco-based Catholic Healthcare West. That year it joined with Catholic Relief Services to operate a hospital in war-torn Angola.

In 1996 DCNHS dropped a proposed merger of its struggling 221-bed Carney Hospital in Boston with Quincy Hospital because the municipally owned Quincy facility was required by law to provide abortions. Instead, DCNHS sold Carney Hospital to Caritas Christi Health Care System (owned by the Boston Roman Catholic archdiocese), one of about a dozen hospital sales by DCNHS in the mid-1990s.

DCNHS reorganized its leadership (creating two new SVP positions — one for system direction and policy, and the other for program development) in 1997 to strengthen and update its programs. In 1998 Sister Irene Kraus, who had founded DCNHS and led it through its expansion, died.

In 1999 DCNHS merged with fellow Catholic caregiver Sisters of St. Joseph Health System, then Michigan's largest healthcare system. The pairing formed the largest Catholic health network in the US, and also the largest not-for-profit health system.

Chair: Sister Xavier Ballance
VC: Sister Jo Ann Cuscurida
President and CEO: Donald A. Brennan
EVP and COO: Douglas D. French
SVP Mission: Sister Kieran Kneaves
SVP Healthcare Innovation and Evaluation:
Marsha A. Ladenburger
SVP Advocacy and External Relations: Susan E. Nestor
SVP Governments and Sponsor Relations:
James E. Small
SVP Finance: Jerry P. Widman
President, Partners First: Kevin P. Conlin
President, DCNHS Foundation: F. Dale Whitten
VP Strategic Planning: Carolyn L. Drummond
VP Purchasing: Jonah Hughes
VP Risk Management: Tim McKivergan
VP Managed Care: David N. Schopp
VP Human Resources: David A. Smith
Director Corporate Communications: John W. Marshall
Auditors: Ernst & Young LLP

LOCATIONS

HQ: 4600 Edmundson Rd., St. Louis, MO 63134
Phone: 314-253-6700   **Fax:** 314-253-6491
Web site: http://www.dcnhs.org

PRODUCTS/OPERATIONS

Facilities
Acute care hospitals
Adult residential facilities
Community Health Centers
Long-term acute care
Long-term care
Psychiatric hospitals
Rehabilitation facilities

COMPETITORS

Allegheny Health, Education & Research
Baylor Health
Beverly Enterprises
Catholic Health East
Catholic Health Initiatives
Catholic Healthcare Partners
Columbia/HCA
Detroit Medical Center
Franciscan Health Partnership
Genesis Health Ventures
HEALTHSOUTH
HMA
Henry Ford Health System
Integrated Health Services
Johns Hopkins Health
Life Care Centers
Mayo Foundation
Mercy Health Services
New York City Health and Hospitals
Quorum Health
Tenet Healthcare
Universal Health Services
Vencor

HISTORICAL FINANCIALS & EMPLOYEES

Not-for-profit FYE: June	Annual Growth	1990	1991	1992	1993	1994	1995	1996	1997	1998	1999
Sales ($ mil.)	4.3%	4,400	5,100	5,900	6,500	7,000	6,200	5,700	5,700	6,170	6,400
Employees	(0.1%)	—	—	—	—	67,400	62,300	61,100	60,000	65,000	67,000

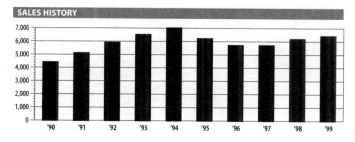

SALES HISTORY

AMPI

Associated Milk Producers Incorporated (AMPI) doesn't have to worry much about spilt milk. Despite what its name implies, the farmers in the New Ulm, Minnesota-based regional dairy cooperative concentrate on solid dairy products, such as cheese, butter, and dry milk.

AMPI has 6,500 member farms in Iowa, Minnesota, Missouri, Nebraska, North Dakota, South Dakota, and Wisconsin. It markets close to 5 billion pounds of dairy products each year, and it has upgraded its 14 plants to produce additional value-added dairy products such as shredded cheese, aseptic-packaged cheese sauces, and individually wrapped butter pats (only one plant produces fluid milk). AMPI produces 60% of all instant milk sold in the US. It is also a major cheddar producer and operates one of the largest butter-packing plants in the US.

The co-op is primarily a private-label producer for retailers and food service customers such as SYSCO. However, AMPI also produces State-brand cheese and butter, which are distributed nationally.

HISTORY

In 1969, faced with declining milk consumption and a subsequent drop in income, about 100 dairy cooperatives in the Midwest and the South merged to form Associated Milk Producers Incorporated (AMPI). AMPI elected John Butterbrodt, from a Wisconsin co-op, as the first president. Co-ops throughout the central US clamored to join, and AMPI became the largest US dairy co-op within two years of its formation.

Almost from the beginning AMPI became embroiled in the two main controversies involving dairy co-ops: monopolistic practices and political contributions. In 1972 consumer advocate Ralph Nader alleged that the three main dairy co-ops — AMPI, Dairymen, and Mid-America Dairymen — had illegally contributed $422,000 to President Nixon's re-election campaign in an attempt to obtain higher price supports (enacted in 1971) and an agreement that the administration would drop antitrust suits against the co-ops. Watergate investigators subpoenaed Nixon's tapes, and AMPI was accused of bribery, destruction of evidence, and attempting to achieve "complete market dominance." In 1974 it pleaded guilty to making illegal political contributions in 1968, 1970, and 1972. By 1975 three former AMPI employees had been convicted of various charges and Butterbrodt had resigned.

The co-op spent the last half of the 1970s quietly reorganizing. In 1982 a suit for monopolistic practices, originally filed in 1971 by the National Farmers Organization (NFO), finally reached the federal courts. The case was decided in favor of AMPI and two other large co-ops, but before the year was out an appeals court reversed the decision, saying AMPI and its co-defendants had conspired to eliminate competitive sellers of milk. (The US Supreme Court subsequently upheld the appeals court ruling.)

AMPI extended its dominance of the industry in 1985 by merging its central region with 2,200 members of Wisconsin-based co-op Morning Glory Farms. (It sold Morning Glory to dairy co-op Foremost Farms USA in 1995.)

Business soured in the early 1990s, and despite successfully lobbying the Department of Agriculture to strengthen dairy price supports, AMPI posted losses. Then it became one of the first targets of a lawsuit stemming from the Family Leave Act: In 1994 the Labor Department sued on behalf of a truck driver in New Mexico who was fired a week after he missed work while his wife was in labor with triplets.

Despite heavy spending in Congress, AMPI watched decades of government support to dairy farmers fall away as the 1996 Farm Bill established free-market agriculture. Faced with falling prices, deregulation, and foreign competition, in 1997 AMPI entered into consolidation talks with three of its dairy co-op brethren: Mid-America Dairymen, Milk Marketing, and Western Dairymen Cooperative. AMPI's Southern Region, which primarily produced fluid milk, decided to join the new co-op, Dairy Farmers of America; members of its Northern Region, which focused on hard products, stayed put, renaming itself North Central AMPI to reduce confusion during the transition. However, the co-op officially readopted the original name in 1999.

High butterfat prices in 1998 helped the co-op post record earnings during its first year after the separation. Amid wild consolidations within the dairy industry, in mid-1999 AMPI made a modest merger with the Glencoe Butter & Produce Association. The small regional cooperative based in Glencoe, Minnesota, brought a cheese production plant and 1,000 new members to AMPI.

President: Wayne Bok
General Manager: Mark Furth
Controller: Ken Spoon
Assistant Manager: Harlen Mamen

LOCATIONS

HQ: Associated Milk Producers Incorporated,
315 N. Broadway, New Ulm, MN 56073
Phone: 507-354-8295   **Fax:** 507-359-8651
Web site: http://www.ampi.com

PRODUCTS/OPERATIONS

Selected Products
Butter
Cheese
Dry milk
Fluid milk
Lactose
Sauces
Whey

COMPETITORS

Dairy Farmers of America
Dean Foods
Foremost Farms
Great Lakes Cheese
Land O'Lakes
Leprino Foods
MMPA

Marathon Cheese
Parmalat Finanziaria
Prairie Farms Dairy
Saputo Group
Schreiber Foods
Suiza Foods

HISTORICAL FINANCIALS & EMPLOYEES

Cooperative FYE: December	Annual Growth	1989	1990	1991	1992	1993	1994	1995	1996	1997	1998
Sales ($ mil.)	(10.5%)	2,987	3,063	2,768	2,835	2,692	2,629	2,554	2,189	928	1,100
Net income ($ mil.)	2.4%	12	(27)	1	(13)	11	1	11	4	9	15
Income as % of sales	—	0.4%	—	0.0%	—	0.4%	0.0%	0.4%	0.2%	0.9%	1.4%
Employees	(10.2%)	4,200	4,500	4,319	4,364	4,199	4,500	4,500	4,500	1,600	1,600

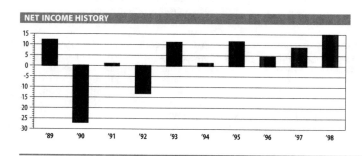

NET INCOME HISTORY

ASSOCIATED WHOLESALE GROCERS

OVERVIEW

Those who work and play well with others are called cooperative; ironically, that might not be the best term for the members of Kansas City, Kansas-based Associated Wholesale Grocers (AWG). Some members of the supermarket cooperative (one of the nation's largest) have wondered if AWG might not be better off as a public company. The co-op is owned by more than 350 retailers who operate about 850 grocery stores, primarily in the Midwest (its Price Chopper franchise is the #1 food chain in the Kansas City metro area). Members each own an equal amount of stock, with end-of-the-year profits passed on in the form of dividends based on how much merchandise they bought. A majority of members

has twice defeated proposals for the cooperative to go public.

AWG supplies members brand-name and private-label food and nonfood items; it also provides services ranging from market research and insurance to loan programs and real estate lease assistance. AWG franchises several store formats, including conventional supermarkets Apple Market and Country Mart as well as the Price Chopper and Price Mart warehouse chains.

The cooperative moved into food retailing with its acquisition of more than 30 Falley's and Food 4 Less stores in Kansas. As a result of consolidation among food chains, wholesalers have bought chains to avoid losing them as customers.

HISTORY

About 20 Kansas City, Kansas-area grocers met in a local grocery in 1924 and organized the Associated Grocers Company to get better deals on purchases and advertising. They elected J. C. Harline president, and each chipped in a few hundred dollars to make their first purchases. It took a while to find a manufacturer who would sell directly to them; a local soap maker was finally convinced, and others gradually followed.

In 1926 the group was incorporated as Associated Wholesale Grocers (AWG). It outgrew two warehouses in four years, finally moving to a 16,000-sq.-ft. facility big enough to add new lines and more products. Membership doubled between 1930 and 1932 as grocers moved from ordering products a year ahead to the new wholesale concept, and members took seriously the slogan: "Buy, Sell, Buy Some More." They met every week to plan how to sell their products, and buyer and advertising manager Harry Small gave sales presentations and advertising ideas (his trade-in plan for old brooms sold more than two train-carloads of brooms in two weeks). Heavy newspaper advertising also paid off; AWG topped $1 million in sales in 1933.

The cooperative made its first acquisition in 1936, buying Progressive Grocers, a warehouse in Joplin, Missouri; a second such warehouse named Associated Grocers was acquired the next year in Springfield, Missouri. AWG continued building and expanding warehouses, and annual sales were at $11 million by 1951.

Louis Fox became CEO in 1956. A stockboy at 14, he owned his own grocery at 26 and was head of a Washington, DC, cooperative before

coming to AWG. Fox introduced cash and stock shares to maximize year-end rebates for members, led several acquisitions, and formed a new subsidiary for financing stores and small shopping centers where AWG members had stores (Supermarket Developers). Sales increased nearly fifteenfold to more than $200 million in his first 15 years. James Basha, who succeeded Fox when he retired in 1984, saw sales reach $2.4 billion by his own retirement in 1992.

Basha was followed by former COO Mike DeFabis, once a deputy mayor of Indianapolis. DeFabis orchestrated several acquisitions, including 41 Kansas City-area stores — most of which were quickly bought by members — from bankrupt Food Barn Stores in 1994 and 29 Oklahoma stores and a warehouse from Safeway spinoff Homeland Stores in 1995 (members bought all the stores).

AWG's nonfood subsidiary, Valu Merchandisers Co., was established in 1995; its new Kansas warehouse began shipping health and beauty aids and housewares the following year to help members battle big discounters. Members narrowly defeated a proposal in late 1996 to convert the cooperative into a public company. Proponents promptly petitioned for a second vote, which was defeated early the next year.

AWG veteran Doug Carolan succeeded DeFabis in 1998, becoming only the fifth CEO in the cooperative's history. The company bought five Falley's and 33 Food 4 Less stores in Kansas and Missouri from Fred Meyer in 1998 for $300 million. In a break with tradition, AWG is operating the stores rather than selling them to members.

Chairman: J. Fred Ball
President and CEO: Doug Carolan
EVP of Marketing: Jerry Garland
EVP of Finance and Administration and CFO:
  Gary Phillips
EVP of Division Operations: Tom Williams
VP and Corporate Controller: Doug Boehmer
VP and General Counsel: Chi Chi Puhl
VP, Secretary, and Treasurer: Joe Campbell
VP of Corporate Sales: Bill Lancaster
VP of Procurement: Dennis Kinser
President and CEO, Benchmark Insurance Companies:
  William R. Morrison
President, Valu Merchandisers: Dick Swain
SVP and Manager, Springfield Division: Maurice Henry
SVP and Manager, Oklahoma City Division: Mike Rand
Executive Corporate Director of Human Resources:
  Frank Tricamo
Executive Director, AWG Brands: Marc Mullins
Director of Human Resources: Kathy Black

LOCATIONS

HQ: Associated Wholesale Grocers Inc.,
  5000 Kansas Ave., Kansas City, KS 66106
Phone: 913-288-1000   **Fax:** 913-288-1508
Web site: http://www.awginc.com

PRODUCTS/OPERATIONS

Selected Private-Label Brands
Always Save
Best Choice

Selected Services

Advertising	Product positioning
Category management	Real estate lease assistance
Employee training	Reclamation
Financial planning	Site acquisition
In-store marketing	Store engineering and
Insurance	construction
Market research and	Store financing
analysis	Store franchise formats
Merchandising advice	Store remodeling
Private-label products	

Selected Store Formats
Apple Market (15,000-25,000-sq.-ft. grocery stores
  designed for neighborhood locations in both rural and
  metropolitan areas)
Cash Saver (designed with fewer perishables to serve
  rural areas)
Country Mart (25,000-45,000-sq.-ft. value-priced stores
  designed for county-seat and medium-sized towns)
Falley's (conventional supermarkets)
Food 4 Less (warehouse stores)
Price Chopper and Price Mart (50,000-92,000-sq.-ft. value-
  priced warehouse stores designed for high-volume areas)
Sun Fresh (40,000-63,000-sq.-ft. stores designed to serve
  medium-to-upper-income customers)
Thriftway (neighborhood locations)

Selected Operations/Subsidiaries
Benchmark Insurance Co.
Supermarket Developers, Inc. (financing for stores and
  supermarkets)
Supermarket Insurance Agency Inc.
Valu Merchandisers Co. (health and beauty supplies,
  general merchandise, and pharmacy products)

COMPETITORS

Affiliated Foods	IGA	Shurfine
Fleming	Kroger	International
Companies	Nash Finch	Spartan Stores
GSC Enterprises	Roundy's	Topco Associates
H.T. Hackney	SUPERVALU	Wal-Mart
Hy-Vee	Schnuck Markets	

HISTORICAL FINANCIALS & EMPLOYEES

Cooperative FYE: December	Annual Growth	1989	1990	1991	1992	1993	1994	1995	1996	1997	1998
Sales ($ mil.)	5.8%	1,919	2,144	2,265	2,404	2,540	2,600	2,970	3,096	3,129	3,200
Employees	5.3%	—	—	—	—	—	—	—	2,797	3,000	3,100

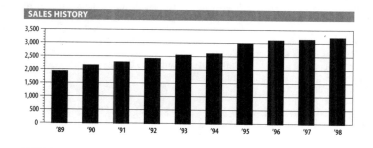

SALES HISTORY

3,500	
3,000	
2,500	
2,000	
1,500	
1,000	
500	
0	'89 '90 '91 '92 '93 '94 '95 '96 '97 '98

BAIN & COMPANY

OVERVIEW

More than 1,000 corporate Eliza Doolittles have retained Bain to stay mainly on the gain. A leading strategic consulting firm, Boston-based Bain & Company, whose consultants are known as "Bainies," is known for becoming intimately involved in its clients' internal affairs. Bain is a generalist, offering a variety of consulting services including business unit, organizational, and corporate strategy; distribution and logistics advice; merger, acquisition, and privatization consulting; and sales and marketing strategy. Bain's clients hail from an array of industries such as media and communications, consumer products and services, financial services, and high tech. The firm has 25 offices in nearly 20 countries. Although founded by the same individuals, Bain & Company and investment firm Bain Capital are separate entities.

Flamboyant chairman Orit Gadiesh has helped Bain, once on the brink of collapse, regain its place as one of the world's most prominent consulting firms. The firm is beefing up its presence in Asia, and it has also started dipping its toe in a new form of remuneration: accepting an equity stake in a client's company as an alternative to more traditional management fees.

HISTORY

Although he had no formal business training, Bill Bain got a job (through a friend) at the Boston Consulting Group (BCG) in 1967. Bain and a group of colleagues defected from BCG and founded Bain & Company in 1973. The firm was so committed to a client that it wouldn't take on other clients in the same industry (the policy was later relaxed). Bain also set itself apart from other firms by helping its clients implement its recommendations. By 1979 it had opened an office in London to serve US clients in Europe.

Bain's strategy of establishing long-term relationships with its clients seemed to attract executives looking for a crutch, a quality that Bain exploited with spectacular results in the 1970s and 1980s. Until 1985 Bill Bain retained total control of the firm (even the other partners did not know how much the firm was making). In 1985 and 1986 he and several partners contributed 30% of the firm to an employee stock option plan (ESOP) and had the ESOP borrow about $200 million to pay for the stock. The loans burdened the firm with substantial debt and precipitated a downturn in its financial well-being.

In the midst of its financial upheaval, Bain's tendency for becoming intimately involved in its clients' affairs backfired during a 1987 UK investigation of Bain client Guinness PLC. It was alleged that Guinness had inflated its stock price, and the resulting inquiry revealed that Bain VP Olivier Roux had continued to draw his Bain salary while employed as finance director of Guinness. Though the episode exposed a serious conflict of interest, Bain was not formally charged with wrongdoing.

Increasing competition combined with an economic downturn during the late 1980s led to a sharp decline in Bain's business. But the debt-ridden firm continued its international expansion, and in 1990 it became one of the first Western consulting firms to open offices in Russia.

By 1991 its employee count had fallen from 1,000 (in 1989) to 550, and Bain was on the verge of collapse. Bill Bain was ousted and Mitt Romney (head of Bain Capital, which had been founded with money from the 1985 ESOP deal) was brought in to revive the ailing firm. Romney recapitalized Bain by pressing the original partners to return most of their holdings. Ownership was then redistributed: About 40% went to the ESOP and 60% to a group of 75 partners. Bill Bain was left with no ownership save a small share of the ESOP.

In 1993, after 16 years as a Bain consultant, the flashy Orit Gadiesh became chairman. Much of the firm's turnaround has been attributed to her leadership (she once worked in military intelligence as a member of the Israeli army). By 1994 the number of Bain consultants had risen to 800, and the firm's financial health had improved.

In 1997 the former chairman of Club Med sued Bain; he claimed that a draft of Bain's study that was critical of him had been circulated. The lawsuit was dismissed in 1998, but that year the firm was hit with another lawsuit from Value Partners, an Italian consulting firm that accused Bain of raiding its Brazilian office and stealing confidential information. The suit was quickly dismissed, but Value Partners refiled the case in a different court that year; Bain's attempt to have that case dismissed failed in 1999.

Chairman: Orit Gadiesh
CFO: Colin Anderson
Worldwide Managing Director: Tom Tierney
Managing Director, London: Crawford Gillies
Managing Director, Munich: Fritz Seikowsky
VP: David Bechhofer
VP: Kim Ogden
Director of Human Resources: Elizabeth Corcoran

LOCATIONS

HQ: 2 Copley Place, Boston, MA 02116
Phone: 617-572-2000   **Fax:** 617-572-2427
Web site: http://www.bain.com

PRODUCTS/OPERATIONS

Selected Consulting Services
Business unit strategy
Corporate strategy
Distribution and logistics
Mergers, acquisitions, and privatization
Organizational strategy
Sales and marketing strategy

Selected Industries Served
Agriculture
Consumer products and services
Financial services
Food and beverages
Health and medical
High technology
Industrial products and construction
Media and communications
Packaging
Transportation, aerospace, and defense
Utilities and environmental

COMPETITORS

American Management
Andersen Consulting
Arthur D. Little
BDO International
Booz, Allen
Boston Consulting
Deloitte Touche Tohmatsu
Ernst & Young
Gemini Consulting
KPMG
Marsh & McLennan
McKinsey & Company
Perot Systems
PricewaterhouseCoopers
Thomas Group
Towers Perrin

HISTORICAL FINANCIALS & EMPLOYEES

Partnership FYE: December	Annual Growth	1989	1990	1991	1992	1993	1994	1995	1996	1997	1998
Sales ($ mil.)	18.5%	—	—	—	—	213	300	375	450	480	499
Employees	8.4%	—	—	—	—	900	1,000	1,200	1,300	1,350	1,350

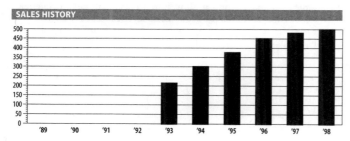

SALES HISTORY

BAIN & COMPANY

BAKER & MCKENZIE

OVERVIEW

How many lawyers does it take to replace a glass ceiling? Whatever the answer, Baker & McKenzie has more than enough. The Chicago-based law firm is the world's largest in number of attorneys, with more than 2,500 lawyers spread out across 60 offices in 35 different countries. It is also one of the first major partnerships to elect a woman to manage the firm. Christine Lagarde was chosen in 1999 to replace outgoing chairman John Klotsche. In addition to closing the gender gap, Lagarde is also one of the youngest partners to lead the firm.

Baker & McKenzie is a global firm offering legal services in areas such as banking, securities, labor, international trade, tax, and technology. With its decentralized structure, the firm employs an advanced computer network to manage its far-flung branches (including Kazakhstan, Poland, Ukraine, and Vietnam). BakerNet provides instant e-mail contact and information sharing between partners; the system also gives clients access to information and contact with their attorneys. The half-century-old firm has handled the legal affairs of such heavy-duty clients as Chase Manhattan, Honeywell, and Ingersoll-Rand.

Despite its size and history, Baker & McKenzie is beginning to face new competition on the global scene. UK firm Clifford Chance has said it will merge with two other practices to create a network larger than Baker's. Meanwhile, the Big Five multinational accounting firms (such as Andersen Worldwide and Ernst & Young) are becoming more active in offering legal advice, and have lured away several of Baker's top tax partners.

HISTORY

Russell Baker traveled from his native New Mexico to Chicago on a railroad freight car to attend law school. Upon graduation in 1925 he started practicing law with his classmate Dana Simpson under the name Simpson & Baker. Inspired by Chicago's role as a manufacturing and agricultural center for the world and influenced by the international focus of his alma mater, the University of Chicago, Baker dreamed of developing an international law practice based in the Windy City. He began developing an expertise in international law, and in 1934 Abbott Laboratories retained him to handle its worldwide legal affairs. Baker was on his way to fulfilling his dream.

Baker joined forces with Chicago litigator John McKenzie in 1949, forming Baker & McKenzie. In 1955 the firm opened its first international office in Caracas, Venezuela, to meet the needs of its expanding US client base. Over the next 10 years it branched out into Asia, Australia, and Europe, with offices in London, Manila, Paris, and Tokyo. Baker's death in 1979 neither slowed the firm's growth nor changed its international character. The next year it expanded into the Middle East and opened its 30th office in 1982 (Melbourne). To manage the sprawling law firm, Baker & McKenzie created the position of chairman of the executive committee in 1984.

In late 1991 the firm dropped the Church of Scientology as a client, losing an estimated $2 million in business. It was speculated that pressure from client Eli Lilly (maker of the drug Prozac, which Scientologists actively oppose) influenced the decision. In 1992 Baker & McKenzie was ordered to pay $1 million for wrongfully firing an employee who later died of AIDS. (The case became the basis for the 1993 film *Philadelphia*.) The firm fought the verdict but eventually settled for an undisclosed amount in 1995.

In 1994 Baker & McKenzie closed its Los Angeles office (the former MacDonald, Halsted & Laybourne; acquired 1988) amid considerable rancor. Also that year, a former secretary at the firm received a $7.1 million judgment for sexual harassment by a partner. (A San Francisco Superior Court judge later reduced the award to $3.5 million.)

John Klotsche, a senior partner from the firm's Palo Alto, California, office was appointed chairman in 1995. The following year the firm began a major expansion into California's Silicon Valley — the first step in an initiative to design services for technology companies around the world. It also expanded its Warsaw, Poland, office through a merger with the Warsaw office of Dickinson, Wright, Moon, Van Dusen & Freman.

In 1998 Baker & McKenzie formed a special unit in Singapore to deal with business generated by the financial troubles in Asia. The opening of offices in Taiwan and Azerbaijan in 1998 brought the firm's total number of offices to 59. Klotsche stepped down in 1999 as the firm celebrated its 50th anniversary. He was replaced by Christine Lagarde.

Chairman Executive Committee: Christine Lagarde, age 43
COO: David A. Yates
CFO: Robert S. Spencer
Chief Information and Technology Officer: Terry L. Crum
General Counsel: Edward J. Zulkey
Director International Administration: Teresa A. Townsend
Director Professional Development and Know-How: Peter F. Smith
Director Special Projects: Suzanne M. Clough
Manager Human Resources: Wilbert Williams
Auditors: Arthur Andersen LLP

LOCATIONS

HQ: 1 Prudential Plaza, 130 E. Randolph Dr., Ste. 2500, Chicago, IL 60601
Phone: 312-861-8800   **Fax:** 312-861-2899
Web site: http://www.bakerinfo.com

PRODUCTS/OPERATIONS

Selected Practice Areas

Banking and finance
  Aircraft and other asset-based finance
  Banking regulatory advice
  Capital markets
  Derivatives
  Export credits
  Global custody
  Loans and credit facilities
Corporate and securities
  Bond and note issues
  Commercial paper and CD issues
  Depositary receipt offerings
  Domestic IPOs
  International equity offerings
International trade
  Antitrust and competition laws
  Customs duties
  Import and export control regulations
  Warranty and limitation of liability provisions
IP, IT, and Communications
  Antipiracy
  Biotechnology and high technology

Dispute resolution
Distribution and franchising
IT and communications
Marketing
Patent prosecution and counseling
Trademarks
Labor and employment
  Foreign transfers of personnel
  Immigration
  Labor, employment, and employee benefits
Tax
  Customs duty
  Domestic and international tax planning
  Financing structures and project finance
  Lobbying on tax matters
  Mergers and acquisitions
  New business operations and joint ventures
  Personal tax, trust, and estate planning
  Transfer pricing planning and defense
  VAT/GST/consumption/ sales tax

COMPETITORS

Andersen Worldwide
Clifford Chance
Deloitte Touche Tohmatsu
Ernst & Young
Jones, Day
KPMG

Kirkland & Ellis
Mayer, Brown & Platt
McDermott, Will
PricewaterhouseCoopers
Sidley & Austin
Skadden, Arps

HISTORICAL FINANCIALS & EMPLOYEES

Partnership FYE: June	Annual Growth	1990	1991	1992	1993	1994	1995	1996	1997	1998	1999
Sales ($ mil.)	8.2%	404	478	504	512	546	594	646	697	785	818
Employees	4.4%	4,736	4,887	4,919	5,054	5,114	5,248	5,680	6,100	6,700	6,900

SALES HISTORY

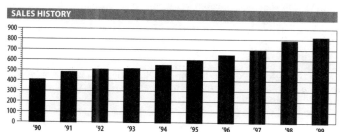

BAKER & MᶜKENZIE

BAKER & TAYLOR CORPORATION

OVERVIEW

Although Baker & Taylor (B&T) is at the top of its industry, it's very quiet about it. The Charlotte, North Carolina-based company is the largest US wholesaler of books to libraries and the nation's #2 book wholesaler overall (after Ingram Book Group).

B&T supplies books, audio books, calendars, and information services to more than 20,000 retailers and 28,000 institutions (mostly schools and public and university libraries). In addition to selling some 50 million books a year, the company sells videos, CDs, audiocassettes, interactive games, CD-ROMs, and software (it carries 40,000 video titles and nearly 100,000 audio titles). More than 25% of retail sales come from Internet retailers such as Amazon.com and barnesandnoble.com, for which the company provides fulfillment. B&T also offers automatic shipping of kids' and adults' books by popular authors (books are mailed as soon as they are published). Its Replica Books unit publishes out-of-print and paperback titles on demand.

It has settled a Justice Department lawsuit alleging that it overcharged libraries but may still face state suits. The company is doubling its warehouse capacity and expanding product offerings to better serve online sellers.

The Carlyle Group, an investment partnership, owns nearly 85% of B&T. Management, employees, and other private investors own the rest.

HISTORY

Baker & Taylor (B&T) traces its roots back to a bindery and subscription publisher founded by David Robinson and B. B. Barber in Hartford, Connecticut, in 1828. A few years later the company opened a bookstore that sold books by other publishers in addition to its own titles; in 1835 it moved to New York. Fifty years later James Baker and Nelson Taylor bought the business and renamed it Baker & Taylor. After Taylor died in 1912, the company stopped publishing in order to concentrate on wholesaling.

B&T moved to New Jersey in 1950. In 1958 it was acquired by the Parents' Institute, publisher of *Parents* magazine. Parents sold B&T to W. R. Grace in 1970, during the period when Grace was assembling an eclectic collection of unrelated companies. Under Grace, B&T's hard-won reputation suffered. Customers complained about incomplete orders, insufficient stock, and poor communications.

Nevertheless, Grace continued to build its media distribution business. In 1986 it bought two video distributors, Sound Video Unlimited and VTR, and software distributor SoftKat. These companies' (renamed Baker & Taylor Video and Baker & Taylor Software) operations remained independent, and customer problems continued. B&T management blamed the parent company, citing Grace's overemphasis on short-term financial performance.

But Grace had its own problems in the late 1980s and early 1990s. Overinvestment in energy and the firm's purchase of a large block of its own stock took it deeply into debt. In 1992 Grace sold B&T to company management and The Carlyle Group. The company then combined the video and software units into Baker & Taylor Entertainment.

After the buyout, B&T began focusing on global markets. It signed an agreement with UK library supplier T. C. Farries and Co. to supply its books, and it released a world edition of its Title Source CD with Book Data, a UK-based bibliographic and marketing information service. This product combined the firm's B&T Link title database with new ordering capabilities.

In 1994 The Carlyle Group unsuccessfully attempted to sell B&T to college bookstore leader Follett. This led to a management shakeup that included the resignation of longtime chairman Gerald Garbacz; Craig Richards became CEO. B&T then completed the overhaul of its 20-year-old fulfillment and distribution systems in 1995. This was part of a larger restructuring that led to the formation of Electronic Business and Information and Library Services units.

B&T's first big contract to perform library purchasing was with the State of Hawaii in 1996. The next year, however, Hawaii slapped the company with a lawsuit, which the US Justice Department later joined, accusing B&T of overcharging public schools, libraries, and federal agencies by $100 million to $200 million from 1983 to 1993. In 1998, 17 states joined the federal government, filing their own lawsuit alleging book overcharges.

The federal suit was settled in 1999 with B&T paying $300 million but admitting no wrongdoing. Soon thereafter, B&T filed to go public.

Chairman: Patrick W. Gross, age 55
Co-Chairman: Joseph R. Wright Jr., age 60
VC: Daniel A. D'Aniello, age 52
CEO and President: Craig M. Richards, age 49, $812,545 pay
EVP; General Manager of Baker & Taylor Entertainment: Richard S. Czuba, age 47
EVP, Chief Administrative Officer, and CFO: Edward H. Gross, age 56, $329,837 pay
EVP, Distribution: Marshall A. Wight, age 48
SVP Electronic Business and Information Services: Robert H. Doran, age 54, $263,052 pay
SVP Human Resources: Claudette Hampton
SVP: Margaret A. Nordstrom, age 50
VP, Marketing: Connie Koury
President, Baker & Taylor Institutional: Gary M. Rautenstrauch, age 46, $302,407 pay (prior to promotion)
President, Baker & Taylor Retailer: James S. Ulsamer, age 49
Auditors: Arthur Andersen LLP

LOCATIONS

HQ: 2709 Water Ridge Pkwy., Charlotte, NC 28217
Phone: 704-357-3500   **Fax:** 704-329-9105
Web site: http://www.baker-taylor.com

PRODUCTS/OPERATIONS

1999 Sales

	$ mil.	% of total
Retail		
Traditional	478	47
Internet	166	16
Institutional	377	37
Total	**1,021**	**100**

Selected Products
Accessories
Bargain books
Calendars
CD-ROM/multimedia
CDs
Children's and young adult's books
Educational software
Hardcover books (trade and academic)
Home office productivity software
Laser discs
Mass-market and trade paperbacks
Music audiocassettes
Spoken word audio
VHS videocassettes
Video games

Selected Information Products
B&T Express Wired (online prepublication information)
Cataloging Database (B&T MARC)
Copy Depth Program
Customized Library Services
Libris 2020 (library automation system)
Replica Books (on-demand printing)
Standing Order Service
Talk Media (audio and video ordering and inquiry system)
Title Source II (CD-ROM and Internet database and ordering software

COMPETITORS

Advanced Marketing
Alliance Entertainment
BH Blackwell Ltd.
Book Wholesalers
Brodart
Chas Levy
East Texas Distributing
Educational Development
Follett
Handleman
Ingram Entertainment
Ingram Industries
Ludington News
Major Video Concepts
Midwest Library Service
Navarre
Publishers Group West
Rentrak
Valley Media

HISTORICAL FINANCIALS & EMPLOYEES

Private FYE: June	Annual Growth	1990	1991	1992	1993	1994	1995	1996	1997	1998	1999
Sales ($ mil.)	6.9%	—	—	—	—	—	784	751	829	883	1,021
Net income ($ mil.)		—	—	—	—	—	(4)	(3)	(3)	53	22
Income as % of sales		—	—	—	—	—	—	—	—	6.0%	2.1%
Employees		—	—	—	—	—	—	—	—	—	2,500

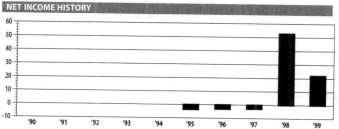

NET INCOME HISTORY

1999 FISCAL YEAR-END
Debt ratio: 38.1%
Return on equity: 100.0%
Cash ($ mil.): 20
Current ratio: 1.02
Long-term debt ($ mil.): 9

BAKER & TAYLOR

BATTELLE MEMORIAL INSTITUTE

OVERVIEW

R&D may stand for random development at Battelle Memorial Institute, one of the world's largest contract research firms. The Columbus, Ohio-based not-for-profit trust was established to perform metallurgy research; however, it has diversified into such areas as agrochemicals, automobiles, chemicals, energy, medical products, and pharmaceuticals.

Through contract research, intellectual property licensing, and joint ventures, Battelle has customers in nearly 30 countries. The institute has been instrumental in developing products such as the photocopy machine, optical digital recording (used on compact discs), and the Universal Product Code (bar codes). It continues to explore such technologies as alternative fuels, advanced medical equipment and processes, and recycling techniques.

Battelle is also a major source of research and development expertise for governments around the world. In the US it serves the departments of Energy, Defense, and Health and Human Services; the Environmental Protection Agency; and nearly 800 other government organizations each year. The institute develops equipment for chemical and biological defense and solutions for environment cleanup and nuclear power plant safety; it has also been active in dismantling stockpiled weapons.

HISTORY

Battelle Memorial Institute was founded with a $1.5 million trust willed by Gordon Battelle, who died in 1923. Battelle was a champion of research for the advancement of humankind, and before taking his father's place as president of several Ohio steel mills, he had funded a former university professor's successful work to extract useful chemicals from mine waste. Battelle's mother, upon her death in 1925, left the institute an additional $2.1 million. The institute opened in 1929.

The institute took on perhaps the most important project in its history in 1944 when it helped an electronics company's patent lawyer, Chester Carlson, find practical uses for his invention, called xerography. Eventually Battelle developed the first photocopy machine, and in 1955 it sold the patent rights for the machine to Haloid (now Xerox) in exchange for royalties.

During WWII Battelle worked on uranium refining for the Manhattan Project, and in the early 1950s it established the world's first private nuclear research facility. The company also set up facilities in Germany and Switzerland.

The tax man came knocking in 1961, questioning the tax-free status of some of Battelle's activities. The organization eventually had to pay $47 million. In 1965 Battelle developed a coin with a copper core and a copper-and-nickel-alloy cladding for the US Treasury.

As the result of a ruling that reinterpreted a clause in Gordon Battelle's will, in 1975 the institute gave $80 million to philanthropic enterprises. This ruling, coupled with the taxes that the organization was still unaccustomed to paying, forced Battelle to re-examine its strategy.

Battelle co-developed the Universal Product Code (the bar code symbol found today on nearly all consumer goods packaging) in the 1970s; the institute also landed a lucrative contract from the US Department of Energy (DOE) to manage its commercial nuclear waste isolation program. The company signed an extension with the DOE in 1992 to run its Pacific Northwest Laboratory (which it has operated since 1965).

An Ohio court in 1997 approved a seven-page agreement with the Battelle Memorial Institute outlining the key principles that must be followed according to Gordon Battelle's will. This agreement replaced the 1975 decree and ended more than 20 years of scrutiny by the state attorney general's office.

In 1998 the DOE awarded a contract for the management and operation of its Brookhaven National Laboratory to Brookhaven Science Associates, a partnership between the State University of New York and Battelle. That year a Battelle contract to dispose of Vietnam War-era napalm drew national attention when subcontractor Pollution Control Industries backed out of the project, citing safety concerns. Under Battelle's direction, Houston-based GNI Group finally started taking the 3.4 million gallons of napalm off the US Navy's hands.

Battelle teamed with the University of Tennessee in 1999 to win a five-year, $2.5 billion contract to operate the US government's Oak Ridge National Laboratory. That year the institute announced several developments in cancer research, including FDA approval to test an inhalation delivery system for treating lung cancer.

Chairman: Willis S. White Jr.
First VC: John J. Hopfield
Second VC: John B. McCoy
President and CEO: Douglas E. Olesen
EVP, Department of Energy Market Sector:
William J. Madia
EVP, Government Market Sectors:
Merwyn R. VanderLind
SVP, CFO, and Treasurer: Mark W. Kontos
SVP and Chief Technology Officer, Core Technology Development: Richard C. Adams
SVP; General Manager, Automotive Technology Market Sector: Donald P. McConnell
SVP; General Manager, Batelle Pulmonary Therapeutics: Dennis B. Cearlock
SVP; General Manager, Chemical Products Market Sector: Benjamin G. Maiden
SVP, Administration, Secretary, and General Counsel: Jerome R. Bahlmann
SVP, Organizational Development: Robert W. Smith Jr.
Director, Human Resources: Bob Lincoln
Auditors: KPMG LLP

LOCATIONS

HQ: 505 King Ave., Columbus, OH 43201
Phone: 614-424-6424   **Fax:** 614-424-5263
Web site: http://www.battelle.org

PRODUCTS/OPERATIONS

Selected Inventions
Cruise control (1960s)
Exploded-tip paintbrush (nylon brush for Wooster Brush Co., 1950)
Golf ball coatings (1965)
Heat Seat (microwaveable heated stadium cushion, 1990s)
Holograms (work began in the 1970s)
Insulin injection pen (for Eli Lilly, 1990s)
Oil spill outline monitor (1992)
PCB-cleaning chemical process (1992)
Photocopy machine (with Haloid, 1940s)
Plastic breakdown process (1990s)
"Sandwich" coins (copper/copper and nickel alloy cladding design for US Treasury, 1965)
SenSonic toothbrush (with Teledyne/WaterPik, 1990s)
Smart cards (cards embedded with tiny computers that store large amounts of information, 1980s)
SnoPake (correction fluid, 1955)
Universal Product Code (co-creator; bar code, 1970s)

COMPETITORS

Aerospace Corporation
Altran Technologies
Computer Sciences
IBAH
Kendle
MIT
MITRE
OEI International
PAREXEL
Quintiles Transnational
Radian
Research Triangle Institute
SAIC
SRI International
Southwest Research Institute
The Charles Stark Draper Laboratory
University of California
Westat

HISTORICAL FINANCIALS & EMPLOYEES

Not-for-profit FYE: September	Annual Growth	1990	1991	1992	1993	1994	1995	1996	1997	1998	1999
Sales ($ mil.)	2.6%	715	774	859	869	958	974	945	946	710	901
Employees	(1.1%)	7,791	8,398	8,553	8,400	8,583	7,500	7,163	7,060	7,250	7,060

1998 is a 9-month fiscal year.

SALES HISTORY

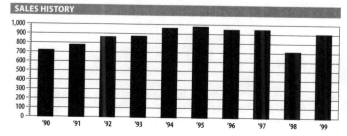

BECHTEL GROUP, INC.

OVERVIEW

Whether it's raising an entire city or razing a nuclear power plant, you can bet the Bechtel Group will be there to bid on the business. The engineering, construction, and project management firm, based in San Francisco, is #2 in the US heavy construction industry (behind Fluor).

Bechtel builds facilities for industries such as aerospace, chemical manufacturing, energy generation and transmission, mining and metals, surface transportation, telecommunications, and water and waste management. Bechtel has made a name for itself on huge projects, such as the building of the entire industrial city of Jubail in Saudi Arabia, and on difficult ones, such as the cleanup of

Chernobyl. It has worked in 140 countries on more than 19,000 projects, including the Hoover Dam. Some two-thirds of its business is outside the US.

In recent years Bechtel has cut costs by standardizing its designs while improving its communications with a worldwide computer network. Bechtel increasingly acts as a private investor in large public-sector projects, and it develops relationships with local suppliers and contractors.

The billionaire Bechtel family controls the company, which is headed by fourth-generation member Riley Bechtel.

HISTORY

In 1898 25-year-old Warren Bechtel left his Kansas farm to grade railroads in the Oklahoma Indian territories, then followed the rails west. Settling in Oakland, California, he founded his own contracting firm. Foreseeing the importance of roads, oil, and power, he won big projects such as the Northern California Highway and the Bowman Dam. By 1925 W.A. Bechtel was the West's largest construction company.

Steve Bechtel (president after his father's death in 1933) won the company projects such as the Hoover Dam and the San Francisco Bay Bridge and WWII defense contracts. Noted for his friendships with influential people, including Dwight Eisenhower, Adlai Stevenson, and Saudi Arabia's King Faisal, Steve developed projects that spanned nations and industries, such as pipelines in Saudi Arabia, Canada, and Australia and numerous power projects. By 1960, when Steve Bechtel, Jr., took over, the company operated on six continents.

In the next two decades, Bechtel worked on transportation projects — such as San Francisco's Bay Area Rapid Transit (BART) system and the Washington, DC, subway system — and power projects, including nuclear plants. After the 1979 Three Mile Island accident, Bechtel tried its hand at nuclear cleanup. With nuclear power no longer in vogue, it focused on other markets, such as mining in New Guinea (gold and copper, 1981-84) and China (coal, 1984). Bechtel's Jubail project in Saudi Arabia, begun in 1976, raised an entire city.

The US recession and rising developing-world debt of the early 1980s sent Bechtel reeling. It cut its workforce by 22,000 and stemmed losses by piling up small projects such as plant modernizations. One disaster was Bechtel's good fortune. When the Chernobyl nuclear plant exploded in 1986, Bechtel became part of the cleanup team.

Riley Bechtel, great-grandson of Warren, became CEO in 1990. He soon profited from another disaster: After the 1991 Gulf War, Bechtel extinguished Kuwait's flaming oil wells and worked on the oil-spill cleanup. During the decade it also worked on such projects as the Channel Tunnel (Chunnel) between England and France, the new airport in Hong Kong, and pipelines in the former Soviet Union.

Bechtel was part of the consortium contracted in 1996 to build a high-speed passenger rail line between London and the Chunnel. International Generating (InterGen), Bechtel's joint venture with Pacific Gas & Electric (PG&E), was chosen to help build Mexico's first private power plant. In 1996 Bechtel bought PG&E's share of InterGen, then sold a 50% stake in InterGen to a unit of Royal Dutch/Shell in early 1997.

That year Bechtel began a venture, Netcon (Thailand), with Lucent to build telecom systems abroad. Bechtel also joined with Dresser (now part of Halliburton), Pacific Enterprises (now Sempra Energy), and Energy Asset Management to buy interests in energy projects in developing regions. In 1998 Bechtel won major contracts to construct a gas production plant in Abu Dhabi, with Technip, and a natural gas pipeline from Turkmenistan to Turkey, with Amoco (now BP Amoco).

In 1999, Bechtel won two billion-dollar contracts with Internet companies: with online grocer Webvan to build a series of automated grocery warehouses in the US and with Equinix for a series of Internet hubs and host centers worldwide.

Chairman and CEO: Riley P. Bechtel
VC: Don Gunther
President and COO: Adrian Zaccaria
SVP and CFO: Georganne Proctor
SVP, Human Resources: Bob Baxter
SVP, Information Systems & Technology:
 Hank Leingang
SVP, External Affairs: Chuck Redman
SVP, Legal and Risk Management: Foster Wollen
**President, Europe, Africa, Middle East, Southwest
 Asia:** John Carter
President, Latin America: Ric Cesped
President, North America: Darrell Donly
President, Asia/Pacific: Ted Kyzer
President, Bechtel Petroleum & Chemical:
 Gary Hammond
President, Bechtel Telecommunications:
 George Conniff
President, Bechtel Technology and Consulting:
 Larry Papay
**President, Bechtel National, Inc.; Bechtel Systems &
 Infrastructure, Inc.:** Lee McIntire
President, Bechtel Enterprises, Inc.: Paul Unruh
Acting President, Bechtel Civil: Bob Baxter
President, Bechtel Nuclear Power: Ken Hess
President, Bechtel Mining and Metals: Dick Harding
Auditors: PricewaterhouseCoopers LLP

LOCATIONS

HQ: 50 Beale St., San Francisco, CA 94105
Phone: 415-768-1234   **Fax:** 415-768-9038
Web site: http://www.bechtel.com

Bechtel Group provides heavy construction design and
construction services in Africa, the Asia/Pacific region,
Europe, Latin America, the Middle East, North America,
and Southwest Asia.

1998 Sales

	% of total
North America	38
Europe, Africa, Middle East	
& Southwest Asia	31
Latin America	19
Asia/Pacific	12
Total	**100**

PRODUCTS/OPERATIONS

Selected Industries Served
Aviation services
Chemicals
Commercial buildings
Environmental and pollution control
Hazardous waste cleanup
Hotels, resorts, and theme parks
Manufacturing
Mining and metals
Petroleum
Pipelines
Ports and harbors
Power
Space and defense
Surface transportation
Telecommunications
Water supply and treatment

Selected Services
Automation technology
Community relations
Environmental health and safety
Equipment operations
International consulting
Labor relations
Project management, engineering, and financing
Worldwide procurement

COMPETITORS

ABB	Morrison Knudsen
Black & Veatch	NKK
Bouygues	Parsons
CH2M Hill	Perini
Chiyoda Corp.	Peter Kiewit Sons'
EMCON	Philipp Holzmann
Eiffage	PowerGen
Enron	RWE
Fluor	Roy F. Weston
Foster Wheeler	Safety-Kleen
HOCHTIEF	Samsung
Halliburton	Schneider
Hyundai Engineering and	Siemens
Construction	Societe Generale
IT Group	d'Entreprises
ITOCHU	Technip
Jacobs Engineering	URS
Kvaerner	Waste Management
Marubeni	

HISTORICAL FINANCIALS & EMPLOYEES

Private FYE: December	Annual Growth	1989	1990	1991	1992	1993	1994	1995	1996	1997	1998
Sales ($ mil.)	10.6%	5,096	5,631	7,526	7,774	7,337	7,885	8,504	8,157	11,329	12,645
Employees	0.8%	27,800	32,500	30,900	30,900	29,400	29,200	29,400	30,000	30,000	30,000

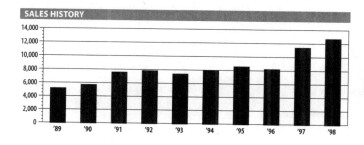

SALES HISTORY

BELK, INC.

OVERVIEW

No need to call in Richard Dawson to settle the Belk family feud. The Belk brood, which has not always brimmed with brotherly love, runs the largest privately owned department store chain in the US. With 260 stores located in 13 southeastern and mid-Atlantic states, the Charlotte, North Carolina-based chain sells moderately priced designer and private-label clothing, cosmetics, and home fashions.

In 1998 Belk streamlined its operations by consolidating its gangly network of 112 separate companies, formed over the past century, into Belk, Inc. While some might say a public offering is the logical next step, chairman John Belk has vowed that will not happen while he is alive. The Belk family owns slightly more than half of the company.

Family feuding nearly toppled the company back in 1952, when founder William Henry Belk died. His six children squabbled over the direction of the company, even suing each other, before making peace. When president Tom Belk died in 1997, the transition went a little smoother: His three sons became the co-presidents, the third generation of Belk brothers to run the company.

HISTORY

William Henry Belk didn't mind being known as a cheapskate. At 26 he opened his first store, New York Racket, in 1888 in Monroe, North Carolina. He nicknamed the tiny shop "The Cheapest Store on Earth" and created the slogan "Cheap Goods Sell Themselves." In 1891 Belk convinced his brother John to give up a career as a doctor and join him in the retail business. The new company, Belk Brothers, opened stores in North and South Carolina, often with partners who were family members or former employees, resulting in many two-family store names such as Belk-Harry and Hudson-Belk.

The Belks formed a partnership with the Leggett family (John's in-laws) in 1920. But feuding between the two families led to a split in 1927. The Leggetts agreed that the Belk family could keep a 20% share of the Leggett stores. John died the next year.

A strict no-credit policy worked in William's favor during the Depression, when he was able to buy out his more lenient competitors for rock-bottom prices. The shrewd businessman grew the chain from 29 stores in 1929 to about 220 stores by 1945, employing concepts such as a no haggling policy and easy returns. William died in 1952.

That year one of his six children, William Henry Jr., opened a Belk-Lindsey store in Florida using a new format that featured, among other things, an Oriental design. Most of his siblings balked at the store's new look, but William Jr. opened another store in 1953 following the same format.

Two years later four of William Jr.'s siblings — John, Irwin, Tom, and Sarah — cut ties with the Florida stores and formed Belk Stores Services to organize their other stores. Angry at the rebuke, William Jr. and another brother, Henderson, sued the rest of the family, but they later dropped the lawsuit. In 1956 the company, with John at the helm, bought out 50-store rival chain Effird.

John had political ambitions and was elected mayor of Charlotte in 1969, despite attempts by his brother William Jr. to foil the campaign. He remained mayor until 1977. Tom became the company's president in 1980.

Belk continued to hold its own in the 1980s against larger department store chains on the prowl for acquisitions. But internal problems continued, as the company was stung by family discord and a loose ownership structure. Some relatives sold Belk stores to competitors such as Proffitt's (now Saks Inc.) and Dillard's. Irwin and his family, discouraged about the company's direction, sold their stock to John. In 1996 the Leggetts came back into the fold when Belk bought out the chain of about 30 stores.

Tom died in 1997 after complications from gall bladder surgery. His three sons, Tim, Johnny, and McKay, stepped up their responsibilities in the company, but as co-presidents they still answer to their uncle, John, the CEO. That year the company closed its struggling 13-store Tags chain of off-price outlets.

In 1998 Belk reorganized its brood and brought all 112 separate corporations under one company. The move is expected to save $8 million to $10 million the first year and $3 million to $5 million annually in upcoming years by streamlining the company's accounting (previously it had to fill out tax forms for all 112 businesses) and other operations. It also will give Belk better access to capital for expansion.

Also in 1998 Belk traded several store locations with Dillard's.

Chairman and CEO: John M. Belk, age 79, $840,840 pay
President, Merchandising and Marketing:
H. W. McKay Belk, age 42, $548,912 pay
President Finance, Systems, and Operations:
John R. Belk, age 40, $548,912 pay
President, Store Divisions and Real Estate:
Thomas M. Belk Jr., age 44, $548,912 pay
EVP, Finance: James M. Berry, age 68
EVP, Secretary, and General Counsel: Ralph A. Pitts,
age 45, $463,385 pay
EVP, Real Estate and Store Planning:
William L. Wilson, age 51
SVP, Treasurer, and Controller: Bill R. Walton, age 50
VP, Personnel: Carolyn McGinnis
Auditors: KPMG LLP

LOCATIONS

HQ: 2801 W. Tyvola Rd., Charlotte, NC 28217
Phone: 704-357-1000   **Fax:** 704-357-1876
Web site: http://www.belk.com

PRODUCTS/OPERATIONS

Store Names	Private Labels
Belk	24Seven
Belk-Beck	Andhurst
Belk-Harry	Home Accents
Belk-Lindsey	J.Khakis
Belk-Matthews	Kim Rogers
Belk-Rhodes	Meeting Street
Belk-Simpson	Nursery Rhyme
Gallant-Belk	Saddlebred
Hudson-Belk	Spa Essentials
Parks-Belk	

COMPETITORS

Dayton Hudson	May
Dillard's	Montgomery Ward
Elder-Beerman Stores	Saks Inc.
Federated	Sears
J. C. Penney	Stein Mart
Jacobson Stores	

HISTORICAL FINANCIALS & EMPLOYEES

Private FYE: January	Annual Growth	1990	1991	1992	1993	1994	1995	1996	1997	1998	1999
Sales ($ mil.)	3.9%	—	—	—	1,662	1,674	1,694	1,685	1,773	1,974	2,091
Net income ($ mil.)	0.3%	—	—	—	56	54	49	44	101	54	57
Income as % of sales	—	—	—	—	3.4%	3.2%	2.9%	2.6%	5.7%	2.8%	2.7%
Employees	(6.2%)	—	—	—	—	—	—	—	25,000	29,000	22,000

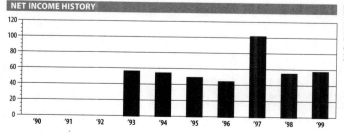

NET INCOME HISTORY

1999 FISCAL YEAR-END

Debt ratio: 33.6%
Return on equity: 7.7%
Cash ($ mil.): 18
Current ratio: 3.41
Long-term debt ($ mil.): 399

BIG FLOWER HOLDINGS, INC.

OVERVIEW

While most paper is made from wood pulp, a lot of newspaper inserts come from a big flower. New York City-based Big Flower Holdings is among the largest commercial printers in the US, and its Treasure Chest Advertising subsidiary is the largest supplier of advertising inserts and circulars in the country. Through its operating subsidiary Big Flower Press Holdings, the company is active in three primary business areas: advertising inserts and newspaper products, direct mail and marketing products, and digital services.

Treasure Chest Advertising (which generates more than 60% of sales) is a leading printer of TV program listings and Sunday comics, serving more than 300 newspapers such as the *Los Angeles Times, The New York Times,* and *The Denver Post.* It also prints advertising inserts for retailers such as OfficeMax, Home Depot, and Wal-Mart. Big Flower's Webcraft subsidiary provides personalized direct mail and marketing products and services. Big Flower also offers retailers and consumer products companies a variety of digital pre-media services, as well as image storage and archiving for packaging and advertising through its Big Flower Digital Services unit. The company operates more than 75 production facilities in the US and the UK.

Known primarily as a commercial printer, Big Flower is repositioning itself as an integrated advertising and marketing business. The company also is focusing on targeted advertising programs and is expanding its online presence through a minority investment in Internet advertising company 24/7 Media.

An investor group including Evercore Capital Partners and Thomas H. Lee Co. owns Big Flower.

HISTORY

Brothers Robert and Paul Milhous founded Treasure Chest Advertising in 1967 to publish the Treasure Chest of Values, a weekly shopping paper. Within five years the company was printing advertising circulars from six plants across the US. In 1982 Treasure Chest began printing color comics and TV program listings. By the early 1990s the Milhouses were ready to sell out. Investment banker Theodore Ammon, who gave up a partnership in Kohlberg Kravis Roberts to strike out on his own, founded BFP Holdings in 1993 and paid $235 million for the company.

In 1994 BFP Holdings acquired two additional operations — Retail Graphic Holding and KTB Associates — which expanded its capacity and customer base in both the advertising insert and newspaper TV magazine segments. It raised about $100 million through an IPO in November 1995. Almost immediately afterward, the newly public company — renamed Big Flower Press Holdings — purchased LaserTech Color (outsourced digital pre-media and content management services). A disastrous Christmas for retailers and high paper prices in 1995 lowered its earnings and sent stock prices to the basement.

In 1996 Big Flower bought direct mail and specialty printer Webcraft Technologies, which focused on fragrance samplers, rub-off promotional games, and lottery tickets. (The lottery unit was sold later that year.) The company also purchased a full-service direct mail company, Scanforms, which increased its customer base among financial services and publishing companies. In addition, it added Internet production services to its repertoire with the acquisition of Pacific Color Connection. Big Flower reached $1 billion in sales in 1996, just three years after its formation.

The following year Big Flower continued its rapid expansion strategy with the purchase of UK-based Olwen Direct Mail Limited, which marked the company's first international acquisition. It also bought two companies, Columbine JDS Systems and Broadcast Systems Software, which diversified Big Flower into broadcast media services. In 1997, the company underwent a legal restructuring; afterward Big Flower Holdings emerged as the parent of Big Flower Press Holdings.

The company's European presence was further expanded in 1998 with the purchase of two prepublication service providers — Production Response Systems and Lifeboat Matey, which operate as the Fusion Group. Also that year the company invested in the Internet advertiser 24/7 Media and acquired a software development and database marketing company (Reach America), a digital prepublication company (Enterton Group), and a marketing services company (ColorStream). In 1999 a group led by leveraged-buyout firm Thomas H. Lee Co. purchased Big Flower for about $800 million.

Chairman: R. Theodore Ammon, age 49, $1,425,000 pay
President and CEO: Edward T. Reilly, age 52, $1,045,000 pay
EVP, Secretary, and General Counsel: Mark A. Angelson, age 48, $968,500 pay
EVP and CFO: Richard L. Ritchie, age 52, $807,500 pay
Chief Executive, Laser Tech Color: Brian W. Mason
Chief Executive, TC Advertising: Donald E. Roland
Chief Executive, Columbine JDS: Wayne M. Ruting
Chief Executive, Webcraft: Theodore D. Sherwin
Manager Human Resources: Linda Brooks
Auditors: Deloitte & Touche LLP

LOCATIONS

HQ: 3 E. 54th St., New York, NY 10022
Phone: 212-521-1600   **Fax:** 212-223-4074
Web site: http://www.cjds.com

PRODUCTS/OPERATIONS

1998 Sales

	$ mil.	% of total
Insert advertising & newspaper	1,102	63
Direct marketing services	283	16
Digital services	273	16
Specialty products & commercial printing	91	5
Adjustments	(9)	—
Total	**1,740**	**100**

Selected Customers

Advertising agencies
  J. Walter Thompson
  Leo Group
Broadcasters
  Fox Broadcasting
  LIN Television
  Meredith
  Turner Broadcasting System
Newspapers
  The Atlanta Journal-Constitution
  The Baltimore Sun
  The Boston Globe
  The Denver Post
  Los Angeles Times
  The Miami Herald
The New York Times
The Philadelphia Inquirer
San Francisco Chronicle
Retailers
  American Drug Stores
  Calvin Klein
  Elizabeth Arden
  Home Depot
  Kmart
  Kraft Foods
  Micron Computer
  OfficeMax
  Rite Aid
  Safeway
  Walgreen
  Wal-Mart

COMPETITORS

ACG Holdings
ADVO
Acxiom
Applied Graphics
Banta
CSG Systems International
Enterprise Software
Experian
Harte-Hanks
infoUSA
Moore Corporation
Quad/Graphics
Quebecor Printing
R. R. Donnelley
Schawk
Standard Register
USCS International
Valassis Communications
Wace Group

HISTORICAL FINANCIALS & EMPLOYEES

Private FYE: December	Annual Growth	1989	1990	1991	1992	1993	1994	1995	1996	1997	1998
Sales ($ mil.)	18.5%	—	—	530	536	555	565	532	1,202	1,377	1,740
Net income ($ mil.)	—	—	—	(4)	4	5	(4)	(14)	(5)	(47)	38
Income as % of sales	—	—	—	—	0.8%	0.8%	—	—	—	—	2.2%
Employees	33.0%	—	—	—	—	—	3,200	4,000	6,410	8,500	10,000

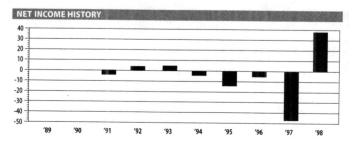

NET INCOME HISTORY

1998 FISCAL YEAR-END

Debt ratio: 85.2%
Return on equity: 37.9%
Cash ($ mil.): 9
Current ratio: 0.98
Long-term debt ($ mil.): 731

BLOOMBERG L.P.

OVERVIEW

Spreading the lowdown on the financial world through virtually every aspect of modern media, Bloomberg is brimming with business information. Foremost among the New York City-based company's products are its Bloomberg proprietary terminals, which provide institutional investors and other users with real-time, around-the-clock news, market data, and analysis. With about 100,000 terminals installed (at a monthly charge of about $1,200 each), Bloomberg ranks behind only #1 Reuters and #2 Bridge Information Systems in the market for such devices. Bloomberg also provides a syndicated news service (Bloomberg News); publishes books and magazines; and broadcasts business information via TV, radio,

and the Internet. Its 700 reporters are stationed around the globe. In addition to the company's media products, Bloomberg also offers the Bloomberg Tradebook (an order-matching system) and the Bloomberg Trading and Bloomberg Portfolio Trading systems.

As competition within the financial information industry intensifies, Bloomberg is beefing up its offerings in the consumer market, particularly through the Internet. Agreements with America Online and CNET will expand the company's presence on the Web. Founder, president, and CEO Michael Bloomberg owns 72% of the company. Merrill Lynch has a 20% ownership interest, and six Bloomberg employees own the remainder.

HISTORY

By the mid-1970s Michael Bloomberg had worked his way up to head of equity trading and sales at New York investment powerhouse Salomon Brothers. He left Salomon in 1981, just after the firm went private, cashing out with $10 million for his partnership interest.

Bloomberg founded Innovative Marketing Systems and spent the next year developing the Bloomberg terminal, which allowed users to manipulate bond data. In 1982 he pitched it to Merrill Lynch, which bought 20 machines. Regular production of the terminals began in 1984, and in 1985 Merrill Lynch invested $39 million in the company to gain a 30% stake. The company prospered during the 1980s boom, and over time the data, not the machines, became the heart of the business, which was renamed Bloomberg L.P. in 1986.

The company weathered the stock market crash of 1987, opening offices in London and Tokyo. Bloomberg made its entry into news-gathering and delivery in 1990 when Bloomberg News began broadcasting on its terminals. The company built its news organization from scratch, hiring away reporters from such publications as *The Wall Street Journal* and *Forbes*. Bloomberg bought a New York radio station in 1992 and converted it to an all-news format. The next year it built an in-house TV studio and created a business news show for PBS. A satellite TV station followed in 1994, along with a personal finance magazine.

In 1995 Bloomberg began offering business information via its Web site. The company also introduced the Bloomberg Tradebook, an electronic securities-trading venue designed to compete with Reuters' Instinet. (In 1997

Tradebook was approved by the SEC for use in connection with some Nasdaq-listed stocks.) Bloomberg also started offering its services to subscribers in a PC-compatible format and selling its data to other news purveyors, such as LEXIS-NEXIS (an online information service).

In 1996 the company went further into financial publishing, issuing *Swap Literacy: A Comprehensive Guide* and *A Common Sense Guide to Mutual Funds.* That year Michael Bloomberg bought back 10% of the company from Merrill Lynch for $200 million, giving Bloomberg L.P. an estimated market value of $2 billion. The company agreed in 1997 to supply the daytime programming for Paxson Communications' New York TV station WPXN.

When Bridge Information Systems bought Dow Jones Markets from Dow Jones in 1998, Bridge surpassed Bloomberg in number of financial information terminals installed, bumping Bloomberg from the #2 spot into third place. But Bloomberg continued expanding its offerings through strategic agreements with Internet companies such as America Online and CNET, and through the introduction of *Bloomberg Money,* a personal finance magazine.

In 1999 Bloomberg secured a deal with the Australian stock exchange that would allow its terminals to facilitate international order routing into the Australian market. The company also expanded its presence in the Spanish-language market through its agreement with CBS Telenoticias to produce a TV news program (*Noticiero Financiero*).

President and CEO: Michael R. Bloomberg, age 57
COO: Susan Friedlander
EVP Syndication: Kathleen Campion
Chief Information Officer: Tom Secunda
Editor Publications: William Inman
Executive Producer, Television and Radio:
Cathy Stevens
Publisher, Bloomberg Magazines and Books:
David Wachtell
Editor in Chief, Bloomberg News: Matthew Winkler
Managing Editor, Television and Radio: John Meehan
General Manager, Bloomberg Radio and Television:
Rich Sabreen
Human Resources: Linda Norris

LOCATIONS

HQ: 499 Park Ave., New York, NY 10022
Phone: 212-318-2000   **Fax:** 212-980-4585
Web site: http://www.bloomberg.com

PRODUCTS/OPERATIONS

Selected Products and Services
Bloomberg (access to Bloomberg information via PCs
and workstations)
Bloomberg API (interface enabling integration of
Bloomberg data into proprietary applications)
Bloomberg Data License (financial database service)
Bloomberg Energy (Web site focusing on energy)
Bloomberg Flat Panel terminal (device that conveys
Bloomberg information via two screens)
Bloomberg Interactive Television (interactive news)
Bloomberg Investimenti (financial publication focusing
on Italian finance)
Bloomberg Magazine (financial magazine)
Bloomberg Money (financial magazine for European
investors)
Bloomberg News (syndicated news service)
Bloomberg Personal Finance (personal finance magazine)
Bloomberg Portfolio Trading System
(asset management tool)
Bloomberg Press (book publishing)
Bloomberg Push Channel (interactive server-push
channel)
Bloomberg Radio (syndicated radio news service)
Bloomberg Television (24-hour news channel and
syndicated reports)
Bloomberg Tradebook (equities trading technology)
Bloomberg Trading System (Bloomberg information
combined with trading technology)
Bloomberg Traveler (access to Bloomberg information via
laptop computers and PCs)
Bloomberg Wealth Manager (magazine for financial
planners and investment advisers)
Bloomberg.com (Web site)

COMPETITORS

Agence France-Presse	Intuit
Associated Press	McGraw-Hill
Bridge Information	Media General
Data Broadcasting	Multex.com
Dialog Corporation	Primark
Dow Jones	Reuters
FactSet	Thomson Corporation
FinancialWeb.com	Time Warner
Forbes	

HISTORICAL FINANCIALS & EMPLOYEES

Private FYE: December	Annual Growth	1989	1990	1991	1992	1993	1994	1995	1996	1997	1998
Estimated sales ($ mil.)	30.1%	140	192	192	290	370	550	650	760	1,300	1,500
Employees	28.4%	—	—	850	1,100	1,800	2,000	2,500	3,000	4,000	4,900

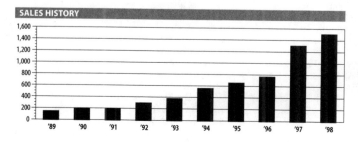

SALES HISTORY

Bloomberg

BLUE CROSS AND BLUE SHIELD

OVERVIEW

The rise of managed health care has had some of its members singing the blues, but Blue Cross and Blue Shield Association still has major market power. The Chicago-based association governs 51 chapters that offer health care coverage to nearly 73 million Americans via indemnity insurance, HMOs, PPOs, point-of-service (POS) plans, and Medicare plans.

While some Blues always faced competition head-on, most received tax benefits for taking all comers. But as lower-cost plans attracted the hale and hearty, the Blues' customers became older, sicker, and more expensive. With their quasi-charitable status and outdated rate structures, many Blues lost market share.

They have fought back by merging among themselves, creating for-profit subsidiaries, forming alliances with for-profit enterprises, or dropping their not-for-profit status and going public — while still using the Blue Cross Blue Shield name. A history of tax breaks complicates some of these efforts and usually requires the creation of charitable foundations. As a result, the umbrella association is becoming a licensing and brand-marketing entity. As industry consolidation threatens their market advantage, many Blues are competing among themselves as they push beyond the boundaries of their home states.

HISTORY

Blue Cross was born in 1929, when Baylor University official Justin Kimball offered schoolteachers 21 days of hospital care for $6 a year. A major plan feature was a community rating system that based premiums on the community claims experience rather than members' conditions.

The Blue Cross symbol was devised in 1933 by Minnesota plan executive E. A. van Steenwyck. By 1935 many of the 15 plans in 11 states used the symbol. Many states gave the plans nonprofit status, and in 1936 the American Hospital Association formed the Committee on Hospital Service (renamed the Blue Cross Association in 1948) to coordinate them.

As Blue Cross grew, state medical societies began sponsoring prepaid plans to cover doctors' fees. In 1946 they united under the aegis of the American Medical Association (AMA) as the Associated Medical Care Plans (later the Association of Blue Shield Plans).

In 1948 AMA thwarted a Blue Cross attempt to merge with Blue Shield. But the Blues increasingly cooperated on public policy matters while competing for members, and each Blue formed a not-for-profit corporation to coordinate its plan's activities.

By 1960 Blue Cross insured about a third of the US. Over the next decade the Blues started administering Medicare and other government health plans, and by 1970 half of Blue Cross' premiums came from government entities.

In the 1970s the Blues adopted such cost-control measures as review of hospital admissions; many plans even abandoned the community rating system. Most began emphasizing preventive care in HMOs or PPOs.

The two Blues finally merged in 1982, but this had little effect on the associations' bottom lines as losses grew.

By the 1990s the Blues were big business; some of the state associations offered officers high salaries and perks but still insisted on special regulatory treatment.

Blue Cross of California became the first chapter to give up its tax-free status when it was bought by WellPoint Health Networks, a managed care subsidiary it had founded in 1992. In a 1996 deal, WellPoint became the chapter's parent and converted it to for-profit status, assigning all of the stock to a public charitable foundation, which received the proceeds of its subsequent IPO. WellPoint also bought the group life and health division of Massachusetts Mutual Life Insurance (better known as MassMutual).

The for-profit switches picked up in 1997. Blue Cross of Connecticut merged with insurance provider Anthem and other mergers followed. Half the nation's Blues formed an alliance called BluesConnect, competing with national health plans by offering employers one nationwide benefits organization. The association also pursued overseas licensing agreements in Europe, South America, and Asia, assembling a network of Blue Cross-friendly caregivers aiming for worldwide coverage.

In 1998 Blues in more than 35 states sued the nation's big cigarette companies to recoup the costs of treating smoking-related illnesses. In a separate lawsuit, Blue Cross and Blue Shield of Minnesota received nearly $300 million from the tobacco industry. In 1999, Anthem moved to acquire or affiliate with Blues in Colorado, Maine, and New Hampshire. The same year, a Georgia Blues plan announced a merger bid with WellPoint.

President and CEO: Patrick G. Hays
EVP Business Alliances: Harry P. Cain II
EVP Systems Development and COO: Scott P. Serota
SVP, Corporate Secretary, and General Counsel:
Roger G. Wilson
SVP Policy, Representation, and Membership Services:
Mary Nell Lehnhard
VP and Chief Administration Officer: Steve Heath
VP Finance and Administration: Ralph Rambach
Human Resources: Bill Colbourne
Auditors: PricewaterhouseCoopers LLP

LOCATIONS

HQ: Blue Cross and Blue Shield Association,
225 N. Michigan Ave., Chicago, IL 60601
Phone: 312-297-6000   **Fax:** 312-297-6609
Web site: http://www.blueshield.com

PRODUCTS/OPERATIONS

1998 Members

	No. (mil.)	% of total
PPO plans	25.7	35
HMO plans	14.2	20
POS plans	6.4	9
Federal health benefits program	3.9	5
Other	22.5	31
Total	**72.7**	**100**

Selected Operations
BlueCard Worldwide (care of US members in foreign
countries)
BluesConnect (nationwide alliance)
Federal Employee Program (federal employees and
retirees)
Health maintenance organizations
Medicare management
Point-of-service programs
Preferred provider organizations

COMPETITORS

Aetna
CIGNA
Foundation Health Systems
Humana
Oxford Health Plans
Prudential
UniHealth
UnitedHealth Group

HISTORICAL FINANCIALS & EMPLOYEES

Association FYE: December	Annual Growth	1989	1990	1991	1992	1993	1994	1995	1996	1997	1998
Sales ($ mil.)	6.8%	56,040	62,566	67,068	70,913	71,161	71,414	74,400	75,200	76,500	94,700
Employees	1.9%	129,000	133,000	138,000	143,000	135,883	146,352	146,000	150,000	150,000	150,000

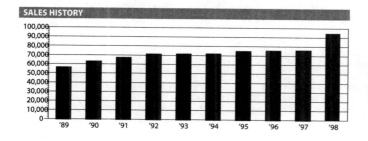

SALES HISTORY

Blue Cross
Blue Shield

BLUE CROSS MASSACHUSETTS

OVERVIEW

Back to black, Blue Cross and Blue Shield of Massachusetts (BCBSMA) is feeling in the pink. The Boston-based health insurer is battling its way back to financial health (selling noncore businesses and reducing staff) after spending recent years in the red.

BCBSMA offers groups and individuals traditional indemnity insurance, HMOs, and medical and dental PPO coverage. It also teams up with other regional Blues to offer plans HMO Blue New England and Blue Choice New England, which feature discounts at some ski resorts. BCBSMA is the state's largest provider of Medigap insurance, which pays for deductibles and costs not covered by Medicare.

Like Blues nationwide, BCBSMA has been hit hard by competition. It is now refocusing on its core business (health insurance) through divestitures and new products. BCBSMA has also expressed interest in forming a regional alliance with other New England Blues.

HISTORY

The predecessor of the Blue Cross Association was founded in Dallas in 1929 to allow teachers to prepay for hospitalization. The idea spread quickly during the Depression. By 1937, when its 26th affiliate was founded in Massachusetts, the organization had already become associated with the Blue Cross logo. Fairly priced by Depression standards, Blue Cross used community ratings, pegging its premiums to care costs in each region rather than underwriting each policyholder or group individually.

Seeing the success of Blue Cross, doctors joined up to offer similar prepayment plans known together as the Blue Shield Association. Doctor participation in Massachusetts was so widespread that members had a nearly unlimited choice of physicians.

Blue Cross and Blue Shield worked almost as one unit in Massachusetts but remained legally separate. At first they limited memberships to groups, but during the 1940s they began accepting individuals. In the 1960s the groups became co-administrators of the state's Medicare program. The Medex program was started in 1966 to supplement Medicare, but later evolved to encompass a state-mandated program for the medically indigent elderly. During the 1970s the companies began creating HMOs, but mostly for rural areas.

The groups continued to dominate Massachusetts health care in the 1980s. By the decade's end, however, the Massachusetts Blues had hit hard times, suffering lost market share, bloated management, and antiquated systems. As Blues in other states merged, competitors repeatedly blocked efforts to join the two Massachusetts organizations. Both Blues lost money from 1986 to 1988.

Efforts to help the situation only made matters worse (a failed upgrade of Blue Cross' information systems was abandoned in 1992 after six years and $100 million). The groups'

efforts to drive harder bargains with hospitals led to cries that the plans were trying to force rejected hospitals out of business.

In 1988 the organizations were at last allowed to merge. William Van Faasen became CEO in 1990, charged with re-engineering BCBSMA. For five years his efforts seemed to work. But the Medex segment was an earnings vacuum, and the new management drew criticism for hefty pay raises.

Blaming Medex, BCBSMA lost $90 million in 1996, which led the state insurance commissioner to step in and oversee its operations.

To make money like a regular health care company, BCBSMA started acting like a regular health care company — it slashed 16% of its workforce, enforced 10% pay cuts for those executives who survived a year-long purge, sold 10 clinics (to MedPartners, now Caremark Rx), and attempted to cancel 7,000 policies.

In 1998 BCBSMA agreed to pay $9.5 million to settle lawsuits that it overcharged Massachusetts subscribers for medical care. It also agreed in 1999 to pay $4.75 million to reimburse the US government for claims paid on people who weren't actually covered by BCBSMA. In the meantime, it created a new health insurance plan, Access Blue (set for launch in 2000), which lets patients see specialists without referrals. The plan has met resistance from hospitals and doctors, who consider its premiums too low to be financially viable.

BCBSMA filed to divide its operations into three companies, a move shot down by state legislators in 1998. Meanwhile, for-profit Blues licensees like Anthem continue to buy Blues (including those in Connecticut and New Hampshire). BCBSMA is pursuing affiliation with other not-for-profit regional Blues, including Blue Cross and Blue Shield of Rhode Island.

Chairman: Milton L. Glass
VC: Laurens MacLure
VC: Sinclair Weeks Jr.
President and CEO: William C. Van Faasen
SVP, Business Planning, Human Resources, Facilities Management: Arthur E. Banks
CFO and Treasurer: Gary D. St. Hilaire
Chief Legal Officer and Assistant Secretary: Sandra J. Carter
Chief of Audit and Controls: William T. Cushing Jr.
Secretary: Fredi Shonkoff
Assistant Treasurer: Keith F. Renaldi
Auditors: KPMG LLP

LOCATIONS

HQ: Blue Cross and Blue Shield of Massachusetts, 100 Summer St., Boston, MA 02110
Phone: 617-832-5000   **Fax:** 617-832-4832
Web site: http://www.bcbsma.com

PRODUCTS/OPERATIONS

1998 Sales

	$ mil.	% of total
Net premium & administrative fee income	1,968	96
Investment income	41	3
Other	32	1
Total	**2,041**	**100**

Services

Access Blue (managed care plan)
Blue Care® Elect-Preferred (managed care plan)
Blue Choice (managed care plan)
Blue Choice New England (regional managed care)
Comprehensive Major Medical (traditional plan)
Dental Blue
Dental Blue PPO
Direct Blue (nongroup plans)
HMO Blue (statewide managed care)
HMO Blue New England (regional managed care)
Medex (Medicare supplement)
Vital Insurance Protection (traditional plan)
Voluntary Dental Blue
Voluntary Dental Blue PPO

COMPETITORS

Aetna
Anthem Insurance
CIGNA
Harvard Pilgrim
Prudential
Tufts Health Plan

HISTORICAL FINANCIALS & EMPLOYEES

Not-for-profit FYE: December	Annual Growth	1989	1990	1991	1992	1993	1994	1995	1996	1997	1998
Sales ($ mil.)	(4.8%)	3,184	3,436	3,257	3,397	3,792	3,595	3,575	3,504	2,123	2,041
Net income ($ mil.)	58.6%	1	30	39	29	54	43	11	(90)	13	64
Income as % of sales	—	—	0.9%	1.2%	0.9%	1.4%	1.2%	0.3%	—	0.6%	3.1%
Employees	(11.5%)	—	—	6,331	6,559	6,171	5,865	5,630	5,500	2,756	2,579

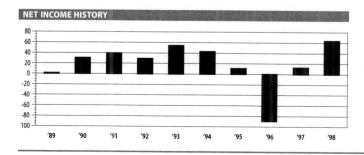

NET INCOME HISTORY

Blue Cross Blue Shield

BLUE CROSS OF MICHIGAN

OVERVIEW

For Detroit-based Blue Cross Blue Shield of Michigan (BCBSM, also known as Michigan Blues), operating a "profitable" not-for-profit is a constant struggle. BCBSM is one of the nation's top Blue Cross Blue Shield health insurance associations, serving more than 4.6 million members, including workers at automakers General Motors and Ford.

BCBSM offerings include Blue Traditional (fee for service), Preferred and Community Blue PPOs, Blue Care Network (HMO), and Blue MedSave (medical savings accounts). It also owns Preferred Provider Organization of Michigan, a for-profit subsidiary that provides private health care management in Indiana, Kentucky, Michigan, and Ohio.

While other Blues have converted to for-profit status or have teamed up with for-profit companies to become more competitive, BCBSM is committed to remaining not-for-profit. Its strategy is to form alliances with other not-for-profit Blue plans to help gain market share and reduce expenses. Although its insurance operations still lose money, BCBSM stays in the black through its investment income.

HISTORY

The history of prepaid medical care began in 1929, when Baylor University Hospital administrator Justin Kimball developed a plan to offer schoolteachers 21 days of hospital care for $6 a year. Fundamental to the plan was a community rating system, which based premiums on the community's claims experience rather than subscribers' conditions.

A similar program was started in Michigan in 1938 when a group of hospitals formed the Michigan Society for Group Hospitalization, which became the Michigan Hospital Service and later became a chapter of the national Blue Cross association. The health care plan was funded by local hospitals and private grants. (A group of private donors, including Oldsmobile automotive founder Ransom Olds, loaned the group $5,000.)

The state insurance commission approved tax-exempt status for the Michigan Blue Cross in 1939. Nine days after opening a three-person office in Detroit, Blue Cross landed its first customer, insurance company John Hancock Mutual Life. John Hancock's Detroit branch manager became the first subscriber, paying $1.90 per month for 21 days of hospitalization coverage for his family of eight.

Due in part to the addition of Chrysler, Ford, and General Motors to its health plans, Blue Cross grew from less than 1 million members in the 1940s to more than 3 million in the 1950s. In 1945 it began to offer coverage for individuals; 14 years later the association started to offer policies to seniors who were ineligible for group coverage. Blue Cross took over operation of Michigan's Medicare program in 1966.

Michigan's Blue Cross merged with longtime partner Blue Shield in 1975 to create Blue Cross Blue Shield of Michigan, with a total of 5 million subscribers. Blue Shield, a prepayment plan that covered doctors' services, had been started in 1939 by the Michigan State Medical Society (a group of Michigan physicians).

As overseas competition forced automakers to cut their employment rolls, Blue Cross Blue Shield of Michigan's membership contracted. BCBSM chairman John McCabe, realizing the need to generate additional revenue, pushed for an end to the company's not-for-profit status in the 1980s but was rejected by the Michigan legislature. This failure was at least partially behind McCabe's resignation in 1987.

The struggling Michigan Blues moved towards profitability in 1994 when the state legislature specially authorized its $291 million purchase of the for-profit State Accident Fund, the state's workers' compensation program. It also lost its large, but hard-to-manage state Medicare contract to Blue Cross Blue Shield of Illinois (now Health Care Service Corporation). In 1996 the company reorganized, with a division for Michigan residents and one for nationwide accounts. In 1997 BCBSM continued its efforts to increase revenue by acquiring private health management company Preferred Provider Organization of Michigan, which operates in Michigan and three nearby states. BCBSM president and CEO Richard Whitmer announced that he was willing to compete with other Blues in bordering states.

In 1998 Blue Cross Blue Shield of Michigan consolidated four regional HMOs into a single statewide HMO, the Blue Care Network. Costs of the merger and growing losses in drug coverage constrained earnings, but were counter-weighted by returns on assets invested in the stock market.

Chairman: Charles L. Burkett
President and CEO: Richard E. Whitmer
EVP and COO: Robert H. Naftaly
SVP and Chief Information Officer: Raymond R. Khan
SVP and General Counsel: Steven C. Hess
SVP, Auto/National Services: Leslie A. Viegas
SVP, Health Care Products and Provider Services:
Marianne Udow
SVP, Human Resources and Administration:
George F. Francis III
SVP, Managed Care; President and CEO, Blue Care Network of Michigan: David B. Siegel
SVP, Michigan Sales and Services: J. Paul Austin
SVP, Strategic Planning and Corporate Communications: Richard T. Cole
VP and CFO: Mark R. Bartlett
VP and Corporate Secretary: Joyce Neumaier
VP and Treasurer: Brenda Ball
President and CEO, Accident Fund: James C. Epolito
Executive Director and CEO, BCBSM Foundation:
Ira Strumwasser
President and CEO, PPOM: Jay J. Levin
Auditors: Deloitte & Touche LLP

LOCATIONS

HQ: Blue Cross Blue Shield of Michigan,
600 E. Lafayette Blvd., Detroit, MI 48226
Phone: 313-225-9000   **Fax:** 313-225-5629
Web site: http://www.bcbsm.com

PRODUCTS/OPERATIONS

Health Care Plans
Blue Care Network (health maintenance)
Blue Choice (point of service)
Blue MedSave (medical savings accounts)
Blue Preferred PPO (preferred provider for
auto industry workers)
Blue Traditional (prepayment)
Community Blue PPO

Subsidiaries
The Accident Fund Company
(workers' compensation coverage)
Blue Care Network of Michigan (HMO)
BCBSM Foundation (philanthropic affiliate)
Preferred Provider Organization of Michigan (health
care management)

COMPETITORS

Aetna
Anthem Insurance
CIGNA
Kaiser Foundation
New York Life
Omnicare
Priority Healthcare
Prudential
UnitedHealth Group

HISTORICAL FINANCIALS & EMPLOYEES

Not-for-profit FYE: December	Annual Growth	1989	1990	1991	1992	1993	1994	1995	1996	1997	1998
Sales ($ mil.)	5.6%	—	—	5,777	6,177	6,193	6,411	6,926	7,001	7,731	8,432
Net income ($ mil.)	(7.0%)	—	—	—	—	120	71	154	101	43	83
Income as % of sales	—	—	—	—	—	1.9%	1.1%	2.2%	1.4%	0.6%	1.0%
Employees	1.2%	—	—	—	—	8,417	8,415	6,500	7,980	8,827	—

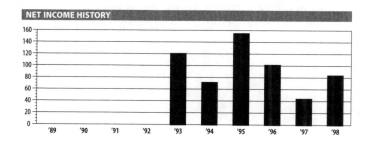

NET INCOME HISTORY

Blue Cross
Blue Shield

BOOZ, ALLEN & HAMILTON INC.

OVERVIEW

Governments all over the world use plenty of Booz. McLean, Virginia-based Booz, Allen & Hamilton provides government agencies and *FORTUNE* 500 companies with international management and technology consulting expertise. The firm operates in two segments: worldwide technology business and worldwide commercial business. Its technology business unit covers such areas as defense and national security, information technology, transportation, and space. The commercial unit is organized into four groups: consumer and engineered products; communications, media, and technology; energy, chemicals, and pharmaceuticals; and financial and health services.

Booz, Allen's gargantuan staff of more than 9,000 covers the US and more than 30 other countries through more than 100 offices. The rising tide of privatization in many world governments has provided an increasing source of consulting work for the company.

HISTORY

Edwin Booz graduated from Northwestern University in 1914 with degrees in economics and psychology and started a statistical analysis firm in Chicago. After serving in the Army during WWI, he returned to his firm, renamed Edwin Booz Surveys. In 1925 Booz hired his first full-time assistant, George Fry, and in 1929 he hired a second, James Allen. By then the company had a long list of clients, including U.S. Gypsum, the *Chicago Tribune,* and Montgomery Ward, which was losing a retail battle with Sears, Roebuck and Co.

In 1935 Carl Hamilton joined the partnership, and a year later it was renamed Booz, Fry, Allen & Hamilton. The firm prospered well into the next decade by providing advice based on "independence that enables us to say plainly from the outside what cannot always be said safely from within," according to a company brochure.

During WWII the firm worked increasingly on government and military contracts. Fry opposed the pursuit of such work for consultants and left in 1942. The firm was renamed Booz, Allen & Hamilton. Hamilton died in 1946, and the following year Booz retired (he died in 1951), leaving Allen as chairman. He successfully steered the firm into lucrative postwar work for clients such as Johnson Wax, RCA, and the US Air Force.

A separate company, Booz, Allen Applied Research, Inc. (BAARINC), was formed in 1955 for technical and government consulting, including missile and weaponry work, as well as consulting with NASA. By the end of the decade, *Time* had dubbed Booz, Allen "the world's largest, most prestigious management consultant firm." The partnership was incorporated as a private company in 1962, and in 1967 Commissioner Pete Rozelle requested its services for the merger of the National Football League and American Football League.

When Allen retired in 1970, Charlie Bowen became the new chairman, and the company went public. However, as the economy stalled during the energy crisis, spending for consultants plunged. Jim Farley replaced Bowen in 1975, and the company was taken private again in 1976. A turnaround was engineered, and the firm was soon helping Chrysler through its historic bailout and developing strategies for the breakup of AT&T.

Booz, Allen again experienced troubles in the 1980s as Farley set up a competition to select his successor. In 1984 Michael McCullough was chosen, but the selection process had taken a toll on morale. McCullough began restructuring the firm along industry lines, creating a department store of services in an industry characterized by boutique houses. The turmoil was too much, and by 1988 nearly a third of the partners had quit.

William Stasior became chairman in 1991 and reorganized Booz, Allen yet again, splitting it down public and private sector lines. James Allen died in 1992, the same year the firm moved to McLean, Virginia. The company began privatization work in the former Soviet Union and in Eastern Europe in 1992 and continued to emphasize government business, including contracts with the IRS (1995) for technology modernization and with the General Services Administration (1996) to provide technical and management support for all federal telecommunications users.

In 1998 the company won a 10-year, $200 million contract with the US Defense Department to establish a scientific and technical data warehouse. Ralph Shrader was appointed CEO in early 1999; Stasior retired as chairman later that year. Booz, Allen is also buying Scandinavian consulting firm Carta.

Chairman and CEO; President, Worldwide Technology Business: Ralph W. Shrader
CFO: Martha Clark Goss
President, Worldwide Commercial Business: Daniel C. Lewis
Chief Human Resources Officer: Joni Bessler

LOCATIONS

HQ: 8283 Greensboro Dr., McLean, VA 22102
Phone: 703-902-5000   **Fax:** 703-902-3333
Web site: http://www.bah.com

Booz, Allen & Hamilton has more than 100 offices in the US and more than 30 other countries.

1999 US Offices

	No.
Virginia	11
Maryland	9
California	4
Florida	4
Texas	4
Virginia	4
New Jersey	3
Pennsylvania	3
Colorado	2
Massachusetts	2
Missouri	2
New York	2
Ohio	2
Alabama	1
Arizona	1
Georgia	1
Illinois	1
Michigan	1
North Carolina	1
Rhode Island	1
South Carolina	1
Washington, DC	1
Total	**61**

PRODUCTS/OPERATIONS

Selected Consulting Services
Commercial Services
Communications, media, and technology
Consumer and engineered products
Energy, chemicals, and pharmaceuticals
Financial and health services

Technology Business Services
Defense and national security
Environment and energy
Information technology
International projects
Management consulting
Telecommunications
Transportation and space

COMPETITORS

American Management
Andersen Consulting
Arthur D. Little
Bain & Company
Boston Consulting
Cap Gemini
Computer Sciences
Day & Zimmermann
Deloitte Touche Tohmatsu
EDS
Ernst & Young
Gemini Consulting
IBM
KPMG
McKinsey & Company
Origin
PricewaterhouseCoopers
SRI International
Towers Perrin

HISTORICAL FINANCIALS & EMPLOYEES

Private FYE: March	Annual Growth	1990	1991	1992	1993	1994	1995	1996	1997	1998	1999
Sales ($ mil.)	13.8%	500	507	530	700	804	989	1,100	1,300	1,400	1,600
Employees	9.1%	4,100	4,100	3,200	5,000	5,481	6,000	6,700	7,500	8,000	9,000

SALES HISTORY

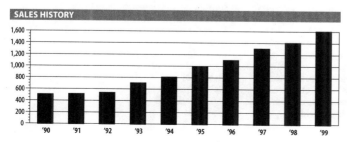

BOOZ·ALLEN & HAMILTON

BORDEN, INC.

OVERVIEW

After giving Elsie the cow and the Cracker Jack boy their pink slips, Borden has reinvented itself as a specialty chemicals company. The Columbus, Ohio-based company, controlled by Kohlberg Kravis Roberts (KKR), has sold its dairy division and its decorative-products unit, as well as its Cracker Jack snack food and Eagle Brand condensed-milk units. Borden is sticking with its pasta brands (including Creamette and Prince), along with its Classico pasta sauces and Wyler's bouillon and dry soups.

Borden operates affiliated salty-snack company Wise Foods, Elmer's Products unit (consumer adhesives), and chemicals divisions (resins, coatings, adhesives, melamine crystal, and specialty inks). It is North America's #1 producer of formaldehyde (followed by Georgia-Pacific and Neste Resins), the bulk of which is used to produce thermosetting resins.

The company is growing its chemicals business through acquisitions. Borden has agreed to buy Spurlock Industries and the chemicals unit of Blagden PLC. Both companies make formaldehyde and resins.

HISTORY

Galveston, Texas, resident Gail Borden Jr. was the founder of one of Texas' first newspapers, the *Telegraph and Texas Register,* in which he headlined the phrase "Remember the Alamo." He was also an inventor whose creations included a portable bathhouse and a nonperishable meat biscuit. By 1853 he had developed a process to preserve milk by condensing it in a vacuum.

Borden located his business in Burrville, Connecticut, in 1857 and called it Gail Borden, Jr., and Company; he formed New York Condensed Milk with grocer Jeremiah Milbank the next year. A big break came with the Civil War, when the US Army ordered 500 pounds of condensed milk. Condensed milk was later carried on Robert Peary's North Pole and Annapurna expeditions. When Borden died in 1874, the company was the leading US milk condenser.

The company incorporated in 1899 and took the name Borden Company in 1919. Between 1928 and 1929 Borden doubled in size and gained operations in ice cream, cheese, and powdered milk. By 1929 it had diversified by buying glue maker Casein.

The company was well-positioned internationally and in the chemicals market by the end of WWII. To reduce dependence on dairy revenues, Borden expanded its chemicals business by buying Columbus Coated Fabrics (1961) and Smith-Douglass (1964). Expansion into snacks began in 1964 with the purchase of Wise Foods and Cracker Jack. In 1979 Borden bought Buckeye and Guy's Food potato chip makers.

In the 1980s Borden spent $1.9 billion on 91 acquisitions, mainly regional makers of snack foods and pasta, but the lack of a centralized manufacturing and selling network slowed growth and resulted in lost market share for many of the company's best-known products. At that time, Borden was the world's largest pasta maker.

By late 1993 Borden had axed CEO Anthony D'Amato, under whose leadership the company's market value had dropped 50% in two years to $2.4 billion. In 1994 Borden sold its food service unit (to Heinz) and several other small food divisions. Later that year Kohlberg Kravis Roberts & Co. (KKR) bought 64% of Borden, paying for it with $2 billion in RJR Nabisco stock, which had been a disappointment to KKR. Eventually, affiliates of KKR owned virtually all of Borden.

Still saddled with debt, in 1996 Borden sold its Global Packaging business to AEP Industries. Borden sold its Borden Foods Corporation and Wise salty-snacks business to other branches of KKR, which kept them affiliated with Borden.

In 1997 Borden sold Cracker Jack to PepsiCo's Frito-Lay. The Borden/Meadow Gold Dairies division was sold to a group led by giant dairy co-op Mid-America Dairymen (now part of Dairy Farmers of America). Also that year the company's Borden Chemical subsidiary acquired Melamine Chemicals, which makes melamine crystals used in adhesives and coatings.

In 1998 it bought the chemicals unit of Sun Coast Industries, which makes specialty resins and compounds. Also in 1998 KKR affiliate BW Holdings, Borden's parent, acquired 92% of Corning Consumer Products, to be managed by Borden. In addition, Borden sold its decorative-products business to buyout firm American Capital Strategies and sold its Eagle Brand, Cremora, ReaLemon, Kava, and None Such grocery brands to startup Eagle Family Foods.

In 1999 Borden agreed to purchase two makers of formaldehyde and resins — Spurlock Industries and the chemicals unit of Blagden PLC (UK).

OFFICERS

Chairman, President, and CEO; Chairman, Corning Consumer Products; Chairman, Borden Foods:
C. Robert Kidder, age 54, $1,647,470 pay
EVP and CFO: William H. Carter, age 45, $565,000 pay
EVP, Corporate Strategy and Development:
Kevin M. Kelley
EVP; Chairman and CEO, Elmer's Products:
Ronald C. Kesselman
EVP; Chairman and CEO, Borden Chemical:
Joseph M. Saggese, age 67, $736,671 pay
SVP Human Resources and Corporate Affairs:
Nancy A. Reardon, age 46, $453,223 pay
SVP and Treasurer: Ronald P. Starkman, age 44
SVP and General Counsel: William F. Stoll Jr., age 50, $441,953 pay
President and CEO, Corning Consumer Products:
Peter Campanella
Chairman and COO, Borden Foods: Peter M. Dunn
Auditors: Deloitte & Touche LLP

LOCATIONS

HQ: 180 E. Broad St., Columbus, OH 43215
Phone: 614-225-4000   **Fax:** —

1998 Sales

	$ mil.	% of total
US	942	67
Canada	142	10
Other countries	316	23
Total	**1,400**	**100**

PRODUCTS/OPERATIONS

1998 Sales

	$ mil.	% of total
Chemicals	1,260	90
Businesses held for sale	37	3
Other	103	7
Total	**1,400**	**100**

Selected Subsidiaries and Affiliates
BCP Finance Corporation
BCP Management, Inc.
Borden Chemical, Inc.
Borden Chemical International, Inc.
Borden Chemical (M.) Sdn. Bhd. (Malaysia)
Borden Chemical UK Ltd.
Borden Chimie, SA (France)
Borden Foods Corporation
Borden International Philippines (98%)
Compania Quimica Borden, SA (Panama)
Corning Consumer Products Company
Elmer's Products Canada, Inc.
Elmer's Products, Inc.
Gun Ei Borden International Resin Co. Ltd. (50%, Japan)
Melamine Chemicals, Inc.
Quimica Borden Espana SA (96%, Spain)
Wise Foods, Inc.

COMPETITORS

Akzo Nobel	Huntsman
American Italian Pasta	ICI
Ashland	Kraft Foods
BASF AG	Lancaster Colony
Bestfoods	Lawter International
Borden Chemicals	M. A. Hanna
Campbell Soup	McWhorter Technologies
Celanese	New World Pasta
ConAgra	Newell Rubbermaid
Dainippon Ink & Chemicals	Procter & Gamble
DuPont	R.J. Reynolds Tobacco
Frito-Lay	Rohm and Haas
General Mills	Sara Lee
Georgia Gulf	Unilever PLC
Georgia-Pacific Group	Valspar
Hormel	

HISTORICAL FINANCIALS & EMPLOYEES

Private FYE: December	Annual Growth	1989	1990	1991	1992	1993	1994	1995	1996	1997	1998
Sales ($ mil.)	(17.1%)	7,593	7,633	6,756	5,872	5,506	5,626	5,944	5,765	3,482	1,400
Net income ($ mil.)	—	(61)	364	295	(364)	(631)	(598)	(366)	82	278	63
Income as % of sales	—	—	4.8%	4.4%	—	—	—	—	1.4%	8.0%	4.5%
Employees	(23.4%)	46,500	46,300	44,000	41,900	41,900	32,300	27,500	20,000	15,000	4,200

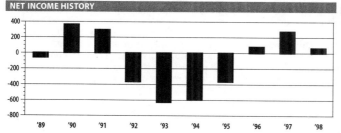

NET INCOME HISTORY

1998 FISCAL YEAR-END
Debt ratio: 86.1%
Return on equity: 14.9%
Cash ($ mil.): 672
Current ratio: 1.05
Long-term debt ($ mil.): 552

BOSE CORPORATION

OVERVIEW

The opposite of a rigid parent, Amar Bose wants his speakers to be heard but not seen. Framingham, Massachusetts-based Bose (rhymes with rose) is the world's #1 speaker maker, with nearly 25% of the market. Bose specializes in high-end audio products used everywhere from homes, cars, and computers to stadiums and chapels.

Founder and owner Bose, still a professor at MIT, keeps his company sharp with unconventional products and methods. The firm stands out by offering such small, yet technologically advanced products as palm-sized cube speakers and compact radios with rich sound; its most famous product is the compact Wave radio with a sound that belies its size. To stay on the cutting edge, Bose invests much of its profits in research and development. In addition to selling its products through retailers and nearly 60 of its own stores, Bose uses sales methods unusual for consumer electronics, such as direct mail.

HISTORY

Music and electronics struck a chord in Amar Bose, the son of an Indian emigrant from Calcutta. As a youngster he studied violin and liked fixing electronic gadgets. A teenaged Bose started a radio repair shop in his basement during WWII that turned out to be the family's main source of income when his father's import business faltered during the war. Bose's interest in electronics led him to college at MIT in 1947.

His quest to develop a better sound system began nearly a decade later when the hi-fi stereo he bought as a reward for doing well in his graduate studies made his violin record sound shrill. MIT allowed Bose to research the topic while he taught there. He formed his namesake company in 1964 and hired as its first employee Sherwin Greenblatt, a former student who later became company president.

Bose discovered that most speaker systems funneled sound directly at the listener, while live concerts sent sound directly and indirectly by bouncing it off walls, floors, and ceilings. He designed a system in which only some speakers are aimed at the listener while others reflect the sounds around the room. Calling the concept "reflected sound," Bose began selling his 901 stereo speakers in 1968.

A feud with *Consumer Reports* showed the arrogant side of the self-made entrepreneur. After the magazine concluded in a 1970 review that Bose speakers created a sound that tended to "wander around the room," Bose sued, claiming product disparagement. (The lawsuit was settled 13 years later when the Supreme Court ruled in favor of *Consumer Reports*.) Bose began making professional loudspeakers in 1972.

After trying and failing to gain market share in Japan throughout the 1970s, in 1978 Bose hired sales executive Sumi Sakura, who convinced 400 Japanese dealers to find space in their jam-packed stores for Bose products.

Sales jumped within months. Bose also turned his attention to car stereos in the 1970s. After promising talks with General Motors in 1979, he risked $13 million and four years developing a stereo that could be custom-designed for cars. The first one was offered in 1983 in a Cadillac Seville. Contracts with other major carmakers followed, usually for their top-of-the-line models.

In the 1980s the company took its technology to TV sets. With an agreeable guinea pig in Zenith, Bose developed a speaker tube that could coil inside the set without adding much bulk. The set was a hit, even with a price tag of more than $1,400 (in 1987). The firm's speakers were also used in several space shuttle flights, beginning in 1992 with *Endeavour*.

The critically acclaimed Wave radio was introduced in 1993 and has been a huge success, even though it is primarily offered through direct mail. A year later Bose acquired professional loudspeaker maker US Sound from Carver. In 1996 it teamed up with satellite TV firm PRIMESTAR to offer the home theater Companion systems. (The systems were discontinued in 1999, dissolving the partnership.) The next year Bose and IBM paired up to upgrade the quality of PC sound systems.

Bose upped the ante on its retail operations in 1997 when it began opening more upscale showcase stores where audiophiles can test sound systems at in-store music theaters. The company began making its sound systems for more mainstream cars, such as the Chevrolet Blazer, the following year. In 1999 Bose began selling its products online and introduced a new version of its popular Wave radio (with a CD player).

Chairman and CEO: Amar G. Bose, age 69
President: Sherwin Greenblatt
VP of Research: Thomas Froeschle
VP: Sumiyoshi Sakura
VP of Engineering: Joseph Veranth
VP of Finance and CFO: Daniel A. Grady
VP of Human Resources: Stephen Pritchard
VP of Manufacturing: Thomas Beeson
VP of Sales: John Geheran
VP of Europe: Nic A. Merks
Secretary: Alexander Bernhard
Treasurer: William R. Swanson
Assistant Secretary: Mark E. Sullivan
Auditors: PricewaterhouseCoopers LLP

LOCATIONS

HQ: The Mountain, Framingham, MA 01701
Phone: 508-879-7330   **Fax:** 508-872-6541
Web site: http://www.bose.com

PRODUCTS/OPERATIONS

Selected Products
Aircraft entertainment systems
Auto sound systems and speakers
Aviation headsets
Custom home audio systems
Home stereo speakers
Marine speakers
Multimedia speakers
Music systems
Outdoor audio systems
PC sound systems
Professional loudspeakers
Radios
Speaker accessories

Selected Brands
131 (marine speakers)
141 (speakers)
151 (environmental speakers)
201, 301, 501, 701, 901 Series (direct/reflecting speakers)
Acoustic Wave (music systems)
Acoustimass (speaker systems)
Auditioner (computer system used to analyze building acoustics based on architectural blueprints)
Jewel Cube (speakers)
Lifestyle (music systems)
Wave radio (compact radio with full stereo sound)
Wave radio (with CD player)

COMPETITORS

Bang & Olufsen Holding	Paradigm Electronics
Boston Acoustics	Philips Electronics
Cambridge SoundWorks	Pioneer
Carver	Polk Audio
Cerwin-Vega	Recoton
Harman International	Ruark Acoustics
Jamo	Snell Acoustics
Kenwood	Sony
Koss	Telex Communications
Matsushita	Yamaha

HISTORICAL FINANCIALS & EMPLOYEES

Private FYE: March	Annual Growth	1990	1991	1992	1993	1994	1995	1996	1997	1998	1999
Sales ($ mil.)	13.3%	—	—	—	450	500	600	700	750	850	950
Employees	4.9%	—	—	—	3,000	3,100	3,100	3,500	4,000	4,000	4,000

SALES HISTORY

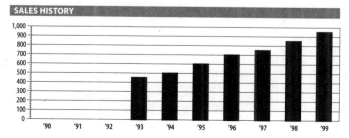

THE BOSTON CONSULTING GROUP

OVERVIEW

Everybody needs a guru, even corporations. Boston Consulting Group (BCG) seeks to be just that — a voice of wisdom and vision in the corporate cosmos of competitive uncertainties. The Boston-based company specializes in high-end consulting for corporate clients, with an emphasis on strategic planning. Concentrating on corporate clients in consumer goods, e-commerce, energy, finance, and telecommunications, the firm applies some of its original consulting concepts, including "time-based competition" (rapid response to change) and "deconstruction" (an end to vertical integration) to clients seeking insight. It employs almost 2,000 consultants in more than 40 offices.

BCG has offices in more than 30 countries; more than half of the firm's revenue comes from outside the US. BCG continues to expand in Asia despite the faltering economy there. The employee-owned firm is also active in the privatization process for companies in Eastern Europe.

HISTORY

In 1953 *Time* magazine named Bruce Henderson one of Pittsburgh's "newsmakers of tomorrow." The magazine proved prophetic as Henderson and his Boston Consulting Group (BCG) went on to be considered pioneers in the consulting world.

After graduating from Harvard Business School and spending 18 years at Westinghouse, Henderson founded the Boston Consulting Group as a one-man operation in 1963. He popularized simple analytical tools for business planning and established BCG as the first consulting "boutique" to specialize purely in strategy. BCG was also ahead of the curve in its approach to expansion; it opened its Japan office in 1965 and three other international offices before opening its second office stateside.

During the 1970s BCG helped popularize the consulting field in part by its willingness to pay large salaries to top business school graduates. Henderson and BCG developed such concepts as the experience curve (the longer a company makes a product, the more cost-efficient its production becomes) and the growth and market-share matrix (a strategy for managing a group of products based on their growth potential). In 1974 Henderson was among the first to utilize new retirement income laws when he placed ownership of the company in the hands of its employees.

BCG's influence waned during the 1980s, when corporate re-engineering and operations-focused planning replaced strategic initiatives. By then many of the firm's innovative concepts had become core subjects at leading business schools, and Henderson retired in 1985 to teach at Vanderbilt, where he continued to develop new ideas. A prolific business writer, he published "The Origin of Strategy" in 1989; the article compared theories of business with Darwin's theories on competition and survival.

In the late 1980s the then-Big-Eight accounting firms became more active in the consulting field (especially in the area of systems integration). As a result BCG avoided areas that would lead it into direct battle with the bigger firms and instead focused its energies on helping its clients get products to market more expeditiously.

In 1992 Henderson died, at the age of 77. The following year BCG formed the joint venture Shanghai-Boston Consulting with Shanghai Jiaotong University and the Bank of Communications. Companies that had streamlined during the 1980s returned their focus to strategy, and major players like BCG and Bain & Co. benefited from the shift in thinking. This and the move toward outsourcing helped BCG's sales shoot up some 20% in 1994. Also that year, however, Ohio's Figgie International filed suit against BCG, claiming that the company was responsible for designing and implementing "flawed programs" and consistently overbilling for its services. The suit was settled out of court in 1995.

In 1997, 23-year BCG veteran Carl Stern was elected CEO by a vote of the firm's 200 worldwide partners. That year surveys of American and European business and engineering school graduates named BCG the second-most desirable firm to work for (after rival McKinsey).

As the rest of the world braced against the Asian economic crisis in 1998, Stern saw the crisis as a boon for the company. BCG shored up its relations with its Asian clients and continued its international expansion. The company furthered this strategy in 1999 with a contract to consult for the Indonesian government on the eventual privatization of more than 150 state-owned companies.

Chairman: John S. Clarkeson
President and CEO: Carl Stern, age 52
CFO: David Parkinson
SVP: Philip B. Evans
SVP: George Stalk
Director Personnel: Kay L. Mosher
Director of Human Resources: Michael Armano

LOCATIONS

HQ: Exchange Place, 31st Fl., Boston, MA 02109
Phone: 617-973-1200   **Fax:** 617-973-1399
Web site: http://www.bcg.com

Boston Consulting Group has offices in more than 30 countries.

US Offices	Kuala Lumpur, Malaysia
Atlanta	Lisbon, Portugal
Boston	London
Chicago	Madrid
Dallas	Melbourne
Los Angeles	Milan, Italy
New York	Monterrey, Mexico
San Francisco	Moscow
Washington, DC	Munich, Germany
	Oslo
International Offices	Paris
Amsterdam	São Paulo
Auckland, New Zealand	Seoul
Bangkok	Shanghai
Bombay	Singapore
Brussels	Stockholm
Budapest, Hungary	Stuttgart, Germany
Buenos Aires	Sydney
Dusseldorf, Germany	Tokyo
Frankfurt	Toronto
Hamburg, Germany	Vienna, Austria
Helsinki, Finland	Warsaw
Hong Kong	Zurich
Jakarta, Indonesia	

PRODUCTS/OPERATIONS

Strategic Planning Services
Branding
Consumer goods and retail
Corporate development
Deconstruction
Electronic commerce
Energy and utilities
Financial services
Globalization
Health Care
High technology
Industrial goods
Information technology
Operational effectiveness
Organization
Pricing

COMPETITORS

Andersen Consulting
Arthur D. Little
Bain & Company
Booz, Allen
Deloitte Touche Tohmatsu
Ernst & Young
Gemini Consulting
KPMG
McKinsey & Company
PricewaterhouseCoopers

HISTORICAL FINANCIALS & EMPLOYEES

Private FYE: December	Annual Growth	1989	1990	1991	1992	1993	1994	1995	1996	1997	1998
Sales ($ mil.)	16.5%	—	—	—	—	340	430	550	600	655	730
Employees	24.6%	—	—	—	—	—	1,246	1,320	1,550	2,000	3,000

SALES HISTORY

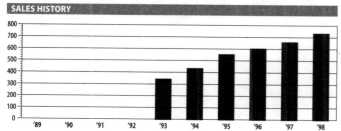

THE BOSTON CONSULTING GROUP

BRIDGE INFORMATION SYSTEMS

OVERVIEW

This Bridge carries savvy investors over the raging sea of financial data. New York City-based Bridge Information Systems is the world's #2 provider of financial information (it's behind Reuters, but ahead of Bloomberg in terms of customer installations). It provides real-time and historical information on stock exchanges from around the world. Bridge targets institutional investors, brokers, exchanges, and other financial professionals, and augments its content with digital feeds, news, transaction services, and workstations.

The company's information requires no proprietary hardware (as does Bloomberg's) but runs on PC-based platforms. Bridge culls information from more than 50 exchanges and 450 news sources; it is active in more than 100 countries, with offices in major cities in Africa, Asia, Europe, North America, South America, and the Pacific Rim.

Bridge's 1998 purchase of Dow Jones Markets, a real-time electronic market data service, tripled the size of the company and helped it jump past Bloomberg in pursuit of Reuters. The company also bought 80,000 installed terminals from Automatic Data Processing (ADP), a deal that gave ADP a minority stake in Bridge.

HISTORY

In 1974 Charles Lebens founded Bridge Data in St. Louis. Lebens' company focused on financial information and targeted investors. The company was a success and grew rapidly until the early 1980s. In 1986 the company considered an IPO (backed by Donaldson Lufkin & Jenrette) but held off because of poor market conditions.

Lebens created Bridge Holding to oversee Bridge Data and his securities brokerage firm, Bridge Trading. In 1987 these two companies combined to form Bridge Information Systems. The company's solid performance drew a slew of investors, including Gateway Venture Partners, a St. Louis venture capital firm that poured some $500,000 into the company. The smooth ride, however, was about to come to an end.

In the early 1990s Bridge ran afoul of the Chicago Board Options Exchange (CBOE) for unauthorized trading activities. Lebens' son John and three other Bridge traders had used company accounts to absorb more than $1 million of personal trading losses incurred over several years. The company was censured $125,000 by the CBOE, and the transgressors were barred from trading. In 1992 Charles Dill took over as CEO, and Lebens was barred from all supervisory authority over trading (though he remained as chairman). Lebens and four other senior officers received disciplinary action letters from the Chicago regulator. In 1993 Lebens and Dill battled for control of the company, but the conflict was ultimately settled when Welsh, Carson, Anderson & Stowe (WCAS) bought Bridge two years later. The $140 million purchase marked the end of a distinct chapter in Bridge's history and brought a swift exit for Lebens, his son, and four other officers whom WCAS forced to resign.

WCAS formed Global Financial Information (GFI) in 1995 to serve as a holding company for its financial information companies, which included Bridge, EJV Partners (fixed-income data), and MarketVision (financial information compiler). With these three companies in its stable, WCAS joined the financial information race with a vengeance. The same year, Thomas Wendel became CEO.

The following year GFI upped its ante and bought Knight Ridder Financial for $275 million. This acquisition gave the company a legitimate news source on global money, capital, and other markets, and furthered its quest to become a legitimate competitor to big names such as Reuters and Bloomberg. In 1996 GFI readopted the name Bridge Information Systems to cover Bridge, EJV Partners, Knight Ridder Financial, and MarketVision.

In 1997 Bridge formed an alliance with Italy's largest financial media group, Il Sole 24 Radiocor, broadening Bridge's services in that country and increasing Radiocor's coverage of international markets. The next year the company bought Dow Jones Markets, a buy that vaulted Bridge past Bloomberg to the #2 spot behind Reuters in the financial information provider race. Also in 1998 the company bought Automatic Data Processing's market-data products and related assets, giving ADP a minority share in Bridge. The following year the company's effort to overtake Reuters was boosted when Reuters lost a key contract with London-based Garban plc, an interdealer bond broker that only recently had begun providing services to Bridge. Garban began directing investors to Bridge and to Bloomberg.

Chairman, President, and CEO: Thomas M. Wendel
CFO: Daryl Rhodes
EVP and General Counsel: Zachary Snow
Manager Human Resources: Julie Brown

LOCATIONS

HQ: Bridge Information Systems, Inc.,
3 World Financial Center, 27th Fl.,
New York, NY 10281
Phone: 212-372-7100   **Fax:** 212-372-7158
Web site: http://www.bridge.com

PRODUCTS/OPERATIONS

Selected Products

Data Products

BridgeFeed (data feed with premium market information)
Global Actions (corporate news worldwide)
Global Cache (real-time database based on Global Ticker)
Global Pricing (market prices and related information)
Global Ticker (real-time broadcast of global market data)

Workstation Products

Activel (customizable tool for managing financial
information)
BridgeStation (Windows or NT-based market data service)

Internet Products

BridgeChannel (real-time, applet-based version of
Bridge data)

COMPETITORS

Bloomberg
FinancialWeb.com
Reuters
Telescan
Thomson Corporation
Track Data

HISTORICAL FINANCIALS & EMPLOYEES

Private FYE: December	Annual Growth	1989	1990	1991	1992	1993	1994	1995	1996	1997	1998
Estimated sales ($ mil.)	67.5%	—	—	—	—	101	115	200	300	400	1,330
Employees	112.1%	—	—	—	—	—	—	—	1,000	1,200	4,500

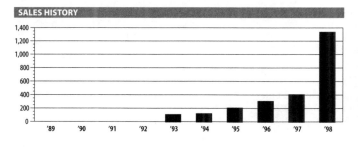

SALES HISTORY

CALPERS

California's public sector retirees already have a place in the sun; CalPERS gives them the money to enjoy it.

The California Public Employees' Retirement System (CalPERS), based in Sacramento, is the largest public pension system in the US, with some $158 billion in assets. It manages retirement and health plans for 2,400 government agencies representing more than a million California employees and retirees and their beneficiaries.

The funds' investments generate 80% or more of CalPERS' annual revenues; the rest comes from member and employer contributions. Because of its size, CalPERS is a power in the investment world and is one of the most active institutional investors in the US on issues such as corporate performance and executive compensation; it even puts out a high-profile list of the worst-performing US companies each year. CalPERS has established itself as a powerful negotiator for such services as insurance; rates established by CalPERS serve as benchmarks for other employers.

The organization has benefited from the bull market of the 1990s, enjoying double-digit returns for five years. The added income has allowed CalPERS to extend its investments to include hedge funds. CalPERS has asked California's legislature to approve plans to increase retirement benefits by some 5%, the first meaningful improvement in nearly 30 years.

Legislation established CalPERS in 1931 to administer a pension fund for state employees. By the 1940s the system allowed other public agencies and some school employees to contract for retirement benefits.

When the Public Employees' Medical and Hospital Care Act was passed in 1962, CalPERS began providing health insurance for members. The fund was managed internally and very conservatively with little exposure to stocks. Despite its slow asset growth, the state saw it as a source of funds to meet its own cash shortfalls.

CalPERS became involved in corporate governance issues in the mid-1980s, when California treasurer Jesse Unruh was outraged by various corporate greenmail schemes. Unruh hired Dale Hanson (formerly with the Wisconsin pension board) as CEO in 1987; under Hanson, CalPERS led the movement to force corporations to be accountable to institutional investors.

In the late 1980s CalPERS moved into real estate and the Japanese stock market. When both crashed around 1990, Hanson came under pressure. CalPERS was twice forced to take major write-downs for its real estate holdings. CalPERS turned to expensive outside fund managers, but its investment performance deteriorated and member services suffered.

Legislation passed in 1990 allowed CalPERS to offer long-term health insurance. In 1991 Governor Pete Wilson tried to take $1.6 billion from CalPERS to help the state meet its budget shortfall. This resulted in legislation preventing future raids. CalPERS made its first direct investment in 1993 when it formed a partnership with energy giant Enron to invest in gas pipelines and similar projects.

With interest rates rising and the bond market crashing, CalPERS in 1994 suffered its worst performance in a decade. That year Hanson resigned amid criticism that his focus on corporate governance had interfered with his running CalPERS. The system moved to an indexing management strategy.

After Hanson left, CalPERS tried being less confrontational with the corporations in which it invested; the pension plan had gained little in terms of performance. CalPERS created a separate office to handle investor issues and launched an International Corporate Governance Program. The next year, because of its activism, CalPERS was uninvited from a Kohlberg Kravis Roberts & Co. investment pool.

In 1996 the system partnered with the Asian Development Bank to invest in the Asia/Pacific region. The next year the organization took a major hit in the Asian financial crisis but used the downturn as an opportunity to expand its position there in undervalued stocks. In 1998 CalPERS pressured foreign companies to adopt more transparent financial reporting methods.

Faced with rising health care costs, in 1999 the system announced it would raise health care premiums almost 10%, heralding possible premium increases across the country. The system also considered looking into bypassing HMOs, and contracting with hospitals and doctors directly.

CEO: James E. Burton
Deputy Executive Officer: James H. Gomez
Assistant Executive Officer, Financial and Administration Services: Vincent P. Brown
Assistant Executive Officer, Governmental Affairs, Planning, and Research: Robert D. Walton
Assistant Executive Officer, Investment Operations: Robert Aguallo
Assistant Executive Officer, Member and Benefit Services: Barbara D. Hegdal
Chief, Human Resources: Tom Pettey
Chief, Information Technology Services Division: Jack Corrie
Chief, Office of Public Affairs: Patricia K. Macht
Chief Actuary: Ronald L. Seeling
Chief Investment Officer: Sheryl Pressler
General Counsel: Kayla J. Gillan
Deputy General Counsel: Linda K. McAtee
Portfolio Manager, Alternative Investments: Richard J. Hayes
Auditors: PricewaterhouseCoopers LLP

LOCATIONS

HQ: California Public Employees' Retirement System, Lincoln Plaza, 400 P St., Sacramento, CA 95814
Phone: 916-326-3000   **Fax:** 916-558-4001
Web site: http://www.calpers.ca.gov

PRODUCTS/OPERATIONS

1998 Assets

	$ mil.	% of total
Cash & equivalents	14,266	9
Treasury & agency securities	5,190	3
Corporate bonds	11,696	8
International bonds	4,786	3
Stocks	92,502	59
Mortgage loans	15,830	10
Real estate equities	6,020	4
Other investments	4,382	3
Receivables	1,899	1
Other assets	72	—
Total	**156,643**	**100**

Programs
CalPERS 457 Public Agency Deferred Compensation Program
Health Benefits Program
Home Loan Program
Judges' Retirement System
Judges' Retirement System II
Legislators' Retirement System
Long-Term Care Program
Volunteer Firefighters' Length of Service Award System

1999 Underperformers List
Circus Circus Enterprises (now Mandalay Resort Group)
Cummins Engine Company, Inc.
Mallinckrodt Inc.
National Semiconductor Corporation
Pacific Century Financial Corporation
Pioneer Natural Resources Company
St. Jude Medical, Inc.
Sierra Health Services, Inc.
Tyson Foods, Inc.

HISTORICAL FINANCIALS & EMPLOYEES

Government-owned FYE: June	Annual Growth	1989	1990	1991	1992	1993	1994	1995	1996	1997	1998
Assets ($ mil.)	17.7%	—	—	—	—	69,484	76,935	90,417	102,797	128,880	156,643
Net income ($ mil.)	19.9%	—	—	—	—	9,111	738	11,622	12,247	19,477	22,594
Income as % of sales	—	—	—	—	—	13.1%	1.0%	12.9%	11.9%	15.1%	14.4%
Employees	8.6%	—	—	—	—	900	1,000	1,037	1,089	1,250	1,250

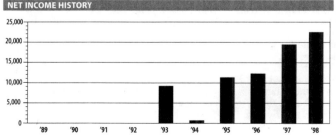

NET INCOME HISTORY

1998 FISCAL YEAR-END
Return on assets: 16.8%
Sales ($ mil.): 27,514

CALIFORNIA STATE UNIVERSITY

OVERVIEW

California State University (CSU) turns students into teachers. Long Beach-based CSU traces its roots to the state's teaching colleges and trains 60% of California's teachers. It vies with New York as the nation's largest university system in terms of enrollment (more than 365,000), and has campuses in 23 cities, including Bakersfield, Los Angeles, San Francisco, and San Jose. The university primarily awards bachelor's and master's degrees in about 240 subject areas, leaving higher levels of study to the University of California (UC) system. It admits the top 33% of students from California's high schools.

CSU is developing strategies to cope with an expected near-doubling of its enrollment — what it calls Tidal Wave II — by the year 2010. The first ripplings are starting already, with 13,000 new students expected to flood the system in 2000-2001. Its San Diego campus already has adopted tougher admission requirements. In addition, CSU plans to offer a distance-education program in which students are taught via teleconferencing and the World Wide Web. Other strategies involve adding a summer semester to create year-long schooling, and redirecting students to campuses that have more room.

HISTORY

In 1862 San Francisco's Normal School, a training center for elementary teachers, became California's first state-founded school for higher education. Six students attended its first classes, but there were 384 by 1866. It later moved to San Jose to escape the bustle of San Francisco.

In the late 1880s State Normal Schools opened in Chico, San Diego, and San Francisco, followed in 1901 by California State Polytechnic Institute, which offered studies in agriculture, business, and engineering. Other new colleges included Fresno State (1911) and Humboldt State (1913). Most of the schools offered four-year programs and admitted any student with eight years of grammar school education.

The Normal Schools were renamed Teachers Colleges in 1921 to reflect their role in teacher education. Two years later the colleges began awarding bachelor of arts degrees in education.

In 1935 the schools were renamed State Colleges and expanded into liberal arts. In 1947 they were authorized to confer master's degrees in education.

After WWII, students on the GI Bill helped increase enrollment, and campuses opened in Los Angeles, Sacramento, and Long Beach. The prospect of the first baby boomers reaching college age prompted the founding of more campuses in the late 1950s. Russia's 1957 launch of Sputnik spurred additional focus on science and math at all education levels. The next year the colleges began awarding master's degrees in subjects unrelated to teacher education.

During the Red Scare, the system's first chancellor, Buell Gallagher, was accused by the press of being soft on communism. Other faculty were subpoenaed to appear before the House Committee on Un-American Activities.

In 1961 the system became the California State Colleges (CSC) and the board of trustees was created, giving the schools more independence from state government. In 1969 student and faculty groups seeking ethnic studies departments went on strike in San Francisco; the unrest closed the campus.

In 1972 CSC became known as the California State University and Colleges. Ten years later it adopted the California State University as its name.

Barry Munitz became chancellor in 1991, taking over a system that had become oppressive due to a heavy-handed administration. Munitz, who came from corporate America, brought his business sense to the university and increased private fund-raising, among other activities. He used words like "consumer" and "product" to describe his job. Munitz also increased tuition, which caused enrollments to drop from 1991-1995.

CSU added two new campuses in 1995, including CSU Monterey Bay, the first military base to be converted into a university since the end of the Cold War.

In 1997 Charles Reed was named to replace Munitz as chancellor, effective the following year. That year CSU proposed the California Educational Technology Initiative (CETI), a plan to build high-speed computer and telephone networks linking its campuses. CETI failed in 1998 after Microsoft and other investors pulled out. In 1999, after lengthy contract negotiations between Reed and faculty members failed to produce accord over teacher salaries and employment conditions, Reed imposed his own merit-based plan. The faculty responded with official rebukes and a vote of no confidence in Reed.

Chairman: William Hauck
VC: Joan Otomo-Corgel
Chancellor: Charles B. Reed
Executive Vice Chancellor and Chief Academic Officer: David Spence
Senior Vice Chancellor Business and Finance: Richard P. West
Vice Chancellor Human Resources: Jackie McCalain
Vice Chancellor University Advancement: Douglas X. Patino
President, California Maritime Academy: Jerry A. Aspland
President, California State Polytechnic University, Pomona: Bob Suzuki
President, California Polytechnic State University, San Luis Obispo: Warren J. Baker
President, CSU, Channel Islands: J. Handel Evans
President, CSU, Fresno: John D. Welty, age 55
President, CSU, Haywood: Norma S. Rees
President, CSU, Sacramento: Donald R. Gerth
President, Humboldt State University: Alistair W. McCrone
President, San Diego State University: Stephen L. Weber
President, San Francisco State University: Robert A. Corrigan
President, San Jose State University: Robert L. Caret
President, Sonoma State University: Ruben Arminana
General Counsel: Christine Helwick, age 52
Auditors: KPMG LLP

LOCATIONS

HQ: 400 Golden Shore, Ste. 330, Long Beach, CA 90802
Phone: 562-985-2740   **Fax:** 562-951-4986
Web site: http://www.calstate.edu

California State University Campuses

California Maritime Academy	Hayward
California Polytechnic State University, San Luis Obispo	Long Beach
	Los Angeles
	Monterey Bay
	Northridge
California State Polytechnic University, Pomona	San Bernardino
	San Marcos
	Stanislaus
California State University Bakersfield	Humboldt State University
	San Diego State University
Channel Islands	San Francisco State University
Chico	San Jose State University
Dominguez Hills	Sonoma State University
Fresno	
Fullerton	

PRODUCTS/OPERATIONS

Selected Majors

Agriculture	Latin American studies
American studies	Mathematics
Asian studies	Nursing
Business administration	Philosophy
Chemistry	Physics
Communications	Psychology
Computer science	Public administration
Economics	Rural and town planning
Education	Theater arts
History	

HISTORICAL FINANCIALS & EMPLOYEES

School FYE: June	Annual Growth	1989	1990	1991	1992	1993	1994	1995	1996	1997	1998
Sales ($ mil.)	3.8%	1,863	2,039	2,099	2,131	2,085	2,121	3,121	3,889	2,522	2,612
Employees	8.5%	18,742	19,163	—	—	33,859	34,779	33,000	37,360	38,512	39,000

SALES HISTORY

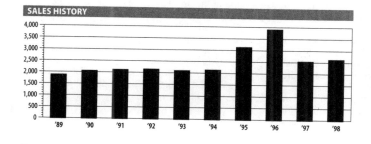

CALTEX CORPORATION

OVERVIEW

Go east, young person, and you'll find Caltex and its petroleum refining and marketing operations. One of the oldest and most successful joint ventures in the history of business, Singapore-based Caltex (formerly Caltex Petroleum) is owned 50-50 by US energy titans Texaco and Chevron.

With operations in more than 60 countries, primarily in Africa, the Asia/Pacific region, and the Middle East, Caltex sells 1.5 million barrels of crude oil and petroleum products per day.

The company has stakes in 13 fuel refineries, two lubricant refineries, 17 lubricant-blending plants, six asphalt plants, and more than 500 ocean terminals and depots. It markets products through 8,000 retail outlets, including 425 Star Mart convenience stores.

Despite the Asian economic downturn, the company is bullish on the Asia/Pacific region — Caltex in 1999 moved its headquarters to Singapore, where it is the country's largest private company.

HISTORY

In the 1930s Standard Oil of California (Socal, now Chevron) had a problem most oil companies would wish for: It had oil reserves in Bahrain with a potential 30,000-barrel-a-day production capacity, but didn't have the refining or marketing network to sell the oil profitably.

While Socal's oil sat idly in the Bahraini soil, Texaco had its own problems. It had a large marketing network in Asia and Africa but lacked a crude supply in the Eastern Hemisphere; it was shipping its products from the US. Enter James Forrestal, head of the American investment bank Dillon Read, with plans for a little matchmaking. Forrestal brought the two companies together, and in 1936 they formed the California-Texas Oil Company (Caltex).

Disrupted by WWII, nonetheless Caltex was to expand quickly, organizing itself by geography. It formed companies in Malaysia, Thailand, and Yemen, and it increased its refining capacity in Bahrain (1945), began building and expanding refineries in other areas (1946), and bought Texaco's European and North African marketing operations (1947). In 1951 Caltex formed a joint venture with Nippon Oil (now called Nippon Mitsubishi Oil) to refine crude oil supplied by Caltex in Japan and bought 50% of Japan's Koa Oil Company.

Caltex sold its European operations to Socal and Texaco in 1967 to concentrate on building its presence in Africa, Asia, and Australasia. A year later Caltex entered South Korea and formed the Honam Oil Refinery (renamed LG-Caltex Oil in 1996) in a partnership with Lucky Chemical (now LG Chemical).

During the 1970s several of Caltex's Arab holdings were nationalized as an OPEC-spawned upheaval shook the oil industry, and in 1978 the Indian government nationalized Caltex Oil Refining (India) Ltd.

In 1980 Caltex tried its hand in the convenience store business, setting up Majik Markets in an Australian venture with US grocer Munford. (Though Caltex had turned the MM stores over to the 7-Eleven franchise by 1990, it later began adding Star Marts to its gas stations.) In 1982 Caltex moved from New York City to Irving, Texas, in the Dallas area. Four years later it began modernizing its refineries in Australia, the Philippines, and Singapore. In 1988 it created Caltex Services Corporation to provide tech support to Caltex companies.

Caltex formed a joint venture for blending and marketing lubricants with Indian oil company IBP in 1993. The next year the company opened offices in Vietnam and Indonesia.

In 1995 company veteran David Law-Smith became CEO. The Japanese government announced plans to lift import restrictions on refined oil in 1996, allowing Caltex to sell to Japanese customers from elsewhere in Asia; Caltex, which had completed a refinery in Thailand, sold its 50% stake in Nippon Oil. That year the company and Shantou Ocean Enterprises announced plans to build China's largest liquid propane gas storage facility.

In 1997 Caltex sold its 40% share of the Bahrain Refining Co. The company also merged its Australian refining and marketing unit with Pioneer International's Ampol unit.

Caltex restructured in 1998, organizing around functions — such as marketing, refining, and trading — rather than geography. It hoped to save about $250 million annually. In 1999 Caltex moved most of its headquarters operations from Texas to Singapore to be closer to its core markets in the Asia/Pacific region, and it changed its name from Caltex Petroleum to plain ol' Caltex to acknowledge the importance of non-petroleum operations, particularly the Star Marts. Law-Smith retired, and SVP Jock McKenzie became CEO. Caltex also sold its stake in Koa Oil to Nippon Mitsubishi Oil that year.

Chairman and CEO: Jock McKenzie
EVP: Guy J. Camarata
CFO: Malcolm J. McAuley
VP, Secretary, and General Counsel: Frank W. Blue
VP; Head of Worldwide Trading, Singapore:
  Leo G. Lonergan
VP Human Resources: Stephen H. Nichols
VP: Shariq Yosufzai
Auditors: KPMG LLP

LOCATIONS

HQ: 30 Raffles Place, Caltex House, 048622, Singapore
Phone: +65-533-3000   **Fax:** +65-439-1711
US HQ: 125 E. John Carpenter Fwy., Irving, TX 75062
US Phone: 972-830-1000   **US Fax:** 972-830-1081
Web site: http://www.caltex.com

PRODUCTS/OPERATIONS

Selected Products
Asphalt/Bitumen
Automotive fuel
Automotive lubes
Aviation fuel
Commercial lubes
Industrial oils
LPG
Marine and railroad fuel
Motorcycle oils
Specialty products

Selected Subsidiaries and Affiliates
American Overseas Petroleum Ltd. (coordinates
  activities of P. T. Caltex Pacific Indonesia)
LG-Caltex Oil Corp. (50%, refining, South Korea)
P. T. Caltex Pacific Indonesia (oil and gas exploration)
Star Petroleum Refining Co. Ltd. (64%, Thailand)

COMPETITORS

7-Eleven	Mitsubishi
Amerada Hess	Occidental
BHP	Petronas
BP Amoco	Royal Dutch/Shell
Coastal	SK Corporation
Devon Energy	TOTAL FINA
ENI	USX-Marathon
Elf Aquitaine	Unocal
Exxon Mobil	Woolworths
Kerr-McGee	

HISTORICAL FINANCIALS & EMPLOYEES

Joint venture FYE: December	Annual Growth	1989	1990	1991	1992	1993	1994	1995	1996	1997	1998
Sales ($ mil.)	4.5%	11,507	15,147	15,445	17,281	15,409	14,751	15,067	18,166	18,357	17,174
Net income ($ mil.)	(14.9%)	609	601	839	720	720	689	899	1,193	846	143
Income as % of sales	—	5.3%	4.0%	5.4%	4.2%	4.7%	4.7%	6.0%	6.6%	4.6%	0.8%
Employees	0.3%	—	7,700	7,700	7,600	7,800	8,000	7,000	7,300	7,600	7,900

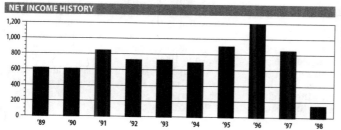

NET INCOME HISTORY

1998 FISCAL YEAR-END
Debt ratio: 17.5%
Return on equity: 3.2%
Cash ($ mil.): 178
Current ratio: 0.70
Long-term debt ($ mil.): 930

CALVIN KLEIN INC.

OVERVIEW

"Marky Mark" Wahlberg's underwear and Brooke Shields' implied lack thereof made everyone aware of their Calvins. New York City-based Calvin Klein designs men's, women's, and children's clothing and accessories. About 90% of sales come from its licensed lines, which include underwear and jeans (by Warnaco); sportswear; several fragrances, including Obsession and cK One (by Unilever); and accessories. Calvin Klein also licenses more than 40 outlet stores worldwide. As the retail environment for upscale fashion has languished in recent years, so have the sales of the company's licensed products, particularly fragrances.

Almost as well known as the clothes are Calvin Klein's advertisements, created in-house by CRK Advertising. The company's erotic campaigns continue to remain controversial: In 1999 it canceled two multimillion-dollar ad campaigns for children's underwear after being blasted for promoting pedophilia. Following the footsteps of retailers such as The Gap, Calvin Klein has been targeting children's lines for growth.

Co-founders Calvin Klein (VC) and Barry Schwartz (chairman and CEO) own the company, but Calvin Klein is currently shopping for a new owner or partner. After missing the IPO craze among fashion houses in the 1990s, the founders hope the current fashion consolidation frenzy can provide the firm with the cash needed to expand.

HISTORY

After five years designing for other Seventh Avenue fashion houses, Calvin Klein went out on his own in 1968, bankrolled with $10,000 from childhood friend Barry Schwartz, who handled the business. That year a Bonwit Teller executive stumbled into Klein's small showroom, leading to a $50,000 order. Klein expanded from coats into sportswear in 1970. Schwartz, realizing that coats only sold during one season, helped the company expand into the more lucrative sportswear market by only selling coats to buyers who also bought the other line.

Nurturing the aura of exclusivity, Calvin Klein kept his outlets few. He also helped kill polyester, which he said was slimy. The designer's look became so influential by 1975 that *Vogue* was calling it "a definitive picture of the American look." The 1978 kidnapping of Klein's daughter was rumored to be a publicity stunt. (The kidnapper, a sitter, eventually pled guilty.)

Klein introduced his designer jeans in a self-directed commercial in 1980. He paid 15-year-old Brooke Shields $500,000 to suggest that she was pantiless beneath her Calvins. Sales of designer jeans peaked in 1982. In the early 1980s Klein introduced gender-bending boxer shorts for women, complete with a fly. In an effort to increase profits, Calvin Klein purchased its jeanswear licensee, Puritan Fashions, for $60 million in 1983. Two years later Klein touted his first fragrance, Obsession, with a slew of ads featuring nude models.

The company signed a pact with Marchon Eyewear in 1991 to make Calvin Klein sunglasses and eyewear (rolled out in 1992). Pal David Geffen bailed the company out of $62 million in junk bond debt (stemming from the Puritan purchase) in 1992 and helped Klein license his underwear business to Warnaco. In the early 1990s Klein benefited when the youth market suddenly turned on to his clothes — not only the baggy, low-slung jeans for the LA County-jail look but the requisite underwear (with CK all over it) showing under them. The youthful resurgence also led the designer to shift down from the kind of exclusive fashions sold at Bergdorf Goodman to a more casual, universal look.

Calvin Klein hired Armani veteran Gabriella Forte as president and COO in 1994; she was instrumental in giving the Calvin Klein name a strong global licensing presence. Also in 1994 the company opened its first retail store in Tokyo. The next year Calvin Klein introduced its home collection (including blankets, pillows, towels, and rugs) in department stores.

In the mid-1990s the company drew criticism for using models who looked anorexic, underaged, and drugged. Critics charged Klein was contributing to a trend in advertising known as "heroin chic." New advertising in 1998 focused on a more wholesome lifestyle, with healthier looking models in outdoor settings. But it didn't take the firm long to wind up back in the hot seat when it used children in an underwear campaign, which was withdrawn in 1999.

Also in 1999, shortly after Forte announced she was leaving, Calvin Klein began shopping for a merger opportunity with another "high profile" company.

Chairman and CEO: Barry Schwartz
VC: Calvin Klein
President and COO: Tom Murry
Corporate President, Finance and Administration:
Richard Martin
SVP Licensing: Robin Orlick
SVP Marketing: Harlan Bratcher, age 43
President, Calvin Klein Cosmetics: Paulanne Mancuso
SVP and General Counsel, Calvin Klein Cosmetics:
Maria Chiclana

LOCATIONS

HQ: 205 W. 39th St., 4th Fl., New York, NY 10018
Phone: 212-719-2600   **Fax:** 212-730-4818

PRODUCTS/OPERATIONS

Products
Accessories
Apparel
Coats
Eyewear
Fragrances
Home furnishings
Hosiery
Shoes
Sleepwear
Socks
Swimwear
Underwear
Watches

Brands
Calvin Klein (collections for women, men, and the
home; cosmetics; and underwear)
cK (collections for men and women; jeans for women,
men, and kids)
cK One (fragrances)
Eternity (fragrances)
Obsession (fragrances)

COMPETITORS

Donna Karan
Estée Lauder
Gucci
Jil Sander
Joe Boxer
Jones Apparel
LVMH
Nautica Enterprises
Polo
Prada
Tommy Hilfiger

HISTORICAL FINANCIALS & EMPLOYEES

Private FYE: December	Annual Growth	1989	1990	1991	1992	1993	1994	1995	1996	1997	1998
Estimated sales ($ mil.)	(5.2%)	—	—	—	220	280	177	127	141	150	160
Employees	5.4%	—	—	—	—	—	—	—	900	900	1,000

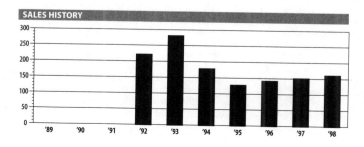

SALES HISTORY

C&S WHOLESALE GROCERS INC.

OVERVIEW

C&S Wholesale Grocers is working its way up the food chain. Based in Brattleboro, Vermont, the company is one of the largest food wholesalers in the nation. C&S Wholesale Grocers sells more than 53,000 products — ranging from dairy products and locally grown produce to groceries and nonfood items — to more than 4,000 supermarkets, military bases, wholesale clubs, and even Wal-Mart stores, from Maine to Maryland.

Unlike some wholesalers, such as fellow giants SUPERVALU and Fleming Companies, the privately owned company owns no retail outlets (it says it doesn't want to compete with its customers). It targets medium-sized and large chains that most wholesalers ignore. C&S Wholesale Grocers handles inventory tracking, warehouse, and distribution operations and can offer better prices because of high-volume buying. Chains account for 85% of the company's sales; independent stores benefit because the wholesaler carries a much wider selection of products than these stores would have access to otherwise. C&S Wholesale Grocers supports its independents with advertising programs and other services.

Vermont's largest company, the wholesaler has been rapidly adding new customers, both chains (such as the troubled Pathmark stores) and independents. As its customer base has increasingly drifted toward the Mid-Atlantic, the company has been expanding its facilities southward as well. It has facilities in Connecticut, Maryland, Massachusetts, New Jersey, New York, and Vermont.

C&S Wholesale Grocers is owned by chairman, president, and CEO Richard Cohen, grandson of the founder.

HISTORY

Israel Cohen and Abraham Siegel began C&S Wholesale Grocers in 1918 in Worcester, Massachusetts. Cohen ran the company for more than 50 years after buying out Siegel in 1921. It became a family concern in 1972 when Cohen turned the company over to his son Lester, who soon brought in his sons, Jim and Rick.

C&S Wholesale Grocers expanded over the years, growing along with its customers. It had $98 million in sales in 1981, the year its skyrocketing growth began. Also in 1981 Rick, now the company's chairman, president, and CEO, engineered a move to Brattleboro, in southern Vermont, where it had better access to interstate highways and a larger workforce.

Six years later warehouse employees said that they were being underutilized; they asked for more work. In response, Rick set up self-managed teams of three to eight employees who would act as small business units responsible for a customer's order from the time it was received to when it was delivered. Team members were paid for the amount of time they worked and were given bonuses for error-free operations and penalties for errors or damaged goods. His plan saw an immediate response in terms of increased sales, and by 1992 C&S Wholesale Grocers had more than $1 billion in sales. Rick bought out his father in 1989 and the next year became the company's single shareholder when he bought out his brother.

C&S Wholesale Grocers started its produce business in 1990 (by 1994 it was the major purchaser of locally grown fruits and vegetables) and began making plans to build an 800,000-sq.-ft. refrigerated warehouse near a scenic highway in Brattleboro. However, it ran up against environmentalists and Vermont's Act 250 environmental impact law, and eventually dropped its original plan, opting instead to expand at its headquarters.

In 1992 the wholesaler offered plans for a smaller, revised warehouse, but again met opposition. After a two-year battle, C&S Wholesale Grocers gave up and said it would build elsewhere. (Most of its employees and warehouses are now in Massachusetts and New Jersey.)

The following year C&S Wholesale Grocers welcomed 127 Grand Union stores and several East Coast Wal-Mart stores as customers. The next year the company picked up another 103 Grand Union stores; Grand Union said it was closing two distribution centers and shifting distribution to C&S Wholesale Grocers in a deal worth $500 million a year. A $650 million-per-year contract with Edwards stores was inked in 1996, the year C&S Wholesale Grocers' sales topped $3 billion.

The company acquired ice-cream distributor New England Frozen Foods in 1997. Continuing its move toward the mid-Atlantic region, C&S Wholesale Grocers took over the distribution and supply operations of New Jersey-based grocery chain Pathmark in 1998 for $60 million. In 1999 C&S Wholesale Grocers announced it would purchase Star Markets' wholesale division.

Chairman, President, and CEO: Richard B. Cohen
SVP and CFO: Brenda Edgerton
SVP Human Resources: Mitch Davis
SVP and General Counsel: Mark Gross
SVP Strategic Planning: William Hamlin
SVP Sales: Larry Newton
SVP Grocery and Frozen Procurement: Bob Palmer
SVP Management Information Systems: Walter Pong
SVP Perishable Procurement: George Semanie
SVP Operations: Nat Silverman

LOCATIONS

HQ: Old Ferry Rd., Brattleboro, VT 05301
Phone: 802-257-4371   **Fax:** 802-257-6727

PRODUCTS/OPERATIONS

Selected Customers
A&P
Big Y Foods
BJ's Wholesale Club
Edwards Super Food Stores
Food Mart
Giant
Grand Union
Mayfair Super Markets
Pathmark
Putney General Store
Safeway
Stop & Shop
Victory Markets
Wal-Mart

COMPETITORS

Bozzuto's
Di Giorgio
Fleming Companies
SUPERVALU
Wakefern Food

HISTORICAL FINANCIALS & EMPLOYEES

Private FYE: September	Annual Growth	1990	1991	1992	1993	1994	1995	1996	1997	1998	1999
Sales ($ mil.)	24.1%	—	—	1,335	1,867	1,837	2,650	3,348	3,665	5,120	6,050
Employees	21.9%	—	—	1,000	1,300	1,500	2,000	2,850	3,000	3,800	4,000

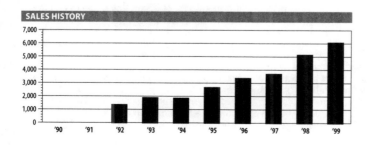

SALES HISTORY

CARGILL, INCORPORATED

On the global corporate battlefield, Cargill is the US's highest-ranking private. The largest private corporation in the US, Wayzata, Minnesota-based Cargill has diversified operations including commodities trading (grain, coffee, and petroleum); food processing; financial trading; futures brokering; seed, feed, and fertilizer producing; shipping; and steelmaking. In addition to making ingredients used in many food products, Cargill has its own food brands, including Honeysuckle White and

Riverside (poultry), Sunny Fresh (processed eggs), and Gerkens (cocoa).

Cargill has 29 subsidiaries with operations in more than 1,000 locations in about 60 countries; it trades in about 130 others. The company is the US's #1 grain exporter and one of the world's largest food processors. Its Excel unit slaughters about one-fifth of US cattle.

About 100 descendants of the founders own about 85% of Cargill.

William W. Cargill founded Cargill in 1865 when he bought his first grain elevator, in Conover, Iowa. He and his brother Sam bought grain elevators all along the Southern Minnesota Railroad in 1870, just as Minnesota was becoming an important shipping route. Sam and a third brother, James, expanded the elevator operations while William worked with the railroads to monopolize transport of grain to markets and coal to farmers.

Around the turn of the century, William's son William S. invested in a number of ill-fated projects. William W. found that his name had been used to finance the projects; shortly afterward, he died of pneumonia. Cargill's creditors pressed for repayment, which threatened to bankrupt the company. John MacMillan, William W.'s son-in-law, took control and rebuilt Cargill. It had recovered by 1916 but lost its holdings in Mexico and Canada. MacMillan opened offices in New York City (1922) and Argentina (1929), expanding grain trading and transport operations.

In 1945 Cargill bought Nutrena Mills (animal feed) and entered soybean processing; corn processing began soon after and grew with the demand for corn sweeteners. In 1954 Cargill benefited when the US began making loans to help developing countries buy American grain. Subsidiary Tradax, established in 1955, became one of the largest grain traders in Europe. A decade later Cargill began trading sugar by purchasing sugar and molasses in the Philippines and selling them abroad.

Cargill made its finances public in 1973 (as a requirement for its unsuccessful takeover bid of Missouri Portland Cement), revealing it to be one of the US's largest companies, with $5.2 billion in sales. In the 1970s it expanded into coal, steel, and waste disposal and became a major force in metals processing, beef, and salt production.

In the early 1990s Cargill began selling

branded meats and packaged foods directly to supermarkets. To placate family heirs who wanted to take Cargill public, CEO Whitney MacMillan, grandson of John, created an employee stock plan in 1991 that allowed shareholders to cash in their shares. He also boosted dividends and reorganized the board, reducing the family's control. MacMillan retired in 1995 and nonfamily member Ernest Micek became CEO and chairman.

The firm bought Akzo Nobel's North American salt operations in 1997, becoming the #2 US salt company, behind Morton (acquired by Rohm and Haas in 1999).

Taking advantage of the high prices being paid for seed companies, in 1998 Cargill sold its foreign seed operations to Monsanto for $1.4 billion. (A tangle over misappropriated seed technology later led Cargill to refund at least $200 million to Monsanto.) Adding to its poultry operations, Cargill purchased turkey processor Plantation Foods that year. Internationally, the company became the manager of Toshoku, a bankrupt Japanese food trader (which it plans to buy). It also bought 60% of the Venezuelan grain and cereals business of commodities giant Bunge International.

In 1999 Cargill bought the #2 US grain export operation from Continental Grain in a deal estimated between $300 to $450 million (the firms agreed to sell some facilities to assuage antitrust interest). Both companies handle about 35% of US total grain sales and over 40% of US corn sales.

Cargill reported depressed earnings during fiscal 1998 and 1999, in part because of weaker foreign markets. Micek resigned as CEO in 1999 (but remained chairman) and was replaced by Warren Staley. Also in 1999 Cargill fessed up to misappropriating some genetic seed material from rival Pioneer Hi-Bred, killing its $650 million deal to sell its North American seed assets to Germany's AgrEvo.

Chairman: Ernest S. Micek
VC: F. Guillaume Bastiaens
VC and CFO: Robert L. Lumpkins
President and CEO: Warren R. Staley, age 57
EVP: David W. Raisbeck
Corporate VP, General Counsel, and Secretary:
James D. Moe
Corporate VP, Human Resources: Nancy Siska

LOCATIONS

HQ: 15407 McGinty Rd. West, Wayzata, MN 55391
Phone: 612-742-7575   **Fax:** 612-742-7393
Web site: http://www.cargill.com

Cargill and its subsidiaries and affiliates have more than 1,000 locations in 59 countries and operate in about 130 others.

PRODUCTS/OPERATIONS

Selected Operations

Agriculture
Animal feed
Canola, cotton, forage, and sunflower seeds
Fertilizer

Financial Markets
Asset Investment & Finance Group (capitalization of partner firms, credit-intensive assets, portfolio finance, and principal investment)
Cargill Technical Services (consultancy, management, natural resource management, rural development, and technical assistance)
Financial Markets Group (financial instrument trading, money markets, trade and structured finance, and value investing)

Food Processing
Bulk and packaged oils (baking, frying, margarine, and salad dressing)
Cargill Cacau (cocoa and cocoa products)
Cargill Salt
Citric acid
Corn- and wheat- wet milling (produce corn syrups, glucose, and dry sweeteners)
Ethanol
Excel Corporation (beef and pork processing and sales)
Poultry (production, processing, marketing)
Soybeans

Industrial
Cargill Steel and Wire (chain link fencing, concrete reinforcing wire, flat-rolled steel, industrial wire, and wire mesh)
North Star Steel (steel minimills)
Steel

Trading
Cargill Investor Services (CIS, futures/futures options broker and risk management consultant)
Cargill Marine and Terminal
Cargo Carriers (operates jumbo dry and liquid cargo barges)
G&M Stevedoring
Greenwich Marine (ocean shipping)
Hohenberg Bros (cotton trading)
Ralli Bros. and Coney (cotton trading)
Rogers Terminal & Shipping (stevedoring services)

COMPETITORS

ADM	Dole	Nippon Steel
Ag Processing	Dow Chemical	Novartis
Agribrands	DuPont	Nucor
International,	E D & F	Perdue
Inc.	Eridania	Pioneer Hi-Bred
Ajinomoto	Beghin-Say	Rohm and Haas
BASF AG	Farmland	Sara Lee
Bethlehem Steel	Industries	Saskatchewan
Cenex Harvest	General Mills	Wheat Pool
States	Heinz	Smithfield Foods
Chiquita Brands	Hormel	Tate & Lyle
ConAgra	IBP	USX-U.S. Steel
ContiGroup	Koch	
Corn Products	Mitsubishi	
International	Monsanto	

HISTORICAL FINANCIALS & EMPLOYEES

Private FYE: May	Annual Growth	1990	1991	1992	1993	1994	1995	1996	1997	1998	1999
Sales ($ mil.)	1.4%	44,000	49,100	46,800	47,100	47,135	51,000	56,000	56,000	51,400	50,000
Net income ($ mil.)	5.4%	372	382	450	358	571	671	902	814	468	597
Income as % of sales	—	0.8%	0.8%	1.0%	0.8%	1.2%	1.3%	1.6%	1.5%	0.9%	1.2%
Employees	4.8%	55,200	60,000	63,500	70,000	70,700	73,300	76,000	79,000	80,600	84,000

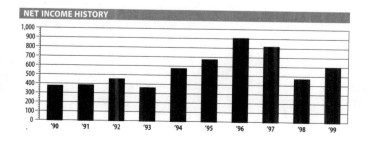

NET INCOME HISTORY

CARLSON COMPANIES, INC.

OVERVIEW

Carlson Companies' customers can eat, drink, and make merry at more than 1,100 locations (cruise ships, hotels, resorts, restaurants) worldwide. The Minnetonka, Minnesota-based hospitality giant also provides travel and marketing services. The company's Carlson Leisure Group is one of the US' largest leisure travel-services providers. Commercial travel services are provided through Carlson Wagonlit Travel (#3 after American Express and Japan Travel Bureau), an Amsterdam-based corporation co-owned by France's Accor hotel and hospitality company, which operates in more than 3,000 locations in about 140 countries. Carlson merged its UK operations with giant Thomas Cook. The company also provides travel services to Neiman Marcus, and trains travel agents through its US-based Carlson Travel Academies.

Carlson Hospitality Worldwide operates and franchises about 550 Radisson Hotels, Country Inns & Suites, and Regent International Hotels, but owns few hotels outright. Carlson Restaurants Worldwide owns or franchises more than 500 T.G.I. Friday's restaurants in Asia, Europe, Mexico, the Middle East, and the US. (The company is selling a minority stake in its restaurant operations.) This division has begun targeting international expansion and is developing new restaurants, including Italianni's and Friday's Front Row Sports Grill. Carlson Marketing Group provides marketing consulting, database, and motivational training services.

Before his death in early 1999, company founder Curtis Carlson — who headed the company for 60 years — turned over the executive reins of the privately held firm (one of the US' largest) to his eldest daughter, Marilyn Carlson Nelson. Nelson is second only to Hewlett Packard's Carly Fiorina as the world's top-ranking female CEO (based on company size).

HISTORY

Curtis Carlson, the son of Swedish immigrants, graduated from the University of Minnesota in 1937 and went to work selling soap for Procter & Gamble in the Minneapolis area. In 1938, as a sideline, he borrowed $55 and formed Gold Bond Stamp Company to sell trading stamps. His wife, Arleen, dressed as a drum majorette and twirled a baton to promote the concept. By 1941 the company had 200 accounts. Business was slowed by WWII, but took off in the 1950s. By 1960 the company was a cash cow, and it began investing in other enterprises, including travel agencies, business promotion, and employee motivation programs.

In 1962 Carlson bought the Radisson Hotel in Minneapolis. He expanded the chain in Minnesota and in 1970 ventured outside the state with the purchase of a Denver hotel from Hyatt. In 1973 Gold Bond became Carlson Companies. Carlson diversified into restaurants by buying the 11-unit T.G.I. Friday's (1975), a dining and fern bar chain, and Country Kitchen International (family restaurants).

In 1978 Carlson bought his first travel agency, Ask Mr. Foster, and the next year he bought Colony Resorts (hotel and condominium management company) from its founder, Peter Ueberroth (later baseball commissioner).

Carlson Companies slowed the pace of its acquisitions in the 1980s. Hired in 1984, Juergen Bartels changed the hospitality division's strategy from building and owning hotels to franchising and managing them. This enabled Carlson to weather the crash that followed the 1980s hotel overbuilding boom. T.G.I. Friday's went public to fund expansion in 1983, but Carlson kept a 76% interest and reacquired all outstanding shares in 1990. That year and the next, Carlson bought two UK travel agencies, A.T. Mays (1990) and Smith Travel (1991). The company entered the cruise ship business in 1992, when it launched the luxury liner SSC *Radisson Diamond*.

The company made a major international advance in 1994 when it formed a joint venture, Carlson Wagonlit Travel, with France's Accor, giving it exposure in more than 120 countries. In 1997 Carlson expanded into the luxury hotel business when it bought Regent International from Four Seasons. Also that year Carlson Wagonlit Travel was formally incorporated as a separate, Netherlands-based company. In 1998 Curtis Carlson appointed his daughter, Marilyn, as the company's chief executive, but retained the title of chairman. In 1999 the company merged its UK leisure travel business with Thomas Cook's international leisure travel and financial services business. Also that year Curtis Carlson died of a stroke; Marilyn became chairwoman. The company later filed to spin off its T.G.I. Friday's unit as Carlson Restaurants Worldwide.

OFFICERS

Chairman, President, and CEO: Marilyn Carlson Nelson
EVP and CFO: Martyn R. Redgrave
SVP Legal, Secretary, and General Counsel:
Lee Bearmon
SVP Human Resources: Terry M. Butorac
SVP and Chief Information Officer: Rex L. Carter
VP Public Relations and Communications:
Douglas R. Cody
VP and Treasurer: John M. Diracles Jr.
VP Tax: Darrel M. Hamann
VP and Controller: Bruce L. Paulsen
President and CEO, Carlson Hospitality Worldwide:
Curtis C. Nelson
President and CEO, Carlson Marketing Group:
James J. Ryan
President and CEO, Carlson Wagonlit Travel:
Jon Madonna
**President and CEO, Carlson Leisure Group and
Carlson Leisure Group-U.K.:** Michael Batt
President and CEO, Carlson Real Estate:
Dean A. Riesen
President, CEO Regent Hotels Worldwide, Inc.:
Paul Hanley
CFO, Carlson Restaurants Worldwide, Inc.: Jeff Warne
CFO, Carlson Leisure Group: John M. Dignan
**EVP Finance, and Operations Carlson Marketing
Group:** Robert A. Ross
SVP and CFO, Carlson Wagonlit Travel:
Olivier de Surville
VP and General Manager, Gold Points: Harold Schrum
Auditors: Arthur Andersen LLP

LOCATIONS

HQ: 701 Carlson Pkwy., Minnetonka, MN 55459
Phone: 612-540-5000   **Fax:** 612-449-2219
Web site: http://www.carlson.com

PRODUCTS/OPERATIONS

Carlson Hospitality Worldwide
Carlson Lifestyle Living (resort-style residential
community)
Carlson Restaurants Worldwide
Carlson Vacation Ownership
Country Inns & Suites By Carlson
Radisson Hotels Worldwide
Radisson Seven Seas Cruises
Regent International Hotels

Carlson Leisure Group
Carlson Destination Marketing Services
Carlson Leisure Fulfillment Services (membership-based
travel program)
Carlson Travel Academies (travel training)
Carlson Wagonlit Travel Associates/Travel Agents
International
Neiman Marcus Travel Services
Thomas Cook (22%, UK travel agencies)

Carlson Marketing Group
Direct marketing
Event and sports marketing
Loyalty marketing
Performance improvement
Carlson Wagonlit Travel
business travel (joint venture with Accor)
Gold Points Corporation
(customer incentive program)

COMPETITORS

Advantica Restaurant	O'Charley's
Group	Prandium
American Express	Rank
Bass	Sandals Resorts
Brinker	Starwood Hotels & Resorts
Darden Restaurants	Worldwide
Hilton	TRT Holdings
Hyatt	The Restaurant Co.
Maritz	WorldTravel
Marriott International	Wyndham International
Metromedia	

HISTORICAL FINANCIALS & EMPLOYEES

Private FYE: December	Annual Growth	1989	1990	1991	1992	1993	1994	1995	1996	1997	1998
Estimated sales ($ mil.)	16.3%	2,000	2,200	2,300	3,200	3,500	3,900	4,500	4,900	6,600	7,800
Employees	10.1%	—	68,000	70,000	49,350	41,000	65,000	69,000	65,462	68,530	147,000

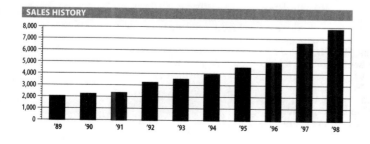

SALES HISTORY

CARLSON WAGONLIT TRAVEL

OVERVIEW

History was bunk for Henry Ford, but for Carlson Wagonlit Travel it was a bunk bed. Minnetonka, Minnesota-based Carlson Wagonlit (pronounced Vah-gon-LEE) Travel descends from Europe's Wagons-Lits (literally, sleeping cars) company, which was founded by the creator of the Orient Express, and from the US's oldest travel agency chain (Ask Mr. Foster). Carlson Wagonlit Travel is the third-largest travel company in the world behind American Express and Japan Travel Bureau (which are virtually tied for the #1 position). The company manages business travel from about 3,000 locations in more than 140 countries.

Carlson Wagonlit Travel is co-owned by France's Accor Group (motel and hotel franchises, travel and tourism services) and the US's Carlson Companies. Carlson Companies is a service conglomerate whose nonbusiness travel operations include hospitality (it franchises Radisson Hotels, T.G.I. Friday's and Italianni's restaurants, and luxury cruise lines) and marketing services (motivational and incentive programs for businesses).

HISTORY

Belgian inventor Georges Nagelmackers' first enterprise was adding sleeping compartments to European trains in 1872. Nagelmackers later created the Orient Express. Over the years his Wagons-Lits company expanded its mission (and modified its spelling) to become Wagonlit Travel.

While Nagelmackers was establishing his business in Europe, across the Atlantic Ocean Ward G. Foster was giving out steamship and train schedules from his gift shop facing the stately Ponce de Leon Hotel in St. Augustine, Florida. As legend has it, hotel patrons with pressing travel questions were directed to Foster's shop with: "Ask Mr. Foster. He'll know."

In 1888 he founded Ask Mr. Foster Travel (it became the oldest travel agency in the US). By 1913 the company had offices located in pricey department stores and in the lobbies of upscale hotels and resorts throughout the country. After 50 years at the helm, Foster sold his business in 1937, three years before his death.

After suffering hard times during WWII and into the 1950s, the company changed hands again in 1957 when Donald Fisher and Thomas Orr, two Ask Mr. Foster shareholders, bought controlling interests for $157,000. In 1972 Peter Ueberroth (Major League Baseball commissioner and Los Angeles Olympic Organizing Committee president) bought the company. Ueberroth sold it seven years later, in 1979, to Carlson Companies, Inc., Carlson Wagonlit's parent. In 1990 Ask Mr. Foster became Carlson Travel Network.

Also in 1990 Carlson Companies acquired the UK's A.T. Mays, the Travel Agents — a leading UK seller of vacation and tour packages. By 1992 Carlson Companies, besides adding a travel agency a day to the 2,000-plus it already owned, was adding a new hotel every 10 days.

Europe's Wagonlit Travel and the US's Carlson Travel Network joined forces in 1994 to pursue expansion efforts. Under a dual-president ownership, the parent companies owned operations in specific world regions. The two companies began developing new business technology and expanded into new business markets throughout the world. In 1994 the venture acquired Germany's Brune Reiseburo travel agency and opened a branch office in Moscow.

Through 1995 and 1996 acquisitions targeted the Asia/Pacific region, including Hong Kong's and Japan's Dodwell Travel and the corporate travel business of Singapore's Jetset Travel. It also formed a partnership with Traveland, an Australian travel agency.

In 1997 Wagonlit Travel and Carlson Travel Network finalized the merger of their business activities operations, renamed Carlson Wagonlit Travel.

The following year the new company acquired Florida's Travel Agents International, with more than 300 franchised operations and $600 million in annual sales.

Also in 1998 Jon Madonna, formerly vice chairman of The Travelers Group, replaced Travis Tanner as CEO. The following year three travel agencies in eastern Canada consolidated under the Carlson Wagonlit Travel brand, creating the largest travel network in that region.

The same year, Carlson Companies founder and Carlson Wagonlit Travel chairman Curtis Carlson died.

OFFICERS

President and CEO: Jon Madonna
EVP Global Sales and Account Management:
Liliana Frigerio
EVP Products and Services: Jim Giancola
EVP North America Operations: Dean Hatton
EVP and CFO: Clive Hole
EVP EMEA Operations and Regions: Richard Lovell
EVP North America Sales and Account Management:
Ron Merriman
EVP Latin America: Ross Mersinger
VP Industry Relations, Worldwide: Gary Alexander
VP Finance, Americas: Tim Hennessy
Chief Information Officer: Loren Brown
President, Europe, Middle East, and Africa:
Herve Gourio
President, Asia/Pacific: Geoffrey Marshall

LOCATIONS

HQ: 701 Carlson Pkwy., Minnetonka, MN 55459
Phone: 612-212-5000   **Fax:** 612-212-1288
Web site: http://www.carlsonwagonlit.com

PRODUCTS/OPERATIONS

Selected Services
Carlson Wagonlit Travel Services (advice, information, reservations)

COMPETITORS

American Express
Japan Travel Bureau
Maritz
Rosenbluth International
WorldTravel

HISTORICAL FINANCIALS & EMPLOYEES

Joint venture FYE: December	Annual Growth	1989	1990	1991	1992	1993	1994	1995	1996	1997	1998
Sales ($ mil.)	7.6%	—	—	—	—	—	—	—	9,500	10,600	11,000
Employees	0.2%	—	—	—	—	—	—	—	20,000	20,000	20,100

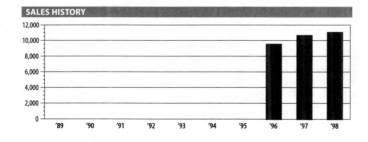

SALES HISTORY

CARQUEST CORP.

OVERVIEW

Searching for a sensor, solenoid, or switches? CARQUEST can steer you in the right direction. The auto parts distribution group, based in Lakewood, Colorado, sells its own line of auto parts (made by Moog Automotive, Gabriel, and Dana, among others) to jobbers and wholesalers for eventual resale to professional repair centers, service stations, dealerships, and, to a lesser degree, do-it-yourself (DIY) customers. CARQUEST is owned by nine warehouse distributors.

The company's roughly 60 warehouse distribution centers (DCs) service more than 4,000 distributor-owned and independent jobbers in the US and Canada. General Parts, its largest distributor, serves more than 2,700 stores across the US and Canada from about 40 DCs. The average CARQUEST store carries about 15,000 parts, while a DC carries some 150,000 items.

To strengthen ties with service shops, CARQUEST offers the Tech-Net Professional Service program. The program, available for an annual fee, includes 20 minutes of diagnostic hotline service per month (additional time is available), as well as a full guarantee on parts, a CARQUEST credit card, direct-mail material, signs, training information, business management courses, computer services, and advertising assistance.

Consolidation in the aftermarket industry has blurred the lines of distribution between wholesalers and retailers, causing all segments of the industry to scramble for ways to gain or maintain market share. CARQUEST focuses on professional mechanics (who account for more than 70% of sales), but it is being squeezed as retailers such as AutoZone look beyond their regular DIY customers for a piece of the commercial pie. At the same time, chains such as The Pep Boys - Manny, Moe & Jack are chipping away at service stations' business by offering parts and service.

HISTORY

Even though he didn't know the auto parts business, Temple Sloan recognized America's infatuation with the automobile and started distributor General Parts in 1961 at age 21. By 1972 he had acquired enough warehouse space to supply not only his hometown of Raleigh but the entire state of North Carolina. Determined to get bigger faster, Sloan studied auto parts kingpin Genuine Parts, digging through its annual reports and uncovering tricks of the trade, while working on a few of his own. To compete in what was then a fast-growing industry, Genuine Parts had created a marketing alliance, NAPA, that used mass buying power to garner better pricing and service from manufacturers that often wouldn't recognize individual companies.

Sloan recruited friends and fellow distributors Dan Bock, president of Bobro Products, and Joe Hughes, president of Indiana Parts Warehouse, and together they formed CARQUEST in 1974. The company was designed to help jobbers (middlemen between distributors and mechanics) being threatened by retailers attempting to get a piece of the commercial business market traditionally served by jobbers. CARQUEST began recruiting other distributors and achieved first-year sales of $29 million. In the first five years, almost 1,500 jobbers committed to CARQUEST. Leadership rotated among distributor members until Bock became president in 1984.

As CARQUEST grew, the need for a unifying private-label line became apparent. In the 1970s it developed the Proven Value line of do-it-yourself-oriented products such as oils and filters. The establishment of the CARQUEST brand in the mid-1980s gave the company complete control over quality, coverage, price, and promotions, giving CARQUEST jobbers an advantage in the marketplace. Private-label sales grew from 20%-25% of business to 70% by 1996.

That year CARQUEST relocated its national headquarters from Tarrytown, New York, to Lakewood, Colorado, and Peter Kornafel became president and CEO, replacing Bock, who stayed active in the company. Kornafel had been president of Hatch Grinding, a Denver distributor that merged with General Parts in 1996. The next year the firm moved into Canada, as General Parts bought half of the McKerlie-Millen subsidiary of Acklands (more than 400 parts stores) for $75 million. In 1998 CARQUEST launched Tech-Net Professional Service, a program for service stations and other installers that offers benefits such as signs, business training, and computer services.

Also in 1998 CARQUEST added about 150 new stores to its network when General Parts bought bankrupt APS Holding. In 1999 General Parts bought The Parts Source, which included 41 Ace Auto Parts stores in Florida.

President, CEO, and CFO: Peter Kornafel
EVP: Daniel Bock
Director Human Resources: Louise Veasman

LOCATIONS

HQ: 12596 W. Bayaud Ave., Ste. 400,
Lakewood, CO 80228
Phone: 303-984-2000 **Fax:** 303-984-2001
Web site: http://www.carquest.com

PRODUCTS/OPERATIONS

Member Warehouse Distributors
A.E. Lottes
Auto Parts Wholesale
Automotive Warehouse, Inc.
BWP Distributors, Inc.
CARQUEST CANADA, Ltd. (50%-owned by Acktion
Corp., 50%-owned by General Parts)
Gabriel
General Parts, Inc.
Muffler Warehouse
Southern Auto Supply
Straus-Frank Company

Selected Manufacturers of CARQUEST Products
Airtex
American Driveline
Autoline Industries
Cardone Industries
Dana
Federal
Federal Mogul Corporation
Maremont/Arvin
Moog Automotive
NEAPCO
Standard Motor Products
Wells Manufacturing Corp.
WIX

COMPETITORS

AutoZone
CSK Auto
Dayton Hudson
Genuine Parts
Hahn Automotive Warehouse
Pep Boys
Sears
Wal-Mart

HISTORICAL FINANCIALS & EMPLOYEES

Private FYE: December	Annual Growth	1989	1990	1991	1992	1993	1994	1995	1996	1997	1998
Sales ($ mil.)	17.5%	—	—	—	734	860	860	940	1,200	1,300	1,400
Employees	34.6%	—	—	—	—	—	—	26,000	26,000	35,000	35,000

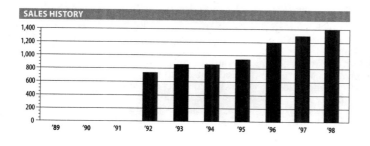

SALES HISTORY

CATHOLIC HEALTH EAST

OVERVIEW

Although lamentations over numbers led to the exodus of some religious health care providers, it was the genesis of Catholic Health East.

Based in Newtown Square, Pennsylvania, the company is the product of the tripartite merger of Allegany Health System, Eastern Mercy Health System, and Sisters of Providence Health System. It is the third-largest religious health system in the US (Ascension Health, formerly Daughters of Charity National Health System, leads the way, followed by Catholic Health Initiatives).

The company carries out its mission of serving the poor and the old through more than 30 hospitals, some 30 nursing homes, 20 independent- and assisted-living facilities, and five behavioral health facilities. The company's services for the elderly include hospice care, adult day care, and home health services. Catholic Health East is governed by a board composed of nine sisters and nine secular health care professionals.

The merger that created the company is a product not only of the hospital industry trend toward gigantism, but of a problem unique to the Catholic health systems: keeping both the faith and the bottom line intact now that the orders can no longer depend on low-cost services from a dwindling number of members. Catholic Health East's high-minded mission to hold down costs in order to provide patient care has collided with drives to unionize its hospitals. It has also run into controversy when, in adding secular community hospitals to its system, it brings women's health services into conformity with the Church's position on reproductive issues.

HISTORY

It was three easy pieces that made up Catholic Health East in 1997. Allegany Health System, Eastern Mercy Health System, and Sisters of Providence Health System operated almost entirely in separate, but adjacent, geographic areas on the East Coast, overlapping only in Florida.

Catholic Health East's history goes as far back as 1831, when the Sisters of Mercy was founded in Dublin, Ireland, by Catherine McAuley, who established a poorhouse using her inheritance. Some of the sisters hopped the Pond in 1843, establishing the first Catholic hospital in the US, the Mercy Hospital of Pittsburgh, four years later. Over the years the Sisters of Mercy expanded throughout the US. By 1991 there were 25 Sisters of Mercy congregations; they united that year under the newly formed Institute of the Sisters of Mercy of the Americas.

The Sisters of Providence came from Kingston, Ontario, to found the first hospital in Holyoke, Massachusetts. Having established their own ministry, the sisters in Holyoke became a separate congregation in 1892. The congregation expanded slowly, moving into North Carolina in 1956, eventually forming the Sisters of Providence Health System.

A Polish nun, Mother Colette Hilbert, formed a new congregation in Pittsburgh in 1897 after the other members of her former parish were recalled to Poland. The new congregation entered health care in 1926, establishing a home for the elderly in New York City. In honor of Hilbert's favorite saint, the order became the Franciscan Sisters of St. Joseph in 1934.

The Franciscan Sisters of St. Joseph and the Sisters of Mercy united to form the ministry that became Pittsburgh Mercy Health System in 1983. In 1986 the congregations formed Eastern Mercy Health System as a holding company for the health concern. The consolidation served to cut costs, as well as to preserve the organization's religious mission.

The Franciscan Sisters of Allegany congregation got its start in 1859 teaching children in Buffalo, New York. In 1883 the order took over St. Elizabeth Hospital in Boston, expanding its health care services ministry throughout New York, New Jersey, and Florida by the 1930s. In 1986 the sisters organized the operations as Allegany Health System.

In the early 1990s Catholic health care systems underwent a round of consolidation. Allegany Health Systems and Eastern Mercy Health Systems combined services, aiming to lower costs through economies of scale.

The mid-1990s also brought consolidation, but this time operational costs weren't the major problem; Catholic health systems across the nation were facing a shortage of sisters. To have a sufficient number of sisters to keep the "Catholic" in Catholic health care, the three health systems merged in 1997, becoming Catholic Health East.

The company continued to acquire, including Mercy Health in Miami (1998) and a suffering, secular Cooper Health System in Camden, New Jersey (1999).

Chairman: Edward J. Connors
President and CEO: Daniel F. Russell
EVP and CFO: C. Kent Russell
EVP, Mid-Atalantic Division: Robert V. Stanek
EVP, Mission Integration: Sister Juliana Casey
EVP, Northeast Division: Sister Kathleen Popko
EVP, Southeast Division: Howard W. Watts
EVP, System Integration and Development:
Stanley T. Urban
VP, Communications: Sal Foti
VP, Human Resources: George Longshore
Assistant to the President/CEO: Eileen Forbes

LOCATIONS

HQ: 14 Campus Blvd., Ste. 300,
Newtown Square, PA 19073
Phone: 610-355-2000 **Fax:** 610-355-2050
Web site: http://www.chenet.org

1998 Facilities

	Hospitals	Nursing	Residential	Behavioral
Alabama	1	1	3	—
Connecticut	—	2	3	—
Florida	9	3	2	—
Georgia	2	—	—	—
Maine	1	—	—	1
Massachusetts	1	5	2	3
New Jersey	2	—	—	—
New York	7	13	4	1
North Carolina	—	1	4	—
Pennsylvania	8	2	2	—
Total	**31**	**27**	**20**	**5**

PRODUCTS/OPERATIONS

1998 Sales

	% of total
Medicare	42
Managed care	20
Medicaid	10
Commercial insurance	7
Physician practices	2
Other	20
Adjustments	(1)
Total	**100**

Divisions

Northeast
Catholic Health System (Buffalo, NY)
Mercy Community Health System of Maine (Portland)
Mercycare System of Care (Albany, NY)
Sisters of Providence Health System (Holyoke, MA)
St. James Mercy Health System (Hornell, NY)

Mid-Atlantic
Mercy Health System (Bala Cynwyd, PA)
Our Lady of Lourdes Health Care Services (Camden, NJ)
Pittsburgh Mercy Health System (Pittsburgh)

Southeast
BayCare Health Systems (Clearwater, FL)
Intracoastal Health System (West Palm Beach, FL)
Holy Cross Health Ministries (Fort Lauderdale, FL)
Mercy Hospital (Miami)
Mount Sinai-St. Francis Nursing and Rehabilitation
Center (Miami)
Saint Joseph's Health System (Atlanta)
St. Mary's Health Care Services (Athens, GA)

Long Term Care
Mercy Community Health (West Hartford, CT)
Mercy Medical (Daphne, AL)
Mercy Uihlein Health Corporation (Lake Placid, NY)
St. Joseph of the Pines (Southern Pines, NC)

Supporting Congregations
Franciscan Sisters of Allegany (St. Bonaventure, NY)
Franciscan Sisters of St. Joseph (Hamburg, NY)
Sisters of Mercy (Albany, NY)
Sisters of Mercy (Baltimore)
Sisters of Mercy (Buffalo, NY)
Sisters of Mercy (Hartsdale, NY)
Sisters of Mercy (Merion, PA)
Sisters of Mercy (Pittsburgh)
Sisters of Mercy (Portland, ME)
Sisters of Mercy (Rochester, NY)
Sisters of Mercy (West Hartford, CT)
Sisters of Providence (Holyoke, MA)

COMPETITORS

Ascension
Bon Secours Health
Columbia/HCA
Foundation Health
Systems

Franciscan Health
Partnership
Kaiser Foundation
Quorum Health

HISTORICAL FINANCIALS & EMPLOYEES

Not-for-profit FYE: December	Annual Growth	1989	1990	1991	1992	1993	1994	1995	1996	1997	1998
Sales ($ mil.)	18.6%	—	—	—	—	—	—	—	2,700	3,000	3,800
Employees	41.3%	—	—	—	—	—	—	—	—	31,838	45,000

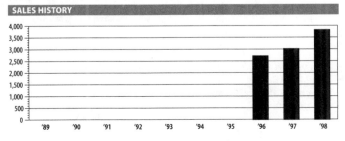

SALES HISTORY

CATHOLIC HEALTH EAST

CATHOLIC HEALTH INITIATIVES

OVERVIEW

"And he sent them out to preach the Kingdom of God and to heal the sick" (Luke 9:2). Denver-based Catholic Health Initiatives (CHI) is the #2 Roman Catholic health care system in the US by sales, behind Ascension Health (formed by the 1999 merger of Daughters of Charity National Health System and Sisters of St. Joseph Health System). Sponsored by 12 different congregations, the not-for-profit organization serves more than 70 communities in 22 states. It operates about 70 hospitals and more than 50 long-term-care facilities.

CHI has to deal with the conundrum facing many Catholic health systems: Their religious mission — to care for the "unserved and underserved" (and underinsured) members of its communities — is financially uncompetitive. CHI is able to offset the expense of its mission by also providing health care to the general public and by making business decisions more often associated with secular business (cutting staff, centralizing functions, and driving harder bargains with medical suppliers by consolidating purchasing operations with other Catholic health care institutions). Success has proved even more difficult to obtain because of its 70% interest in Centura Health, a money-losing joint venture with PorterCare Adventist Health System; Centura was formed to give the not-for-profits more clout against competitors in the Denver market.

As a reflection of its divine purpose in a mundane health care market, the company's 12-member governing board is comprised of six religious and six lay officers.

HISTORY

Faced with fewer women entering the religious orders that have traditionally provided health care, three major Roman Catholic health care organizations (Franciscan Health System, Sisters of Charity Health Care Systems, and Catholic Health Corporation) agreed to merge in 1995. Supported by a number of different religious congregations, the systems saw the merger as an opportunity to create a more efficient national health care system.

In 1860 the Sisters of St. Francis established a hospital in Philadelphia, laying the foundation for what would eventually become a larger health care organization. In 1981 Franciscan Health System was formally established to be a national holding company for Catholic hospitals and related organizations. By the mid-1990s the system consisted of 12 member and two affiliate hospitals and 11 long-term-care facilities located in the mid-Atlantic states and the Pacific Northwest.

The Sisters of Charity Health Care Systems was incorporated in 1979 as a multi-institutional health care network co-sponsored by the Sisters of Charity of Cincinnati and the Sisters of St. Francis Perpetual Adoration of Colorado Springs. By the mid-1990s the system included 20 hospitals in Colorado, Kentucky, Nebraska, New Mexico, and Ohio.

Catholic Health Corporation was formed in 1980 as a result of the collaboration of three congregations, one of the first such health care partnerships between religious communities within the Roman Catholic Church in the US.

By 1996 this coalition was operating 100 health care facilities in 12 states.

The development of modern managed care health care systems put pressure on the smaller Catholic hospital operations, so the three systems established CHI in 1996 as a national entity serving five geographic regions. Patricia Cahill, a lay health care veteran who previously served the Archdiocese of New York, was appointed president and CEO of CHI.

In its first major acquisition since its founding in 1996, CHI absorbed the 10-hospital Sisters of Charity of Nazareth Health Care System, based in Nazareth, Kentucky, in 1997. That year CHI and Alegent Health formed provider network Midwest Select with nearly 200 hospitals; the Omaha, Nebraska-based operation markets discounted rates to businesses.

In 1997 CHI and the Daughters of Charity formed for-profit joint venture Catholic Healthcare Audit Network to provide operational, financial, compliance, and information systems audits, as well as due diligence reviews. CHI also formed insurance joint venture NewCap Insurance Company with the Daughters of Charity and Catholic Health East; the company will allow CHI to operate independently of commercial insurers.

CHI made a secular tie-in with the University of Pennsylvania Health System in 1998, whereby five Catholic hospitals would offer care through the university's system. The next year CHI announced its first loss, due to lackluster performance in the Midwest.

Chairwoman: Maryanna Coyle
President and CEO: Patricia A. Cahill
SVP Operations: C. Kregg Hanson
SVP Finance and Treasury: Geraldine M. Hoyler
Chief Administrative Officer: Michael Fordyce
SVP Legal Services and General Counsel:
Paul G. Neumann
SVP Mission: Diana G. Bader
SVP Strategy and Business Development: John F. DiCola
**SVP Information Technology and Performance
Improvement:** Margaret M. McCarthy
SVP National Communications: Joyce M. Ross
SVP Operations: Dan Sinnott
COO: Kevin Lofton
Auditors: Ernst & Young LLP

LOCATIONS

HQ: 1999 Broadway, Ste. 2605, Denver, CO 80202
Phone: 303-298-9100   **Fax:** 303-298-9690

Catholic Health Initiatives operates health care facilities
in 22 states.

1998 Facilities

	No.
Colorado	17
Oregon	11
Minnesota	11
Nebraska	9
North Dakota	9
Iowa	8
Kentucky	7
Pennsylvania	7
South Dakota	6
Washington	6
New Mexico	5
Ohio	5
Arkansas	4
Delaware	3
Kansas	2
Missouri	2
Wisconsin	2
California	1
Idaho	1
Maryland	1
New Jersey	1
Tennessee	1
Total	**119**

PRODUCTS/OPERATIONS

Supporting Congregations
Benedictine Sisters of Mother of God Monastery
(Watertown, SD)
Congregation of the Dominican Sisters of St. Catherine
of Siena (Kenosha, WI)
Franciscan Sisters (Little Falls, MN)
Nuns of the Third Order of St. Dominic (Great Bend, KS)
Sisters of Charity of Cincinnati
Sisters of Charity of Nazareth (Bardstown, KY)
Sisters of the Holy Family of Nazareth, Immaculate
Conception Province, Philadelphia
Sisters of Mercy of the Americas, Regional Community
of Omaha (NE)
Sisters of the Presentation of the Blessed Virgin Mary
(Fargo, ND)
Sisters of St. Francis of Colorado Springs
Sisters of St. Francis of the Immaculate Heart of Mary
(Hankinson, ND)
Sisters of St. Francis of Philadelphia

COMPETITORS

BJC Health
Beverly Enterprises
Catholic Healthcare Partners
Columbia/HCA
HMA
Life Care Centers
Mayo Foundation
Tenet Healthcare

HISTORICAL FINANCIALS & EMPLOYEES

Not-for-profit FYE: June	Annual Growth	1990	1991	1992	1993	1994	1995	1996	1997	1998	1999
Sales ($ mil.)	31.1%	—	—	—	985	1,116	3,800	3,755	4,002	4,500	5,000
Employees	—	—	—	—	—	—	—	—	—	44,000	—

SALES HISTORY

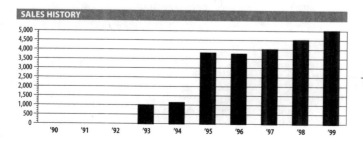

CATHOLIC HEALTH
INITIATIVES

CATHOLIC HEALTHCARE WEST

OVERVIEW

Faced with skyrocketing health care costs, diminishing health care spending, and a host of problems related to its growth, Catholic Healthcare West (CHW) is operating on a wing and a prayer. The organization is the Golden State's #2 hospital group (Tenet Healthcare is #1).

San Francisco-based CHW has a network of more than 45 hospitals in California, Arizona, and Nevada; seven physician groups; two retirement homes; and an alliance with Scripps-Health, a large San Diego HMO. With both clergy and laity on its governing board, CHW has grown by consolidating hospitals owned by

Roman Catholic women's religious orders, as well as non-Catholic institutions. These affiliations have raised some hackles because Catholic doctrine opposes abortion, most forms of birth control, and in vitro fertilization.

The rapid expansion that made CHW a name in the California health care industry also left it bloated. Rising health care costs and trouble with its physician management groups have cut deeply into earnings. Management casualties (including Richard Kramer, the architect of CHW's growth) occurred as CHW tried to regain profitability by reorganizing.

HISTORY

Catholic Healthcare West traces its history to 1857, when the Sisters of Mercy founded St. Mary's Hospital in San Francisco. The order expanded in the San Francisco area, and in 1986 the Sisters of Mercy (Burlingame community) merged their hospitals with those of the Sisters of Mercy (Auburn community, near Sacramento). The resulting organization had one retirement home and 10 hospitals stretching from the Bay Area to San Diego. Declining membership in Roman Catholic religious orders, combined with consolidation in the field, had led the orders to believe that their only route to survival lay in merging.

The new organization, confronted by rising medical costs, slow payers, and merger expenses, saw its combined net income drop from nearly $58 million in 1986 to $20 million in 1988. One of the hardest-hit CHW affiliates was Mercy Healthcare Sacramento, which lost $4.2 million between 1986 and 1987. In 1988 Mercy Healthcare restructured along regional lines.

The next year the Sisters of St. Dominic brought two hospitals into the alliance. In 1990 CHW started its Community Economic Assistance Program to provide grants to human services and health care agencies. In its first year the program donated $220,000 to 16 organizations.

CHW continued to add new facilities, including AMI Community Hospital in Santa Cruz, California, in 1990. Since CHW already owned the area's only other acute care hospital, Dominican Santa Cruz Hospital, CHW in 1993 was ordered not to acquire any more acute care hospitals in Santa Cruz County for 10 years without FTC approval.

As the trend to managed care became a stampede in the 1990s, CHW moved more into preventive care and began reining in costs

through productivity improvement plans. It continued to add hospitals, including tax-supported institutions trying to compete with such national for-profit systems as Columbia/HCA.

The network increased its medical clout in 1994 by allying with San Diego-based Scripps-Health, one of the state's largest HMO systems. In 1995 the Daughters of Charity Province of the West realigned its six-hospital operation with CHW. The next year the Dominican Sisters (California), the Dominican Sisters of St. Catherine of Siena (Wisconsin), and the Sisters of Charity of the Incarnate Word allied their California hospitals with CHW. New community hospitals included Bakersfield Memorial, Sierra Nevada Memorial (Grass Valley), Sequoia Hospital (Redwood City), and Woodland Healthcare.

In 1996 the tension between charity and cost-consciousness became apparent when union members staged a walkout to protest nonunion outsourcing of vocational nursing, housekeeping, and kitchen jobs. This dispute was settled, but CHW continued to be a target for union organizers, with a bitter battle against the Service Employees International Union starting in 1998.

CHW agreed in 1996 to merge with Samaritan Health Systems, Arizona's largest health care provider (a move that would have made CHW one of the US's top five providers), but the deal fell apart in 1997. That year the company acquired Emergency Physicians Medical Group, a provider of emergency room services. In 1998 CHW merged with UniHealth, a hospital group with eight facilities in Los Angeles and Orange counties. Mounting costs forced CHW to post a loss, and in 1999 it eliminated some managerial positions and reorganized to recover.

Interim President and CEO: Phyllis Hughes
EVP and COO: Larry Wilson
EVP: Bridget McCarthy
SVP and CFO: Jack Burgis
SVP and Chief Information Officer: David M. Bowen
SVP Financial Services: Vince Schmitz
SVP Legal Services and General Counsel:
Robert Johnson
SVP Mission Services: Bernita McTernan
SVP Operations: Anna Mullins
SVP Public Policy: J. Michael Gallagher
VP Administration and Director Care Management:
Denise Allen
VP Business Development: Raymond Nelson
VP Finance: Mary Connick
VP Home Health Services: Meg Piscitelli
VP Strategy and Marketing: David Berg
Auditors: Arthur Andersen LLP

LOCATIONS

HQ: 1700 Montgomery St., Ste. 300,
San Francisco, CA 94111
Phone: 415-438-5500   **Fax:** 415-438-5724
Web site: http://www.chw.edu

Catholic Healthcare West operates hospitals in Arizona, California, and Nevada.

1999 Facilities

	no.	% of total
California	46	96
Arizona	1	2
Nevada	1	2
Total	**48**	**100**

PRODUCTS/OPERATIONS

Sponsoring Organizations
Daughters of Charity, Province of the West
Dominican Sisters of San Rafael
Franciscan Sisters of the Sacred Heart of Frankfort, IL
Sisters of Charity of the Incarnate Word of Houston, TX
Sisters of Mercy, Auburn and Burlingame Regional
Communities
Sisters of St. Catherine of Siena of Kenosha, WI
Sisters of St. Dominic of Adrian, MI
Sisters of St. Francis of Penance and Christian Charity
of Redwood City

Physician Groups
Folsom Sierra Medical Group
Lassen Medical Group
MedClinic Medical Group
Personal Choice Medical Group
San Francisco Medical Group
Sierra Care/Sierra Nevada
Western Medical Associates

COMPETITORS

Adventist Health
Carondelet Health
Catholic Health Initiatives
Columbia/HCA
Foundation Health Systems
Kaiser Foundation
Los Angeles County Department of Health
Memorial Health Services
PacifiCare
Samaritan Health
Sutter Health
Tenet Healthcare
Triad Hospitals
UCSF Stanford Health
WellPoint Health Networks

HISTORICAL FINANCIALS & EMPLOYEES

Not-for-profit FYE: June	Annual Growth	1990	1991	1992	1993	1994	1995	1996	1997	1998	1999
Sales ($ mil.)	16.5%	1,113	1,253	1,464	1,633	2,584	2,674	2,688	2,749	3,301	4,400
Net income ($ mil.)	6.4%	47	59	87	45	91	99	160	36	73	82
Income as % of sales	—	4.2%	4.7%	5.9%	2.8%	3.5%	3.7%	6.0%	1.3%	2.2%	1.9%
Employees	9.5%	16,836	18,506	18,806	17,451	17,618	20,000	21,495	17,451	20,000	38,000

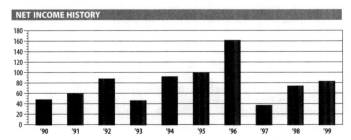

NET INCOME HISTORY

Catholic Healthcare West

CENEX HARVEST STATES

OVERVIEW

Why can't we all just get along? Cenex Harvest States Cooperatives thinks grain producers can. Based in Inver Grove Heights, Minnesota, the cooperative (formed by the 1998 merger of Harvest States Cooperatives and CENEX) is a network of farming supply, grain marketing, and food production operations. Owned by about 300,000 individual farmers and members of local co-ops in 17 central and western states, it is the #2 agricultural co-op in the nation.

Cenex Harvest States derives most of its sales from its grain trading activities (purchasing, selling, and arranging transfer), mainly in corn, wheat, and soybeans. The co-op also operates wheat mills, which grind semolina and durum wheat for use in pastas, and processes soybeans into animal feed and food such as margarine, mayonnaise, and salad dressings. In addition, the company supplies fuel, operates 160 farm supply stores called Agri-Service Centers, and provides insurance and financial services.

As is common in a business where cooperation is key, Cenex Harvest States conducts several of its operations via partnership. Through a joint venture with the Land O'Lakes dairy cooperative, the co-op supplies crop-protection products, plant food, and technology services. The company's soybeans are used in products manufactured by Ventura Foods, a joint venture with Japan's Mitsui & Co. Country Energy, a joint venture with Farmland Industries, markets and distributes petroleum products to the cooperative's customers.

HISTORY

To help farmers through the struggle of the Great Depression, the Farmers Union Terminal Association (a grain marketing association formed in 1926) created the Farmers Union Grain Terminal Association (GTA) in 1938. With loans from the Farmers Union Central Exchange (later known as CENEX) and the Farm Credit Association, the organization operated a grain elevator in St. Paul, Minnesota. By 1939 GTA had 250 grain-producing associations as members.

In the early 1940s GTA leased terminals in Minneapolis and Washington state and built others in Wisconsin and Montana. In 1942 it got into the milling business by creating Amber Milling when it took over a Minnesota flour mill. The next year GTA began managing farming insurance provider Terminal Agency and started the GTA News and Views radio station. (The station went off the air in 1968.) In 1958 the association bought 57 elevators and feed plants from the McCabe Company.

Adding to its value-added operations in 1960, GTA bought the Honeymead soybean plant. The next year the co-op acquired Minnesota Linseed Oil. GTA joined other co-ops in building a grain elevator that opened at the port of New Orleans in 1968. In a bid for more efficient waterway shipping, GTA teamed with other co-ops again in 1974 to purchase river transportation co-op Agri-Trans.

After a drought in 1977, the company focused more on its food processing operations. That year it acquired Jewett & Sherman (later Holsum Foods), which helped transform the company into a major provider of olives, jams, jellies, salad dressings, and syrups.

In 1983 GTA combined with North Pacific Grain Growers, a Pacific Northwest co-op incorporated in 1929, to form Harvest States Cooperatives. Harvest States grew by acquiring companies in the early and mid-1990s. It bought salad dressing makers Albert's Foods, Great American Foods, and Saffola Quality Foods; soup stock producer Private Brands; and margarine and dressings manufacturer and distributor Gregg Foods.

The company started a joint venture to operate the Ag States Agency agricultural insurance company in 1995. The next year the co-op's Holsum Foods division and Mitsui & Co.'s edible oils unit, Wilsey Foods, merged to form Ventura Foods, a distributor of margarines, oils, spreads, and other food products. Harvest States' sales were down in 1997 due to decreased grain volume, but higher grain prices kept the co-op's earnings unaffected.

Harvest States merged in 1998 with Minnesota-based CENEX, a 16-state agricultural supply co-op that had been founded in 1931 as Farmers Union Central Exchange. (Among CENEX's major operations was a farm inputs, services, marketing, and processing joint venture with dairy cooperative Land O'Lakes formed in 1987.) CENEX CEO Noel Estenson took the helm of the resulting co-op, Cenex Harvest States Cooperatives, which soon formed petroleum joint venture Country Energy with Farmland Industries.

In 1999 Cenex Harvest States and Farmland agreed to merge their entire operations. However, when put to a vote by Cenex members, the proposal failed by a narrow margin.

CEO: Noel K. Estenson
President and General Manager: John D. Johnson, age 50, $900,000 pay
SVP Corporate Administration and Public Affairs (HR): Allen J. Anderson
SVP Corporate Planning: Patrick Kluempke
President, Cenex/Land O'Lakes Agronomy Co.: Al Giese
EVP, Country Energy: Leon Westbrook
Group VP Finance: Thomas F. Baker, age 56, $391,200 pay
Group VP Wheat Milling: Gary A. Pistoria, age 57, $304,200 pay
Group VP, Oilseed Processing and Refining Division: James Tibbetts, age 49, $288,000 pay
Group VP Grain and Agri-Services: Michael H. Bergeland, age 53
Auditors: Deloitte & Touche LLP

LOCATIONS

HQ: Cenex Harvest States Cooperative, 5500 Cenex Dr., Inver Grove Heights, MN 55077
Phone: 651-451-5151   **Fax:** 651-451-5568
Web site: http://www.cenexharveststates.com

PRODUCTS/OPERATIONS

1999 Sales

	$ mil.	% of total
Grain merchandising		
Wheat	1,170	18
Soybeans	1,010	16
Corn	896	14
Other	233	4
Energy	1,346	21
Argonomy	594	9
Feed & farm supples	548	8
Grain processing	532	8
Other	106	2
Total	**6,435**	**100**

Selected Joint Ventures

Ag States Benefits, LLC (a joint venture between Ag States Agency and the Insurance Cooperative Association of Wisconsin)
Cenex/Land O'Lakes Agronomy Co. (a joint venture with Land O'Lakes to manufacture and distribute plant food, distribute crop-protection products, and provide technical services)
Imperial, Inc. (formulates crop-protection products)
RSA MicroTech (micronutrient sales organization)
Country Energy, LLC (a joint venture with Farmland Industries to market and distribute refined fuels, propane, and lubricants)
Harvest States-Farmland Specialty Feeds (a joint venture with Farmland Industries to produce and market pet food)
TEMCO (a joint venture with Continental Grain to produce and export feed grains for overseas customers)
Ventura Foods, LLC (a joint venture that combines the operations of Harvest States' Holsum Foods division with the Wilsey Foods subsidiary of Mitsui & Co. Ltd. of Tokyo to produce vegetable-oil based products for the food service industry and for retail sales)

Other Operations

Accounting and information management
Farm financing
Farm supplies
Feed products and ingredients
Futures and option services
Grain merchandising
Insurance
Soybean crushing and refining
Wheat milling

COMPETITORS

ADM	ContiGroup
Ag Processing	Dakota Growers
Agway	Farmland Industries
Andersons	GROWMARK
Barilla	General Mills
Bartlett & Company	Louis Dreyfus
Cargill	Riceland Foods
Central Soya	Scoular
ConAgra	

HISTORICAL FINANCIALS & EMPLOYEES

Cooperative FYE: August	Annual Growth	1990	1991	1992	1993	1994	1995	1996	1997	1998	1999
Sales ($ mil.)	9.7%	—	3,072	3,482	3,482	3,898	5,121	8,236	7,109	5,607	6,435
Net income ($ mil.)	20.0%	—	20	31	32	35	45	51	53	57	86
Income as % of sales	—	—	0.7%	0.9%	0.9%	0.9%	0.9%	0.6%	0.7%	1.0%	1.3%
Employees	2.0%	—	—	—	—	—	—	2,428	2,178	2,404	2,576

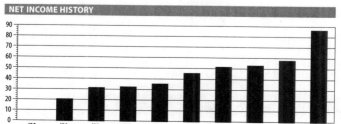

NET INCOME HISTORY

1999 FISCAL YEAR-END
Debt ratio: 28.0%
Return on equity: 13.8%
Cash ($ mil.): 76
Current ratio: 1.21
Long-term debt ($ mil.): 461

Cenex Harvest States

THE CITY UNIVERSITY OF NEW YORK

CUNY is the big "U" in the Big Apple. The sizable City University of New York (CUNY) has an undergraduate and graduate enrollment that exceeds 200,000; the university also teaches some 150,000 students in adult- and continuing-education programs. CUNY's 21 campuses span New York City's five boroughs. The university has 10 senior colleges, six community colleges, a doctoral-level graduate school, a four-year technical college, and law and medical schools. It offers more than 900 programs, from traditional liberal arts curricula to specialized, career-oriented courses. Notable CUNY alumni include novelist Oscar

Hijuelos, General Colin Powell, comedian Jerry Seinfeld, and 11 Nobel laureates.

CUNY is the nation's biggest urban university system and is making some big changes. The university has decided to limit remedial classes in order to improve the quality and reputation of CUNY, but critics say the plan will hurt the low income and minority students who make up much of the college's population. In an additional push for national prestige, the college announced plans to hire more than 300 full-time teaching and research staff. Adjunct professors presently account for more than half of the university's 12,700 faculty members.

The New York State Legislature first created a municipal college system in New York City in 1926, when it formed the New York City Board of Higher Education to manage the operations of the City College of New York and Hunter College. City College's roots were established in 1847 when New York passed a referendum creating the Free Academy, a tuition-free school. Hunter College was founded in 1870 as a women's college, and it was the first free teacher's college in the US.

In 1926 the Board of Higher Education authorized City College to create the Brooklyn Collegiate Center, a two-year men's college; Hunter established a similar two-year women's branch in Brooklyn. Four years later the schools merged to create the Brooklyn College of the City of New York, the city's first public, coed liberal arts college. Other schools added to the municipal system included Queens College (1937), New York City Community College (1947), Staten Island Community College (1955), Bronx Community College (1957), and Queensborough Community College (1958).

In 1961 the state legislature renamed New York City's municipal college system the City University of New York (CUNY) and ordered its board of trustees to expand the system's facilities and scope. One of the first actions was to create a graduate school.

CUNY chartered a number of new schools during the 1960s, including Richmond College (1965), York College (1966), Medgar Evers College (1968), and several community colleges. In 1964 CUNY took over management of the New York State Institute of Applied Arts and Sciences (renamed New York City Technical College) and established the John Jay College of Criminal Justice. CUNY

became affiliated with Mount Sinai School of Medicine in 1967.

Despite its expansion, the university system had difficulty keeping up with demand, particularly after 1970, when it established an open admissions policy for all New York City high school graduates. Richmond College and Staten Island Community College became the College of Staten Island in 1976. Both CUNY and the City of New York ran into serious financial problems in the mid-1970s, spelling the end of CUNY's tradition of free undergrad tuition for New York City residents. To increase state financial support for CUNY, the legislature signed the City University Governance and Financing Act in 1979.

In 1983 the City University School of Law held its first classes. The following year the state board of regents authorized CUNY to offer a doctor of medicine degree. CUNY's law school received accreditation from the American Bar Association in 1992.

After several years of budget cuts, and with enrollment increasing steadily, CUNY declared a state of financial emergency in 1995. The following year New York's Governor George Pataki proposed new budget cuts, and in 1997 he called for tuition hikes. In 1998 CUNY's board of trustees introduced a resolution calling for the elimination of remedial education programs at the senior college level; the move was challenged by professors and civil rights groups who sued. The state Board of Regents approved the plan in 1999, and most remedial classes will be phased out by 2001, barring further legal challenge. Some remedial programs will continue to be offered on a limited basis.

Chairman: Herman Badillo
Chancellor: Matthew Goldstein
Interim Deputy Chancellor: Patricia Hassett
Interim Vice Chancellor for Budget, Finance, and Information Services: Sherry Brabbam
Vice Chancellor for Academic Affairs: Lousie Mirrer
Vice Chancellor for Facilities Planning, Construction, and Management: Emma Espino Macari
Vice Chancellor for Faculty and Staff Relations: Brenda Richardson Malone
Vice Chancellor for University Relations: Jay Hershenson
University Dean for Academic Affairs: Russell K. Hotzler
University Dean for Adult and Continuing Education: John Mogulescu
Interim University Dean for Student Affairs and Enrollment Services: Lester Jacobs
University Dean for Instructional Technology and Information Services: Michael Ribaudo
University Dean for Research and Acting President of the Research Foundation: Alvin Halpern
Acting University Dean for The Executive Office: Robert Ptachik
Special Counsel to the Chancellor: Dave Fields
Acting General Counsel and Acting Vice Chancellor for Legal Affairs: Roy Moskowitz
Director of HR: James Demby
Auditors: KPMG LLP

LOCATIONS

HQ: 535 E. 80th St., New York, NY 10021
Phone: 212-794-5555   **Fax:** 212-794-5590
Web site: http://www.cuny.edu

PRODUCTS/OPERATIONS

1998 Funding Sources

	$ mil.	% of total
Government appropriations	750.0	42
Tuition & other revenue	579.0	32
Government grants & contracts	317.1	18
Other	138.1	8
Total	**1,784.2**	**100**

Senior Colleges
Bernard M. Baruch College
Brooklyn College
City College
City University Graduate Center
CUNY Law School at Queens College
College of Staten Island
Herbert H. Lehman College
Hunter College
John Jay College of Criminal Justice
Medgar Evers College
New York City Technical College
Queens College
York College

Community Colleges
Borough of Manhattan Community College
Bronx Community College
Eugenio Maria de Hostos Community College
Fiorello H. LaGuardia Community College
Kingsborough Community College
Queensborough Community College

HISTORICAL FINANCIALS & EMPLOYEES

School FYE: June	Annual Growth	1989	1990	1991	1992	1993	1994	1995	1996	1997	1998
Sales ($ mil.)	1.9%	—	—	—	—	—	1,655	1,722	1,756	1,729	1,784
Employees	2.8%	—	—	—	—	—	—	25,800	25,800	27,900	28,000

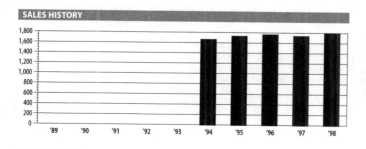

SALES HISTORY

CLARK USA, INC.

OVERVIEW

Like Clark Kent shedding his business suit and eyeglasses, Clark USA has sold its petroleum marketing operations to become a lean, mean, refining machine. The St. Louis-based company is among the top independent oil refiners in the US.

Clark USA refines crude oil to produce gasoline, diesel, aviation fuel, and petrochemicals. It owns two refineries in Illinois, one in Ohio, and one in Texas. Overall refining capacity is more than 540,000 barrels of crude oil per day.

To focus on higher-margin refinery operations, the company has sold its nearly 700 company-run gas station/convenience stores, located in Illinois, Indiana, Michigan, Missouri, Ohio, and Wisconsin, and its 200 franchised sites, as well as the Clark brand name. (Clark USA plans to change its name.)

An affiliate of the Blackstone Group investment firm owns 68% of Clark and controls 79% of the voting rights. Occidental Petroleum owns 31% and holds a 20% voting stake.

HISTORY

Emory Clark founded Clark Oil in 1932 with a single gas station in Milwaukee. According to company legend, Clark was given the station when the original owner could not pay for the construction work Clark carried out on the facility. Clark Oil expanded through the Midwest in the 1930s, branching into Minnesota in 1939 and Missouri in 1940.

The firm acquired a refinery in the Chicago suburb of Blue Island, Illinois, in 1945. Extensive remodeling to the facility, which supplied pipeline terminals throughout the Midwest, boosted capacity to 70,000 barrels per day. In 1967 Clark Oil acquired a 35,000-barrel-per-day refinery in Wood River, Illinois.

Increased refining capacity led to rapid growth in the late 1960s; the company opened as many as 100 stations per year in its expanded market areas (including Iowa, North Dakota, and Kansas). In 1968 Clark Oil acquired 122 Owens gas stations; by the following year, the company was operating gas stations in 13 states.

In 1981, trading firm Apex Oil of St. Louis paid $500 million for the company, whose name was now Clark Oil and Refining Corp. However, Apex ran into trouble in the 1980s when high debt and a prolonged industry slump forced it to cut down its refining operations, fire workers, and close gas stations. By the time Apex and Clark filed for bankruptcy protection in 1988, Clark's chain of gas station/convenience stores had been reduced from 1,800 to 950.

Toronto-based Horsham Corp. partnered with AOC Limited Partnership to form Clark USA in 1988 as a holding company to acquire the assets of Clark Oil and Refining Corp. In 1992 Horsham bought out AOC's 40% stake in Clark, and the company became a wholly owned subsidiary of the Canadian company. That year Clark veteran Paul Melnuk was appointed president and CEO of the company.

Clark Oil and Refining Corp. became Clark Refining & Marketing in 1993. It launched a new logo and upgraded its retail operations, adopting the On-The-Go moniker for its gas station/convenience stores.

Horsham backed down from a Clark public offering in 1994 because of weak market conditions. Instead, it sold a 40% stake the next year (later diluted to 31%) to Tiger Management to help Clark purchase a 200,000-barrel-per-day refinery in Port Arthur, Texas, from Chevron. Horsham also sold minority stakes in Clark to Gulf Resources and Occidental Petroleum. The Port Arthur refinery purchase more than doubled Clark's refining capacity but unanticipated expenses related to upgrading it dragged Clark into the red.

Clark acquired 10 suburban-Chicago gasoline and convenience stores in 1996. The next year Clark acquired 48 Hop-In gas stations/convenience stores in Michigan from Canada's Silicorp. To pay down debt, Clark sold its wholesale fuel distribution business to a unit of Petroleum Heat and Power.

Tiger Management sold its stake in 1997; Horsham, now named TrizecHahn, increased its 46% stake to 65%, but finally said goodbye to Clark, selling its stake to Blackstone Group for $135 million.

Atlantic Richfield Company veteran Bill Rusnack was named CEO of Clark USA in 1998. That year the company sold its minority interests in the Southcap, Chicap, Wolverine, and Westshore pipelines, and bought an Ohio refinery from British Petroleum (now BP Amoco).

In 1999 Clark sold its convenience store and gasoline operations, along with the Clark brand name, to an Apollo Management affiliate in a $230 million deal. Clark tried to buy a 295,000 barrel-per-day refinery in Wood River, Illinois, from Equilon Enterprises, but the companies were unable to reach agreement.

Chairman: Marshall A. Cohen, age 64
President, CEO, and COO: William C. Rusnack, age 54, $570,077 pay
EVP Corporate Development and CFO: Maura J. Clark, age 40, $408,847 pay
Secretary: John T. Bernbom, age 54
Controller and Treasurer: Dennis R. Eichholz, age 45
Director Corporate Human Resources: Juli Sherman
Auditors: Deloitte & Touche LLP

LOCATIONS

HQ: 8182 Maryland Ave., St. Louis, MO 63105
Phone: 314-854-9696   **Fax:** 314-854-1580
Web site: http://www.clarkusa.com

PRODUCTS/OPERATIONS

1998 Operating Income

	% of contribution
Refining	76
Retail marketing	24
Total	**100**

COMPETITORS

7-Eleven
ARCO
BP Amoco
Chevron
Coastal
Equilon Enterprises
Exxon Mobil
Marathon Ashland Petroleum
Motiva Enterprises
Phillips Petroleum
QuikTrip
Sunoco
TOTAL FINA
Tosco
Ultramar Diamond Shamrock

HISTORICAL FINANCIALS & EMPLOYEES

Private FYE: December	Annual Growth	1989	1990	1991	1992	1993	1994	1995	1996	1997	1998
Sales ($ mil.)	10.2%	—	—	—	2,254	2,265	2,441	4,487	5,073	4,337	4,043
Net income ($ mil.)	—	—	—	—	1	(7)	8	(37)	(56)	(108)	(30)
Income as % of sales	—	—	—	—	0.0%	—	0.3%	—	—	—	—
Employees	3.3%	—	—	—	—	5,700	5,700	7,000	7,400	7,500	6,700

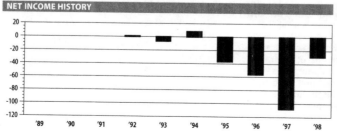

NET INCOME HISTORY

1998 FISCAL YEAR-END
Debt ratio: 99.8%
Return on equity: —
Cash ($ mil.): 154
Current ratio: 1.55
Long-term debt ($ mil.): 981

CLUBCORP, INC.

OVERVIEW

It's always tee time at ClubCorp. The Dallas-based holding company is the world's largest operator of private clubs and resorts. The company owns or manages a collection of about 230 resorts, country club and golf facilities, and city clubs spanning more than a dozen countries. Under the leadership of billionaire founder and chairman Robert Dedman (recognized by *Forbes* magazine as one of the 400 wealthiest Americans), Club-Corp's properties have grown to include Mission Hills Country Club near Palm Springs, California, and North Carolina's Pinehurst Resort and Country Club (site of the 1999 US Open). ClubCorp also owns 25% of ClubLink, a leading Canadian developer and operator of golf courses.

In addition to its portfolio of clubs and resorts, ClubCorp has a 30% stake in PGA European Tour Courses, an operator of tournament golf courses across Europe. As a complement to its club and resort operations, ClubCorp has developed ClubHaven.com, a virtual private club on the Internet.

Although it has secured its place as the largest operator of private clubs and resorts, ClubCorp continues executing its expansion strategy. It acquired more than 20 properties from The Meditrust Companies in 1999, and its joint venture with Jack Nicklaus has broken ground on a handful of the 36 new golf courses that it plans to develop. Dedman and his family own 75% of ClubCorp; investment firm The Cyress Group, 15%.

HISTORY

Though his childhood in Depression-era Arkansas was dominated by intense poverty, ClubCorp founder Robert Dedman knew how to dream big. At a young age he vowed to become "very, very rich," and the scrappy Dedman embarked on achieving that goal by earning a college scholarship, obtaining a law degree, and eventually launching a flourishing Dallas law practice.

Dedman's law firm was successful, but he realized that it wouldn't bring him the $50 million he wanted to earn by age 50. In 1957 he formed Country Clubs, Inc., to venture into the country club business. At that time, doctors and lawyers working on a volunteer basis were managing most clubs, and Dedman believed his new company could bring professional management expertise to these facilities. The company opened its first country club, Dallas' Brookhaven Country Club, in 1957. Through the subsequent purchase of 20 more clubs, Country Clubs refined its management style, implementing unique practices such as reducing playing time on the golf course and developing specialized training for club staff.

In 1965 the company expanded into city and athletic clubs and assumed the Club Corporation of America name. The expansion drive that followed fueled a 30% growth rate that the company maintained from the 1960s through the 1980s. In 1985 the company was restructured and divided into a handful of separate companies owned by the newly formed Club Corporation International holding company.

In 1988 the company bought an 80% interest in Franklin Federal Bancorp. The bank's club properties had initially caught his eye,

but Dedman also believed that the 400,000 members of his clubs might prove fertile ground for the marketing of financial services. In 1996, however, Club Corporation International sold the financial institution to Norwest. Although Franklin Federal was turning a profit, losses from investment in derivatives, coupled with the bank's inability to compete with larger competitors, prompted the company to sell the bank and refocus on its core club and resort business.

In 1996 Japanese cookie-maker Tohato sued the company, claiming that it intentionally mismanaged the Pinewild Country Club. Pinewild was owned by Tohato, managed by Club Corporation International, and located next door to Club Corporation International's Pinehurst Resort and Country Club. Tohato alleged that the company's mismanagement was part of a scheme to eventually buy Pinewild at a reduced price. The nasty legal wrangling that ensued cast a pall over the impending 1999 US Open at Pinehurst.

In 1998 the company was reincorporated as ClubCorp International, Inc. It expanded its international base that year by purchasing nearly 30% of PGA European Tour Courses. The company also entered into a joint venture with Jack Nicklaus to develop three dozen new golf courses.

The company shortened its moniker to ClubCorp in 1999. Among the additions ClubCorp made to its holdings that year were 22 properties acquired from The Meditrust Companies. The company also increased its ownership of Canadian club developer ClubLink to 25%.

Chairman: Robert H. Dedman Sr., age 72, $342,689 pay
President and CEO: Robert H. Dedman Jr., age 41, $850,165 pay
COO: James M. Hinckley, age 42, $579,440 pay
EVP and CFO: James P. McCoy Jr., age 52
EVP (HR): Albert Chew III, age 44
EVP: Mark W. Dietz, age 44
EVP: James E. Maser, age 44
EVP: Gerry Smith
EVP, Secretary, and Chief Legal Officer: Terry A. Taylor, age 42
SVP and Controller: Pete Little
COO, International: Robert H. Johnson, age 51
VP: Darlene Jo Harris
Treasurer: John Massey
Auditors: KPMG LLP

LOCATIONS

HQ: 3030 LBJ Fwy., Ste. 700, Dallas, TX 75234
Phone: 972-243-6191   **Fax:** 972-888-7700
Web site: http://www.clubcorp.com

PRODUCTS/OPERATIONS

1998 Sales

	$ mil.	% of total
Country club & golf facilities	375.1	44
City clubs	255.5	30
Resorts	172.6	20
Other	29.7	4
Corporate services & eliminations	18.4	2
Total	**851.3**	**100**

Selected Clubs

Aspen Glen Club (CO)
Barton Creek Country Club (TX)
Cascades Golf Club (VA)
The Currituck Club (NC)
Diamante Country Club (AK)
Firestone Country Club (OH)
Glen Oaks Country Club (IA)
Granite Bay Golf Club (CA)
Kingwood Country Club (TX)
Pinehurst (NC)
Quail Hollow Country Club (OH)
Southern Trace (LA)
Stonebridge Country Club (TX)

COMPETITORS

American Golf
Club Med
Divot Golf
Golf Trust of America
Hilton
Hyatt
National Golf Properties
NorthStar Capital Investment
ResortQuest International
Sandals Resorts
Silverleaf Resorts
Starwood Hotels & Resorts Worldwide

HISTORICAL FINANCIALS & EMPLOYEES

Private FYE: December	Annual Growth	1989	1990	1991	1992	1993	1994	1995	1996	1997	1998
Sales ($ mil.)	1.8%	—	—	751	884	1,200	773	761	784	840	851
Net income ($ mil.)	12.5%	—	—	—	19	41	15	(11)	29	122	38
Income as % of sales	—	—	—	—	2.1%	3.4%	1.9%	—	3.7%	14.5%	4.5%
Employees	9.8%	—	—	—	12,000	13,000	19,200	19,800	19,000	20,000	21,000

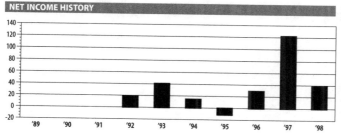

NET INCOME HISTORY

1998 FISCAL YEAR-END

Debt ratio: 38.5%
Return on equity: 8.8%
Cash ($ mil.): 72
Current ratio: 1.11
Long-term debt ($ mil.): 256

COLUMBIA UNIVERSITY

OVERVIEW

Columbia University in the City of New York is one of the pearls in the educational ocean. Its origins predate the American Revolution, qualifying the private university as the oldest institution of higher learning in New York and the fifth oldest in the country. With more than 22,000 students, the university's main campus is spread across 32 acres in the Morningside Heights section of Manhattan.

While best known for its graduate and professional schools in areas such as journalism, law, and medicine, Columbia also has gained renown for its Columbia College, the Ivy League's smallest undergraduate school. The university grants undergraduate degrees in 65 subjects, while graduate students may earn Master of Arts and professional degrees in 183 subjects and Master of Philosophy and Doctor

of Philosophy degrees in 91 subjects. Among Columbia's 7,200 faculty members (about 38% are full-time) are 58 Nobel laureates. With a strong reputation for research, the university ranks #1 in collecting funds through patents and royalties.

Columbia also has forged affiliations with nearby institutions such as Barnard College, Teachers College, and Union Theological Seminary. Columbia-Presbyterian Medical Center, the result of a more than 70-year partnership between Columbia and The Presbyterian Hospital, helped pioneer the concept of academic medical centers.

After weathering some lean years during the 1970s and 1980s, Columbia University is experiencing a rebirth that has boosted both its academic and fiscal reputations.

HISTORY

Created by royal charter of King George II of England, the university was founded in 1754 as King's College. Its first class of eight students met in a schoolhouse adjacent to Trinity Church (located in what is now Manhattan). The university's earliest students included Alexander Hamilton and John Jay. In 1784 King's College was renamed Columbia College, a name that symbolized the patriotic mind-set of the age.

The college moved to 49th Street and Madison Avenue in 1849. The School of Law was created in 1858, followed by the School of Engineering and Applied Science's predecessor in 1864. The Graduate School of Arts and Sciences was established in 1880, and Columbia became affiliated with Barnard College in 1889.

Columbia College became Columbia University in 1896. The following year it moved to its present location on Manhattan's Upper West Side, on the former site of the Bloomingdale Insane Asylum. (Columbia retained its original site, on which Rockefeller Center was built, until selling it in 1985.)

Columbia continued to expand during the early 20th century. In 1912 it added the School of Journalism with funding from publishing magnate Joseph Pulitzer. Other additions included the School of Business (1916), the School of Public Health (1921), and the School of International and Public Affairs (1946).

Dwight Eisenhower became president of Columbia in 1948, retaining the position until becoming president of the US in 1953. During the late 1960s Columbia gained a reputation

for student political action, and in 1968 students closed down the university for several days in protest of the Vietnam War.

Facing financial woes, an escalating New York City crime rate, and contention among its faculty, Columbia struggled to maintain its reputation during the 1970s and 1980s. With this challenge as a backdrop, the university continued to evolve, welcoming its first coeducational freshman class in 1983.

By 1991, still facing economic pressures and reductions in government research spending, Columbia was forced to cut costs, eliminating its linguistics and geography departments. George Rupp became Columbia's president in 1993. In 1996 Columbia took over operation of the controversial Biosphere 2 laboratory in Arizona (the university had been associated with the lab since 1994, when it formed a consortium with other universities to overhaul the ailing science experiment).

By the late 1990s Columbia had begun to recover from its financial and academic decline. Under the leadership of President Rupp, the university improved its fund-raising efforts and became more selective in student admissions. In 1999 Microsoft founder Bill Gates donated $150 million to Columbia's School of Public Health for research into the prevention of death and disability from childbirth in developing countries. That same year, Columbia created Morningside Ventures, a for-profit company focused on producing educational materials.

Chairman: Stephen Friedman
President: George Rupp
Provost and Dean Faculties: Jonathan R. Cole
EVP Administration: Emily Lloyd
EVP Finance: John Masten
VP Student Services: Mark Burstein
VP and Dean Arts and Sciences: David Cohen
VP Human Resources: Colleen M. Crooker
VP Investments: Bruce M. Dresner
VP Development and Alumni Relations:
Richard K. Naum
VP Health Sciences and Dean Medicine: Herbert Pardes
VP University Budget and Financial Planning:
Jon Rosenhein
VP Public Affairs: Alan J. Stone
Deputy VP Information Services: Robert W. Juckiewicz
Secretary: R. Keith Walton
Treasurer and Controller: Patricia L. Francy
Ombuds Officer: Marsha L. Wagner
General Counsel: Elizabeth J. Keefer
Auditors: Deloitte & Touche LLP

LOCATIONS

HQ: 2690 Broadway, New York, NY 10027
Phone: 212-854-1754 **Fax:** 212-749-0397
Web site: http://www.columbia.edu

PRODUCTS/OPERATIONS

Selected Undergraduate Schools
Columbia College
School of Engineering and Applied Science
School of General Studies

Selected Graduate Schools
College of Physicians and Surgeons
Graduate School of Arts and Sciences
School of Architecture, Planning & Preservation
School of Business
School of Dental & Oral Surgery
School of Engineering & Applied Science
School of International and Public Affairs
School of Journalism
School of Law
School of Nursing
School of Public Health
School of Social Work
School of the Arts

Selected Continuing Education and Special Programs
ACCESS (Customized Corporate Training Programs)
Advanced Information Technology Management
Program (AITM)
American Language Program
Auditing Program
Business Careers Initiative
Computer Technology & Applications Program
Creative Writing Center
Foreign Language: Credit, Noncredit,
Conversation Groups
High School Programs
Lifelong Learners Program
Postbaccalaureate Classics Program
Postbaccalaureate Psychology Program
Postbaccalaureate TESOL Program (teaching English as
a second language)
Postgraduate Nondegree Program
Second-Majors Program
Special Students Program
Study-Away programs (Beijing; Berlin; Paris; and
Scandiano, Italy)
Summer Session
Visiting Students Program

HISTORICAL FINANCIALS & EMPLOYEES

School FYE: June	Annual Growth	1989	1990	1991	1992	1993	1994	1995	1996	1997	1998
Sales ($ mil.)	7.2%	775	841	898	953	1,032	1,103	1,160	1,234	1,339	1,448
Employees	1.1%	—	—	—	—	—	14,639	16,565	16,300	17,930	15,300

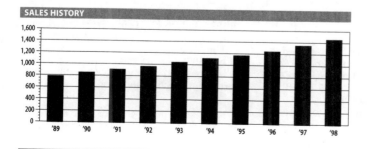

SALES HISTORY

COMARK, INC.

OVERVIEW

You can't always get what you want. But when it comes to computers, Comark promises that you can get what you need. The Bloomingdale, Illinois-based company is the nation's top privately held supplier of information technology (IT) goods and services. Comark resells some 10,000 products, including computers, software, peripherals, communications devices, networking gear, and backup storage devices. Among the company's more than 500 suppliers are top hardware manufacturers — Hewlett-Packard, IBM, and Compaq brands are its biggest sellers — and software leaders such as Lotus, Microsoft, and Novell. Comark also makes its own line of PCs, Plus Data. The company is owned by co-founders and co-CEOs Philip Corcoran and Chuck Wolande.

Known for keeping close ties to its customers, Comark supports its sales with system design and maintenance, networking, help desk, staffing, and other services. It caters to the largest corporations in the US, but also counts on government agencies, educational institutions, value-added resellers and other organizations to make up a significant portion of sales.

Company spokesman Mike Singletary, a former Chicago Bear and a Pro Football Hall of Fame inductee, is leading Comark's rush toward the top spot in its industry. As the IT marketplace continues to grow more sophisticated, Comark has stayed in the game by adding to its products and services, as well as by expanding its marketing internationally; its goal is to generate a third of its sales overseas.

Comark is also expanding through alliances with leading IT companies; Comark engineers are certified by leading vendors such as IBM, Compaq, and HP. Such moves have kept its annual growth rate since 1991 at nearly 50%.

HISTORY

Comark, originally called Communications Marketing, was founded in 1977 by former St. Mary's College (Minnesota) fraternity brothers Phil Corcoran and Chuck Wolande. After college Corcoran took a job at Memorex, where he was in charge of finding small companies to distribute Memorex products. Wolande, unable to get into medical school, went to work for Jefferson Electric as a gopher. Corcoran came up with a plan to form a distribution company of his own, and talked Wolande into sharing the project. The pair quit their jobs and began operations from a spare room in a neighbor's warehouse that stored corrugated cardboard boxes.

Starting with a single supplier (Memorex) and working 12-hour days (each had a goal of 30 calls a day), Corcoran and Wolande were able to sell about $100,000 worth of products by the end of their first year. Soon they began adding employees, and by 1979 sales had topped $1 million.

The company's turning point came in 1981, when IBM debuted the PC. Comark quickly added computers to its product list, getting in on the ground floor of an industry that was on the verge of explosive growth. The following year Hewlett-Packard became a Comark supplier for printers and printing supplies. Epson joined the Comark lineup in 1985, and IBM products were added in 1989.

Comark's business continued to expand with the information technology tidal wave.

The company added Compaq and Toshiba as suppliers in 1990. Comark formed its Corporate Services Division in 1992 and enjoyed sales that year of more than $170 million.

In 1992 Compaq chose several companies, including Comark affiliate USA FLEX, to sell PCs by mail. Comark opened its first satellite office, in Minneapolis, in 1994. The next year it added an office in Miami.

In 1996 the company sold USA FLEX to computer catalog retailer Micro Warehouse for $100 million. That year Comark opened a 175,000-sq.-ft. distribution center in Hanover Park, Illinois (near Chicago), where it stocks more than $100 million in products.

Comark celebrated its twentieth anniversary in 1997 by topping $1 billion in sales while keeping its 20-year profitability streak intact. That year the company was chosen to participate in IBM's authorized assembler program. Also in 1997 Comark added offices in Georgia, New Jersey (serving the New York City area), Oregon, Tennessee, and Virginia.

The company opened its Milwaukee office in 1998. Industry trade magazine *Computer Reseller News* ranked Comark #1 among general business value-added resellers that year. Also in 1998 Comark was one of three firms chosen by the US Army for a blanket purchase agreement for computer products.

Chairman and Co-CEO: Phil Corcoran
President and Co-CEO: Chuck Wolande
CFO: Dave Keilman
VP Corporate Sales: Greg Stinsa
VP Corporate Service: Scott Daley
VP Service Sales: Karen Chiappetta
Manager Recruiting: Eileen Sirrell

LOCATIONS

HQ: 444 Scott Dr., Bloomingdale, IL 60108
Phone: 630-924-6670   **Fax:** 630-924-6684
Web site: http://www.comark.com

PRODUCTS/OPERATIONS

Products
CD-ROMs
CPU upgrades
Desktop computers
Fax machines
Monitors
Networking products
Operating systems
Portable computers
Printer supplies
Printers and plotters
Scanners
Servers
Software
Surge protection
Tape backup and other
    memory
Video boards
Workstations

Services
Asset management
Custom system
    configuration

Hardware maintenance
Help desks
Internet and e-commerce
Network design
NT migration
Year 2000 compliance

Selected Suppliers
3Com
Adaptec
Canon
Cisco Systems
Compaq
Hewlett-Packard
IBM
Microsoft
NEC
Nikon
Novell
Samsung
Sony
Toshiba
Xerox

Divisions
Comark Capital (leasing services for companies)
Comark Corporate Sales
Comark Federal Systems
Comark Government and Education Sales
Comark Technology Services (system support)

COMPETITORS

CDW Computer Centers
CHS Electronics
CompUSA
CompuCom
ENTEX
En Pointe
InaCom

Ingram Micro
Merisel
Micro Electronics
Micro Warehouse
MicroAge
Systemax
Tech Data

HISTORICAL FINANCIALS & EMPLOYEES

Private FYE: December	Annual Growth	1989	1990	1991	1992	1993	1994	1995	1996	1997	1998
Sales ($ mil.)	37.8%	—	—	—	—	297	411	563	782	1,100	1,478
Employees	29.3%	—	—	—	—	—	472	605	670	900	1,320

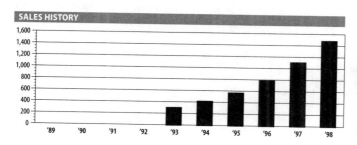

SALES HISTORY

CONSUMERS UNION

OVERVIEW

Consumers Union of United States (CU) can make or break new products almost as fast as the average 8-year-old. The Yonkers, New York-based not-for-profit organization publishes the monthly *Consumer Reports* magazine (4.6 million subscribers) and a subscriber Web site (330,000 paid subscribers), which rates products ranging from candy bars to cars. CU also reaches consumers through its newsletters, books and videos, car and insurance pricing services, TV and radio programs, and its children's magazine, *Zillions*. The organization testifies before legislative and regulatory entities and files lawsuits on behalf of consumers. CU is governed by an 18-member board, and the organization's Consumer Policy Institute conducts research and education projects on issues such as air pollution, biotechnology, food safety, and right-to-know laws.

CU derives revenue from sales of its publications, from car and insurance pricing services, and from contributions, grants, and fees. To preserve its independence, CU accepts no advertising and does not permit its ratings or comments to be used commercially. It maintains 50 laboratories within its National Testing and Research Center in Yonkers. In addition to conducting its own product testing, CU gathers product information by surveying the readers of its publications.

A major legal battle is shaping up between CU and several SUV makers who claim that *Consumer Reports* defamed them with negative vehicle reviews. Some analysts say that the case will harm CU's credibility regardless of the outcome and may inhibit the willingness of the media to print negative product reviews.

HISTORY

In 1926 engineer Frederick Schlink organized a "consumer club" (in White Plains, New York), which distributed lists of recommended and non-recommended products. The lists led to the founding of Consumers' Research and a magazine devoted to testing products.

Schlink moved the group to Washington, New Jersey, in 1933. In 1935 three employees formed a union. Schlink fired them. Faced with another strike that year, Schlink accused the strikers of being "Red" and responded with strikebreakers and armed detectives. The next year the strikers set up their own organization, the Consumers Union of United States (CU).

CU's first magazine, *Consumers Union Reports*, came out three months later and rated products that the fledgling organization could afford to test, such as soap and breakfast cereals. Subsequent issues focused on food and drug regulation and working conditions for women in textile mills.

The organization drew the wrath of both *Reader's Digest* and *Good Housekeeping* (which accused it in 1939 of prolonging the Depression). The next year the House Un-American Activities Committee put CU on its list of suspect organizations. CU cut staff and dropped "Union" from its magazine title, but circulation remained low until after WWII.

By 1950, however, Americans began consuming again, helping to boost circulation to almost 400,000. During the 1950s CU published a series of reports on the health hazards of smoking.

In 1960 CU helped found the International Organization of Consumers Unions (now Consumers International) to foster the consumer movement worldwide. Rhoda Karpatkin was hired as publisher in 1974. During the 1970s CU established consumer advocacy offices in California, Texas, and Washington, DC.

Recession and an increase in not-for-profit mailing rates caused the organization to lose money in the early 1980s. CU looked to its readers, who donated more than $3 million. The organization was hit by a 13-week strike in 1984 by union members calling for more say in management.

In 1996 CU slapped "not acceptable" ratings on the Isuzu Trooper and the Acura SLX. The next year the National Highway Traffic Safety Administration declared that CU's testing procedure of the Trooper was flawed, but CU stood by its tests of the vehicle.

CU hit another bump in 1998 when it was compelled to retract a story on the nutritional value of Iams and Eukanuba pet food. Admitting its test results were incorrect, CU's retraction of the story was something of a rarity — its last retraction had occurred almost 20 years earlier when the organization retracted a story on condoms.

In 1999 the company published its first review of e-commerce sites. CU also defended itself in court against allegations by Isuzu and Suzuki that their companies were defamed through negative reviews by *Consumer Reports*. The cases are pending.

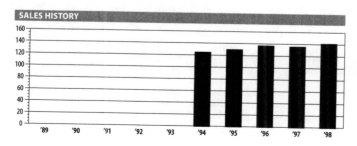

CONTIGROUP COMPANIES, INC.

OVERVIEW

Talk about going against the grain. New York City-based ContiGroup Companies (CGC, formerly Continental Grain) has gotten out of the business in which it literally made its name. CGC was once the US's #2 grain exporter, but grain accounted for only one-fourth of the company's income before its commodities marketing business was bought in 1999 by Cargill.

CGC's largest business is ContiAgriIndustries, the world's #1 cattle feeder and one of the top pork and poultry producers in the US.

It also has interests in flour milling and animal feed and nutrition. CGC owns about 78% of publicly traded ContiFinancial, a consumer and commercial finance company specializing in home equity loans. CGC's investment arm, ContiInvestments, has interests in real estate, shipping, fund management, and natural resources.

Chairman emeritus Michel Fribourg (the great-great-grandson of ContiGroup's founder) and his family own the company.

HISTORY

Simon Fribourg founded a commodity trading business in Belgium in 1813. It operated domestically until 1848, when a drought in Belgium caused it to buy large stocks in Russian wheat.

As the Industrial Revolution swept across Europe and populations shifted to cities, people consumed more traded grain. In the midst of such rapid changes, the company prospered.

After WWI, Russia, which had been Europe's primary grain supplier, ceased to be a major player in the trading game, and Western countries picked up the slack. Sensing the shift, Jules and Rene Fribourg reorganized the business as Continental Grain and opened its first US office in Chicago in 1921.

Throughout the Depression the company bought US grain elevators wherever it could find them, often at low prices. Through its purchases, Continental Grain built a North American grain network that included major locations like Kansas City, Missouri; Nashville, Tennessee; and Toledo, Ohio.

In Europe, meanwhile, the Fribourgs were forced to endure constant political and economic upheaval, often profiting from it (they supplied food to Republican forces during the Spanish Civil War). When Nazis invaded Belgium in 1940, the Fribourgs were forced to flee, but they reorganized the business in New York City after the war.

Following the war, Continental Grain pioneered US grain trade with the Soviets. The company went on a buying spree in the 1960s and 1970s, acquiring Allied Mills (feed milling, 1965) and absorbing many agricultural and transport businesses, including Texas feedlots, a bakery, and the Quaker Oats agricultural products unit.

During the 1980s Continental Grain sold its baking units (Oroweat and Arnold) and its commodities brokerage house and, amid an agricultural bust, formed ContiFinancial and other financial units.

Michel Fribourg stepped down as CEO in 1988 and was succeeded by Donald Staheli, the first nonfamily-member CEO. Soon after, Continental Grain realigned its international grain and oilseeds operations into the World Grain and Oilseeds Processing Group under the leadership of Michel's son Paul.

The company entered a grain-handling and selling joint venture with Scoular in 1991. Three years later Staheli added the title of chairman, and Paul became president. Continental Grain sold a stake in ContiFinancial (its most profitable business, including home equity loans and investment banking) to the public in 1996. Also in 1996 the firm formed ContiInvestments, an investment arm geared toward the parent company's areas of expertise.

That year Continental Grain and an overseas affiliate (Arab Finagrain) agreed to pay the US government $35 million, which included a $10 million fine against Arab Finagrain, to settle a fraud case involving commodity sales to Iraq.

Paul succeeded Staheli as CEO in 1997. The company bought Campbell Soup's poultry processing units that year, and in 1998 it bought a 51% stake in pork producer/processor Premium Standard Farms, adding those operations (Texas and Missouri) to its own Missouri swine production business. Meanwhile, ContiFinancial diversified into retail home mortgage and home equity lending, among other areas.

Continental Grain sold its commodities marketing business in July 1999 to #1 grain exporter Cargill, though antitrust restrictions excluded seven facilities from the deal. With its grain operations gone, in 1999 the company renamed itself ContiGroup Companies and began to focus on its ContiAgriIndustries, ContiFinancial, and ContiInvestments units. In October 1999 the firm placed its US Animal Nutrition Division (Wayne Foods) up for sale to better focus on its main industrial units.

Chairman Emeritus: Michel Fribourg, age 82
Chairman and CEO: Paul J. Fribourg
CFO: Michael J. Zimmerman
EVP Human Resources and Information Technology:
Teresa McCaslin
CEO, ContiIndustries: Vart Adjemian
VP and General Counsel: Lawrence G. Weppler

LOCATIONS

HQ: 277 Park Ave., New York, NY 10172
Phone: 212-207-5100   **Fax:** 212-207-2910
Web site: http://www.contigroup.com

PRODUCTS/OPERATIONS

Major Business Units

ContiAgriIndustries
Animal feed and nutrition
Aquaculture
Beef production
Cattle feeding
Flour milling
Pork processing and production
Poultry processing and production

ContiFinancial Corporation (78%)
Auto financing
Commercial mortgages
Home equity loans

ContiInvestments, LLC
Fund management
Natural resources
Real estate
Shipping

COMPETITORS

ADM
Ag Processing
Agribrands International, Inc.
Cactus Feeders
Cargill
Cenex Harvest States
ConAgra
Farmland Industries
Gold Kist
Household International
IBP
IMC Mortgage
Pilgrim's Pride
Purina Mills
Smithfield Foods
The Associates
Tyson Foods

HISTORICAL FINANCIALS & EMPLOYEES

Private FYE: March	Annual Growth	1990	1991	1992	1993	1994	1995	1996	1997	1998	1999
Estimated sales ($ mil.)	(3.8%)	14,850	15,000	15,000	15,000	15,000	14,000	15,000	16,000	15,000	10,500
Employees	(0.4%)	14,500	14,500	14,750	14,700	15,500	16,000	16,000	16,800	17,500	14,000

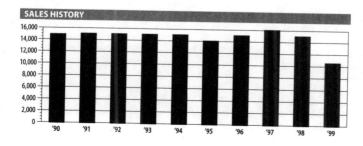

SALES HISTORY

COX ENTERPRISES, INC.

OVERVIEW

Like an octopus at an all-you-can-eat buffet, Cox Enterprises has a lot on its plate. The Atlanta-based company is one of the US's largest media conglomerates, with interests in newspapers, radio, and broadcast and cable TV. Cox publishes 16 daily newspapers (including its flagship, *The Atlanta Journal-Constitution*) and 15 weeklies and shoppers. It owns 11 broadcast TV stations and owns or operates nearly 60 radio stations through its 70% stake in Cox Radio. In addition, the company owns about 80% of Cox Communications, one of the largest cable systems in the US with nearly 5 million subscribers, and provides telecommunications services (local and long-distance telephone, data transport network) to a variety of businesses. Cox's Manheim Auctions (more

than 80 traditional and Internet auctions) is the nation's largest used-car auction company.

With the growth of wireless communications and the Internet, Cox is sticking with its strategy of finding opportunity in emerging technologies. Its Cox Media Interactive operates a network of 28 online city sites, including Access Atlanta and InsideNewOrleans.com. The company is also a leader in digital television (its WSB-TV station in Atlanta was one of the first in the nation to offer digital programming) and provides Internet access to nearly 70,000 customers.

The company is owned by Barbara Cox Anthony (mother of CEO James Kennedy) and Anne Cox Chambers, daughters of founder James Cox.

HISTORY

James Middleton Cox dropped out of school in 1886 at age 16 and worked as a teacher, reporter, and congressional secretary before buying the *Dayton Daily News* in 1898. He acquired the nearby *Springfield Press-Republican* in 1905 and soon took up politics. Cox served two terms in the US Congress (1909-1913) and three terms as Ohio governor (1913-1915; 1917-1921). In 1920 he was the Democratic candidate for president, with running mate Franklin D. Roosevelt, but he lost to rival Ohio publisher Warren Harding. In 1923 Cox bought the *Miami Daily News* and founded WHIO, Dayton, Ohio's first radio station. He bought Atlanta's WSB ("Welcome South, Brother"), the South's first radio station, in 1939, and in 1948 he added WSB-FM and WSB-TV, the South's first FM and TV stations. The next year Cox started WHIO-FM and WHIO-TV, Dayton's first FM and TV stations. *The Atlanta Constitution* joined his collection in 1950. When Cox died in 1957, his company owned seven newspapers, three TV stations, and several radio stations.

Cox Enterprises expanded its broadcast interests in the late 1950s and early 1960s. It was one of the first major broadcasting companies to enter cable TV when it purchased a system in Lewistown, Pennsylvania (1962). The Cox family's broadcast properties were placed in publicly held Cox Broadcasting in 1964. Two years later, its newspapers were placed into privately held Cox Enterprises, and the cable holdings became publicly held Cox Cable Communications. The broadcasting arm diversified, buying Manheim Services

(auto auctions, 1968) and Kansas City Automobile Auction (1969).

Cox Broadcasting bought TeleRep, a TV advertising sales firm, in 1972. Cox Cable was in nine states and had 500,000 subscribers by 1977, when it rejoined Cox Broadcasting. The broadcasting company changed its name to Cox Communications in 1982; the Cox family took the company private again in 1985 and combined it with Cox Enterprises. James Kennedy, the founder's grandson, became chairman in 1987.

In 1991 Cox merged its Manheim unit with the auto auction business of Ford Motor Credit and GE Capital. It formed Sprint Spectrum LP, a partnership with long-distance operator Sprint and cable leviathans TCI (now part of AT&T) and Comcast in 1994 to bundle telephone service, cable TV, and other communication services. (Sprint bought Cox out in 1999.) The next year Cox bought Times Mirror's cable TV operations for $2.3 billion and folded those systems and its own into a new, publicly traded company, Cox Communications Inc. In 1996 the company formed Cox Interactive Media to expand its presence on the Internet.

Cox acquired two Seattle TV stations in 1997. In 1998 Manheim began an auction Web site for automobile wholesalers and Cox Interactive Media introduced interactive classified advertising Web sites.

The company entered into a joint venture with MP3.com in 1999 to develop and run a number of music-related Web sites.

Chairman and CEO: James C. Kennedy, age 51
President and COO: David E. Easterly, age 56
EVP and CFO: Robert C. O'Leary
SVP Administration: Timothy W. Hughes
President and CEO, Manheim Auctions:
Dennis G. Berry
President and CEO, Cox Communications, Inc.:
James O. Robbins
President, Cox Newspapers: Jay R. Smith
President, Cox Broadcasting: Nicholas D. Trigony
President, Cox Interactive Media: Peter M. Winter
SVP Operations, Cox Communications:
Margaret A. Bellville
VP Tax: Preston B. Barnett
VP Business Development and Planning:
Dean H. Eisner
VP and Chief Information Officer: Scott A. Hatfield
VP and Treasurer: Richard J. Jacobson
VP New Media: William L. Killen Jr.
VP Human Resources: Marybeth H. Leamer
VP Materials Management: Michael J. Mannheimer
VP Legal Affairs and Secretary: Andrew A. Merdek
VP Public Policy: Alexander V. Netchvolodoff
VP Marketing and Communication: John C. Williams

HQ: 1400 Lake Hearn Dr., Atlanta, GA 30319
Phone: 404-843-5000   **Fax:** 404-843-5109
Web site: http://www.CoxEnterprises.com

Cox Enterprises operates in Canada, France, Puerto Rico, the UK, and the US.

Top Cable System Clusters
Hampton Roads, VA
Las Vegas
New England
New Orleans
Omaha, NE
Orange County, CA
Pensacola-Fort Walton Beach, FL
Phoenix
San Diego
Tucson-Sierra Vista, AZ

Selected Daily Newspapers
The Atlanta Journal-Constitution
Austin American-Statesman (Texas)
The Daily Reflector (Greenville, NC)
The Daily Sentinel (Grand Junction, CO)
The Daily Sentinel (Nacogdoches, TX)
Dayton Daily News (Ohio)
Longview News-Journal (Texas)
The Lufkin Daily News (Texas)
Palm Beach Post (Florida)

Selected Television Stations
KIRO, Seattle
KTVU, San Francisco-Oakland
WFTV, Orlando, FL
WHIO, Dayton, OH
WPXI, Pittsburgh
WSB-TV, Atlanta
WSOC, Charlotte, NC

Selected Cable and Television Operations
Cox Communications, Inc. (80%, cable
television operator)
Harrington, Righter & Parsons (sales representation)
MMT Sales (sales representation)
TeleRep, Inc. (sales representation)

AT&T
Advance Publications
Bell Atlantic
Belo
Cablevision Systems
Comcast
Dow Jones
E. W. Scripps
GTE
Gannett
Hearst
Infinity Broadcasting
Knight Ridder
MediaOne Group
New York Times
News Corp.
SBC Communications
Time Warner
Tribune
Viacom
Vodafone AirTouch
Walt Disney
Washington Post

Private FYE: December	Annual Growth	1989	1990	1991	1992	1993	1994	1995	1996	1997	1998
Sales ($ mil.)	11.7%	1,973	2,094	2,323	2,495	2,675	2,939	3,806	4,591	4,936	5,355
Employees	10.6%	22,487	24,864	29,943	30,865	31,000	37,000	38,000	43,000	50,000	55,500

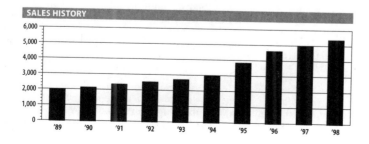

SALES HISTORY

DAIRY FARMERS OF AMERICA

OVERVIEW

Dairy Farmers of America (DFA) seeks strength in numbers — big numbers. As the nation's largest dairy cooperative, DFA rides herd on about 25,000 members in 45 states, and it controls 22% of the US milk supply, or an annual pool nearing 40 billion pounds of milk. The Kansas City, Missouri-based co-op was formed by the 1997 merger of Mid-America Dairymen (previously the #1 milk co-op), the Southern Region of Associated Milk Producers, Milk Marketing, and Western Dairymen Cooperative. These partners in cream sell fluid milk, cheese, butter, and other dairy products to wholesale and retail customers worldwide. DFA also provides marketing, research and development, and legislative lobbying on behalf of its members.

In addition to retail sales of dairy products under dozens of national, regional, and private labels (it owns the trademark to Elsie the Cow and the Borden name for dairy products), DFA supplies shredded mozzarella to pizza chains and produces Frito-Lay's cheese dips, infant formula, and Starbucks' Frappuccino coffee drink.

American dairy farmers face an uncertain future due to consolidation in the retail industry, dissolving government milk price supports, and increased foreign competition. To better compete with large food manufacturers and other dairy processors, DFA has invested heavily in facilities and joint ventures to process its fluid milk into value-added products. DFA will own about 34% of a joint venture it's forming with Suiza Foods to create the #1 US fluid milk processor.

HISTORY

Mid-America Dairymen (Mid-Am), the largest of the cooperatives that merged to form Dairy Farmers of America (DFA), was born in 1968. At that time, several midwestern dairy co-ops banded together to attack common economic problems, such as reduced government subsidies, price drops resulting from a rising milk surplus, dealer consolidation, and improvements in production, processing, and packaging. The merging organizations — representing 15,000 dairy farmers — were Producers Creamery Company (Springfield, Missouri), Sanitary Milk Producers (St. Louis), Square Deal Milk Producers (Highland, Illinois), Mid-Am (Kansas City, Missouri), and Producers Creamery Company of Chillicothe (north central Missouri).

During the early 1970s Mid-Am struggled with internal restructuring. Most dairy farmers and co-ops were hit hard by the energy crisis and the government's decision to allow increased dairy imports in 1973, the same year the US Justice Department filed an antitrust suit against Mid-Am. (A judge cleared the co-op 12 years later.)

In 1974 Mid-Am lost almost $8 million on revenues of $625 million, chalked up to record-high feed prices, a weakened economy, a milk surplus, and a massive inventory loss. Co-op veteran Gary Hanman was named CEO that year. Over the next two years, Mid-Am cut costs, sold corporate frills, downsized management, and began marketing more of its own products under the Mid-America Farms label, thus reducing dependency on commodity sales.

Mid-Am expanded its research and development efforts throughout the 1980s. After 20 years of fighting, in 1991 Mid-Am, along with two other co-ops, reached a $21.4 million settlement of an antitrust suit filed by the National Farmers Organization.

The co-op opened its services to farmers in California and New Mexico in 1993, and a series of mergers in 1994 and 1995 nearly doubled its size. In 1997 it purchased some of Borden's dairy operations, including rights to the valuable Elsie the Cow and Borden's trademarks.

Wary of falling milk prices, Mid-Am merged with Western Dairymen Cooperative, Milk Marketing, and the Southern Region of Associated Milk Producers at the end of 1997 to form DFA. Hanman moved into the seat of CEO at the new co-op. DFA partnered in a joint venture with the #1 US dairy processor, Suiza Foods, after Suiza bought former DFA partner Land-O-Sun Dairies. Late in 1998 the co-op entered a second joint venture (25% stake) with Suiza Foods that combined that company's northeastern dairy operations with DFA's. Another joint venture with Suiza followed in mid-1999.

DFA added California Gold (more than 330 farmers) and Independent Cooperative Milk Producers Association (730 dairy farmer members in Michigan and parts of Ohio and Indiana) in 1998 and early 1999. Later in 1999, in another joint venture with Suiza, DFA agreed to sell its 50% stake in the US's #3 fluid milk processor, Southern Foods, in exchange for 34% of a new company to be called Suiza Fluid Dairy Group.

Chairman: Herman M. Brubaker
President and CEO: Gary E. Hanman
EVP: Don Schriver
CFO: Jerry Bos
VP Marketing and Planning: John Wilson
VP Special Projects: Jim Carroll
VP Human Resources and Administration: Ray Silver
VP Industry and Joint Venture Relations: Bob Wallace
Auditors: Deloitte & Touche LLP

LOCATIONS

HQ: 10220 N. Executive Hills Blvd.,
     Kansas City, MO 64190
Phone: 816-801-6455   **Fax:** 816-801-6456
Web site: http://www.dfamilk.com

PRODUCTS/OPERATIONS

Selected Products
Butter
Cheese dips
Cheeses
Condensed milk
Cream
Dehydrated dairy products
Nonfat dry milk
Shelf-stable nutritional beverages
Whey products

COMPETITORS

AMPI
California Dairies Inc.
Dairylea
Danone
Darigold
Dean Foods
Foremost Farms
Galaxy Foods
Kraft Foods
Lactalis
Land O'Lakes
Leprino Foods
Nestlé
Parmalat Finanziaria
Prairie Farms Dairy
Saputo Group
Schreiber Foods
Suprema Specialties

HISTORICAL FINANCIALS & EMPLOYEES

Cooperative FYE: December	Annual Growth	1989	1990	1991	1992	1993	1994	1995	1996	1997	1998
Sales ($ mil.)	16.9%	1,798	1,863	1,752	1,868	1,826	2,491	3,681	4,085	3,818	7,325
Employees	6.1%	3,100	—	—	3,600	3,500	3,000	3,100	3,200	5,300	5,300

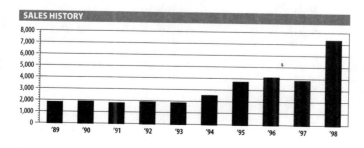

SALES HISTORY

DART CONTAINER CORPORATION

OVERVIEW

Dart Container's cups runneth over and over and over. The world's #1 maker of foam cups and food containers, with about half the world market, Dart Container is the money machine of the secretive and contentious Dart family. Based in Mason, Michigan, the company has more than a dozen manufacturing plants and four recycling centers. To undercut competition, the company makes its own feedstocks and machines and uses its own trucks for distribution.

Dart Container makes more than 400 products, including foam cups and disposable dinnerware and cutlery for hospitals, schools,

and restaurants. The firm sells its recycled polystyrene to companies that make such items as insulation material and egg cartons.

The king of cups has a simple strategy — secrecy. The cup-making machine developed by the Darts was never patented to avoid revealing how it works. Most of its factory workers have never seen the machines, and the firm's salespeople are not allowed inside the plants. After years of legal battles, the Darts have reached an agreement regarding alleged discrepancies in the family inheritance. The terms of the settlement are, of course, secret.

HISTORY

William F. Dart founded a Michigan firm to make steel tape measures in 1937. Dart's son William A. started experimenting with plastics in 1953, and in the late 1950s the two devised a cheap way to mold expandable polystyrene and built a cup-making machine. Dart Container was incorporated in Mason, Michigan, in 1960 and shipped its first cups that year. By the late 1960s the rising demand for plastic-foam products sparked an increase in R&D. In 1970 the company built a plant in Corona, California.

It was a family feud in the making in 1974, as William F. divided the business among his grandsons — Tom, Ken, and Robert — in separate trusts that named William A. trustee for all. Tom branched out in 1975 and founded oil and gas company Dart Energy, which was later absorbed into Dart Container. William F. died the next year. Following the oil market crash of the early 1980s, Tom went through a sticky divorce and admitted to cocaine abuse. His father temporarily removed him as head of Dart Energy in 1982, and the next year the entire family underwent group psychiatric counseling.

The family reorganized its assets in 1986, giving Ken and Robert the cup business and Tom the energy business plus $58 million in cash. In 1987 Ken began to swell the family fortune with a series of successful investments. Better tax rates motivated Dart family members to move to Sarasota, Florida, in 1989. They set up shop in an unmarked building behind a sporting-goods store. By the late 1980s Dart Container commanded more than 50% of the worldwide market for foam cups.

In 1990 the company paid $250,000 to settle a factory worker's minority discrimination lawsuit. The next year Ken bought 11% of the

Federal Home Loan Mortgage Corp. (Freddie Mac), as well as portions of Salomon and Brazil's foreign debt. According to Tom, that year Ken also financed brain research in hopes of finding a way to keep his brain alive after the death of his body in an attempt to avoid future estate taxes.

Tom sued his brothers and father in 1992 for allegedly cheating him out of millions in trust money in the 1986 reorganization. Ken turned a $300 million investment into $1 billion by selling the Freddie Mac shares. The next year he and Robert renounced their US citizenship to avoid paying taxes. Ken also made a failed attempt to block the restructuring of Brazil's debt (of which Dart owned 4%). That year Ken's new $1 million Sarasota home was firebombed (the case remains unsolved), and Robert moved to Britain, where he soon filed for divorce.

Ken began hiring bodyguards, and he moved his family to the Cayman Islands in 1994. Dart shelled out $230,000 to settle yet another discrimination case. In 1995 Tom was fired from Dart Energy, and Ken tried — and failed — to return to the US as a diplomat of Belize. In 1996 Tom accused Judge Donald Owens of being biased in favor of William A. The judge succumbed to the pressure in 1997 and removed himself from the proceedings, only to be ordered back on the case by Michigan's Court of Appeals. The lawsuit was settled in 1998 before going to trial, but the terms were kept secret. The following year saw yet another series of lawsuits for the container company. Dart Container has filed an appeal to an IRS demand to pay $29.8 million in back taxes and late penalties.

President: Kenneth B. Dart
VP of Administration: Jim Lammers
Treasurer: William Myer
Director of Human Resources: Mark Franks
Manager of Facilities Engineering: Wayne Fox

HQ: 500 Hogsback Rd., Mason, MI 48854
Phone: 517-676-3803   **Fax:** 517-676-3882
Web site: http://www.dartcontainer.com

Selected Products
Bowls
Containers
Cups
Cutlery
Lids
Plates
Recycled polystyrene pellets

Selected Services
CARE (Cups Are REcyclable) Program (provides
    densifier to larger customers to compact their
    polystyrene, which Dart then picks up)
Foam-Recycling (four plants in Canada, Florida,
    Michigan, and Pennsylvania and a drop-off site
    in Georgia)
Recycla-Pak (provides small-volume businesses with
    cup-shipping containers that double as recycling bins)

EarthShell
Fort James
Huhtamaki Van Leer
Huntsman
Jim Pattison Group
NOVA Chemicals
Pactiv

Smurfit-Stone Container
Sonoco Products
Sweetheart Cup
Temple-Inland
Tetra Laval
VIAG

Private FYE: December	Annual Growth	1989	1990	1991	1992	1993	1994	1995	1996	1997	1998
Estimated sales ($ mil.)	13.8%	—	—	464	475	600	800	1,000	1,000	1,000	1,150
Employees	8.9%	—	—	—	3,000	3,750	3,600	4,300	4,300	5,000	5,000

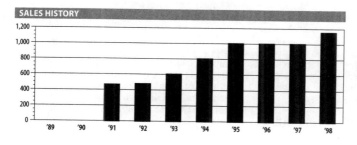

SALES HISTORY

DATEK ONLINE HOLDINGS CORP.

OVERVIEW

Despite having more trouble with the *federales* than the badgeless bandits in *The Treasure of the Sierra Madre*, Datek is going for gold in online trading.

Iselin, New Jersey-based Datek Online Holdings is hoping to get a solid foothold on the growing market through its Datek Online Brokerage Services (among the top five behind #1 Charles Schwab), as well as The Island ECN (an alternative electronic trading venue that rivals Reuters's Instinet). The brokerage has 250,000 active accounts, which make 70,000 transactions daily, charging about $10 for trades up to 5,000 shares. Datek's operations also include Datek Online Clearing Corp., which clears trades for other brokers, and financial software developer Big Think. Datek clients can trade in any NYSE, Nasdaq, or AMEX stock, as well as in financial tools ranging from mutual funds to margin investments.

Flush with a $300 million infusion by investors including Bernard Arnault and TA Associates (Microsoft co-founder Paul Allen bowed out due to pending investigations of the firm), Datek hopes to elevate The Island ECN to a full-fledged (for-profit) stock exchange and expand financial products offered by its brokerage.

HISTORY

Aaron Elbogen and George Weinberger founded Datek Securities in 1970. The firm led an unremarkable existence for its first 15 years, serving as a small-time broker and investment banker. Datek set out on the path to notoriety during the Black Monday market crash of 1987, when some Nasdaq market makers ignored small trades, choosing to protect their own interests at the expense of individual investors. That spurred Nasdaq's parent, the National Association of Securities Dealers (NASD), to institute the Small Order Execution System (SOES), which automatically executes orders of less than 1,000 trades. About that time Datek hired the swashbrokering Sheldon Maschler, a veteran of the notorious failed penny-stock firm First Jersey Securities. Maschler had once drawn fines totaling $10,000 for using "gross, vile, and disgusting" language on the trading floor.

Under Maschler, Datek joined other small, wily traders (like All-Tech Investment Group's Harvey Houtkin) in using the SOES system to capitalize on pokey market makers who failed to update their quotes to match the market. Dubbed "SOES bandits," Datek drew the ire, and sanctions, of the big time market makers (mostly larger brokerages) who dominate Nasdaq's governing board. Datek and its ilk claimed to be a force for efficiency in a clubby market skewed in favor of the market makers. Maschler became the nemesis of then-Nasdaq president Joseph Hardiman. In 1995 he disguised himself as a sports reporter at a press conference and got into a shouting match with Hardiman over a proposed substitute to the SOES system. In 1998, after leaving Datek, Maschler was implicated in an alleged penny-stock scam.

The software enabling the so-called SOES banditry was designed by Jeffrey Citron (hired out of high school in 1988) and Joshua Levine. The software evolved into Datek's The Island ECN trading system. Citron and Peter Stern formed Datek's online brokerage subsidiary in 1996, launching The Island ECN the same year. As Datek Online grew, it helped Datek distance itself from its notorious past. However, all distance is relative — in 1998 the firm sold the trading operations associated with the SOES high jinks to Heartland Securities, owned by Datek founder Elbogen and Maschler's son Erik, who also owned a share of Datek. Also that year the company acquired Big Think, which developed software for Datek. Despite the image scrubbing, the company had to postpone IPO plans when *The New York Times* revealed the SEC was investigating Datek.

Datek took to the soap again, in 1999, hiring Waterhouse Securities (now TD Waterhouse Group) co-founder Edward Nicoll to head up Datek Online Brokerage. That year Datek became the first online brokerage censured by the SEC, and was compelled to hire an outside consultant to review its financial procedures for failing to maintain minimum balances to cover customer trades (the company attributes the shortfall to math errors).

The company's worries about the tenability of a public offering dissipated later that month, when a group of investors including French luxury-goods billionaire Bernard Arnault (LVMH Moet Hennessy Louis Vuitton) and TA Associates ponied up $300 million. Through Vulcan Ventures, Microsoft co-founder Paul Allen had intended to chip in also, but investigations into whether Datek engaged in money laundering and illegal trading practices prompted him to withdraw; Arnault provided another $30 million to cover Allen's pullout.

Chairman and CEO: Edward J. Nicoll
President, COO, and CFO: John Grifonetti
President, Datek Online Brokerage Services:
John Mullin
President, Datek Online Clearing: Ralph Sorrentino
EVP, Datek Online Brokerage Services: Alex Goor
Chief Technology Officer; President, Big Think:
Peter Stern
VP Marketing; VP, Big Think: Robert Bethge
Human Resources Representative: Dana Gershgorn

LOCATIONS

HQ: 399 Thornall St., Edison, NJ 08837
Phone: 732-516-8000   **Fax:** 732-548-7668
Web site: http://www.datek.com

PRODUCTS/OPERATIONS

Subsidiaries
Big Think (in-house software development)
Datek Online Brokerage Services
(online discount brokerage)
Datek Online Clearing Corp. (trade clearing services)
The Island ECN (computerized trading system)

COMPETITORS

Ameritrade
Charles Schwab
DLJdirect
E*TRADE
FMR
Morgan Stanley Dean Witter
National Discount Brokers Group
Quick & Reilly/Fleet
Reuters
Siebert Financial
TD Waterhouse Securities

HISTORICAL FINANCIALS & EMPLOYEES

Private FYE: December	Annual Growth	1989	1990	1991	1992	1993	1994	1995	1996	1997	1998
Estimated sales ($ mil.)	87.5%	—	—	—	—	—	—	—	—	40	75
Employees	74.5%	—	—	—	—	—	—	—	—	216	377

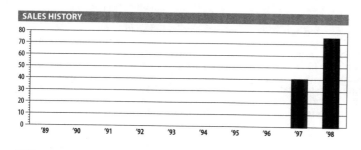

SALES HISTORY

DELOITTE TOUCHE TOHMATSU

OVERVIEW

There's more than a touch of teamwork at Deloitte Touche Tohmatsu (DTT), known in the US as Deloitte & Touche LLC. The New York City-based firm operates in more than 130 countries, using industry specialists to provide auditing, accounting, and consulting services. Its consulting specialties include strategic planning, information technology, financial management, and productivity. The commodification of the auditing side of the business (whose driving force has moved from relationships to pricing) has spurred the growth of the consulting side.

The 1998 merger of Price Waterhouse and Coopers & Lybrand into PricewaterhouseCoopers (and the proposed but abandoned pairing of Ernst & Young and KPMG International) made size more important than ever. The PricewaterhouseCoopers combination dropped DTT to last place among the Big Five, prompting the company to begin an aggressive new advertising campaign.

HISTORY

In 1845 William Deloitte opened an accounting office in London. At first he solicited business from bankrupts. The growth of joint stock companies and the development of stock markets in the mid-19th century created a need for standardized financial reporting and fueled the rise of auditing. Deloitte moved into the new field. The Great Western Railway appointed him as its independent auditor (the first anywhere) in 1849.

In 1890 John Griffiths, who became a partner in 1869, opened the company's first US office in New York City. Four decades later, branches had opened throughout the US. In 1952 the firm partnered with Haskins & Sells, which operated 34 US offices.

Deloitte aimed to be the "Cadillac, not the Ford" of accounting. The firm, which became Deloitte Haskins & Sells in 1978, began shedding its conservatism as competition heated up; it was the first of the Big Eight firms, for example, to use aggressive ads.

In 1984 Deloitte Haskins & Sells tried to merge with Price Waterhouse. The deal was dropped after Price Waterhouse's UK partners objected.

The Big Eight accounting firms became the Big Six in 1989 when Ernst & Whinney merged with Arthur Young to become Ernst & Young. Also that year Deloitte Haskins & Sells joined the flamboyant Touche Ross (founded, 1899) to become Deloitte & Touche. Touche Ross's Japanese affiliate's name, Ross Tohmatsu (founded 1968) rounded out the current name. The merger was engineered by Deloitte's Michael Cook and Touche's Edward Kangas, in part to unite the former firm's US and European strengths with the latter's Asian presence. Cook continued to oversee US operations with Kangas presiding over international operations. Many affiliates, particularly in the UK, rejected the merger and defected to competing firms.

As auditors were increasingly held accountable for the financial results of their clients, legal action soared. In the 1990s Deloitte was sued because of its actions relating to Drexel Burnham Lambert junk-bond king Michael Milken, the failure of several savings and loans, and clients' bankruptcies.

Nevertheless, in 1995 the SEC chose Michael Sutton, the firm's national director of auditing and accounting practice, as its chief accountant. That year DTT formed Deloitte & Touche Consulting to consolidate its US and UK consulting operations; its Asian consulting operations were later added to the group to facilitate regional expansion.

In 1996 the firm formed a corporate fraud unit (with special emphasis on the Internet) and bought PHH Fantus, the leading corporate relocation consulting company. The next year Deloitte and Thurston Group (a Chicago-based merchant bank) teamed up to form NetDox, a system for delivering legal, financial, and insurance documents via the Internet. In 1997 amid a new round of mergers in the industry, rumors swirled that a merger of DTT and Ernst & Young had been scrapped because the firms could not agree on relative ownership of the two firms' partners. DTT disavowed plans to merge and launched an ad campaign directly targeted against its rivals.

In 1998 the firm's overseas expansion was hit by the Asian economic crisis, but the silver lining of the situation was a rise in restructuring and workout consulting. In 1999 the firm sold its accounting staffing service unit (Re:sources Connection) to its managers and Evercore Partners, citing possible conflicts of interest with its core audit business. Also that year Kangas stepped down as CEO and was succeeded by James Copeland, and Deloitte Consulting decided to sell its computer programming subsidiary to CGI Group.

Chairman: Edward A. Kangas
CEO: James E. Copeland Jr.
COO: J. Thomas Presby
CFO: William A. Fowler
Chairman, Deloitte & Touche LLP:
Douglas M. McCracken, age 50
**Chief Executive and Senior Partner, Deloitte & Touche
(UK):** John P. Connolly
CEO, Deloitte & Touche Consulting Group Global:
Pasquale Loconto
National Director U. S. International Operations:
Tom Schiro
Director Communications: David Read
Director Finance: Gerald W. Richards
Director Human Resources: Martyn Fisher
**National Director Human Capital and Actuary Practice,
Deloitte & Touche LLP:** Ainar D. Aijala Jr.
**National Director Human Resources, Deloitte &
Touche LLP:** James H. Wall
**National Director Marketing, Communications, and
Public Relations, Deloitte & Touche LLP:**
Gary Gerard
National Director Operations, Deloitte & Touche LLP:
William H. Stanton
Counsel: Joseph J. Lambert
General Counsel, Deloitte & Touche LLP:
Philip R. Rotner

LOCATIONS

HQ: 1633 Broadway, New York, NY 10019
Phone: 212-492-4000   **Fax:** 212-492-4154
Web site: http://www.deloitte.com

Deloitte Touche Tohmatsu operates through about 700 offices in more than 130 countries.

PRODUCTS/OPERATIONS

Selected Services
Accounting and auditing
Information technology consulting
Management consulting
Mergers and acquisitions consulting
Tax advice and planning

Selected Representative Clients
Allstate
DaimlerChrysler
General Motors
Merrill Lynch
MetLife
Microsoft
Mitsubishi
Nortel Networks
Procter & Gamble
Sears

Selected Affiliates
Akintola Williams & Co. (Cameroon)
Braxton Associates
C. C. Chokshi & Co. (India)
D&T Corporate Finance Europe Ltd. (UK)
Deloitte & Touche Central Europe (Czech Republic)
Deloitte & Touche Consulting Group/ICS
Hans Tuanakotta & Mustofa (Indonesia)
The IDOM Group
Nautilus Indemnity Holdings Ltd. (Bermuda)
Shawki & Co. (Egypt)
Tohmatsu & Co. (Japan)

COMPETITORS

Andersen Worldwide   H&R Block
Arthur D. Little   KPMG
BDO International   Marsh & McLennan
Booz, Allen   McKinsey & Company
Boston Consulting   PricewaterhouseCoopers
EDS   Towers Perrin
Ernst & Young   Watson Wyatt
Gemini Consulting
Grant Thornton
International

HISTORICAL FINANCIALS & EMPLOYEES

Partnership FYE: August	Annual Growth	1990	1991	1992	1993	1994	1995	1996	1997	1998	1999
Sales ($ mil.)	10.8%	4,200	4,500	4,800	5,000	5,200	5,950	6,500	7,400	9,000	10,600
Employees	4.7%	59,700	56,000	56,000	56,000	56,600	59,000	63,440	65,000	82,000	90,000

SALES HISTORY

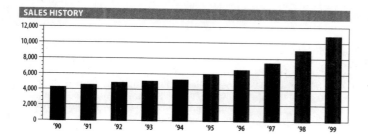

**Deloitte &
Touche**

DFS GROUP LIMITED

OVERVIEW

DFS Group would have been wise to heed the old Japanese proverb, "Even monkeys fall from trees." Based in San Francisco, DFS (Duty Free Shoppers) has been the dexterous 900-lb. gorilla of duty-free retailing, with more than 150 stores in airports, hotels, and downtown locales, mostly along the Pacific Rim. Catering to international travelers (particularly the Japanese, who account for more than 70% of sales), it sells high-quality, brand-name clothing, liquor, perfume, tobacco, jewelry, and other goods.

The company's reliance on the Japanese, who were grounded by the Asian currency crisis, hurt sales and forced it to shift focus to non-airport stores. To reduce its dependence on duty-free retailing, DFS is exploring new store formats in resort and downtown locations with cheaper rents. These Galleria centers contain upscale specialty stores, designer boutiques, and an entertainment complex. DFS also manages the US and Asian operations of Sephora, a chain of cosmetics and perfume stores worldwide.

LVMH Moet Hennessy Louis Vuitton owns 61% of DFS and supplies it with Christian Dior perfumes and clothing, among other luxury goods; co-founder Robert Miller owns the remaining 39% of the company.

HISTORY

Charles Feeney and Robert Miller were classmates at Cornell University's School of Hotel Administration in the mid-1950s. They started a business in Europe in the late 1950s selling duty-free liquor and foreign cars to tourists and US servicemen. By 1960 the business had moved to Asia, where Feeney and Miller opened offices near US Air Force and Navy bases.

By the early 1960s the company, by then known as Duty Free Shoppers (DFS), opened its first duty-free stores at the Hong Kong and Honolūlu international airports, where sales boomed. But DFS was in dire financial straits by 1965 after the US government eased restrictions on duty-free liquor (DFS's main merchandise) and allowed US car manufacturers to sell on military bases. To salvage the operation, Feeney and Miller in 1966 sold lawyer Anthony Pilaro and British accountant Alan Parker each 10% of the company.

Overseas travel from Japan skyrocketed after the 1964 Tokyo Olympics, when travel restrictions on the Japanese were lifted. DFS targeted Japanese tourists because of the huge amounts they spent while traveling and their penchant for expensive designer goods. In 1968 it opened its first non-airport location in downtown Hong Kong.

Feeney and Miller had handed day-to-day operations over to others by the early 1980s, and DFS had opened airport stores in Alaska, Guam, Los Angeles, Saipan, San Francisco, and Singapore. In 1983 Adrian Bellamy was appointed chairman and CEO.

In 1987 and 1988 the company opened new stores in Australia and New Zealand after learning that Japanese newlyweds were going there instead of Hawaii. Also in the late 1980s, DFS opened new stores at airports in Atlanta, Boston, Dallas, New York, and other US airports as well as in the UK at Gatwick Airport. In 1989 the company tried to renew its contract at the San Francisco airport but was outbid by rival Allders International. DFS switched to selling general merchandise there and opened one of its first department stores in downtown San Francisco.

DFS entered Canada in 1990 with a five-year contract at Toronto's Pearson International Airport. The Persian Gulf War curtailed international travel in 1991 and sales dropped about 15%. The sales slump halted plans for European expansion and led DFS to close its London stores. In 1994 the company opened its first multi-department Galleria store in Guam.

Myron Ullman, former chairman and CEO of Macy's, replaced Bellamy as chairman and CEO of the company in 1995. That year, despite Miller's protests, co-founder Feeney, Parker, and Pilaro sold their stakes in DFS (totaling 61%) to luxury goods conglomerate LVMH Moet Hennessy Louis Vuitton. (The sale of Feeney's stake revealed that he had secretly donated $600 million to charity and had created two foundations holding $3.5 billion more.) After rejecting the aid of an outside arbitrator, Miller said in 1997 that he would not only hold onto his share of DFS but would also return to more active duty with the company. Later in 1997 LVMH bought Sephora, a chain of cosmetics and fragrance specialty stores.

Saks Holdings' COO, Brian Kendrick, succeeded Ullman as CEO in 1998. DFS opened its much-ballyhooed Sephora flagship store in Rockefeller Center in Manhattan in 1999. In November 1999 Edward Brennan took the helm from Kendrick, who left to join Asbury Automotive Group.

OFFICERS

Chairman: Myron Ullman III
President and CEO: Edward J. Brennan
CFO: Caden Wang
EVP Human Resources and Merchandise Planning: James Wiggett
SVP Human Resources: Peggy Tate

LOCATIONS

HQ: 525 Market St., 33rd Fl., San Francisco, CA 94105
Phone: 415-977-2700   **Fax:** 415-977-2956
Web site: http://www.dfsgroup.com

PRODUCTS/OPERATIONS

Selected Merchandise and Services
Beauty makeovers
Cosmetics
Designer apparel
Fragrances
Gifts
Golf accessories
Jewelry
Leather items
Liquor
Massages
Specialty foods
Tobacco
Watches

COMPETITORS

BAA
Federated
Hermes
King Power
Little Switzerland
Neiman Marcus
Nordstrom
Saks Inc.
Shiseido
Tiffany
Vendome Luxury Group

HISTORICAL FINANCIALS & EMPLOYEES

Private FYE: December	Annual Growth	1989	1990	1991	1992	1993	1994	1995	1996	1997	1998
Sales ($ mil.)	(5.6%)	2,650	2,300	2,300	2,150	2,600	2,600	3,000	2,689	2,240	1,574
Employees	(10.9%)	—	—	—	—	—	13,500	10,000	9,300	8,600	8,500

SALES HISTORY

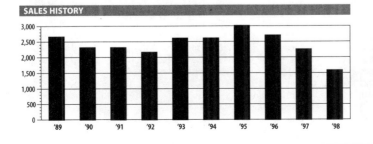

DHL WORLDWIDE EXPRESS

OVERVIEW

By bus, boat, or bicycle, from Albania to Kyrgyzstan, Qatar to Zimbabwe, DHL Worldwide Express delivers. The Redwood City, California-based privately held company is the world leader in cross-border express deliveries, ahead of FedEx and UPS.

DHL operates an integrated global delivery network through two main companies. DHL Airways serves the US market, and Brussels-based DHL International goes everywhere else. Overall, DHL links more than 225 countries. The company operates a fleet of more than 200 aircraft and 13,500 delivery vehicles.

DHL is expanding its logistics management services, which include Internet tracking and order fulfillment.

DHL International partners with its investors to share facilities and routes. Deutsche Post and Lufthansa each own 25% of DHL International, and Japan Airlines owns 6%; company founders own 21%. DHL has announced that it is considering an IPO of a 23% stake in DHL International held by two investment trusts. (DHL International owns 25% of DHL Airways; private investors own the rest.)

HISTORY

In 1969 co-workers Adrian Dalsey (the "D" in DHL Worldwide Express), Larry Lee Hillblom (the "H"), and Robert Lynn (the "L") were looking for a way to improve the turnaround time for ships in ports. Their brainstorm was to fly shipping documents to ports for examination and processing before the ship arrived. This idea rapidly developed into an express delivery service between California and Hawaii, and Bank of America became a major customer.

Service was expanded to the Philippines in 1971. The next year the three original investors asked Hong Kong entrepreneur Po Chung to help them form DHL International, a global delivery network. Chung had no previous experience in the express delivery business, but he pioneered a simplified rate structure and the single network concept, which required that the company take full responsibility for picking up and delivering the package. By the end of 1972, service was extended to Australia, Hong Kong, Japan, and Singapore.

From its Pacific Basin origins, DHL expanded worldwide in the 1970s, moving into Europe in 1974, Latin America in 1977, and the Middle East and Africa in 1978.

An agreement with hotel franchisor Hilton in 1980 to provide daily pickup and international delivery garnered new outlets for DHL. The next year Hillblom, just retired from active management of the company, moved to the Pacific island of Saipan.

Having focused on its international network during its early years, DHL invested heavily in developing a delivery network within the US in 1983. It also extended its service to Eastern Europe. In 1985 — the year UPS and FedEx also began providing international express delivery — DHL and Western Union entered a venture to transmit documents by e-mail. The next year DHL established the first air express venture in China. Dalsey ran the company until his retirement in the mid-1980s (he died in 1994).

In 1990 DHL International sold 12.5% (later increased to more than 55%) of the company to Japan Airlines, Lufthansa (Germany), and Japanese securities firm Nissho Iwai (which sold back its stake in 1999). Through its new owners, DHL boosted its customer base and improved its expertise in dealing with Japanese and German clients.

Hillblom died in a 1995 plane crash in the Pacific Ocean, after having survived a crash two years earlier. The company bought back the 25% stake in DHL International that had been owned by his estate. Distribution of his $500 million fortune — much of which was to go for medical research — was delayed by lawsuits, and part of the estate was ordered given to four DNA-linked children born to barmaids in the Pacific Islands where Hillblom retired.

In 1996 DHL opened a gateway in Moscow, and in 1997 the company became one of the first international air carriers to serve North Korea. Deutsche Post acquired a 25% stake in DHL International in 1998. Lynn, DHL's last living co-founder, died that year.

In 1999 the company opened a bigger service center in Silicon Valley (its largest US center); began work on its larger, fully automated North American hub in Cincinnati; and formed an alliance with the US Postal Service guaranteeing a priority mail service across the Atlantic.

Also that year Japan Airlines reduced its stake in DHL International to 6% (from 26%), and DHL announced that it planned an IPO of a 23% stake in DHL International held by two investment trusts.

Executive Chairman: Patrick Lupo
CEO: Rob Kuijpers
SVP, Sales and Marketing: Jeff Corbett
SVP, Field Services and Customer Service:
  Larry Hughes
SVP, Network Transportation: Steve Waller
Chairman, DHL Airways: Patrick Foley
CEO, DHL Airways: Victor Guinasso, age 44
CEO, Asia Region, DHL International: Charles Longley
CFO: Simon Clayton, age 42
SVP, Secretary, and General Counsel, DHL Airways:
  Jed Orme
SVP, Human Resources, DHL Airways: Garry Sellers
SVP, Finance and CFO, DHL Airways: William Smartt
Director, Group Central Support: Bob Parker
Country Manager, Singapore: Charles Chan

HQ: 333 Twin Dolphin Dr., Redwood City, CA 94065
Phone: 650-593-7474 **Fax:** 650-593-1689
Web site: http://www.dhl.com

DHL Worldwide Express operates 33 hubs and about
3,000 stations in more than 225 countries.

Stations

	No.	% of total
Europe & Africa	1,470	50
Asia/Pacific	793	27
The Americas	595	20
Middle East	96	3
Total	**2,954**	**100**

Selected Services
Customs clearance
Desktop Shipping Services
DHLNET (electronic tracking and tracing system)
DHL Worldwide Priority Express (worldwide transport of
  non-document goods)
International Document Service (overnight service to
  major destinations)
Same Day Service (next-flight-out delivery for critical
  shipments)
USA Overnight
WorldMail (sorting and delivery of international mail)
Worldwide Express Logistics

Major Operating Companies
DHL Airways, Inc.
DHL International, Ltd. (Brussels, serving
  non-US markets)

Air Express
Airborne Freight
American Freightways
Bilspedition
CNF Transportation
Circle International
Consolidated Delivery
Expeditors International
FDX
Fritz
Pittston BAX
Ratos
SAirGroup
Stinnes
TNT Post Group
U.S. Postal Service
UPS
USFreightways

Private FYE: December	Annual Growth	1989	1990	1991	1992	1993	1994	1995	1996	1997	1998
Estimated sales ($ mil.)	11.4%	1,900	2,000	2,200	2,800	3,000	3,100	3,800	4,200	4,800	5,000
Employees	13.1%	20,000	23,000	25,000	28,000	34,000	35,000	40,000	50,000	59,200	60,486

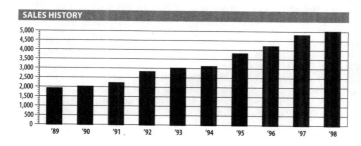

SALES HISTORY

DISCOVERY COMMUNICATIONS, INC.

OVERVIEW

With shows such as *Cleopatra's Palace* and *Live From a Shark Cage,* Discovery Communications, Inc. (DCI), knows that documentaries should be anything but boring. The Bethesda, Maryland-based company is a leading producer of original nonfiction programming, serving some 320 million homes in about 145 countries. Its Discovery Channel reaches more than 75 million households in the US and, along with The Learning Channel (which offers programming on science, history, and human behavior to nearly 70 million homes), generates most of DCI's sales. DCI also owns Animal Planet ("all animals, all the time"), The Travel Channel (world cultures, travel ideas and advice), and Discovery People (news and entertainment), as well as seven digital cable channels (including the newly launched and much-ballyhooed

Discovery Health Channel). The company showcases original and third-party programming.

Building on its name brand, DCI creates original programming, games, and activities for its Web site and publishes videos, books, and CD-ROMs. The company also operates more than 100 retail stores under the Discovery Channel and Nature Company names. In addition, it has teamed with travel agency Rosenbluth International to launch Discovery Travel, which will create and market vacations to locales featured by DCI's programming. DCI is also the largest shareholder of online retailer petstore.com.

AT&T's Liberty Media Group owns 49% of the company; Cox Communications, about 24%; Advance Publications, 24%; DCI founder and CEO John Hendricks, the rest.

HISTORY

John Hendricks, a history graduate who wanted to expand the presence of educational programming on TV, founded Cable Educational Network in 1982. Three years later he introduced the Discovery Channel. Devoted entirely to documentaries and nature shows, the channel premiered in 156,000 US homes. Within a year, the Discovery Channel had 7 million subscribers and a host of new investors, including Cox Cable Communications and Tele-Communications (now AT&T Broadband & Internet Services). It expanded its programming from 12 hours to 18 hours a day in 1987.

Discovery continued to attract subscribers, reaching more than 32 million by 1988. The next year it launched Discovery Channel Europe to more than 200,000 homes in the UK and Scandinavia. In 1990 the company began selling home videos and entered the Israeli market. The following year Discovery Communications, Inc. (DCI), was formed to house the company's operations. Also that year the company bought The Learning Channel (TLC, founded in 1980). The company revamped TLC's programming and in 1992 introduced a daily, six-hour, commercial-free block of children's programs. The next year it introduced its first CD-ROM title, *In the Company of Whales,* based on the Discovery Channel documentary.

In 1994 DCI increased its focus on international expansion. That year it moved into Asia, Latin America, the Middle East, North Africa, Portugal, and Spain. The next year the company introduced a Web site. It also began selling

company merchandise such as CD-ROMs and videos with the purchase of the Discovery Store chain (renamed Discovery Channel Store). In 1996 DCI solidified its move into the retail sector with the acquisition of The Nature Company and Scientific Revolution chains. Also that year it launched its third major cable channel, Animal Planet.

The company continued expanding internationally throughout the mid-1990s, establishing operations in Australia, Canada, India, New Zealand, and South Korea (1995); Africa, Brazil, Germany, and Italy (1996); and Japan and Turkey (1997). Also in 1997 DCI added to its stable of cable channels with the purchase of 70% of Paxson Communications' Travel Channel (it acquired the rest in 1999). The company's 1997 original production *Titanic: Anatomy of a Disaster* attracted 3.2 million US households, setting a network ratings record.

The following year DCI and the British Broadcasting Network launched Animal Planet in Asia through a joint venture and agreed to market and distribute new cable channel BBC America. It also took a 50% stake in CBS's Eye on People. Later in 1998 it bought the rest of the channel from CBS and renamed it Discovery People.

In 1999 DCI spent $330 million launching its new health and fitness channel, Discovery Health. Also that year it formed partnerships with high-speed online service Road Runner (to provide interactive information and services to Road Runner customers) and Rosenbluth Travel (to provide vacation packages based on DCI programming).

Founder, Chairman, and CEO: John Hendricks
President and COO: Judith McHale
EVP and CFO: Greg Durig
SVP; CFO, Discovery Networks: Robert E. Buenting Jr.
SVP and General Manager - Animal Planet:
W. Clark Bunting
SVP and General Manager - Travel Channel:
Jay R. Feldman
SVP Human Resources: Pandit Wright
SVP Public Policy & Communications: Donald A. Baer
President, Discovery Networks, US: Johnathan Rodgers
President, Discovery Networks International:
Dawn McCall
President, Discovery Enterprises Worldwide:
Michela English
SVP Interactive Media, Discovery Enterprises Worldwide: Andrew Sharpless
SVP Operations and Administration, Discovery Networks, US: Jo Ann Burton
SVP Children's Programming, Discovery Networks, US and SVP Children's Products, Discovery Enterprises Worldwide: Majorie Kaplan
VP and General Manager, Discovery Online Networks:
Bill Allman
Director Communications, Discovery Networks, US:
Katherine Urbon
Director E-Commerce: Jackie Chorney
Director and Executive Producer, Travel Channel Online: Harry Moxley

LOCATIONS

HQ: 7700 Wisconsin Ave., Bethesda, MD 20814
Phone: 301-986-0444   **Fax:** 301-771-4064
Web site: http://www.discovery.com

PRODUCTS/OPERATIONS

Cable Channels and US Subscribers
Animal Planet (49.3 million)
The Discovery Channel (76.4 million)
Discovery Digital Networks (4 million)
 Discovery Civilization Channel
 Discovery en Espanol
 Discovery Health Channel
 Discovery Home & Leisure Channel
 Discovery Kids Channel
 Discovery Science Channel
 Discovery Wings Channel
Discovery People (11 million)
The Learning Channel (69.6 million)
The Travel Channel (30.3 million)

COMPETITORS

A&E Networks
BET
CPB
Coldwater Creek
Dorling Kindersley
NBC
National Geographic
Natural Wonders
News Corp.
Time Warner
Toys
Viacom
Walt Disney

HISTORICAL FINANCIALS & EMPLOYEES

Private FYE: December	Annual Growth	1989	1990	1991	1992	1993	1994	1995	1996	1997	1998
Sales ($ mil.)	84.1%	—	—	—	—	52	200	452	662	860	1,100
Employees	45.6%	—	—	—	—	—	400	500	1,900	3,000	1,800

SALES HISTORY

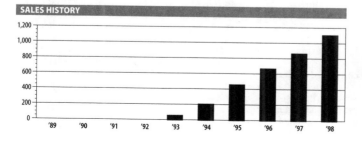

DOMINO'S PIZZA, INC.

OVERVIEW

Creating its own definition of the domino effect, Domino's Pizza has spread a craving for pizza across the globe. Ann Arbor, Michigan-based Domino's is the world's #1 pizza delivery company and the #2 pizza chain overall (behind TRICON's Pizza Hut). The company boasts in excess of 6,200 stores (almost 90% are franchised) in more than 60 countries. Toppings vary from place to place — refried beans are popular in Mexico, while pie-lovers elsewhere favor pickled ginger (India), green

peas (Brazil), canned tuna and corn (UK), and squid (Japan).

Domino's has built its reputation on speedy delivery (it focuses solely on delivery and has no "eat-in" restaurants), but the company also has begun to emphasize the quality of its fare. Domino's founder Thomas Monaghan, a devout Catholic, retired from the company in 1998 to concentrate on his religious activities. He sold 93% of his company to Boston-based investment firm Bain Capital.

HISTORY

Thomas Monaghan's early life was one of hardship. After growing up in an orphanage and numerous foster homes, Monaghan spent his young adult life experimenting, trying everything from a Catholic seminary to a stint in the Marine Corps.

In 1960 Monaghan borrowed $500 and bought DomiNick's, a failed pizza parlor in Ypsilanti, Michigan, which he operated with the help of his brother James. In 1961 James traded his share in the restaurant to his brother for a Volkswagen Beetle, but Thomas pressed on, learning the pizza business largely by trial and error. After a brief partnership with an experienced restaurateur with whom he later had a falling out, Monaghan developed a strategy to sell only pizza and to locate stores near colleges and military bases. In 1965 the company changed its name to Domino's.

In the 1960s and 1970s, Monaghan endured setbacks that brought the company to the brink of bankruptcy. Among these were a 1968 fire that destroyed the Domino's headquarters and a 1975 lawsuit from Domino Sugar maker Amstar Corporation for trademark infringement. But the company won the ensuing legal battles and by 1978 it was operating 200 stores.

In the 1980s Domino's grew phenomenally. Between 1981 and 1983 the company doubled its number of US stores to 1,000; it went international in 1983, opening a store in Canada. The company's growth brought Monaghan a personal fortune. In 1983 he bought the Detroit Tigers baseball team and amassed one of the world's largest collections of Frank Lloyd Wright objects.

Domino's expansion continued in the mid-1980s. With sales figures mounting, the company introduced pan pizza (its first new product) in 1989. That year Monaghan put Domino's up for sale, but his practice of

linking his personal and professional finances had gotten both the founder and company into such dire fiscal straits that no one wanted to buy the chain. Monaghan removed himself from direct management in 1989 and installed a new management group.

When company performance began to slide, Monaghan returned in 1991, having experienced a religious rebirth. He sold off many of his private holdings (including his resort island and his baseball team, which went to cross-town pizza rival Michael Ilitch of Little Caesar) to reinvigorate the company and reorganize company management.

In 1989, a Domino's driver, trying to fulfill the company's 30-minute delivery guarantee, ran a red light and collided with another car. The resulting $79 million judgment against the company in 1993 prompted Domino's to drop its famous 30-minute policy and replace it with a satisfaction guarantee.

Domino's introduced Buffalo Wings (chicken wings doused with hot sauce) in 1994, began a national advertising push for its Ultimate Deep Dish pizza the next year, and launched its Roma Herb flavored-crust pizza in 1996. The company revamped its logo and store interiors with a new look in 1997.

In 1998 Domino's introduced a delivery bag with a patented heating system designed to keep pies hot and crispy. Later that year, prompted by his decision to devote more time to religious pursuits, Monaghan retired from the business he had guided for nearly 40 years. He sold 93% of his company to investment firm Bain Capital. David Brandon, former CEO of sales promotion company Valassis Communications, replaced Monaghan as chairman and CEO in 1999.

Chairman, President, and CEO: David A. Brandon
EVP Finance and Administration and CFO:
Harry J. Silverman, age 40, $3,345,116 pay
EVP Marketing and Product Development:
Cheryl A. Bachelder, age 42, $2,092,957 pay
EVP Domino's Pizza International: J. Patrick Doyle
EVP Corporate Operations: Patrick Kelly, age 46
EVP Franchise Operations: Stuart Mathis, age 43,
$2,143,185 pay
EVP Distribution: Michael D. Soignet, age 39,
$2,078,993 pay
SVP and Treasurer: Steve Benrubi
SVP Franchise Administration: Jim Stansik
VP Human Resources: Robert Clayton
VP Corporate Communications: Tim McIntyre
VP Training and Quality Compliance:
Patricia Moore Thomas
Chief Information Officer: Timothy Monteith
Auditors: Arthur Andersen LLP

LOCATIONS

HQ: 30 Frank Lloyd Wright Dr., Ann Arbor, MI 48106
Phone: 734-930-3030   **Fax:** 734-668-1946
Web site: http://www.dominos.com

PRODUCTS/OPERATIONS

1998 Sales

	$ mil.	% of total
Domestic distribution	599	51
Corporate stores	410	35
Domestic franchise royalties	112	9
International	56	5
Total	**1,177**	**100**

COMPETITORS

Burger King
CEC Entertainment
CKE Restaurants
Godfather's Pizza
KFC
LDB Corp
Little Caesar
McDonald's
Papa John's
Pizza Hut
Pizza Inn
Round Table Pizza
Sbarro
Subway
Uno Restaurant
Wendy's
Whataburger

HISTORICAL FINANCIALS & EMPLOYEES

Private FYE: December	Annual Growth	1989	1990	1991	1992	1993	1994	1995	1996	1997	1998
Sales ($ mil.)	7.7%	—	—	—	—	—	875	905	970	1,045	1,177
Net income ($ mil.)	382.4%	—	—	—	—	—	0	25	20	61	77
Income as % of sales	—	—	—	—	—	—	0.0%	2.8%	2.0%	5.8%	6.5%
Employees	—	—	—	—	—	—	—	—	—	—	14,200

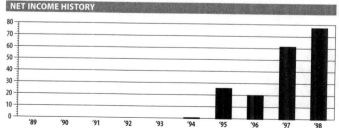

NET INCOME HISTORY

1998 FISCAL YEAR-END
Debt ratio: 100.0%
Return on equity: —
Cash ($ mil.): 0
Current ratio: 0.84
Long-term debt ($ mil.): 720

DOW CORNING CORPORATION

OVERVIEW

With health consequences of silicone gel breast implants still under debate, Dow Corning is experiencing side effects. Facing thousands of claims by women that they have been injured by the company's breast implants, Auburn, Michigan-based Dow Corning (a 50-50 joint venture between chemical titan Dow Chemical and glass giant Corning) is operating under bankruptcy protection.

The company produces more than 10,000 products made of silicone, a polymer developed by Dow Corning scientists in the 1940s. The polymer combines the chemical- and temperature-resistant properties of glass with the versatility of plastic. It is used in such products as nipples for baby bottles, sealants for the construction industry, capsules for drugs, and needle lubricants. Silicone's hard crystalline form, silicon (not produced by Dow Corning), is used as the basic chip on which semiconductors are assembled.

Although the breast-implant case has dragged on for nearly a decade, Dow Corning expects a settlement with 170,000 claimants to finally get the company out from under bankruptcy protection.

HISTORY

Dow Corning was founded in 1943 as a joint venture between Dow Chemical and Corning Glass Works. Corning, founded by Amory Houghton in 1875, provided Thomas Edison with glass for the first lightbulbs. It developed Pyrex heat-resistant glass in 1915.

Using pioneering silicone research by British chemist F. S. Kipping, Corning made its first silicone resin samples in 1938. It teamed with a group of Dow Chemical scientists also working on silicone products in 1940. Dow Chemical president Willard Dow and Corning Glass Works president Glen Cole shook hands on the idea of a joint venture in 1942, and 10 months later Dow Corning was formed. Its first product, the engine grease DOW CORNING 4, enabled B-17s to fly at 35,000 feet for eight hours without their engines shorting out (a major contribution to the Allied war effort). In 1945 DOW CORNING 35 (an emulsifier used in tire molds) and Pan Glaze (which made baking pans stick-proof and easier to clean) were instant successes on the home front.

Dow Corning expanded rapidly in international markets and in 1960 set up Dow Corning International to handle sales and technical service in markets outside North America. By 1969 the company also had operations in Asia, Europe, and Latin America.

Dow Corning's first breast implants went on the market in 1964. By the mid-1970s biocompatible products (made mostly from silicone and accepted as compatible with the human body) were in wide use in artificial hearts, heart valves, and other medical devices. Since 1964 Dow Corning and other silicone makers have sold silicone breast implants to more than a million women in the US. In the early 1980s breast-implant recipients began suing Dow Corning and other implant makers, claiming that the silicone gel in the implants leaked and caused health problems such as disfigurement, autoimmune diseases, and chronic pain. Dow Corning, the leading implant maker, defended the devices as safe. Dow stopped making implants in 1992, after the Food and Drug Administration called for a moratorium on silicone gel implants.

In 1993 Baxter International, Bristol-Myers Squibb, and Dow Corning offered $4.2 billion to settle thousands of claims. The corporation declared bankruptcy in 1995 to buy time for financial reorganization. Also that year Dow Chemical was stripped by a federal judge of its protection from direct liability and was later ordered to pay a Nevada couple $4.1 million in damages (other jurisdictions did not follow suit). Dow Corning sold its Polytrap polymer technology to Advanced Polymer, maker of polymer-based pharmaceutical delivery systems, in 1996. The following year the company sold Bisco Products, its silicone-foam business, to Rogers Corporation for $12 million. Also in 1997 Dow Corning opened its first plant in China.

Dow Corning's $3.7 billion bankruptcy reorganization plan, offered in 1997, allowed for $2.4 billion to be set aside to end most implant lawsuits against the corporation. However, a federal bankruptcy judge found that the proposal was full of legal flaws and refused to allow claimants to vote on it. In 1998 Dow Corning upped the ante to $4.4 billion — $3 billion to the silicone claimants and the rest to creditors. Both sides later agreed to a $3.2 billion compensation package with payments of $10,000 to $250,000. Late in 1999, the plan received the approval of a bankruptcy judge and creditors.

Chairman: Richard A. Hazleton
President and CEO: Gary Anderson
EVP: Siegfried Haberer
VP Planning and Finance and CFO:
John W. Churchfield
VP, Secretary, and General Counsel: James R. Jenkins
Director Human Resources: Gifford Brown

LOCATIONS

HQ: 2200 W. Salzburg Rd., Midland, MI 48686
Phone: 517-496-4000 **Fax:** 517-496-8240
Web site: http://www.dowcorning.com

PRODUCTS/OPERATIONS

Selected Products

Aerospace
Seals and gaskets
Windshield and canopy gasket sealants

Automotive
Sealants and adhesives
Specialty lubricants

Chemicals and Petrochemicals
Processing aids
Silane coupling agents

Electrical/Electronics
Coatings for circuit boards
Compounds for potting and protecting semiconductors
Varnishes

Maintenance, Repair, and Engineering
Adhesives and sealants
Antifoams
Greases
Surfactants

Paints and Coatings
Additives, resins, and intermediates for high-
performance paints, enamels, finishes, and coatings

Textiles and Nonwovens
Antifoams and softeners for textile processes
Waterproofing treatments

COMPETITORS

3M
Aventis
Baxter
Bristol-Myers Squibb
CK Witco
Degussa-Huls
Exxon Mobil
GE
Lexington Precision
Shin-Etsu Chemical
Th. Goldschmidt
Wacker-Chemie

HISTORICAL FINANCIALS & EMPLOYEES

Joint venture FYE: December	Annual Growth	1989	1990	1991	1992	1993	1994	1995	1996	1997	1998
Sales ($ mil.)	5.6%	1,575	1,720	1,845	1,956	2,044	2,205	2,493	2,532	2,644	2,568
Net income ($ mil.)	2.7%	163	171	153	(72)	(287)	(7)	(31)	222	238	207
Income as % of sales	—	10.3%	9.9%	8.3%	—	—	—	—	8.8%	9.0%	8.0%
Employees	2.9%	6,988	7,328	7,598	8,600	8,000	8,300	8,500	8,900	9,100	9,000

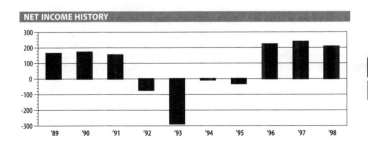

NET INCOME HISTORY

DOW CORNING

DREAMWORKS SKG

OVERVIEW

Steven Spielberg, Jeffrey Katzenberg, and David Geffen had a Dream and now it Works. Universal City, California-based DreamWorks SKG is the brainchild of the three Hollywood moguls, who formed the multimedia company in 1994. Spielberg oversees the live-action movies, which include 1998's Oscar-winning WWII epic *Saving Private Ryan* and the critically acclaimed *American Beauty* (1999). Katzenberg heads up the animation division, responsible for such films as *The Prince of Egypt* and *Antz,* while Geffen runs DreamWorks Records, producing albums for dozens of artists such as George Michael and Randy Travis. The company also produces TV shows (*Spin City*), develops interactive software in a joint venture with Microsoft, and is a partner with SEGA and

Universal Studios in 14 SEGA GameWorks video arcades.

A former production executive at Disney, Katzenberg is essentially DreamWorks' CEO, handling the day-to-day operations (as Spielberg is often out directing films for the company). The company's bid to build a new studio failed, and DreamWorks' current offices are located at Universal Pictures, where Spielberg has hung his hat for many years.

Film projects include *What Lies Beneath* (starring Harrison Ford) and the animated adventure *Chicken Run* (featuring the voice of Mel Gibson). DreamWorks also has a hand in online venture POP.com, co-owned with Ron Howard's Imagine Entertainment and Microsoft co-founder Paul Allen's Vulcan Ventures (Vulcan owns a stake in DreamWorks).

HISTORY

Before pooling their collective talents in 1994, Steven Spielberg, Jeffrey Katzenberg, and David Geffen had each established an impressive track record. Spielberg had spawned such blockbusters as *Jaws,* the *Indiana Jones* trilogy, and *Jurassic Park.* Katzenberg had guided Walt Disney's return to animation (*The Lion King, Aladdin*) before a falling out with Disney CEO Michael Eisner. Music guru Geffen had helped make superstars of the Eagles and Nirvana.

A high-tech who's who embraced the SKG dream. Microsoft invested around $30 million to develop video games, while Microsoft co-founder Paul Allen shelled out nearly $500 million for a stake in the new company. Soon DreamWorks had arranged a $100 million programming deal with ABC and a 10-year HBO licensing agreement worth an estimated $1 billion, and co-founded a $50 million animation studio with Silicon Graphics. DreamWorks then announced plans in 1995 to build the first new studio since the 1930s, just outside of Los Angeles in Playa Vista.

DreamWorks started with television in 1996, producing a string of flops before finding success with the Michael J. Fox comedy *Spin City.* Later that year the company released the first record under its new label, a dud from pop star George Michael, and it announced its partnership with SEGA and MCA (now Universal Studios) to develop SEGA GameWorks (video arcade super-centers featuring SEGA titles and games designed by Spielberg). The company finally released its

first three movies in 1997 (*The Peacemaker, Amistad,* and *Mouse Hunt*) to mixed critical reviews and mediocre box office performance. Combined with DreamWorks' less-than-stellar offerings in TV and music, buzz began to circulate that the meeting of the minds at DreamWorks wasn't all it was cracked up to be.

But DreamWorks started showing signs of life in 1998 with the comet disaster film *Deep Impact* and Spielberg's Oscar-winning *Saving Private Ryan,* the highest grossing film of the year. It also introduced its first two animated films that year, *Antz* and *The Prince of Egypt,* both successful. DreamWorks finished the year with the highest average gross per film of all the major studios.

After facing a multitude of environmental protests, cost overruns, and construction delays since announcing the project, DreamWorks scrapped its Playa Vista studio plans in 1999. Around the same time, Katzenberg settled his high-profile lawsuit against Disney over a bonus owed him when he resigned. Later that year DreamWorks joined with Imagine Entertainment and Vulcan Ventures to create POP.com, a Web site offering digital short films and streaming video features. It also announced a four-picture deal with Academy Award-winning animation firm Aardman Animations, with which it co-produced *Chicken Run* (due in 2000), and showed continued success in theaters with *American Beauty.*

Partner: David Geffen
Partner, Interim Head, Production: Jeffrey Katzenberg
Partner: Steven Spielberg
CFO: Ronald L. Nelson
Senior Executive, DreamWorks Consumer Products:
Brad Globe
Senior Executive, Business and Legal Affairs:
Helene Hahn
Senior Executive, Sales: Don Harris
Senior Executive, Television Division: Dan McDermott
Senior Executive, DreamWorks SKG Music: Mo Ostin
**Senior Executive, Strategic Marketing, Public
Relations and Special Projects:** Terry Press
Feature Executive: Laurie MacDonald
Feature Executive: Walter Parkes
President, Feature Animation: Ann Daly
**Supervisor, Exhibitor Relations and In-Theater
Marketing:** Patricia Gonzalez
Supervisor, Music Publishing: Chuck Kaye
Supervisor, Sales, Western States: Noel Kendall
Supervisor, Sales, Eastern States: Joe Sabatino
Supervisor, Central Region: Jim Smith
Supervisor, Distribution: Jim Tharp
Director, Human Resources: Pierre Towns
Auditors: Ernst & Young LLP

HQ: 100 Universal Plaza, Bungalow 477,
Universal City, CA 91608
Phone: 818-733-7000   **Fax:** 818-733-9918
Web site: http://www.dreamworks.com

Selected Titles of DreamWorks Interactive
Boombots
Jurassic Park: The Lost World
Jurassic Park: Warpath
Medal of Honor
SkullMonkeys
Small Soldiers
Small Soldiers: Squad Commander
T'ai Fu
Trespasser

Selected Films of DreamWorks Pictures
American Beauty (1999)
Amistad (1997)
Antz (1998)
Deep Impact (1998)
The Love Letter (1999)
Mouse Hunt (1997)
Paulie (1998)
The Peacemaker (1997)
The Prince of Egypt (1998)
Saving Private Ryan (1998)
Small Soldiers (1998)

Selected Artists of DreamWorks Records
Buckcherry
George Michael
Morphine
Randy Newman
Chris Rock
Henry Rollins
Elliott Smith
Randy Travis
Rufus Wainwright

Selected Show of DreamWorks Television
Spin City

Activision	Nintendo
Carsey-Werner	Pixar
Electronic Arts	Sony
GT Interactive	Time Warner
King World	Universal Studios
Lucasfilm	Viacom
MGM	Virgin Group
News Corp.	Walt Disney

Private FYE: December	Annual Growth	1989	1990	1991	1992	1993	1994	1995	1996	1997	1998
Estimated sales ($ mil.)	—	—	—	—	—	—	—	—	—	—	1,000
Employees	—	—	—	—	—	—	—	—	—	—	1,600

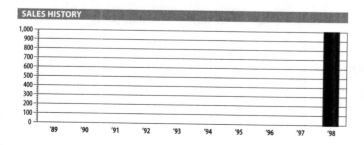

E. & J. GALLO WINERY

"We don't want most of the business," E. & J. Gallo Winery chairman Ernest Gallo has said. "We want it all." A longtime producer of cheap jug wine, such as Carlo Rossi and Gallo and fortified favorites such as Thunderbird, the world's largest wine maker has also siphoned market share from upscale rivals by branching into more profitable middle- and premium-priced wines, including Gallo Sonoma. The Modesto, California-based winery also sells premium wines such as Turning Leaf and Gossamer Bay without mentioning the Gallo name to distance them from their common cousins.

Already the leader in US table wines, with about 25% of the market, Gallo sells wine in more than 85 countries and is the leading US wine exporter. (It is the top brand in the UK.) Gallo cultivates 4,000-plus acres over five vineyards in prestigious Sonoma County, California, alone and buys grapes from other area growers. Gallo sells nearly 35 brands over a wide price range, from alcohol-added wines and wine coolers to a growing number of upscale varietals that fetch up to $60 a bottle.

The founding Gallo family owns the company.

HISTORY

Ernest, Julio, and Joe, the three sons of Joe Gallo Sr., left Italy for San Francisco around 1906. Joe Sr. started selling wine and, after marrying the daughter of a commercial wine maker, began growing grapes. During Prohibition, Joe Sr. sent his grapes to Chicago, where Ernest and Julio sold them for use in legal home wine making.

Near the end of Prohibition, Joe Sr. and his wife were found dead in an apparent murder-suicide. In 1933 Ernest and Julio started their own business, E. & J. Gallo Winery, selling through their Chicago grape contacts. Gallo soon became a popular local brand.

Ernest ran the business end, assembling a large distribution network and building a national brand, while Julio made the wine and Joe worked for them. In the early 1940s Gallo opened bottling plants in Los Angeles and New Orleans, using screw-cap bottles, which then seemed more hygienic and modern than corks. Gallo lagged during WWII, when alcohol was diverted for the military. Under Julio's supervision, it began upgrading its planting stock and refining its wine-making technology.

In the 1950s US wine tastes were generally unsophisticated, and sweet wines such as Italian Swiss Colony were sales leaders. In an attempt to take this market, Gallo introduced Thunderbird, a fortified wine (its alcohol content boosted to 20%), in 1957. In the 1960s Gallo spurred its growth by advertising heavily and keeping prices low. It introduced Hearty Burgundy, a jug wine, in 1964, along with Ripple. Gallo introduced the carbonated, fruit-flavored Boone's Farm Apple Wine in 1969, creating an interest in "pop" wines that lasted for a few years.

The company in 1974 introduced its first varietal wines, bearing the name of the grape from which they were made. In the 1970s

Gallo field workers switched unions, from the United Farm Workers to the Teamsters. Repercussions included protests and boycotts, but sales were largely unaffected. From 1976 to 1982 Gallo operated under an FTC order limiting its control over wholesalers. The order was lifted after the industry's competitive balance changed.

Through the 1970s and 1980s, Gallo expanded its production of varietals; in 1988 it began adding vintage dates to the wines' labels. But it also kept a hand in the lower levels of the market, introducing Bartles & Jaymes wine coolers.

Gallo began a legal battle in 1986 with Joe over the use of the Gallo name. After working for his brothers for years, Joe had been eased out and had started a dairy farm to make cheese. In 1992 he lost the use of his name for commercial purposes. Julio died the next year when his jeep overturned on a family ranch.

Heublein, maker of Jose Cuervo tequila, sued Gallo in 1995 for selling a "margarita" cooler without tequila; the companies settled the case in 1996 when Gallo agreed to downplay the "margarita" theme. Further litigation followed that year when rival Kendall-Jackson sued Gallo for trademark infringement over Gallo's new wine brand, Turning Leaf, claiming Gallo copied its Vintner's Reserve bottle and label. A jury ruled in Gallo's favor in 1997; a federal appeals court supported that decision in 1998.

Gina Gallo, Julio's granddaughter and a company wine maker, broke the firm's publicity-shy tradition in 1999 by appearing in national advertising to promote its more expensive wines.

Chairman: Ernest Gallo
Co-President: James E. Coleman
Co-President: Joseph E. Gallo
Co-President: Robert J. Gallo
EVP, Marketing: Albion Fenderson
EVP and General Counsel: Jack B. Owens
VP, Controller, and Assistant Treasurer: Tony Youga
VP, Human Resources: Mike Chase
VP, Information Systems: Kent Kushar
VP, Media: Sue McClelland
VP, National Sales: Gary Ippolito
VP and Secretary: Charles M. Crawford

LOCATIONS

HQ: 600 Yosemite Blvd., Modesto, CA 95354
Phone: 209-341-3111   **Fax:** 209-341-3569
Web site: http://www.gallo.com

PRODUCTS/OPERATIONS

Selected Labels

Anapamu	Gallo Hearty Burgundy
André	Gallo Sonoma
Ballatore	Gossamer Bay
Bartles & Jaymes	Hornsby's Cider
Boone's Farm	Indigo Hills
Burlwood	Laguna Ranch
Carlo Rossi	Livingston Cellars
Copperidge	Marcelina
E & J Brandy	Night Train Express
E & J Superior Reserve	Peter Vella
VSOP (brandy)	Rancho Zabaco
Ecco Domani	The Reserve Cellars of
Eden Roc	Ernest & Julio Gallo
Ernest & Julio Gallo	Ripple
Ernest & Julio Gallo	Sheffield
Northern Sonoma Estate	Thunderbird
Fairbanks	Tott's
Frei Ranch	Turning Leaf
Gallo	Wild Vines
Gallo Estate	William Wycliff

COMPETITORS

Allied Domecq	LVMH
Asahi Breweries	Pernod Ricard
Bacardi-Martini	R.H. Phillips
Beringer	Ravenswood Winery
Brown-Forman	Robert Mondavi
Canandaigua Brands	Seagram
Chalone Wine	Sebastiani Vineyards
Concha y Toro	Sutter Home
Diageo	UST
Foster's Brewing	Wine Group
Kendall-Jackson	

HISTORICAL FINANCIALS & EMPLOYEES

Private FYE: December	Annual Growth	1989	1990	1991	1992	1993	1994	1995	1996	1997	1998
Estimated sales ($ mil.)	4.6%	1,000	1,050	1,100	1,000	1,100	980	1,100	1,200	1,300	1,500
Employees	6.0%	2,950	3,000	3,000	3,000	4,000	4,000	4,000	5,000	5,000	5,000

SALES HISTORY

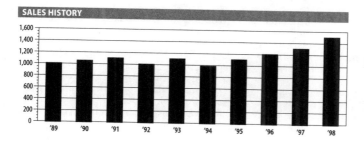

EBSCO INDUSTRIES INC.

OVERVIEW

EBSCO Industries has taken the idea of diversification to the extreme: Among the conglomerate's 80 sales, service, and manufacturing subsidiaries are magazine subscription and fulfillment firms, a fishing lure manufacturer, a rifle manufacturer, a company that sells specialty office and computer furniture, and another that manages real estate for the company. Birmingham, Alabama-based EBSCO's main businesses revolve around the publishing industry: EBSCO operates a leading subscription management agency and is one of the largest publishers of information online and on CD-ROM. It also prints magazines, publishes educational materials, and provides such services as sales, promotion, telemarketing, and fulfillment to other publishers.

EBSCO provides bulk subscription services for print and electronic journals, technical reports, books, and other publications to schools, libraries, and professional offices. It also owns commercial printers and supplies bindery and packaging products.

Among EBSCO's more eclectic subsidiaries are promotional products manufacturers Four Seasons and Vitronic; PRADCO, which makes fishing tackle; Valley Joist, which produces steel construction materials; Vulcan Industries, which makes point-of-purchase displays; Knight & Hale, which makes game calls for hunters; and specialty furniture makers H. Wilson and Luxor.

Founder and chairman Elton Stephens and his family own EBSCO.

HISTORY

During the 1930s Elton Stephens put himself through college selling magazine subscriptions door-to-door. Although he later earned a law degree, Stephens thought he could make more money selling magazines. After WWII broke out, Stephens and his wife, Alys, formed Military Service Co. in 1944 to sell magazines, binders, and display racks to the US military.

Early in his career Stephens suggested that he'd like to own five companies so that he'd have a fallback if one failed. He set about fulfilling his wish, forming Metal Fabricators and Finishers (now Vulcan Industries) in 1946, Vulcan Binder & Cover (now Vulcan Information Packaging) in 1947, and Vulcan Enterprises (now Directional Advertising Services) in 1954. In 1958 the Stephens' businesses were combined under the name EBSCO Industries, Inc. (the name is a contraction of Elton B. Stephens Company). In 1960 EBSCO acquired Chicago's Hanson-Bennett Magazine Agency, and in 1967 it bought Los Angeles' National Publications and binder manufacturer The Burkhardt Co. of Detroit.

Stephens retired as president of the company in 1971, and his son, J. T., took the job. The following year EBSCO bought the Franklin Square Agency and Ziff-Davis' international subscription service, doubling the volume of EBSCO Subscription Services. EBSCO started its Publisher Promotion and Fulfillment service and added operations in Europe in 1975.

EBSCO acquired Valley Joist (metal construction products) in 1976 and H. Wilson Co. (audiovisual and computer furniture) in 1977. EBSCO Curriculum Materials and EBSCO

Reception Room Subscription Services were formed in 1979 and 1980, respectively. Purchases in 1980 included Oklahoma-based Metro Press (now EBSCO Graphics), Cincinnati's National Billiard, and Arkansas-based PRADCO (fishing lures).

In 1981 Elton began a second career at age 70 when he founded Alabama Bancorp.

Under J. T.'s direction, EBSCO continued to grow through acquisitions and startups. It bought Four Seasons (promotional clothing and other items, 1983) and NSC International (binding and laminating products, 1984). The company formed electronic database publisher EBSCO Electronic Information (now EBSCO Publishing, 1986) and bought Bomber Bait (1988), merging it into PRADCO.

After a short breather, the company acquired Luxor (school and library furniture) in 1992. That year the various Vulcan operations were combined in a new facility in Moody, Alabama. The company acquired Dynamic Information (later EBSCO Document Services) in 1994. The following year it bought Northeast Looseleaf (now part of Vulcan Information Packaging), and in 1996 it formed EBSCO Magazine Express.

The next year EBSCO bought Fred Arbogast, maker of the Jitterbug and Hula Popper fishing lures, and hunting game-call maker Knight & Hale. In 1998 the company bought Network Support, a Canadian maker of document imaging and management software, and closed down its document delivery unit. The following year EBSCO Publishing revealed Searchasaurus, an online search engine for children.

Chairman: Elton B. Stephens
President and CEO: James T. Stephens
VP and CFO: Richard L. Bozzelli
VP Administration: Jean S. Mallette
VP and Chief Accounting Officer: Carol Matthews
Johnson
VP; General Manager, EBSCO Curriculum Materials:
H. Douglas Allison
VP; General Manager, EBSCO Publishing:
Timothy R. Collins
VP; General Manager, EBSCO Realty:
Elton B. Stephens Jr.
**VP; General Manager, EBSCO Subscription Services
Division:** F. Dixon Brooke Jr.
VP; General Manager, EBSCO Telemarketing Service:
N. Robert Cortellino
**VP; General Manager, Information Systems and
Services:** John R. Fitts
VP; General Manager, Military Science: Mac Chandler
**VP; General Manager, Publisher Promotion and
Fulfillment:** Tambra A. McKerley
VP; General Manager, Publisher's Warehouse:
William F. Haver
**VP Marketing; General Manager, EBSCO Reception
Room Subscription Services:** Jack H. Breard Jr.
VP Personnel: John Thompson
VP Communications: Joe K. Weed

HQ: 5724 Hwy. 280 East, Birmingham, AL 35242
Phone: 205-991-6600   **Fax:** 205-995-1636
Web site: http://www.ebscoind.com

Selected Operations

Manufacturing
EBSCO Graphics (commercial printer)
EBSCO Media (commercial printer)
Four Seasons and Vitronic (promotional products)
H. Wilson Co. (audiovisual and computer furniture)
Knight & Hale (game calls for hunting)
Luxor (specialty furniture for offices, schools)
Modern Muzzleloading (rifle manufacturing)
PRADCO (fishing lures, fishing line, and related products)
Valley Joist (steel joists, girders for construction industry)
Vulcan Industries (point-of-purchase displays; specialty
contract painting services)
Vulcan Information Packaging (binders, tabs, and
packaging for albums, software, and videotapes)
Wayne Industries (point-of-purchase advertising and signs)

Sales and Service
Directional Advertising Services (marketing in reception
rooms and other reading areas)
EBSCO Information Services (document delivery,
publishing, and subscription services)
EBSCO Magazine Express (direct-marketing subscription
agency)
EBSCO Publishing (database publishing and information
retrieval services)
EBSCO Telemarketing Service (telemarketing services)
EBSCOhost (database access)
Kinescope Interactive (multimedia marketing services)
Military Service Company (producer and manufacturers'
representative serving military base exchanges)
NSC International (binding and laminating systems)
Publisher Promotion and Fulfillment
Relais International (interlibrary loan management)
Vulcan Service/Periodical Sales (magazine subscriptions)

ACI Telecentrics	Devon Group	Roanoke Electric
AMREP	General Binding	Steel
APAC Customer	Johnson	RoweCom
Services	Worldwide	SITEL
Bowne	McGraw-Hill	Scholastic
Brunswick	Moore	TeleSpectrum
Champion	Corporation	Thomson
International	Quebecor	Corporation
Dai Nippon	R. R. Donnelley	U.S. Office
Printing	Reed Elsevier	Products

Private FYE: June	Annual Growth	1990	1991	1992	1993	1994	1995	1996	1997	1998	1999
Estimated sales ($ mil.)	10.4%	—	—	—	—	—	—	900	1,000	1,000	1,210
Employees	1.6%	—	—	—	—	—	—	4,000	4,000	4,000	4,200

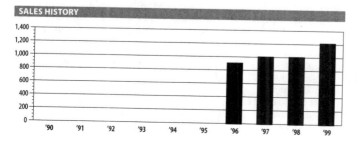

SALES HISTORY

EBSCO
Industries,
Inc.

EDWARD J. DEBARTOLO

OVERVIEW

Real estate holdings, gambling, horse racing, a felony conviction, and warring siblings surrounded by a storied NFL franchise — sounds like an old episode of *Dallas*. But the story of The Edward J. DeBartolo Corporation takes place in Youngstown, Ohio (where the company is based), via San Francisco (where the company owns the 49ers football team). The company also owns a racetrack (Louisiana Downs in Bossier City), and 11% of Simon Property Group (SPG), North America's largest public real estate company.

The saga of the DeBartolo family concerns chairman and CEO Denise DeBartolo York and her brother, former CEO Eddie DeBartolo Jr., children of the company's eponymous founder.

Eddie's guilty plea in 1998 to charges of failing to report a felony led to his ouster and a lawsuit from his sister to recover a $94 million debt from him. Eddie countersued, and after much wrangling, a tentative agreement has been reached whereby Denise DeBartolo York will take the company name, the 49ers, and the racetrack, and Eddie DeBartolo will receive other real estate holdings and stock.

Before the gambling fraud probe became public, San Francisco voters approved a $100 million bond issue to help finance a $525 million stadium/shopping mall (built by the Mills Corporation and SPG) for the 49ers. Until the company's ownership issues are settled, those plans have been put on ice.

HISTORY

Edward J. DeBartolo left his stepfather's paving business in 1944 and established the company that bears his name. DeBartolo's foresight about the growth of the suburbs led him to build one of the first strip-style malls outside California, the Belmont Plaza near Youngstown, Ohio, in 1949. Over the next 15 years, the company built 45 more strip centers throughout the US. In the 1960s DeBartolo became one of the first to develop large, covered regional malls in many parts of the nation. DeBartolo opened the Louisiana Downs racetrack in 1974 and moved the company into the sports business in 1977 when he helped his son, Edward Jr. (Eddie), buy the San Francisco 49ers.

When the management of Allied Stores asked DeBartolo to help fend off a bid by real estate developer Robert Campeau, DeBartolo thought that control of Allied's department store chains would provide anchor stores for his mall developments and loaned Campeau $150 million for the takeover instead. Two years later DeBartolo borrowed $480 million and lent it to Campeau for his acquisition of Federated Department Stores.

The company reached its zenith in the late 1980s (opening the Rivercenter in San Antonio and Lakeland Square in Florida), but Campeau was in trouble — the highly leveraged Allied and Federated went bankrupt and threatened to take DeBartolo with them. As part of the bankruptcy settlement, DeBartolo took a 60% interest in California-based Ralphs supermarket (since sold) and started selling off assets in 1991 to cover the loan he made to Campeau and the company's own $4 billion debt. The firesale included his

private jet, three malls, two office buildings, a 50% stake in Higbee's department stores, and the Rivercenter.

Edward DeBartolo died in 1994. His daughter, Denise DeBartolo York, became chairman, and his son, Eddie (who was also chairman and CEO of the 49ers) became president and CEO. Eddie reshuffled the company's assets with most of its real estate holdings turned into DeBartolo Realty, a real estate investment trust that went public that year, raising $575 million. Mounting tensions between the siblings intensified in 1995 when Eddie formed DeBartolo Entertainment, his own separate company in the gaming business (Denise tried to distance the family business from Eddie's new company in a press release). DeBartolo Realty merged with Simon Property Group the following year.

Eddie ran into trouble with the law in 1997 when an investigation revealed that he had paid former Louisiana governor Edwin Edwards $400,000 in an effort to obtain a riverboat gambling license for DeBartolo Entertainment. Eddie pleaded guilty to felony charges of concealing wrongdoing the next year, was fined $2 million, and stepped down from DeBartolo Corp. The NFL then fined Eddie another $1 million and banned him from the 49ers in 1999. Later that year Denise sued Eddie for debt owed to the company, and he countersued. The parties have reached a tentative agreement dividing the company's assets between them. DeBartolo Corp. also sold two of its racetracks (Thistledown and Remington Park) in 1999.

OFFICERS

Chairman and CEO: Marie Denise DeBartolo York
SVP and CFO: Lynn E. Davenport
EVP: John C. York II
General Manager, San Francisco 49ers: Bill Walsh
Head Coach, San Francisco 49ers: Steve Mariucci
Human Resources: Linda Pearce

LOCATIONS

HQ: The Edward J. DeBartolo Corporation,
7620 Market St., Youngstown, OH 44512
Phone: 330-965-2000   **Fax:** 330-965-2077

PRODUCTS/OPERATIONS

Selected Holdings
Louisiana Downs (horse racetrack, Bossier City)
San Francisco 49ers (NFL franchise)
Simon Property Group (11%, real estate company)

COMPETITORS

Atlanta Falcons
Carolina Panthers
Fair Grounds
General Growth Properties
JMB Realty
Kimco Realty
New Orleans Saints
Players
Rouse
St. Louis Rams

HISTORICAL FINANCIALS & EMPLOYEES

Private FYE: June	Annual Growth	1989	1990	1991	1992	1993	1994	1995	1996	1997	1998
Estimated sales ($ mil.)	(10.9%)	—	—	—	500	525	550	230	220	250	250
Employees	1.3%	—	—	—	—	—	3,800	3,000	3,000	3,000	4,000

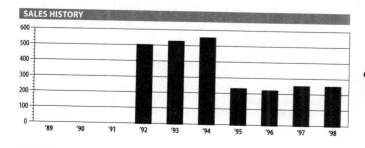

SALES HISTORY

EMPIRE BLUE CROSS

OVERVIEW

To convert or not to convert? That's Empire Blue Cross and Blue Shield's question. Serving more than 4 million customers in eastern New York and northern New Jersey, the New York City-based company is the largest health care provider in its market. The company offers traditional indemnity, HMO, PPO, and EPO (exclusive provider organization offering no out-of-network benefits) plans for individuals and groups. Empire offers Blue Card, a national program giving certain members access to enrolled providers across the US. It also has dental, pharmacy, and vision care plans.

A licensee of the Blue Cross and Blue Shield Association, Empire was traditionally an insurer of last resort. In exchange for covering otherwise uninsurable people, Empire received quasi-charitable status and generous state tax breaks. But increased competition through consolidation has reduced its market share, and Empire now wants to convert to for-profit status to be more competitive.

The conversion plan has to contend with state legislation that appears to block such a move, as well as with consumer advocates' concerns about the fate of Empire's older, sicker, and poorer clientele (and about the use of public funds to build the value of a for-profit company). Empire responds with plans to set up a charitable foundation — which would initially own the company's stock — to provide health care for New York's uninsured population.

HISTORY

Prepaid medical care was born in 1929 when Baylor University Hospital administrator Justin Kimball began offering hospital care coverage to teachers for $6 a year. Kimball's plan — to stabilize hospital costs while encouraging people to insure themselves — eventually developed into the national Blue Cross and Blue Shield Association.

Empire's story began in 1934 when the Associated Hospital Service (AHS Blue Cross) was created to provide hospital insurance in New York. It had more than 40,000 members at the end of its first year, and 2.2 million members by 1945. In 1936 the organization that would later become Blue Cross of Northeastern New York was founded as the Associated Hospital Service Capital District (AHSCD).

In 1940 not-for-profit Medical Expense Fund began providing payment for doctors' services. Four years later it merged with AHS affiliate Community Medical Care to create United Medical Service (UMS). UMS signed up 1.5 million members in just four years. It joined the national Blue Shield Association in 1949 and became New York Blue Shield.

AHSCD became a contractor with the US military's CHAMPUS insurance program in 1956 and began using the name Blue Cross of Northeastern New York in 1965. In 1966 the federal government selected AHS Blue Cross to help manage New York State's Medicare program. In the early 1970s the association created an HMO to challenge the managed care companies that were crowding into its territory.

AHS Blue Cross and New York Blue Shield merged to form the Blues of Greater New York in 1974. Finally, in 1985 the Blues of Greater New York and Blue Cross of Northeastern New York merged to form Empire.

The 1990s were rocky, as Empire lost younger, healthier members to managed care companies offering lower rates. In 1992 and again in 1995, the US Senate investigated Empire, uncovering mismanagement and fraud. In 1997 former CFO Jerry Weissman (fired in 1993) was convicted of lying to the Senate in 1992 about Empire's financial problems. His successor, Michael Stocker, cut costs and boosted managed care membership.

In 1996 Empire created for-profit subsidiaries Family HealthChoice (an HMO, now Empire Health Choice) and Family Health Assurance (an accident and health insurer, now Empire Health Choice Assurance), then announced plans to convert to for-profit status. That year New York ended Empire's preferred status and deregulated hospital rates (Empire had been exempt from a 13% hospital surcharge), forcing all insurers to compete on equal footing.

In 1997 regulators approved the company's purchase of Central National Life Insurance Co. of New Jersey, giving Empire a foothold in that state and a license to sell health insurance in seven more states. Empire posted a loss that year because of rising claims against its HMOs and startup costs for its Medicare supplement. To offset the loss, it applied in 1998 to raise its HMO rates by almost 21%. In 1999 the firm started a cost-containment program to track patients and suggest treatment options to their doctors.

OFFICERS

Chairman: Philip Briggs
President and CEO: Michael A. Stocker
SVP and CFO: John W. Remshard
SVP and Chief Information Officer:
William B. O'Loughlin
SVP and General Counsel: Linda V. Tiano
SVP, Corporate Development: Kenneth O. Klepper
SVP, Human Resources and Services:
S. Tyrone Alexander
SVP, Operations, Managed Care, and Sales:
Gloria M. McCarthy
SVP, Sales and National Accounts: Joseph Berardo Jr.
VP and Chief Actuary: Michael W. Fedyna
VP and Chief Medical Officer: William J. Osheroff
VP and COO: Raymond Khan
VP and Chief Underwriter: J. Michael Feehan
VP, Albany Operations: John F. Early
VP, Auditing: John M. Furka
VP, Communications: Deborah Bohren
VP, Contracting and Network Development:
Connie C. Poirier
VP, Fraud Investigation and Detection: Louis Parisi
VP, Medical Management: Angelo V. Dascoli
Corporate Secretary: Peter Liria Jr.
Auditors: Ernst & Young LLP

LOCATIONS

HQ: Empire Blue Cross and Blue Shield,
1 Rural Trade Center, New York, NY 10048
Phone: 212-476-1000   **Fax:** 212-476-1281
Web site: http://www.empirehealthcare.com

PRODUCTS/OPERATIONS

1998 Sales

	$ mil.	% of total
Premiums earned	3,065	93
Administrative services	152	5
Investment income	60	2
Total	**3,277**	**100**

Products and Services

Managed Care Products
BlueChoice HMO
BlueChoice Senior Plan
Direct Connection EPO
Direct Connection HMO
Empire Deluxe PPO
Empire Dental Preferred PPO
BlueChoice Workers Compensation

Indemnity Products
CompreCare
Empire Dental TraditionPLUS Medicare Supplement
Prescription Drug
TraditionPLUS Hospital
Wraparound

For-Profit Subsidiaries
Empire HealthChoice Assurance, Inc. (accident and
health insurance)
Empire HealthChoice, Inc. (HMO)
Empire Health Plans Assurance, Inc. (credit life,
accident, and health insurance)

COMPETITORS

Aetna
Anthem Insurance
CIGNA
Foundation Health Systems
Health Insurance of New York
Oxford Health Plans
Prudential
Travelers
UnitedHealth Group
WellCare Management

HISTORICAL FINANCIALS & EMPLOYEES

Not-for-profit FYE: December	Annual Growth	1989	1990	1991	1992	1993	1994	1995	1996	1997	1998
Sales ($ mil.)	(9.3%)	—	—	—	—	5,338	4,798	4,088	3,401	3,277	3,277
Net income ($ mil.)	(14.3%)	—	—	—	—	91	(49)	44	11	52	42
Income as % of sales	—	—	—	—	—	1.7%	—	1.1%	0.3%	1.6%	1.3%
Employees	(6.1%)	—	—	—	—	8,215	7,900	6,821	6,099	6,000	6,000

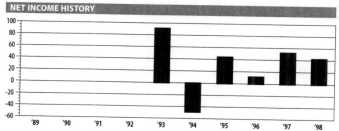

NET INCOME HISTORY

1998 FISCAL YEAR-END
Debt ratio: 12.6%
Return on equity: 11.8%
Cash ($ mil.): —
Current ratio: —
Long-term debt ($ mil.): 55

Blue Cross
Blue Shield

ENCYCLOPAEDIA BRITANNICA, INC.

OVERVIEW

Gone are the days of students paying their way through college by selling *Britannica*s door-to-door. Based in Chicago, the publisher of the oldest and largest English-language general encyclopedia and of *Merriam-Webster's* dictionaries has closed the book on in-home sales in North America and the UK. Instead, Encyclopaedia Britannica is peddling encyclopedias online and in stores.

As part of its new strategy to remain competitive in the digital age, the company has created a new subsidiary, Britannica.com, that houses all of the firm's electronic and online products. Britannica.com now offers its encyclopedia database to online users free of charge. The electronic products subsidiary also offers a multimedia CD-ROM version of the

Encyclopaedia Britannica, featuring 73,000 full-length articles and some 30,000 integrated Web sites, as well as a free online dictionary service. In addition, Britannica.com operates a self-described "thinking person's" search engine, which includes about 130,000 Web sites hand-picked by Britannica's editors, based on the sites' usefulness and accuracy. It also offers selected articles from about 70 popular newspapers and magazines such as *Newsweek*.

Britannica's print products include the original 32-volume *Encyclopaedia Britannica,* and a new 12-volume "ready reference" version. It also publishes the *Britannica Atlas, Great Books of the Western World,* and dictionaries under the *Merriam-Webster* name.

Swiss financier Jacob Safra owns the firm.

HISTORY

Encyclopaedia Britannica was founded in Scotland in 1768 by engraver Andrew Bell and printer and bookseller Colin Macfarquhar. The first edition was released volume-by-volume between 1768 and 1771. It included articles by Benjamin Franklin (on electricity) and John Locke (on human understanding). From the late 1700s to the mid-1800s, the encyclopedia grew from 10 to 22 volumes and developed a reputation for quality.

American businessmen Horace Hooper and Walter Jackson purchased the company in 1901 and established the Encyclopaedia Britannica Company in the US. It published the first *Britannica Book of the Year* in 1913. Hooper's golfing partner, Sears chairman Julius Rosenwald, bought the company in 1920. After a failed attempt to market the *Britannica* through Sears' mail-order catalog and retail stores, Rosenwald assembled a national sales force to sell the books door-to-door. Former piano salesman Louis Schoenewald led the effort.

Encyclopaedia Britannica began printing the *Britannica Junior* (later the *Children's Britannica*) for schoolchildren in 1934. Ownership was transferred in 1943 to the University of Chicago and university VP William Benton (of Benton & Bowles Advertising Agency fame). Benton built up a nationwide sales force with a hard-sell reputation. Britannica released its first foreign-language encyclopedia in 1957, the *Enciclopedia Barsa,* in Spanish.

The company acquired G. & C. Merriam, publisher of *Webster's Third New International Dictionary,* in 1964. Britannica bought out rival *Compton's Encyclopedia* in the mid-1970s. The firm led the industry with the 1989 release of

Compton's MultiMedia Encyclopedia. However, in the midst of a 40% drop in sales from 1990 to 1994, it sold Compton's NewMedia division to Chicago's Tribune Company. This move took Britannica completely out of the CD-ROM business just before the market exploded. It belatedly re-entered electronic publishing in 1994 when it released the *Britannica* CD, which provides access to the entire 32-volume *Encyclopaedia Britannica* on a single CD-ROM for half the price of the printed version. Britannica Online became available in 1994-1995.

A *Britannica* lover since childhood, Jacob Safra and his group paid $135 million in 1996 to purchase the financially struggling company from the not-for-profit William Benton Foundation. The company cut its prices and ceased its door-to-door marketing in 1996 and a year later agreed to sell both its CD-ROM and print encyclopedias in retail stores. Also in 1997 Britannica lured publisher Paul Hoffman away from Walt Disney's successful *Discover* magazine, and the company began offering Britannica Internet Guide (BIG), a free Internet search engine.

In 1998 Britannica added more information, guest columns, and other features to BIG and renamed it eBlast (it changed the Web site's name again to Britannica the following year). Also that year it began marketing a 12-volume encyclopedia set. In 1999 the company created a new subsidiary, Britannica.com, to house all of the company's electronic and Internet products and services. CEO Don Yannias resigned his post and took the reigns of the new digital subsidiary, allowing Hoffman to take over as the parent's new big cheese.

Chairman: Jacob E. Safra
CEO: Paul Hoffman
EVP, Secretary, and General Counsel: William J. Bowe
SVP Worldwide Marketing: John Halberg
Publisher, Merriam-Webster: John Morse
VP Finance Operations: Richard Anderson
VP and Executive Producer New Media: Peter Esmonde
VP Online Services Marketing: Joan Julian
VP Information Technology: Harold Kester
VP Human Resources: Karl Steinberg
CEO, Britannica.com: Don Yannias
Controller: Helen Townsend
Director Strategic Marketing Planning:
Diana Simeon Spadoni
Managing Director Art and Cartography: Barbra Vogel

LOCATIONS

HQ: 310 S. Michigan Ave., Chicago, IL 60604
Phone: 312-347-7000   **Fax:** 312-347-7399
Web site: http://corporate.britannica.com

PRODUCTS/OPERATIONS

Selected Products

Electronic

Britannica CD 99 Multimedia Edition
Britannica CD 99 Standard Edition
Britannica CD Ultimate Reference Suite
Britannica Online
Britannica Profiles Black History
Discovering Dinosaurs

Print

1998 Great Ideas Today
1999 Medical and Health Annual
1999 Yearbook of Science and the Future
The Annals of America
Britannica Atlas
Britannica Book of the Year
Britannica First Edition Replica Set
Britannica Ready Reference
Encyclopaedia Britannica (32-volume set)
Encyclopaedia Britannica Reference Suite
Encyclopaedia Universalis
Great Books of the Western World

Merriam-Webster, Inc.
Merriam-Webster Online
Merriam-Webster's Biographical Dictionary
Merriam-Webster's Collegiate Dictionary
Merriam-Webster's Collegiate Thesaurus
Merriam-Webster's Elementary Dictionary
Merriam-Webster's Geographical Dictionary
Merriam-Webster's Intermediate Dictionary
Merriam-Webster's School Dictionary
Merriam-Webster's School Thesaurus
Webster's Third New International Dictionary,
Unabridged

Selected Current and Past Contributors

Isaac Asimov
Marie Curie
Michael Ellis DeBakey
W.E.B. Du Bois
Albert Einstein
Benjamin Franklin
Sigmund Freud
Milton Friedman
Lillian Gish
Thor Heyerdahl
Thomas Henry Huxley
John Locke
John Muir
Linus Pauling
Carl Sagan
George Bernard Shaw
Lorado Taft
Leon Trotsky
Alfred North Whitehead

COMPETITORS

Berkshire Hathaway
Dorling Kindersley
Excite@Home
Franklin Electronic
 Publishers
Grolier
Harcourt General
Havas
Houghton Mifflin
IBM
Lycos

McGraw-Hill
Microsoft
Nam Tai
PRIMEDIA
Pearson
Thomson Corporation
Time Warner
Tribune Education
Viacom
Yahoo!
go.com

HISTORICAL FINANCIALS & EMPLOYEES

Private FYE: September	Annual Growth	1989	1990	1991	1992	1993	1994	1995	1996	1997	1998
Sales ($ mil.)	(9.2%)	—	650	627	586	540	453	400	375	325	300
Employees	(13.2%)	—	1,247	1,260	1,100	1,000	900	800	700	400	400

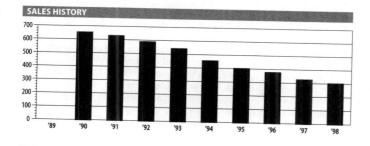

SALES HISTORY

17 68

ENTERPRISE RENT-A-CAR

OVERVIEW

You won't catch anybody sprinting through an airport for Enterprise Rent-A-Car.

St. Louis-based Enterprise oversees the biggest US car rental fleet — about 370,000 vehicles — but avoids the industry's crowded business-traveler segment. The company stays close to home, serving the local market. Most of its customers need a car because of an accident or repair to their own vehicles; some use Enterprise cars for short business or leisure trips. By charging rates that are up to 30% lower than most airport car rental companies and offering extra services, such as free customer pickup, Enterprise has carved a niche in a competitive industry. It has more than 3,700 offices in Canada, Germany, the UK, and the US. Billionaire founder Jack Taylor and his family control the company (son Andrew is president and CEO).

In addition to renting cars, Enterprise leases vehicles and manages fleets for other companies (Enterprise Fleet Services), and it sells cars, both new (ELCO Chevrolet) and used (Enterprise Car Sales). Through its Enterprise Capital Group, the company owns such diverse businesses as Betallic Balloon (maker of Mylar balloons), Elite (supplier of hotel and motel goods), and Keefe Supply (supplier of food to prisons).

HISTORY

Jack Taylor, a WWII-veteran US Navy fighter pilot, in 1957 hit on the idea that leasing cars might be an easier way to make money than selling them. At the time Taylor was the sales manager for a Cadillac dealership in St. Louis. Taylor's idea sounded good to his boss, Arthur Lindburg, who agreed to set Taylor up in the leasing business. In return for a 50% pay cut, Taylor received 25% of the new enterprise, called Executive Leasing, which began in the walled-off body shop of a car dealership.

In the early 1960s Taylor started renting cars for short periods as well as leasing them. When his leasing agents expressed annoyance with the rental operation, Taylor turned that business over to Don Holtzman. Holtzman realized that his 17-car rental operation was too little to take on industry giants like Hertz and Avis; instead, he concentrated on the "home city" or replacement market. He offered competitive rates to insurance adjusters who needed to find cars for policyholders whose cars were damaged or stolen. Propelled by court decisions that required casualty companies to pay for loss of transportation, Taylor expanded from his St. Louis base in 1969 with a branch office in Atlanta. Since another car leasing outfit in Georgia was already named Executive, Taylor changed the name of his company to Enterprise Rent-A-Car.

The company expanded into Florida and Texas in the early 1970s, targeting garages and body shops that performed repairs for insured drivers. Oil price shocks of that period compelled Taylor to diversify his operations. In 1974 Enterprise acquired Keefe Coffee and Supply, a supplier of coffee, packaged foods, and beverages to prison commissaries. To service *FORTUNE* 1000 companies wanting to lease or buy more than 50 vehicles, the company started Enterprise Fleet Services in 1976.

Enterprise acquired Courtesy Products in 1980, and the following year sales reached the $100 million mark. It acquired ELCO Chevrolet in 1986, the same year it formed Crawford Supply. Taylor bought out the Lindburg family's interest in Enterprise the next year. In 1989 Enterprise decided to compete with the major players on their own turf by raising brand recognition among consumers with a national TV campaign that focused on an older and higher-income audience by showing its commercials exclusively on CBS. Also in the late 1980s, the company began targeting "discretionary rentals" to families with visiting relatives or with children home for the holidays.

Taylor's son, Andrew, became CEO of Enterprise in 1991, and sales topped $1 billion for the first time. By 1994 sales had passed $2 billion, and the company had expanded into Canada and the UK. By 1996 Enterprise had a fleet of more than 300,000 vehicles. That year it opened groups in Bristol, Leeds, Leicester, Newcastle, and Oxford in the UK. In 1997 the company opened locations in Ireland, Munich, Scotland, and Wales.

In 1998 Enterprise battled other rental firms over use of the advertising tagline, "We'll pick you up," which it had trademarked. Rent-A-Wreck lost a court case over the matter; Hertz settled with Enterprise over use of the term.

Chairman: Jack C. Taylor
President and CEO: Andrew C. Taylor
SEVP and COO: Donald L. Ross
EVP: William F. Holekamp
EVP and CFO: John T. O'Connell
SVP Fleet Services: Richard V. Snyder
SVP and Chief Information Officer: William W. Snyder
SVP North American Operations: Pam Nicholson
SVP International Operations: Greg Stubblefield
VP Human Resources: Ed Adams
VP Rental: Jeff Brummett
VP and General Manager, Access Catalog:
Mark J. DeRousse
VP and General Manager, Betallic Balloon:
Robert A. Boedeker
VP and General Manager, Boone Valley Golf Club:
Roger E. Null
VP and Director Operations, Crawford Supply:
John A. Spesia
VP and General Manager, Keefe Supply: David C. Kruse
President, Enterprise Capital Group:
Douglas A. Albrecht
President and General Manager, ELCO Chevrolet:
Mark S. Hadfield
Manager Media Relations: Christy Conrad
Assistant VP Marketing: Callaway Ludington
Auditors: Ernst & Young LLP

LOCATIONS

HQ: 600 Corporate Park Dr., St. Louis, MO 63105
Phone: 314-512-5000   **Fax:** 314-512-4706
Web site: http://www.enterprise.com

PRODUCTS/OPERATIONS

Subsidiaries
ELCO Chevrolet Inc. (car dealership, St. Louis)
Enterprise Capital Group
  Access Catalog (supplier of electronics, clothing, and
    other goods to prisons)
  The Bernard Company (maker of robes and spa wear
    for hotels and motels)
  Betallic Balloon Co. (maker of Mylar balloons)
  Boone Valley Golf Club, Inc. (country club, St. Louis)
  Courtesy Products (supplier of in-room coffee and tea
    for hotel patrons, Cafe Valet)
  Elite Cos. (supplier of hotel and motel goods such as
    irons, ironing boards, vanity items, clock radios)
  Keefe Supply Co. (supplier of food products to prison
    commissaries)
    Crawford Supply (supplier of hygiene products and
      other goods to prisons)
  Riddell Footwear (owns a license to make footwear
    under the Riddell brand name)
Enterprise Car Sales (used car sales)
Enterprise Fleet Services (vehicle leasing)

Vehicle Classes Offered
Compact
Economy
Full size
Intermediate
Luxury
Premium
Sport utility
Standard
Van

COMPETITORS

AMERCO
Airways Transportation
  Group
AutoNation
Budget Group
Cendant
Dollar Thrifty Automotive
  Group
Hertz
Penske
Rent-A-Wreck
Rollins Truck Leasing
Ryder
SYSCO

HISTORICAL FINANCIALS & EMPLOYEES

Private FYE: July	Annual Growth	1990	1991	1992	1993	1994	1995	1996	1997	1998	1999
Sales ($ mil.)	20.4%	889	1,022	1,124	1,659	2,108	2,464	3,127	3,680	4,180	4,730
Employees	25.3%	5,241	7,750	8,500	14,000	18,500	21,703	28,806	35,182	37,000	40,000

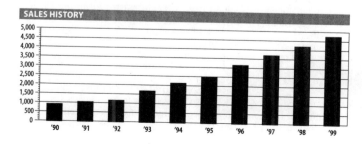

SALES HISTORY

ENTEX INFORMATION SERVICES

OVERVIEW

Once upon a time just having computers earned a business respect; now a company has to make the most of them. Enter ENTEX. Headquartered in Rye Brook, New York, ENTEX Information Services takes customers through the entire process of setting up or revamping their computer systems — from purchasing the necessary hardware and software to installing the equipment and training users. ENTEX also provides help desk support and on-site maintenance.

Once the US's largest privately held supplier of computer equipment and PC systems integration services, ENTEX has sold its resale products division to focus on providing higher-margin IT services. The company's outsourced management services unit manages about 800,000 PC desktops worldwide, a duty that generates about three-fifths of the company's sales. But ENTEX is expanding its consulting offerings, which include network design, implementation, and e-commerce.

An investor group led by chairman Dort Cameron owns 74% of ENTEX. Microsoft and IBM also have small stakes in the company.

HISTORY

David Norman founded Dataquest in 1972, building it into a top research company over the next six years. He then sold the business to consumer research organization ACNielsen, staying on as CEO. After four years he realized he would never run family-managed Nielsen, so he struck out on his own again.

In 1982 the entrepreneurial Norman wrote a 15-page business plan detailing a PC retail chain; in eight weeks he raised $3.5 million to start Businessland. His next goal was a deal with IBM, but Big Blue had a policy of not working with startups and initially no one would talk to him. Norman persisted and eventually IBM capitulated. He began opening stores and raised $21 million in additional capital by January 1983. That year he made a $50 million public stock offering. After its third full year, Businessland showed sales of $267 million and a small profit.

Norman then made a series of poor decisions that included angering Compaq head Joseph "Rod" Canion, buying the now-defunct ComputerCraft retail chain, and selling the NeXT computer while excluding its chief rival, Sun Microsystems' workstation. By 1991 Businessland had suffered five straight losing quarters. Norman attempted a comeback, slashing costs and laying off 1,000 workers, but that year JWP Inc. acquired Businessland.

JWP, a 100-year-old New York-based company, entered the information services industry in 1987 with its subsidiary JWP Information Systems. JWP (for Jamaica Water Properties) was originally a waterworks operator that evolved, by 1987, into a provider of building maintenance for large corporate and government clients.

In 1990 JWP Information Systems acquired Micro Financial, a four-store West Coast PC retailer. The following year it purchased Businessland and was renamed JWP Businessland. The acquisition contributed to JWP's loss of almost $500 million in less than two years and led to its ultimate bankruptcy. Faced also with a construction industry slump, the parent company in 1993 decided to sell the unit. Two potential buyers emerged: Dallas-based PC dealer CompuCom Systems and an investor group led by Dort Cameron (formerly with securities firm Drexel Burnham Lambert) that included JWP Businessland management. The subsidiary ended up in the hands of the latter.

Renamed ENTEX (short for Enterprise Technologies), the company quickly increased its presence in the growing computer network integration business. It consolidated three warehouses into one facility with an automated inventory control system and increased its on-site technical support staff. ENTEX began selling Texas Instruments notebooks and printers in 1994.

ENTEX acquired computer reseller Random Access and the L.E.A.D. Group of Detroit in 1995. The next year it purchased computer network services firm FCP Technologies, and named John McKenna CEO. McKenna went to work changing ENTEX's focus from reselling hardware to providing services.

After considering a public stock offering in 1996, the company was rumored to be up for sale in 1997. ENTEX insisted it was only looking for investors to fund its growth.

With PC integrators Info Products Europe and Otsuka Shokai, ENTEX formed The Global Alliance Personal Computer Services LLC in 1998 to foster ventures with other partners. After dividing its products and services businesses, ENTEX in 1999 sold its $2 billion resale products business to hardware sales and services company CompuCom Systems. The restructuring caused a loss for fiscal 1999.

Chairman: Dort A. Cameron III, age 54, $400,000 pay
CEO: John A. McKenna Jr., age 44, $425,000 pay
President: Kenneth A. Ghazey, age 43, $366,827 pay
SVP and Chief Information Officer:
Spencer McIlmurray, age 45
SVP, CFO and Treasurer: Michael G. Archambault,
age 47, $246,854 pay
SVP, General Counsel and Assistant Secretary:
Lynne A. Burgess, age 49
SVP, Consulting Services: Peter Van Zant
SVP, Human Resources: Kim Nathanson, age 43
SVP, Outsourcing Services: Lou Schiavone
VP and Controller: Shirley S. Mehta, age 45
VP, Training and Organizational Development:
Jon Couture
Auditors: KPMG LLP

LOCATIONS

HQ: Entex Information Services, Inc.,
6 International Dr., Rye Brook, NY 10573
Phone: 914-935-3600   **Fax:** 914-935-3650
Web site: http://www.entex.com

PRODUCTS/OPERATIONS

Services
Consulting
Groupware design
Help desk support
Internetworking development
Network management
Project management
System migrations and upgrades
Total cost of ownership assessment

Managed Staffing
Desktop support
Help desk
Maintenance
Warranty services

Outsourcing (ENCare)
Asset management
Help desk problem resolution
Installations, moves, adds, and changes
Mobile computing management
PC maintenance
Server and network maintenance

COMPETITORS

Amdahl	Getronics
Andersen Consulting	IBM
Cap Gemini	InaCom
CompuCom	Ingram Micro
Computer Horizons	International Network
Computer Sciences	Services
DecisionOne	Perot Systems
Deloitte Touche Tohmatsu	PricewaterhouseCoopers
EDS	Technology Solutions
Ernst & Young	Unisys
GE	

HISTORICAL FINANCIALS & EMPLOYEES

Private FYE: June	Annual Growth	1990	1991	1992	1993	1994	1995	1996	1997	1998	1999
Sales ($ mil.)	(15.1%)	—	—	—	—	1,095	1,473	2,148	2,481	2,457	484
Net income ($ mil.)		—	—	—	—	(3)	(29)	(26)	2	18	(101)
Income as % of sales		—	—	—	—	—	—	—	0.1%	0.7%	—
Employees	3.8%	—	—	—	—	—	5,000	6,200	7,500	8,200	5,800

NET INCOME HISTORY

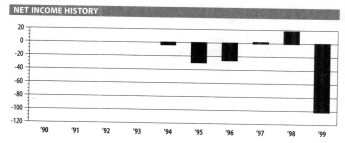

1999 FISCAL YEAR-END
Debt ratio: 100.0%
Return on equity: —
Cash ($ mil.): 13
Current ratio: 0.80
Long-term debt ($ mil.): 124

EQUITY GROUP INVESTMENTS

OVERVIEW

Equity Group Investments is the apex of financier Sam Zell's pyramid of business holdings. The Chicago-based private investment group controls a multi-billion dollar mix of businesses, including real estate investment trusts (REITs), restaurants, and cruise ships. Zell's REITs are #1 in office property (Equity Office Properties Trust), apartments (Equity Residential Properties Trust), and land leased to manufactured home owners (Manufactured Home Communities).

A prowess for finding and turning around distressed companies has earned Zell the nickname "Grave Dancer." Equity Group Investments has rescued many companies floundering in bankruptcy and often buys during downturns. Many acquisitions are made through the Zell/Chilmark Fund.

Ironically, Equity Group Investments may have become the kind of behemoth Zell once belittled. The company has been hit hard by the recent REIT downturn, and the size of its portfolio makes it vulnerable to market. To appease disgruntled shareholders, Zell is restructuring his REITs, selling less valuable properties and using the proceeds for more acquisitions. He is also considering an infusion of private money for Equity Office Properties Trust, a move that could both raise the stock price of that company and make funds available for future buys. Zell is eyeing expansions in Asia, Latin America, and elsewhere by raising capital for his latest fund, Equity International Properties.

HISTORY

Sam Zell's first business endeavor was photographing his eighth-grade prom. In 1953 he graduated to reselling 50-cent *Playboy* magazines to schoolmates at a 200% markup.

While at the University of Michigan in the 1960s, Zell teamed with fraternity brother Robert Lurie to manage off-campus student housing. In graduate school, they invested in residential properties and after graduation formed Equity Financial and Management Co. Their collection of distressed properties grew in the 1970s as Zell made the deals and Lurie made them work. Zell's hands-off management style had its drawbacks, however: In 1976 Zell and three others (including his brother-in-law) were indicted on federal tax-related charges after selling a Reno, Nevada, hotel and apartment complex. The charges were later dropped against Zell and another defendant (only the brother-in-law was convicted).

In the 1980s tax-law changes led the team to begin buying troubled companies. They started in 1983 with Great American Management and Investment Inc., a foundering real estate manager they turned into an investment vehicle. Other targets included Itel (1984, now Anixter International) and oil and gas company Nucorp (1988, now part of insurer CNA Surety). The true attraction in many of these acquisitions, however, lay in tax-loss carryforwards that could be applied against future earnings.

Lurie died in 1990, after which Zell began to consolidate his power and ease out old friends. (Lurie's estate still owns shares of many Zell enterprises.) That year Zell and David Schulte formed the Zell/Chilmark Fund, which soon owned or controlled such companies as Schwinn (sold 1997), Sealy (sold 1997), and Revco (sold 1997). Among the fund's failures was West Coast retailer Broadway Stores, which Zell bought out of bankruptcy in 1992; when California's slumping economy prevented a rapid turnaround, Zell sold it (once again near bankruptcy) in 1995.

Starting in 1987, Zell formed four real estate funds with Merrill Lynch; six years later, both Equity Residential Properties Trust and Manufactured Home Communities went public. As REITs became popular with investors, more trusts began vying for distressed assets — Zell's traditional lifeblood. In 1997 Zell melded four of his commercial real estate funds into another REIT, Equity Office Properties Trust, and took it public.

In 1998, as investors and financiers looked for fresh opportunities, Zell launched Equity International Properties, a fund targeting acquisitions in Latin America and elsewhere. That year a civil racketeering suit brought against Zell by former executive Richard Perlman shed light on "handshake" loans to top executives and other informal business deals.

In 1999 Zell sold Jacor Communications to radio industry consolidator Clear Channel Communications. Equity Group Investments remains diversified, however: That year Equity Office Properties teamed with venture capital firm Kleiner Perkins Caufield & Byers to form Broadband Office to offer Internet and phone services to Zell's tenants and those of other property owners.

Chairman: Samuel Zell
President and CEO: Sheli Z. Rosenberg
COO: Donald J. Liebentritt
VP, Treasurer, and Controller: Greg Stegimen
VP Human Resources: Dan Harris
President and CEO, Anixter International and Great American Management and Investment: Rod F. Dammeyer

HQ: Equity Group Investments, Inc., L.L.C.,
2 N. Riverside Plaza, Ste. 600, Chicago, IL 60606
Phone: 312-454-1800   **Fax:** 312-454-0610

Selected Affiliates
American Classic Voyages Co. (cruises)
Anixter International, Inc. (communications network equipment)
Capital Trust, Inc. (commercial real estate finance)
Chart House Enterprises, Inc. (restaurants)
Davel Communications Group, Inc. (pay-telephone operator)
Equity International Properties (overseas buyout fund)
Equity Office Properties Trust (office property REIT)
Equity Residential Properties Trust (apartments REIT)
Manufactured Home Communities, Inc. (mobile home communities REIT)
Matria Healthcare (disease management services)
Transmedia Network (consumer savings programs)
Zell/Chilmark Fund L.P. (investment vulture fund)

AMLI Residential	Goldman Sachs
Apollo Advisors	JMB Realty
Avalonbay Communities	KKR
BRE Properties	Security Capital
Blackstone Group	Thomas Lee
Camden Property	Trammell Crow
Carlyle Group	Trump
Clayton, Dubilier	

ERNST & YOUNG INTERNATIONAL

OVERVIEW

Accounting may actually be the oldest profession, and Ernst & Young is one of the oldest practitioners. The New York-based concern has more than 660 offices in over 130 countries. Ernst & Young is the fourth-largest of the Big Five accounting firms (PricewaterhouseCoopers is #1).

The company's audit and accounting business provides internal audit and accounting advice and oversight. The firm has one of the world's largest tax practices, particularly serving the needs of multinational clients that have to comply with multiple local tax laws. Ernst & Young's consulting services concentrate on corporate operations and information technology.

Most of the leading accounting firms have moved strongly into consulting in response to growing competition and legal entanglements from evolving audit standards. Ernst & Young has followed this trend, which may be reversing as questions arise about the independence of auditors who also consult. The company is in talks to sell its management consulting business to French consultantcy Cap Gemini Group SA.

HISTORY

The 1494 publication in Venice of Luca Pacioli's *Summa di Arithmetica* — the first published work dealing with double-entry bookkeeping — boosted the accounting profession, but it wasn't until the 19th century that the industry took off.

Frederick Whinney joined the UK firm of Harding & Pullein in 1849. R. P. Harding reputedly had been a hatmaker whose business ended up in court. The ledgers he produced were so clear that he was advised to take up accounting, which was a growth field as stock companies proliferated.

Whinney became a name partner in 1859 and was followed into the business by his sons. The firm became Whinney, Smith & Whinney in 1894. The name lasted until 1965.

After WWII Whinney, Smith & Whinney formed an alliance with the American firm of Ernst & Ernst (founded in Cleveland in 1903 by brothers Alwin and Theodore Ernst). The alliance, which recognized that the accountants' business clients were getting larger and becoming more international, provided that each firm would operate on the other's behalf within their respective markets.

Whinney merged with Brown, Fleming & Murray in 1965 to become Whinney Murray. The firm continued to form joint ventures with other accounting firms to provide services.

In 1979 Whinney Murray and Turquands Barton Mayhew — itself the product of a merger that began with a cricket match — united with Ernst & Ernst to form Ernst & Whinney, a firm with an international scope.

But Ernst & Whinney wasn't done merging. Ten years later, when it was the fourth-largest accounting firm, it merged with #5 Arthur Young, which had been founded by Scotsman Arthur Young in 1895 in Kansas City. Long known as "old reliable," Arthur Young fell on hard times in the 1980s because its audit relationships with failed S&Ls led to expensive litigation.

The new firm of Ernst & Young faced a rocky start. In 1990, it fended off rumors of collapse. The next year it slashed payroll, even thinning its partner roster. Ernst & Young agreed in 1992 to pay $400 million for allegedly mishandling the audits of four failed S&Ls.

Exhausted by the legal battles, in 1994 the firm replaced its pugnacious general counsel, Carl Riggio, with the more cost-conscious Kathryn Oberly.

In the mid-1990s Ernst & Young concentrated on its consulting services, adding several new information software products. It also grew through acquisitions. In 1996 the firm bought Houston-based Wright Killen & Co., a petroleum and petrochemicals consulting firm, to form Ernst & Young Wright Killen. It also entered new alliances that year with Washington-based ISD/Shaw, which provides banking industry consulting, and India's Tata Consulting, among others.

In 1997 Ernst & Young was sued for a record $4 billion for its alleged failure to effectively handle the 1993 restructuring of the defunct Merry-Go-Round Enterprises retail chain (it settled the suit for $185 million in 1999). On the heels of a merger deal between Coopers & Lybrand and Price Waterhouse, Ernst & Young agreed in 1997 to merge with KPMG International. At Ernst & Young's suggestion, however, the firms called off the deal in 1998, citing the costly, time-consuming, and uncertain regulatory process they faced.

In 1999 Ernst & Young launched a worldwide media blitz aimed at raising awareness of the firm's full range of services. That year the firm reached a settlement in lawsuits regarding accounting errors at Informix and Cendant, and sold its UK and Southern African trust and fiduciary businesses to Royal Bank of Canada.

Chairman: Philip A. Laskawy
Senior VC: William L. Kimsey
VC Assurance and Advisory Services: John F. Ferraro
VC Consulting Services: Antonio Schneider
VC Finance, Technology, and Administration:
Hilton Dean
VC Global Accounts: David A. Reed
VC Human Resources: Lewis A. Ting
VC Intrastructure: John G. Peetz Jr.
**VC Regional Integration and Entrepreneurial Growth
Companies:** Jean-Charles Raufast
VC Regional Integration and Planning:
Richard N. Findlater
VC Tax and Legal Services: Andrew B. Jones
Executive Partner: Paul J. Ostling
National Director SALT Practice and Procedure:
Prentiss Willson Jr.
General Counsel: Kathryn A. Oberly

LOCATIONS

HQ: 787 7th Ave., New York, NY 10019
Phone: 212-773-3000   **Fax:** 212-773-6350
Web site: http://www.eyi.com

Ernst & Young has more than 660 offices in over 130
countries.

PRODUCTS/OPERATIONS

Representative Clients
American Express
BankAmerica
Coca-Cola
Eli Lilly
Exxon Mobil
Hanson
Hoover's, Inc.
Knight Ridder
Lockheed Martin
Marubeni
McDonald's
Time Warner
US Postal Service
USF&G
Wal-Mart

COMPETITORS

American Management
Andersen Worldwide
Arthur D. Little
BDO International
Bain & Company
Booz, Allen
Boston Consulting
Computer Sciences
Deloitte Touche Tohmatsu
EDS
Grant Thornton International
IBM
KPMG
Marsh & McLennan
McKinsey & Company
Perot Systems
Policy Management Systems
PricewaterhouseCoopers
Towers Perrin

HISTORICAL FINANCIALS & EMPLOYEES

Partnership FYE: September	Annual Growth	1990	1991	1992	1993	1994	1995	1996	1997	1998	1999
Sales ($ mil.)	10.7%	5,006	5,406	5,701	5,839	6,020	6,867	7,800	9,100	10,900	12,510
Employees	5.3%	61,591	61,173	58,900	58,377	61,287	68,452	72,000	79,750	85,000	97,800

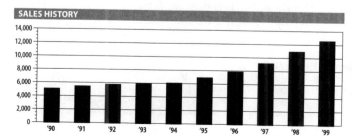

SALES HISTORY

≡II ERNST & YOUNG

FARMLAND INDUSTRIES, INC.

OVERVIEW

Farmland Industries helps its members farm land industriously. The Kansas City, Missouri-based enterprise is the #1 agricultural cooperative in the US and a major player in agribusiness worldwide, exporting agricultural products (primarily grain) to more than 90 countries.

Farmland is owned by 1,500 local co-ops, comprising about 600,000 farmers in the US, Canada, and Mexico. In addition to processing members' crops, the co-op's operations include fertilizer plants, a petroleum refinery, grain elevators, feed mills, barges, 4,400 railcars, 1,000-plus trucks, and nearly 2,000 trailers. The co-op processes and markets beef and pork through its Farmland National Beef Packing and Farmland Foods subsidiaries. Farmland also has more than 60 joint ventures and alliances, including Country Energy (petroleum distribution) and Farmland Hydro (phosphate production).

HISTORY

US agriculture has always been sensitive to boom-and-bust cycles and to the ups and downs of raw commodity prices. After a golden age of supplying food for a world torn by WWI, the industry had a hard time during the 1920s. In 1929 President Herbert Hoover called a special session of Congress to deal with farm issues, resulting in passage of the far-reaching Agricultural Marketing Act (AMA). The act encouraged the formation of cooperatives as one means of bringing order to the marketplace, but a record grain harvest in 1928 and 1929 foiled its intent. The glut ground down prices, and later the Depression (and drought) dried up markets.

By the time of the AMA, Union Oil Company, Farmland Industries' predecessor, was already in the works. Union Oil was formed in 1929 to provide petroleum supplies to farmers in a period of rapid agricultural mechanization. In the early 1930s, as the government sought to regulate supply by introducing payments for taking land out of production, Union Oil increased the range of its co-op activities. It changed its name to Consumers Cooperative Association in 1935.

Farming did not revive until WWII, though price controls and supports remained an important feature of agricultural policy. Throughout this period the performance of Consumers Cooperative's growing membership of primary producers and local co-ops remained tied to raw commodity prices. In 1959, however, to decrease its reliance on commodity prices, Consumers Cooperative bought a pork processing plant in Denison, Iowa, and began making Farmbest meat products. It was a success, and four years later the co-op opened another plant in Iowa Falls. In 1966 Consumers Cooperative became Farmland Industries, and in the 1970s it expanded into beef production. However, when prices and consumption declined, it exited the field.

Overzealous expansion by American farmers in the 1970s was followed in the 1980s by an industrywide crisis. When the farm economy went down, it hurt the co-op's sales of inputs such as fertilizers. Cheap fertilizer imports, low crude oil prices, and high natural gas prices also took their toll, and the co-op lost more than $210 million in 1985 and 1986. James Rainey took over as CEO in 1986 and turned the operation around. Farmland began placing a greater emphasis on food processing and marketing, otherwise known as outputs.

Harry Cleberg succeeded Rainey in 1991. The co-op had stopped handling grains in 1985, after a period of volatile prices, but it profitably re-entered the market in 1992. The next year it bought the Tradigrain unit of British Petroleum (now BP Amoco). The purchase led Farmland into markets outside the US. Also in 1993 the co-op resumed beef processing and expanded its pork processing facilities. Farmland formed a joint venture in 1995 with fertilizer producer Mississippi Chemical (Farmland Trinidad Limited) and acquired the OhSe and Roegelein lunch meat brands from Hudson Foods.

In 1996 the co-op formed a joint venture with Strauss Veal Feeds to make specialty feeds. The next year Farmland formed OneSystem, a joint venture with Ernst & Young, to manage its data systems. The co-op also combined its meat and livestock businesses in 1997. The company formed partnerships in 1998 with ConAgra (Concourse Grain, grain marketing) and Cenex Harvest States Cooperatives (Country Energy, energy products) and absorbed SF Services, an agricultural cooperative. Farmland's income fell in 1998 due to low prices on many of its key products.

Farmland and Cenex's early 1999 discussions yielded an agreement to merge their entire operations. Farmland members approved the deal, but Cenex members voted it down by a narrow margin. Undeterred, Cenex officers announced they would keep talks open with Farmland for future merger attempts.

Chairman: Albert J. Shivley
VC and VP: Jody Benzer
President and CEO: H. D. Cleberg
EVP and CFO: Terry M. Campbell
SVP and Corporate Secretary: Bernard L. Sanders
EVP and COO, Grain and Grain Processing Businesses: John F. Berardi
EVP and COO, Meats Group: Gary E. Evans
EVP and COO, Ag Input Businesses: Robert W. Honse
VP Government Relations: William R. Allen Jr.
VP and Controller: Merl Daniel
VP System Strategic Planning: Gerald Leeper
VP Human Resources: Holly D. McCoy
VP; Co-President, Country Energy: Ken D. Otwell
VP; President, Pork Division: George H. Richter
VP Crop Production: Stan Riemann
VP and Treasurer: Jeff Roberts
VP Administration: Drue M. Sander
VP Transportation: Fred E. Schrodt
VP; President, Feed and Grain Processing: Michael T. Sweat
VP and General Counsel: Robert B. Terry
Auditors: KPMG LLP

LOCATIONS

HQ: 3315 N. Oak Trafficway, Kansas City, MO 64116
Phone: 816-459-6000   **Fax:** 816-459-6979
Web site: http://www.farmland.com

PRODUCTS/OPERATIONS

1999 Sales

	$ mil.	% of total
Grain marketing	4,167	39
Food marketing	3,756	35
Crop production	1,002	9
Petroleum	954	9
Feed	576	6
Other	254	2
Total	**10,709**	**100**

Selected Subsidiaries and Joint Ventures

Concourse Grain, LLC (grain alliance with ConAgra)
Country Energy, LLC (energy products alliance with Cenex Harvest States Cooperatives)
Farmers Chemical Co. (fertilizer production)
Farmland-Atwood, LLC (50%, with ConAgra; risk management services)
Farmland Foods (99%, 11 food processing plants)
Farmland Hydro, LP (50%, with Norsk Hydro; phosphate fertilizer manufacturing)
Farmland Industrias SA de CV (marketing support services, Mexico)
Farmland Insurance Agency, Inc.
Farmland National Beef Packing Co., LP (76%)
Farmland Securities Co. (broker-dealer)
Farmland Transportation, Inc. (brokerage)
Heartland Wheat Growers LP (79%, wheat gluten and starch processing)
National Carriers, Inc. (79%, transportation brokerage)
OneSystem Group, LLC (50%, with Ernst & Young; information technology)
SF Phosphates Limited Co. (50%, fertilizer manufacturing)
SF Services Inc. (farm supply cooperative)
Tradigrain SA (international grain trading)
WILFARM, LLC (50%, with Wilbur-Ellis Co.; pesticides)

COMPETITORS

ADM	Hormel
Ag Processing	IBP
Agway	IMC Global
American Foods	JR Simplot
CF Industries	Keystone Foods
Cargill	Monsanto
Cenex Harvest States	Rose Packing
ConAgra	Royal Dutch/Shell
ContiGroup	Smithfield Foods
Exxon Mobil	Southern States
Gold Kist	Transammonia

HISTORICAL FINANCIALS & EMPLOYEES

Cooperative FYE: August	Annual Growth	1990	1991	1992	1993	1994	1995	1996	1997	1998	1999
Sales ($ mil.)	13.7%	3,378	3,638	3,429	4,723	6,678	7,257	9,789	9,148	8,775	10,709
Net income ($ mil.)	(13.0%)	49	43	62	(30)	74	163	126	135	59	14
Income as % of sales	—	1.4%	1.2%	1.8%	—	1.1%	2.2%	1.3%	1.5%	0.7%	0.1%
Employees	11.4%	6,691	7,126	7,616	8,155	12,000	12,700	14,700	14,600	16,100	17,700

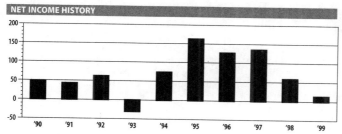

NET INCOME HISTORY

1999 FISCAL YEAR-END
Debt ratio: 45.8%
Return on equity: 1.5%
Cash ($ mil.): 0
Current ratio: 1.32
Long-term debt ($ mil.): 808

FEDERAL RESERVE BANK (NY)

OVERVIEW

Where do banks go when they need a loan? To the Federal Reserve System (known as the Fed), and if they're in or around New York (or in Puerto Rico, or the US Virgin Islands), they go to the Federal Reserve Bank of New York, the largest of the 12 Federal Reserve District Banks.

The New York Fed, like its sister Fed banks, provides regulatory oversight and examination of the banks in its district. It ensures that they maintain adequate reserves, provides for electronic funds transfer and transaction settlement, and, by setting the interest rates for interbank borrowing, controls the money supply under the direction of the Federal Reserve Board (chaired by Alan Greenspan).

But the New York Fed also oversees foreign exchange transactions, maintains relationships with foreign governments and central banks, provides assistance to developing countries' banking systems, and compiles the statistics on which the Fed bases its interest rate policies.

Like the other Federal Reserve Banks, the New York Fed is owned by commercial banks in its district. National banks must own stock in their Federal Reserve Bank, though it is optional for state-chartered banks.

HISTORY

When New York's Knickerbocker Trust Company failed in 1907, it brought on a panic that was stemmed by J. P. Morgan, who strongarmed his fellow bankers into supporting shaky New York banks. The incident showed the need for a central bank.

Morgan's actions sparked fears of his economic power and spurred congressional efforts to establish a central bank. After a six-year struggle between eastern money interests and populist monetary reformers, the 1913 Federal Reserve Act was passed. Twelve Federal Reserve districts were created, but the economic dominance of New York ensured that it would be the most powerful.

In WWI the Treasury Department forced the Fed Banks to buy Treasury bonds at low interest; this sparked a wartime inflation that collapsed when the Fed later raised rates. Benjamin Strong, head of the New York bank dominated the Fed during the 1920s, acting in 1923 to counter the effects of a European flood of gold into the US. After he died in 1928, the system began drifting. It lowered rates, prompting members to borrow cheaply from the Fed to make loans for stock speculation. This set the stage for the 1929 crash.

During the Depression and WWII, the Fed again yielded to the demands of the Treasury to buy bonds. But after WWII it sought independence, cultivating Congress to help free it from the Treasury's demands. This effort was led by chairman William McChesney Martin, with the assistance of New York bank president Alan Sproul, who was also a rival for the chairmanship. Martin diluted Sproul's influence by governing by consensus with the other bank leaders.

In the postwar boom the Fed was fairly successful in managing the economy, but it was stymied by inflation starting in the late 1960s. In the early 1970s the New York bank also faced the collapse of the fixed currency exchange-rate system and the growth of currency trading. Its role as foreign currency trader became even more crucial as the dollar's value eroded in the face of rising oil prices and a slowing economy.

The US suffered from double-digit inflation in 1979 as President Jimmy Carter appointed New York Fed president Paul Volcker as chairman. Volcker, believing that raising interest rates a few points would not suffice, allowed the banks to raise their discount rates and increased bank reserve requirements to reduce the money supply. By the time inflation eased, Ronald Reagan was president.

During the 1980s and 1990s, US budget fights limited the options for controlling the economy through spending decisions, so the Fed's actions became more important. The higher profile brought calls for more access to the Fed's decision-making processes. And although the system is self-funding, the banks made a show of cutting costs and closing offices. While the US economy seemed immune to the Asian currency crisis of 1997 and 1998, the Federal Reserve remained relatively quiescent. But when Russia defaulted on some of its bonds in 1998, leading to the near-collapse of hedge fund Long-Term Capital Management, the New York Federal Reserve Bank brokered a bailout by the fund's lenders and investors.

This led in 1999 to new guidelines for banks' risk management. Also that year the bank began closing its few consumer service teller windows, which sold savings bonds and exchanged old cash for new.

Chairman: John C. Whitehead
President: William J. McDonough
First VP: Jamie B. Stewart Jr., age 54
EVP and Director of Research and Research and Market Analysis: Stephen G. Cecchetti
EVP, Administrative Services: Suzanne Cutler
EVP, Automation and Systems Services: Israel Sendrovic
EVP, Bank Supervision: Chester B. Feldberg
EVP, Emerging Markets and International Affairs: Terrence J. Checki
EVP, Financial Services: Kathleen A. O'Neil
EVP, Legal and General Counsel: Thomas C. Baxter Jr.
EVP, Markets: Peter R. Fisher
SVP and Branch Manager, Buffalo: Carl W. Turnipseed
SVP, Audit and General Auditor: David Sheehe
SVP, Advisory and Technical Services: Christine M. Cumming
SVP, Banking Applications: Betsy B. White
SVP, Banking Trends: Fred C. Herriman Jr.
SVP, Foreign Exchange: Dino Kos
SVP, Integration Management: Pauline Chen
SVP, Office of Regional and Community Affairs and Public Information: Peter Bakstansky
SVP, Supervision Support: Elaine D. Mauriello
Auditors: PricewaterhouseCoopers LLP

LOCATIONS

HQ: Federal Reserve Bank of New York,
33 Liberty St., New York, NY 10045
Phone: 212-720-5000   **Fax:** 212-720-7459
Web site: http://www.ny.frb.org

PRODUCTS/OPERATIONS

1998 Assets

	$ mil.	% of total
Cash & equivalents	4,221	2
Government securities	201,503	93
Foreign governments' securities	4,002	2
Other securities	3,202	1
Recoverables & receivables	745	—
Receivables	1,965	1
Other assets	1,786	1
Total	**217,424**	**100**

1998 Sales

	$ mil.	% of total
Interest on US government securities	9,803	93
Interest on foreign currencies	89	1
Other interest	1	—
Service income	99	1
Reimbursable services to government agencies	58	1
Foreign currency gains	380	4
Government securities gains	17	—
Other	35	—
Total	**10,482**	**100**

Selected Services
Bank reserves depository
Bank supervision and regulation
Check and transfer clearance
Economic research and analysis
Foreign currency exchange and settlement

HISTORICAL FINANCIALS & EMPLOYEES

Member-owned banking authority FYE: December	Annual Growth	1989	1990	1991	1992	1993	1994	1995	1996	1997	1998
Assets ($ mil.)	8.8%	101,408	125,233	130,253	123,485	160,707	170,655	183,893	186,483	197,870	217,424
Net income ($ mil.)	3.3%	7,545	8,494	8,108	6,964	6,215	7,625	9,519	8,550	8,230	10,080
Income as % of assets	—	7.4%	6.8%	6.2%	5.6%	3.9%	4.5%	5.2%	4.6%	4.2%	4.6%
Employees	(1.0%)	3,935	3,963	4,070	4,238	4,294	4,192	3,100	3,119	3,600	3,600

NET INCOME HISTORY

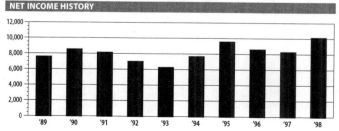

1998 FISCAL YEAR-END

Equity as % of assets: 1.1%
Return on assets: 4.8%
Return on equity: 440.2%
Long-term debt ($ mil.): —
Sales ($ mil.): 10,482

FELD ENTERTAINMENT, INC.

OVERVIEW

Clowning around is Feld Entertainment's business. The company, which pitches its main tent in Vienna, Virginia, owns the Ringling Bros. and Barnum & Bailey Circus and, you guessed it, evens runs its own Clown College. The original circus travels the world in two troupes, performing in local arenas, while a third troupe presents a more upscale version of the circus under the big top. One of the world's largest producers of live family entertainment, Feld Entertainment also produces nine touring ice shows, including Walt Disney's World on Ice, and Las Vegas magicians Siegfried & Roy. Its shows draw about 25 million people each year and have been seen in 44 countries.

Multimillionaire owner Kenneth Feld, however, has more important concerns than how many clowns can be squeezed into a VW Bug. A very hands-on CEO, Feld oversees every show personally and is pushing the company into new markets, including television and the Internet.

HISTORY

When five-year-old Irvin Feld found a $1 bill in 1923, he told his mother, "I'm going to buy a circus." He started by working the sideshows of traveling circuses before settling in Washington, DC, in 1940. Feld, who was white, opened the Super Cut-Rate Drugstore in a black section of the segregated city with the backing of the NAACP. His store stocked records, and in 1944 he opened the Super Music City record store and started his own record company, Super Disc. Feld and his brother Israel also began promoting outdoor concerts by Super Disc acts. When rock and roll became popular in the 1950s, Feld promoted Chubby Checker and Fats Domino, among others.

Feld came a step closer to his dream in 1956 when he began managing the Ringling Bros. and Barnum & Bailey Circus for majority owner John Ringling North. North's circus traced its roots back to 1871 and P. T. Barnum's Grand Traveling Museum, Menagerie, Caravan, and Circus. Barnum's circus merged with James Bailey's circus in 1881, creating Barnum & Bailey. In 1907 Bailey's widow sold Barnum & Bailey to North's uncles, the Ringling brothers, who had started their circus in 1884.

Among Feld's suggestions to North was moving the circus out from under the big top and into air-conditioned arenas, saving $50,000 a week because 1,800 roustabouts were no longer needed to set up tents. Feld continued to promote music acts, but he suffered a serious blow in 1959 when three of his stars — Buddy Holly, Ritchie Valens, and J. P. Richardson (the Big Bopper) — died in a plane crash.

Feld's dream of owning a circus finally was realized in 1967 when he and investors paid $8 million for Ringling Brothers. He fired most of the circus' performers and opened a Clown College to train new ones. Feld bought a German circus the following year to obtain animal trainer Gunther Gebel-Williams. He then split the circus into two units in 1969 so he could book it in two parts of the country at the same time and double his profits. Feld took the company public that year.

Feld and the other stockholders sold the circus to Mattel in 1971 for $47 million in stock; Feld stayed on as manager and held on to the lucrative concession business, Sells-Floto. Feld persuaded Mattel to buy the Ice Follies, Holiday on Ice, and the Siegfried & Roy magic show in 1979. Mattel sold the circus back to Feld in 1982 for $22.5 million, along with the ice shows and the magic show. Feld died two years later, and his son Kenneth became head of the company. A chip off the old block, Kenneth fired almost all the circus performers when he took over.

Feld bought the rights to the Wizard of Oz ice show from Turner Entertainment in 1994, and in 1996 the company changed its name to Feld Entertainment. A constant target of animal rights activists, Feld began backing conservation efforts on behalf of the endangered Asian elephant, a crucial part of the circus. The company established the Center for Elephant Conservation in Florida in 1995.

Under increasing pressure as the company's creative guru and managerial boss, Feld hired Turner Home Entertainment executive Stuart Snyder as president and COO in 1997, so he could focus on the creative side of the business. That focus produced P.T. Barnum's Kaleidoscape in 1999, a pricier version of the original circus featuring specialty acts, gourmet food, plush seats, audience interaction, and for the first time since 1956, it's performed under a tent. That year Stuart announced his resignation to take a post with USA Networks.

Chairman and CEO: Kenneth Feld, age 51
EVP and General Counsel: Jerome S. Sowalsky
VP and CFO: Mike Ruch
VP Human Resources: Richard Felsenstein
VP International Sales and Business Development:
  Robert McHugh

LOCATIONS

HQ: 8607 Westwood Center Dr., Vienna, VA 22182
Phone: 703-448-4000   **Fax:** 703-448-4100
Web site: http://www.ringling.com

PRODUCTS/OPERATIONS

Selected Attractions
Grease on Ice
P.T. Barnum's Kaleidoscape
Ringling Bros. and Barnum & Bailey Circus
Siegfried & Roy
Walt Disney's World on Ice
The Wizard of Oz on Ice

COMPETITORS

Cirque du Soleil
Clyde Beatty-Cole Brothers Circus
Great American Circus
Hannaford Family Circus
Ice Capades
Pickle Family Circus

HISTORICAL FINANCIALS & EMPLOYEES

Private FYE: January	Annual Growth	1990	1991	1992	1993	1994	1995	1996	1997	1998	1999
Estimated sales ($ mil.)	4.3%	—	—	—	500	570	600	625	550	630	645
Employees	0.0%	—	—	—	2,500	2,500	2,500	2,500	2,500	2,500	2,500

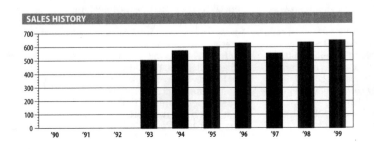

SALES HISTORY

ENTERTAINMENT, INC.

FMR CORP.

OVERVIEW

FMR Corp. is *semper fidelis* (ever faithful) to its core business. The Boston-based financial service conglomerate, better known as Fidelity Investments, is the world's #1 mutual fund company. With more than 15 million investors, FMR manages some 280 funds, including Magellan (the US's largest).

Magellan's growing bulk raises the question of whether the leviathan fund can retain the nimbleness that historically gave it such impressive growth. FMR's nonfund products include online brokerage, life insurance, real estate management, and retirement services.

As Congress dismantles Depression-era restrictions on financial and insurance companies, FMR is opening Fidelity Personal Trust Company, a savings and loan that will provide trust services.

Chairman Ned Johnson has shuffled management and slimmed down nonfund assets amid sagging performance in a bull market. The Johnson family controls 49% of FMR; company executives control the rest. Abigail Johnson, Ned's daughter and heir apparent, is the largest single shareholder with about 25%.

HISTORY

In 1930 Fidelity Fund was formed by Anderson & Cromwell, a Boston money management firm. Edward Johnson became president of Fidelity Fund in 1943, when it had $3 million invested in Treasury bills. Johnson diversified into stocks, and by 1945 the fund had grown to $10 million. In 1946 he established Fidelity Management and Research to act as investment adviser to Fidelity Fund.

In the early 1950s Johnson hired Gerry Tsai, a young immigrant from Shanghai, to analyze stocks. He put Tsai in charge of Fidelity Capital Fund in 1957. Tsai's brash, go-go strategy in such speculative stocks as Xerox and Polaroid paid off; when he left to form his own fund in 1965, he was managing more than $1 billion.

The Magellan Fund started in 1962. The firm entered the corporate pension plans market (FMR Investment Management) in 1964, retirement plans for self-employed individuals (Fidelity Keogh Plan) in 1967, and foreign investors (Fidelity International) in 1968.

Holding company FMR was formed in 1972, and that year Johnson gave control of Fidelity to his son Ned, who vertically integrated FMR by selling directly to customers rather than through brokers. The next year he formed Fidelity Daily Income Trust, the first money market fund to offer check writing.

Peter Lynch was hired as manager of the Magellan Fund in 1977. During his 13-year tenure, Magellan grew from $20 million to $12 billion in assets and outperformed all other mutual funds. Fidelity Brokerage Services was established in 1978, making Fidelity the first mutual fund company to offer discount brokerage services.

In 1980 the company launched a nationwide branch network and in 1986 entered the credit card business. The Wall Street crash of 1987 forced its Magellan Fund to liquidate almost $1 billion in stock in a single day. That year FMR moved into insurance by offering variable life, single premium, and deferred annuity policies. In 1989 the company introduced the low-expense Spartan Fund, targeted toward large, less-active investors.

Magellan's performance faded in the early 1990s, and the fund dropped from #1 performer in the industry to #3. FMR founded London-based COLT Telecom in 1993. In 1994 Ned Johnson gave his daughter and heir apparent, Abigail, a 25% stake in FMR.

Jeffrey Vinik resigned his position as manager of Magellan in 1996, one of more than a dozen fund managers to leave the firm that year and the next. Robert Stansky then took the helm of the $56 billion fund. Magellan had been criticized as being too large to be managed well, and FMR decided the next year to close it to new shareholders. That year, for the first time in its history, Fidelity hired an outside group, Bankers Trust (now part of Deutsche Bank), to manage its index mutual funds.

The company continued to do the management shuffle in 1998. Robert Pozen took over as head of mutual funds from Gary Burkhead, who moved to the CEO slot at the institutional group. Meanwhile, James Curvey moved from venture capital to oversee corporate daily operations. FMR sold Capital Publishing, which produced *Worth* magazine, in 1998 (after selling Wentworth art galleries in 1997). FMR also made its first steps into Japan and expanded its presence in Canada in 1998.

In 1999 the firm formed a joint venture with Charles Schwab; Donaldson, Lufkin & Jenrette; and Spear, Leeds & Kellogg to form and electronic communications network (ECN) to trade Nasdaq stocks online. That year Fidelity signed a deal with Internet portal Lycos to help develop the company's Powerstreet online brokerage.

OFFICERS

Chairman and CEO: Edward C. Johnson III
President and COO: James C. Curvey
VC; President, Fidelity Personal Investments and Brokerage Group: J. Gary Burkhead
SVP and Chief of Administration and Government Affairs: David C. Weinstein
EVP and CFO: Stephen P. Jonas
VP and General Counsel: Lena G. Goldberg
President, Fidelity Corporate Systems and Services: Mark A. Peterson
President, Fidelity Investments Systems: Donald A. Haile
President, Fidelity-Wide Processing: Chuck Griffith
President, Fidelity Corporate Real Estate: Ronald C. Duff
President, Fidelity Security Services: George K. Campbell
EVP, Fidelity Investments Human Resources: Ilene B. Jacobs
President, Fidelity Management and Research Company: Robert C. Pozen
President and Chief Investment Officer, Strategic Advisors: William V. Harlow
President, Fidelity Investments Institutional Retirement Group: Robert L. Reynolds
President, Fidelity Investments Institutional Services: Kevin J. Kelly
President, Fidelity Ventures: Timothy T. Hilton
President, Fidelity Capital: Steven P. Akin
President, Fidelity International Limited: Barry R. J. Bateman
SVP, Fidelity Management & Research Company: Abigail P. Johnson, age 37
Auditors: PricewaterhouseCoopers LLP

LOCATIONS

HQ: 82 Devonshire St., Boston, MA 02109
Phone: 617-563-7000   **Fax:** 617-476-6150
Web site: http://www.fidelity.com

PRODUCTS/OPERATIONS

Subsidiaries
Fidelity Brokerage Group
  Fidelity Brokerage Technology Group
  Fidelity Investment Advisor Group
  National Financial Correspondent Services
Fidelity Capital
  BostonCoach
  Devonshire Custom Publishing
  Fidelity Capital Telecommunications & Technology
    COLT Telecom Group (nearly 60%)
  Fidelity Technology Solutions
  Fidelity Ventures
  J. Robert Scott
  NetSuite Development
  Pembroke Real Estate
  Seaport Hotel at the World Trade Center
  World Trade Center Boston
Fidelity Financial Intermediary Services
Fidelity International Limited
  Fidelity Brokerage Services Japan LLC
Fidelity Investments Institutional Retirement Group
  Fidelity Group Pensions International
  Fidelity Institutional Retirement Services Company
  Fidelity Investments Tax-Exempt Services Company
Fidelity Investments Institutional Services Company
Fidelity Investments Life Insurance Company
Fidelity Investments Retail Group
  Fidelity Investments Premium Assets Group
Fidelity Technology & Processing Group
Strategic Advisers, Inc.

COMPETITORS

AXA Financial	Hearst	Paine Webber
Aetna	John Hancock	Prudential
Alliance Capital	Lehman Brothers	Quick &
Ameritrade	Marsh &	Reilly/Fleet
Barclays	McLennan	Raymond James
Charles Schwab	MassMutual	Financial
Citigroup	Merrill Lynch	T. Rowe Price
Datek Online	MetLife	TD Waterhouse
Dow Jones	Morgan Stanley	Securities
E*TRADE	Dean Witter	TIAA-CREF
First Union	Northwestern	USAA
Goldman Sachs	Mutual	Vanguard Group

HISTORICAL FINANCIALS & EMPLOYEES

Private FYE: December	Annual Growth	1989	1990	1991	1992	1993	1994	1995	1996	1997	1998
Sales ($ mil.)	22.6%	1,083	1,272	1,474	1,824	2,570	3,530	4,277	5,080	5,878	6,770
Net income ($ mil.)	26.7%	53	32	89	125	225	315	431	423	536	446
Income as % of sales	—		4.9%	2.5%	6.0%	6.9%	8.8%	8.9%	10.1%	8.3%	9.1%	6.6%
Employees	17.6%	6,500	7,000	7,700	9,000	12,900	14,600	18,000	23,300	25,000	28,000

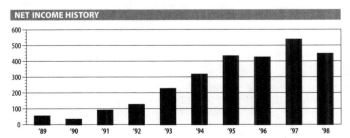

NET INCOME HISTORY

Fidelity Investments®

FOLLETT CORPORATION

OVERVIEW

No folly found in Follett's foray into text-books. River Grove, Illinois-based Follett is the #1 operator of US college bookstores, with more than 500 stores (operated through retail division Follett College Stores) serving campuses in 48 states and Canada. In addition to books, campus stores sell products such as clothing: Follett buyers are on call to place orders for in-demand emblem apparel at the moment a college team wins a big game. Other higher education services include Custom Academic Publishing (formerly known as CAPCO, which Follett acquired), which secures copyright permissions and publishes custom college coursepacks.

Follett also brings books to the younger set. It is the top US wholesaler and distributor of used textbooks to elementary and high schools. Follett Library Resources supplies books and audiovisual materials to libraries at more than 45,000 schools. Follett collaborates with LSSI (Library Systems & Services) to provide library management services (in 1997 it took over management of California's Riverside County Library System). Follett Software develops software for use in elementary and secondary schools.

The company has capitalized on the growing trend of universities farming out bookstore operations to independent operators. Adding to its bevy of campus bookstores, it signed a contract in 1998 to build a $5 million bookstore at the University of Texas at Arlington. Follett is owned and managed by the Follett family, which has controlled the firm for four generations.

HISTORY

Follett began in 1873 as a small bookstore opened by the Rev. Charles Barnes in his Wheaton, Illinois, home. By 1893 a recession had rocked the business, and Barnes sought investment from his wife's family, for which he gave up controlling interest. Sales topped $237,000 in 1899.

Initially hired by Barnes in 1901 to help move the store to a new location in Chicago, 18-year-old C. W. Follett stayed on as both salesman and stock clerk. Barnes retired the following year, and left the business to his son William and his father-in-law, John Wilcox, who was a major shareholder. In 1917 Follett bought into the company when William moved to New York (he started what became one of Follett's biggest competitors, Barnes & Noble), and renamed it J. W. Wilcox & Follett Company. Wilcox died in 1923, and Follett bought the Wilcox family shares and shortened the name to Wilcox & Follett.

Follett's four sons were brought into the business, and each son was instrumental in shaping the company's future. Garth created Follett Library Resources, a wholesale service for libraries. Dwight started the elementary textbook publishing division. But Robert would have the most influence: He began wholesaling college textbooks, which led to the establishment of Follett College Stores and Follett Campus Resources.

Wilcox & Follett expanded throughout the Depression. During WWII it began publishing kids' books, which were in demand because of a metal toy shortage. C. W. died in 1952 and Dwight took over. In 1957 the firm organized into divisions; Follett Corporation was created as the parent company. During the 1960s Follett developed the first multiracial textbook series. Dwight built the company to $50 million in annual sales by 1977, when he retired. His son Robert succeeded him and led Follett through tremendous growth in the 1980s.

In 1983 the company sold its publishing division to Esquire Education Group; using funds from this sale, it began acquiring college bookstore chains such as Campus Services. In 1989 Follett developed Tom-Tracks, a computerized textbook system for college bookstores. In 1990 the company acquired Brennan College Service, adding 57 stores to its chain. Robert's son-in-law Richard Traut, named chairman in 1994, was the first person without the Follett name to hold that position. By that year Tom-Tracks had been installed in over 500 bookstores across the country. Also in 1994 the company introduced Sneak Preview Plus, a CD-ROM product designed to enhance the acquisition process in libraries.

The company acquired used-textbook reseller Western Textbook Exchange (1996), juvenile-book distributor Book Wholesalers (1997), and coursepack printer CAPCO (1998). In 1998 Ken Hull replaced Richard Litzsinger as CEO. Also in 1998 the Follett Campus Resources unit agreed to pay the University of Tennessee $380,000 after the school discovered that the firm had been underpaying students in a book-buyback program for several years.

Chairman, President and CEO: Kenneth Hull
VC: Mark Litzsinger
SVP Internet Marketing: Tim Dorgan
SVP Human Resources: Richard Ellspermann
VP Finance and CFO: Kathryn Stanton
Auditors: Arthur Andersen LLP

LOCATIONS

HQ: 2233 West St., River Grove, IL 60171
Phone: 708-583-2000   **Fax:** 708-452-9347
Web site: http://www.follett.com

PRODUCTS/OPERATIONS

Company Divisions

Higher Education Group
Custom Academic Publishing Company (custom
  coursepacks)
Follett Campus Resources (used-textbook supplier)
Follett College Stores Corporation (college bookstore
  operations)
Follett Express Sales (textbook distributor)

Library Group
Book Wholesalers, Inc. (juvenile-book distributor)
Follett Library Resources (wholesaler to K-12 libraries)

School Group
Follett Educational Services (K-12 textbook and
  workbook distributor)
Follett Software Company (K-12 library services)
Library Systems & Services (LSSI; library management,
  operation)

COMPETITORS

Baker & Taylor
Barnes & Noble College Bookstores
Bigwords.com
Data Research
Educational Development
Ingram Industries
Kinko's
VarsityBooks.com
Wallace's Bookstores

HISTORICAL FINANCIALS & EMPLOYEES

Private FYE: March	Annual Growth	1990	1991	1992	1993	1994	1995	1996	1997	1998	1999
Sales ($ mil.)	14.9%	343	432	549	612	646	713	811	916	1,073	1,200
Employees	7.4%	4,200	5,758	6,198	6,500	6,800	7,200	7,500	8,000	7,500	8,000

SALES HISTORY

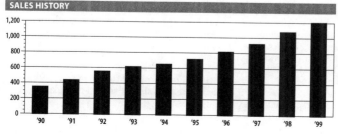

THE FORD FOUNDATION

OVERVIEW

As one of the US's largest philanthropic organizations with some $11.1 billion in assets, The Ford Foundation can afford to be generous. The New York City-based not-for-profit foundation provides financial support (grants or loans) to individuals and institutions in the US and abroad that meet its stated goals of strengthening democratic values, reducing poverty and injustice, promoting international cooperation, and advancing human achievement.

The Ford Foundation gives to a variety of causes that fall under one of three subsets: Asset Building and Community Development (designed to help expand opportunities for the poor and reduce hardship); Peace and Social Justice (promotes peace and the rule of law, human rights, and freedom); and Education, Media, Arts, and Culture (aimed at strengthening education and the arts and at building identity and community).

The foundation is governed by an international board of trustees and no longer has stock in Ford Motor Company or ties to the Ford family. Funds are derived solely from a diversified investment portfolio that includes publicly traded equity and fixed-income securities.

HISTORY

Henry Ford and his son Edsel gave $25,000 to establish The Ford Foundation in Michigan in 1936, followed the next year by 250,000 shares of nonvoting stock in the Ford Motor Company. The foundation's activities were limited mainly to Michigan until the deaths of Edsel (1943) and Henry (1947) made the foundation the owner of 90% of the automaker's nonvoting stock (catapulting the endowment to $474 million, the US's largest).

In 1951, under a new mandate and president (Paul Hoffman, former head of the Marshall Plan), Ford made broad commitments to the promotion of world peace, the strengthening of democracy, and the improvement of education. Early education program grants overseen by University of Chicago chancellor Robert Maynard Hutchins ($100 million between 1951 and 1953) helped establish major international programs (e.g., Harvard's Center for International Legal Studies) and the National Merit Scholarships.

Under McCarthyite criticism for its experimental education grants, the foundation in 1956 granted $550 million (after selling 22% of its Ford shares to the public) to noncontroversial recipients: 600 liberal arts colleges, 3,500 not-for-profit hospitals, and 44 private medical schools. The organization's money set up the Radio and Television Workshop (1951); public TV support became a foundation trademark.

International work, begun in Asia and the Middle East (1950) and extended to Africa (1958) and Latin America (1959), focused on education and rural development. The foundation also supported the Population Council and research in high-yield agriculture with The Rockefeller Foundation.

In the early 1960s Ford targeted innovative approaches to employment and race relations. McGeorge Bundy (former national security adviser to President John F. Kennedy), named president of the foundation in 1966, increased the activist trend with grants for direct voter registration; the NAACP and the Urban League; public-interest law centers serving consumer, environmental, and minority causes; and housing for the poor.

The early 1970s saw support for black colleges and scholarships, child care, and job training for women, but by 1974 inflation, weak stock prices, and overspending had eroded assets. Programs were cut, but continued support for social justice issues led Henry Ford II to quit the board in 1976.

Under lawyer Franklin Thomas (named president in 1979), Ford established the nation's largest community development support organization, Local Initiatives Support. Thomas, the first African-American to lead the foundation, was a catalyst in a series of meetings between white and black South Africans in the mid-1980s.

Thomas stepped down in 1996, and EVP Susan Berresford, the new president, consolidated the foundation's grant programs into its three main areas: Asset Building and Community Development; Peace and Social Justice; and Education, Media, Arts, and Culture. Despite criticism from both the right and the left, in 1997 Ford announced $50 million in new projects — its largest project announcement ever — focusing on increasing international grants and programs that help people help themselves. The next year the Lilly Endowment (started by drugmaker Eli Lilly) surpassed Ford as the US's largest charitable organization, a title held by Ford for 30 years. In 1999 Ford dropped to the #4 spot behind the David and Lucile Packard Foundation, Lily, and Gates.

LOCATIONS

HQ: 320 E. 43rd St., New York, NY 10017
Phone: 212-573-5000   **Fax:** 212-599-4584
Web site: http://www.fordfound.org

PRODUCTS/OPERATIONS

Program Area Grants

Asset Building and Community Development
Community and Resource Development
  Agricultural productivity
  Community revitalization
  International economics and development
  Land and water management
  Research and policy
  Rural community development
Economic Development
  Economic revitalization
  Employment generation
  Research and policy
Human Development and Reproductive Health
  Community involvement
  Dissemination of information and public education
  Ethics, law, and policy
  Fair start for children
  Social science and research training
  Welfare and teen pregnancy

Education, Media, Arts, and Culture
Education, Knowledge, and Religion
  Access and equity
  Teaching and scholarship
Media, Arts, and Culture
  Artistic creativity and resources
  Cultural preservation, vitality, and interpretation
  Media and public policy

Peace and Social Justice
Government and Civil Society
  Civic participation
  Criminal justice
  Governmental structures and functions
  Philanthropy
  Public policy analyses
  Strengthening public service
Human Rights and International Cooperation
  Access to social justice/legal services
  Civil and political liberties
  Development cooperation
  Human rights, education, scholarship and
    dissemination of information
  International human rights law
  International relations
  Peace and security
  Refugees' and migrants' rights
  US foreign policy

HISTORICAL FINANCIALS & EMPLOYEES

Foundation FYE: September	Annual Growth	1989	1990	1991	1992	1993	1994	1995	1996	1997	1998
Assets ($ mil.)	6.1%	5,672	5,291	6,158	6,367	6,821	6,475	7,373	8,177	9,579	9,655
Employees	0.4%	561	559	568	590	590	597	587	570	574	580

ASSET HISTORY

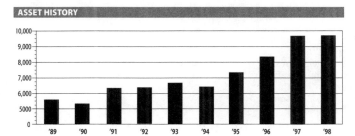

FORD FOUNDATION

FRY'S ELECTRONICS, INC.

OVERVIEW

Fry's Electronics keeps its customers angry but entertained. The legendary San Jose, California-based chain — known just as much for its cranky customer service as for its merchandise — has 16 stores, most of them in the Golden State, yet ranks among the largest US computer retailers.

Its mammoth stores, some swallowing 200,000 sq. ft., cater to the intensely technical shopper. Fry's outlets (a regular stop on bus tours) stock more than 10,000 low-priced electronic items and are known for their whimsical decor and displays. Each follows a theme, from *Alice in Wonderland* to a UFO crash site. The geek-gaws range from silicon chips to potato chips, from *Byte* to *Playboy,* and high-speed PCs (plus software and peripherals) to No-Doz (and other over-the-counter drugs).

But Fry's unfriendly reputation has left it a target of the Better Business Bureau and the subject of gripe-filled Web sites. Employees are searched at the end of each day as an antitheft measure (a concern that also keeps Fry's products stacked on the sales floor due to the elimination of stock rooms). Customers hoping to return items must abide by a process known internally as the "double H," for hoops and hurdles. One manager of an anti-Fry's Web site has likened the experience to a bizarre game of S&M that keeps customers coming back for more abuse.

Media-stonewalling brothers John (president and CEO), David (chief information officer), and Randy Fry (EVP) own the company, which continues aggressive expansion. John Fry, a mathematician who collects the writings of Nobel Prize winners for fun, is a bona fide cheapskate who hires computer-illiterate sales clerks for a pittance and accepts the resulting high turnover.

HISTORY

The Fry brothers — David, John, and Randy — wear genes stitched of retailing. Their father, Charles, started Fry's Food Stores supermarket chain in the 1950s in South Bay, California. The 40-store chain was sold for $14 million in 1972 before Charles Fry's progeny heard the retail calling.

Charles gave each of his sons $1 million. His oldest, John, who had gained technical expertise while running the supermarket's computer system, convinced his siblings of the viability of a hard-core computer retail store. The brothers pooled their funds and in 1985 started the first in Sunnyvale, California, along with Kathryn Kolder (VP). They added a store in Fremont in 1988; the Palo Alto store was completed two years later with an adjacent corporate headquarters.

John mixed his supermarket sales experience with a sharp marketing acumen, selling prime shelf space at smart prices to suppliers. He stocked the stores with everything for a computer user's survival and slashed prices. The first Los Angeles-area store opened in 1992; a second one opened the following year.

Hiring an ex-Lucasfilm designer, John spent $1 million on each location, draping stores in medieval castle, Mayan temple, Wild West saloon, and other individual fantasy themes.

In 1994 the Los Angeles computer retail market began to see increased competition from nationwide discount computer superstores. The next year Fry's responded by opening a new store in Woodland Hills with an *Alice in Wonderland* motif. It was the first Southern California Fry's Electronics store to offer appliances and an expanded music department.

The chain continued to gain notoriety for the contempt it seemed to show its customers. Local Better Business Bureaus started ranking Fry's "unsatisfactory" because the stores would not respond to complaints. Visitors were usually met with security guards, scores of hidden surveillance cameras, and employees who were promised bonuses for talking customers out of cash returns.

Still the company thrived, turning over its inventories twice as fast as competitors. One customer who sued Fry's for injuries allegedly received at the hands of store security guards went back for deals soon thereafter. Fry's went on an expansion frenzy in 1996, opening new California stores in Burbank, San Jose, and Anaheim. Moving beyond its Pacific roots, the company in 1997 spent $118 million to buy six of Tandy's failed Incredible Universe retail mega-outlets in Arizona, Oregon, and Texas. The company also won a legal battle with Frenchy Frys, a Seattle vending machine maker, for the right to own and use "frys.com" (it has not yet created a Web site with this URL). The company in 1998 continued to restructure its new stores into Fry's outlets.

President and CEO: John Fry
EVP and General Manager: Randy Fry
SVP of Merchandising: Raymond G. Navarrete
VP of Business Development (HR): Kathryn Kolder
Chief Information Officer: David Fry

LOCATIONS

HQ: 600 Brokaw Rd., San Jose, CA 95112
Phone: 408-487-4500   **Fax:** 408-487-4700

Fry's Electronics has stores in Arizona, California, Oregon, and Texas.

Store Locations
Anaheim, CA
Arlington, TX
Burbank, CA
Campbell, CA
Dallas
Fountain Valley, CA
Fremont, CA
Manhattan Beach, CA
Palo Alto, CA
Sacramento, CA
San Diego
San Jose, CA
Sunnyvale, CA
Tempe, AZ
Wilsonville, OR
Woodland Hills, CA

PRODUCTS/OPERATIONS

Selected Computer Products
Computer chips
Motherboards
PCs
Peripherals
Software

Other Products
Audio CDs
Beer
Coffee makers
Digital mixers
Fax machines
Magazines
Over-the-counter medicines
Potato chips
Razors
Soda
Stereos
Telephones
Telescopes
Televisions
Video systems

COMPETITORS

BUY.COM	InaCom
Best Buy	Insight Enterprises
Beyond.com	Micro Electronics
CDW Computer Centers	Micro Warehouse
Circuit City	MicroAge
CompUSA	Multiple Zones
Creative Computers	International
Cyberian Outpost	Office Depot
Dell Computer	PC Connection
Egghead	Staples
Gateway	Systemax
Good Guys	Tandy

HISTORICAL FINANCIALS & EMPLOYEES

Private FYE: December	Annual Growth	1989	1990	1991	1992	1993	1994	1995	1996	1997	1998
Sales ($ mil.)	38.0%	—	—	—	—	250	327	414	535	950	1,250
Employees	25.2%	—	—	—	—	1,300	1,500	1,500	2,000	4,000	4,000

SALES HISTORY

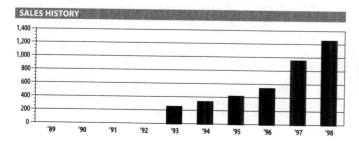

GENAMERICA CORPORATION

OVERVIEW

The General is being subordinated. Despite plans to fully demutualize after its 1997 restructuring into a mutual/stock hybrid, St. Louis-based GenAmerica Corporation (formerly General American Life Insurance) is being acquired by Metropolitan Life Insurance Company (MetLife). General American Mutual Holding Company holds GenAmerica, which in turn owns General American Life Insurance and 11 other insurance and financial service subsidiaries operating in North and South America, Europe, and Asia. The reorganization was intended to allow more flexibility to raise capital and fund acquisitions.

GenAmerica subsidiaries sell primarily individual life and health insurance, but other operations include Consultec (government health program administration), Cova Corporation (annuities), NaviSys (formerly Genelco, third-party technology services and claims

administration), Reinsurance Group of America (reinsurance), and Walnut Street Securities (securities brokerage).

To expand its financial services offerings, GenAmerica merged investment management subsidiary GAIMCO with Conning & Company. The resulting Conning Corporation offers institutional asset management and research services; GenAmerica owns about 65% of Conning, which went public in 1997.

GenAmerica had been planning to convert to a full stock company in 1999; a sudden and massive exodus of investors from General American Life Insurance, however, threatened its capital reserves and forced it to seek regulatory protection from the Missouri Insurance Department. No longer able to convert on its own, GenAmerica began seeking strategic partners; MetLife agreed to purchase the company.

HISTORY

In 1892 the Safety Fund Life Association was founded in Missouri as a mutual insurer. Later, the firm became a stock company, changed its name to Missouri State Life Insurance, and invested heavily in commercial real estate and farmland in the 1920s.

By 1929 Missouri State Life was the third-largest stock insurer in the US. Four years later, at the nadir of the Depression, it became the largest US life outfit to fail. The Morris Plan Co., a financial organization led by John D. Rockefeller's son-in-law, David Milton, bought Missouri State Life for $2 million and renamed it General American.

To preserve the rights of policyholders (necessary to fulfill an agreement with the state of Missouri), the new management imposed a lien on 50% of the reserve value of each policy and charged policyholders interest on the lien, which boosted the firm's depleted reserves and allowed it to pay death benefits in full. General American entered the farming and real estate businesses after the default of many of its agricultural mortgage investments. At one point, General American's agricultural holdings made it the largest US cotton producer.

In 1936, after the company was pressured to contribute to Missouri politicians, Milton bailed out, leaving the company's future in doubt; management reacted by mutualizing General American, a process that took 10 years.

In the 1950s the industry boomed; life and medical sales soared. The company became an investor in and an originator of residential and

commercial real estate loans. The firm started processing Medicare claims in 1966.

In the 1970s the company diversified, founding Genelco (insurance software) and entering the reinsurance business. The 1980s saw the rise of General American's health care operations, which contributed to lower profits in 1987 and 1988. It also entered the financial services arena, buying Walnut Street Securities.

General American launched its GenCare HMO subsidiary in a 1991 IPO and followed that with the 1993 IPO of Reinsurance Group of America. In 1995 it bought Xerox's life insurance businesses and sold its remaining interest in GenCare. The firm formed a joint venture with Security Mutual Life Insurance Company in 1996, expanding General American's presence in the New York market.

The company formed a mutual holding company in 1997 and began doing business as GenAmerica. In 1999 the company's partner in a short-term funding agreement joint venture, ARM Financial, was unable to meet its obligations; the return of these obligations to GenAmerica caused a ratings drop and threatened a run by investors. To protect its policyholders, the company placed itself under the supervision of the Missouri Department of Insurance. GenAmerica agreed to be acquired by Metropolitan Life Insurance, which also agreed to secure the debt, and to sell its group health business to a US subsidiary of The Great-West Life Assurance Company.

Chairman, President, and CEO, GenAmerica and
  General American Life Insurance: Richard A. Liddy
CFO: David L. Herzog
VP and Associate General Counsel:
  Matthew P. McCauley
VP and Controller: John W. Barber
VP, Secretary, and General Counsel:
  Robert J. Banstetter
VP Corporate Relations: Charles L. Larance
VP Human Resources: Marcia S. McMillian
Chief Technology Officer: Bruce B. Brodie
Treasurer and Corporate Actuary: E. Thomas Hughes
EVP, General American Life Insurance; Chairman,
  GenMark and Walnut Street Securities; President,
  Collaborative Strategies: Kevin Eichner
EVP Group Life and Health, General American Life
  Insurance: Warren J. Winer
VP and CFO, Group Life and Health, General American
  Life Insurance: Trevor E. Holland
VP and Chief Information Officer, Individual
  Information Systems, General American Life
  Insurance: Randall C. Poppell
VP Finance and CFO, Individual Line, General
  American Life Insurance: Mark M. Hopfinger
VP Group Business Segment, General American Life
  Insurance: Michael P. Ingrassia
VP Group Information Systems, General American Life
  Insurance: Walter T. Schultz
VP Group Operations, General American Life
  Insurance: Karen A. Smith
VP Individual Operations, General American Life
  Insurance: Deborah J. Walters
Auditors: KPMG LLP

HQ: 700 Market St., St. Louis, MO 63101
Phone: 314-231-1700   Fax: 314-525-6444
Web site: http://www.genamerica.com

1998 Assets

	$ mil.	% of total
Cash & equivalents	619	2
US Treasuries	21	—
Treasury & agency securities	1,274	5
Mortgage-backed securities	1,841	6
Corporate bonds	7,217	25
Other securities	878	3
Mortgage loans	2,338	8
Real estate	130	—
Policy loans	2,151	7
Other investments	409	2
Assets in separate account	5,287	18
Recoverables & receivables	785	3
Other assets	5,999	21
Total	**28,949**	**100**

1998 Sales

	$ mil.	% of total
Premiums	2,285	59
Investments	1,144	29
Other income	444	11
Commissions	41	1
Total	**3,914**	**100**

AXA Financial
Allmerica Financial
Conseco
Jefferson-Pilot
John Hancock
Liberty Mutual
Life Re
MONY
MassMutual

New York Life
Northwestern Mutual
Pacific Mutual
Principal Financial
Provident Mutual
Prudential
The Hartford
Torchmark
USAA

Mutual company FYE: December	Annual Growth	1989	1990	1991	1992	1993	1994	1995	1996	1997	1998
Assets ($ mil.)	20.1%	5,583	6,103	6,742	7,296	8,618	9,574	12,434	19,113	24,010	28,949
Net income ($ mil.)	20.0%	22	33	58	37	42	(14)	237	83	96	113
Income as % of assets	—	0.4%	0.5%	0.9%	0.5%	0.5%	—	1.9%	0.4%	0.4%	0.4%
Employees	11.8%	—	—	—	—	2,700	2,200	2,200	4,339	4,085	4,725

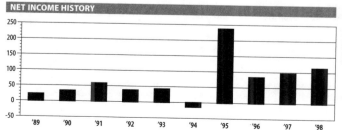

NET INCOME HISTORY

1998 FISCAL YEAR-END
Equity as % of assets: 4.5%
Return on assets: 0.4%
Return on equity: 9.1%
Long-term debt ($ mil.): 216
Sales ($ mil.): 3,914

General American
LIFE INSURANCE COMPANY

GIANT EAGLE INC.

OVERVIEW

Giant Eagle has taken wing to new haunts beyond its hometown of Pittsburgh. The food wholesaler and supermarket chain has more than 200 company-owned and franchised stores, and it is the #1 chain in Pittsburgh and Cleveland. As with other birds of the retailing feather, Giant Eagle's stores carry private-label merchandise (Eagle Valley and Giant Eagle) and nonfood items; many have pharmacies and banks, and some offer ready-to-eat meals. The company also provides wholesale goods (Butler

Refrigerated Meats) to hundreds of supermarkets. Giant Eagle is owned by the families of its five founders.

The grocer hasn't been immune to the consolidation bug among food retailers. The addition of Riser Foods (35 stores) helped it fend off aggressive rival Royal Ahold, which runs the Finast chain in eastern Ohio. Giant Eagle has converted Riser's Rini-Rego Stop-n-Shop stores to its banner.

HISTORY

When Joe Porter, Ben Chait, and Joe Goldstein sold their chain of 125 Eagle grocery stores in Pittsburgh to Kroger in 1928, a term in the agreement stated that the men would have to leave the grocery business for three years. In retrospect, Kroger should have made the term last for the length of their lives, because in 1931 the three men joined the owners of OK Grocery — Hyman Moravitz and Morris Weizenbaum — and launched a new chain of grocery stores called Giant Eagle. Eventually, the chain would knock Kroger out of the Pittsburgh market.

Although slowed by the Great Depression, the chain expanded, fighting large rivals like Acme, A&P, and Kroger for Pittsburgh's food shoppers. The stores were mom-and-pop operations with over-the-counter service until they began converting to self-service during the 1940s. Store sizes expanded to nearly 15,000 sq. ft. in the 1950s. During that time Giant Eagle, with about 30 stores, launched Blue Stamps in answer to Green Stamps and other loyalty programs.

Giant Eagle phased out trading stamps in the 1960s in lieu of everyday low prices. To accommodate its growth, in 1968 the company acquired a warehouse in Lawrenceville, Pennsylvania, that more than doubled its storage area. Also that year the company opened its first 20,000-sq.-ft. Giant Eagle store.

During the inflationary 1970s Giant Eagle introduced generic items and began offering the Food Club line, a private-label brand, in conjunction with wholesaler Topco. The chain continued its steady expansion, and by 1979 it had become Pittsburgh's leading supermarket chain, as chains like Kroger, Acme, and A&P were leaving the city.

In 1981 the company, with 52 stores, acquired Tamarkin, a wholesale and retail chain in Youngstown, Ohio, part-owned by the Monus family. The purchase moved it into the

franchise business, and later that year the first independent Giant Eagle store opened in Monaca, Pennsylvania (outside Pittsburgh).

The Tamarkin purchase brought together Michael Monus and Giant Eagle CEO David Shapira, grandson of founder Goldstein. In 1982 they created Phar-Mor, a deep-discount drugstore chain (Wal-Mart's Sam Walton once said it was the only competitor he truly feared). From a single store in Niles, Ohio, Phar-Mor grew rapidly to 310 outlets in 32 states in the early 1990s.

Phar-Mor president Monus helped found the World Basketball League (WBL) in 1987 and became the owner of three teams. In 1992 an auditor discovered two unexplainable Phar-Mor checks to the WBL totaling about $100,000. From that discrepancy, investigators uncovered three years of overstated inventories and a false set of books; Shapira (who was also CEO of Phar-Mor), Giant Eagle owners (the company had a 50% stake in Phar-Mor until 1992), and other investors had been duped to the tune of over $1 billion. Shapira fired Monus and his cronies on July 31, 1992. The next day the WBL folded; three days later Phar-Mor began a massive downsizing, and two weeks after that Phar-Mor filed for Chapter 11 bankruptcy. A mistrial in 1994 couldn't save Monus from prison; he was reindicted and sentenced to 20 years in 1995. Giant Eagle took a financial hit from Phar-Mor's losses, but the company, which had grown to more than 130 stores in three states, was not permanently damaged.

In 1997 Giant Eagle made its largest acquisition, buying Riser Foods, a wholesaler (American Seaway Foods) with 35 company-owned stores under the Rini-Rego Stop-n-Shop banner. The stores were converted to the Giant Eagle banner in 1998 (another 18 independent Stop-n-Shop stores were also converted).

OFFICERS

Chairman and CEO: David S. Shapira
VC: Anthony Rego
President and COO: Raymond Burgo
SVP and CFO: Mark Minnaugh
VP Personnel: Raymond A. Huber

LOCATIONS

HQ: 101 Kappa Dr., Pittsburgh, PA 15238
Phone: 412-963-6200   **Fax:** 412-963-0374
Web site: http://www.gianteagle.com

1998 Stores

	No.
Ohio	
Cleveland	53
Youngstown	32
Akron/Canton	16
Pennsylvania	
Pittsburgh	78
Johnstown/Altoona	10
Erie	8
West Virginia	7
Total	**204**

PRODUCTS/OPERATIONS

Selected Services
Bakery
Banking services
Childcare
Deli department
Dry cleaning
Fresh seafood
Greeting cards
Pharmacy
Photo developing
Ready-to-eat meals
Ticketmaster outlet
Video rental

Private Labels
Eagle Valley
Giant Eagle

COMPETITORS

Dave's Supermarkets
Heinen's
IGA
Kroger
Royal Ahold
SUPERVALU
Wal-Mart
Weis Markets

HISTORICAL FINANCIALS & EMPLOYEES

Private FYE: June	Annual Growth	1990	1991	1992	1993	1994	1995	1996	1997	1998	1999
Estimated sales ($ mil.)	10.6%	—	1,950	2,000	2,000	2,000	2,100	2,200	3,800	4,050	4,360
Employees	13.8%	—	—	—	11,800	7,200	7,200	12,000	19,200	25,000	25,600

SALES HISTORY

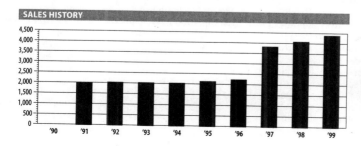

GOLD KIST INC.

OVERVIEW

Will a high-protein diet help Gold Kist shape up? Atlanta-based agricultural cooperative Gold Kist is a top US poultry processor, with 31,000 members (farmers and other co-ops) and operations in 11 states, primarily in the South. Poultry operations account for the bulk of its business. Gold Kist divides its operations into cooperative broiler divisions, each with its own chicken flocks, hatcheries, feed mill, and processing plant. It markets whole and cut-up chickens, chicken parts, and other processed products under brands such as Gold Kist Farms and Young 'n Tender to fast-food and grocery chains, school systems, and the military, among others.

Gold Kist is shedding other agricultural operations to focus on its food production, which also includes pork processing and catfish breeding. The firm's Agri-Services division once included wholesale and retail farm supplies. A difficult market (including a reduction

in the number of farm operators) led Gold Kist in 1998 to sell some Agri-Services assets, including 100 farm supply stores in the South and Southwest, peanut and grain buying stations, and feed mills, to Southern States Cooperative. Gold Kist also sold Southern States its cotton gins as it phases out most of its cotton operations.

The company's protein production isn't limited to poultry, pork, and fish. Its Young Pecan Company (a partnership with Young Pecan Shelling Company) is the #1 US pecan processor. Through Golden Peanut Company (a partnership with Archer-Daniels-Midland and Alimenta), Gold Kist processes and markets peanuts and peanut by-products in the US and overseas. Additional operations include financing for farmers (subsidiary AgraTrade Financing) and metal design and fabrication (subsidiary Luker).

HISTORY

Georgia native David Brooks, a University of Georgia agronomy professor from the age of 19, left teaching to form Georgia Cooperative Cotton Producers Association in 1933. A Depression-era creation, Brooks saw the Carrollton, Georgia cotton marketing cooperative as a way to improve the economic well-being of its members through collective price bargaining and the elimination of middlemen. By the end of its first year, Georgia Cotton Producers had grown from 13 members to about 7,000. The co-op expanded into neighboring states during the 1930s and subsequently dropped "Georgia" from its official name.

The cooperative diversified in the 1940s and 1950s. During WWII, the enterprise made ammunition at its fertilizer plants. Cotton Producers moved into pecan production in 1951 under the Gold Kist label. It also established itself as a major exporter of agricultural products, setting up sales offices in Europe in the late 1940s and Asia and the Middle East in the 1950s. The Gold Kist moniker was slowly adopted as the co-op's name over the next 20 years. When Brooks stepped down from full-time leadership in 1968, Gold Kist was the South's largest farm cooperative.

In the late 1970s the energy crisis, bad harvests, and other factors led to a decline in cooperatives, including Gold Kist, which posted a loss in 1980. As part of a diversification strategy, the co-op founded Golden Poultry in 1982 to run the Georgia-based broiler complex

acquired earlier that year by Agri International, another of its subsidiaries. In 1986, in a major affront to traditionalists (who saw co-ops as only member-owned institutions), Gold Kist spun off 27% of Golden Poultry (the first farmer-owned cooperative to make such a move). North Carolina-based Carolina Golden Products (a poultry processor partnership between Gold Kist and Golden Poultry) was merged into the company that year.

Gold Kist opened its Russellville, Alabama, facility in 1990, increasing its processed-chicken production capacity by half and entering the fast-food market. The company also expanded several plants. The co-op continued to hedge its bets through diversification in the early 1990s, moving into pork and pet food processing and catfish farming. It also beefed up exports (from about $46 million in 1990 to more than $70 million in 1995).

In 1997 Gold Kist acquired the stake in Golden Poultry it did not already own. Although low poultry prices and troubled foreign markets hit the company hard in 1998, Gold Kist continued its plan to focus on food, selling its wholesale and retail farm supply assets — including 100 stores as well as grain buying stations and cotton gins — to the Southern States agricultural cooperative.

Chairman: Fred N. Norris Jr.
CEO: Gaylord O. Coan, age 63, $1,018,269 pay
President and COO: John Bekkers, age 54, $836,538 pay
CFO and Treasurer: Stephen O. West, age 53
SVP Planning and Administration: Michael A. Stimpert, age 55, $430,577 pay
VP Communications: Paul G. Brower, age 60
VP Human Resources: William A. Epperson, age 60
VP Pork and Aquaculture: John K. McLaughlin, age 61
VP Information Services: Michael F. Thrailkill, age 51
VP Science and Technology: Allen C. Merritt, age 53
VP Marketing and Sales: Jerry L. Stewart, age 59, $357,500 pay
VP Operations, Poultry Group: Donald W. Mabe, age 45, $319,569 pay
VP, Purchasing Division: Marshall Smitherman, age 57
Controller: W. F. Pohl Jr., age 49
General Counsel, VP, and Secretary: J. David Dyson, age 52
Auditors: KPMG LLP

LOCATIONS

HQ: 244 Perimeter Center Pkwy. NE, Atlanta, GA 30346
Phone: 770-393-5000   **Fax:** 770-393-5262
Web site: http://goldkist.com

PRODUCTS/OPERATIONS

Selected Subsidiaries and Partnerships
AgraTrade Financing, Inc. (financing to farmers for poultry and pork facilities)
Golden Peanut Company (joint venture with Archer Daniels Midland and Alimenta)
Luker Inc. (metal fabricating firm, including design and installation services)
Young Pecan Company (joint venture with Young Pecan Shelling Company)

Selected Brands
Big Value
Early Bird
Gold Kist Farms
Medallion
Young 'n Tender

COMPETITORS

Cagle's
ConAgra
ContiGroup
Farmland Industries
Foster Poultry
Perdue
Pilgrim's Pride
Sanderson Farms
Tyson Foods
WLR Foods
Zacky Farms

HISTORICAL FINANCIALS & EMPLOYEES

Cooperative FYE: June	Annual Growth	1990	1991	1992	1993	1994	1995	1996	1997	1998	1999
Sales ($ mil.)	4.5%	1,185	1,259	1,301	1,401	1,561	1,689	1,956	2,289	1,651	1,766
Net income ($ mil.)	4.3%	42	33	(2)	27	34	12	37	12	(103)	61
Income as % of sales	—	3.6%	2.6%	—	1.9%	2.2%	0.7%	1.9%	0.5%	—	3.5%
Employees	3.8%	—	—	—	14,000	14,000	15,700	16,500	17,500	18,000	17,500

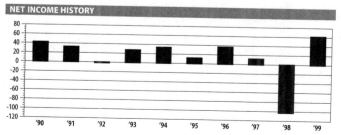

NET INCOME HISTORY

Debt ratio: 40.1%
Return on equity: 25.5%
Cash ($ mil.): 21
Current ratio: 1.39
Long-term debt ($ mil.): 187

GOLDEN STATE FOODS

OVERVIEW

Some companies have archenemies; food processor and distributor Golden State Foods has an arch-friend: McDonald's. The fast-food giant with the golden arches is Golden State Foods' only customer. Headquartered in Irvine, California, the company is one of McDonald's largest suppliers, providing individual restaurants with more than 130 products (beef, ketchup, mayonnaise, salad dressing). Golden State Foods operates 12 production plants and distribution centers in Australia, Egypt, and the US, and delivers goods to more than 2,000 McDonald's units (McDonald's has about 25,000).

McDonald's and its suppliers have established symbiotic relationships. Golden State Foods adheres to McDonald's standards and gears most of its operations toward furthering the restaurant chain's interests. The company serves McDonald's without the benefit of a long-term, written contract, but McDonald's is known for its loyalty to its suppliers.

Investment firm Yucaipa owns 70% of Golden State, and management company Wetterau Associates owns most of the remainder. Those firms bought Golden State in 1998 from its management, which kept a small stake in the company.

HISTORY

In 1947 William Moore founded Golden State Meat, a small meat-supply business that served restaurants and hotels in the Los Angeles area. In 1954 he added several new clients to his business — franchisees of a new chain of hamburger stands called McDonald's that was founded in San Bernardino, California in 1948. In 1961 Ray Kroc, a franchisee from Illinois, bought out the founding McDonald brothers, and the next year he moved to California to oversee a massive expansion in that state.

Moore and Kroc met, were mutually impressed, and became friends. At first Moore tried to get Kroc to buy him out, but Kroc's view of McDonald's did not include micromanaging its supply operations. He wanted to find suppliers the company could trust, and preferred smaller ones that weren't intent on breaking into the retail market. Golden State's relationship with McDonald's was sealed by a handshake between Kroc and Moore.

Moore and a partner bought a McDonald's franchise in 1965; two years later they had five. When Moore's partner died, McDonald's bought the units back for stock, which Moore later sold, using the proceeds to finance a new meat processing plant and warehouse. In 1969 Golden State Meat incorporated as Golden State Foods.

In 1972, after the new facilities were completed, Moore introduced the idea of total distribution. In addition to processing and distributing meat (by now delivered as frozen patties rather than fresh meat, which had limited delivery ranges in the 1950s and 1960s), Moore began supplying most of the needs of the McDonald's stores, making and delivering ketchup, mayonnaise, packaging, and syrup base for soft drinks. This allowed clients to reduce the number of weekly deliveries they received from as many as 30 to about three. The company went public in 1972, and two years later it dropped all of its other clients to cater exclusively to McDonald's.

Golden State grew in the 1970s, supplying a large share of the millions of McDonald's hamburgers sold every day. Moore died in 1978. Soon thereafter, a group of executives led by newly appointed CEO James Williams began exploring the possibility of taking the company private. In 1980, with backing from Butler Capital, they paid $29 million for the company, which then had sales of $330 million.

During the next decade Golden State expanded its relationship with McDonald's (and with the buying co-ops that supply stores operated by franchisees), opening facilities in other parts of the country. In 1990 the owners of Golden State tried to cash out by putting the company up for sale, but they withdrew it from the market within two years.

Golden State moved its headquarters from Pasadena to Irvine in 1992. In 1996 the company opened a distribution center in Portland, Oregon, and international expansion followed.

Yucaipa and Wetterau Associates, whose management hails from a major midwestern food wholesaler sold to SUPERVALU in 1992, bought Golden State in 1998 for about $400 million. The purchase represented Yucaipa's first significant acquisition outside the supermarket arena. James Williams, who had been with Golden State Foods for 38 years and served as its CEO for more than two decades, resigned in 1999. He was replaced by Mark Wetterau.

CEO: Mark S. Wetterau
President: Richard W. Gochnauer
SVP Finance and Secretary: Gene L. Olson
Office Manager: Joe Soran
Director Human Resources: Ron Childers

LOCATIONS

HQ: Golden State Foods Corporation,
    18301 Von Karman Ave., Ste. 1100,
    Irvine, CA 92612
Phone: 949-252-2000   **Fax:** 949-252-2080

PRODUCTS/OPERATIONS

Selected Products
Beef patties
Buns
Ketchup
Jelly
Lettuce
Mayonnaise
Onions
Salad dressing
Sundae toppings

COMPETITORS

Alliant Foodservice
AmeriServe
Foodbrands America
International Multifoods
JR Simplot
Keystone Foods
MBM
Martin-Brower
SYSCO
Sara Lee
Services Group
Shamrock Foods
U.S. Foodservice

HISTORICAL FINANCIALS & EMPLOYEES

Private FYE: December	Annual Growth	1989	1990	1991	1992	1993	1994	1995	1996	1997	1998
Estimated sales ($ mil.)	5.8%	960	1,026	1,013	1,032	1,160	1,260	1,340	1,450	1,500	1,600
Employees	1.2%	1,620	1,700	1,700	1,700	1,700	1,700	1,700	2,000	2,000	1,800

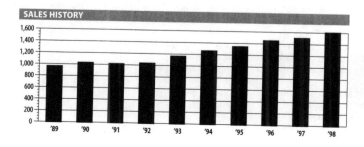

SALES HISTORY

GOYA FOODS, INC.

OVERVIEW

Called frijoles or habicuelas, beans are beans, and Goya's got 'em. Based in Secaucus, New Jersey, family-owned and -operated Goya Foods makes more than 850 Hispanic and Caribbean grocery products, including a variety of canned and dried beans, packaged meats, olives and olive oil, specialty rices, seasonings, plantain and yuca chips, tropical fruit nectars, and a line of frozen Caribbean entrées. Goya is one of the largest Hispanic-owned companies in the US. It's owned and operated by one of the richest US Hispanic families. President and CEO Joseph Unanue is son of the founder; eight third-generation members of the Unanue family work at the company.

Goya has historically served the Hispanic foods market in the Northeast and Florida with mostly Cuban, Dominican, and Puerto Rican customers. However, in response to demographic changes and in pursuit of greater market share, the company is adding products geared toward the tastes of Hispanics in California and the Southwest with roots in Mexico and Central and South America. Additionally, a growing interest in ethnic foods among non-Hispanics is strengthening Goya's sales. Yet, it faces competition from food giants, such as Campbell Soup, who are releasing lines of Hispanic specialties, as well as food manufacturers from Mexico who are turning north to tap the deeper pocketbooks of US consumers. Goya is responding with its own crossover aims — the company wants to be as recognized in Anglo homes as it is in the Hispanic market.

HISTORY

Immigrants from Spain by way of Puerto Rico, the husband and wife team of Prudencio Unanue and Carolina Casal founded Unanue & Sons in New York City in 1936. The couple imported sardines, olives, and olive oil from Spain, but when the Spanish Civil War (1936-1939) interrupted supply lines, they began importing from Morocco.

In 1949 the company established a cannery in Puerto Rico; the Puerto Rican imports were distributed to a local market of immigrants from the West Indies. Each of the couple's four sons eventually joined the family business, and in 1958 the firm relocated to Brooklyn. The company took its current name in 1962 when the family bought the Goya name — originally a brand of sardines — for $1.

The oldest Unanue son, CEO Charles, was fired from Goya in 1969 — and subsequently cut out of Prudencio's will — when he spoke out about an alleged tax evasion scheme. (Legal wrangling between Charles and the rest of the family continued into the 1990s.) Goya moved to its present New Jersey headquarters in 1974.

Another son, Anthony, died in 1976, as did Prudencio. That year Joseph, another sibling, was named president and CEO. Along with his brother Frank, president of Goya Foods de Puerto Rico, he began a cautious expansion campaign by adding traditional products to the company's existing line of Latin Caribbean and Spanish favorites.

Buoyed by the growing popularity of Mexican food, in 1982 Goya began distributing its products in Texas, targeting the region's sizable Mexican and Central American population. At first, the move proved a disaster. Goya's products were not suited to the Mexican palate, which generally preferred spicier flavors. Likewise, a similar strategy to capture a portion of Florida's huge Cuban market share initially met with only moderate success, but Goya persevered, eventually turning the tables in its favor.

During the 1980s the company also attempted to woo the non-Hispanic market. While Goya's cream of coconut — a key ingredient in pina coladas — found a broader market, its ad campaign featuring obscure actress Zohra Lampert did little to attract a large following of non-Hispanic customers.

Success in that market came in the 1990s. America's interest in the reportedly healthier "Mediterranean diet" boosted sales of Goya's extra virgin olive oil. Recommendations for low-fat, high-fiber diets prompted the company's launch of the "For Better Meals, Turn to Goya" advertising campaign — its first in English — in 1992.

In 1995 the company released a line of juice-based beverages. The next year Goya sponsored an exhibition of the works of the Spanish master Goya at the New York Metropolitan Museum of Art. Continuing its efforts to reach out to non-Hispanics and English-dominant Hispanics, in 1997 the company began including both English and Spanish on the front of its packaging. To lure more snackers, in 1998 Goya added yuca (aka cassava) chips to its line, which already included plantain chips.

President and CEO: Joseph A. Unanue
CFO: Miguel Lugo
President, Goya Foods de Puerto Rico:
Francisco J. Unanue
VP Marketing: Conrad O. Colon
VP Computer Information Services: David Kinkela
VP Purchasing: Joseph Perez
VP Sales: Tony Santamaria
Controller: Tony Diaz
Director Public Relations: Rafael Toro
Manager Personnel: Karmen A. Reccio
General Counsel: Carlos Ortiz
Assistant Public Relations: Jeanette Ojeda
Auditors: Deloitte & Touche LLP

LOCATIONS

HQ: 100 Seaview Dr., Secaucus, NJ 07096
Phone: 201-348-4900   **Fax:** 201-348-6609
Web site: http://www.goyafoods.com

PRODUCTS/OPERATIONS

Selected Beverages
Jamaican-style ginger beer
Malta goya
Pina colada mix
Tropical fruit nectars
Tropical fruit sodas
Tropi-Cola champagne sodas

Selected Foods and Other Products
Canned beans
Cheese
Chorizos
Corn masa mix
Cornmeal
Devotional candles
Dried beans
Flan
Flavorings and spices
Frozen Caribbean entrees
Guacamole
Guava paste
Imported sardines
Imported Spanish olive oil
Mexican specialty items
Plantain chips
Rice specialty mixes
Salsas
Stuffed olives
Vegetable oil
Yuca chips

COMPETITORS

American Rice
Authentic Specialty Foods
Bestfoods
Borden
Chiquita Brands
ConAgra
Del Monte
Diageo
Dole
Frito-Lay
Herdez
Hormel
Industrial Bimbo
International Home Foods
McCormick
Nestlé
Pro-Fac
Riceland Foods
Riviana Foods
Seneca Foods
Tri Valley Growers
Unilever

HISTORICAL FINANCIALS & EMPLOYEES

Private FYE: May	Annual Growth	1990	1991	1992	1993	1994	1995	1996	1997	1998	1999
Sales ($ mil.)	9.0%	300	330	410	453	480	528	560	600	620	653
Employees	4.3%	1,500	1,500	1,500	1,800	2,000	2,000	2,200	3,000	3,000	2,200

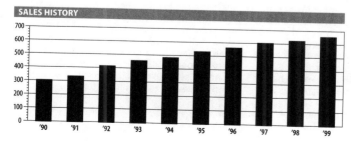

SALES HISTORY

GOYA. FOODS, INC.

GRANT THORNTON INTERNATIONAL

Grant Thornton International — it's everywhere your business ought to be. The Chicago-based partnership offers accounting and management consulting through some 580 offices in 93 countries. Member firms elect representatives to an international policy board that runs the day-to-day operations of the accounting company, which is #7 in the world. (It ranks behind the Big Five accounting firms — PricewaterhouseCoopers, Andersen Worldwide, KPMG International, Ernst & Young International, and Deloitte Touche Tohmatsu — and #6 BDO International.)

The consolidation of the Big Five prompted Grant Thornton International and other second-tier firms to enter such niche areas as

information technology and corporate finance. And while the Big Five focus on large corporations, Grant Thornton locks in on midsized companies, helping them not only with accounting, audit, and tax issues, but also with growth strategies. It is facing new competitors for its target market, with such firms as H&R Block and American Express adding accounting, tax planning, and consulting services.

Despite the difficulties caused by regulatory and cultural differences, accounting firms around the world are attempting to establish global standard practices. On a smaller scale, Grant Thornton's member firms are working to increase cross-border cooperation by pooling resources and cutting costs.

Alexander Grant, an accountant from Cameron, Missouri, and William O'Brien founded Alexander Grant & Co. in 1924. They built their accounting firm in Chicago and concentrated on providing services to clients in the Midwest.

In the 1950s and 1960s, the company began expanding both domestically and internationally. Sticking to its midwestern roots, Alexander Grant & Co. focused on companies involved in manufacturing and distribution.

In 1973 O'Brien died. In 1979 the company began publishing its well-known (and sometimes controversial) index of state business climates. That year it also tried — but failed — to merge with fellow second-tier accounting firm Laventhol & Horwath. The next year Grant Thornton International was formed when Alexander Grant & Co. and its British affiliate, Thornton Baker of England, combined their offices around the world to form a global network. The UK and US companies, however, kept their respective names.

The 1980s brought turmoil and change for the firm. In the wake of financial scandals, investors and the government held accounting firms liable for their audits. Along with the (then) Big Six, Alexander Grant & Co. was hit with several lawsuits alleging fraudulent statements and cover-ups. One suit marred the firm's squeaky-clean reputation and caused dozens of clients to jump ship: Just days after Alexander Grant issued it a clean audit, a Florida trading firm was shut down by the SEC. Jilted investors sued to reclaim the money they'd lost, and Alexander Grant settled for $160 million. Executive partner Robert Kleckner and chairman Herbert Dooskin also

left the company; although both executives denied they left because of the scandal, their departures stranded Alexander Grant without leadership during a critical time.

Meanwhile, the company merged with Fox & Co. to create the US's ninth-largest accounting firm. With partners leaving (and taking clients) following auditing scandals, Fox looked to the merger to shore up its reputation. But Alexander Grant's own auditing troubles led some Fox partners and clients to flee from the merged company.

After the fallout from the lawsuits and the merger, the company began rebuilding, taking on new clients, reclaiming ones it had lost, and refocusing on midsized companies. In 1986 both Alexander Grant & Co. and Thornton Baker took the Grant Thornton name to emphasize their work in both accounting and consulting.

The recession in the early 1990s reduced accounting revenues but increased demand for management consulting services. As political and economic barriers fell during the decade, Grant Thornton International grew. The firm expanded overseas, entering emerging markets in Africa, Asia, Europe, and Latin America. In 1998 the Big Six became the Big Five; Grant Thornton added refugee firms and partners to its global network. In 1999 the firm's US branch flirted with consolidation, entertaining merger offers from H&R Block and PricewaterhouseCoopers. Instead, the US branch announced plans to reposition itself as a corporate services firm to better compete.

OFFICERS

Chairman, International Policy Board and Divisional Director, Europe, Middle East, and Africa:
David C. McDonnell
Managing Director: Robert A. Kleckner
Divisional Director, Asia Pacific: Gabriel Azedo
Divisional Director, North America and Caribbean:
Richard Delaney
Treasurer: Louis A. Fanchi
CEO, Grant Thornton LLP: Domenick J. Esposito
National Director Human Resources, Grant Thornton LLP: Debbie Pastor

LOCATIONS

HQ: Prudential Plaza, Ste. 800,
130 E. Randolph St., Chicago, IL 60601
Phone: 312-856-0001   **Fax:** 312-861-1340
Web site: http://www.gti.org

Grant Thornton International has offices in 93 countries in Africa, Asia, Europe, North America, and South America.

1998 Sales

	$ mil.	% of total
Europe, Middle East & Africa	627	42
North America & Caribbean	503	33
Asia/Pacific	311	21
Central & South America	65	4
Total	**1,506**	**100**

PRODUCTS/OPERATIONS

1998 Sales

	% of total
Auditing & accounting	56
Tax	19
Other (includes consulting, recovery, forensics, legal investigations & corporate finance)	25
Total	**100**

Selected Services
Accounting
Auditing
Consulting
Corporate finance searches
Information technology
International tax planning
Lead advisory

COMPETITORS

American Express
American Management
Andersen Worldwide
Arthur D. Little
BDO International
Bain & Company
Booz, Allen
Boston Consulting
Centerprise Advisors
Deloitte Touche Tohmatsu
Ernst & Young
H&R Block
IBM
KPMG
McGladrey & Pullen
McKinsey & Company
Policy Management Systems
PricewaterhouseCoopers

HISTORICAL FINANCIALS & EMPLOYEES

Partnership FYE: December	Annual Growth	1989	1990	1991	1992	1993	1994	1995	1996	1997	1998
Sales ($ mil.)	8.3%	—	—	—	—	—	—	—	1,285	1,405	1,506
Employees	5.0%	—	—	—	—	—	—	—	18,300	18,562	20,160

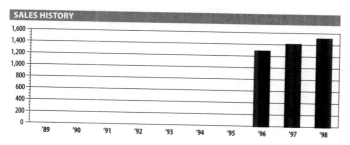

SALES HISTORY

Grant Thornton
International

GRAYBAR ELECTRIC COMPANY, INC.

OVERVIEW

Graybar Electric Company raises the bar for other distributors. With more than 100,000 items from thousands of manufacturers, the St. Louis-based company is a top distributor of electrical and communications products. Graybar also provides equipment leasing and financing through subsidiary Graybar Financial Services.

Graybar Electric's traditional market has been the construction industry, but rapid changes in telecommunications have prompted the company to solidify its relationships with major vendors such as Lucent and GE.

Customers include electrical contractors (who make up nearly 40% of sales), industrial plants, power utilities, and telecommunications providers.

The company uses technology to bring down supply, distribution, and inventory costs. It uses electronic data interchange and supplier-assisted inventory management and urges its suppliers to bar-code all products. Graybar Electric grows by targeting national and international accounts. The *FORTUNE* 500 company is owned by its more than 8,000 employees.

HISTORY

After serving as a telegrapher during the Civil War, Enos Barton borrowed $400 from his widowed mother in 1869 and started an electrical equipment shop in Cleveland with George Shawk. Later that year Elisha Gray, a professor of physics at Oberlin College who had several inventions (including a printing telegraph) to his credit, bought Shawk's interest in the shop, and the firm moved to Chicago, where a third partner joined.

The company incorporated as the Western Electric Manufacturing Co. in 1872, with two-thirds of the company's stock held by two Western Union executives. As the telegraph industry took off, the enterprise grew rapidly, providing equipment to towns and railroads in the burgeoning western US.

Gray and his company missed receiving credit for inventing the telephone in 1875 when Gray's patent application for a "harmonic telegraph" reached the US Patent Office a few hours after Bell's application for his telephone. However, the telephone and the invention of the lightbulb in 1879 opened new doors for Western Electric. The company began to grow into a major corporation, selling and distributing a variety of electrical equipment, including electric bells and batteries, telegraph keys, and fire-alarm boxes. By 1900 the firm was the world's #1 maker of telephone equipment.

Western Electric formed a new distribution business in 1926, Graybar Electric Co. (from "Gray" and "Barton"), the world's largest electrical supply merchandiser. In 1929 employees bought the company from Western Electric for $3 million in cash and $6 million in preferred stock. During the 1930s it marketed a line of appliances and sewing machines under the Graybar name.

In 1941 the company bought the outstanding shares of stock from Western Electric for $1 million. Graybar Electric was an important link between manufacturers and US defense needs during WWII. Its men and equipment wired the Panama Canal with telephone cable; it also helped the US military during the Korean conflict and the Vietnam War.

By 1980 Graybar Electric had reached nearly $1.5 billion in sales. However, its business was hurt when construction slowed in the late 1980s and the early 1990s, and the company reorganized in 1991, closing regional offices and cutting jobs. Rebounding in 1992 as the US economy improved, Graybar acquired New Jersey-based Square Electric Co.

Graybar Electric celebrated its 125th anniversary (its 65th as an employee-owned business) in 1994. That year the company acquired a minority interest in R.E.D. Electronics, a Canadian data communications and computer networking company, and realigned its operations into two business segments: electrical products and communications and data products.

In 1995 Graybar Electric formed the Solutions Providers Alliance with wholesale distributors Kaman Industrial Technologies, VWR Scientific Products, and Vallen Corporation. The national and international network provides products and services to the companies' maintenance, repair, and operations customers. In 1996 AT&T's Global Procurement Group named the company as one of only three suppliers for its electrical products. The next year Graybar Electric upped its stake in one of its Canadian operations, Harris & Roome Supply Limited.

In 1998 Graybar Electric opened a subsidiary in Chile. Also that year the company formed at joint venture called Graybar Financial Services with Newcourt Financial (formerly AT&T Capital).

OFFICERS

President and CEO: Carl L. Hall, age 61, $703,234 pay
SVP, Electrical Business: Richard H. Haney, age 56,
$339,908 pay
SVP, CommData Business: Robert A. Reynolds Jr.,
age 50, $339,908 pay
VP and Comptroller: John R. Seaton, age 64,
$360,791 pay
VP and Treasurer: John W. Wolf, age 59, $311,076 pay
VP Electrical Marketing: Charles R. Udell, age 54
VP, General Counsel, and Secretary: Thomas F. Dowd,
age 55
VP Human Resources: Jack F. Van Pelt, age 60
VP Operations: Golden W. Harper, age 62
District VP, Boston District: William L. King, age 63
District VP, Chicago District: Richard A. Cole, age 49
District VP, Northeastern District: Gerard J. McCrea,
age 59
District VP, Richmond District: Thomas S. Gurganous,
age 49
District VP, Seattle District: John C. Loff, age 49
District VP, Southeastern Comm/Data District:
Richard D. Offenbacher, age 48
Auditors: Ernst & Young LLP

LOCATIONS

HQ: 34 N. Meramec Ave., St. Louis, MO 63105
Phone: 314-512-9200   **Fax:** 314-512-9453
Web site: http://www.graybar.com

PRODUCTS/OPERATIONS

1998 Sales

	% of total
Electrical contractors	38
Telecommunications companies	29
Industrial plants	26
Power utilities	4
Integrated supply	2
Other	1
Total	**100**

COMPETITORS

All-Phase
Anixter International
Arrow Electronics
Avnet
Consolidated Electrical
Cooper Industries
Eaton
Emerson
Framatome
GE
Kent Electronics
Matsushita
Molex
Pioneer-Standard Electronics
Premier Farnell
Rexel
SPX
Siemens
Tech Data
Tyco International
W.W. Grainger
WESCO International
Wyle Electronics

HISTORICAL FINANCIALS & EMPLOYEES

Private FYE: December	Annual Growth	1989	1990	1991	1992	1993	1994	1995	1996	1997	1998
Sales ($ mil.)	7.9%	1,894	1,885	1,735	1,894	2,033	2,356	2,765	2,991	3,338	3,744
Net income ($ mil.)	18.9%	13	12	10	10	15	19	37	45	53	60
Income as % of sales	—	0.7%	0.6%	0.5%	0.5%	0.7%	0.8%	1.3%	1.5%	1.6%	1.6%
Employees	5.7%	4,800	4,900	4,729	4,700	5,100	5,500	6,200	6,600	7,200	7,900

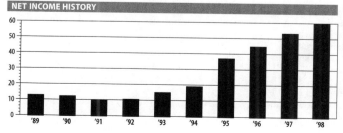

NET INCOME HISTORY

1998 FISCAL YEAR-END
Debt ratio: 47.6%
Return on equity: 21.7%
Cash ($ mil.): 20
Current ratio: 1.77
Long-term debt ($ mil.): 270

GraybaR

THE GREEN BAY PACKERS, INC.

OVERVIEW

Say cheese! Given the playoff success of the Green Bay Packers over the last six seasons (including two Super Bowl appearances and one championship), the team's fans (or "Cheeseheads," as they're affectionately known) have plenty to smile about. Since 1960, every game played on the frozen tundra of Lambeau Field in Green Bay, Wisconsin, has been sold out, thanks to the team's adoring, cheddar-cheese-chapeau-wearing fans, some of whom are also shareholders. The legendary team is organized as a not-for-profit corporation that is publicly owned by more than 100,000 shareholders and governed by 45 directors and a seven-person executive committee. Its shares do not appreciate or pay dividends, and if the team is ever liquidated, proceeds go to the Green Bay Packers Foundation.

In the modern world of big-money sports, the Packers, who play in the NFL's smallest market, are able to hold their own because of the league's TV contracts and revenue sharing. But the franchise is falling behind in stadium revenues with a 40-year-old facility with limited luxury boxes and club seating (from which other NFL teams derive millions in revenue). The Packers and the city of Green Bay now must decide whether to renovate Lambeau Field or replace it.

HISTORY

In 1919 Curly Lambeau and George Calhoun met in the newsroom of the *Green Bay Press-Gazette* to organize a football team. After talking Lambeau's employer, Indian Packing Company, into buying equipment for the team, its name naturally became the Packers. The team's revenues came from fans passing the hat at games. The team became so successful and popular that coach Lambeau and two packing plant officials obtained a franchise from the new National Football League in 1921. Receipts didn't cover expenses, and the franchise folded at the end of the season.

When Lambeau and other backers repurchased the franchise again in 1922 for $250, bad weather was almost the team's downfall. After a rainout, its insurance company wouldn't pay off; a storm later that year threatened to cancel another game and ruin the team. A. B. Turnbull, a *Press-Gazette* executive who was the first Packers president, convinced merchants in Green Bay to underwrite the team; the Packers became a corporation, and the game was played.

The Packers' first stock offering followed in 1923, raising $5,000. The Packers went on to win three straight championships from 1929 to 1931, but its winning ways couldn't stem the tide of bad fortune. In 1934 the Packers lost a $5,000 lawsuit to a fan who fell from the bleachers. The club's insurance company went out of business, and the Packers were forced into receivership. Green Bay merchants raised $15,000 through the second stock sale in 1935 to revive the corporation.

Championships in 1936, 1939, and 1944 kept the team popular, but didn't seem to help financially. A 1949 intra-squad game raised $50,000 to keep the team afloat, and a 1950 stock drive (the team's third) raised an additional $118,000. Lambeau resigned from the Packers in 1950, and the team's football fortunes were temporarily sacked. Then came Vince Lombardi in 1959.

The legendary coach, known for his "winning isn't everything — it's the only thing" mantra, commanded a team that dominated the NFL in the 1960s, winning five championships and the first two Super Bowls in 1967 and 1968 (Super Bowl winning teams now receive the Vince Lombardi Trophy.) City Stadium (built in 1957) was renamed Lambeau Field after Lambeau's death in 1965. Lombardi left coaching for the front office in 1968, and the team struggled to regain its luster during dismal seasons in the 1970s and 1980s.

In 1989 Bob Harlan, a former sports publicist who joined the Packers as assistant general manager in 1971, became president and CEO. Harlan named Ron Wolf general manager in midseason 1991, and Wolf hired Mike Holmgren as head coach in 1992. With the help of three-time NFL MVP quarterback Brett Favre, Holmgren led the team to the playoffs for six straight seasons from 1993 to 1998, including the Packers' third Super Bowl victory in 1997. The Packers returned to the Super Bowl the following year, but lost to the Denver Broncos.

The team raised more than $20 million for stadium improvements through its fourth stock offering in 1998. Holmgren then left the Packers after the 1998 season for a head coach/general manager job with the Seattle Seahawks. He was replaced by former Philadelphia Eagles head coach Ray Rhodes.

Rhodes was later fired after only one season when the Packers failed to make the playoffs for the first time since 1992.

President and CEO: Robert E. Harlan, age 63
EVP and General Manager: Ron Wolf, age 61
SVP Adminstration: John Jones, age 47
VP and General Counsel: Lance Lopes, age 36
VP Player Personnel: Ken Herock
Executive Director Public Relations: Lee Remmel, age 75
Director Administrative Affairs: Mark Schiefelbein
Director Tickets: Mark Wagner
Marketing Director: Jeff Cieply
Auditors: Wipfli Ullrich Bertelson LLP

LOCATIONS

HQ: 1265 Lombardi Ave., Green Bay, WI 54304
Phone: 920-496-5700   **Fax:** 920-496-5738
Web site: http://www.packers.com

PRODUCTS/OPERATIONS

Titles
Super Bowl Champions (1967-68, 97)
NFL Champions (1929-31, 36, 39, 44, 61-62, 65-67)
NFC Champions (1997-98)
NFC Central Division Champions (1972, 95-97)
NFC Wild Card (1993-94, 98)

COMPETITORS

Chicago Bears Football Club
Detroit Lions
Minnesota Vikings
Tampa Bay Buccaneers

HISTORICAL FINANCIALS & EMPLOYEES

Not-for-profit FYE: March	Annual Growth	1990	1991	1992	1993	1994	1995	1996	1997	1998	1999
Sales ($ mil.)	14.6%	30	42	45	54	66	62	70	75	82	103
Employees	7.2%	51	54	62	72	74	80	82	90	92	95

SALES HISTORY

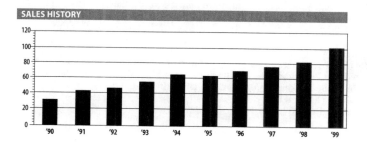

GUARDIAN INDUSTRIES CORP.

OVERVIEW

You won't catch Guardian Industries off guard against the fast break — or any other kind of break. Auburn Hills, Michigan-based Guardian is the world's fourth-largest glassmaker. The company is owned by billionaire William Davidson, who also owns the Detroit Pistons basketball team and Detroit Shock women's basketball team, along with the Detroit Vipers hockey team. Guardian tries to slam dunk the competition through its low-cost production of fiberglass, exterior car trim, and flat glass used by the construction and auto industries.

Guardian produces windows, windshields, doors, and mirrors using float technology (floating molten glass on molten tin to create pristine, high-clarity glass). Its Guardian Fiberglass subsidiary sells its fiberglass insulation under such leading brand names as True Value and Ace Hardware.

Guardian and other large US makers of flat glass had none other than Bill Clinton sticking up for them in a 1999 summit meeting with Japanese Prime Minister Keizo Obuchi. The two statesmen inked a pact that will allow both countries to exchange information while investigating suspected antitrust practices. Historically, a cartel of Japanese glassmakers (including Asahi Glass, Nippon Sheet Glass, and Central Glass) has kept American companies dividing up a mere 2% share of Japan's $3 billion glass market.

HISTORY

Guardian Glass began as a small maker of car windshields in Detroit in 1932 during the Depression. The company spent the 1930s and 1940s building its business to gain a foothold in glassmaking, historically one of the world's most monopolized industries. In 1949 PPG Industries and Libbey-Owens-Ford (now owned by the UK's Pilkington) agreed to stop their alleged monopolistic activity. William Davidson took Guardian Glass over from his uncle in 1957. As company president, he tried to boost the firm's standing in the windshield niche, but PPG and Libbey-Owens-Ford refused to sell him raw glass. That year Guardian Glass filed for bankruptcy to reorganize.

The company emerged from bankruptcy in 1960 (the same year Pilkington developed the float process for glassmaking), and in 1965 it was hit with its first patent-infringement suit. Three years later the firm went public, changed its name to Guardian Industries, and was refused a license to use Pilkington's float technology. Guardian began an aggressive acquisition strategy in 1969, and in 1970 it hired Ford Motor's top glass man (who knew the float process) and proceeded to build its first float-glass plant in Michigan. PPG sued Guardian in 1972. Davidson bought the Detroit Pistons in 1974. His do-or-die style might best be illustrated by the 1979 firing of Piston's coach Dick Vitale, who claims Davidson axed him on his own front doorstep while a curbside limo waited with the motor running.

In 1980 Guardian started making fiberglass and began hiring former Manville workers who could duplicate that company's patented technology for fiberglass insulation. In 1981 Manville successfully sued Guardian. Guardian opened a Luxembourg plant in 1981. Pilkington sued Guardian in 1983 (the case was settled out of court three years later). Davidson took Guardian private again in 1985, and in 1988 he bought an Indiana auto trim plant. That year he also built The Palace of Auburn Hills sports arena.

The 1990s brought more international expansion for Guardian, with new plants in India, Spain, and Venezuela. It also set up a distribution center in Japan, a country known for its tight control of the glass industry. In 1992 Guardian bought OIS Optical Imaging Systems, a maker of computer display screens. Guardian moved its headquarters to Auburn Hills, Michigan, in 1995. Its 1996 purchase of Automotive Moulding boosted its position in the auto plastics and trim market. In 1997 some 30 class-action lawsuits that alleged price-fixing were filed against the top five US glassmakers, including Guardian. The US Justice Department is conducting a separate investigation into the matter.

Guardian booted its OIS Optical Imaging Systems unit in 1998, citing ongoing losses. The fiberglass subsidiary bought 50% of Builder Marts of America, ushering Guardian into the market for lumber and roofing products. That year Davidson made a failed attempt to buy the Tampa Bay Lightning hockey team. In 1999 Guardian announced that it was pursuing a deal to buy majority ownership of jointly owned Siam Guardian Glass Ltd. from Siam Cement Plc, the company's partner in Thailand.

President and CEO: William Davidson
Group VP Finance and CFO: Jeffrey A. Knight
Director of Human Resources: Bruce Cummings

LOCATIONS

HQ: 2300 Harmon Rd., Auburn Hills, MI 48326
Phone: 248-340-1800   **Fax:** 248-340-2395
Web site: http://www.guardian.com

PRODUCTS/OPERATIONS

Selected Products and Services

Architectural Glass
Custom fabrication
Entrances and storefronts
Float glass
Insulating glass
Laminated glass
Mirrors
Patterned glass
Reflective coated glass
Tempered glass

Automotive Systems
Bodyside (mud flaps, wheel covers)
Front and rear end (grilles, rub strips)
Side window (door frame mouldings)
Windshield (window surround mouldings)

Guardian Fiberglass
Fiberglass insulation

Retail Auto Glass
Auto glass repair
Auto glass replacement
Insurance claim processing

COMPETITORS

Apogee Enterprises
Asahi Glass
CRH
Corning
Donnelly
Johns Manville
Nippon Sheet Glass
Owens Corning
PPG
Pilkington
Safelite Glass
Saint-Gobain
Vitro

HISTORICAL FINANCIALS & EMPLOYEES

Private FYE: December	Annual Growth	1989	1990	1991	1992	1993	1994	1995	1996	1997	1998
Estimated sales ($ mil.)	11.1%	—	—	1,050	1,200	1,200	1,500	1,700	1,900	2,000	2,200
Employees	7.0%	—	—	—	10,000	9,000	10,000	12,000	13,000	14,000	15,000

SALES HISTORY

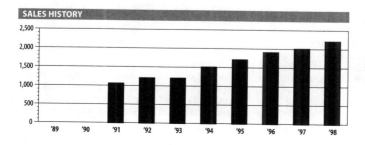

GUARDIAN LIFE INSURANCE

OVERVIEW

When your guardian angel fails you, there's Guardian Life Insurance Company of America. The New York City-based mutual company boasts more than 2.7 million policyholding owners.

Guardian offers life insurance, disability income insurance, and, more recently, retirement programs. The company has been expanding its traditional employee health indemnity plans to encompass a wider variety of disability, dental, and vision benefits. It is doing this primarily through acquisitions.

In the retirement area, Guardian has long offered the Park Avenue group of mutual funds and annuity products, managed by its Guardian Investor Services. To meet competition in the quickly deregulating financial services area, the company is building its wealth management capabilities to tap the baby boomer preretirement market. It has created a broker-dealer, Park Avenue Securities, and launched Guardian Trust Company, to offer trust and investment management services.

As part of these initiatives, Guardian has been on the move to improve customer service and to raise its profile through national advertising.

HISTORY

Hugo Wesendonck came to the US from Germany in 1850 to escape a death sentence for his part in the abortive 1848 revolution. After working in the silk business in Philadelphia, he moved to New York City, which was home to more ethnic Germans than any city save Berlin and Vienna.

In 1860 Wesendonck and other expatriates formed an insurance company to serve the German-American community. Germania Life Insurance was chartered as a stock mutual, which paid dividends to shareholders and policy owners. Wesendonck was its first president.

The US Civil War blocked the Guardian's growth in the South, but the company expanded in the rest of the US and its territories and by 1867 even operated in South America.

After the Civil War, many insurers foundered from high costs. Wesendonck battled this by implementing strict cost controls and limiting commissions, allowing the company to continue issuing dividends and rebates on its policyholders' premiums.

In the 1870s Germania opened offices in Europe, and for the next few decades much of the company's growth was there. By 1910, 46% of sales originated in Europe. The company's target clientele in the US decreased between the 1890s and WWI as German immigration slowed, and its market share dropped from ninth in 1880 to 21st in 1910.

During WWI the company lost contact with its German business. Prodded by anti-German sentiment in the US, the company changed its name to The Guardian Life Insurance Company of America in 1917. After WWI, the company began winding down its German business (a process that lasted until 1952).

In 1924 Guardian began mutualizing but could not complete the process until 1944 because of probate problems with a shareholder's estate.

After WWII, Guardian offered noncancelable medical insurance (1955) and group insurance (1957). The company formed Guardian Investor Services in 1969 to offer mutual funds; two years later it established Guardian Insurance & Annuity to sell variable contracts. In 1989 it organized Guardian Asset Management to handle pension funds.

In 1993, as indemnity health costs rose, the company moved into managed care via its membership in Private Health Care Systems, a consortium of commercial insurance carriers offering managed health care products and services. This allowed Guardian to offer HMO and PPO products.

Guardian entered a joint marketing agreement in 1995 with Physicians Health Services (an HMO), which contracts with physicians and hospitals in the New York tri-state area. In 1996 the company acquired Managed Dental Care of California and bought an interest in Physicians Health Services.

In the late 1990s, facing deregulation and consolidation in the financial services area and the threat posed by the demutualization of some of its largest competitors, Guardian formulated a strategy of adding depth to its employee benefits lines and breadth to its wealth management lines.

In 1999 Guardian formed its broker-dealer subsidiary and received a thrift license to facilitate creation of a trust business. Employee benefit actions included the purchase of First Commonwealth (managed dental care) and Amalgamated Insurance's New York State nonunion-worker disability benefits business. Also that year the company's national advertising campaign was dealt a blow when it lost a legal battle to force tiny, Wisconsin-based National Guardian Life to change its name.

President and CEO: Joseph D. Sargent
EVP and CFO: Peter L. Hutchings
EVP and Chief Investment Officer: Frank J. Jones
EVP Equity Products: John M. Smith
EVP Individual Markets and Group Pensions:
Dennis J. Manning
EVP: Edward K. Kane
SVP and Chief Actuary: Armand M. de Palo
SVP and Chief Marketing Officer: Franklin E. Sorrentino
SVP Financial Management and Control:
Stephen A. Scarpati
SVP Group Insurance: Gary B. Lenderink
SVP Human Resources and Administrative Support:
Douglas C. Kramer
SVP Taxes and Reinsurance Pools: Thomas G. Kabele
VP and Chief Information Officer: Thomas J. Baker
VP and Controller: John Cifu
VP and Corporate Secretary: Joseph A. Caruso
VP and General Counsel: John Peluso
VP Disability Insurance: John M. Sawyer
VP Reinsurance: Jeremy Starr
Auditors: PricewaterhouseCoopers LLP

LOCATIONS

HQ: The Guardian Life Insurance Company of America,
7 Hanover Sq., New York, NY 10004
Phone: 212-598-8000   **Fax:** 212-919-2790
Web site: http://www.theguardian.com

PRODUCTS/OPERATIONS

1998 Assets

	$ mil.	% of total
Cash & equivalents	800	3
Mortgage-backed securities	730	3
Bonds	10,243	40
Stocks	3,053	12
Real estate	49	—
Policy loans	1,028	4
Other investments	140	1
Assets in separate account	8,841	34
Receivables	888	3
Other assets	82	—
Total	**25,854**	**100**

1998 Sales

	$ mil.	% of total
Premiums	7,186	84
Net investment income	865	10
Service fees	216	3
Other	232	3
Total	**8,499**	**100**

Subsidiaries

Guardian Asset Management Corp.
Guardian Baillie Gifford, Ltd. (UK)
Guardian Insurance & Annuity Co.
Guardian Investor Services Corp.
Guardian Reinsurance Services Corp.
Managed Dental Care of California
Managed DentalGuard of Texas
Park Avenue Life Insurance Co.
Park Avenue Securities LLC

COMPETITORS

AXA Financial
Aetna
Allstate
American General
Anthem Insurance
CIGNA
CNA Financial
Charles Schwab
Citigroup
FMR
General Re
John Hancock
Liberty Mutual
MassMutual
Merrill Lynch
MetLife
New York Life
Northwestern Mutual
Oxford Health Plans
Pacific Mutual
Paine Webber
Principal Financial
Prudential
The Hartford
Transamerica
USAA
UnitedHealth Group
WellPoint Health
Networks

HISTORICAL FINANCIALS & EMPLOYEES

Mutual company FYE: December	Annual Growth	1989	1990	1991	1992	1993	1994	1995	1996	1997	1998
Assets ($ mil.)	16.2%	6,715	7,523	8,861	10,271	12,336	13,567	15,811	18,196	22,089	25,854
Net income ($ mil.)	2.0%	134	236	186	132	249	144	125	173	299	160
Income as % of assets	—	2.0%	3.1%	2.1%	1.3%	2.0%	1.1%	0.8%	1.0%	1.4%	0.6%
Employees	4.3%	3,420	6,845	7,175	7,502	7,126	7,602	5,322	5,155	4,800	—

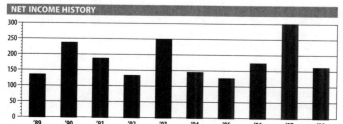

NET INCOME HISTORY

1998 FISCAL YEAR-END

Equity as % of assets: 6.0%
Return on assets: 0.7%
Return on equity: 18.8%
Long-term debt ($ mil.): —
Sales ($ mil.): 8,499

GUARDIAN™

HALLMARK CARDS, INC.

OVERVIEW

Hallmark Cards is the #1 producer of warm fuzzies. The Kansas City, Missouri-based company's greeting cards (sold under brand names such as Hallmark, Shoebox, and Ambassador) are sold in more than 47,000 US retail stores. About 7,500 of these stores bear the Hallmark or Hallmark Gold Crown name, but the company owns less than 5% of these stores, and the rest are franchised. Hallmark cards are distributed internationally in more than 100 countries.

While personal expression products bring in about three-quarters of Hallmark's revenue, the company has diversified into a host of other areas. Hallmark owns Binney & Smith, makers of Crayola brand crayons and markers, and mall-based portrait studio chain Picture People (with more than 180 studios across 19 states). The company also produces television movies through is Hallmark Entertainment unit and offers Keepsake brand ornaments. Through its Web site, Hallmark.com, Hallmark offers electronic greeting cards.

Not resting on well-engraved laurels, Hallmark has announced its intention to triple its revenue by 2010. While it plans to continue expanding its greeting card empire, the company is also intent on stretching its reach into markets such as gifts and family entertainment. Members of the Hall family (including chairman Donald Hall, son of founder Joyce Hall) own two-thirds of Hallmark; company employees own the remainder.

HISTORY

Eighteen-year-old Joyce Hall started selling picture postcards from two shoe boxes in his room at the Kansas City, Missouri, YMCA in 1910. His brother Rollie joined him the next year, and the two added greeting cards (made by another company) to their line in 1912. The brothers opened Hall Brothers, a store that sold postcards, gifts, books, and stationery, but it was destroyed in a 1915 fire. The Halls got a loan, bought an engraving company, and produced their first original cards in time for Christmas.

In 1921 a third brother, William, joined the firm, which started stamping the backs of its cards with the phrase "A Hallmark Card." By 1922 Hall Brothers had salespeople in all 48 states and had begun offering gift wrap. The firm began selling internationally in 1931.

Hall Brothers patented the "Eye-Vision" display case for greeting cards in 1936 and sold it to retailers across the country. The company aired its first radio ad in 1938. The next year it introduced a friendship card, displaying a cart filled with purple pansies. The card became the company's best-seller. During WWII Joyce Hall convinced the government not to curtail paper supplies, arguing that his greeting cards were essential to the nation's morale.

The company opened its first retail store in 1950. The following year marked the first production of *Hallmark Hall of Fame,* TV's longest-running dramatic series and winner of more Emmy awards than any other program. Hall Brothers changed its name to Hallmark Cards in 1954.

Hallmark introduced paper party products and started putting *Peanuts* characters on cards in 1960. Donald Hall, Joyce Hall's son, was appointed CEO in 1966. The following year the company began construction of Crown Center, which surrounded company headquarters in Kansas City. Disaster struck in 1981 when two walkways collapsed at the Crown Center's Hyatt Regency hotel, killing 114 and injuring 225.

Joyce Hall died in 1982, and Donald Hall became both chairman and CEO. Hallmark acquired Binney & Smith (Crayola Crayons, Magic Marker) in 1984. It introduced Shoebox Greetings, a line of nontraditional cards, in 1986. Irvine Hockaday replaced Donald Hall as CEO in 1986 (Donald Hall continued as chairman).

The company joined with Information Storage Devices in 1993 to market recordable greeting cards. It unveiled its Web site, Hallmark.com, in 1996 and began offering electronic greeting cards. That year Hallmark and Microsoft signed a five-year agreement to create personal expression products.

In 1997 Binney & Smith created a children's television series, *Crayola Kids Adventures,* featuring many product tie-ins. Hallmark's 1998 acquisition of UK-based Creative Publications boosted the company into the top spot in the British greeting card market. The following year the company acquired portrait studio chain Picture People and Christian greeting card maker DaySpring Cards. Hallmark also introduced Warm Wishes, a line of 99-cent cards. In the face of e-greetings competition, Hallmark began offering all electronic cards free of charge.

OFFICERS

Chairman: Donald J. Hall
President and CEO: Irvine O. Hockaday Jr.
President and CEO, Binney & Smith: Mark Schwab
President and CEO, Hallmark Entertainment:
  Robert Halmi Jr.
VP Administration and CFO: Robert J. Druten
VP Public Affairs and Communications: Steve Doyal
VP Human Resources: Ralph N. Christensen
Manager Corporate Media Relations: Julie O'Dell
Auditors: Arthur Andersen LLP

LOCATIONS

HQ: 2501 McGee St., Kansas City, MO 64108
Phone: 816-274-5111   **Fax:** 816-274-5061
Web site: http://www.hallmark.com

PRODUCTS/OPERATIONS

Selected Products
Albums
Calendars
Christmas ornaments
Collectibles
Electronic greetings
Gift wrap
Gifts
Greeting cards
Party goods
Personal expression software
Puzzles
Stickers
Writing paper

Selected Brands
Ambassador (greeting cards)
Hallmark Business Expressions (business greeting cards)
Keepsake Ornaments (holiday and other collectibles)
Mahogany (products celebrating African-American
  heritage)
Party Express (party products)
Shoebox (greeting cards)
Tree of Life (products celebrating Jewish heritage)

Selected Subsidiaries
Binney & Smith (Crayola brand crayons and markers)
DaySpring Cards (Christian greeting cards)
Hallmark Entertainment (television, movies, and home
  video production)
The Picture People (portrait studio chain)
Tapper Candles

COMPETITORS

American Greetings
Andrews McMeel Universal
Blue Mountain Arts
Blyth Industries
CPI Corp.
CSS Industries
Dixon Ticonderoga
Egreetings

Gibson Greetings
Olan Mills
PCA International
Syratech
Time Warner
Viacom
Walt Disney

HISTORICAL FINANCIALS & EMPLOYEES

Private FYE: December	Annual Growth	1989	1990	1991	1992	1993	1994	1995	1996	1997	1998
Sales ($ mil.)	5.1%	2,487	2,742	2,850	3,100	3,400	3,800	3,400	3,600	3,700	3,900
Employees	5.3%	13,213	13,877	13,202	12,487	12,600	12,800	12,100	12,600	12,554	20,945

SALES HISTORY

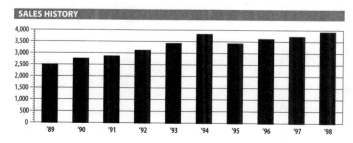

HARPO, INC.

OVERVIEW

Daytime talk queen Oprah Winfrey has 33 million loyal subjects. Her popular show is just one of the ventures produced by her Chicago-based company, Harpo ("Oprah" spelled backwards). Winfrey is one of the wealthiest African-American women in the US and consistently ranks as one of the most powerful and highest-paid entertainers. Her empire is built upon the success of *The Oprah Winfrey Show,* the highest-rated talk show in TV history, which is seen in more than 200 US markets and about 142 international markets. The company also produces films (she acts in some of them) for both TV (*Oprah Winfrey Presents)* and the big screen (*Beloved).*

After more than a dozen years at the top, Winfrey saw her program fall to second place in the ratings in 1998 behind Jerry Springer's trash TV talk show (which she called a "vulgarity circus"). Railing against the degeneration of the medium, Winfrey started a new show format called "Change Your Life TV," which aims to improve viewers' lives by focusing on spirituality and personal empowerment

(more poets and pop psychology, fewer prostitutes and porno queens). Critics charge that Winfrey is merely preaching to her audience through the show's new platform — criticism she dismisses.

Winfrey's innovative ideas have led to numerous Emmys (she won the academy's lifetime achievement award in 1998). Oprah's Book Club, in which she discusses books on the show, has the power to push a novel to the top of best-seller lists. Her reach is widening: Winfrey, along with TV producer Marcy Carsey (*3rd Rock From the Sun, That '70s Show*) and former Nickelodeon executive Geraldine Laybourne, is a key partner in the highly anticipated Oxygen cable TV station for women. Harpo will contribute original programming to the venture, scheduled to debut in 2000. Oxygen has also staked out a spot on the Internet with a variety of Web sites. Winfrey has also inked a deal with publisher Hearst Corp. to launch a magazine in 2000 that will focus on such topics as relationship advice, health care issues, and fashion trends.

HISTORY

Oprah Winfrey began her broadcasting career (she was originally a speech and performing arts student) in 1973 at age 19 as a news anchor at Nashville's WTVF-TV. Three years later she became an evening news co-anchor in Baltimore, where she was recruited to co-host WJZ-TV's local talk show *People Are Talking.* At first station management was apprehensive about Winfrey (a black, overweight woman in a field usually reserved for white, appearance-oriented males), but positive viewer response and healthy Nielsen ratings put their fears to rest. In the early 1980s Winfrey moved to Chicago to host ABC affiliate WLS-TV's *AM Chicago,* which quickly became the city's top morning talk show. (It was later renamed *The Oprah Winfrey Show.)*

In 1986 Winfrey's agent, Jeffrey Jacobs (now Harpo president and COO), secured syndication rights to the show and started distributing it through King World Productions. Harpo Entertainment was founded that year. Winfrey's 1985 performance in Steven Spielberg's *The Color Purple* won her an Oscar nomination. The academy nod helped boost her ratings when *Oprah* debuted nationally in 1986 in 138 cities. In 1988 Winfrey obtained full ownership of the program. Two years later Harpo Films was created, and Winfrey bought a

Chicago studio to produce *Oprah.* (The economically challenged Chicago neighborhood where her studio is located went from shabby to shiny after Winfrey's move.) In 1996 she introduced Oprah's Book Club, a show segment in which she selects a book for viewers to read and then discusses on a future show.

Texas cattlemen sued Winfrey after a 1996 show on the UK outbreak of mad cow disease, claiming she had caused a drop in beef futures prices (Winfrey didn't emphasize that the disease had not appeared in the US). But jurors ruled in her favor in early 1998. Also that year Winfrey renewed her contract with King World Productions until the 2001-02 TV season.

In 1998 Winfrey agreed to produce original programming for Oxygen, a new cable network for women, in exchange for an equity stake in the company. Oxygen also will acquire the rights to reruns of *The Oprah Winfrey Show* in 2002. CBS bought King World Productions in 1999; the deal gives Winfrey, a King World stockholder, a $100 million stake in CBS. (CBS subsequently agreed to a buyout offer from media giant Viacom, owner of Paramount Pictures.) Also that year Winfrey announced plans to launch a magazine in 2000 with Hearst Corp.

Chairman and CEO: Oprah Winfrey
President and COO: Jeffrey Jacobs
CFO: Doug Pattison
President, Harpo Productions: Tim Bennett
EVP, Harpo Films: Kate Forte
Director of Media and Corporate Relations:
Deborah Johns
Director of Human Resources: Bernice Smith
Director of Development, Harpo Films: Valerie Scoon

LOCATIONS

HQ: 110 N. Carpenter St., Chicago, IL 60607
Phone: 312-633-1000   **Fax:** 312-633-1976
Web site: http://www.oprah.com

PRODUCTS/OPERATIONS

Selected Operations
Harpo Films
  Feature films (for The Walt Disney Company)
  Oprah Winfrey Presents (TV movies)
Harpo Productions
  The Oprah Winfrey Show
Harpo Video
Oxygen (cable station for women; Harpo will provide
  original content)

COMPETITORS

BET	Time Warner
Lifetime	Tribune
NewStar Media	USA Networks
News Corp.	Viacom
Sony	dick clark productions

HISTORICAL FINANCIALS & EMPLOYEES

Private FYE: December	Annual Growth	1989	1990	1991	1992	1993	1994	1995	1996	1997	1998
Sales ($ mil.)	7.5%	—	—	—	105	110	120	130	140	150	162
Employees	7.1%	—	—	—	—	135	141	166	176	175	190

NET INCOME HISTORY

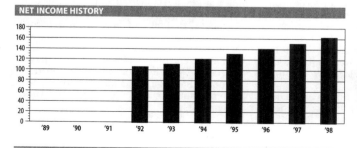

HARVARD UNIVERSITY

OVERVIEW

Many parents dream of sending their kids to Harvard; some even dream of being able to afford it — $34,350 a year for tuition, fees, and board. Located primarily in Cambridge, Massachusetts, Harvard is the oldest college in the US and one of the world's most prestigious educational institutions. The private, coeducational school consists of Harvard College (undergraduate) and 10 graduate schools (including the John F. Kennedy School of Government and renowned law, medicine, business, and public health schools), as well as the Division of Continuing Education. The women's undergraduate college, Radcliffe, remained legally separate until a 1999 agreement formally merged the two schools.

Harvard is oriented toward its graduate programs, with almost 11,000 students enrolled in postgrad courses; undergraduate enrollment is just over 6,700. Still, at both levels Harvard is among the US' most competitive universities. Its alumni include Vice President Al Gore, John Adams, T. S. Eliot, Ralph Waldo Emerson, Helen Keller, John F. Kennedy, Franklin and Theodore Roosevelt, Oliver Wendell Holmes, and Gertrude Stein.

Harvard's reputation for academic excellence is well-founded. More than 30 Harvard faculty members have won Nobel Prizes over the years. Harvard's endowment ($14 billion) is the largest of any US university.

HISTORY

In 1636 the General Court of Massachusetts appropriated 400 pounds sterling for the establishment of a college. The first building was completed at Cambridge in 1639 and was named for John Harvard, who had willed his collection of about 400 books and half of his land to the school. The first freshman class had four students.

During its first 150 years, Harvard adhered to the education standards of European schools, with emphasis on classical literature and languages, philosophy, and mathematics. It established its first professorship in 1721 (the Hollis Divinity Professorship) and soon after added professorships in mathematics and natural philosophy. In 1783 the school appointed its first professor of medicine.

Harvard updated its curriculum in the early 1800s, after professor Edward Everett returned from studying abroad with reports of the modern teaching methods in Germany. The university established the Divinity School in 1816, the Law School in 1817, and two schools of science in the 1840s.

In 1869 president Charles Eliot began engineering the development of graduate programs in arts and sciences, engineering, and architecture. He raised standards at the medical and law schools and laid the groundwork for the Graduate School of Business Administration and the School of Public Health. Radcliffe College was founded as "Harvard Annex" in 1879, 15 years after a group of women had begun studying privately with Harvard professors in rented rooms.

Harvard's enrollment, faculty, and endowment grew tremendously throughout the 20th century. The Graduate School of Education

opened in 1920, and the first undergraduate residential house opened in 1930. In the 1930s and 1940s, the school established a scholarship program and a general education curriculum for undergraduates. During WWII Harvard and Radcliffe undergraduates began attending the same classes.

A quota limiting the number of female students was abolished in 1975, and in 1979 Harvard introduced a new core curriculum. Princeton-educated Neil Rudenstine became president in 1991 and vowed to cut costs and to seek additional funding so that no one should be denied a Harvard education for financial reasons.

Harvard made dubious headlines during its 1994-95 academic year, enduring a bank robbery in Harvard Square, three student suicides, and one murder-suicide. The following year Harvard paid a fine of $775,000 after the US Attorney's Office claimed the school's pharmacy had not properly controlled drugs, including antidepressants and codeine cough syrup. The fine was the largest ever paid in the US under the Controlled Substance Act.

In 1998 Harvard's endowment fund acquired insurance services firm White River in one of the largest direct investments ever made by a not-for-profit institution. Also that year the school altered some of its graduation processes and introduced stress-reducing programs in the wake of another student suicide.

At the end of the 1999 school year, Harvard agreed to absorb the undergraduate operations of Radcliffe, which becomes the Radcliffe Institute for Advanced Study to focus on gender issues.

OFFICERS

President: Neil L. Rudenstine
Provost: Harvey V. Fineberg
VP Government, Community, and Public Affairs:
Paul Grogan
VP Finance: Elizabeth Huidekoper
VP Alumni Affairs and Development:
Thomas M. Reardon
VP and General Counsel: Anne Taylor
VP Administration: Sally H. Zeckhauser
Treasurer: D. Ronald Daniel
Director Human Resources: Mary Cronin
Auditors: PricewaterhouseCoopers LLP

LOCATIONS

HQ: Massachusetts Hall, Cambridge, MA 02138
Phone: 617-495-1000   **Fax:** 617-495-0754
Web site: http://www.harvard.edu

PRODUCTS/OPERATIONS

Schools and Colleges
Harvard Business School
Harvard College
Harvard Divinity School
Harvard Law School
Harvard Medical School
Harvard School of Dental Medicine
Harvard School of Public Health
Graduate School of Arts and Sciences
Graduate School of Design
Graduate School of Education
John F. Kennedy School of Government

Selected Affiliated Institutions
Arnold Arboretum
Dumbarton Oaks
Harvard Institute for International Development
Harvard University Art Museums
Harvard Yenching Institute
Joint Center for Housing Studies
Nieman Foundation
Radcliffe Institute for Advanced Study
Villa I Tatti (Florence, Italy)

HISTORICAL FINANCIALS & EMPLOYEES

School FYE: June	Annual Growth	1990	1991	1992	1993	1994	1995	1996	1997	1998	1999
Sales ($ mil.)	5.7%	1,083	1,143	1,210	1,306	1,377	1,467	1,519	1,565	1,679	1,788
Employees	20.9%	2,121	2,206	11,000	11,000	11,000	11,100	12,150	12,782	9,701	—

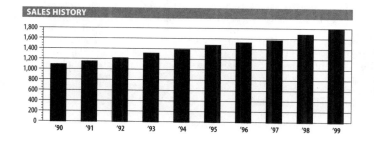

SALES HISTORY

HAWORTH INC.

OVERVIEW

Designers at Haworth sit at their cubicles and think about . . . more cubicles. Holland, Michigan-based Haworth is the #3 US maker of office furniture, trailing only #1 Steelcase and #2 Herman Miller. It offers a full range of furniture known for its innovative design, including partitions, desks, chairs, tables, and storage products. The company sells its products in more than 70 countries worldwide through more than 1,200 dealers. Haworth, known as an aggressive competitor, has been expanding its presence in Europe, mostly through acquisitions.

The Haworth family, including chairman Richard Haworth, the founder's son, owns the company.

HISTORY

Gerrard Haworth, an industrial arts high school teacher in Holland, Michigan, started a woodworking business in his garage in 1938. Gerrard hoped to garner some extra money to pay for his children's education: His efforts were successful, and 10 years later the business had grown to the point where he decided to take his hobby full time.

He quit his teaching job and applied for a bank loan, but as he had no business experience, he was turned down. Undaunted, Gerrard took out a mortgage on his house, received a $10,000 loan from his father, and started Modern Products in 1948. The fledgling company employed only six workers, but that changed two years later when Modern Products received a contract with the United Auto Workers in Detroit. The contract called for an innovative product: a "bank partition" — a partition constructed with wood below but with glass at the top. Believing other companies would want these partitions, Gerrard concentrated on their production. His hunch was correct, and Modern Products boomed throughout the 1950s, gaining a national presence by the decade's end.

Another Haworth, Gerrard's son Richard, went to work for the company in the 1960s, starting with sweeping floors but rising quickly to VP of research and development. When competitor Herman Miller introduced a set of movable panels, shelves, and desktops, it was Richard who developed the counterstroke for Modern Products, creating an insulated movable panel that also reduced noise. The insulated panels started shipping in 1971, helping fuel the company's continued growth.

Four years later, Richard — who would visit competitors' showrooms and take apart their furniture surreptitiously — invented, developed, and patented an even more innovative panel, this one with electrical wiring inside. These panels, called Uni-Group, eliminated the need to call electricians in for rewiring, boosting sales by millions — and ushering in the age of cubicles for office workers everywhere. Also in 1975 Modern Products changed its name to Haworth; the next year Gerrard became chairman and made Richard president.

As president, Richard was at the helm during Haworth's most explosive period of growth; not only was the office furniture industry booming during the 1980s, but Haworth was growing at more than twice the industry's rate. The company expanded overseas as well, setting up a European division after buying German chair maker Comforto (1988). Seeking to emulate Haworth's success with the pre-wired electrical panel, competitor Steelcase introduced its own version. Haworth, claiming patent infringement, sued Steelcase in 1985, lost in 1988, but then successfully appealed in 1989. Haworth filed a similar patent claim against Herman Miller three years later.

With the office furniture industry tightening in the late 1980s (due in part to a glut of used office supplies), Haworth turned to its international markets. The company purchased two Portuguese furniture makers in 1991 and French and Italian companies (Ordo and Castelli, respectively) the next year. Haworth continued to expand its business line through domestic acquisitions as well, acquiring Globe Business Furniture in 1992 and United Chair and Anderson Hickey three years later.

Haworth's patents on pre-wired partitions entered public domain in 1994. In 1996 and 1997 it had a successful resolution of both its lawsuits against its top two competitors: Herman Miller settled out of court in 1996 for about $44 million, and the next year Steelcase was ordered to pay $211.5 million, one of the largest judgments in patent-litigation history.

In May 1999 Haworth expanded its international presence with its purchase of office furniture companies in Germany (dyes, Nestler, Roder, and Art Collection) and Spain (Kemen).

OFFICERS

Chairman: Richard G. Haworth
President and CEO: Gerald B. Johanneson
VP Finance: Calvin W. Kreuze
VP Human Resources: Nancy Teutsch

LOCATIONS

HQ: 1 Haworth Center, Holland, MI 49423
Phone: 616-393-3000   **Fax:** 616-393-1570
Web site: http://www.haworth.com

PRODUCTS/OPERATIONS

1998 Sales

	% of total
Desk & panel systems	50
Seating	25
Metal desks, files & storage cabinets	15
Wood desks & tables	10
Total	**100**

Selected Products and Brands

Desk and panel systems (Causeway, Correspondent, Nomade, PLACES, PREMISE, RACE, Tango, and UniGroup)

Seating (Accolade, Catalyst, Improv, Penelope, Plia, System 26)

Metal desks, files, and storage cabinets (950 Series, PLACES, PREMISE)

Wood desks and tables (410 Series, Crossings, Nottingham, Sit-to-Stand, Tactis, Tripoli, Varia, and Wellsley)

COMPETITORS

Boise Cascade Office Products
Bush Industries
Facom
HON INDUSTRIES
Herman Miller
Kimball International
Knoll
O'Sullivan Industries
Sauder Woodworking
Shelby Williams
Steelcase

HISTORICAL FINANCIALS & EMPLOYEES

Private FYE: December	Annual Growth	1989	1990	1991	1992	1993	1994	1995	1996	1997	1998
Sales ($ mil.)	12.8%	—	—	650	655	800	1,005	1,150	1,360	1,510	1,540
Employees	8.9%	—	—	—	6,000	7,000	7,400	8,900	9,000	10,000	10,000

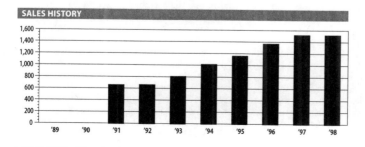

SALES HISTORY

H. E. BUTT GROCERY COMPANY

OVERVIEW

H. E. Butt Grocery Company (H-E-B) is the real "king of the hill" of the Texas Hill Country, and then some. The #1 food retailer in Austin, its home base of San Antonio, and Corpus Christi, H-E-B is by far the largest private company in Texas and one of the nation's largest regional supermarket chains. The company operates more than 260 supermarkets, mostly in South and Central Texas. Among those stores are about 90 small-sized H-E-B Pantry stores that serve mostly rural towns between Southeast Texas and Southwest Louisiana. In addition to a full line of groceries, about one-quarter of its stores have Gas 'N Go outlets. H-E-B also operates facilities for processing milk, meat, ice cream, and baked goods. The founding Butt family owns the chain.

The company is familiar with the tastes of Latinos (about half of its market is Hispanic), and H-E-B expanded south to Mexico before deciding to move into North Texas (H-E-B's headquarters is actually closer to Mexico than it is to Dallas). As part of that expansion, the company has moved into Monterrey's more affluent neighborhoods, and it also has opened a discount supermarket under the Economax name. The company plans to add more stores in Mexico, growing from about five stores to roughly 40 supermarkets there over five years. It also plans to open it first store in the Dallas/Fort Worth area in 2000.

HISTORY

Charles C. Butt and his wife, Florence, moved to Kerrville, in the Texas Hill Country, in 1905, hoping the climate would help Charles' tuberculosis. Since Charles was unable to work, Florence began peddling groceries door-to-door for A&P. Later that year she opened a grocery store, C. C. Butt Grocery. However, Florence, a dyed-in-the-wool Baptist, refused to carry such articles of vice as tobacco. The family lived over the store, and all three of the Butt children worked there. The youngest son, Howard, began working in the business full time in his teens and took over the business after WWI.

By adopting modern marketing methods such as price tagging (and deciding to sell tobacco), the Butts earned enough to begin expanding. In 1927 Howard opened a second store in Del Rio in West Texas, and over the next few years he opened other stores in the Rio Grande Valley. The company gained patron loyalty by making minimal markups on staples. It moved from Kerrville to Harlingen, Texas, in 1928 (it moved to Corpus Christi, Texas, in 1940 and to San Antonio in 1985).

The company began manufacturing foods in the 1930s, and it invested in farms and orchards. In 1935 Howard (who had adopted the middle name Edward) rechristened the chain the H. E. Butt Grocery Company (H-E-B). He put his three children to work for the company, grooming son Charles for the top spot after Howard Jr. took over the H. E. Butt Foundation from his mother.

While other chains updated their stores during the 1960s, H-E-B plodded. Howard Sr. resigned in 1971 and Charles took over, bringing in fresh management. But this was not enough. Studies showed that the reasons for its lagging market share were its refusal to stock alcohol and its policy of Sunday closing. H-E-B abandoned these policies in 1976. It also drastically lowered its prices, undercutting competitors and driving many independents out of business. Winning the price wars, H-E-B emerged the dominant player in its major markets.

H-E-B's first superstore, a 56,000-sq.-ft. facility offering general merchandise, photofinishing, and a pharmacy, opened in Austin, Texas, in 1979, and it concentrated on building more superstores over the next decade. It also installed in-store video rentals and added 35 freestanding Video Central locations.

In 1988 H-E-B launched its Pantry division, which remodeled and built smaller supermarkets mostly in rural Texas towns. Three years later it used San Antonio to launch another format, the 93,000-sq.-ft. H-E-B Marketplace, which included restaurants. In 1993 the company sold 33 video stores to Oregon-based Hollywood Entertainment. It opened the upscale Central Market in Austin in 1994 with 2,500 domestic and imported wines, more than 500 varieties of produce, and 500 kinds of cheese.

Chairman and CEO Charles retired as president in 1996, and James Clingman became the first nonfamily member to assume the office. That year H-E-B opened its first non-Texas store, in Lake Charles, Louisiana. In 1997 it opened its first Mexican store, in Monterrey, and launched a home meal replacement store-in-store called Great's! In 1998 H-E-B opened a discount supermarket in Monterrey under the Economax banner. As supermarket giant Safeway entered the Texas market in 1999, H-E-B unveiled ramped-up aspirations to expand in Mexico — where profit margins are higher — with six to eight new stores per year.

Chairman and CEO: Charles C. Butt
President and COO: James F. Clingman
SVP Marketing: Scott McClelland
SVP Human Resources: Diane Peck
CFO and Chief Administrative Officer:
John C. Brouillard
President, Pantry Food Division: Bob Loesler
President, Foods and Drugs: Harvey Mabry
VP Store Operations, San Antonio: Paul Madura
VP Finance: Alan Markert
VP and Secretary: Wesley D. Nelson
VP, Austin Region: Hal Collett
VP, North/West Region: Martin Otto
VP, Border Division: Greg Souquette
VP, Gulf Coast Region: Jeff Thomas
Auditors: Arthur Andersen LLP

LOCATIONS

HQ: 646 S. Main Ave., San Antonio, TX 78204
Phone: 210-938-8000   **Fax:** 210-938-8169
Web site: http://www.heb.com

PRODUCTS/OPERATIONS

Private labels
H-E-B
Hill Country Fare

Store formats
Gas 'N Go (gas stations)
H-E-B (large supermarkets)
H-E-B Central Market (upscale supermarket with
expanded organic and gourmet foods)
H-E-B Marketplace (large supermarkets with specialty
departments)
H-E-B Pantry (small supermarkets)

Selected Services and Programs
H-E-B Education 2000 (stores linked with schools to
promote educational goals)
H-E-B Food Bank (food donations to Texas food banks)
H-E-B Science Treehouse (an interactive educational
play area adjacent to San Antonio's Witte Museum)
H-E-B Volunteer Corps (employee involvement in
charitable organizations)

COMPETITORS

7-Eleven	Gigante
Albertson's	IGA
Brookshire Brothers	Kmart
Brookshire Grocery	Kroger
Carrefour	Randall's
Comerci	Rice Food Markets
Costco Companies	Soriana
Drug Emporium	Tosco
Eckerd	Wal-Mart
Fiesta Mart	Walgreen
Food Lion	Whole Foods

HISTORICAL FINANCIALS & EMPLOYEES

Private FYE: October	Annual Growth	1989	1990	1991	1992	1993	1994	1995	1996	1997	1998
Sales ($ mil.)	12.6%	2,586	2,900	3,162	3,204	4,500	4,844	5,137	5,800	6,500	7,500
Employees	18.9%	9,485	10,000	12,000	12,000	19,772	25,000	25,000	42,000	45,000	45,000

SALES HISTORY

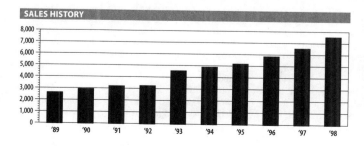

HEALTH CARE SERVICE

OVERVIEW

Headquartered in Chicago, mutually owned Health Care Service Corporation (HCSC) is made up of Blue Cross Blue Shield of Illinois (that state's oldest and largest health insurer) and Blue Cross and Blue Shield of Texas (about 25% the size of its counterpart). The Blue Cross and Blue Shield Association licenses its name to HCSC, which uses the brand to offer indemnity insurance, managed care programs, prescription drug plans, Medicare supplement insurance, dental and vision coverage, life and disability insurance, retirement plans, and workers' compensation.

Health Care Service Corporation covers federal employees in Illinois and Texas through the Federal Employee Program, a contract with the US government. It also offers insurance and medical financial services through such subsidiaries as FDL, Preferred Financial Corporation, and Nichold Company.

To better compete in the health care industry and to benefit from economies of scale, HCSC is looking to form alliances within the Blue Cross Blue Shield family. Health Care Service Corporation, as a mutual, can easily convert to for-profit status, unlike other Blues that have received tax breaks for decades and are compelled to treat their assets as a public trust, at least to some degree.

HISTORY

The seeds of the Blue Cross organization were sown in 1929, when an official at Baylor University Hospital in Dallas began offering schoolteachers 21 days of hospital care for $6 a year. Fundamental to its coverage was a community rating system, which based premiums on the community's claims experience rather than subscribers' conditions.

In 1935 Elgin Watch Co. owner Taylor Strawn, Charles Schweppe, and other Chicago civic leaders pooled resources to form Hospital Services Corporation to provide the same type of coverage. (The company adopted the Blue Cross symbol in 1939.) Employees of the Rand McNally cartography company were the first to be covered by the plan.

Soon, four similar plans were launched in other Illinois towns. Between 1947 and 1952, Hospital Services Corporation and these other four joined forces, offering coverage nearly statewide.

Meanwhile, Blue Shield physician's fee plans in several cities were incorporated as Illinois Medical Service. Hospital Services Corporation and Illinois Medical Service operated independently but shared office space and personnel.

A 1975 change in state legislation let the entities merge to become Health Care Service Corporation, which offered both Blue Cross and Blue Shield coverage. Following the merger, the company's board of directors (which had been primarily composed of care providers) became dominated by consumers, which helped HCSC become more responsive to its members.

For the next six years, the state denied HCSC any rate increases, leaving it with a frighteningly low $12 million in reserves in 1982. HCSC achieved statewide market presence in 1982 when it merged with Illinois' last independent Blue Cross plan, Rockford Blue Cross. In 1986, as managed care swept through the health care industry, only 14% of HCSC's members were enrolled in managed care plans. HCSC created its Managed Care Network Preferred point-of-service plan in 1991; the idea caught on with both employers and individuals and enrollment skyrocketed. By 1994 more than two-thirds of the company's subscribers participated in some sort of managed care plan. That year HCSC picked up Medicare payment processing for the state of Michigan after the Michigan Blues relinquished the increasingly onerous contract.

In 1995 HCSC and Blue Cross and Blue Shield of Texas (BCBST) formed an affiliation they hoped would culminate in a merger. The move would give the combined company $6 billion in sales and reserves of more than $1 billion. Consumer groups in Texas objected to the merger, claiming that Texas residents own BCBST and that Texans should be compensated for the transfer of ownership — especially since BCBST, unlike HCSC, had received state tax breaks for decades in exchange for accepting all applicants. (A Texas judge ruled in favor of the merger in 1998.)

Citing high risks and low margins, HCSC in 1997 dropped its Medicare payment processing contract, which it had held for some 30 years. The next year HCSC agreed to pay $144 million after it pleaded guilty to covering up its poor performance in processing Medicare claims.

In 1999 HCSC agreed to buy Aetna's NylCare of Texas, giving it large, profitable HMOs in Houston and Dallas.

PRODUCTS/OPERATIONS

1998 Assets

	$ mil.	% of total
Cash & equivalents	572	23
Treasury & agency securities	258	10
Corporate bonds	300	12
Stocks	87	4
Real estate	282	11
Other investments	354	14
Receivables	609	24
Other assets	47	2
Total	**2,509**	**100**

1998 Sales

	$ mil.	% of total
Limited risk	3,763	48
Premiums	2,910	38
HMO	1,034	13
Investments	94	1
Other	18	—
Total	**7,819**	**100**

Selected Products and Services
Dental insurance
Disability insurance
Indemnity insurance
Life insurance
Managed health care plans
Supplemental Medicare coverage
Prescription drug coverage
Retirement plans
Vision insurance
Workers' compensation

Selected Subsidiaries
American Capital Life Insurance Company
BCI HMO, Inc.
Dental Benefits, Inc.
Dental Network of America
Empire Benefit Services, Inc.
FDL (Fort Dearborn Life Insurance)
Midwest Group Insurance Agency
Multiple Insurance Services Corp.
Siouxland Insurance Consultants
Hallmark Services
HCSA, Inc.
Healthcare Benefits, Inc.
Industry Savings Plan, Inc.
Medical Life Insurance Agency
Medlease Company
Nichold Company
NIF Management, Inc.
Preferred Financial Corporation
Health Care Consulting Services, Inc.
MedLease Company
Rio Grande HMO, Inc.
Third Coast Holding Company
Third Coast Insurance Company
Third Coast Insurance Service Company
Trailblazer Insurance Company
Update Benefit Services, Inc.

COMPETITORS

AFLAC	Kaiser Foundation
Aetna	Mutual of Omaha
CIGNA	New York Life
Guardian Life	Prudential
Humana	UnitedHealth Group

HISTORICAL FINANCIALS & EMPLOYEES

Mutual company FYE: December	Annual Growth	1989	1990	1991	1992	1993	1994	1995	1996	1997	1998
Assets ($ mil.)	15.4%	—	796	960	1,111	1,314	1,452	1,621	1,749	1,864	2,509
Net income ($ mil.)	(14.2%)	—	170	61	69	98	166	139	89	71	50
Income as % of assets	—	—	21.4%	6.4%	6.2%	7.5%	11.4%	8.6%	5.1%	3.8%	2.0%
Employees	0.9%	—	—	—	—	—	—	5,600	5,650	5,700	—

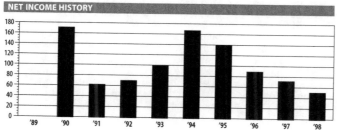

NET INCOME HISTORY

1998 FISCAL YEAR-END
Equity as % of assets: 45.5%
Return on assets: 2.3%
Return on equity: 4.7%
Long-term debt ($ mil.): 0
Sales ($ mil.): 7,819

Blue Cross
Blue Shield

THE HEARST CORPORATION

OVERVIEW

Like legendary founder William Randolph Hearst's castle, The Hearst Corporation is sprawling. New York City-based Hearst owns 12 daily newspapers (*San Francisco Examiner, Houston Chronicle*) and 12 weeklies; about 20 US consumer magazines (*Cosmopolitan, Popular Mechanics, Esquire*); stakes in cable TV networks (A&E, ESPN); TV and radio stations (through Hearst-Argyle Television); a features and comic syndicate; and business publishers. Hearst plans to either sell the *Examiner* or fold it into the *San Francisco Chronicle* once it completes its purchase of the rival newspaper from Chronicle Publishing Company.

Although it no longer owns Hearst Castle (deeded to the State of California in 1951), the company has extensive real estate holdings. Hearst is also active in a realm of which its founder never dreamed: the Internet. Its online interests include Women.com Networks.

The company is owned by the Hearst family, but managed by a board of trustees (per William Randolph Hearst's will). Upon his death, Hearst left 99% of the company's common stock to two charitable trusts controlled by a 13-member board that includes five family and eight non-family members. The will includes an *in terrorem* clause that allows the trustees to disinherit any heir who contests it.

HISTORY

William Randolph Hearst, son of a California mining magnate, started as a reporter, having been expelled from Harvard in 1884 for playing jokes on professors. In 1887 he became editor of the *San Francisco Examiner,* which his father had obtained as payment for a gambling debt. In 1895 he bought the *New York Morning Journal* and competed against the *New York World,* owned by Joseph Pulitzer, Hearst's first employer. The "yellow journalism" resulting from that rivalry characterized American-style reporting at the turn of the century.

Hearst branched into magazines (1903), film (1913), and radio (1928). Also during this time, it created the Hearst International News Service (it was sold to E.W. Scripps' United Press in 1958 to form United Press International). The Hearst organization pioneered film journalism throughout the 1920s with the Hearst-Selig News Pictorial. In 1935 the company was at its peak, with newspapers in 19 cities (nearly 14% of total US daily and 24% of Sunday circulation), the largest syndicate (King Features), international news and photo services, 13 magazines, eight radio stations, and two motion picture companies. Two years later Hearst relinquished control of the company to avoid bankruptcy, selling movie companies, radio stations, magazines, and, later, most of his San Simeon estate to reduce debt. (Hearst's rise and fall inspired Orson Welles' 1941 film *Citizen Kane.*)

In 1948 Hearst became the owner of one of the US's first TV stations, WBAL-TV in Baltimore. When Hearst died in 1951, company veteran Richard Berlin became CEO. Berlin sold off failing newspapers but also moved into television and acquired more magazines.

Frank Bennack, president and CEO since 1979, expanded the company, acquiring newspapers, publishing firms (notably William Morrow, 1981), TV stations, magazines (*Redbook,* 1982; *Esquire,* 1986), and 20% of cable sports network ESPN (1991). Hearst branched into video via a joint venture with Capital Cities/ABC (1981) and helped launch the Lifetime and Arts & Entertainment cable channels (1984).

In 1990 Hearst teamed up with *Izvestia* to start a newspaper in Russia. The following year the company launched a New England news network with Continental Cablevision. In 1992 Hearst brought on board former Federal Communications Commission chairman Alfred Sikes, who quickly moved the company onto the Internet with the opening of the Hearst New Media Center at its New York headquarters in 1994. In 1996 Randolph A. Hearst (the sole surviving son of the founder) passed the title of chairman to nephew George Hearst. Broadcaster Argyle Television merged with Hearst's TV holdings in 1997 to form publicly traded Hearst-Argyle Television.

In 1999 Hearst combined its HomeArts Web site with Women.com to create one of the largest online networks for women (Women.com Networks then went public). It also announced joint-venture projects with Walt Disney's Miramax Films (entertainment magazine *Talk*) and Oprah Winfrey's Harpo Entertainment. In 1999 the company sold its book publishing operations (Avon Books, William Morrow & Co.) to News Corp.'s HarperCollins unit. It also agreed to buy the *San Francisco Chronicle* from rival Chronicle Publishing. Hearst will either sell the *Examiner* or fold it into the other paper. The company also announced it would form a joint venture distribution company with rival Condé Nast.

Chairman: George R. Hearst Jr.
President and CEO: Frank A. Bennack Jr.
EVP and COO: Victor F. Ganzi
Chairman and Co-CEO, Hearst-Argyle Television:
Bob Marbut, age 64
President, Hearst Magazines: Cathleen P. Black
President, King Features Syndicate: T. R. Shepard III
VP; President, Hearst Newspapers: George B. Irish,
age 53
**VP; Group Head, Hearst Entertainment and
Syndication:** Raymond E. Joslin
VP; President, Hearst New Media and Technology:
Alfred C. Sikes
VP; President and Co-CEO, Hearst-Argyle Television:
John G. Conomikes, age 66
VP and CFO: Ronald J. Doerfler
VP and Chief Legal and Development Officer:
James M. Asher
VP and General Counsel: Jonathan E. Thackeray
VP Human Resources: Ruth Diem
SVP and Group Publishing Director, Hearst Magazines:
Anne S. Fuchs
SVP and Chief Marketing Officer, Hearst Magazines:
Michael A. Clinton

LOCATIONS

HQ: 959 8th Ave., New York, NY 10019
Phone: 212-649-2000   **Fax:** 212-765-3528
Web site: http://www.hearstcorp.com

PRODUCTS/OPERATIONS

Selected Operations
Broadcasting
Hearst-Argyle Television (56%)

Entertainment and Syndication
A&E Television Networks (37.5%, with ABC & NBC)
The History Channel
ESPN (20%)
King Features Syndicate
Lifetime Entertainment Services (50%, with ABC)

Interactive Media
Talk City (5%, online communities)
Women.com Networks (48%, Internet site geared
towards women)

Magazines
Cosmopolitan
Esquire
Good Housekeeping
Harper's Bazaar
House Beautiful
Marie Claire (with Marie
Claire Album)
Popular Mechanics
Redbook
SmartMoney (with Dow
Jones)
Talk (joint venture with
Disney's Miramax unit)
Town & Country

Major Newspapers
Albany Times Union (New York)
Beaumont Enterprise (Texas)
Edwardsville Intelligencer (Illinois)
Houston Chronicle
Huron Daily Tribune (Michigan)
Laredo Morning Times (Texas)
Midland Daily News (Michigan)
Midland Reporter-Telegram (Texas)
Plainview Daily Herald (Texas)
San Antonio Express-News
San Francisco Examiner
Seattle Post-Intelligencer

COMPETITORS

Advance Publications
Belo
Bertelsmann
Bloomberg
CBS
Chronicle Publishing
Cox Enterprises
E. W. Scripps
Freedom Communications
Gannett
Hachette Filipacchi
Knight Ridder
McGraw-Hill
MediaNews
New York Times
News Corp.
PRIMEDIA
Reader's Digest
Reed Elsevier
Time Warner
Times Mirror
Tribune
Viacom
Walt Disney
Washington Post

HISTORICAL FINANCIALS & EMPLOYEES

Private FYE: December	Annual Growth	1989	1990	1991	1992	1993	1994	1995	1996	1997	1998
Sales ($ mil.)	1.4%	2,094	2,138	1,888	1,973	2,174	2,299	2,513	2,568	2,833	2,375
Employees	(0.4%)	14,000	13,950	14,000	13,000	13,500	14,000	14,000	14,000	15,000	13,555

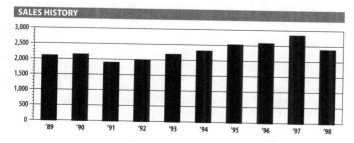

SALES HISTORY

The Hearst Corporation

HICKS, MUSE, TATE & FURST INC.

OVERVIEW

These Texas Hicks know an investment pool ain't no cement pond. Dallas-based Hicks, Muse, Tate & Furst creates investment pools in the form of limited partnerships. Investors consist mostly of pension funds but also include financial institutions and wealthy private investors such as Texas' Hunt family. The firm generally targets underperforming niche companies and builds them up through add-on investments. Unlike other investment firms, Hicks, Muse does not manage acquired companies; instead, it uses outside managers.

Traditionally diversified, Hicks, Muse has of late been tuning in a media empire. Its AMFM (formerly Chancellor Media) and Capstar Broadcasting radio groups are merging to create the US's largest radio group. The firm also has stakes in TV, broadcasting towers, outdoor advertising, and movie theaters.

Hicks, Muse is following a similar strategy in Latin America, where one of its funds has acquired cable-TV and radio stations and outdoor advertising interests. That fund also invests in Portugal and Spain.

Partners Tom Hicks, John Muse, Charles Tate, and Jack Furst own the firm.

HISTORY

The son of a Texas radio station owner, Thomas Hicks became interested in leveraged buyouts as a member of First National Bank's venture capital group. Hicks and Robert Haas formed Hicks & Haas in 1984; the next year it bought Hicks Communications, a radio outfit run by Hicks' brother Steven. The firm's biggest coup was its mid-1980s buy of several soft drink makers, including Dr Pepper and Seven-Up. Hicks & Haas took Dr Pepper/Seven-Up public just 18 months after merging the two companies, earning $600 million for just 50% of its equity. In all, the firm turned $88 million of investor funding into $1.3 billion. The pair split up in 1989; Hicks wanted to raise a large pool to invest, but Haas preferred to work deal by deal.

Hicks raised $250 million in 1989 and teamed with John Muse, a former Prudential Securities banker. Early investments included Life Partners Group (life insurance, 1990; sold to Conseco in 1996). In 1991 Charles Tate, formerly of Morgan Stanley, and Jack Furst, of First Boston, became partners.

Hicks joined brother Steven again in 1992, forming Gulfstar Communications to buy radio stations in the Southwest. The following year Hicks, Muse helped form Chancellor Broadcasting to target top US radio markets.

As part of its buy-and-build strategy, Hicks, Muse bought DuPont's connector systems unit (renamed Berg Electronics, sold 1998) in 1993, adding six more companies and nearly doubling Berg's earnings. Not all deals went so well: The firm failed to turn bankrupt brewer G. Heileman (bought in 1994) around, selling it to Stroh in 1996 for almost $100 million less than it had paid for it.

In 1995 Hicks, Muse, its Marcus Cable affiliate (folded into Charter Communications in 1999), and Goldman Sachs bought half of Sammons Communications' cable-TV systems.

The firm failed in its 1995 attempt, through Chancellor, to buy Robert Sillerman's SFX Broadcasting, whose president and COO was Steve Hicks. The firm's broadcasting buys boomed in 1996, though, when new legislation allowed ownership of up to eight stations in a single market. Shortly thereafter, Hicks, Muse formed Capstar Broadcasting (headed by Steve Hicks) to buy middle-market stations; the firm expanded into TV by forming Sunrise Television; and Chancellor went public.

After the 1994 peso crash left Mexican companies cash-starved, Hicks, Muse finally gained entry into Latin America. Also that year Hicks, Muse bought International Home Foods from American Home Products.

In 1997 Chancellor merged with Evergreen Media, forming Chancellor Media (renamed AMFM in 1999), and Gulfstar merged into Capstar.

The next year the firm continued buying both US and Latin American media companies. Hicks, Muse teamed with Kohlberg Kravis Roberts to form the largest US theater chain by merging KKR's Act III Cinemas with newly purchased Regal Cinemas. Investing in undervalued industries, it moved into the depressed energy field (Triton Energy) and announced plans to begin a $1.5 billion European fund.

In 1999 Hicks, Muse backed away from energy investments, canceling a planned investment in Coho Energy. The firm won a bidding war with Candover Investments over UK food group Hillsdown Holdings. That year the company took advantage of low real estate investment trust values and agreed to buy Walden Residential Properties, bought one-third of Grupo Minsa, a Mexican corn flour maker, and agreed with Nabisco Holdings to buy the UK's United Biscuits.

Chairman and CEO: Thomas O. Hicks
President: Charles W. Tate
COO: John R. Muse, age 47
CFO: Darron Ash
General Counsel: Michael Salem
Treasurer: Dave Knickel
Human Resources Manager: Lynita Jessen

LOCATIONS

HQ: 200 Crescent Ct., Ste. 1600, Dallas, TX 75201
Phone: 214-740-7300   **Fax:** 214-720-7888

PRODUCTS/OPERATIONS

Selected Holdings

Capstar (59%, radio stations in midsized markets)
Chancellor Media (15%, radio stations in large markets)
CEI Citicorp Holding (40%, telecommunications and
  publishing)
Circo Craft Co. (printed circuit boards, Canada)
The Forward Group PLC (printed circuit boards, UK)
Grupo MVS SA (pay-TV provider and radio station
  owner, Mexico)
Grupo Vidrio Formas (69%, glass container supplier,
  Mexico)
Hedstrom Corp. (playground equipment)
Home Interiors & Gifts, Inc. (direct-selling of decorative
  accessories and gift items)
International Home Foods (Chef Boyardee, Jiffy Pop
  popcorn, and PAM cooking spray)
International Wire Holdings Corp. (wire and wire
  harnesses, cable)
LIN Television
Marcus Cable Co. (19%, cable TV)
Olympus Real Estate Corp. (real estate equity and
  mortgage investments)
OmniAmerica Wireless LP (broadcast towers)
RCN Corp.(fiberoptic telecommunications networks)
Seguros Commercial America (13%, insurance, Mexico)
Sunrise Television Corp. (small-market television
  stations)
Traffic (49%, broadcasting, Brazil)
Triad Systems Corp. (computer systems for auto parts
  stores)

COMPETITORS

Berkshire Hathaway
Clayton, Dubilier
Equitex
Equity Group Investments
Haas Wheat
Heico
Investcorp
Jordan Company
KKR
Leonard Green
Texas Pacific Group
Thomas Lee
Vestar Capital Partners
Wingate Partners

HIGHMARK INC.

OVERVIEW

Highmark is walking the tightrope between high-minded and high income. The Pittsburgh-based company — the result of the union between the Medical Service Association of Pennsylvania (Pennsylvania Blue Shield) and Veritus (Blue Cross of Western Pennsylvania) — provides medical coverage to almost 6 million customers, primarily in Pennsylvania. Highmark also offers dental, vision, life, casualty, and other health insurance, as well as such community service programs as the Western Pennsylvania Caring Foundation, which offers free health care coverage to children whose parents earn too much to qualify for public aid but too little to afford private programs.

Highmark aims to grow in order to compete with for-profit leviathans like Aetna and UnitedHealth. The growth strategy irks critics (many of which are smaller healthcare providers) worried that the organization already has too much market power (it has 60% of the Western Pennsylvania market). Growth plans may include going public and becoming a for-profit organization, raising concerns that Highmark could focus on its capitalistic mission (maximizing returns) at the expense of its Blue Cross/Blue Shield mission (being the insurer of last resort).

Highmark continues to operate in Western Pennsylvania under the Highmark Blue Cross Blue Shield name and as Pennsylvania Blue Shield statewide. National subsidiaries include United Concordia Companies (dental coverage) and Highmark Life and Casualty Group (disability and life insurance).

HISTORY

Highmark was created from the merger of Blue Cross of Western Pennsylvania (founded in 1937) and Pennsylvania Blue Shield, created in 1964 when the Medical Service Association of Pennsylvania (MSAP) adopted the Blue Shield name.

The Pennsylvania Medical Society, in conjunction with the state of Pennsylvania, had formed MSAP to provide medical insurance to the poor and indigent. MSAP borrowed $25,000 from the Pennsylvania Medical Society to help set up its operations, and Chauncey Palmer (who had originally proposed the organization) was named president. Individuals paid 35 cents per month, and families paid $1.75 each month to join MSAP, which initially covered mainly obstetrical and surgical procedures.

Enrollment declined during WWII as many members left the state to support the war effort. In 1945 Arthur Daugherty (who served until his death in 1968) replaced Palmer as president and helped MSAP recruit major new accounts, including the United Mine Workers and the Congress of Industrial Organizations. MSAP in 1946 became a chapter of the national Blue Shield association, which was started that year by the medical societies of several states to provide prepaid health insurance plans.

In 1951 MSAP signed up the 150,000 employees of United States Steel, bringing its total enrollment to more than 1.6 million. Growth did not lead to prosperity, though, as the organization had trouble keeping up with payments to its doctors. This shortfall in funds led MSAP to raise its premiums in 1961, at which point the state reminded the association of its social mission and suggested it concentrate on controlling costs instead of raising rates.

MSAP changed its name to Pennsylvania Blue Shield in 1964. Two years later the association began managing the state's Medicare plan and in 1966 started the 65-Special plan to supplement Medicare coverage. In the 1970s Pennsylvania Blue Shield again could not keep up with the cost of paying its doctors, which led to more rate increases and closer scrutiny of its expenses. Competition increased in the 1980s as HMOs cropped up around the state. Pennsylvania Blue Shield fought back by creating its own HMO plans — some of which it owned jointly with Blue Cross of Western Pennsylvania — in the 1980s.

After years of slowly collecting noninsurance businesses, Blue Cross of Western Pennsylvania changed its name to Veritus in 1991 to reflect the growing importance of its for-profit operations.

In 1996 Pennsylvania Blue Shield overcame physicians' protests and state regulators' concerns to merge with Veritus. The company adopted the name Highmark to represent its standards for high quality; it took a loss as it failed to meet cost-cutting goals and suffered early-retirement costs related to the merger consolidation. To gain support for the merger, Highmark sold for-profit subsidiary Keystone Health Plan East to Independence Blue Cross in 1997.

In 1999 Highmark announced it had the urge to merge with and acquire other Blues.

Chairman: John A. Shaffer
VC: John A. Carpenter
President and CEO: John S. Brouse
EVP Government Business and Corporate Affairs:
George F. Grode
Group EVP Health Insurance Operations:
James Klingensmith
EVP Strategic Business Development:
Kenneth R. Melani
EVP Health Services: David M. O'Brien
EVP Sales: Carl W. Smollinger Jr.
SVP and General Auditor: Elizabeth A. Farbacher
SVP Operations: Gino A. Francavilla
SVP Finance and CFO: Robert C. Gray
SVP Government Business: Marilyn Koch
SVP Business Development: Daniel J. Lebish
SVP and Chief Information Officer:
Donald L. Morchower
SVP Managed Care Development: Michael A. Romano
SVP Resources Management (HR):
Thomas C. Sommers
SVP Provider Affairs: Sandra R. Tomlinson
SVP, Corporate Secretary, and General Counsel:
Gary R. Truitt
SVP Community Affairs: Aaron A. Walton
Assistant Secretary: Carrie J. Pecht
Auditors: PricewaterhouseCoopers LLP

LOCATIONS

HQ: 5th Avenue Place, 120 5th Ave.,
Pittsburgh, PA 15222
Phone: 412-544-7000   **Fax:** 412-544-8368
Web site: http://www.highmark.com

PRODUCTS/OPERATIONS

1998 Sales

	$ mil.	% of total
Premiums	6,961	92
Investments	141	2
Gain on investments	113	1
Other	328	5
Total	**7,543**	**100**

Subsidiaries

Alliance Ventures, Inc. (integrated health care systems)
Caring Foundation of Central Pennsylvania (joint venture Capital Blue Cross)
Caring Foundation of Northeastern Pennsylvania (joint venture with Blue Cross of Northeastern Pennsylvania)
Health Benefits Management, Inc. (joint venture with Capital Blue Cross)
Health Education Center, Inc.
HealthGuard of Lancaster, Inc.
Highmark Dental
United Concordia Companies, Inc.
Highmark Life and Casualty Group, Inc.
Highmark Vision
Clarity Vision, Inc.
Davis Vision, Inc.
Independence Blue Cross and Pennsylvania Blue Shield Caring Foundation for Children (joint venture with Independence Blue Cross)
Insurer Physician Services Organization, Inc.
Inter-County Health Plan, Inc. (joint venture with Independence Blue Cross)
Inter-County Hospitalization Plan, Inc. (joint venture with Independence Blue Cross)
Keystone Health Plan Central, Inc. (joint venture with Capital Blue Cross)
Keystone Health Plan West, Inc. (HMO serving Western Pennsylvania)
Standard Property Corporation
Veritus Medicare Services (Part A Medicare claims processing)
Western Pennsylvania Caring Foundation for Children
Xact Medicare Services (Part B Medicare claims processing)

COMPETITORS

Aetna
CIGNA
Guardian Life
Humana
New York Life
Prudential
UnitedHealth Group

HISTORICAL FINANCIALS & EMPLOYEES

Not-for-profit FYE: December	Annual Growth	1989	1990	1991	1992	1993	1994	1995	1996	1997	1998
Sales ($ mil.)	13.1%	—	2,822	3,168	3,083	3,113	3,221	3,367	6,619	7,405	7,544
Net income ($ mil.)	(2.3%)	—	75	101	141	132	128	43	(50)	101	62
Income as % of sales	—	—	2.7%	3.2%	4.6%	4.2%	4.0%	1.3%	—	1.4%	0.8%
Employees	13.6%	—	—	—	—	—	7,200	8,000	10,500	12,000	12,000

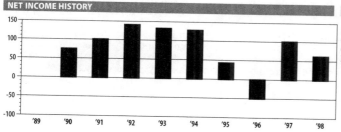

NET INCOME HISTORY

1998 FISCAL YEAR-END
Debt ratio: 9.6%
Return on equity: 3.2%
Cash ($ mil.): 287
Current ratio: 0.00
Long-term debt ($ mil.): 216

HUNTSMAN CORPORATION

OVERVIEW

Petrochemical production and charitable giving make up the chemistry of Huntsman Corporation, the #1 privately held US chemical firm. Salt Lake City-based Huntsman makes industrial chemicals, petrochemicals, and specialty chemicals used by the chemical, plastics, detergent, personal care, rubber, and packaging industries.

Huntsman's products include polypropylene, a plastic used in products ranging from electronics to lawn furniture; surfactants used in detergents and personal products; expandable resins such as molded polystyrene for insulation; and protective packaging. Huntsman Packaging also produces printed and laminated films used in food packaging, medical products, and other items.

The company has sold its foam-packaging business and most of its styrenics business. CEO and chairman Jon Huntsman, a devout Mormon philanthropist and cancer survivor, has said that he exited the styrenics business (in the US and Europe) to concentrate on his charitable activities and to pay down debt. The company nearly doubled its size, however, when it bought much of the bulk chemicals business of the UK's Imperial Chemical Industries. Mr. Huntsman has said he's interested in making another multi-billion dollar acquisition in early 2000 to stay competitive in the consolidating chemical industry.

Mr. Huntsman has given hundreds of millions of dollars to educational and charitable causes and medical research, including committing a billion dollars to Utah's Huntsman Cancer Institute.

HISTORY

First exposed to the use of plastics in the manufacture of egg cartons, Jon Huntsman spent three frustrating years at Dow Chemical. Then he and his brother Blaine raised $300,000 and received a $1 million loan from Hambrecht & Quist to found Huntsman Container in 1970. When chemical supplies began to run short, Huntsman sold the company to Keyes Fiber in 1976.

After six years, half spent doing missionary work for the Mormon Church, Huntsman took over polystyrene operations and set his sights on an underused Shell plant in Ohio. With oil and gas titan Atlantic Richfield's backing, Huntsman convinced Shell and a bank to lend him the balance of the purchase price and formed Huntsman Chemical in 1983.

With the acquisition of Hoechst Celanese's polystyrene business in 1986, Huntsman became the #1 producer of styrene in the US. That year Huntsman formed a joint venture with General Electric Plastics. In 1987 Huntsman sold 40% of Huntsman Chemical for $52 million and then acquired a New Jersey polypropylene plant from Shell. Huntsman re-entered the packaging business in 1989 by acquiring Keyes, the European firm that had once been a part of Huntsman Container.

In 1991 hamburger dynasty McDonald's succumbed to environmentalist pressure and ceased to use the Huntsman-developed polystyrene clamshell containers, and as a result Huntsman lost about 10% of its business. The company acquired packaging assets from Goodyear Tire and Rubber in 1992 and named the new subsidiary Huntsman Packaging. The

following year Huntsman acquired Mobil's unit that made polyethylene bakery bags. Also in 1993 Huntsman bought 50% of Chemplex Australia Limited from Consolidated Press Holdings (controlled by Australian tycoon Kerry Packer). Huntsman and Packer joined forces again in 1994 to buy most of Texaco's unprofitable petrochemical operations (renamed Huntsman Corporation) for $1 billion, which doubled Huntsman's size and added 24 plants in 12 countries.

Huntsman bought Eastman Chemical's worldwide polypropylene business in 1994. The next year it formed a joint venture with Texaco to operate Texaco's worldwide lubricant-additives line. That year Huntsman reacquired the 17% stake held by the Great Lakes Chemical, the only stock in the company held by outsiders.

In 1996 Huntsman placed all of his businesses under a single entity, the Huntsman Corporation. In 1997 the company bought the last of Texaco's chemicals operations, moving Huntsman into the propylene oxide market. Huntsman also bought packaging maker Rexene that year. To expand its Latin American packaging operations, the company bought Blessings Corporation in 1998.

Also in 1998 Huntsman sold its polystyrene and styrene monomer businesses in the US and Europe to NOVA Chemicals; it retained its expandable polystyrene unit when federal regulators objected to its sale. In 1999 the company bought Imperial Chemical Industries' polyurethane, aromatics, titanium dioxide, petrochemical, and olefins businesses.

Chairman and CEO: Jon M. Huntsman Sr.
President and COO: Peter R. Huntsman
SVP and CFO: J. Kimo Esplin
SVP Legal: Robert Lence
VP Glycols and Maleic: Thomas Fisher
VP Human Resources: William Chapman
VP Manufacturing, Chemicals: Mike Kern
VP Olefins and Performance Chemicals:
Donald Stanutz
VP Research and Development, Information Systems,
and Quality: Nathan Hubbard
President and CEO, Huntsman Packaging:
Richard P. Durham
Auditors: Deloitte & Touche LLP

LOCATIONS

HQ: 500 Huntsman Way, Salt Lake City, UT 84108
Phone: 801-532-5200   **Fax:** 801-584-5781
Web site: http://www.huntsman.com

PRODUCTS/OPERATIONS

Selected Products
Expandable resins (molded polystyrene for residential,
commercial, and industrial insulation; protective
packaging; insulated food containers)
Plastic compounds and colorants
Polypropylene (durable plastic used in the manufacture
of automobiles, clothing, electronics, lawn furniture,
and packaging materials)
Printed and laminated polyethylene and polypropylene
films
Specialized amines
Surfactants (detergents, shampoo)

Selected Joint Ventures
CONDEA-Huntsman GmbH & Co. KG (automobile
parts, boat hulls, and marble bath fixtures; Germany)
Huntsman Chemical Company Australia Limited (joint
venture with Consolidated Press Holdings)
Polystyrene Australia (joint venture with Dow Chemical
(Australia) Ltd.)

COMPETITORS

Akzo Nobel	Hercules
American Home Products	ICI
BASF AG	Lyondell Chemical
BP Amoco	Millennium Chemicals
Bayer AG	Mitsubishi
Chevron	Novartis
Degussa-Huls	Occidental
Dow Chemical	Owens Corning
DuPont	PPG
Eastman Chemical	Phillips Petroleum
Elf Aquitaine	Rhône-Poulenc
Exxon Mobil	Rohm and Haas
Formosa Plastics	Shanghai Petrochemical
Henkel	Union Carbide

HISTORICAL FINANCIALS & EMPLOYEES

Private FYE: December	Annual Growth	1989	1990	1991	1992	1993	1994	1995	1996	1997	1998
Sales ($ mil.)	18.6%	—	1,325	—	—	1,850	3,400	4,300	4,500	4,750	5,200
Employees	21.8%	1,700	2,000	2,850	3,900	5,000	8,100	8,000	8,000	9,550	10,000

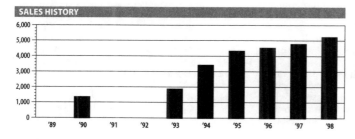

SALES HISTORY

HUNTSMAN

HYATT CORPORATION

OVERVIEW

Chicago-based Hyatt is high at the top of the list of major US hotel operators, with a few other rivals, such as Marriott and Hilton. Hyatt manages or licenses more than 110 full-service luxury hotels and resorts in North America and the Caribbean through its Hyatt Hotels; Hyatt International, a separate company, operates 80 hotels and resorts in 35 countries. In addition, Hyatt manages casinos at several of its hotels and runs a retirement community subsidiary called Classic Residence by Hyatt.

Hyatt caters to business travelers, convention-goers, and upscale destination-oriented vacationers. The company offers specially designed Business Plan rooms with fax machines and 24-hour access to copiers, printers, and other business necessities. Camp Hyatt targets family travelers with educational games, activities, and programs for children.

Led by chairman, president, and CEO Thomas Pritzker, the company is owned by the Pritzker family, one of the US's wealthiest families (its net worth is estimated by *Forbes* at nearly $14 billion).

HISTORY

In 1881 Nicholas Pritzker left Kiev for Chicago, where his family's ascent to the ranks of America's wealthiest families began.

Nicholas' son A. N. left the family law practice in the 1930s and began investing in a variety of businesses. He turned a 1942 investment (Cory Corporation) worth $25,000 into $23 million by 1967.

After WWII, A. N.'s son Jay followed in his father's wheeling-and-dealing footsteps. In 1953, with the help of his father's banking connections, Jay purchased Colson Company and recruited his brother Bob, an industrial engineer, to restructure a company that made tricycles and US Navy rockets. By 1990 Jay and Bob had added 60 industrial companies, with annual sales exceeding $3 billion, to the entity they called the Marmon Group.

In 1957 Jay bought a hotel called Hyatt House, located near the Los Angeles airport, from Hyatt von Dehn. Jay added five locations by 1961 and hired his gregarious youngest brother, Donald, to manage the hotel company.

Hyatt went public in 1967, but the move that opened new vistas for the hotel chain was the purchase that year of an 800-room hotel in Atlanta that both Hilton and Marriott had turned down. John Portman's design, incorporating a 21-story atrium, a large fountain, and a revolving rooftop restaurant, became a Hyatt trademark.

The Pritzkers formed Hyatt International in 1969 to operate hotels overseas, and the company grew rapidly in the US and abroad during the 1970s. Donald Pritzker died in 1972, and the family decided to take the company private in 1979.

Much of Hyatt's growth in the 1970s came from contracts to manage, under the Hyatt banner, hotels built by other investors. When Hyatt's cut on those contracts shrank in the 1980s, it launched its own hotel and resort developments under Nick Pritzker, a cousin to Jay and Bob. In 1988, with US and Japanese partners, it built the Hyatt Regency Waikoloa on Hawaii's Big Island for $360 million — a record for a hotel.

Through Hyatt subsidiaries, the Pritzkers bought bedraggled Braniff Airlines in 1983 as it emerged from bankruptcy. After a failed 1987 attempt to merge the airline with PanAm, the Pritzkers sold Braniff in 1988. Hyatt opened Classic Residence by Hyatt, a group of upscale retirement communities, in 1989.

In 1993 Hyatt sold the majority of its 85% interest in Ticketmaster to Paul Allen, co-founder of Microsoft. Hyatt joined Circus Circus (now Mandalay Resort Group) in 1994 to launch the *Grand Victoria*, the nation's largest cruising gaming vessel, at Elgin, Illinois. The next year, as part of a new strategy to manage both freestanding golf courses and those near Hyatt hotels, the company opened its first freestanding course: an 18-hole par 71 championship course on Aruba.

Hyatt Regency hotels hosted both the Republican (San Diego) and the Democratic (Chicago) national conventions in 1996. That year Hyatt said it would build a 500-room resort and casino, with a Jack Nicklaus championship golf course running through it, at Lake Las Vegas — a development on a man-made lake 17 miles from town.

In 1997 the company acquired hotels in Atlanta, San Francisco, and Miami as part of a plan to buy up to 30 hotels by the year 2000. President Thomas Pritzker, Jay's son, took over as chairman and CEO of Hyatt following his father's death in early 1999. The company continues to expand through acquisitions and new resort construction.

Chairman, President and CEO; Chairman Hyatt International Corporation: Thomas J. Pritzker, age 48
VC; Chairman and President, Hyatt Development Corporation; President, Hyatt Equities: Nicholas J. Pritzker, age 53
SVP Finance and Adminstration: Frank Borg
Chairman and President, Classic Residence by Hyatt: Penny S. Pritzker, age 39
President, Hyatt Hotel Corporation: Doug Geoga
President, Hyatt International Corporation: Bernd Chorengel
EVP, Hyatt Development Corporation: Scott D. Miller
EVP, Hyatt Hotels Corporation: Ed Rabin
SVP, Human Resources, Hyatt Hotels Corporation: Linda Olson
SVP Sales, Hyatt Hotels Corporation: Chuck Floyd
SVP Marketing, Hyatt Hotels Corporation: Tom O'Toole
Divisional VP (Eastern), Hyatt Hotels Corporation: Alex Alexander
Divisional VP (Southern), Hyatt Hotels Corporation: Tim Lindgren
Divisional VP (Resorts), Hyatt Hotels Corporation: Victor Lopez
Divisional VP (Western), Hyatt Hotels Corporation: John Orr
Divisional VP (Central), Hyatt Hotels Corporation: Steve Sokal
Associate General Counsel: Mary Catherine Sexton

LOCATIONS

HQ: 200 W. Madison St., Chicago, IL 60606
Phone: 312-750-1234   **Fax:** 312-750-8550
Web site: http://www.hyatt.com

PRODUCTS/OPERATIONS

Selected Operations
Camp Hyatt (designed for the needs of traveling families)
Classic Residence by Hyatt (upscale retirement communities)
Hyatt Hotels and Resorts
Hyatt Vacation Ownership (time-share resorts)
Regency Casinos

COMPETITORS

Accor
Bass
Canadian Pacific
Carlson
Carnival
Cendant
Four Seasons Hotels
Granada Group
Helmsley
Hilton
Hilton Group
Host Marriott
Loews
Marriott International
Rank
Ritz Carlton
Sandals Resorts
Starwood Hotels & Resorts Worldwide
Trump
Walt Disney

HISTORICAL FINANCIALS & EMPLOYEES

Private FYE: January	Annual Growth	1990	1991	1992	1993	1994	1995	1996	1997	1998	1999
Estimated sales ($ mil.)	1.0%	3,101	2,915	1,350	1,460	950	1,240	2,500	2,900	3,250	3,400
Employees	4.2%	55,195	49,820	51,275	52,275	47,000	54,000	65,000	80,000	80,000	80,000

SALES HISTORY

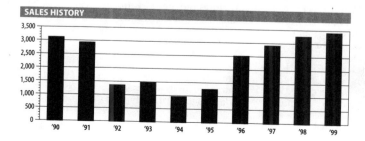

IGA, INC.

OVERVIEW

Independent grocers have found they can boost their business by being a little less independent. More than 3,600 stores belong to Chicago-based IGA (which stands for "Independent Grocers Alliance" or "International Grocers Alliance"). The alliance is the world's largest voluntary supermarket network, with stores in 47 states and about 30 countries. Collectively, its members are one of the largest food operations in terms of sales in North America.

IGA is owned by 18 marketing and distribution companies worldwide, including Fleming Companies and SUPERVALU. In addition to flying the IGA Red Oval banner and having access to IGA Brand private-label products, members receive advertising and marketing services, educational programs, and volume discounts through the food distributors that control it. Roughly 200 rural stores in the alliance also sell gas.

The association continues its expansion overseas. The first US grocer to go into China and Singapore, IGA is now looking to move into Europe, focusing on signing up independent food retailers in Poland.

HISTORY

IGA was founded in Chicago in 1926 by a group led by accountant Frank Grimes. During the 1920s chains began to dominate the grocery store industry. Grimes, an accountant for many grocery wholesalers, saw an opportunity to develop a network of independent grocers that could compete with the burgeoning chains. Grimes and five associates — Gene Flack, Louis Groebe, W. K. Hunter, H. V. Swenson, and William Thompson — created IGA.

Their idea was to "level the playing field" for independent grocers and chain stores by taking advantage of volume buying and mass marketing. IGA originally acted as a purchasing agent for its wholesalers but eventually passed that duty to the wholesalers. The group's first members were Poughkeepsie, New York-based grocery distributor W. T. Reynolds Company and the 69 grocery stores it serviced.

IGA focused on adding distributors and retailers, and it soon added wholesaler Fleming-Wilson (now Fleming Companies) and Winston & Newell (now SUPERVALU). In 1930 it hired Babe Ruth as a spokesman; other celebrity endorsers during the period included Jackie Cooper, Jack Dempsey, and Popeye. IGA also sponsored a radio program called the *IGA Home Town Hour.*

In 1945 the company introduced the Foodliner format, a design for stores larger than 4,000 sq. ft. The next year IGA introduced the 30-ft.-by-100-ft. Precision Store — designed so customers had to pass all the other merchandise in the store to get to the dairy and bread sections.

Grimes retired as president in 1951. He was succeeded by his son, Don, who continued to expand the company. Don was succeeded in 1968 by Richard Jones, head of IGA member J. M. Jones Co.

Thomas Haggai was named chairman of the company in 1976. A Baptist minister, radio commentator, and former CIA employee, Haggai had come to the attention of Grimes in 1960 when he praised Christian Scientists in one of his radio broadcasts. Grimes, a Christian Scientist, asked Haggai to speak at an IGA convention and eventually asked him to join the IGA board. Haggai, who became CEO in 1986, tightened the restrictions for IGA members, weeding out many of the smaller, low-volume mom-and-pop stores making up much of the group's network.

Haggai also began a push for international expansion. In 1988 the organization signed a deal with Japanese food company C. Itoh (now ITOCHU) to open a distribution outlet in Tokyo. The company moved into Australia that year and into the Papua New Guinea market in 1990.

Three years later IGA began an international television advertising campaign, a first for the supermarket industry. The group licensed grocery stores in four Caribbean countries in 1994 and signed a deal to enter China. Additionally, IGA launched its first line of private-label products for an ethnic food market, introducing several Mexican food products.

The company signed a partnership in 1995 with Singapore's largest grocery store chain, NTUC Fairprice Co-operative, thereby gaining 47 stores in Singapore. In 1996 IGA opened stores in Hawaii and South Africa, and the next year it opened a store in Brazil. In 1998 the group developed a new format for its stores that included on-site gas pumps.

SUPERVALU signed 54 independent grocery stores to the IGA banner in August 1999; the stores are located primarily in Mississippi and Arkansas and Trinidad in the Caribbean.

OFFICERS

Chairman and CEO: Thomas S. Haggai
SVP: Duane Martin, age 32
VP, Benefit Trust: Ronald Bujko
VP, IGA International: Paul Goelzer
VP, IGA Brand and Equipment: Patrick Sylvester
VP, Communications & Events: Barbara G. Wiest
Director, Public Relations: Shannan Blagg
Human Resources: Juanita Brodkorb
Auditors: Arthur Andersen

LOCATIONS

HQ: 8725 W. Higgins Rd., Chicago, IL 60631
Phone: 773-693-4520   **Fax:** 773-693-1271
Web site: http://www.igainc.com

PRODUCTS/OPERATIONS

Distributors/Owners
Bozzuto's, Inc.
C.I. Foods Systems Co., Ltd.
The Copps Corp.
Davids Ltd.
Fairway Foods of Michigan, Inc.
Fleming Companies, Inc.
Foodland Associated Ltd.
Great North Foods
IGA Brasil
IGA South Africa
Ira Higdon Grocery Co.
McLane Polska
Merchants Distributors, Inc.
Nash Finch Co.
Pearl River Distribution Ltd.
SUPERVALU INC.
Tripifoods, Inc.
W. Lee Flowers & Co., Inc.

Selected Joint Operations and Services
Advertising
Community service programs
Equipment purchase
IGA Brand (private-label products)
IGA Grocergram (in-house magazine)
Internet services
Marketing
Merchandising
Red Oval Family (manufacturer/IGA collaboration on sales and marketing efforts and other activities)
Volume buying

COMPETITORS

A&P
Albertson's
Associated Wholesale Grocers
BJs Wholesale Club
C&S Wholesale
Daiei
Delhaize
George Weston
H-E-B
Hannaford Bros.
Ito-Yokado
Kroger
Meijer
Penn Traffic
Publix
Roundy's
Royal Ahold
Safeway
Spartan Stores
Topco Associates
Wakefern Food
Wal-Mart
Winn-Dixie

HISTORICAL FINANCIALS & EMPLOYEES

Association FYE: December	Annual Growth	1989	1990	1991	1992	1993	1994	1995	1996	1997	1998
Estimated sales ($ mil.)	6.3%	10,400	11,100	11,500	15,900	16,500	17,000	17,100	16,800	18,000	18,000
Employees	(10.9%)	—	—	—	—	—	—	130,000	128,000	135,000	92,000

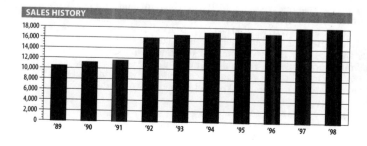

SALES HISTORY

IMG

Show me the money! The world's largest sports talent and marketing agency, Cleveland-based IMG (headed by founder Mark McCormack, the "original Jerry Macguire") is credited with having invented the field of sports management. Along with representing some of the most talented athletes of our age (Wayne Gretzky, Pete Sampras, Tiger Woods), the company serves more than 700 clients including artists such as Placido Domingo and Itzhak Perlman, and models Tyra Banks and Niki Taylor.

While representing VIP clients may be how IMG (the acronym stands for International Management Group) gained its fame, IMG is involved in several other aspects of sports promotion. IMG's Trans World International division produces and distributes thousands of hours of sports TV programming each year.

IMG also gives many of its clients venues in which to compete by promoting more than 1,000 sporting events annually. When athletes need training, they can take advantage of IMG's sports academies (Florida's Bollettieri Sports Academy) scattered around the world. The company also represents corporate clients and organizations (Kennedy Space Center, Rock and Roll Hall of Fame), acts as a literary agent, and is active in real estate, golf course design, and financial consulting.

IMG is steadily building its international profile. It helped to establish a Chinese basketball league and has worked toward the international commercialization of other sports such as cricket (India), golf (Australia), and rugby (Europe). Founder Mark McCormack owns IMG.

In the 1950s when former amateur golfer Mark McCormack went to Yale Law School, he didn't desert golf entirely. In his free time he set up paid exhibitions for pro golfers he knew from his days on the links. In 1960 one of these players, Arnold Palmer, asked McCormack to manage his finances, so he could concentrate on his game. McCormack went above and beyond the call of duty, signing Palmer to endorsement deals and licensing his name and image. In two years Palmer's annual income skyrocketed from $60,000 to more than $500,000 — a fiscal triumph that would be the bedrock of IMG's business. Throughout the early and mid-1960s, IMG signed up more big-name golfers, as well as stars from other sports such as Jackie Stewart (car racing) and Jean-Claude Killy (skiing).

The addition of international stars such as Stewart (Scotland), Killy (France), and Gary Player (South Africa) allowed IMG access to global markets. In the late 1960s, as television began to bring sports and its stars into living rooms around the world, IMG used its clients to promote products and services internationally.

In 1967 McCormack created a new division of IMG — Trans World International (TWI), a TV production company that filmed and distributed sporting events. The next year IMG signed a contract with Wimbledon's organizers to coordinate video and television licensing. TWI would go on to become a key part of IMG's operations, eventually producing thousands of hours of original sports programming worldwide.

IMG's entrepreneurial spirit came to the forefront with a vengeance in the 1980s. In addition to managing athletes, sporting events, and sponsors, the company began to skip the middleman and create the sports event itself. In 1983 IMG debuted the Skins Game, a golf invitational featuring four of the sport's top athletes playing for high stakes. IMG also created Saturday afternoon sports staples such as *The Superstars* and *The Battle of the Network Stars*, shows that featured sports or TV stars competing in a series of events like the tug-o-war and obstacle courses.

By the 1990s McCormack had situated IMG to take advantage of almost every aspect of televised sports events: Typically, an IMG event involved working with the athletes, the sponsor or sponsors, the event itself, and the television distribution rights. The company continued to expand its clientele beyond sports, adding names such as musician Itzhak Perlman and model Niki Taylor. By 1997 IMG also counted the Rock and Roll Hall of Fame, the Americas Cup, and the Mayo Clinic as clients.

In 1998 IMG teamed up with Chase Capital Partners to form IMG/Chase Sports Capital, a private equity fund expected to raise some $200 million to invest in the sports industry. The next year IMG demonstrated a well-honed knack for capitalizing on its clients' appeal by staging a televised golf matchup between Tiger Woods and David Duval.

Chairman and CEO: Mark H. McCormack
SVP Finance: Arthur J. LaFave
VP Human Resources: Dan Lewis

LOCATIONS

HQ: 1360 E. 9th St., Ste. 100, Cleveland, OH 44114
Phone: 216-522-1200   **Fax:** 216-522-1145

PRODUCTS/OPERATIONS

Selected Clients
Andre Agassi
Tyra Banks
Placido Domingo
Wayne Gretzky
Martina Hingis
Nancy Lopez
Martina Navratilova
Mark O'Meara
Arnold Palmer
Itzhak Perlman
Rebecca Romijn-Stamos
Pete Sampras
Monica Seles
Niki Taylor
Tiger Woods

Selected Sporting Events Produced
ITT LPGA Tour Championship
Office Depot Father Son Challenge
Skins Games
The Transamerica Seniors
World Championships of Women's Golf
The World Match Play

Selected Sports Academies
Bollettieri Sports Academy
David Leadbetter Golf Academy

COMPETITORS

Creative Artists
DIRECTV
Dentsu
Golden Bear Golf
International Creative Management
Interpublic Group
ProServe
SFX Entertainment
TBA
United Talent
WPP Group
Walt Disney
William Morris
Worldwide Entertainment & Sports

HISTORICAL FINANCIALS & EMPLOYEES

Private FYE: December	Annual Growth	1989	1990	1991	1992	1993	1994	1995	1996	1997	1998
Estimated sales ($ mil.)	3.2%	—	—	—	—	—	—	1,000	1,000	1,100	1,100
Employees	9.9%	—	—	—	—	—	—	1,600	1,959	2,000	2,125

SALES HISTORY

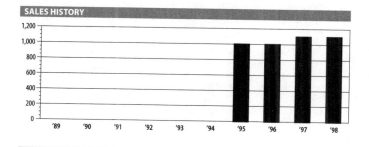

INGRAM INDUSTRIES INC.

OVERVIEW

Book 'em, Martha. Billionaire Martha Ingram heads Nashville-based Ingram Industries, whose Ingram Book Group is the US's largest wholesale distributor of trade books and audiobooks to retailers and a leading distributor to libraries. Ingram Book, through its some 11 fulfillment centers, can distribute 115 million titles a year. It serves some 32,000 retail outlets and represents over 12,000 publishers.

Although Ingram Book accounts for just over half of Ingram Industries' sales, the company also operates Ingram Marine Group, which ships grain, ore, and other products through its 2,600 barges, and Ingram Insurance

Group, which offers high-risk auto insurance in about 10 states through Permanent General Insurance.

Ingram Industries has undergone dramatic makeovers in the last few years. It spun off its largest segment, Ingram Micro (the world's largest distributor of microcomputer products), in 1996 and Ingram Entertainment (the US's top distributor of videotapes) in 1997.

Martha Ingram is America's wealthiest active businesswoman, and she and her family own and run Ingram Industries. The Ingram family controls nearly 85% of Ingram Micro's voting stock.

HISTORY

Orrin Ingram and two partners founded the Dole, Ingram & Kennedy sawmill in 1857 in Eau Claire, Wisconsin, on the Chippewa River, about 50 miles upstream from the Mississippi River. By the 1870s the company, renamed Ingram & Kennedy, was selling lumber as far downstream as Hannibal, Missouri.

Ingram's success was noticed by Frederick Weyerhaeuser, a German immigrant in Rock Island, Illinois, who, like Ingram, had worked in a sawmill before buying one of his own. In 1881 Ingram and Weyerhaeuser negotiated the formation of Chippewa Logging (35%-owned by up-river partners, 65%-owned by down-river interests), which controlled the white pine harvest of the Chippewa Valley. In 1900 Ingram paid $216,000 for 2,160 shares in the newly formed Weyerhaeuser Timber Company. Ingram let his sons and grandsons handle the investment and formed O.H. Ingram Co. to manage the family's interests. He died in 1918.

In 1946 Ingram's descendants founded Ingram Barge, which hauled crude oil to the company's refinery near St. Louis. After buying and then selling other holdings, in 1962 the family formed Ingram Corp., consisting solely of Ingram Barge. Brothers Bronson and Fritz Ingram (the great grandsons of Orrin) bought the company from their father, Hank, before he died in 1963, and in 1964 they bought half of Tennessee Book, a textbook distributing company founded in 1935. In 1970 they formed Ingram Book Group to sell trade books to bookstores and libraries.

Ingram Barge won a $48 million Chicago sludge-hauling contract in 1971, but later the company was accused of bribing city politicians with $1.2 million in order to land the contract. The brothers stood trial in 1977 for

authorizing the bribes; Bronson was acquitted, but the court convicted Fritz on 29 counts. Before Fritz entered prison (he served 16 months of a four-year sentence), he and his brother split their company. Fritz took the energy operations and went bust in the 1980s. Bronson took the barge and book businesses and formed Ingram Industries.

This acquisitive, technologically savvy new company formed computer products distributor Ingram Computer in 1982 and between 1985 and 1989 bought all the stock of Micro D, a computer wholesaler. Ingram Computer and Micro D merged to form Ingram Micro. In 1992 it acquired Commtron, the world's #1 wholesaler of prerecorded videocassettes, and merged it into Ingram Entertainment.

When Bronson died in mid-1995, his wife Martha became chairman (she had been the company's PR director) and began a dramatic restructuring. Ingram Industries closed its non-bookstore rack distributor (Ingram Merchandising) in 1995 and sold its oil-and-gas machinery subsidiary (Cactus Co.) in 1996. It spun off Ingram Micro in 1996, followed in 1997 by Ingram Entertainment. Ingram Industries purchased Christian books distributor Spring Arbor that year and also introduced an on-demand book publishing service (Lightning Print).

The company in late 1998 agreed to sell its book group to Barnes & Noble for $600 million, but the companies killed the deal in mid-1999 when it appeared that the FTC would do the same. With customers and competitors increasing distribution capacity in the western US, a resulting drop in business led Ingram Industries to cut more than 100 jobs at an Oregon warehouse in 1999.

Chairman: Martha Ingram, age 62
VC; Chairman, Ingram Book Group: John R. Ingram, age 36
President and CEO: Orrin H. Ingram II, age 37
VP, CFO, and Treasurer: Robert W. Mitchell
VP and Controller: Mary K. Cavarra
VP: Richard B. Patton
President, Ingram Periodicals: Julie Burns
President, Ingram Library Services and Ingram International: Martin Keeley
President and CEO, Ingram Book Group: Michael Lovett
President, Spring Arbor Distributors: Frances Salamon
Chief Administrative Officer, Spring Arbor Distributors: Steven Little
Human Resources: Dennis Delaney

LOCATIONS

HQ: 1 Belle Meade Place, 4400 Harding Rd., Nashville, TN 37205
Phone: 615-298-8200   **Fax:** 615-298-8242
Web site: http://www.ingrambook.com

PRODUCTS/OPERATIONS

Selected Operations

Ingram Book Group
Ingram Book Company (wholesaler of trade books and audiobooks)
Ingram Customer Systems (computerized systems and services)
Ingram International (international distribution of books and audiobooks)
Ingram Library Services (distributes books, audiobooks, and videos to libraries)
Ingram Periodicals (direct distributor of specialty magazines)
Ingram Publisher Services (distribution services for publishers)
Lighting Print (on-demand printing)
Retailer Services (book distributor to nontraditional book market)
Spring Arbor Distributors (product and services for Christian retailers)
White Bridge Communications (consumer marketing programs for publishers and retailers)

Ingram Insurance Group
Permanent General Insurance Co. (automobile insurance in California, Georgia, Indiana, Louisiana, Mississippi, Ohio, South Carolina, Tennessee, and Wisconsin)
Tennessee Insurance Company (insures Ingram affiliates)

Ingram Marine Group
Ingram Barge (ships grain, ore, and other products)
Ingram Materials Co. (produces construction materials such as sand and gravel)

COMPETITORS

Advanced Marketing
Allstate
American Commercial Lines
American Financial
Baker & Taylor
Chas Levy
Kirby
Progressive Corporation
SAFECO
State Farm
Thomas Nelson
Times Publishing

HISTORICAL FINANCIALS & EMPLOYEES

Private FYE: December	Annual Growth	1989	1990	1991	1992	1993	1994	1995	1996	1997	1998
Sales ($ mil.)	(3.0%)	2,640	2,677	3,422	4,657	6,163	8,010	11,000	1,463	1,796	2,000
Employees	3.9%	4,600	5,400	6,526	8,407	9,658	10,000	13,000	5,300	6,362	6,500

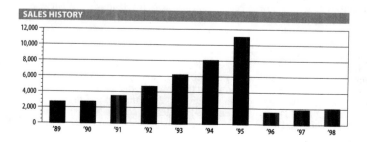

SALES HISTORY

TEAMSTERS

OVERVIEW

The International Brotherhood of Teamsters is trying to turn over a new leaf. One of the US's largest and best-known labor unions, the Washington, DC-based Teamsters represents approximately 1.4 million members, including truckers, United Parcel Service workers, warehouse employees, cab drivers, airline workers, and factory and hospital employees. The Teamsters (an AFL-CIO affiliate) negotiates with employers for contracts that guarantee its members fair promotion policies, health coverage, job security, and other benefits. It has about 650 local chapters in the US, Canada, and Puerto Rico.

Elected in 1998, Teamsters chief James P. Hoffa (son of late, notoriously unfindable union leader Jimmy Hoffa) is attempting to usher in a new era for the controversial union. Hoffa wants the Teamsters to police themselves and put an end to the close governmental supervision under which the union operated throughout the 1990s. Toward that end he has hired Edwin Stier, a former federal prosecutor, to head a new in-house anti-corruption program.

HISTORY

In 1903 two rival team-driver unions, the Drivers International Union and the Teamsters National Union, merged to form the International Brotherhood of Teamsters. Led by Cornelius Shea, the Teamsters established headquarters in Indianapolis. Daniel Tobin (president for 45 years, starting in 1907) demanded that union locals obtain executive approval before striking. Membership expanded from the team-driver base, prompting the union to add Chauffeurs, Stablemen, and Helpers to its name (1909).

Following the first transcontinental delivery by motor truck (1912), the Teamster deliverymen traded their horses for trucks. The union then recruited food processing, brewery, and farm workers, among others, to augment Teamster effectiveness during strikes. In 1920 it joined the American Federation of Labor.

Until the Depression the Teamsters was still a small union of predominantly urban deliverymen. Then Farrell Dobbs, a Trotskyite Teamster from Minneapolis, organized the famous Minneapolis strikes in 1934 to protest local management's refusal to allow the workers to unionize. Workers clashed with police and National Guard units for 11 days before management acceded to the workers' demands. The strikes demonstrated the potential strength of unions, and Teamsters membership swelled. Although union power ebbed during WWII, the union continued to grow. In 1953 the union moved its headquarters to Washington, DC.

The AFL-CIO expelled the Teamsters in 1957 when Teamster ties to the mob became public during a US Senate investigation. New Teamsters boss Jimmy Hoffa eluded indictment and took advantage of America's growing dependence on trucking to negotiate the powerful National Master Freight Agreement (1964). Hoffa also organized industrial workers. He used a union pension fund to make mob-connected loans and was later convicted of jury tampering and sent to prison. In 1975, four years after his release, Hoffa vanished without a trace and is believed to have been the victim of a Mafia hit.

The Teamsters rejoined the AFL-CIO in 1987. The union settled a 1988 lawsuit filed by the Justice Department's antiracketeering forces by allowing government appointees to discipline corrupt union leaders, help run the union, and oversee its elections.

The 1991 election of self-styled reformer Ronald Carey (he received 49% of the vote) seemed to portend real changes for the union; each of his six predecessors had been accused of or imprisoned for criminal activities. However, membership dropped by 40,000 in both 1991 and 1992.

In 1996 Carey won re-election as union president over rival James P. Hoffa (whom Carey accused of having ties to organized crime). A 15-day strike by the Teamsters' UPS employees in 1997 led to the delivery company's agreement to combine part-time jobs into 10,000 new full-time positions. That year Carey's re-election was overturned amid a campaign finance investigation that netted guilty pleas from three Carey associates, and the Teamsters leader was disqualified from running for re-election in 1998. Carey was officially expelled from the Teamsters by the federal government, and Hoffa won the 1998 election over Tom Leedham (who was backed by the union's reform wing). Promising to fight corruption, Hoffa's leadership cracked down on local chapters that had bad reputations. The Teamsters also began an investigation into the reasons why its treasury decreased from $154 million to $1 million from 1991 to 1998.

General President: James P. Hoffa
General Secretary-Treasurer: Tom Keegel
VP At-Large: Randy Cammack
VP At-Large: Chester Glanton
VP At-Large: Tom O'Donnell
VP At-Large: Fred Gegare
VP At-Large: Ralph Taurone
Eastern Region VP: Jack Cipriani
Eastern Region VP: John Murphy
Eastern Region VP: Dan Desanti
Eastern Region VP: Richard Volpe
Southern Region VP: Ken Wood
Western Region VP: Chuck Mack
Western Region VP: Jon Rabine
Western Region VP: Jim Santangelo
Director Human Resources: Adam Downs

Trade Divisions
Airline
Automobile Transportation
Bakery and Laundry
Brewery and Soft Drink
Building Material and Construction
Dairy
Freight
Industrial Trades
Motion Picture and Theatrical Trade
Newspaper, Magazine, and Electronic Media
Parcel and Small Package
Port
Public Employees
Tank Haul
Trade-Show and Convention Centers
Warehouse

HQ: International Brotherhood of Teamsters,
25 Louisiana Ave. NW, Washington, DC 20001
Phone: 202-624-6800   **Fax:** 202-624-6918
Web site: http://www.teamster.org

Labor union FYE: December	Annual Growth	1988	1989	1990	1991	1992	1993	1994	1995	1996	1997
Sales ($ mil.)	1.2%	—	—	—	83	78	74	82	89	90	89
Employees	—	—	—	—	—	—	—	—	—	—	—

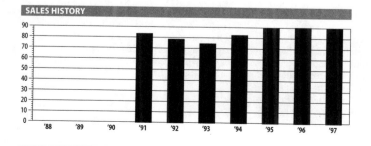

INTERNATIONAL DATA GROUP

OVERVIEW

A million dollars says Microsoft king Bill Gates has at least one International Data Group (IDG) magazine on his coffee table. Through its print products, Internet magazines, e-mail newsletters, and other media, the Boston-based company is one of the the world's leading high-tech publishers.

Subsidiary IDG Communications is the world's #1 publisher of computer-related periodicals (ahead of Ziff-Davis and CMP Media), with more than 290 magazines (including *Computerworld* and *PC World*) and newspapers and more than 225 technology-related Web sites. More than 90 million people in 75 countries read IDG publications each month. IDG Books Worldwide (75%-owned) prints some 1,000 titles (including the popular how-to series . . . *For Dummies* and . . . *SECRETS*)

in 36 languages. Subsidiary International Data Corporation leads the industry in information technology market research and analysis with offices in 41 countries. In addition, IDG sponsors about 170 conferences, trade shows, and other events for the computer industry, provides integrated marketing services for information technology companies, and offers computer training courses.

Founder and chairman Patrick McGovern, who has a net worth of $1.5 billion and is listed as one of the 400 richest Americans in *Forbes,* owns about 65% of IDG; employees own the rest. Over the years McGovern — known as "Chairman Pat" — has dressed up as Ben Franklin for employees in Boston and as Confucius for employees in China.

HISTORY

Patrick McGovern began his publishing career at the *Philadelphia Bulletin* as a paper boy. As a teenager in the 1950s he was inspired by Edmund Berkeley's book *Giant Brains; or Machines That Think.* He built a computer and won a scholarship to MIT. There he edited the first computer magazine, *Berkeley's Computers and Automation.*

McGovern was inspired to start a market research service (International Data Corporation) after he interviewed the president of computer pioneer UNIVAC for *Computers and Automation* in 1964. Three years later he began International Data Group with the launch of an eight-page tabloid, *Computerworld.* He introduced his new paper at a computer trade show. Within a few weeks it had 20,000 subscribers. By 1968 IDG had $1 million in annual sales.

IDG began publishing in Japan in 1971, then expanded to Germany in 1975 and Brazil the next year. By 1990, following the collapse of communism, the company had started 10 publications in Russia and Eastern Europe.

Two teenage hackers, angry because they didn't receive a free poster with the IDG publication *Gamepro,* broke into the company's voice mail system in 1990 and erased orders from customers and messages from writers. The prank cost IDG as much as $2.4 million in lost revenues and additional expenses.

Beset by competition from the mushrooming computer magazine marketplace in 1993, several of IDG's magazines, including *InfoWorld, Macworld,* and *PC World,* began losing ad pages. The company began an incentive program tied

to its new online service to help stem advertiser attrition. In 1995 IDG said it would cease publication of *AmigaWorld.*

That year, as part of IDG's move toward Internet-based services, it bought a stake in online software companies Architect Software (now Excite@Home) and Netscape (now owned by America Online). Along with former IDG officer Axel Leblois, it also bought Boston-based publisher World Times.

IDG's new products in 1996 included *Netscape World; The Web,* a magazine covering the Internet; and more than 30 e-mail newsletters providing computer industry news. The company also bought *PC Advisor,* the UK's fastest-growing computer magazine.

IDG kicked off its Global Web Advertising Network online ad placement service in 1997 and had more than 135 sites in the network by year's end. That year IDG merged *Macworld* with rival Ziff-Davis' *MacUser* in a joint venture called Mac Publications. Other ventures for the year included WebShopper, an online service for computer buyers, and new magazine *Solutions Integrator.*

In 1998 IDG pledged $1 billion in venture capital for high-tech startups in China. It also introduced new publications in China, including a Chinese edition of *Cosmopolitan* (with Hearst Magazines) and *China Computer Reseller World.* Later that year the company spun off 25% of IDG Books to the public.

Chairman: Patrick J. McGovern
President and CEO: Kelly P. Conlin
COO: James Casella
SVP: Peter C. Horan
President, CEO and Publisher, Computerworld:
  Michela O'Connor Abrams
President and CEO, Infoworld: Stephen Moylan
SVP and Publishing Director, InfoWorld: Bob Maund
President, Marketing Services Group: Bernie Theobald
VP and Corporate Controller: Ted Bloom
VP Taxation: Jayne Enos
VP Finance: Jim Ghirardi
VP Corporate Services: Marion Kibbee
VP Human Resources: Tom Mathews
VP Technology: Robert M. Metcalf
Director Corporate Communications: Alys R. Creighton
Auditors: Deloitte & Touche LLP

LOCATIONS

HQ: 1 Exeter Plaza, 15th Fl., Boston, MA 02116
Phone: 617-534-1200   **Fax:** 617-659-8642
Web site: http://www.idg.com

PRODUCTS/OPERATIONS

Selected Periodicals
China Infoworld
Computer Sweden
ComputerPartner Benelux
Computerworld
Computerworld Australia
Computerworld Canada
eMediaweekly
Informatica Chile
InfoWorld
Le Monde Informatique (France)
Macworld
Macworld Poland
Network World
PC World
PC World China Weekly
PC World East Africa
PC World Hong Kong
PC World India
PC World Vietnam
Publish
Sety Russia
Solutions Integrator

Selected Book Brands and Series
3D Visual series
Bible series
. . . For Dummies series
For Kids & Parents
For Teachers
Novell Press
. . . SECRETS series
. . . Simplified series
Teach Yourself . . . VISUALLY series

COMPETITORS

America Online	Official Information
Asian Sources	Company
Dynamic Graphics	Penton Media
Freeman Companies	Phillips International
Future Network	SOFTBANK
Gartner Group	Southam
Havas	Upside Media
HyperMedia	Yahoo!
Magnamedia Verlag	internet.com
McGraw-Hill	

HISTORICAL FINANCIALS & EMPLOYEES

Private FYE: September	Annual Growth	1990	1991	1992	1993	1994	1995	1996	1997	1998	1999
Sales ($ mil.)	17.1%	620	780	840	880	1,100	1,400	1,700	1,876	2,050	2,560
Employees	13.6%	3,812	4,200	4,500	5,000	7,200	8,200	8,500	9,500	11,500	12,000

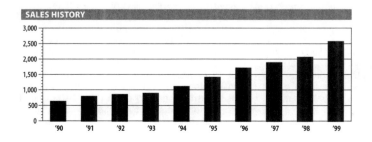

SALES HISTORY

IRIDIUM LLC

OVERVIEW

"From Greenland's icy mountains, from India's coral strand," as the hymn goes, and from anywhere else for that matter, you can make and receive calls on an Iridium phone. The Washington, DC-based consortium operates a $5 billion satellite communications system that allows paging and wireless telephony anywhere in the world. Founded by Motorola, the primary technology partner and 18% owner, the consortium is made up of 19 telecom and industrial companies, including Lockheed Martin, Raytheon, SK Telecom, and Sprint.

Iridium began commercial operations in 1998 but has had trouble getting off the ground. It has cut prices for its phones and service in half but has failed to make subscriber goals set by its creditors. After defaulting on $1.5 billion in loans, Iridium has filed for bankruptcy protection.

The Iridium project is a global network of 66 low-earth-orbit (LEO) satellites linked to 15 ground stations called gateways. Motorola-made LEOs, combined with existing wireless

infrastructure, allow Iridium's 20,000 customers to roam worldwide and remain accessible from a single phone number. Iridium has distribution agreements with service providers and roaming partners, including AT&T Wireless, Japan's DDI, and Telecom Italia; the system is licensed in almost 140 countries.

Although the phones work in remote locations, they don't always function well inside buildings, cars, or anywhere else that prohibits a line of sight with the satellites. Made by Motorola and consortium partner Kyocera, the phones are also clunky, weighing about a pound and having a large antenna. Because satellites run out of fuel and burn up in the atmosphere in about five years, Iridium would also need to launch a new network by 2003.

These problems don't sit well with Iridium's key markets, international business travelers and companies operating in remote areas. The US Department of Defense, the firm's largest customer, has built its own gateway in Hawaii to reduce access costs.

HISTORY

The Iridium idea was seeded in 1985 when Motorola engineer Bary Bertiger's wife tried unsuccessfully to use her cellular phone to call home from the Bahamas. Exasperated, she asked her husband why there couldn't be a phone system that would work anywhere.

Bertiger discussed this question with colleagues Ray Leopold and Ken Peterson. After rejecting several terrestrial designs, the trio began research in 1987 on a constellation of low-earth-orbiting (LEO) satellites that could communicate with each other and with phones worldwide. In 1988 Leopold came up with a key design element: a network of earth stations connecting the satellites to existing phone systems.

The original plan called for 77 LEOs, and engineer Jim Williams named the project Iridium, after the 77th element on the periodic table. (By 1992 the system required only 66 satellites, but the name stuck.)

Motorola chairman Robert Galvin approved the project, and in 1990 the firm announced it at simultaneous press conferences in Beijing, London, Melbourne, and New York. After the Iridium proposal was submitted, the FCC invited others to apply to share an internationally allocated spectrum for non-geostationary mobile telephony systems. Other submissions included Loral/Qualcomm's Globalstar and TRW's Odyssey.

A series of contentious FCC-led meetings

between rival companies led to a recommendation to share the mobile satellite service (MSS) band. Motorola requested separate spectrum for Iridium, and in 1994 the FCC acceded, granting exclusive rights to the upper range of the band. The FCC licensed Iridium the next year, and Iridium LLC was formed. In 1996 Edward Staiano, who had led Motorola's cell phone unit, was named CEO.

Iridium World Communications was formed as a public investment vehicle, and its 1997 IPO raised $240 million. Beginning in 1997, the constellation of satellites (including spares) was deployed using US, Russian, and Chinese launch vehicles. Despite technical setbacks (including the failure of two satellites) and a delay in the kick-off date, the Iridium network began commercial service in late 1998.

In 1999 Motorola won a $219 million Department of Defense contract for Iridium, but customer count lagged and technological glitches remained. Staiano resigned under pressure and was temporarily replaced by John Richardson. Iridium subsequently moved to dismiss 15% of its workforce and reorganize its marketing operations. Unable to meet subscriber goals set by its creditors, Iridium filed for bankruptcy protection in 1999. Later that year Motorola paid $750 million to banks holding Iridium's debt.

Chairman: Robert W. Kinzie, age 65, $490,080 pay
VC: Richard L. Lesher, age 65
**CEO, Iridium LLC and Iridium World
  Communications:** John A. Richardson
Interim CFO: David R. Gibson
EVP Marketing and Distribution: Mauro Sentinelli,
  age 52, $500,000 pay
SVP Business Operations: Mark Gercenstein, age 47
SVP Network Operations: O. Bruce Dale, age 56
VP, General Counsel, and Secretary: F. Thomas Tuttle,
  age 56, $352,292 pay
VP Global Gateway Relations: Lauri J. Fitz-Pegado,
  age 43
Assistant Director (HR): Barbara Murkel
Auditors: KPMG LLP

LOCATIONS

HQ: 1575 Eye St. NW, Washington, DC 20005
Phone: 202-408-3800   **Fax:** 202-408-3801
Web site: http://www.iridium.com

PRODUCTS/OPERATIONS

Member Companies
American International Group, Inc.
Iridium Africa Corporation
Iridium Canada, Inc.
Iridium SudAmerica Corporation
Iridium Middle East Corporation
Iridium China (Hong Kong) Ltd.
Iridium India Telecom Limited
Iridium Italia S.p.A.
Khrunichev State Research and Production Space Center
Lockheed Martin Corporation
Motorola, Inc.
Nippon Iridium (Bermuda) Limited
Pacific Asia Communications Ltd.
Raytheon Company
SK Telecom
South Pacific Iridium Holdings Limited
Sprint Iridium, Inc.
Thai Satellite Telecommunications Co., Ltd.
Vebacom Holdings, Inc.

Subsidiaries
Iridium Aero Acquisition Sub, Inc.
Iridium Geolink LLC
Iridium Operating LLC
  Iridium Canada Facilities Inc.
  Iridium Capital Corporation
  Iridium Facilities Corporation
  Iridium IP LLC
  Iridium (Potomac) LLC
  Iridium Roaming LLC
Iridium Promotions Inc.
Iridium World Communications Ltd.

COMPETITORS

Alcatel	ICO Global
American Mobile Satellite	Communications
Asia Satellite	INTELSAT
Telecommunications	Mobile Communications
COMSAT	ORBCOMM
Constellation	PanAmSat
Communications	Pasifik Satelit
Eutelsat	Philippine Long Distance
Globalstar	Teledesic
Hughes Electronics	

HISTORICAL FINANCIALS & EMPLOYEES

Consortium FYE: December	Annual Growth	1989	1990	1991	1992	1993	1994	1995	1996	1997	1998
Sales ($ mil.)	—	—	—	—	0	0	0	0	0	0	0
Net income ($ mil.)	—	—	—	—	(9)	(12)	(15)	(24)	(76)	(294)	(1,253)
Income as % of sales	—	—	—	—	—	—	—	—	—	—	—
Employees	62.9%	—	—	—	—	—	—	—	202	417	536

NET INCOME HISTORY

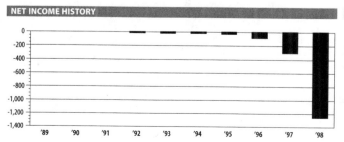

1998 FISCAL YEAR-END

Debt ratio: 86.0%
Return on equity: —
Cash ($ mil.): 25
Current ratio: 0.19
Long-term debt ($ mil.): 2,940

THE IRVINE COMPANY INC.

OVERVIEW

At The Irvine Company, everything is going according to plan. *Master* plan, that is.

The Newport Beach, California-based Irvine Company creates master-planned communities in well-heeled Orange County (of which the company owns some 54,000 acres). The communities are built to exacting specifications by contractors who buy the land for them from The Irvine Company.

The company's land is called Irvine Ranch and includes the US's largest planned community, Irvine. The modest metropolis has more than 200,000 residents (but no cemetery) and some 250,000 jobs, primarily in such white-collar industries as biotech, computers, and engineering. Agriculture — including avocados, citrus, and other cash crops — takes up about 15% of Irvine Ranch.

The Irvine Company's portfolio includes about 40 million sq. ft. of residential, commercial, and industrial space, including two hotels, five marinas, and three golf courses. The University of California, Irvine, is built on company-donated land, and the firm's Irvine Spectrum development is the largest university-affiliated research park in the US. The Irvine Company also owns Irvine Apartment Communities, a real estate investment trust (REIT) that owns some 70 apartment complexes in the Irvine Ranch area, as well as in San Diego, San Jose, and Los Angeles.

Chairman Donald Bren, the company's sole owner, has continued the Irvine Foundation's master plan, which calls for gradual development of rigorously planned communities. The plan — which has so far helped form the communities of Tustin, Newport Coast, Newport Ridge, and Newport Beach, in addition to centerpiece Irvine — is set for completion around 2025.

HISTORY

A wholesale merchant in San Francisco during the gold rush, James Irvine and two others assembled vast holdings in Southern California in the mid-1800s by buying out the debts of Mexican and Spanish land-grant holders. Irvine's son James Jr. bought out the other partners in 1876 and incorporated the ranch of more than 120,000 acres as part of an agribusiness empire.

James Jr. ran the ranch and company until the 1930s, when the death of his son, James III, prompted him to put 54% of the land into a foundation. Much of the rest was sold. James III's wife, Athalie, and daughter Joan inherited 22% of Irvine.

In 1959 company president Myford Irvine, a grandson of James I and uncle to Joan, was found dead from two shotgun wounds. Officials ruled it a suicide, but others weren't so sure.

The company donated land in 1964 for the construction of the University of California, Irvine. (The campus was later used as the setting for *Battle for the Planet of the Apes*.)

The 1960s also saw the Irvine Foundation forming its definitive master plan for prearranged communities; the plan was designed to anticipate and control growth, with provisions for green space and a mix of pricing levels.

Superrich firebrand Joan, who had long accused foundation officers of serving their own interests at the expense of other stockholders, lobbied Congress in the late 1960s to change tax laws pertaining to the foundation. Along with a group of investors led by Donald Bren, Alfred Taubman, and Herbert Allen, Joan trumped a bid by Mobil and in 1977 gained control of the company.

In 1983, when California's real estate market went sour, Bren bought out the other investors, purchasing a majority interest. Joan returned to court to protest the price, gaining extra money when the court valued the land at $1.4 billion.

In the 1990s Bren sought cash from his holdings by offering some developments as publicly traded REITs.

Orange County's notoriously record-setting bankruptcy in 1994 (the county lost $1.6 billion in risky investments) threatened the value of The Irvine Company's property portfolio, most of which is located in Orange County. Thanks in part to a frothy economy and $640 million in settlements from brokerage firms, Orange County and The Irvine Company were spared another 1983-esque bust.

In 1996 the company redeemed all outstanding stock held by minority shareholders, leaving Bren the sole owner. As part of its expansion into R&D, retail, and office properties in the Silicon Valley area, Irvine opened an office in San Jose, California the next year. In 1998 the company opened its Eastgate Technology Park in San Diego with Sun Microsystems as its anchor resident. An industry-wide slide in REIT stock prices prompted Bren to take Irvine Apartment Communities private in 1999, paying just at or below its asset value.

Chairman and President: Donald L. Bren, age 67
VC and CFO: Michael D. McKee
VC: Raymond L. Watson
EVP Corporate Affairs: Gary H. Hunt
EVP Investment Properties Group: Richard G. Sim
SVP Corporate Development: Monica Florian
SVP Human Resources: Bruce Endsley
SVP Urban Planning and Design: Robert N. Elliott
VP Corporate Communications: Paul Kranhold
VP Government Relations: Franz Wisner
President and CEO, Irvine Apartment Communities:
Clarance W. Barker
President, Irvine Community Development Company:
Joseph D. Davis

LOCATIONS

HQ: 550 Newport Center Dr., Newport Beach, CA 92660
Phone: 949-720-2000   **Fax:** 949-720-2501
Web site: http://www.irvineco.com

PRODUCTS/OPERATIONS

Selected Divisions
Corporate Affairs
Finance and Corporate Administration
Investment Properties Group
  Irvine Commercial Land Sales
  Irvine Finance and Business Properties (hotels,
    marinas, and golf courses)
  Irvine Industrial Company (8.0 million sq. ft. of
    industrial and technology-oriented space)
  Irvine Office Company (5.7 million sq. ft. of office space)
  Irvine Retail Properties Company (5 million sq. ft. of
    shopping centers and retail sites)
Irvine Apartment Communities, Inc. (apartment REIT)
Irvine Community Development Company

COMPETITORS

C.J. Segerstrom & Sons
Castle & Cooke
Goldrich & Kest
Kaufman & Broad
MBK Real Estate
Newhall Land and Farming
Spieker Properties

HISTORICAL FINANCIALS & EMPLOYEES

Private FYE: June	Annual Growth	1989	1990	1991	1992	1993	1994	1995	1996	1997	1998
Sales ($ mil.)	7.8%	—	550	500	700	800	800	700	710	816	1,000
Employees	(4.8%)	—	350	350	300	200	200	200	190	200	236

SALES HISTORY

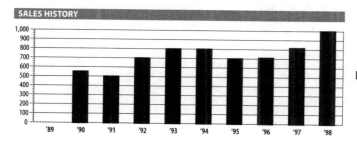

THE IRVINE COMPANY

J. CREW GROUP INC.

OVERVIEW

After more than a decade of hanging with the college crowd, J. Crew Group is trying to graduate. Hemmed by the stagnant growth of its catalog operations, the New York City-based company has sold or closed two of its noncore catalog businesses, Popular Club Plan and Clifford & Wills, leaving it with only its namesake operations. With its J. Crew catalog division struggling, the company is hoping its profitable retail outlets, as well as the Internet, will make it a more stable and well-rounded retailer.

With a brand that is sometimes used as an adjective ("That's very J. Crew!"), the company generally focuses on young, college-educated professionals. Timeless casuals, jeans, and other durables account for about 60% of sales. Most of those sales come from its 110 retail and outlet stores in the US and 67 stores in Japan (through a partnership with Itochu). The rest of its sales come from 33 magazine-quality catalog editions that reach about 75 million people each year. Items available from the J. Crew catalog are generally priced between $12 and $100, while the retail stores, usually located in upscale malls, carry higher-priced apparel. Merchandise is produced primarily by Asian contractors (60%); the rest comes equally from the US and Europe.

Faced with poor growth prospects for its catalog segment, J. Crew plans to add about 20 stores a year. Emily Cinader Woods, daughter of founder Arthur Cinader, owns about 20% of the company. Investment firm Texas Pacific Group owns about 62%.

HISTORY

Although the J. Crew Group started in 1983, the Cinader family's participation in the mail-order catalog business extends back to 1947, when Arthur Cinader's father, Mitchell, along with Saul Charles, founded the Popular Club Plan, a mail-order catalog selling ladies' apparel, furniture, and kitchen supplies.

After inheriting the Popular Club Plan, Arthur observed the remarkable growth in the early 1980s of The Talbots, L.L. Bean, and other clothing catalogs. In 1983 he established his own classic apparel catalog as J. Crew, a name that connoted casual, collegiate clothing. First-year sales were about $3 million. The following year Arthur offered a job to his eldest daughter, Emily, a recent college graduate. Her first decision was to ban polyester from all J. Crew clothes. Although early catalogs included clothing from a number of manufacturers, Emily, as the company's chief designer, moved the company to selling its own brand exclusively. J. Crew's early unisex styles were shaped by her desire to wear some of the same clothes she wore while growing up, such as her brother's chinos. Also in 1984 Arthur started the Clifford & Wills catalog operation (low-priced women's clothing). J. Crew catalog sales grew rapidly during the mid-1980s.

Costs were hurt in 1989 when the United States Postal Service increased its rates by 30%. Emily, then 28, became president of the J. Crew catalog division and launched a risky expansion into retail, with its first store in New York City. Later in 1989 J. Crew unveiled an ambitious store-opening plan (50 stores in five years). However, a weakened economy and sharp competition slowed growth. The company signed an agreement with Itochu to open stores in Japan in 1993.

High executive turnover also stunted growth, possibly attributable to the rough-edged style of Arthur. President and COO Arnold Cohen stepped down in 1993. His replacement, Robert Bernard, resigned in 1996, and Arthur took on his duties.

In an effort to recapitalize the struggling company, the Texas Pacific Group bought its stake in J. Crew the following year, with an eye on taking it public when its performance improved. At that time, Arthur retired and Emily succeeded her father as J. Crew's chair. In 1998 J. Crew attributed a loss of $27 million to disappointing mail-order sales caused by the strike and a warm fall and winter. The company dismissed 10% of its workforce to reduce overhead costs that year. Also that year J. Crew sold its Popular Club Plan to catalog firm Fingerhut Companies (the company had tried to sell it as early as the late 1980s).

Speaking of losing popularity, CEO Howard Socol fell out of favor and left the company in early 1999 after less than a year on the job. Mark Sarvary, former president of Nestlé Frozen Foods, succeeded him. Also in 1999 J. Crew ceased its Clifford & Wills catalog and agreed to sell it to Spiegel.

Chair and Chief Designer: Emily Cinader Woods, age 38, $2,000,000 pay
CEO: Mark Sarvary, age 40
SVP Women's Design: Scott Formby, age 37, $499,158 pay
SVP New Media and Strategic Planning: Scott R. Gilbertson, age 30
SVP; General Manager, Mail Order: Walter Kilough, age 44
SVP and Chief Information Officer: Thomas A. Lesica, age 39
SVP and CFO: Scott M. Rosen, age 40
SVP; General Merchandising Manager, Retail: Carol Sharpe, age 44, $499,158 pay
VP, General Counsel, and Corporate Secretary: Barbara K. Eisenberg, age 53
VP and Corporate Controller: Nicholas Lamberti, age 56
President of Stores: Richard M. Anders, age 42
President, Mail Order: Trudy Sullivan, age 49, $540,000 pay
Auditors: KPMG LLP

LOCATIONS

HQ: 770 Broadway, New York, NY 10003
Phone: 212-209-2500   **Fax:** 212-209-2666
Web site: http://www.jcrew.com

1999 Stores

	No.
California	15
New York	12
Florida	6
Massachusetts	6
Pennsylvania	6
Texas	6
New Jersey	5
Connecticut	4
Georgia	4
Illinois	4
Colorado	3
Indiana	3
Maryland	3
Washington	3
Other	30
Total	**110**

PRODUCTS/OPERATIONS

1999 Sales

	$ mil.	% of total
J. Crew brands	626	76
Other	198	24
Total	**824**	**100**

COMPETITORS

AnnTaylor
Benetton
Calvin Klein
Dayton Hudson
Dillard's
Federated
The Gap
Guess?
Hartmarx
Intimate Brands
J. C. Penney
L.L. Bean
Lands' End
The Limited
Liz Claiborne
Loehmann's
Marks & Spencer
May
Men's Wearhouse
Nautica Enterprises
Neiman Marcus
Nordstrom
Polo
Saks Inc.
Sears
Spiegel
Talbots
Tommy Hilfiger

HISTORICAL FINANCIALS & EMPLOYEES

Private FYE: January	Annual Growth	1990	1991	1992	1993	1994	1995	1996	1997	1998	1999
Sales ($ mil.)	11.3%	314	354	466	571	647	738	746	809	834	824
Net income ($ mil.)	—	—	—	—	14	12	15	6	13	(27)	(15)
Income as % of sales	—	—	—	—	2.5%	1.9%	2.0%	0.9%	1.6%	—	—
Employees	16.2%	2,300	2,550	2,700	3,670	4,479	5,413	5,600	6,100	6,200	8,900

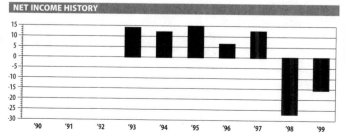

NET INCOME HISTORY

1999 FISCAL YEAR-END
Debt ratio: 100%
Return on equity: —
Cash ($ mil.): 10
Current ratio: 1.93
Long-term debt ($ mil.): 283

J.CREW

JM FAMILY ENTERPRISES, INC.

OVERVIEW

The Moran family's car is probably a Lexus. Based in Deerfield Beach, Florida, JM Family Enterprises is a privately owned holding company with about a dozen automotive-related businesses (including JM Lexus, the nation's largest-volume Lexus retailer, in Margate, Florida). It is Florida's second-largest private company, after Publix Super Markets.

Southeast Toyota Distributors, JM's primary subsidiary, operates the world's #1 Toyota distribution franchise, delivering Toyota and Lexus vehicles to more than 160 dealers in Alabama, the Carolinas, Florida, and Georgia. Among its other subsidiaries, JM&A Group provides insurance and warranty services to retailers nationwide. World Omni Financial handles leasing, dealer financing, and other financial services for US auto dealers.

JM is owned by the family of billionaire founder and chairman Jim Moran. Pat Moran, Jim's daughter and company CEO and president, is one of the top female business owners in the US.

HISTORY

Jim Moran first became visible as "Jim Moran, the Courtesy Man" in Chicago TV advertisements in the 1950s. At that time he ran Courtesy Motors, where he was so successful as the world's #1 Ford dealer that *Time* magazine put his picture on its cover in 1961.

Moran had entered the auto sales business after fixing up and selling a car for more than three times the price he had paid for it. That profit was much better than what he made at the Sinclair gas station he had bought, so he opened a used-car lot. Later, he moved to new-car sales when he bought a Hudson franchise (Ford had rejected him).

Seeing the promise of TV advertising, in 1948 Moran pioneered the forum for Chicago car dealers, not only as an advertiser and program sponsor but also as host of a variety show and a country/western music barn dance. The increased visibility positioned Moran as Hudson's #1 dealer, but the sales tactics at Courtesy Motors earned an antitrust suit that was settled out of court.

In 1955 Moran started with Ford and, with his TV influence as host of *The Jim Moran Courtesy Hour,* he became the world's #1 Ford dealer in his first month.

He moved to Florida in 1966 after being diagnosed with cancer and given one year to live. Successfully fighting the disease, he bought a Pontiac franchise and later started Southeast Toyota Distributors. In 1969 he formed JM Family Enterprises.

Legal problems cropped up in 1973 when the IRS investigated a Nassau bank serving as a tax haven for wealthy Americans. Moran and three Toyota executives were linked to the bank, and in 1978 Moran was indicted for tax fraud. When an immunity deal fell through, Moran pleaded guilty to seven tax fraud charges in 1984 and was sentenced to two years (suspended), fined more than $12 million, and ordered to perform community service. Moran's legal problems threatened his association with Toyota and were blamed for causing his stroke in 1983.

JM's legal problems continued in the 1980s, partly because of the imposition of auto import restrictions. To get more cars to sell, some Southeast Toyota managers encouraged auto dealers to file false sales reports. Some North Carolina dealers resisted and one sued, settling out of court for $22 million. Other dealers alleged racketeering and fraud on the part of Southeast Toyota, and by the beginning of 1994, JM had paid more than $100 million in fines and settlements for cases stretching back to 1988. In spite of that, Toyota renewed its contract with the company in 1993, a year ahead of schedule.

Pat Moran succeeded her father as JM president in 1992. Between 1991 and 1994 three suits were filed against Jim and Southeast Toyota alleging racism against blacks in establishing Toyota dealerships. All three suits were settled.

Jim teamed with Wayne Huizenga in 1996 to launch a national chain of used-car megastores under the name AutoNation USA, which Jim expected would draw buyers to his own auto dealerships. (AutoNation USA's first store was built just two blocks from JM's Coconut Creek Lexus Dealership.) Jim's interest in AutoNation USA was converted into a small percentage (less than 5%) of Republic Industries stock after Huizenga merged AutoNation into waste hauler Republic Industries (now called AutoNation) in 1997.

In late 1998 JM embarked on a national strategy to expand its presence outside the Southeast, establishing an office in St. Louis that handles indirect consumer leasing.

Chairman: James M. Moran
President and CEO: Patricia Moran
COO and General Counsel: Collin Brown
EVP and CFO: Jim Foster
EVP Human Resources: Gary L. Thomas
Auditors: Arthur Andersen LLP

LOCATIONS

HQ: 100 NW 12th Ave., Deerfield Beach, FL 33442
Phone: 954-429-2000　　　**Fax:** 954-429-2244

PRODUCTS/OPERATIONS

Selected Subsidiaries

Finance and Leasing
World Omni Financial Corp.

Insurance, Marketing, Consulting, and Related Companies
Fidelity Insurance Agency
JM&A Group (auto service contracts, insurance)
　Courtesy Insurance Co.
　Fidelity Acceptance Corp.
　Fidelity Warranty Services Inc.
　JM&A Group
　JMIC Life Insurance Co.

Retail Car Sales
JM Lexus

Vehicle Processing and Distribution
Southeast Toyota Distributors, Inc.

Selected Affiliates

Executive Incentives & Travel
Petro Chemical Products

COMPETITORS

CarMax
Gulf States Toyota
Hendrick Automotive
Holman Enterprises
Island Lincoln-Mercury
Morse Operations
United Auto Group

HISTORICAL FINANCIALS & EMPLOYEES

Private FYE: December	Annual Growth	1989	1990	1991	1992	1993	1994	1995	1996	1997	1998
Sales ($ mil.)	12.6%	2,134	2,295	2,400	2,600	3,500	4,200	4,500	5,100	5,400	6,200
Employees	3.4%	2,226	2,107	2,300	2,300	2,300	2,000	2,000	3,000	2,900	3,000

SALES HISTORY

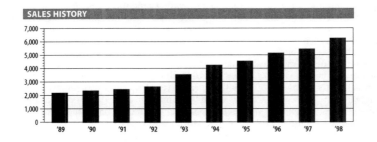

JM FAMILY
ENTERPRISES, INC.

JOHN HANCOCK MUTUAL LIFE

OVERVIEW

John Hancock Mutual Life Insurance has products designed to offer comfort in your old age and security to your survivors.

The Boston-based company's largest business is life insurance, but as baby boomers move toward retirement age, the company has put more emphasis on retirement savings products. These include annuities, proprietary mutual funds, and long-term-care insurance. One of the largest investors in the US, John Hancock offers institutional asset management services, providing clients with specialty funds in such industries as timber and agriculture.

John Hancock is demutualizing (converting to a stock company) by early 2000, and is trying to clean up its image before its IPO. The company's name has been tainted by policyholder lawsuits and a lobbying scandal that just won't go away. Even its association with the Olympics has been tarred by the Salt Lake City bribery scandal. To distance the insurer from the problems surrounding the Games, company president David D'Alessandro has been loudly calling for members of the International Olympic Committee to resign.

HISTORY

In 1862 Albert Murdock and other Boston businessmen founded John Hancock Mutual Life Insurance Company, named after a signer of the Declaration of Independence. The firm added agents in Connecticut, Illinois, Missouri, and Pennsylvania in 1865.

The following year the policyholder-owned company began making annual distributions of surplus to paid-up members. It became the first US mutual life insurer to offer industrial insurance (small-face-value weekly premium life insurance) in 1879. Hancock was also a pioneer in granting dividends and cash surrender values (the amount returned to the policyholder when a policy is canceled) with industrial insurance. In 1902 its weekly premium agencies began selling annual premium insurance.

Hancock added annuities in 1922, group insurance in 1924, and individual health insurance in 1957. In 1968 it formed John Hancock Advisers (mutual funds) and John Hancock International Group Program (group health and life insurance overseas). It added property/casualty insurance operations (with Sentry Insurance) in the early 1970s.

Despite these forays into new areas, Hancock's mainstay remained whole-life insurance. In the late 1970s, as interest rates soared, members borrowed on their policies at low rates to invest at higher rates, draining company funds. This convinced the company that it had to diversify.

It did so through acquisitions, including brokerages and bond specialists. Other business additions included equipment leasing, universal life, and credit cards. The company also made risky direct investments in the booming real estate market.

Despite the new business lines, Hancock's position in the industry declined during the 1980s. In the 1990s the company was hit by a downturn in the real estate industry that forced it to establish hefty reserves against defaults, which contributed to declining earnings. As a result, it sold its banking and credit card operations, as well as its property/casualty business.

Hancock expanded overseas by acquiring interests in insurers in Singapore and Thailand. (In 1998 the company also began collaborating with Vietnam Insurance Company to operate in that country.) John Hancock was among many insurers subjected to increased fraud scrutiny in the mid-1990s. In 1994 it agreed to pay more than $1 million in federal and state fines for treating Massachusetts state senators to sports events and dinners over a six-year period (a policyholder suit about this is outstanding).

But the problems went deeper. In 1996 Hancock was fined $1 million by the State of New York because agents persuaded consumers that life insurance policies were retirement savings products. To help restore public trust, the company fined and laid off agents and altered their compensation plans. But problems continued in 1997 when Massachusetts began investigating the company in the wake of the settlement of a deceptive-sales class-action policyholder civil suit. (In 1999 the company announced it would spend more than $700 million to settle that lawsuit, started in 1995.)

John Hancock initiated new sales strategies to bypass agents entirely, including direct mail, telemarketing, and online (through a pact with Microsoft). It sold its health care operations to WellPoint Health Networks in 1997. The next year the company's policyholders voted to demutualize. In 1999 John Hancock was among the first insurers approved to sell life insurance in China.

OFFICERS

Chairman and CEO: Stephen L. Brown
VC and Chief Investment Officer: Foster L. Aborn
President and COO: David F. D'Alessandro, age 48
CFO: Thomas E. Moloney
EVP Corporate Sector: Diane M. Capstaff
SVP and Controller: Earl W. Baucom
SVP Business Insurance Group: Nancy F. Bern
SVP and Demutualization Project Director:
  John M. DeCiccio
SVP Real Estate Investment Group: Edward P. Dowd
SVP Mergers and Acquisitions: John T. Farady
SVP Alternative Channels and Product Management:
  Kathleen M. Graveline
SVP Corporate Law, Corporate Compliance, and Deputy
  General Counsel: Bruce E. Skrine
VP Human Resources: A. Page Palmer
Chief Information Officer: Robert F. Walters
General Counsel: Richard S. Scipione
Chairman and CEO, John Hancock International
  Holdings: Derek Chilvers
SVP John Hancock Signature Services: David A. King
SVP Signator Financial Network: Robert A. Marra
Auditors: Ernst & Young LLP

LOCATIONS

HQ: John Hancock Mutual Life Insurance Company,
  200 Clarendon St., Boston, MA 02117
Phone: 617-572-6000   **Fax:** 617-572-6451
Web site: http://www.jhancock.com

PRODUCTS/OPERATIONS

1998 Assets

	$ mil.	% of total
Cash & equivalents	1,395	2
Bonds	24,875	37
Stocks	2,347	3
Mortgage loans	8,716	13
Real estate	1,885	3
Policy loans	1,826	3
Assets in separate account	24,042	36
Other assets	1,993	3
Total	**67,079**	**100**

1998 Sales

	$ mil.	% of total
Premiums, annuity considerations & pension fund contributions	10,116	74
Net investment income	3,118	23
Other income	419	3
Total	**13,653**	**100**

Services
Banking services
Commercial real estate loans
Group retirement funds
Guaranteed investment contracts
Life insurance and annuities
Long-term-care insurance
Mutual funds

Selected Subsidiaries and Affiliated Companies
ENERGY Investors Management, Inc.
First Signature Bank & Trust Company
Hancock Natural Resource Group, Inc.
  Hancock Agricultural Investment Group
  Hancock Timber Resource Group
Hancock Venture Partners, Inc.
Independence Investment Associates Inc.
JHM Capital Management, Inc.
John Hancock Advisers, Inc.
John Hancock Life Insurance Company of America
Maritime Life (of Canada)
The Maritime Life Assurance Company (Canada)
NM Capital Management, Inc.
Patriot Group, Inc., Boston
Sovereign Asset Management Corporation

COMPETITORS

AIG	Kemper	Northwestern
AXA Financial	Insurance	Mutual
Allmerica	Lincoln National	Phoenix Home
Financial	MONY	Life
American	MassMutual	Principal
General	Merrill Lynch	Financial
Charles Schwab	MetLife	Prudential
Conseco	Morgan Stanley	Prudential plc
FMR	Dean Witter	TIAA-CREF
GenAmerica	Mutual of Omaha	Transamerica
Guardian Life	National Life	
Hartford	Insurance	
Jefferson-Pilot	New York Life	

HISTORICAL FINANCIALS & EMPLOYEES

Mutual company FYE: December	Annual Growth	1989	1990	1991	1992	1993	1994	1995	1996	1997	1998
Assets ($ mil.)	8.4%	32,344	35,332	38,105	41,242	46,468	49,805	54,505	58,361	62,125	67,079
Net income ($ mil.)	11.7%	232	224	233	141	199	183	341	314	414	627
Income as % of assets	—	0.7%	0.6%	0.6%	0.3%	0.4%	0.4%	0.6%	0.5%	0.7%	0.9%
Employees	(7.2%)	15,655	16,000	16,500	13,903	16,500	16,000	7,996	9,453	6,362	7,959

NET INCOME HISTORY

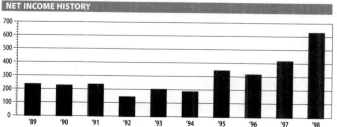

1998 FISCAL YEAR-END

Equity as % of assets: 7.5%
Return on assets: 0.9%
Return on equity: 13.9%
Long-term debt ($ mil.): 0
Sales ($ mil.): 13,653

JOHNSON PUBLISHING COMPANY

OVERVIEW

Johnson Publishing really caters to the *Jet* set. The Chicago-based company publishes a variety of black-oriented magazines, including its flagship *Ebony* (with a circulation of 1.75 million), as well as *Jet* and *Ebony South Africa*. It's one of the largest minority-owned businesses in the US and the nation's largest black-owned publisher. Johnson Publishing also produces a line of hair care products (Supreme Beauty) and cosmetics (Fashion Fair) marketed for African-American consumers, and each year

it hosts the Ebony Fashion Fair, a traveling fashion show that raises money for charities in 175 cities. The company's book division features titles by black authors (Doris Saunders' *Special Moments in African-American History 1955-1996*).

Johnson Publishing is owned and controlled by founder and CEO John Johnson and his family. Johnson's daughter and heir apparent, Linda Johnson Rice, handles the day-to-day operations as president and COO.

HISTORY

John H. Johnson launched his publishing business in 1942 while he was still in college in Chicago. The idea for a black-oriented magazine came to him while he was working part-time for Supreme Life Insurance Co. of America, where one of his jobs was to clip magazine and newspaper articles about the black community. Johnson used his mother's furniture as collateral to secure a $500 loan, then mailed $2 charter subscription offers to potential subscribers. He received 3,000 replies and used the $6,000 to print the first issue of *Negro Digest,* patterned after Reader's Digest. Circulation was 50,000 within a year.

In 1945 Johnson started *Ebony* magazine, which gained immediate popularity and is still the company's premier publication. Johnson launched *Jet* in 1951, a pocket-sized publication containing news items and features. For 20 years, *Ebony* and *Jet* were the only national publications targeting blacks in the US.

In the early days Johnson was unable to obtain advertising, so he formed his own Beauty Star mail-order business and advertised its products (dresses, wigs, hair care products, and vitamins) in his magazines. He won his first major account, Zenith Radio, in 1947; Johnson landed Chrysler in 1954, only after sending a salesman to Detroit every week for 10 years.

By the 1960s Johnson had become one of the most prominent black men in the US. In 1963 he posed with John F. Kennedy to publicize a special issue of *Ebony* celebrating the Emancipation Proclamation. In 1972 US magazine publishers named him Publisher of the Year. His first magazine, *Negro Digest* (renamed *Black World*), became known for its provocative articles, but its circulation dwindled from 100,000 to 15,000. Johnson retired the magazine in 1975.

In 1973 Johnson launched *Ebony Jr!* (since discontinued), a magazine designed to

provide "positive black images" for black pre-teens. Unable to find the proper makeup for his *Ebony* models, Johnson founded his own cosmetics business, Fashion Fair Cosmetics, that year. Fashion Fair competed successfully against Revlon (which introduced cosmetic lines for blacks) and another black cosmetics company, Johnson Products (unrelated) of Chicago. By 1982 Fashion Fair sales were more than $30 million.

The company got into broadcasting in 1972 when it bought Chicago radio station WGRT (renamed WJPC; that city's first black-owned station). It added WLOU (Louisville, Kentucky) in 1982 and WLNR (Lansing, Illinois; relaunched in 1991 as WJPC-FM) in 1985. By 1995, however, it had sold all of its stations.

Johnson and the company sold their controlling interest in the last minority-owned insurance company in Illinois (and Johnson's first employer), Supreme Life Insurance, to Unitrin (a Chicago-based life, health, and property insurer) in 1991. That year the company and catalog retailer Spiegel announced a joint venture to develop fashions for black women. The two companies launched a mail-order catalog called *E Style* in 1993 and an accompanying credit card the next year.

Johnson Publishing teamed with several South African companies in 1995 to launch its South African edition of *Ebony*. In 1996 Johnson was awarded the Presidential Medal of Freedom. The next year, however, circulation of *Ebony* fell 7% as mainstream magazines began covering black issues more thoroughly and a host of new titles appeared. In response, the company restructured its ventures and closed its *E Style* catalog. Johnson Publishing retired *Ebony Man* (launched in 1985) in 1998:

Chairman, Publisher, and CEO: John H. Johnson
President and COO: Linda Johnson Rice
Secretary and Treasurer; Producer and Director,
  Ebony Fashion Fair: Eunice W. Johnson
VP Finance: Treka Owens
Editor, Ebony Magazine: Lerone Bennett Jr.
Editor, Jet Magazine: Sylvia Flanagan
VP, Fashion Fair Cosmetics: J. Lance Clark
Controller: Gregory Robertson
Director Personnel: LaDoris Foster

LOCATIONS

HQ: Johnson Publishing Company, Inc.,
  820 S. Michigan Ave., Chicago, IL 60605
Phone: 312-322-9200   **Fax:** 312-322-0918
Web site: http://www.ebony.com

PRODUCTS/OPERATIONS

Selected Operations

Fashion and Beauty Aids
Ebony Fashion Fair (traveling fashion show)
Fashion Fair Cosmetics
Supreme Beauty Products Co.

Publishing
Johnson Publishing Co. Book Division
Magazines
  Ebony
  Ebony South Africa (joint venture run
    through EBCO subsidiary, 85%)
  Jet

COMPETITORS

Advance Publications
Amway
Avon
BET
Essence Communications
Estée Lauder
Forbes
Hearst
L'Oréal
Mary Kay
Perrigo
Revlon
Soft Sheen Products
Time Warner

HISTORICAL FINANCIALS & EMPLOYEES

Private FYE: December	Annual Growth	1989	1990	1991	1992	1993	1994	1995	1996	1997	1998
Sales ($ mil.)	4.9%	241	252	261	274	294	307	316	326	361	372
Employees	1.2%	2,370	2,382	2,710	2,785	2,600	2,662	2,680	2,702	2,677	2,647

SALES HISTORY

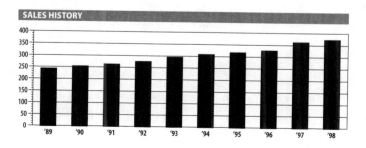

THE JONES FINANCIAL COMPANIES

OVERVIEW

"The Wal-Mart of Wall Street" is most at home on Main Street. St. Louis-based The Jones Financial Companies is a limited partnership and the parent of Edward D. Jones & Co., one of the largest brokerage branch networks in the world, with some 4,600 offices in the US, Canada, and the UK. The company's brokers cater to individual investors, especially retired persons and small-business owners; most of its one-person offices are in rural communities, small cities, and suburbs.

Brokers at Edward D. Jones sell relatively low-risk investment vehicles (municipal, government, and corporate bonds; established stocks; and high-quality mutual funds) and preach a conservative buy-and-hold approach. The company also sells insurance and engages

in investment banking for such clients as Wal-Mart and public agencies. The firm embraces technology, maintaining one of the industry's largest satellite networks (including a dish for each office).

Preferring to build its brokers from the ground up, the firm accepts applicants with no previous experience, trains them extensively, and monitors investment patterns to prevent account churning and investments in risky low-cap stocks. Before they are given such luxuries as office space, assistants, or even a computer, new brokers must make 1,000 cold calls in their chosen community.

John Bachmann, managing partner of Edward D. Jones, has said the company has no plans to go public.

HISTORY

Jones Financial got its start in 1871 as bond house Whitaker & Co. In 1922 Edward D. Jones (no relation to the Edward D. Jones of Dow Jones fame) opened a brokerage service in St. Louis. In 1943 the two firms merged.

Jones' son Edward "Ted" Jones Jr. joined the firm in 1948. Under Ted's leadership (and against his father's wishes), the company focused on rural customers, opening its first branch in Mexico, Missouri, in 1955 and beginning its march across small-town America. Ted took over as managing partner in 1968, masterminding the company's small-town expansion. (The Wal-Mart comparison is apt; Ted Jones and Sam Walton were good friends.)

Almost from the start, the firm hammered home a conservative investment message focusing on blue-chip stocks and bonds. It expanded steadily throughout the years, adding offices with such rural addresses as Cedarburg, Wisconsin, and Paris, Illinois.

In the 1970s Edward D. Jones moved into underwriting with clients including Southern Co., Citicorp, and Humana. (It got burned in the mid-1980s on one such deal, when the SEC accused the company of fraud in a bond offering for life insurer D.H. Baldwin Co., which later filed for bankruptcy.)

The company's technological bent was spurred in 1978 after its Teletype network couldn't handle the demand generated by the firm's 220 offices. As a stopgap, the company nixed use of the Teletype for stock quotes, telling its brokers to call Merrill Lynch's toll-free number instead.

Managing partner John Bachmann took over from Ted Jones in 1980. (Bachmann started at

the company as a janitor.) A follower of management guru Peter Drucker, Bachmann inculcated the company's brokers with Drucker's customer- and value-oriented principles.

Edward D. Jones began moving into the suburbs and into less-than-posh sections of big cities in the mid-1980s. In 1986 the company started a mortgage program, but the plan was never successful and was ended in 1988. The company weathered the 1987 stock market crash (many brokerages did not), albeit with thinner profit margins.

In 1990 Ted Jones died. The first half of the decade was a time of great expansion for the company as it doubled its number of offices. In 1993 the company opened an office in Canada.

In 1994 Jones Financial diversified into banking with the acquisition of Columbia, Missouri-based thrift Boone National. The move gave Jones the ability to offer trust and mortgage services to its clients, which helped sales as it started facing competition from Merrill Lynch in its small-town niche. The company's rapid expansion and relatively expensive infrastructure (all those one-person offices add up) began to eat at the bottom line, and in 1995 Bachmann stopped expansion so the firm could catch its breath.

In 1997 Edward D. Jones moved overseas, opening its first offices in the UK, a prime expansion target for the company. The next year the firm teamed up with Mercantile Bank to offer small-business loans. In 1999 Jones resumed its expansionist push, adding offices in all its markets.

Managing Partner: John W. Bachmann, age 60, $193,750 pay
General Partner and CFO: Steven Novik, age 49
General Partner and Director Human Resources:
Michael R. Holmes Sr., age 40
General Partner Banking Services:
Connie M. Silverstein
General Partner, Canada Division: Gary D. Reamey
General Partner Compliance: Pam Cavness
General Partner Financial Services: Patricia Hannum
General Partner Fixed Income: Kevin Flatt
General Partner Headquarters Administration:
Robert Virgil Jr., age 64
General Partner Information Systems:
Richie L. Malone, age 50, $153,750 pay
General Partner Insurance and Annuities:
Merry Mosbacher
General Partner Investment Advisory: Heidi Whitfield
General Partner Investment Banking:
Daniel A. Burkhardt
General Partner Marketing: Douglas E. Hill, age 54, $153,750 pay
General Partner Operations: Darryl W. Pope, age 59
General Partner Public Relations and Advertising:
Mary Beth Heying
General Partner Public Relations and Advertising:
Colleen Raley
General Partner Research: Dave Otto
General Partner Sales and Hiring: John Sloop
General Partner Sales Management: James D. Weddle, $153,750 pay
Auditors: Arthur Andersen LLP

LOCATIONS

HQ: The Jones Financial Companies, L.P., LLP,
12555 Manchester Rd., St. Louis, MO 63131
Phone: 314-515-2000 **Fax:** 314-515-2622

PRODUCTS/OPERATIONS

1998 Sales

	$ mil.	% of total
Commissions		
Mutual funds	529	37
Insurance	178	12
Listed	171	12
Principal transactions	148	10
OTC	81	5
Interest & dividends	118	8
Investment banking	52	4
Money market fees	44	3
Gain on investment	41	3
IRA custodial services fees	16	1
Other	72	5
Total	**1,450**	**100**

Selected Subsidiaries
EDJ Holding Co., Inc.
EDJ Leasing Co., LP
Edward D. Jones & Co. Canada Holding Co., Inc.
Edward D. Jones & Co., LP (broker-dealer)
Edward D. Jones Ltd. (UK)
EJ Insurance Agency Holding LLC
EJ Mortgage LLC
Edward Jones Mortgage (50%)
LHC, Inc.
Unison Capital Corp., Inc.
Passport Research Ltd. (50%, money market mutual fund adviser)
Unison Investment Trust

COMPETITORS

A.G. Edwards
Charles Schwab
Citigroup
FleetBoston
Merrill Lynch
Morgan Stanley Dean Witter
Paine Webber
Raymond James Financial
TD Waterhouse Securities
U. S. Bancorp Piper Jaffray
Wells Fargo

HISTORICAL FINANCIALS & EMPLOYEES

Private FYE: December	Annual Growth	1989	1990	1991	1992	1993	1994	1995	1996	1997	1998
Sales ($ mil.)	17.3%	—	—	—	557	642	661	722	952	1,135	1,450
Net income ($ mil.)	21.4%	—	—	—	62	66	54	58	93	114	199
Income as % of sales	—	—	—	—	11.2%	10.3%	8.2%	8.1%	9.8%	10.1%	13.7%
Employees	13.7%	—	—	—	—	8,330	7,418	11,717	12,148	13,691	15,795

NET INCOME HISTORY

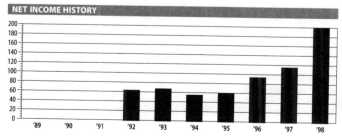

1998 FISCAL YEAR-END

Debt ratio: 8.6%
Return on equity: 53.4%
Cash ($ mil.): 144
Current ratio: 0.00
Long-term debt ($ mil.): 42

Edward**Jones**
INVESTMENTS

J.R. SIMPLOT COMPANY

OVERVIEW

J.R. Simplot is McDonald's primary french fry supplier, and that's no small potatoes. Named after its founder, Boise, Idaho-based agribusiness giant J.R. Simplot is one of the world's largest processors of frozen potatoes, making 2 billion pounds of fries, hash browns, and nuggets annually. The spuds sprouted other businesses, including cattle ranches and feedlots (which use feed made from potato peels), fertilizer operations, and mining.

Frozen french fries are the biggest item on J.R. Simplot's food service menu; it also offers frozen vegetables, fruits, entrees, and ground beef products. The company's US retail food products are limited to J.R. Simplot-brand frozen potato products and the MicroMagic

line of microwaveable sandwiches and snacks. Its Minerals and Chemical Group mines phosphates (for fertilizer and feed) and silica. Additionally, J.R. Simplot is building its presence down under through acquisitions of several Australian food processors.

Three of J. R. "Jack" Simplot's children and one grandchild oversee the family-owned company through the "Office of the Chair." ("They've not done as good as I'd hoped," he has groused.) Officially retired since 1994, the elder Simplot remains one of the wealthiest Americans. After amassing a mountain of potato money, the spudillionaire moved on to semiconductors and invested heavily in Boise-based Micron Technology.

HISTORY

J. R. Simplot was born in Dubuque, Iowa, in 1909. His family moved to the frontier town of Declo, Idaho, about a year later. Frustrated with school and an overbearing father, Simplot dropped out at age 14 and moved to a local hotel, where he made money by paying cash for teachers' wage scrip, at 50 cents on the dollar. Simplot then got a bank loan using the scrip as collateral and moved into farming, first by raising hogs and then by growing potatoes. He met Lindsay Maggart, a leading farmer in the area, who taught him the value of planting certified potato seed, rather than potatoes.

Simplot purchased an electric potato sorter in 1928 and eventually dominated the local market by sorting for neighboring farms. By 1940 his company, J.R. Simplot, operated 33 potato warehouses in Oregon and Idaho. The company moved into food processing in the 1940s, first by producing dried onions and other vegetables for Chicago-based Sokol & Co. and later by producing dehydrated potatoes. Between 1942 and 1945 J.R. Simplot produced over 50 million pounds of dehydrated potatoes for the US military. During the war the company also expanded into fertilizer production, cattle feeding, and lumber. It moved to Boise, Idaho, in 1947.

In the 1950s J.R. Simplot researchers developed a method for freezing french fries. In the mid-1960s Simplot persuaded McDonald's founder, Ray Kroc, to go with his frozen fries, a handshake deal that practically guaranteed Simplot's success in the potato processing industry. By the end of the 1960s, Simplot was the largest landowner, cattleman, potato grower, and employer in the state of Idaho. He also had established fertilizer plants, mining operations, and

other businesses in 36 states, as well as in Canada and a handful of other countries.

During the oil crisis of the 1970s, J.R. Simplot began producing ethanol from potatoes. However, Simplot's empire-building was not without its rough edges. In 1977 he pleaded no contest to federal charges that he failed to report his income, and the next year he was forced to settle charges that he manipulated Maine potato futures.

The company entered the frozen fruit and vegetable business in 1983. Other ventures included using wastewater from potato processing for irrigation and using cattle manure to fuel methane gas plants.

In 1992 J.R. Simplot acquired a stake in the Marbran Group, a private Mexican processor of frozen broccoli and cauliflower for export to the US and Japan. The company also set up a Chinese joint venture in the 1990s to provide processed potatoes to McDonald's and other customers in East Asia.

The company bought the giant ZX cattle ranch near Paisley, Oregon, in 1994. Simplot retired from the board of directors in 1994 to become chairman emeritus; Stephen Beebe was named president and CEO. The 1995 acquisition of Pacific Dunlop lead to the creation of Simplot Australia, one of the largest food processors in Australia. Its 1997 stock swap with I. & J. Foods Australia enlarged the subsidiary's frozen food menu.

J.R. Simplot consolidated its Australian operations in 1998 to upgrade plants and reduce costs. In 1999 the company sold its Simplot Dairy Products cheese business to France's Besnier Group, the largest dairy company in the European Union.

Chairman Emeritus: J. R. Simplot
Office of the Chair: Don J. Simplot
Office of the Chair: Gay Simplot
Office of the Chair: J. E. Simplot
Office of the Chair: Scott R. Simplot
President and CEO: Stephen A. Beebe
SVP Finance and CFO: Dennis Mogensen
President, Agriculture Group: Tom Basabe
President, Minerals and Chemical Group:
Larry Hinderager
President, Diversified Products Group: Ray G. Kaufman
President, Food Group: Jim Munyon
VP, Secretary, and General Counsel: Ronald N. Graves
VP Human Resources: Ted Roper
VP and Treasurer: Tom Sorge
VP Public Relations: Fred Zerza
Treasurer: James D. Crawford

LOCATIONS

HQ: 1 Capital Center, 999 Main St., Ste. 1300,
Boise, ID 83702
Phone: 208-336-2110   **Fax:** 208-389-7515
Web site: http://www.simplot.com

PRODUCTS/OPERATIONS

Major Operating Groups
Agriculture Group
  Cattle feeding
  Crop production
  Ranching
Diversified Products Group
  Animal feed and supplements
  Commodities
  Construction contracting
  Dry pet food
  Seeds and beans
  Transportation services
Food Group
  Avocado products
  Fresh potatoes
  Frozen fruits and vegetables
  Frozen potatoes
Minerals and Chemical Group
  Agricultural chemicals
  Agricultural fertilizer
  Animal feed phosates
  Industrial chemicals
  Silica products
  Turf fertilizers and chemicals

Other Operations
Corporate Information Systems
Jacklin Seed (grass seed production)
Simplot Aviation (in-company flight services)
Simplot SunGro (vegetables, fruit, and ornamental
  plants production)
SSI Food Services, Inc. (meat processing and packaging)

US Retail Brands
J.R. Simplot (frozen potato products)
MicroMagic (microwavable sandwiches and fries)
Pride Feeds (animal feed)
Simplot's BEST (lawn and garden products)

COMPETITORS

Bartlett & Company	IBP
Cactus Feeders	IMC Global
Cargill	Koch
ConAgra	McCain Foods
Del Monte	Michael Foods
Farmland Industries	Penford
Friona Industries	Potash Corporation
GFI America	Pro-Fac
Heinz	

HISTORICAL FINANCIALS & EMPLOYEES

Private FYE: August	Annual Growth	1990	1991	1992	1993	1994	1995	1996	1997	1998	1999
Sales ($ mil.)	7.9%	—	—	1,600	1,700	2,100	2,200	2,700	2,800	2,800	2,730
Employees	4.9%	—	—	—	9,000	10,000	10,000	13,000	12,000	12,000	12,000

SALES HISTORY

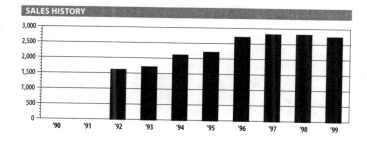

KAISER FOUNDATION HEALTH PLAN

OVERVIEW

This Kaiser isn't German, but it still reigns — as the largest not-for-profit HMO in the US.

Oakland, California-based, Kaiser Foundation Health Plan has an integrated care model, offering both hospital and physician care, through a network of hospitals and physician practices operating under the Kaiser Permanente name. Kaiser serves nearly 9 million members in 18 states and the District of Columbia.

Kaiser once had sole possession of the HMO market, but now faces increased competition from such for-profit care providers as Aetna, CIGNA, and UnitedHealth Group, which do not face the dilemma of operating hospitals while trying to contain costs by limiting admissions. Back-to-back losses have prompted Kaiser to raise rates, divest underperforming units, and pursue enrollment growth through alliances.

HISTORY

Henry Kaiser — shipbuilder, war profiteer, builder of the Hoover and Grand Coulee Dams, and founder of Kaiser Aluminum — was a bootstrap capitalist who did well by doing good. A high school dropout from upstate New York, Kaiser moved to Spokane, Washington, in 1906 and went into road construction. During the Depression, he headed the consortium that built the great WPA dams.

It was in building the Grand Coulee dam that, in 1938, Kaiser teamed with Dr. Sidney Garfield. Garfield had devised a prepayment health plan in 1933 for workers on California public works projects.

In WWII Kaiser moved into steelmaking and shipbuilding, turning out some 1,400 bare-bones Liberty ships (at the rate of 1 per day at peak production). On the theory that healthy workers produce more than sick ones, Kaiser called on Garfield to set up onsite clinics, funded by the US government as part of operating expenses. Garfield was released from military service by President Roosevelt for the purpose.

After the war, the clinics became war surplus. Kaiser and his wife bought them — at a 99% discount — through the new Kaiser Hospital Foundation. His vision was to provide the public with low-cost, prepaid medical care. He created the Health Plan — the self-supporting entity that would administer the system — and the Group Medical Organization, Permanente (named after Kaiser's first cement plant site).

He then endowed the Health Plan with $200,000. This health plan, the classic HMO model, was criticized by the medical establishment as socialized medicine performed by "employee" doctors.

But the plan flourished, becoming California's #1 medical system. In 1958 Kaiser retired to Hawaii and started his health plan there. But physician resistance limited national growth; HMOs were illegal in some states well into the 1970s.

As health care costs rose, Congress legalized HMOs in all states. Kaiser expanded in the 1980s; as it moved outside its traditional geographic areas the company contracted for space in hospitals rather than building them. Growth slowed as competition increased.

Some health care costs in California fell in the early 1990s as more medical procedures were performed on an outpatient basis. Specialists flooded the state, and as price competition among doctors and hospitals heated up, many HMOs landed advantageous contracts. Kaiser, with its own highly paid doctors, was unable to realize the same savings and was no longer the best deal in town. Its membership stalled.

To boost membership and control expenses, in 1996 Kaiser instituted a controversial program in which nurses earned bonuses for cost-cutting. Critics said the program could lead to a decrease in care quality; Kaiser later became the focus of investigations into wrongful death suits linked to cost-cutting in California (where it has since beefed up staffing and programs) and Texas (where it has agreed to pay $1 million in fines).

In 1997, to fend off for-profit competitors, Kaiser and Washington-based Group Health Cooperative of Puget Sound formed Kaiser/Group Health to handle the companies' administrative services in the Northwest. Kaiser also tried to boost membership by lowering premiums, but the strategy proved *too* effective: Costs linked to an unwieldy 20% enrollment surge brought a loss in 1997 — Kaiser's first annual loss ever. A second year in the red prompted Kaiser to sell its Texas operations to Sierra Health Services. It also entered the Florida market via an alliance with Miami-based AvMed Health Plan. In 1999 Kaiser announced plans to sell its unprofitable Northeast and North Carolina operations.

Chairman and CEO: David M. Lawrence
President and COO: Richard G. Barnaby
EVP and CFO: L. Dale Crandall
SVP and Chief Information Officer:
Timothy E. Sullivan
SVP and General Counsel: Kirk E. Miller
SVP Government Relations: Steven R. Zatkin
SVP Labor/Management Partnerships: Gary Fernandez
SVP New Business Development: James A. Lane
SVP Strategic Development and Human Resources:
James B. Williams
VP Communications: James H. Hill
Chief Administrative Officer: Robert M. Crane
EVP and President, Southwest Division:
William A. Gillespie
EVP and Chief Marketing Officer, Medicare and Commercial Operations: Kathy Swenson

LOCATIONS

HQ: Kaiser Foundation Health Plan, Inc.,
1 Kaiser Plaza, Oakland, CA 94612
Phone: 510-271-5910   **Fax:** 510-271-6493
Web site: http://www.kaiserpermanente.org

Kaiser Foundation Health Plan operates in 18 states and the District of Columbia.

1998 Membership

	No.
California	5,800,000
Central East	734,000
Northeast	617,000
Northwest	440,000
Rocky Mountain	433,000
Southeast	372,000
Hawaii	212,000
Total	**8,608,000**

PRODUCTS/OPERATIONS

1998 Membership

	% of total
Private-sector employees	59
State/local government employees	18
Individuals	10
Federal government employees	9
Education employees	4
Total	**100**

Selected Operations

Kaiser Foundation
Kaiser Foundation Health Plan (health coverage)
Kaiser Foundation Hospitals (community hospitals and outpatient facilities)
Kaiser Foundation Research Institute
Permanente Medical Groups

Permanente Medical Groups
Kaiser Foundation Health Plan of Georgia, Inc.
Kaiser Foundation Health Plan of Hawaii, Inc.
Kaiser Foundation Health Plan of North Carolina, Inc.
Kaiser Foundation Health Plan of the Northeast, Inc.
Kaiser Permanente California
Kaiser Permanente Colorado Denver/Boulder
Kaiser Permanente Colorado Springs
Kaiser Permanente Kansas City
Kaiser Permanente Mid-Atlantic States
Kaiser Permanente Northwest
Kaiser Permanente Ohio

COMPETITORS

Aetna
CIGNA
Catholic Health East
Catholic Health Initiatives
Catholic Healthcare Network
Catholic Healthcare Partners
Catholic Healthcare West
Columbia/HCA

Foundation Health Systems
Humana
Oxford Health Plans
PacifiCare
Sierra Health
UnitedHealth Group
WellPoint Health Networks

HISTORICAL FINANCIALS & EMPLOYEES

Not-for-profit FYE: December	Annual Growth	1989	1990	1991	1992	1993	1994	1995	1996	1997	1998
Sales ($ mil.)	9.5%	6,857	8,443	9,823	11,032	11,930	12,268	12,290	13,241	14,500	15,500
Net income ($ mil.)	—	159	381	486	796	848	816	550	265	(270)	(288)
Income as % of sales	—	2.3%	4.5%	4.9%	7.2%	7.1%	6.7%	4.5%	2.0%	—	—
Employees	3.2%	—	—	—	82,858	84,885	84,845	85,000	90,000	100,000	100,000

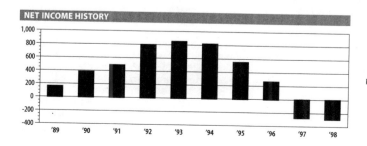

NET INCOME HISTORY

KAISER PERMANENTE

KEMPER INSURANCE COMPANIES

OVERVIEW

Kemper fi! Long Grove, Illinois-based The Kemper Insurance Companies offers personal, risk management, and commercial property/casualty insurance products and services through Lumbermens Mutual Casualty Company and other subsidiaries. Kemper's Commercial Lines Group provides workers' compensation and property coverage lines, and the Personal Lines Group offers auto and homeowners insurance. The growing Risk Management Group offers casualty and related services to large businesses.

Over the past two years, Kemper has been realigning its operations — selling its reinsurance operations, building its specialty casualty business, adding coverage for health care equipment, acquiring companies involved in workers' compensation and surety bonds, and getting involved in claims management software. The company is realigning into four operational units (business, individuals and families, international, and casualty) to improve agents' and brokers' accessibility to the products.

HISTORY

James Kemper started Lumbermens Mutual in 1912 to provide workers' compensation coverage to Illinois lumberyard owners. The 26-year-old insurance agent perceived a niche when yard owners complained that insurers were overcharging by lumping lumberyards in with the more dangerous logging business. The next year Kemper expanded into fire insurance for lumberyards by founding National Underwriters. Lumbermens began growing, adding offices in Philadelphia, Boston, and Syracuse, New York. By 1921 the company was based in Chicago.

Lumbermens was one of the first auto insurers in the US, and in 1926 it formed American Motorists Insurance Co. specifically for personal and commercial auto insurance. In the early 1930s the firm added boiler and machinery, surety bond, and inland marine coverage. After a receptionist began greeting callers with "Kemper Insurance," Lumbermens subsidiaries all began to be known as the "Kemper companies."

The Kemper family was active in philanthropy, founding a traffic safety institute at Northwestern University in the 1930s and endowing a scholarship fund.

In 1957 Lumbermens began offering marine coverage. The Kemper companies grew to include Federal Kemper Life Assurance in 1961 and American Protection Insurance the next year. In 1964 it introduced Highly Protected Risk commercial coverage.

In 1967 Lumbermens, responding to concerns about how a mutual company could own so many subsidiaries, formed public holding company Kemperco (later Kemper Corp.) in which Lumbermens owned controlling interest. In 1981, at age 94, James Kemper died.

Like many other companies, Kemper Corp. set its sights in the 1980s on becoming a financial services powerhouse, buying three

brokerages. As cyclic losses inherent in property/casualty insurance dragged down earnings growth, the company in 1989 began selling those operations back to Lumbermens for stock, decreasing Lumbermens' interest in Kemper Corp. (Property/casualty premiums had dropped from 60% of operating income in 1980 to 49% in 1981 and continued to fall until 1985.)

Additionally, reorganization gave separate management and boards of directors to Kemper Corp. and Kemper National Insurance Cos. (formed by Lumbermens Mutual Casualty Company, American Motorists Insurance Company, and American Manufacturers Mutual Insurance Company). In 1992 the companies' chairmanships were separated as well. Kemper Insurance (originally Kemper National) was formed just in time to be pummeled by the longest and costliest string of natural disasters in the 20th century.

Kemper Corp., meanwhile, became a financial services company with mutual fund offerings. In 1995 it spun off its brokerage unit, and in 1996 it was bought by Insurance Partners and Zurich Insurance Group (now Zurich Financial).

Kemper Insurance, meanwhile, was devastated by the 1994 bond crash; earnings sank again in 1996 when the company bolstered environmental and asbestos reserves. Toward the end of the decade, the firm began realigning its insurance offerings, acquiring specialty coverage players (including Integrated DisAbility Management in 1997, Eagle Insurance in 1998, and Universal Bonding in 1999) and selling Kemper Reinsurance to GE Capital (1998). In 1999 Kemper took advantage of continuing deregulation when it announced plans to open LMC, a thrift serving Illinois. Kemper joined forces with Sumitomo Marine & Fire to sell discounted insurance products to Japanese corporations.

Chairman and CEO: David B. Mathis
President and COO: William D. Smith
EVP and CFO: Walter L. White
EVP: Dale S. Hammond
EVP: James S. Kemper III
EVP: Elizabeth M. Lindner
EVP: Peter M. Mooney
SVP: Alan J. Baltz
SVP: Ronald E. Greco
SVP: William A. Hickey
SVP: Mural R. Josephson
SVP: Robert A. Lindemann
SVP: Mark A. Mallonee
SVP Administration: Frederic C. McCullough
SVP: Mark D. O'Brien
SVP: Jack E. Scott
SVP: Kenneth C. Simmons
President and CEO, Kemper National Services:
David K. Patterson
President and CEO, Kemper Casualty Company:
Dennis P. Kane
President, Business Customer Group:
Douglas A. Batting
Auditors: KPMG LLP

LOCATIONS

HQ: The Kemper Insurance Companies,
1 Kemper Dr., Long Grove, IL 60049
Phone: 847-320-2000   **Fax:** 847-320-2494
Web site: http://www.kemperinsurance.com

PRODUCTS/OPERATIONS

Subsidiaries and Affiliates
American Manufacturers Mutual Insurance Company
Eagle Insurance Group (specialty workers'
compensation)
GreatLand Insurance (commercial insurance)
Kemper Auto & Home (personal property/casualty)
Kemper Cost Management (health care equipment
insurance)
Kemper Environmental (commercial and environmental
insurance and services)
Kemper Professional (individual professional liability)
Kemper Underwriting Brokers (excess casualty coverage)
Kempes (professional liability, public entity, and
property/casualty)
Lou Jones & Associates (contract surety bonds)
Lumbermens Mutual Casualty Company
Pyramid Services (medical claims software)
Universal Bonding Insurance Company (small-contract
surety bonds)

COMPETITORS

AIG
Acordia
Allstate
American Family Insurance
American Financial
American Safety Insurance
CNA Financial
Chubb
Liberty Mutual
Mutual of Omaha
Prudential
Reliance Group Holdings
St. Paul Companies
Travelers

HISTORICAL FINANCIALS & EMPLOYEES

Mutual company FYE: December	Annual Growth	1989	1990	1991	1992	1993	1994	1995	1996	1997	1998
Assets ($ mil.)	6.7%	6,640	7,330	8,190	8,460	9,137	8,956	9,023	8,962	9,834	9,810
Net income ($ mil.)	6.3%	157	(71)	41	86	119	25	169	19	222	227
Income as % of sales	—	2.4%	—	0.5%	1.0%	1.3%	0.3%	1.9%	0.2%	2.3%	2.3%
Employees	—	—	—	—	—	9,000	8,295	8,837	10,068	9,500	9,000

SALES HISTORY

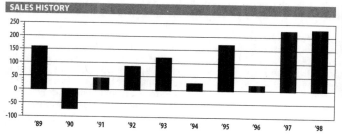

1998 FISCAL YEAR-END

Equity as % of assets: 26.2%
Return on assets: 2.3%
Return on equity: 9.2%
Long-term debt ($ mil.): —

KING RANCH, INC.

OVERVIEW

King Ranch's property is Texas-sized (not really, but it is larger than all of Rhode Island). The company's 825,000-acre namesake ranch still conducts the farming and ranching that made it famous, but the dwindling demand for beef has made it more dependent on oil and gas royalties, fruit and sugar cane farming in Florida, and tourist dollars (from sightseers, hunters, and birdwatchers). The operations are managed from its Houston corporate headquarters.

Considered the birthplace of the American ranching industry, King Ranch also has introduced the new highly fertile breed of beef cattle: the King Ranch Santa Cruz, which is one-fourth Gelbvieh, one-fourth Red Angus, and one-half Santa Gertrudis. About 55,000 cattle still roam the land, but raising animals isn't the only thing King Ranch cottons to — this sprawl of four noncontiguous ranches is also one of the US's largest cotton producers.

Like a good western movie, some things ride into the sunset at King Ranch. The company sold its 670-acre Kentucky Thoroughbred breeding and racing farm, as well as most of its foreign ranches, and is selling its primary oil and gas subsidiary. About 85 descendants of the company's founder, Richard King, own King Ranch.

HISTORY

King Ranch was founded in 1853 by former steamboat captain Richard King and his wife Henrietta, the daughter of a Brownsville, Texas, missionary. On the advice of his friend Robert E. Lee, King used his steamboating profits and occasional strong-arm tactics to buy land — miles of flat, brush-filled, coastal plain and desert south of Corpus Christi, Texas, valued at pennies an acre.

The next year King relocated the residents of an entire drought-ravaged village to the ranch and employed them as ranch hands, known ever after as *kinenos* ("King's men"). The Kings built their homestead in 1858 at a site recommended by Lee.

King Ranch endured attacks from Union guerrillas during the Civil War and Mexican bandits after the war. Times were tough, but King was up to the challenge, always traveling armed and with outriders.

In 1867 the ranch used its famed Running W brand for the first time. After King's death in 1885, Robert Kleberg, who married King's daughter Alice, managed the 1.2 million-acre ranch for his mother-in-law. Henrietta died in 1925 and left three-fourths of the ranch to Alice. Before Robert's death in 1932, control of the ranch passed to sons Richard and Bob. In 1933 Bob negotiated an exclusive oil and gas lease with Houston-based Humble Oil, which later became part of Exxon.

While Richard served in Congress, Bob ran the ranch. He developed the Santa Gertrudis, the first breed of cattle ever created in the US, by crossing British shorthorn cattle with Indian Brahmas. The new breed was better suited to the hot, dry South Texas climate.

Bob made King Ranch a leading breeder of quarter horses, which worked cattle, and Thoroughbreds, which he raced. He bought Kentucky Derby winner Bold Venture in 1936 and a Kentucky breeding farm in 1946; that year a King Ranch horse, Assault, won racing's Triple Crown.

When Bob died in 1974, the family asked James Clement, husband of one of the founders' great-granddaughters, to become CEO and bypassed Robert Shelton, a King relative and orphan whom Bob had raised as his own son. Shelton severed ties with the ranch in 1977 over a lawsuit he filed against Exxon, and partially won, alleging underpayment of royalties.

Under Clement, King Ranch became a multinational corporation. In 1980 it formed King Ranch Oil and Gas (also called King Ranch Energy) to explore for and produce oil and gas in five states and the Gulf of Mexico. In 1988 Clement retired, and Kimberly-Clark executive Darwin Smith became the first CEO not related to the founders. Smith left after one year, and the reins passed to petroleum geologist Roger Jarvis and then to Jack Hunt in 1995.

With the help of scientists, in the early 1990s the company developed a leaner, more fertile breed of the Santa Gertrudis called the Santa Cruz.

In 1998 Stephen "Tio" Kleberg, the only King descendant still actively working the ranch, was pushed from the saddle of daily operations to a seat on the board. King Ranch sold its Kentucky horse farm in 1998 and teamed up with Collier Enterprises that year to purchase citrus grower Turner Foods from utility holding company FPL Group. In 1999 King Ranch agreed to sell King Ranch Energy to St. Mary Land and Exploration Co. for $60 million.

HISTORICAL FINANCIALS & EMPLOYEES

Private FYE: December	Annual Growth	1989	1990	1991	1992	1993	1994	1995	1996	1997	1998
Estimated sales ($ mil.)	7.2%	160	160	165	330	250	250	250	250	300	300
Employees	8.0%	350	350	350	700	700	700	700	700	700	700

SALES HISTORY

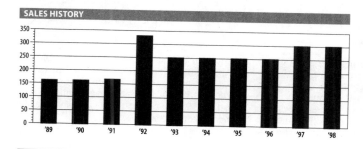

KINGSTON TECHNOLOGY COMPANY

OVERVIEW

Kingston Technology is sharpening its memory. The Fountain Valley, California-based company is a leading maker of memory boards that increase the capacity and speed of printers and computers, from notebooks to servers. Kingston makes processor upgrades, storage peripherals (including hard drives), networking equipment (adapters, hubs, routers), and housings for storage products. The company also offers contract manufacturing services for semiconductor and PC manufacturers. Kingston sells worldwide, primarily through resellers and distributors.

Co-founders John Tu and David Sun promote a casual atmosphere wherein all employees are treated as members of an extended family. The two promote teamwork and equality, occupying cubicles like the rest of the staff and encouraging employees to abandon ties in favor of jeans. They also play different roles in the company family — Tu as the public figure and Sun as the operational force.

With continued volatility in the memory market, the company has boosted its flash memory line to include products for a new generation of digital devices, including palmtop computers, digital cameras, digital phones, and personal digital assistants. Kingston is also expanding geographically, with manufacturing facilities in Asia and Europe.

In 1999 Tu and Sun repurchased Japanese computer conglomerate SOFTBANK's 80% stake in Kingston for less than half what SOFTBANK paid for it in 1996.

HISTORY

Kingston Technology was founded in 1987 by Shanghai-born John Tu and Taiwan-born David Sun, who had both moved to California in the 1970s. The pair met in 1982 and started a memory upgrade company called Camminton Technology in Tu's garage. At first they carried around memory chips in the back seats of their cars. Sales had reached $9 million by 1986, when they sold the business to high-tech firm AST Research for $6 million. The two invested their money in stock market futures but suffered heavy losses when the market crashed in 1987.

That year PC makers were producing computers that lacked the memory needed to run the latest, hottest software, so Tu and Sun sprang into action. With just $4,000 in cash, they started another company that converted inexpensive, outdated chips into memory upgrades. Tu, who was educated in Europe, wanted to call the company Kensington after the gardens in London. A mouse pad company had that name, so Kingston was chosen.

Tu had doubts about the new company and bet Sun a Jaguar that it wouldn't survive the first year of operations. Sun won the car (which he later gave to a veteran employee who dreamed of owning one) and within two years the company had sold nearly $40 million worth of products. In 1989 Kingston began making memory system upgrades and a year later started producing processor upgrades.

The company was #1 on *Inc.* magazine's list of fastest-growing private US companies in 1992. The next year Kingston began marketing networking and storage products. Its vendor-friendly policy paid off that year, when the demand for semiconductors exceeded the supply. Suppliers kept shipping to the company as orders from other buyers were delayed.

Demand for Kingston's upgrades kicked in when Microsoft launched the Windows 95 operating system, leading many consumers to boost the power of their computers so they could run the software. In addition, the company increased production capacity by expanding its US facilities.

Kingston joined with Legend Technology Limited in 1996 to develop computers for the emerging Chinese market. It also launched a processor upgrade giving a 486-based computer system the processing power of a 75 MHz Pentium chip. That year SOFTBANK paid $1.5 billion for 80% of the company but promised to preserve its culture and retain all management — including Tu and Sun — and employees. Kingston workers received bonuses totaling $100 million.

In 1997 Kingston opened a European headquarters in the UK. Asian competitors continued pricing pressures through that year and by mid-1998 the company had cut its prices several times. That year Kingston opened its first foreign manufacturing facility, in Ireland, and later in 1998 it established one in Taiwan. Also in 1998, in a unique arrangement suggesting that SOFTBANK overpaid when it bought Kingston, Tu and Sun agreed to forgo SOFTBANK's final $333 million payment. The following year Tu and Sun bought back SOFTBANK's stake for about $450 million. Also in 1999 the company opened a manufacturing plant in Malaysia.

President and CEO: John Tu
CFO: Henri Tchen
VP Administration (HR): Daniel Hsu
VP Engineering: David Sun
VP Marketing: Gary MacDonald
Director Internet Enterprise Group: Benjamin Chou

LOCATIONS

HQ: 17600 Newhope St., Fountain Valley, CA 92708
Phone: 714-435-2600   **Fax:** 714-435-2699
Web site: http://www.kingston.com

PRODUCTS/OPERATIONS

Selected Products

Hard Drives
Card-type hard disk drives (DataPak)
Notebook hard drive replacement (StrataDrive Plus)

Memory
Flash memory (DataCard and DataFlash)
Memory modules and add-on boards

Networking
Adapters
Hubs
Print servers
Routers
Switches

Processor Upgrades
CPU upgrades (TurboChip)

Storage Products
Cables and terminators (internal and external SCSI
  cables and terminators)
External chassis with removable device enclosures
  (Rhino Jr.)
External enclosures (Data Silo)
Removable drive enclosures (Data Express)
Stackable external expansion chassis (Data Stacker)

Other
Standard memory modules (ValueRAM)

COMPETITORS

3Com
AMD
ASD Group
Cabletron
Centennial Technologies
Cisco Systems
Hyundai Electronics
Intel
Macronix International
Matsushita-Kotobuki
Micron Technology
NEC
Newbridge Networks
Nortel Networks
PNY Technologies
S3
SUPERMICRO Computer
Samsung
SanDisk
Sharp
Simple Technology
Unigen
Viking Components

HISTORICAL FINANCIALS & EMPLOYEES

Private FYE: December	Annual Growth	1989	1990	1991	1992	1993	1994	1995	1996	1997	1998
Sales ($ mil.)	44.5%	37	88	141	251	489	800	1,300	2,100	1,000	1,000
Employees	29.4%	—	—	110	175	255	310	450	547	663	670

SALES HISTORY

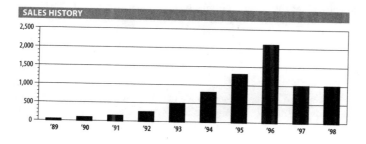

KINKO'S, INC.

OVERVIEW

Ask someone what they're doing at Kinko's and they might respond, "Makin' copies." But they might also say they're sending documents around the world electronically, shipping packages, videoconferencing, getting business cards or forms printed, checking e-mail, or even accessing the Internet. Ventura, California-based Kinko's began as a one-store, campus-oriented copy shop and has evolved into an entrepreneurial "branch office" for small offices and home businesses. Although the small office/home office market accounts for most of the company's sales, it also provides digital document services to medium and large corporations.

Kinko's operates a global chain of more than 1,000 stores in Australia, Canada, China, Japan, the Netherlands, South Korea, the United Arab Emirates, and the US. It operates in the UK through a joint venture with the Virgin Group. The company's 24-hour-a-day, seven-day-a-week service centers keep up with the latest technologies so that Kinko's customers can focus on their businesses. Its aggressive expansion strategy includes plans to open about 100 stores annually. Founder and chairman Paul Orfalea, who has announced his intention to take the company public, owns 32% of Kinko's.

HISTORY

Kinko's is the creation of Paul Orfalea, a dyslexic who failed second grade and who was inappropriately placed for six weeks in a school for the mentally retarded. The red-haired, Afro-sporting Orfalea (nicknamed Kinko) started selling pencils and spiral notebooks on the campus of the University of California at Santa Barbara in 1970. When he saw a 10-cents-a-page photocopy machine in the library, he decided selling copies would be even better. The self-described hippie borrowed $5,000 that year and opened his first Kinko's shop in a former taco stand near the university. He sold school supplies and made copies on a wheeled copy machine that had to be moved outside because the shop was so small.

Orfalea opened a second California store in San Luis Obispo in 1972, and in the mid-1970s he started providing custom publishing materials for colleges. His innovative approach caught on, and by 1980 he had 80 stores in operation, mostly located near colleges and universities.

In 1983 Kinko's opened its first store outside the US, in Canada, and in 1985 it opened its first 24-hour store, in Chicago. The company moved to Ventura, California, in 1988 and shifted its focus to the growing home office market in 1989 following the loss of a $1.9 million copyright-infringement suit for photocopying texts for professors. By 1990 Kinko's had 420 stores.

Kinko's began positioning itself as "Your Branch Office" in 1992. The next year it teamed up with telecommunications company Sprint and introduced videoconferencing services in 100 stores.

By 1995 all locations had high-speed digital color copiers and printers. Kinko's opened an office in South Korea that year and launched Kinkonet, its electronic communications network. The company teamed up with UUNET (now owned by MCI WorldCom) in 1996 to make Internet access available at its stores.

Until that year Orfalea was the sole owner of 110 stores and had partnership arrangements with more than 120 other entrepreneurs, a relationship that allowed Orfalea to control the company's rapidly growing network, while giving plenty of incentive for local expansion. This relaxed style of management also led to some unprofitable operations.

To remedy this, Kinko's went corporate in 1996, selling about 30% of the company to buyout firm Clayton, Dubilier & Rice for $219 million; the funds are being used for new technology and to expand both in the US and overseas. As part of the deal, Kinko's established a single, unified corporation, rolling into it all of the decentralized joint venture, corporate, and partnership companies operating under the Kinko's name.

In 1997 the company made its first acquisition ever, buying document management company Electronic Demand Publishing, making it the core of its corporate document unit. Also that year the company opened its first branch in China. In 1998 Kinko's opened its first stores in the UK (through a joint venture with the Virgin Group) and in the Middle East. The next year it began offering Internet-based custom printing services through an alliance with online print services firm iPrint.com. Also that year the company joined with greeting card producer Hallmark to allow customers to create their own invitations and other documents using Hallmark products.

Chairman: Paul J. Orfalea
President and CEO: Joseph Hardin Jr.
CFO: Bennett Nusbaum
SVP Quality: Jim Warren
VP Business Development: Brad Krause
VP Human Resources: Paul Rostron
President, Eastern Division: Scott Seay
President, Kinko's International: Michael Cohn
President, Western Division: Tom Parrish
Chief Technology Officer: Robert Meltzer
Director Public Relations: Laura McCormick

LOCATIONS

HQ: 255 W. Stanley Ave., Ventura, CA 93002
Phone: 805-652-4000   **Fax:** 805-652-4347
Web site: http://www.kinkos.com

PRODUCTS/OPERATIONS

Selected Products and Services
Binding and finishing services
Business and specialty papers
Computer rentals
Conference room rental
Custom printing
Digital printing
E-mail
Fax services
FedEx and UPS services
Folding
Free local phone calling
Instant posters and banners
Internet access
Laminating
Laser printing
Office supplies
Overhead transparencies
Photocopying (black-and-white, color, full-service, self-
   service, oversize)
Pick up and delivery
Presentation materials
Scanning
Videoconferencing

COMPETITORS

Champion Industries
Devon Group
Franchise Services
IKON
Mail Boxes Etc.
Merrill
Office Depot
OfficeMax
PIP
Pitney Bowes
Staples
TRM
Xerox

HISTORICAL FINANCIALS & EMPLOYEES

Private FYE: June	Annual Growth	1990	1991	1992	1993	1994	1995	1996	1997	1998	1999
Estimated sales ($ mil.)	13.1%	—	—	—	—	—	1,100	1,350	1,500	1,600	1,800
Employees	7.1%	—	—	—	—	—	19,000	23,000	24,000	24,000	25,000

SALES HISTORY

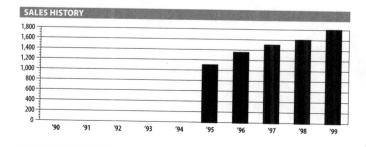

KOCH INDUSTRIES, INC.

OVERVIEW

Among really big privately owned businesses, Koch (pronounced "coke") is the real thing. Wichita, Kansas-based Koch Industries, which has extensive operations in oil and gas, agriculture, and chemicals, is the second-largest private company in the US, after grain merchant Cargill.

Koch's petroleum operations include the purchasing, gathering, and trading of crude oil. The company's two refineries in Minnesota and Texas process about 540,000 barrels of crude a day, making it a leading producer of gasoline and petrochemicals. Koch also owns gas gathering systems and about 35,000 miles of pipeline between Texas and Canada, and it purchases, processes, and markets natural gas liquids.

Agricultural businesses include Purina Mills,

the leading commercial animal feed producer in the US, and cattle ranches in Kansas, Montana, and Texas. Both Koch and Purina Mills have been hurt by the slump in the farm economy, however. Purina Mills has filed for bankruptcy protection, and Koch is expected to give up its ownership when the company reorganizes.

Through its 50% ownership of the KoSa joint venture with Mexico's Saba family, Koch is one of the world's leading polyester producers. Koch also produces paraxylene and high-octane missile fuels. Other lines of businesses include asphalt production, dry bulk ocean transport of minerals, and the manufacture of equipment for the chemical industry.

Brothers Charles and David Koch own the family-run enterprise.

HISTORY

Fred Koch grew up poor in Texas and worked his way through MIT. In 1928 Koch developed a process to refine more gasoline from crude oil, but when he tried to market his invention, the major oil companies sued him for patent infringement. Koch eventually won the lawsuits (after 15 years in court), but the controversy made it tough to attract many US customers. In 1929 Koch took his process to the USSR but, disenchanted with Stalinism, he returned home to become a founding member of the anticommunist John Birch Society.

Koch launched Wood River Oil & Refining in Illinois (1940) and bought the Rock Island refinery in Oklahoma (1947). Though he would later sell the refineries, he folded the remaining purchasing and gathering network into Rock Island Oil & Refining.

After Koch's death in 1967, his 32-year-old son Charles took the helm and renamed the company Koch Industries in honor of his father. With the help of his father's confidant, Sterling Varner, Charles began a series of acquisitions, adding petrochemical and oil trading service operations.

During the 1980s Koch was thrust into various arenas, legal and political. Charles' brother David, also a Koch Industries executive, ran for US vice president on the Libertarian ticket in 1980. That year the other two Koch brothers, Frederick and William (David's fraternal twin), launched a takeover attempt, but Charles retained control, and William was fired from his job as VP.

The brothers traded lawsuits, and in a 1983 settlement Charles and David bought out the dissident family members for just over

$1 billion. William and Frederick continued to challenge their brothers in court, claiming they had been shortchanged in the deal (the two estranged brothers eventually lost their case in 1998). In 1987 they even sued their mother over her distribution of trust fund money.

Despite this legal wrangling, Koch Industries continued to expand, purchasing a Corpus Christi, Texas, refinery in 1981. It expanded its pipeline system, buying Bigheart Pipe Line in Oklahoma (1986), and two systems from Santa Fe Southern Pacific (1988).

In 1991 Koch purchased the Corpus Christi marine terminal, pipelines, and gathering systems of Scurlock Permian (a unit of Ashland Oil). In 1992 the company bought United Gas Pipe Line (renamed Koch Gateway Pipeline) and its pipeline system extending from Texas to Florida.

Koch acquired Glitsch International (a maker of separation equipment) from engineering giant Foster Wheeler in 1997, a move that strengthened Koch's engineering services presence worldwide. It also acquired USX-Delhi Group, a natural gas processor and transporter.

In 1998 Koch bought Purina Mills, the largest US producer of animal feed, and formed the KoSa joint venture with Mexico's Saba family to buy Hoechst's Trevira polyester unit. Lethargic energy and livestock prices in 1998 and 1999, however, led Koch to lay off several hundred employees, sell its feedlots, and divest portions of its natural gas gathering and pipeline systems. Purina Mills filed for bankruptcy protection in 1999.

Chairman and CEO: Charles G. Koch
President and COO: William W. Hanna
EVP: Richard H. Fink
EVP Chemical Technology: David H. Koch
EVP Finance and Administration and Treasurer:
F. Lynn Markel
EVP International: Joe W. Moeller
EVP Operations: Bill R. Caffey
EVP and Special Counsel: Donald L. Cordes
SVP Capital Services: Paul W. Brooks
SVP Chemicals: Cy S. Nobles
SVP Gas Liquids: S. E. Odell
SVP Crude Oil and Energy Services: Kyle D. Vann
VP Agriculture: D. E. Watson
VP Capital Services: J. C. Pittenger
VP Chemical Technology: John M. Van Gelder
VP Human Resources: Paul Wheeler
VP Information Technology: M. Brad Hall
VP, Koch Industries and Koch Petroleum Group:
Seth Vance
Auditors: KPMG LLP

LOCATIONS

HQ: 4111 E. 37th St. North, Wichita, KS 67220
Phone: 316-828-5500   **Fax:** 316-828-5739
Web site: http://www.kochind.com

PRODUCTS/OPERATIONS

Selected Operations
Koch Agriculture Group
  Koch Beef Company (livestock and ranches)
  Purina Mills (animal feed)
Koch Capital Services Group (financial and capital
  market management)
Koch Chemicals Group
  Koch Chemicals (paraxylene)
  KoSa (polyester, 50%)
  Koch Microelectronic Service Company
  (semiconductor chemicals)
  Koch Specialty Chemicals (high-octane missile fuel)
Koch Chemical Technology Group (specialty equipment
  and services for refining and chemical industry)
Koch Energy Group
  Koch Energy Trading
  Koch Gateway Pipeline Company
  Koch Midstream Enterprises (gas gathering systems
  and pipelines)
Koch Gas Liquids Group
Koch Mineral Services Group (bulk ocean transportation
  and fuel supply)
Koch Petroleum Group (crude oil and refined products)
  Koch Materials Company (asphalt)
Koch Ventures Group (investment in noncore businesses)

COMPETITORS

ADM	King Ranch
Ashland	Lyondell Chemical
Avista	Motiva Enterprises
BP Amoco	Occidental
Cargill	PEMEX
Chevron	PG&E
Coastal	Peabody Group
Columbia Energy	Phillips Petroleum
Conoco	Reliant Energy
ContiGroup	Royal Dutch/Shell
Duke Energy	Southern Company
Dynegy	Statoil Energy
EOTT Energy Partners	Sunoco
Elf Aquitaine	Tosco
Enron	Tractebel
Entergy	USX-Marathon
Equilon Enterprises	Ultramar Diamond
Exxon Mobil	Shamrock
Imperial Oil	UtiliCorp
Kerr-McGee	Williams Companies

HISTORICAL FINANCIALS & EMPLOYEES

Private FYE: December	Annual Growth	1989	1990	1991	1992	1993	1994	1995	1996	1997	1998
Sales ($ mil.)	9.1%	16,000	17,190	19,250	19,914	20,000	23,725	25,200	30,000	36,200	35,000
Employees	8.0%	8,000	9,300	10,000	12,000	12,000	12,000	12,500	13,000	15,600	16,000

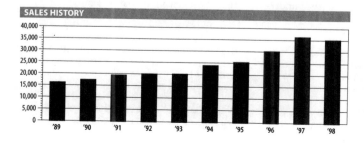

SALES HISTORY

KOCH

KOHLBERG KRAVIS ROBERTS & CO.

OVERVIEW

The master of the 1980s buyout universe, Kohlberg Kravis Roberts (KKR) has shed its hostile takeover image for a kinder, gentler buy-and-build strategy. Providing investment vehicles for some of the country's largest investors, New York City-based KKR assembles funds to buy low and sell high. An active investor, it supervises or installs new management and revamps strategy and corporate structure, selling underperforming units or adding new ones. KKR profits not only from its direct interest in these companies but also from fund and company management fees (about 20% of the investment). Cousins Henry Kravis and George Roberts are the senior partners in the firm.

Since 1976 KKR has invested some $13 billion in about 75 companies, with investors receiving returns of around 23%. However, not all its investments have been stellar. The 1987 fund, from which it financed its infamous RJR Nabisco acquisition, earned investors about 10% returns (and the return on the investment itself was rumored to be a lower, possibly negative, figure).

As private equity funds become mainstream investment tools, competition for buyouts has increased. KKR is investing in niche companies (such as movie multiplexes), paying more for acquisitions that may not net hefty returns. KKR has launched a European buy-out fund to pick up bargains as companies there shed bloated operations.

HISTORY

In 1976 Jerome Kohlberg left investment bank Bear Stearns to form his own leveraged buyout firm. With him he brought protégé Henry Kravis and Kravis's cousin George Roberts. They formed Kohlberg Kravis Roberts & Co.

Kohlberg believed LBOs, by giving management ownership stakes in their companies, would yield better results. KKR orchestrated friendly buyouts funded by investor groups and debt. The firm's first buyout was machine-toolmaker Houdaille Industries in 1979.

KKR lost money on its 1981 investment in the American Forest Products division of Bendix. But by 1984 the firm had raised its fourth fund and made its first $1 billion buyout, of Wometco Enterprises.

The next year KKR turned mean with a hostile takeover of Beatrice. The deal depended on junk bond financing devised by Drexel Burnham Lambert's Michael Milken and on the sale of pieces of the company. KKR funded the buyouts of Safeway Stores and Owens-Illinois in 1986, Jim Walter Homes in 1987, and Stop & Shop in 1988 (sold in 1996 to Royal Ahold).

Unhappy with the firm's hostile image, Kohlberg left in 1987 to form Kohlberg & Co. His suit against KKR over the alleged undervaluing of companies in relation to his departure settlement was resolved for an undisclosed amount.

The Beatrice LBO triggered a rash of similar transactions as the financial industry sought fat fees. The frenzy culminated in 1988 with the $31 billion RJR Nabisco buyout, which brought KKR $75 million in fees.

As the US slid into recession in 1989, LBOs dwindled and KKR turned to managing its acquisitions. A $3 billion additional investment in debt-ridden RJR Nabisco doubled KKR investors' equity stakes but halved returns.

The firm also did some bottom feeding. In 1991 KKR joined with what is now Fleet Boston to buy Bank of New England. The next year it picked up 47% of what is now Advantica Restaurant Group, owner of Denny's (sold 1997).

KKR made its first international foray in 1993 with Russian truck maker Kamaz (it later stalled when Kamaz refused to pay management fees). The next year KKR freed itself from the RJR morass by swapping its investment in RJR for troubled food maker Borden.

In the latter half of the decade, KKR reaped mixed results on its investments in a mix of companies, including what is now Spalding Holdings (sporting goods and Evenflo baby products), supermarket chain Bruno's, and KinderCare Learning Centers. The $600 million KKR had sunk into magazine group K-III (now PRIMEDIA) between 1990 and 1994 didn't revive interest in the stock, and KKR failed to turn around Bruno's, sending it into bankruptcy in 1998. Disgruntled investors complained about low returns, and in 1996 KKR kicked activist megafund CalPERS out of its investor ranks.

In 1998 KKR's niche buying continued when it joined with Hicks, Muse, Tate & Furst to buy Regal Cinemas, which it combined with Act III to form the biggest theater chain in the US. The next year KKR departed from course and unveiled online mortgage lender Nexstar Financial, its first company built from the ground up. With PRIMEDIA's shares in the cellar, KKR may sell parts of the media conglomerate.

OFFICERS

Founding Partner: Henry R. Kravis
Founding Partner: George R. Roberts
General Partner: Edward Gilhuly
General Partner: Perry Golkin
General Partner: James H. Greene Jr.
General Partner: Robert I. MacDonnell
General Partner: Michael W. Michelson
General Partner: Paul E. Raether
General Partner: Scott Stuart
General Partner: Michael T. Tokarz
Managing Director, Europe: Johannes Huth, age 38
Office Manager (HR): Sandy Cisneros
Auditors: Deloitte & Touche LLP

LOCATIONS

HQ: 9 W. 57th St., Ste. 4200, New York, NY 10019
Phone: 212-750-8300   **Fax:** 212-750-0003

PRODUCTS/OPERATIONS

Largest LBO Deals	Final value
	$ mil.
RJR Nabisco	30,600
Beatrice	6,100
Safeway	5,340
Borden	4,640
Owens-Illinois	3,640

Selected Investments

Accuride Corp. (90%, wheels and rims)
Amphenol Corp. (74%, cables and connectors)
Birch Telecom (35%, telecommunications)
Borden, Inc. (diversified manufacturing)
Boyds Collection Inc. (collectibles)
Bristol West Group (nonstandard auto insurance)
CAIS Internet Inc. (17%, high-speed Internet service)
Corning Consumer Products (92%, housewares)
Evenflo (51%, products for infants and children)
Idex Corp. (29%, pumps)
KinderCare (83%, day care and preschool)
Nexstar Financial (online mortgage lender)
Owens-Illinois (23%, containers)
PRIMEDIA, Inc. (86%, publishing)
Spalding Holdings (89%, sporting goods)
TI Group (5%, specialized engineering)
Walter Industries (26%, residential construction,
    mortgages, and diversified manufacturing)
Willis Corroon Group (80%, insurance brokerage)

COMPETITORS

AEA Investors
American Financial
Apollo Advisors
Bear Stearns
Berkshire Hathaway
Blackstone Group
Carlyle Group
Clayton, Dubilier
Equity Group Investments
Forstmann Little
GE Capital
Goldman Sachs
Haas Wheat
Heico
Hicks, Muse
Interlaken Investment
Investcorp
Jordan Company
Lehman Brothers
Leonard Green
MacAndrews & Forbes
Merrill Lynch
Salomon Smith Barney
    Holdings
Texas Pacific Group
Thomas Lee
Veronis, Suhler
Vestar Capital Partners
Wasserstein Perella
Wingate Partners

KOHLER CO.

OVERVIEW

Kohler sits on the throne of the global bathroom business. Based in Kohler, Wisconsin, the 96% family-owned firm is the US market leader for bathroom fixtures.

In the US its products are sold under brand names such as Ann Sacks (ceramic tile, marble, stone products, and antique building materials), Kallista (bathroom and kitchen fixtures), Kohler and Sterling (plumbing products), Robern (mirrored cabinets), and Canac (kitchen and bathroom cabinets). European brands include Jacob Delafon and Neomediam plumbing products and Sanijura bath cabinetry and related products.

But Kohler's 44 manufacturing facilities don't just make plumbing. The company also makes small engines, generators, and electrical systems and produces furniture under the Baker and McGuire names. Additional interests include a luxury Wisconsin resort (The American Club), golf courses, a wilderness preserve, and design showrooms.

Herbert Kohler Jr., the founder's grandson, is reorganizing the company to gain even more control, a move that is being fought by some shareholders (both inside and outside the Kohler family), as they feel the shares have been undervalued. Kohler and his sister, Ruth, control more than 70% of the company.

HISTORY

Kohler & Silberzahn was founded in Sheboygan, Wisconsin, in 1873 by 29-year-old Austrian immigrant John Kohler and partner Charles Silberzahn. That year they purchased a small iron foundry that made agricultural products for $5,000 from Kohler's father-in-law. In 1880, two years after Silberzahn left the firm, its machine shop was destroyed by fire.

The company introduced enameled plumbing fixtures in the rebuilt factory in 1883. The design caught on, and the business sold thousands of sinks, kettles, pans, and bathtubs. By 1887, when Kohler was incorporated, enameled items accounted for 70% of sales. By 1900 the 250-person company received 98% of its sales from enameled iron products. That year, shortly after John Kohler began building new facilities near Sheboygan (which later became the company village of Kohler), he died at age 56. More trouble followed: Kohler's new plant burned down in 1901, and two of the founder's sons died — Carl at age 24 in 1904 and Robert at age 35 in 1905.

Eldest surviving son Walter built a boarding hotel to house workers and introduced other employee-benefit programs. He also set up company-paid workmen's compensation before the state made it law in 1917.

By the mid-1920s, when Kohler premiered colors in porcelain fixtures and added brass fittings and vitreous china toilets and washbasins to its line, it was the #3 plumbing-product company in the US. As a testament to the design quality of its products, Kohler items were displayed at the New York Museum of Modern Art in 1929. The company also began developing products that would grow in importance in later decades: electric generators and small gasoline engines. During the

1950s Kohler's engines virtually conquered Southeast Asia, where they were used to power boats, drive air compressors, and pump water for rice paddies in Vietnam and Thailand. While strikes against Kohler in 1897 and 1934 had been resolved quickly, a 1954 strike against the firm lasted six years. The strike gave Kohler the dubious honor of enduring the longest strike in US history.

Small-engine use grew in the US in the 1960s, and Kohler's motors were used in lawn mowers, construction equipment, and garden tractors. The founder's last surviving son, Herbert (a child from John Kohler's second marriage), died in 1968. Under the leadership of Herbert's son, Herbert Jr. (appointed chairman 1972), Kohler expanded its operations, buying Sterling Faucet (1984); Baker, Knapp & Tubbs (1986); and Jacob Delafon (1986). More recent acquisitions include Sanijura, a French bathroom furniture maker (1993); Osio, an Italian enamel bath maker (1994); Robern, a maker of mirrored cabinets (1995); Holdiam, a French bath, whirlpool, and sink maker (1995); and Canac, a Canadian cabinetmaker (1996).

Hoping to capitalize on the growing plumbing market in China, Kohler entered into four joint ventures in that country in 1996 and 1997. In 1998 several family and non-family shareholders claimed a reorganization plan unfairly forced them out and undervalued their stock. Legal battles over the stock's fair price continued in 1999. On a lighter note, that year the company unveiled RiverBath, a $6,600, 72" diameter round bathtub that emulates river currents — complete with a small waterfall.

OFFICERS

Chairman and President: Herbert V. Kohler Jr.
Group President, Power Systems: George R. Tiedens
Group President, Interiors and General Counsel:
Natalie A. Black
SVP Technical Services: Dale E. Snyder
SVP Finance: Jeffery P. Cheney
Corporate Secretary: William J. Drew
Corporate Controller: Clyde W. Kometer
Group VP, Hospitality and Real Estate: Alica Hubbard
President, Kitchen and Bath Group: David Kohler
President, Ann Sacks Tile & Stone: Ann G. Sacks
President, Baker, Knapp & Tubbs: Christian G. Plasman
President, Canac: Brian D. Magee
President, Kohler Asia: Bernhard H. Langel
President, Kohler Europe: Gerard Dieudonne
President, McGuire Furniture: Sarah H. Garcia
President, Robern: Patrick D. Albregts
President, Sterling Plumbing: Barbara A. Koren
VP, International Power Systems Group:
Otto R. Kopietzki
Director General, Sanijura: Charles Hajiaaj
Sector Executive, Cabinetry & Tile: S. Tracy Coster
Auditors: Arthur Andersen LLP

LOCATIONS

HQ: 444 Highland Dr., Kohler, WI 53044
Phone: 920-457-4441   **Fax:** 920-457-9064
Web site: http://kohlerco.com

PRODUCTS/OPERATIONS

Selected Business Units, Brands, and Products

Ann Sacks Tile & Stone
Architectural tile
Terra cotta

Furniture
Baker Furniture
McGuire Furniture Company

Kitchen and Bath Products
Cabinets and vanities
  Canac (bathroom and kitchen cabinetry)
  Robern (lighting and mirrored bath cabinetry)
  Sanijura (vanities and other bath furniture)
Plumbing products
  Jacob Delafon (bathtubs, faucets, lavatories, and toilets)
  Kohler (bath and shower faucets, baths, glass showers
    and shower doors, kitchen and bathroom sinks and
    faucets, toilets)
  Neomediam (bathroom and kitchen plumbing)
  Kallista (bathroom and kitchen sinks and faucets)
  Sterling (bathing fixtures, faucets, sinks)

Kohler Engines
Commercial turf
Consumer lawn and garden
Industrial, construction, and commercial

Kohler Generators
Home standby
Industrial standby and prime power product line
Power System Controls
Automatic transfer switches
Generator controls

COMPETITORS

American Standard	Klaussner Furniture
Armstrong World	Group
Bassett Furniture	LADD Furniture
Black & Decker	Leggett & Platt
Briggs & Stratton	Masco
Chicago Faucet	Mueller Industries
Cooper Industries	NIBCO
Crane	Newell Rubbermaid
Dal-Tile	Premark
Dyson-Kissner-Moran	Tecumseh Products
Fortune Brands	U.S. Industries
Gerber Plumbing Fixtures	Waxman
Honda	Yamaha

HISTORICAL FINANCIALS & EMPLOYEES

Private FYE: December	Annual Growth	1989	1990	1991	1992	1993	1994	1995	1996	1997	1998
Estimated sales ($ mil.)	6.7%	1,343	1,349	1,400	1,350	1,450	1,600	1,850	2,020	2,210	2,400
Employees	2.6%	14,300	14,796	13,794	13,778	14,257	14,500	15,000	18,000	18,000	18,000

SALES HISTORY

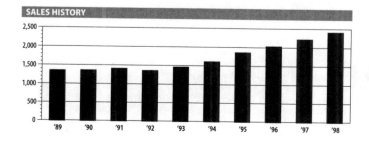

KPMG INTERNATIONAL

OVERVIEW

KPMG is taking off the gloves in its struggle for leadership in the bare-knuckle field of international accountancy. The third-largest of the Big Five accounting firms (after PricewaterhouseCoopers and Andersen Worldwide), Montvale, New Jersey-based KPMG International is forging a 21st Century identity as the technological champion in its field.

Traditionally a confederation of accounting firms based in more than 150 nations, KPMG is strengthening ties between its more than 800 offices and organizing them into two groups, KPMG Americas (North and South America and Australasia), and KPMG Europe (Europe, Africa, Asia, and the Middle East).

KPMG is the only one of the Big Five whose practice is larger outside the US.

Even more radically, KPMG plans to take its US consulting business public. KPMG, the most Internet savvy of the accounting/consulting firms, hopes that a major investment in its online-related services will distinguish it from the pack. Cisco Systems is investing about $1 billion for about 20% of the new entity (should it receive regulatory clearance). This plan, as well as KPMG's move into legal services, particularly in the UK, has raised concerns about the conflict of interest involved in auditing companies that consulting or legal groups may view as potential clients.

HISTORY

Peat Marwick was founded in 1911, when William Peat, a London accountant, met James Marwick on a westbound Atlantic crossing. University of Glasgow alumni Marwick and Roger Mitchell had formed Marwick, Mitchell & Company in New York in 1897. Peat and Marwick agreed to ally their firms temporarily, and in 1925 they merged permanently as Peat, Marwick, Mitchell, & Copartners.

In 1947 William Black became senior partner, a position he held until 1965. He guided the firm's 1950 merger with Barrow, Wade, Guthrie, one of the US's oldest firms, and built its consulting practice. Peat Marwick restructured its international practice as PMM&Co. (International) in 1972 and reformed it as Peat Marwick International in 1978.

The following year several European accounting firms led by Klynveld Kraayenhoff (the Netherlands) and Deutsche Treuhand (Germany) discussed forming an international accounting federation. Needing an American member, the European firms encouraged the merger of two American firms founded around the turn of the century, Main Lafrentz and Hurdman Cranstoun. Main Hurdman & Cranstoun soon joined the Europeans to form Klynveld Main Goerdeler (KMG), named after two of the member firms and the chairman of Deutsche Treuhand, Reinhard Goerdeler. Other members were C. Jespersen (Denmark), Thorne Riddel (Canada), Thomson McLintok (UK), and Fides Revision (Switzerland).

Peat Marwick merged with KMG in 1987 to form Klynveld Peat Marwick Goerdeler (KPMG). KPMG lost 10% of its business owing to the departure of competing client companies.

In 1990 the firm began consolidating operations, cutting the number of partners. This brought a flood of departures, which the firm attempted to stem by emphasizing increased profit per partner.

In the 1990s the Big Six fell victim to legal actions resulting from the belief that auditors should actively search for clients' accounting misdeeds instead of simply certifying the proper form of accounts. Among KPMG's problems were suits stemming from its audits of defunct S&Ls and litigation relating to the bankruptcy of Orange County, California (settled for $75 million in 1998).

Despite these setbacks, the firm continued growing; it expanded its consulting division with the acquisition of Barefoot, Marrinan & Associates, a banking consultancy, in 1996.

In 1997, after Price Waterhouse and Coopers & Lybrand announced their merger, KPMG and Ernst & Young announced one of their own. But fears that regulators would find the merger anticompetitive and that the two cultures would clash led the firms to abandon the effort in 1998.

The creation of PricewaterhouseCoopers (PwC) and competition in the consulting sides of the Big Five brought a realignment of loyalties in their separate national practices. KPMG Consulting lost its Belgian group to PwC and its French group to Computer Sciences Corporation. Its Canadian consulting group was nearly wooed away by Andersen Worldwide's audit group. (The plan was foiled by the ever-sullen Andersen Consulting group and by KPMG's promises of more money to build the business.) It was against this background that the reorganization and the alliance with Cisco Systems took place. In addition to the cash infusion, Cisco agreed to let KPMG provide installation and system management to Cisco's customers.

Chairman; Chairman and CEO, KPMG LLP:
Stephen G. Butler
CEO: Paul C. Reilly
CFO: Joseph E. Heintz
Regional Executive Partner, Americas: Lou Miramontes
Regional Executive Partner, Asia/Pacific: John Sim
Regional Executive Partner, Europe, Middle East, and Africa: Colin Holland
International Managing Partner, Assurance:
Hans de Munnik
International Managing Partner, Consulting:
Jim McGuire
International Managing Partner, Financial Advisory Services: Gary Colter
International Managing Partner, Infrastructure and Resources: Don Christiansen
International Managing Partner, Markets:
Alistair Johnston
International Managing Partner, Tax and Legal:
Hartwick Lubmann
Deputy Chairman, KPMG LLP: Robert W. Alspaugh
VC, Consulting, KPMG LLP: Randolph C. Blazer
Chief Marketing Officer, KPMG LLP:
Timothy R. Pearson
General Counsel, KPMG LLP: Claudia L. Taft
Partner, Human Resources, KPMG LLP:
Timothy P. Flynn

LOCATIONS

HQ: Burgemeester Rijnderslaan 20,
1185 MC Amstelveen, The Netherlands
Phone: +31-20-656-6700   **Fax:** +31-20-656-6777
US HQ: 345 Park Ave., New York, NY 10154
US Phone: 212-758-9700   **US Fax:** 212-758-9819
Web site: http://www.kpmg.com

PRODUCTS/OPERATIONS

Selected Areas of Industry Expertise
Banking and finance
Building and construction
Energy and natural resources
Government
Health care and life sciences
Industrial products
Information, communications, and entertainment
Insurance
Retail and consumer products
Transportation

Representative Clients
Aetna U.S. Healthcare
Apple Computer
AT&T Broadband & Internet Services
Bankers Trust
City of New York
Motorola
NBC
Oxford Health Plans
PepsiCo
Pfizer
PhyCor
Smithsonian Institution
Tenet
Wells Fargo

COMPETITORS

Andersen Worldwide	Gemini Consulting
Aon	H&R Block
Arthur D. Little	Hewitt Associates
BDO International	IBM
Bain & Company	Marsh & McLennan
Booz, Allen	McKinsey & Company
Boston Consulting	Perot Systems
Deloitte Touche Tohmatsu	PricewaterhouseCoopers
EDS	Towers Perrin
Ernst & Young	Watson Wyatt

HISTORICAL FINANCIALS & EMPLOYEES

Partnership FYE: September	Annual Growth	1990	1991	1992	1993	1994	1995	1996	1997	1998	1999
Sales ($ mil.)	9.6%	5,368	6,011	6,150	6,000	6,600	7,500	8,100	9,200	10,600	12,200
Employees	3.1%	77,300	75,000	73,488	76,200	76,200	72,000	77,000	83,500	85,300	102,000

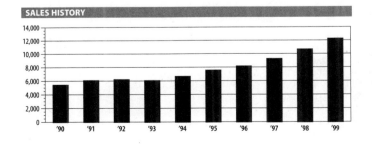

SALES HISTORY

LAND O'LAKES, INC.

OVERVIEW

Land O'Lakes makes lakes o' dairy products. Through more than 1,000 community cooperatives, Arden Hills, Minnesota-based Land O'Lakes serves 300,000 farmers and ranchers in 29 states. The cooperative — the #2 US dairy co-op, behind Dairy Farmers of America — produces packaged milk, margarine, dips, sour cream, and a variety of cheeses, including several under the Alpine Lace name. The company's oldest product, Land O'Lakes butter, is the leading US brand.

In addition to its Dairy division, the co-op's Agricultural Services division produces alfalfa seed and is the #3 livestock feed producer in the US. It also supplies members with fertilizers and chemical crop protection products. The division's offerings have evolved from low-cost feed programs to providing animal production systems to independent producers.

In response to a tight consumer packaged goods market, changes in the agriculture business, and the rapidly consolidating dairy market, Land O'Lakes is positioning itself as a national player with member co-ops coast to coast. In addition, through joint ventures, Land O'Lakes is expanding both its Dairy and Ag Services divisions at home and overseas.

HISTORY

In the old days, grocers sold butter from communal tubs and it often went bad; therefore, the widespread distribution of dairy products had to await the invention of fast, reliable transportation. By 1921 the necessary transportation was available. That year about 320 dairy farmers in Minnesota formed the Minnesota Cooperative Creameries Association and launched a membership drive with $1,375 mostly borrowed from the US Farm Bureau.

The co-op arranged joint shipments for members; imposed strict hygiene and quality standards; and aggressively marketed its sweet cream butter nationwide, packaged for the first time in the familiar box of four quarter-pound sticks. A month after the co-op's New York sales office opened, it was ordering 80 shipments a week.

Minnesota Cooperative Creameries, as part of its promotional campaigns, ran a contest in 1924 to name that butter. Two contestants offered the winning name — Land O'Lakes. The distinctive Indian Maiden logo first appeared about the same time, and in 1926 the co-op changed its name to Land O'Lakes Creameries. By 1929, when it began supplying feed, its market share approached 50%.

During WWII, civilian consumption dropped, but the co-op increased production of dried milk, which was easily transported and provided food for soldiers and newly liberated concentration camp victims.

In the 1950s and 1960s, Land O'Lakes added ice cream and yogurt producers to its membership and fought margarine makers, yet butter's market share continued to melt. The co-op diversified in 1970 through acquisitions, adding feeds and agricultural chemicals. Two years later Land O'Lakes threw in the towel and came out with its own margarine. Despite the decreasing use of butter nationally, the co-op's market share grew.

Land O'Lakes formed a marketing joint venture, Cenex/Land O'Lakes Agronomy, with fellow co-op CENEX in 1987. As health consciousness bloomed in the 1980s, Land O'Lakes launched reduced-fat products, such as Country Morning Blend (60% butter and 40% margarine) and light sour cream. However, as margarine consumption declined in the mid-1990s, the company scaled down its production and launched a line of no-fat sour cream dips. It also purchased a cheese plant in California and doubled its capacity. Land O'Lakes began ramping up its international projects at the same time: It built a feed mill in Taiwan, introduced a line of feed products in Mexico, and established feed and cheese operations in Poland.

In 1997 Land O'Lakes gained strength in the eastern US when it merged with the 3,600-member Atlantic Dairy Cooperative. It bought low-fat cheese producer Alpine Lace Brands for $60 million that year. Then Land O'Lakes firmed up the West Coast when California-based Dairyman's Cooperative Creamery Association joined in 1998. Also in 1998 the co-op formed a joint venture with Novartis Seeds, a division of drug firm Novartis, to develop specialty corn hybrids.

Cenex/Land O'Lakes Agronomy bought Terra Industries' $1.7 billion distribution business (400 farm supply stores, seed and chemical distribution operations, partial ownership of two chemical plants) in 1999.

Chairman: Stan Zylstra
President and CEO: John E. Gherty
EVP and COO, Agricultural Operations:
Duane Halverson
EVP and COO, Dairy Foods: Chris Policinski
EVP and COO, Dairy Foods: Jack Prince
Group VP and CFO: Ronald O. Ostby
VP Public Affairs: Bob Dever
VP Research, Technology, and Engineering:
David Hettinga
VP Human Resources: Jack Martin
VP and General Counsel: John Rebane
Auditors: KPMG LLP

LOCATIONS

HQ: 4001 Lexington Ave. North, Arden Hills, MN 55126
Phone: 651-481-2222 **Fax:** 651-481-2022
Web site: http://www.landolakesinc.com

PRODUCTS/OPERATIONS

Selected Products

Agricultural Supplies and Services
Animal feeds
Crop protection products
Plant food
Seeds

Dairy Products
Butter
Cheese (including Alpine Lace)
Cream
Flavored butter
Light butter
Margarine
Milk
Sour cream

COMPETITORS

ADM
AMPI
California Dairies Inc.
Cargill
Dairy Farmers of America
Darigold
Dean Foods
Foremost Farms
Kraft Foods
Marathon Cheese
Monsanto
Nabisco Holdings
Parmalat Finanziaria
Pioneer Hi-Bred
Prairie Farms Dairy
Purina Mills
Saputo Group
Schreiber Foods
Suiza Foods

HISTORICAL FINANCIALS & EMPLOYEES

Cooperative FYE: December	Annual Growth	1989	1990	1991	1992	1993	1994	1995	1996	1997	1998
Sales ($ mil.)	9.0%	2,377	2,415	2,458	2,562	2,733	2,859	3,014	3,486	4,195	5,174
Net income ($ mil.)	8.1%	34	37	54	57	47	75	121	119	95	69
Income as % of sales	—	1.4%	1.5%	2.2%	2.2%	1.7%	2.6%	4.0%	3.4%	2.3%	1.3%
Employees	3.4%	4,800	4,600	4,900	5,000	5,700	5,500	5,500	5,500	5,500	6,500

NET INCOME HISTORY

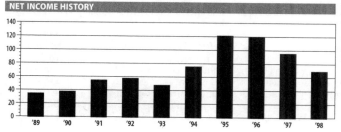

1998 FISCAL YEAR-END

Debt ratio: 30.8%
Return on equity: 10.4%
Cash ($ mil.): 4
Current ratio: 1.34
Long-term debt ($ mil.): 347

THE LEFRAK ORGANIZATION

OVERVIEW

There's a whole lotta shaking going on, and it's The Lefrak Organization that's moving the earth. The Rego Park, New York-based building firm is one of the US's largest private landlords with some 61,000 apartments in the New York boroughs and New Jersey, an additional 30,000 units under management, and millions of square feet of commercial space. The company is concentrating a new building boom on its Newport City development, a community of apartments, office towers, and stores on the waterfront in Jersey City across the Hudson River from Manhattan. Lefrak is racing to finish a 14-story office building on the site to take advantage of the strong real estate market.

Lefrak's flagship development, 5,000-unit

Lefrak City in Queens, has been home to successive waves of ethnic groups seeking a better life. The company also has holdings in oil exploration (Lefrak Oil & Gas Organization) and entertainment (Lefrak Entertainment operates LMR, the record label that launched Barbra Streisand). It also owns stage and movie theaters and produces TV, movies, and Broadway shows.

Chairman Samuel LeFrak, famed for his interpretation of the Golden Rule ("he who has the gold makes the rules"), is an active philanthropist, supporting the Guggenheim Museum. He also sponsored the oceanographic studies of Jacques Cousteau.

HISTORY

Harry Lefrak and his father, both builders, came to the US from Palestine around 1900. They began building tenements to house the flood of immigrants then pouring into New York City. In 1905 they started what is now known as The Lefrak Organization. It diversified into glass and for some time provided raw material for the workshops of Louis Comfort Tiffany. After WWI the glass factory was sold, and the company expanded into Brooklyn, where it developed housing and commercial space in Bedford-Stuyvesant, among other areas.

Samuel, Harry's son, began working in the business early, assisting tradesmen at building sites. He then attended the University of Maryland and returned to the business.

After WWII business took off, as the company began building low-cost housing. Samuel took over the company in 1948. To keep down expenses, Samuel bought clay and gypsum quarries, as well as forests, and operated his own lumber mills and cement plants, eventually achieving 70% vertical integration of his operations.

The 1950s building boom was in part spurred by new laws in New York authorizing the issue of state bonds for financing low-interest construction loans, which Lefrak used to build more than 2,000 apartments in previously undeveloped coastal sections of Brooklyn. At its peak, Lefrak turned out an apartment every 16 minutes for rents as low as $21 per room.

In 1960 Lefrak broke ground for Lefrak City, a 5,000-apartment development built on 40 acres in Queens, which featured air-conditioned units and rented for $40 per room.

The next decade brought a real estate slump

that endangered the organization's next project, Battery Park. Lefrak issued public bonds to save it. Samuel also picked up a few more properties during this period, and he capitalized the "F" in his family name but not the company name. (He later said that he did this to distinguish himself from other Lefraks at his club who had been posted for nonpayment of dues.)

Samuel's son Richard became increasingly involved in the business in the 1980s as the organization began an even bigger project — the 4,000-acre Newport City development, with 9,000 apartments and retail and commercial space.

The company bought 200 oil fields in 1994 to build up its reserves of gas and home-heating oil.

Meanwhile, Lefrak City had "turned," as its original Jewish occupants sought still greener fields. As occupancy dropped, the company relaxed its tenant screening, and the development deteriorated (it was subsequently tagged with the sobriquet "Crack City"). In the 1990s, however, it began attracting a mix of African, Jewish, and Central Asian immigrants, whose disciplined, tightly knit communities improved the development's safety and equilibrium.

Construction of the company's Newport project continued in 1997 and 1998, as the company broke ground on a new office building. Lefrak also announced plans to build a hotel on the site and has scheduled construction of another rental building in 1999. The entire development is expected to be finished in 2008, but two Manhattan stalwarts — Cigna and US Trust — have already announced plans to move employees to the Newport site.

OFFICERS

CEO: Samuel J. LeFrak
COO and CFO: Richard S. LeFrak
SVP Marketing: Edward Cortese
VP and General Counsel: Howard Boris
VP Commercial: Marsilia Boyle
VP Commercial: Irwin Granville
VP: Harrison LeFrak
VP Management: Charles Mehlman
VP Construction-Engineering: Anthony Scavo
Director Human Resources: Mitchell Ingerman
Auditors: Lewis Goldberg

LOCATIONS

HQ: 97-77 Queens Blvd., Rego Park, NY 11374
Phone: 718-459-9021 **Fax:** 718-897-0688
Web site: http://www.lefrak.com

PRODUCTS/OPERATIONS

Energy
Lefrak Oil & Gas Organization (300 properties)

Entertainment
Lefrak Entertainment Co.

Real Estate
Commercial Space (10 million sq. ft.)
Manhattan (40 W. 57th St., Gateway Plaza at Battery
Park City, James Tower)
Newport City
Queens/Brooklyn/Westchester

Residential (200,000 units)
Residential Apartments
Newport, Jersey City, Waterfront (about 10,000 units)
Presidential Plaza
Riverside
Manhattan
Gateway Plaza at Battery Park City (2,200 units)
Other
Lefrak City, Queens (5,000 units)
Mount Vernon, NY
New Brunswick, NJ

Residential Condo and Co-op Properties
Brooklyn Co-ops
Bay Ridge
Bensonhurst
Flatbush
Park Slope
Sheepshead Bay
Queens Co-ops
Elmhurst
Flushing
Forest Hills
Key Gardens
Rego Park
Woodside

Retail (7 million sq. ft.)

COMPETITORS

Alexander's
Dyson-Kissner-Moran
Helmsley
Sunoco
Tishman Realty
Trammell Crow
Trump

HISTORICAL FINANCIALS & EMPLOYEES

Private FYE: November	Annual Growth	1989	1990	1991	1992	1993	1994	1995	1996	1997	1998
Sales ($ mil.)	(0.5%)	2,875	2,900	3,100	3,200	3,200	3,100	3,300	3,500	3,400	2,750
Employees	(1.3%)	18,000	18,000	18,000	18,000	18,000	17,500	17,400	17,500	18,000	16,000

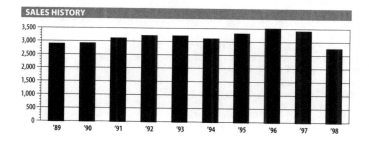

SALES HISTORY

THE LEO GROUP, INC.

OVERVIEW

The Leo Group (formerly Leo Burnett) became an advertising giant by cultivating a string of icons now known to nearly every American with an appetite and a television set. Over more than six decades, the Chicago-based company has created such characters as the Jolly Green Giant (developed for Minnesota Valley Canning, which later changed its corporate name to match the character's), the Marlboro Man, Kellogg's Tony the Tiger, and the Pillsbury Doughboy (hee-hee!!).

Today, the employee-owned agency serves a select list of about 30 clients, including Pillsbury (now parent of Green Giant), Keebler Foods, and Walt Disney. Many of its clients have been with the company for decades. The Leo Group has a network of offices in more than 70 countries, and offers a variety of specialized services through subsidiaries such as Starcom Worldwide (media buying and planning), Giant Step (interactive services), and VIGILANTE (urban marketing).

While the company has been as solid as its distinguished legacy, The Leo Group has struggled recently with the perception that the agency is staid and out of touch. It also struggles against larger rivals such as conglomerates Omnicom and Interpublic. To meet this challenge, The Leo Group has agreed to merge with MacManus Group and form a new company, BDM, with operations in 90 countries and revenues of almost $2 billion. Dentsu, Japan's #1 ad agency, will also own a minority stake in BDM.

HISTORY

In 1935 Leo Burnett left Erwin Wasey & Company, then one of the US's top ad agencies, to start his own firm. He opened his office in Chicago with eight staffers, three clients (Minnesota Valley Canning, Hoover, and Realsilk Hosiery), and a bowl of red apples on the receptionist's desk as a gesture of hospitality. Though some said Burnett would soon be selling his apples rather than giving them away, the agency opened its first office in New York in 1941. In 1944, the firm landed Pillsbury Mill's Farina account, an assignment that quickly grew to other baking products. Billings surpassed $10 million in 1947.

Shunning the flashy sophistication of many New York firms, Burnett instead tried to convey the "inherent drama" of a product. This strategy proved itself most successful with Philip Morris, which hired the agency in 1954 to boost sales of one of its minor brands — Marlboro. Burnett successfully repositioned the brand from its distinctly feminine image into one of rugged masculinity, culminating in the rollout of the Marlboro Country campaign in 1964.

By 1962 the agency had offices in Detroit, Hollywood, New York, and Toronto. That year it expanded overseas, buying an interest in British firm Legget Nicholson and Partners. In 1967 Burnett bought D. P. Brother & Co. of Detroit, gaining Oldsmobile as a client. Leo Burnett retired from management in 1967 (he died in 1971) and was succeeded by Phillip Schaff. The agency grew throughout the 1970s by improving the sales of its existing clients rather than adding many new ones. However, in the 1980s the agency adopted a slightly more aggressive approach and wrestled the McDonald's account from Needham. Still, the firm's client list remained relatively short.

In 1992 Richard Fizdale, who had worked his way up from copywriter, became chairman and CEO. A year later he turned CEO duties over to William Lynch, Burnett's president. Pressured by conglomerates such as Interpublic and Omnicom, the agency began adding services, particularly in the electronic area. In 1996 it bought an interest in Giant Step Productions to create online and Web site home pages and advertising.

In 1997 the company ousted Lynch and COO James Jenness, and Fizdale returned to the position of CEO. That year the agency lost much of McDonald's creative business after its failed "Campaign 55" promotion, but it tried to recoup by buying a 49% stake in London's cutting-edge Bartle Bogle Hegarty agency.

The next year Leo Burnett acquired Cartwright Williams, Australia's leading independent direct marketer, and entered the technology-marketing field with the acquisition of Chicago-based TFA Communications. It also called off merger talks with MacManus Group, but started negotiating a partnership with Dentsu. In 1999 Burnett shifted to a holding company structure and renamed itself The Leo Group. It renewed talks with MacManus Group and the firms agreed to merge and form a new company called BDM. Dentsu will also own a minority stake in the new firm. MacManus chairman Roy Bostock and incoming Leo Group CEO Roger Haupt will retain those positions at BDM. Also in 1999 The Leo Group won business from Scandinavian Airlines System and Delta Air Lines, its two largest worldwide airline accounts since losing United.

OFFICERS

Chairman and CEO: Richard B. Fizdale
VC and COO (CFO): Roger A. Haupt
VC and Chief Administrative Officer: Chris Kimball
VC and Chief Creative Officer: Michael B. Conrad
VC Client Services Worldwide: Kerry M. Rubie
President: James G. Oates
EVP and Chief Information Officer: Richard W. Capps
EVP and Director Research Worldwide: Josh McQueen
EVP; CEO, Starcom Worldwide: Jack M. Klues
SVP Corporate Affairs Worldwide: Walter R. Petersen
VP Human Resources: Cathy Norris
Chief Creative Officer, Leo Burnett USA:
 Cheryl R. Berman
Chairman and CEO, Leo Burnett Connaghan and May,
 Australia/New Zealand: Stan May
VC, Europe, Middle East and Africa: Reiner Erfert
Group President, Europe, Middle East, Africa, and Asia
 Pacific: Jeffrey J. Fergus
Group President, Latin America:
 Giacomo Zandomenego
Group President, North America: Linda S. Wolf
President and CEO, Leo Burnett Toronto:
 James R. McKenzie
CFO Starcom Worldwide: Frank Voris
Director Brand Planning Worldwide: Neil Cassie

LOCATIONS

HQ: 35 W. Wacker Dr., Chicago, IL 60601
Phone: 312-220-5959   **Fax:** 312-220-3299
Web site: http://www.leoburnett.com

PRODUCTS/OPERATIONS

Selected Services
Advertising
Brand consulting
Direct marketing
Event marketing
Interactive media services
Market research
Media buying
Promotional services
Public relations

Selected Clients
Allstate Insurance Cos.
Andersen Worldwide
BP Amoco
The Coca-Cola Company
Delta Air Lines
Eli Lilly & Company
Hallmark Cards, Inc.
Keebler Foods Company
Kellogg Company
Kraft Foods, Inc.
Maytag Corporation
McDonald's
Nintendo of America
Oldsmobile (a division of General Motors)
Philip Morris Incorporated
The Pillsbury Company
The Procter & Gamble Company
United Distillers North America
The Walt Disney Company

COMPETITORS

Dentsu
Grey Advertising
Interpublic Group
MacManus Group
Omnicom Group

Publicis
Saatchi & Saatchi
True North
WPP Group
Young & Rubicam

HISTORICAL FINANCIALS & EMPLOYEES

Private FYE: December	Annual Growth	1989	1990	1991	1992	1993	1994	1995	1996	1997	1998
Sales ($ mil.)	7.7%	487	538	577	560	622	678	781	866	878	950
Employees	5.2%	—	—	6,314	4,250	6,581	6,308	6,950	8,000	8,170	9,029

SALES HISTORY

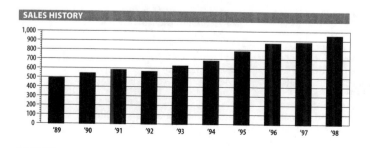

LEVI STRAUSS & CO.

OVERVIEW

Levi Strauss & Co. (LS&CO.) has been caught with its pants down in the minds of America's tastemakers: teenagers. The company that invented denim jeans is now trying to reinvent itself. San Francisco-based LS&CO. is the world's largest maker of brand-name clothing. It sells jeans, casual wear, and sportswear under the Levi's, Dockers, and Slates names.

The Levi's brand accounts for about two-thirds of LS&CO.'s business, but its historical influence in the jeans world has faded. As the jeans market became more competitive, LS&CO. spent most of the 1990s pursuing corporate enlightenment rather than following fashion — namely the baggy, wide-leg preferences of the swelling US teenage population. LS&CO., which sells more than 85% of its jeans through department stores, also failed to respond to the rising popularity of more youth- and fashion-oriented retailers. Sales and profits have fallen as a result, and the company's US market share, which topped 30% when the 1990s began, has slipped to 14%.

To undo the financial damage, LS&CO. has moved to close 29 US, Canadian, and European plants. To restore its image with the liberal-spending youth market, LS&CO. has boosted its marketing efforts in hipper venues, such as the Internet and concert halls, and it has begun designing more expensive, fashion-forward products. LS&CO. has also begun looking for executive talent from outside its ranks.

The family-owned company is controlled by chairman Robert Haas — a great-great-grandnephew of LS&CO.'s founder — and three relatives.

HISTORY

Levi Strauss arrived in New York City from Bavaria in 1847. In 1853 he moved to San Francisco to sell dry goods to the gold rushers. Shortly after, a prospector told Strauss of miners' problems in finding sturdy pants. Strauss made a pair out of canvas for the prospector; word of the rugged pants spread quickly.

Strauss continued his dry-goods business in the 1860s. During this time he switched the pants' fabric to a durable French cloth called serge de Nimes, soon known as denim. He colored the fabric with indigo dye and adopted the idea from Nevada tailor Jacob Davis of reinforcing the pants with copper rivets. In 1873 Strauss and Davis produced their first pair of waist-high overalls (later known as jeans). The pants soon became de rigueur for lumberjacks, cowboys, railroad workers, oil drillers, and farmers.

Strauss continued to build his pants and wholesaling business until he died in 1902. Levi Strauss & Co. (LS&CO.) passed to four nephews who carried on their uncle's jeans business while maintaining the company's philanthropic reputation.

After WWII, Walter Haas and Peter Haas (a fourth-generation Strauss family member) assumed leadership of LS&CO. In 1948 they ended the company's wholesaling business to concentrate on Levi's clothing. In the 1950s Levi's jeans ceased to be merely functional garments for workers: They became the uniform of American youth. In the 1960s LS&CO. added women's attire and expanded overseas.

The company went public in 1971. That year it added a women's career line and bought Koret sportswear (sold in 1984). By the mid-1980s profits declined. Peace Corps veteran-turned-McKinsey consultant Robert Haas (Walter's son) grabbed the reins at LS&CO. in 1984 and took the company private the next year. He also instilled a touchy-feely corporate culture often at odds with the bottom line.

In 1986 LS&CO. introduced Dockers casual pants. The company's sales began rising in 1991 as consumers forsook designer duds of the 1980s for more practical clothes. However, LS&CO. missed out on the birth of another trend: the split between the fashion sense of US adolescents and their Levi's-loving, baby boomer parents.

In 1996 the company introduced Slates dress slacks. That year LS&CO. bought back nearly one-third of its stock from family and employees for $4.3 billion. Grappling with slipping sales and debt from the buyout, in 1997 LS&CO. closed 11 of its 37 North American plants, laying off 6,400 workers and 1,000 salaried employees; it granted generous severance packages even to those earning minimum wage.

In 1998, LS&CO. added a third of its European plants to the closures list.

LS&CO. revealed in 1999 that it would close 11 of 22 remaining North American plants. Meanwhile, LS&CO. unleashed several new jeans brands that eschewed the company's one-style-fits-all approach of old.

In September 1999 Haas handed his CEO title to Pepsi executive Philip Marineau. An administrative shakeup soon followed.

Chairman: Robert D. Haas
CEO: Philip Marineau
SVP, Human Resources: Donna J. Goya
SVP and General Counsel: Albert F. Moreno
SVP and CFO: William B. Chiasson
President, Levi Strauss Europe, Middle East and Africa: Joe Middleton
President, Levi Strauss Asia/Pacific: John Anderson
President, Levi's (USA): James Capon
Chief Information Officer: Linda S. Glick
Director Public Affairs: Dan Chew
President, Dockers and Slates (USA): Bobbi Silten
VP, Human Resources Americas: Karen Hanna
Auditors: Arthur Andersen LLP

LOCATIONS

HQ: 1155 Battery St., San Francisco, CA 94111
Phone: 415-501-6000   **Fax:** 415-501-3939
Web site: http://www.levistrauss.com

Levi Strauss & Co. manufactures and sells its branded jeans, sportswear, and dress pants through retail locations and company-owned outlets in more than 60 countries.

1998 Sales

	% of total
The Americas	65
Europe, Middle East & Africa	29
Asia/Pacific	6
Total	**100**

PRODUCTS/OPERATIONS

Selected Brand Names
501
Dockers Classic
Dockers Equipment For Legs
Dockers K-1
Dockers Premium
L2
Red Line
Red Tab Basics
Red Tab Dry Goods
Red Tab Elesco
Silver Tab
Slates
Slates Collection
Sta-Prest
Vintage

Operating Divisions
Asia/Pacific Division
Levi Strauss Europe
Levi Strauss, the Americas
  Levi Strauss & Co. (Canada) Inc.
  Levi Strauss Argentina
  Levi Strauss Mexico
  Levi Strauss U.S.

COMPETITORS

Bugle Boy
Calvin Klein
Fruit of the Loom
Guess?
Haggar
J. C. Penney
J. Crew
NIKE
OshKosh B'Gosh
Oxford Industries
Polo
The Gap
Tommy Hilfiger
VF
Warnaco Group

HISTORICAL FINANCIALS & EMPLOYEES

Private FYE: November	Annual Growth	1989	1990	1991	1992	1993	1994	1995	1996	1997	1998
Sales ($ mil.)	5.7%	3,628	4,247	4,903	5,570	5,892	6,074	6,707	7,140	6,900	6,000
Employees	(0.4%)	31,000	31,000	32,100	34,200	36,400	36,500	37,700	37,000	37,000	30,000

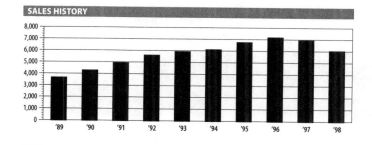

SALES HISTORY

LIBERTY MUTUAL

OVERVIEW

Businesses that want freedom from the tyranny of employees' medical bills have made Boston-based Liberty Mutual Insurance the US's leading workers' compensation insurer. The insurer also offers personal property/casualty coverage (homeowners and auto insurance), retirement products, and group and individual life insurance to local, regional, and national customers. Other services include risk-prevention management, consulting, and physical rehabilitation centers.

The 1990s have meant diversification for the firm, which has expanded its publicly traded Liberty Financial subsidiary with numerous acquisitions. Liberty Financial offers fixed and variable annuities, mutual funds, and investment advice through several asset management firms (the best known of these is Stein Roe & Farnham).

Other diversification efforts include Liberty International, which provides insurance and occupational health and safety services in such countries as Canada, Japan, Mexico, Singapore, and the UK.

HISTORY

The need for financial aid to workers injured on the job was recognized in Europe in the late 19th century but did not make its way to the US until a workers' compensation law for federal employees was passed in 1908. Massachusetts was one of the first states to enact similar legislation. Liberty Mutual was founded in Boston in 1912 to fill this newly recognized niche.

Liberty Mutual followed the fire insurance practice of taking an active part in loss prevention. It evaluated clients' premises and procedures and recommended ways to prevent accidents. The company rejected the budding industry practice of limiting medical fees, instead studying the most effective ways to reduce the long-term cost of a claim by getting the injured party back to work.

In 1942 the company acquired the United Mutual Fire Insurance Company (founded 1908, renamed Liberty Mutual Fire Insurance Company in 1949). The next year it founded a rehabilitation center in Boston to treat injured workers and to test treatments.

In the 1960s and 1970s Liberty Mutual expanded its line to include life insurance (1963), group pensions (1970), and IRAs (1975).

Seeking to increase its national presence, the company formed Liberty Northwest Insurance Corporation in 1983. It continued expanding its offerings, with new subsidiaries in commercial, personal, and excess lines and, in 1986, by moving into financial services by buying Stein Roe & Farnham (founded 1958).

The expansion/diversification strategy seemed to work. Earnings between 1984 and 1986 more than tripled. Then came the downturn: Recession was followed by a string of natural disasters, and Liberty Mutual's income fell sharply between 1986 and 1988. In 1992 and 1993 the company lost suits to Coors and Outboard Marine for failing to back the companies in environmental litigation cases.

Liberty Mutual restructured in 1994, withdrawing from the group health business and reorganizing claims operations into two units: Personal Markets and Business Markets. The next year it gained a foothold in the UK when it received permission to invest in a Lloyd's of London syndicate management company.

The company expanded its financial services operations in 1995 and 1996, merging its Liberty Financial subsidiary with the already-public Colonial Group; it also acquired American Asset Management and Newport Pacific Management.

In a soft workers' compensation market, the company tried to build its position through key market acquisitions. In 1997 Liberty Mutual acquired bankrupt workers' comp provider Golden Eagle Insurance of California; the next year the firm bought Florida's Summit Holding Southeast. Mutual funds were also on the shopping list: Purchases included Société Générale's US mutual funds unit, led by international money dean Jean-Marie Eveillard. The firm also played suitor to high-performance trust fund SIFE; the $450 million proposal was rebuffed as ungenerous. In 1998 the company was slammed by increased claims — many related to a Condé Nast Building construction accident that shut down New York City's Times Square that summer. Liberty Mutual acquired erstwhile competitor Employers Insurance of Wausau that year.

In 1999 the company bought Guardian Royal Exchange's US operations. In a new international initiative that year, Liberty Mutual bought 70% of Singapore-based insurer Citystate Holdings (to be renamed Liberty Citystate) as its foothold in Asia.

Chairman, Liberty Mutual Insurance Co. and Liberty Mutual Fire Insurance Co.: Gary L. Countryman
President and CEO: Edmund F. Kelly
EVP: John B. Conners
EVP: William G. Gourley
EVP: Gary R. Gregg
EVP: Gary P. Lia
EVP: Thomas C. Ramey
EVP: Edward G. Troy
SVP and CFO: J. Paul Condrin III
SVP: J. Michael Ashwood
SVP: James D. Barret
SVP: James A. Dupont
SVP: Robert J. Brautigam
SVP: James J. Colbert
SVP: John M. Collins
SVP: Terry L. Connor
SVP: Thomas P. Coyne
SVP: Lawrence B. Dorman
SVP: Thomas J. Driscoll
VP and Manager of Human Resources and Administration: Helen Sayles
Auditors: Ernst & Young LLP

LOCATIONS

HQ: Liberty Mutual Insurance Companies, 175 Berkeley St., Boston, MA 02117
Phone: 617-357-9500   **Fax:** 617-350-7648
Web site: http://www.libertymutual.com

PRODUCTS/OPERATIONS

Subsidiaries
Liberty International
  Liberty ART SA (Argentina)
  Liberty Citystate (Singapore)
  Liberty International Canada
  Liberty International Risk Services
  Liberty Mexico Seguros
  Liberty Mutual Insurance Company (Japan)
  Liberty Mutual Insurance Company (UK) Ltd.
  Liberty Seguros SA (Colombia)
  Paulista de Seguros (Brazil)
  Seguros Caracas (Venezuela)
Liberty Financial Companies
  The Colonial Group
  Crabbe Huson Group
  Independent Financial Marketing Group
  Keyport Life Insurance Co.
  Liberty Asset Management Co.
  Newport Pacific Management, Inc.
  Progress Investment Management Co.
  Stein Roe & Farnham
Liberty Mutual Group
  Colorado Casualty Insurance Co.
  CUNA Mutual
  Employers Insurance of Wausau
  Golden Eagle Insurance Co.
  Liberty Mutual Research Center for Safety and Health (research facility)
  Merchants and Business Men's Mutual Insurance Co.
  Montgomery Mutual Insurance Companies
  Summit Holding Southeast, Inc.

COMPETITORS

20th Century	MassMutual
AIG	MetLife
Allstate	New York Life
CIGNA	Northwestern Mutual
Charles Schwab	Progressive Corporation
Citigroup	Prudential
Fremont General	SAFECO
GenAmerica	St. Paul Companies
The Hartford	State Farm
Lincoln National	T. Rowe Price

HISTORICAL FINANCIALS & EMPLOYEES

Mutual company FYE: December	Annual Growth	1989	1990	1991	1992	1993	1994	1995	1996	1997	1998
Assets ($ mil.)	12.1%	17,924	18,836	19,704	20,216	20,544	20,644	21,791	22,690	25,230	26,254
Net income	8.6%	117	164	149	217	321	451	457	474	412	245
Income as % of assests	—	0.7%	0.9%	0.8%	1.1%	1.6%	2.2%	2.1%	2.1%	1.6%	0.9%
Employees	11.7%	—	—	—	19,000	22,000	22,000	23,000	23,000	23,000	24,000

NET INCOME HISTORY

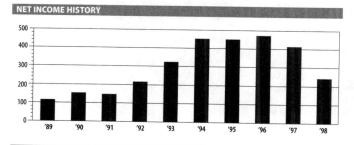

LIBERTY TRAVEL, INC.

OVERVIEW

Liberty Travel doesn't mix business and pleasure. The Ramsey, New Jersey-based travel agency is the nation's leading private leisure travel company. It is one of the only large agencies to focus almost entirely on leisure rather than business travel. The company offers trips to more than 250 destinations, including Colorado Rockies ski excursions, Alaskan cruises, and family vacations to Walt Disney World. Liberty specializes in package deals, in which various aspects of a trip (travel and hotel accommodations, meals, rental cars, tours, and activities) are sold in combinations for less than they would cost if purchased individually. The company operates about 200 offices throughout the Northeast and in Florida.

Liberty Travel conducts its business as a true retail operation. A majority of the company's offices are open seven days a week. Its agents rely entirely on commission, and the company stresses salesmanship, providing a comprehensive training program that includes computer training as well as "vacation class," which cover products and customer service. The agency is also redesigning its offices to be more enticing to clients. (In order to keep costs low, Liberty manufactures its own office furnishings.) In addition, the company is in the midst of an aggressive acquisition program in which it is looking for agencies to buy within a 10-mile radius of existing Liberty offices. Unlike most travel agencies, Liberty does not franchise; it owns all of its offices.

Liberty Travel's GOGO Worldwide Vacations division offers wholesale packages to other travel agencies through some 90 offices across the US.

HISTORY

Gilbert Haroche and Fred Kassner began Liberty Travel in 1951 in New York City. From the beginning, the company was unusual. Offices were open from 9 a.m. to 9 p.m. Monday through Friday and from 10 a.m. to 5 p.m. Saturdays and Sundays, unlike most travel agencies, which kept somewhat closer to bankers' hours. At first Haroche and Kassner offered package trips to local resorts, but soon they began encouraging their clients to go to Miami, even in the hottest months. The two men were successful in getting hotel owners to guarantee them rooms in the peak season if they could fill the rooms at other times. They used the term "package trip" to cover not only the rooms but also sightseeing tours and rental cars, combining vacation elements at a lower price than if they had been purchased individually. They also began booking airplane seats in volume, and soon were offering "deluxe economy vacations," vacation packages with upscale accommodations at discount prices that combined airfare and hotel room rates.

GOGO Worldwide Vacations began in 1955 as GOGO Tours, with packages to Florida and Puerto Rico. The company prided itself on offering affordable vacations to the average working family. As disposable income grew, GOGO added the Bahamas and the Caribbean and eventually included other US, Canadian, and European destinations, as well as trips to South America and parts of Asia.

During the intense competition and fare wars of the 1980s, Liberty joined other travel agencies in charging fees for canceled or revised itineraries. The company also made an early foray into self-ticketing by installing video-display kiosks in New York City shopping centers.

GOGO began upgrading its "Kmart of travel" image in 1995. Since GOGO Tours conjured up images of escorted tours, the company changed its name to GOGO Worldwide Vacations to reflect the more global — and upscale — nature of its packages. The next year it added a hotel rating system and introduced FIRST (Future in Reservation Systems Technology), a real-time booking system available to agents 24 hours a day, seven days a week; FIRST eventually is expected to account for more than 35% of volume.

In 1996 Liberty announced plans to open 15 offices a year, a goal it achieved for the next two years. It received more than 1,000 inquiries after announcing it wanted to buy a number of small- to medium-sized travel agencies. In 1997 GOGO began its Intimate Hotels of the Caribbean showcase of some 170 smaller, independent hotels, inns, and guest houses in 28 locations in the Bahamas, Belize, Bermuda, and the Caribbean. Following the trend toward sales over the Internet, both Liberty and GOGO began in 1998 to allow customers to browse and book vacations through their Web site.

Co-founder Fred Kassner died in late 1998.

President and CEO: Gilbert Haroche
SVP Finance: Richard Cowlan
SVP Marketing: Michelle Kassner
VP, GOGO Worldwide Vacations: Mike Norton
VP Information Services: Bill Hughes
VP Strategic Planning: Orest Rusynko
VP Sales: Cathy Peleaz
Director of Human Resources: Patt Harmes

LOCATIONS

HQ: 69 Spring St., Ramsey, NJ 07446
Phone: 201-934-3500   **Fax:** 201-934-3651
Web site: http://www.libertytravel.com

Liberty Travel has about 200 offices, primarily on the East Coast. GOGO Worldwide Vacations, its sister company, has about 90 offices in major cities throughout the US.

Selected Destinations

Bahamas	Cozumel
Belize	Huatulco
Bermuda	Manzanillo
Canada	Puerto Vallarta
Alberta	US
British Columbia	California
Quebec	Colorado
Caribbean	Florida
Aruba	Hawaii
Barbados	Maine
Cayman Islands	Nevada
Dominican Republic	New Mexico
Jamaica	New York
Puerto Rico	Pennsylvania
St. John	South Carolina
St. Lucia	Texas
St. Maarten	Utah
St. Martin	Vermont
St. Thomas	Virginia
Costa Rica	Wyoming
Mexico	
Acapulco	
Cancun	

PRODUCTS/OPERATIONS

Selected Products and Services
Activities and entertainment
Cruises
Domestic and foreign destinations
Family vacations
Honeymoons
Rental cars
Reservation confirmation
Ski trips
Tours
Vacation planning

COMPETITORS

AAA
Accor
American Express
Carlson Wagonlit
Carnival
Empress Travel
Globus/Cosmos
Pleasant Holidays
Rosenbluth International
Royal Caribbean Cruises
WorldTravel

HISTORICAL FINANCIALS & EMPLOYEES

Private FYE: December	Annual Growth	1989	1990	1991	1992	1993	1994	1995	1996	1997	1998
Sales ($ mil.)	3.3%	—	—	—	—	—	—	—	1,236	1,297	1,320
Employees	0.0%	—	—	—	—	—	—	—	—	1,700	1,800

SALES HISTORY

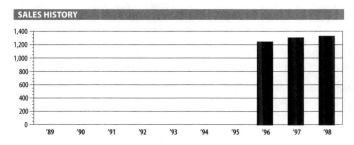

LIFESTYLE FURNISHINGS

OVERVIEW

LifeStyle Furnishings International wants consumers to choose their sofas the same way they choose their clothing: to make a fashion statement. The High Point, North Carolina-based furniture maker has eight principal brands, including the moderately priced Lexington and Universal lines and the more upscale Henredon and Drexel Heritage lines. Stressing style, it also sells furniture bearing the names of designers better known for clothing (such as Ralph Lauren and Alexander Julian), celebrities (Arnold Palmer); and institutions (Smithsonian). The #2 maker of home furnishings in the US (behind Furniture Brands International), LifeStyle sells bedroom, living room, and dining room furniture, plus lamps, mirrors, outdoor furniture, and decorative fabric. Furniture represents about 88% of sales; fabric accounts for the rest.

The company sells its products through some 22,000 independent retailers, 1,500 galleries within stores, department stores, specialty shops, and more than 80 independent stores that sell only LifeStyle products. Its products are also sold through 13 company-owned Beacon Hill designer-exclusive showrooms and through contract distribution channels.

Building supply manufacturer Masco holds a 15% stake in LifeStyle, managers own about 21%, and a Citibank venture capital unit controls the rest.

HISTORY

LifeStyle Furnishings International was the result of remodeling by its former owner, Michigan-based Masco. The leading US maker of faucets, kitchen cabinets, and other home products, Masco branched into the furniture business in 1986. The company brought brand recognition to the home improvement market (it introduced Delta and Peerless faucets) and saw a similar opportunity in furniture. Masco believed customers would select furniture by name to reflect their individual tastes and styles. The company thought it could quickly make a mark in the fragmented market.

Masco started by buying, rather than building, furniture companies, most in North Carolina. In 1986 it purchased the first member of its furniture family, Henredon, a well-known manufacturer of medium- and high-priced wood and upholstered furniture. Within months Masco scooped up Drexel Heritage. The following year it bought Lexington Furniture. (Masco spent $1 million on computerized routing machines to eliminate a six-month backlog of furniture orders at Lexington.) In 1989 the company took the top spot in the US furniture industry with its $550 million acquisition of Universal Furniture, the #1 supplier of dining room furniture. It also began signing big-name designers (Alexander Julian, artist Bob Timberlake, and others) to create furniture lines. Masco maintained the brands' identities and sought ways to strengthen the group, such as through added buying power.

Trying to create a niche, Masco started its own furniture brand, Lineage, aimed at the middle-income customer. Unveiled in 1991, the line contained eclectic pieces to fit certain lifestyles: "casual living," "gracious living," and "special places." But Lineage fell flat, in part because the custom designs turned out to be too expensive and too unusual for the middle market. Meanwhile, furniture competitors saw Masco as an arrogant intruder that never understood the furniture industry.

On the heels of its divestitures of other non-core interests and disappointed that its furniture division never earned the anticipated profit margin, Masco cleaned house again in 1996. It sold off the furniture unit as LifeStyle Furnishings International for $1.1 billion — a half-billion-dollar loss — to a group of investors led by a venture capital arm of Citibank. But Masco did not cut the apron strings completely. It retained a 15% stake in the company, and Wayne Lyon, who had been Masco's president and COO, left to lead the venture, planning to continue building brand recognition and to accelerate the manufacturing cycle.

The company restructured in 1997 and 1998, closing about 10 manufacturing and distribution plants and laying off 5,000 employees (about 15% of its workforce), mostly from its Universal Furniture operations in Asia.

In 1998 LifeStyle moved its headquarters from Thomasville to High Point, North Carolina. The company filed to go public that year but opted to hold off on an IPO until market conditions become more comfy. LifeStyle restructured some of its operations to reduce order-to-ship times and inventories in 1998 and 1999.

OFFICERS

Chairman, President, and CEO: Wayne B. Lyon, age 66,
$685,731 pay
EVP Operations: Donald L. Barefoot, age 44,
$429,900 pay
EVP: Alan D. Cole, age 49, $429,900 pay
VP, General Counsel, and Secretary:
Douglas C. Barnard, age 40, $227,027 pay
VP Human Resources: William J. Frakes
VP, Treasurer, and CFO: Ronald J. Hoffman, age 54,
$235,335 pay
Auditors: PricewaterhouseCoopers LLP

LOCATIONS

HQ: LifeStyle Furnishings International Ltd.,
4000 Lifestyle Ct., High Point, NC 27265
Phone: 336-878-7000 **Fax:** 336-878-7015

LifeStyle Furnishings International makes and
distributes its products at about 70 facilities in North
America, Asia, and Europe.

1998 Sales

	$ mil.	% of total
US	1,853	93
Pacific Rim	87	4
Europe & other regions	67	3
Total	**2,007**	**100**

PRODUCTS/OPERATIONS

1998 Sales

	$ mil.	% of total
Fine furniture	1,876	88
Fabric	268	12
Adjustments	(137)	—
Total	**2,007**	**100**

Selected Products

Accent items
Bedroom sets
Chairs
Dining room sets
Family room sets
Home entertainment centers
Home furnishings fabrics
Home office case goods
Lamps
Living room sets
Mirrors
Outdoor furniture
Recliners
Sleeper sofas
Sofas
Tables

Selected Brands

Home Furnishings	Fabrics
Benchcraft	Ametex
Berkline	Beacon Hill
Drexel Heritage	Ramm, Son & Crocker
Henredon	Robert Allen
La Barge	Sunbury
Lexington	
Maitland-Smith	
Universal	

COMPETITORS

Ashley Furniture
Industries
Bassett Furniture
Bush Industries
Chromcraft Revington
DMI Furniture
Ethan Allen
F. Schumacher
Flexsteel
Furniture Brands
International

Klaussner Furniture
Group
Knoll
LADD Furniture
La-Z-Boy
O'Sullivan Industries
P/Kaufman
Sauder Woodworking
Stanley Furniture

HISTORICAL FINANCIALS & EMPLOYEES

Private FYE: December	Annual Growth	1989	1990	1991	1992	1993	1994	1995	1996	1997	1998
Sales ($ mil.)	2.6%	—	—	—	—	1,764	1,898	1,993	1,997	1,969	2,007
Net income ($ mil.)	—	—	—	—	—	(26)	(24)	(16)	7	(22)	71
Income as % of sales	—	—	—	—	—	—	—	—	0.3%	—	3.5%
Employees	0.0%	—	—	—	—	—	—	—	—	30,000	30,000

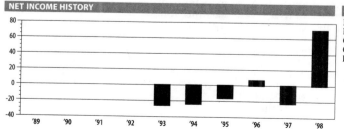

NET INCOME HISTORY

1998 FISCAL YEAR-END
Debt ratio: 38.9%
Return on equity: 15.2%
Cash ($ mil.): 8
Current ratio: 2.91
Long-term debt ($ mil.): 312

LITTLE CAESAR ENTERPRISES, INC.

OVERVIEW

I saw, I called, they came (with pizzas). Headquartered in Detroit, Little Caesar Enterprises' pizza chain boasts roughly 4,500 restaurants in a dozen countries, ranking it #3 in size behind TRICON's Pizza Hut (#1) and Domino's (#2). Little Caesar is part of Ilitch Ventures, a company formed in 1999 to oversee the businesses owned by Mike and Marian Ilitch. Among Ilitch Ventures' other holdings are the NHL's Detroit Red Wings, Major League Baseball's Detroit Tigers, and indoor soccer team the Detroit Rockers.

Little Caesar has made its mark on the pizza world through its bold and wacky advertising, most notably for its two-for-one "Pizza! Pizza!" deal. But the discount pizza aspect of its reputation has translated into slumping sales. To add insult to injury, the company is also facing new competition from up-and-comer Papa John's (the #4 US pizza chain). Little Caesar has reacted by launching a campaign to emphasize quality. It has also temporarily closed some 300 stores in markets such as Dallas and Baltimore so that it can remodel the locations and test drive-thrus. The formation of Ilitch Ventures also represented a departure for the Ilitch family: It marked the first time the family named an outside board of directors. A non-family member, Richard Peters, was also appointed Ilitch Ventures' CEO.

HISTORY

In 1959 Michael and Marian Ilitch sank $10,000 of their savings into their first pizza operation in Garden City, Michigan, a Detroit suburb. Michael, the son of Macedonian immigrants, wanted to name the operation Pizza Treat, but Marian suggested that the name reflect his behavior (like a little Caesar). They opened a second location in 1961, and the next year they sold their first franchise.

Little Caesar grew to more than 50 outlets during the 1960s. In 1974 the company initiated its two-for-one marketing concept. (It coined the phrase "Pizza! Pizza!" in 1979.) Little Caesar installed drive-through windows at its quick-serve locations and a pizza conveyor oven that increased pizza production in 1997.

By 1980 there were 226 Little Caesar units. During the 1980s the chain opened its first college campus restaurant, at the University of Oklahoma, and its first hospital restaurant, at Mt. Carmel Mercy Hospital in Detroit. The 500th Little Caesar outlet was established by 1984; two years later there were 1,000. Sales took off exponentially after a national ad campaign in 1988.

Profits from pizza sales allowed the Ilitchs to expand the scope of their operations. In 1982 they acquired the Detroit Red Wings hockey team for $8 million and reopened the renovated, 4,804-seat Fox Theatre in downtown Detroit as part of a $50 million complex that serves as the company's headquarters.

In 1985 the company formed Little Caesars Love Kitchen, a not-for-profit restaurant on wheels that delivers pizzas donated by local franchise owners to soup kitchens and shelters in the US and Canada.

Mike Ilitch fulfilled a lifelong dream in 1992 by acquiring the Detroit Tigers from Domino's magnate Tom Monaghan. (Ilitch had played on a Tiger farm team from 1952 to 1955 until a leg injury sidelined him.) In a joint venture with Kmart, the company opened 400 Pizza Stations inside Kmart stores that year. The alliance was expanded in 1997 when the two companies agreed to open Little Caesar outlets in an additional 1,000 Kmart stores.

Little Caesar began providing delivery from many of its stores in 1995, but when the service increased their costs, many franchisees dropped deliveries (some continue to deliver). In 1996 the company opened the first of 50 planned Little Caesar units in Wal-Mart stores and added such items as turkey, stuffing, and mashed potatoes to the menu.

In 1998, amid declining sales and franchisee complaints, Little Caesar brought in a new advertising agency (True North's Bozell) and implemented a plan to emphasize quality. It also announced a makeover plan for its stores. A class-action lawsuit brought by franchisees claiming that Blue Line Distribution, a Little Caesar subsidiary, sold food to them at inflated prices was dismissed later that year.

Bringing in outside management for the first time, in 1999 the Ilitchs formed Ilitch Ventures, a holding company that oversees their businesses. Little Caesar observed its 40th anniversary that year, but sagging sales put a damper on the celebration.

OFFICERS

Chairman and CEO: Michael Ilitch
VC: Marian Ilitch
VC: Denise Ilitch
COO: Harsha V. Agadi
CFO: James Weissenborn
VP Corporate Communications: Sue Sherbow
VP Human Resources: Darrel Snygg
Director of Risk Management: C. Michael Healy

LOCATIONS

HQ: 2211 Woodward Ave., Detroit, MI 48201
Phone: 313-983-6000   **Fax:** 313-983-6494
Web site: http://www.littlecaesars.com

Little Caesar Enterprises has restaurants in Aruba, Canada, the Czech Republic, the Dominican Republic, Ecuador, Egypt, Guam, Guatemala, Honduras, Iceland, Japan, the Philippines, Puerto Rico, Slovakia, South Korea, Turkey, and the US.

PRODUCTS/OPERATIONS

Selected Menu Items
Antipasto
Caesar salad
Crazy bread
Crazy sauce
Italian cheese bread
Pizza (small, medium, large, extra large, giant, and by the slice)
Soft drinks
Sub sandwiches

COMPETITORS

Burger King
CEC Entertainment
CKE Restaurants
Domino's Pizza
Godfather's Pizza
LDB Corp
McDonald's
Papa John's
Pizza Hut
Pizza Inn
Round Table Pizza
Sbarro
Subway
Uno Restaurant
Wendy's

HISTORICAL FINANCIALS & EMPLOYEES

Subsidiary FYE: December	Annual Growth	1989	1990	1991	1992	1993	1994	1995	1996	1997	1998
Sales ($ mil.)	(0.9%)	—	—	—	—	—	—	621	617	619	605
Employees	—	—	—	—	—	—	—	—	—	—	90,000

SALES HISTORY

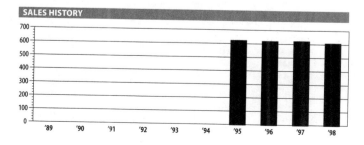

Little Caesars

L.L. BEAN, INC.

OVERVIEW

Although Leon Leonwood Bean didn't live in a shoe, he did make his living by selling them. Headquartered in Freeport, Maine, L.L. Bean was the first national mail-order house (and now the largest) to specialize in outdoor goods (such as the original Maine Hunting Shoe, which started the company). L.L. Bean publishes 50 catalogs a year and operates its flagship retail store on Main Street in Freeport (which attracts 3.5 million visitors annually and is open 24 hours a day, 365 days a year). It also sells its wares through 10 outlet stores in the US, 20-plus stores in Japan, and through its Web site. The company offers more than 16,000 items ranging from outdoor apparel to sporting goods to household furnishings, most of which carry the L.L. Bean label. It makes more than 300 of its products (such as shoes, tote bags, luggage) in Maine.

L.L. Bean's famous customer service is exemplified by its liberal return policies and perpetual replacement of the rubber soles of its Maine Hunting Shoe. The company also offers seminars and events on such topics as fly fishing, sea kayaking, and outdoor photography. Faced with intense competition from rivals such as Lands' End, L.L. Bean plans to grow by adding full-price retail stores, including a 75,000-sq.-ft. store in the Washington, DC, area. It also has launched Freeport Studio, a more fashion-conscious women's catalog.

The company is controlled by the family of its founder.

HISTORY

Leon Leonwood Bean started out as a storekeeper in Freeport, Maine. Tired of wet, leaky boots, he experimented with various remedies and in 1911 came up with the Maine Hunting Shoe, a boot with rubber soles and feet and leather uppers. It became his most famous product.

From its outset in 1912, Bean's company was a mail-order house. The first batch of boots was a disaster: Almost all of them leaked. But Bean's willingness to correct his product's defects quickly, at his own expense, saved the company.

Maine's hunting licensing system, implemented in 1917, provided the company with a mailing list of affluent recreational hunters in the Northeast, and that year Bean opened a showroom to accommodate the customers stopping by his Freeport workshop.

Bean cultivated the image of the folksy Maine guide, offering durable, comfortable, weather-resistant clothes and reliable camping supplies. In 1920 Bean built a store on Main Street in Freeport. L.L. Bean continued to grow and add products, even during the Depression, and sales reached $1 million in 1937.

During WWII Bean helped design the boots used by the US military, and his company manufactured them, thus remaining afloat as the war years and rationing brought cutbacks in materials and outdoor activities. He began keeping the retail store open 24 hours a day in 1951, noting that he had "thrown away the keys." Bean added a women's department three years later.

Sales rose to $2 million in the early 1960s and were at $4.8 million when Bean died in 1967 at age 94. (He had resisted growing the business bigger, saying, "I'm eating three meals a day; I can't eat four.") The new president was Bean's grandson Leon Gorman, who had started with L.L. Bean in 1960. His early attempts at updating the mailing operations (mailing labels typed by hand and correspondence kept in cardboard boxes) had been vetoed by his grandfather. Gorman brought in new people and made improvements, including automating the mailing systems, improving the manufacturing systems, and targeting new, nonsporting markets (such as women's casual clothes).

L.L. Bean continued its transition by targeting more of its classic customer profile — upper-middle-class college graduates — and sales grew about 20% annually for most of the 1980s. By 1989, however, sales had slowed and growth flattened as the national economy slumped and imitators carried away market share.

Unsolicited catalog orders had been coming in from Japan since the late 1980s, so in 1992 L.L. Bean began a joint venture with SEIYU and Matsushita Electric Industrial. Their first store opened that year (the company opened a catalog and service center in Japan in 1995). L.L. Kids began in 1993.

In 1996 the company began an online shopping service. Sparked by the success of its L.L. Kids division, which grew 300% in four years, the company opened a separate children's store in Freeport the next year. In 1999 L.L. Bean introduced Freeport Studio, a more fashion-forward catalog for women, and announced plans to begin opening full-price retail outlets in the US.

President and CEO: Leon A. Gorman
SVP Advertising and Direct Marketing:
Chris McCormick
SVP Operations: Bob Paquin
SVP Finance and Administration: Lee Surace
VP Sources: Rol Fessenden
VP Total Quality and Human Resources: Bob Peixotto
SVP and General Manager Retail Stores: Bill Shea
Auditors: PricewaterhouseCoopers LLP

LOCATIONS

HQ: Casco St., Freeport, ME 04033
Phone: 207-865-4761   **Fax:** 207-552-6821
Web site: http://www.llbean.com

PRODUCTS/OPERATIONS

Selected Catalogs
L.L. Bean
L.L. Kids (children's wear and accessories)
Outdoors (seasonal outdoor wear and accessories)
Fly Fishing (equipment, outer wear, and accessories)
Traveler (clothing, luggage, and accessories)
Home (linens, pillows, and decorating)
Corporate Sales (custom embroidered clothing
 and luggage)
Outdoor Discovery Schools (classes and symposiums)
Freeport Studio (fashionable women's apparel
 and accessories)

Selected Products
Home and garden accessories
Outdoor classes
Outer wear
Men's, women's, and children's casual apparel
Sports gear and apparel
Shoes and boots
Travel apparel and luggage

COMPETITORS

American Eagle Outfitters
American Retail
Bass Pro Shops
Brylane
Cabela's
Coldwater Creek
Coleman
Columbia Sportswear
Dayton Hudson
Dillard's
Federated
J. C. Penney
J. Crew
J. Jill Group
Johnson Worldwide
Lands' End
Levi Strauss
Lost Arrow
May
Montgomery Ward
Nautica Enterprises
North Face
Orvis Company
OshKosh B'Gosh
REI
Sears
Spiegel
Sports Authority
Sportsman's Guide
Talbots
The Gap
The Limited
Timberland
Venator Group

HISTORICAL FINANCIALS & EMPLOYEES

Private FYE: February	Annual Growth	1990	1991	1992	1993	1994	1995	1996	1997	1998	1999
Sales ($ mil.)	6.3%	615	617	632	743	867	976	1,078	1,040	1,068	1,070
Employees	2.5%	3,200	3,200	3,300	3,500	3,500	3,800	3,800	3,500	3,600	4,000

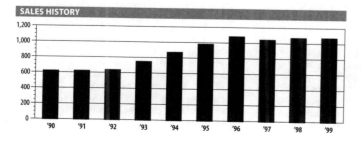

SALES HISTORY

L.L.Bean

LONG JOHN SILVER'S

OVERVIEW

Ahoy, matey! Long John Silver's may be the biggest pirate in the quick-service seafood ocean, but its galleon came close to sinking during the 1990s when the financially seasick company didn't have enough loot to cover its debts. On the verge of being plundered, the Lexington, Kentucky-based company was swabbing its deck with Chapter 11 bankruptcy notices when landlubber A&W Restaurants came to its rescue in 1999. A&W bought the chain, created holding company Yorkshire Global Restaurants, and now both Long John Silver's and A&W are Yorkshire subsidiaries.

Struggling to regain its sea legs, the Long John Silver's chain spans more than 1,270 franchised or company-owned restaurants across the US and Singapore. Each week, nearly 4 million hungry seafood fans set sail for its nautical-themed restaurants to feast on menu items such as batter-dipped fish, chicken, clams, shrimp, sandwiches, salads, and desserts.

Long John Silver's is planning to expand internationally and also is branching into co-branding with other restaurants.

HISTORY

Long John Silver's traces its roots to Jerome Lederer's White Tavern Shoppe hamburger stand, which opened in Shelbyville, Kentucky, in 1929. Lederer had amassed 13 White Tavern Shoppes by WWII, but shortages in supplies and employees caused by the war prompted the closing of 10 locations.

In 1946 Lederer founded Jerrico Inc. and established Jerry's Five and Dime, a Lexington, Kentucky-based restaurant that offered 15-cent roast beef sandwiches. The following year Jerry's Five and Dime replaced its unsuccessful roast beef sandwiches with hamburgers.

Jerrico was one of the first companies to expand its operations through franchising; by 1957 there were seven Jerry's restaurants. Throughout the 1960s the company experimented with a variety of restaurant concepts, including sandwiches (Lott's), full-service seafood (Davy's Dock), general full-service dining (Governor's Table), and Spanish food (Don Q's). Lederer died in 1963, and Jerrico's CEO Warren Rosenthal became the company's owner.

In 1969 Jerrico went public. Also that year Rosenthal suggested a quick-service seafood restaurant as an alternative to the pizza, hamburger, and fried chicken fast-food chains. Jerrico established Long John Silver's Fish & Chips (inspired by Robert Louis Stevenson's pirate character from *Treasure Island*).

Long John Silver's cast a wide net and had about 200 restaurants across the US by the end of 1971. Two years later the chain changed its name to Long John Silver's Seafood Shoppes to show that it served more than fish and chips. By the end of the 1970s, Long John Silver's had 1,000 restaurants (about half franchised), and by the mid-1980s the chain accounted for 75% of Jerrico's sales.

In the late 1980s a recession and the high price of fish led to reduced earnings for the 1,500-unit Long John Silver's chain. The company was bought out by senior management and two New York investment firms (Castle Harlan and DJS-Inverness) for $620 million in 1989. Jerrico sold its other restaurant chains, and the company took the name Long John Silver's Restaurants. Rosenthal departed the company.

In the early 1990s Long John Silver's began offering broiled and grilled fare for health-conscious consumers and added drive-through windows at some locations. Despite efforts to lure new customers, the restaurant chain experienced flat sales during this time, primarily because of increased competition from non-seafood chains.

The company expanded into nontraditional locations in 1993 when it established a kiosk in Louisville, Kentucky's General Electric plant. It continued opening kiosks over the next several years, mostly on college campuses.

In 1994 Triarc, parent of Arby's fast-food restaurants, announced plans to buy Long John's, but the deal eventually fell through. Former Kentucky Fried Chicken president John Cranor was appointed CEO in 1996.

Still drowning in debt left over from the 1989 LBO, in 1996 Long John Silver's restructured its debt, closed three divisional offices, and jettisoned 130 employees. The following year it shuttered more than 130 restaurants.

In 1998 the company filed for bankruptcy. After A&W Restaurants acquired Long John Silver's in 1999, it created holding company Yorkshire Global Restaurants, and both chains became Yorkshire subsidiaries. A&W chairman and CEO Sidney Feltenstein replaced John Cranor as Long John Silver's CEO. The company closed 28 underperforming stores that same year.

Chairman and CEO: Sidney J. Feltenstein
President and COO: Ron Powell
SVP, Controller, and Chief Accounting Officer:
  Mark Plummer
SVP Franchise Operations: Alan Caldwell
SVP Human Resources: Michael Allen
SVP Marketing: Kevin Armstrong
SVP Procurement: Rick Jenkins
SVP Product and Operation Processes: Mark Sievers
SVP and Treasurer: Gregory M. Jasko
SVP, Secretary, and General Counsel: Forrest Ragsdale

LOCATIONS

HQ: Long John Silver's Restaurants, Inc.,
  Kincaid Towers, 300 W. Vine St.,
  Lexington, KY 40508
Phone: 606-388-6000   **Fax:** 606-388-6363
Web site: http://www.ljsilvers.com

PRODUCTS/OPERATIONS

Selected Menu Items

Baked fish	Desserts
Batter-dipped fish	Salads
Breaded fish	Sandwiches
Chicken	Shrimp
Clams	

COMPETITORS

AFC Enterprises	Jack in the Box
Advantica Restaurant	Landry's Seafood
Group	McDonald's
Arthur Treacher's	Shoney's
Boston Chicken	Sonic
Burger King	Subway
CKE Restaurants	TRICON
Checkers Drive-In	Triarc
Chick-fil-A	Wendy's
Dairy Queen	Whataburger

HISTORICAL FINANCIALS & EMPLOYEES

Subsidiary FYE: June	Annual Growth	1990	1991	1992	1993	1994	1995	1996	1997	1998	1999
Sales ($ mil.)	(7.0%)	—	—	830	628	642	646	634	583	500	500
Employees	(5.2%)	—	—	—	19,245	18,100	18,000	18,500	18,500	13,462	14,000

SALES HISTORY

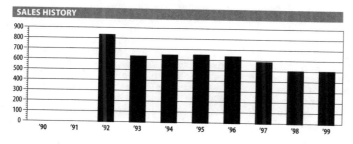

MACANDREWS & FORBES

OVERVIEW

Ron Perelman banks on glamour and thrift. The cigar-smoking financier's New York City-based MacAndrews & Forbes Holdings owns 83% of Revlon (cosmetics) and a 34% stake in the nation's #2 thrift, Golden State Bancorp. The company also has major stakes in M&F Worldwide (licorice extract), Panavision (motion picture cameras), and Sunbeam (small appliances and Coleman camping gear).

Perelman had a passing fancy with being a media marvel, but lately he has been stoked on improving his cash position and paying down debt — hence his IPO of Revlon (1996), the sale of The Coleman Company to Sunbeam (1998), and the pending sale of two of Revlon's noncore units. He made a hefty profit when he sold his Mafco Consolidated Group's stake in Consolidated Cigar Holdings to French tobacco manufacturer Société Nationale d'Exploitation Industrielle des Tabacs et Allumettes (Seita) in 1999.

HISTORY

Ron Perelman grew up working in his father's Philadelphia-based conglomerate, Belmont Industries, but he left at the age of 35 to seek his fortune in New York. In 1978 he bought 40% of jewelry store operator Cohen-Hatfield Industries. The next year Cohen-Hatfield bought a minority stake in MacAndrews & Forbes (licorice flavoring). Cohen-Hatfield acquired MacAndrews & Forbes in 1980.

Two years later MacAndrews & Forbes bought 82% of Technicolor, a motion picture processor (sold 1988). In 1984 Perelman reshuffled his assets to create MacAndrews & Forbes Holdings, which acquired control of Pantry Pride, a Florida-based supermarket chain, in 1985. Pantry Pride then bought Revlon for $1.8 billion with the help of convicted felon Michael Milken. After Perelman acquired Revlon, he added several other cosmetics vendors, including Max Factor and Yves Saint Laurent's fragrance and cosmetic lines.

In 1988 MacAndrews & Forbes agreed to invest $315 million in five failing Texas savings and loans (S&Ls), which Perelman combined and named First Gibraltar (sold to BankAmerica, now Bank of America, in 1993). The next year MacAndrews & Forbes bought The Coleman Company, a maker of outdoor equipment.

With a growing reputation for buying struggling companies, revamping them, and then selling them at a higher price, Perelman bought Marvel Entertainment Group (Marvel Comics) in 1989 and took it public in 1991. That year he sold Revlon's Max Factor and Betrix units to Procter & Gamble for over $1 billion.

MacAndrews & Forbes acquired 37.5% of TV infomercial producer Guthy-Renker and SCI Television's seven stations and merged them to create New World Television. That company was combined with TV syndicator Genesis Entertainment and TV production house New World Entertainment to create New World Communications Group, which Perelman took public in 1994. That year MacAndrews & Forbes and partner Gerald J. Ford bought Ford Motor's First Nationwide, the US's fifth-largest S&L at that time.

Subsidiaries Mafco Worldwide and Consolidated Cigar Holdings merged with Abex (aircraft parts) to create Mafco Consolidated Group in 1995. Also that year New World and Hachette Filipacchi teamed up to buy entertainment magazine *Premiere*.

Following diminishing comic sales, Perelman placed Marvel in bankruptcy in 1996. He lost control of the struggling company the next year after a federal judge ruled that Marvel bondholders could foreclose on the 80% of company stock that backed their bonds, allowing the bondholders (led by corporate raider Carl Icahn) to oust the board.

Also in 1997 First Nationwide bought California thrift Cal Fed Bancorp for $1.2 billion. In addition, Perelman sold New World to Rupert Murdoch's News Corp. and announced plans to refinance Revlon's $1.15 billion debt. He then bought the 15% of Mafco Consolidated that he didn't already own for $15 million.

In 1998 Perelman orchestrated a $1.8 billion deal in which First Nationwide merged with Golden State Bancorp to form the US's second-largest thrift, retaining the Golden State Bancorp name. Sunbeam bought Perelman's stake in Coleman that year, making Perelman a major Sunbeam shareholder. Also in 1998 MacAndrews & Forbes bought a 72% stake in Panavision (movie camera maker, later increased to 91%), invested in WeddingChannel.com, and sold its 64% stake in Consolidated Cigar to French tobacco giant Seita (netting Perelman a smoking $350 million profit).

Still burdened by debt, Revlon announced in 1999 that it would sell its professional products and Latin American noncore brands.

OFFICERS

Chairman and CEO: Ronald O. Perelman, age 56
VC: Donald G. Drapkin, age 51
VC: Howard Gittis
SVP: James T. Conroy

LOCATIONS

HQ: MacAndrews & Forbes Holdings Inc.,
  35 E. 62nd St., New York, NY 10021
Phone: 212-688-9000   **Fax:** 212-572-8400

PRODUCTS/OPERATIONS

Selected Holdings
Golden State Bancorp (34%, #2 US thrift)
Mafco Consolidated Group
  M&F Worldwide Corp. (32%, licorice extract)
Panavision (91%, movie cameras)
Revlon Inc. (83%, cosmetics and personal care products)
Sunbeam Corporation (about 37%, small appliances and
  Coleman camping gear)
WeddingChannel.com

COMPETITORS

Alberto-Culver
Amway
Avon
Bank of America
Body Shop
Brunswick
Chattem
Colgate-Palmolive
Cosmair
Estée Lauder
Golden West Financial
Kellwood
LVMH
Mary Kay
Procter & Gamble
Unilever
Washington Mutual
Wells Fargo

HISTORICAL FINANCIALS & EMPLOYEES

Private FYE: December	Annual Growth	1989	1990	1991	1992	1993	1994	1995	1996	1997	1998
Sales ($ mil.)	(0.9%)	5,325	5,381	4,521	3,496	2,748	3,030	4,413	6,196	6,071	4,900
Employees	(8.6%)	44,000	44,000	38,100	25,700	23,500	22,328	22,800	30,000	29,854	19,500

SALES HISTORY

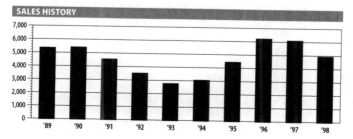

REVLON

THE MACMANUS GROUP

Over the years, The MacManus Group has helped add a little Cheer, Joy, and Zest to our lives. The New York City-based advertising and marketing holding company is one of the advertising firms closely allied with consumer products maker Procter & Gamble (P&G), which gave us Cheer laundry detergent, Joy dishwashing liquid, and Zest soap. MacManus' flagship agency, D'Arcy Masius Benton & Bowles (which now does business under the shortened moniker D'Arcy), has nearly 130 offices in 75 different countries. MacManus also operates agencies The Kaplan Thaler Group and N.W. Ayer & Partners (the nation's oldest ad agency), media buying unit MediaVest Worldwide, and public relations arm Manning, Selvage & Lee. In addition to P&G, MacManus'

other top clients include Burger King, Coca-Cola, and General Motors.

While the company's close relationship with P&G provides it with a steady stream of business, MacManus is pitted against much larger firms (like Omnicom and Interpublic) for other business. To remain strong in the market, the company has agreed to merge with fellow P&G shop The Leo Group (formerly Leo Burnett) to form a new firm called BDM. The combined operation, with MacManus chairman and CEO Roy Bostock serving as chairman, should rank in the top five globally. Japanese ad giant Dentsu will take a 20% stake in BDM, which also is planning a public stock offering sometime in 2000. Privately held MacManus is owned by a group of executives, with Bostock reportedly owning about 10%.

The MacManus Group traces its roots to 1906 when William D'Arcy founded D'Arcy Advertising in St. Louis. With Coca-Cola as an early client, the firm's success attracted other major accounts, including Anheuser-Busch in 1914 and General Tire in 1916. In 1931 D'Arcy launched its signature Christmas campaign for Coca-Cola, featuring Santa with a Coke. It also came up with the slogan "The Pause That Refreshes" in the 1930s. But in 1951 Coca-Cola dropped D'Arcy in favor of McCann-Erickson, a firm with greater access to international markets. D'Arcy bounced back with new clients, including Standard Oil and Royal Crown Cola.

In the 1960s the company launched the red and blue Budweiser label (1965), which became an industry icon. The loss of Royal Crown Cola (1969) and McDonald's (1970) put D'Arcy in financial difficulties, and in 1971 it merged with MacManus, John & Adams, a Detroit-based agency that counted 3M and General Motors among its clients. (MacManus, Inc., founded in 1911 by image advertising pioneer Theodore MacManus, had joined with John & Adams in 1934.) In 1973 the company changed its name to D'Arcy-MacManus, Masius (DM&M) after merging with Masius, Wynn-Williams, a UK agency founded as Masius & Ferguson in 1943. The expanded company pursued international expansion and by 1984 had 46 offices worldwide.

The next year DM&M merged with Benton & Bowles, the company formed when William Benton and Chester Bowles opened their first office in New York City in 1929. General Foods and Procter & Gamble had been early clients.

Both founders had left the company by 1941. Benton & Bowles later opened its first international office, in London, in 1958, and then in 1972 established subsidiary Medicus Communications, acquired public relations firm Manning, Selvage & Lee in 1979, and formed the B&B Direct partnership in 1981. Benton & Bowles' 1985 union with DM&M was the largest merger in advertising at the time.

D'Arcy Masius Benton & Bowles (DMB&B) streamlined its operations in the 1980s. In 1989 Roy Bostock, who had been president of B&B, rose to CEO; the next year he was named chairman. During the early 1990s the firm gained a reputation as a "bridesmaid agency" in the US after it failed to win high-profile accounts such as Burger King, IBM, and Pan Am. In 1996 DMB&B changed its name to MacManus and acquired the venerable N.W. Ayer (founded in 1869). Media subsidiary TeleVest landed the US account for Procter & Gamble in 1997 — the largest assignment in the history of advertising (valued at $1 billion).

In 1998 MacManus began talks with Leo Burnett about merging their media buying operations. Those talks broke down, and MacManus formed MediaVest Worldwide from its media buying units the next year. Also in 1999, Avon Products, which had selected MacManus as its single global agency the year before, pulled its creative account from the company. Later MacManus and Leo Burnett (renamed The Leo Group) were again in the news announcing plans to merge into one company called BDM.

OFFICERS

Chairman and CEO: Roy J. Bostock
VC, COO, and CFO: Craig D. Brown
Chairman and CEO, D'Arcy: Arthur Selkowitz
President and CEO, Clarion Marketing & Communications: Lance Smith
Co-President and CEO, D'Arcy TransAtlantic: John F. P. Farrell
President, D'Arcy Americas: Paulo Salles
EVP and Executive Director Corporate and Public Affairs, D'Arcy: Tricia Kennedy
EVP and CFO, D'Arcy: Scott van der Helder
Regional CEO, D'Arcy Asia/Pacific: Garry Titterton
EVP, Global Marketing Director, and Chief Branding Officer, D'Arcy TranAtlantic: Susan Gianinno
SVP Human Resources, D'Arcy: Leslie Engel
Worldwide Account Director; General Motors, Mananging Director, D'Arcy Detroit: Patrick Sherwood

LOCATIONS

HQ: 1675 Broadway, New York, NY 10019
Phone: 212-468-3622   **Fax:** 212-468-4385
Web site: http://www.dmbb.com

PRODUCTS/OPERATIONS

Selected Clients
American Family Life Insurance
Burger King
Coca-Cola
Ernst & Young
General Motors
Mars, Inc.
Philip Morris
The Pillsbury Company
Procter & Gamble
Royal Philips Electronics
Scotts Worldwide
Trans World Airlines

Subsidiaries
Blue Marble
Bromley, Aguilar & Associates
Clarion Marketing and Communications
D'Arcy Masius Benton & Bowles
The Kaplan Thaler Group
Manning, Selvage & Lee
MediaVest Worldwide
Medicus Group International
N. W. Ayer & Partners
Sherry Group

COMPETITORS

Dentsu
Grey Advertising
Havas Advertising
Interpublic Group
Leo Group
Omnicom Group
Publicis
SFM Media
Saatchi & Saatchi
True North
WPP Group
Young & Rubicam

HISTORICAL FINANCIALS & EMPLOYEES

Private FYE: December	Annual Growth	1989	1990	1991	1992	1993	1994	1995	1996	1997	1998
Sales ($ mil.)	8.6%	—	—	498	524	554	608	714	754	843	890
Employees	5.2%	—	—	—	—	5,904	6,405	6,333	7,500	7,620	7,619

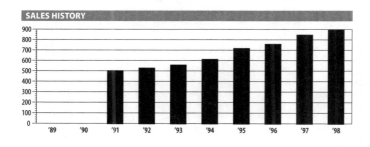

SALES HISTORY

MAJOR LEAGUE BASEBALL

OVERVIEW

By all accounts, the 1998 baseball season was out of the park. Bolstered by the home run race between Mark McGwire and Sammy Sosa, as well as the New York Yankees' terrific winning season, Major League Baseball (MLB) enjoyed one of the finest years in its long history. Based in New York City, MLB has 30 franchises, which play baseball in two leagues, the National and American. It also has about 180 minor league teams.

The 1998 season may have helped erase almost all of the bitter memories associated with the 1994-95 players' strike, but baseball still has some off-the-field problems. Although the teams do share some broadcasting revenues, gate receipts, and licensing rights, a fiscal disparity is growing between large-market and small-market teams. Big-market teams like the Yankees and Los Angeles Dodgers have payrolls of more than $90 million, while such teams as the Minnesota Twins and Montréal Expos have payrolls under $15 million (a figure equivalent to Dodgers pitcher Kevin Brown's annual salary).

Exacerbating the chasm between payroll and, by extension, talent, is an atmosphere where teams are owned by large conglomerates such as Walt Disney (Anaheim Angels), Time Warner (Atlanta Braves), and News Corp. (Dodgers), giving these franchises even deeper pockets which they can use to lure World Series-caliber players. MLB Commissioner Bud Selig has vowed to address the problem.

HISTORY

Abner Doubleday designed the diamond, Alexander Joy Cartwright placed the bases 90 feet apart, Henry Chadwick wrote the first book of rules, and baseball was born. The popularity of this new sport during the mid-19th century led to the 1869 formation of the first professional team, the Cincinnati Red Stockings. William Hulbert, owner of the Chicago White Stockings, formed the National League of Professional Baseball Clubs in 1876.

Competing leagues sprang up and folded, but the Western League (formed in 1892) survived by offering higher salaries to National League players to lure them away. Renamed the American League in 1900, it had spirited away more than 100 players by 1901, including star pitcher Cy Young, and soon was drawing more fans than the National League. In 1903 the two sides agreed to work together by having the two league champions meet in the World Series.

The sport flourished until 1920's "black sox" scandal, in which eight Chicago White Sox players were accused of taking bribes to throw the 1919 World Series. The teams' owners, looking to clean up the game's image, hired Judge Kenesaw Mountain Landis as baseball's first commissioner.

A joint committee of owners and players introduced a number of reforms in 1947, including a player pension fund. The players' unhappiness with the pension plan led to the 1954 formation of the Major League Baseball Players' Association (MLBPA).

Players and owners signed baseball's first collective-bargaining agreement in 1968, giving the players a voice in policy making. During the 1970s the players began to gain more power. In 1972 they called their first strike, a 13-day walk-out that won an improved pension plan. Four years later the players won the right to free agency. A seven-week strike interrupted the 1981 season.

In the mid-1980s most free agents found the market for their services dried up, and salary increases slowed down. The MLBPA accused the owners of conspiring to keep the price of free agents down, and in 1990 the owners agreed to a settlement of $280 million in collusion damages. MLB Commissioner Fay Vincent resigned in 1992. The players began a 232-day strike in August 1994, prompted by the franchise owners' decision to unilaterally restrict free agency and withdraw salary arbitration. MLB's revenues and income plummeted. In 1995 both the owners and the players' union approved a new collective-bargaining agreement.

While healing from the last strike, MLB still lacks team spirit. In 1997 owners bitterly rejected marketing chief Greg Murphy's proposed deal with NIKE and Reebok. (At the same time Yankees owner George Steinbrenner was reaching his own deal with adidas, an action which earned him suspension from the MLB executive committee.)

In 1998 St. Louis Cardinals' Mark McGwire and Chicago Cubs' Sammy Sosa entertained huge crowds as they raced to break Roger Maris' single season home run record of 61. McGwire took the top spot with 70 homers for the year, while Sosa slammed 66 out of the park. A 1999 labor dispute resulted in 22 umpires losing their jobs. Later that year MLB signed a new six-year, $800 million TV contract with ESPN, ending its contract dispute with the network.

OFFICERS

Commissioner: Allan H. Selig
President and COO: Paul Beeston
CFO: Jeffrey White
President, American League: Gene Budig
President, National League: Leonard S. Coleman
Executive Director of Baseball Operations:
William Murray
Executive Director of Human Resources: Wendy Lewis
Executive Director of Public Relations: Richard Levin
Director of Government Relations: Alan C. Sobba
Auditors: Ernst & Young LLP

LOCATIONS

HQ: Office of the Commissioner,
245 Park Ave., New York, NY 10167
Phone: 212-931-7800   **Fax:** 212-949-8636
Web site: http://www.majorleaguebaseball.com

PRODUCTS/OPERATIONS

Major League Baseball Teams

American League	National League
Central	Central
Chicago White Sox	Chicago Cubs
Cleveland Indians	Cincinnati Reds
Detroit Tigers	Houston Astros
Kansas City Royals	Milwaukee Brewers
Minnesota Twins	Pittsburgh Pirates
East	St. Louis Cardinals
Baltimore Orioles	East
Boston Red Sox	Atlanta Braves
New York Yankees	Florida Marlins
Tampa Bay Devil Rays	Montréal Expos
Toronto Blue Jays	New York Mets
West	Philadelphia Phillies
Anaheim Angels	West
Oakland Athletics	Arizona Diamondbacks
Seattle Mariners	Colorado Rockies
Texas Rangers	Los Angeles Dodgers
	San Diego Padres
	San Francisco Giants

Subsidiaries and Affiliates

Major League Baseball Properties Inc.
Major League Scouting Bureau

COMPETITORS

NBA
NFL
NHL
PGA

HISTORICAL FINANCIALS & EMPLOYEES

Association FYE: October	Annual Growth	1989	1990	1991	1992	1993	1994	1995	1996	1997	1998
Sales ($ mil.)	11.0%	1,241	1,337	1,537	1,663	1,775	1,134	1,411	1,847	2,216	3,174
Employees	7.5%	—	—	—	—	150	150	170	200	200	—

SALES HISTORY

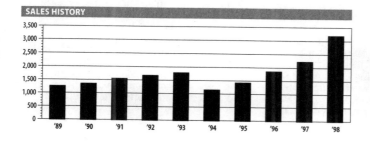

MAJOR LEAGUE BASEBALL

MARITZ INC.

Organizing trips, making employees happy and productive, and collecting data are all in a day's work for Maritz. The St. Louis-based company, which has 240 offices in North America and Europe, operates in three areas: travel services, employee motivation services, and marketing services. The Maritz Travel Company, one of the nation's leading travel firms, provides corporate travel services, consulting, and event management. The company also has a majority stake in GTM, a travel agency with about 1,250 offices in more than 40 countries.

The company's employee motivation and incentive programs help clients improve quality control and customer satisfaction. Maritz is also one of the largest custom market research providers in the US, specializing in telecommunications and automotive research; it also operates test kitchens and a shopper service to study retail service standards, and conducts consumer surveys (called "Maritz Polls"). The company's customers include Dell, Brunswick, and ARCO.

Maritz has continued to grow through acquisitions in its three core businesses. In 1998 chairman William Maritz, grandson of the company's founder, relinquished his CEO title to his son Stephen, who was already serving as president. The Maritz family owns the company.

Edward Maritz, an entrepreneur of Swiss-French descent, founded the E. Maritz Jewelry Manufacturing Company in St. Louis in 1894. By 1900 the wholesaler and manufacturer of men's and women's jewelry was supplying retail jewelers across the South and West. By 1921 Maritz had become a major importer of Swiss watches, which it sold to retail jewelers under the Merit, Cymrex, and Record brands. In the 1920s the company added diamond jewelry and silverware to its product mix. Edward Maritz died in 1929.

To drum up new business during the Depression, Edward's son James began trying to sell watches and jewelry to large corporations for use as sales and service awards, pioneering the incentive market. The first sale for a nationwide employee incentive campaign was to Caradine Hat, a St. Louis hatmaker, in 1930. In 1948 Maritz handled a $2 million incentive program for Chevrolet.

In 1950 the Maritz family split the business into two operations. Brother Lloyd handled the jewelry business (it went out of business around 1960); James took over the incentive operations, which flourished. In the 1950s James expanded his company's offerings to include merchandise awards, and in 1958, travel incentive awards (arranged through the newly acquired Holiday House Travel Center of Detroit). The enterprise adopted the corporate name Maritz Inc. in 1961. During the 1960s and early 1970s, Maritz made a series of acquisitions closely allied with its motivation endeavors, including Lee Creative Research, the nucleus of what would become its market research operations (1973). The organization expanded internationally with the opening of Maritz offices in the UK and Mexico in 1974.

In 1980 the company acquired the Wilding division of Bell & Howell, which it merged with another unit to form Maritz Communications Co. James died in 1981. Maritz beefed up its travel operations in the 1980s, acquiring corporate travel agency Traveler's Service (St. Louis, 1981), Byfield Travel (Chicago, 1984), Beverly Hills Travel (Los Angeles, 1986), and Travel Counselors International (Virginia, 1986).

These acquisitions led to record sales in 1989, but sliding results began to slide in the early 1990s prompted the company to streamline its operations by cutting overlapping units. After a family boardroom tussle in 1993, William Maritz expanded his control of the company by buying out his sister's 50% stake in the company and putting his two sons on the board. His son Stephen Maritz subsequently took over as president.

As part of its international expansion strategy, Maritz acquired The Research Business Group, the UK's largest independently owned marketing research firm (1993), and BLC, the largest performance-improvement company in France (1994). In 1997 the company established an office in Manila, its first in Asia.

In 1998 William Maritz stepped down as CEO and retained the title of chairman; his son Stephen succeeded him. In 1998 and 1999 the company boosted its international presence with acquisitions in Canada (group travel firm Partners in Performance, marketing research firm Thompson Lightstone & Co.) and the Netherlands (Maritz B.V.).

Chairman: William E. Maritz
VC, President, and CEO: W. Stephen Maritz
SEVP and CFO: James W. Kienker
SEVP and Chief Administrative Officer:
 Jeffrey D. Reinberg
SEVP: Norman L. Schwesig
SEVP, Secretary, and General Counsel: Henry S. Stolar
SVP: Michael M. Boland
SVP: John R. Chalker
SVP Human Resources: Terry L. Goring
SVP Information Resources: Gilbert L. Hoffman
SVP: Ronald P. Lipovsky
SVP: John F. Risberg
SVP: William T. Rogers

LOCATIONS

HQ: 1375 N. Highway Dr., St. Louis, MO 63099
Phone: 636-827-4000   **Fax:** 636-827-5505
Web site: http://www.maritz.com

PRODUCTS/OPERATIONS

Services
Marketing Research
  Custom marketing research
  Customer satisfaction and customer value analysis
  Data collection (focus groups, telephone interviews,
    test kitchens)
Performance Improvement
  Communications
  Learning systems
  Measurement and feedback
  Research and assessment
  Rewards and recognition
  Solution design
Travel
  Business meetings
  Consulting services
  Corporate travel management
  Group travel services
  Special events
  Technology services

COMPETITORS

ACNielsen
American Express
Carlson Wagonlit
Franklin Covey
Gallup
Harris Interactive
IMS Health
Information Resources
J.D. Power
Japan Travel Bureau
NFO Worldwide
Navigant International
Opinion Research
Rosenbluth International
Thomas Cook
Thomson Travel Group
WorldTravel

HISTORICAL FINANCIALS & EMPLOYEES

Private FYE: March	Annual Growth	1990	1991	1992	1993	1994	1995	1996	1997	1998	1999
Sales ($ mil.)	9.3%	—	—	1,184	1,173	1,260	1,442	1,078	1,795	2,010	2,200
Employees	1.6%	—	—	—	—	6,000	6,080	6,410	7,000	7,500	6,500

SALES HISTORY

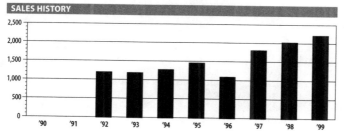

THE MARMON GROUP, INC.

OVERVIEW

"The more the merrier" could well be The Marmon Group's motto. A worldwide association of more than 100 manufacturing and service companies, Chicago-based Marmon is one of the largest private conglomerates in the US. Marmon units operate about 550 facilities in more than 40 countries. Each company works under its own management, and a small corporate office (fewer than 100 employees) oversees and pulls together the conglomerate, acting as combination CFO, tax lawyer, accountant, and broker to member companies.

Marmon companies make medical products, mining equipment, railway equipment, indus-

trial materials and components, industrial and consumer products, transportation equipment, building and commercial products, and water-treatment products. Services include marketing and distribution, contract rail switching, and consumer credit information.

Marmon tacked on more than 30 new companies in 1998, largely to complement existing businesses in fields such as the manufacture of medical products and wire and cable and the distribution of pipes and tubes. Marmon is owned by Chicago's Pritzker family, which also owns the Hyatt hotel chain.

HISTORY

Although the history of The Marmon Group officially begins in 1953, the company's roots are in the Chicago law firm Pritzker and Pritzker, started by Nicholas Pritzker in 1902. Through the firm the family made connections with First National Bank of Chicago, which A. N. Pritzker, Nicholas' son, used to get a line of credit to buy real estate. By 1940 the firm had stopped accepting outside clients to concentrate on the family's growing investment portfolio.

In 1953 A. N.'s son Jay used his father's connections to get a loan to buy Colson Company, a small, money-losing manufacturer of bicycles, hospital equipment, and other products. Jay's brother, Robert, a graduate of the Illinois Institute of Technology, took charge of Colson and turned it around. Soon Jay began acquiring more companies for his brother to manage.

In 1963 the brothers paid $2.7 million for about 45% of the Marmon-Herrington Company (whose predecessor, Marmon Motor Car, built the car that in 1911 won the first Indianapolis 500). The family now had a name for its industrial holdings — The Marmon Group.

It became a public company in 1966 when it merged with door- and spring-maker Fenestra. However, Jay began to take greater control of the group through a series of stock purchases, and by 1971 The Marmon Group was private once again.

A year earlier, in 1970, the group acquired a promising industrial pipe supplier, Keystone Tubular Service (which later became Marmon/Keystone). In 1973 Marmon began to acquire stock in Cerro Corp., which had operations in mining, manufacturing, trucking, and real estate; by 1976 the group had bought all of Cerro, thereby tripling its revenues. The brothers sold Cerro's trucking subsidiary, ICX, in 1977 and bought organ maker

Hammond Corp., along with Wells Lamont, Hammond's glove-making subsidiary.

Marmon acquired conglomerate Trans Union in 1981. Trans Union brought many operations, including railcar and equipment leasing, credit information services, international trading, and water- and wastewater-treatment systems. Jay acquired Ticketmaster in 1982.

The Pritzkers made a foray into the airline business in 1984 by buying Braniff Airlines. After unsuccessfully bidding for Pan Am in 1987, they sold Braniff in 1988. Disappointments in other Pritzker businesses didn't slow Marmon, which added to its transportation equipment business in 1984 with Altamil, a maker of products for the trucking and aerospace industries.

To mark its 40th anniversary, the company sponsored a car, the Marmon Wasp II, at the 1993 Indianapolis 500. That year the Pritzkers sold 80% of Ticketmaster to Microsoft cofounder Paul Allen but retained a minority interest. Marmon sold Arzco Medical Systems in 1995 and Marmon/Keystone acquired Anbuma Group, a Belgian steel tubing distributor.

The Anbuma purchase and Marmon/Keystone's 1997 acquisition of UK tube distributor Wheeler Group exemplify Marmon's practice of building strength through acquisitions in its established markets. In 1998 Marmon purchased more than 30 companies, chiefly as complements to existing operations. Also that year the Chinese government gave Marmon/Keystone permission to open a business development office in Beijing.

Jay Pritzker died in 1999, and the company announced that his title of chairman will not be filled.

HISTORICAL FINANCIALS & EMPLOYEES

Private FYE: December	Annual Growth	1989	1990	1991	1992	1993	1994	1995	1996	1997	1998
Sales ($ mil.)	5.1%	3,841	3,846	3,867	4,008	4,319	5,302	6,083	5,776	6,003	6,032
Net income ($ mil.)	6.0%	206	125	126	145	207	281	307	305	316	348
Income as % of sales	—	5.4%	3.3%	3.3%	3.6%	4.8%	5.3%	5.0%	5.3%	5.3%	5.8%
Employees	3.8%	25,074	26,705	27,050	27,000	27,700	28,000	30,000	35,000	33,000	35,000

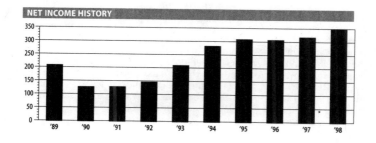

NET INCOME HISTORY

MARMON

MARS, INC.

OVERVIEW

Mars knows chocolate sales are nothing to snicker at. The McLean, Virginia-based company is the US's #2 candy maker, after Hershey, and one of the nation's largest private companies. Mars' products include M&M's, Snickers, 3 Musketeers, Dove, Milky Way, Skittles, Twix, and Starburst candies. In addition, the company offers ice-cream versions of several of its candy bars; Combos and Kudos snacks; Uncle Ben's rice (the #1 brand); and pet food under the names Kal Kan, Pedigree, and Whiskas. It also manufactures drink vending equipment and electronic coin changers and related equipment.

The company, while surpassed in the US by Hershey, is ahead of its rival internationally. Mars stays virtually debt-free and uses its profits for international expansion. It now sells its products in more than 100 countries on five continents.

Co-presidents and brothers Forrest Mars Jr. and John Mars, along with their sister, VP Jacqueline Mars Vogel, own the secretive enterprise, making the Mars family one of the richest in the country.

HISTORY

Frank Mars invented the Milky Way candy bar in 1923 after his previous three efforts at the candy business left him bankrupt. After his estranged son Forrest graduated from Yale, Mars hired him to work at his candy operation. When Forrest demanded one-third control of the company and Frank refused, Forrest moved to England with the foreign rights to Milky Way and started his own company (Food Manufacturers) in the 1930s. He made a sweeter version of Milky Way for the UK, calling it a Mars bar. Forrest also ventured into pet food with the 1934 purchase of Chappel Brothers (renamed Pedigree). At one point he controlled 55% of the British pet food market.

During WWII, Forrest returned to the US and introduced Uncle Ben's rice (the world's first brand-name raw commodity) and M&M's (a joint venture between Forrest and Bruce Murrie, son of the then-Hershey president). The idea for M&M's was borrowed from British Smarties, for which Forrest obtained rights (from Rowntree Mackintosh) by relinquishing similar rights to the Snickers bar in some international markets. The ad slogan "Melts in your mouth, not in your hand" (and the candy's success in non-air-conditioned stores and war zones) made the company an industry leader. Mars introduced M&M's Peanut in 1954. It was one of the first candy companies to sponsor a television show — *Howdy Doody* in the 1950s.

Forrest merged his firm with his deceased father's company in 1964, after buying his dying half sister's controlling interest in the firm (he renamed the business Mars at her request). The merger was the end of an alliance with Hershey, who had supplied Frank with chocolate since his Milky Way inception.

In 1968 Mars bought Kal Kan. In 1973 Forrest, then 69 years old, delegated his company responsibility to sons Forrest Jr. and John. Five years later the brothers, looking for snacks to offset dwindling candy sales from a more diet-conscious America, bought the Twix chocolate-covered cookie brand. During the late 1980s they bought ice-cream bar maker Dove Bar International and Ethel M Chocolates, producer of liqueur-flavored chocolates, a business their father had begun in his retirement.

Hershey passed Mars as the US's largest candy maker in 1988 when it acquired Cadbury Schweppes' US division (Mounds and Almond Joy). In response to the success of Hershey's Symphony Bar, Mars introduced its dark-chocolate Dove bar in 1991. Other product debuts in the early 1990s included peanut butter, mint, and almond M&M's and Milky Way Dark.

The company entered the confectionery market in India in 1989 by building a $10 million factory there. By 1994 Mars was still losing market share to Hershey; Forrest Jr. was blasted as "Worst Marketer" by the *Delaney Report* for it.

In 1996 the company opened a confectionery processing plant in Brazil and introduced low-fat Starburst Fruit Twists and Starburst Jellybeans (to appeal to fat-conscious snackers). To help improve sales, the next year Mars began new ad campaigns, including M&M's spots featuring comedian Dennis Miller.

Mars pulled the plug on its VO2 Max energy bar in 1998 amid complaints that its taste fell considerably short of Snickers. The company introduced new products such as M&M Crispy and Uncle Ben's Rice Bowl meals in the late 1990s. Forrest Sr. died in July 1999, spurring rumors that Mars would go public or be sold. In October 1999 the company agreed to partner with Dreyer's to make premium ice cream products, including Snickers Ice Cream and M&M's Chocolate and Vanilla Ice Creams, for sale in the spring of 2000.

Co-President and CEO: Forrest E. Mars Jr.
Co-President: John F. Mars
VP and Treasurer: Vito J. Spitaleri
VP: Jacqueline Mars Vogel
Secretary: Ed J. Stegemann

LOCATIONS

HQ: 6885 Elm St., McLean, VA 22101
Phone: 703-821-4900   **Fax:** 703-448-9678
Web site: http://www.mars.com

PRODUCTS/OPERATIONS

Selected Products

Candy	Ice-Cream Bars
3 Musketeers	3 Musketeers
Bounty Bar	DoveBars
Dove	M&M Ice Cream
Ethel M Chocolates	Cookie Sandwiches
Maltesers	Milky Way
M&M's Almond	Snickers
M&M's Crispy	Starburst Ice Bars
M&M's Peanut	
M&M's Peanut Butter	**Pet Food**
M&M's Plain	Bounce
Mars	Brekkies
Milky Way	Cesar
Milky Way Dark	Chappy
Milky Way Lite	Dine
Mint M&M's	Frolic
Opal Fruit	Kal Kan
Revels	KiteKat
Skittles	Pedigree
Snickers	Sheba
Starburst	Trill
Starburst	Waltham
Fruit Twists	Whiskas
Starburst	
Jellybeans	**Snacks**
Twix	Combos
	Kudos

Rice and Other Food and Drinks
Dolmio sauces
Flavia drinks
Masterfoods condiments and sauces
Suzi Wan Chinese food
Uncle Ben's Chef's Recipe
Uncle Ben's Converted Rice
Uncle Ben's Country Inn Rice
Uncle Ben's Hearty Soups
Uncle Ben's Long Grain & Wild Rice
Uncle Ben's Original Brown Rice
Uncle Ben's Rice Bowls

Other Products
Automated payment systems
Coin changers
Drink vending equipment
Exelpet pet accessories
Handheld scanning devices
Lockets medicated lozenges
Tunes medicated lozenges

COMPETITORS

Ben & Jerry's	Lindt & Sprungli
Blue Bell	Meiji Seika
Cadbury Schweppes	Nabisco Holdings
Campbell Soup	Nestlé
Colgate-Palmolive	Pillsbury
ConAgra	Quaker Oats
Doane Pet Care Company	Ralston Purina
ERLY Industries	Riviana Foods
Ezaki Glico	Russell Stover
Ferrero	See's Candies
General Mills	Tootsie Roll
Grupo Corvi	UIS
Heinz	Unilever
Hershey	Wrigley
Kraft Foods	

HISTORICAL FINANCIALS & EMPLOYEES

Private FYE: December	Annual Growth	1989	1990	1991	1992	1993	1994	1995	1996	1997	1998
Estimated sales ($ mil.)	6.6%	8,450	9,100	11,000	12,500	13,000	12,500	13,000	13,000	15,000	15,000
Employees	3.0%	23,000	26,000	28,000	28,000	27,000	28,000	28,000	28,000	28,500	30,000

SALES HISTORY

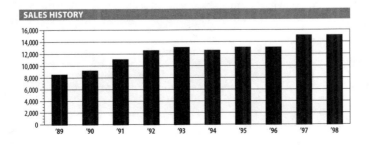

MARY KAY INC.

OVERVIEW

Mary Kay promoted Girl Power before any of the Spice Girls were even born. The Dallas-based company, the US's #2 direct seller of beauty products (after Avon), aims to empower its primarily female employees through careers that allow them ample time for their families. Mary Kay sells more than 200 products in eight product categories: facial skin care, cosmetics, body care, nail care, men's skin care, fragrances, nutritional supplements, and sun protection. Some 500,000 direct-sales consultants demonstrate Mary Kay products in small group settings in the US and 28 other countries.

Founded by a woman — Mary Kay Ash — for women, Mary Kay has an overwhelmingly female workforce. Although Ash stands by her original goal of providing financial and career opportunities for women, men exert quite a bit of power at the company: Mary Kay's chairman/CEO and CFO are men.

The company gives bonuses each year, ranging from jewelry to the company's trademark pink Cadillacs. Management is also eligible for phantom stock options, wherein a price is assigned by the company (based on financial benchmarks) to fictional shares, which employees cash in after a period of time. Ash is known for her religious nature as well as generosity. The company's credo has always been "God first, family second, career third."

Ash and her family own most of Mary Kay.

HISTORY

Before founding her own company in 1963, Mary Kay Ash worked as a Stanley Home Products sales representative. Impressed with the alligator handbag awarded the top saleswoman at a Stanley convention, Ash was determined to win the next year's prize — and she did. Despite that accomplishment and having worked at Stanley for 11 years, a male assistant she had trained was made her boss after less than a year on the job. Tired of not receiving recognition, Ash and her second husband used their life savings ($5,000) to go into business for themselves. Although her husband died of a heart attack shortly before the business opened, Ash forged ahead with the help of her two grown sons.

She bought a cosmetics formula invented years earlier by a hide tanner. (The mixture was originally used to soften leather, but the tanner noticed how the formula made his hands look younger, and he began applying the mixture to his face, with great results.) Ash kept her first line simple — 10 products — and packaged her wares in pink to contrast with the typical black and red toiletry cases of the day. Ash also enlisted consultants, who held "beauty shows" with five or six women in attendance. Mary Kay grossed $198,000 in its first year.

The company introduced men's skin care products in 1965. Ash bought a pink Cadillac the following year and began awarding the cars as prizes three years later. (By 1981 orders were so large — almost 500 — that GM dubbed the color "Mary Kay Pink.")

Ash became a millionaire when her firm went public in 1968. Mary Kay grew steadily through the 1970s. International operations began in 1971 in Australia, and over the next 25 years the company entered 24 more countries, including nations in Asia, Europe, Central and South America, and the Pacific Rim.

Sales plunged in the early 1980s, along with the company's stock prices (from $40 to $9 between 1983 and 1985). Ash and her family reacquired Mary Kay in 1985 through a $375 million LBO. Burdened with debt, the firm lost money in the late 1980s. Mary Kay took a number of steps to boost sales and income, doing a makeover on the cosmetics line and advertising in women's magazines again (after a five-year hiatus) to counter its old-fashioned image. The company also introduced recyclable packaging. In 1989 Avon rebuffed a buyout offer by Mary Kay, and both companies halted animal testing. (Mary Kay ended its tradition of giving fur coats as bonuses in 1997.)

Mary Kay introduced a bath and body product line in 1991, and its Skin Revival System, launched in 1993, raked in $80 million in its first six months on the market. It began operations in Russia that year; sales there reached $25 million by 1995.

In 1998 the company began selling through retail outlets in China because of a government ban on direct selling. Changing with the times, Mary Kay added a white sport utility vehicle and new shades of pink to its fleet of 10,000 GM cars that year.

Chairman John Rochon was named CEO in 1999. Also in 1999 Mary Kay launched *Women & Success* (a magazine for consultants) and Atlas (its electronic ordering system).

Chairman Emeritus: Mary Kay Ash
Chairman and CEO: John P. Rochon
CFO: David Holl
EVP Marketing: Curran Dandurand
EVP Manufacturing: Dennis Greaney
SVP and Chief Scientific Officer: Myra O. Barker
SVP Information Systems: Trey Bradley
SVP Global Human Resources: Darrell Overcash
General Counsel: Brad Glendening
Manager Organization Effectiveness: Susan Chaffin
Auditors: PricewaterhouseCoopers LLP

LOCATIONS

HQ: 16251 Dallas Pkwy., Dallas, TX 75001
Phone: 972-687-6300   **Fax:** 972-687-1609
Web site: http://www.marykay.com

Mary Kay employs about 500,000 direct-sales consultants who sell the company's merchandise in 29 countries in Asia, Australia, Europe, North America, and South America.

Selected Countries

Argentina	Mexico
Australia	New Zealand
Brazil	Norway
Brunei	Portugal
Canada	Russia
Chile	Singapore
China	Spain
Czech Republic	Sweden
El Salvador	Taiwan
Finland	Thailand
Germany	UK
Guatemala	Ukraine
Hong Kong	Uruguay
Japan	US
Malaysia	

PRODUCTS/OPERATIONS

Selected Product Lines

Body care	Nutritional supplements
Cosmetics	for men
Facial skin care	Nutritional supplements
Fragrances	for women
Men's skin care	Sun protection
Nail care	

Selected Brand Names

Acapella	LipSync
Angelfire	Mary Kay
Belara	Private Spa
Cybershine	Rub-A-Dub Bubble
Daily Benefits for Men	Skin Management
Daily Benefits for Women	Sun Essentials
Elige	Terme d'Isola
Eyesicles	Tribute
Genji	Triple-Action
Indulge	Visible-Action
Journey	

COMPETITORS

Alberto-Culver	Johnson & Johnson
Allou	L'Oréal
Amway	Merle Norman
Avon	Nu Skin
BeautiControl Cosmetics	Perrigo
Body Shop	Procter & Gamble
Carson, Inc.	Reliv
Clarins	Renaissance Cosmetics
Colgate-Palmolive	Revlon
Coty	Schwarzkopf & DEP
Del Labs	Scott's Liquid Gold
Dial	Shaklee
Estée Lauder	Shiseido
Garden Botanika	Sunrider
Helen of Troy	ThermoLase
Herbalife	Unilever
Intimate Brands	Wella

HISTORICAL FINANCIALS & EMPLOYEES

Private FYE: December	Annual Growth	1989	1990	1991	1992	1993	1994	1995	1996	1997	1998
Sales ($ mil.)	9.3%	450	487	520	613	737	850	950	1,000	1,050	1,000
Employees	10.7%	1,400	1,722	1,900	2,100	2,400	2,400	2,800	3,000	3,500	3,500

SALES HISTORY

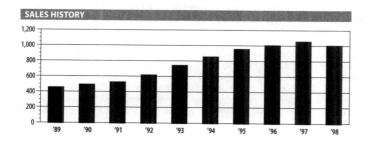

MASHANTUCKET PEQUOT GAMING

OVERVIEW

Mashantucket Pequot Gaming Enterprise has taken the Pequot tribe (with roughly 600 members) from intense poverty to its position as the wealthiest tribe in the US. Established by the Mashantucket Pequot Tribal Nation, Mashantucket Pequot Gaming Enterprise owns the Foxwoods Resort Casino in Ledyard, Connecticut, which is the largest casino in the world and is said to be the most profitable. The casino complex offers nearly 6,000 slot machines, 350 gaming tables, three hotels, about 20 restaurants and lounges, and a string of retail shops. About 50,000 people visit the casino each day.

As a sovereign nation, the Pequot tribe is not obligated to report its finances, but estimates of Foxwoods' annual revenues exceed $1 billion (more than 50% comes from slot machines). The state of Connecticut receives 25% of slot machine revenues.

In addition to its gaming operations, the Pequot tribe owns Pequot River Shipworks (shipbuilding), Fox Navigation (high-speed ferries), and the Pequot Pharmaceutical Network (mail-order pharmaceuticals). It also owns three Connecticut hotels (the Hilton Hotel in Mystic, the Norwich Inn & Spa in Norwich, Randall's Ordinary Inn in North Stonington) and is the part-owner of two golf courses. The Pequot tribe has established the Mashantucket Pequot Museum and Research Center dedicated to Indian life and history.

Richard Hayward, the tribe member who ushered the Pequots through the birth of their casino and the phenomenal changes in their fortunes, lost his bid for re-election as chairman of the tribe's governing body in 1998 (he was, however, elected vice chairman). The election followed a 1997 shakeup in top management of Pequot business concerns and coincided with increasingly strained relations between the Pequots and other tribes and towns near the Foxwoods Resort Casino.

HISTORY

Once a powerful tribe, the Pequots were virtually wiped out in the 17th century by disease and attacks from colonists who wanted their land and fur trade. Some 350 years later, Richard "Skip" Hayward, a pipefitter making $15,000 a year, led a bitter fight for federal recognition of his nearly extinct Mashantucket Pequot tribe. In 1983 the US government officially recognized the tribe.

The 1988 Indian Gaming Regulatory Act opened the door for legal gambling on reservations, but tribes still had to negotiate with state governments for authorization. Hayward hired G. Michael "Mickey" Brown as a consultant and lawyer. Brown took the tribe's legal battle to the US Supreme Court, which eventually ruled that the Pequots could build a casino. When some 30 banks turned down the Pequots for a construction loan, Brown introduced Hayward and his tribe to Lim Goh Tong, billionaire developer of the successful Gentings Highlands Casino resort in Malaysia. Tong invested $60 million, and the Foxwoods casino opened in 1992.

Hayward became the chief of a seven-member tribal council that serves as the board of directors, and Brown brought in Alfred J. Luciani as president of Foxwoods. Luciani stayed less than a year at Foxwoods, resigning because of what he called philosophical differences with some council members, particularly VC Kenneth Reels.

Brown took over as president in 1993. Although Foxwoods grew rapidly, Brown often wrestled with members of the tribal council over how the business should be run. In 1996 Reels and council members went to the police with allegations of financial misconduct by Brown and his management team. Nothing was proven. The next year Brown rehired Luciani to oversee the development of the Pequot Tower hotel.

In mid-1997 both Luciani and Brown were ousted under pressure from the tribal council. It was discovered that in 1993 Brown purchased stock in a company that did business with Foxwoods, and Luciani accepted a $377,000 loan in 1992 from a vendor. Although not illegal, these transactions were considered a conflict of interest by the tribal council. Luciani was terminated and Brown resigned without comment. Shortly afterward Bob Levitt, a VP for hotel services, gave his notice. The Pequots hired a new management team and Floyd "Bud" Celey, a veteran of Hilton Hotels, was appointed CEO.

In 1998 the Pequots opened the Mashantucket Pequot Museum and Research Center. When tribal elections were held later that year, Kenneth Reels was elected chairman of the Pequot's tribal governing body, ousting Hayward from the position he had held for more than 20 years. Hayward was elected vice chairman.

OFFICERS

Chairman, Tribal Council: Richard A. Hayward
VC, Tribal Council: Kenneth Reels
CEO: Floyd M. Celey Jr.
SVP Human Resources: Larry Fowler
SVP Finance: John O'Brien
Director Public Relations: Michael Dutton

LOCATIONS

HQ: Mashantucket Pequot Gaming Enterprise Inc.,
Rte. 2, Mashantucket, CT 06339
Phone: 860-312-3000   **Fax:** 860-312-1599
Web site: http://www.foxwoods.com

PRODUCTS/OPERATIONS

Selected Foxwoods Resort Attractions

Entertainment	The Fast Food Court
Championship boxing	The Fast Food Kiosk
Cinedrome Dance Club	The Festival Buffet
The Fox Theatre	Fox Harbour
Turbo Ride	Golden Dragon
Gaming tables	Han Garden
Baccarat	High Stakes Cafe
Bingo	Java Hut
Blackjack	Pizza Plus
Caribbean Stud	Scoops
Craps	Soft Spot
Keno	Sports Bar
Let it Ride	Veranda Cafe
Poker	Retail shops
Roulette	Atrium
Ultimate Race Book	Beads, Bells & Cowerie
Hotels	Shells
Grand Pequot Tower	Casino Boutique
Great Cedar Hotel	Foxwoods Logo Store
Two Trees Inn	Indian Nations
Restaurants and lounges	Outpost
360 Bar	Pequot Tower Gift Shop
Aces Up Lounge	Sports Center
Al Dente	Two Trees Inn Gift Shop
Atrium Lounge	Wampum Center
The Bistro	Winners
Branches	Woodland Flower Shop
Cedars Steak House	Slot machines
The Deli	

Selected Pequot Tribe Holdings

Fox Navigation (New London, CT, and Liberty Landing, NJ)
Hilton Hotel (Mystic, CT)
Mashantucket Pequot Gaming Enterprise Inc. (Ledyard, CT)
The Mashantucket Pequot Museum and Research Center (Mashantucket, CT)
The Norwich Inn & Spa (Norwich, CT)
The Pequot Pharmaceutical Network (Ledyard, CT)
Pequot River Shipworks (New London, CT)
Randall's Ordinary Inn (North Stonington, CT)

COMPETITORS

Aztar
Boyd Gaming
Connecticut Lottery
Greate Bay
Harrah's Entertainment
MGM Grand
Mandalay Resort Group
Mirage Resorts
New York State Lottery
Park Place Entertainment
Starwood Hotels & Resorts Worldwide
Sun International Hotels
Trump Hotels & Casinos

HISTORICAL FINANCIALS & EMPLOYEES

Private FYE: September	Annual Growth	1989	1990	1991	1992	1993	1994	1995	1996	1997	1998
Estimated sales ($ mil.)	0.0%	—	—	—	—	1,000	1,000	1,030	1,100	1,000	1,000
Employees	4.8%	—	—	—	—	9,100	10,000	11,000	12,000	11,180	11,500

SALES HISTORY

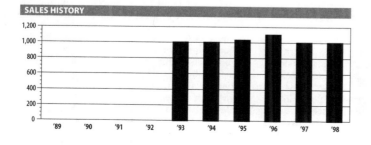

MASSACHUSETTS MUTUAL LIFE

OVERVIEW

You could say MassMutual is a stock-tease. After flirting with the idea of demutualizing or of forming a mutual holding company to issue stock (which it hasn't done since 1866), the management of Springfield, Massachusetts-based Massachusetts Mutual Life Insurance Company has decided to keep things collective.

Through more than 1,200 offices in the US, MassMutual primarily sells pension products and life and disability insurance. Its Investment Group offers investment management products (securities and real estate) and includes subsidiaries OppenheimerFunds (mutual fund management), David L. Babson & Company (individual and institutional investor services), MassMutual Trust Company (trust services), and Cornerstone Real Estate (real estate equities management).

MassMutual International is exporting the company's operations worldwide; it markets products that emphasize the company's traditional expertise, such as individual coverage and institutional money management. The company has established subsidiaries in Argentina, Bermuda, Chile, and Luxembourg.

HISTORY

Insurance agent George Rice formed Massachusetts Mutual in 1851 as a stock company based in Springfield. The firm converted to a mutual in 1867. For its first 50 years the company sold only individual life insurance, but after 1900 it branched out, offering first annuities (1917) and then disability coverage (1918).

The early 20th century was rough on MassMutual, which was forced to raise premiums on new policies during WWI, then faced the high costs of the 1918 flu epidemic. The firm endured the Great Depression despite policy terminations, expanding its product line to include income insurance. In 1946 MassMutual wrote its first group policy, for Louisville's Brown-Forman Distillers, maker of Jack Daniel's. By 1950 the company had diversified into medical insurance.

MassMutual began investing in stocks in the 1950s, switching from fixed-return bonds and mortgages for higher returns. It also decentralized and in 1961 began automating operations. By 1970 the company had installed a computer network linking it to its independent agents. During this period, whole life insurance remained the dominant product.

With interest rates increasing during the late 1970s, many insurers diversified by offering high-yield products like guaranteed investment contracts funded by high-risk investments. MassMutual resisted as long as it could, but as interest rates soared to 20%, the company experienced a rash of policy loans, which led to a cash crunch. In 1981, with its policy growth rate trailing the industry norm, MassMutual developed new products, including UPDATE, which offered higher dividends in return for adjustable interest on policy loans.

In the 1980s MassMutual reduced its investment in stocks (to about 5% of total investments by 1987), allowing the company to emerge virtually unscathed from the 1987 stock market crash.

The company changed its course in 1990 and entered financial services. It bought a controlling interest in mutual fund manager Oppenheimer Management, paying some $22 million for stock in the parent company and loaning it $44 million. MassMutual announced in 1993 that, with legislation limiting rates, it would stop writing new individual and small-group policies in New York.

The next year the company targeted the neglected family-owned business niche. MassMutual continued this policy in 1995 by becoming a founding sponsor of the American Alliance of Family-Owned Businesses and rolled out new whole life products aimed at small businesses. That year it bought David L. Babson & Company, a Massachusetts-based investment management firm, and opened life insurance companies in Chile and Argentina.

In 1996 MassMutual merged with Connecticut Mutual. It also acquired Antares Leveraged Capital Corp. (commercial finance) and Charter Oak Capital Management (investment advisory services). The next year MassMutual sold its Life & Health Benefits Management subsidiary to WellPoint Health Networks.

Still in the mood to merge, the company entered discussions with Northwestern Mutual Life Insurance in 1998, but culture clashes terminated the talks. Also that year the company helped push through legislation that would allow insurers to issue stock through mutual holding companies, a move which MassMutual itself contemplated but then set aside in 1999. That year the firm planned to issue securities in Europe; it also opened new offices in such locales as Bermuda and Luxembourg and bought the Argentina operations of Jefferson-Pilot.

Chairman: Thomas B. Wheeler
President and CEO: Robert J. O'Connell
EVP and CFO: Joseph M. Zubretsky
EVP and Chief Information Officer: Peter J. Daboul
EVP and Chief Investment Officer: Gary E. Wendlandt
EVP and General Counsel, Law and Individual Accumulation; President and CEO, C.M. Life Insurance and MML Bay State Life Insurance: Lawrence V. Burkett Jr.
EVP International Operations; President and CEO, MassMutual International: Daniel J. Fitzgerald
EVP Life Insurance Sales and Marketing: John B. Davies
EVP Life Insurance Services: James E. Miller
EVP Retirement Services: John V. Murphy
SVP Life Insurance Sales and Marketing: Paul D. Adornato
SVP Corporate Human Resources: Susan A. Alfano
SVP Retirement Services: Frederick C. Castellani
SVP and Deputy General Counsel, Law and Federal Government Relations: Kenneth S. Cohen
SVP Corporate Services: Colin C. Collins
SVP Information Systems: Nancy A. Dalessio
SVP Large Corporate Markets: Anne Melissa Dowling
President, MassMutual Trust Company: Frank Barone
VP State Government Relations: John L. Abbott
VP Corporate Strategy: Paul T. Pasteris
Auditors: PricewaterhouseCoopers LLP

HQ: Massachusetts Mutual Life Insurance Company, 1295 State St., Springfield, MA 01111
Phone: 413-788-8411   **Fax:** 413-744-6005
Web site: http://www.massmutual.com

1998 Assets

	$ mil.	% of total
Cash & equivalents	1,256	2
Bonds	25,929	39
Mortgage loans	6,043	9
Real estate	1,740	3
Policy loans	5,399	8
Other investments	2,370	3
Assets in separate account	22,940	34
Other assets	1,302	2
Total	**66,979**	**100**

1998 Sales

	$ mil.	% of total
Premium income	8,462	72
Net investment	3,044	26
Other	222	2
Total	**11,728**	**100**

Selected Subsidiaries
MassMutual Holding Company, Inc.
Antares Capital Corporation (commercial finance)
Charter Oak Capital Management, Inc. (insurance investment advice)
Cornerstone Real Estate Advisers, Inc.
David L. Babson & Company, Inc. (institutional investment services)
OppenheimerFunds, Inc. (mutual funds)

AIG	Liberty Mutual
AXA Financial	Mellon Financial
Allianz	Merrill Lynch
Allstate	MetLife
American Financial	Nationwide Insurance
American General	New York Life
CIGNA	Northwestern Mutual
CNA Financial	Paine Webber
Citigroup	Principal Financial
Conseco	Prudential
FMR	St. Paul Companies
Guardian Life	State Farm
The Hartford	TIAA-CREF
Jefferson-Pilot	Torchmark
John Hancock	Transamerica

Mutual company FYE: December	Annual Growth	1989	1990	1991	1992	1993	1994	1995	1996	1997	1998
Assets ($ mil.)	11.5%	25,062	27,507	29,582	31,495	34,699	35,720	38,632	55,752	61,069	66,979
Net income ($ mil.)	10.9%	142	101	180	116	139	93	159	239	262	359
Income as % of assets	—	0.6%	0.4%	0.6%	0.4%	0.4%	0.3%	0.4%	0.4%	0.4%	0.5%
Employees	—	—	—	—	—	—	—	—	—	—	7,885

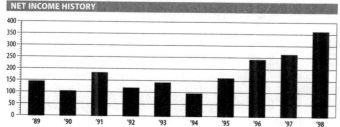

NET INCOME HISTORY

1998 FISCAL YEAR-END
Equity as % of assets: 4.8%
Return on assets: 0.6%
Return on equity: 11.8%
Long-term debt ($ mil.): —
Sales ($ mil.): 11,728

MassMutual®

MASTERCARD

OVERVIEW

MasterCard International hopes to master the market, but it has a ways to go: its approximately 25% share of the payments market is about half that of the leader, Visa. Based appropriately enough in Purchase, New York, MasterCard has cards for shoppers buying on credit (MasterCard) and for debt-shy consumers paying via debit (Maestro and MasterMoney). It is working hard amid growing competition to make its electronic smart card (Mondex) the industry standard. MasterCard is owned by the 23,000 financial institutions that issue its cards; the company markets the brand, provides the transaction authorization network, and collects fees from members. Its cards are accepted at 16 million global locations.

Long considered more downmarket than Visa, MasterCard is working to add affluent users (the World MasterCard offers 24-hour concierge services). And it has hopes in the field of smart cards (single use or refillable chip-based cards used as cash) through its 51%-owned subsidiary Mondex International. Smart cards are common in Europe but have met consumer resistance in the US. MasterCard is launching smart card initiatives in Asia and moving into wireless e-commerce.

MasterCard's quest for market share in the 1990s has been hurt by revolving-door management and past problems with its European affiliate, Europay. However, the decision of Citigroup, one of the US's largest card issuers, to shift most of its credit card business to MasterCard may help.

HISTORY

A group of bankers formed The Interbank Card Association (ICA) in 1966 to establish authorization, clearing, and settlement procedures for bank credit card transactions. This was particularly important to banks left out of the rapidly growing BankAmericard (later Visa) network sponsored by Bank of America.

By 1969, ICA was issuing the Master Charge card throughout the US and had formed alliances in Europe and Japan. In the mid-1970s ICA modernized its system, replacing telephone transaction authorization with a computerized magnetic strip system.

ICA had members in Africa, Australia, and Europe by 1979. That year the organization changed its name (and the card's) to MasterCard to reflect both its enlarged function as an integrated payment services company and its global identity.

In 1980 Russell Hogg became president when John Reynolds resigned after disagreeing with the board over company performance and direction. Hogg made major organizational changes and consolidated data processing in St. Louis. MasterCard began offering debit cards (1980), traveler's checks (1981), and other services.

MasterCard issued the first credit cards in China in 1987. The next year it bought Cirrus, then the world's largest ATM network. It also secured Eurocard (now Europay) to supervise MasterCard's European operations and help build the brand.

Hogg resigned in 1988 after disagreements with the board and was succeeded by Alex Hart. In 1991 the Maestro debit card was unveiled.

The 1990s were marked by trouble in Europe: The Europay pact hadn't resulted in the boom MasterCard had hoped for, customer service was below par, and competition was keen. Alex Hart retired in 1994 and was succeeded by Eugene Lockhart, who tackled the European woes. Lockhart considered ending the relationship, but worked things out with Europay, which began improving service and recognition. By the end of the decade, Europay was locked in a vicious battle to undercut Visa's market share through lower fees.

MasterCard in 1995 invested in UK-based Mondex International (now 51% owned by MasterCard International), maker of electronic, set-value, refillable smart cards. But US consumer resistance to cash cards and competition in the more advanced European market delayed growth in this area.

Lockhart resigned in 1997 and was succeeded by former head of overseas operations Robert Selander. The next year the Justice Department sued MasterCard and Visa for prohibiting member banks from issuing competing credit cards, such as American Express' Optima. That year MasterCard and Visa came under scrutiny for attempting to create a debit card industry monopoly; Wal-Mart and other retailers have sued the two over the requirement to accept debit cards. Both cases are still pending.

Yet another management upheaval began in 1999 as the company moved to streamline its organizational structure and shift away from geographical divisions. It also said member banks could boost visibility by putting their logos on card fronts and moving MasterCard's logo to the back.

OFFICERS

Chairman: Donald L. Boudreau
President and CEO: Robert W. Selander
SEVP, Customers: Alan J. Heuer
SEVP, Strategic Ventures: William I. Jacobs
SEVP, Technology: Jerry McElhatton
SEVP, Central Resources: Christopher D. Thom
EVP; President Emeritus, Asia/Pacific Region:
James A. Cassin
EVP: Richard N. Child
EVP, Human Resources: Michael W. Michl
EVP: G. Henry Mundt III
EVP: Jean F. Rozwadowski
EVP; President, Asia/Pacific Region: Andre Sekulic
EVP: Joseph V. Tripodi
SVP, Office of the CEO: Elizabeth A. Baltz
SVP, Audit: Andrew L. Cheskis
SVP and CFO: Frank J. Cotroneo
SVP, Global Planning and Analysis: Mary C. Johnsson
SVP, Electronic Commerce: Art Kranzley
SVP, Corporate Secretary, and General Counsel:
Robert E. Norton Jr.
SVP, Global Communications: David A. Ruth
Auditors: PricewaterhouseCoopers LLP

LOCATIONS

HQ: MasterCard International Incorporated,
2000 Purchase St., Purchase, NY 10577
Phone: 914-249-2000 **Fax:** 914-249-4206
Web site: http://www.mastercard.com

MasterCard International provides services in more than
220 countries.

1998 Gross Dollar Volume

	% of total
US	47
Asia/Pacific	26
Europe	19
Latin America	4
Canada	3
Middle East & Africa	1
Total	**100**

PRODUCTS/OPERATIONS

1998 Sales

	$ mil.	% of total
Operations fees	609	49
Member assessments	579	46
Other	69	5
Total	**1,257**	**100**

Products
Maestro (debit card)
MasterCard (credit card including standard, Gold,
Platinum, and World cards, as well as business,
business debit, corporate, corporate fleet, corporate
purchasing, and executive cards)
MasterCard Global Service (telephone services)
MasterCard OnLiNE (risk management tools)
MasterCard/Cirrus ATM network
Member Protection Program
Mondex (chip-based electronic cash card)

COMPETITORS

American Express
Morgan Stanley Dean Witter
Visa

HISTORICAL FINANCIALS & EMPLOYEES

Private FYE: December	Annual Growth	1989	1990	1991	1992	1993	1994	1995	1996	1997	1998
Sales ($ mil.)	18.2%	—	329	375	451	540	665	816	946	1,090	1,257
Net income ($ mil.)	48.5%	—	—	—	—	—	12	21	71	40	57
Income as % of sales	—	—	—	—	—	—	1.8%	2.6%	7.6%	3.6%	4.6%
Employees	13.0%	—	—	—	1,300	1,975	2,000	2,025	2,357	2,400

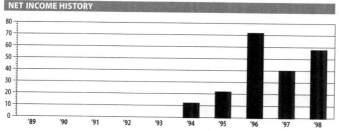

NET INCOME HISTORY

1998 FISCAL YEAR-END

Debt ratio: 26.6%
Return on equity: 28.9%
Cash ($ mil.): 150
Current ratio: 1.34
Long-term debt ($ mil.): 82

MAYO FOUNDATION

OVERVIEW

Mayo can whip up a medical miracle. Rochester, Minnesota-based Mayo Foundation manages the Mayo Clinic, the world-famous private medical facility. Its multidisciplinary team approach to health care attracts some 400,000 patients a year, including such notables as Ronald and Nancy Reagan and the late King Hussein of Jordan. Affluent patients who can pay — well — for treatment (and who may contribute to the endowment) help subsidize care for those who can't pay.

In addition to the Mayo Clinic, the foundation operates two other Rochester hospitals — Saint Marys and Rochester Methodist. It has clinics in Scottsdale, Arizona, and Jacksonville, and operates 13 hospitals in Iowa, Minnesota, and Wisconsin. At the University of Minnesota, the foundation's education programs include the Mayo Graduate School of Medicine and the Mayo School of Health-Related Sciences.

With managed care limiting patients' ability to use its facilities, Mayo forms referral alliances with hospital groups, HMOs, and other groups. Its charter prevents it from raising prices to compensate for rising health care costs, so the foundation commercializes medical technology, publishes medical literature, and invests in other medical startups to increase income.

HISTORY

In 1845 William Mayo came to the US from England. He was a doctor, veterinarian, river boatman, surveyor, and newspaper editor before settling in Rochester, Minnesota, in 1863.

When a tornado struck Rochester in 1883, Mayo took charge of a makeshift hospital. The Sisters of St. Francis offered to build a hospital to replace the one lost in the disaster if Mayo would head the staff. He agreed reluctantly. Not only were hospitals then associated with the poor and insane, but his affiliation with the sisters raised eyebrows among Protestants and Catholics.

Saint Marys Hospital opened in 1889. Mayo's sons William and Charles, who were beginning their medical careers, helped him. After the elder Mayo retired, the sons ran the hospital. Although the brothers accepted all medical cases, they made the hospital self-sufficient by attracting patients who could pay. They did this by pioneering in specialization at a time when physicians were jacks-of-all-medical-trades.

The emphasis on specialization attracted other physicians, and by 1907 the practice was known as "the Mayo's clinic." The brothers, in association with the University of Minnesota, established the Mayo Foundation for Medical Research (now the Mayo Graduate School of Medicine), the world's first program to train medical specialists, in 1915.

In 1919 the brothers transferred the clinic properties and miscellaneous financial assets, primarily from patient care profits, into the Mayo Properties Association (renamed the Mayo Foundation in 1964). Under the terms of the endowment, all Mayo Clinic medical staff members became salaried employees. In 1933 the clinic established one of the first blood banks in the US. Both brothers died in 1939.

Part of the Association's mission was to fund research. In 1950 two Mayo researchers won a Nobel Prize for developing cortisone, used to treat rheumatoid arthritis. The foundation opened its second medical school, the Mayo Medical School, in 1972.

In the 1980s, under pressure from insurers to cut hospital admissions and stays, the foundation diversified with for-profit ventures. In 1983 Mayo began publishing the *Mayo Clinic Health Letter,* its first subscription publication for a general audience, and the *Mayo Clinic Family Health Book*. It also began providing specialized lab services to other doctors and hospitals. The addition of Rochester Methodist Hospital to the Mayo Clinic/St. Marys group was also a response to financial pressures and created the largest not-for-profit medical concern in the country. Following the money south as affluent folks retired, the foundation opened clinics in Jacksonville (1986); Scottsdale, Arizona (1987); and in nearby Phoenix (1998).

Seeking to expand care in its home market, Mayo in 1992 formed the Mayo Health System, a regional network of health care facilities and medical practices. In 1996 former patient Barbara Woodward Lips left her $127.9 million estate to the foundation, the largest bequest in its history.

In the late 1990s the foundation increasingly looked to corporate partnerships to help defray the costs and expand the scope of its research activities. In 1998 and 1999 Mayo expanded overseas, opening nonmedical regional offices to build its presence in Asia, the Middle East, and Mexico.

OFFICERS

Chairman, Board of Trustees: Francis D. Fergusson
President and CEO: Robert R. Waller
CFO and Treasurer: David R. Ebel
VP; Chair, Executive Committee: Michael B. Wood
VP and Director for Education:
Richard M. Weinshilboum
VP and Chief Administrative Officer: John H. Herrell
Chief Development Officer: David W. Lawrence
Secretary; Chair, Planning and Public Affairs:
Robert K. Smoldt
General Counsel: Jill A. Beed
Chair, Board of Governors, Mayo Clinic Jacksonville:
Leo F. Black
Chair, Board of Governors, Mayo Clinic Rochester:
Robert R. Hattery
Chair, Board of Governors, Mayo Clinic Scottsdale:
Michael B. O'Sullivan
Chair, Human Resources: Marita Heller
**Chair, Department of Radiation Oncology, Mayo Clinic
Scottsdale:** Michele Y. Halyard
Director for Development: E. Rolland Dickson
Director, Mayo Clinic Cancer Center:
Franklyn G. Prendergast
Administrator, Mayo Clinic Rochester:
Sharon E. Dunemann

LOCATIONS

HQ: 200 1st St. SW, Rochester, MN 55905
Phone: 507-284-2511   **Fax:** 507-284-0161
Web site: http://www.mayo.edu

PRODUCTS/OPERATIONS

1998 Sales

	% of total
Rochester Medical Center	47
Mayo Regional Practices	20
Jacksonville Medical Center	9
Scottsdale Medical Center	6
Investments	4
Mayo Medical Laboratories	4
Research	4
Contributions	2
Other	4
Total	**100**

Mayo Publications

Publications for Patients
Inside Mayo Clinic (Rochester)
The Mayo Checkup (Jacksonville)
*Mayo Clinic Complete Book of Pregnancy
  & Baby's First Year*
Mayo Clinic Family Health Book
Mayo Clinic Guide to Self-Care
Mayo Clinic Health Letter
Mayo Clinic Heart Book
Mayo Clinic on Arthritis
Mayo Clinic Women's HealthSource
Perspectives on Mayo
Update (Scottsdale)

Publications for Physicians
Clinical Update
Mayo Clinic Cardiology Review
Mayo Clinic Proceedings
Mayo Medical Laboratories Communique
Mayo Medical Laboratories Interpretive Handbook
Medical Update (Jacksonville)

COMPETITORS

Allina Health
Ascension
Catholic Health Initiatives
Catholic Healthcare Partners
Columbia/HCA
Detroit Medical Center
HEALTHSOUTH
HMA
Henry Ford Health System
Johns Hopkins Health
Memorial Sloan-Kettering
Mercy Health Services
Methodist Health Care
New York City Health and Hospitals
Rush System for Health
SSM Health Care
ScrippsHealth
Tenet Healthcare
UCSF Stanford Health
Universal Health Services

HISTORICAL FINANCIALS & EMPLOYEES

Not-for-profit FYE: December	Annual Growth	1989	1990	1991	1992	1993	1994	1995	1996	1997	1998
Sales ($ mil.)	9.4%	1,058	1,181	1,323	1,490	1,579	1,873	2,189	2,348	2,566	2,370
Employees	7.4%	17,165	17,836	18,775	20,615	21,770	21,856	25,433	28,671	30,497	32,531

SALES HISTORY

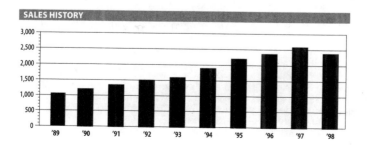

MCCRORY CORPORATION

OVERVIEW

Like horror hero Freddy Krueger, McCrory refuses to die. The most recent incarnation of the York, Pennsylvania-based chain operates about 175 variety stores under the names H. L. Green, McLellan, McCrory, J. J. Newberry, and T.G.& Y. Most of the stores are in the northeastern US, but some are in Arizona, New Mexico, Oregon, Texas, and Washington state.

McCrory's flourished in the five-and-dime heyday of the 1950s and 1960s. However, during the past two decades it has lost customers to malls and large discount chains and has struggled for survival. Although the company operated under bankruptcy protection for

nearly six years, it has outlived discount brethren Ben Franklin (bankrupt in 1996) and Woolworth (closed in 1997).

At its largest McCrory had 1,300 stores; it emerged from bankruptcy in 1997 with 159. Meshulam Riklis, who controlled the company as it descended into Chapter 11, bought the remaining stores out of bankruptcy through his HGG Acquisition Corp. for $51 million. He used $35 million of that to repay a loan he had made the company and the remainder to pay administrative claims (stiffing other creditors). To improve sales, McCrory is refurbishing stores and expanding its grocery selection.

HISTORY

John McCrorey opened his first variety store in Scottdale, Pennsylvania, in 1882. In 1897 he joined forces with Sebastian Kresge (founder of Kmart) and opened five-and-dime stores in Memphis and Detroit, until their eventual split up in 1899. By 1915 the McCrory chain (which dropped the "e," supposedly to save money on signs) went on to grow to more than 125 stores.

McCrory went bankrupt during the Depression. In 1936 Morrow Brothers acquired stakes in McCrory and another chain, McLellan Stores. As part of Morrow's United Stores Corp., McCrory's image improved with new stores and displays, and by the 1950s it was a leader in the five-and-dime industry. McCrory and McLellan, which were 37%-owned by United Stores, merged in 1959. Later that year the operations of retailer H. L. Green Co. were added, giving United Stores control of 850 outlets. During the early 1960s Meshulam Riklis bought stakes in United Stores and H. L. Green, gaining control of McCrory.

Born in Istanbul, Turkey, and raised in Palestine, Riklis came to the US in 1947. After a stint as a stockbroker, in 1957 he gained control of Rapid-American, an office machine and greeting card company. Rapid-American was used to take over other firms, including the McCrory chain in 1960. By 1963 poor earnings had forced Riklis to sell everything except a 51% stake in McCrory.

Riklis rebuilt Rapid-American, whose holdings included the McCrory-McLellan-Green operations. In 1972 Rapid-American acquired J. J. Newberry and merged its 439 stores with its other retail operations as G. McNew. But the move failed to revive sales; in 1975 the operations were renamed McCrory and several poorly performing stores were closed. The next year McCrory acquired the operations of variety store operator W. T. Grant. Rapid-American gained

full control of McCrory, which by then had 883 stores. Meanwhile Riklis romanced entertainer Pia Zadora (30 years his junior), whom he married in 1977. (They divorced in 1995.)

By the early 1980s McCrory was again struggling, and Riklis hired aggressive managers and offered incentives to raise sales. The effort was briefly effective, but by the end of the decade, the company was again on the skids and Riklis' other holdings were strapped with debt. To fund more acquisitions, Riklis engineered a series of cash-generating schemes, including transfers of assets from Rapid-American to Riklis Family Corp. Several deals involved Riklis in controversy.

For example, he drew criticism for his role in the 1986 Guinness takeover of liquor producer United Distillers Company. Riklis, Ivan Boesky, and others bought Guinness stock, raising the price just as it was being used to acquire United Distillers. Riklis-owned distiller Schenley depended on continued US distribution rights of Dewar's, a Distillers' brand, after the takeover. Amid the ensuing stock-manipulation lawsuits, Guinness chief Ernest Saunders resigned, but Riklis escaped legal entanglements after selling Schenley at a loss to Guinness in 1987. In 1989 McCrory acquired 130 G.C. Murphy stores and 25 Bargain World stores from Ames Department Stores for $77.6 million.

The company was again in trouble by the early 1990s. The chain, which had 1,000 stores by 1991, began closing more stores. By the time McCrory and McCrory Parent Corp. (the successor to Rapid-American) went bankrupt in 1992, there were 810 stores. It remained in bankruptcy, closing stores, until early 1997. That year Riklis' HGG Acquisition Corp. acquired 159 McCrory stores. In 1998 McCrory began refurbishing select outlets.

Chairman and CEO: Meshulam Riklis
President: Ted Watkins
SVP and Treasurer: Paul Weiner
General Counsel (HR): John Gaunt

LOCATIONS

HQ: 2955 E. Market St., York, PA 17402
Phone: 717-757-8181   **Fax:** 717-699-4099

PRODUCTS/OPERATIONS

Store Chains
H. L. Green
J. J. Newberry
McCrory
McLellan
T.G.& Y.

COMPETITORS

Ames
Bradlees
CVS
Dollar Tree
Family Dollar Stores
Kmart
Target Stores
Wal-Mart
Walgreen

HISTORICAL FINANCIALS & EMPLOYEES

Private FYE: January	Annual Growth	1989	1990	1991	1992	1993	1994	1995	1996	1997	1998
Sales ($ mil.)	(26.6%)	—	—	1,519	1,363	1,161	1,024	840	604	447	175
Employees	(42.2%)	—	—	—	—	—	—	11,300	8,900	5,800	2,184

SALES HISTORY

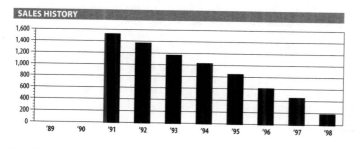

MCKINSEY & COMPANY

OVERVIEW

If you're not good enough to make partner at McKinsey & Company, cheer up — you still could become chairman of American Express. McKinsey, the world's leading management consultant firm, is based in New York City and has about 74 offices in 38 countries. The company, with an old boys' network that reaches to the top of some of the world's largest companies, has been compared to the Mafia. Distinguished alumni include business guru Tom Peters, American Express chairman and CEO Harvey Golub, IBM chairman and CEO Louis Gerstner, and former CBS chairman and CEO Michael Jordan.

The Firm (as it is known to insiders) provides services in strategy, overall organization, policy, profit and costs, research and development, and management information, among other areas. It is also beefing up its capabilities in information technology, an area on which the consulting industry is increasingly focused. Its customers are primarily private companies, but McKinsey also serves government organizations, foundations, and associations. Additionally, the company runs the McKinsey Global Institute, an independent research group that generates original research on economic, social, and geopolitical issues.

McKinsey's cachet comes from its devotion to the bottom line, meticulous data-gathering methods, discretion, and a carefully cultivated mystique. These principles have forged its reputation as an unquestionable source of reliable, objective advice. The Firm's partners must survive a rigorous up-or-out weeding process in which failure to advance to ever-higher levels means dismissal. The company is owned by its partners and led by a managing director.

HISTORY

McKinsey & Company was founded in Chicago in 1926 by University of Chicago accounting professor James McKinsey, a pioneer in the field of management. The company evolved from an auditing practice of McKinsey and his partners, Marvin Bower and A. T. Kearney, who began analyzing business and industry and offering advice. McKinsey died in 1937; two years later, Bower, who headed the New York office, and Kearney, in Chicago, split the firm. Kearney renamed the Chicago office A. T. Kearney & Co., and Bower kept the McKinsey name and built up a collegial practice structured like a law firm.

Bower focused on the big picture instead of on specific operating problems, helping boost billings to $2 million by 1950. He hired staff straight out of prestigious business schools, reinforcing the firm's theoretical bent. Bower implemented a competitive up-or-out policy requiring employees who are not continually promoted to leave the firm. Only 20% of associates become partners; only 10% become directors.

Before becoming president in 1953, Dwight Eisenhower asked McKinsey to find out exactly what it was that the government did.

By 1959 Bower had opened an office in London, followed by others in Amsterdam; Dusseldorf, Germany; Melbourne; Milan, Italy; Paris; and Zurich. In 1964 the company founded *The McKinsey Quarterly,* a management journal written primarily by McKinsey consultants. When Bower retired in 1967, sales were $20 million, and McKinsey was the #1 management consulting firm. During the 1970s it faced stiff competition from firms with newer approaches and lost market share. In response, then-managing director Ronald Daniel started specialty practices and expanded international operations.

The consulting boom of the 1980s was spurred by mergers and buyouts. By 1988 the firm had 1,800 consultants, sales were $620 million, and 50% of billings came from overseas.

The recession of the early 1990s hit white-collar workers, including consultants. McKinsey, scrambling to upgrade its technical side, bought Information Consulting Group (ICG), its first acquisition. But the corporate cultures did not meld, and most ICG people left by 1993.

In 1994 the company elected its first managing director of non-European descent, Indian-born Rajat Gupta, to a three-year term, which was later extended. Two years later the traditionally hush-hush firm found itself at the center of that most public 1990s arena, the sexual discrimination lawsuit. A female ex-consultant in Texas sued, claiming McKinsey had sabotaged her career.

In 1998 McKinsey partnered with Northwestern University and the University of Pennsylvania to establish a world-class business school in India. The following year, a survey of graduating seniors in Europe, the UK, and the US named the company as their ideal employer.

Managing Director: Rajat Gupta
CFO: Donna Rosenwasser
Director Research and Information Systems:
Jane M. Kirkland
Director Communications: Stuart Flack
Director Personnel: Jerome Vascellaro
General Counsel: Jean Molino

LOCATIONS

HQ: 55 E. 52nd St., New York, NY 10022
Phone: 212-446-7000   **Fax:** 212-446-8575
Web site: http://www.mckinsey.com

PRODUCTS/OPERATIONS

Selected Areas of Practice
Aerospace and defense
Automotive
Banking and securities
Business technology (information technology)
Business-to-business marketing
Chemicals
Consumer industries and packaged goods
Continuous relationship marketing
Corporate finance
Corporate strategy
Electronics
Environment
Foreign affiliated companies
Information technology and systems
Insurance
Latin American desk
Marketing
Microeconomics
Operational effectiveness
Payors and providers
Pharmaceuticals and medical products
Post-merger management
Pricing
Pulp and paper
Purchasing and supply management
Retail
Sales force and channel management
Strategic alliances
Telecommunications
Transportation

COMPETITORS

Andersen Consulting
Arthur D. Little
Bain & Company
Booz, Allen
Boston Consulting
Deloitte Touche Tohmatsu
EDS
Ernst & Young

Gemini Consulting
IBM
KPMG
Marsh & McLennan
Perot Systems
PricewaterhouseCoopers
Towers Perrin

HISTORICAL FINANCIALS & EMPLOYEES

Private FYE: December	Annual Growth	1989	1990	1991	1992	1993	1994	1995	1996	1997	1998
Sales ($ mil.)	16.4%	635	900	1,050	1,230	1,300	1,500	1,800	2,100	2,200	2,500
Employees	10.7%	4,000	4,500	4,500	5,500	5,560	6,000	6,050	7,100	8,500	10,000

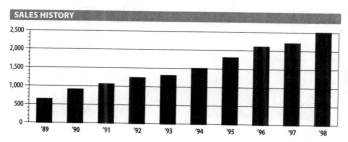

SALES HISTORY

McKinsey&Company, Inc.

MEIJER, INC.

OVERVIEW

After "behemoth: something of monstrous size or power," the dictionary might add, "example — a Meijer store." Grand Rapids, Michigan-based Meijer (pronounced "Meyer") has about 130 combination grocery and general merchandise stores averaging 200,000 to 250,000 sq. ft. (about the size of four regular grocery stores) in Illinois, Indiana, Kentucky, Michigan, and Ohio.

Although the discount superstore format is most often referred to in conjunction with Wal-Mart Stores, Meijer is its pioneer. In addition to selling groceries (which account for one-third of the sales floor), including private-label products, typical Meijer stores have about 40 departments, such as a bakery, bank, pharmacy, photo lab, and food court; hardware, toys, and apparel sections; and pet and garden centers. Most stores also sell gasoline and have multiple in-store restaurants.

It makes itself known to potential customers in its new locales with an advertising blitzkrieg that includes large newspaper inserts and thousands of promotional videos that can be redeemed at stores for phone cards. Rivals like Kroger are forced to answer Meijer's low prices — a gallon of milk for 99 cents — with promotional pricing of their own.

The Meijer family owns the company.

HISTORY

Dutch immigrant and barber Hendrik Meijer opened Thrift Market in Greenville, Michigan, in 1934 with the help of his wife, Gezina; son, Fred; and daughter, Johanna. Next to his barbershop was a vacant space that he owned but, because of the Depression, was unable to rent out. He bought $338.76 in merchandise on credit and started his own grocery store. Meijer had 22 competitors in Greenville alone, but his dedication to low prices (he and Fred often traveled long distances to find bargains) attracted customers. In 1935, to encourage self-service, Meijer placed 12 wicker baskets at the front of the store and posted signs that read, "Take a basket. Help yourself."

A second store was opened in 1942. The company added four more in the 1950s and began a supermarket chain in western Michigan. In 1962 Meijer — then with 14 stores — opened the first one-stop shopping Meijer Thrifty Acres store, similar to a hypermarket another operator had opened in Belgium a year earlier. By 1964, the year that Hendrik died and Fred took over, three of these general merchandise stores were operating. The company entered Ohio in the late 1960s.

Many of the Meijer stores were equipped with gasoline pumps in the late 1970s. However, a 1978 law prohibiting the sale of gasoline and alcohol at the same site forced the company to separate the two operations.

In the early 1980s Meijer bought 14 Twin Fair stores in Ohio, 10 of them in Cincinnati. But it sold the stores by 1987 after disappointing results. Meijer had greater success in Columbus, Ohio, where it opened one store that year and immediately captured 20% of the market. In 1988 the company began keeping most stores open 24 hours a day.

Meijer annihilated competitors in Dayton, Ohio, in 1991, when it opened four stores that year. The company entered the Toledo market in 1993 with four stores; after one year it had taken 11.5% of the market. A foray into the membership warehouse market was abandoned in 1993, just a few months after they had opened, when Meijer said it would close all seven SourceClub warehouses in Michigan and Ohio.

The company entered Indiana in 1994, opening 16 stores in less than two years; it also reached an agreement with McDonald's to open restaurants in several stores. The first labor strike in Meijer's history hit four stores in Toledo that year, leading to pickets at 14 others. Union officials accused the company of using intimidation tactics by its hiring of large, uniformed men in flak jackets and combat boots as security guards, but after nine weeks Meijer agreed to recognize the workers' newly attained union affiliation.

In 1995 the company opened 13 stores, including its first in Illinois. It re-entered the Cincinnati market in 1996, announcing the opening of two new stores there by mailing 80,000 videos to residents. By the end of the year, Meijer had a total of five stores in Cincinnati and had entered Kentucky.

Meijer opened a central kitchen in Indiana to prepare deli salads and some vegetables and process orange juice for its stores in 1997. It opened its first two stores in Louisville, Kentucky, the following year. Meijer broke into the tough Chicago-area market with its first store in 1999.

Senior Chairman: Fred Meijer, age 79
Co-Chairman: Doug Meijer
Co-Chairman: Hank Meijer
President: Jim McLean
SVP of Human Resources: Windy Ray
SVP and General Counsel: Bob Riley
SVP of Finance and Administration: Jim Walsh
VP of Finance and Treasurer: Joan Garety
**Director of Technology Services, Advertising, and
e-Commerce:** Russ Cole
Director of Advertising Group: Paul Smardo
Director of Corporate Trade Development: Tom Vilella
Director of Corporate Relations: John Zimmerman

LOCATIONS

HQ: 2929 Walker Ave. NW, Grand Rapids, MI 49544
Phone: 616-453-6711   **Fax:** 616-791-2572
Web site: http://www.meijer.com

PRODUCTS/OPERATIONS

Selected Meijer Store Departments

Apparel	Health and beauty
Auto supplies	products
Bakery	Home fashions
Banking	Jewelry
Books	Lawn and garden
Bulk foods	Nutrition centers
Coffee shop	Pets and pet supplies
Computer software	Pharmacy
Delicatessen	Photo lab
Electronics	Portrait studio
Floral	Produce
Gas station	Service meat and seafood
The Grand Food Fair (food	Sporting goods
court)	Tobacco
Hardware	Toys

COMPETITORS

A&P	IGA
ALDI	Kmart
Albertson's	Kroger
Ames	Marsh Supermarkets
CVS	Penn Traffic
D&W Food Centers	Phar-Mor
Dayton Hudson	SUPERVALU
Dollar General	Schottenstein Stores
Dominick's	Seaway Food Town
Eagle Food	Wal-Mart
Family Dollar Stores	Walgreen
Fleming Companies	Winn-Dixie
Home Depot	

HISTORICAL FINANCIALS & EMPLOYEES

Private FYE: January	Annual Growth	1990	1991	1992	1993	1994	1995	1996	1997	1998	1999
Sales ($ mil.)	12.0%	3,000	3,700	5,370	5,390	4,250	5,160	5,640	6,000	6,900	8,300
Employees	9.9%	37,000	42,700	50,000	60,000	65,000	70,000	65,000	73,000	77,000	86,200

SALES HISTORY

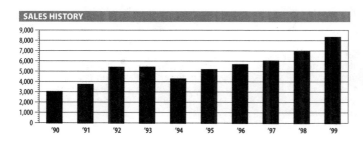

MENARD, INC.

If sticks and stones break bones, what can two-by-fours and two-inch nails do? That is what Eau Claire, Wisconsin-based Menard is wondering now that #1 home improvement giant The Home Depot is hammering away at its home turf. The third-largest home improvement chain in the US (after The Home Depot and Lowe's), Menard runs about 135 Menards stores in nine upper-midwestern states. Although its outlets are typically smaller than those of The Home Depot, the stores offer a similar selection of products by building large warehouses adjacent to stores and then quickly restocking merchandise when it's sold. The chain's merchandise is laid out on easy-to-reach, supermarket-styled shelves rather than twenty-foot high racks common to lumberyards. That shopper-friendly approach has helped it find a niche with consumers scared away by large warehouse retailers. Billionaire founder John Menard owns and runs the chain; other family members are engaged in its everyday operations.

To help keep expenses low and prices cheap, Menard makes some of its product lines, including countertops, picnic tables, and doors, at its own manufacturing facility. It also cuts costs by buying overruns, products that are overproduced and sold at discounted prices.

In addition to his home improvement chain, Menard owns Team Menard, an Indy car racing team.

HISTORY

John Menard was the oldest of eight children on a Wisconsin dairy farm. To pay for attending the University of Wisconsin at Eau Claire, he and some fellow college students built pole barns in the late 1950s. Learning that other builders had trouble finding lumber outlets that were open on the weekends, Menard began buying wood in bulk and selling it to them. He added other supplies in 1960 and sold his construction business in 1970 as building supply revenues became his chief source of income.

He founded Menard in 1972 as the do-it-yourself craze was beginning, but he wanted an operation run more like mass merchandiser Target, with easy-to-reach shelves, wide aisles, and tile floors rather than the cold, cumbersome layout used by lumberyards. To offer a wide selection of merchandise within a relatively small amount of space, Menard built warehouses and stockrooms behind the stores so he could restock merchandise quickly.

Menard's vision worked, and he began building his midwestern empire, often acquiring abandoned retail sites that were inexpensive and in good locations. By 1986 Menard was in Iowa, Minnesota, North and South Dakota, and by 1990 it had 46 stores. In the early 1990s Menard began enlarging its operations to serve the ever-growing number of stores, opening a huge warehouse and distribution center and a manufacturing facility that made doors, Formica countertops, and other products. It entered Nebraska in 1990 and opened its first store in Chicago the next year. By 1992 there were more than 60 Menards stores.

That year Menard made the *National Enquirer* with a story about the firing of a store manager who had built a wheelchair-accessible home for his 11-year-old daughter with spina bifida, violating a company theft-prevention policy forbidding store managers to build their own homes. The company insisted that the man was fired in part because of poor work performance.

Menard continued to expand to new areas, operating stores in Indiana and Michigan by 1992. As it continued expanding in the Chicago area, it offered varying store formats, ranging from a full line of building materials to smaller Menards Hardware Plus stores. By 1994 Menard had 85 stores, many bigger than 100,000 sq. ft.

In 1995 and 1996, the company was plagued with lawsuits filed by customers charging false arrest and imprisonment for shoplifting. In one incident, an on-duty police officer who was apprehending a shoplifting suspect at a store was even stopped and searched.

Competition also heated up during that time. The Home Depot's push into the Midwest — including opening several stores directly across the street from Menards — spurred Menard to fight back by lowering prices and opening nearly 40 stores. The fight forced smaller chains like Handy Andy out of business.

In 1997 Menard and his company were fined $1.7 million after dumping bags of toxic ash from the company's manufacturing facility at residential trash pick-up sites rather than at properly regulated outlets (it had been fined for similar violations in 1989 and 1994). In response to a price war initiated by The Home Depot, in 1998 Menard dropped sales prices by 10%.

President and CEO: John R. Menard
CFO and Treasurer: Earl R. Rasmussen
Manager Operations: Larry Menard
Director Human Resources: Terri Jain
Senior Merchandiser: Ed Archibald

LOCATIONS

HQ: 4777 Menard Dr., Eau Claire, WI 54703
Phone: 715-876-5911　　**Fax:** 715-876-5901

PRODUCTS/OPERATIONS

Operations
Menards (home improvement stores)
Midwest Manufacturing and Distributing (Menard-brand
  products)

COMPETITORS

84 Lumber	Payless Cashways
Ace Hardware	Sears
Carolina Holdings	Sherwin-Williams
Do it Best	Sutherland Lumber
The Home Depot	TruServ
Lanoga	Wal-Mart
Lowe's	Wickes
Montgomery Ward	

HISTORICAL FINANCIALS & EMPLOYEES

Private FYE: January	Annual Growth	1990	1991	1992	1993	1994	1995	1996	1997	1998	1999
Estimated sales ($ mil.)	19.1%	—	—	—	1,400	1,750	2,300	2,700	3,200	3,700	4,000
Employees	7.0%	—	—	—	—	5,000	5,800	6,534	7,000	7,000	7,000

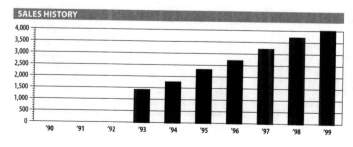

SALES HISTORY

MENARDS

METROMEDIA COMPANY

OVERVIEW

Metromedia has a large stake in steak. Billionaire investors John Kluge and Stuart Subotnick run the East Rutherford, New Jersey-based company through a partnership. The firm is the franchisor for three of the nation's best-known steak houses: Bonanza, Ponderosa Steakhouse, and Steak and Ale, as well as the Bennigan's pub-style restaurant chain. Under the Metromedia Restaurant Group banner, the company has more than 1,000 restaurants in the US and internationally. One of the nation's largest private companies, Metromedia owns controlling

interests in telecom firms Metromedia International Group (MIG) and Metromedia Fiber Network, and energy broker Metromedia Energy (formerly CPM Energy).

Its aging fleet of family-oriented restaurants (most were started in the 1960s) were not top performers during much of the 1990s, partly as a result of increased competition from steak house upstarts like Outback Steakhouse. With an influx of funds from a recent refinancing, the company is updating its Bennigan's and Steak and Ale concepts. It is also expanding through new franchising agreements.

HISTORY

German immigrant John Kluge, born in 1914, came to Detroit at age eight with his mother and stepfather. At Columbia University he studied economics and (to the chagrin of college administrators) poker, building a tidy sum with his winnings by graduation. Kluge worked in Army intelligence during WWII. After the war he bought WGAY radio in Silver Spring, Maryland, and went on to buy and sell other small radio stations.

Kluge began to diversify, entering the wholesale food business in the mid-1950s. In 1959 he purchased control of Metropolitan Broadcasting, including TV stations in New York City and Washington DC, and took it public. He renamed the company Metromedia in 1960.

Metromedia added independent stations — to the then-legal limit of seven — in other major markets, paying relatively little compared to network affiliate prices. The stations struggled through years of infomercials but thrived in the late 1970s and early 1980s. Metromedia's stock price rose from $4.50 in 1974 to more than $500 in 1983. The company also acquired radio stations, the Harlem Globetrotters, and the Ice Capades.

In 1983 Kluge bought paging and cellular telephone licenses across the US. He later acquired long-distance carriers in Texas and Florida. In 1984 Metromedia went private in a $1.6 billion buyout and began to sell off its assets in 1985. It sold its Boston TV station to Hearst and its six other TV stations to Rupert Murdoch for a total of $2 billion. In 1986 it sold its outdoor advertising firm, nine of its 11 radio stations, and the Globetrotters and Ice Capades. Kluge then sold most of the company's cellular properties to SBC Communications. In 1990 it sold its New York cellular

operations to LIN Broadcasting and its Philadelphia cellular operations to Comcast.

Building what Kluge envisioned as his steak house empire, the firm bought the Ponderosa steak house chain (founded in the late 1960s) in 1988 from Asher Edelman and later added Dallas-based USA Cafés (Bonanza steak houses, founded 1964) and S&A Restaurant Corp. (Steak and Ale, founded 1966; Bennigan's, founded 1976). Also in 1988 Kluge rescued friend Arthur Krim, whose Orion Pictures was threatened by Viacom, by buying control of the filmmaker.

Kluge's grand steak house vision did not come to fruition. Increased competition squeezed profits at Ponderosa and Bonanza. The restaurant group was also plagued by management shakeups, aging facilities, food-quality issues, and even bad press. (Bennigan's was ranked the worst casual dining chain in the US in a 1992 Consumer Reports poll.)

In 1989 Kluge merged Metromedia Long Distance with the long-distance operations of ITT. Renamed Metromedia Communications in 1991, the company merged with other long-distance providers to become MCI WorldCom. (Kluge sold his 16% of MCI WorldCom to the public in 1995.)

Kluge created MIG in 1995 by merging Orion Pictures, Metromedia International Telecommunications, MCEG Sterling (film and television production), and Actava Group (maker of Snapper lawn mowers and sporting goods). Metromedia Restaurant Group announced a $190 million refinancing agreement for S&A Restaurant Corp. in 1998, which will be used in an aggressive restaurant expansion and refurbishing plan. The company also closed 28 unprofitable restaurants in 1998 and launched a franchise program to grow its Bennigan's and Steak and Ale chains.

Chairman, President, and CEO: John W. Kluge
EVP; President and CEO, Metromedia International Group: Stuart Subotnick
SVP Finance: Robert A. Maresca
SVP, Secretary, and General Counsel: Arnold L. Wadler
SVP; President, Kluge and Company: Silvia Kessel
SVP; President, Metromedia Restaurant Group: Michael Kaufman
VP and Controller: David Gassler
Director of Human Resources: Jamie Smith

LOCATIONS

HQ: 1 Meadowlands Plaza, East Rutherford, NJ 07073
Phone: 201-531-8000 **Fax:** 201-531-2804
Web site: http://www.metromediarestaurants.com

PRODUCTS/OPERATIONS

Subsidiaries and Affiliates
Metromedia Energy, Inc. (energy and long-distance telephone service)
Metromedia Fiber Network, Inc. (competitive local-exchange carrier)
Metromedia International Group (telecommunications)
Metromedia Restaurant Group (Bennigan's, Bonanza, Ponderosa, Steak and Ale restaurants)

COMPETITORS

AT&T	Lone Star Steakhouse
Applebee's	MCI WorldCom
BT	O'Charley's
Bell Atlantic	Outback Steakhouse
Brinker	Prandium
Buffets	Ryan's Family Steak
Carlson Restaurants	Houses
Worldwide	Sizzler
Champps Entertainment	Sprint
Darden Restaurants	The Restaurant Co.
Deutsche Telekom	

HISTORICAL FINANCIALS & EMPLOYEES

Private FYE: December	Annual Growth	1989	1990	1991	1992	1993	1994	1995	1996	1997	1998
Estimated sales ($ mil.)	(2.6%)	2,530	2,220	1,896	1,804	1,900	2,000	1,900	1,900	1,950	2,000
Employees	0.0%	—	—	—	—	—	—	—	—	63,000	63,000

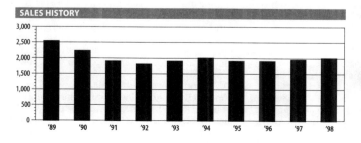

SALES HISTORY

METLIFE INSURANCE

OVERVIEW

MetLife is ditching the dog and taking it to the Street.

New York-based mutual Metropolitan Life Insurance (MetLife) has scaled back its use of long-time spokesbeagle Snoopy to gussy up its image in advance of its planned demutualization. Despite all the change, the #2 US insurer by assets (after Prudential) still sells whole and term life insurance, variable policies, and annuities around the world through approximately 45,000 agents. MetLife also provides such financial services as proprietary mutual funds to help affluent customers manage their retirement plans. The company offers investment advisory services to businesses and institutions and sells property/casualty insurance to individuals.

MetLife would like to demutualize *and* descandalize. The company is dogged by lawsuits alleging churning, that is, customers being urged to buy unnecessary new policies; many of these it settled (without admitting wrongdoing, of course) to the tune of $1.7 billion. Several other leading insurance companies have undergone similar scrutiny.

HISTORY

New York merchant Simeon Draper tried to form National Union Life and Limb Insurance to cover Union soldiers in the Civil War, but investors were scared away by heavy casualties. After several reorganizations and name changes, the enterprise emerged in 1868 as Metropolitan Life Insurance (MetLife), a stock company.

Sustained at first by business from mutual assistance societies for German immigrants, MetLife went into industrial insurance with workers' burial policies. The firm was known for its aggressive sales methods. Agents combed working-class neighborhoods, collecting small premiums. This nickel-and-dime business could be particularly profitable because if a worker missed one payment, the company could cancel the policy and keep all premiums paid, a practice outlawed in 1900.

MetLife became a mutual company (owned by its policyholders) in 1915 and began offering group insurance two years later.

After a period of conservative management under the Eckers family from 1929 to 1963, MetLife began to change, dropping industrial insurance in 1964. It started offering automobile and homeowners insurance in 1974.

The company began to diversify in the 1980s. It bought State Street Research & Management (1983), Century 21 Real Estate (1985, sold 1995), London-based Albany Life Assurance (1985), and Allstate's group life and health business (1988). In 1987 the company took over the annuities segment of the failed Baldwin United Co., and it expanded into Spain and Taiwan in 1988. During the early 1990s, the company reemphasized insurance, adding such new products as long-term-care insurance.

In 1993 MetLife was hit by charges of improper sales practices in 13 states, including misrepresentation of life insurance policies as retirement accounts and churning (persuading policyholders to replace old policies with more expensive ones). Legal fees, fines, and refunds in these cases exceeded $100 million; bad publicity had a chilling effect on policy sales. MetLife addressed the crisis by instituting new training and sales practices. (In 1998 it agreed to pay an additional $25 million civil penalty to settle the federal investigation.)

In 1996 MetLife bought New England Mutual Life Insurance, expanding its customer base to include wealthier middle-class customers (it also sought to obliterate its 1995 loss by retroactively restating results on combined sales).

MetLife's problems continued in 1996 and 1997 with a suit over its sales of insurance to Americans in Europe and another relating to the alleged mischaracterization of universal life insurance policies. The company also became the target of a churning investigation in Florida (ongoing in 1999) and of suits filed in several states alleging deceptive sales practices.

In 1997 MetLife acquired Los Angeles-based Security First Group (annuity contracts for public employees). In 1998 it sold its UK insurance operations and its Canadian business, then cut 10% (more than 1,900) of its administrative employees.

In 1999 MetLife followed the industry trend of pinpoint acquisitions and divestitures (buying and selling single product lines rather than whole companies). Deals included agreements to buy The St. Paul Companies' personal insurance business (nearly doubling that unit's size) and the individual disability lines of Lincoln National Life and to sell its managed vision care benefits operations to Cole National Corporation. MetLife also formed an asset management joint venture with Japanese life insurer Asahi Mutual Life Insurance and agreed to buy fellow insurer GenAmerica.

The company agreed in 1999 to pay $1.7 billion to settle policyholder lawsuits stemming from the misselling allegations. Late that year, MetLife filed to sell a 31% stake in the company to the public.

OFFICERS

Chairman, President and CEO: Robert H. Benmosche, age 55, $723,847 pay
VC and CFO: Stewart G. Nagler, age 56, $614,770 pay
VC and Chief Investment Officer: Gerald Clark, age 55, $614,770 pay
President, Client Services and Chief Administrative Officer: William J. Toppeta, age 50
President, Individual Business: James M. Benson, age 52, $600,000 pay
President, Institutional Business: C. Robert Henrikson, age 52, $500,000 pay
SEVP and General Counsel: Gary A. Beller, age 60
SEVP: John H. Tweedie, age 54
SVP Human Resources: Lisa M. Weber, age 36
SEVP; President and CEO, Metlife Property and Casualty Insurance Company: Catherine A. Rein, age 56
EVP and Chief Actuary: Judy E. Weiss, age 47
Auditors: Deloitte & Touche LLP

LOCATIONS

HQ: Metropolitan Life Insurance Company,
1 Madison Ave., New York, NY 10010
Phone: 212-578-2211   **Fax:** 212-578-3320
Web site: http://www.metlife.com

PRODUCTS/OPERATIONS

1998 Assets

	$ mil.	% of total
Cash & equivalents	3,301	2
Treasury & agency securities	7,747	4
Foreign government securities	3,601	2
Mortgage-backed securities	26,979	13
Corporate bonds	48,588	23
Stocks	2,340	1
Mortgage loans	16,827	8
Real estate	6,287	3
Policy loans	5,600	3
Separate account assets	58,350	26
Other assets	35,726	15
Total	**215,346**	**100**

1998 Sales

	$ mil.	% of total
Investment income	10,228	38
Premiums		
Institutional	5,101	19
Individual	4,381	16
Auto & home	1,403	5
International	618	2
Investment gains	2,021	8
Fees	1,360	5
Other	1,965	7
Total	**27,077**	**100**

Selected Affiliates

Financing and Investment
MetLife Funding, Inc.
MetLife Securities, Inc.
Nvest, LP
State Street Research & Management Company

Insurance
Afore Genesis Metropolitan, SA (Mexico)
Genesis Seguros Generales, SA (Spain)
Hyatt Legal Plans
Metropolitan Tower Life Insurance Co.
New England Life Insurance Co.
Security First Life Insurance Co.
Texas Life Insurance Co.

Investment Management
GFM International Investors (UK)

Real Estate
Farmers National Co.
SSR Realty Advisors, Inc.

COMPETITORS

AFLAC	GEICO	Pacific Mutual
AIG	Guardian Life	Principal
AXA Financial	John Hancock	Financial
Aetna	Liberty Mutual	Prudential
Allstate	Lincoln National	State Farm
American	MassMutual	TIAA-CREF
General	Mutual of Omaha	The Hartford
Aon	New York Life	Transamerica
CIGNA	Northwestern	USAA
CNA Financial	Mutual	

HISTORICAL FINANCIALS & EMPLOYEES

Mutual company FYE: December	Annual Growth	1989	1990	1991	1992	1993	1994	1995	1996	1997	1998
Assets ($ mil.)	6.5%	—	—	—	—	—	167,569	183,138	189,276	202,776	215,346
Net income ($ mil.)	85.3%	—	—	—	—	—	114	699	853	1,203	1,343
Income as % of assets	—	—	—	—	—	—	0.1%	0.4%	0.5%	0.6%	0.6%
Employees	—	—	—	—	—	—	—	—	—	—	42,300

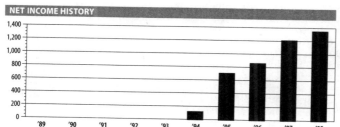

NET INCOME HISTORY

1,400
1,200
1,000
800
600
400
200
0

'89 '90 '91 '92 '93 '94 '95 '96 '97 '98

1998 FISCAL YEAR-END
Equity as % of assets: 6.9%
Return on assets: 0.6%
Return on equity: 9.3%
Long-term debt ($ mil.): 2,903
Sales ($ mil.): 27,077

MetLife®

MTA

OVERVIEW

Getting around New York City is the goal of natives and tourists alike. Getting them around is the goal of the Metropolitan Transportation Authority (MTA), the largest provider of public transportation in the US.

Serving almost 6 million people a day, New York City's MTA operates buses in all five boroughs (the Bronx, Brooklyn, Manhattan, Queens, and Staten Island), provides subway service to all but Staten Island, and operates the Staten Island Railway. The authority also provides bus and railway service to Connecticut and Long Island and maintains toll bridges and tunnels.

The MTA, a public-benefit corporation chartered by the New York Legislature, is working to become more self-sufficient. It has cut expenses and raised sales (with a 25 cent increase in fares), and it is selling off noncore operations such as its freight line. The MTA has also automated electronic fare and toll collection with its MetroCard and E-ZPass.

Meanwhile, ridership is up, crime is down, and the MTA is continuing its efforts to make the system safer and easier to use. It has placed maps on all its buses and begun to allow late-night passengers to request stops at non-designated bus stops, and — hold on to your seat — new subway trains will even feature stops announced in a clear, understandable voice. MTA is beginning a one-fare program permitting free bus and subway transfers. It has also announced a $1.7 billion improvement plan, pending approval by regulators and the public.

HISTORY

Mass transit began in New York City in the 1820s and 1830s with the introduction of horse-drawn stagecoaches run by small private firms. By 1832 a horse-drawn railcar operating on Fourth Avenue offered a smoother and faster ride than its street-bound rivals.

By 1864 residents were complaining that horsecars and buses were overcrowded and that drivers were intolerably rude. (Horsecars were transporting 45 million passengers annually.) In 1870 a short subway under Broadway was opened to the public, but it was never more than an amusement. Elevated steam railways were built, but people resisted them because of the smoke, noise, and danger from explosions. Cable cars provided a limited transit solution in the 1880s, and by the 1890s electric streetcars became important.

Construction of the first commercial subway line was completed in 1904. It was operated by Interborough Rapid Transit Co. (IRT), which leased the primary elevated rail line in 1903 and had effective control of rail transit in Manhattan and the Bronx. In 1905 IRT merged with the Metropolitan Street Railway, which operated almost all surface railways in Manhattan, giving the new firm almost complete control of the city's rapid transit. Public protests led the city to grant licenses to Brooklyn Rapid Transit (later BMT), creating the Dual System. The two rail firms quickly covered most of the city.

By the 1920s the transit system was again in crisis, largely because the two lines were not allowed to raise their five-cent fares. With the IRT and BMT in receivership in 1932, the city decided to own and operate part of the rail system and organized the Independent (IND) rail line. Pressure for public ownership and operation of the transit system resulted in the city's purchase of all of IRT's and BMT's assets in 1940 for $326 million.

In 1953 the legislature created the New York City Transit Authority, the first unified system. In 1968, two years after transit workers walked out for higher wages and left the city in a virtual gridlock, the Metropolitan Transit Authority began to coordinate the city's transit activities with other commuter services.

The 1970s and 1980s saw the city's transit infrastructure and service deteriorate while crime, accidents, graffiti, and fares rose. But by the early 1990s a multibillion-dollar modernization program had begun to make noticeable improvements: Subway stations were repaired, graffiti was removed from trains, and service was extended. By 1994 the agency said subway crime was down 50% from 1990, and ridership had increased.

The MTA set up a five-year plan in 1995 to cut expenses by $3 billion. Only 18 months later and already two-thirds of the way to reaching the goal, the authority said it would cut another $230 million and return the savings to customers as fare discounts. The agency agreed in 1996 to sell the freight operations of the Long Island Rail Road. The next year it began selling its one-fare/free-transfer MetroCard Gold.

In 1998 the MTA capital program completed the $200 million restoration of the Grand Central Terminal. The next year the MTA ordered 500 new clean-fuel buses and proposed a $1.7 billion bond program for transit improvements.

Chairman: E. Virgil Conway
First VC: Daniel T. Scannell
Executive Director: Marc V. Shaw
Deputy Executive Director and CFO:
Stephen V. Reitano
Deputy Executive Director, Corporate Affairs and Communications: Christopher P. Boylan
Deputy Executive Director, Operations and Chief of Staff: Forrest R. Taylor
Deputy Executive Director, Planning and Development: Susan L. Kupferman
Deputy Executive Director, Secretary, and General Counsel: Mary J. Mahon
President, MTA Bridges and Tunnels: Michael C. Ascher
President, MTA Long Island Bus: Neil Yellin
President, MTA Long Island Rail Road:
Thomas F. Prendergast
President, MTA Metro-North Railroad: Peter A. Cannito
President, MTA New York City Transit:
Lawrence G. Reuter
Head Human Resources: Dave Knapp
Auditor General: Nicholas DiMola
Auditors: PricewaterhouseCoopers LLP

HQ: Metropolitan Transportation Authority,
347 Madison Ave., New York, NY 10017
Phone: 212-878-7174   **Fax:** 212-878-0186
Web site: http://www.mta.nyc.ny.us

1998 Sales

	$ mil.	% of total
Operating revenues	2,848	50
State/regional taxes	1,319	23
Tolls	884	15
Local subsidies	329	6
State subsidies	209	4
Other subsidies	25	—
Other revenues	93	2
Total	**5,707**	**100**

1998 Agency Statistics

Rolling Stock
Long Island Bus: 317 buses
Long Island Rail Road: 1,086 railcars
Metro-North Railroad: 851 railcars
New York City Transit bus system: 4,172 buses
New York City Transit subway system: 5,799 railcars

Annual Revenue Vehicle Miles
Long Island Bus: 9.3 million
Long Island Rail Road: 56.5 million
Metro-North Railroad: 42.7 million
New York City bus system: 91.5 million
New York City subway system: 309.8 million
Staten Island Railway: 1.9 million

Number of Lines or Routes
Long Island Bus: 53
Long Island Rail Road: 11
Metro-North Railroad: 6
New York City Transit bus routes: 227
New York City Transit subway system: 25
Staten Island Railway: 1

Route Miles
Long Island Bus: 684
Long Island Rail Road: 595
Metro-North Railroad: 758
New York City Transit bus system: 1,671
New York City Transit subway system: 656
Staten Island Railway: 14

Government-owned FYE: December	Annual Growth	1989	1990	1991	1992	1993	1994	1995	1996	1997	1998
Sales ($ mil.)	2.9%	4,426	4,727	4,701	4,845	5,036	5,189	5,005	5,381	5,511	5,707
Net income ($ mil.)	—	—	—	—	(173)	(136)	(156)	(154)	440	(93)	(7)
Income as % of sales	—	—	—	—	—	—	—	—	8.2%	—	—
Employees	(1.7%)	67,302	65,960	64,119	63,868	64,838	65,465	58,201	56,551	57,563	57,551

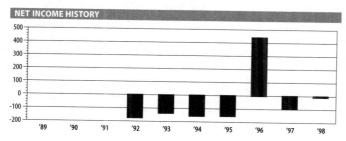

NET INCOME HISTORY

1998 FISCAL YEAR-END
Debt ratio: 45.8%
Return on equity: —
Cash ($ mil.): 46
Current ratio: 1.17
Long-term debt ($ mil.): 11,799

MICRO ELECTRONICS, INC.

OVERVIEW

"We're not greedy," says Micro Electronics co-founder, owner, and president John Baker. "We don't need it all" — just a healthy chunk of the computer, software, and peripheral sales market.

Hilliard, Ohio-based Micro Electronics, which operates about a dozen Micro Center chain stores, has declared itself a leader by means of its "technical retailing" concept. Micro Center is the largest of Micro Electronics' seven divisions. Its stores (which average 45,000 sq. ft.) carry about 36,000 products in 700 different categories. Store departments include books, education, Macintosh products, mobile computing, name brand systems, peripherals, and software. The company typically locates its stores in major cities with high-tech centers, office complexes, and universities.

Micro Center's technical retailing strategy includes intensive training for salespeople. Customer surveys helped the company create its version of a computer department store (featuring a dozen departments divided by

business and home, education, and entertainment interests), which consistently wins industry accolades.

Other Micro Electronics divisions include WinBook, which makes notebook computers and provides a technical support Web site; PowerSpec, which makes desktop computers (the company eliminates marketing and other overhead by building computers and selling them through its own stores); MEI/Micro Center, a mail-order operation; Corporate Sales Micro Center; and Micro Center Computer Education, which has taught hundreds of thousands of students everything from general computing to programming and support.

Micro Electronics is touting new products such as the WinBook XL laptop with a CD-ROM for under $1,000 and the under-$700 PowerSpec PC. Baker has been approached to sell the company or take it public, but he has refused because of his belief in his long-term business plan.

HISTORY

John Baker had studied agricultural economics, taken pharmacy classes, and worked in the insurance business before becoming interested in computers in 1976, when he read an article about microcomputing. Determined to learn more, he took a job with a Radio Shack store in Columbus, Ohio. By 1980 Baker was a store manager, but he was given a choice of quitting or being fired after a disagreement with the company over how to market computer equipment. That year he and another Radio Shack refugee, Bill Bayne, pooled their resources ($35,000) and opened the first Micro Center, in the same mall. The store was a success and within a few years had grown from 1,200 to 44,000 sq. ft. The resulting company, Micro Electronics, soon added mail-order and manufacturing operations.

The company established its Corporate Sales Micro Center subsidiary in 1983 to provide hardware, software, and services to large purchasers such as corporations and institutions.

Early on Micro Electronics began making private-label computers, but it left the business in 1985 after having trouble with the FCC (which the company has not elaborated on). In 1986 Micro Center stores added a computer education department, which evolved into the company's Micro Center Computer Education unit. The company

returned to the private-label market in 1987, making Laser brand computers.

By 1988 there were only two Micro Center stores, both in Ohio. Initially, Baker expanded the company slowly, insisting that the business finance its growth internally, without significant debt. "What grows fast, dies fast," he has said. "We won't die fast."

Growth of Micro Electronics' retail operations picked up speed in the 1990s. In 1991 the company started conducting in-store customer surveys to help maximize sales through well-designed store layouts.

Micro Electronics opened a direct marketing unit in 1993 for its WinBook computers. The company's Laser Computer brand was replaced by the PowerSpec brand in 1994. Micro Center opened a store in Houston that year and a location in Dallas the following year.

Micro Electronics' sales topped $1 billion for the first time in 1996. That year the company moved to its new 200,000-sq.-ft. headquarters near Columbus, Ohio, and added its first store in the Chicago area. In 1998 Micro Center filed a lawsuit against two former employees charging misappropriation of trade secrets. The suit claims that the ex-employees started a competing company and then began advertising heavily to lure WinBook Micro Center customers away.

CEO: Dale Brown
President: John Baker
CFO: James Koehler
Director of Human Resources: Deanna Lyon

LOCATIONS

HQ: 4119 Leap Rd., Hilliard, OH 43026
Phone: 614-850-3000   **Fax:** 614-850-3001
Web site: http://www.microelectronics.com

Micro Electronics operates 13 Micro Center stores
in the US.

Micro Center Stores
Atlanta
Boston
Chicago
Cincinnati
Cleveland
Columbus, OH
Dallas
Houston
Long Island, NY
Los Angeles
Philadelphia
Santa Clara, CA
Washington, DC

PRODUCTS/OPERATIONS

Micro Center Store Departments
Accessories
Books
Education
Furniture
Macintosh products
Mobile computing
PC hardware
PC systems
Peripherals
Service
Software
Technical support

Micro Center Computer Education Courses
Accounting and finance
Databases
Desktop publishing and graphics
Integration
Internet
Macintosh computers
Microsoft certification
Novell networking
Operating systems and environments
PCs
Programming and support
Project management
Spreadsheets
Word processing

COMPETITORS

BUY.COM
Best Buy
CDW Computer Centers
Circuit City
CompUSA
Creative Computers
Cyberian Outpost
Dell Computer
Egghead
Fry's Electronics
Gateway
InaCom
Insight Enterprises
Micro Warehouse
MicroAge
Multiple Zones
  International
Office Depot
OfficeMax
PC Connection
Staples
Systemax
Tandy

HISTORICAL FINANCIALS & EMPLOYEES

Private FYE: December	Annual Growth	1989	1990	1991	1992	1993	1994	1995	1996	1997	1998
Estimated sales ($ mil.)	20.7%	—	—	—	400	515	780	930	1,000	1,110	1,235
Employees	13.8%	—	—	—	900	980	980	1,800	2,600	1,800	1,950

SALES HISTORY

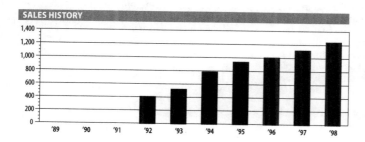

MICRO CENTER

MILLIKEN & COMPANY INC.

From outer space to tennis courts, Milliken & Company is part of the fabric of society. The Spartanburg, South Carolina-based company is one of the largest US textile companies; its more than 48,000 textile and chemical products include finished fabrics for space suits, rugs, and carpets, as well as other woven and knitted fabrics used in automobiles, sails, tennis balls, and computer ribbons. The company also produces braided polyester cords (used in tires) and a fabric finish for clothes and tablecloths (Visa). Milliken operates more than 65 plants worldwide. It has acquired some 1,500 patents and operates an extensive textile research center.

The company's chemicals are used in dyes, plastics, petroleum products, textiles, and other industrial applications. Milliken's chemicals help keep carpets clean, give color to Crayola crayons and markers, and provide durability for car dashboards. Milliken also makes clarifiers for the plastics and polypropylene industries.

Milliken has about 200 shareholders (most from the Milliken family), but Roger Milliken, brother Gerrish, and cousin Minot control the company. Roger, a strong supporter of conservative causes, has led the company since 1947.

HISTORY

Seth Milliken and William Deering formed a company in 1865 to become selling agents for textile mills in New England and the South. Deering left the partnership and in 1869 founded Deering Harvester (now Navistar).

Milliken set up operations in New York before the turn of the century, began buying the accounts receivables of cash-short textile mill operators, and invested in some of the companies. He also allied himself with leaders in the Spartanburg, South Carolina, area.

In his position as agent and financier, Milliken was able to spot failing mills. He bought out the distressed owners at a discount and soon became a major mill owner himself. In 1905 Milliken and his allies waged a bitter proxy fight and court case to win control of two mills, earning Milliken a fearsome reputation.

H. B. Claflin, a New York dry-goods wholesaler that also operated department stores, owed money to Milliken. When Claflin went bankrupt in 1914, Milliken got some of the stores, which became Mercantile Stores. The Milliken family retained about 40% of the chain (sold to Dillard's in 1998).

Roger Milliken, grandson of the founder, became the president of the company in 1947 and ruled with a firm hand. He fired his brother-in-law W. B. Dixon Stroud in 1955, and none of Roger's children, nephews, or nieces have ever been allowed to work for the company. The workers at Milliken's Darlington, South Carolina, mill voted to unionize in 1956. The next day Milliken closed the plant, beginning 24 years of litigation that ended at the US Supreme Court. Milliken settled with its workers for $5 million.

In the 1960s the company introduced Visa, a finish for easy-care fabrics. Milliken launched its Pursuit of Excellence program in 1981. The program stressed self-managed teams of employees and has since eliminated 700 management positions. Roger also emphasizes research, training, and new technology. The company adapted quickly to automation. Tom Peters dedicated his 1987 bestseller, *Thriving on Chaos,* to Roger.

Away from that limelight, Milliken is (and has always been) a secretive, closely held business. In 1989 that secrecy and family control were threatened when members of the Stroud branch of the family sued the company in the Delaware courts and then sold a small number of shares to Erwin Maddrey and Bettis Rainsford, executives of Milliken competitor Delta Woodside. The courts ruled in favor of Milliken in 1992; Maddrey and Rainsford were required to sign confidentiality agreements before receiving Milliken information.

The company introduced Fashion Effects, a process that allowed it to customize drapery designs, in 1991. In 1993 Roger financially backed opponents of NAFTA.

In 1995 the company's largest factory, in La Grange, Georgia, was destroyed by fire; it was rebuilt the next year. Despite the fire, Milliken is recognized as an industry leader in voluntary plant safety.

Milliken is also known — less fondly — by competitors for its unofficial motto: "Steal shamelessly." Woven-filament maker NRB sued Milliken in 1997 for corporate spying. Milliken settled the case out of court in 1998, but that year industrial textile maker Johnston Industries filed a similar lawsuit.

In 1999, Milliken announced plans to build a new clarifying agents plant in South Carolina.

Chairman and CEO: Roger Milliken
President and COO: Thomas J. Malone
CFO: John Lewis
VP Human Resources: Tommy Hodge
Director Public Affairs: Richard Dillard
Auditors: Arthur Andersen LLP

LOCATIONS

HQ: 920 Milliken Rd., Spartanburg, SC 29304
Phone: 864-503-2020 **Fax:** 864-503-2100
Web site: http://www.milliken.com

PRODUCTS/OPERATIONS

Selected Products
Area rugs (Milliken Modular Carpets)
Automotive airbag fabric
Automotive upholstery
Carpet and carpet tiles (Milliken Place Custom Carpets)
Carpet cleaner (Capture)
Colorants and tints (Versatint, Reactint, Blazon)
Duct tape reinforcement
Easy-care fabrics (Visa)
Elastic fabrics
Entrance mats (KEX)
Grass-catcher bag fabric
Impression fabrics for computer printer ribbons
Knit and woven apparel fabrics
Lining fabrics
Machinery filters
Napery fabrics
Nylon fabric for sails
Packing reinforcement materials
Shop towels
Specialty chemicals
Stretch fabrics (Lycra)
Tennis ball felt
Textured yarns
Tire cord
Unfinished fabrics
Uniform fabrics

COMPETITORS

Asahi Chemical Industry
Avondale Incorporated
Beaulieu Of America
Burlington Industries
Chargeurs
Collins & Aikman
Dixie Group
Dow Chemical
DuPont
Galey & Lord
Interface
JPS Industries
Johnston Industries
Mohawk Industries

Pillowtex
Polymer Group
R. B. Pamplin
Reliance Industries
Samsung
Shaw Industries
Spartan Mills
Springs Industries
Texfi Industries
Thomaston Mills
Unifi
Union Carbide
WL Gore
WestPoint Stevens

HISTORICAL FINANCIALS & EMPLOYEES

Private FYE: November	Annual Growth	1989	1990	1991	1992	1993	1994	1995	1996	1997	1998
Estimated sales ($ mil.)	2.4%	2,500	2,498	2,400	2,640	2,707	2,706	2,800	3,000	3,200	3,100
Employees	1.5%	14,000	14,000	14,000	14,000	14,000	13,500	13,500	15,000	16,000	16,000

SALES HISTORY

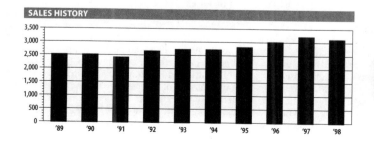

MONTGOMERY WARD

OVERVIEW

Montgomery Ward Holding is hoping for a brighter future now that it's owned by General Electric unit GE Capital. Chicago-based Montgomery Ward Holding operates Montgomery Ward & Co., with more than 250 full-line department stores across 32 states. The company's primary offerings of clothing, housewares, and furniture are aimed at middle-income female shoppers.

Lost between discounters such as Wal-Mart and fashion-forward specialty stores like The Gap, Montgomery Ward is searching for a more appealing identity. The company's lack of top brand-name merchandise and its dowdy image have all contributed to its woes. To beat out the dust, it is rolling out a brighter store format under the zippier "Wards" banner and upgrading its apparel. As part of its turnaround plan, Montgomery Ward has closed more than 100 under-performing stores.

HISTORY

Thank Aaron Montgomery Ward for fixed retail prices. Before he started the world's first general merchandise mail-order concern, consumers haggled to buy everything from a pair of white cotton socks to a tiller. In 1872 Ward provided customers with an inexpensive way to shop with his single-sheet "catalog" offering 163 items. Ward's brother-in-law George Thorne became his partner in 1873.

Thorne bought a controlling interest in the company in 1893. By 1900 its sales had fallen behind Chicago rival Sears, Roebuck (founded 1893). Profits surpassed $1 million for the first time in 1909, and the following year Thorne retired, leaving five sons in control of the company. In 1913 Ward died; Charles Thorne became president. Montgomery Ward went public in 1919.

Robert Wood, a former army general, was brought in to run the company after WWI. Although Wood wanted to develop retail stores, Montgomery Ward remained in the mail-order business. In 1924 Wood left for Sears, where his retail plans were better accepted. The company opened its first retail store two years later in Plymouth, Indiana, and expanded to about 550 stores in 1930.

Sewell Avery became CEO in 1931. Known as "Gloomy Sewell" because of his pessimistic economic outlook, Avery turned the chain around in the 1930s by closing stores and cutting unprofitable lines. The retailer took its place in holiday history in 1939 when copywriter Robert May created Rudolph the Red-Nosed Reindeer for a poem the stores handed out to children (the beloved song wasn't written until 1949).

Avery, who had correctly predicted the Depression, was convinced a recession would follow WWII and canceled expansion plans, thereby missing the postwar boom. He refused to open any new stores between 1941 and 1955, when he resigned after losing a proxy fight. As a result, Montgomery Ward's sales shrank 10%

during the 10 years following the war; Sears' sales doubled.

In 1966 the company founded The Montgomery Ward Insurance Group, which later became Signature Group. Montgomery Ward merged with Container Corporation of America two years later. Mobil Oil acquired control of the company between 1974 and 1976 and made huge loans to it in hopes of making it profitable.

Montgomery Ward shuttered 300 catalog stores and closed its catalog operations in 1985. That year Mobil put it up for sale and brought in Bernard Brennan to lead the company. In 1988 GE Capital helped finance a $3.8 billion LBO led by Brennan and other senior managers and simultaneously bought Montgomery Ward's credit card business.

The company formed its Montgomery Ward Direct catalog business in 1991 (sold 1996). It bought Lechmere, a northeastern 24-store retailer of appliances and consumer electronics, in 1994. Between 1993 and 1995 four people held the post of president, whereby Brennan's fiery temper was said to be the cause of the turnover. Earnings dropped almost 90% in 1995.

Former Toys "R" Us executive Roger Goddu came in as chairman and CEO of Montgomery Ward in 1996. Failing to renegotiate $1.4 billion in loans, the firm filed for bankruptcy in mid-1997 and closed nearly 100 stores, including all of its 33 Lechmere and 11 Electric Avenue & More outlets (more store closings have followed since). In an attempt to revitalize the chain, Montgomery Ward introduced a new store format with the new "Wards" moniker in 1998.

In August 1999 the company emerged from Chapter 11 after being acquired by GE Capital, which gave up $1 billion in claims against Wards. As part of the deal, the Financial Assurance unit of GE Capital acquired Montgomery Ward's Signature Group direct marketing arm.

Chairman and CEO; Chairman and CEO, Montgomery Ward & Co.: Roger V. Goddu, age 48, $1,350,000 pay
EVP Home, Montgomery Ward & Co.: Thomas G. Grimes
EVP Secretary and General Counsel; EVP - Secretary and General Counsel, Montgomery Ward & Co.; President, Montgomery Ward Properties: Spencer H. Heine, age 56, $525,000 pay
EVP Men's, Children's Apparel, and Shoes, Montgomery Ward & Co.: Tom Austin
EVP Women's Apparel and Fine Jewelry, Montgomery Ward & Co.: Lou Caporale
EVP Appliances, Electronics, Automotive, Montgomery Ward & Co.: Alan E. DiGangi
EVP Store Operations, Montgomery Ward & Co.: Kevin Freeman, age 48, $525,000 pay
EVP and CFO, Montgomery Ward & Co.: Thomas J. Paup
SVP Finance, Montgomery Ward & Co.: Don Civgin
SVP Human Resources, Montgomery Ward & Co.: Sherry Harris
VP Governmental Affairs & Corporate Communications, Montgomery Ward & Co.: Chuck Knittle
Auditors: Arthur Andersen LLP

HQ: Montgomery Ward Holding Corp., Montgomery Ward Plaza, Chicago, IL 60671
Phone: 312-467-2000   **Fax:** 312-467-3975
Web site: http://www.mward.com

1998 Stores

	No.
California	49
Texas	37
Illinois	17
Maryland	15
Florida	12
Michigan	12
Virginia	12
Pennsylvania	11
Other	87
Total	**252**

Subsidiaries
Montgomery Ward & Co. (department stores)

Selected Departments
Apparel
Appliances
Automotive (Auto Express car care centers)
Electronics
Fine jewelry
Furniture
Home fashions
Housewares
Lawn and garden

Ames
AutoZone
Bed Bath & Beyond
Belk
Best Buy
Bon-Ton Stores
Circuit City
Costco Companies
Dayton Hudson
Dillard's
Filene's Basement
Fred Meyer
J. C. Penney
Kmart
Kohl's
Levitz
Ross Stores
Schottenstein Stores
Sears
Service Merchandise
Spiegel
TJX
Tandy
The Gap
Venator Group
Wal-Mart
Zale

Private FYE: December	Annual Growth	1989	1990	1991	1992	1993	1994	1995	1996	1997	1998
Sales ($ mil.)	(4.4%)	5,461	5,584	5,654	5,781	6,002	7,038	7,085	6,620	5,386	3,634
Net income ($ mil.)	—	151	153	135	100	101	117	11	(237)	(1,152)	(971)
Income as % of sales	—	2.8%	2.7%	2.4%	1.7%	1.7%	1.7%	0.2%	—	—	—
Employees	(3.4%)	67,000	66,300	62,400	62,300	51,350	58,600	55,000	58,100	58,400	49,000

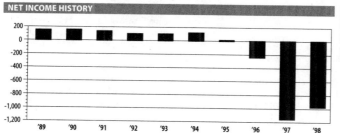

Debt ratio: 0.0%
Return on equity: —
Cash ($ mil.): 61
Current ratio: 0.88
Long-term debt ($ mil.): 46

MOTIVA ENTERPRISES LLC

OVERVIEW

Low oil prices and stiff competition provided the motivation to create Motiva Enterprises. The Houston-based company combines the eastern and Gulf Coast US refining and marketing operations of oil majors Texaco, Shell Oil (the US arm of Royal Dutch/Shell), and Saudi Aramco. The venture has absorbed Texaco and Saudi Aramco's previous joint venture, Star Enterprise. Motiva, the second-largest gasoline retailer in the US behind BP Amoco, operates about 14,200 Shell and Texaco gas stations in 26 northeastern and southeastern states.

With a long-term agreement with Saudi Aramco for crude oil supply, Motiva has holdings in almost 50 product terminals and operates three refineries on the Gulf Coast and one in Delaware. Shell Oil owns 35% of Motiva, and Texaco and Saudi Aramco's Saudi Refining each own 32.5%.

Pushing a marketing strategy more familiar to the food business than the oil world, Motiva market products under both the Texaco and Shell brands, often in competition for the same car-driving consumer. The motive behind the formation of Motiva and sister company Equilon, a similar venture that merged Shell's and Texaco's downstream businesses in the Midwest and West, was to cut $800 million in annual operating costs by eliminating overlapping outlets and taking other consolidation measures.

HISTORY

Although Motiva was not created until 1998, two of its key players, Texaco and Saudi Aramco, had been doing business together in various ventures since 1936. But they had never tried anything on the scale of the Star Enterprise joint venture agreement signed in London by Texaco CEO James Kinnear and Saudi Oil Minister Hisham Nazer in late 1988. The deal, valued at nearly $2 billion, was the largest joint venture of its kind in the US.

The agreement to create Star Enterprise sprang, in part, from Texaco's tumultuous ride following its purchase of Getty Oil in 1984. Texaco was sued by Pennzoil for pre-empting Pennzoil's bid for Getty, and Pennzoil won a $10.5 billion judgment in 1985. Texaco filed for bankruptcy in 1987 and eventually settled with Pennzoil for $3 billion.

In 1988 Texaco emerged from bankruptcy after announcing a reorganization. However, corporate raider Carl Icahn had begun buying up Texaco's stock in a bid to take control of the company. Icahn wanted five seats on Texaco's board, and he was only defeated after Texaco's management announced the deal with Saudi Aramco at a stockholder meeting.

Texaco got a much-needed injection of cash, and Saudi Aramco gained a steady US outlet for its supply of crude. The Saudis had been at odds with their OPEC partners for several years, and in late 1985 then-Saudi Oil Minister Sheikh Yamani and Saudi Aramco began increasing production, leading to an oil price crash in 1986. Nazer replaced Yamani and changed Saudi Aramco's strategy. To secure market share, the Saudis started signing long-term supply contracts.

The deal with Texaco gave Saudi Aramco a 50% interest in Texaco's refining and marketing operations in the East and on the Gulf Coast — about two-thirds of Texaco's US downstream operations — including three refineries and its Texaco-brand stations. In return, the Saudis paid $812 million cash and provided three-fourths of Star's initial inventory, about 30 million barrels of oil. They also agreed to a 20-year, 600,000-barrel-a-day commitment of crude. Each company named three representatives to Star's management.

The new company soon initiated a modernization and expansion program: It acquired 65 stations, built 30 new outlets, and remodeled another 172 during 1989. In 1994, the company began franchising its Texaco-brand Star Mart convenience stores. By mid-1995 it had sold 30 franchises.

Facing a more competitive oil marketing environment in the US, Shell Oil approached Texaco in 1996 with the possibility of merging some of their operations. In 1998 Shell and Texaco formed Equilon Enterprises, a joint venture that combined their western and midwestern refining and marketing activities.

Later that year Shell and Texaco/Saudi Aramco (Star Enterprises) formed Motiva to merge the companies' refining and marketing businesses on the East Coast and Gulf Coast. Shell and Texaco also formed two more Houston companies as satellite firms for Motiva and Equilon: Equiva Trading Company, a general partnership that provides supplies and trading services, and Equiva Services, which provides support services. L. Wilson Berry, the former president of Texaco Refining and Marketing, took over as CEO of Motiva.

In 1999 Motiva and Equilon together bought 15 product terminals from Clark USA.

President and CEO: L. Wilson Berry
CFO: William M. Kaparich
VP Human Resources: Jerry Bean
VP Sales and Marketing: Larry Burch
VP Commercial Marketing and Distribution:
Ralph Grimmer
VP Portfolio Planning and Development: Lori Herlin
General Counsel: Rick Frazier
Chief Diversity Officer: Redia Anderson

HQ: 910 Louisiana St., Houston, TX 77002
Phone: 713-277-8000   **Fax:** 713-241-4044

Motiva operates about 14,200 Shell and Texaco gas
stations in 26 northeastern and southeastern US states.

Major Areas of Operation
Alabama
Arkansas
Connecticut
Delaware
Florida
Georgia
Louisiana
Maryland
Massachusetts
Mississippi
New Hampshire
New Jersey
North Carolina
Pennsylvania
Rhode Island
Tennessee
Texas
Vermont
Virginia

Refineries
Convent, Louisiana
Delaware City, Delaware
Norco, Louisiana
Port Arthur, Texas

1998 Retail Outlets

	No.	% of total
Company-owned & leased	2,325	16
Company-owned & operated	610	4
Other	11,265	80
Total	**14,200**	**100**

7-Eleven
BP Amoco
Chevron
CITGO
Cumberland Farms
Dairy Mart
Equilon Enterprises
Exxon Mobil
Gulf Oil
Marathon Ashland Petroleum
Racetrac Petroleum
Sunoco
Tosco
Ultramar Diamond Shamrock
Valero Energy
Wawa

Joint venture FYE: December	Annual Growth	1989	1990	1991	1992	1993	1994	1995	1996	1997	1998
Sales ($ mil.)	—	—	—	—	—	—	—	—	—	—	5,371
Net income ($ mil.)	—	—	—	—	—	—	—	—	—	—	78
Income as % of sales	—	—	—	—	—	—	—	—	—	—	1.5%
Employees	—	—	—	—	—	—	—	—	—	—	3,750

Debt ratio: 27.1%
Return on equity: —
Cash ($ mil.): 25
Current ratio: 1.15
Long-term debt ($ mil.): 1,425

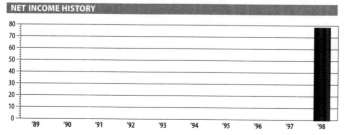

MTS, INCORPORATED

OVERVIEW

Whether pop music rocks your world or Broadway tunes set your feet a-tappin', MTS offers a Tower of choices. Sacramento, California-based MTS — owner of Tower Records — is the second-largest music retailer in the US (after Musicland). It operates about 225 music, book, and video stores in 17 countries, including 40 stores in Japan. The privately held company also publishes free music magazines such as *Pulse!* (US). MTS was founded by self-described "aging hippie" Russell Solomon (majority owner), who in 1998 passed tower-guarding duties to his son Michael (for whom the company is named).

Pioneers of specialty retailing's superstore concept, Tower Records stores go beyond best-sellers to address a variety of tastes. Although MTS has fewer stores than other major music chains, it is known for broad

selection and high volume. US stores (mainly located in big cities or college towns) sell an average of more than 70,000 CDs daily. Unlike other specialty retailers, managers at each store select the titles for their stores (many company managers began as clerks).

The chain has faced increasing competition from discounters (such as Wal-Mart, which sells more limited selections of CDs but at lower prices), from industry consolidation, and from the growing crowd of online retailers. MTS is dealing with the tough domestic scene by expanding in Asia and Latin America (international stores bring in about 40% of sales) and online (including its own shopping site). MTS plans to expand its book selling business and open stores in new US cities and is considering a public stock offering.

HISTORY

Russell Solomon confiscates neckties from visiting executives (he scorns corporate stuffiness) and displays them outside his office. Solomon began selling used jukebox records in 1941 in his father's Tower Cut Rate Drug Store at age 16. He joined the Army after dropping out of high school and went back to work in his father's store after his 1946 discharge. In 1952 he took over the record inventory from his father's store and began wholesaling, setting up record departments in drugstores and department stores.

Solomon's record wholesaling business went broke and creditors forced him to liquidate in 1960. Days later, with $5,000 from his father, Solomon incorporated MTS (named after Solomon's son Michael T.) and then opened the first Tower Records in Sacramento, California. A month later a second Sacramento store was born. The first Tower Books opened in 1963, adjacent to one of the record stores.

By the 1967 "Summer of Love," Solomon was noticing the diverse musical tastes of the flower children who hung out in his stores, from the fuzzed-out blues wail of Jimi Hendrix to the mellow yellow sounds of Donovan. With the music business exploding, he figured serving the market would require stocking stores with a huge selection. In 1968 the first store outside Sacramento was opened, Tower Records' landmark Columbus Street store in San Francisco. At the time it was the largest record store in the US. Much of its inventory consisted of surplus goods from

record manufacturers who were glad to move the stuff.

In 1970 Tower Records opened in Los Angeles on the Sunset Strip. The company started expanding outside California in 1976, mainly in the West. MTS opened its first overseas store in 1979 (Japan). The first Tower Video opened in Sacramento in 1981; three more opened the next year. The East Coast got its first Tower Records in 1983 (New York City); at the time the 35,000-sq.-ft. store was the world's largest. That year the company debuted *Pulse!* magazine, an in-store freebie with record reviews and artist interviews. Its real expansion began in 1989; by 1994 Tower Records had more than doubled its stores with 127 outlets. That year it opened its first multimedia store, offering books, videos, records, and CD-ROMs under one roof.

MTS opened the largest record shop in the world (an eight-floor megastore in Tokyo) and the first WOW! superstore (a joint venture with electronics retailer The Good Guys) in Las Vegas in 1995. That year it started selling CDs on the Internet via America Online; it added its own online store in 1996. Tower Records became Malaysia's first international music chain in 1997 when it opened a store in the country's capital, Kuala Lumpur. In 1998 MTS had its first public offering, selling $110 million in bonds to raise money for expansion. Also in 1998 president and CEO Russell passed his title to Michael.

Chairman: Russell Solomon, age 74, $1,243,260 pay
President and CEO: Michael T. Solomon, age 51,
$505,024 pay
EVP and COO: Stanley L. Goman, age 51, $310,395 pay
EVP, CFO, Secretary, and Treasurer:
DeVaughn D. Searson, age 55, $416,177 pay
Chief Advertising Officer and EVP:
Christopher S. Hopson, age 47
SVP Far East Operations: Keith Cahoon, age 43,
$192,897 pay
SVP European Operations: Andy D. Lown, age 34
VP: David Solomon
Manager Human Resources: Shauna Pompei
Auditors: PricewaterhouseCoopers LLP

LOCATIONS

HQ: 2500 Del Monte St., Bldg. C,
West Sacramento, CA 95691
Phone: 916-373-2500　　　**Fax:** 916-373-2535
Web site: http://www.towerrecords.com

MTS has about 225 Tower stores in Argentina, Canada,
Colombia, Hong Kong, Ireland, Israel, Japan, Malaysia,
Mexico, the Philippines, Singapore, South Korea,
Taiwan, Thailand, the UK, and the US.

1999 Sales

	$ mil.	% of total
US	616	60
Japan	313	31
UK	66	6
Other countries	31	3
Total	**1,026**	**100**

US Locations

Arizona	Michigan
California	Nevada
Colorado	New Jersey
District of Columbia	New York
Georgia	Oregon
Hawaii	Pennsylvania
Illinois	Tennessee
Louisiana	Texas
Maryland	Virginia
Massachusetts	Washington

PRODUCTS/OPERATIONS

Selected Operations

Music magazines
Bounce (Japan)
Latin Pulse! (South America)
Pass (Asia, excluding Japan)
Pulse! (US)
Top (UK)

Stores
Tower Books
Tower Records
Tower Video
WOW! superstore (jointly operated with The Good Guys)

COMPETITORS

Amazon.com
Barnes & Noble
Bertelsmann
Best Buy
Blockbuster
Books-A-Million
Borders
CDnow
Circuit City
Costco Companies
Crown Books
EMI Group
Hastings Entertainment
Hollywood Entertainment
Kmart
Movie Gallery
Musicland
Target Stores
Trans World Entertainment
Virgin Group
WH Smith
Wal-Mart
Wherehouse Entertainment

HISTORICAL FINANCIALS & EMPLOYEES

Private FYE: July	Annual Growth	1990	1991	1992	1993	1994	1995	1996	1997	1998	1999
Sales ($ mil.)	6.6%	—	—	—	699	809	951	1,001	992	1,008	1,026
Net income ($ mil.)	—	—	—	—	15	17	15	10	4	10	(8)
Income as % of sales	—	—	—	—	2.1%	2.1%	1.6%	1.0%	0.4%	1.0%	—
Employees	5.0%	—	—	—	—	—	—	—	6,800	7,200	7,500

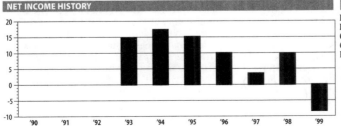

NET INCOME HISTORY

1999 FISCAL YEAR-END
Debt ratio: 70.8%
Return on equity: __
Cash ($ mil.): 25
Current ratio: 1.80
Long-term debt ($ mil.): 280

MUTUAL OF OMAHA

OVERVIEW

In the wild kingdom that is today's insurance industry, The Mutual of Omaha Companies wants to distinguish itself from the pack. But the venerable insurer is not immune to the health industry's upheaval. Increased cost-mindedness among clout-wielding managed care organizations has put traditional indemnity insurers — which have less power to bargain for lower-cost services — at a disadvantage, as have state laws mandating coverage for persons regardless of underwriting policy. So, Mutual of Omaha is exiting the health business in some areas and is adding managed care services. It is focused on growing its health care networks internally, rather than by acquisition, to ensure its standards are met. These networks are largely in underserved rural areas, where the firm has kept a strong presence. Coverage includes alternative treatments such as chiropractic and acupuncture. Other services include disability coverage, employee health, mutual funds, pension plans, homeowner and auto coverage, and brokerage.

Mutual of Omaha is involved in wildlife conservation and protection. Starting with sponsorship of the long-running *Mutual of Omaha's Wild Kingdom,* this interest has evolved into a grant and scholarship program run by the company's Wildlife Heritage Center.

HISTORY

Charter Mutual Benefit Health & Accident Association got its start in Omaha, Nebraska, in 1909. A year later, half of its founders quit, leaving a group headed by pharmaceuticals businessman H. S. Weller in charge. He tapped C. C. Criss as principal operating officer, general manager, and treasurer. Criss brought in his wife, Mabel, and brother Neil to help run the business.

Formed to offer accident and disability protection at a time when there were many fraudulent benefit societies, Charter Mutual Benefit Health faced consumer resistance that slowed growth in its first 10 years. By 1920 it was licensed in only nine states. Experience helped it refine its products and improve its policies' comprehensibility. By 1924 the firm had more than doubled its penetration, gaining licensing in 24 states.

The US was nearing the depths of the Depression when Weller died in 1932. Criss succeeded him as president. The stock crash had brought a steep decline in the value of the firm's asset base, and premium income dropped (accompanied by an increase in claims). Even so, Mutual Benefit Health expanded its agency force, the scope of its benefits, and its operations. It went into Canada in 1935 and began a campaign to obtain licensing throughout the US.

By 1939 the company was licensed in all 48 states. During WWII it wrote coverage for civilians killed or injured in acts of war in the US (including Hawaii) and Canada. With paranoia running high and consumer goods in short supply, the insurance industry boomed during the war (and payouts on stateside act-of-war claims were low to nonexistent). Criss retired in 1949.

Gearing up its post-war sales efforts, in 1950 the company changed its name to Mutual of Omaha and adopted its distinctive chieftain logo. During the 1950s it added specialty accident and group medical coverage. In 1963 it made an advertising coup when it launched *Mutual of Omaha's Wild Kingdom.* Hosted by zoo director Marlin Perkins and, later, naturalist sidekick Jim Fowler, the show was one of the most popular nature programs of all time. Later that decade the company added investment management to its services.

Changes in the health care industry during the 1990s led Mutual of Omaha to de-emphasize its traditional indemnity products in favor of building managed care alternatives such as HMOs. In 1993 it joined with Alegent Health System to form managed care company Preferred HealthAlliance. Mutual of Omaha also stopped writing new major medical coverage in such states as California, Florida, New Jersey, and New York, where state laws made providing health care onerous. This led the company to cut its workforce by about 10% in 1996.

In 1997 the company introduced a medical savings account program and a new, bundled 401(k) plan. It sold its Canadian insurance operations in 1998 to Royal Bank of Canada and discontinued its Tele-Trip flight-accident insurance line. In 1999 it bought out Alegent's interest in their joint venture and entered the credit card business (offering First USA Visa cards). The company also began offering critical illness insurance (patients diagnosed with certain serious illnesses receive one lump-sum payment of up to $750,000).

OFFICERS

Chairman and CEO: John W. Weekly
President and COO; President, United World Life Insurance: John A. Sturgeon
EVP and Chief Actuary: Cecil D. Bykerk
EVP, Chief Investment Officer, and Treasurer: John L. Maginn
EVP and Comptroller: Tommie D. Thompson
EVP and Executive Counsel: Lawrence F. Harr
EVP and General Counsel: Thomas J. McCusker
EVP Corporate Services and Corporate Secretary: M. Jane Huerter
EVP Customer Service Operation; President, Companion Life Insurance: Kimberly S. Harm
EVP Federal Government Affairs: William C. Mattox
EVP Group Benefit Services: Randall C. Horn
EVP Health Care Management: Stephen R. Booma
EVP Human Resources: Robert B. Bogart
EVP Individual Operation: James N. Plato
EVP Information Services: James L. Hanson
EVP: G. Ronald Ames

LOCATIONS

HQ: The Mutual of Omaha Companies,
Mutual of Omaha Plaza, Omaha, NE 68175
Phone: 402-342-7600 **Fax:** 402-351-2775
Web site: http://www.mutualofomaha.com

PRODUCTS/OPERATIONS

1998 Assets

	$ mil.	% of total
Bonds	9,242	70
Stocks	916	7
Mortgage loans	599	5
Cash & equivalents	272	2
Other	2,202	16
Total	**13,231**	**100**

1998 Sales

	% of total
Health	44
Investments	20
Annuities	19
Life	17
Total	**100**

Selected Services and Products
Annuities
Dental insurance
Disability insurance
Individual life and health insurance
Long-term-care insurance
Major medical
Mutual funds
Property/casualty coverage

Selected Subsidiaries and Affiliates
Companion Life Insurance Co.
innowave (water purification products)
Kirkpatrick, Pettis, Smith, Polian (brokerage)
Mutual of Omaha Insurance Company
Mutual of Omaha Investor Services (mutual funds)
Omaha Property and Casualty Insurance Co.
United of Omaha Life Insurance Co.
United World Life Insurance Co.

COMPETITORS

AXA Financial	Liberty Mutual
Aetna	MONY
Allstate	MassMutual
American National Insurance	Morgan Stanley Dean Witter
Blue Cross	New York Life
CIGNA	Northwestern Mutual
CNA Financial	Prudential
Guardian Life	State Farm
John Hancock	USAA

HISTORICAL FINANCIALS & EMPLOYEES

Mutual company FYE: December	Annual Growth	1989	1990	1991	1992	1993	1994	1995	1996	1997	1998
Assets ($ mil.)	9.4%	—	—	—	7,714	8,600	9,551	10,659	11,726	12,639	13,231
Net income ($ mil.)	10.4%	—	—	—	65	94	82	122	105	181	117
Income as % of assets	—	—	—	—	0.8%	1.1%	0.9%	1.1%	0.9%	1.4%	0.9%
Employees	(1.5%)	—	—	—	—	7,665	8,330	8,163	7,047	7,309	7,111

NET INCOME HISTORY

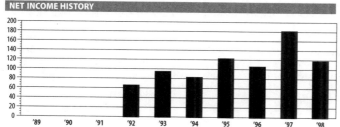

1998 FISCAL YEAR-END
Equity as % of assets: 15.5%
Return on assets: 1.0%
Return on equity: 5.8%
Long-term debt ($ mil.): —
Sales ($ mil.):

MUZAK LIMITED LIABILITY

OVERVIEW

The king of background music has stepped into the foreground. Seattle-based Muzak — best known for anti-psychotic, instrumental renditions of pop songs — now deals primarily in "foreground" music (pop songs in their original form). The company offers businesses about 60 channels of music in 10 genres (jazz, Latin, popular contemporary), delivered primarily by satellite. From its library of more than one million songs, customers can choose a format that complements their marketing approach or design their own programming. Its varied clients include The Gap, McDonald's, and Nordstrom.

In addition to providing music, Muzak offers video programming, as well as in-store and phone messaging systems. The company also sells, installs, and services related equipment like receivers and speakers. Muzak sells its services all across the US through 35 company-owned affiliate offices and 73 independent affiliates. The company also does business in 11 other countries. Media investment firm ABRY Partners owns nearly 70% of the private company; AMFM (formerly Chancellor Media) owns 23%.

HISTORY

Muzak is the brainchild of George Squier, a two-star US Army general and West Point graduate who devoted much of his army career to scientific pursuits. In 1922 he patented a system for transmitting phonograph music over electrical lines and sold the rights to utility North American Company. Together they formed a subsidiary called Wired Radio to begin testing the system in Cleveland. The service initially offered three channels from news to dance music and cost $1.50 a month. In 1934 Squier coined the term Muzak ("muz" from music and "ak" from Kodak, his favorite company) before he died that year. The company moved to New York in 1936.

During the 1930s Muzak was used in then-newfangled elevators to calm nervous riders (hence the term "elevator music"). Waddill Catchings, then president, came up with the idea of designating each song with a stimulus code in order to target certain times with tempos that would soothe the listener. In 1938 Warner Bros. bought the company, but sold it the next year to US Senator William Benton. The company almost went belly-up until experiments showed that music could increase productivity, and during WWII Muzak systems were installed in factories, arsenals, and shipyards. Muzak even tested its programming's effect on animals: The company found that cows produced more milk when *Blue Danube* was piped into a dairy in McKeesport, Pennsylvania.

After the war the company continued to work on Stimulus Progression — the idea of regulating worker productivity through music. Muzak accompanied Neil Armstrong

to the moon in 1969 as it played through the speakers of the *Apollo XI* spaceship.

In 1972 Teleprompter bought the company and began distributing its music via satellite. Westinghouse (later CBS) bought Teleprompter in 1981. Unsure of its odd subsidiary (Westinghouse was never able to make any money with Muzak), it sold the company to Chicago media magnate and department store heir Marshall Field V for $45 million in 1986. Field bought Seattle-based Yesco, a producer of "foreground" music for restaurants and stores, and merged the two the next year. Led by Yesco's management, Muzak began updating its sound to appeal to baby boomers weaned on rock and roll. Like Westinghouse, Field also failed to make the firm profitable. He sold Muzak to its management and New York investment firm Centre Capital in 1992. That year it started offering ancillary services such as a retail marketing program called Superlink.

In 1996 the company called off plans to go public. Saddled with debt from the buyout and mounting losses, it ousted CEO John Jester in 1997 and replaced him with William Boyd, who discontinued Muzak's ancillary services to focus on its core music business. During 1998 the company began buying competitors and its own independent affiliates. In 1999 Muzak merged with Audio Communications Network, a Muzak franchiser owned by media investment firm ABRY Partners. It also bought Data Broadcasting's InStore Satellite Network, a music and ad business.

OFFICERS

Chairman: Steven Hicks, age 48
President and CEO: William A. Boyd, age 57, $342,017 pay
COO: Charles A. Saldarini, age 55, $286,014 pay
CFO and Treasurer: Brad D. Bodenman, age 35
SVP: Steven M. Tracy, age 48, $141,008 pay
VP: David Unger, age 42, $93,750 pay
VP: Royce G. Yudkuff, age 43
VP Affiliate Sales and Development: Jack D. Craig, age 63
VP Audio Architecture: D. Alvin Collis, age 46
VP Marketing: Kenneth F. Kahn, age 37, $144,008 pay
VP National Sales: Dino J. DeRose, age 38, $150,217 pay
VP Operations: Richard Chaffee, age 54
VP and Secretary: Peni Garber, age 36
VP Video Imaging: Bruce McKagan, age 48
Human Resources Director: Geanie Willis
Auditors: PricewaterhouseCoopers LLP

LOCATIONS

HQ: Muzak Limited Liabilty Company,
2901 3rd Ave., Ste. 400, Seattle, WA 98121
Phone: 206-633-3000   **Fax:** 206-633-6210
Web site: http://www.muzak.com

PRODUCTS/OPERATIONS

1998 Sales

	$ mil.	% of total
Music-related services	65.9	66
Equipment sales & services	33.8	34
Total	**99.7**	**100**

Selected Products
Audio Architecture (business music programming)
Audio Marketing (on-hold and in-store messaging)
InStore Satellite Network (music and advertising)
Video Imaging (in-store video programming)

Selected Music Formats
Classical
Country
Jazz
Latin
Mature Adult
Oldies
Popular Contemporary
Popular Contemporary Instrumentals
Urban
Specialty

Selected Video Formats
Children
  Bounce (cartoons and sing-alongs for preschoolers)
  Go (cartoons and music videos)
Sports
  Edge (MBA, NBA, and NFL highlights and bloopers)
  Xtreme (snowboarding, surfing, and skateboarding)
Total Music
  FrenchTrax (French music videos)
  Hitline (dance and top 40)
  Latin Trax (contemporary Latin music)
  Pop Mellow (pop vocals and instrumentals)
  Pop Moderate (80s and 90s)
  Street Soundz (hip-hop and R&B)
  Top Trax (alternative and top 40)
Variety
  Look (music and fashion)
  Pulse (music, fashion, and lifestyles)
  Pure Country (music and interviews)
  Snap (music, sports, and lifestyles)
  Spectrum (comedy, music, sports, and trivia)

Selected Equipment and Services
Closed circuit television systems
In-store messaging systems
Intercom systems
Paging systems
Sound masking
Sound systems
Telephone messaging systems
Video system design

COMPETITORS

AEI Music Network
Liberty Digital
PlayNetwork

HISTORICAL FINANCIALS & EMPLOYEES

Private FYE: December	Annual Growth	1989	1990	1991	1992	1993	1994	1995	1996	1997	1998
Sales ($ mil.)	8.6%	—	—	56	55	59	83	87	87	91	100
Net income ($ mil.)	—	—	—	(10)	(6)	(4)	(7)	(6)	(11)	(13)	(12)
Income as % of sales	—	—	—	—	—	—	—	—	—	—	—
Employees	13.3%	—	—	—	—	—	—	715	751	667	1,041

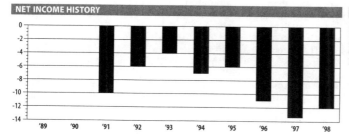

NET INCOME HISTORY

1998 FISCAL YEAR-END
Debt ratio: 100.0%
Return on equity: —
Cash ($ mil.): 3
Current ratio: 0.83
Long-term debt ($ mil.): 103

muzak

NASD

You've heard of a fund of funds? Well now there's a market of markets.

The National Association of Securities Dealers (NASD) has merged its NASD Automated Quotations (Nasdaq) stock market (the US's #2 securities market) with #3 American Stock Exchange (AMEX) to form the Nasdaq-Amex Market Group. Although they operate separately, the combination broadens NASD's share of the securities market and allows it to offer listing companies and investors a choice of auction (AMEX) or electronic trading (Nasdaq). Nasdaq and AMEX have more companies listed (5,000 and 800, respectively) than the New York Stock Exchange's 3,100, but the NYSE's $12 trillion market capitalization is much higher than Nasdaq's ($2.5 trillion) or AMEX's ($152 million).

The Nasdaq-AMEX merger follows years of controversy about the relative fairness of auction and electronic trading. Under Nasdaq's electronic system, market makers can control trading; they also pocket spreads between the buying and selling prices, giving them an incentive to keep the spreads large.

NASD separates its regulatory and market operations into two units (per SEC orders): NASD Regulation governs trading (virtually all US securities traders are NASD members). The Nasdaq-Amex Market Group operates the AMEX and Nasdaq. The NASD is also launching a European subsidiary, to be called Nasdaq Europe.

The NASD was founded in 1939 as a self-regulating entity for OTC securities traders, who traded directly with companies or with market makers authorized to trade their stock. Traders shopped by phone to get the best price from the market makers, and up-to-date OTC quotes were unobtainable. The organization set trading qualifications, administered licensing tests, set standards for underwriting compensation, and disciplined wayward traders.

In 1963 the SEC asked the NASD to develop an automated OTC quotations system. Work began in 1968 on facilities based in Trumbull, Connecticut, and Rockville, Maryland. The system went online in 1971 and soon turned into an electronic trading medium because it made dealer quotes more competitive and instantly visible. By late 1972 volume exceeded 2 billion shares, and two years later the Nasdaq claimed a share volume nearly one-third of the NYSE's. By 1980 it reported having almost 60% of the NYSE's volume; however, Nasdaq counted both sides of many trades.

In 1975 Congress gave NASD responsibility for regulating the municipal securities market and asked the SEC to develop a national market system for share trading. The SEC handed the task to NASD. The market started trading in 1982 with 40 stocks, establishing a two-tier system: one for the crème de la crème, such as MCI (now MCI WorldCom) and Microsoft, and one for smaller or newer issues. The system's continually updated, newer-than-new technology made it a model for other exchanges.

To improve responsiveness to small investors, NASD instituted the SOES (small order entry system) after the 1987 stock crash, when many traders bailed themselves out before executing customer sell orders. Some dealers (called SOES bandits) began using the new system for themselves by making frequent small trades, thus increasing the market's volatility. The problem persisted and led to an SEC investigation resulting in dealers being required to execute small customer orders along with their own at the best prices. (The situation also made Nasdaq vulnerable to the NYSE's contention that auction exchanges are more fair to investors.)

But NASD teetered between appeasing the public and looking out for its own. In 1997 it proposed to cap investor arbitration awards at $750,000 regardless of actual damages. This met with criticism; arbitration had been instituted in 1987 because parties could receive remedies comparable to those available in court.

Reform-minded Wall Streeter Frank Zarb took over NASD in 1997. Nasdaq and AMEX soon began discussing an alliance, completing the deal in 1998. NASD reluctantly complied when the SEC asked it to join the NYSE in real-time trade price reporting. It also announced a plan in 1999 to join with SOFTBANK to build a Japanese version of Nasdaq.

Facing competition from such for-profit, around-the-clock electronic communications networks (ECNs) as The Island ECN and Archipelago, NASD prepared in 1999 to spin Nasdaq off from the Nasdaq-Amex Market Group as a for-profit exchange (the NYSE made similar plans), with AMEX remaining part of NASD. Also that year the Nasdaq announced it would extend official pricing to 6:30 p.m. Eastern time in response to the growth of after-hours trading, and agreed to share listings with the Hong Kong Stock Exchange.

Chairman and CEO: Frank G. Zarb
President; EVP, American Stock Exchange:
Richard G. Ketchum
**COO and CFO; Acting President, American Stock
Exchange:** Salvatore F. Sodano
**EVP and Chief Information Officer, National
Association of Securities Dealers and American
Stock Exchange:** Gregor S. Bailar
EVP Global Sales and Member Affairs: John N. Tognino
EVP Strategic Development Administration:
John L. Hilley
SVP and Corporate Controller: Todd T. Diganci
SVP and General Counsel: T. Grant Callery
SVP and Treasurer: James R. Allen
SVP Economic Research: Steven Dean Furbush
SVP Human Resources: Diane E. Carter
**SVP Individual Investor Services and Chief
Administrative Officer:** Michael D. Jones
SVP Internal Review: Daniel S. Shook
VP Administrative Services: Catherine C. Tighe
VP Economic Research: Michael Edleson
VP Year 2000 Program: William D. Bone
President, Nasdaq International: John T. Wall
**President, NASD Regulation; EVP, American Stock
Exchange:** Mary L. Schapiro
President, Nasdaq Stock Market: Alfred R. Berkeley III
**COO and EVP Law and Regulatory Policy, NASD
Regulation:** Elisse B. Walter
Auditors: Ernst & Young LLP

LOCATIONS

HQ: National Association of Securities Dealers, Inc.,
1735 K St. NW, Washington, DC 20006
Phone: 202-728-8000   **Fax:** 202-293-6260
Web site: http://www.nasd.com

PRODUCTS/OPERATIONS

1998 Sales

	$ mil.	% of total
Transaction service fees	307.4	41
Issuer fees	139.7	19
Member assessments	92.1	12
Registration fees	80.1	11
Regulatory fees & fines	49.2	7
Other	71.0	10
Total	**739.5**	**100**

Selected Subsidiaries
NASD Regulation, Inc. (securities trading regulation)

The Nasdaq-Amex Market Group
American Stock Exchange LLC
Nasdaq International
The Nasdaq Stock Market, Inc. (National Association
of Securities Dealers Automated Quotations system)
Securities Dealers Insurance Co., Inc. (fidelity bond
reinsurance for NASD members)
Securities Dealers Risk Purchasing Group
(professional liability insurance for NASD members)

Selected Products
Fixed Income Pricing System (electronic junk bond
trading system)
The Portal Market (electronic private placement system)
StockWatch (automated trading analysis system)

COMPETITORS

Archipelago
Bloomberg
E*TRADE
EASDAQ
Goldman Sachs
Instinet
Island ECN
NYSE

HISTORICAL FINANCIALS & EMPLOYEES

Not-for-profit FYE: December	Annual Growth	1989	1990	1991	1992	1993	1994	1995	1996	1997	1998
Sales ($ mil.)	18.3%	163	183	216	264	332	372	438	556	634	740
Net income ($ mil.)	21.7%	8	7	27	35	39	21	17	55	36	47
Income as % of sales	—	4.9%	3.8%	12.5%	13.2%	11.7%	5.6%	3.9%	9.9%	5.7%	6.4%
Employees	6.0%	1,712	1,771	1,890	1,991	2,145	2,328	2,000	2,218	2,200	2,900

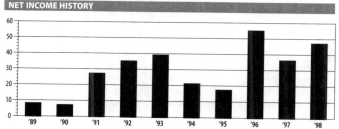

NET INCOME HISTORY

1998 FISCAL YEAR-END

Debt ratio: 5.3%
Return on equity: 11.1%
Cash ($ mil.): 143
Current ratio: 1.74
Long-term debt ($ mil.): 25

NBA

OVERVIEW

The New York City-based National Basketball Association (NBA) is looking to rebound from a less than stellar 1998-99 season that saw a contentious lockout and the retirement of its most popular player, Michael Jordan. The league features 29 teams, including two Canadian clubs, playing in the Eastern and Western Conferences. The third-largest US sports league (behind the National Football League and Major League Baseball), the NBA also operates the Women's NBA and is active in consumer products, network television, and new media projects.

During the 1998-99 season, team owners instigated a lockout, claiming that the previous bargaining agreement with players was unprofitable for many teams. When a compromise finally was reached, three months of the season had been lost. The end of the lockout also saw the end of the Jordan era, as the superstar hung up his jersey and retired from the Chicago Bulls. Post-lockout, post-Jordan attendance is down some 6% (excluding novelty events). It also doesn't help that the average ticket price for an NBA game (about $48) is the most expensive in professional sports.

HISTORY

Basketball was invented by Dr. James Naismith, a physical education teacher at the International YMCA Training School in Springfield, Massachusetts. In 1891 Naismith nailed peach baskets at either end of the school's gymnasium, gave his students a soccer ball, and created what has become one of the most popular games in the world.

In the beginning many YMCAs deemed the game too rough and banned it, so basketball was limited to armories, gymnasiums, barns, and dance halls. To pay the rent for the use of the hall, teams began charging spectators fees for admission, and leftover cash was divided among the players. The first pro basketball game was played in 1896 in Trenton, New Jersey.

In 1946 a group of arena owners looking to fill their halls when their hockey teams were on the road formed the Basketball Association of America. It merged in 1949 with the midwestern National Basketball League to form the 17-team National Basketball Association (NBA).

Six teams dropped out in 1950. The league got an unexpected boost the next year when a point-shaving scandal rocked college basketball. The bad publicity for the college game made the pros look relatively clean, and it helped attract more fans. Another boost came through innovation. In 1954 the league introduced a 24-second shot clock, which sped up the game and increased scoring.

Basketball finally began to come into its own in the late 1950s and 1960s, thanks to the popularity of such stars as Wilt Chamberlain, Bill Russell, and Bob Cousy. In 1967 a rival league, the American Basketball Association (ABA), appeared on the scene with its red, white, and blue basketball. Salaries escalated

as the two leagues competed for players. In 1976 the leagues merged.

By the early 1980s the NBA was suffering major image problems (drugs, fighting, racial issues) and began to wane in popularity. In 1980, 17 of its 23 teams lost money. The league was resuscitated by exciting new players such as Magic Johnson, Larry Bird, and Michael Jordan, and, in 1984, a new commissioner, David Stern. Although increased commercialism drives some purists crazy, big-name players like Jordan, Dennis Rodman, and Shaquille O'Neal have helped sell the NBA's most important commodity — sport as entertainment.

Stern went to work cleaning up the league's image and financial problems, pushing through a strict antidrug policy and a salary cap (the first such cap in major US sports). He also signed major marketing deals with such sponsors as Coca-Cola and McDonald's. In 1995 the NBA added its first two non-US teams, the Vancouver Grizzlies and the Toronto Raptors, and Jordan came out of retirement to lead the Chicago Bulls to championships in 1996, 1997, and 1998. The year 1997 also saw the launch of the Women's NBA (WNBA).

In 1998 the NBA and Rank Group's Hard Rock Café unit agreed to build a chain of 10 NBA City basketball-themed restaurants (six outside the US), the first of which opened in mid-1999 at Universal Studios' theme park and resort in Orlando, Florida. On July 1, 1998, the NBA owners voted to lock out players, leading to the first work stoppage in the NBA's 52-year history. The dispute lasted six months, and the NBA's 1998-99 season was pared down to 50 games from the standard 82. In conjunction with the start of the 1999-2000 season, the NBA launched NBA.com TV, a 24-hour basketball network available to DIRECTV subscribers.

Commissioner: David J. Stern
Deputy Commissioner and COO: Russell T. Granik
EVP and Chief Legal Officer: Jeffrey A. Mishkin
SVP Basketball Development: Steve Mills
SVP Basketball Operations: Rod Thorn
SVP Business Affairs: Harvey Benjamin
SVP Consumer Products: Christopher Heyn
SVP Finance: Robert Criqui
SVP International Group: Paul E. Zilk
SVP Media Programs: Barry Frey
SVP NBA Players and Administration: John T. Rose II
SVP Team Operations: Paula Hanson
VP Organizational Development: Marcia Sells
President, Women's National Basketball Association:
Val Ackerman
President and COO, NBA Entertainment: Adam Silver
President, NBA Television and New Media Ventures:
Ed Desser
**SVP International Television and Business
Development, NBA Entertainment:** Heidi Ueberroth
**SVP Programming and Broadcasting, NBA
Entertainment:** Gregg Winik
Human Resources: Patrica E. Swedin

LOCATIONS

HQ: Olympic Tower, 645 5th Ave., New York, NY 10022
Phone: 212-407-8000   **Fax:** 212-754-6414
Web site: http://www.nba.com

The National Basketball Association broadcasts its games
to nearly 200 countries.

PRODUCTS/OPERATIONS

Eastern Conference

Atlantic Division	Central Division
Boston Celtics	Atlanta Hawks
Miami Heat	Charlotte Hornets
New Jersey Nets	Chicago Bulls
New York Knicks	Cleveland Cavaliers
Orlando Magic	Detroit Pistons
Philadelphia 76ers	Indiana Pacers
Washington Wizards	Milwaukee Bucks
	Toronto Raptors

Western Conference

Midwest Division	Pacific Division
Dallas Mavericks	Golden State Warriors
Denver Nuggets	Los Angeles Clippers
Houston Rockets	Los Angeles Lakers
Minnesota Timberwolves	Phoenix Suns
San Antonio Spurs	Portland Trail Blazers
Utah Jazz	Sacramento Kings
Vancouver Grizzlies	Seattle SuperSonics

WNBA

Eastern Conference	Western Conference
Charlotte Sting	Houston Comets
Cleveland Rockers	Los Angeles Sparks
Detroit Shock	Minnesota Lynx
New York Liberty	Phoenix Mercury
Orlando Miracle	Sacramento Monarchs
Washington Mystics	Utah Starzz

COMPETITORS

Major League Baseball
NFL
NHL

HISTORICAL FINANCIALS & EMPLOYEES

Association FYE: August	Annual Growth	1990	1991	1992	1993	1994	1995	1996	1997	1998	1999
Sales ($ mil.)	5.9%	—	606	843	999	1,030	1,259	1,403	1,664	1,874	956
Employees	22.1%	—	—	—	—	450	550	650	850	1,000	—

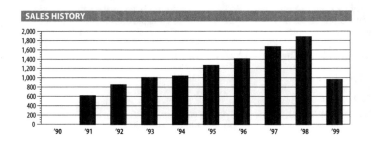

NATIONAL FOOTBALL LEAGUE

Football combines two things that Americans love: violence and the committee meeting. Little wonder then that the New York City-based National Football League (NFL) is the nation's most popular professional sports league, and the most watched sport on TV (stock car racing is second).

The NFL consists of 31 teams (a 32nd team in Houston is on the way) divided into two conferences: the American Football Conference and the National Football Conference. Though run as separate businesses, teams share their revenues with each other (for example, visiting teams receive 34% of gate receipts). The league acts as a trade association for franchise owners to promote the sport, license team names and logos, collect dues and royalties, and develop new programs. NFL Properties, the NFL's merchandising arm, generates about $2 billion a year in revenues.

Even though its TV ratings are declining, the NFL in 1998 brokered a generous TV deal, giving the league $2.2 billion a year for eight years. The league has seen success in attracting young fans.

HISTORY

A descendant of the English game of rugby, American football was developed in the late 1800s. Walter Camp, a player from Yale University, is generally credited with creating the rules that changed rugby into a new game, including adding a system for downs and scoring.

Professional teams sprang up in the 1890s, but the pro game was relatively unorganized until 1920, when several teams banded together to form the American Professional Football Association. Of the 14 teams that finished the original season, only two remain in today's NFL: the Chicago Bears (then known as the Decatur Staleys) and the Arizona Cardinals (originally the Chicago Cardinals). By 1922, when it changed its name to the National Football League, the group had grown to 18 teams.

During the 1930s the NFL shrank as the nation struggled through the Depression, but it began to rebound late in the decade. The first televised NFL game, between the Brooklyn Dodgers and the Philadelphia Eagles, was broadcast in 1939 to about 1,000 New York TV sets.

The league, which had been centered in the Midwest and East, began to go national in 1946 when the Cleveland Rams moved to Los Angeles. In 1950 the NFL swallowed up three teams from a defunct rival league, including San Francisco, Baltimore, and Cleveland.

Pete Rozelle, the general manager of the Los Angeles Rams, was named league commissioner in 1960. Two years later he negotiated the first league-wide television contract, inking a deal with CBS for $4.65 million. The NFL began to take advantage of other sources of revenue in 1963 when it formed licensing arm NFL Properties.

In 1966 the NFL agreed to merge with the upstart American Football League, boosting its roster to 24 teams. The two leagues agreed to meet in an end-of-season matchup in the beginning of 1967. (Called the AFL-NFL World Championship Game, it would not be known as the Super Bowl until 1969.) The league reorganized in 1969, creating the American Football Conference (AFC) and the National Football Conference (NFC).

By the late 1970s, the NFL had come into its own. The Super Bowl was routinely attracting 70-80 million viewers, and football passed baseball as America's favorite sport. In 1982 a jury ruled against the NFL in its effort to block the Oakland Raiders from moving to Los Angeles, and the ruling opened the way for the movement of several teams during the 1980s and 1990s. Rozelle retired in 1989; he was replaced by Paul Tagliabue, an attorney who had excelled in basketball at Georgetown University.

In 1994 the league lured Sara Levinson away from MTV to become president of NFL Properties, making her the highest-ranking woman in sports. The former MTV president was given the task of reproducing the NBA's success in attracting younger viewers. The NFL added the Carolina Panthers and the Jacksonville Jaguars to the league roster in 1995. In 1998 the NFL signed television contracts with FOX, ESPN, CBS, and ABC worth $17.6 billion over eight years. The league also concluded a players' collective bargaining agreement to last through 2003. The Cleveland Browns returned to the NFL in 1999 as an expansion team after a four-year absence. The Browns' televised debut was the league's highest-rated opener in cable TV history, even though the team was clobbered by Pittsburgh 43-0. The NFL also awarded the league's 32nd franchise to Houston, which has been without a team for three years following the Oilers' defection to Tennessee after the 1996-97 season, for $700 million plus $310 million to build a new stadium.

Commissioner: Paul J. Tagliabue
President and COO: Neil Austrian
CFO: Thomas E. Spock
EVP and League Counsel: Jeff Pash
EVP Labor Relations; Chairman, NFLMC:
Harold Henderson
EVP League and Football Development: Roger Goodell
SVP Broadcast Planning: Dennis Lewin
SVP Communications and Government Affairs:
Joe Browne
VP Player and Employee Development: Lem Burnham
President and CEO, NFL Europe: Oliver Luck
President, NFL Enterprises: Ron Bernard
President, NFL Properties: Sara Levinson
SVP and Managing Director, NFL International:
Douglas Quinn, age 37
Senior Director Human Resources and Administration:
John Buzzeo
Auditors: Arthur Andersen LLP

LOCATIONS

HQ: 280 Park Ave., New York, NY 10017
Phone: 212-450-2000   **Fax:** 212-681-7573
Web site: http://www.nfl.com

PRODUCTS/OPERATIONS

American Football Conference

Central Division	Miami Dolphins
Baltimore Ravens	New England Patriots
Cincinnati Bengals	New York Jets
Cleveland Browns	**Western Division**
Jacksonville Jaguars	Denver Broncos
Pittsburgh Steelers	Kansas City Chiefs
Tennessee Titans	Oakland Raiders
Eastern Division	San Diego Chargers
Buffalo Bills	Seattle Seahawks
Indianapolis Colts	

National Football Conference

Central Division	New York Giants
Chicago Bears	Philadelphia Eagles
Detroit Lions	Washington Redskins
Green Bay Packers	**Western Division**
Minnesota Vikings	Atlanta Falcons
Tampa Bay Buccaneers	Carolina Panthers
Eastern Division	New Orleans Saints
Arizona Cardinals	St. Louis Rams
Dallas Cowboys	San Francisco 49ers

Selected Business Units
NFL Enterprises (media development)
NFL Films (highlight packages)
NFL Properties (licensing, marketing, promotions, and
publishing)

COMPETITORS

FIFA
Major League Baseball
NBA
NHL
PGA

HISTORICAL FINANCIALS & EMPLOYEES

Not-for-profit FYE: March	Annual Growth	1990	1991	1992	1993	1994	1995	1996	1997	1998	1999
Sales ($ mil.)	13.3%	—	—	—	—	1,753	1,730	2,059	2,331	2,448	3,271
Employees	—	—	—	—	—	—	—	—	—	400	—

SALES HISTORY

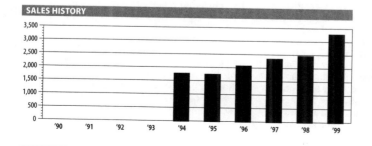

NATIONAL GEOGRAPHIC SOCIETY

OVERVIEW

If your only brush with the National Geographic Society involves maneuvering around the stacks of yellow magazines wedged into every nook and cranny of Grandma's attic, you might be surprised to learn what the organization's been up to lately. Still publishing its flagship *National Geographic* magazine (with about 9 million member/subscribers), the Washington, DC-based not-for-profit organization has branched across the media spectrum to enhance our familiarity with all things geographic. For-profit subsidiary National Geographic Ventures has expanded the organization's presence on television and the Web and in map-making and retail. The company also owns 25% of the National Geographic Channel, a cable channel it operates jointly with NBC and Fox.

While the National Geographic Society has stretched its reach across media, it hasn't abandoned its roots. It continues to fund geographic expeditions (7,000 such treks have been financed by the organization) and sponsors exhibits, lectures, and education programs.

As competition from relative newcomers such as Discovery Communications increases, the commercialization of the National Geographic Society is accelerating. In 1998 the organization created its National Geographic Enterprises Group to license its name for use on consumer products such as games and toys.

HISTORY

In 1888 a group of scientists and explorers gathered at the Cosmos Club in Washington, DC, to form the National Geographic Society. Gardiner Hubbard was its first president. The organization mailed the first edition of its magazine, dated October 1888, to 165 members. The magazine was clothed in a brown cover and contained a few esoteric articles, such as "The Classification of Geographic Forms by Genesis." The organization's tradition of funding expeditions began in 1890 when it sent geologist Israel Russell to explore Alaska. It began issuing regular monthly editions of *National Geographic* in 1896.

Following Hubbard's death in 1897, his son-in-law, inventor Alexander Graham Bell, became president. Aiming to boost the magazine's popularity, he hired Gilbert Grosvenor (who later married Bell's daughter) as editor. Grosvenor turned the magazine from a dry, technical publication to one of more general interest.

Under Grosvenor the magazine pioneered the use of photography, including rare photographs of remote Tibet (1904), the first hand-tinted colored photos (1910), the first underwater color photos (1920s), and the first color aerial photographs (1930).

The organization sponsored Robert Peary's trek to the North Pole in 1909 and Hiram Bingham's 1912 exploration of Machu Picchu in Peru. It expanded into cartography with the creation of a maps division in 1915. Grosvenor became president in 1920.

By 1930 circulation was 1.2 million (up from 2,200 in 1900). Grosvenor's policy of printing only "what is of a kindly nature . . . about any country or people" resulted in two articles that were criticized for their kindly portrayal of pre-war Nazi Germany (however, National Geographic maps and photographs were used by the US government for WWII intelligence). That policy eased over the years, and in 1961 a *National Geographic* article described the growing US involvement in Vietnam.

Grosvenor retired in 1954 after 55 years with the organization. His son Melville Bell Grosvenor, who became president and editor in 1957, accelerated book publishing and created a film unit that aired its first TV documentary, *Americans on Everest,* in 1965. Melville retired in 1967.

Melville's son Gilbert Melville Grosvenor took over as president in 1970. The organization debuted its *National Geographic Explorer* television series in 1985. National Geographic branched into commercial ventures in 1995 when it created for-profit subsidiary National Geographic Ventures to expand its presence on television and the Internet, as well as in maps and retail.

Grosvenor became chairman in 1996, and Reg Murphy took over as president. Murphy shook up the organization by laying off nearly a quarter of its staff and stepping up its profit-making activities. National Geographic branched into cable television in 1996 when it partnered with NBC to launch a documentary channel (Fox bought into the partnership three years later).

John Fahey replaced Murphy as president in 1998. The following year, the organization unveiled its *Adventure* magazine. To fight a circulation decline, the company began offering *National Geographic* on newsstands for the first time in 1999.

Chairman: Gilbert M. Grosvenor
VC: Reg Murphy
President and CEO: John M. Fahey Jr., age 47
SVP and CFO: Christopher A. Liedel
SVP Law, Business, and Government Affairs:
Terrence B. Adamson
SVP Publications: Nina D. Hoffman
SVP: Robert B. Sims
VP and Treasurer: H. Gregory Platts
VP: Bernard B. Callahan
VP: Michael J. Cole
VP: Kitty Carroll Hoffman
Chairman, Committee for Research and Exploration:
Peter Raven, age 62
President, National Geographic Television:
Timothy T. Kelly
President, National Geographic Ventures:
C. Richard Allen
Editor, National Geographic Magazine: William L. Allen
Executive Director, Education Foundation:
Lanny M. Proffer
Managing Editor, National Geographic: Robert L. Booth
Managing Director, NG Interactive: Lawrence R. Lux
Associate Editor, National Geographic: Robert M. Poole
Human Resources: Robert E. Howell

LOCATIONS

HQ: 1145 17th St. NW, Washington, DC 20036
Phone: 202-857-7000   **Fax:** 202-775-6141
Web site: http://www.nationalgeographic.com

PRODUCTS/OPERATIONS

Selected Operations
Books
  Everest: Mountain Without Mercy
  Eyewitness to the 20th Century
  National Geographic: The Photographs
  Satellite Atlas
CD-ROMs
  GeoBee Challenge
    Maps: The War Series
    Photo Gallery
    Trip Planner Platinum 2000
Globes and maps
Magazines
  Adventure
  National Geographic
  Traveler
Sponsorship of expeditions, lectures, and education
  programs
Television
  National Geographic Channel (25%, cable channel)
  National Geographic Explorer
Travel products
  Alarm clocks
  Binoculars
  Language translators
Videos

COMPETITORS

Discovery Communications
Dorling Kindersley
Educational Insights
Encyclopaedia Britannica
Environmental Systems Research
Lonely Planet
Natural Wonders
Rand McNally
Time Warner
World of Science

HISTORICAL FINANCIALS & EMPLOYEES

Not-for-profit FYE: December	Annual Growth	1989	1990	1991	1992	1993	1994	1995	1996	1997	1998
Sales ($ mil.)	2.6%	426	437	436	453	423	419	423	401	489	537
Employees	(6.7%)	2,628	2,526	2,189	2,005	1,700	1,493	1,551	1,300	1,214	1,410

SALES HISTORY

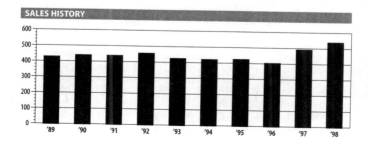

NATIONAL
GEOGRAPHIC
SOCIETY

NATIONAL HOCKEY LEAGUE

OVERVIEW

Contrary to popular humor, you don't have to go to a fight to see a hockey match break out in the NHL. Nevertheless, for the New York City-based National Hockey League's 28 US and Canadian teams, there's plenty of opportunity for fisticuffs in each game. Hockey is the fourth most popular of professional sports in North America, with clubs organized in two conferences with three divisions each. Seven minor and semi-pro hockey leagues also fly under the NHL banner.

The NHL has undergone rapid expansion in the 1990s. Revenues have increased markedly over the past few seasons, and the league signed a new five-year TV deal with ABC and ESPN (beginning with the 2000-01 season). But the NHL still has a long way to go to catch up to its professional counterparts. Commissioner Gary Bettman's top priorities involve changing the slow, low-scoring image of the game (rule changes the past two seasons have helped improve the pace), and preventing a mass evacuation of Canadian teams to US cities (the weak Canadian dollar and high taxes make it extremely difficult for Canadian teams to compete with US franchises).

HISTORY

The National Hockey League traces its heritage back to 1893, when the Stanley Cup (donated by Lord Stanley, Earl of Preston and Governor General of Canada) was first awarded to the Montréal Amateur Athletic Association hockey club of the Amateur Hockey Association of Canada. The National Hockey Association (NHA) was the first professional league to award the Cup (a large silver chalice with a new layer added each year, passed to the winning team and engraved with the names of that team's players) in 1910. The NHA folded in 1917 when feuding brought the need for a new image. That year Frank Calder, a British scholar and former sports journalist who came to Canada to be a soccer player, decided to keep the NHA's teams intact, rename the organization the National Hockey League (NHL), and appoint himself president. The league consisted of four teams that played a 22-game schedule.

The original Ottawa Senators (the team went under in 1934 and re-emerged as an expansion team in 1992) were the league's first dynasty, winning four Cups from 1920-27. The NHL added its first US team in 1925 when the Boston Bruins joined the league, and the 1920s saw continued expansion, but the NHL never became a solid league as numerous teams joined up and dropped out during the decade. During WWII hordes of players went to war, forcing the NHL to field teams whose players were too young, too old, or barely able to take the ice. The league almost shut down, but the Canadian government encouraged play to continue, claiming it boosted national morale.

The Montréal Canadiens (winners of 24 Stanley Cups, more than any other franchise by far) dominated the NHL for most of the next three decades. The NHL, after representing a small number of teams for many years, launched its largest expansion in league history in 1967 when six US-based franchises joined up. The league expanded to 21 teams in 1979 by absorbing its rival professional league, the World Hockey Association. US interest in the sport stagnated for many years, however, as it was largely considered a Canadian sport, and its reputation for brutal violence turned off many fans. The NHL tried to put an end to its slugfest image by implementing new rules in 1992, reducing violent play and emphasizing a quicker game based on skill and style.

Several expansion teams (Anaheim, Florida, Tampa Bay, Ottawa, San Jose) were added to the NHL throughout the 1990s, a decade marred by the only major labor dispute in the league's history. Team owners instituted a player lockout in 1994 over escalating salaries, delaying the season and ultimately failing in their goal of implementing a salary cap (the current contract between the players' union and owners runs through 2004). In 1997 the NHL added four new expansion teams (Atlanta; Columbus, Ohio; Minnesota; and Nashville), introducing them over a four year period (Columbus and Minnesota will begin play in 2000).

The league hoped to use exposure from professional players competing for the first time at the 1998 Winter Olympics games in Nagano, Japan, to boost popularity. But limited, late-night coverage thwarted its plan, and the sport's image was further tarnished when the US hockey team trashed its dorm rooms after a loss. Later that year NHL team owners agreed to a $600 million, five-year television contract with Walt Disney's ABC and ESPN starting with the 2000-01 season.

Commissioner: Gary B. Bettman
EVP and COO: Jon Litner
SVP: Richie Woodworth
VP and CFO: Craig Harnett
VP Human Resources: Janet A. Meyers
VP Marketing: Ed Horne
Auditors: PricewaterhouseCoopers LLP

LOCATIONS

HQ: 1251 Avenue of the Americas, 47th Fl.,
New York, NY 10020
Phone: 212-789-2000   **Fax:** 212-789-2020
Web site: http://www.nhl.com

The National Hockey League has 22 teams in the US and six in Canada.

PRODUCTS/OPERATIONS

Eastern Conference

Atlantic Division	**Southeast Division**
New Jersey Devils	Atlanta Thrashers
New York Islanders	Carolina Hurricanes
New York Rangers	Florida Panthers
Philadelphia Flyers	Tampa Bay Lightning
Pittsburgh Penguins	Washington Capitals

Northeast Division
Boston Bruins
Buffalo Sabres
Montréal Canadiens
Ottawa Senators
Toronto Maple Leafs

Western Conference

Central Division	**Pacific Division**
Chicago Blackhawks	Mighty Ducks of Anaheim
Detroit Red Wings	Dallas Stars
Nashville Predators	Los Angeles Kings
St. Louis Blues	Phoenix Coyotes
	San Jose Sharks

Northwest Division
Calgary Flames
Colorado Avalanche
Edmonton Oilers
Vancouver Canucks

Minor and Semi-Pro Leagues
American Hockey League
Central Hockey League
East Coast Hockey League
International Hockey League
United Hockey League
West Coast Hockey League
Western Professional Hockey League

COMPETITORS

Championship Auto Racing
Indy Racing League
Major League Baseball
NASCAR
NBA
NFL
PGA

HISTORICAL FINANCIALS & EMPLOYEES

Association FYE: June	Annual Growth	1990	1991	1992	1993	1994	1995	1996	1997	1998	1999
Sales ($ mil.)	19.6%	—	—	—	—	604	763	728	1,099	1,336	1,476
Employees	27.3%	—	—	—	—	110	150	200	257	289	—

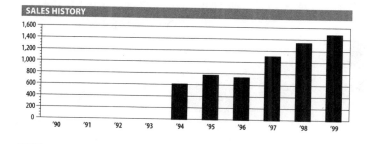

SALES HISTORY

AMTRAK

OVERVIEW

Is Amtrak the little engine that couldn't? The Washington, DC-based National Railroad Passenger Corporation, better known as Amtrak, is a private, for-profit company — that can't seem to make a profit. Amtrak, which has a monopoly on US intercity passenger rail service and serves 44 states, carries 21 million passengers each year. Amtrak is now governed by the seven-member Reform Board (which until 1997 was a nine-member board of directors) established by Congress. The board consists of the Secretary of Transportation and six other members appointed by the President and approved by the Senate.

Almost wholly owned by the US Department of Transportation, Amtrak will receive a projected $600 million in operating subsidies from the federal government for 1999. Amtrak needs the subsidies: It hasn't once turned a profit in its nearly 30-year history. To change that, Congress approved a one-time $2.3 billion capital expenditure that Amtrak is using to establish a new, high-speed commuter rail service between Boston and Washington, DC (with more planned outside the Northeast) and to improve infrastructure, equipment, and customer service. It is also adding revenues by carrying mail and time-sensitive cargo to help free itself from federal support by 2002.

Amtrak faces many challenges to be self-sustaining, not to mention profitable: competition from low-cost airlines, almost 30 years of massive debts, and increasing political pressure to straighten up and fly right.

HISTORY

US passenger train travel peaked in 1929, with 20,000 trains in operation. But the spread of automobiles, bus service, and air travel cut into business, and by the late 1960s only about 500 passenger trains remained running in the US. Railroad CEOs saw the end coming and let service and equipment decay dramatically. In 1970 the combined losses of all private train operations exceeded $1.8 billion in today's dollars. That year Congress passed the Rail Passenger Service Act, which created Amtrak to preserve America's passenger rail system. Although railroads were offered stock in the corporation for their passenger equipment, most just wrote off the loss.

Amtrak began operating in 1971 with 1,200 cars, most built in the 1950s. Although the company lost money from the outset ($153 million in 1972), it continued to be bankrolled by Uncle Sam, despite much criticism. Amtrak ordered its first new equipment in 1973, the year it also began taking over stations, yards, and service staff. The company didn't own any track until 1976, when it purchased hundreds of miles of right-of-way track in the Northeast Corridor (NEC), from Boston to Washington, DC.

After a 1979 study showed Amtrak passengers to be by far the most heavily subsidized travelers in the US, Congress ordered the company to better utilize its resources. The 1980s saw Amtrak leasing its rights-of-way along its tracks in the NEC to telecommunications companies, which installed fiber-optic cables, and beginning mail and freight services for extra revenue.

In the early 1990s Amtrak faced a number of challenges: Midwest flooding, falling airfares, and safety concerns over a number of rail accidents, particulary the 1993 wreck of the Sunset Limited near Mobile, Alabama, in which 47 people were killed (the worst accident in Amtrak's history). In 1994 Amtrak's Board of Directors (at Congress' behest) adopted a strategic plan to be free of federal support by 2002. Facing a $200 million shortfall, the company attempted to streamline in 1995 by splitting into three segments: Northeast Corridor, Intercity, and Amtrak West. It also began planning high-speed trains for its heavily traveled East Coast routes.

Aided by $2.3 billion in capital expenditure funds authorized by Congress in 1997, Amtrak finalized agreements to purchase the high-speed cars and locomotives central to its self-sufficiency plan. It also began increasing its freight hauling and had its first profitable product line: the Metroliner route between New York and Washington, DC.

Amtrak's board of directors was replaced by Congress in 1997 with a seven-member Reform Board appointed by the President. Chairman and president Thomas Downs resigned that year, claiming exhaustion, and was replaced in 1998 by Governor Tommy Thompson of Wisconsin (chairman), former Massachusetts governor and presidential candidate Michael Dukakis (VC), and president and CEO George Warrington. In 1998 Amtrak also saw its passenger revenues pass the $1 billion mark for the first time in its history.

Amtrak in 1999 announced plans to introduce its Acela high-speed service in the Northeast.

Chairman: Gov. Tommy G. Thompson
VC: Michael S. Dukakis
President and CEO: George D. Warrington
CFO: Alfred S. Altschul
President, Northeast Corridor Division: Stan Bagley Jr.
President, Amtrak Intercity: Lee Bullock
President, Amtrak West: Gilbert O. Mallery
VP Labor: Joseph M. Bress
VP Marketing and Sales: Richard P. Donnelly
VP and General Counsel: Sarah Duggin
VP Government Affairs: Thomas J. Gillespie Jr.
VP Human Resources: Lorraine A. Green
VP Reservations, Sales, and Customer Relations:
  Anne W. Hoey
VP Operations: Ron Scolaro
Acting Corporate Secretary: Barbara Richardson

PRODUCTS/OPERATIONS

1998 Sales

	$ mil.	% of total
Passenger related		
Transportation	928	41
430B services	83	4
Food & beverage	73	3
Commuter operating	260	11
Reimbursable	91	4
Commuter fees	74	3
Mail baggage & express	83	4
Real estate	35	1
Freight	18	1
Other	98	4
Federal payments	542	24
Total	**2,285**	**100**

LOCATIONS

HQ: National Railroad Passenger Corporation,
  60 Massachusetts Ave. NE, Washington, DC 20002
Phone: 202-906-3000   **Fax:** 202-906-3306
Web site: http://www.amtrak.com

COMPETITORS

AMR
America West
Burlington Northern
 Santa Fe
Coach USA
Continental Airlines
Delta
FDX
Greyhound
Metra
Northwest Airlines

Port Authority of NY & NJ
Roadway Express
Schneider National
Southwest Airlines
TWA
U.S. Postal Service
UAL
UPS
US Airways
Union Pacific
Yellow Corporation

HISTORICAL FINANCIALS & EMPLOYEES

Government-owned FYE: September	Annual Growth	1989	1990	1991	1992	1993	1994	1995	1996	1997	1998
Sales ($ mil.)	7.6%	—	1,269	1,308	1,359	1,325	1,403	1,497	1,555	1,674	2,285
Net income ($ mil.)	—	—	(665)	(703)	(722)	(712)	(731)	(808)	(764)	(762)	(353)
Income as % of sales	—	—	—	—	—	—	—	—	—	—	—
Employees	0.2%	—	—	—	23,741	24,000	24,000	24,100	23,000	23,000	24,000

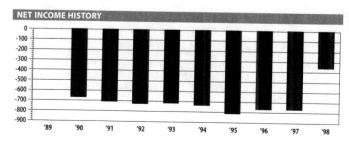

NET INCOME HISTORY

1998 FISCAL YEAR-END
Debt ratio: 26.0%
Return on equity: —
Cash ($ mil.): 684
Current ratio: 1.40
Long-term debt ($ mil.): 1,536

NATIONWIDE INSURANCE

OVERVIEW

Call it truth in advertising — Columbus, Ohio-based mutual Nationwide Insurance Enterprise (which now answers simply to Nationwide) has offices throughout the US.

Nationwide offers property/casualty policies (#6 in the US), life insurance and financial services, managed health care, and commercial insurance. The company sells property/casualty and life insurance through affiliates that include Nationwide Life and Farmland Mutual. It also sells policies in Germany (Neckura), Puerto Rico, and the US Virgin Islands.

The company owns about 80% of Nationwide Financial Services (NFS), which it spun off in 1997 to give Nationwide Life, the principal asset of NFS, access to capital markets the mutual parent does not have.

With its commitment to acquisition as the best way to introduce new products and distribution channels, the company is putting its money where its mouth is. It made more than 10 acquisitions in 1998 and 1999, chief among them ALLIED Group, a multi-line insurer.

HISTORY

In 1919 members of the Ohio Farm Bureau Federation, a farmers' consumer group, established their own automobile insurance company. (As rural drivers, they didn't want to pay city rates.) To get a license from the state, the company, called Farm Bureau Mutual, needed 100 policyholders. It gathered more than 1,000. Founder Murray Lincoln headed the company until 1964.

The insurer expanded into Delaware, Maryland, North Carolina, and Vermont in 1928, and in 1931 it began selling auto insurance to city folks. It expanded into fire insurance in 1934 and life insurance the next year.

During WWII growth slowed, although the company had operations in 12 states and Washington, DC, by 1943. It diversified in 1946 when it bought a Columbus, Ohio, radio station. By 1952 the firm had resumed expansion and changed its name to Nationwide.

The company was one of the first auto insurance companies to use its agents to sell other financial products, adding life insurance and mutual funds in the mid-1950s. Nationwide General, the country's first merit-rated auto insurance firm, was formed in 1956.

Nationwide established Neckura in Germany in 1965 to sell auto and fire insurance. Four years later the company bought GatesMcDonald, a provider of risk, tax, benefit, and health care management services. It organized its property/casualty operations into Nationwide Property & Casualty in 1979.

The company experienced solid growth throughout the 1980s by establishing or purchasing insurance firms, among them Colonial Insurance of California (1980), Financial Horizons Life (1981), Scottsdale (1982), and, the largest, Employers Insurance of Wausau (1985). Wausau wrote the country's first workers' compensation policy in 1911.

Earnings were up and down in the 1990s as the company invested in Wausau and in consolidating office operations. Nationwide set up an ethics office in 1995, a time of increased scrutiny of insurance industry sales practices, and made an effort to hire more women as agents. In 1996 the Florida Insurance Commission claimed the company discriminated against customers on the basis of age, gender, health, income, marital status, and location. Nationwide countered that the allegations originated from displeased agents.

In 1997 the company settled a lawsuit by agreeing to stop its redlining practices (it avoided selling homeowners' insurance to urban customers with homes valued at less than $50,000 or more than 30 years old, which allegedly discriminated against minorities). It also dropped a year-old sales quota system that was under investigation.

Nationwide began to narrow its focus on its core businesses that year. It spun off Nationwide Financial Services, sold its West Coast Life Insurance unit to insurance holding company Protective Life, and sold its radio stations to broadcast company Jacor Communications.

In a move to boost the western expansion of its property/casualty business, in 1998 Nationwide purchased ALLIED Group and sold its Wausau subsidiary to Liberty Mutual. The next year the company bought AXA subsidiary PanEuroLife to expand its European market and bought CalFarm (agricultural insurance in California) from Zenith National. It also sold its ALLIED Life operations to Swiss Re. The company's discrimination woes came back to haunt it in 1999, and it created a $750,000 fund to help residents in poor Cincinnati neighborhoods buy homes. Nationwide also opened 20 new sales offices in minority Texas communities that year.

Chairman and CEO: Dimon R. McFerson
President; President and COO, Nationwide Mutual, Nationwide Mutual Fire, and Nationwide Property and Casualty Insurance: Galen R. Barnes
President and COO, Nationwide Financial Services and Nationwide Life: Joseph J. Gasper
EVP and CFO: Robert A. Oakley
EVP and Chief Investment Officer: Robert J. Woodward Jr.
SVP and Chief Communications Officer: John R. Cook Jr.
SVP and Chief Information Technology Officer: Richard D. Headley
SVP and General Counsel: Patricia R. Hatler
SVP Human Resources: Donna A. James
Chairman, Nationwide General: Willard J. Engel
Chairman, Nationwide Mutual Insurance: Arden L. Shisler
Chairman, Nationwide Life and Nationwide Life and Annuity: David O. Miller
Chairman, Nationwide Mutual Fire: James F. Patterson
Chairman, Nationwide Property & Casualty: Nancy C. Thomas
Auditors: KPMG LLP

LOCATIONS

HQ: Nationwide Insurance Enterprise,
1 Nationwide Plaza, Columbus, OH 43215
Phone: 614-249-7111　　**Fax:** 614-249-7705
Web site: http://www.nationwide.com

PRODUCTS/OPERATIONS

1998 Assets

	$ mil.	% of total
Cash & equivalents	1,398	1
Bonds	27,082	28
Stocks	5,300	5
Mortgage loans & real estate	6,329	7
Assets in separate account	51,328	52
Other assets	6,843	7
Total	**98,280**	**100**

1998 Sales

	$ mil.	% of total
Life, health & annuity premiums	13,634	54
Property/casualty premiums	8,116	32
Investment income	2,547	10
Other	1,004	4
Total	**25,301**	**100**

Selected Subsidiaries and Affiliates

ALLIED Group (property/casualty)
Farmland Insurance Companies (commercial services)
GatesMcDonald & Company (workers compensation, other lines)
Insurance Intermediaries (insurance services)
Morley Financial Services (long-term savings)
Nationwide Agency (property/casualty)
Nationwide Agribusiness
Nationwide Financial Services, Inc. (80%)
Nationwide General Insurance Company (property/casualty)
Nationwide Indemnity Company (property.casualty)
Nationwide Health Plans, Inc.
Nationwide Life Companies (long-term savings and life)
Nationwide Mutual Fire Insurance Company (property/casualty)
Nationwide Mutual Insurance Company (property/casualty)
Nationwide Property and Casualty Insurance Company (property/casualty)
Nationwide Realty Investors
Neckura Insurance Companies (Germany)
PanEuroLife (international operations)

COMPETITORS

AXA Financial
Allstate
American Financial
Blue Cross
CIGNA
CNA Financial
Citigroup
Guardian Life
John Hancock
Liberty Mutual
MassMutual
MetLife
New York Life
Northwestern Mutual
Pacific Mutual
Principal Financial
Prudential
St. Paul Companies
State Farm
The Hartford
Transamerica
USAA
UnitedHealth Group

HISTORICAL FINANCIALS & EMPLOYEES

Mutual company FYE: December	Annual Growth	1989	1990	1991	1992	1993	1994	1995	1996	1997	1998
Assets ($ mil.)	16.4%	25,044	27,848	32,779	37,582	42,213	47,696	57,420	67,624	83,214	98,280
Net income ($ mil.)	15.6%	261	148	393	69	501	445	183	250	1,031	963
Income as % of assets	—	1.0%	0.5%	1.2%	0.2%	1.2%	0.9%	0.3%	0.4%	1.2%	1.0%
Employees	3.1%	25,000	26,000	27,000	32,500	32,583	32,600	32,949	33,184	29,051	32,815

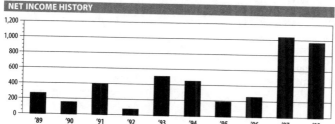

NET INCOME HISTORY

1998 FISCAL YEAR-END

Equity as % of assets: 11.2%
Return on assets: 1.1%
Return on equity: 9.5%
Long-term debt ($ mil.): 298
Sales ($ mil.): 25,301

NEW COLT HOLDING CORP.

OVERVIEW

The Colt .45 may have won the West, but it took a New York investment firm to save New Colt Holding from a post-Cold War decline in weapons sales and tough foreign competition.

The West Hartford, Connecticut-based company makes the non-inebriating brand of Colt .45, along with other handguns, semiautomatic rifles, and military assault weapons, through subsidiaries Colt's Manufacturing and Colt Rifles. Its products are sold to the US and international governments and to commercial distributors. New Colt also owns military weapons manufacturer Saco Defense and licenses its name to a variety of other companies, such as Encore Software (for Encore's Wild West Shootout game).

With the firearms industry taking cover from lawsuits filed by cities and counties across the US, New Colt is discontinuing a number of cheaper handguns it makes for the consumer market (including its 9mm pistols and double-action revolvers). It is also focusing on its "smart gun" technology that makes it impossible for anyone other than a weapon's owner to fire it. The company spun off its smart gun division as iColt.

Investment firm Zilkha & Co., which owns about 83% of New Colt, has been reviving the company since 1994 when it bought the firm out of bankruptcy.

HISTORY

After waiting four years for a patent, Samuel Colt started the Patent Arms Manufacturing Company in 1836 to make his revolutionary handgun, a revolver. The newfangled gun was slow to catch on (the company went bankrupt in 1842), but it gained fame after being adopted by the Texas Rangers. The US Army delegated Capt. Samuel Walker to work with Colt to improve the design, and sales of the resulting "Walker Colt" enabled Colt to set up a factory in Hartford, Connecticut.

In 1851 the company was the first American manufacturer to open a plant in England. Patent Arms Manufacturing was renamed Colt's Patent Fire Arms Manufacturing Co. four years later. Colt was a millionaire when he died in 1862 at age 47.

Colt's introduced the six-shot Colt .45 Army Model, "the gun that won the West," in 1873. More products followed, including machine guns and automatic pistols designed by inventor John Browning. Colt's widow sold the firm to an investor group in 1901.

Business boomed during both world wars, but by the 1940s labor strife and outmoded equipment began to take a toll, and Colt's lost money during the last years of WWII. In 1955 the struggling firm was acquired by conglomerate Penn-Texas. In 1959 Colt's patented the M-16 assault rifle; in 10 years it sold a million to the US military.

During the Vietnam War the company flourished, but the 1980s brought low-end competition and shrinking defense orders. Colt's sales were hurt when the US government replaced the Colt .45 as the official sidearm for the armed forces. A three-year strike prompted the Army to shift its M-16 contract to FN Herstal in 1988.

Two years later Colt's was acquired by private investors and a Connecticut state pension fund and was renamed Colt's Manufacturing Co. Sales remained flat, however, forcing the company to seek bankruptcy protection in 1992. There Colt's remained until New York investment firm Zilkha & Co. bailed it out in 1994, reorganizing the company as New Colt Holding. The new management made an offer for rival FN Herstal in 1997, but the deal was blocked by the Belgian government and fell through. Late that year the company won a contract to supply M-4 rifles to the Army.

New Colt bought military weapons specialist Saco Defense, maker of MK 19 and Striker grenade launchers, in 1998. Also that year Steven Sliwa succeeded retiring CEO Ronald Stewart.

As US cities began suing Colt's Manufacturing and other makers of firearms in attempts to recover safety and health expenses attributed to gun violence, the company stepped up lobbying in 1999 and said it would increase gun safety efforts, including development of its "smart gun" technology.

A restructuring began in 1999 that will end most of New Colt's consumer handgun business. It also spun off its smart gun technology as a separate company, iColt. Sliwa left to head iColt, and retired Lt. Gen. William Keys was named president and CEO of New Colt. Also in 1999 New Colt bought Ultra-Light Arms, a maker of upscale hunting rifles.

Chairman: Donald Zilkha
President and CEO: William Keys
CFO: Thomas Gilboy
Manager, Human Resources: Rae Holmes

LOCATIONS

HQ: 545 New Park Ave., West Hartford, CT 06110
Phone: 860-236-6311   **Fax:** 860-244-1442
Web site: http://www.colt.com

PRODUCTS/OPERATIONS

Selected Products and Brands
Commercial rifles
  Colt accurized rifles
  Match target rifles
Law enforcement
  AR15
  Carbine
  Colt accurized rifles
  Commando
  M-16
  M203 Grenade Launchers
  M-4 Carbine
  Match target rifles
  Submachine guns
Performance products
  Colt XS Series
  Gold Cup Trophy
  Special Combat Government Competition
Personal protection
  Colt Defender
  M1991A1
Western
  Colt Cowboy
  Model Ps

COMPETITORS

Action Arms
BAE SYSTEMS
Beretta
Browning Arms
Crosman
FN Manufacturing
Glock
Herstal
Magnum Research
Mauser-Werke
Navegar
Remington Arms
SIG
Saf T Lok
Springfield Inc.
Sturm, Ruger
Tomkins

HISTORICAL FINANCIALS & EMPLOYEES

Private FYE: December	Annual Growth	1989	1990	1991	1992	1993	1994	1995	1996	1997	1998
Sales ($ mil.)	4.3%	—	—	—	—	—	—	—	—	92	96
Employees	0.0%	—	—	—	—	—	—	—	—	700	700

SALES HISTORY

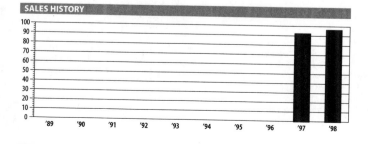

NUMMI

Like a Samurai assembly worker with American roots, Fremont, California-based New United Motor Manufacturing, Inc., (NUMMI) — a 50-50 joint venture between General Motors (GM) and Toyota — has the capacity to make 240,000 cars and 150,000 pickups a year. The lineup includes Tacoma pickups and Corolla sedans made for Toyota (about 60% of vehicles), and Chevrolet Prizms (near-twins to Corollas, formerly called Geos) made for GM. NUMMI makes the light pickups Toyota sells in North America; specially designed for the American market, the Toyota Tacoma is made only at the NUMMI plant.

Begun as an experiment to see if Japanese management techniques emphasizing team decision-making would work in the US, NUMMI is a success story. Toyota builds more vehicles (rather than transporting them) in the markets it serves, as a way to reduce costs. NUMMI's production methods are considered to be among the world's most efficient, and industrial surveyor Harbour and Associates consistently ranks the plant as one of North America's most productive.

As Prizm sales falter — Chevrolet sold less than 50,000 of the models last year — GM and Toyota are teaming up at NUMMI to develop vehicles designed to use alternative fuels (electric, fuel cell, hybrid gasoline-electric).

HISTORY

Rivals General Motors (GM) and Toyota spawned New United Motor Manufacturing (NUMMI); they figured if you can't beat the competition, join forces. In the early 1980s GM was sagging in the small-car market and Japan's Toyota wanted to build cars in the US to ease trade tension. GM head Roger Smith and Toyota chairman Eiji Toyoda met in 1982 to discuss ways to achieve their goals.

After a year of negotiations, the two companies announced their partnership at the Fremont, California plant, which GM had closed in 1982. Toyota put up $100 million and GM provided the plant (valued at $89 million) and $11 million cash. The companies also raised $350 million to build a stamping plant.

To gain FTC approval, the companies agreed to limit the venture to 12 years, make no more than 250,000 cars a year for GM, and refrain from sharing strategic information. In 1984 the FTC approved the deal and NUMMI was born.

The Fremont plant had a reputation for poor labor relations, and Toyota originally refused to rehire any of the workers from the plant; after prolonged negotiations with the UAW, it agreed to hire 50% plus one of the former workers. From the outset the company was different, with fewer management layers and a blurred distinction between blue- and white-collar workers.

NUMMI's first car, a Chevy Nova, rolled off the assembly line in late 1984. The company began producing the Corolla FX, a two-door version of the four-door Nova, in 1986. NUMMI earned kudos for high worker morale and productivity and was selected that year as a case study on positive labor-management relations for the International Labor Organization Conference.

Despite its success on some fronts, NUMMI's sales slid during the late 1980s. It had earned a reputation for high-quality cars, but it struggled with high overhead and the Nova's weak sales. In 1988 NUMMI halted production of the Nova and the Corolla FX and built the Geo Prizm and the Corolla sedan.

By late 1989, the company's production numbers had begun to rebound. In 1990 NUMMI began a major expansion as it geared up to build Toyota's half-ton pickup. In 1991 its first Toyota 4X2 pickup (the Toyota Hi-Lux) rolled off the assembly line, and in 1992 NUMMI began making the Toyota 4X4 pickup.

In 1993 the FTC approved an indefinite extension of the original 12-year GM-Toyota agreement. Also that year NUMMI began building the Toyota Xtracab, an extended version of Toyota's pickup and began construction of a plastics plant to build bumper coverings for Prizms and Corollas. It also expanded the paint, body welding, and assembly plant facilities.

Though Toyota had produced half of its North America-bound pickups in Japan and half in the US for years, it shifted all compact truck production to the NUMMI plant with the 1995 launch of the Tacoma. NUMMI built its three-millionth vehicle in 1997 and marked the event by donating three vehicles to charitable agencies in the Fremont area. Toyota introduced an updated 1998 Tacoma compact pickup, and GM changed the name of the Geo Prizm to the Chevrolet Prizm. In 1999 the parent companies agreed to a five-year partnership to develop and possibly produce alternative fuel vehicles.

President and CEO: Kanji Ishii
EVP: Gary Convis
VP Human Resources: Gregg Vervais
VP, Legal, Environment, and Governmental Affairs and Corporate Secretary: Patricia Pineda
VP Production Control and Quality Assurance: Akio Toyoda
Treasurer and General Manager Finance: Y. Toyoda
Comptroller and General Manager General Affairs: Mark Mathews
General Manager Production Control: Bill Borton
General Manager Purchasing: Linda McColgan
General Manager Quality Control: John Nogy
General Manager Body Shop and Stamping: Robert O'Leary
Director Engineering: Gary Twisselmann
Director Plant Operations: Jesse Wingard

LOCATIONS

HQ: New United Motor Manufacturing, Inc., 45500 Fremont Blvd., Fremont, CA 94538
Phone: 510-498-5500   **Fax:** 510-770-4010
Web site: http://www.nummi.com

PRODUCTS/OPERATIONS

Products
Chevrolet Prizm (sedan)
Toyota Corolla (sedan)
Toyota Tacoma (pickup truck; standard & extended cabs)

COMPETITORS

DaimlerChrysler
Fiat
Ford
Fuji Heavy Industries
Honda
Hyundai
Isuzu
Kia Motors
Mack Trucks
Mazda
Mitsubishi
Nissan
Saab Automobile
Suzuki
Volkswagen

HISTORICAL FINANCIALS & EMPLOYEES

Joint venture FYE: December	Annual Growth	1989	1990	1991	1992	1993	1994	1995	1996	1997	1998
Estimated sales ($ mil.)	13.5%	—	—	—	2,200	2,700	3,700	4,500	4,700	4,600	4,699
Employees	3.2%	—	—	—	3,969	4,300	4,500	4,800	4,700	4,800	4,800

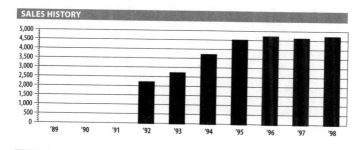

SALES HISTORY

NYC HEALTH AND HOSPITALS

OVERVIEW

This dinosaur is having trouble in the cold climate of managed care and stringent cost controls for the medical industry.

New York City Health and Hospitals Corporation (HHC) is looking for ways to evolve into a new beast. The company, which administers New York's municipal health service, is the US's largest such system, with facilities in all five boroughs. It operates 11 acute care hospitals (including Bellevue, the nation's oldest public hospital), as well as community clinics, diagnostic and treatment centers, long-term-care facilities, and the city's correctional medical services. MetroPlus is the system's HMO.

In recent years HHC has lost paying patients to newer, better-equipped facilities, and it is left caring for a deluge of medically indigent and Medicaid patients, who tend to be sicker than the general population since they wait longer to seek care.

To cut costs, HHC is focusing on preventative and primary care. The corporation believes community clinics, wellness programs, and other services will reduce patients' reliance on more expensive hospital-based care. HHC is also trying to switch Medicaid patients over to its HMO to decrease its dependence on uncertain government funding.

HISTORY

The City of New York created a Hospitals Department in 1929 to manage its hospitals for the poor. During the Depression, more than half of the city's residents were eligible for subsidized care, and its public hospitals operated at full capacity.

Four new hospitals opened in the 1950s, but the city was already having trouble maintaining its existing facilities and attracting staff, as young doctors opted to serve at private, insurance-supported hospitals catering to the middle class. Meanwhile, advances in medical technology and increased demand for skilled nurses made hospitals more expensive to operate. The advent of Medicaid in 1965 was a boon for the system because it brought in federal money.

In 1969 the city created the New York City Health and Hospitals Corporation (HHC) to manage its public health care system — and, it was hoped, to distance it from the political arena. But HHC was still dependent on the city for funds, arousing criticism from those who wanted the corporation to be more autonomous. A 1973 state report claimed "the people of New York City are not materially better served by the Health and Hospitals Corporation than by its predecessor agencies."

City budget shortfalls in the mid-1970s led to cutbacks at HHC, including a nearly 20% staff cut. During the latter part of the decade, several hospitals closed and some services were discontinued. After his election as mayor in 1978, Ed Koch gained more control over HHC's operations. Struggles between his administration and the system led three HHC presidents to resign by 1981. That year Koch crony Stanley Brezenoff assumed the post and helped transform HHC into a city pseudo-department.

The early 1980s brought greater prosperity to the city's health care system. Reimbursement rates and collections procedures improved, allowing HHC to upgrade its record-keeping and its ambulatory and psychiatric care programs. However, as the decade closed, sharp increases in AIDS and crack addiction cases strained the system, and a sluggish economy decreased city funding. Criticism mounted in the early 1990s, with allegations of wrongful deaths, dangerous facilities, and lack of Medicaid payment controls. HHC lost patients to managed care providers, and revenues plummeted. In 1995 a city panel recommended that the city radically revamp the system.

Faced with declining revenues and criticism from Mayor Rudolph Giuliani that HHC was "a jobs program," the company began cutting jobs and consolidating facilities in 1996. Under Giuliani's direction, HHC agreed to sell Coney Island Hospital that year and began seeking buyers for its Elmhurst and Queens hospital centers. The following year the New York State Supreme Court struck down Giuliani's privatization efforts, saying the City Council had a right to review and approve each sale. In 1998 Giuliani continued to seek to restructure HHC, and the agency itself contended it was making progress toward its restructuring goals, which were aimed at giving HHC more autonomy as well as more fiscal responsibility. In anticipation of a budget shortfall that year, the system laid off some 900 support staff employees. In 1999 the state court of appeals ruled HHC could not legally lease or sell its hospitals.

Chairperson: Rosa M. Gil
President: Luis R. Marcos
SVP Communications and Marketing:
Jane D. Zimmerman
SVP Corporate Planning, Community Health, and Intergovernmental Relations: LaRay Brown
SVP Finance and Capital and CFO: Rick Langfelder
SVP Medical and Professional Affairs and Behavioral Health: Van Dunn
SVP, Brooklyn Staten Island Family Health Network; Executive Director, Kings County Hospital Center: Jean Leon
SVP, Generations Plus Health Network; Executive Director, Metropolitan Hospital Center: Jose Sanchez
SVP, North Bronx HealthCare Network; Executive Director, Jacobi Medical Center: Joseph S. Orlando
SVP, Northern Manhattan Network: John Palmer
SVP, Queens Health Network; Executive Director, Elmhurst Hospital Center: Pete Velez
SVP, South Manhattan Network; Executive Director, Bellevue Hospital Center: Carlos Perez
VP Human Resources and Workforce Development: Pamela S. Silverblatt
Corporate Executive Director Operations: Frank J. Cirillo
Executive Director, Coney Island Hospital: William P. Walsh
General Counsel: Elizabeth St. Clair
Auditors: KPMG LLP

HQ: New York City Health and Hospitals Corporation, 125 Worth St., Ste. 510, New York, NY 10013
Phone: 212-788-3339 **Fax:** 212-788-3348
Web site: http://www.ci.nyc.ny.us/html/hhc

HHC Networks

Brooklyn Staten Island Family Health Network
East New York Diagnostic & Treatment Center
Kings County Hospital Center
Sea View Hospital Rehabilitation Center and Home

Coney Island Hospital

Generations Plus Health Network
Lincoln Medical and Mental Health Center
Metropolitan Hospital Center
Morrisania Diagnostic & Treatment Center
Segundo Ruiz Belvis Diagnostic & Treatment Center

North Bronx Network
Jacobi Medical Center
North Central Bronx Hospital

North Brooklyn Network
Cumberland Diagnostic & Treatment Center
Woodhull Medical and Mental Health Center

Northern Manhattan Network
Harlem Hospital Center
Renaissance Diagnostic & Treatment Center

Queens Health Network
Elmhurst Hospital Center
Neponsit Health Care Center
Queens Hospital Center

South Manhattan Network
Bellevue Hospital Center
Coler/Goldwater Memorial Hospital
Gouverneur Nursing Facility/Diagnostic & Treatment Center

Carondelet Health
Catholic Healthcare Network
Catholic Medical Center of Brooklyn & Queens
Columbia University
Columbia/HCA
Cornell University
Franciscan Health Partnership

Memorial Sloan-Kettering
Montefiore Medical
Mount Sinai
NYU
North Shore-Long Island Jewish Health System
Rockefeller University

Government-owned FYE: June	Annual Growth	1990	1991	1992	1993	1994	1995	1996	1997	1998	1999
Sales ($ mil.)	3.0%	—	—	—	3,468	3,949	4,134	4,460	4,069	3,835	4,131
Employees	(5.8%)	—	—	—	—	45,000	41,711	35,000	33,000	31,600	33,403

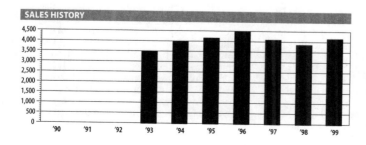

NEW YORK LIFE INSURANCE

OVERVIEW

New York Life Insurance has been in the Big Apple since it was just a tiny seed.

The New York City-based insurer is adding products but holding onto its core business of selling life insurance and annuities. Through New York Life International, it is reaching new markets, especially in Asia where the life insurance market is not as mature.

As customers focus more on retirement rather than death benefits, New York Life has added financial products and services, such as mutual funds and securities brokerage for individuals. It has also turned its asset management skills into a profit center by offering its services to institutional investors. Other lines of business include special group policies sold through the AARP and to contractors working for the federal government.

After state legislators failed to approve a mutual holding company structure, New York Life announced it would not follow its rivals in demutualizing for fear of being gobbled up in a merger. The insurer will instead use its considerable war chest (from divestitures) to build its international and asset management operations.

HISTORY

In 1841 actuary Pliny Freeman and 56 New York businessmen founded Nautilus Insurance Co., the third US mutual (policyholder-owned) company. It began operating in 1845 and became New York Life in 1849.

By 1846 the company had the first life insurance agent west of the Mississippi River. Although the Civil War disrupted its southern business, New York Life honored all its obligations and renewed lapsed policies when the war ended. By 1887 the company had developed its branch office system.

By the turn of the century, the company had established the NYLIC Plan for compensating agents, which featured a lifetime income after 20 years of service (discontinued in 1991). New York Life had moved into Europe in the late 1800s but withdrew after WWI.

In the early 1950s the company simplified insurance forms, slashed premiums, and updated mortality tables from the 1860s. In 1956 it became the first life insurance firm to use data-processing equipment on a large scale.

In the 1960s New York Life helped develop variable life insurance, which featured variable benefits and level premiums. The company added variable annuities in 1968. Steady growth continued until the late 1970s, when high interest rates led to heavy policyholder borrowing. Jarred by the outflow of money, New York Life sought to make its products more competitive as investments.

The company formed New York Life and Health Insurance Co. in 1982. It acquired MacKay-Shields Financial, which oversees its MainStay mutual funds, in 1984. That year NYLIFE Realty offered the company's first pure investment product, a real estate limited partnership. When the limited partnerships proved riskier than most insurance customers bargained for, investors sued New York Life; in 1996 the company negotiated a plan to liquidate the partnerships and reimburse investors.

Expansion continued in 1987 when it bought a controlling interest in Hillhouse Associates Insurance (a third-party administrator of insurance plans) and Madison Benefits Administrators (group insurance programs). The company also acquired Sanus Corp. Health Systems.

New York Life formed an insurance joint venture in Indonesia in 1992 and entered South Korea and Taiwan. The next year it bought Aetna UK's life insurance operations.

In 1994 New York Life increased its health care holdings, adding ETHIX Corp. (utilization review) and Avanti Health Systems (physician practice management). After allegations of churning (agents padding commissions by inducing customers to buy more expensive policies), New York Life overhauled its sales practices in 1994, then settled the resulting lawsuit for $300 million in 1995. Next came claims that agents had not properly informed customers of the vulnerability of "vanishing premium" policies to interest-rate changes. In 1997 agents were accused of not properly notifying customers that they might be entitled to share in the settlement. Some agents lashed out at New York Life, claiming they were fired so New York Life wouldn't have to pay them retirement benefits.

In 1998, feeling the one-two punch of decreasing margins in health care and consolidation in the insurance industry, New York Life sold its health insurance operations and announced plans to demutualize — a move which was prevented when state legislators failed to pass laws legalizing the structure. In 1999 the company planned to buy two Mexican insurance companies, including Seguros Monterrey Aetna SA, that nation's #2 life insurer.

OFFICERS

Chairman, President, and CEO: Seymour Sternberg
VC: Frederick J. Sievert
EVP; Chairman and CEO, New York Life Asset Management and MacKay Shields Financial: Ravi Akhoury
EVP and CFO: Howard I. Atkins
EVP; Chairman and CEO, New York Life International: Gary G. Benanav
EVP and Chief Investment Officer: Richard M. Kernan Jr.
EVP and Secretary: George J. Trapp
SVP and Treasurer: Jay S. Calhoun
SVP and Controller: Richard D. Levy
SVP and General Counsel: Michael J. McLaughlin
SVP and Chief Actuary: Stephen N. Steinig
SVP and General Auditor: Thomas J. Warga
SVP: Frank M. Boccio
SVP: Jefferson C. Boyce
SVP: Patrick G. Boyle
SVP: Judith E. Campbell
SVP: Marc J. Chalfin
SVP: Jessie M. Colgate
SVP Human Resources: Richard A. Hansen
Auditors: PricewaterhouseCoopers LLP

LOCATIONS

HQ: New York Life Insurance Company,
51 Madison Ave., New York, NY 10010
Phone: 212-576-7000   **Fax:** 212-576-8145
Web site: http://www.newyorklife.com

PRODUCTS/OPERATIONS

1998 Assets

	$ mil.	% of total
Cash & equivalents	4,377	5
Bonds	55,019	61
Stocks	4,949	5
Mortgage loans	8,050	9
Real estate	784	1
Policy loans	5,626	6
Assets in separate account	8,311	9
Other assets	3,251	4
Total	**90,367**	**100**

1998 Sales

	$ mil.	% of total
Premiums	11,444	62
Net investment income	5,647	31
Other income	1,259	7
Total	**18,350**	**100**

Selected Operations

Asset Management
MacKay Shields Financial Corp. (manager of the MainStay mutual funds)
Monitor Capital Advisors, Inc. (third-party mutual fund management)
NYLife Distributors, Inc. (securities broker-dealer)

Individual Operations
New York Life Insurance and Annuity Corporation (individual life insurance and annuities)

International Operations
New York Life International, Inc.

Special Markets
NYLIFE Administration Corp. (long-term care and other specialty programs)
New York Life Benefit Services, Inc. (retirement benefits administration)

COMPETITORS

AEGON
AXA Financial
Allianz
Allstate
American General
American National Insurance
CIGNA
CNA Financial
Charles Schwab
Citigroup
Fortis
Guardian Life
Jefferson-Pilot
John Hancock
Kemper Insurance
MONY

MassMutual
Merrill Lynch
MetLife
Morgan Stanley Dean Witter
Mutual of Omaha
Northwestern Mutual
Paine Webber
Principal Financial
Prudential
State Farm
T. Rowe Price
TIAA-CREF
The Hartford
Transamerica

HISTORICAL FINANCIALS & EMPLOYEES

Mutual company FYE: December	Annual Growth	1989	1990	1991	1992	1993	1994	1995	1996	1997	1998
Assets ($ mil.)	7.6%	46,648	50,126	54,066	59,169	66,791	68,926	74,281	78,809	84,067	90,367
Net income ($ mil.)	33.2%	57	290	280	271	368	404	625	579	650	753
Income as % of assets	—	0.1%	0.6%	0.5%	0.5%	0.6%	0.6%	0.8%	0.7%	0.8%	0.8%
Employees	(4.4%)	19,438	18,200	18,848	—	—	8,130	8,442	12,190	12,570	13,000

NET INCOME HISTORY

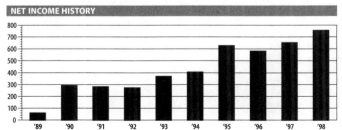

1998 FISCAL YEAR-END

Equity as % of assets: 6.2%
Return on assets: 0.8%
Return on equity: 14.8%
Long-term debt ($ mil.): 0
Sales ($ mil.): 18,350

NEW YORK STATE LOTTERY

OVERVIEW

The New York State Lottery is the king of the hill, the top of the heap. The Schenectady-based lottery is the largest state lottery in the US and the nation's second oldest (after New Hampshire). It has raised some $17 billion for the Empire State since it was started in 1967. More than 17,000 retailers sell tickets for its various games of chance, which include numbers games such as Lotto and Take Five, as well as instant-win games such as Break the Bank and Joker's Wild. The lottery also has some 14,000 online terminals in operation, which are maintained by Rhode Island-based GTECH Holdings.

Of the money collected through the lottery, about half is returned to players in prizes, while the state's education system receives almost 40%. The remaining funds go for operating costs and commissions for retailers. In addition to education, proceeds from the lottery have helped pay for the construction of New York City Hall, as well as bridges, canals, ferries, and roads for the state.

Despite its position as the nation's largest, the New York lottery faces the same pressures as many other state lotteries. Sales have decreased over the past few years due to competition from other gambling outlets, such as casinos and racing, as well as from rival lotteries in neighboring states offering larger jackpots through multistate drawings. The lottery also is facing increased criticism from anti-gaming forces who claim the games — most notably the state's Keno-style Quick Draw game (which can be played in bars and taverns) — take advantage of problem gamblers.

HISTORY

In the mid-1960s the New York state legislature succeeded in sending a lottery amendment to voters, and 60% of New Yorkers voted in favor of the amendment in 1966. Lottery sales began in 1967 with a raffle-style drawing game. In its first year of operation, the lottery contributed more than $26 million to the state's education fund.

New York introduced its first instant game in 1976, with sales topping $18 million the first week. The state debuted its six-of-six lotto game two years later. Sales were slow until 1981, when Louie "the Light Bulb" Eisenberg — the state's first lottery celebrity — won $5 million, the largest single-winner prize at that time.

GTECH Holdings won the contract to operate New York's lottery terminal sales in 1987. The Quick Pick option — through which a terminal chooses a player's numbers — was introduced in 1989, as was a new lotto game and the state's first online computer terminal game. The largest individual prize to date, $35 million, was won in 1990 by autoworker Antonio Bueti. The biggest jackpot, $90 million, was split among nine players in 1991.

Through the mid-1990s, however, lackluster lottery sales were blamed on the Persian Gulf War, the recession, and poor publicity. During 1993 and 1994, lottery management revamped the state's lottery infrastructure and redesigned some games. The investment paid off in October 1994 when lotto fever pushed a jackpot to $72.5 million. During the height of the frenzy, sales reached $46,000 a minute.

Quick Draw, which lets players choose numbers every five minutes, was added in 1995. Sales of the game topped $1 million on the second day, and soon it was grossing nearly $12 million a week. Real estate mogul Donald Trump unsuccessfully sued to stop Quick Draw, claiming that it was more addictive than (his) casinos and would encourage organized crime. That year the New York State Lottery became the first to reach $3 billion in sales in a single year.

In 1996 the state pulled its Quick Draw advertising after critics complained it encouraged compulsive gambling. Lottery officials replaced enticing ads with advertising stressing the lottery's benefits to state education. The lottery was the subject of a sting operation that year led by Gov. George Pataki to crack down on lottery vendors selling tickets to minors. In 1997 the lottery spawned its own game show with the debut of *NY Wired,* a half-hour weekly program pitting vendor representatives against each other for cash prizes given to audience members and schools.

With sales slipping, the state left longtime ad partner DDB Needham Worldwide in 1998 (now DDB Worldwide) and signed a $28 million contract with Grey Advertising. Lottery Director Jeff Perlee resigned the next year. He was replaced by Margaret DeFrancisco, who helped drum up sales with Millennium Millions, a lottery game with a multimillion dollar drawing on New Year's Eve 1999.

Director: Margaret R. DeFrancisco
Director Financial Management: Jerry Woitkoski
Director Marketing and Sales: Connie H. Laverty
Director of Gaming Systems: Daniel J. Codden
Director Regulation and Compliance: Diane Scala
Regional Director, Long Island: James Benoit
Regional Director, Western New York:
Joanne Thompson
Regional Director, Central New York: William Lonczak
Regional Director, New York City: Charles O'Donnell
General Counsel: Stephen M. Dolan
Director Human Resources: Charlie Titus
Special Assistant: Art DelSignore
Auditors: KPMG LLP

LOCATIONS

HQ: 1 Broadway Center, Schenectady, NY 12301
Phone: 518-388-3300 **Fax:** 518-388-3368
Web site: http://www.nylottery.org

PRODUCTS/OPERATIONS

1999 Sales By Game

	% of total
Instant	25
Lotto	20
Numbers	19
Quick Draw	13
Win 4	12
Take Five	10
Pick 10	1
Total	**100**

1999 Sales Allocations

	% of total
Prizes	51
School aid	38
Retailer commissions	6
Administrative costs	3
Contractor fees	2
Total	**100**

Selected Games

Numbers games	Instant-win games
Lotto	Break the Bank
New York Numbers	Casino Royale
Pick 10	Joker's Wild
Quick Draw	Nifty 50
Take Five	Quick 7's
Tax Free Million	Race for Cash
Win 4	Saratoga 1-2-3
Win for Life	Tax Free Million
	Wheel of Fortune

COMPETITORS

Connecticut Lottery
Massachusetts State Lottery
Multi-State Lottery
New Hampshire Lottery
New Jersey Lottery
Pennsylvania Lottery
Vermont Lottery

HISTORICAL FINANCIALS & EMPLOYEES

Government-owned FYE: March	Annual Growth	1990	1991	1992	1993	1994	1995	1996	1997	1998	1999
Sales ($ mil.)	7.1%	2,058	2,134	2,063	2,360	2,369	3,028	3,752	4,136	4,185	3,831
Employees	5.6%	211	246	231	233	241	239	310	340	350	345

SALES HISTORY

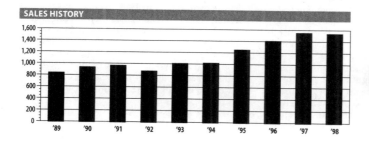

NEW YORK STOCK EXCHANGE, INC.

OVERVIEW

Bulls and bears and boards, oh my!

The New York Stock Exchange (NYSE), aka the Big Board, is the US's oldest and the world's largest stock market. NYSE's more than 3,100 listings include most large US companies. The member-owned, not-for-profit corporation also attracts many foreign companies seeking the liquidity available only in US markets.

In a John Henry-esque battle, NYSE is touting its humanity-driven auction exchange — where stock prices are set largely by a throng of traders in an area the size of a football field — against the electronic exchange run by archrival Nasdaq. (The NYSE is scurrying to find ways to trade Nasdaq stocks on the NYSE board, and vice versa.) The Big Board also faces competition from foreign exchanges and such electronic communications networks (ECNs) as The Island and Instinet. Even though NYSE argues that such trades hamper investors' ability to see the market big picture, the exchange accommodates brokers making large-block trades off the floor.

To better compete, the NYSE is planning to go public as a for-profit company. Proceeds from an IPO might be used to buy any of the several systems vying to become new exchanges. A for-profit NYSE would also be able to make more decisive management decisions without interference from major members (many of whom also happen to hold stakes in competing ECNs).

HISTORY

To prevent a monopoly on stock sales by securities auctioneers, 24 New York stockbrokers and businessmen agreed in 1792 to avoid "public auctions," to charge a commission on sales of stock, and to "give preference to each other" in their transactions (to form their own monopoly). The Buttonwood Agreement, named after a tree on Wall Street under which they met, established the first organized stock market in New York. (Traders excluded from this exchange continued dealing on the streets of New York until 1921 and later formed the American Stock Exchange.) The Bank of New York was the first corporate stock traded under the Buttonwood tree.

In 1817 the brokers created the New York Stock & Exchange Board, a stock market with set meeting times. The NYS&EB began to require companies to qualify for trading (listing) by furnishing financial statements in 1853. Ten years later the board became the New York Stock Exchange.

Stock tickers began recording trades in 1867, and two years later the NYSE consolidated with competitors the Open Board of Brokers and the Government Bond Department. Despite repeated panics and recessions in the late 1800s, the stock market remained unregulated until well into the 20th century.

In the 1920s the NYSE installed a centralized stock quote service. Post-war euphoria brought a stock mania that fizzled in October 1929, when the market crashed. The subsequent Depression brought investigation and federal regulation to the securities industry.

The NYSE registered as an exchange in 1934. In 1938 it reorganized, with a board of directors representing member firms, non-member brokers, and the public; it also hired its first full-time president, member William McChesney Martin. As a self-regulating body, the NYSE policed the activities of its members.

The NYSE began electronic trading in the 1960s; in 1968 it broke 1929's one-day record for trading volume (16 million shares). It became a not-for-profit corporation in 1971.

Despite upgrades, technology was at least partly to blame for the 1987 crash: A cascade of large sales triggered by computer programs fueled the market's fall. NYSE's income suffered, leading to a $3 million loss in 1990.

In 1995 Richard Grasso became the first NYSE staff employee ever to become chairman. The NYSE followed the other US stock markets in 1997 by switching trade increments from one-eighth point to the narrower one-sixteenth point (known as a "teenie" by arbitrageurs). New circuit-breaker rules halted trading on October 27 when the Dow Jones Industrial Average dropped 550 points in a day (The NYSE increased the trigger to 1,050 points in 1999).

The NYSE used a veiled threat to win itself the promise of some growing space (New York City isn't likely to let its financial industry move to New Jersey unless the price tag is *really* exorbitant). In 1999 the exchange named Karen Nelson Hackett as its first woman governor. The Big Board announced its plans to go public in 2000 in the face of the impending extension of trading hours and the threat of competition from a new crop of alternative trading venues known as ECNs; the exchange extended its official pricing until 6:30 p.m. EST in response as well.

Chairman and CEO: Richard A. Grasso
President and COO: William R. Johnston
Group EVP Competitive Position: Catherine R. Kinney
Group EVP International and Research:
Georges L. Ugeux
Group EVP Operations: Robert G. Britz
Group EVP Regulatory: Edward A. Kwalwasser
EVP and General Counsel: Richard P. Bernard
EVP Market Operations and Real Estate and Facilities:
Richard A. Edgar
EVP Market Structure: Donald J. Solodar
SVP and Corporate Secretary: James E. Buck
SVP Communications: Robert T. Zito
SVP Finance: Keith R. Helsby
SVP Floor Operations: Anne E. Allen
SVP Government Relations: Sheila C. Bair
SVP Human Resources: Frank Z. Ashen
SVP New Listings and Client Service:
Noreen M. Culhane
SVP Public Affairs: David P. Lambert
SVP Strategic Planning and Chief Economist:
James L. Cochrane
SVP Technology: William A. Bautz
Treasurer: James F. Sullivan
Auditors: PricewaterhouseCoopers LLP

LOCATIONS

HQ: 11 Wall St., New York, NY 10005
Phone: 212-656-3000 **Fax:** 212-656-2126
Web site: http://www.nyse.com

PRODUCTS/OPERATIONS

1998 Sales

	$ mil.	% of total
Listing fees	296	41
Trading fees	124	17
Market data fees	112	15
Regulatory fees	93	13
Facility & equipment fees	42	6
Membership fees	7	1
Other	55	7
Total	**729**	**100**

Services
Market regulation
Member regulation
Securities clearing
Securities depository
Securities information
Securities trading sponsorship

Subsidiaries and Affiliates
Depository Trust Co. (35%)
National Securities Clearing Corp. (33%)
Options Clearing Corp. (minority interest)
Securities Industry Automation Corp. (67%, owned with
American Stock Exchange)

COMPETITORS

Archipelago
Bloomberg TRADEBOOK
CBOE
Chicago Mercantile Exchange
E*TRADE
Instinet
Investment Technology
Island ECN
Knight/Trimark Group
NASD
NYFIX

HISTORICAL FINANCIALS & EMPLOYEES

Not-for-profit FYE: December	Annual Growth	1989	1990	1991	1992	1993	1994	1995	1996	1997	1998
Sales ($ mil.)	8.5%	349	349	375	418	445	452	501	562	639	729
Net income ($ mil.)	36.9%	6	(3)	12	41	54	44	57	74	86	101
Income as % of sales	—	1.7%	—	3.2%	9.8%	12.1%	9.7%	11.3%	13.3%	13.5%	13.9%
Employees	0.0%	—	—	—	—	1,500	1,450	1,450	1,475	1,475	1,500

NET INCOME HISTORY

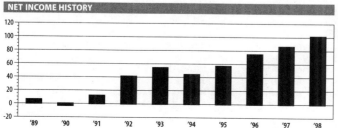

1998 FISCAL YEAR-END

Debt ratio: 0.0%
Return on equity: 15.5%
Cash ($ mil.): 7
Current ratio: 2.85
Long-term debt ($ mil.): 0

NORTHWESTERN MUTUAL LIFE

OVERVIEW

Better safe than sorry is more than a corporate policy, it's what Northwestern Mutual Life Insurance offers almost 3 million policyholders — a safety net against becoming disabled, dying too young, or living too long. Owned by its policyholders, the Milwaukee-based company operates nationwide and is one of the 10 largest US life insurers, with a network of some 7,500 agents. Targeting professionals and small businesses, the company sells life insurance, health and retirement products, fixed and variable annuities, and mutual funds. Northwestern also owns Robert W. Baird & Co., a Milwaukee-based investment bank.

The firm has a solid reputation in the life insurance industry and is known for its employee training programs. Agents are loyal to the company's products, which are added only after prudent consideration.

Although the company was prominent in the push to let Wisconsin insurers demutualize by forming mutual holding companies, Northwestern apparently has no immediate plans to join its peers in going public. The contrarian company has largely stayed out of the diversification frenzy, though it does plan to form a trust company and expand overseas.

HISTORY

In 1854, at age 72, John Johnston, a successful New York insurance agent, moved to Wisconsin to become a farmer. Three years later Johnston returned to the insurance business when he and 36 others began Mutual Life Insurance (changed to Northwestern Mutual Life Insurance in 1865). From the beginning the company's goal was to become better, not bigger.

In 1907, partly in response to a federal investigation of the insurance industry, Northwestern appointed policyholders to evaluate its operations. This five-person committee, whose members change annually, still operates today, publishing a summary of its findings in the annual report.

The company continued to offer level-premium life insurance in the 1920s, while competitors offered new types of products. As a result, Northwestern's insurance-in-force ranking fell between 1918 and 1946.

The company automated in the late 1950s and introduced the Insurance Service Account (ISA) in 1962, whereby all policies owned by a family or business could be combined into one monthly premium and paid with pre-authorized checks. In 1968 Northwestern inaugurated Extra Ordinary Life (EOL), which combined whole and term life insurance, using dividends to convert term to paid-up whole life each year. EOL soon became the company's most popular product.

Suffering from a low profile, in 1972 the insurer kicked off its "The Quiet Company" ad campaign during the summer Olympics. The ads worked; public awareness of Northwestern jumped. But even in advertising, the company was staid; a revamped Quiet Company campaign made a return Olympic appearance 24 years later in another effort to raise the public's consciousness.

In the 1980s Northwestern began financing leveraged buyouts, gaining direct ownership of companies. Investments included two-thirds of flooring maker Congoleum (with other investors); it also bought majority interests in Milwaukee securities firm Robert W. Baird (1982) and mortgage guarantee insurer MGIC Investment (1985; now reduced to about 18%).

The firm remained largely immune to the 1980s mania for fast money and high-risk diversification. Instead, it devoted itself almost religiously to its core business, despite indications that it was a shrinking market.

In the early 1990s new life policy purchases slowed and the agency force declined — ominous developments, since insurers make their premium income on retained policies, and continued sales are crucial to growth. Northwestern took steps to reverse the trend, adding more administrative support for its agents, using database marketing to target new customers, and increasing the cross-selling of products to its current customer base. The result was a record-setting 1996.

With the financial services industry consolidating, Northwestern in 1997 moved into the mutual fund business by setting up its nine Mason Street Funds. The expansion continued with the 1999 acquisition of Frank Russell Co., a pension management firm. The acquisition gave Northwestern a foothold in global investment management and analytical services (the Russell 2000 index). Although many mutuals are converting to stock ownership to take advantage of the industry consolidation trend, Northwestern Mutual plans to bankroll its own growth rather than demutualizing.

President and CEO: James D. Ericson
EVP, Secretary, and General Counsel: John M. Bremer
EVP Accumulation Products and Long Term Care:
  Peter W. Bruce
EVP Life and Disability Income Insurance:
  Edward J. Zore
EVP; President, Northwestern International Holdings, Inc: Robert E. Carlson
SVP and Chief Actuary: William C. Koenig
SVP Agencies: William H. Beckley
SVP Government Relations: Frederic H. Sweet
SVP Insurance Operations and Chief Compliance Officer: Deborah A. Beck
SVP Life Marketing: Richard L. Hall
SVP Public Markets: Mark G. Doll
VP and Controller: Gary E. Long
VP Annuity and Accumulation Products:
  Meridee J. Maynard
VP Communications: W. Ward White
VP Compliance/Best Practices: Robert J. Berden
VP Corporate Planning and Development:
  Martha M. Valerio
VP Human Resources: Susan A. Lueger
VP New Business: Steven T. Catlett
Auditors: PricewaterhouseCoopers LLP

LOCATIONS

HQ: The Northwestern Mutual Life Insurance Company,
720 E. Wisconsin Ave., Milwaukee, WI 53202
Phone: 414-271-1444   **Fax:** 414-299-7022
Web site: http://www.northwesternmutual.com

PRODUCTS/OPERATIONS

1998 Assets

	$ mil.	% of total
Bonds	36,990	47
Stocks	6,576	8
Mortgage loans	12,250	16
Real estate	1,481	2
Policy loans	7,580	10
Other investments	1,839	2
Separate accounts	9,966	13
Other assets	1,313	2
Total	**77,995**	**100**

1998 Sales

	$ mil.	% of total
Premiums	8,943	66
Net investment income	4,536	34
Total	**13,479**	**100**

Selected Subsidiaries
Frank Russell Company (investment management and securities brokerage)
Mason Street Funds (mutual funds)
Robert W. Baird & Co. Incorporated (asset management)

COMPETITORS

AXA Financial	Merrill Lynch
Alliance Capital	MetLife
American General	Morgan Stanley Dean
CIGNA	Witter
CNA Financial	Mutual of Omaha
Citigroup	Nationwide Insurance
Conseco	New York Life
FMR	Pacific Mutual
Fortis	Principal Financial
GenAmerica	Prudential
Guardian Life	T. Rowe Price
John Hancock	TIAA-CREF
Liberty Mutual	The Hartford
MONY	Transamerica
MassMutual	

HISTORICAL FINANCIALS & EMPLOYEES

Mutual company FYE: December	Annual Growth	1989	1990	1991	1992	1993	1994	1995	1996	1997	1998
Assets ($ mil.)	11.8%	28,515	31,389	35,757	39,679	44,061	48,112	54,876	62,680	71,081	77,995
Net income ($ mil.)	9.0%	372	143	227	244	330	279	459	620	689	809
Income as % of assets	—	1.3%	0.5%	0.6%	0.6%	0.7%	0.6%	0.8%	1.0%	1.0%	1.0%
Employees	3.7%	2,970	3,050	3,100	3,298	3,500	3,300	3,344	3,513	3,818	4,117

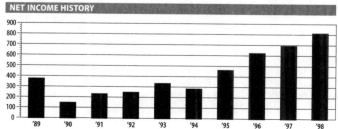

NET INCOME HISTORY

1998 FISCAL YEAR-END
Equity as % of assets: 6.1%
Return on assets: 1.1%
Return on equity: 18.3%
Long-term debt ($ mil.): —
Sales ($ mil.): 13,749

Northwestern Mutual Life

NORTHWESTERN UNIVERSITY

OVERVIEW

Near the city of big shoulders is a place that shapes broad minds. Located in the Chicago suburb of Evanston, Northwestern University is widely recognized as one of the country's top learning institutions, serving more than 17,700 full- and part-time students through two campuses. Its 240-acre main campus is home to most of Northwestern's 12 schools and colleges, while some 2,300 students take graduate work at its 20-acre Chicago campus. The downtown location serves as home to Northwestern's School of Law, Medical School, and McGaw Medical Center. With tuition and expenses running more than $30,000 a year, more than 60% of undergraduates receive some form of financial aid from the school.

Among Northwestern's top ranked programs are its law school, medical school, and its engineering program. Its J. L. Kellogg Graduate School of Management is ranked second in the nation by *U.S. News and World Report*. Its journalism and drama programs produced such alumni as Charlton Heston, Gary Marshall, and Julia Louis-Dreyfus. Current US Supreme Court Justice John Paul Stevens is also a former Wildcat. Northwestern is home to several research centers, continuing education services though University College, and community outreach programs. The university also supports 18 intercollegiate athletic programs. It is the only private institution in the Big 10 conference.

Like other major research campuses, Northwestern is undergoing a building boom as it expands to meet the challenges of the dawning century. Plans call for 10 new buildings by 2001, including a $100 million biomedical research center in Chicago. Along with physical expansion, the school's endowment has also swelled to more than $2.8 billion, and its drive to raise $1 billion, Campaign Northwestern, has pulled in more than $800 million in donations since launching in 1998.

HISTORY

Northwestern University's Methodist founders met in 1850 to create an institution of higher learning serving the original Northwest Territory. The university was chartered in 1851, and two years later it acquired 379 acres of property north of Chicago on Lake Michigan. The town of Evanston was later named after John Evans, one of the school's founders.

Classes began in the fall of 1855 with two professors and 10 students. By 1869 Northwestern had more than 100 students and began to admit women. In 1870 Northwestern signed an affiliation agreement with the Chicago Medical College (founded 1859), and three years later it joined with the original University of Chicago (no relation to the current institution) to create the Union College of Law. When the University of Chicago closed in 1886 due to financial difficulties, Northwestern took control of the law school. The university reorganized in 1891, consolidating its affiliated professional schools (dentistry, law, medicine, and pharmacy) into the university.

By 1900 Northwestern had become the third-largest university in the US (after Harvard and Michigan), with an enrollment of 2,700. During the 1920s the university created the Medill School of Journalism, named for Joseph Medill, founder of the Chicago Tribune. In 1924 the school's athletic teams adopted the nickname Wildcats, and two years later the university completed the primary buildings that form its Chicago campus. Northwestern suffered a drop in enrollment during the Depression, but after WWII it saw student numbers swell as veterans took advantage of the GI Bill. Expansion continued throughout the 1960s and 1970s.

In 1985 the school and the City of Evanston began developing a research center to attract more high-tech industries to the area. The university's graduate school of business achieved national prominence in 1988 after it was ranked #1 in the US by *Business Week*. In 1995 Henry Bienen, a dean at Princeton, became the school's 15th president. That same year, Northwestern's football team, forever the doormat of the Big 10, achieved national fame when it won the conference championship.

In 1998 faculty member Professor John Pople won the Nobel Prize in Chemistry, the first Nobel Prize awarded to a faculty member while teaching at the university. To help pay for needed expansion, Bienen launched Campaign Northwestern that year with the goal of raising $1 billion. The university also decided to close its dental school by 2001. Northwestern won a significant legal battle in 1998 when a judge ruled that the university was not obligated to pay a faculty member simply because he had been granted tenure.

LOCATIONS

HQ: 633 Clark St., Evanston, IL 60208
Phone: 847-491-3741　　　**Fax:** 847-491-8406
Web site: http://www.nwu.edu

PRODUCTS/OPERATIONS

1998 Sales

	$ mil.	% of total
Tuition & fees	339	37
Grants & contracts	199	22
Investment income	125	14
Private gifts	89	10
Sales & services	73	8
Auxiliary services	55	6
Professional fees	23	2
Other	4	1
Scholarship & fellowship payout	(91)	—
Total	**816**	**100**

Selected Undergraduate Colleges and Schools
Medill School of Journalism
Robert McCormick School of Engineering and Applied
Sciences
School of Education and Social Policy
School of Music
School of Speech
University College (extension)
Weinberg College of Arts and Sciences

Selected Graduate Schools
The Graduate School
J. L. Kellogg Graduate School of Management
Medill School of Journalism
Medical School
Robert McCormick School of Engineering and
Applied Sciences
School of Education and Social Policy
School of Law
School of Music
School of Speech

Selected Research Centers and Institutes
Banking Research Center
Center for Biotechnology
Center for Catalysis and Surface Science
Center for Circadian Biology and Medicine
Center for Mathematical Studies in Economics and
Management Science
Center for Reproductive Science
Center for the Study of Ethical Issues in Business
Center for Quantum Devices
Center for Quality Engineering and Failure Prevention
Heizer Center for Entrepreneurial Studies
Institute for Environmental Catalysis
Institute for Health Services Research and
Policy Studies
Institute for Neuroscience
Institute for Policy Research
Institute for the Learning Sciences
Kellogg Environmental Research Center
Materials Research Center
Program of African Studies
Science and Technology Center for Superconductivity
Traffic Institute
Transportation Center

HISTORICAL FINANCIALS & EMPLOYEES

School FYE: August	Annual Growth	1989	1990	1991	1992	1993	1994	1995	1996	1997	1998
Sales ($ mil.)	5.5%	502	515	550	587	628	676	708	779	721	816
Employees	1.2%	—	—	—	—	5,650	5,650	5,800	5,800	5,978	5,985

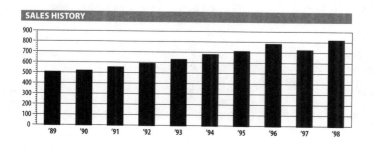

SALES HISTORY

OCEAN SPRAY CRANBERRIES, INC.

OVERVIEW

It's not just sour grapes: Ocean Spray Cranberries knows that cranberries can go sour too. Based in Lakeville-Middleboro, Massachusetts, the company — a marketing cooperative owned by more than 900 cranberry and grapefruit growers in the US and Canada — controls 60% of the cranberry juice market and makes the US's leading brand of canned and bottled juices. Surplus harvests of cranberries and competition from store brands have cut into its market share and forced layoffs.

The company made its name through a quest for quality (only berries that pass a series of bounce tests rate the blue-and-white wave logo) and successful marketing that elevated the fruit's status from Thanksgiving staple to designer ingredient. To expand beyond the berry's traditional role, Ocean Spray has featured the fruit in a cornucopia of drinks (Cran-Grape, Cranapple) and chewy snacks (Craisins), and cranberries now show up in co-branded cookies and cereal. Promotion efforts have been aided by research showing that cranberry juice can reduce urinary tract infections.

HISTORY

Ocean Spray Cranberries traces its roots to Marcus Urann, president of the Cape Cod Cranberry Company. In 1912 Urann, who became known as the "Cranberry King," began marketing a cranberry sauce that was packaged in tins and could be served year-round. Inspired by the sea spray that drifted off the Atlantic and over his cranberry bogs, Urann dubbed his concoction Ocean Spray Cape Cod Cranberry Sauce.

It didn't take long for other cranberry growers to make their own sauces, and rather than compete, the Cranberry King consolidated. In 1930 Urann merged his company with A.D. Makepeace Company and with Cranberry Products, forming a national cooperative called Cranberry Canners, Inc.

Urann became president and began trying to expand cranberry demand with new products. In 1933 the company introduced a juice, and in 1939 it introduced cranberry syrup. During the 1940s it added growers in Wisconsin, Oregon, and Washington state and, to reflect its new scope, changed its name to National Cranberry Association.

Canadian growers were added to the fold in 1950. Urann retired in 1955, and two years later the co-op introduced its first frozen products. To take advantage of the popular Ocean Spray brand name, in 1959 the company changed its name to Ocean Spray Cranberries.

Two weeks before Thanksgiving that year, the US Department of Health mistakenly announced that aminotriazole, a herbicide used by some cranberry growers, was linked to cancer in laboratory rats. Sales of what consumers called "cancer berries" plummeted, and Ocean Spray nearly folded. However, the US government came to the rescue with subsidies in 1960, and the company stayed afloat.

The scare convinced Ocean Spray it needed to cut its dependence on seasonal demand, and it began to diversify more aggressively into the juice business. The company sweetened its cranberry juice cocktail and went on to introduce a heavily promoted new line of juices blending cranberries with apples, grapes, and other fruits.

Ocean Spray expanded into grapefruit growing in 1976, allowing Florida's Indian River Ruby Red grapefruit growers to join the co-op. It introduced the first juice box, a brick-shaped container with an attached straw, in 1981. The company acquired Milne Food Products, a manufacturer of fruit concentrates and purees, in 1985, and three years later it signed a Japanese distribution deal with food company POKKA.

In 1992 Ocean Spray entered a distribution and drink-development joint venture with PepsiCo, and the next year the companies introduced a line of fruit drinks for the "New Age" beverage market. However, clashing corporate cultures ended the drink-development pact in 1995. To maintain its edge in a growing but increasingly competitive market, Ocean Spray automated plants and allied with food giants to create cranberry-flavored treats such as cookies (Nabisco, 1993) and cereal (Kraft Foods, 1996). Former rugby player Thomas Bullock became president and CEO in 1997.

In 1998 Ocean Spray introduced Wellfleet Farms (later renamed Ocean Spray Premium), a line of 100% juice blends, to compete with rivals such as former co-op member Northland Cranberries, and it bought a stake in Nantucket Allserve, maker of Nantucket Nectars.

Back-to-back bumper harvests in 1997 and 1998 led to lower cranberry prices. As a result, in 1999 the company announced its third round of layoffs since 1997 (bringing the total to 600, or nearly one-fourth of its workforce). Amid criticism that Ocean Spray has been unable to compete effectively with for-profit rivals, CEO Thomas Bullock plans to leave his post in 2000.

Chairman: Craige I. Scott
President and CEO: Thomas E. Bullock
EVP and COO: Kevin B. Murphy
SVP Grower Relations and CFO: John P. Henry
SVP Brand Development: Lynn A. Rotando
VP, Secretary, and General Counsel: Jim O'Shaughnessy
VP: John W. Emerson
VP Operations: Kevin Kavanaugh
VP Research and Development: Lawrence Kuzminski
VP International: Malcolm R. Lloyd
SVP Operations/Value Chain: Nancy McDermott
VP Marketing: David L. Murphy
VP Manufacturing: Tripta Sarin
Treasurer: Christopher H. Perry
Manager Corporate Communications and Public Affairs: John M. Lawlor
Auditors: Deloitte & Touche LLP

LOCATIONS

HQ: 1 Ocean Spray Dr., Lakeville-Middleboro, MA 02349
Phone: 508-946-1000 **Fax:** 508-946-7704
Web site: http://www.oceanspray.com

PRODUCTS/OPERATIONS

Selected Juices

Apple juice	Lightstyle Cran Raspberry
Black Cherry Blast	Lightstyle Cranberry
Cran Blueberry	Mandarin Magic
Cran Cherry	¡Mango Mango!
Cran Currant	Mauna La'i Island Guava
Cran Grape	Mauna La'i Paradise
Cran Mango	Passion
Cran Raspberry	Mega Melon
Cran Strawberry	Orange juice
Cran Tangerine	Pink Grapefruit
Cranapple	Reduced Cran Raspberry
Cranberry Juice Cocktail	Reduced Cranapple
Cranicot	Reduced Cranberry Juice
Crantastic (fruit punch)	Cocktail
Crazy Kiwi Passion	Ruby Red & Mango
Grapefruit juice	Ruby Red & Tangerine
Kiwi Strawberry	Grapefruit
Lightstyle Cran Grape	Ruby Red Grapefruit
Lightstyle Cran Mango	

Other Products
Craisins (sweetened dried cranberries)
Cran Raspberry sauce
Fresh cranberries
Jellied cranberry sauce
Whole cranberry sauce

COMPETITORS

Cadbury Schweppes
Clement Pappas
Cliffstar
Coca-Cola
Dole
Florida's Natural
National Grape Co-op
Northland Cranberries
Philip Morris
Triarc
Tropicana Products

HISTORICAL FINANCIALS & EMPLOYEES

Cooperative FYE: August	Annual Growth	1989	1990	1991	1992	1993	1994	1995	1996	1997	1998
Sales ($ mil.)	5.8%	889	942	974	1,091	1,168	1,221	1,361	1,433	1,438	1,480
Employees	2.2%	1,940	2,200	2,200	2,200	2,300	2,300	2,300	2,300	2,300	2,350

SALES HISTORY

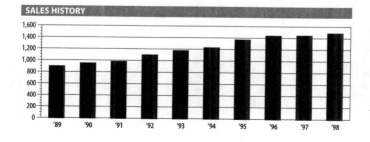

THE OHIO STATE UNIVERSITY

OVERVIEW

Ohio State University's first class consisted of 24 students. Today, the University (OSU) is the state's largest institution of higher learning and has the nation's second-largest single-campus enrollment (about 48,000 students at its Columbus campus), behind The University of Texas at Austin. OSU also runs four regional campuses and two agricultural institutes in Ohio. The university has a non-teaching staff of more than 14,000 and a 4,500-member faculty that teaches classes in 176 undergraduate majors and 220 graduate fields.

Famous alumni include children's author R. L. Stine, golfer Jack Nicklaus, and country singer Dwight Yoakum. In 1998 William Kirwan (from the University of Maryland) succeeded President Gordon Gee, who is credited with boosting the university's academic reputation and starting OSU's successful drive to a $1 billion endowment.

HISTORY

In 1870 the Ohio legislature, prompted by Gov. Rutherford B. Hayes, agreed to establish the Ohio Agricultural and Mechanical College in Columbus on property provided by the Morrill Act of 1862 (the land-grant institution act, which gave land to states and territories for the establishment of colleges). After a heated battle — and an eight-to-seven board of trustees vote — over whether the college should teach only agricultural and mechanical arts or foster a broad-based liberal arts curriculum, the college opened in 1873 offering agriculture, ancient languages, chemistry, geology, mathematics, modern languages, and physics to its first class of 24 students. Two years later the school appointed its first female faculty member. The Ohio State University became the school's name in 1878; that year it graduated its first class. OSU graduated its first female student the next year.

OSU grew dramatically, adding schools of veterinary medicine (1885), pharmacy (1885), law (1891), and dairy sciences (1895). It awarded its first Masters of Arts degree in 1886.

The university continued to expand in the early 20th century, with enrollment surpassing 3,000 in 1908; by 1923 it had reached 10,000. New schools were added in education (1907), medicine and dentistry (1913), and commerce and journalism (1923). During WWI Ohio State designated part of its campus as training grounds and established the only college schools in the nation for airplane and balloon squadrons. Ohio Stadium was dedicated in 1922.

During the Great Depression Ohio State cut back salaries and course offerings. In the 1940s the school geared for war once again by establishing radiation and war research labs, as well as programs and services for students who were drafted. OSU captured its first national football championship in 1942.

The 1950s ushered in the era of legendary OSU football coach Woody Hayes. Hayes led his beloved Buckeyes to three national championships and nine Rose Bowl appearances before he was discharged for striking a Clemson player in 1978. The 1950s also saw the addition of four regional campuses at Lima, Mansfield, Marion, and Newark.

In the early 1960s the university was engaged in internal free-speech battles. By the end of that decade, enrollment had surpassed 50,000. OSU opened its School of Social Work in 1976.

In 1986 OSU and rival Michigan shared the Big 10 football conference title. Enrollment at OSU topped 54,000 in 1990 but then began declining. In response, the university tried to cut costs and beef up revenues. One way was through alliances: In 1992 it teamed with research group Battelle to develop a testing system for new drugs for the Food and Drug Administration. But when more savings were needed in 1995 and 1996, the university began streamlining operations, merging journalism and communications, and consolidating several veterinary departments. However, it also approved the creation of a new school of public health to provide education in environmental health, epidemiology, and health care management and financing.

But sports were not forgotten, and in 1996 OSU broke ground on the $84 million Schottenstein Center, a multipurpose facility for the university's basketball and ice hockey teams (named after its chief benefactor, the Jerome Schottenstein family).

In 1997 President Gordon Gee announced that he was leaving OSU for Brown University. The next year William Kirwan from the University of Maryland came on board as president of OSU. In 1999 the University surpassed $1 billion in its "Affirm Thy Friendship" public contribution campaign, which was initiated in 1995.

President: William E. Kirwan
EVP and Provost: Edward J. Ray
SVP for Business and Finance: William Shkurti
VP Agricultural Administration and Executive Dean:
Bobby D. Moser
VP for University Development: Jerry A. May
VP for Graduate Studies and Dean of the Graduate
School: Susan L. Huntington
VP Health Sciences: Manuel Tzagournis
VP Student and Urban/Community Affairs:
David Williams II
Interim VP Research: William A. Baeslack III
Associate VP Human Resources: Larry M. Lewellen
Secretary of the Board of Trustees, Special Assistant to
the President for Government Relations:
William Napier
Executive Assistant to the President and General
Counsel: Virginia Trethewey
Auditors: Deloitte & Touche LLP

LOCATIONS

HQ: 1800 Cannon Dr., Columbus, OH 43210
Phone: 614-292-6446   **Fax:** 614-292-2387
Web site: http://www.osu.edu

The Ohio State University has five campuses in
Columbus, Lima, Mansfield, Marion, and Newark, and
two agricultural centers in Wooster.

1999 Enrollment

	No. of students	% of total
Columbus	48,003	87
Other campuses	6,986	13
Total	**54,989**	**100**

PRODUCTS/OPERATIONS

Selected Colleges and Schools
College of the Arts
  School of Music
College of Biological Sciences
College of Dentistry
College of Education
College of Engineering
  Austin E. Knowlton School of Architecture
College of Food, Agricultural, and Environmental
  Sciences
  School of Natural Resources
College of Human Ecology
College of Humanities
College of Law
College of Mathematical and Physical Sciences
College of Medicine and Public Health
  School of Allied Medical Professions
College of Nursing
College of Optometry
College of Pharmacy
College of Social and Behavioral Sciences
  School of Journalism and Communication
  School of Public Policy and Management
College of Social Work
College of Veterinary Medicine
Max M. Fisher College of Business

HISTORICAL FINANCIALS & EMPLOYEES

School FYE: June	Annual Growth	1990	1991	1992	1993	1994	1995	1996	1997	1998	1999
Sales ($ mil.)	2.2%	—	—	1,656	1,409	1,506	1,575	1,531	1,630	1,749	1,923
Employees	(0.0%)	—	—	29,565	29,576	29,658	29,500	29,266	29,000	31,268	29,502

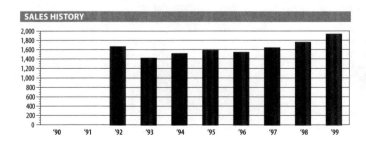

SALES HISTORY

PACIFIC MUTUAL HOLDING

OVERVIEW

Pacific Mutual Holding is into cross-breeding. The Newport, California-based insurer is now a mutual holding company that owns stock holding company Pacific LifeCorp, which is the parent of Pacific Life Insurance, the Golden State's largest life insurer. Pacific Mutual's conversion from a pure mutual to a mutual holding company gives it more flexibility and the option of an IPO; meanwhile, policyholders retain ownership of the company, but hold no stock.

Pacific Life sells individual insurance, pension products, and annuities. Its subsidiaries include PM Group Life (employee health and life insurance), Pacific Mutual Distributors (brokerage services), Pacific Mezzanine Investors (portfolio management), and World-Wide Reassurance (reinsurance operations based in the UK). Affiliate PIMCO Advisors Holdings, of which Pacific Life owns 31%, is an investment management partnership; German insurer Allianz is buying a majority stake in PIMCO, with Pacific Life retaining its investment.

HISTORY

Pacific Mutual began business in 1868 in Sacramento, California, as a stock company. Its board was dominated by California business and political leaders, including three of the "Big Four" who created the Central Pacific Railroad (Charles Crocker, Mark Hopkins, and Leland Stanford) and three former governors (Stanford, Newton Booth, and Henry Huntley Haight). Stanford (founder of Stanford University) was the company's first president and policyholder.

By 1870 Pacific Mutual was selling life insurance throughout most of the western US. Expansion continued in the early 1870s into Colorado, Kentucky, Nebraska, New York, Ohio, and Texas. The company ventured into Mexico in 1873 but sold few policies. It had more luck in China, accepting its first risk there in 1875, and in Hawaii, where it started business in 1877. In 1881 Pacific Mutual moved to San Francisco.

When Leland Stanford died in 1893, his widow and eponymous university, though rich in assets, found themselves struggling through a US economic depression. The benefit from Stanford's policy kept the university open until the estate was settled.

In 1905 Conservative Life bought the firm. The Pacific Mutual name survived the acquisition just as its records survived the fire that ravaged San Francisco after the 1906 earthquake. Pacific Mutual then relocated to Los Angeles.

The company squeaked through the Depression after a flood of claims on its noncancellable disability income policies, which forced Pacific Mutual into a reorganization plan initiated by the California insurance commissioner (1936). After WWII, Pacific Mutual entered the group insurance and pension markets.

After 83 years as a stock company and an eight-year stock purchasing program, Pacific Mutual became a true mutual in 1959.

Pacific Mutual relocated to Newport Beach in 1972. During the 1980s it built up its financial services operations, including its Pacific Investment Management Co. (PIMCO, founded 1971). The company was in trouble even before the stock crash of 1987 because of health care costs and over-investment in real estate. That year it brought in CEO Thomas Sutton, who sold off real estate and emphasized HMOs and fee-based financial services.

In the 1990s the company cut costs and increased its fee income. PIMCO Advisors, L.P. was formed in 1994 when PIMCO merged with Thomson Advisory Group. The merger gave Pacific Mutual a retail market for its fixed-income products, a stake in the resulting public company, and sales that offset interest rate variations and changes in the health care system.

The company assumed failed Confederation Life Insurance Co.'s corporate-owned life insurance business and merged insolvent First Capital Life into Pacific Life as Pacific Corinthian Life in 1997. That year Pacific Mutual became the first top-ten US mutual to convert to a mutual holding company, thus allowing it the option of issuing stock to fund acquisitions. Because the firm remained partially mutual, however, policyholders retained ownership but got no shares of Pacific LifeCorp, its new stock company.

In an attempt to compete with one-stop financial service behemoths such as Citigroup, Pacific Mutual began selling annuities through a Compass Bank subsidiary in 1998. The next year Allianz agreed to buy a majority stake in PIMCO Advisors, but Pacific Mutual would retain its 31% interest. Also in 1999 the firm made plans to acquire controlling interests in broker-dealer M. L. Stern and investment adviser Tower Asset Management.

Chairman and CEO, Pacific Mutual Holding, Pacific LifeCorp, and Pacific Life Insurance Company: Thomas C. Sutton
President, Pacific Mutual Holding, Pacific LifeCorp, and Pacific Life Insurance Company: Glenn S. Schafer
SVP and CFO, Pacific Mutual Holding and Pacific Life Insurance Company: Khanh T. Tran
SVP and General Counsel, Pacific Mutual Holding and Pacific Life Insurance Company: David R. Carmichael
EVP, Pacific Life Annuities: Bill Robinson
EVP Marketing, Pacific Life Individual Insurance: John A. Jarboe
EVP, Pacific Life Individual Insurance: Lynn C. Miller
EVP, Pacific Life Institutional Products Group: Daryle G. Johnson
EVP, Pacific Life Real Estate Division: Michael S. Robb
EVP, Pacific Life Securities Division: Larry J. Card
SVP Administration, Pacific Life Annuities: Bill Doomey
SVP Business Development, Pacific Life Institutional Products Group: John E. Milberg
SVP Financial, Pacific Life Individual Insurance: S. Gene Schofield
SVP Financial, Pacific Life Institutional Products Group: John D. Murray
SVP Human Resources, Pacific Life Insurance Company: Anthony J. Bonno
SVP Operations, Pacific Life Individual Insurance: James T. Morris
SVP Portfolio Management, Pacific Life Securities Division: Raymond J. Lee
SVP Public Affairs, Pacific Life Insurance Company: Robert G. Haskell
SVP Strategic Planning and Development, Pacific Life Insurance Company: Marc S. Franklin
VP Sales, Pacific Life Annuities Division: Dewey P. Bushaw

HQ: Pacific Mutual Holding Company, 700 Newport Center Dr., Newport Beach, CA 92660
Phone: 949-640-3011   Fax: 949-219-7614
Web site: http://www.pacificlife.com

1998 Assets

	$ mil.	% of total
Cash & equivalents	150	—
Bonds	13,617	34
Stocks	547	1
Mortgage loans	2,789	7
Policy loans	3,901	10
Other investments	1,221	3
Assets in separate account	15,844	40
Other assets	1,815	5
Total	**39,884**	**100**

1998 Sales

	$ mil.	% of total
Policy fees	525	19
Premiums	515	18
Investments	1,333	47
Commissions	220	8
Other	216	8
Total	**2,809**	**100**

AXA Financial
Acordia
Aetna
Blue Cross
CIGNA
Charles Schwab
Citigroup
Foundation Health Systems
GenAmerica
Guardian Life
John Hancock
Liberty Mutual
Lincoln National
MONY

MassMutual
MetLife
New York Life
Northwestern Mutual
PacifiCare
Principal Financial
Provident Mutual
Prudential
St. Paul Companies
StanCorp Financial Group
State Farm
Transamerica
WellPoint Health Networks

Mutual company FYE: December	Annual Growth	1989	1990	1991	1992	1993	1994	1995	1996	1997	1998
Assets ($ mil.)	18.5%	8,630	9,783	10,650	11,547	13,346	14,728	17,589	27,065	34,009	39,884
Net income ($ mil.)	27.0%	28	32	78	79	119	81	85	167	176	242
Income as % of assets	—	0.3%	0.3%	0.7%	0.7%	0.9%	0.5%	0.5%	0.6%	0.5%	0.6%
Employees	1.5%	2,364	2,412	2,385	2,265	2,400	2,400	2,700	2,750	3,422	2,700

Equity as % of assets: 5.8%
Return on assets: 0.7%
Return on equity: 10.8%
Long-term debt ($ mil.): —
Sales ($ mil.): 2,809

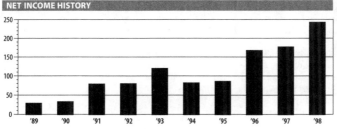

PACIFIC MUTUAL

PARSONS CORPORATION

OVERVIEW

No village vicar, this Parsons shepherds a flock of construction projects from Abu Dhabi to Venezuela. One of the world's largest engineering and construction firms, the Pasadena, California-based company has three main groups: transportation, energy and chemicals, and infrastructure and technology.

Parsons provides construction, program, and project management services, as well as engineering, planning, and design. The company's transportation projects have included rail systems, bridges, and highways, and it has

designed power plants, overseen the cleanup of hazardous nuclear waste, and built airports, dams, resorts, and shopping centers. Parsons can count the California Institute of Technology, Disney, the government of Greece, and all major US rail transit authorities as clients.

The company, which is owned by its employees, has diversified in order to compete in every major region of the world. In many places privatization has opened the door for Parsons to bid on government contracts.

HISTORY

Ralph Parsons, the son of a Long Island fisherman, was born in 1896. At age 13 he started his first business venture, a garage and machine shop, which he operated with his brother. After a stint in the US Navy, Parsons joined Bechtel as an aeronautical engineer. The company changed its name to Bechtel-McCone-Parsons Corporation in 1938. However, Parsons later sold his shares in that company and left in 1944 to start his own design and engineering firm, the Ralph M. Parsons Co., after splitting with partner John McCone (who later headed the CIA).

Parsons Co. expanded into the chemical and petroleum industries in the early 1950s. During that decade it oversaw the building of several natural gas and petroleum refineries overseas, including the world's largest, in Lacq, France.

In the early 1960s the company began working in Kuwait, which later proved to be one of its biggest markets. By 1969 Parsons had built oil refineries for all of the major oil companies, designed launch sites for US missiles, and constructed some of the largest mines in the world. In 1969 the company went public. With annual sales of about $300 million, it ranked second only to Bechtel in the design and engineering field. Ralph Parsons died in 1974.

The company built oil and gas treatment and production plants in Alaska in the 1970s. In 1978 the company reorganized itself into The Parsons Corporation and RMP International. It went private in 1984 as The Parsons Corporation, taking advantage of a new tax law that favored corporations with employee stock ownership plan (ESOPs). Not all employees were happy, though. Several groups sued, maintaining that they had little say in the decision, that the plan disproportionately benefited

executives, and that the buyout left the ESOP with all of the debt but no decision-making power. A Labor Department investigation later exonerated Parsons executives.

Parsons had just finished work on a power plant in Kuwait when Iraq invaded in 1990. Several employees were detained by the Iraqis but were released shortly before the US entered the Persian Gulf War. Two years later the company was hired by Kuwait Oil to rebuild some of the country's demolished infrastructure.

In 1995 Parsons acquired Gilbert/Commonwealth, an engineering company that specializes in designing nuclear power plants. The purchase, Parsons' first since 1988, was part of an effort to bolster Parsons' ability to compete for power plant projects in industrializing countries, such as Indonesia and China. That year Parsons was awarded a contract to help build the Seoul International Airport, one of the largest airport projects in the world.

James McNulty, who had led the company's infrastructure and technology group, replaced Leonard Pieroni as CEO in 1996 after Pieroni died in the Bosnia plane crash that also claimed the life of US Secretary of Commerce Ronald Brown. Later that year a Parsons-led consortium won a $164.5 million contract for infrastructure projects in Bosnia.

Parsons restructured in 1997 to focus on energy, transportation, and infrastructure projects. A Parsons/Inelectra joint venture won a $150 million construction contract in 1998 to develop Cerro Negro's heavy oil production facilities in Venezuela, and the next year Parsons was chosen to manage construction of a $5 billion refinery in Bahrain, a $1.4 billion gas plant in Saudi Arabia, and a $1 billion polyethylene project in Abu Dhabi.

Chairman, President, and CEO: James F. McNulty
SVP and CFO: Curtis A. Bower
President, Parsons Europe, Middle East, Africa, and South Asia: Dean K. Allen
President, Parsons Infrastructure and Technology Group: Frank A. DeMartino
President, Parsons Energy and Chemicals Group: William E. Hall
President, Parsons Asia Pacific: Peter F. Hedges
President, Parsons Transportation Group: Robert S. O'Neil
President, Parsons Latin America: J. Douglas Pitts
VP Human Resources: Shirley Gaufin
VP Construction: Ronald Laime

LOCATIONS

HQ: 100 W. Walnut St., Pasadena, CA 91124
Phone: 626-440-2000   **Fax:** 626-440-2630
Web site: http://www.parsons.com

PRODUCTS/OPERATIONS

Selected Projects and Services

Parsons Energy and Chemicals Group
Fossil plants
Hydroelectric projects
Nuclear reactors
Oil and gas production and gas treatment
Petrochemical and chemical plants
Refining
Transmission and distribution systems

Parsons Infrastructure and Technology Group
Aviation
Commercial
Environmental
Federal
Industrial/manufacturing
Infrastructure
Institutional
Mobile source air quality
Water resources

Parsons Transportation Group
Advanced technology
Construction management/construction engineering
Design/building
Highways
Intelligent transportation systems
Long-span structures
Major investment studies
Program management
Railroads/commuter railroads
Systems engineering; railroads/transit
Traffic and transportation planning
Urban transit

COMPETITORS

ABB
BE&K
Bechtel
Berger Group
Black & Veatch
Day & Zimmermann
Fluor
Foster Wheeler
Gilbane
Granite Construction
Halliburton
Hyundai Engineering and Construction
ICF Kaiser
IT Group
Jacobs Engineering
Michael Baker
Morrison Knudsen
Peter Kiewit Sons'
Raytheon
Stone & Webster
Turner Corporation
Tutor-Saliba
URS
Waste Management

HISTORICAL FINANCIALS & EMPLOYEES

Private FYE: December	Annual Growth	1989	1990	1991	1992	1993	1994	1995	1996	1997	1998
Sales ($ mil.)	6.9%	879	1,002	1,303	1,556	1,547	1,597	1,467	1,600	1,263	1,600
Employees	3.6%	8,000	9,500	10,000	10,000	10,000	9,500	10,600	10,000	10,400	11,000

SALES HISTORY

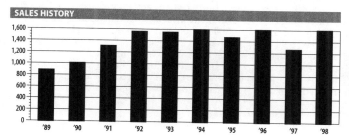

PATHMARK STORES, INC.

OVERVIEW

What seemed like a fairy tale at first was not to be. Pathmark Stores hoped to be revived with the kiss of capital from the Dutch prince of food retailing, Royal Ahold, but the story ended sadly in 1999 when Royal Ahold backed out of a deal to buy the company. The Carteret, New Jersey-based supermarket chain once thrived on its large, well-stocked stores and prime locations (its 130-plus stores are located in the densely populated area ranging from Philadelphia to New York). But competitors arrived with newer, cleaner, and sometimes bigger stores, and interest debt has hobbled the chain, which has reported losses throughout

most of the decade. Merrill Lynch owns about 80% of the company.

A pioneer of larger-than-average stores selling nonfood items as well as food, Pathmark has remained loyal to the superstore format (its stores average 52,800 sq. ft.) while making changes to keep up with the times. Typical stores have pharmacies, videocassette rentals, and bakeries, and the company has been adding banking centers at nearly three-fourths of its outlets. Pathmark also offers over 3,000 generic and private-label items under the No Frills, Pathmark, and Pathmark Preferred brands.

HISTORY

After WWII, supermarket operators in New York and New Jersey formed the Wakefern cooperative to combat chain grocers. Members enjoyed enhanced buying power and, with some stores sharing the name ShopRite, extended advertising reach. Three participants in the cooperative — Alex Aidekman, Herbert Brody, and Milton Perlmutter — combined in a smaller group to form Supermarkets Operating Co. in 1956. The operating company's stores continued to use the ShopRite name and Wakefern cooperative's services. Supermarkets Operating merged with publicly traded General Supermarkets in 1966 to become Supermarkets General Corp.

Supermarkets General left Wakefern two years later and renamed its stores Pathmark. It branched into small-town department stores that year with the purchase of Genung's, which operated chains under the names Steinbach (New Jersey) and Howland (New York and New England). In 1969 it bought Baltimore department store retailer Hochschild, Kohn & Co. and the six-store Rickel home improvement chain.

The company grew steadily in the 1970s and 1980s, pioneering large supermarket and grocery/drug combinations in densely populated areas of Connecticut, New Jersey, New York, and Pennsylvania. Among its acquisitions were Boston's Purity Supreme, operator of Purity Supreme stores; Heartland grocery stores; and Li'l Peach convenience stores (1984, sold 1991). Supermarkets General opened superstores under both the Pathmark and Purity Supreme names in 1985. The next year Aidekman stepped down as chairman, and the company sold its department stores.

Expansion of Supermarkets General slowed when the Haft family's Dart Group made a

$1.62 billion raid on the company in 1987. Merrill Lynch Capital Partners stepped in with an LBO, retaining control of Supermarkets General after the company was taken private. By this time Pathmark's once heralded stores were gathering a reputation for being dirty and outmoded.

In an effort to take the company public, in 1993 Supermarkets General spun off the Rickel Home Center chain (it was sold in 1994 to investment firm Eos Partners). The supermarket chain, now called Pathmark Stores, underwent a $1.4 billion recapitalization but eventually gave up its plan to go public because executives believed shares would not garner a worthy price.

Pathmark sold 30 of its 36 freestanding drugstores to Rite Aid in 1995 for $60 million and closed five; the last one closed in 1996. Jack Futterman retired as chairman and CEO that year. Board member John Boyle took over for Futterman until James Donald, formerly with Safeway and Wal-Mart Stores, was named chairman, president, and CEO late that year. One of Donald's first acts, in early 1997, was to eliminate about one-fourth of the positions at Pathmark's headquarters (about 300 jobs). The company then closed a dozen New Jersey and Pennsylvania stores.

Burdened by debt, Pathmark sold its distribution business to C&S Wholesale Grocers for $60 million plus an additional $44 million in inventory in 1998. The chain also closed the last of its stores in Connecticut that year.

In late 1999 Royal Ahold axed its planned purchase of Pathmark after it was unable to satisfy the FTC's antitrust concerns.

OFFICERS

Chairman, President, and CEO: James L. Donald,
age 45, $1,350,000 pay
EVP, Marketing and Distribution: Eileen Scott, age 46,
$402,600 pay
EVP, Operations: John Sheehan, age 41, $402,600 pay
SVP and Controller: Joseph W. Adelhardt, age 52
SVP, Retail Development: Harvey M. Gutman, age 53,
$326,494 pay
SVP, Administration: Robert Joyce, age 53, $359,210 pay
SVP, Secretary, and General Counsel: Marc A. Strassler,
age 50
SVP, CFO, and Treasurer: Frank Vitrano, age 43
VP and General Counsel, Real Estate:
Myron D. Waxberg, age 65
Director, Human Resources: Kevin Kane
Auditors: Deloitte & Touche LLP

LOCATIONS

HQ: 200 Milik St., Carteret, NJ 07008
Phone: 732-499-3000 **Fax:** 732-499-3072
Web site: http://www.pathmark.com

PRODUCTS/OPERATIONS

1999 Stores

	No.
Super Centers	129
Conventional	3
Total	**132**

Selected Departments
Bakery
Banking
Cheese shop
Delicatessen
Health and beauty care
Perishables
Pharmacy
Seafood
Service delicatessen
Videocassette rentals

Private-Label Brands
No Frills
Pathmark
Pathmark Preferred

COMPETITORS

A&P
Ahold USA
Albertson's
BJs Wholesale Club
CVS
Costco Companies
Grand Union
IGA
King Kullen Grocery
Kmart
Red Apple Group
Rite Aid
Wakefern Food
Wal-Mart
Walgreen
Weis Markets

HISTORICAL FINANCIALS & EMPLOYEES

Private FYE: January	Annual Growth	1990	1991	1992	1993	1994	1995	1996	1997	1998	1999
Sales ($ mil.)	(4.4%)	5,475	4,481	4,378	4,340	4,207	4,189	4,182	3,711	3,696	3,655
Net income ($ mil.)	—	(74)	(18)	(197)	(623)	(132)	39	33	(21)	(36)	(29)
Income as % of sales	—	—	—	—	—	—	0.9%	0.8%	—	—	—
Employees	(6.9%)	51,000	46,000	31,000	27,000	28,000	29,000	31,000	29,700	28,000	26,700

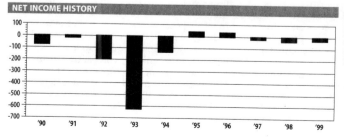

NET INCOME HISTORY

1999 FISCAL YEAR-END
Debt ratio: 100.0%
Return on equity: —
Cash ($ mil.): 8
Current ratio: 0.86
Long-term debt ($ mil.): 1,259

PENSION BENEFIT GUARANTY

OVERVIEW

Even in these days of the 401(k), some retired Americans still rely on their pensions. The Pension Benefit Guaranty Corporation (PBGC) makes sure they can. Washington, DC-based PBGC is a government corporation that insures some 44,000 single-company pension funds and 2,000 multi-employer plans (collective-bargaining agreements involving two or more employers); all together, these plans cover about 42 million workers. Governed by a board that includes the secretaries of labor, commerce, and the treasury, PBGC audits pension plans to spot those that are at risk. It is funded by employer-paid insurance premiums (about $19 per employee), as well as investment income, assets from administered plans, and recoveries from companies with terminated plans.

PBGC terminates pension plans when it determines that a company can no longer pay benefits; it can take up to 30% of a company's assets to ensure that pension obligations are met. When PBGC takes over a failed plan, it pays the individual pensioner covered by the plan about $36,000 annually.

Many companies are moving from traditional defined benefit pension plans to so-called defined contribution plans, usually reducing the benefits of long-time workers in the process. Workers and their advocates criticize the switched plans, but they don't come under PBGC's jurisdiction unless they fail.

HISTORY

The Employment Retirement Income Security Act (ERISA) of 1974 established the Pension Benefit Guaranty Corporation (PBGC) to protect workers' pension benefits. The poor economy of the day guaranteed PBGC plenty of business. By 1975 more than 1,000 companies were unable to meet pension obligations. Other companies tried to avoid entering the system by terminating their plans before a 1996 deadline; the Supreme Court in 1980 upheld PBGC's contention that these companies were obligated to pay benefits to vested workers.

ERISA's provisions initially let companies voluntarily terminate their plans by paying PBGC a portion of their assets; many companies took this route until Congress limited the provision. Pensions faced a new threat in the late 1980s, as many buyout deals were structured to use company pension plans as part of their funding; Congress put a stop to that practice in 1990.

Companies found themselves caught between conflicting requirements of the PBGC (ever watchful for underfunded pension plans) and the IRS (which penalized overfunded plans). PBGC's deficit grew as it took on more and more pension payment liabilities; companies continued to jeopardize plans by using funds for other purposes. On behalf of 40,000 workers, PBGC in 1988 sued companies that allegedly terminated their plans illegally between 1976 and 1981 (the suit was settled in 1995 for $100 million.)

In 1989 new director James Lockhart began airing PBGC's plight, claiming that the pension system would follow the savings and loan industry into collapse. In the early 1990s his predictions seemed reasonable; PBGC's deficit was driven sky-high by such bankruptcies as Pan Am (1991), TWA, and Munsingwear (1992). Under Lockhart's guidance, the PBGC began publishing the "iffy fifty" — the 50 most underfunded pensions in the country. Critics countered that underfunded plans did not necessarily end in failure.

Martin Slate succeeded Lockhart in 1993 and toned down the Chicken Little rhetoric, although that year PBGC announced that underfunding had nearly doubled between 1987 and 1992. Help arrived in the form of 1994's Retirement Protection Act, which put some teeth into pension laws. Under the reforms, PBGC required some employers to notify workers and retirees about the funding of their plans; it also changed the rules for annual reporting to the PBGC. The next year President Bill Clinton vetoed the budget bill, which would have allowed companies to take money from their pension plans.

Slate died in 1997 and David Strauss took over. After two decades in the red, PBGC in 1998 marked its third consecutive year in the black. The organization was sued by several former Pan Am workers who claimed PBGC had shorted their benefits. That year PBGC announced that LTV, the giant steel company that went bankrupt in 1993, could resume monthly pension payments to retired workers.

In 1999 PBGC defended itself against critics who claimed it took too long to determine benefits from bankrupt companies and often required pensioners to repay thousands of dollars that had been paid in estimated benefits, sometimes over the course of several years.

Chairman: Alexis M. Herman
Executive Director: David M. Strauss
Deputy Executive Director and COO: Joseph Grant
Deputy Executive Director and CFO:
  N. Anthony Calhoun
Chief Negotiator: Andrea E. Schneider
Director Budget: Henry R. Thompson
Director Communications and Public Affairs:
  Judith Welles
Director Contracts and Controls Review: Marty Boehm
Director Corporate Policy and Research:
  Stuart A. Sirkin
Director Facilities and Services: Janet Smith
Director Financial Operations: Hazel Broadnax
Director Human Resources: Sharon Barbee-Fletcher
Director Information Resources Management:
  Cristin M. Birch
Director Insurance Operations: Bennie Hagans
Director Participant and Employer Appeals:
  Harriet D. Verburg
Director Procurement: Robert Herting
Assistant Executive Director Legislative Affairs:
  Judy Schub
General Counsel: James J. Keightley
Auditors: PricewaterhouseCoopers LLP

LOCATIONS

HQ: Pension Benefit Guaranty Corporation,
  1200 K St. NW, Washington, DC 20005
Phone: 202-326-4040   **Fax:** 202-326-4042
Web site: http://www.pbgc.gov

PRODUCTS/OPERATIONS

1998 Assets

	$ mil.	% of total
Cash & equivalents	714	4
Bonds	11,242	61
Stocks	6,051	33
Other investments	74	—
Receivables	291	2
Other assets	4	—
Total	**18,376**	**100**

1998 Sales

	$ mil.	% of total
Investments	2,251	69
Premiums	999	31
Total	**3,250**	**100**

HISTORICAL FINANCIALS & EMPLOYEES

Government-owned FYE: September	Annual Growth	1989	1990	1991	1992	1993	1994	1995	1996	1997	1998
Assets ($ mil.)	20.7%	—	—	—	—	—	8,659	10,848	12,548	15,910	18,376
Net income ($ mil.)	1.2%	—	—	—	—	—	1,578	920	1,116	2,707	1,653
Income as % of assets	—	—	—	—	—	—	18.2%	8.5%	8.9%	17.0%	9.0%
Employees	2.2%	—	—	—	—	—	687	660	764	750	750

NET INCOME HISTORY

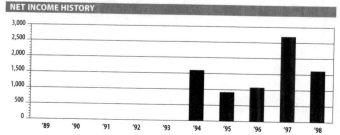

1998 FISCAL YEAR-END

Equity as % of assets: 20.1%
Return on assets: 19.0%
Return on equity: 71.8%
Long-term debt ($ mil.): —
Sales ($ mil.): 3,250

PENSKE CORPORATION

OVERVIEW

His eyes are on the finish line — and the bottom line. Roger Penske, known to be lead-footed and a hard-driving executive, heads closely held Detroit-based Penske Corporation, which operates nearly 10 automotive and transportation businesses.

The company's Penske Truck Leasing Company (79%-owned by GE Capital) is the US's #2 truck-rental operation, after Ryder. Penske also operates Penske Automotive and UnitedAuto Group (UAG), the second-largest publicly traded auto group (behind Wayne Huizenga's AutoNation). Penske Automotive's six dealerships, which include Longo Toyota (the US's largest Toyota dealer), are concentrated in Southern California; UAG has more than 60 dealerships in 16 states. Penske also owns nearly half of heavy-duty engine maker Detroit Diesel, as well as a 15% stake in Diesel Technology (Robert Bosch owns the rest), which makes electronic fuel-injection systems. The company owns Penske Auto Centers, with about 650 in-store automotive service centers at Kmart.

Penske just can't seem to resist that new-car smell. The company has sold its racetrack interests and picked up a 38% stake in UAG, which despite $3.3 billion in annual sales has been losing money. Roger Penske now heads UAG and holds a 57% stake in Penske Corporation.

HISTORY

As a teen, Roger Penske earned money by repairing and reselling cars. At 21 he entered his first auto race; he was running second when his car overheated. His winning ways, however, were soon apparent, and in 1961 *Sports Illustrated* named him race car driver of the year.

Nonetheless, in 1965 Penske went looking for a day job. With a $150,000 loan from his father, he bought a Chevrolet dealership in Philadelphia and retired from racing to avoid loading his balance sheet with steep life-insurance premiums for the CEO. Penske teamed with driver Mark Donohue in 1966 to form the Penske Racing Team. Donohue died in a crash in 1975, but team Penske continued.

In 1969 Penske started a regional truck-leasing business, incorporated under the name Penske. Six years later the company bought the Michigan International Speedway. In 1978 Penske and fellow racing team owner Pat Patrick started the race-sponsoring organization Championship Auto Racing Teams (CART). In 1982 Penske's truck-leasing business formed a joint venture with rental company Hertz to form Hertz Penske Truck Leasing.

Racing legend Al Unser Sr. surprised Indy 500 watchers in 1987 by driving a car borrowed from an exhibition in a hotel lobby to a first place finish for the Penske Racing Team. Penske had established auto dealerships in Pennsylvania and Ohio in the early 1970s, and he expanded his auto chain in the 1980s by acquiring dealerships in California, including Longo Toyota in 1985.

In 1988 Penske bought 80% of GM's Detroit Diesel engine-making unit, which had a market share of only 3% and had lost some $600 million over the previous five years. Penske trimmed $70 million from the unit's budget by firing 440 salaried employees, streamlining manufacturing processes, and cutting administration expenses. Detroit Diesel's market share doubled in its first two years as a Penske unit. Also in 1988 Penske purchased Hertz's stake in Hertz Penske Truck Leasing, which it later combined with the truck-rental division of appliance maker General Electric to create Penske Truck Leasing.

By 1993 Detroit Diesel's market share had grown to more than 25%. That year the engine maker went public.

Penske bought 860 Kmart auto centers for $112 million in 1995. The company's racing business, Penske Motorsports, went public in 1996, but Penske retained a 55% stake in the company. Also that year Penske bought Truck-Lite, Quaker State's automotive lighting unit.

In 1997 Penske Truck Leasing formed Penske Logistics Europe to offer information systems and other integrated logistics services on that continent. The next year it formed a logistics joint venture with Brazil-based Cotia Trading to serve US-based clients in the South American market, and Penske Logistics Europe opened a pan-European transport routing center in the Netherlands. In 1999 Penske sold its Penske Motorsports operations, which included racetracks in California, Michigan, North Carolina, and Pennsylvania, to International Speedway. The same year Penske invested about $83 million for a 38% stake in car retailer UnitedAuto Group (UAG). Penske became the company's CEO that year, too.

Chairman and CEO: Roger S. Penske
President and COO: Timothy D. Leuliette
EVP: Walter P. Czarnecki
EVP Administration (HR): Paul F. Walters
EVP and Assistant Secretary: Robert H. Kurnick Jr.
EVP, General Counsel, and Secretary:
Lawrence N. Bluth
SVP, Corporate Finance: J. Patrick Conroy
President and CEO, Penske Auto Centers:
James M. Wheat
President, Penske Truck Leasing: Brian Hard
VP and Assistant Secretary: James H. Harris
VP, Information Technology: Stephen Pickett
VP, Communications: Dan R. Luginbuhl
Auditors: Deloitte & Touche LLP

HQ: 13400 Outer Dr. West, Detroit, MI 48239
Phone: 313-592-5000   **Fax:** 313-592-5256
Web site: http://www.penske.com

Subsidiaries and Affiliates
Davco, Inc. (fuel filters and engine accessories)
Detroit Diesel (46%, heavy-duty motor manufacturing)
Diesel Technology (15%, fuel-injection system
manufacturing)
Penske Auto Centers, Inc. (retail auto-service outlets
at Kmart)
Penske Automotive (retail auto sales)
Penske Truck Leasing Co. LP (21%, truck rental
and leasing)
Penske Logistics Europe (tracking and integrated
logistics support)
Truck-Lite (automotive lighting, harness
systems, accessories)
UnitedAuto Group (38%, retail auto sales)

AMERCO
AutoNation
BFGoodrich
Cummins Engine
DaimlerChrysler
Discount Tire
Fiat
General Motors
Isuzu
Mack Trucks
Navistar
PACCAR
Prospect Motors
Rollins Truck Leasing
Ryder
Volvo

Private FYE: December	Annual Growth	1989	1990	1991	1992	1993	1994	1995	1996	1997	1998
Sales ($ mil.)	11.2%	2,300	2,500	2,530	2,800	3,250	3,287	3,900	5,200	5,800	6,000
Employees	12.5%	9,700	9,800	9,800	10,906	11,500	16,000	16,700	25,000	28,000	28,000

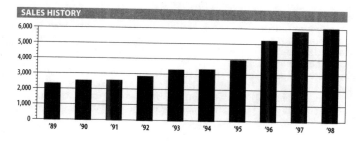

PERDUE FARMS INCORPORATED

OVERVIEW

Bird is the word at Perdue Farms, the leading chicken producer in the Northeast and near the top of the pecking order of all US poultry companies. Each week the Salisbury, Maryland-based company supplies supermarkets, restaurants, and other customers with some 42 million pounds of chicken products and 3.5 million pounds of turkey products. It sells its products primarily in the East, Midwest, and South, and it exports to more than 30 countries.

Perdue is vertically integrated: It hatches the eggs, grows the birds, and then processes and ships the meat. The company processes grain to make its own feeds and vegetable oils. Perdue also turns poultry by-products into pet food ingredients. In recent years the company has doubled the size of its food service division and has placed greater emphasis on value-added chicken products.

The family-owned company is headed by James Perdue, who — like his famous father, Frank, had before him — appears in its advertisements. Perdue produces its own breed of chicken, the skin of which is a distinct yellow color, resulting from a diet that includes marigold petals.

HISTORY

If asked which came first, the chickens or the eggs, the Perdue family will tell you the eggs did. Arthur Perdue, a railroad express worker, bought 23 layer hens in 1920 and started supplying the New York City market with eggs from a henhouse in his family's backyard in Salisbury, Maryland. His son Frank joined the business in 1939.

The Perdues sold broiling chickens to major processors, such as Swift and Armour, in the 1940s and pioneered chicken crossbreeding to develop new breeds. The family started contracting with farmers in the Salisbury area in 1950 to grow broilers for them. Frank became president of the company in 1952. The next year it began mixing its own feed.

Frank persuaded his father to borrow money to build a soybean mill in 1961. (Arthur had not willingly gone into debt in his previous 40-plus years in the poultry industry.) The soybean mill was part of Frank's plan to vertically integrate the company — with grain storage facilities, feed milling operations, soybean processing plants, mulch plants, hatcheries, and 600 contract chicken farmers — to counter the threat of processors buying chickens directly from farmers rather than through middlemen like the Perdues. To differentiate their products, the Perdue name was applied to packages on retail meat counters in 1968.

Two years later the company began a breeding and genetic research program. During the following years Frank transformed himself from country chicken salesman to media poultry pitchman when the company decided to use him as spokesperson in its print, radio, and TV ads. Catchy slogans ("It takes a tough man to make a tender chicken") combined with Frank's whiny voice and sincere face helped sales. As Perdue Farms expanded geographically into new eastern markets such as Philadelphia, Boston, and Baltimore, it acquired the broiler facilities of other processors.

In 1983 James Perdue, Frank's only son, joined the company as a management trainee. In 1984 Perdue added processors in Virginia and Indiana and introduced turkey products. Two years later it acquired Intertrade, a feed broker, and FoodCraft, a food equipment maker. However, after enjoying a rising demand for poultry by a health-conscious society in the 1970s and early 1980s, the company found its sales leveling off in the late 1980s. When North Carolina fined Perdue for unsafe working conditions in 1989, the company increased its emphasis on safety.

James, who had become chairman of the board in 1991, replaced his folksy father in 1994 as the company's spokesman in TV ads. In the early 1990s Perdue's management determined future sales growth lay in food service, international sales, and prepared foods; therefore, the poultry company quietly began laying the groundwork to support these new markets.

Perdue launched its Cafe Perdue entree meal kits in 1997. The following year it purchased Italian entree maker De Luca and food service poultry processor Gol-Pak. Also in 1998, through a joint venture, Perdue opened a poultry processing plant in Shanghai, China.

Early in 1999 the company purchased Advantage Foods, a poultry processor specialized in deboning chicken for portion-control chicken breasts. Later in 1999 Perdue announced it would build a plant to convert chicken manure into pelletized fertilizer to alleviate some of the environmental strain on the area around its chicken farms.

Chairman and CEO: James A. Perdue
President and COO: Robert Turley
CFO: Michael Cooper
VP of Corporate Affairs: Tom Moyers
VP of Environmental Service: Keith Rinehart
VP of Food Service and Prepared Foods: Randy Day
VP and General Manager, Grain and Oilseed Division:
 Dick Willey
VP of Human Resources: Rob Heflin
VP of Retail Poultry Operations: Larry Winslow
VP of Retail, Sales, and Marketing: Steve Evans

LOCATIONS

HQ: Old Ocean City Rd., Salisbury, MD 21804
Phone: 410-543-3000   **Fax:** 410-543-3874
Web site: http://www.perdue.com

PRODUCTS/OPERATIONS

Selected Poultry Products and Brands

Fresh Poultry
Chicken parts (Prime Parts)
Ground chicken
Roasters, turkeys, and Cornish hens (Oven Stuffer)
Seasoned chicken
Skinless, boneless poultry cuts (Fit'n Easy)
Turkey burgers
Turkey sausage

Fully Cooked Poultry
Carved chicken breast (Short Cuts)
Chicken and turkey breast entrees (Cafe Perdue)
Chicken Parmesan
Chicken with BBQ Sauce
Perdue Individually Frozen Chicken
Rotisserie-style chicken (Tender Ready, food service)

Other Brands
Chef's Choice
Cookin' Good
Shenandoah

Other Products
Commercial aquaculture feeds
Pet food ingredients
Vegetable oils

COMPETITORS

AJC International
Cagle's
Cargill
ConAgra
ContiGroup
Gold Kist
Hormel
Pilgrim's Pride
Rocco Enterprises
Sanderson Farms
Seaboard
Smithfield Foods
Townsends
Tyson Foods
WLR Foods

HISTORICAL FINANCIALS & EMPLOYEES

Private FYE: March	Annual Growth	1990	1991	1992	1993	1994	1995	1996	1997	1998	1999
Sales ($ mil.)	9.6%	1,100	1,000	1,239	1,300	1,600	1,700	2,100	2,200	2,200	2,515
Employees	6.1%	12,080	12,500	12,500	13,300	18,600	18,600	19,000	18,000	18,000	20,500

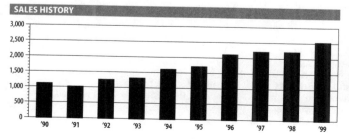

SALES HISTORY

PETER KIEWIT SONS', INC.

OVERVIEW

By building everything from tunnels to high-rises, Peter Kiewit Sons' has become a heavyweight in the heavy construction industry. The Omaha, Nebraska-based company is one of the largest general contractors in the US. About half of its projects are in transportation, including airports, bridges, highways, mass transit systems, and railroads. It also constructs commercial buildings, dams and tunnels, water treatment and sewage facilities, mining and petroleum infrastructure, and heating and cooling systems.

Operating through 22 district offices, the firm has projects in 43 US states and the District of Columbia, Puerto Rico, and Canada. It specializies in design-build projects and often works through joint ventures. Half of its business comes from government contracts.

The construction business has the undivided attention of Kiewit these days after it divested its energy assets and spun off its telecommunications and computer services businesses as Level 3 Communications. The company has kept its construction contract to build Level 3's vast national fiber-optic network.

Kiewit has no trouble answering to both its shareholders and its employees — they are one and the same. The company is 100% owned by current and former employees and Kiewit family members.

HISTORY

Born to Dutch immigrants, Peter Kiewit and brother Andrew founded Kiewit Brothers, a brickyard, in 1884 in Omaha, Nebraska. By 1912 two of his sons worked at the yard, which was named Peter Kiewit & Sons. When Peter Kiewit died in 1914, his son Ralph took over and the firm took the name Peter Kiewit Sons'. Another son, Peter, joined Ralph at the helm in 1924 after dropping out of Dartmouth and later took over.

During the Depression, Kiewit managed huge federal public works projects, and in the 1940s it focused on war-related emergency construction projects. It began coal mining in Wyoming in 1943.

One of the firm's most difficult projects was top-secret Thule Air Force Base in Greenland, above the Arctic Circle. For more than two years 5,000 men worked around the clock, beginning in 1951; the site was in development for 15 years. In 1952 the company won a contract to build a $1.2 billion gas diffusion plant in Portsmouth, Ohio. It also became a contractor for the US interstate highway system (begun in 1956).

Peter Kiewit died in 1979, after stipulating that the largely employee-owned company should remain under employee control and that no one employee could own more than 10%. His 40% stake, when returned to the company, transformed many employees into millionaires. Walter Scott Jr., whose father had been the first graduate engineer to work for the Kiewit company, took charge. Scott was to make his mark by parlaying money made from construction into spectacularly successful investments.

When the construction industry slumped, Kiewit began looking for other investment opportunities, and in 1984 it acquired packaging company Continental Can Co. (selling off non-core insurance, energy, and timber assets). Continental was saddled with a 1983 class action lawsuit alleging that it had plotted to close plants and lay off workers before they were qualified for pensions. In 1991 Kiewit agreed to pay $415 million to settle the lawsuit. In the face of a consolidating packaging industry, the company sold Continental in the early 1990s.

In 1986 Kiewit loaned money to a business group to build a fiber-optic loop in Chicago; by 1987 it had launched MFS Communications to build local fiber loops in downtown districts. In 1992 Kiewit split its business into two: the construction group, which was strictly employee-owned; and a diversified group, to which it added a controlling stake in phone and cable TV company C-TEC in 1993. That year Kiewit took MFS public; by 1995 it had sold all its shares, and the next year MFS was bought by telecom giant WorldCom (now MCI WorldCom).

In 1996 Kiewit assisted CalEnergy (now MidAmerican Energy) in a hostile $1.3 billion takeover of the UK's Northern Electric. Kiewit got stock in CalEnergy and a 30% stake in the UK electric company, all of which it sold to CalEnergy in 1998.

That year Kiewit spun off its diversified holdings (telecom and computer services) into Level 3 Communications. Scott, who had been hospitalized the year before by a blood clot in his lung, stepped down as CEO, and Ken Stinson, CEO of Kiewit Construction Group, took over Peter Kiewit Sons'.

In 1999 the more focused Kiewit acquired a majority interest in Pacific Rock Products, a construction materials firm in Canada.

Chairman Emeritus: Walter Scott Jr.
Chairman and CEO: Kenneth E. Stinson,
$2,070,835 pay
VC and EVP: William L. Grewcock, $496,415 pay
EVP and CFO: Kenneth Jantz
President, Kiewit Pacific: Richard Geary
EVP: Richard W. Colf, $511,350 pay
EVP: Allan K. Kirkwood, $654,885 pay
EVP: George B. Toll Jr., $990,921 pay
VP Human Resources: Brad Chapman
Auditors: PricewaterhouseCoopers LLP

LOCATIONS

HQ: 1000 Kiewit Plaza, Omaha, NE 68131
Phone: 402-342-2052 **Fax:** 402-271-2829
Web site: http://www.kiewit.com

Peter Kiewit Sons' has projects in more than 40 US
states, the District of Columbia, Puerto Rico, and
Canada.

1998 Sales

	$ mil.	% of total
US	3,306	97
Canada	77	2
Other countries	20	1
Total	**3,403**	**100**

Office Locations

Alaska	Massachusetts
Alberta, Canada	Nebraska
Arizona	Nevada
British Columbia, Canada	New Jersey
California	New Mexico
Colorado	Ontario, Canada
Florida	Quebec, Canada
Georgia	Texas
Hawaii	Utah
Illinois	Washington
Maryland	

PRODUCTS/OPERATIONS

1998 New Contracts

	% of total
Transportation (highways, bridges, airports, railroads & mass transit)	48
Commercial buildings	21
Water supply	8
Sewage & waste disposal	6
Mining	5
Dams	5
Power, heat & cooling	3
Oil & gas	3
Other	1
Total	**100**

COMPETITORS

ABB
Bechtel
Black & Veatch
Bovis Construction
Chicago Bridge and Iron
EMCOR
Fluor
Foster Wheeler
Granite Construction
Halliburton
ITOCHU
Jacobs Engineering
Mannesmann AG
Morrison Knudsen
Parsons
Perini
Raytheon
Skanska
Turner Corporation
Tutor-Saliba
Whiting-Turner
Williams Companies

HISTORICAL FINANCIALS & EMPLOYEES

Private FYE: December	Annual Growth	1989	1990	1991	1992	1993	1994	1995	1996	1997	1998
Sales ($ mil.)	8.0%	1,701	1,917	2,086	2,020	2,179	2,991	2,902	2,904	2,764	3,403
Net income ($ mil.)	13.5%	92	108	49	181	261	110	244	221	155	288
Income as % of sales	—	5.4%	5.6%	2.3%	9.0%	12.0%	3.7%	8.4%	7.6%	5.6%	8.5%
Employees	10.6%	—	—	8,000	7,600	10,620	14,000	14,300	14,000	16,200	16,200

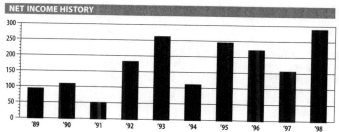

NET INCOME HISTORY

1998 FISCAL YEAR-END
Debt ratio: —
Return on equity: 42.9%
Cash ($ mil.): 227
Current ratio: 1.82
Long-term debt ($ mil.): —

PORT AUTHORITY OF NY AND NJ

OVERVIEW

The Port Authority of New York and New Jersey bridges the often-troubled waters between the two states — and helps with other transportation needs of the almost 16 million people who live and work in the metropolitan area. The New York City-based, bistate agency operates and maintains tunnels, bridges, airports, a commuter rail system, shipping terminals, and other facilities within the Port District, an area surrounding the Statue of Liberty that consists of five boroughs and 12 counties in the two states. The Port Authority also develops and manages two industrial parks and two commercial developments. A self-supporting public agency, the Port Authority receives no state or local tax money, relying on tolls, fees, and rents. The governors of the two states each appoint six of the 12 members of the board of commissioners and review the board's decisions.

The Port Authority's facilities include such international symbols of transportation and commerce as the George Washington Bridge, the Holland and Lincoln tunnels, LaGuardia and John F. Kennedy airports, the New York-New Jersey Port, and the World Trade Center. The Port Authority Trans-Hudson Corp. (PATH) rapid-transit system carries more than 70% of the rail passengers entering New York from New Jersey.

The Port Authority's growth strategy includes building new marine terminals and distribution facilities to capture a larger share of the growing North American maritime cargo market. The agency has been repeatedly criticized by New York City Mayor Rudolph Giuliani, who claims that the agency favors its New Jersey facilities at the expense of those in New York, primarily the airports. Giuliani has proposed legislation to place control of LaGuardia and JFK airports in City Hall hands.

HISTORY

New York and New Jersey spent much of their early history fighting over their common waterways. In 1921 a treaty creating a single, bistate agency, the Port of New York Authority, was ratified by the New York and New Jersey state legislatures.

The agency struggled at first, although its early projects, such as the Goethals Bridge (1928, linking Staten Island to New Jersey), were far from timid. It merged with the Holland Tunnel Commission in 1930, which brought a steady source of revenue. In 1931 the George Washington Bridge (spanning the Hudson River from Manhattan to New Jersey) was completed. The Lincoln Tunnel (also linking Manhattan to New Jersey) opened in 1937.

After WWII the Port Authority broadened its focus to include commercial aviation. In 1947 the agency took over LaGuardia Airport, and the next year it dedicated the New York International Airport (renamed John F. Kennedy International Airport in 1963).

As trucking supplanted railroads in the late 1950s, The Port Authority experimented with more-efficient ways of transferring cargo. In 1962 it built the first containerport in the world. That year the agency acquired a commuter rail line connecting Newark to Manhattan, which became the Port Authority Trans-Hudson (PATH).

In the early 1970s the Port Authority completed the World Trade Center. The agency changed its name to the Port Authority of New York and New Jersey in 1972, reflecting its role in mass transit between the two states. Critics, however, frequently assailed the agency for inefficiency and pork-barrel politics. In 1993 terrorists detonated a truck bomb in the World Trade Center, but within a year the building had largely recovered.

George Marlin became executive director in 1995. He cut operating expenses for the first time since 1943, saving $100 million in 1996 through budget cuts and layoffs while avoiding hikes in tolls and fares. A privatization proponent, Marlin sold the World Trade Center's Vista Hotel to Host Marriott and arranged for the sale of other nontransportation businesses. He stepped down in 1997, and Robert Boyle took the post. That year the agency broke ground on the $1.2 billion Terminal 4 at JFK International Airport.

In 1998 the Port Authority authorized a $930 million design and construction contract for a light-rail line to JFK International Airport. New York City Mayor Rudolph Giuliani proposed legislation in 1999 to place the Port Authority's LaGuardia and JFK airports under City Hall jurisdiction.

Chairman: Lewis M. Eisenberg
VC: Charles A. Gargano
Executive Director: Robert E. Boyle
Deputy Executive Director: Ronald H. Shifton
Chief of Staff: Louis J. LaCapra
COO: Ernesto L. Butcher
CFO: Charles F. McClafferty
Chief Technology Officer: Gregory G. Burnham
Director Aviation: Robert J. Kelly
Director Business and Job Opportunity:
Michael G. Massiah
Director Corporate Communications: Carolyne Bowers
Director Corporate Policy and Planning: Cruz C. Russell
Director Government and Community Relations:
Richard Codd
Director Human Resources: Paul Segalini
Director Port Commerce: Lillian C. Borrone
Director Procurement: Michael J. Rienzi
Director Tunnels, Bridges, and Terminals:
Kenneth P. Philmus
Director World Trade: Alan L. Reiss
Comptroller: Margaret R. Zoch
General Counsel: Jeffrey S. Green
Auditors: Deloitte & Touche LLP

LOCATIONS

HQ: The Port Authority of New York and New Jersey,
67 West, 1 World Trade Center, New York, NY 10048
Phone: 212-435-7000   **Fax:** 212-435-4660
Web site: http://www.panynj.gov

PRODUCTS/OPERATIONS

1998 Sales

	$ mil.	% of total
Air terminals	1,230	52
Interstate transportation	626	26
World Trade Center	320	14
Port commerce	111	5
Economic development	74	3
Total	**2,361**	**100**

Selected Locations

Aviation
Downtown Manhattan Heliport (New York)
John F. Kennedy International Airport (New York)
LaGuardia Airport (New York)
Newark International Airport (New Jersey)
Teterboro Airport (New Jersey)

Port Commerce
Auto Marine Terminal (Bayonne, New Jersey)
Brooklyn-Port Authority Marine Terminal (New York)
Howland Hook Marine Terminal (New York)
Port Newark/Elizabeth Marine Terminal (New Jersey)
Red Hook Container Terminal (New York)

Tunnels, Bridges, and Terminals
Bayonne Bridge (Staten Island to Bayonne, New Jersey)
George Washington Bridge (Manhattan to Ft. Lee,
New Jersey)
George Washington Bridge Bus Terminal
Goethals Bridge (Staten Island to Elizabeth, New Jersey)
Holland Tunnel (Manhattan to Jersey City, New Jersey)
Lincoln Tunnel (Manhattan to Union City, New Jersey)
Outerbridge Crossing (Staten Island to Perth Amboy,
New Jersey)
Port Authority Bus Terminal (Manhattan)

Other
The Port Authority Trans-Hudson System (PATH, rail
transportation between New York and New Jersey)
World Trade Center (office complex, Manhattan)

COMPETITORS

Amtrak
Helmsley
Lefrak Organization
MTA
Ogden
Reckson Associates Realty
Tishman Realty
Trump

HISTORICAL FINANCIALS & EMPLOYEES

Government-owned FYE: December	Annual Growth	1989	1990	1991	1992	1993	1994	1995	1996	1997	1998
Sales ($ mil.)	5.0%	1,527	1,691	1,857	1,934	1,921	1,980	2,083	2,154	2,206	2,361
Net income ($ mil.)	12.0%	108	31	60	144	108	153	177	199	282	299
Income as % of sales	—	7.1%	1.8%	3.2%	7.4%	5.6%	7.7%	8.5%	9.2%	12.8%	12.7%
Employees	(3.5%)	9,950	9,700	9,500	9,500	9,350	9,200	9,250	8,100	7,500	7,200

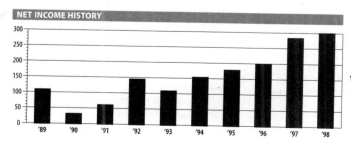

NET INCOME HISTORY

THE PORT AUTHORITY OF NY & NJ

PRICEWATERHOUSECOOPERS

OVERVIEW

Mergers make for strange bedfellows, especially in the cutthroat world of accounting. PricewaterhouseCoopers (PwC), formed from the 1998 merger of the fourth- and sixth-largest Big Six accounting firms, is now the world's largest professional services company — having displaced Andersen International from its decades-long stay at the top. The New York City-based partnership provides accounting, auditing, and consulting services from more than 850 offices in about 150 countries. PwC's offerings include auditing, accounting and tax advice, information technology and human resource consulting, and business process outsourcing. It also offers legal services through a worldwide network of affiliated law firms.

The merger of Price Waterhouse and Coopers & Lybrand was prompted by the need to offer seamless services to its multinational clientele. In addition the two firms wanted to bring their respective strengths under one roof. Price Waterhouse was strong in the media, entertainment, and utility industries, and Coopers & Lybrand excelled in telecommunications and mining. By consolidating into PwC, the firms whittled the Big Six down to the Big Five and created a professional services behemoth with annual revenues of $15 billion.

As Anderson Worldwide and Deloitte & Touche have already done, PriceWaterhouseCoopers is considering splitting its auditing and consulting operations into separate businesses to maintain auditing objectivity.

HISTORY

In 1850 Samuel Price founded an accounting firm in London, and in 1865 he took on Edwin Waterhouse as a partner. The firm and the industry expanded rapidly, thanks to the growth of stock exchanges that required uniform financial statements from listees. By the late 1800s Price Waterhouse (PW) had become the world's best-known accounting firm.

US offices were opened in the 1890s, and in 1902 United States Steel chose the firm as its auditor. PW benefited from tough, new audit requirements instituted after the 1929 stock market crash. The firm was given the prestigious job in 1935 of handling balloting for the Academy Awards. In 1946 it started a management consulting service.

PW's dominance slipped in the 1960s, although by 1970 it still retained 100 *FORTUNE* 500 companies as clients. PW came to be viewed as the most traditional and formal of the major firms, even though it tried to show more aggressiveness in the 1980s.

In 1992 Touche Ross (the UK arm of Deloitte Touche Tohmatsu) acting as bankruptcy liquidator, sued PW for $11 billion to recover losses from the failure of Bank of Credit & Commerce International. The amount was later reduced.

Coopers & Lybrand, the product of a 1957 transatlantic merger, wrote the book on auditing. Lybrand, Ross Bros. & Montgomery was formed in 1898 by William Lybrand, Edward Ross, Adam Ross, and Robert Montgomery. In 1912 Montgomery wrote *Montgomery's Auditing*, the bible of accounting.

Cooper Brothers began in 1854 when William Cooper, the oldest son of a Quaker banker, formed his accountancy at 13 George Street in London. His brothers joined the firm, which became Cooper Brothers & Company in 1861. Cooper Brothers branched out after WWI to Liverpool (1920), Brussels (1921), New York (1926), and Paris (1930).

In 1957 Lybrand joined with Cooper Brothers to form Coopers & Lybrand. During the 1960s the firm expanded into employee benefits consulting and began evaluating clients' systems of internal control. In the 1970s the firm focused on integrating computer technology into the auditing process.

Coopers & Lybrand dropped from the top to fifth in the Big Six during the 1980s as competitors merged. After the savings and loan debacle of the 1980s, investors and the government wanted accounting firms held liable not only for the form of audited financial statements, but for their veracity.

In 1997 Coopers & Lybrand proposed a merger with Price Waterhouse, which happened the next year. In 1999 PwC wrapped up old Coopers & Lybrand business when it settled SEC charges relating to a 1991 Arizona bond bid-rigging scheme involving former governor Fife Symington.

That year the company expanded internationally through associations with firms in Italy and Belgium and garnered publicity with its audit of Russia's corruption-riddled central bank. PwC held merger talks with Grant Thornton LLP, but they fell through. Also in 1999 the firm announced it would cut 1,000 jobs to reduce administrative costs and replace obsolete positions with e-business consultants.

Chairman: Nicholas G. Moore
CEO: James J. Schiro
Global CFO: Marcia Cohen
Global Service Line Leader: Willard W. Brittain
Global Geography Leader: Rolf Windmoller
Global Industries Leader: Peter A. Smith
Global Human Capital Leader: William K. O'Brien
Global Operations Leader: Geoffrey E. Johnson
Global Risk Management Leader: Ian Brindle
Global Consumer and Industrial Products Leader:
Thomas W. Cross
Global Financial Services Leader: Rocco J. Maggiotto
Global Energy and Mining Leader: James G. Crump
**Global Technology, Information, Communications, and
Entertainment Leader:** Francis A. Doyle
Global Services Leader: Bruce W. Hucklesby
**Global Assurance and Business Advisory Services
Leader:** Amyas C.E. Morse
Global Business Process Outsourcing Leader:
John C. Barnsley
Global Financial Advisory Services Leader:
Raymond A. Ranelli
Global Human Resources Solutions Leader:
Reed A. Keller
Global Insurance Industry Services Leader:
Jeremy Scott
Global Management Consulting Services Leader:
Scott C. Hartz

HQ: 1301 Avenue of the Americas, New York, NY 10019
Phone: 212-596-7000   **Fax:** 212-259-1301
Web site: http://www.pwcglobal.com

Selected Services
Audit and business
advisory
Corporate finance
Corporate recovery
Dispute analysis
Management consulting
Outsourcing
Tax and legal

Representative Clients
Alcoa
American International
Group
Anheuser-Busch
AT&T
Avon
Bristol-Myers Squibb
Campbell Soup
Caterpillar
Chase Manhattan
Chevron
CIGNA
Compaq
Dun & Bradstreet
DuPont

Eastman Kodak
Ericsson
Exxon
Fiat
Ford
Goodyear
Hewlett-Packard
IBM
Johnson & Johnson
J.P. Morgan
Kmart
3M
NationsBank
New York Life
NIKE
Nippon Telegraph and
Telephone
Philip Morris
Shell Oil
Toshiba
Unilever
United Technologies
Walt Disney
W. R. Grace

American Management
Andersen Worldwide
Atos
BDO International
Bain & Company
Booz, Allen
Boston Consulting
Deloitte Touche Tohmatsu
EDS
Ernst & Young
Gemini Consulting

Getronics
H&R Block
Hewitt Associates
IBM
ICL
KPMG
Marsh & McLennan
McKinsey & Company
Perot Systems
Towers Perrin
Watson Wyatt

Partnership FYE: June	Annual Growth	1990	1991	1992	1993	1994	1995	1996	1997	1998	1999
Sales ($ mil.)	20.3%	2,900	3,603	3,781	3,890	3,980	4,460	5,020	5,630	15,000	15,300
Employees	14.3%	46,406	49,461	48,600	48,781	50,122	53,000	56,000	60,000	140,000	155,000

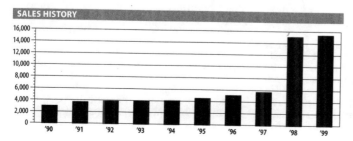

THE PRINCIPAL FINANCIAL GROUP

OVERVIEW

The Principal Financial Group makes financial security its guiding principle.

The Des Moines, Iowa-based group is the umbrella organization for a variety of financial service providers that offer pension products and services (the company is a top 401(k) plan administrator), mortgage financing, and other products, including mutual funds, annuities, and investment advice. Its flagship unit is Principal Life Insurance (The Principal), which provides life, health, dental, and disability insurance. To compete with banks encroaching on the company's territory, subsidiary Principal Bank offers online banking.

With some 250 offices around the world,

Principal Financial aims to become a global player in retirement services, targeting Australia, Brazil, Japan, and the UK. In the US, the company is focused on small to mid-sized businesses and institutional asset management. It formed Capital Management in 1999 to offer institutional asset management to endowments, foundations, and other clients.

In 1998 the company reorganized as a mutual insurance holding company to gain better access to capital (increasingly important as the insurance industry consolidates). The company is using its existing war chest to expand both at home and abroad and has not yet issued any stock.

HISTORY

Principal Financial was founded as the Bankers Life Association in 1879 by Edward Temple, a Civil War veteran and banker. Life insurance became popular after the war, but some dishonest insurers canceled customers' policies before they had to pay out benefits. Bankers Life, an assessable association (members shared the cost of death benefits as the claims arose), was intended to provide low-cost protection to bankers and their families. The company soon began offering life insurance to nonbankers, but it refused to insure women because of the high mortality rate among mothers during childbirth.

Bankers Life relied on volunteer workers until 1893. By 1900 it was operating in 21 states. Temple died in 1909, and two years later the company converted to a legal reserve mutual life insurance company with a new name: the Bankers Life Company. The conversion scared many customers away, however. About 50,000 policies were lost over the next three years. In 1915 Bankers Life began insuring women.

WWI slowed growth, and the 1918-1919 influenza epidemic, which struck and killed many policyholders, hit the company hard. The Depression also stunted growth. In 1941 the firm started offering group life insurance, and during WWII it became a major force in that area.

Bankers Life grew through the 1950s and 1960s, adding individual accident and health insurance (1952) and other products. In 1968 it began offering variable annuities for profit-sharing plans and mutual funds, forming what have since become Princor Financial Services and Principal Management. In 1977 Bankers Life introduced an adjustable life insurance

product, which allowed policyholders to change both premium costs and coverage.

In 1986 the company made a few name changes, renaming its holding company The Principal Financial Group and its largest unit Principal Mutual Life Insurance. That year Principal Financial acquired Eppler, Guerin & Turner, the largest independent stock brokerage firm in the Southwest.

In 1993 Principal Financial was issued Mexico's first new insurance license in 50 years; subsequent expansion has included Argentina, China, and Spain.

In 1996 Principal Financial expanded its health care operations, purchasing the St. Louis branch of health insurer MetraHealth (the rest had been acquired by what is now UnitedHealth Group in 1995) and Maryland-based third-party administrator The Admar Group. The next year the company bought the 76,000-member FHP of Illinois health plan from PacifiCare Health Systems. Despite this fast buildup, Principal Financial decided to exit the direct provision of health care and agreed later in 1997 to sell these operations to Coventry Corporation in exchange for a 40% stake in the renamed Coventry Health Care.

Continuing to refocus, the company in 1998 sold its Principal Financial Securities brokerage to EVEREN Capital (which First Union acquired in 1999) in favor of building a franchise in mortgage banking through the acquisition of ReliaStar Mortgage. The company also began offering online banking services. Also that year Principal Financial converted to a mutual holding structure, though it made no move to issue stock. The company bought Bankers Trust Australia Group in 1999.

OFFICERS

Chairman and CEO: David J. Drury
President: J. Barry Griswell
SVP and CFO: Michael H. Gersie
SVP and Chief Information Officer: Carl C. Williams
SVP and General Counsel: Gregg R. Narber
SVP Human Resources: Thomas J. Gaard
SVP; President, Principal International:
Norman R. Sorensen, age 53
SVP: John E. Aschenbrenner
SVP: Paul F. Bognanno
SVP: C. Robert Duncan
SVP: Dennis P. Francis
SVP: Thomas J. Graf
SVP: Robb B. Hill
SVP: Mary A. O'Keefe
SVP: Richard L. Prey
SVP: Robert A. Slepicka
VP and Corporate Secretary: Joyce Nixson Hoffman
President, Mutual Fund Division: Jan Jobe, age 48
Auditors: Ernst & Young LLP

LOCATIONS

HQ: 711 High St., Des Moines, IA 50392
Phone: 515-247-5111 **Fax:** 515-246-5475
Web site: http://www.principal.com

PRODUCTS/OPERATIONS

1998 Assets

	$ mil.	% of total
Cash & equivalents	461	1
Mortgage-backed securities	2,748	4
Corporate bonds	17,137	23
Stocks	1,102	1
Mortgage loans	13,286	18
Real estate	2,691	3
Policy loans	25	—
Other investments	349	1
Assets in separate account	29,009	39
Other assets	7,135	10
Total	**73,943**	**100**

1998 Sales

	$ mil.	% of total
Premiums, annuities & other considerations	3,409	44
Investment income	2,821	37
Policy & contract charges	780	10
Realized capital gains	466	6
Commissions & other income	221	3
Total	**7,697**	**100**

Selected Subsidiaries
The Admar Group, Inc.
Dental-Net, Inc.
HealthRisk Resource Group, Inc.
Principal Bank
Principal Capital Management, LLC
Principal Financial Services, Inc.
Principal International, Inc.
Principal Consulting (India) Private Limited
Principal Insurance Company (Hong Kong) Limited
Principal International Argentina, S.A.
Principal International de Chile, S.A.
Principal International Espana, S.A. de Seguros de Vida
Principal International (Asia) Limited
Principal Mexico Compania de Seguros, S.A. de C.V.
PT Asuransi Jiwa Principal Indonesia
Principal Life Insurance Company
Principal Mutual Holding Company
Principal Residential Mortgage, Inc.
Professional Pensions, Inc.
Trustar Retirement Services

COMPETITORS

AFLAC	The Hartford	Northwestern
A.G. Edwards	John Hancock	Mutual
AXA Financial	Liberty Mutual	Pacific Mutual
Allstate	MONY	Paine Webber
CIGNA	MassMutual	Prudential
CNA Financial	Merrill Lynch	St. Paul
Charles Schwab	MetLife	Companies
Chubb	Morgan Stanley	State Farm
Citigroup	Dean Witter	State Street
GEICO	New York Life	T. Rowe Price
Guardian Life		Vanguard Group

HISTORICAL FINANCIALS & EMPLOYEES

Mutual company FYE: December	Annual Growth	1989	1990	1991	1992	1993	1994	1995	1996	1997	1998
Assets ($ mil.)	12.9%	24,825	27,541	31,499	35,125	40,072	44,117	51,268	59,142	67,054	73,943
Net income ($ mil.)	14.2%	210	234	330	237	212	152	263	526	454	693
Income as % of assets	—	0.8%	0.8%	1.0%	0.7%	0.5%	0.3%	0.5%	0.9%	0.7%	0.9%
Employees	4.7%	11,101	12,139	12,153	12,825	13,583	16,275	17,392	17,010	17,637	16,837

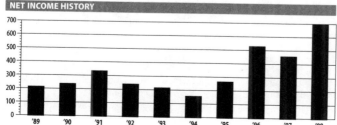

NET INCOME HISTORY

1998 FISCAL YEAR-END
Equity as % of assets: 7.7%
Return on assets: 1.0%
Return on equity: 12.7%
Long-term debt ($ mil.): —
Sales ($ mil.): 7,697

the**Principal**
Financial Group

THE PRUDENTIAL INSURANCE CO.

OVERVIEW

Prudential is caught between the Rock of its mutual company status and the hard place of demutualization. Newark, New Jersey-based Prudential Life Insurance Company of America, the #1 life insurer in the US (MetLife is #2) and fourth-largest worldwide, is converting from a mutual to a stock company despite the potential danger of a takeover.

Prudential's sale of its health care operations — once a substantial jewel in its crown — to Aetna is an indication it is serious about its main business, individual life insurance.

Additionally, its wealth accumulation businesses (asset management, brokerage services, mutual funds — it has a joint venture with Japanese bank Mitsui — and other investment products) remain compromised by past sales abuses such as "churning" (Prudential is paying out over $2 billion to resolve customer claims). Other lines include individual property/casualty insurance, credit cards, a national real estate brokerage franchise, relocation services, and group life and disability.

HISTORY

In 1873 John Dryden founded the Widows and Orphans Friendly Society in New Jersey to sell workers industrial insurance (low-face-value weekly premium life insurance). He changed the name in 1875 to The Prudential Friendly Society, taking the name from England's Prudential Assurance Co. The next year he visited the English company and copied some of its methods, such as recruiting agents from its targeted neighborhoods. The company adopted its current name in 1877.

Prudential added ordinary whole life insurance in 1886. By 1900 the company was selling more than 2,000 such policies annually and had 3,000 agents in eight states. In 1896 the J. Walter Thompson advertising agency designed Prudential's Rock of Gibraltar logo.

The company issued its first group life policy in 1916 (Prudential became a major group life insurer in the 1940s). In 1928 Prudential introduced an Accidental Death Benefit, which cost it an extra $3 million in benefits the next year alone (death claims rose drastically early in the Depression).

In 1943 Prudential mutualized. The company began decentralizing operations in the 1940s. Later the company introduced a Property Investment Separate Account (PRISA), which gave pension plans a real estate investment option. By 1974 Prudential was the US's group pension leader.

The insurer acquired securities brokerage The Bache Group (now Prudential Securities) in 1981. Bache's forte was retail investments, an area expected to blend well with Prudential's insurance business. Under George Ball, Pru Bache tried to become a major investment banker — but failed. In 1991 Ball resigned, leaving losses of almost $260 million and numerous lawsuits relating to the selling of real estate limited partnerships.

Despite the 1992 settlement of the real estate partnership suits, Prudential remained under scrutiny by several states because of "churning," a process in which agents generated commissions by inducing policyholders to trade up to more expensive policies. In 1995 Prudential's board brought in new management to fix the problem. This group, under former Chase Manhattanite Arthur Ryan, not only acted to bring sales under control but also began shedding company units such as reinsurance and mortgage servicing and decided to sell its $6 billion real estate portfolio.

In 1996 regulators from 30 states found that Prudential knew about the churning earlier than it had admitted, had not stopped them, and had even promoted wrongdoers. A 1997 settlement called for the company to pay restitution. The estimated cost, more than $2 billion, was thought to be less than the losses customers had suffered.

The real estate divestitures began in 1997 with the sales of its property management unit and Canadian commercial real estate business (the next year it sold its landmark Prudential Center complex in Boston).

In 1998, as the pace of convergence in the financial services industry picked up (including the arrival of Citigroup), Prudential announced plans to become publicly traded by the year 2001 at the latest. Making good on its promise to focus on insurance, the company also agreed to sell its health care operations to Aetna; the deal went through the next year. Also in 1999 Prudential paid $62 million to resolve more churning claims, revamped itself into international, institutional, and retail divisions, and trimmed job rolls at headquarters. That year the company's Prudential Securities bought investment firm Volpe Brown Whelan.

OFFICERS

Chairman and CEO: Arthur F. Ryan
EVP Financial Management: E. Michael Caulfield
EVP Human Resources: Michele S. Darling
EVP Operations and Systems: Robert C. Golden
EVP Corporate Governance: Mark B. Grier
EVP Institutional: Jean D. Hamilton
EVP International Investments and Global Marketing Communications: Rodger A. Lawson
EVP International Insurance: Kiyofumi Sakaguchi
EVP Individual Financial Services: John V. Scicutella
President and CEO, Prudential Securities Incorporated: Hardwick Simmons
EVP Global Asset Management: John R. Strangfeld
Chief Investment Officer: William M. Bethke
CFO: Richard J. Carbone
SVP and General Counsel: John M. Liftin
SVP and Chief Auditor: Thomas J. Carroll
VP and Secretary: Susan L. Blount
VP and Treasurer: C. Edward Chaplin
VP and Controller: Anthony Piszel
Auditors: Deloitte & Touche LLP

LOCATIONS

HQ: The Prudential Life Insurance Company of America, 751 Broad St., Newark, NJ 07102
Phone: 973-802-6000   **Fax:** 973-367-8204
Web site: http://www.prudential.com

PRODUCTS/OPERATIONS

1998 Assets

	$ mil.	% of total
Cash & equivalents	3,738	1
Trading account	8,888	3
Treasury & agency securities	6,337	2
Mortgage-backed securities	8,130	3
Corporate bonds	76,064	27
Mortgage loans	16,495	6
Policy loans	7,476	3
Other investments	38,348	14
Assets in separate account	81,621	29
Receivables	10,142	4
Other assets	22,183	8
Total	**279,422**	**100**

1998 Sales

	$ mil.	% of total
Net investment income	9,520	35
Premiums income	9,024	33
Investment gains	2,630	10
Policy charges & fees	1,462	5
Commissions & other	4,451	17
Total	**27,087**	**100**

Business Lines

Diversified Group (banking, real estate, marketing, database resources)
Individual Insurance Group (individual and group life, property/casualty, annuities, mutual funds, pension products)
International Insurance Group
Private Asset Management Group (in-house and third-party investment management)
Prudential HealthCare Group (group life and health products and HMOs; being sold to Aetna)
Prudential Investments (individual and institutional investment management)
Prudential Securities Group (securities brokerage)

COMPETITORS

AEGON
AXA Financial
Aetna
Allstate
American Financial
CIGNA
Charles Schwab
Chubb
Citigroup
FMR
GE
Guardian Life

The Hartford
John Hancock
Liberty Mutual
MassMutual
Merrill Lynch
MetLife
New York Life
Northwestern Mutual
Principal Financial
State Farm
TIAA-CREF

HISTORICAL FINANCIALS & EMPLOYEES

Mutual company FYE: December	Annual Growth	1989	1990	1991	1992	1993	1994	1995	1996	1997	1998
Assets ($ mil.)	6.1%	163,967	169,046	189,148	199,625	218,440	211,902	219,380	229,063	259,482	279,422
Net income ($ mil.)	4.5%	743	113	2,280	347	879	(1,175)	579	1,078	610	1,106
Income as % of assets	—	0.5%	0.1%	1.2%	0.2%	0.4%	—	0.3%	0.5%	0.2%	0.4%
Employees	(7.9%)	105,063	104,847	103,284	101,000	105,534	99,386	92,966	83,000	80,000	50,000

NET INCOME HISTORY

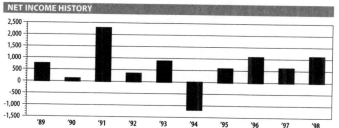

1998 FISCAL YEAR-END

Equity as % of assets: 7.3%
Return on assets: 0.4%
Return on equity: 5.5%
Long-term debt ($ mil.): 4,734
Sales ($ mil.): 27,087

PUBLIX SUPER MARKETS, INC.

OVERVIEW

What's eating at Winn-Dixie Stores and other supermarket chains located in Florida? Publix Super Markets. The Lakeland, Florida-based company is one of the nation's largest grocers, with about 600 stores (about 80% are located in Florida; the rest are in Alabama, Georgia, and South Carolina). Its stores, which range from 27,000-60,000 sq. ft., have been expanding beyond the standard food fare. Many now offer specialty services, including pharmacies, bank branches, and gourmet meals such as prepared sushi — some even provide valet parking. By emphasizing service and a family-friendly image rather than price, Publix has grown faster and been more profitable than Winn-Dixie and other rivals. Employees own about 85% of the firm, and its officers and directors, including the founding Jenkins family, own the rest.

While winning Florida's shoppers, Publix has lost a few legal battles brought by its employees. It settled two suits (over gender and race discrimination) but currently is embroiled in more suits alleging it discriminated against women and blacks.

HISTORY

George Jenkins, age 22, resigned as manager of the Piggly Wiggly grocery in Winter Haven, Florida, in 1930. With money he had saved to buy a car, he opened his own grocery store, Publix, next door to his old employer. The small store prospered despite the Depression, and in 1935 Jenkins opened another Publix in the same town.

Five years later, after the supermarket format had become popular, Jenkins closed his two smaller locations and opened a new Publix Market, a modern marble, tile, and stucco edifice. With pastel colors and electric-eye doors, it was also the first US store to feature air conditioning.

Publix Super Markets bought the All-American chain of Lakeland, Florida (19 stores), in 1944 and moved its corporate headquarters to that city. The company began offering S&H Green Stamps in 1953, and in 1956 it replaced its original supermarket with a mall featuring an enlarged Publix and a Green Stamp redemption center. Publix expanded into South Florida, opening a store in Miami, then buying and converting seven former Grand Union stores in 1959. It began selling stock to employees in the late 1950s.

As Florida's population grew, Publix continued to expand, opening its 100th store in 1964. The company launched a discount chain, Food World, in 1970 (sold in the mid-1980s). Publix was the first grocery chain in the state to use bar-code scanners — all its stores had the technology by 1981. The company beat Florida banks in providing ATMs and during the 1980s opened debit card stations.

Publix continued to grow in the 1980s, safe from takeover attempts because of its employee ownership. In 1988 the firm bought stores from Kroger and installed the first automated checkout systems in South Florida, giving patrons an always-open checkout lane.

The chain stopped offering Green Stamps in 1989, and most of the $19 million decrease in Publix advertising expenditures was attributed to the end of the 36-year promotion. That year, after almost six decades, "Mr. George" — as founder Jenkins was known — stepped down as chairman in favor of his son Howard. (George died in 1996.)

In 1991 Publix opened its first store outside Florida, in Georgia, as part of its plan to become a major player in the Southeast. Publix entered South Carolina in 1993 with one supermarket; it also tripled its presence in Georgia to 15 stores.

The United Food and Commercial Workers Union began a campaign in 1994 against alleged gender and racial discrimination in Publix's hiring, promotion, and compensation policies. The next year the union claimed the company was rewrapping and redating meats not sold by their "sell by" dates.

Publix opened its first store in Alabama in 1996. That year a federal judge allowed about 150,000 women to join a class-action suit filed in 1995 by 12 women who had sued Publix charging that the company consistently channeled female employees into low-paying jobs with little chance for good promotions. The case, said to be the biggest sex discrimination lawsuit ever, was set to go to trial, but in 1997 the company paid $82.5 million to settle that suit and another $3.5 million to settle a complaint of discrimination against black applicants and employees.

Publix promised to change its promotion policies and to work with employees on their careers; however, two more lawsuits alleging discrimination against women and blacks were filed later in 1997 and 1998.

OFFICERS

Chairman and CEO: Howard M. Jenkins, age 47, $411,870 pay
Chairman of the Executive Committee: Charles H. Jenkins Jr., age 55, $480,895 pay
VC: Barney Barnett
President: W. Edwin Crenshaw, age 48, $416,904 pay
EVP: Hoyt R. Barnett, age 55
EVP: William H. Vass, age 49, $473,792 pay
CFO and Treasurer: David P. Phillips, age 39
SVP: Tina P. Johnson, age 39
SVP: James J. Lobinsky, age 59
SVP and CIO: Daniel M. Risener, age 58
VP: Jesse L. Benton, age 56
VP: Glenn J. Eschrich, age 54
VP: William V. Fauerbach, age 52
VP: John R. Frazier, age 49
VP: M. Clayton Hollis Jr., age 42
VP: Mark R. Irby, age 43
VP: Thomas M. McLaughlin, age 48
VP: Robert H. Moore, age 56
VP: Thomas M. O'Connor, age 51
VP Human Resources: James H. Rhodes II, age 54
Auditors: KPMG LLP

LOCATIONS

HQ: 1936 George Jenkins Blvd., Lakeland, FL 33815
Phone: 941-688-1188   **Fax:** 941-284-5532
Web site: http://www.publix.com

Publix Super Markets has three dairy processing plants in Deerfield Beach and Lakeland, Florida; and in Lawrenceville, Georgia; and a deli plant and a bakery in Lakeland. Publix operates seven distribution centers in Florida (Boynton Beach, Deerfield Beach, Jacksonville, Lakeland, Miami, Orlando, and Sarasota) and one in Georgia (Lawrenceville).

1998 Stores

	No.
Florida	471
Georgia	91
South Carolina	21
Alabama	3
Total	**586**

PRODUCTS/OPERATIONS

Selected Supermarket Departments
Bakery
Banking
Dairy
Deli
Floral
Groceries
Health and beauty care
Housewares
Meat
Pharmacy
Photo processing
Produce
Seafood

Foods Processed
Baked goods
Dairy products
Deli items

COMPETITORS

Albertson's	Nash Finch
Bruno's	Rite Aid
Costco Companies	Royal Ahold
Fleming Companies	Ruddick
Food Lion	Smart & Final
Hannaford Bros.	Walgreen
IGA	Wal-Mart
Ingles Markets	Whole Foods
Jitney-Jungle	Winn-Dixie
Kroger	

HISTORICAL FINANCIALS & EMPLOYEES

Private FYE: December	Annual Growth	1989	1990	1991	1992	1993	1994	1995	1996	1997	1998
Sales ($ mil.)	9.4%	5,386	5,758	6,140	6,664	7,473	8,665	9,393	10,431	11,224	12,067
Net income ($ mil.)	12.7%	129	149	158	166	184	239	242	265	355	378
Income as % of sales	—	2.4%	2.6%	2.6%	2.5%	2.5%	2.8%	2.6%	2.5%	3.2%	3.1%
Employees	6.9%	64,037	66,756	68,606	73,000	82,000	90,000	95,000	103,000	111,000	117,000

NET INCOME HISTORY

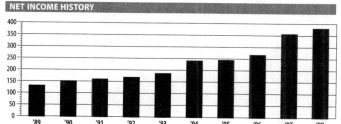

1998 FISCAL YEAR-END

Debt ratio: 0.0%
Return on equity: 17.4%
Cash ($ mil.): 669
Current ratio: 1.47
Long-term debt ($ mil.): 0

QUAD/GRAPHICS, INC.

OVERVIEW

One thing keeps Quad/Graphics in the black — ink. The Pewaukee, Wisconsin-based company is the nation's #1 privately owned printer of catalogs, magazines, books, inserts, and other commercial products. It provides comprehensive pre-press, press, and post-press services from 18 printing facilities for clients such as *Time, Newsweek*, Lillian Vernon, Hanover Direct, and McGraw-Hill. The company, which offers 100% digital imaging capabilities, operates internationally through joint ventures in Argentina, Brazil, and Poland.

Quad is one of the most employee- and community-oriented companies in the industry. The firm is known for its employee parties and provides on-site day care centers, health clubs, and medical clinics. In addition, it sponsors sports leagues (softball, bowling), provides interest-free auto loans, and awards college scholarships to employees' children. Quad/Graphic's Windhover Fund manages the philanthropic distribution of 5% of the company's pretax profit for social, cultural, and educational projects.

Founder and president Harry Quadracci and company employees own Quad/Graphics.

HISTORY

Ink runs in Harry V. Quadracci's family. His father, Harry R., founded his own printing business — Standard Printing — in Racine, Wisconsin, in 1930, when he was 16. Four years later Quadracci sold out to William A. Krueger. Though he worked to build Krueger into a major regional printer, the elder Quadracci had little equity in the company.

In the 1960s son Harry V. joined Krueger as a company lawyer. Within a few years he had worked his way up to plant manager. Krueger was a union shop, and in those days unions dictated the work rules and often salary levels. In 1970 there was a three-and-a-half-month strike. At odds with new management and reportedly dissatisfied with the way Krueger caved in to union demands and the adversarial relationship between company and union, the younger Quadracci left (not voluntarily, it is said).

After 18 months of unemployment, in 1971 Quadracci formed a limited partnership with 12 others to get a loan to buy a press, which was installed in a building in Pewaukee, Wisconsin. The next year his father joined the company as chairman. Within two years the partners had recouped their initial investment, but the business' future remained in question until about 1976. One of its most innovative moves was to make its delivery fleet drivers into entrepreneurs by requiring them to find cargo to haul on their return trips after making their deliveries.

Working on a shoestring, Quadracci hired inexperienced workers and trained them, moving them up as the company grew. The need to improvise fostered a flexibility that Quadracci institutionalized by keeping management layers flat and remaining accessible to his employees. Beginning in 1974, Quadracci rewarded his workers with equity in the company.

In the 1980s Quad/Graphics' commitment to technology enabled it to offer better service than many of its competitors could. It was also immune to the merger-and-acquisition fever of the time. Free of acquisition debt, the company had excellent credit and was able to finance equipment upgrades with bank loans. Quad expanded by opening a plant in Saratoga Springs, New York (1985), and buying a plant in Thomaston, Georgia (1989).

But there were missteps, such as its 1985 attempt to break into the newspaper coupon insert business dominated by Treasure Chest Advertising. Quad/Graphics sold that operation three years later. The company could not avoid the national economic downturn that began about that time, which forced it to lay off employees in the late 1980s and early 1990s and prompted it to reduce weekend overtime pay (from double time to time-and-a-half). The firm was also hit when a major customer consolidated its printing outside the Midwest. In response, Quad/Graphics increased its capacity in other regions of the US during the 1990s.

In 1996 the company bought 40% of Argentinean printer Anselmo L. Morvillo. Benefiting from the UPS strike and changes in the postal regulations, in 1997 Quad/Graphics expanded its shipping services with Parcel/Direct, targeting parcels for large shippers such as catalog merchants, in cooperation with the US Postal Service. Also that year it created a joint venture color printing firm with Brazil's Folha Group.

In 1998 Quad/Graphics expanded its international reach, agreeing to a joint venture in Poland. The next year the company was awarded the pre-press business of Condé Nast magazines.

President: Harry V. Quadracci
SVP Sales and Administration: Carl L. Bennett
VP Finance and CFO: John C. Fowler
VP Employee Services: Emmy M. LaBode
**VP Manufacturing and Technology; President,
    Quad/Tech:** Thomas A. Quadracci
Auditors: Arthur Andersen LLP

LOCATIONS

HQ: W. 224 N. 3322 DuPlainville Rd.,
    Pewaukee, WI 53072
Phone: 414-566-6000   **Fax:** 414-691-7814
Web site: http://www.qg.com

PRODUCTS/OPERATIONS

Selected Services
Binding and finishing
Color correction
Design
Desktop production
Direct mailing
Imaging and photography
Ink jetting
Integrated circulation
Mailing and distribution
Mailing list management
Parcel fulfillment
Printing
Scanning

COMPETITORS

Applied Graphics
Arandell
Banta
Big Flower Holdings
Consolidated Graphics
Dai Nippon Printing
Devon Group
Merrill
Quebecor Printing
R. R. Donnelley
Taylor Corporation

HISTORICAL FINANCIALS & EMPLOYEES

Private FYE: December	Annual Growth	1989	1990	1991	1992	1993	1994	1995	1996	1997	1998
Sales ($ mil.)	15.7%	376	454	509	582	703	801	1,002	1,042	1,200	1,400
Employees	10.3%	4,550	5,077	5,369	6,400	6,800	7,500	8,444	9,500	11,000	11,000

SALES HISTORY

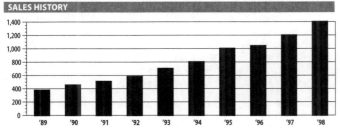

RAND MCNALLY & COMPANY

OVERVIEW

Rand McNally lets you know where you stand. The largest commercial mapmaker in the world, the Skokie, Illinois-based company is known for its flagship *Rand McNally Road Atlas* — one of the best-selling travel products in the world (more than 15 million copies are sold annually). In addition to maps and atlases, Rand McNally produces travel and reference software (*TripMaker, StreetFinder*) and educational products for classrooms (globes, maps). The company sells travel products (software, luggage) through its 22 retail stores across the US, and via its virtual store on the Internet. Rand McNally offers custom cartographic services and, through subsidiary Transportation

Data Management, makes mileage and routing software for the transportation industry. Its Premium and Incentive Division makes custom products for promotions. The company also makes maps for the Canadian market through its Allmaps unit.

Rand McNally sold a number of subsidiaries in 1997 and renewed its focus on geographic information. Controlling interest in the formerly family-owned company was sold to AEA Investors later that year, a move that paved the way for growth in mapmaking. The company has been buying smaller, regional mapmakers in keeping with that strategy.

HISTORY

Rand McNally was founded by William Rand and Andrew McNally in 1856. In 1864 the pair bought the job-printing department of the *Chicago Tribune*, and they eventually expanded into the printing of railroad tickets and schedules. They published their first book, a Chicago business directory, in 1870.

In 1872 the company printed its first map for the *Railway Guide*. Rand McNally later expanded into publishing paperback novels (popular among train travelers), and by 1891 annual sales topped $1 million.

During the 1890s McNally bought Rand's share of the business, and the company branched into printing school textbooks. Rand McNally's first photo auto guide was issued in 1907, and the company introduced its first complete US road atlas in 1924.

When Hitler invaded Poland in 1939, Rand McNally's New York stock of European maps sold out in one day. WWII necessitated the revision of a number of maps — a challenge that the company continued to face throughout the 20th century. (Rand McNally's map sales slowed in 1991 and 1992 when the breakup of the Soviet Union rendered its maps outdated.)

Although the company had abandoned adult fiction and nonfiction in 1914, it reentered the field in 1948 when a company official persuaded explorer Thor Heyerdahl to write a book for the company about his adventures. First published in 1950, Heyerdahl's *Kon-Tiki* sold more than a million copies in its first six years.

Rand McNally produced its first four-color road atlas in 1960, and during the 1970s it began publishing travel guides for Mobil Oil. The next decade the company published

several new road atlases to fill the void created when gas stations discontinued their practice of giving away free road maps. Rand McNally sold its textbook publishing business to Houghton Mifflin in 1980, and five years later it began computerizing its cartography operation.

The company introduced *TripMaker*, a CD-ROM vacation-planning program, in 1994. That year Rand McNally won a contract to create maps for a *Reader's Digest* atlas and formed a joint venture with Italian publisher De Agostini to provide geographic information for print and electronic media. The company debuted its StreetFinder street-level software in 1995 and created its Cartographic and Information Services division in 1996.

The next year, as part of a plan to focus on mapmaking and providing geographic information, Rand McNally sold a number of its subsidiaries (Book Services Group, DocuSystems Group). AEA Investors bought a controlling interest in the company later in 1997, bringing an end to more than 140 years of McNally family control (though it did retain a minority stake). While Rand McNally was still profitable, the sale to AEA underscored the challenges facing the company: Growth in earnings had slowed, and technological changes (Internet maps and software) had altered the mapmaking industry.

Rand McNally expanded in 1999 with acquisitions of mapmakers Thomas Bros. Maps and King of the Road Map Service. Later that year Henry Feinberg resigned as chairman and CEO. Richard Davis was appointed CEO, and John Macomber became chairman.

Chairman: John D. Macomber
President and CEO: Richard J. Davis
SVP and CFO: Larry Gyenes
VP and General Counsel: Deborah Lipoff
VP Business Development: Russell L. Voisin
VP Human Resources: Mary Lynn Smedinghoff
VP New Business Development and Chief Technologist:
Michael W. Dobson
VP Operations: Dennis R. Decock
VP Retail: Vicky Donnowitz
VP Sales: Bob S. Amico
VP and General Manager, randmcnally.com:
Christopher Heivly
Group Controller: Dave Jones
Director Information Services: Ken Levin
Auditors: Arthur Andersen LLP

LOCATIONS

HQ: 8255 N. Central Park Ave., Skokie, IL 60076
Phone: 847-329-8100   **Fax:** 847-329-6361
Web site: http://www.randmcnally.com

Rand McNally has operations in California, Florida,
Illinois, Kentucky, and Washington. It has retail stores
in 13 states and international operations in Canada.

Selected Rand McNally Retail Store Locations

Boston	Oak Brook, IL
Bethesda, MD	Palm Beach Gardens, FL
Chicago	Philadelphia
Costa Mesa, CA	San Diego
Dallas	San Francisco
Glendale, CA	Schaumburg, IL
Honolulu	Short Hills, NJ
Houston	Skokie, IL
Los Angeles	St. Louis
McLean, VA	Troy, MI
New York City	
Northbrook, IL	

PRODUCTS/OPERATIONS

Selected Print Products
Business Travelers' Road Atlas
Commercial Atlas and Marketing Guide
Easy-to-Read Travel Atlas
Motor Carriers' Road Atlas
Rand McNally Road Atlas
The Thomas Guides

Selected Software
New Millennium World Atlas Deluxe Edition
Rand McNally GPS Satellite Receiver
StreetFinder Deluxe 2000 & GPS Receiver
StreetFinder Deluxe 2000 Edition
TripMaker Deluxe 2000 Edition
TripMaker/StreetFinder 2000 Value Pack
World Watch Screen Saver Software

COMPETITORS

AAA
Analytical Surveys
Banyan Systems
Barnes & Noble
Borders
DeLorme
Educational Insights
Encyclopaedia Britannica
Environmental Systems Research
Expedia
Globe Pequot
Langenscheidt
Lonely Planet
MapInfo
MapQuest.com
Michelin
National Geographic
Piersen Graphics
TravRoute
Vicinity

HISTORICAL FINANCIALS & EMPLOYEES

Private FYE: December	Annual Growth	1989	1990	1991	1992	1993	1994	1995	1996	1997	1998
Sales ($ mil.)	(3.8%)	247	262	307	342	395	438	469	163	175	175
Employees	(14.3%)	4,000	4,200	4,000	4,000	4,000	4,200	4,650	1,000	1,000	1,000

SALES HISTORY

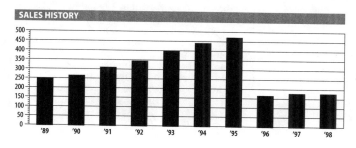

RAND McNALLY

RANDALL'S FOOD MARKETS, INC.

OVERVIEW

Spilt milk isn't worth crying over, but spilt market share has made Houston-based Randall's Food Markets a little teary. Owned by Safeway, one of the largest food retailers in the US, Randall's operates more than 115 supermarkets under the Randalls, Tom Thumb, and Simon David banners. Known for offering slightly upmarket shopping in wealthier neighborhoods, all of its stores are located in three of Texas' four biggest markets: Austin, Dallas/Fort Worth, and Houston.

Tom Thumb and Randalls once led Dallas and Houston, respectively, in market share, and Randalls had the #2 spot in Austin. However, competition from supermarket giants Albertson's and Kroger has dropped the company into the #2 spots in Big D and Houston and into the #3 spot in Austin (where Texas-based H. E. Butt Grocery is #1).

Investment group Kohlberg Kravis Roberts exchanged a 62% stake in the company for a 7% stake in Safeway.

HISTORY

Robert Randall Onstead first entered the grocery business in the mid-1950s when he went to work for his father-in-law, who owned three Houston grocery stores. In 1966, using $85,000 of mostly borrowed money, Onstead, Randall Barclay, and Norman Frewin purchased two Minimax stores in Houston. They renamed them Randall's Food Markets and within three months weekly sales at the two stores rose from $18,000 to $38,000. Less than two years later, the men added a third store.

As Houston grew in the 1970s, the company grew with it. By 1983 it had 25 locations in the city, and its market share had risen from 4% to 11% since 1978. Randall's had blossomed during this time because of Onstead's strategy of copying the smaller gourmet stores becoming popular in the eastern US, then locating his stores in upper-class and upper-middle-class neighborhoods. In 1984 Onstead expanded into nearby Pasadena and Galveston, and Houston market share rose to 16%. By 1985 Randall's had 29 stores in operation. That year the company introduced its first of many flagship stores — upscale, specialty supermarkets with amenities such as coffee bars.

By 1986 Randall's, with more than $600 million in annual sales, was second in Houston only to Kroger. The next year the company debuted its New Generation store format, expanding upon the produce selection in conventional stores. Having saturated the upscale markets in Houston, Onstead decided to lure middle-income families with the new design and new locations. By 1991 the company had $1 billion in sales and, with a 21% market share and 44 stores, had surpassed its main competitor.

The next year Randall's made its first big regional jump when it acquired Cullum Cos., a highly leveraged Dallas-based supermarket operator that ran 79 stores, consisting of 36 Tom Thumb-Page food-and-drug-combination outlets, 26 Tom Thumb supermarkets, 16 Page Drug stores, and a Drug Plus outlet. Cullum was founded in 1948 by Charles and Bob Cullum with the purchase of five supermarkets; it acquired Page Drugs in 1968 and was the area's leading food chain at the time of its sale. In 1993 Randall's expanded its presence in Austin by acquiring 12 supermarkets from AppleTree, which was operating under Chapter 11.

From the founding of the chain in 1966, Onstead had steadfastly refused to stock his stores with beer or wine, citing his father-in-law's alcoholism. When Randall's purchased Tom Thumb, however, it inherited that chain's beer and wine categories, and competition led to management's difficult 1994 decision to allow stores under the Randalls name to stock alcoholic beverages. Two years later Randall Onstead, Robert's son, became CEO.

With Randall's saddled with debt from its earlier purchases, investment firm Kohlberg Kravis Roberts bought a 62% stake in the company for $225 million in 1997. That year Randall's decided to close approximately 20 stores, taking a charge of nearly $33 million, and settled a suit over its employee stock-option plan, choosing to pay out more than $11 million.

Robert passed the role of chairman to Randall in 1998. Also in 1998 Randall's terminated its contact with Fleming Companies, which provided it with about 25% of its merchandise, and announced it would move to self-distribution in 1999. In September 1999 Safeway bought the company in a $1.8 billion cash and stock deal. Along with the acquisition, Randall stepped down, replaced by Frank Lazaran, formerly an SVP of sales at Randall's.

President: Frank Lazaran, age 41, $186,923 pay (prior to promotion)
SVP Real Estate and Assistant Secretary: Joe R. Rollins, age 43
SVP Store Operations; President, Dallas Division: D. Mark Prestidge, age 40, $196,443 pay
VP and Controller: Curtis D. McClellan
VP Human Resources: Judy Ward
VP Information Technology: Ray Walsh
Auditors: Deloitte & Touche LLP

LOCATIONS

HQ: 3663 Briarpark, Houston, TX 77042
Phone: 713-268-3500   **Fax:** 713-268-3602
Web site: http://www.randalls.com

1998 Stores

	No.
Dallas/Fort Worth	53
Houston	50
Austin	12
Total	**115**

PRODUCTS/OPERATIONS

Store Concepts
Conventional store (food and drug combination, approximately 50,600 sq. ft.)
Flagship (upscale specialty goods, approximately 57,800 sq. ft.)
New Generation (expanded perishable sections; approximately 65,400 sq. ft.)

Selected In-Store Services
Bakery
Bank
Coffee shop
Deli
Dry cleaning
Film processing
Floral
Meat and seafood department
Pharmacy
Prepared meals
Produce
Video rental

Private-Label Lines
President's Choice
Remarkable
Value Time

COMPETITORS

7-Eleven	H-E-B
Albertson's	Hollywood Entertainment
Blockbuster	Kmart
Brinker	Kroger
Brookshire Brothers	Minyard Food Stores
Brookshire Grocery	Rice Food Markets
Drug Emporium	Tosco
Eckerd	Walgreen
Fiesta Mart	Wal-Mart
Food Lion	Whole Foods
Gerland's Food Fair	Winn-Dixie

HISTORICAL FINANCIALS & EMPLOYEES

Subsidiary FYE: June	Annual Growth	1990	1991	1992	1993	1994	1995	1996	1997	1998	1999
Sales ($ mil.)	4.0%	—	—	—	2,038	2,305	2,328	2,369	2,345	2,419	2,585
Net income ($ mil.)	78.2%	—	—	—	1	(4)	0	19	(41)	21	42
Income as % of sales	—	—	—	—	0.1%	—	0.0%	0.8%	—	0.9%	1.6%
Employees	(0.3%)	—	—	—	18,000	21,000	22,000	22,000	17,067	18,368	17,650

NET INCOME HISTORY

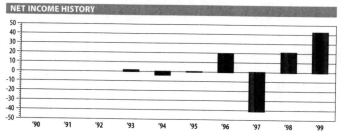

1999 FISCAL YEAR-END

Debt ratio: 55.1%
Return on equity: 16.8%
Cash ($ mil.): 28
Current ratio: 0.99
Long-term debt ($ mil.): 332

THE ROCKEFELLER FOUNDATION

OVERVIEW

Supporter of the arts and promoter of global concerns, or elitist destroyer of American values and propagandist for the New World Order? The Rockefeller Foundation, one of the oldest and wealthiest private charitable organizations in the world, is viewed as both in the fiercely partisan American political scene. Based in New York City, the organization supports grants, fellowships, and conferences for programs it hopes will lead to a better world. These programs include initiatives in Africa to foster gender equity, agricultural programs to increase crop yields in developing nations, vaccination programs, equal opportunity grants, global environment studies, arts and humanities projects, and population control (family planning). The foundation also provides grants

for international security programs to promote the nonproliferation of nuclear, chemical, and biological weapons and to foster democracy around the globe.

The foundation's science-based programs concentrate on reducing poverty, disease, malnutrition, unwanted pregnancies, and illiteracy in developing nations and also seek to develop a global environmental strategy. President Gordon Conway is changing its organizational structure to focus on food, work, health, and creativity.

The foundation maintains no ties to the Rockefeller family or its other philanthropies. An independent board of trustees sets program guidelines and approves all expenditures.

HISTORY

Oil baron John D. Rockefeller, one of America's most criticized capitalists, was also one of its pioneer philanthropists. Before founding The Rockefeller Foundation in 1913, he funded the creation of The University of Chicago (with $36 million over a 25-year period) and formed organizations for medical research (1901), the education of southern African-Americans (1903), and hookworm eradication in the southern US.

Rockefeller turned the control of the foundation over to his son John D. Rockfeller Jr. in 1916. The younger Rockefeller separated the foundation from the family's interests and established an independent board. (The board later rejected a proposal from John Sr. to replace school textbooks that he claimed promoted Bolshevism.)

In the mid-1920s the foundation started conducting basic medical research. In 1928 it absorbed several other Rockefeller philanthropies, adding programs in the natural and social sciences and the arts and humanities. During the 1930s the foundation developed the first effective yellow fever vaccine (1935), continued its worldwide battles against disease, and supported pioneering research in the field of biology. Other grants supported the performing arts in the US and social science research. During WWII it supplied major funding for nuclear science research tools (spectroscopy, X-ray diffraction).

After the war, with an increasing number of large public ventures modeled after the foundation (e.g., the UN's World Health Organization) taking over its traditional physical and natural sciences territory, the organization

dissolved its famed biology division in 1951. The following year emphasis swung to agricultural studies under chairman John D. Rockefeller III. The organization took wheat seeds developed at its Mexican food project to Colombia (1950), Chile (1955), and India (1956); a rice institute in the Philippines followed (1960). The Green Revolution sprouted 12 more developing-world institutes.

In the 1960s the foundation began dispatching expertise to African and Latin American universities in an effort to raise the level of training at those institutions. The long bear market of the 1970s caused the foundation's assets to drop to a low of $732 million (1977).

In 1990 the organization set up the Energy Foundation, a joint effort with the MacArthur Foundation and the Pew Charitable Trusts, to explore alternate energy sources.

Alice Stone Ilchman, president of Sarah Lawrence College, was elected chairman of the board of trustees in 1995, succeeding John Evans. In the mid-1990s the Republican-led Congress launched three probes into the foundation and several other not-for-profits over allegations of political activities that could jeopardize their tax status.

In 1998 Gordon Conway, a British agricultural ecologist, became the foundation's 12th (and first non-American) president. He implemented a retooling of the organization's programs in 1999. He also led an effective campaign against bioengineering giant Monsanto's plan to market "sterile seeds" that do not regenerate.

Chairman: Alice Stone Ilchman
President: Gordon Conway
Corporate Secretary: Lynda Mullen
Treasurer and Chief Investment Officer:
Rosalie J. Wolfe
Comptroller: Charles J. Lang
Director Agricultural Sciences: Robert W. Herdt
Director for Communications: Denise A. Gray-Felder
Director Administration and Budget (CFO): Sally Ferris
Director Equal Opportunity: Julia I. Lopez
Director Arts and Humanities: Mikki Shepard
Director Population Sciences: Steven W. Sinding
Manager Information Technology: Fernando Mola-Davis
Manager Fellowship Office: Joseph R. Bookmyer
Manager Office Services: Cora L. Springer
Manager Records and Library Services:
Meredith S. Averill
Manager Human Resources: Charlotte N. Church
Team Director, Health Sciences: Timothy Evans
Associate VP African Initiatives and Acting Director for Global Environment: Joyce L. Moock
Auditors: Ernst & Young LLP

LOCATIONS

HQ: 420 5th Ave., New York, NY 10018
Phone: 212-869-8500 **Fax:** 212-764-3468
Web site: http://www.rockfound.org

PRODUCTS/OPERATIONS

1998 Assets

	$ mil.	% of total
Stocks	2,064	61
Corporate bonds	439	13
Treasury & agency securities	375	11
Cash & equivalents	203	6
Other investments	192	6
Other assets	67	2
Other securities	18	1
Total	**3,358**	**100**

1998 Grants

	$ mil.	% of total
Equal opportunity	22	19
Global environment	20	17
Agricultural sciences	16	14
Population sciences	15	13
Health sciences	14	11
Arts & humanities	13	11
African initiatives	6	5
Building democracy	4	3
International security	2	2
Other	6	5
Total	**118**	**100**

Divisions and Programs
Equal Opportunity
Agricultural Sciences
Population Sciences
Global Environment
Arts and Humanities
Health Sciences
African Initiatives
Building Democracy
International Security

HISTORICAL FINANCIALS & EMPLOYEES

Foundation FYE: December	Annual Growth	1989	1990	1991	1992	1993	1994	1995	1996	1997	1998
Assets ($ mil.)	9.1%	—	—	2,172	2,152	2,375	2,216	2,540	2,767	3,132	3,358
Employees	0.8%	—	—	142	142	147	137	130	152	149	150

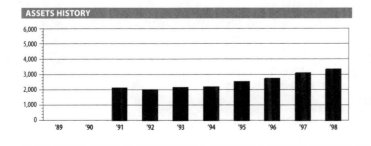

ASSETS HISTORY

ROLL INTERNATIONAL

OVERVIEW

Frankly, Scarlett, you deserve a commemorative plate. So thought husband-and-wife team Stewart and Lynda Rae Resnick, owners of the world's top collectibles company, The Franklin Mint. That frippery firm is part of the couple's Los Angeles-based Roll International, which also owns Paramount Farms (processes pistachios), Paramount Citrus (California-based citrus products), and Teleflora (floral wire service). Roll also operates The Franklin Mint Museum, which has displayed such pop culture items as Jacqueline Kennedy Onassis' triple-strand faux pearl necklace.

Based near Philadelphia and with operations in 16 countries, The Franklin Mint is the centerpiece of the Resnicks' empire. (It has no connection to the US Mint.) The company develops up to 1,200 products each year and has sold everything from *Gone With the Wind* figurines and *Star Trek* chess sets to limited-edition Monopoly games and Elvis Presley commemorative plates. The Franklin Mint produces many of its wares under licensing agreements with the likes of the Vatican, The Coca-Cola Company, and Rolls-Royce, among others. Products are sold by mail order, through its Web site, and in company-owned and independent retail outlets.

HISTORY

Stewart Resnick, a UCLA Law School graduate, is recognized as the financial and organizational brains of Roll International. Lynda Rae, an art lover and marketing guru, started her own advertising agency when she was 19 years old. Each had established careers when they married in the early 1970s. Together they have built their company through a series of acquisitions.

Among the Resnicks' first purchases was Teleflora, which they bought in 1979. Originally called Telegraph Delivery Service, Teleflora had been founded in 1934 by Edwin Douglas. The Resnicks also bought alarm company American Protection Industries (API), which they set up as their holding company.

In 1985 the Resnicks acquired The Franklin Mint from Warner Communications (now Time Warner) for around $167 million. Founded in 1964 by Joseph Segal (who in 1986 started the QVC television shopping network) as General Numismatics, the company originally focused on coins and other metal objects. It went public in 1965 and changed its name to The Franklin Mint in 1968. The Franklin Mint was purchased by Warner in 1981, but it failed to prosper. The Resnicks, who had been eyeing the company for some time, saw a greater opportunity in the collectibles market rather than in coins and greatly expanded that part of the business. In 1991 The Franklin Mint turned its first profit since 1987.

The Resnicks bought Mobil's Apex Orchards, an almond and pistachio grower in the San Joaquin Valley, in 1986. The next year they added the California agribusinesses of Texaco to their holdings. (Texaco had become owner of the Central California operations when it acquired Getty Oil in 1984.) The Resnicks formed their agribusiness unit, Paramount Farms, in 1989. That year they sold API; however, they retained the name until 1993, when they renamed their holding company Roll International, after another agricultural company they had acquired.

The couple had planned to take The Franklin Mint public in 1992, but its poor earnings prior to 1991 and a cool IPO market changed their minds. Instead they focused on expanding the mint's line of collectibles through licensing agreements and added commemorative plates to their line. In the early 1990s the company began opening The Franklin Mint retail stores. In 1993 Paramount Farms and the Pistachio Producers of California teamed up to form the CAL-PURE marketing co-op, offering pistachios under the Sunkist name.

The Franklin Mint had 50 gallery shops in US shopping centers and more than $600 million in US sales by 1996. The following year Teleflora bought Redbook Florist Services, giving it more subscribers (though still lower sales) than rival floral company FTD.

Also in 1997 Lynda bought the high-collared "Elvis dress" worn by the late Diana, Princess of Wales, for more than $150,000 to display in The Franklin Mint Museum. A memorial fund for Diana sued The Franklin Mint in 1998, charging it with unauthorized use of the princess' image on various items. That year the Resnicks looked into selling the company, reportedly because its legal problems had tarnished Lynda's standing among American socialites. In 1999 Lynda was named a trustee for the Aspen Institute, a high-brow intellectual group for societal leaders.

Co-Chairman: Lynda R. Resnick
Co-Chairman, President, and CEO; President, Paramount Farms: Stewart A. Resnick
CFO: Robert A. Kors
President, The Franklin Mint: Adam Berger
President and CEO, Teleflora: Gregg Coccari
VP and General Counsel: Jean Cooper
VP Finance and Accounting and Secretary: Peter R. Gurney

LOCATIONS

HQ: Roll International Corporation,
11444 W. Olympic Blvd., 10th Fl.,
Los Angeles, CA 90064
Phone: 310-966-5700   **Fax:** 310-914-4747

PRODUCTS/OPERATIONS

Selected Franklin Mint Licenses
The Coca-Cola Company
General Motors
Graceland
Milton Bradley
National Football League
National Wildlife Federation
Paramount
Parker Brothers
Rolls-Royce
Turner Entertainment Co.
Twentieth Century Fox
The Vatican
Warner Bros.

COMPETITORS

1-800-FLOWERS.COM
Action Performance
Boyds Collection
Brown-Forman
Collectibles USA
Department 56
Enesco Group
FTD
Gerald Stevens
John Sanfilippo & Son
Knickerbocker
ML Macadamia Orchards
Sun-Diamond Growers
Zindart

HISTORICAL FINANCIALS & EMPLOYEES

Private FYE: December	Annual Growth	1989	1990	1991	1992	1993	1994	1995	1996	1997	1998
Sales ($ mil.)	8.1%	778	785	925	960	1,180	1,300	1,360	1,280	1,511	1,570
Employees	4.8%	4,900	4,900	7,200	7,500	7,500	7,500	7,700	7,500	7,500	7,500

SALES HISTORY

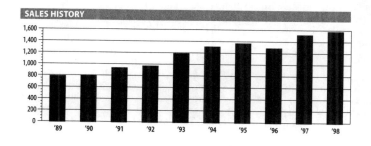

ROSENBLUTH INTERNATIONAL

OVERVIEW

Rosenbluth International makes billions by keeping its customers second. The Philadelphia-based travel company, brought to prominence by CEO Hal Rosenbluth's 1992 book *The Customer Comes Second* (after employees), is a leader in US travel sales. The company arranges travel for corporate clients from 1,300 offices in more than 25 countries. Services include En Route Service, a 24-hour traveler's aid operation; Global Executive Traveller Programme, which offers hotel discounts; and an air charter service. Rosenbluth also provides some ancillary services such as valet parking near Philadelphia International Airport. The company has jumped into the burgeoning online travel industry through its purchase of a majority stake in Biztravel.com. The company is owned by the Rosenbluth family.

Rosenbluth is noted for its cutting-edge information technology, such as its VISION data management systems and DACODA yield information system. The company focuses primarily on corporate business, which allows it to make money on corporate fees rather than airline commissions. Rosenbluth is also known for its employee-friendly management style, which the company claims leads to better customer service. It periodically holds get-togethers that combine elements of pep rallies, corporate retreats, and revival meetings. In Rosenbluth culture, meeting rooms are "thought centers," sick days are "family responsibility days," and orientation for new employees concludes with a high tea served by the CEO. The company established the salmon as its corporate mascot to honor its contrarian philosophy of "swimming against the current."

HISTORY

In 1892 Marcus Rosenbluth began selling immigration packages from his storefront shop to neighbors in Philadelphia's Brewerytown. After collecting $50 in various currencies, he arranged passage for an immigrant family's European relative to Ellis Island, often greeting the American-to-be personally and helping complete forms in the new language.

Rosenbluth's travel company rode out the ups and downs of two world wars and the emerging commercial airline industry. By the time Rosenbluth's great-grandson Hal Rosenbluth came aboard in 1974, the mostly consumer leisure travel agency was making just over $20 million a year. In the year of airline deregulation (1978), a lightbulb came on as Hal Rosenbluth observed reservation agents working on the company's corporate accounts (about $5 million). He soon demoted himself from vice president to reservations agent and began steering the company toward corporate accounts.

Prior to deregulation, airlines focused on service; fares were regulated by law and rarely changed. Businesses were mostly interested in who could deliver their tickets the fastest. With deregulation, fares changed with dizzying frequency. Yield management replaced service. Travelers needed help sorting through the confusion, and Rosenbluth saw the opportunity to meet their needs.

In the early 1980s, accounts with Bethlehem Steel and DuPont helped Rosenbluth gain a national presence. A less than ecstatic reception in Atlanta in 1985 (the year Hal Rosenbluth became president) motivated the company to upgrade its high-tech pricing and reservations system and lure corporate accounts with promises of savings and good service. In 1988 Rosenbluth sought to grow overseas by forming Rosenbluth International Alliance (RIA), a network of independent business travel agencies.

In 1992 the company took flight when Hal Rosenbluth's book (and company) attracted a national following. Rosenbluth abandoned RIA in 1993 (buying some of the businesses and setting up new ones) when it found it could not control the quality of service it offered to multinationals. Crunched by low air fares, the company began reorganizing operations in 1994 along the lines of a family farm, breaking up the company into 100-plus independent branches serving specific clients and regions. It also laid off about 10% of its workers.

In 1996 the company geared itself for global growth by forming a strategic alliance with The Sabre Group to integrate the two companies' online reservations systems.

In 1998 Rosenbluth bought Philips Reisbureau, the travel agency owned by Dutch giant Philips Electronics. The purchase earned Rosenbluth another $200 million a year in airline ticket sales. Also that year Hal Rosenbluth (along with Diane McFerrin Peters, who collaborated on his earlier book) published another leadership book titled *Good Company: Caring as Fiercely as You Compete*. In 1999 the company teamed with Discovery Communications to create and market trips inspired by shows on Discovery networks Animal Planet, Travel Channel, TLC, and Discovery Channel.

Chairman and CEO: Hal F. Rosenbluth
President and COO: Alex Wasilov
SVP and CFO: Robert M. Infarinato
VP Operations and Organizational Development:
Kathy Veit
VP Business Development: Ron DiLeo
VP Business Development: Robert McGurk
VP Business Development: R. Timothy Small
**Acting VP Business Development, Europe, Middle
East, Africa, India, Australia, New Zealand:**
Pieter Reider
VP and Chief Travel Scientist:
Danamichele Brennan O'Brien
VP and Corporate Controller: Jeff Petrick
VP Human Resources Development: Cecily Carel
VP Marketing and Chief Information Officer:
Neal Bibeau
**VP Multinational Accounts, Sales, and Supplier
Relations:** Joe Terrion
VP Multinational Accounts and Sales: Linda Ritter
VP Supplier Relations: Michael Boult
VP, Asia Pacific: Edward Lau
VP, Latin America: Enrique Felgueres Jr.

LOCATIONS

HQ: 2401 Walnut St., Philadelphia, PA 19103
Phone: 215-977-4000   **Fax:** 215-977-4028
Web site: http://www.rosenbluth.com

PRODUCTS/OPERATIONS

Selected Services
Air charter
Airport (on-site travel agencies; 3 locations)
Airport Valet Parking (Philadelphia)
Biztravel.com (majority stake; Internet travel sales for
business customers)
En Route (24-hour emergency telephone)
Global Executive Traveller Programme (hotel discounts)
The Rivery (corporate retreat)
Total Client Satisfaction Center (customer service)

COMPETITORS

American Express
Carlson Wagonlit
Japan Travel Bureau
Maritz
WorldTravel

HISTORICAL FINANCIALS & EMPLOYEES

Private FYE: December	Annual Growth	1989	1990	1991	1992	1993	1994	1995	1996	1997	1998
Sales ($ mil.)	3.0%	—	—	—	—	—	—	3,200	3,500	4,000	3,500
Employees	0.0%	—	—	—	—	—	—	—	4,500	4,500	4,500

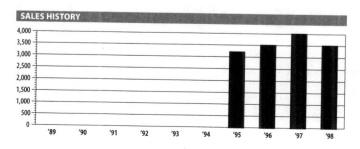

SALES HISTORY

ROTARY INTERNATIONAL

OVERVIEW

The rotary phone may be gone, but Rotary International is still going strong. The Evanston, Illinois-based service organization has a membership of nearly 1.2 million (predominantly men, although women are its fastest-growing segment) in about 30,000 clubs across 161 countries. With the motto "Service Above Self" as its banner, Rotary International is active in addressing a variety of issues including AIDS, hunger, and polio. Through the not-for-profit Rotary Foundation, the organization invests $90 million each year in international education and humanitarian programs (funds are raised through voluntary contributions). Rotary International also sponsors Interact clubs for secondary school students, as well as a network of about 6,500 Rotaract clubs for members ages 18-30.

Membership in Rotary clubs is by invitation only. Each club strives to include one representative from each business, profession, and institution in its community. Governed by a 19-member board, the organization maintains offices worldwide.

Along with other service organizations, Rotary International has been confronted with a new issue — social and attitudinal trends that have made it more difficult to attract new members. While Rotary International has fared better than some counterparts, a decline in civic-mindedness and the fact that corporations no longer stress membership in service organizations present new challenges for the organization.

HISTORY

On February 23, 1905, lawyer Paul Harris met with three friends in an office in Chicago's Unity Building. Inspired by the fellowship and tolerance of his boyhood home in Wallingford, Vermont, Harris proposed organizing a men's club to meet periodically for the purpose of camaraderie and making business contacts. The new endeavor was organized as the Rotary Club of Chicago (the name arose from the club's custom of rotating its meeting place) and had 30 members by the end of the year.

As additional clubs followed, the organization assumed its role as a civic and service organization (the installation of public comfort stations in Chicago's City Hall was one of its first projects). At the first convention of the National Association of Rotary Clubs in 1910, Harris was elected president. International clubs soon followed, and by 1921 there were Rotary clubs on each continent.

In 1932, while struggling to revive a company with financial difficulties, Rotarian Herbert Taylor devised a statement of business ethics that later became the Rotarian mantra. Taylor's "4-Way Test" consisted of the following questions: "Is it the truth? Is it fair to all concerned? Will it build goodwill and better friendships? Will it be beneficial to all concerned?"

During WWI Rotary clubs promoted war relief and peace fund efforts. Following WWII the clubs assisted in efforts to aid refugees and prisoners of war. The extent of Rotarian involvement in international issues became clear when 49 members assisted in drafting the United Nations Charter in 1945.

The first significant contributions to The Rotary Foundation followed Harris' death in 1947. These funds formed the bedrock for the foundation's programs, and in 1965 the foundation created its Matching Grants and Group Study Exchange programs. Rotary International also welcomed younger members in the 1960s by creating its Interact and Rotaract clubs in 1962 and 1968, respectively.

The largest meeting of Rotarians occurred in 1978 when almost 40,000 members attended the organization's Tokyo convention. But controversy was fast approaching the male-only organization. In 1978 a California Rotary club defied the male-only requirement and admitted two women. Claiming that the club had violated the organization's constitution, Rotary International revoked the club's charter. A lengthy court battle ensued, and a series of appeals landed the issue on the docket of the US Supreme Court. In 1987 the court ruled that the all-male requirement was discriminatory. Two years later, Rotary International officially did away with its all-male status.

In the 1990s membership in Rotary clubs grew, but at a slower pace than in the organization's past. Mary Wolfenberger was appointed the organization's first female CFO in 1993 (resigned 1997). In 1998 Rotary International joined with the United Nations to launch a series of humanitarian service projects in developing areas. In 1999 the organization spearheaded events to help flood victims in North Carolina and refugees in the Balkans.

President: Carlo Ravizza
VP: Abraham I. Gordon
Chairman, The Rotary Foundation: Bill Huntly
Treasurer: William D. Boyd
Controller: Laurie Carami
Director Corporate Services: Mark A. Garazaglia
Director Human Resources: C. Engblom
President-Elect: Frank J. Devlyn

LOCATIONS

HQ: 1 Rotary Center, 1560 Sherman Ave.,
Evanston, IL 60201
Phone: 847-866-3000   **Fax:** 847-866-9732
Web site: http://www.rotary.org

PRODUCTS/OPERATIONS

Selected Issues Addressed
AIDS
Drug-abuse prevention
Environment
Family
Hunger
Literacy
Polio
Potable water
Urban violence prevention
Youth

Selected Programs
Educational programs
  Ambassadorial Scholarships
  Group Study Exchange (GSE)
  Rotary Friendship Exchange
  Rotary Grants for University Teachers
Humanitarian grants
  Carl P. Miller Discovery Grants
  Grants for Rotary Volunteers
  Health, Hunger and Humanity (3-H)
  Matching Grants
  New Opportunities Grants
  Peace Program Grants
  PolioPlus Program

HISTORICAL FINANCIALS & EMPLOYEES

Not-for-profit FYE: June	Annual Growth	1989	1990	1991	1992	1993	1994	1995	1996	1997	1998
Sales ($ mil.)	9.9%	31	40	46	51	52	59	60	62	72	73
Employees	(2.2%)	487	532	—	554	617	450	350	400	400	400

SALES HISTORY

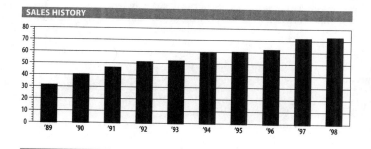

ROUNDY'S, INC.

OVERVIEW

Yippee-ti-yi-yo! Roundy's has rounded up a herd of independent grocers and is supplying them with name-brand and private-label food and general merchandise. The Pewaukee, Wisconsin-based wholesaler is a cooperative of nearly 60 members, which operate about 120 supermarkets primarily in Wisconsin, but also in Illinois. Roundy's also distributes to nearly 700 other independent grocery stores in 12 states throughout the Midwest and South. (Co-op operations account for nearly 40% of sales.) Roundy's offers its members and customer stores a host of support services, including accounting and inventory control, advertising, and store financing. Co-op members own all of the voting shares (about 72% of the total company); employees and other investors control the rest.

Roundy's also owns about 20 supermarkets, more than half of which are Pick 'n Save or Park & Save warehouse stores offering complete food and general merchandise lines at discounted prices. The rest are limited assortment Mor For Less stores and conventional supermarkets (under the Buy Low Foods, Park & Shop, and Price Less banners).

HISTORY

Migration from the eastern US and overseas was boosting Milwaukee's ranks when William Smith, Judson Roundy, and Sidney Hauxhurst formed grocery wholesaler Smith, Roundy & Co. in 1872. Smith left the firm in 1878 for his first of two terms as Wisconsin's governor, and William Peckham joined the enterprise, which was then renamed Roundy, Peckham & Co. Two years later Charles Dexter joined the company, by then operating in five midwestern states and running a manufacturing business. An 1892 fire in Milwaukee destroyed the firm's headquarters, but within a week it had a new office and was back in operation.

The wholesaler became Roundy, Peckham & Dexter Co. in 1902, following the death of Hauxhurst (Roundy died in 1907). The company introduced its first private-label product — salt — in 1922. In 1929 Dexter (then 84) came up with a plan to further market the Roundy's name by offering cooking demonstrations. Cookbooks handed out to attendees encouraged them to buy Roundy's-brand goods.

Roy Johnson, who joined the company in 1912 as a "sample boy," was named president near the end of the Depression. In the 1940s the wholesaler acquired smaller companies in the region. The company became Roundy's in 1952 when Roundy, Peckham & Dexter was bought by a group comprising hundreds of Wisconsin grocery retailers. Johnson remained head of the new company until his death in a car wreck in 1962. James Aldrich led the company for the next 11 years.

In 1970 Roundy's started Insurance Planners, which offered insurance to retailers. Vincent Little became president of the company in 1973. Two years later Roundy's began a real estate subsidiary (Ronco Realty) and opened its first Pick 'n Save Warehouse Foods store. It offered a limited selection and minimal service but still drew large recession-era crowds with its low prices.

The company expanded in the 1980s through the purchase of distributors in Indiana, Michigan, Ohio, and Wisconsin. The acquisitions included Cardinal Food Group in 1984 and Viking Foods in 1985. Expansion hurt profits, and dividends were suspended in 1984 and 1985. In the late 1980s several Pick 'n Save stores opened throughout Wisconsin and other midwestern states. Owners grew suspicious of Little's accounting practices and the special treatment given a Roundy's-owned store run by his son, and in 1986 they forced him out of his president and CEO positions. John Dickson replaced him.

By 1994 Pick 'n Save had vastly upgraded its image — one store sold $1,000 cognac and featured an $18,000 cappuccino machine. However, sales dropped off for the third straight year. Roundy's and rival wholesaler Spartan Stores announced merger plans in late 1994 but called off the deal seven weeks later. COO Gerald Lestina was named CEO in 1995, replacing Dickson, who continued as chairman. Dickson died later that year.

Roundy's did not pay its members a dividend in 1995 as it made an effort to offset losses in Michigan and Ohio. To ease those losses, in 1997 the company closed 12 poorly performing stores in those states and merged its other out-of-state facilities. A year later a fire destroyed its Evansville, Indiana, warehouse; the company rebuilt the facility in 1999. Also in 1999 Roundy's purchased three supermarkets in Indiana from Kroger and The John C. Groub Company. It also agreed to buy two grocery chains, Mega Marts and Ultra Mart, which together operate 24 Pick n' Save stores, mainly in Wisconsin.

President and CEO: Gerald F. Lestina, age 56, $494,000 pay
VP, Real Estate: Roger W. Alswager, age 50
VP, Advertising: Londell J. Behm, age 48
VP, Wholesale: Ralph D. Beketic, age 52, $236,600 pay
VP, Administration: David C. Busch, age 50
VP, Secretary and Treasurer: Edward G. Kitz, age 45
VP, Planning and Information Services:
Charles H. Kosmaler Jr., age 55
VP, Human Resources: Debra A. Lawson, age 43
VP, Distribution: John E. Paterson, age 51
VP and CFO: Robert D. Ranus, age 58, $295,750 pay
VP, Sales and Development: Michael J. Schmitt, age 50, $208,000 pay
VP, Marketing: Marion H. Sullivan, age 52, $223,600 pay
Auditors: Deloitte & Touche LLP

LOCATIONS

HQ: 23000 Roundy Dr., Pewaukee, WI 53072
Phone: 414-547-7999 **Fax:** 414-547-4540
Web site: http://www.roundys.com

PRODUCTS/OPERATIONS

1998 Sales

	% of total
Independent retailers	50
Co-op members	39
Company-owned stores	11
Total	**100**

Selected Private and Controlled Labels
Buyers' Choice
Old Time
Roundy's
Shurfine

Product Lines
Bakery goods
Dairy products
Dry groceries
Fresh produce
Frozen foods
General merchandise
Meats

Selected Services
Centralized bakery
purchasing
Financing
Group advertising
Insurance
Inventory control
Merchandising
Ordering assistance
Point-of-sale support
Pricing programs
Purchasing reports
Real estate services
Retail accounting
Retail training
Store development
Store engineering

COMPETITORS

A&P
Albertson's
Associated Wholesale
Grocers
Central Grocers
Cooperative
Certified Grocers Midwest
Costco Companies
Dominick's
Eagle Food
Fleming Companies

GSC Enterprises
Hy-Vee
IGA
Kmart
Kroger
Meijer
Nash Finch
Spartan Stores
SUPERVALU
Topco Associates
Wal-Mart

HISTORICAL FINANCIALS & EMPLOYEES

Cooperative FYE: December	Annual Growth	1989	1990	1991	1992	1993	1994	1995	1996	1997	1998
Sales ($ mil.)	0.4%	—	2,501	2,534	2,491	2,480	2,462	2,488	2,579	2,611	2,579
Net income ($ mil.)	6.9%	—	7	7	7	8	7	9	10	11	12
Income as % of sales	—	—	0.3%	0.3%	0.3%	0.3%	0.3%	0.4%	0.4%	0.4%	0.5%
Employees	(0.8%)	—	5,520	5,300	5,088	4,884	4,775	4,839	5,481	5,071	5,193

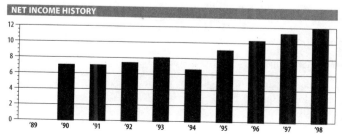

NET INCOME HISTORY

1998 FISCAL YEAR-END

Debt ratio: 36.8%
Return on equity: 9.8%
Cash ($ mil.): 72
Current ratio: 1.36
Long-term debt ($ mil.): 73

RUSSELL STOVER CANDIES INC.

OVERVIEW

What do Barbie, Snoopy, and peanut butter and jelly have in common? They've all played a role in the revitalization of Russell Stover Candies, the largest maker of boxed chocolates in the US. The Kansas City, Missouri-based company (the #3 confectioner in the US, after Hershey and Mars) now produces individually wrapped sweets, including candy bars and peanut butter and jelly cups — ideal for Halloween, a holiday previously ignored by the boxed chocolatier. Its Whitman's affiliate makes Russell Stover's best-selling assortment, the famous Whitman's Sampler. (Most of the company's sales come from various samplers.)

Russell Stover also makes Pangburn's candy, including the Millionaires brand.

Some treats are adorned by licensed characters such as Barbie, Elvis, Looney Tunes, and the Peanuts gang. The delectables are sold in supermarkets, card and gift shops, drugstores, mass merchandisers, and about 50 Russell Stover Candies retail stores. Although Halloween is the biggest selling season for candy makers, it is only Russell Stover's third-biggest holiday, after Christmas and Valentine's Day. Co-presidents Tom and Scott Ward and their mother and sister own the company.

HISTORY

Russell William Stover began selling Mrs. Stover's Bungalow Candies with his wife, Clara, in 1923. Russell had more than 10 years of experience in the candy industry, including a 1921-23 partnership with Christian Nelson, who created the I-Scream bar (chocolate-coated ice cream). Russell changed the name to Eskimo Pie, and the two did well selling the patented item until look-alikes started popping up; the patent was eventually declared invalid, and Russell sold his interest and moved to Denver.

There the Stovers' homemade candies were an instant hit, and by 1925 they were selling their candies in seven local stores. That year they opened candy factories in Denver and in Kansas City, Missouri, to keep up with demand. With Russell as president and Clara as VP, Mrs. Stover's flourished through the rest of the decade and even managed to turn a profit during the lean times of the Depression. A third factory opened in Lincoln, Nebraska, in 1942, and the company's name was changed to Russell Stover Candies a year later.

By the time Russell died in 1954, the company was selling about 11 million pounds of candy a year through about 2,000 department stores and 40 Russell Stover Candies shops. The Stover family and partners carried on until 1960, when they sold the business to Louis Ward, then president of the Ward Paper Box Co., for about $7 million.

Evidently Ward enjoyed boxing chocolates more than making boxes, because he took the company national, expanding sales on the East Coast and building a factory in Clarksville, Virginia, in 1969. Ward maintained the use of higher-cost small-batch production processes and continued, in many cases, using recipes unchanged since the 1940s. The firm used marketing to sweeten its sales in the 1970s and 1980s, introducing heart-shaped boxes, cherry cordials, and miniature chocolates. By the mid-1980s Russell Stover was the king of boxed chocolates; content with their sales, candy-bar makers had conceded the markets for gift and seasonal chocolates. The company soon diversified into a wide range of Easter items, including chocolate-covered creme eggs and Easter basket gift packs. In the late 1980s Russell Stover began roasting its own nuts and established a candy school.

In 1993 the senior Ward retired after suffering a stroke, and his sons stepped in to run things. That year the company acquired Whitman's Candies, a 152-year-old confectioner with about $85 million in annual sales. Candy-bar sales had flattened in the early 1990s, and big players such as Mars and Hershey began going after Russell Stover's market by introducing boxed chocolate products and dressing up products in seasonal colors and shapes.

The Ward brothers fought back. They began licensing the rights to use artwork and cartoon characters in 1994 and opened new plants in Abilene (1995) and Iola, Kansas (1997). The firm introduced bagged candy the following year.

Russell Stover acquired the trademarks of bankrupt Pangburn Candy Co., makers of Millionaires-brand boxed chocolates, for $4.5 million in 1999. It also completed a 462,000-sq.-ft. candy plant and kitchen in Corsicana, Texas, the company's fourth new plant in three years. In November 1999 Russell Stover abandoned its offer to buy the Rocky Mountain Chocolate Factory candy chain after being unable to agree on a price.

Chairman, Co-President and CEO: Thomas S. Ward
Co-President and VP Finance: Scott H. Ward
CFO: Dick Masinton
VP Manufacturing: Robert G. Maack
Director Personnel (HR): Robinn S. Weber

LOCATIONS

HQ: 4900 Oaks St., Kansas City, MO 64112
Phone: 816-842-9240   **Fax:** 816-842-5593

PRODUCTS/OPERATIONS

Selected Licensed Characters

Barbie
Batman and Robin
Bugs Bunny
Daffy Duck
DC Comics

Elvis
Looney Tunes
Peanuts
Super Heroes

Selected Products

Almond Delights
Assorted (Caramels,
  Chocolates, Cremes,
  and Whips)
Assortments (Clara Stover,
  Dark Chocolate, Fussy
  Chocolate, Milk
  Chocolate, and Truffle)
Butter Nut Toffee
Caramel & Granola
Caramel & Peanuts
Cherry Blimps
Cherry Cordials
Chocolate Covered Nuts
Coconut Clusters
Cookies N Cream Bar
English Caramel Tin
French Chocolate Mints
Fruit Flavored Jellies
Fudge (Chocolate,
  Pecan, Vanilla Pecan,
  and Walnut)
George Washington
  Cherries
German Chocolate Fudge
Home Fashioned Favorites
Honey Roasted
  Peanut Delight
MC Caramel Bar
Medallions (Almond,
  Peanut, and Pecan)
Messenger Boys

Millionaires (regular
  and sugar free)
Miniature Chocolates
Mint Patties
Nut Chewy & Crisp
PB & Grape Jelly Cup
PB & Red Raspberry Cup
Peanut Delights
Peanuts Caramel &
  Granola Peg Bag
Peanuts Caramel &
  Peanuts Peg Bag
Peanuts Milk Chocolate
  Caramel & Granola Bag
Pecan Delights
Pectin Jelly Beans
Rocky Mallow Box
Sampler (Assorted
  Chocolates, Assorted
  Creams, Chocolate
  Covered Nuts, Dark
  Chocolate, Milk
  Chocolate, and Truffles)
Soft Creamy Caramel
  Squares
Sugar Free MC Pecan
  Delights
Sugar Free Pecan
  Delight Bar
Toffee Stick Box
Truffle Golf Balls
Vermont Pecan Roll

COMPETITORS

Archibald Candy
Cadbury Schweppes
Campbell Soup
Chase General
Ferrero
Hershey
Lindt & Sprungli
Mars

Mr. Bulky Treats & Gifts
Nestlé
Rocky Mountain Chocolate
See's Candies
Sherwood Brands
Tootsie Roll
World's Finest Chocolate

HISTORICAL FINANCIALS & EMPLOYEES

Private FYE: February	Annual Growth	1990	1991	1992	1993	1994	1995	1996	1997	1998	1999
Sales ($ mil.)	18.4%	—	—	—	—	—	—	—	442	510	620
Employees	3.3%	—	—	—	—	—	—	—	5,900	6,000	6,300

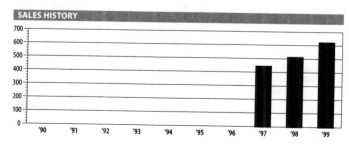

SALES HISTORY

Russell Stover

SALVATION ARMY USA

The name Salvation Army may only ring a bell with you around Christmas, but the Salvation Army USA is always working. Active as a church and a charity, the organization serves more than 27 million people each year. The Alexandria, Virginia-based organization's many programs help alcoholics, drug addicts, battered women, the elderly, the homeless, people with AIDS, prison inmates, teenagers, and the unemployed. It also provides disaster relief in the US and abroad. The Salvation Army usually tops the list of US not-for-profits in terms of donations received: Including gifts and food, the contributions hover above $1 billion annually.

Along with promoting charity, the Salvation Army seeks to save souls. As an evangelical church, it preaches the message of salvation through Jesus Christ. Before joining the organization and becoming a soldier (a lay member), one must sign an agreement known as the "Articles of War," a commitment to the avoidance of gambling, debt, and profanity and to abstention from alcohol, tobacco, and other recreational drugs. The organization counts some 450,000 people worldwide as soldiers.

Officers (the ordained clergy) are expected to wear their uniforms at all times and to work full-time for the Salvation Army. They receive no salary; instead, they are compensated with a housing and clothing allowance, a car, 80% of their medical expenses, and a limited stipend.

The Salvation Army USA is only one of scores of national Salvation Army organizations around the world, which report to the group's global leader, General Paul Rader, at its international headquarters in the UK.

HISTORY

William Booth (1829-1912) started preaching the gospel as a Wesleyan Methodist in the UK, but the church expelled him because he insisted on preaching outside and to everyone, including the poor. In 1865 he moved to the slums of London's East End and attracted large crowds with his volatile sermons. Opposition to his message of universal salvation for drunks, thieves, prostitutes, and gamblers often caused riots. In fact, the first women in the organization wore bonnets designed with a dual purpose in mind — warmth and protection from flying objects.

At a meeting in 1878, a sign was used referring to the "Salvation Army." Booth adopted the reference as both the name and the style of his organization. Members became soldiers, evangelists were officers, and Booth was referred to as "General." Prayers became knee drills, and contributions were called cartridges.

The Salvation Army marched across the Atlantic to the US in 1880, led by seven women and one man. Women have always played an active role in the Salvation Army, both as officers and soldiers. Booth's wife, Catherine Mumford, was a leading suffragette, and Booth advocated equal rights for women.

In 1891 a crab pot was placed on a San Francisco street to collect donations, with a sign reading "Keep the Pot Boiling." The idea led to the Salvation Army's annual Christmas kettle program.

During WWI the organization became famous for the doughnuts that it served the doughboys fighting on the front lines. After some internal dissension, the Salvation Army took its only public political stance in 1928 with the endorsement of Herbert Hoover for his support of Prohibition during his presidential campaign. The charity opened its first home for alcoholics in 1939, in Detroit.

After WWII the Salvation Army began using such radio and TV programs as *Heartbeat Theater* and *Army of Stars* to spread its message.

Over the years the Salvation Army has provided assistance to victims of hurricanes, floods, and earthquakes. Volunteers rendered almost 70,000 service hours in the aftermath of the Oklahoma City bombing in 1995, counseling more than 1,600 victims and family members, helping with funeral arrangements, and providing food, clothing, and travel assistance. Indicative of the organization's readiness and extensive reach, its volunteers were helping victims in Guam within minutes of the 1997 Korean Air plane crash.

The Salvation Army was quickly on the scene after a Jonesboro, Arkansas, shooting incident in 1998 when four students and one teacher were killed by fellow students. Its mobile canteens served 800 lunches and 700 dinners to students, parents, teachers, and others in the hours following the tragedy. Later that year the organization received the largest donation in its history — $80 million from Joan Kroc, wife of McDonald's co-founder Ray Kroc.

OFFICERS

General (International Director): Paul A. Rader
Chairman National Advisory Board:
Steven S. Reinemund
Commissioner (National Commander):
Robert A. Watson
Colonel (National Chief Secretary): John M. Bate
Lieutenant Colonel (National Treasurer and Secretary Business Administration): Larry E. Bosh
Lieutenant Colonel (National Secretary for Personnel):
Myrtle V. Ryder
Commissioner (Southern Territorial Commander):
John Busby
Commissioner (Western Territorial Commander):
David Edwards
Commissioner (Central Territorial Commander):
Harold D. Hinson
Commissioner (Eastern Territorial Commander):
Doris Noland
Commissioner (Eastern Territorial Commander):
Joseph J. Noland
Commissioner (National President Women's Organizations): Alice Watson
Auditors: PricewaterhouseCoopers LLP

LOCATIONS

HQ: 615 Slaters Ln., Alexandria, VA 22314
Phone: 703-684-5500 **Fax:** 703-684-3478
Web site: http://www.salvationarmyusa.org

PRODUCTS/OPERATIONS

Selected Services
Adult rehabilitation centers
Christmas sharing (aid for needy families, the elderly, and homeless people)
Community centers
Counseling
Day care centers for adults and children
Disaster services
Domestic violence programs
Emergency family services (financial assistance)
Group homes
Home League (women's programs)
Homeless shelters
Inmate/prisoner services (spiritual material, Bible courses, and job training programs)
Job referrals
League of Mercy (visitation program to correctional facilities, hospitals, nursing homes, and private residences; distribution of toilet articles, periodicals, and Bibles in institutions)
Maternal services
Substance abuse services (detoxification, residential and outpatient care)
Summer camps (for low-income children and senior citizens)
Summer reading programs
Thrift stores
Tutoring at-risk students
Youth services (Boys' and Girls' Clubs)

COMPETITORS

Goodwill

HISTORICAL FINANCIALS & EMPLOYEES

Not-for-profit FYE: September	Annual Growth	1989	1990	1991	1992	1993	1994	1995	1996	1997	1998
Sales ($ mil.)	8.0%	—	—	1,216	1,287	1,398	1,355	1,421	2,070	2,525	2,078
Employees	0.2%	—	—	—	—	—	39,591	38,999	44,626	40,770	39,883

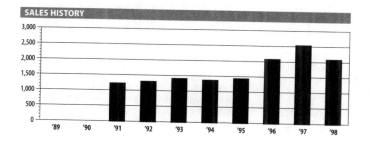

SALES HISTORY

S&P COMPANY

OVERVIEW

For those who consider Coors Light or Miller Genuine Draft too froufrou, there are the brews of S&P. Based in Mill Valley, California, S&P (no, not the financial service) owns a stable of nonpremium beers through its Pabst Brewing Company. Its brands include Pabst, Pearl, Falstaff, and Olympia. The company added Old Milwaukee, Heileman's Old Style, Schlitz, and Colt 45 to its ice chest with its 1999 purchase of Stroh Brewery's brands. S&P also owns commercial and residential real estate in California.

S&P's founder, Paul Kalmanovitz, bought past-their-prime breweries and rode the brands down, allocating few resources to upgrading breweries, developing new products, or advertising the old ones. Instead, he used the breweries' cash to buy real estate. Of the breweries S&P bought, only a Pearl plant in Texas and an Olympia plant in Washington are still brewing. (It also has a plant in China.) Most of S&P's production is contracted out to other brewers, such as Miller Brewing, though the company itself offers contract and specialty brewing services from its Pearl brewery.

Since the deaths of Kalmanovitz and his wife, Lydia, S&P has been run by former Howard Hughes counsel William Bitting, the trustee for a charitable trust. If a challenge to Lydia's will fails and the trust takes ownership of S&P as she directed, federal law will require the trust to give up control of the company within five years.

HISTORY

Born in Poland in 1905, Paul Kalmanovitz went to sea and jumped ship in Philadelphia in 1926. After moving to California, he worked as a handyman and driver for film magnate Louis B. Mayer and then bought an auto shop and a bar. During WWII, he and partner Nathan Sherry (the "S" in S&P) bought bars around Union Station in Los Angeles (a major transit point for troops). Kalmanovitz bought out Sherry and bought restaurants and nightclubs before buying his first brewery, bankrupt Maier Brewing Co., in 1958. In 1971 he bought (and then dismantled) General Brewing.

Falstaff Brewing caught his eye in 1975. Falstaff began in 1917 when Joseph Griesedieck bought Forest Park Brewing Company. Falstaff later acquired other breweries, including Fred Krug Brewery (1935), Narragansett (1966), and Ballantine (1972). Once S&P took control, it cut Falstaff's annual advertising budget from $2.6 million to $23,000 and later closed its breweries.

S&P bought the Pearl brewery in 1978. Pearl was founded in 1885 when several San Antonio businessmen bought City Brewery and began producing Pearl beer. The name was changed to Pearl Brewing Company in 1952, and in 1961 it acquired Goetz Brewing and its Country Club Malt Liquor and Goetz Pale Near Beer brands.

In a 1985 takeover, Kalmanovitz acquired Pabst, which had begun in 1844 when Jacob Best and his sons began making beer in Milwaukee as Best & Company. Phillip Best's son-in-law Frederick Pabst joined in 1864, and by 1868 Best was the biggest brewer in Milwaukee. It was renamed Pabst Brewing Co. in 1889 and was the US's #1 beer through the turn of the century, with sales throughout the US, across Europe, and as far afield as China. During Prohibition, Pabst sold tonic, malt syrup, and cheese. Fred Pabst, Frederick's son, bought new equipment and merged with Premier Malt Products Company when Prohibition was winding down. By the 1970s Pabst was the US's #3 brewer, its decline attributed to its failure to introduce new brands. In 1983 Pabst acquired Olympia Brewing Co. (founded 1896).

Kalmanovitz plowed the profits of his eroding beer interests into real estate until he died in 1987. His wife, Lydia, died seven years later. After her death, relatives attempted to gain larger shares of the estate, charging, among other things, that Lutz Issleib and William Bitting (trustees of the Kalmanovitz's) had influenced her to change her will and had kept her isolated.

Financial information obtained from court filings revealed that Pabst was losing money. S&P closed the antiquated Milwaukee plant in 1996 and farmed all Pabst production out to rival brewer Stroh, throwing about 400 Pabst workers out of their jobs. That year the company also stopped paying retirement benefits for more than 700 retirees. (After a class-action suit, S&P agreed in 1998 to pay $66 million to a pension fund over the next 15 years.) Also in 1998 Pabst chairman Issleib retired, and S&P moved the making of Pabst back to Milwaukee via a five-year contract with Miller Brewing.

Meanwhile, members of the Kalmanovitz family appealed the dismissal of their challenge to Lydia's will. In 1999 S&P bought several beverage brands and a Pennsylvania brewery from Stroh in a $500 million deal. Miller Brewing bought two Stroh brands (Henry Weinhard's, Mickeys), as well as the Olde English 800 and Hamm's brands from Pabst.

Co-Chairman, CEO, EVP, and General Counsel;
  President, Pabst: William M. Bitting
Co-Chairman, SVP, and Secretary: Bernard Orsi
VP Finance, Pearl Brewing: Barry Harris
Director Industrial Relations, Pearl Brewing and Pabst
  Brewing: Gary Lewitzke
Director Quality Assurance: Ken Tucker

LOCATIONS

HQ: 100 Shoreline Hwy., Bldg. B, Ste. 395,
  Mill Valley, CA 94941
Phone: 415-332-0550   Fax: 415-332-0567

PRODUCTS/OPERATIONS

Products

Falstaff
  Ballantine Premium
    Lager
  Falstaff Beer
  Falstaff NA
  Haffenreffer Malt Liquor
Olympia
  Olympia Dry
  Olympia Genuine Draft
  Olympia Gold Light
  Olympia Ice
  Olympia Lager
  Olympia Light Lager
Pabst
  Bull Ice
  Champale
  Colt 45 Malt Liquor
  Goebel
  Heileman's Old Style
  Lone Star
  McSorley's
  Old Milwaukee
  Old Style
  Pabst Blue Ribbon

Pabst Cold Filtered Ice
  Draft
Pabst Genuine Draft
Pabst Light
Pabst NA
Rainier
Red Bull Malt Liquor
St. Ides
Schaefer
Schlitz Malt Liquor
Schmidt's
Silver Thunder
Special Export
Stroh's
Woodchuck Draft Cider
Pearl
  Country Club Malt
    Liquor
  Goetz Pale
  NA
  Pearl Light
  Pearl Premium Lager
  Texas Pride Lager

COMPETITORS

Adolph Coors
Anheuser-Busch
Miller Brewing

HISTORICAL FINANCIALS & EMPLOYEES

Private FYE: June	Annual Growth	1990	1991	1992	1993	1994	1995	1996	1997	1998	1999
Estimated sales ($ mil.)	11.3%	—	—	566	628	595	600	550	550	500	1,200
Employees	(20.6%)	—	—	—	2,800	2,400	1,300	1,604	1,600	1,500	700

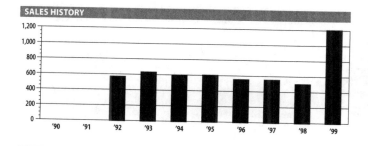

SALES HISTORY

SAS INSTITUTE INC.

OVERVIEW

"Who Dares Wins" is the motto of the British special military force, the SAS. It could also be the motto of Cary, North Carolina-based SAS Institute, the world's largest privately held software company, with 3.5 million users in 120 countries. The company makes decision support, data warehousing, and data mining software that enables corporations to gather, manage, and analyze voluminous amounts of information in order to make better business decisions. Customers such as Coca-Cola, Home Depot, and the US Environmental Protection Agency use its SAS System to find patterns in customer purchases, create mailing lists for repeat buyers, and target new business. SAS Institute also offers integrated software and support packages for such applications as financial reporting and consolidation, oil and gas analysis, clinical trials analysis, and information technology service management.

Co-founder, president, and CEO James Goodnight, who spends most mornings churning software code, continues to expand the company's product line. SAS is among industry leaders in research and development, reinvesting more than 30% of its sales. The company's customer renewal rate is 98%, although its software is licensed annually, freeing clients to walk away at the end of a year's contract.

With on-site medical care, discounted homes in a subdivision owned by Goodnight, and M&Ms for everyone on Wednesdays, SAS maintains an employee turnover rate of below 4% (the industry average is 20%). Executives say the money is better spent on perks than training new replacement workers.

Goodnight owns two-thirds of the company and fellow founder John Sall, an SVP, owns the remaining one-third.

HISTORY

SAS Institute was started in 1976 by North Carolina State University professors James Goodnight and John Sall. The two had developed their own mainframe statistical analysis system (SAS) to analyze agricultural data around the state. Its popularity grew at other southern campuses, enabling the two professors to go out on their own.

Inc. magazine named SAS one of the US's fastest-growing private companies in 1982. The company began rewriting SAS System software in 1984 to make it independent of hardware systems. While rewriting the package in C language, the company ran into a problem — none of the commercial C compilers supported the IBM 370 mainframe architecture. SAS Institute then began developing MultiVendor Architecture in C to enable the package to be hardware- and platform-independent. That year Intel sold its SYSTEM 2000 DBMS to SAS.

SAS acquired Lattice Inc., a prominent maker of C language code translators, in 1986 to assist in the adaptation of SAS software to the PC environment. The next year the complete version of SAS System for the PC was released, and in 1988 the company unveiled systems for UNIX platforms.

In 1989 SAS released JMP software for the Apple Macintosh, developed a cooperative software program with IBM, and began offering consulting services. By 1990 the company had completed its redesign of all SAS System software so it would be completely hardware-independent in the mainframe and minicomputer platforms. SAS Institute also introduced a new menu-driven, task-oriented interface to the SAS System that enabled access to those with limited computer experience.

The company released its first vertical market product for the pharmaceuticals and biotechnology industries in 1992, and the next year it introduced software for building customized executive information systems. In 1994 SAS released a version of its SAS/Access communications software, which ties its data analysis tools more closely to client/server applications. By that year almost all of the top 100 companies in the *FORTUNE* 500 had site license agreements for SAS software.

In 1996 SAS delivered Orlando II, a version of the SAS System with considerably expanded data warehousing capabilities. The following year it acquired Abacus Concepts' StatView software, a market-leading statistical analysis program for the life sciences. It also teamed up with Hewlett-Packard to create the Data Insight and Discovery Center, a data mining lab for financial services firms seeking information about their customers.

In 1998 SAS formed an alliance with business and information technology consulting firm American Management Systems to offer customized data warehousing and decision support systems to their clients.

President and CEO: James H. Goodnight, age 56
SVP: John Sall
VP Finance: Greyson Quarles
VP Human Resources: David Russo
VP Information Systems: Charlie Dunham
VP Sales and Marketing, North America:
 Barrett R. Joyner
Director, Asia/Pacific Operations: Lee Richardson
Director, Business Solutions Division: Richard Roach
Director, Corporate Controller/Finance: David Davis
**Director, Risk-Management Center, SAS Institute
 Japan:** Peter Fuchs
Manager, Western Regional Sales and Marketing:
 Hillary Freeman

HQ: SAS Campus Dr., Cary, NC 27513
Phone: 919-677-8000   **Fax:** 919-677-4444
Web site: http://www.sas.com

SAS Institute has offices, subsidiaries, and distributors
in about 50 countries worldwide.

1998 Sales

	% of total
North America	53
Europe, Middle East & Africa	36
Asia/Pacific & Latin America	11
Total	**100**

1998 Sales

	% of total
Software licensing	95
Other	5
Total	**100**

Selected SAS System Applications
Applications development
Business planning
Claims reservation
Clinical research
Computer performance evaluation
Credit analysis
Customer relationship management
Data entry, retrieval, and management
Database marketing
Decision support
Executive information systems
Financial consolidation and reporting
Forecasting
Geographic reporting
Guided data analysis
Human resources management
Management science
Market research
Network information system management
Operations research
Performance management
Petroleum exploration and production data integration
Portfolio analysis
Project management
Quality improvement
Report writing and graphics
Risk management
Statistical and mathematical analysis

Ardent Software	Oracle
Attachmate	Progress Software
Cognos	SAP
Computer Associates	SPSS
IBM	Sybase
Inprise	System Software
Microsoft	Associates
Novell	

Private FYE: December	Annual Growth	1989	1990	1991	1992	1993	1994	1995	1996	1997	1998
Sales ($ mil.)	17.5%	206	240	295	366	420	482	562	653	750	871
Employees	11.6%	1,970	2,237	2,386	2,600	2,897	3,260	4,138	4,500	5,108	5,400

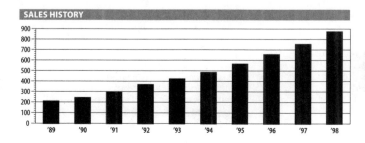

SALES HISTORY

S.C. JOHNSON & SON, INC.

OVERVIEW

The Karate Kid might use S.C. Johnson & Son's Pledge to wax on, wax off. The Racine, Wisconsin-based maker of household cleaning, insect control, personal care, and storage products has not stopped trying to polish off the competition. S.C. Johnson is one of the world's largest makers of consumer chemical specialty products, including Drano drain cleaner, Glade air freshener, Edge shaving gel, OFF! insect repellent, Pledge furniture cleaner, Raid household insecticide, Shout stain remover, and Windex cleaner. It recently introduced Allercare, a line of products that control dust mites.

S.C. Johnson's commercial products division (Johnson Wax Professional and Johnson Polymer) has been spun off as a separate private company owned by the Johnson family, SC Johnson Commercial Markets. The family has interests in Johnson International (banking, finance, and insurance) and Johnson Worldwide (camping equipment). Descendants of the founder's daughter own almost 40% of the firm. Chairman Samuel Johnson, great-grandson of the company's founder and one of the US's richest people, and his immediate family own 60% of S.C. Johnson.

HISTORY

S.C. Johnson was founded in Racine, Wisconsin, in 1886 by Samuel C. Johnson, a carpenter whose customers were as interested in his floor wax as they were in his parquet floors. Forsaking carpentry, Johnson began to manufacture floor care products. The company, named S.C. Johnson & Son in 1906, began establishing subsidiaries worldwide in 1914. By the time Johnson's son and successor, Herbert Johnson, died in 1928, annual sales were $5 million. Herbert Jr. and his sister, Henrietta Lewis, received 60% and 40% of the firm, respectively. The original section of S.C. Johnson's headquarters, designed by Frank Lloyd Wright and called "the greatest piece of 20th century architecture" in the US, was finished in 1939.

In 1954, with $45 million in annual sales, Herbert Jr.'s son Samuel Curtis Johnson joined the company as new products director. Two years later it introduced Raid, the first water-based insecticide, and soon thereafter, OFF! insect repellent. Each became a market leader. The company unsuccessfully attempted to diversify into paint, chemicals, and lawn care during the 1950s and 1960s. The home care products section prospered, however, with the introduction of Pledge aerosol furniture polish and Glade aerosol air freshener.

Samuel became president after Herbert Jr. suffered a stroke in 1965. He started a recreational products division that was bought by the Johnson family in 1986. That company went public in 1987 as Johnson Worldwide Associates, with the family retaining control. In 1975 the firm banned the use of the chlorofluorocarbons (CFCs) in its products, three years before the US government banned CFCs.

The company launched Edge shaving gel and Agree hair products in the 1970s but had few products as successful in the 1980s. It

moved into real estate with Johnson Wax Development (JWD) in the 1970s, but sold JWD's assets in the late 1980s.

S. Curtis Johnson, Samuel's son, joined the company in 1983. In 1986 S.C. Johnson bought Bugs Burger Bug Killers, moving into commercial pest control; in 1990 it entered into an agreement with Mycogen to develop biological pesticides for household use.

During the 1990s S.C. Johnson began preservation efforts on its aging Racine headquarters (listed on the National Register of Historic Places). In 1993 it bought Drackett, bringing Drano and Windex to its product roster along with increased competition from heavyweights like Procter & Gamble and Clorox. That year S.C. Johnson sold the Agree and Halsa lines to DEP. In 1996 it launched a line of water-soluble pouches for cleaning products that allow work to be done without touching hazardous chemicals. President William Perez became CEO the next year.

S.C. Johnson bought Dow Chemical's Dow-Brands unit, maker of bathroom cleaner (Dow), plastic bags (Ziploc), and plastic wrap (Saran Wrap), for $1.2 billion in 1998. It then sold off other Dow brands (cleaners Spray 'N Wash, Glass Plus, Yes, and Vivid) to the UK's Reckitt & Colman to settle antitrust issues. With wax acounting for only a small fraction of sales, it also decided to drop the mention of wax from its ads and logos.

In 1999 S.C. Johnson sold its skin care line, including Aveeno, to Johnson & Johnson. That year also brought about the introduction of two new products, Allercare (for control of dust mites) and Pledge Grab-It (electrostatically charged cleaning sheets). In late 1999 the company spun off its commercial operations as a separate private company controlled by the Johnson family.

Chairman: Samuel C. Johnson
President and CEO: William D. Perez
VC: H. Fisk Johnson
President Americas and South Asia: Joseph T. Mallof
President and Regional Director, Consumer Products Asia/Pacific: John R. Buerkle
President and Regional Director, Europe and Africa/Near East: Steven P. Stanbrook
EVP and Group Managing Director Atlantic Cluster: Pedro Cleza
EVP North American Consumer Products: David L. May
SVP Worldwide Consumer Products Research, Development and Engineering: John H. Berschied Jr.
SVP General Counsel & Secretary: David Hecker
SVP Worldwide Corporate Affairs: Jane M. Hutterly
SVP Worldwide Human Resources: Gayle P. Kosterman
SVP and CFO: W. Lee McCollum
SVP Worldwide Manufacturing & Procurement: Nico J. Meiland
VP Human Resources, North American Consumer Products: Wesley A. Coleman
VP Customer Service and Logistics Management: David C. Henry
VP and Chief Information Officer: Daniel E. Horton
VP Corporate Treasurer: William H. Van Lopik
VP Corporate Controller: Jeffrey M. Waller

LOCATIONS

HQ: 1525 Howe St., Racine, WI 53403
Phone: 414-260-2000 **Fax:** 414-260-2133
Web site: http://www.scjohnsonwax.com

S.C. Johnson & Son has operations in more than 50 countries worldwide.

Selected Countries with Manufacturing Facilities

Argentina	India	South Africa
Australia	Indonesia	South Korea
Brazil	Japan	Spain
Canada	Kenya	Taiwan
Chile	Mexico	UK
China	The Netherlands	Ukraine
Egypt	Nigeria	US
Ghana	The Philippines	Venezuela
Greece	Saudi Arabia	Vietnam

PRODUCTS/OPERATIONS

Principal North American Brand Names

Air Care
Allercare
Glade

Home Cleaning
Bathroom/Drain
　Drano
　Scrubbing Bubbles
　Soap Scum & Mildew
　Toilet Duck
　Vanish
Cleaners
　Fantastik
　Windex
Floor Care
　Armstrong
　Brite
　Fine Wood
　Future
　Glo-Coat
　Pledge
　Step Saver
Furniture Care
　Favor
　Jubilee
　Klean 'n Shine
　Pledge
Laundry/Carpet Care
　Glory
　Shout

Other Products
Brillo
End Bac
Goddard's
Lifeguard
Mr. Muscle
SC Johnson Paste Wax
Wall Power Wall Washer

Home Storage
Handi-Wrap
Saran Wrap
Slide-Loc
Ziploc

Insect Control
Insecticides
　Raid
　Raid Max
Repellents
　Deep Woods OFF!
　OFF!
　OFF! Skintastic

Personal Care
Men's Grooming Aids
　Edge
Women's Shave
　Skintimate

COMPETITORS

3M	Lilly Industries
Amway	Pactiv
Blyth Industries	Procter & Gamble
Church & Dwight	Reckitt Benckiser
Clorox	Sara Lee
Colgate-Palmolive	Shaklee
Dial	Unilever
DuPont	USA Detergents
Gillette	Yankee Candle
IWP International	

HISTORICAL FINANCIALS & EMPLOYEES

Private FYE: June	Annual Growth	1990	1991	1992	1993	1994	1995	1996	1997	1998	1999
Estimated sales ($ mil.)	3.8%	3,000	3,400	3,300	3,550	3,800	4,000	4,000	4,300	5,000	4,200
Employees	(3.4%)	13,000	13,600	13,400	13,100	13,100	13,400	12,100	12,500	13,200	9,500

SALES HISTORY

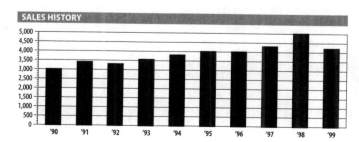

SCHNEIDER NATIONAL

Big trucks are wheeling hefty sales for Schneider National, the US's largest truckload carrier. Hauling out of Green Bay, Wisconsin, Schneider National transports customers' cargo from the Shaky Side (trucker slang for the West Coast) to the Dirty Side (the East Coast). The Schneider Van division is the most recognizable of the groups, with more than 14,000 trucks and about 40,000 trailers in bright orange wrappers (paint), providing one-way, long-haul, single-load trucking — 5,000 cargo shipments daily — throughout the US, Canada, and parts of Mexico.

The Schneider Dedicated Operations unit supplies customers with their personal Schneider fleet, including trucks, trailers, and drivers. Other divisions include Schneider Bulk (liquid chemical transport), Schneider Specialized (trailers and hauling services for unique shipments), and Schneider Intermodal (containers and trailers designed for use on rail or over the road). The company also acts as a middleman through Schneider Brokerage, which finds carriers for shippers, and Schneider Finance,

which sells and leases truck equipment.

Schneider also rides the information superhighway. A big contributor to company revenues (about 30%) is its Schneider Logistics subsidiary, which cuts shipping costs of large US and European customers by finding efficient ways to use their supply chain, shipping routes, and carriers. Schneider Logistics has its own real-time tracking system, which customers can use to find out exactly where their cargo is via Internet.

Schneider has set the industry standard with satellite-tracking systems onboard trucks, allowing dispatchers to contact drivers in minutes with the details of their next shipment. Largely nonunionized, Schneider provides its more than 20,000 employees (13,000 truckers, or "associates," as the company calls them) with incentive packages and a democratic workplace in which everyone is encouraged to make suggestions. Company owner and CEO Donald Schneider, son of the company founder, is known for hard work and humility that has kept Schneider National in the hammer lane.

A. J. "Al" Schneider bought a truck in 1935 with money earned from selling the family car. He drove the truck for three years, got another, and then leased them both to another firm. Becoming general manager of Bins Transfer & Storage in 1938, Schneider bought the company that year and changed the name to Schneider Transport & Storage. In 1944 Schneider stopped storing household goods and continued as an intrastate carrier in Wisconsin through the 1950s, transporting food and household goods. The Interstate Commerce Commission granted its first interstate license to Schneider in 1958.

Al's son Donald joined the company as general manager in 1961, and in 1962 the company dropped "Storage" from its name to become Schneider Transport. The 1960s also saw the first of many acquisitions. Donald became CEO in 1973, overseeing more acquisitions and the creation of Schneider National as a holding company for the organization. Donald also saw to the installation of computerized control systems, the first of many technical innovations Schneider would use in its trucks.

With the Motor Carrier Act's passage in 1980, restrictions eased and interstate shipping opened up. Schneider (and its competitors) saw the sky as the limit and founded Schneider Communications, a long-distance provider, in 1982. Eager to escape the

Teamsters' thrall, but choosing not to go head-to-head with the powerful union, Schneider formed Schneider National Carriers as a nonunion company out of three 1985 acquisitions, which signed on new recruits, while Schneider Transport remained unionized. Schneider focused on guaranteeing on-time delivery in the deregulated market: In 1988 Schneider became the first trucking company to install a satellite-tracking system in its trucks, setting the industry standard.

Schneider further expanded its services in the 1990s, starting with Schneider Specialized Services for carrying difficult items. By 1993 some two-thirds of *Fortune* 500 companies used Schneider, and the company formed Schneider Logistics to help companies streamline their shipping operations. It sold Schneider Communications to Frontier Communications in 1995. The company continued buying other trucking firms, mainly to acquire their drivers for its expanding fleet, and in 1998, to increase its driver retention, Schneider increased wages for experienced drivers (after competitor J.B. Hunt raised its wages in 1997).

The company expanded its operations in 1998 through the acquisition of trucking firms Landstar Poole and Buider's Transport. In 1999 Schneider acquired the glass-transportation business of A. J. Meler & Rigging.

OFFICERS

President: Donald J. Schneider
CFO: Tom Gannon
VP Human Resources: Tim Fliss
Chief Information and Logistics Officer: Chris Lofgren

LOCATIONS

HQ: 3101 S. Packerland Dr., Green Bay, WI 54313
Phone: 920-592-5100   **Fax:** 920-592-3252
Web site: http://www.schneider.com

PRODUCTS/OPERATIONS

Schneider National Products and Services

Schneider Brokerage
Dry van/refrigerated
Flatbed/open equipment

Schneider Bulk

Schneider Dedicated Operations
Logistics
Carrier management and coordination
Cross-dock management
Logistics engineering and analysis
Mode selection
Return container program
Warehousing services

Schneider Finance
Leasing
Purchasing

Schneider Intermodal
Optimodal
Truckrail

Schneider Specialized

Schneider Van

Schneider Logistics Products and Services

Carrier Management
Claims management
Load tendering
Negotiation
Payment
Performance reporting
Selection
Tracking and tracing loads

Dedicated Carriage Components
Custom-designed equipment
Customized operations solutions
Dedicated tractors and drivers
Two-way satellite communication

Freight Management Associates
Account managers
Customer accounting managers
General managers
Logistics analysts
Logistics engineers
Transportation managers

Schneider Track and Trace (STAT)

SUMIT (Schneider Utility for Managing Integrated Transportation)

Supply Chain Analysis
Carrier optimization
Carrying cost analysis
Consolidation
Cube optimization
Dedicated operations analysis
Distribution center location analysis
Dynamic route creation
Mode optimization
Static route design

COMPETITORS

Burlington Northern Santa Fe	Landstar System
Cannon Express	M.S. Carriers
Celadon	Norfolk Southern
CHR	Roadway Express
CSX	Ryder
Intrenet	Union Pacific
J. B. Hunt	Werner

HISTORICAL FINANCIALS & EMPLOYEES

Private FYE: December	Annual Growth	1989	1990	1991	1992	1993	1994	1995	1996	1997	1998
Sales ($ mil.)	15.3%	—	—	1,000	1,066	1,175	1,325	1,700	2,156	2,510	2,711
Employees	6.0%	—	—	—	12,000	13,950	15,300	15,500	17,550	16,500	17,000

SALES HISTORY

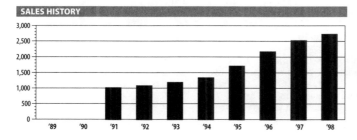

SCHWAN'S SALES ENTERPRISES, INC.

OVERVIEW

As Homer Simpson says, "Mmmm, pizza." Schwan's Sales Enterprises is the #2 US frozen pizza maker, selling the Tony's, Red Baron's, and Freschetta brands. (Kraft Foods is #1.) The Marshall, Minnesota, private company also sells Chicago Town pizza in Western Europe and supplies schools and other institutional cafeterias with frozen pizza and sandwiches. In addition, Schwan's maintains a home delivery system that brings 250 frozen food products, such as fish, fruit, ice cream, juice drink concentrates, meats, pizza, sandwiches, and vegetables, directly to customers. The company delivers across the 48 mainland states.

Schwan's Lyon Financial Services subsidiary leases equipment, including office and medical equipment, and provides asset-based lending and financial management. Subsidiary SSE Manufacturing makes some of the company's food products.

The secretive family of late founder Marvin Schwan (who gave no interviews after 1982) owns Schwan's. Marvin's children settled a 1995 lawsuit filed against their uncle, Alfred Schwan, and a friend of their father's for mismanagement of the estate in 1997; details of the settlement are unknown.

HISTORY

Paul Schwan bought out his partner in their dairy in 1948 and began manufacturing ice cream using his own recipes. His son, Marvin Schwan, delivered for the dairy for a few years. After attending a two-year college, Marvin came back in 1950 to work at the dairy full-time. Two years later he began using his delivery experience to take advantage of the increase in homes with freezers. He bought an old truck for $100 and began a rural route selling ice cream to farmers. He quickly developed a loyal customer base and expanded to two routes the following year.

In the 1960s the company diversified with two acquisitions: a prepared sandwich company and a condensed fruit juice company. A new holding company, Schwan's Sales Enterprises, was established in 1964. Schwan's began delivering pizza the next year. Paul died in 1969.

Deciding that frozen pizza was not a fad, Marvin bought Kansas-based Tony's Pizza in 1970 and quickly rose to the top of the new industry. In the late 1970s Schwan's entered the commercial leasing business, and it later added more leasing companies under the Lyon Financial Services umbrella.

The company entered the institutional pizza market in the mid-1980s and bought out competitors Sabatasso Foods and Better Baked Pizza. Schools liked Schwan's use of their government surplus cheese to make pizzas, which the company then sold to the schools at a discount.

In 1992 the company bought two Minnesota-based food companies: Panzerotti, a stuffed pastry business, and Monthly Market, a specialty retailer that sells groceries to fund-raising groups. It also began selling its pizzas in the UK. The next year Schwan's bought Chicago

Brothers Frozen Pizza, a San Diego-based company specializing in deep-dish pizza.

Marvin died of a heart attack in 1993 at age 64, with his worth estimated at more than $1 billion. The previous year he had willed two-thirds of the company's stock to a charitable Lutheran trust, which was to be bought out by Schwan's after his death. In 1994 his brother, Arthur, and Marvin's friend Lawrence Burgdorf made arrangements to have the company repurchase the foundation's shares for a total of $1.8 billion. But Marvin's four children filed a lawsuit in 1995 against their uncle and Burgdorf over the action. They claimed the men did not have the financial health of the company at heart and were divided in their loyalty. The children, on the other hand, were called money-hungry and callous to their father's last wishes. (The case was settled in 1997 but no information was released.)

A rash of salmonella poisoning was linked to the company's ice-cream products in 1994. (An investigation revealed the contamination came from leased trucks.) Two years later the company introduced Freschetta, its version of a rising-crust style of pizza, to compete with Kraft Food's fast-selling DiGiorno pizza as well as restaurant delivery and carryout pizza. In 1997 Schwan's began selling Tony's pizza in Malaysia and rising-crust pizza in Europe.

Lenny Pippin became the company's fourth CEO in 1999, replacing Alfred, who remained as chairman. Also in 1999 Schwan's launched its improved pasta products featuring new packaging and an additional vegetarian flavor. Schwan's exited the Canadian market at the end of 1999 due to perennial losses.

OFFICERS

Chairman: Alfred Schwan
President and CEO: M. Lenny Pippin
CFO: Dan Herrmann
VP Human Resources: Dave Jennings

LOCATIONS

HQ: 115 W. College Dr., Marshall, MN 56258
Phone: 507-532-3274 **Fax:** 507-537-8226
Web site: http://www.schwans.com

PRODUCTS/OPERATIONS

Selected Products
Alaskan crab legs
Beef & bean burrito
Breaded chicken
Breaded shrimp
Burgers
Fish
Fruits
Ice cream
Juice drink concentrates
Lasagna
Meats
Mozzarella sticks
Pizza
  (Chicago Town,
  Freschetta, Red
  Baron, Tony's)

Polish sausage
Sandwiches
Steaks
Sweet & sour chicken
Vegetables

Selected Brands
Camden Creek Bakery
Coyote Grill
Crockett's
Little Charlie's
Minh

Selected Subsidiaries and Operations
Chicago Brothers Pizza
Lyon Financial Services (commercial leasing)
  BCL Capital (office equipment and technology)
  Secured Funding (medical equipment)
  Spectrum Commercial Services (asset-based lending,
    accounts receivable factoring)
  Stellar Financial Services (financial information
    management)
  Synergy Resources (small-ticket banking equipment)
  The Manifest Group (small-ticket office equipment)
  Universal Leasing, Inc. (tractor-trailer)
Red Baron School Food Service
Schwan's Fine Foods (retail)
Schwan's Frozen Foods (wholesale)
Schwan's Ice Cream (manufacturing, parlors, and
  wholesale)
Schwan's Sales (wholesale)
SSE Manufacturing

COMPETITORS

Aurora Foods
Celentano Brothers
ConAgra
Domino's Pizza
Heinz
Kraft Foods
Little Caesar

McLane
Nation Pizza Products
Nestlé
Piemonte Foods
Pillsbury
SYSCO
TRICON

HISTORICAL FINANCIALS & EMPLOYEES

Private FYE: December	Annual Growth	1989	1990	1991	1992	1993	1994	1995	1996	1997	1998
Estimated sales ($ mil.)	8.0%	—	—	1,680	1,780	2,100	2,200	2,350	2,500	2,900	2,875
Employees	0.0%	—	—	—	—	6,000	6,000	6,000	6,000	6,000	6,000

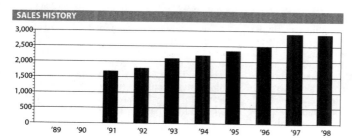

SALES HISTORY

SCIENCE APPLICATIONS

OVERVIEW

See what happens when you apply yourself? San Diego-based Science Applications International Corporation (SAIC) offers technical and related R&D services to government and corporate customers. The company furnishes computer systems integration, technology development, systems engineering, operational support, medical information systems, environmental remedial actions, and energy plant monitoring systems.

Through some 30 years of sales and earnings growth, SAIC has transformed itself from a defense contractor with few peers into a tech firm ably competing with top players. The company owns Telcordia Technologies (formerly AT&T research unit Bellcore), and is the controlling shareholder of Network Solutions, the former registrar of Internet domain names (the Web addresses that end in ".com" and ".net," for example).

Employees (many of whom are now millionaires) own more than 90% of SAIC, whose stock is internally traded. Founder and chairman Robert Beyster asserts that employee ownership has been key to the company's success. And since the US government still accounts for about half of SAIC's work, it probably doesn't hurt that the company's board includes retired Admiral and former National Security Agency director Bobby Ray Inman and retired US Army General Wayne Downing.

HISTORY

Physicist Robert Beyster, who worked at Los Alamos National Laboratory in the 1950s, was hired by General Atomic in 1957 to establish and manage its Traveling Wave Linear Accelerator. When the company was sold to Gulf Oil in 1968, research priorities changed and Beyster left. He founded Science Applications Inc. (SAI) the following year and landed consulting contracts from Los Alamos and Brookhaven National Laboratories.

During the first year Beyster instituted an employee ownership plan in which stock became available to all those judged to be doing a superior job. Beyster's idea was to share the success of SAI and to raise capital. (His stake, then 100%, has dropped to about 2%.)

In 1970 sales neared $1 million. That year the company established an office in Washington, DC. Despite a recession, SAI continued to grow during the 1970s. Its policy was to support new researchers for their first year, after which they had to bring in enough work to support their position or be released. This policy created an entrepreneurial atmosphere but also fostered cloistered divisions.

Sales rose to $100 million by 1979. The following year SAI restructured, becoming a subsidiary of Science Applications International Corporation, a new holding company.

During the 1980s defense buildup, an emphasis on high-tech weaponry and SAI's high-level Pentagon connections (directors have included former defense secretaries William Perry and Melvin Laird and former CIA director John Deutch) brought in contracts for submarine warfare systems, artificial intelligence work, and technical development for the Strategic Defense Initiative ("Star Wars"). These larger contracts required a greater concentration of resources, so SAI reorganized again.

SAI merged into SAIC in 1984, and by the following year a new layer of management was added to coordinate the company's autonomous divisions. Cost-consciousness in Washington and new competition put added pressure on the company. Nevertheless, growth continued.

As defense spending slowed with the end of the Cold War, SAIC began casting a wider net. By 1991 computer systems integration and consulting accounted for 25% of sales. That year SAIC pleaded guilty to fraud charges relating to a government contract and paid $1.3 million in fines.

SAIC made several purchases during the mid-1990s, including transportation communications firm Syntonic, Internet domain name registrar Network Solutions, Inc. (NSI), and government think tank Aerospace Corp. In 1997 SAIC acquired Bellcore (the research lab of the regional Bells, now Telcordia Technologies), sold Science Applications International Technologies (rugged computers and displays), and reduced its stake in NSI through a public offering (SAIC sold additional shares in 1999). SAIC formed several alliances in 1998, including a joint venture with Rolls-Royce to service the aerospace, energy, and defense industries.

The next year the company continued expanding its information technology (IT) services with acquisitions. It bought Critical Path Software (enterprise resource planning software and IT services), the customer relationship management business of Elite Information Group (formerly Broadway & Seymour), and Boeing's Information Services unit.

Chairman, President, and CEO: J. Robert Beyster, age 74, $1,323,077 pay
CEO, Telcordia Technologies: R. C. Smith, age 57, $1,150,012 pay
EVP: J. E. Glancy, age 53, $765,007 pay
EVP: J. H. Warner Jr., age 58, $641,930 pay
SVP and CFO: W. A. Roper Jr., age 53, $608,528 pay
EVP: D. A. Cox, age 51
EVP: S. D. Rockwood, age 56
EVP: R. A. Rosenberg, age 64
EVP: E. A. Straker, age 61
EVP Corporate Development: D. P. Andrews, age 54
SVP and Treasurer: D. W. Baldwin, age 46
SVP and Controller: P. N. Pavlics, age 38
SVP and General Counsel: D. E. Scott, age 42
SVP Administration and Secretary: J. D. Heipt, age 56
SVP Human Resources: Bernard Theull
Auditors: PricewaterhouseCoopers LLP

LOCATIONS

HQ: Science Applications International Corporation, 10260 Campus Point Dr., San Diego, CA 92121
Phone: 858-546-6000   **Fax:** 858-546-6800
Web site: http://www.saic.com

PRODUCTS/OPERATIONS

Selected Services

Energy
Information systems
Plant monitoring systems
Project management
Quality assurance
Reliability engineering evaluations
Safety evaluations
Security
Technical reviews

Environmental
Feasibility studies
Monitoring
Regulatory compliance support and training
Remedial actions and investigations
Sampling
Site assessments
Technology evaluations

Health
Medical information systems
Research support services
Technology development

Information Technology
Domain name registration
Information protection and e-business security

Intranet consulting and network design
IT outsourcing

National Security
Advanced research
Management support services
Operational support services
Systems engineering and integration
Technical support services
Technology development

Telecommunications
Consulting and engineering services
Network design and implementation
Software development and enhancements

Other Services
Automated toll collection
Computer and information security
Material control
NASA engineering support
Undersea data collection, transmission, and analysis

COMPETITORS

Affiliated Computer
Andersen Consulting
BTG
Ball Corporation
Battelle Memorial
Bechtel
Booz, Allen
Cap Gemini

Computer Sciences
DynCorp
EDS
IBM
IT Group
Keane
Litton Industries
Lockheed Martin
MITRE
McKesson HBOC

Northrop Grumman
Raytheon
Shared Medical Systems
TRW
Tetra Tech
Thermo
TerraTech
Unisys

HISTORICAL FINANCIALS & EMPLOYEES

Private FYE: January	Annual Growth	1990	1991	1992	1993	1994	1995	1996	1997	1998	1999
Sales ($ mil.)	18.6%	1,022	1,163	1,285	1,504	1,671	1,922	2,156	2,402	3,089	4,740
Net income ($ mil.)	19.2%	31	33	34	38	42	49	57	64	85	151
Income as % of sales	—	3.0%	2.8%	2.6%	2.5%	2.5%	2.6%	2.7%	2.7%	2.7%	3.2%
Employees	13.8%	11,000	12,000	13,510	15,839	17,800	20,500	21,100	22,600	30,300	35,200

NET INCOME HISTORY

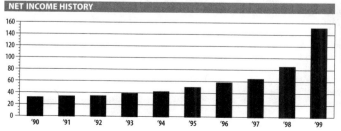

1999 FISCAL YEAR-END

Debt ratio: 11.7%
Return on equity: 16.4%
Cash ($ mil.): 389
Current ratio: 1.25
Long-term debt ($ mil.): 143

SEALY, INC.

Sealy is a slumbering giant. The Trinity, North Carolina-based company is North America's #1 maker of bedding products. Sealy's mattresses and box springs are sold under such brands as Sealy Posturepedic and Stearns & Foster through more than 7,000 retail outlets, including furniture stores, mass merchandisers, and department stores. It also licenses the Sealy name to makers of other bedding products (pillows, comforters) and non-bedroom furnishings (sofas, recliners). Most of Sealy's sales come from the US, but its products are also sold abroad, largely through licensees.

Like Serta and Simmons, the runners-up in the US mattress industry, Sealy is privately held. It is majority-owned by investment firm Bain Capital, Sealy management, and other investors. Bain Capital has a controlling interest in the 240-store bedding chain Mattress Discounters.

Daniel Haynes, a cotton gin builder, first made a new, more resilient type of cotton-filled mattress in 1881 in Sealy, Texas. In 1889 he patented a machine to mass produce his increasingly popular product. Haynes sold manufacturing rights to firms in other cities, and in 1906 he sold his patents to a Texas firm that renamed itself Sealy.

Earl Edwards, an advertising executive at the new company, made some wake-up calls. He expanded Sealy by advertising in national magazines and finding licensees to open mattress factories. By 1920 the company had 28 licensed plants.

Sealy didn't lose too much sleep during the Depression; in fact, it successfully launched a button-free innerspring mattress. When doctors in the 1940s advised that people with back problems sleep on firm mattresses, Sealy designed the Orthopedic Firm-O-Rest; it was renamed the Posturepedic in 1950 after the FTC banned the use of the medical term "orthopedic" in brand names.

In the 1950s Sealy sprung out geographically (it added Canadian licensees in 1954) and financially (sales quintupled to $48 million during the decade). During the 1960s it became the first mattress firm to advertise on prime-time TV.

The princess had her uncomfortable pea; Sealy had The Ohio Mattress Company, one of its independent licensees. In the 1950s Ohio Mattress began entering other licensees' territories and lowering its prices to force its new rivals to sell out. In 1963 Ernest Wuliger succeeded his father as president of Ohio Mattress and began an expansion campaign. He acquired a Sealy licensee in Texas and Oklahoma in 1967, but Sealy bought some of the licensees that Wuliger wanted. The Supreme Court found Sealy guilty that year of antitrust violations regarding price-fixing and exclusive territories. Still, by the end of the 1960s, Sealy had sales of $113 million and additional international licensees.

Wuliger took Ohio Mattress public in 1970. The next year Wuliger began a series of antitrust lawsuits against Sealy that lasted fifteen years. Ohio Mattress acquired bedding maker Stearns & Foster (1983) and Woodstuff Manufacturing (1985). In 1986 the legal bedding battle ended, and Ohio Mattress was awarded $77 million. Instead, in 1987 Ohio Mattress opted to buy Sealy and all but one of Sealy's nine US licensees. It acquired the holdout licensee's Sealy license later in 1987 and became the leading mattress manufacturer.

Investment firm Gibbons Goodwin van Amerongen led a $965 million LBO of Ohio Mattress in 1989; it renamed the company Sealy in 1990. From 1991 to 1993 Sealy changed owners twice, ending up with investment fund Zell/Chilmark. Right after the LBO, Wuliger — and many of Wuliger's top managers — resigned due to conflicts with the new owners. Malcolm Candlish, who had been appointed president and COO during the LBO, was promoted to CEO. In 1992, however, Candlish resigned, citing disagreements with new directors. Sealy brought in Lyman Beggs to replace Candlish.

In 1995 the company began exporting to South Korea, and in 1996 it launched operations in Mexico. Beggs was replaced that year by Ronald Jones, former head of Masco Home Furnishings. In 1997 investment firm Bain Capital bought a majority stake in Sealy. Sealy also sold its Samuel Lawrence bedroom furniture unit (formerly Woodstuff Manufacturing) that year.

The company in 1998 created a Spanish subsidiary, announced plans for a Brazilian plant, and relocated from Ohio to North Carolina. Sealy lost $34 million in fiscal 1998 due to early debt repayment and employee compensation related to the Bain Capital buyout.

In 1999 Bain Capital bought a controlling interest in the US's top mattress retailer, Mattress Discounters — good news for Sealy, which is Mattress Discounters' only outside supplier.

Chairman, President, and CEO: Ronald L. Jones,
age 56, $1,203,710 pay
Corporate VP Research and Development:
Bruce G. Barman, age 53
Corporate VP Human Resources: Jeffrey C. Claypool,
age 51
**Corporate VP/General Manager, Domestic Bedding
Group:** Gary T. Fazio, age 48, $337,776 pay
Corporate VP/General Manager, Domestic Bedding:
Douglas E. Fellmy, age 49, $325,196 pay
**Corporate VP Technology, Planning, and Operations
Support:** James Goughenour, age 61
Corporate VP Sales and Marketing: David J. McIlquham,
age 44, $341,281 pay
Corporate VP/General Manager, International Group:
Lawrence J. Rogers, age 50, $290,669 pay
Corporate VP Finance: Richard F. Sowerby, age 44
Corporate VP, General Counsel, and Secretary:
Kenneth L. Walker, age 50
Corporate VP Administration: E. Lee Wyatt, age 46
Auditors: KPMG LLP

LOCATIONS

HQ: 1 Office Pkwy., Trinity, NC 27370
Phone: 336-861-3500   **Fax:** 336-861-3501
Web site: http://www.sealy.com

PRODUCTS/OPERATIONS

Brand Names
Sealy BackSaver
Sealy Correct Comfort
Sealy Kids
Sealy OrthoZone
Sealy Posture Premier
Sealy Posturematic
Sealy Posturepedic
Sealy Posturepedic Crown Jewel
Stearns & Foster

COMPETITORS

Premier Bedding Group
Select Comfort
Serta
Simmons
Spring Air

HISTORICAL FINANCIALS & EMPLOYEES

Private FYE: November	Annual Growth	1989	1990	1991	1992	1993	1994	1995	1996	1997	1998
Sales ($ mil.)	5.5%	—	—	—	—	683	698	654	698	805	891
Net income ($ mil.)	—	—	—	—	—	26	29	20	(1)	7	(34)
Income as % of sales	—	—	—	—	—	3.8%	4.2%	3.0%	—	0.9%	—
Employees	1.4%	—	—	—	—	4,844	4,345	4,520	4,875	5,456	5,193

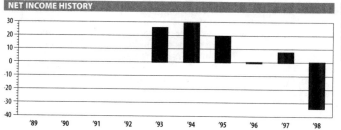

NET INCOME HISTORY

1998 FISCAL YEAR-END
Debt ratio: 100.0%
Return on equity: —
Cash ($ mil.): 11
Current ratio: 1.32
Long-term debt ($ mil.): 682

SEMATECH, INC.

OVERVIEW

SEMATECH is the seminal research organization for semiconductor production. The Austin, Texas-based industry consortium — whose name stands for "semiconductor manufacturing technology"— funds research in areas such as design, front-end processes, lithography, and interconnect systems to improve semiconductor manufacturing techniques. The organization is credited with updating the equipment used in American factories and helping US chip makers recover their global-dominance (they own almost half of the world market). Its members include US chip makers Advanced Micro Devices, IBM, Intel, Lucent (including its Bell Labs unit), Motorola, and Texas Instruments. Subsidiary International SEMATECH includes chip makers from Asia (but none from Japan) and Europe. Each member company sends several employees to Texas to work on group projects.

When government funding came to an end in 1996, SEMATECH knew it had to evolve or become extinct. It widened its focus to issues facing chip companies worldwide (generally, how to make chips smaller, faster, and cheaper), formed an international branch, and increased its dues to cover lost funding. The organization even went so far as to form ties with Japan's own semiconductor research consortium, SELETE (Semiconductor Leading Edge Technologies, Inc.). While those moves helped revive Sematech's fortunes, challenges remain. Some members object to the inclusion of foreign firms, expansion that detracts from individual member goals, and consortium dues ($10 million to $15 million annually). Charter member National Semiconductor has bowed out of the organization, and Motorola, the #3 chip maker worldwide, has announced plans to leave. But other members — including US firms Intel (the world's dominate chipmaker), Advanced Micro Devices, IBM, Hewlett-Packard, Conexant, and Lucent, and Europe's STMicroelectronics — say they'll remain consortium members.

HISTORY

The semiconductor (Bell Labs' transistor) was invented in the US in 1947, and for the next several decades the US dominated the industry. However, by 1986 Japan had overtaken the US as world leader in chip manufacturing. Enter the Semiconductor Industry Association (SIA), a US chip industry trade group. The US firms were being out-engineered by Japanese companies using new technologies and improved manufacturing techniques. SIA directors, led by Robert Noyce (co-inventor of the semiconductor and an Intel founder), formed SEMATECH in 1987 with $100 million per year for five years from the US Department of Defense's Defense Advance Research Projects Agency, and another $100 million per year from 14 member companies.

Noyce died in 1990 and ex-Xerox research executive Bill Spencer was named CEO. While SEMATECH made technological advances, critics complained that it benefited only the largest companies, which dominated the agenda; in the early 1990s Micron Technology and LSI Logic (the two smallest members) and Harris Corp. all dropped out.

SEMATECH's government funding was extended in 1992, but it was lowered to $90 million a year. That year the US became #1 in semiconductor manufacturing again. Many credited SEMATECH's focus on new manufacturing techniques for the turnaround.

In 1994 SEMATECH announced that it would phase out its federal backing. Saying the main challenge to US chip makers was no longer foreign competition, but the limits of manufacturing technology, two years later the organization invited European and Asian manufacturers to join an initiative to convert semiconductor wafers from eight to 12 inches (300mm). In 1997 Mark Melliar-Smith was named CEO; Spencer remains chairman. International doors opened wider in 1998 when five companies from Asia and Europe formed the new International SEMATECH subsidiary, and companies like Hyundai Electronics and Taiwan Semiconductor joined. That year National Semiconductor left SEMATECH, citing financial difficulties.

In 1999 Motorola, concerned about the organization's international push, gave the required two years notice that it would withdraw. Compaq — which became a member when it acquired Digital Equipment (but not that company's chip operations) in 1997 — also made plans to leave. Sematech was instrumental in two major chip industry developments implemented in 1999: migration to 300 millimeter (12-in.) silicon wafers and adoption of copper interconnect technology.

Chairman: William J. Spencer
President and CEO: Mark Melliar-Smith
CFO: Dan Damon
VP and COO: Frank Robertson
VP and Chief Administrative Officer: David Saathoff
VP, Corporate Services: Ann Marett
Director, 300mm Programs: Ashwin Gatahlia
Director, Advanced Technology: Bob Werner
Director, ATDF and Facilities: Chris McDonald
Director, Environment, Safety, and Health: Bob Duffin
Director, Front End Process: Rinn Cleavelin
Director, Human Resources: Susan Sandberg
Director, Interconnect: Paul Wineberger
Director, Internal Technical Support: Ray Delk
Director, Lithography, International SEMATECH:
  Gerhard Gross
Director, Manufacturing Methods: Vern Reynolds
Director, Supplier Relations: David Anderson
General Counsel: Robert Falstad
Auditors: PricewaterhouseCoopers LLP

HQ: 2706 Montopolis Dr., Austin, TX 78741
Phone: 512-356-3500   **Fax:** 512-356-3086
Web site: http://www.sematech.org

Research and Development Programs
300mm wafers
Advanced technologies
Advanced tool development facilities
Design
Environment, safety, and health
Front-end processes
Interconnect
Lithography
Manufacturing methods

SEMATECH Members
Advanced Micro Devices
Compaq
Conexant
Hewlett-Packard
IBM
Intel
Lucent Technologies
Motorola
Texas Instruments

International SEMATECH Members
Hyundai (South Korea)
Infineon Technologies (Germany)
Philips Electronics (The Netherlands)
STMicroelectronics (France)
Taiwan Semiconductor Manufacturing

Battelle Memorial
MCC
MIT
SAIC
SRI International
Southwest Research Institute
University of California

SKADDEN, ARPS

OVERVIEW

Attorneys at Skadden, Arps, Slate, Meagher & Flom have probably heard every lawyer joke in circulation, and they are laughing all the way to the bank. The New York City-based law firm is one of the largest in the world and #1 in the US in terms of revenue. It has some 1,340 attorneys, including nearly 300 partners, operating from 31 offices in Asia, Australia, Europe, and North America. Skadden, Arps is widely known for its mergers and acquisitions (M&A) practice, but it also offers services in tax, communications, international trade, insurance, real estate, labor law, and other areas. The firm's clients include individuals and government agencies, as well as nearly 200 *FORTUNE* 500 companies.

The firm has been credited with changing the practice of corporate law into a fiercely competitive business. When "white shoe" lawyers on Wall Street were hesitant to tread into the uncivilized region of corporate takeovers, Skadden, Arps went for it. With a sharp attorney named Joe Flom leading the way, the firm forged into new territory and virtually pioneered the business of mergers and acquisitions (along the way it invented what is now known as the retainer). From the late 1970s through the 1980s, Skadden, Arps was involved in almost every important M&A case in the US.

HISTORY

Marshall Skadden, Leslie Arps, and John Slate hung out their shingle in New York City on April Fool's Day, 1948. Skadden and Arps came from a Wall Street law firm, and Slate had been counsel to Pan American World Airways. Without the reputation and connections of the established New York law firms, the firm found work one case at a time from referrals, handling mainly commercial, corporate, and litigations work. Skadden died in 1958.

Denied the luxury of steady clients, the firm was forced to be innovative and, at times, unorthodox. Joe Flom, who had joined as the firm's first associate, specialized in corporate law and proxy fights. During the 1960s, when tender offers and hostile takeovers increased, many of the more venerable firms referred clients engaged in the undignified corporate raids to Flom to preserve their gentlemanly reputations. In 1968 Congress passed the Williams Act, which regulated tender offers, thus making them legitimate.

As corporations and lawyers realized that aggressive legal tactics helped win corporate takeover battles, it also became apparent that Joe Flom was the expert. In the early 1970s, as takeover fights became more frequent, Skadden, Arps earned more than just respect. Earnings came not just from some of the highest hourly rates in the industry, but from hefty retainers — on the theory that association with Flom would scare raiders off. The only other name that could strike such fear in people's hearts was Marty Lipton of the rival takeover specialist firm Wachtell, Lipton, Rosen & Katz.

The firm used its success in mergers and acquisitions to build its practice in other areas. In the early 1980s it branched into bankruptcy, product liability, and real estate law. By then it had opened offices in Boston; Chicago; Los Angeles; Washington, DC; and Wilmington, Delaware.

Arps died in 1987. With the boom in mergers and acquisitions (M&A) activity and bankruptcies in the late 1980s, the firm grew to almost 2,000 lawyers in 1989. Then came the recession, and M&A work virtually dried up. Skadden, Arps responded by shedding more than 500 lawyers — 207 of them partners — between 1989 and 1990. It also scrambled to diversify and expand internationally.

As takeover activity rebounded in the mid-1990s, the diversification strategy actually began to work against Skadden, Arps, since profits didn't skyrocket like those of M&A specialist firms, hurting morale among some partners.

In 1995 the firm opened an office in Singapore to coordinate its Asian business, signaling that city's growing importance as a financial center. In 1997 two-thirds of the firm's Beijing team defected to a rival firm. Headquarters shrugged it off and flew in replacements.

The following year Skadden, Arps won one of its highest profile cases when the sexual harassment suit brought against President Clinton by Paula Jones was thrown out. In the first half of 1999, Skadden, Arps was involved in 82 announced M&A deals, including the $75 billion merger of oil companies Exxon and Mobil, and DuPont's $7.7 billion buy of the portion of seed company Pioneer Hi-Bred International it didn't already own.

Executive Partner: Robert C. Sheehan
Finance Director: Karl Duchek
Senior Partner, Corporate Practice: Roger S. Aaron
Senior Partner: Lynn R. Coleman
Senior Partner: Thomas J. Schwarz
Managing Partner, Asian Practice: Jonathan F. Pedersen
Managing Partner, Austrian Practice: Rainer K. Wachter
Managing Partner, Boston: Louis A. Goodman
Managing Partner, European Practice: Bruce M. Buck
Managing Partner, Houston: Lyndon C. Taylor
Managing Partner, Los Angeles: Rand S. April
Managing Partner, Newark: Robert J. Del Tufo
Managing Partner, New York: Irene A. Sullivan
Managing Partner, Singapore: Jeffrey S. Christie
Managing Partner, Washington: Neal S. McCoy
Managing Partner, Wilmington: Rodman Ward Jr.
Partner: Joseph H. Flom
Director Legal Hiring: Carol Lee H. Sprague

LOCATIONS

HQ: Skadden, Arps, Slate, Meagher & Flom,
919 3rd Ave., New York, NY 10022
Phone: 212-735-3000   **Fax:** 212-735-2000
Web site: http://www.skadden.com

Skadden, Arps has offices in Asia, Australia, Europe, and
North America.

US Offices	International Offices
Boston	Beijing
Chicago	Brussels
Houston	Frankfurt
Los Angeles	Hong Kong
New York City	London
Newark, NJ	Moscow
Palo Alto, CA	Paris
San Francisco	Singapore
Washington, DC	Sydney
Wilmington, DE	Tokyo
	Toronto

PRODUCTS/OPERATIONS

Selected Areas of Practice
Alternative dispute resolution
Antitrust
Banking and institutional investing
Communications
Corporate compliance
Corporate finance
Derivative financial products
Employee benefits and executive compensation
Energy
Environment
Financial institution regulation
Gaming
Government enforcement
Health care
Insurance
Intellectual property
International arbitration
International trade
Investment companies, advisers, and broker-dealers
Labor and employment law
Litigation
Mergers & acquisitions
Political law
Real estate
Tax
Trusts and estates
Utilities
White-collar crime

COMPETITORS

Baker & McKenzie	Robins, Kaplan
Cahill Gordon	Shearman & Sterling
Cleary, Gottlieb	Simpson Thacher
Clifford Chance	Sullivan & Cromwell
Cravath, Swaine	Wachtell, Lipton
Davis Polk	Weil, Gotshal
Debevoise & Plimpton	White & Case
Jones, Day	

HISTORICAL FINANCIALS & EMPLOYEES

Partnership FYE: December	Annual Growth	1989	1990	1991	1992	1993	1994	1995	1996	1997	1998
Sales ($ mil.)	7.4%	518	503	490	440	478	582	635	710	826	890
Employees	0.8%	—	3,000	3,200	3,000	3,200	3,100	3,000	3,150	3,000	3,200

SALES HISTORY

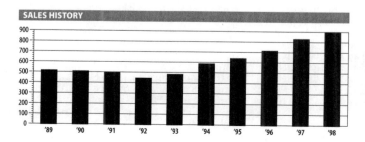

SKADDEN
ARPS
SLATE
MEAGHER &
FLOM

SKIDMORE, OWINGS & MERRILL, LLP

OVERVIEW

More than the SOM of its parts, SOM (short for Skidmore, Owings & Merrill) is one of the largest architecture and engineering firms in the world. The Chicago-based partnership also provides interior design and site and space planning. Although it made its reputation with its signature high-rises, including the Sears Tower, SOM also takes on institutional projects such as airports and schools, interior design work, and renovation projects for older buildings. It has offices in five US cities, London, and Hong Kong.

One of the stalwarts of modernist design, SOM has used its reputation for innovation (though some critics sniff that it has lost its creative distinction and become the IBM of architectural firms) to put its stamp on cities throughout Asia. Its biggest Asian project is the 88-story Jin Mao hotel and office tower in the financial district of Shanghai. However, in the wake of the Asian financial crisis, SOM has turned its attention to the US market.

HISTORY

While studying and working in Paris in 1929, Louis Skidmore met two architects involved in planning the 1933-1934 Century of Progress Exposition in Chicago. He arranged to be appointed chief designer for the exposition and asked Nathaniel Owings, his brother-in-law, to assist him, thus beginning their professional association.

After the exposition, the two pursued separate paths, only to come together again in 1936 to found a small design firm in Chicago bearing their names. Trading on corporate relationships developed at the exposition, the two men soon had enough work for three draftsmen.

The next year the firm opened a New York office to serve a client, American Radiator Company. The New York presence and its experience at the Chicago exposition made Skidmore & Owings a logical choice to work on the New York World's Fair of 1939-1940. Gordon Bunshaft came on in 1937 and spent the next 42 years with the firm, becoming one of its most famous and influential architects. By 1939, when architectural engineer John Merrill joined the firm, it had developed a reputation for clean, functional design.

In 1940 Skidmore & Owings won the contract that brought it to national prominence — designing the defense community of Oak Ridge, Tennessee, home of part of the Manhattan (atomic bomb) Project.

After WWII, the firm, now Skidmore, Owings & Merrill (SOM), grew rapidly, gaining such commissions as Mount Zion Hospital in San Francisco, Lever House in New York City, and the H.J. Heinz vinegar plant in Pittsburgh. By 1950 the company's modernistic style had become so distinctive that SOM was the first architectural firm granted an exhibition at New York's Museum of Modern Art. Two years later SOM had 14 partners and four offices.

The 1960s saw more noteworthy commissions, including IBM's Armonk, New York, headquarters and the University of Illinois at Chicago. In 1962 SOM received the first architectural excellence award for firms given by the American Institute of Architects. In the 1970s the firm's presence was keenly felt in Chicago, where, under the modernist influence of architect Bruce Graham, SOM designed the John Hancock building, the Sears Tower, Northwestern University's library, and Baxter Travenol's headquarters.

By the mid-1980s SOM had 47 partners and 1,400 other employees in nine offices. It opened its first foreign office in London in 1986. That decade SOM's old-fashioned commitment to modernism in the face of postmodernism hurt its bottom line. By the time it adapted, the building boom of the 1980s had gone bust. Several offices closed and half of SOM's staff was laid off in 1990. To survive, SOM's first chairman, David Childs (appointed in 1991), cut costs and perks. He also steered the firm toward institutional work and integrating design services for clients, instead of separating work by specialties. Meanwhile as some second-generation stars retired, their retirement draws were a drain on company finances. SOM renegotiated with some retired partners, but others (including John Merrill's son) sued in 1996.

In 1997 the Asian financial crisis halted some projects, and SOM began focusing more on work in the US. Nonetheless, SOM was chosen to design the 52-story PBCom Tower in Makati City, the Philippines. In an ironic turn of events, award-winning designer Joseph Gonzalez resigned after 20 years with the firm when SOM learned that he was not licensed. In 1998 SOM was developing Shanghai's Jin Mao hotel complex, the San Francisco International Airport Terminal, and a 2,000-foot skyscraper that would return the title of "World's Tallest Building" to Chicago.

CEO: John H. Winkler
CFO: Joseph Dailey
Director Personnel: Carol Able
Auditors: Arthur Andersen LLP

LOCATIONS

HQ: 224 S. Michigan Ave., Ste. 1000, Chicago, IL 60604
Phone: 312-554-9090   **Fax:** 312-360-4545
Web site: http://www.som.com

PRODUCTS/OPERATIONS

Services
Architecture
Building services engineering
Civil engineering
Graphics
Interior design
Landscape architecture
Structural engineering
Urban design and planning

Types of Projects
Airports/transportation
Convention centers
Cultural and performing arts facilities
Educational facilities
Financial institutions
Health care facility design
Hotels and resorts
Large-scale and mixed-use projects
Office buildings
Renovation and restoration

Selected Projects
AT&T Corporate Center (Chicago, 1989)
Bank of America (San Francisco, 1971)
Banque Lambert (Brussels, 1965)
Brunswick Building (Chicago, 1965)
Chase Manhattan Bank (New York, 1961)
Equitable Life Assurance Society Office Building
   (Chicago, 1965)
Haj Terminal at International Airport (Jeddah, Saudi
   Arabia; 1982)
Hirshhorn Museum and Sculpture Garden (Washington,
   DC; 1974)
Hong Kong Convention and Exhibition Center (1997)
Inland Steel (Chicago, 1956)
Jin Mao Building (Shanghai, 1998)
John Hancock Center (Chicago, 1970)
LBJ Library (University of Texas, Austin; 1971)
Lever House (New York, 1952)
Library at Northwestern University (Evanston, IL; 1971)
Lincoln Center for the Performing Arts, Library-
   Museum (New York, 1965)
Manufacturers Hanover Trust Company Bank and Office
   Building (New York, 1954)
New York City Building (1939 World's Fair)
Oak Ridge defense community (Tennessee, 1942-46)
One Shell Plaza (Houston, 1971)
San Francisco International Airport Terminal (1998)
Sears Tower (Chicago, 1974)
Spiegel Headquarters (Downers Grove, IL; 1992)
University of Illinois at Chicago (1965)
US Air Force Academy (Colorado Springs, CO; 1962)
USG Building (Chicago, 1992)
Vila Olimpica (Barcelona, Spain; 1992)
Weyerhaeuser Headquarters (Tacoma, WA; 1971)
Worldwide Plaza (New York, 1991)

COMPETITORS

A. Epstein & Sons	Jacobs Engineering
AECOM	Loebl Schlossman & Hackl
Einhorn Yaffee Prescott	McClier
Architecture	Murphy/Jahn
Ellerbe Beckett	Perkins & Will
FFNS	STV
Holabird and Root	Takenaka

HISTORICAL FINANCIALS & EMPLOYEES

Partnership FYE: September	Annual Growth	1988	1989	1990	1991	1992	1993	1994	1995	1996	1997
Sales ($ mil.)	(5.8%)	152	149	134	92	63	68	79	87	82	88
Employees	(8.7%)	1,702	1,632	1,602	804	687	746	733	800	800	850

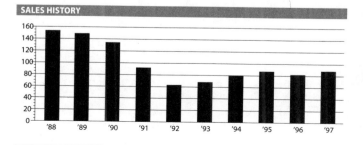

SALES HISTORY

SMITHSONIAN INSTITUTION

OVERVIEW

Attics are notorious for being full of old (and odd) stuff. The Smithsonian Institution — known as "the nation's attic" — is no different, except that the stuff in its 16 museums and galleries, zoo, and research facilities is of interest to people other than the owner. About 23 million people each year visit the world's largest museum, in Washington, DC. It has more than 140 million items (only a small portion of which are on display at any one time), from the flag that inspired Francis Scott Key to write "The Star-Spangled Banner" to the ruby slippers worn by Judy Garland in *The Wizard of Oz*. Smithsonian exhibits also include art, fossils, historical documents, gardens, and audio and video recordings.

Most Smithsonian facilities are on the National Mall between the Washington Monument and the Capitol. The Smithsonian is headed by a board of regents that includes Vice President Al Gore, Chief Justice William Rehnquist, six members of Congress, and eight private citizens.

The Smithsonian receives just over half its revenues (more than $380 million) from the federal government. The institution, which does not charge admission fees at most of its attractions, is also active in soliciting contributions from individuals, corporations, and foundations.

HISTORY

In 1826 English chemist James Smithson wrote a proviso to his will that would lead to the creation of the Smithsonian Institution. When he died in 1829, he left his estate to his nephew, Henry James Hungerford, with the stipulation that if Hungerford died without heirs, the estate would go to the US to create "an Establishment for the increase and diffusion of knowledge among men." Hungerford died in 1835 without any heirs, and the US government inherited more than $500,000 in gold.

Congress squandered the money after it was received in 1838, but perhaps feeling pangs of guilt, covered the loss. The Smithsonian was finally created in 1846 and Princeton physicist Joseph Henry was named as its first secretary. That year it established the Museum of Natural History, the Museum of History and Technology, and the National Gallery of Art.

In 1858 the Smithsonian's National Museum was developed around the collection of the US Patent Office. The Smithsonian continued to expand, adding the National Zoological Park in 1889 and the Smithsonian Astrophysical Observatory in 1890.

The Freer Gallery, a gift of industrialist Charles Freer, opened in 1923. In 1937 the National Gallery was renamed the National Collection of Fine Arts, and a new National Gallery, created with Andrew Mellon's gift of his art collection and a building, opened in 1941. The Air and Space Museum was established in 1946.

More museums were added in the 1960s, including the National Portrait Gallery (1962) and the Anacostia Museum (exhibits and materials on African-American history, 1967). The Kennedy Center for the Performing Arts was opened in 1971. In 1980 the Collection of Fine Arts was renamed the National Museum of American Art, and the Museum of History and Technology was renamed the National Museum of American History.

The Smithsonian placed its first-ever contribution boxes in four of its museums in 1993. A planned exhibit featuring the *Enola Gay* — the plane that dropped the atomic bomb on Hiroshima — created a firestorm in 1994 with critics charging that the exhibit downplayed Japanese aggression and US casualties in WWII. The original exhibit was canceled in 1995, the director of the Air and Space Museum resigned, and a scaled-down version of the exhibit premiered.

The Smithsonian has received large contributions from private donors. In 1994 the Mashantucket Pequot tribe gave $10 million from its casino operations for a planned American Indian museum, and prolific electronics inventor Jerome Lemelson donated $10.4 million in 1995.

The museum celebrated its sesquicentennial in 1996 amid news that $500 million in repairs were needed over the next 10 years.

In 1997 California real estate developer Kenneth Behring gave the largest cash donation ever to the museum — $20 million for the National Museum of Natural History. Short of funds, the Smithsonian had to cut back on its 150th anniversary traveling exhibit that year. In 1998 the Smithsonian announced a $26 million renovation for the National Museum of Natural History. Also that year it signed an agreement with Mandalay Television Pictures and Showtime Networks to produce made-for-TV movies.

Provost: J. Dennis O'Connor
Inspector General: Thomas D. Blair
CFO: Rick R. Johnson
Secretary: I. Michael Heyman
Director Government Relations: Donald Hardy
Director Human Resources: Carolyn E. Jones
Director Communications: David J. Umansky
Director Planning, Management, and Budget:
L. Carole Wharton
**Director, Freer Gallery of Art and Arthur M. Sackler
Gallery:** Milo C. Beach
Director, National Museum of Art: Elizabeth Broun
Director, National Museum of American History:
Spencer R. Crew
Director, Hirshhorn Museum and Sculpture Garden:
James T. Demetrion
Director, National Air and Space Museum:
Donald D. Engen
Director, National Portrait Gallery: Alan M. Fern
Director, National Museum of Natural History:
Robert W. Fri
Director, National Zoological Park:
Michael H. Robinson
**Publisher, Smithsonian Magazine and Air & Space
Smithsonian Magazine:** Ronald C. Walker
General Counsel: John E. Huerta
Under Secretary: Constance B. Newman
Auditors: KPMG LLP

LOCATIONS

HQ: 1000 Jefferson Dr. SW, Washington, DC 20560
Phone: 202-357-2700   **Fax:** 202-786-2377
Web site: http://www.si.edu

PRODUCTS/OPERATIONS

Selected Facilities
Anacostia Museum and Center for African American
History & Culture
Archives of American Art
Arthur M. Sackler Gallery
Arts and Industries Building
Center for Folklife Programs and Cultural Studies
Conservation and Research Center
Cooper-Hewitt, National Design Museum (New York City)
Freer Gallery of Art
Hirshhorn Museum and Sculpture Garden
Marine Station at Link Port
National Air & Space Museum
National Museum of African Art
National Museum of American Art
National Museum of American History
National Museum of Natural History
National Museum of the American Indian (New York City)
National Portrait Gallery
National Postal Museum
National Zoological Park
Renwick Gallery
Smithsonian Astrophysical Observatory
Smithsonian Center for Materials Research and Education
Smithsonian Environmental Research Center
Smithsonian Institution Archives
Smithsonian Institution Libraries
Smithsonian Tropical Research Institute

HISTORICAL FINANCIALS & EMPLOYEES

Not-for-profit FYE: September	Annual Growth	1989	1990	1991	1992	1993	1994	1995	1996	1997	1998
Sales ($ mil.)	3.3%	578	595	656	706	730	605	750	703	729	774
Employees	0.4%	6,000	6,300	6,700	6,800	6,800	6,671	6,600	6,487	6,469	6,500

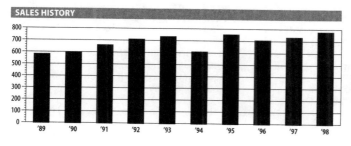

SALES HISTORY

SMITHSONIAN INSTITUTION

SPARTAN STORES, INC.

OVERVIEW

Like the Spartans before it, Spartan Stores is not one to walk away from a fight, especially a food fight. The Grand Rapids, Michigan-based wholesaler supplies food and general merchandise to more than 470 independent grocery stores and about 9,600 convenience stores, mostly in Michigan, but also in eight other states as far away as Georgia. Spartan distributes more than 40,000 items in every food line except baked foods and deli items (which its customers receive from partner Lipari Foods). Tobacco products and candy account for most of its sales to convenience stores. Its offerings include more than 2,000 private-label items under the Spartan, HomeHarvest, and Save Rite names. In addition to support services, such as advertising and coupon redemption, Spartan offers its customers a broad range of insurance options.

Spartan once operated as a cooperative, and it is still primarily owned by about 240 customers (employees and management also own shares). To better equip its customers for the ever-combative food business, the company has eliminated purchase-based rebates and is using the increased capital to expand through acquisitions. To that end, it has purchased eight Ashcraft's Markets in central Michigan. Spartan is also eyeing possible acquisitions in Ohio and Indiana and is considering going public.

HISTORY

Making dinner in the early 1900s often required several shopping stops: the grocer for canned goods, a butcher for meat, and yet another place for produce. Eventually the big grocery chains began offering one-stop shopping, not to mention better prices because of their greater buying power. Worrying about how to compete, in 1917 approximately 100 small grocers met in Grand Rapids, Michigan, to discuss organizing a cooperative; almost half of those formed the Grand Rapids Wholesale Grocery Co. The stores remained independent, operating under different names but achieving economies of scale and volume buying through the co-op. They also began developing a variety of services for member stores. Sales topped $1 million in 1934.

Over the years the company expanded beyond its Grand Rapids origins. In 1950 it formed subsidiary United Wholesale, which served independent grocers on a cash-and-carry basis. It acquired the Grand Rapids Coffee Company in 1953. The next year the co-op launched its first private-label item, Spartan Coffee, with a green Spartan logo reminiscent of the Michigan State University mascot. The company changed its name to Spartan Stores in 1957.

Spartan entered retailing in the early 1970s when it bought 19 Harding's stores. It became a for-profit company in 1973 but continued to provide rebates to customers based on their purchases. Spartan began offering insurance to its customers in 1979.

Concerned about the direction of the company, customers named Patrick Quinn, formerly a VP at a small chain of grocery stores, as president and CEO in 1985. Quinn began seeking acquisitions, but talks to acquire the Eberhard Foods chain and Viking Food Stores collapsed in 1985 and 1987, respectively.

To focus on the wholesale business, and to avoid any appearance of conflict of interest in both supplying member stores and operating competing stores, Spartan sold its 23 retail stores between 1987 and 1994, giving customer stores the first option on them. It entered the convenience store wholesale business with its 1987 acquisition of L&L/Jiroch. Two years later the co-op acquired Associated Grocers of Michigan (later known as Capistar; closed in 1996).

Sales topped $2 billion in 1991. Spartan expanded its convenience store operations in 1993 by buying J.F. Walker, a convenience store wholesaler. The next year it announced plans to merge with Roundy's, a Wisconsin-based wholesale food co-op, which would have created the third-largest food wholesale company; however, the deal fell through soon after.

Despite record sales in 1996, a $46 million restructuring charge that included extensive technological improvements led to a $21.7 million loss, the largest in the company's history. The following year Jim Meyer, who had joined Spartan in 1973, replaced the retiring Quinn as president and CEO. Also in 1997 the company stopped giving its customers rebates, finally doing away with the last remnants of its co-op years. In an effort to expand its operations, in 1998 Spartan re-entered retailing by acquiring eight Ashcraft's Markets formerly owned by company members.

Chairman: Russell H. VanGilder Jr., age 65
VC: Parker T. Feldpausch, age 67
President, CEO and Treasurer: James B. Meyer, age 53, $371,540 pay
VP Development: Charles Fosnaugh, age 49, $200,980 pay
VP Information Technology: David deS. Couch, age 48, $168,260 pay
VP Logistics: Michael D. Frank, age 47, $154,405 pay
VP Sales: J. Kevin Schlosser, age 49, $138,500 pay
VP Human Resources: Richard Deming, age 54
General Counsel and Assistant Secretary: Alex J. DeYonker, age 49
Secretary: Roger L. Boyd, age 53
Director Corporate Communications and Public Affairs: Mary Dechow
Manager Recruiting, Selection and Planning: Margarita Hernandez
Auditors: Deloitte & Touche LLP

LOCATIONS

HQ: 850 76th St. SW, Grand Rapids, MI 49518
Phone: 616-878-2000   **Fax:** 616-878-8802
Web site: http://www.spartanstores.com

PRODUCTS/OPERATIONS

1999 Sales

	$ mil.	% of total
Distribution	2,680	99
Insurance	16	1
Real estate & finance	11	—
Adjustments	(35)	—
Total	**2,672**	**100**

Selected Services
Accounting and tax preparation services
Coupon redemption and product reclamation services
Human resource services
Information services
Insurance services
Marketing, promotion, and advertising assistance
Real estate and finance services
Site identification and market analysis
Store planning and development

COMPETITORS

A&P
Advantage Logistics Michigan
Alex Lee
Associated Wholesale Grocers
Certified Grocers Midwest
Costco Companies
Eby-Brown
Fleming Companies
GSC Enterprises
IGA
Kmart
Kroger
Meijer
Nash Finch
Purity Wholesale Grocers
Roundy's
SUPERVALU
Shurfine International
Topco Associates
Wal-Mart

HISTORICAL FINANCIALS & EMPLOYEES

Private FYE: March	Annual Growth	1990	1991	1992	1993	1994	1995	1996	1997	1998	1999
Sales ($ mil.)	4.0%	—	—	2,024	2,041	2,172	2,495	2,521	2,475	2,489	2,672
Net income ($ mil.)	16.1%	—	—	5	6	7	9	(22)	10	14	15
Income as % of sales	—	—	—	0.3%	0.3%	0.3%	0.4%	—	0.4%	0.6%	0.6%
Employees	7.2%	—	—	—	2,300	2,940	3,200	3,000	3,100	2,900	3,500

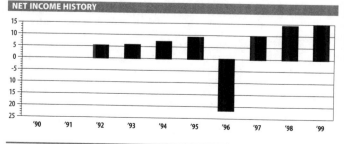

NET INCOME HISTORY

1999 FISCAL YEAR-END
Debt ratio: 69.0%
Return on equity: 12.6%
Cash ($ mil.): 44
Current ratio: 1.77
Long-term debt ($ mil.): 270

SPECIALTY FOODS CORPORATION

OVERVIEW

Specialty Foods wants to live on bread (and cookies) alone. The #3 cookie maker (after Nabisco and Keebler), its brands include Archway and Mother's, as well as Mrs. Wheatley's, Bakery Wagon, and Marie Lu. Its Metz Baking wholesale bakery subsidiary, which The Earthgrains Company is buying, produces breads, rolls, and sweet goods under brands such as Country Hearth, D'Italiano, and Taystee. The company's bakery distribution system consists of a network of direct-to-the-store delivery routes across 45 states. Specialty Foods also owns about 45 Boudin Sourdough Bakery & Café outlets, located mainly in California.

Created by a group of Texas investors to buy

eight major American food firms ranging from pickles to tobacco, the Deerfield, Illinois-based private holding company bit off more than it could chew, then found its selection hard to swallow and later acquisitions indigestible. After bingeing and purging noncore businesses, Specialty Foods has settled on a steady acquisition diet of bakery companies.

Investment facilities run by Texas billionaire Robert Bass and J. Taylor Crandall own about 55% of the company; Dallas-based investors Robert Haas and Douglas Wheat together own about 13%. Other major shareholders include Union Bank of Switzerland and Donaldson, Lufkin & Jenrette.

HISTORY

Specialty Foods was founded in June 1993 when a group of investors, including Texas billionaire Robert Bass, J. Taylor Crandall, Robert Haas, and Douglas Wheat, teamed up to buy the North American food businesses of Beledia (the Netherlands), a subsidiary of Belgium's Artal Group. The $1.1 billion LBO, the largest of 1993, included eight companies (all acquired by Beledia over the previous seven years).

The companies, with combined annual revenues of about $2 billion, were B&G (New Jersey; pickles, peppers, and spices), Burns & Ricker, (New Jersey, snack foods), Gordon's Wholesale (Iowa; candy, tobacco, and foodstuffs distributor; sold 1994), H&M Food Systems (Texas, specialty prepared meats), Metz Baking Company (Iowa, wholesale baker), Stella Foods (Wisconsin, specialty Italian cheese), Mother's Cake & Cookie Co. (California, cookies), and the Pacific Coast Baking Co., which owned Gai's Seattle French Baking Co. and San Francisco French Bread Company (one of the nation's leading wholesale producers of sourdough French bread and operator of the Boudin Sourdough Bakery and Café chain).

Recruiting a number of executives from Kraft Foods, Specialty Foods named Thomas Herskovits (former president of Kraft's Frozen Products and Dairy Groups) its new president and CEO. Herskovits said acquisitions would drive future growth, with expectations that the company would become a $4 billion firm within five years.

Acquisitions after Specialty Foods' inception included Design Foods (1993), The Bagel Place (1994), and Chicago-area bakeries and the New York Style Bagel Chip Co. (1995). However, sales stayed fairly flat in 1994 and 1995, contrary to the company's expectations. As a result,

Specialty Foods took a $253 million write-down in 1995.

Faced with a high cholesterol debt load and a smorgasbord of problems — falling meat prices, rising grain prices, and the loss of large customers — Specialty Foods hired Merrill Lynch in 1996 to sell its noncore businesses. An agreement was made to sell Mother's, but the subsidiary's poor fourth quarter results caused the deal to be called off.

Herskovits resigned that year and was replaced by COO Paul Liska, who resigned a year later. Lawrence Benjamin, head of the Stella Foods subsidiary, took Liska's place in 1997.

In 1996 and 1997 Specialty Foods unloaded businesses, including B&G, Burns & Ricker, the bagel businesses, Gai's Seattle French Baking Co., San Francisco French Bread Company, and Stella Foods (to Montréal-based Saputo Group). The company whipped up a new batch of acquisitions in 1998 starting with Archway Cookies, which made it the nation's third-largest cookie baker.

Strengthening its presence in Southern California, Specialty Foods purchased the San Diego Bread Company (variety breads and private-label sourdough) in 1998. Subsidiary Metz Bakery expanded its presence in midwestern markets with the 1998 purchases of Clear Lake Bakery in Iowa, Grandma Sycamore's in Utah, and a bakery from Eagle Food Centers in Illinois; it added Grocers Baking Company in Michigan in 1999.

Fully focused on its bakery business, in 1999 Specialty Foods announced it would sell its H&M Food Systems to US beef giant IBP. In November 1999 the company agreed to sell Metz Baking to The Earthgrains Company for $625 million.

Chairman: Robert B. Haas, age 51
President and CEO: Lawrence S. Benjamin, age 43, $1,696,000 pay
VP and CFO: Robert L. Fishbune, age 43, $550,000 pay
VP, Human Resources: John R. Reisenberg
VP and General Counsel, Business Units: David E. Schreibman, age 31
Chairman, Metz Baking: Henry J. Metz, age 48, $600,500 pay (prior to promotion)
President and CEO, H&M Food Systems: William D. Day, age 44, $828,000 pay
President and CEO, Mother's Cake & Cookie: Patrick J. O'Dea, age 37, $520,000 pay
President, André-Boudin Bakeries: Lawrence J. Strain, age 46
Auditors: KPMG LLP

LOCATIONS

HQ: 520 Lake Cook Rd., Ste. 550, Deerfield, IL 60015
Phone: 847-405-5300   **Fax:** 847-267-0015

PRODUCTS/OPERATIONS

Companies and Brands
André-Boudin Bakeries, Inc. (specialty bread cafés)
Archway Cookies, Inc.
Metz Baking Company (name-brand and private-label breads, buns, rolls, and sweet goods)
  Country Hearth
  D'Italiano
  Egekvist
  Grandma Sycamore's
  Holsum
  Master
  Old Home
  Taystee
Mother's Cake & Cookie Co.
  Bakery Wagon
  Marie Lu
  Mother's
  Mrs. Wheatley's
San Diego Bread Company

COMPETITORS

Bestfoods
Campbell Soup
Earthgrains
Flowers Industries
George Weston
Industrial Bimbo
Interbake Foods
International Multifoods
Interstate Bakeries
Keebler
Lance
McKee Foods
Nabisco Holdings
Sara Lee
Tasty Baking

HISTORICAL FINANCIALS & EMPLOYEES

Private FYE: December	Annual Growth	1989	1990	1991	1992	1993	1994	1995	1996	1997	1998
Sales ($ mil.)	(5.5%)	939	1,170	1,383	1,637	1,998	1,979	1,975	1,661	920	742
Net income ($ mil.)	—	(7)	(7)	3	(11)	(14)	(21)	(270)	(447)	91	(46)
Income as % of sales	—	—	—	0.2%	—	—	—	—	—	9.9%	—
Employees	(8.3%)	—	—	—	14,000	13,100	13,900	14,000	11,000	8,250	8,300

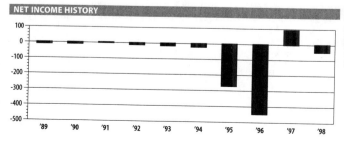

NET INCOME HISTORY

1998 FISCAL YEAR-END
Debt ratio: 100.0%
Return on equity: —
Cash ($ mil.): 6
Current ratio: 1.17
Long-term debt ($ mil.): 820

STANFORD UNIVERSITY

OVERVIEW

One of the premier universities in the US, Stanford University is the West Coast's answer to the Ivy League. The Stanford, California-based private university awards undergraduate degrees in humanities and sciences, Earth sciences, and engineering, and also allows undergraduates to pursue individually designed degree programs. Its graduate programs encompass fields of study such as business, engineering, law, and medicine. One of the top US research universities, Stanford boasts 2,300 externally sponsored research projects and a host of research laboratories, centers, and institutes. Its $4.7 billion endowment ranks among the six largest university endowments in the US. Stanford's athletic programs span 33 varsity sports.

Stanford has more than 14,000 students (47% undergraduate, 53% graduate), and for the 13% of applicants who are admitted, the estimated annual tab for an undergraduate's tuition, books, and living expenses is more than $33,500. The university's nearly 1,600-member faculty (including 16 Nobel Laureates and 20 Medal of Science winners) enhances the university's stature, as do its numerous ties to Silicon Valley companies headed by individuals with close ties to the university (3Com, Cisco Systems, Hewlett-Packard, Sun Microsystems, Yahoo!).

Stanford has curbed increases in tuition rates and relaxed financial aid requirements to attract students from middle-income families.

HISTORY

In 1885 Leland Stanford Sr. and his wife, Jane, established Leland Stanford Junior University in memory of their son Leland Jr., who had died of typhoid at age 15. Stanford made his fortune selling provisions to California gold miners and as a railroad magnate whose Central Pacific Railroad built tracks eastward and eventually completed the transcontinental railway. Stanford also served as California's governor and as a US senator.

The Stanfords donated more than 8,000 acres of land from their own estate to establish an unconventional university, one that was both coeducational and nondenominational. Stanford opened its doors in 1891 to a freshman class of 559 students. It awarded its first degrees four years later, and among the graduates was future US president Herbert Hoover.

Leland Stanford Sr. died in 1893, and in 1903 Jane Stanford turned the university over to the board of trustees. After weathering significant damage in 1906 from the Great San Francisco Earthquake, the university established a law school in 1908 and its medical school five years later.

During WWI the university mobilized half of its students into the Students' Army Training Corps. The School of Education was established in 1917, followed by the School of Engineering and Graduate School of Business eight years later. In 1933 a rule limiting the number of women admitted to Stanford was abolished.

Wallace Sterling, who became president of the university after WWII, initiated the transformation of Stanford into a world-class institution with a reputation for teaching and research. Under Sterling the university

initiated development on the Stanford Research Park.

In 1958 Stanford opened its first overseas campus (near Stuttgart, Germany), and the Stanford Medical Center was completed the following year. The university created a computer science department in 1965 and two years later opened the Stanford Linear Accelerator Center dedicated to physics research.

Donald Kennedy became president in 1980. During his tenure, it was revealed that Stanford had overcharged the Office of Naval Research for indirect costs associated with research. The scandal led to Kennedy's resignation in 1992, and in 1994 the Office of Naval Research and the university settled a related lawsuit for $1.2 million and a stipulation that Stanford had not committed any wrongdoing. Gerhard Casper succeeded Kennedy as president.

In 1997 Stanford and the University of California at San Francisco combined their teaching hospitals in a public/private merger. Two years later, after the controversial experiment had harmed both hospitals' financial picture, the merger was terminated, and the two hospitals agreed to go their separate ways.

In 1999 Casper announced his intention to resign as president effective in August 2000. Later that year, Former Stanford professor and Netscape co-founder Jim Clark donated $150 million to support Stanford's biomedical engineering and sciences program. His donation was the university's largest since its founding grant.

OFFICERS

Chairman Board of Trustees: Robert M. Bass
President: Gerhard Casper
Provost: John Hennessy
VP Business Affairs and CFO: Mariann Byerwalter
VP Development: John B. Ford
VP Medical Affairs and Dean School Medicine:
Eugene Bauer
CEO, Stanford Management Co.: Laurance R. Hoagland
Vice Provost and Dean Institutional Planning, Learning Technology, and Extended Education:
Geoffrey M. Cox
Vice Provost and Dean Research and Graduate Policy:
Charles H. Kruger
Vice Provost and Dean Student Affairs: James Montoya
Vice Provost Budget and Auxiliaries Management:
Timothy Warner
Vice Provost Faculty Development: Patricia Jones
Vice Provost Undergraduate Education: John Braveman
Chief Information Officer: Raman Khanna
Director Government and Community Relations:
Larry N. Horton
Director Human Resources: Peggy Hiraoka
Director Office Campus Relations: Sally Dickson
President, Stanford Alumni Association: William Stone
Director University Communications: Alan Acosta
General Counsel: Michael Roster

LOCATIONS

HQ: 857 Serra St., Stanford, CA 94305
Phone: 650-723-2300   **Fax:** 650-725-0247
Web site: http://www.stanford.edu

PRODUCTS/OPERATIONS

1998 Sales

	$ mil.	% of total
Sponsored research	635	41
Student income	266	17
Investment income	264	17
Special program fees	132	8
Auxiliary activities	116	8
Expendable gifts	78	5
Other	67	4
Total	**1,558**	**100**

Selected Schools
Graduate and undergraduate
  School of Earth Sciences
  School of Engineering
  School of Humanities and Sciences
Graduate
  Graduate School of Business
  School of Education
  School of Law
  School of Medicine

Selected Laboratories, Centers, and Institutes
Center for Economic Policy Research
Center for Materials Research
Center for the Study of Language and Information
Edward L. Ginzton Laboratory
Institute for International Studies
Institute for Research on Women and Gender
Stanford Humanities Center
W.W. Hansen Experimental Physics Laboratory

Selected Medical Research Facilities
Center for Biomedical Ethics
Program in Molecular and Genetic Medicine
Sleep Disorders Center
Stanford Center for Research in Disease Prevention

Selected National and International Research Centers
Center for Advanced Study in the Behavioral Sciences
Department of Plant Biology in the Carnegie Institution
  of Washington
National Bureau of Economic Research

Other Selected Research Facilities
Hoover Institution on War, Revolution and Peace
Hopkins Marine Station
Iris & B. Gerald Cantor Center for Visual Arts
Jasper Ridge Biological Preserve
Stanford Linear Accelerator Center
Stanford University Libraries

HISTORICAL FINANCIALS & EMPLOYEES

School FYE: August	Annual Growth	1989	1990	1991	1992	1993	1994	1995	1996	1997	1998
Sales ($ mil.)	4.3%	—	—	—	—	1,262	1,243	1,171	1,416	1,474	1,558
Employees	4.7%	—	—	—	—	—	—	—	8,702	8,677	9,500

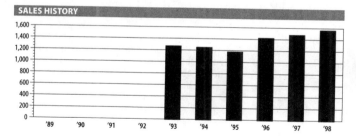

SALES HISTORY

Stanford University

STATE FARM

Don't expect State Farm Mutual Automobile Insurance to host a hurricane party for all its good neighbors.

The Bloomington, Illinois-based company has sought to limit its risk by segregating operations in such disaster-prone states as Florida. The #1 property/casualty insurer in the US also provides accident, health, and life insurance and annuities. Through approximately 16,500 independent agents, State Farm insures about 20% of the automobiles on US roads and some 11 million of the nation's homes.

Competition has increased with the fall of barriers between the banking, securities, and insurance industries. State Farm's not-so-secret weapon is a federal savings bank charter that lets agents offer deposit accounts, CDs, mortgages, auto and home equity loans, and other financial products in Illinois, Missouri, and (eventually) Arizona.

Since its founding, the company has been run by two families, the Mecherles (1922-54) and the Rusts (1954-present).

HISTORY

Retired farmer George Mecherle formed State Farm Mutual Automobile Insurance in Bloomington, Illinois, in 1922. State Farm served only members of farm bureaus and farm mutual insurance companies, charging a one-time membership fee and a premium to protect an automobile against loss or damage.

Unlike most competitors, State Farm offered six-month premium payments. The insurer billed and collected renewal premiums from its home office, relieving the agent of the task. In addition, State Farm determined auto rates by a simple seven-class system, while competitors varied rates for each model.

State Farm in 1926 started City and Village Mutual Automobile Insurance to insure non-farmers' autos; it became part of the company in 1927. Between 1927 and 1931 it introduced borrowed-car protection, wind coverage, and insurance for vehicles used to transport schoolchildren.

State Farm expanded to California in 1928 and formed State Farm Life Insurance the next year. In 1935 it established State Farm Fire Insurance. George Mecherle became chairman in 1937, and his son Ramond became president. In 1939 George challenged agents to write "A Million or More (auto policies) by '44." State Farm saw a 110% increase in policies.

During the 1940s State Farm focused on urban areas after most of the farm bureaus formed their own insurance companies. In the late 1940s and 1950s, it moved to a full-time agency force.

Homeowners' coverage was added to the insurer's offerings under the leadership of Adlai Rust, who led State Farm from 1954 until 1958, when Edward Rust took over. He died in 1985 and his son, Edward Jr., now holds the top spot.

Between 1974 and 1987 the insurer was hit by several gender discrimination suits (a 1992 settlement awarded $157 million to 814 women). State Farm has since tried to hire more women and minorities.

Disasters in the early 1990s, including Hurricane Andrew and the Los Angeles riots, proved costly. The 1994 Northridge earthquake alone generated more than $2.5 billion in claims and contributed to a 72% decline in earnings.

State Farm — the top US home insurer since the mid-1960s — canceled 62,500 residential policies in South Florida in 1996 to cut potential hurricane loss an estimated 11%. In response, Florida's insurance regulators rescinded a previously approved rate hike. That year the company agreed to open more urban neighborhood offices to settle a discrimination suit brought by the Department of Housing and Urban Development, which accused State Farm of discriminating against potential customers in minority-populated areas.

Legal trouble continued. In 1997 State Farm settled with a California couple who alleged the company forged policyholders' signatures on forms declining coverage and concealed evidence to avoid paying earthquake damage claims. That year a policyholder sued to keep State Farm from "wasting company assets" on President Clinton's legal defense against Paula Jones' sexual harassment charges (Clinton held a State Farm personal liability policy).

Relations with its sales force already rocky, State Farm in 1998 proposed to reduce up-front commissions and cut base pay in favor of incentives for customer retention and cross-selling. Reduced auto premiums and increased catastrophe claims from across the US eroded State Farm's bottom line that year. A federal thrift charter obtained in 1998 let the company launch banking operations the next year.

State Farm is appealing a 1999 Illinois state court judgment that it pay $1.2 billion to policyholders for using aftermarket parts in auto repairs.

Chairman and CEO: Edward B. Rust Jr.
VC, President, and COO: Vincent J. Trosino
VC, CFO, and Treasurer: Roger S. Joslin
EVP and Chief Administrative Officer:
James E. Rutrough
EVP and Chief Agency and Marketing Officer:
Charles R. Wright
SVP and General Counsel: Kim M. Brunner
SVP Investments: Paul Eckley
SVP Investments: Kurt G. Moser
SVP: John P. Coffey
SVP: Barbara Cowden
SVP: Jack W. North
VP, Secretary, and Counsel: Laura Sullivan
VP Human Resources: Arlene Hogan
President and CEO, State Farm Federal Savings Bank:
Stanley R. Ommen
EVP and Chief Administrative Officer, State Farm Fire and Casualty Company: W. Donald Sullivan
EVP and Chief Administrative Officer, State Farm Life Insurance: Roger Tompkins
Auditors: PricewaterhouseCoopers LLP

LOCATIONS

HQ: State Farm Mutual Automobile Insurance Company,
1 State Farm Plaza, Bloomington, IL 61710
Phone: 309-766-2311   **Fax:** 309-766-3621
Web site: http://www1.statefarm.com

PRODUCTS/OPERATIONS

1998 Assets

	$ mil.	% of total
Cash & equivalents	521	1
Bonds	27,116	36
Stocks	28,701	39
Other investments	10,712	14
Other assets	7,529	10
Total	**74,579**	**100**

1998 Sales

	$ mil.	% of total
Premiums	24,824	90
Investments & other	2,882	10
Total	**27,706**	**100**

Lines of Business

Accident and health
Automobile insurance
Homeowners' insurance
Life insurance
Reinsurance
Thrift banking
  Auto loans
  CDs
  Deposit accounts
  Home equity loans
  Mortgages

Selected Affiliates and Subsidiaries

State Farm County Mutual Insurance Company of Texas
State Farm Financial Services
State Farm Fire and Casualty Company
State Farm Florida Insurance Company
State Farm General Insurance Company
State Farm Indemnity Company
State Farm Life and Accident Assurance Company
State Farm Life Insurance Company
State Farm Lloyds
State Farm Mutual Automobile Insurance Company

COMPETITORS

AIG	MetLife
Allstate	Nationwide Insurance
American Family	Progressive Corporation
Insurance	Prudential
Berkshire Hathaway	SAFECO
GEICO	Travelers
The Hartford	USAA
Liberty Mutual	Zurich Financial Services

HISTORICAL FINANCIALS & EMPLOYEES

Mutual company FYE: December	Annual Growth	1989	1990	1991	1992	1993	1994	1995	1996	1997	1998
Assets ($ mil.)	9.2%	35,493	37,508	42,676	43,603	47,537	48,842	54,756	60,892	69,442	74,579
Net income ($ mil.)	13.3%	419	372	1,317	1,780	1,742	485	972	2,343	2,450	1,013
Income as % of assets	—	1.2%	1.0%	3.1%	4.1%	3.7%	1.0%	1.8%	3.8%	3.5%	1.3%
Employees	4.1%	52,236	55,133	58,113	60,768	64,520	70,220	71,437	71,612	72,655	76,257

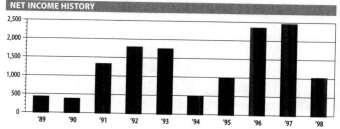

NET INCOME HISTORY

1998 FISCAL YEAR-END
Equity as % of assets: 55.3%
Return on assets: 1.4%
Return on equity: 2.6%
Long-term debt ($ mil.): —
Sales ($ mil.): 27,706

STATE UNIVERSITY OF NEW YORK

OVERVIEW

More than a third of New York's college students direct their feet to the SUNY side of the street. The State University of New York, based in Albany, is virtually deadlocked with California State University as the largest public university system in the US. SUNY has an enrollment of about 370,000 students distributed across its 64 campuses. About 95% of its undergrads pay the in-state tuition of $3,400, less than half that of out-of-state tuition.

At the heart of the SUNY system are 30 community colleges. The system also has 13 university colleges and four university centers offering undergraduate, graduate, postgraduate, and research programs, as well as a network of colleges located on other university campuses. Its specialized colleges include maritime studies, forestry, optometry, and technology. SUNY offers students more than 300 overseas academic programs and sponsors exchange students from more than 50 countries.

Incoming chancellor Robert King is expected to use his background as the governor's budget director to help SUNY deal with its troubled teaching hospitals, which have cost the system $78 million.

HISTORY

State University of New York's roots in public higher education can be traced to several institutions founded in the 19th century: 29 public colleges that acted independently of one another. At the time there were no public liberal arts colleges or research universities in the state.

In 1844 the legislature authorized the creation of the Albany Normal School, which was charged with educating the state's secondary school teachers. Other normal schools were founded between 1861 and 1889 in Brockport, Buffalo, Cortland, Fredonia, Geneseo, New Paltz, Oneonta, Oswego, Plattsburgh, and Potsdam.

In 1846 the legislature chartered the University of Buffalo and authorized academic, theological, legal, and medical studies, but at its formation the new school was solely a medical college. Its first chancellor was the future US president Millard Fillmore, who had been one of the biggest proponents of the school. By the late 1800s the school had expanded to offer degrees in pharmacy, dentistry, and law.

In the early 1900s the state established several agricultural colleges, including schools in Canton (1907), Alfred (1908), Morrisville (1910), Farmingdale (1912), and Cobleskill (1916). The state also set up several schools as units of Cornell University, including colleges of veterinary medicine (1894), agriculture (1909), home economics (1925), and industrial and labor relations (1945).

After WWII, veterans began to fill US colleges and universities, taking advantage of the GI Bill to secure a college education. The legislature set up SUNY in 1948 and appointed a board of trustees charged with coordinating the state public colleges into a single body and establishing four-year liberal arts colleges, professional and graduate schools, research centers, and other facilities deemed necessary.

During the late 1940s and the 1950s, SUNY went through the process of pulling together the separate colleges now under its banner. It also founded New York's first community colleges and public liberal arts colleges. Enrollment began to take off in the late 1950s, jumping from 30,000 in 1955 to 63,000 in 1959.

In the 1960s SUNY greatly expanded its community college system, expanded and transformed its colleges of education into colleges of arts and science, and created four graduate centers. By the early 1970s SUNY had more than 320,000 students. But after the rapid growth of the previous decade, the 1970s brought budget constraints that led to higher tuition, reduced enrollment goals, and employment cutbacks.

SUNY's enrollment grew slowly during the 1980s, reaching more than 400,000 by 1990. In the early 1990s the system began implementing SUNY 2000, a plan that called for increasing access to education and diversifying undergraduate studies, among other plans. Following his election in 1994, Governor George Pataki proposed more than $550 million in cuts to the SUNY system.

In 1997 John Ryan replaced Thomas Bartlett as chancellor. The following year SUNY became the exclusive sponsor of The College Channel, a guide to colleges and college life aimed at high school juniors and seniors and broadcast by Channel One, a PRIMEDIA-owned satellite channel that reaches 12,000 middle- and high schools each day. In 1999 the governor's budget director, Robert King, was named chancellor to replace Bartlett, who retired.

Chairman: Thomas F. Egan
Chancellor Emeritus: John W. Ryan
Chancellor: Robert King, age 52, $250,000 pay
Provost and Vice Chancellor Academic Affairs: Peter D. Salins
Executive Vice Chancellor: Donald G. Dunn
Vice Chancellor Finance and Business: Brian T. Stenson
Vice Chancellor and Secretary: John J. O'Connor
Associate Vice Chancellor Government Relations: Molly McKeown
Associate Vice Chancellor Marketing and Enrollment Management: David L. Farren
Associate Vice Chancellor Public Relations: Jon R. Sorensen
Associate Vice Chancellor University Life: William J. Murabito
Associate Provost Advanced Learning and Information Services: Christine E. Haile
Associate Provost Community Colleges: William Gehring
Associate Provost Comprehensive Colleges: Jennifer A. Clarke
Associate Provost Engineering and Technical Education: Robert Kraushaar
Associate Provost Hospital and Clinical Services: Peter T. Pileggi
Associate Provost Opportunity Programs: Robert D. James
University Controller: Patrick J. Wiater
University Auditor: John H. Murphy
President University Faculty Senate: Joseph G. Flynn
Auditors: KPMG LLP

LOCATIONS

HQ: State University Plaza, Albany, NY 12246
Phone: 518-443-5555 **Fax:** 518-443-5321
Web site: http://www.suny.edu

PRODUCTS/OPERATIONS

SUNY Colleges of Technology
Alfred
Canton
Cobleskill
Delhi
Morrisville
University Colleges of Technology

Health Science Centers
Brooklyn
Syracuse

Specialized Colleges
College of Environmental Science and Forestry
College of Optometry
College of Technology at Farmingdale
Institute of Technology at Utica/Rome
Maritime College

Statutory Colleges
College of Agriculture and Life Sciences at Cornell University
College of Human Ecology at Cornell University
College of Veterinary Medicine at Cornell University
College of Ceramics at Alfred University
School of Industrial and Labor Relations at Cornell University

University Centers (research and graduate studies)
Albany
Binghamton
Buffalo
Stony Brook

University Colleges (undergraduate and graduate studies)

Brockport	Old Westbury
Buffalo State	Oneonta
Cortland	Oswego
Empire State	Plattsburgh
Fredonia	Potsdam
Geneseo	Purchase
New Paltz	

Selected Affiliated Organizations
Construction Fund
The Research Foundation of SUNY
SUNY Business Officer's Association
SUNY Computer Officer's Association
Task Force on Postsecondary Education and Disabilites

HISTORICAL FINANCIALS & EMPLOYEES

School FYE: June	Annual Growth	1989	1990	1991	1992	1993	1994	1995	1996	1997	1998
Sales ($ mil.)	4.9%	3,034	3,113	3,307	3,407	3,692	4,018	4,167	4,136	4,244	4,564
Employees	3.8%	47,934	48,347	49,598	47,514	47,574	48,194	52,000	55,000	56,135	65,000

SALES HISTORY

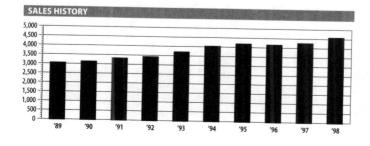

STATER BROS. HOLDINGS INC.

OVERVIEW

David felled one Goliath, but could he have toppled three? That's the task ahead of Colton, California-based Stater Bros. Holdings. With 112 supermarkets in five heavily populated Southern California counties, the company is not exactly tiny (and it is adding nearly 45 stores it bought from Albertson's and its newly acquired Lucky chain). But its foes — highly profitable Albertson's, burgeoning Fred Meyer (with the Ralph's and Food 4 Less chains; now part of Kroger), and Safeway (Vons) — are the biggest names in the US supermarket industry.

Stater Bros. is owned by La Cadena Investments, a general partnership consisting of Stater Bros. chairman, president, and CEO Jack Brown and other top company executives.

Competition from the grocery giants has put a strain on the company's profit margins and sales. To distinguish itself from rivals, the chain refuses to offer promotional games and frequent shopper cards, boasting everyday low prices instead. Stater Bros. owns 50% of milk and juice processor Santee Dairies and is planning to expand into San Diego County.

HISTORY

In 1936, at age 23, Cleo Stater and his twin brother, Leo, mortgaged a Chevrolet to make a down payment on a modest grocery store where Cleo had been working for five years in their hometown of Yucaipa, California. Later that year the brothers bought their second grocery in the nearby community of Redlands. Their younger brother, Lavoy, soon joined them to help build the company. In 1938 the brothers opened the first Stater Bros. market in Colton; by 1939 they had a chain of four stores.

The small, family-owned grocery chain continued to grow. In 1948 Stater Bros. opened its first supermarket (which was several times larger than its other stores and had its own parking lot), in Riverside. By 1950 the company had 12 stores.

Stater Bros. consolidated its offices and warehouse in Colton in the early 1960s and continued its expansion into nearby communities. By 1964 it operated 27 supermarkets in 18 cities in Los Angeles, Orange, Riverside, and San Bernardino Counties. In 1968 the brothers sold the company's 35 stores to Long Beach, California-based petroleum services provider Petrolane for $33 million. Lavoy succeeded Cleo as president.

As a division of Petrolane, Stater Bros. kept growing. In the 1970s the company introduced a new store design that had an expanded sales area but required less land and a smaller building. The number of stores more than doubled (to over 80) between 1968 and 1979, when Lavoy retired.

Ron Burkle, VP of Administration for Petrolane, and his father, Joe, president of Stater Bros., attempted to buy the chain for $100 million in 1981. Infuriated by the low bid, Petrolane fired Ron and demoted his father, who left that year. Jack Brown was named president in his place. Petrolane sold the chain in 1983 to La Cadena Investments, a private company that included Brown and other top Stater Bros. executives.

Leo died in 1985. That year the company went public to reduce debt from the 1983 LBO and to provide funds for an extensive expansion plan. It also incorporated as Stater Bros. Inc. In 1986 a proxy fight for control of the company erupted between Brown's La Cadena group and chairman Bernard Garrett, who owned about 41% of Stater Bros. Brown had been suspended as president and CEO (Joe Burkle returned in his place), but Los-Angeles-based investment firm Craig Corp. bought Garrett's stake and Brown returned; he was later elected chairman. That year Stater Bros. also became a co-owner in Santee Dairies with Hughes Markets.

The next year Craig and Stater Bros. executives took the grocery chain private again. Burkle bought a 9% stake in Craig in 1989 through Yucaipa Capital Partners. Also in 1987 Craig reduced its stake in Stater Bros., transferring some stock to La Cadena. Stater Bros. Holdings Inc. was created as a parent company for the grocery chain.

Stater Bros. expressed an interest in buying rival Alpha Beta stores when they were put up for sale, but Yucaipa Companies bought them in 1991. Craig considered selling its stake in Stater Bros. in 1992; it finally sold its half of the company to La Cadena in 1996.

In 1997 the company became Southern California's first grocery chain to use the state's new electronic benefits transfer system. In 1998 Stater Bros. announced it would spend $15 million to open its first three stores in San Diego County. In mid-1999 Stater Bros. acquired 33 Albertson's and 10 Lucky stores (as well as one store site) as part of rival Albertson's acquisition of American Stores.

Chairman, President, and CEO: Jack H. Brown
EVP: Donald Baker, age 57
SVP Finance and CFO: Dennis N. Beal
Group SVP Development: H. Harrison Lightfoot
Group SVP Human Resources: A. Gayle Paden
VP Corporate Affairs: Susan Atkinson
VP Human Resources: Kathy Finazzo
Secretary: Bruce D. Varner
Auditors: Ernst & Young LLP

LOCATIONS

HQ: 21700 Barton Rd., Colton, CA 92324
Phone: 909-783-5000   **Fax:** 909-783-3930

Stater Bros. Holdings operates more than 110
supermarkets in Southern California.

1998 Stores

	No.
San Bernardino County	46
Riverside County	35
Orange County	16
Los Angeles County	13
Kern County	2
Total	**112**

PRODUCTS/OPERATIONS

Selected Departments and Products
Bakery
Convenience foods
Dairy products
Delicatessen
Fresh produce
Frozen foods
General merchandise
Meats
Seafood

Business Affiliations
Santee Dairies, Inc. (50%, dairy processing)
Stater Bros. Development, Inc. (supermarket
construction and shopping center maintenance and
management)
Stater Bros. Markets (retail supermarkets)

COMPETITORS

7-Eleven
Albertson's
Arden Group
Costco Companies
Fred Meyer
Longs
Safeway
Smart & Final
Trader Joe's Co
Wal-Mart
Walgreen
Whole Foods

HISTORICAL FINANCIALS & EMPLOYEES

Private FYE: September	Annual Growth	1990	1991	1992	1993	1994	1995	1996	1997	1998	1999
Sales ($ mil.)	2.7%	—	—	1,538	1,526	1,540	1,580	1,705	1,718	1,726	1,850
Employees	6.3%	—	—	8,500	9,800	10,000	9,800	8,900	8,900	8,700	13,000

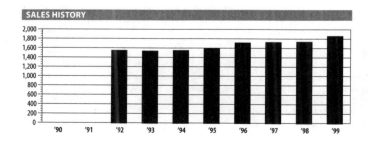

SALES HISTORY

SUBWAY

OVERVIEW

They're called heros, hoagies, and poor-boys, but co-founder Fred DeLuca calls his foot-long submarine sandwiches easy money. Milford, Connecticut-based Subway has more franchises — some 14,000 restaurants in nearly 75 countries — than any other company except McDonald's. Each location offers hot and cold sandwiches, chips, salads, kids' meals, freshly baked cookies and buns, and beverages; restaurants are also free to add menu items to fit local tastes and customs. The company franchises nearly 12,000 Subway restaurants in the US and has locations that range from freestanding units and shopping centers to airports, colleges, and sports arenas. President DeLuca and co-founder Peter Buck own the company, which features DeLuca's mother as its treasurer.

Because the initial franchise cost is relatively low and operations are simple (minimum space requirements and no cooking on the premises except for baking bread), Subway is one of the fastest-growing franchises in the world. In the past decade the chain has added more than 10,000 stores.

However, the picture is not all rosy. Franchisees criticize the company for its 8% royalty fee, the highest in fast-food franchising. Subway also gets involved in more legal disputes than its top seven competitors combined; its problems include not only discontented franchisees, but also landlords and regulators.

HISTORY

In 1965, 17-year-old Fred DeLuca dreamed of becoming a doctor and worked as a stockboy in a Bridgeport, Connecticut, hardware store to earn college tuition. It wasn't enough, so he cornered family friend Peter Buck at a backyard barbecue and asked for advice. Buck, a nuclear physicist, suggested DeLuca start a submarine sandwich shop and put up $1,000 to get him started.

In 1965 when the summer was coming to an end, DeLuca rented a small location in a remote area of Bridgeport for $165 a month, opened Pete's Super Submarines, and began selling foot-long sandwiches. On the first day the sandwiches were so popular that DeLuca hired customers to help him behind the counter; by the end of the day, he had sold out of all his supplies. The sandwiches continued to be popular for a while, but within a few months the shop started losing money and DeLuca and Buck found that selling submarine sandwiches was a seasonal business. They decided they could create an illusion of success by opening a second location and then a third. The third store was finally successful, partly because of its more visible location and increased marketing and partly because of a new name — Subway.

DeLuca and Buck had set a goal of 32 shops open by 1975, but they had only 16 by 1974. They realized that the only way they could reach their goal in one year was to license the Subway name. The first franchise opened that year, in Wallingford, Connecticut, and there were 32 by the following year's end. The partners hit 100 by 1978 and 200 by 1982, and DeLuca set a new goal: 5,000 Subway shops by 1994. The first international Subway opened in Bahrain in 1984, and Subway was opening more than a dozen stores a week in the late 1980s. DeLuca hit his goal by 1990, well ahead of schedule.

Menu changes have been few, although Subway has added hot sandwiches, veggie sandwiches, salads, and round-bun deli sandwiches. With its limited menu, the company kept equipment needs to a minimum, although Subway did have to design a special oven to fit into narrow spaces.

Over the years DeLuca has tried several other franchise concepts, including We Care Hair (budget styling salons), Cajun Joe's (spicy fried chicken), and Q Burgers, but none have taken off.

A Federal Trade Commission investigation against the company was dropped in 1993, but Subway lost a $1.4 million battle over franchise rights in 1994. That year Subway opened the first of 200 restaurants planned for Russia by 2005, and in 1995 it announced plans to open 2,000 sandwich shops in railway stations in China by 1999. Subway opened its 11,000th restaurant in 1995.

A multimillion dollar contract with the Navy Exchange System gave Subway the right in 1997 to develop Subway restaurants on more than 100 naval installations around the world. The following year Subway scratched chicken breast sandwiches from its Ohio stores' menus after Tyson Foods (one of Subway's major suppliers) recalled a batch of chicken that was feared to be undercooked. In 1999 the company opened its 14,000th restaurant in Mount Gambier, Australia.

OFFICERS

Chairman: Peter Buck
President and CEO: Frederick A. DeLuca
Treasurer: Carmela DeLuca
Controller: Tom Hislop
Director of Human Resources: Wendy Kopazna
Director of Sales: Don Fertman

LOCATIONS

HQ: 325 Bic Dr., Milford, CT 06460
Phone: 203-877-4281   **Fax:** 203-876-6695
Web site: http://www.subway.com

PRODUCTS/OPERATIONS

Selected Menu Items

Breakfast Sandwiches
Bacon and Egg
Cheese and Egg
Ham and Egg
Western Egg

Cold Subs and Deli Style Sandwiches
Classic Italian B.M.T.
Cold Cut Trio
Ham
Roast Beef
Subway Club
Subway Seafood and Crab
Tuna
Turkey Breast and Ham
Veggie Delite

Hot Subs
Meatball
Roasted Chicken Breast
Steak & Cheese
Subway Melt

Salads
Tuna
Turkey Breast
Veggie Delight

Wraps
Chicken Parmesan Ranch
Steak & Cheese
Turkey Breast & Bacon

COMPETITORS

7-Eleven
Advantica Restaurant
  Group
American Restaurant
  Group
Blimpie
Boston Chicken
Burger King
CKE Restaurants
Casey's General Stores
Chick-fil-A
Dairy Queen
Domino's Pizza
Fresh Choice
Jack in the Box

Jerry's Famous Deli
Little Caesar
McDonald's
Miami Subs
Panera Bread
Quizno's
Schlotzsky's
Shoney's
TRICON
Tosco
Triarc
Wall Street Deli
Wawa
Wendy's

HISTORICAL FINANCIALS & EMPLOYEES

Private FYE: December	Annual Growth	1989	1990	1991	1992	1993	1994	1995	1996	1997	1998
Systemwide sales ($ mil.)	7.1%	—	—	—	—	2,200	2,400	2,600	2,700	3,300	3,100
Employees	—	—	—	—	—	—	—	—	—	—	—

SALES HISTORY

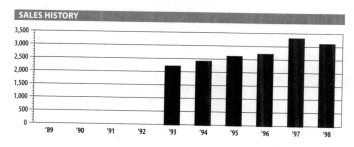

SUNKIST GROWERS, INC.

OVERVIEW

Sunkist is ripe in the minds of shoppers. One of the most recognized brands in the US, the Sunkist name on fruit-bowl staples commands higher prices in supermarkets. Sherman Oaks, California-based citrus cooperative Sunkist Growers counts more than 6,500 California and Arizona farmers as its members/owners. The co-op markets fresh oranges, lemons, grapefruit, and tangerines, as well as citrus juice and peel products. The familiar ink-stamped Sunkist name is now only on lemons; its other fruits wear stickers naming the variety, unique retail code, and the brand logo to make retail checkout easier.

The co-op's Processed Products division turns the fruit that doesn't meet fresh market standards into juices and oils used in food products. Sunkist has licensing agreements with companies in over 50 countries. Through those agreements, the Sunkist name and logo appear on scores of beverages and other products, such as flowers and snacks. The co-op's fruits are exported around the world; Japan and Hong Kong are its largest export customers. Sunkist is eyeing new markets in China, Argentina, and elsewhere.

HISTORY

Sunkist Growers was founded in the early 1890s as the Pachappa Orange Growers, a group of California citrus farmers determined to control the sale of their fruit. Success attracted new members, and in 1893 the Southern California Fruit Exchange was born. The name "Sunkissed" was coined by an ad copywriter in 1908, and it was soon reworked into "Sunkist" and registered as a trademark, becoming the first brand name for a fresh produce item. Eventually the co-op renamed itself after its popular brand: It became Sunkist Growers in 1952. Sunkist began licensing its trademark to other companies in the early 1950s.

As early as 1916 efforts to increase consumption of citrus included designing and marketing glass citrus juicers and encouraging homemakers to "Drink an Orange." The co-op also promoted the practice of putting lemon slices in tea or water and funded early research on the health benefits of vitamins (vitamin C in particular). In 1925 tissue wrappers gave way to stamping the Sunkist name directly on each piece of fruit.

Although Sunkist pioneered bottled orange juice in 1933, its efforts to market juices were never as successful as its Florida competitors. Florida oranges are drippy and dowdy and thus better suited for juicing. Capitalizing on this aspect, Florida growers dominated the market for fresh and frozen juice.

In 1937 Congress created a system of citrus shipment quotas and limits (known as "marketing orders") that ultimately proved most beneficial to large citrus cooperatives. By the early 1990s the marketing order system was under political attack, and in 1992 the Justice Department filed civil prosecution against Sunkist, alleging that the co-op had reaped unfair extra

profits by surpassing its lemon shipment limits. In 1994, after much legal wrangling, the quotas were abolished and the Justice Department dropped its case against Sunkist.

Inconveniently warm weather and increasing competition from imported citrus marked the harvests of 1996. That year the co-op had trouble maintaining discipline among its members, as some undercut Sunkist price levels, while others flooded the market to sell their fruit at the higher early market prices, creating a supply surplus. Also that year the co-op relinquished the marketing of all Sunkist juices in North America to Florida-based Lykes Bros. in a licensing agreement.

To woo younger consumers, usually conservative Sunkist launched a Web site in 1997 featuring Scurvy Boy — a hipster with green hair and bad teeth who is transformed by eating oranges. The site proved popular enough to engender new versions of Scurvy Boy in 1998 and 1999.

The co-op agreed to distribute grapefruit in 1998 from Florida's Tuxedo Fruit, giving Sunkist a winter grapefruit supply and increasing its year-round consumer a-peel. Also in 1998 Russell Hanlin, Sunkist president and CEO since 1978, was succeeded by Vince Lupinacci. Lupinacci, who had held positions with Pepsi and Six Flags, became the first person from outside the citrus business to hold Sunkist's top post.

Despite increased competition from imported Latin American, South African, and Spanish crops, a damaging California freeze, and the ill effects of El Niño, Sunkist sold 90 million cartons of fresh citrus in 1998, the greatest volume in its history.

Chairman Emeritus: Ralph E. Bodine
Chairman Emeritus: Thomas N. Dungan
Chairman Emeritus: John V. Newman
Chairman: James H. Mast
VC: John M. Dickenson III
VC: Dan S. Dunlap
VC: Al Williams
President and CEO: Vincent Lupinacci
SVP Law and General Counsel: Thomas M. Moore
VP Processed Products and Research and Technical Services: Owen W. Belletto
VP Finance and Administration: H. B. Flach
VP Fresh Fruit Marketing: Richard J. Mead
VP Corporate Relations and Counsel: William K. Quarles
Secretary: Linda D. Shepler
Treasurer and Controller: Richard G. French
Director Human Resources: John R. McGovern
Auditors: Deloitte & Touche LLP

LOCATIONS

HQ: 14130 Riverside Dr., Sherman Oaks, CA 91423
Phone: 818-986-4800   **Fax:** 818-379-7405
Web site: http://www.sunkist.com

1998 Sales

	% of total
US	77
Other countries	23
Total	**100**

PRODUCTS/OPERATIONS

1998 Fruit Production

	cartons (thou.)
Oranges	
Navel & other	38,105
Valencia	24,844
Lemons	19,497
Grapefruit	6,060
Tangerines	1,942
Total	**90,448**

1998 Sales

	$ mil.	% of total
Fresh fruit		
Domestic	616	58
Export	297	28
Fruit products	108	10
Other	48	4
Total	**1,069**	**100**

COMPETITORS

Alico
Chiquita Brands
Dole

HISTORICAL FINANCIALS & EMPLOYEES

Cooperative FYE: October	Annual Growth	1989	1990	1991	1992	1993	1994	1995	1996	1997	1998
Sales ($ mil.)	0.0%	934	1,066	956	1,029	1,093	1,005	1,096	1,025	1,075	1,069
Employees	(1.7%)	1,200	1,000	1,000	900	1,200	1,138	1,150	878	813	875

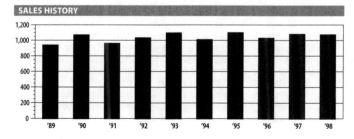

SALES HISTORY

TIAA-CREF

The Teachers Insurance and Annuity Association-College Retirement Equities Fund (TIAA-CREF) is learning new math. The New York City-based organization no longer has tax-exempt status, but is still operated as if it were a not-for-profit — with a twist. It continues to provide benefits for some 2 million members of the academic community, making it the US's largest pension fund provider. Thanks to the loosening of restrictions it faced as a not-for-profit, TIAA-CREF is also spreading outside academia's ivied confines. TIAA-CREF now has two major operating units. Retirement Services continues the historical core business of offering members financial advice, investment information, pensions, and annuities. TIAA-CREF Enterprises targets the general public with such offerings as mutual funds, tuition financing, and education IRAs; this unit also includes TIAA-CREF Trust (trusts, estate planning, investment management).

TIAA-CREF is known for active (and choosy) investing. It's not afraid to use its clout to sway — or even replace — portfolio companies' management. It is cautious in its underwriting and minimizes vulnerability to commercial real estate cycles through scrupulous selection (holdings include a 27% stake in the Mall of America).

With $15 million, the Carnegie Foundation for the Advancement of Teaching in 1905 founded the Teachers Insurance and Annuity Association (TIAA) in New York City to provide retirement benefits and other forms of financial security to employees of educational and research organizations. When Carnegie's original endowment was found to be insufficient, another for $1 million reorganized the fund into a defined contribution plan in 1918. TIAA was the first portable pension plan, letting participants change employers without losing benefits and offering a fixed annuity. The fund required infusions of Carnegie cash until 1947.

In 1952 TIAA CEO William Greenough pioneered the variable annuity, based on common stock investments, and created the College Retirement Equities Fund (CREF) to offer it. Designed to supplement TIAA's fixed annuity, CREF invested participants' premiums in stocks. CREF and TIAA were subject to New York insurance (but not SEC) regulation.

During the 1950s, TIAA led the fight for Social Security benefits for university employees and began offering group total disability coverage (1957) and group life insurance (1958).

In 1971 TIAA-CREF began helping colleges boost investment returns from endowments, then moved into endowment management. It helped found a research center to provide objective investment information in 1972.

For 70 years retirement was the only way members could exit TIAA-CREF. Their only investment choices were stocks through CREF or a one-way transfer into TIAA's annuity accounts based on long-term bond, real estate, and mortgage investments. In the 1980s CREF indexed its funds to the S&P average.

By 1987's stock crash, TIAA-CREF had a million members, many of whom wanted more protection from stock market fluctuations. After the crash, Clifton Wharton (the first African-American to head a major US financial organization) became CEO; the next year CREF added a money market fund, for which the SEC required complete transferability, even outside TIAA-CREF. Now vulnerable to competition, TIAA-CREF became more flexible, adding investment options and long-term-care plans.

John Biggs became CEO in 1993. After the 1994 bond crash, TIAA-CREF began educating members on the ABCs of retirement investing, hoping to persuade them not to switch to flashy short-term investments and not to panic during such cyclical events as the crash.

In 1996 the company went international, buying interests in UK commercial and mixed-use property. TIAA-CREF filed for SEC approval of more mutual funds in 1997. Although Federal tax legislation took away TIAA-CREF's tax-exempt status in 1997, the change was made without decreasing annuity incomes for the year.

The status change let TIAA-CREF offer no-load mutual funds to the public in 1998. A trust company and financial planning services were added; all new products were sold at cost. TIAA-CREF in 1998 became the first pension fund to force out an entire board of directors (that of sputtering cafeteria firm Furr's/Bishop's). When prospective buyers didn't bite on asking prices, TIAA-CREF in 1999 pulled several real estate properties (including Mall of America) from the market. Also that year TIAA-CREF's crusade to curb "dead hand" poison pills (an antitakeover defense measure) found favor with the shareholders of Bergen Brunswig, Lubrizol, and Mylan Laboratories.

Chairman, President, and CEO: John H. Biggs
VC and Chief Investment Officer: Martin L. Leibowitz
EVP and General Counsel: Charles H. Stamm
EVP Consulting Services: David A. Shunk
EVP, Corporate Management Information Systems: James A. Wolf
EVP External Affairs: Don Harrell
EVP Human Resources: Matina S. Horner
EVP Finance and Planning: Richard L. Gibbs
EVP Marketing: Deanne J. Shallcross
EVP Retirement Administration: Mary Ann Werner
President and CEO, TIAA-CREF Life Insurance: Thomas G. Walsh
President, Retirement Services: John A. Putney Jr.
President, TIAA-CREF Enterprises: John J. McCormack
President, TIAA-CREF Trust: Joseph J. Gazzoli
EVP CREF Investments and TIAA-CREF Investment Management: Scott C. Evans
EVP TIAA Investments and TIAA-CREF Investment Management: John A. Somers
VP and Corporate Secretary: E. Laverne Jones
Auditors: Deloitte & Touche LLP

LOCATIONS

HQ: Teachers Insurance Annuity Association-College Retirement Equities Fund,
730 3rd Ave., New York, NY 10017
Phone: 212-490-9000   **Fax:** 212-916-6231
Web site: http://www.tiaa-cref.org

PRODUCTS/OPERATIONS

1998 TIAA Assets

	$ mil.	% of total
Cash & equivalents	512	—
Bonds	69,068	68
Stocks	1,257	1
Mortgages	20,249	20
Real estate	6,099	6
Other investments	1,513	1
Other assets	3,518	4
Total	**102,216**	**100**

1998 CREF Assets

	$ mil.	% of total
Cash & equivalents	175	—
Bonds	12,402	8
Stocks	133,800	91
Other assets	1,175	1
Total	**147,552**	**100**

1998 Sales

	$ mil.	% of total
Capital gains	24,286	53
Premiums & other	9,516	21
Investment income	9,669	21
Annuity dividend additions	2,428	5
Total	**45,899**	**100**

Subsidiaries
TIAA-CREF Enterprises (for the general public)
TIAA-CREF Retirement Services (for educators only)
TIAA-CREF Trust Co. FSB (trust services)

COMPETITORS

AXA Financial
Aetna
American Express
American General
Berkshire Hathaway
CIGNA
Charles Schwab
Citigroup
FMR
FleetBoston
John Hancock
MassMutual

Merrill Lynch
MetLife
New York Life
Northwestern Mutual
Principal Financial
Prudential
T. Rowe Price
Transamerica
U.S. Global Investors
USAA
Vanguard Group

HISTORICAL FINANCIALS & EMPLOYEES

Not-for-profit FYE: December	Annual Growth	1989	1990	1991	1992	1993	1994	1995	1996	1997	1998
Sales ($ mil.)	21.6%	—	—	—	—	—	—	—	31,024	41,437	45,899
Employees	5.5%	—	—	—	—	—	—	—	4,490	4,920	5,000

SALES HISTORY

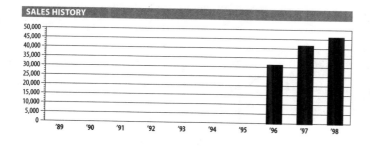

TENNESSEE VALLEY AUTHORITY

OVERVIEW

The Tennessee Valley Authority (TVA) is *not* an expert on Tennessee attractions such as Dollywood and the Grand Ole Opry, but it is an authority on power generation. The Knoxville-based federal corporation is the US's largest electricity generator and the sole power wholesaler, by law, in an 80,000-sq.-mi. territory that includes most of Tennessee and portions of six neighboring states. Established during the Depression as part of the New Deal, the TVA began as an effort to spur economic development in its area.

The TVA works with 159 locally owned power distributors who supply power to more than 7 million consumers. It manages the Tennessee River system (the US's fifth-largest) for power production, flood control, and more.

The TVA's rates are among the nation's lowest, which would-be competitors attribute to more than $1 billion a year in indirect subsidies resulting from the TVA's exemption from federal and state income and property taxes. Moreover, the TVA's government affiliation allows it to arrange loans at favorable rates. To prepare for deregulation, the TVA is implementing a 10-year business plan that includes cutting its $27 billion debt in half.

HISTORY

In 1924 the Army Corps of Engineers completed construction (begun in 1918) of the Wilson Dam on the Tennessee River at Muscle Shoals, Alabama, to provide power for two WWI-era nitrate plants. With the war long since ended, the question of what to do with the facilities became a political football.

Legislation creating a regional federal agency to take control of the plants and manage the waterways of the Tennessee Valley made it through Congress but was vetoed. Not until 1933, after Franklin Roosevelt became president, was the Tennessee Valley Authority (TVA) created by an act of Congress. New Dealers saw the TVA as a way to revitalize the regional economy through flood control, improved navigation, and power generation. Power companies claimed the agency was unconstitutional, but in 1939 a federal court ruled against them. By that time the agency had five hydroelectric facilities and five under construction and had acquired power lines.

During the 1940s the TVA supplied power for the war effort, including the Manhattan Project in Oak Ridge, Tennessee. Between 1945 and 1950 Tennessee Valley power usage nearly doubled. Although it continued to add dams, the TVA couldn't keep up with postwar power demand, so in 1949 it began construction of its first coal-fired unit. Some members of Congress questioned whether non-hydroelectric plants fit with the agency's mission, and a task force recommended in 1955 that the TVA be dissolved. The TVA survived, but its funding was cut back.

In 1959 the TVA Act was amended so that the TVA could sell bonds. The agency no longer received direct government appropriations for its power operations and had to pay back what it had received from the government in the past.

The agency began to build its first nuclear plant, Browns Ferry, in Alabama in 1967. The TVA planned an ambitious nuclear program of 17 units, but skyrocketing costs forced it to raise rates and cut maintenance to its coal-fired plants, which led to breakdowns. In 1985 five operating reactors had to be shut down because of safety concerns.

In 1988 former auto industry executive Marvin Runyon was appointed chairman of the agency. "Carvin' Marvin" cut layers of management, sold three airplanes, and got rid of peripheral businesses, saving $400 million a year. Runyon left the TVA to head the postal service in 1992. He was replaced by Craven Crowell, who began preparing the TVA for competition in the retail power market, including taking a one-time charge of $136 million in 1995 to encourage 2,500 employees to leave.

The TVA ended its nuclear construction program in 1996 after it brought two nuclear units on line within three months, a first for a US utility. The next year Crowell proposed ending TVA's annual $106 million government appropriation for nonpower projects. TVA also raised its rates for the first time in 10 years, planning to use the extra funds to reduce its debt. In response to a lawsuit filed by neighboring utilities, the TVA agreed to stop "laundering" power by using third parties to sell it outside the agency's legally authorized area.

But despite its preparations for competition, the TVA continued its tradition of promoting its region. In 1999 the agency finished installing almost $2 billion in scrubbers and other equipment at its coal-fired plants so that it could buy Kentucky coal along with cleaner Wyoming coal. Allegedly the TVA hadn't installed enough scrubbers: The EPA ordered the TVA to stop making major overhauls on old coal plants that had been exempted from the Clean Air Act, extending the plants' lives without making environmental improvements.

Chairman: Craven Crowell
President and COO: O. J. Zeringue
EVP Financial Services and CFO: David N. Smith
EVP, Resource Group: Kate Jackson
EVP, Customer Service and Marketing Group:
  Mark O. Medford
EVP, Transmission and Power Supply Group:
  William Museler
EVP and Chief Nuclear Officer: John Scalice
**EVP Business Services and Chief Administrative
  Officer:** Norm A. Zigrossi
SVP Human Resources: Wally Tanksley
VP Communications: Steve Bender
General Counsel: Edward S. Christenbury
Auditors: PricewaterhouseCoopers LLP

LOCATIONS

HQ: 400 W. Summit Hill Dr., Knoxville, TN 37902
Phone: 423-632-2101   **Fax:** 423-632-6783
Web site: http://www.tva.gov

PRODUCTS/OPERATIONS

1998 Electricity Sales

	$ mil.	% of total
Municipalities & cooperatives	5,554	83
Industries	523	8
Federal agencies	556	8
Other	96	1
Total	**6,729**	**100**

1998 Electricity Marketed

	kWh (mil.)	% of total
Municipalities & cooperatives	123,330	76
Federal agencies	21,293	13
Industries	18,514	11
Total	**163,137**	**100**

1998 Electric-Generating Capacity

	MW	% of total
Fossil	15,003	53
Nuclear	5,620	20
Hydroelectric	5,491	19
Combustion turbine	2,384	8
Total	**28,498**	**100**

Selected Nonpower Programs
Economic development
Environmental Research Center
Land Between the Lakes Recreation Area
Water, wildlife, and land stewardship

COMPETITORS

AEP	Duke Energy
Allegheny Energy	Entergy
Ameren	Illinova
Carolina Power & Light	LG&E Energy
Cinergy	Oglethorpe Power
Conectiv	Southern Company
Dominion Resources	

HISTORICAL FINANCIALS & EMPLOYEES

Government-owned FYE: September	Annual Growth	1989	1990	1991	1992	1993	1994	1995	1996	1997	1998
Sales ($ mil.)	2.9%	5,287	5,339	5,136	5,065	5,276	5,401	5,375	5,693	5,552	6,729
Net income ($ mil.)	(9.7%)	559	(387)	286	120	311	151	10	61	8	233
Income as % of sales	—	10.6%	—	5.6%	2.4%	5.9%	2.8%	0.2%	1.1%	0.1%	3.5%
Employees	(8.6%)	26,700	28,392	24,870	19,493	18,974	19,027	16,559	16,021	14,500	13,818

NET INCOME HISTORY

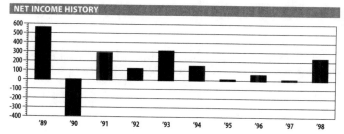

1998 FISCAL YEAR-END

Debt ratio: 82.0%
Return on equity: 4.7%
Cash ($ mil.): 451
Current ratio: 0.38
Long-term debt ($ mil.): 23,020

TEXAS A&M UNIVERSITY

OVERVIEW

Don't even think about trying to douse the Aggie school spirit. Renowned for their enthusiasm and school traditions, students at the namesake school of The Texas A&M University System don't mind standing for an entire football game or saluting the school mascot (a pooch named Reveille). But behind the fervor is solid education: College Station, Texas-based Texas A&M University System teaches more than 90,000 students at nine universities. Texas A&M in College Station is the largest campus, with an enrollment exceeding 44,500. A&M also operates eight state agencies

and a health sciences center (including Baylor College of Dentistry in Dallas).

The Texas A&M University System has been expanding its academic and physical reach. It is adding a branch in San Antonio (the branch will be located at Palo Alto College in San Antonio's south side but could eventually become a separate campus). The system is also fighting to add a law school to its ranks: It established an affiliation with Houston's South Texas College of Law (a private institution) in 1998, but faced opposition from the Texas Higher Education Coordinating Board, which oversees public higher education in Texas.

HISTORY

The Texas Constitution of 1876 created an agricultural and mechanical college and stated that "separate schools shall be provided for the white and colored children, and impartial provisions shall be made for both." The white school, the Agricultural and Mechanical College of Texas (later Texas A&M), began instruction that year. Texas A&M was a men's school at first, and membership in its Corps of Cadets was mandatory. The Agricultural and Mechanical College of Texas for Colored Youth (later Prairie View A&M) opened in 1878.

To help fund the agricultural colleges and The University of Texas, the Legislature established the Permanent University Fund in 1876 to hold more than 1 million acres of land in West Texas as an endowment. An additional 1 million acres was added in 1883.

When the Santa Rita well on university lands in West Texas struck oil in 1923, money flowed into the Permanent University Fund's coffers. Under the provisions of the constitution, The University of Texas got two-thirds of the income, and A&M got the rest.

The Texas A&M College System, established in 1948, originally included Texas A&M, Prairie View A&M, Tarleton State, and Arlington State (now The University of Texas at Arlington; it dropped out in 1965). In 1963 it changed its name to The Texas A&M University System.

Texas A&M went co-ed in 1963, and membership in the Corps became voluntary in 1965. Enrollment jumped from about 8,000 in 1963 to more than 35,000 by the mid-1980s. Texas A&M University at Galveston was created in 1962 as the Texas Maritime Academy, but its roots go back to a school of seamanship and navigation founded in 1931.

The system grew quickly in 1989 when it added Texas A&I University (now Texas A&M University-Kingsville), Corpus Christi State (now Texas A&M University-Corpus Christi), and Laredo State University (now Texas A&M International). West Texas State College in Canyon — which was founded in 1910 and reached university status in 1963 — joined the system in 1990 and became West Texas A&M University in 1993.

The 91-year-old Baylor College of Dentistry (in Dallas) and East Texas State University, well-known for training future teachers, joined the A&M system in 1996 (East Texas State was divided into Texas A&M University-Commerce and Texas A&M-Texarkana). In 1997 the system opened the first portion of the $82 million George Bush Presidential Library and Museum.

In early 1998 the system signed an alliance with the private South Texas College of Law in Houston, which was opposed by the Texas Higher Education Coordinating Board. (In 1999 a judge ruled that the two schools had to discontinue their affiliation.) That year, Texas Instruments donated $5.1 million to the system (one of the largest donations in the institution's history) for the creation of an analog technology program. Chancellor Barry Thompson announced his retirement effective in 1999, and the system named former Army general Howard Graves as his replacement.

Tragedy struck the College Station campus later that year when logs being stacked for the annual bonfire celebrating the University of Texas-Texas A&M football game collapsed and killed 12 people. Clinging to the 90-year tradition, many Aggies past and present insisted the bonfire go on in future years.

Chairman, Board of Regents: Don Powell
VC, Board of Regents: Fredrick D. McClure
Chancellor: Howard D. Graves, age 59
Deputy Chancellor: Jerry Gatson
Vice Chancellor Agriculture and Life Sciences:
Edward A. Hiler
Vice Chancellor Business Services (CFO): Tom D. Kale
Vice Chancellor Engineering: C. Roland Haden
Vice Chancellor Facilities Planning and Construction:
Wesley E. Peel
Vice Chancellor Governmental Affairs:
Stanton C. Calvert
Vice Chancellor Health Affairs: Jay Noren
Vice Chancellor Planning and System Integration:
Walter V. Wendler
Deputy Chancellor, Academic and Student Affairs:
Leo Sayavedra
Associate Vice Chancelllor Human Resources:
Patti Couger
President, Prairie View A&M University:
Charles A. Hines
President, Tarleton State University: Dennis P. McCabe
President, Texas A&M International University:
J. Charles Jennett
President, Texas A&M University: Ray M. Bowen
President, Texas A&M University-Corpus Christi:
Robert R. Furgason
President, Texas A&M University-Kingsville:
Marc Cisneros
President, West Texas A&M University: Russell Long
Auditors: Texas State Auditor

LOCATIONS

HQ: The Texas A&M University System,
John B. Connally Bldg., 301 Tarrow, 3rd Fl.,
College Station, TX 77843
Phone: 409-845-3211   **Fax:** 409-845-5406
Web site: http://tamusystem.tamu.edu

PRODUCTS/OPERATIONS

Fall 1999 Enrollment

Texas A&M University	43,442
Texas A&M University-Commerce	7,913
West Texas A&M University	6,651
Tarleton State University	7,433
Texas A&M University-Kingsville	5,843
Texas A&M University-Corpus Christi	6,606
Prairie View A&M University	6,271
Texas A&M International University	3,212
Texas A&M University-Texarkana	1,152
Texsa A&M University-Galveston	1,288
Other	880
Total	**90,691**

Selected Texas A&M University System Components
Health Science Center
  Baylor College of Dentistry
  College of Medicine
  Graduate School of Biomedical Sciences
  Institute of Biosciences and Technology
  School of Rural Public Health
Universities
  Prairie View A&M University
  Tarleton State University
  Texas A&M International University
  Texas A&M University
  Texas A&M University-Commerce
  Texas A&M University-Corpus Christi
  Texas A&M University-Kingsville
  Texas A&M University-Texarkana
  West Texas A&M University
State Agencies
  Texas Agricultural Experiment Station
  Texas Agricultural Extension Service
  Texas Engineering Experiment Station
  Texas Engineering Extension Service
  Texas Forest Service
  Texas Transportation Institute
  Texas Veterinary Medical Diagnostic Laboratory
  Texas Wildlife Damage Management Service

HISTORICAL FINANCIALS & EMPLOYEES

School FYE: August	Annual Growth	1989	1990	1991	1992	1993	1994	1995	1996	1997	1998
Sales ($ mil.)	5.8%	804	1,079	1,073	1,172	1,212	1,287	1,299	1,425	1,550	1,695
Employees	5.8%	14,076	14,802	15,228	15,670	15,966	16,367	20,000	22,600	22,800	23,300

SALES HISTORY

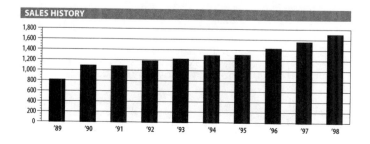

TEXAS LOTTERY COMMISSION

OVERVIEW

The lotto dough of Texas ranks among the biggest three. The Austin-based Texas Lottery Commission oversees the third-largest state-run lottery in the US, behind New York and Massachusetts. Created in 1991, it has generated more than $7 billion for the state's coffers. The lottery offers four numbers games, including Lotto Texas, Pick 3, Cash 5, and Texas Million, as well as an ever-changing variety of "scratchers," the instant-win tickets sold through retailers and more than 1,400 vending machines leased from Cincinnati-based Interlott Technologies. More than 55% of ticket sales is paid out in prizes, while the state's Foundation School Fund gets about 30%. The remaining money goes to cover administration costs and to pay commissions to retailers.

Despite its size and stature, the Lone Star lottery has been on the losing end more often than not in recent times. A 17% dip in sales in 1998 was blamed on reduced advertising and lower prize payouts mandated by the legislature. But sales have continued to decline even after prize levels were restored in 1999. An effort later that year to generate larger Lotto jackpots by decreasing the odds of winning was rejected due to public criticism. The lottery also has been at the center of a several lawsuits concerning its main contractor, GTECH Holdings. The gaming company has settled two suits brought by former lottery directors who claimed that their criticism of GTECH cost them their jobs.

HISTORY

A state lottery had been an issue in Texas for years before it was discussed in earnest in the mid-1980s. Falling oil and gas revenues had plunged the state into a recession, raising the specter of tax increases. In 1985 the state budget had a shortfall of $1 billion; that figure tripled by 1987. Adding fuel to the fire, the Texas Supreme Court ruled in 1989 that Texas had to change the way it funded public schools to avoid penalizing poor school districts. The ruling forced the state to seek new sources of revenue. In 1991 Governor Ann Richards called a special session of the legislature to deal with the fiscal crisis, and House Bill 54 was passed, creating the state lottery. The measure was approved by 64% of voters.

In May of 1992, Richards bought the symbolic first ticket at an Austin feed store (it was not a winner). Fourteen hours later Texans had spent nearly $23 million on tickets — breaking the California Lottery's first-day sales record — and had won $10 million in prizes. More than 102 million tickets were sold the first week. GTECH Holdings was awarded a five-year contract that year for lotto operations. Lotto Texas started in November with a winner taking nearly $22 million. By the end of fiscal 1992, lotto sales in Texas had topped $1 billion. In its first 15 months, it contributed $812 million to the state's coffers.

In March 1994 five winners split a record $77 million jackpot. By that autumn sales had surpassed $5 billion. In November a Mansfield, Texas, gas station owner picked up the largest single-winner jackpot, $54 million. By the end of 1994, Texas had the largest state lottery in the US. Cumulative sales topped $8 billion in mid-1995. In its first 37 months of operation, the Texas Lottery contributed $2.5 billion to the state's general fund. Cash 5 debuted that year, and instant ticket vending machines were installed at some sites.

In 1996 lottery director Nora Linares was dismissed following allegations that one of her friends received $30,000 from GTECH as a "hunting consultant." When a GTECH official was convicted in New Jersey of taking kickbacks from a lobbyist, questions were raised concerning payments to GTECH's Texas lobbyist, former Texas Lieutenant Governor Ben Barnes. In 1997 Texas canceled its contract with GTECH to operate the lottery through 2002 and reopened bidding; GTECH filed suit to enforce the contract. Executive director Lawrence Littwin later was dismissed by the commission. Littwin sued GTECH, claiming the company had gotten him fired (the case was settled in 1999). Linda Cloud, his replacement, reinstated GTECH's contract. That same year the Texas legislature voted to increase the amount going to the state and to reduce prize payouts.

Lottery sales fell sharply in 1998, due in part to the reduced prize money. To combat suffering sales, the legislature reversed itself the next year and restored the level of prize payouts. The commission proposed lengthening the odds of winning to create larger jackpots, but public outcry scuttled the plan.

Chairwomen Texas Lottery Commission: Harriet Miers
Commissioner: C. Thomas Clowe
Commissioner: Anthony Sadberry
Executive Director: Linda Cloud
Deputy Executive Director: Patsy Henry
Director Communications: Keith Elkins
Director Financial Administration: Bart Sanchez
Director Information Technology: Robert Bell
Director Human Resources: Jim Richardson
Director Lottery Operations: Gary Grief
Director Marketing: Toni Smith
Director Security: Mike Pitcock
General Counsel: Kimberly Kiplin
Manager Intergovernmental Affairs: Nelda Trevino
Auditors: Deloitte & Touche LLP

LOCATIONS

HQ: 611 E. 6th St., Austin, TX 78701
Phone: 512-344-5000   **Fax:** 512-344-5490
Web site: http://www.txlottery.org

PRODUCTS/OPERATIONS

Selected Games
Lottery games
  Cash 5
  Lotto Texas
  Pick 3
  Texas Million
Scratch-off games
  9's In A Line
  12 Ways to Celebrate
  Break the Bank
  Cash Vault
  Double Doubler
  Gold Fever
  Jack O Lantern Cash
  Jackalope Loot
  Lucky Duck
  Scratch Happy
  Ten Gallon Tripler
  Texas 2000
  Touchdown
  Turkey Tripler
  Wild Card Cash

COMPETITORS

Louisiana Lottery
Multi-State Lottery
New Mexico Lottery

HISTORICAL FINANCIALS & EMPLOYEES

Government-owned FYE: August	Annual Growth	1989	1990	1991	1992	1993	1994	1995	1996	1997	1998
Sales ($ mil.)	31.7%	—	—	—	594	1,863	2,772	3,052	3,449	3,761	3,106
Net income ($ mil.)	30.1%	—	—	—	250	660	932	1,014	1,101	1,421	1,213
Income as % of sales	—	—	—	—	42.1%	35.4%	33.6%	33.2%	31.9%	37.8%	39.0%
Employees	0.5%	—	—	—	325	325	325	325	325	304	335

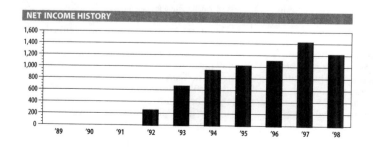

NET INCOME HISTORY

TEXAS PACIFIC GROUP

OVERVIEW

He may not be the Oracle of Omaha, but David Bonderman is certainly no Trickster from Texas. Like investor Warren Buffett, Bonderman's Texas Pacific Group (TPG) invests in brands, buying and resuscitating consumer and *luxe* labels.

The firm's holdings include wineries (Beringer), food (Del Monte), clothing (J. Crew), motorcycles (Ducati), and technology (Motorola spinoff ON Semiconductor). Specialty funds include the Newbridge partnerships (overseas investments) and Colony Capital (real estate). TPG is an active investor, often taking control of the firms in which it invests. It profits not only from the rise in value of its holdings but also from fund management.

TPG goes where other firms fear to tread, targeting perennial losers that offer the potential for big payoffs. With buying opportunities drying up in the US, the firm is leading the way overseas, where bloated European companies are shedding operations that are ripe for revitalization.

HISTORY

The story of Texas Pacific Group is largely the story of David "Bondo" Bonderman. The magna cum laude Harvard law grad — an ardent Democrat and former law professor — built a reputation as an adviser who helped Texas billionaire Robert Bass rack up triple-digit returns.

After some 10 years with Bass, Bonderman struck out on his own in 1992. James Coulter, recruited to the Bass organization straight out of Stanford University's business school, went with him. They were joined by William Price, a former Bain & Company consultant who advised Bonderman on some of his Bass deals. Also joining the firm were Richard Schifter (airlines background) and David Stanton (technology expertise).

Bonderman raised eyebrows in 1993 when TPG affiliate Air Partners recapitalized Continental Airlines, then in its second bankruptcy. At the time the airline industry was losing billions, and Bonderman was a little-known quantity. After an extensive restructuring and management shakeup, Bonderman turned Continental into the US's #5 airline, logging record profits for four consecutive quarters.

This type of deal would become Bonderman's modus operandi: Jumping into troubled waters shunned by others, turning the company around, then (often) selling his interest for a profit. Of the head-rolling that frequently occurs after buyouts, Bonderman once said, "Generally speaking, you like to dance with the girl that brung you, and if you can't, sometimes you have to shoot her." In 1994 Bonderman worked similar magic with bankrupt America West Airlines. As with Continental, TPG sold shares in a second offering that made millions for TPG (and Bonderman).

While the health care industry was debating reform in 1994, Bonderman seized the opportunity to buy a majority share in managed care company PPOM (sold in 1997). In 1995 TPG's Colony Capital teamed up with Virgin Group to buy 116 MGM Cinemas and bring the multiplex boom to the UK.

After watching Robert Mondavi become the first major winery to go public in 1993, TPG bought Nestlé's debt-ridden Wine World Estates in 1996 (with an assist from California investment group Silverado Partners), renamed it Beringer Wine Estates Holdings, and took it public in 1997 in an IPO twice as big as Mondavi's.

After failing to buy troubled upscale retailer Barneys in 1997, it bought clothier J. Crew Group. In an era of falling petroleum prices, TPG gambled on Appalachian energy company Belden & Blake and teamed with Genesis Health Ventures and Cypress Group to buy a stake in ailing elder care operator Multicare. It also bought Del Monte Foods, the world's #1 maker of canned fruits and vegetables (taking it public in 1999).

Bonderman and Air Partners in 1998 sold their interest in Continental to Northwest Airlines. Following its strategy of buying turnarounds, TPG threw lifelines to HMO Oxford Health Plans (1998) and struggling psychiatric care company Magellan Health Services (1999). The firm also built its technology holdings, investing in integrated circuits maker Zilog (1998) and leading a management buyout of Motorola's Semiconductor Components Group (now ON Semiconductors).

The group jumped in a Europen hotbed of investment activity, taking a majority stake in Punch Taverns Group, which is buying some 3,600 pubs from Allied Domecq; TPG in 1999 bought the Bally fashion house and a stake in Italian scooter maker Piaggio. TPG failed, however, to turn around Favorite Brands; the investment firm agreed to sell the marshmallow and candy maker to Nabisco.

CEO and Managing Partner: David Bonderman
Managing Director: James G. Coulter
Managing Director: William S. Price
Managing Director: Richard P. Schifter
CFO: Jim O'Brien
Administrative Manager: Michelle Reese

LOCATIONS

HQ: 201 Main St., Ste. 2420, Fort Worth, TX 76102
Phone: 817-871-4000   **Fax:** 817-871-4010

PRODUCTS/OPERATIONS

Selected Holdings
America West Airlines (51%)
Belden & Blake Corp. (oil and gas)
Beringer Wine Estates Holdings (52%)
Del Monte Foods Company (42%)
Denbury Resources Inc. (33%, oil and gas)
Ducati Motor SpA (28%)
Favorite Brands International Inc.
Genesis Health Ventures Inc. (11%)
GlobeSpan Semiconductor Inc.
J. Crew Group Inc. (62%)
Korea First Bank (through Newbridge Capital)
Magellan Health Services Inc. (20%)
MGM Cinemas
ON Semiconductor
Oxford Health Plans, Inc. (16%)
Paradyne Networks, Inc. (40%)
Piaggio (10%)
Punch Taverns Ltd. (70%)
Ryanair Holdings (airlines)
Zilog Inc. (semiconductors)

COMPETITORS

AEA Investors	Hicks, Muse
Berkshire Hathaway	Jordan Company
Blackstone Group	KKR
Clayton, Dubilier	Keystone
Goldman Sachs	Sevin Rosen Funds
Haas Wheat	Thomas Lee
Heico	Wingate Partners

TISHMAN REALTY & CONSTRUCTION

OVERVIEW

The Tishman name has been a constant in New York state for the last century. Tishman Realty & Construction, descendant of a company founded in 1898 to build tenements, now controls more than 220 million sq. ft. of office, retail, and other properties; it also built such landmarks as the World Trade Center and Disney's EPCOT Center in Orlando, Florida. Its E Walk entertainment and hospitality development is under construction in New York City. Subsidiaries include Tishman Realty Corporation, which finances the firm's activities and

offers investment banking; Tishman Real Estate Services (TRESCO), a real estate planner and development manager; and Tishman Construction Corporation.

Chairman and CEO John Tishman has expanded the company beyond its Big Apple origins both geographically and in scope, most notably through its partnership with the Walt Disney Company to build hotels and theme parks in Florida.

Tishman Realty & Construction Company is owned by the Tishman family.

HISTORY

Julius Tishman escaped the Russian pogroms of the late 19th century by immigrating to the US in 1885. Five years later he opened a store in Newburgh, New York. In 1898, as eastern European immigrants inundated New York City, Tishman began using the proceeds of his store to build tenements on the Lower East Side. He named his business Julius Tishman & Sons. By the 1920s, the firm had moved uptown and upscale, building luxury apartment buildings. The firm went public in 1928 as Tishman Realty & Construction Company, with the family retaining an ownership stake. Julius was chairman; his son David was CEO.

The pitfalls of going public were soon obvious. The offering raised less than $2 million, not enough to finance projects, and because the stock market favored profit generation over asset appreciation, the company was undervalued. When the Depression hit, David's involvement as a director of the Bank of the United States and the family's participation in bad loans made by the bank forced the firm to sell assets. Tishman's lenders, including insurer Metropolitan Life, took over some of its buildings, leaving the firm to manage them. In the 1930s and 1940s the company focused mainly on managing its properties. It continued its construction operations on a contract basis for the Federal Housing Authority.

After WWII Tishman moved away from residential development and into office construction. During this period the company suffered from internal succession struggles. David's younger brothers Paul and Norman began jockeying for position to replace him as CEO; in 1948, David chose Norman to succeed him, and Paul resigned to form his own construction company. Paul's nephew John became head of the firm's construction arm.

By the early 1950s, Tishman had moved into

managment and leasing services, and expanded nationally, opening offices in Chicago and Los Angeles. In 1962 David Tishman relinquished his chairmanship to Norman, who was in turn replaced as CEO by his brother Bob. Under Bob's leadership, Tishman divested residential properties to focus on office space, mostly company-owned.

Tishman was hit hard by recession in the 1970s. By then various family members were itching to fulfill their own ambitions. In 1976, Bob took the company private again, selling off the firm's New York assets, and split the company into Tishman Speyer Properties (headed by Bob and son-in-law Jerry Speyer); Tishman Management and Leasing Corporation (now part of Grubb & Ellis); and Tishman Realty & Construction (headed by John and promptly bought by the Rockefeller Center Corporation).

John Tishman bought back Tishman Realty & Construction in 1980 and steered it into high profile partnerships with the likes of the Walt Disney Company. He also added project management and real estate investment finance services. In New York City, the firm focused on construction projects rather than development. In the late 1980s and early 1990s, as the New York real estate market slumped, Tishman took up projects like prisons, public buildings, and renovations, and developed hotels and resorts in the US and Japan.

In 1996, Tishman refocused on its New York market, breaking ground on office building, hotel, and entertainment complex projects. The firm's new ready-for-anything approach was further reflected in 1999 when it was tapped to managed the latest phase of renovation at Carnegie Hall and began converting a San Diego shipyard into a hotel and marina.

Chairman and CEO: John Tishman
President, Tishman Realty Corp.: William J. Sales
CFO: Larry Schwarzwalder
EVP: Daniel R. Tishman
SVP: Richard M. Kielar
Director Human Resources: Christine Smith

LOCATIONS

HQ: 666 5th Ave., New York, NY 10103
Phone: 212-399-3600   **Fax:** 212-397-1316

PRODUCTS/OPERATIONS

Selected Subsidiaries
Tishman Construction Corp. (construction operations)
Tishman Hotel Corp. (hotel & property management)
Tishman Interiors Corp. (tenant build-out needs)
Tishman Real Estate Management Co. (property
   management for third-party clients)
Tishman Real Estate Services Co. (TRESCO, real estate
   planning & project management)
Tishman Research Corp. (industry consulting)
Tishman Technologies Corp. (development &
   construction for high-tech & financial tenants)
Tishman Urban Development Corp.
   (new development projects)

COMPETITORS

CB Richard Ellis
Cushman & Wakefield
Gilbane
Grubb & Ellis
JMB Realty
Jones Lang LaSalle
Lefrak Organization
Lincoln Property
Reckson Associates Realty
Starrett Corporation
Trammell Crow
Trump
Turner Corporation

HISTORICAL FINANCIALS & EMPLOYEES

Private FYE: June	Annual Growth	1990	1991	1992	1993	1994	1995	1996	1997	1998	1999
Sales ($ mil.)	5.2%	—	668	500	527	540	572	580	650	937	1,005
Employees	7.8%	—	—	—	510	575	575	600	620	650	800

SALES HISTORY

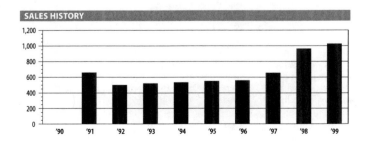

TOPCO ASSOCIATES INC.

OVERVIEW

The motto of Topco Associates, "We're better together," is more than a feel-good slogan; it's the company's way of doing business. The Skokie, Illinois-based company is a cooperative-buying organization that primarily serves food retailers. The co-op purchases more than 7,000 private-label items from manufacturers, and its members sell them under Topco brands such as Food Club, Top Care, and Top Crest, among others, and under their own brands. Products offered include frozen food, regional dairy and bakery items, cheese, groceries, health and beauty products, general merchandise, and pharmaceutical items. It also offers perishables such as processed and fresh meat, seafood, poultry, deli items, produce, and floral items. About 25% of Topco's sales come from fresh meat alone. In addition to private-label products, the co-op also offers members national brand products through its World Brands division and purchases warehouse equipment and supplies.

Private-label products are attractive to grocers because they provide better profit margins than name-brand items; they're attractive to customers because they're cheaper.

Topco is owned by 27 retailers, two food service companies, and one cooperative. Its size enables it to purchase large volumes of products at lower prices than its member-owners could get if they bought the goods on their own. Most of Topco's members are in the US (ranging from Seattle-based Quality Food Centers to Pittsburgh-based Giant Eagle), but it also has members in Israel, Japan, and Puerto Rico. Among the support services Topco offers its members are packaging design, financial and administrative assistance, and coupon processing. The co-op offers marketing and merchandising support through Daymon Associates. Topco also has a staff of over 30 who are responsible for ensuring the quality of products.

HISTORY

Food Cooperatives was founded in Wisconsin in 1944 to procure dairy bags and paper products during wartime shortages. A few years later it merged with Top Frost Foods, with which it had some common members. In 1948 the name Topco Associates was adopted (created by combining the word "Top" from Top Frost with the "Co" in Cooperatives). The member companies involved in the merger included Alpha Beta, Big Bear Stores, Brockton Public Market, Fred Meyer, Furr's, Hinky Dinky, Penn Fruit Company, and Star Markets.

Topco initially sold basic commodities to private-label retailers. It added fresh produce in 1958 and expanded its product line further in 1960, moving into general merchandise, health and beauty care items, and store equipment. In 1961, when the company moved its headquarters to Skokie, Illinois, revenues topped the $100 million mark. In the 1960s other leading supermarkets, including Giant Eagle, King Soopers, McCarty-Holman, and Tom Thumb, joined Topco.

Also that decade it came under attack from the Justice Department when it was accused of antitrust activity in granting its members exclusive distribution rights for Topco-branded products. In 1972 the Supreme Court ruled against Topco. It then agreed to sell products under the private labels of its members.

In the late 1970s the company introduced Valu Time, the first nationally marketed line of branded generic products. This concept was then adopted by many US supermarkets. By 1979 Topco surpassed $1 billion in annual revenues.

By the end of the 1980s, Topco's membership had expanded to include Randall's, Riser Foods, Pueblo International, Schnuck Markets, and Smith's Food & Drug Centers. In 1988 it introduced World Classics, a premium line of high-volume, high-margin products that are promoted as national brands.

During the early 1990s Topco ran through a number of CEOs. In 1990 Robert Seelert replaced 10-year CEO Marcel Lussier. In 1992 John Beggs took over, and the next year current CEO Steven Rubow was handed the reins. The early 1990s also saw rapid growth, with 20 new members bringing the company's total to 46 by 1995 (its members later declined in number through acquisition and consolidation). Topco also expanded internationally, with the membership of Oshawa Group in Canada and the associate membership of SEIYU in Japan that year.

The company also lured upscale Kings Super Markets away from distributor White Rose in 1995. Two years later the company chose Schneider Logistics to manage its freight transportation. Topco began offering members utility accounting and natural gas services through Illinova Energy Partners in 1998.

Chairman: Charles D'Amour
President and CEO: Steven K. Lauer
SVP Member Development and Creative Services: Kenneth H. Guy
SVP Branded Goods: Daniel F. Mazur
SVP Perishables: Russell Wolfe
VP Human Resources: Ronald Ficks
VP Produce and Floral Operations: Fred Tsuhura
VP Non-Foods: Curt Maki
VP Dairy: Laird Snelgrove
VP Meat Operations: Rick Findlay
Treasurer: Kathy Runice
Controller: Debbie Byers

LOCATIONS

HQ: 7711 Gross Point Rd., Skokie, IL 60077
Phone: 847-676-3030   **Fax:** 847-933-9429
Web site: http://www.topcoess.com

PRODUCTS/OPERATIONS

Selected Private-Label Brands

Food Club	Paws Professional
GreenMark	Top Care
Jungle Land	Top Crest
Kingston	Top Fresh
Maxxi	Top Frost
Mega	Valu Time

Selected Member Companies
Ace Hardware
Big Y Foods
Blue Square-Israel
Dillon Companies
Eagle Food Centers
F.A.B.
Fred W. Albrecht Grocery Co.
Furr's Supermarkets
Giant Eagle
Gooding's Supermarkets
Haggen
Jitney-Jungle Stores of America
Kings Super Markets
K-Va-T Food Stores
Lowes Food Stores
Meijer
Penn Traffic
Premier Foodservice Distributors of America
Pueblo Xtra International
Quality Food Centers
Randall's Food Markets
Schnuck Markets
Schultz Sav-O Stores
THE SEIYU
Smith's Food & Drug Centers
Star Markets
Ukrop's Super Markets
Weis Markets

COMPETITORS

Loblaw
Shurfine International
Unified Western Grocers

HISTORICAL FINANCIALS & EMPLOYEES

Cooperative FYE: March	Annual Growth	1990	1991	1992	1993	1994	1995	1996	1997	1998	1999
Sales ($ mil.)	5.8%	2,400	2,600	2,900	3,000	3,500	3,700	3,900	3,700	3,900	4,000
Employees	(0.5%)	375	400	400	375	400	375	390	400	365	359

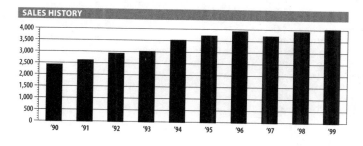

SALES HISTORY

TOWERS PERRIN

OVERVIEW

Towers Perrin is an imposing figure on the landscape of management consulting. One of the world's largest consultants, the company focuses on three primary areas: human resources and general management services, employee benefit services, and health industry consulting. It serves some 10,000 clients worldwide, including about 65% of the 500 biggest global companies and more than 70% of the top 1,000 US firms. The company's Tillinghast-Towers Perrin division provides insurance, financial, and risk management services, and its Towers Perrin Reinsurance unit assists clients with the placement of their reinsurance programs.

Towers Perrin's philosophy is, "Prescription without diagnosis is malpractice"; it provides the industrialized world with reports analyzing everything from workplace diversity to executive pay to health care costs. Its studies are costly but all-encompassing — consultants spend months watching a company operate and talking with countless employees before proposing solutions (unless they issue boilerplate recommendations, as at least one unit was found doing in the mid-1990s).

Towers Perrin is owned by company executives and other principal employees.

HISTORY

In 1934 Towers, Perrin, Forster & Crosby (TPF&C) was formed in Philadelphia by John Towers, Charles Perrin, H. Walter Forster, Arthur Crosby, H. Pratt Weaver, and Walter Chase (all former partners in predecessor firm Henry W. Brown and Company, which was founded in 1871). TPF&C specialized in reinsurance, pensions, and other employee benefits consulting. Among its initial clients were General Foods and International Harvester. Business prospered in the 1930s as companies wrestled with newly enacted Social Security and minimum-wage laws. TPF&C's reinsurance division was particularly busy in London with brokers active among Lloyd's syndicates. In 1938 Walter Forster, considered "the father of pension planning," was named president.

TPF&C expanded its consulting business with a move into Chicago in 1946 and beyond US borders with a move into Montréal 10 years later. In the 1960s the firm bought companies, added offices, and expanded services to include compensation and organization consulting in response to proliferation of federal employment laws. Revenues grew from $4 million in 1960 to $14 million in 1969.

Quentin Smith was named CEO in 1972 and intensified the company's growth through acquisition. TPF&C moved from Philadelphia to New York City in 1975.

In 1983 TPF&C moved into general management consulting with the purchase of Cresap, McCormick & Paget, which was formed in 1946, and garnered notice for the number of consultants it graduated into the CEO and chairmanship ranks at major corporations.

TPF&C, continuing to bulk up in an effort to keep up with first-tier competitors, bought insurance actuarial consultancy Tillinghast,

Nelson & Warren in 1986. The next year TPF&C changed its name to Towers Perrin.

A consulting industry slump in the early 1990s, partly because of a lack of new federal legislation, prompted a 10% staff cut at Towers Perrin in 1991. The company expanded into workplace diversity consulting in 1992. An internal restructuring produced unprofitable projects and led to staff resignations, surprising at a firm traditionally noted for low turnover.

Benefit and actuarial consulting specialist Buck Consultants, a company one-quarter the size of Towers Perrin, made a blustering bid to buy Towers Perrin in 1994. Towers Perrin, which had been trying to buy Buck for years, rejected the maneuver; one company executive called it "the goofiest thing we've ever seen."

Reports surfaced that some Towers Perrin customers who paid high fees between 1994 and 1996 for workplace diversity recommendations received 100-page reports containing identical generic suggestions and plans. Most clients accepted the proposals, although Westinghouse Electric returned its diversity report and Nissan USA retained a new consulting firm.

The company has continued to expand through acquisition, particularly outside the US and in health care services. Its purchases include health care adviser Partners Consulting Group in 1997 and Canadian management consulting firm Tandem International and Atlanta-based change management firm Miller/Howard Consulting Group, both in 1998. In 1999 Towers Perrin was appointed investment consultant to The Monetary Authority of Singapore, which plans to place $10 billion with fund managers over the next three years.

Chairman and CEO: John T. Lynch
CFO: Patrick Gonnelli
Chief Administrative Officer: Ron Giesinger
Managing Director Administration and Operations:
Marvin Greene
**Managing Director Change Management and
Communication Services:** Patricia Milligan
Managing Director General Management Services:
Jeffrey Schmidt
Managing Director Global Employee Benefits Services:
Alan Dugan
Managing Director Global Retirement Services:
Robert Hogan
Managing Director Health and Welfare Services:
Mark Mactas
**Managing Director People Performance and Rewards
Services:** Don Lowman
Managing Director Strategic Growth and Development:
Bruce Pittenger
Managing Director, Tillinghast-Towers Perrin:
Mike Tuohy
**Managing Director, Tillinghast-Towers Perrin
Worldwide Life Practice:** Tricia Guinn
CEO, Towers Perrin Reinsurance: Bill Eyre
COO, Towers Perrin Reinsurance: Dan Collello
Director Human Resources: Ken Ranftle

HQ: 335 Madison Ave., New York, NY 10017
Phone: 212-309-3400   **Fax:** 212-309-0975
Web site: http://www.towers.com

Selected Services
Employee Benefits
  Benefit administration
  Benefit strategy
  Plan management
Health Industry Consulting
Human Resources & General Management
  Business strategy
  Change management
  Organization strategy
  People strategy
Other
  Financial services, risk management & actuarial
    consulting (Tillinghast-Towers Perrin)
  Reinsurance consulting (Towers Perrin Reinsurance)

Selected Publications
AlfaBeta (Canadian investment issues & pension funds)
Custody World (custody information)
Focus (Canadian human resource strategies)
Health Industry Research Report (industry analysis)
Integration Advisor (current & emerging health
  care issues)
Pensions & Benefits Today (Canadian pension
  & benefits)
Perspectives on Management Pay
  (executive compensation)
Perspectives on Total Rewards (total rewards series)
SuperNews (Australian superannuation plans)
Total Health Management News Digest (health benefits)
Towers Perrin Monitor (client newsletter)
Worldwide Pay and Benefits Headlines

Andersen Consulting	Hewitt Associates
Aon	J & H Marsh & McLennan
Bain & Company	KPMG
Booz, Allen	Marsh & McLennan
Boston Consulting	McKinsey & Company
Deloitte Touche Tohmatsu	PricewaterhouseCoopers
Ernst & Young	Watson Wyatt

Private FYE: December	Annual Growth	1989	1990	1991	1992	1993	1994	1995	1996	1997	1998
Sales ($ mil.)	8.6%	—	—	—	686	705	709	767	822	855	1,125
Employees	5.9%	—	—	—	—	4,730	5,000	5,000	5,050	6,361	6,314

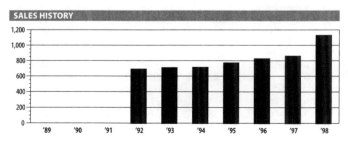

Towers Perrin

THE TRUMP ORGANIZATION

OVERVIEW

Like a bizarre flashback to the 1980s, the stock market is booming, Tom Wolfe has written a book about excess and greed, and The Donald is proving it's all in the art of the deal. Through his New York City-based Trump Organization, Donald J. Trump owns and develops several pieces of prime NYC real estate, including Trump International Hotel and Tower, 40 Wall St., and half-ownership of the Empire State Building. He is also the new owner of the GM Building (now the General Motors Building at Trump International Plaza), has completed two of 16 planned residential towers at Trump Place, and is raising the world's tallest residential building, the 90-story Trump World Tower.

Meanwhile, Trump continues to have some ownership in the projects that made him famous, such as Trump Tower, Trump Plaza, and Trump Palace. Beyond Manhattan, Trump owns the Mar-A-Lago resort in Palm Beach, Florida. He also has a 42% stake in, and is chairman of, the publicly traded Trump Hotels & Casino Resorts, which operates three Atlantic City casinos — Trump Taj Mahal, Trump Plaza, and Trump Marina — as well as the Trump Indiana Riverboat casino.

The Donald continues to excel on the strength of his deal-making prowess; the flamboyant tycoon is renowned for setting up real estate partnerships in which other people put up most of the cash while he retains most of the control. In the Trump World Tower, for example, he has invested $6.5 million, while Korean firm Daewoo has pumped in more than $58 million. Trump has also profited from his famous moniker — which he has trademarked — and his public image.

HISTORY

The third of four children, Donald Trump was the son of a successful builder in Queens and Brooklyn. After graduating from the Wharton School of Finance in 1968, his first job was to turn around a 1,200-unit foreclosed apartment complex in Cincinnati that his father had purchased for $6 million with no money down. Managing the Cincinnati job gave Trump a distaste for the nonaffluent; he wanted to get to Manhattan to meet all the right people.

Operating as the Trump Organization, he took options on two Hudson River sites in 1975 for no money down and began lobbying the city to finance his construction of a convention center. The center was built, but not by Trump, who nevertheless got about $800,000 and priceless publicity. He and hotelier Jay Pritzker turned the Commodore Hotel near Grand Central Station into the Grand Hyatt Hotel in 1975. Trump married fashion model Ivana Zelnicek two years later.

In 1981 he built the posh Trump Tower on Fifth Avenue and proceeded to wheel and deal himself into eighties folklore. In 1983 he bought the New Jersey Generals football team in the upstart USFL (the league folded in 1986). That year he joined with Holiday Inn to build the Trump Casino Hotel (now Trump Plaza) in Atlantic City using public-issue bonds (he bought out Holiday Inn's interest in 1986), and he acquired the Trump Castle from Hilton in 1985. In 1987, he ended up with the unfinished Taj Mahal in Atlantic City, then the world's largest casino, after a battle with Merv Griffin for Resorts International (Griffin won). He bought the Plaza Hotel in Manhattan in 1988, and the Eastern air shuttle (renamed the Trump Shuttle) the next year.

As the 1990s dawned, though, Trump's balance sheet was loaded with about $3 billion in debt. At the same time, his marriage to Ivana broke up in a splash of publicity. Trump's 70 creditor banks consolidated and restructured his debt in 1990. He married Marla Maples in 1993. (They divorced in 1998).

In 1995 Trump formed Trump Hotels & Casino Resorts and took it public. He also paid a token $10 for 40 Wall St. (now home to American Express). The next year he sold his half-interest in the Grand Hyatt Hotel to the Pritzker family and unloaded more than $1.1 billion of his debt by selling the Taj Mahal and Trump's Castle to Trump Hotels. That year Trump bought the Miss Universe, Miss USA, and Miss Teen USA beauty pageants.

In 1997 he published *The Art of the Comeback*, a followup to *The Art of the Deal* (1987), and started work on Trump Place, a residential development on New York's Upper West Side. He teamed with Conseco in 1998 to buy the famed General Motors Building for $800 million. (Trump chipped in between $15 and $20 million.) That year he also announced plans to build the Trump World Tower (a 90-story residential building scheduled to open in 2001), and began pre-selling units in 1999.

Chairman, President, and CEO: Donald J. Trump, age 52
CFO: Allen Weisselberg
EVP Acquisitions and Finance: Abraham Wallach
VP Finance: John P. Burke, age 51
VP Human Resources: Norma Foerderer
Corporate Secretary: Rhona Graff-Riccio
General Counsel: Bernard Diamond
Auditors: Arthur Andersen LLP

LOCATIONS

HQ: 725 5th Ave., New York, NY 10022
Phone: 212-832-2000   **Fax:** 212-935-0141

PRODUCTS/OPERATIONS

Trump Hotels & Casino Resorts, Inc.
Plaza Associates (entity that owns Trump Plaza)
    Trump Plaza (555-room hotel/casino; Atlantic City, NJ)
    Trump Plaza East (349-room hotel/casino)
    Trump Plaza West (500-room hotel/casino)
Trump Indiana (mooring for a 37,000-square-foot yacht casino; Buffington Harbor, IN)
Trump Taj Mahal (hotel/casino; Atlantic City, NJ)
Trump Marina (casino resort; Atlantic City, NJ)

Other Holdings
40 Wall Street
Empire State Building (50%)
General Motors Building at Trump International Plaza
Mar-A-Lago (private club; Palm Beach, FL)
Miss Teen USA pageant
Miss Universe pageant
Miss USA pageant
Trump Casino Services
Trump Enterprises Inc.
Trump International Hotel and Tower
Trump Palace
Trump Parc
Trump Tower (apartment tower and retail space)

COMPETITORS

Alexander's	Millennium Partners
Aztar	Park Place Entertainment
Greate Bay	Port Authority of NY & NJ
Harrah's Entertainment	Ritz Carlton
Helmsley	Rouse
Hyatt	Starwood Hotels & Resorts
Lefrak Organization	Worldwide
Marriott International	Tishman Realty
Mashantucket Pequot Gaming	Vornado

HISTORICAL FINANCIALS & EMPLOYEES

Private FYE: December	Annual Growth	1989	1990	1991	1992	1993	1994	1995	1996	1997	1998
Estimated sales ($ mil.)	21.1%	1,359	1,494	1,340	1,400	2,000	2,750	4,000	6,000	6,500	6,900
Employees	(1.6%)	25,000	25,000	20,000	17,000	15,000	15,000	19,000	19,000	22,000	22,000

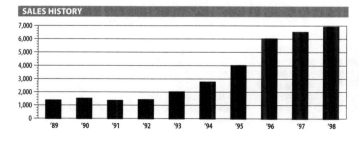

SALES HISTORY

TRUMP

TRUSERV CORPORATION

OVERVIEW

To survive against home improvement giants like The Home Depot and Lowe's, Chicago-based TruServ is relying on pure service. The company is the world's #1 hardware cooperative, serving about 10,000 independent retailers throughout the US and Canada. Its True Value, Coast to Coast, and ServiStar chains sell lumber and building materials, home and garden supplies, and hardware. (Coast to Coast and ServiStar are being converted to the True Value banner.) The firm also operates the Taylor Rental Center and Grand Rental Station chains and serves the Home & Garden Showplace and V&S chains.

In addition, TruServ manufactures paint and paint applicators. (Its Cary, Illinois, paint factory is the largest in North America.)

TruServ was formed with the marriage of Cotter & Company (wholesaler to the True Value chain) and SERVISTAR COAST TO COAST (operator of Coast to Coast hardware stores and several other chains). The merger has given members — many of them mom-and-pop outlets — more buying clout to compete against the do-it-yourself mega-retailers. Members, who own the cooperative and receive stock and cash dividends, also receive retail advice and advertising support.

HISTORY

In 1916, 12-year-old John Cotter started working part-time in a St. Paul, Minnesota, hardware store. By the time Cotter became a traveling hardware salesman in 1928, the rise of catalog houses like Sears and chain stores such as Woolworth's had already begun to put pressure on neighborhood hardware stores, and some hardware retailers had formed wholesale cooperatives to help lower costs.

Cotter and associate Ed Lanctot began pitching the wholesale co-op idea in 1947 to small-town and suburban hardware retailers, and by early 1948 they had enrolled 25 merchants for $1,500 each. Cotter became chairman of the new firm, Cotter & Company. By 1949 it had 84 member-retailers and sales of $385,000.

The co-op created the Value & Service (V&S) store trademark in 1951 to emphasize the advantages of an independent hardware store. By 1956 sales hit $1 million a month and 700,000 customers were receiving its catalogs.

Acquisitions included the 1963 purchase of Chicago-based wholesaler Hibbard, Spencer, Bartlett, giving Cotter 400 new members and the well-known True Value trademark, which soon replaced V&S signs.

Four years later Cotter broadened its focus by buying the General Paint & Chemical Company (Tru-Test paint). The V&S name was revived in 1972 for a five-and-dime store co-op, V&S Variety Stores. John's son Daniel became president in 1978.

John died in 1989. By that time there were almost 7,000 True Value Stores, but the "big boxes" (such as The Home Depot and Lowe's) had become powers in the industry. Cotter moved into Canada in 1992 by acquiring hardware distributor and store operator Macleod-Stedman, which had more than 275 outlets.

Juggling variety-store and hardware merchandise and delivering very small amounts of merchandise to a lukewarm co-op membership did not allow for economies of scale, so in 1995 the company quit its manufacturing operations and its US variety stores (though it still serves variety stores in Canada), tightened membership requirements, and introduced new services.

Two years later Cotter formed TruServ by merging with hardware wholesaler SERVISTAR COAST TO COAST. SERVISTAR had its origins in the nation's first hardware co-op — American Hardware Supply, which was founded in Pittsburgh in 1910 by M. R. Porter, John Howe, and E. S. Corlett. Over the years the co-op entered a variety of markets, including lumber and building materials, nursery, rental, automotive, and commercial and industrial interests. By 1988, the year it changed its name to SERVISTAR, the co-op topped $1 billion in sales.

SERVISTAR expanded in the upper Midwest and on the West Coast in 1990 when it acquired the assets of the Coast to Coast chain (founded in 1928 as a franchise hardware store in Minneapolis); SERVISTAR brought Coast to Coast out of bankruptcy two years later, making it a co-op. Merging its 1992 acquisition of Taylor Rental Center with its Grand Rental Station stores in 1993 made SERVISTAR the #1 general rental chain. In 1996 it consolidated Coast to Coast's operations into its own and changed its name to SERVISTAR COAST TO COAST.

President Don Hoye was promoted to CEO of the company in 1999. To streamline the combined Cotter and SERVISTAR companies, in 1999 TruServ announced it would cut 15% of its corporate staff by year-end and consolidate its hardware store chains under the True Value banner.

PRODUCTS/OPERATIONS

1998 Sales

	% of total
Lumber & building materials	30
Hardware goods	18
Farm & garden	15
Electrical & plumbing	13
Painting & cleaning	11
Appliances & housewares	8
Sporting goods & toys	5
Total	**100**

Selected Operations
Coast to Coast
Grand Rental Station
Home & Garden Showplace
Induserve Supply
ServiStar
Taylor Rental Center
True Value
V&S

COMPETITORS

84 Lumber	McCoy
Ace Hardware	Menard
Akzo Nobel	Payless Cashways
Benjamin Moore	Reno-Depot
Carolina Holdings	Sears
Do it Best	Sherwin-Williams
Hertz	Sutherland Lumber
Home Depot	United Rentals
HomeBase	Valspar
Kmart	Wal-Mart
Lanoga	Wickes
Lowe's	Wolohan Lumber

HISTORICAL FINANCIALS & EMPLOYEES

Cooperative FYE: December	Annual Growth	1989	1990	1991	1992	1993	1994	1995	1996	1997	1998
Sales ($ mil.)	9.2%	2,059	2,135	2,140	2,356	2,421	2,574	2,437	2,442	3,332	4,328
Net income ($ mil.)	(11.6%)	67	55	59	61	57	60	59	52	43	20
Income as % of sales	—	3.2%	2.6%	2.8%	2.6%	2.4%	2.3%	2.4%	2.1%	1.3%	0.5%
Employees	5.6%	4,200	4,200	4,200	4,400	4,400	4,200	4,186	3,825	5,800	6,500

NET INCOME HISTORY

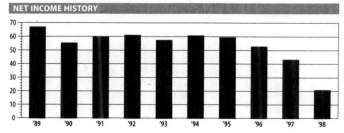

1998 FISCAL YEAR-END

Debt ratio: 47.2%
Return on equity: 5.4%
Cash ($ mil.): 2
Current ratio: 1.26
Long-term debt ($ mil.): 317

TY INC.

OVERVIEW

Ty Inc.'s Beanies aren't so weenie. The Westmont, Illinois-based company makes Beanie Babies, the plush collectibles that are small in size but big in stature. The plastic-pellet-filled creatures, have a cult-like following among kids and adults alike. In addition to the more than 225 varieties of Beanie Babies in circulation, Ty's products include Pillow Pals (larger, floppier animals), Attic Treasures (stuffed animals), and Beanie Buddies (bigger versions of traditional Beanies).

Beanies are recognizable by their heart-shaped tags, but if the company itself had a tag, it might well be shaped like a brain. Ty's marketing smarts have kept Beanies wildly popular for years rather than for a single holiday season, a la Furby or Tickle Me Elmo. Rather than flood the market with Beanies, Ty sells them only through specialty toy and gift

retailers. It limits production so that supply never outstrips demand.

The firm doesn't advertise, relying instead on the word of mouth that is rampant in Beanie culture. Books, magazines, newsletters, and Web sites stoke collectors' enthusiasm. Some grownups have become famous simply for owning complete collections of Beanies. And Ty's "retirement" of a Beanie can cause its price among collectors to skyrocket from its $5-$7 retail debut to hundreds or even thousands of dollars. This collectors' market — which Ty frowns upon (officially, anyway) — has given many kids a taste of the same sort of stock market action that has enchanted their parents.

Mysterious, gimmicky founder Ty Warner owns Ty, whose success enabled him to pay $275 million in 1999 for the Four Seasons luxury hotel in New York City.

HISTORY

Ty Warner, the son of a plush-toy salesman, started his toy career selling stuffed animals to specialty shops for stuffed bear manufacturer Dakin. Warner left Dakin in 1980, moved to Europe for a few years, and in the mid-1980s returned to the US and founded Ty Inc. It first designed a line of $20, understuffed Himalayan cats, which Warner sold to his old Dakin customers.

Beanie Babies first debuted at a 1993 trade show. In January 1994 the first nine Beanies went on sale — at prices low enough for kids to afford — in Chicago specialty stores. As Warner had learned at Dakin, selling stuffed animals through specialty retailers rather than through mass merchandisers meant bigger profits for suppliers and longer-term popularity. By 1995 there were about 30 different Beanies and Ty's estimated sales were $26 million.

The popularity of Beanies exploded in 1996, first in the Midwest, then along the East Coast, and then across the US. By midyear, Beanies — and the public's mania for getting them before they sold out — were receiving widespread media coverage. Ty heightened the frenzy among collectors when it started announcing Beanie retirements on its Web site in 1997.

McDonald's got on the bandwagon in 1997: The fast-food giant issued some 100 million "teenie" Beanie Babies in a Happy Meal promotion. McDonald's ran out of the toys and had to end the promotion early, causing a public relations mess. McDonald's doubled its toy order in 1998 and teamed up with Ty again in 1999.

In 1998 Ty set up a hotline for consumers to

report counterfeit Beanie Babies. Warner paid $10 million that year for a 7% stake in marketing company Cyrk. In return, Cyrk developed the Beanie Babies Official Club, which turned stores that sell Beanies into "official headquarters" offering club membership kits (membership cards, newsletters, stickers, and so forth). Ty introduced its Attic Treasures and Beanie Buddies lines that year.

By spring 1998 Beanies had become a customs issue at the US-Canadian border, where limits of one imported Beanie per person resulted in tears and fisticuffs. In July Ty decided to raise the personal import limit to 30 Beanies. Also that summer the crowds that turned out for Major League Baseball games featuring Beanie giveaways were 26% bigger than average.

Warner bought the Four Seasons hotel in New York City in 1999, paying the equivalent of the retail price of roughly 46 million Beanies. Further flaunting his big bucks in the Big Apple, Warner uncharacteristically provided auditing documents and correspondence to *The New York Post* indicating that Ty had 1998 profits of more than $700 million — more than the combined profits of toy giants Hasbro and Mattel.

After shocking its followers with an August 1999 announcement that it would retire all the Beanies at the end of the year, Ty held a New Year's weekend Web-site vote (at 50 cents per vote) to determine the fate of the line. To the surprise of no one, the public voted overwhelmingly to continue the Beanies.

President: H. Ty Warner
CFO: Michael W. Kanzler
Director Human Resources: Sharon Salcman

LOCATIONS

HQ: 280 Chestnut, Westmont, IL 60559
Phone: 630-920-1515   **Fax:** 630-920-1980
Web site: http://www.ty.com

PRODUCTS/OPERATIONS

Selected Products

Attic Treasures Collection
Azure
Breezy
Cody
Grant
Peppermint
Ramsey

Beanie Babies
Amber the gold tabby
B.B. Bear the birthday
  bear
Crunch the shark
Derby the horse
Ewey the lamb
Flutter the butterfly
Gigi the poodle
Happy the hippo
Iggy the iguana
Jabber the parrot
Knuckles the pig
Lips the fish
Mystic the unicorn
Peanut the elephant
Pinchers the lobster
Prickles the hedgehog
Roam the buffalo
Scat the cat
Scorch the dragon

Tank the armadillo
Wiser the owl
Ziggy the zebra

Beanie Buddies
Beak the kiwi bird
Chip the cat
Hope the praying bear
Patti the platypus
Quakers the duck
Snort the bull
Twigs the giraffe

Pillow Pals
Ba Ba
Huggy
Paddles
Rusty
Sherbert
Swinger
Woof

Plush
Bears
Cats
Country Cousins
  Collection
Dogs
Wildlife Collection

COMPETITORS

Applause Enterprises
Boyds Collection
Hasbro
Imperial Toy Corp.
Mattel
North American Bear
Play By Play
Russ Berrie
Vermont Teddy Bear

HISTORICAL FINANCIALS & EMPLOYEES

Private FYE: December	Annual Growth	1989	1990	1991	1992	1993	1994	1995	1996	1997	1998
Estimated sales ($ mil.)	242.0%	—	—	—	—	—	—	25	250	400	1,000
Employees	171.4%	—	—	—	—	—	—	50	200	500	1,000

SALES HISTORY

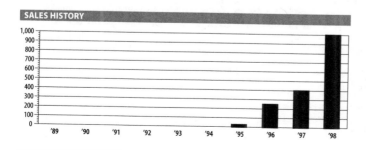

UNIFIED WESTERN GROCERS

OVERVIEW

What do you name a company when two wholesale grocery distributors on the West Coast unite? Unified Western Grocers, of course. Formed when Certified Grocers of California merged with United Grocers in 1999, the Commerce, California-based cooperative supplies food and general merchandise to about 3,700 stores, mostly independents located in Arizona, California, Hawaii, Nevada, and Oregon and supplies select items to a few of the area's big chains, including Lucky and Ralphs. The co-op is owned by members who receive dividends each year based on the amount they purchase.

Unified distributes name-brand groceries, frozen foods, meat, and baked and dairy goods. The co-op also provides a full line of food and nonfood items under private labels Springfield, Gingham, Special Value, La Corona, and Golden Creme. In addition to distribution, which accounts for 98% of sales, the company provides its members support services, including financing, insurance, and store development.

Consolidation and the trend toward self-distribution among food retailers has hurt wholesale grocery distributors. To match the buying power afforded to large supermarket chains and wholesalers, the two co-ops merged to become Unified. The company has begun its own store format, Apple Markets, to replace older stores.

HISTORY

Certified Grocers of California evolved from a group of 15 independent Southern California grocers that formed a purchasing cooperative in 1922 to compete against large grocery chains. Certified Grocers of California incorporated in 1925 and issued stock to 50 members.

In 1928 the co-op merged with a small retailer-owned wholesale company called Co-operative Grocers. It acquired Walker Brothers Grocery in 1929 and nearly tripled the previous year's sales. By 1938 the co-op had grown to 310 members and 380 stores, and sales passed $10 million.

Certified launched a line of private-label products under the Springfield name in 1947. In the early 1950s it added nonfood items and began processing its own private-label coffee and bean products. The co-op added delicatessen items in 1956. During the 1960s and 1970s, Certified added a meat center, a frozen food and deli warehouse, a produce distribution center, a creamery, a central bakery, and a specialty foods warehouse.

In 1989 the co-op opened several membership warehouse stores called Convenience Clubs. The Save Mart and Boys Markets chains left the fold in 1991. The co-op lost about 30% of its business during the next two years, including the Bel Air and Williams Bros. chains. After disappointing returns, in 1992 Certified sold its warehouse stores, cut staff, and consolidated warehouses.

CFO (and former Atlantic Richfield executive) Al Plamann was appointed CEO in 1994, succeeding Everett Dingwell. In 1996 the co-op began to convert its customers' older retail stores to Apple Markets in Southern California. That year revenues dipped as the result of reduced purchases from some supermarkets and the sale in 1996 of one of its subsidiaries, Hawaiian Grocery Stores.

In 1998 member chain Stumps converted to the Apple Markets banner. Faced with a declining customer base, in 1999 Certified merged with United Grocers to form Unified Western Grocers.

Dr. R. Norton, F. L. Freeburg, and A. C. Brinckerhoff founded United Grocers of Oregon in 1915 as a way for grocers in Portland to cooperate in the purchase of merchandise. The next year the co-op had 35 members. In the 1950s United formed a trucking department and established a general merchandise division. The company also grew rapidly in the 1950s through acquisitions, buying Northwest Grocery Company and the Fridegar Grocery Company. In 1963 United formed its frozen food department when it purchased Raven Creamery.

By 1975 the company's Northwest Grocery Company subsidiary had 14 Cash and Carry warehouses that sold goods to small grocers and restaurants. In 1995 the company bought California food distributor Market Wholesale. Three years later United sold its Cash & Carry warehouse-style stores to Smart & Final.

Upon completion of the merger in September 1999, Certified's president and CEO, Plamann, was named to head the new organization.

President and CEO: Alfred A. Plamann, age 56
EVP and COO: Terrence Olsen
Auditors: Deloitte & Touche LLP

HQ: 5200 Sheila St., Commerce, CA 90040
Phone: 323-264-5200   **Fax:** —
Web site: http://www.certifiedgrocers.com

Selected Co-op Members
Alamo Market
Berberian Enterprises, Inc.
Briston Farms Markets, Inc.
Gerrard's, Inc.
Jack Young's Supermarkets
Joe Notrica, Inc.
K. V. Mart Co.
Mac Ber, Inc.
Mar-Val Food Stores, Inc.
Nob Hill General Store, Inc.
Pro & Son's, Inc.
Ralphs Grocery Company
Star Markets Company, Inc.
Super A Foods, Inc.
Super Center Concepts, Inc.

Selected Support Services
Advertising and marketing
General merchandise
Information services
Insurance
Private labels
Real estate development
Store development
Technical services

Albertson's	SUPERVALU
Associated Food	Safeway
Fleming Companies	Services Group
Kroger	Topco Associates
Nash Finch	Wal-Mart

Cooperative FYE: September	Annual Growth	1990	1991	1992	1993	1994	1995	1996	1997	1998	1999
Sales ($ mil.)	(3.8%)	2,696	2,768	2,378	2,007	1,874	1,823	1,949	1,927	1,832	1,894
Net income ($ mil.)	3.1%	2	(5)	(4)	0	(2)	1	2	2	3	3
Income as % of sales	—	0.1%	—	—	—	—	0.0%	0.1%	0.1%	0.2%	0.1%
Employees	3.5%	—	3,000	3,000	2,500	2,600	2,470	2,400	2,400	2,200	3,945

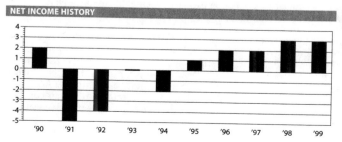

NET INCOME HISTORY

1999 FISCAL YEAR-END
Debt ratio: 64.2%
Return on equity: 3.3%
Cash ($ mil.): 8
Current ratio: 1.55
Long-term debt ($ mil.): 144

UNIFIED
UNIFIED WESTERN GROCERS, INC.

UNITED STATES POSTAL SERVICE

OVERVIEW

Through snow, rain, heat, and gloom of night, the United States Postal Service (USPS) delivers about 40% of the world's mail, more than 190 billion pieces a year. Based in Washington, DC, the independent government agency is overseen by a board of nine governors appointed by the president. The board selects the postmaster general and establishes objectives, goals, and policies, such as postal rates.

With an annual budget that is about 1% of the US gross domestic product, USPS relies on postage and fees to fund its operations. It holds a monopoly on the delivery of nonurgent

letters, but in services that are subject to competition, such as package delivery, it has less than 10% of the market.

After years of losses, the agency has had four consecutive years of profits, placing it in reach of debt-free status. However, USPS has warned that fax machines, the Internet, and e-mail could cut into sales (nearly 80% of which go to pay workers' wages and benefits). To make "snail mail" a little speedier, it has licensed two companies, E-Stamp and Stamps.com, to sell online stamps.

HISTORY

The second-oldest agency of the US government (after Indian Affairs), the Post Office was created by the Continental Congress in 1775. Benjamin Franklin was postmaster general. The postal system came to play a vital role in the development of US transportation.

At that time, postal workers were riders on muddy paths delivering letters with no stamps and no envelopes. Postal rates varied by the length of the letter and the distance it was traveling. Letters were delivered only between post offices. Congress approved the first official postal policy in 1792: Rates ranged from six cents for less than 30 miles to 25 cents for more than 450 miles. Letter carriers began delivering mail in cities in 1794.

First based in Philadelphia, in 1800 the Post Office loaded all of its records, furniture, and supplies into two wagons and went to Washington, DC. In 1829 Andrew Jackson elevated the postmaster general to cabinet rank — it became a means of rewarding political cronies. Mail contracts subsidized the early development of US railroads. The first adhesive postage stamp appeared in the US in 1847.

Uniform postal rates (not varying with distance) were instituted in 1863, the same year free city delivery began. The start of free rural delivery in 1896 jumpstarted road construction in isolated parts of the US. Parcel post was launched in 1913, and new mail-order houses such as Montgomery Ward and Sears, Roebuck flourished.

The famous pledge beginning "Neither snow nor rain ..." — not an official motto — was first inscribed at the main New York City post office in 1914. Scheduled airmail service between Washington, DC, and New York City began in 1918, stimulating the development of commercial air service. The ZIP code was introduced in 1963.

Postal workers grew increasingly militant under work stress. (Franklin's pigeonhole sorting method had barely changed.) A work stoppage in the New York City post office in 1970 spread within nine days to 670 other post offices, and the US Army was deployed to handle the mail. Later that year the Postal Reorganization Act was passed. The new law pulled the postmaster general out of the president's cabinet and made him CEO of an independent agency, the United States Postal Service (USPS). The next year USPS negotiated the first US government collective bargaining labor contract. Express mail service began in 1977, and during this period the service stepped up automation efforts.

In 1995 USPS launched Global Package Link, a program to expedite major customers' shipments to Canada, Japan, and the UK. A year later it overhauled rates, cutting prices for larger mailers who prepared their mail for automation and raising prices for small mailers who didn't.

That year chief marketing officer Loren Smith — architect of a series of ads taking swings at rivals Federal Express (now FDX) and UPS — resigned after an audit showed that he had overspent his $140 million ad budget by nearly $90 million. Shortly thereafter, FDX sued the postal service for false advertising.

Postmaster General Marvin Runyon — whose six-year tenure took the agency from the red into the black — retired in 1998 and was succeeded by USPS veteran William Henderson. The next year the humble stamp took center stage. First, a one-cent hike in the price of first-class postage (proposed in 1997) took effect. Then, in a nod to the Internet Age, USPS allowed two companies, Stamps.com and E-Stamp, to sell stamps from their Web sites.

Chairman: Sam Winters
Postmaster General and CEO: William J. Henderson, age 50
Deputy Postmaster General: Michael S. Coughlin
EVP and COO: Clarence E. Lewis Jr.
SVP and CFO: M. Richard Porras
SVP and General Counsel: Mary S. Elcano
SVP and Chief Marketing Officer: Allen R. Kane
SVP and Chief Technology Officer: Norman E. Lorentz
SVP Labor Relations: John E. Potter
SVP Government Relations: Debrorah K. Willhite
VP Operations Support: Nicholas F. Barranca
VP Corporate Relations: Frank P. Brennan Jr.
VP International Business: James F. Grubiak
VP Human Resources: Yvonne D. Maguire
VP Quality: Don W. Peterson
VP Strategic Planning: Robert A. F. Reisner
VP Tactical Marketing and Sales Development: Gail G. Sonnenberg
VP Customer Relations: John R. Wargo
VP Information Systems: Richard D. Weirich
Chief Postal Inspector: Kenneth J. Hunter
Auditors: Ernst & Young LLP

LOCATIONS

HQ: 475 L'Enfant Plaza, Washington, DC 20260
Phone: 202-268-2000   **Fax:** 202-268-3488
Web site: http://www.usps.gov

PRODUCTS/OPERATIONS

1998 Sales

	$ mil.	% of total
First-class mail	33,983	57
Standard mail	13,753	23
Priority mail	4,150	7
Periodicals	2,072	3
International mail	1,599	3
Express mail	854	1
Mailgram	2	—
Other	3,659	6
Total	**60,072**	**100**

Selected Services
Certified mail
Collection-on-delivery (COD)
Express mail
First-class mail
International mail
Mail forwarding
Money orders
Passport applications
Periodicals
Post office boxes
Postage meters
Priority mail
Registered mail
Return receipt
Special delivery
Standard mail

COMPETITORS

Air Express	FDX
Airborne Freight	Mail Boxes Etc.
CNF Transportation	Pittston BAX
Circle International	Roadway Express
DHL	UPS

HISTORICAL FINANCIALS & EMPLOYEES

Government-owned FYE: September	Annual Growth	1989	1990	1991	1992	1993	1994	1995	1996	1997	1998
Sales ($ mil.)	5.5%	37,979	39,201	43,323	46,151	47,418	49,252	54,294	56,402	58,216	60,072
Net income ($ mil.)	—	61	(874)	(1,469)	(536)	(1,765)	(914)	1,770	1,567	1,264	550
Income as % of sales	—	0.2%	—	—	—	—	—	3.3%	2.8%	2.2%	0.9%
Employees	0.5%	777,715	760,668	748,961	725,290	691,723	728,944	753,384	760,966	765,174	792,041

NET INCOME HISTORY

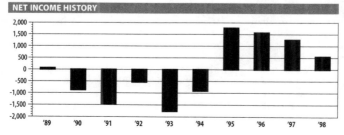

1998 FISCAL YEAR-END
Debt ratio: 100.0%
Return on equity: —
Cash ($ mil.): 395
Current ratio: 0.10
Long-term debt ($ mil.): 2,788

UNITED WAY OF AMERICA

OVERVIEW

United Way of America (UWA) has been described as a mutual fund for charitable causes, and with about 45,000 agencies receiving financial support from UWA's 1,400 local organizations, the epithet seems fitting. Headquartered in Alexandria, Virginia, the not-for-profit organization focuses on health and human services causes. Its local organizations help to fund a multitude of endeavors, including the American Cancer Society, the Arthritis Foundation, Catholic Charities, Girl Scouts, Boy Scouts, the National Easter Seal Society, the National Urban League, and Planned Parenthood. During its

1997-1998 fund-raising year, UWA raised $3.4 billion (nearly 50% came from employee contributions; corporations contributed another 22%). Its administrative expenses average 13% of all funds raised.

Each of the local organizations is an independent entity governed by local volunteers, and UWA acts as a national services and training center, supporting the local organizations with services such as national advertising and research. To advance the understanding of its role, UWA has launched an initiative to raise awareness of how it serves local communities.

HISTORY

The first modern Community Chest was created in 1913, laying the foundation for the practice of allocating funds among multiple causes. Five years later, representatives from 12 fund-raising organizations met in Chicago and established the American Association for Community Organizations, the predecessor of the present-day United Way. Contributing to the community became more widespread in the 1920s, and by 1929 more than 350 Community Chests had been established.

Payroll deductions for charitable contributions debuted in 1943, providing a key conduit for the collection of donations. In 1946 the United Way's predecessor organization initiated a cooperative relationship with the American Federation of Labor and the Congress of Industrial Organizations (which merged to become the AFL-CIO in 1955) to provide services to members of organized labor. (The relationship continues today, with the organizations collaborating on projects such as recruiting members of organized labor to lead health and human services organizations.)

The Uniform Federal Fund-Raising Program was created by executive order of President Dwight Eisenhower in 1957, enabling federal employees to contribute to charities of their choice. (The program later evolved into the Combined Federal Campaign.) Six years later, Los Angeles became the first city to adopt the United Way name when more than 30 local Community Chests and United Fund organizations merged. The national organization, which had been operating under the United Community Funds and Councils (UCFCA) name, adopted the United Way of America (UWA) name in 1970. It established its headquarters in Alexandria, Virginia, the next year.

Congress made its first emergency food and shelter grant to the private sector in 1983, and UWA was selected as its fiscal agent. UWA created its Emergency Food and Shelter National Board Program the same year. In 1984 UWA created the Alexis de Tocqueville Society to solicit larger donations from individuals. The Alexis de Tocqueville Society went on to attract members including Bill Gates and Walter Annenberg.

In 1992 William Aramony, UWA's president for more than two decades, came under fire for his lavish expenditures. After his actions came to light, he resigned the same year. Former Peace Corps head Elaine Chao was tapped to replace him, and in 1995 Aramony was sentenced to seven years in prison for defrauding the organization of about $600,000. Former UWA CFO Thomas Merlo and Stephen Paulachak (former president of a UWA spin-off) were convicted on related charges. After four years spent burnishing UWA's tarnished image, Chao resigned from UWA in 1996, and was succeeded in 1997 by Betty Beene, who had headed UWA operations in Houston and New York's tri-state area.

In an effort to stress the manner in which its local organizations benefit their communities, UWA launched a brand initiative campaign in 1998. The following year UWA's local organization in Santa Clara, California, found itself in serious financial straits when donations began slipping despite its location in the wealthy Silicon Valley. Infoseek (now go.com) founder Steve Kirsch and Microsoft founder Bill Gates chipped in $1 million and $5 million, respectively, to help keep the organization afloat.

Chairman: Dimon R. McFerson
President: Betty S. Beene
Chairman Finance and Audit Committee:
Richard W. Gushman II
Human Resources Chair: Dorothy Myles
Auditors: Arthur Andersen LLP

LOCATIONS

HQ: 701 N. Fairfax St., Alexandria, VA 22314
Phone: 703-836-7100   **Fax:** 703-683-7840
Web site: http://www.unitedway.org

PRODUCTS/OPERATIONS

Selected Programs
AIDS Initiative
Diversity Initiative
Education and Literacy Initiative
Housing Initiatives Program
Mobilization for America's Children
Substance Abuse Initiative

Selected Recipients of United Way Funds
American Cancer Society
American Foundation for the Blind
American Heart Association
American Red Cross
American Social Health Association
The Arc
Arthritis Foundation
Big Brothers/Big Sisters of America
Boy Scouts of America
Boys and Girls Clubs of America
Camp Fire Boys and Girls
Catholic Charities USA
Child Welfare League of America
Council of Jewish Federations
Epilepsy Foundation of America
Evangelical Lutheran Church of America
Family Service America
Girl Scouts of the U.S.A.
Girls, Inc.
Goodwill Industries of America
National Concilio of America
National Council on Alcoholism and Drug Dependence
National Council on Crime and Delinquency
National Easter Seal Society
National Mental Health Association
National Urban League
Planned Parenthood Federation of America
The Salvation Army
Travelers Aid International
United Cerebral Palsy Associations
United Seamen's Service
United Way of America
USO World Headquarters
Visiting Nurse Associations of America
Volunteers of America
YMCA of the U.S.A.
YWCA of the U.S.A.

HISTORICAL FINANCIALS & EMPLOYEES

Not-for-profit FYE: December	Annual Growth	1989	1990	1991	1992	1993	1994	1995	1996	1997	1998
Sales ($ mil.)	1.8%	2,980	3,110	3,170	3,040	3,050	3,078	3,148	3,250	3,400	3,580
Employees	0.0%	—	—	—	—	—	—	—	10,000	10,000	10,000

SALES HISTORY

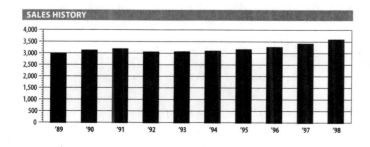

UNIVERSITY OF CALIFORNIA

OVERVIEW

UC is striving not to become known as the "University for Caucasians." Struggling with minority recruitment in an era without affirmative action, Oakland-headquartered University of California (UC) maintains nine primary campuses — Berkeley, Davis, Irvine, Los Angeles, Riverside, San Diego, San Francisco, Santa Barbara, and Santa Cruz. It also plans to open a campus in Merced in 2005. Nearly 175,000 graduate and undergraduate students attend UC.

UC offers academic study areas in more than 150 disciplines. It has three law schools, five medical schools, and one of the nation's leading continuing education programs. In addition, the university manages three national laboratories for the federal government and produces more research leading to patented inventions than any other US university.

In the wake of California's Proposition 209, the UC Board of Regents voted in 1995 to phase out the use of race, ethnicity, or gender in admissions decisions, stirring up a storm of protest. Since then, enrollment of African-Americans and Latinos has dropped. In response, the university guarantees admission to the top 4% of students at each of California's high schools. It also is investing in a number of minority outreach programs.

HISTORY

In 1849 the founders of California's government provided for a state university via a clause in the state's constitution. The origins of the College of California, opened in Oakland in 1869, date back to the Contra Costa Academy, a small school established by Yale alumnus Henry Durant in 1853. Durant ran Contra Costa, and then the college, until 1872. Women were allowed to enter the school in 1870. The college moved to Berkeley and graduated its first class (12 men) in 1873.

As California's economy and population grew, so did its university system. Renamed University of California (UC) in 1879, it had 1,000 students by 1895. Agriculture, mining, geology, and engineering were among its first fields. A second campus was established at Davis in 1905, followed by campuses in San Diego (1912) and Los Angeles (1919).

The Depression brought cutbacks in funding for UC, but the system rebounded in the 1940s. In 1944 it opened its fifth campus, in Santa Barbara, and during WWII it also began gaining recognition for research. With the US government, UC runs the Los Alamos National Laboratory, which, under Robert Oppenheimer, tested the first atomic bomb on July 18, 1945.

Between 1945 and 1965, enrollment quadrupled, spurred by GI Bill-sponsored veterans and a population shift to the West. The state legislature formulated the Master Plan for Higher Education in 1960, which reorganized university administration and established admission requirements. In 1965 campuses were established at Irvine and Santa Cruz.

The first of several important demonstrations in the 1960s at UC Berkeley came in 1964 over the university's attempts to ban political activity on a strip of UC-owned land. The People's Park riot of 1969, touched off when UC tried to close a parcel of land in Berkeley that students had turned into a kind of playground for the counterculture, left one dead and more than 50 wounded.

Aware of the changing demographics of its student body, especially its growing Asian enrollment (28% in 1990), UC Berkeley in 1990 gave the chancellor's job to Chang-Lin Tien — the first person of Asian descent to hold that position at a major US university. A California recession in the early 1990s resulted in budget cuts for UC. Strapped for cash, the university launched a for-profit entity in 1992 to tap, through license agreements, its extensive library of patents.

UC San Diego chancellor Richard Atkinson succeeded Jack Peltason as UC president in 1995, the same year the UC Board of Regents approved the site of a new campus — the university's 10th — in the San Joaquin Valley. That year it voted to phase out race- and sex-based affirmative action. In 1997 the board, in an effort to be competitive with other top universities in recruiting faculty, voted to offer health benefits to the partners of gay employees. Also that year UC created the California Digital Library and began putting its library collection online.

In 1998 entrepreneur Alfred Mann donated $100 million to UC Los Angeles for biomedical research. Admissions of non-Asian-American minorities to the fall freshman classes of UCLA and UC Berkeley fell sharply in 1998. The following year the UC system began guaranteeing admission to the top 4% of students in each of the state's high schools.

Chairman: John G. Davies
President: Richard C. Atkinson
SVP Business and Finance: V. Wayne Kennedy
SVP Academic Affairs and Provost: C. Judson King
VP Agriculture and Natural Resources: W. R. Gomes
VP Budget: Larry Hershman
VP Clinical Services Development: William H. Gurtner
VP Financial Management: Anne C. Broome
VP Health Affairs: Cornelius L. Hopper
VP Legal Affairs and General Counsel: James E. Holst
VP University and External Relations: Bruce B. Darling
Assistant VP Human Resources: Lubbe Levin
Auditors: Deloitte & Touche LLP

HQ: 1111 Franklin St., Oakland, CA 94607
Phone: 510-987-0700   **Fax:** 510-987-0894
Web site: http://www.ucop.edu

University of California has nine main undergraduate and graduate campuses in California and national research laboratories in California and New Mexico.

Main Campuses
UC Berkeley
UC Davis
UC Irvine
UC Los Angeles
UC Riverside
UC San Diego
UC San Francisco
UC Santa Barbara
UC Santa Cruz

1999 Sales

	$ mil.	% of total
Department of Energy Laboratories	3,026	23
State appropriations	2,601	20
Hospitals	1,928	15
Federal appropriations	1,569	12
Student tuition & fees	1,082	8
Educational activities sales	898	7
Private gifts, grants & contracts	651	5
Auxiliary enterprises	615	5
Investment income	327	2
Local government grants & contracts	100	1
Other income	293	2
Adjustments	(16)	—
Total	**13,074**	**100**

Affiliated Institutions
Lawrence Berkeley National Laboratory
Lawrence Livermore National Laboratory
Los Alamos National Laboratory

School FYE: June	Annual Growth	1990	1991	1992	1993	1994	1995	1996	1997	1998	1999
Sales ($ mil.)	8.2%	6,443	6,993	7,394	7,548	7,895	7,958	8,363	9,022	9,375	13,074
Employees	(2.4%)	124,329	129,946	132,279	131,661	132,964	131,660	137,874	130,000	130,000	99,890

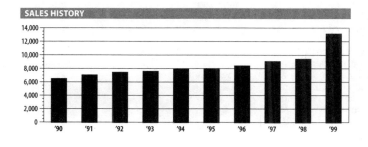

THE UNIVERSITY OF CHICAGO

OVERVIEW

Few institutions sport more impressive ivory towers than the University of Chicago. Located in the Hyde Park-South Kenwood area of the Windy City, the esteemed university lists among its alumni economist Milton Friedman, author Saul Bellow, and *Washington Post* publisher Katharine Graham, and it has been home to 70 Nobel Prize winning scholars, including scientists Enrico Fermi and Robert Millikan.

Its undergraduate college offers divisions of study in biology, the humanities, physical sciences, and social sciences. Among the U of C's five professional schools, its business and law schools are both ranked in the top 10 among US universities by *U.S. News & World Report*. The 12,000 students attending the U of C study primarily at its 200-acre main campus, but the university also has a downtown center for its business school and a campus in Barcelona, Spain. In addition, it operates the Graham

School of General Studies (continuing education programs) and the University of Chicago Press. It has an endowment of $2.6 billion.

Founded in 1891 by John D. Rockefeller, the U of C has long prided itself on the scholarship of its students and faculty as well as its rigorous academic requirements. Students must take a common core curriculum that stresses an exposure to a broad range of arts and sciences. President Hugo Sonnenschein, who has announced his intention to leave the university after the 1999-2000 academic year, came under fire for reducing the number of core classes from 21 to 18 in an effort to increase undergraduate enrollment. Controversy also has surrounded the school's agreement to supply content for Internet distance-learning startup UNext.com, which was founded by U of C trustee Andrew Rosenfield.

HISTORY

The University of Chicago was founded with a $600,000 gift from John D. Rockefeller in 1891. The school took its name from the first U of C, a small Baptist school that operated from 1858-86. Members of the American Baptist Education Society chipped in another $400,000, and land was donated by department store owner Marshall Field. The university opened in 1892 with a faculty of 103 and 594 students. As it grew, the university took over property that had been used in the Columbian Exposition of 1892-93, eventually surrounding the fair's former midway. (The school's football team later earned the nickname "Monsters of the Midway" before withdrawing from intercollegiate play in 1939.)

Only four years after its founding, the university's enrollment of 1,815 exceeded Harvard's. By 1907, 43% of its 5,000 students were women. Robert Maynard Hutchins, president from 1929-51, revolutionized the university and American higher education by insisting on the study of original sources (the Great Books) and competency testing through comprehensive exams. He organized the college and graduate divisions into their present structure, reaffirming the role of the university as a place for intellectual exploration rather than vocational training. In 1942 the U of C ushered in the nuclear age when Enrico Fermi created the first controlled nuclear chain reaction in the school's abandoned football stadium.

From the 1950s through the 1970s, the

university purchased and restored Frank Lloyd Wright's famed Robie House and built the Joseph Regenstein Library (1970). In 1978 Hanna Holborn Gray became the first woman to be named president of a major university. Hugo Sonnenschein succeeded Gray in 1993. The beginning of his tenure coincided with a period of financial difficulty for the school, as increases in costs outpaced revenue growth. In 1996 Sonnenschein announced plans to boost enrollment by as much as 30% in order to invigorate the school's finances.

U of C graduate and former professor Myron Scholes shared the Nobel Prize in economics in 1997. The next year the school announced plans for a $35 million athletics center to be named after Gerald Ratner, a former student who donated $15 million toward construction of the facility. In 1999 the university's Graduate School of Business announced plans to open a permanent campus in Singapore in 2000, becoming the first US business school to have its own facility in Asia. The school later signed on to supply content to Internet distance-learning startup UNext.com, founded by trustee Andrew Rosenfield. Sonnenschein announced his retirement that year, and critics of his plans to attract more undergraduates claimed victory in their fight to restore the school's reputation.

OFFICERS

Chairman, Board of Trustees: Edgar D. Jannotta
President: Hugo F. Sonnenschein
Provost: Geoffrey R. Stone
VP and CFO: Patricia Woodworth
VP Administration and General Counsel:
Arthur M. Sussman
VP and Chief Investment Officer: Philip Halpern
VP Community Affairs: Henry Webber
VP Development and Alumni Relations:
Randy L. Holgate
VP Medical Affairs: Glenn D. Steele Jr.
Associate VP Human Resources: G. Chris Keeley
Secretary, Board of Trustees: Kineret S. Jaffe
Auditors: KPMG LLP

LOCATIONS

HQ: 5801 S. Ellis Ave., Chicago, IL 60637
Phone: 773-702-1234   **Fax:** 773-702-0809
Web site: http://www.uchicago.edu

PRODUCTS/OPERATIONS

Undergraduate Divisions
Biological Sciences
Humanities
New Collegiate Division (interdisciplinary courses)
Physical Sciences
Social Sciences

Graduate Divisions
Biological Sciences and Pritzker School of Medicine
Humanities
Physical Sciences
Social Sciences

Professional Schools
Divinity School
Graduate School of Business
Law School
Harris Graduate School of Public Policy Studies
School of Social Service Administration

Other Schools and Operations
Graham School of General Studies
The Laboratory Schools
Oriental Institute
University of Chicago Press

Selected Libraries
Joseph Regenstein Library (humanities and
social sciences)
John Crerar Library (natural sciences, medicine,
and technology)
D'Angelo Law Library
Harper Memorial Library
School of Social Service Administration Library
Eckhart Library (mathematics, mathematical statistics,
and computer science)
Jones Library (chemistry)

HISTORICAL FINANCIALS & EMPLOYEES

School FYE: June	Annual Growth	1989	1990	1991	1992	1993	1994	1995	1996	1997	1998
Sales ($ mil.)	1.2%	1,134	1,370	1,054	1,113	1,150	1,217	1,313	1,395	1,377	1,507
Employees	1.7%	—	—	—	—	11,800	11,400	10,954	12,000	12,000	12,869

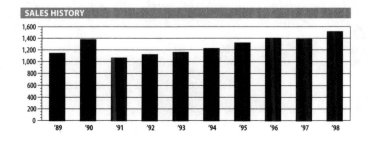

SALES HISTORY

THE UNIVERSITY OF TEXAS

OVERVIEW

Longhorns, Mavericks, and Rattlers, oh my! No, this isn't some kind of southwestern circus; it's The University of Texas (UT) System, one of the largest university systems in the US. More than 148,000 students are enrolled in UT's nine universities, including the largest university in the nation on its flagship Austin campus (more than 49,000 students). The UT system houses six health centers, four medical schools, two dental schools, and seven nursing schools, and spends more than $870 million each year on research. Its $10.2 billion endowment (managed by the University of Texas Investment Management Co.) is the second largest in the country, after Harvard's.

Despite its size and reputation, UT's in-state tuition is among the lowest in the nation for public universities. Its prestigious faculty of more than 13,000 includes seven Nobel laureates and a Pulitzer Prize winner. UT-Austin alone has more than 17,600 non-faculty employees, making it one of the largest employers in Austin. Classes also are offered to students enrolled at UT universities via the Internet through its UT Tele-campus. A search is under way to replace Chancellor William Cunningham, who is resigning in August 2000.

HISTORY

The Texas Declaration of Independence (1836) admonished Mexico for having failed to establish a public education system in the territory, but attempts to start a state-sponsored university were stymied until after Texas achieved US statehood and fought in the Civil War. A new constitution in 1876 provided for the establishment of "a university of the first class," and in 1883 The University of Texas (UT) opened in Austin. Eight professors taught 218 students in two curricula: academics and law.

The school's first building opened in 1884, and in 1891 the university's medical school opened in Galveston. By 1894 UT-Austin had 534 students and a football team. UT opened a graduate school in 1910 and various other colleges over the years. The university added its first academic branch campus when the Texas State School of Mines and Metallurgy (opened in 1914 in El Paso) became part of the system in 1919.

UT's future was secured in 1923 when oil was found on West Texas desert lands that had been set aside by the legislature for educational support. The income from oil production, as well as the proceeds of surface-use leases, became the Permanent University Fund (PUF), from which only interest and earnings on the revenues can be used: two-thirds by UT and one-third by Texas A&M University. UT continued to grow, thanks to the PUF, which topped $100 million by 1940.

UT sported the black eye of racial prejudice (as did many other institutions at the time) when it refused to admit a black student named Heman Sweatt to its law school in 1946. The Supreme Court ordered UT to admit him in 1950, the same year the UT System was

officially organized. Sixteen years later, in one of the nation's most highly publicized crimes, Charles Whitman killed 14 people and wounded 31 others with a high-powered rifle fired from atop the UT-Austin administration tower. The observation deck wasn't closed until 1975, however, after a series of suicides (it was reopened in 1999 with a new iron barrier to prevent further incidents).

In the meantime, UT added a medical center in Dallas and several graduate schools in Austin. The 1960s through the 1980s were a time of geographic expansion for the system as it absorbed other institutions, started several new campuses, and expanded its network of medical centers. In 1996 the UT System became the first public university to establish a private investment management company (University of Texas Investment Management Co.) to invest PUF money (by that time over $9 billion) and other funds.

The race issue reared its head again in 1996 when a Federal court ruled in the Hop-wood decision (named for the plaintiff) that the UT System could no longer use race to determine scholarships and admissions. The decision caused a staggering decline in minority enrollments the following year, the same year the Texas Legislature passed a bill mandating that student athletes meet the same admission requirements as other students. The state moved to offset the drop in minority enrollments with a law that grants admission to the top 10% of graduates from any Texas high school to the state university of their choice. UT Chancellor William Cunningham announced his resignation in 1999, effective in August 2000.

Chairman, Board of Regents: Donald L. Evans
VC, Board of Regents: Rita Crocker Clements
VC, Board of Regents: Tom Loeffler
Executive Secretary, Board of Regents:
Francie A. Fredrick
Chancellor: William H. Cunningham
Executive Vice Chancellor Academic Affairs:
Edwin R. Sharpe
Executive Vice Chancellor Business Affairs:
R. D. Burck
Executive Vice Chancellor Health Affairs:
Charles B. Mullins
Vice Chancellor and General Counsel: Ray Farabee
Vice Chancellor Development and External Relations:
Shirley Bird Perry
Vice Chancellor Federal Relations: Mark Franz
Vice Chancellor Governmental Relations:
Michael D. Millsap
Vice Chancellor Information Technology and Distance Education: Mario J. Gonzalez
President, University of Texas at Arlington:
Robert E. Witt
President, University of Texas at Austin:
Larry R. Faulkner
President, University of Texas at Dallas:
Franklyn G. Jenifer
President, University of Texas at El Paso:
Diana Natalicio
President, University of Texas Pan American:
Miguel A. Nevarez
President, University of Texas of the Permian Basin:
Charles A. Sorber
President, University of Texas at San Antonio:
Ricardo Romo
Auditors: Texas State Auditor

LOCATIONS

HQ: 601 Colorado St., Austin, TX 78701
Phone: 512-499-4200   **Fax:** 512-499-4218
Web site: http://www.utsystem.edu

PRODUCTS/OPERATIONS

University of Texas System Component Institutions

Academic Institutions
The University of Texas at Arlington
(est. 1895; 19,148 students)
The University of Texas at Austin
(est. 1883; 49,034 students)
The University of Texas at Brownsville
(est. 1991; 9,094 students)
The University of Texas at Dallas
(est. 1961; 10,137 students)
The University of Texas at El Paso
(est. 1914; 14,695 students)
The University of Texas Pan American
(Edinburg; est. 1927; 12,520 students)
The University of Texas of the Permian Basin
(Odessa; est. 1969; 2,222 students)
The University of Texas at San Antonio
(est. 1969; 18,607 students)
The University of Texas at Tyler
(est. 1971; 3,392 students)

Health Institutions
The University of Texas Health Science Center at
Houston (est. 1972; 3,170 students)
The University of Texas Health Science Center at San
Antonio (est. 1959; 2,557 students)
The University of Texas Health Center at Tyler
(est. 1947)
The University of Texas M.D. Anderson Cancer Center
(Houston; est. 1941)
The University of Texas Medical Branch at Galveston
(est. 1891; 1,952 students)
The University of Texas Southwestern Medical Center at
Dallas (est. 1943; 1,554 students)

HISTORICAL FINANCIALS & EMPLOYEES

School FYE: August	Annual Growth	1989	1990	1991	1992	1993	1994	1995	1996	1997	1998
Sales ($ mil.)	7.7%	2,564	2,895	4,796	3,433	3,744	4,030	4,300	4,624	4,803	5,244
Employees	2.8%	—	61,936	63,271	67,210	67,985	70,000	72,395	74,364	75,517	77,112

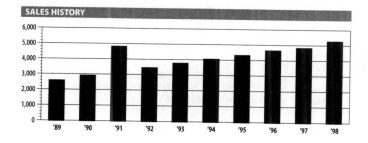

SALES HISTORY

THE UNIVERSITY OF WISCONSIN

OVERVIEW

There is no School of Cheese in the University of Wisconsin System, but there are 13 four-year universities, 13 two-year campuses, and a statewide extension program. Based in Madison, the University of Wisconsin System is one of the largest public university systems in the US, with more than 150,000 students.

The University of Wisconsin at Madison is the system's flagship school and has more than 40,000 students enrolled on its campus. It is ranked in the top 10 US public schools by *U.S. News & World Report* and offers undergraduate, graduate, and postdoctoral studies to its students. The school's graduate program in sociology is considered one of the best in the nation. The system's other major campus is the University of Wisconsin at Milwaukee, with nearly 23,000 students.

About 34% of UW-Madison's annual budget comes from state funds. Aside from student fees and federal programs, the UW Foundation, an independent, not-for-profit operation, is a major provider of funds.

HISTORY

When Wisconsin became a state in 1848, its constitution called for the establishment of a state university. A board of regents was named, and it first established a preparatory school because regents felt Wisconsin's secondary schools were not advanced enough to prepare students for university studies. The school began classes in 1849 with 20 students in the Madison Female Academy Building. The University of Wisconsin's first official freshman class began studies in the fall of 1850. A campus was established a mile west of the state capitol in Madison. By 1854, when it held its first commencement (with two graduates), the school had 41 students.

Enrollment dipped during the Civil War (all but one of the school's senior class joined the army) but soon rebounded, and by 1870 the university had almost 500 students. Meanwhile, it established a school of agriculture (in 1866) and a school of law (1868). The state established normal schools (teachers colleges) in Platteville (1866), Whitewater (1868), Oshkosh (1871), and River Falls (1874).

There was also a teachers' course for women at the university in Madison. However, when John Bascom became president in 1874, he transformed the university into a truly coeducational institution, putting women "in all respects on precisely the same footing" with the men.

While the university at Madison remained Wisconsin's primary seat of learning, the state continued to establish normal schools. It opened institutions in Milwaukee (1885), Superior (1893), Stevens Point (1894), La Crosse (1909), and Eau Claire (1916). The nine normal schools eventually became a system of state colleges called Wisconsin State Universities.

The university at Madison also continued to grow, and by the late 1920s it had almost 9,000 students. WWII brought a drop in enrollment, but afterward it took off, jumping from about 7,000 in 1945 to over 22,000 by the late 1950s. In 1956 a branch, the University of Wisconsin-Milwaukee, was founded. Other branch campuses were established in Green Bay (1965) and Kenosha (1968).

The Madison campus became a focal point for student protests during the Vietnam War. Events came to a head in 1970 when President Fred Harrington resigned during a four-day standoff between students and the National Guard. War protesters also placed a bomb outside Sterling Hall, which housed the Army Math Research Center; the explosion killed one student and injured three others.

The state legislature merged the University of Wisconsin and the Wisconsin State Universities in 1971 to create The University of Wisconsin System. By the early 1980s it had an enrollment of nearly 160,000. However, later that decade it tightened admission standards, and enrollment began to fall.

A property tax reform bill passed by the state legislature in 1994 cut into The University of Wisconsin System's funding the next year. Also in 1997 the system announced it would cut 500 jobs, use more part-time instructors, and increase class sizes to deal with the $43 million it lost in the budget cuts. That year The University of Wisconsin System Board of Regents approved salary increases for the system's president and chancellors, their first pay adjustment since 1994.

In 1998 UW-Madison broke ground on the $22 million Fluno Center for Executive Education, a 100-room dorm, classroom building, and dining hall rolled into one. The next year enrollment at The University of Wisconsin System's two-year colleges broke 10,000 for the first time in five years.

President: Katharine C. Lyall
SVP Administration: David W. Olien
SVP Academic Affairs: David J. Ward
Acting VP Finance: Deborah A. Duncan
Acting VP University Relations: Margaret S. Lewis
Associate VP Academic Affairs: Sharon L. James
Associate VP Budget and Planning: Kathleen R. Sell
Associate VP Human Resources: George H. Brooks
Associate VP Learning and Information Technology:
Edward Meachen
Associate VP Policy Analysis and Research:
Frank Goldberg
Assistant VP Administrative Services: Ellen James
Assistant VP Capital Planning and Budget:
Nancy J. Ives
Assistant VP Multicultural Affairs: Andrea-Teresa Arenas
Director Budget Planning: Joan Westgard
Director Information Services: Nancy Crabb
Director Internal Audit: Ronald L. Yates
Director Public Information: Sharyn Wisniewski
Controller: Mike Kraus
General Counsel: Elizabeth Rindskopf Parker
Treasury Manager and Assistant Trust Officer:
Lori D. Mills
Auditors: State of Wisconsin Legislative Audit Bureau

HQ: The University of Wisconsin System,
Van Hise Hall, 1220 Linden Dr., Madison, WI 53706
Phone: 608-262-2321   **Fax:** 608-262-3985
Web site: http://www.uwsa.edu

University Campuses

Baraboo/Sauk County	Oshkosh
Barron County	Parkside
Eau Claire	Platteville
Fond Du Lac	Richland
Fox Valley	River Falls
Green Bay	Rock County
La Crosse	Sheboygan
Madison	Stevens Point
Manitowoc	Stout
Marathon County	Superior
Marinette County	Washington County
Marshfield/Wood County	Waukesha
Milwaukee	Whitewater

1998 Sales

	$ mil.	% of total
State appropriations	884	35
Tuition & fees	559	22
Federal grants & contracts	341	13
Auxiliary enterprises	204	8
Private gifts, grants & contracts	201	8
Educational activities	150	6
UW Hospital authority	28	1
State grants & contracts	27	1
Federal appropriations	14	1
Endowment income	10	0
Local grants & contracts	8	0
Other	117	5
Total	**2,543**	**100**

School FYE: June	Annual Growth	1989	1990	1991	1992	1993	1994	1995	1996	1997	1998
Sales ($ mil.)	3.1%	1,836	1,995	2,110	2,226	2,309	2,442	2,556	2,612	2,399	2,543
Employees	(1.8%)	28,920	29,379	29,656	30,090	30,269	30,341	30,410	28,626	25,399	25,500

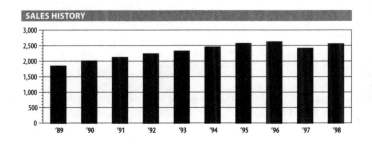

The University of Wisconsin System

USAA

OVERVIEW

Whether the country is at war or at peace, USAA's relationship with the US military stands firm.

With more than 3 million customers, the San Antonio-based mutual company primarily serves military personnel (95% of military officers are members) and their families, as well as select government employees, such as FBI and DEA agents. In addition to property /casualty and life insurance, USAA operates USAA Capital Corporation (CAPCO) as an umbrella organization that offers several services through subsidiaries. These include discount brokerage and investment management (both available to nonmembers), banking, and real

estate development. The company also sells merchandise (jewelry, major appliances, electronic and consumer goods) in seasonal catalogs and offers long-distance telephone services through USAA Alliance Services.

A unique insurance institution, USAA attracts policyholders largely by word of mouth from the loyal, close-knit military community, keeping costs down and creating a customer base of officers with high job and wage security. However, the downsizing of the armed forces has driven the USAA to extend membership eligibility to active-duty enlisted personnel in 48 states, the District of Columbia, and overseas.

HISTORY

In 1922 a group of 26 US Army officers gathered in a San Antonio hotel and formed their own automobile insurance association. The reason? As military officers who often moved, they had a hard time getting insurance because they were considered transient. So the officers decided to insure each other. Led by Major William Garrison, who became the company's first president, they formed the United States Army Automobile Insurance Association.

In 1924, when US Navy and Marine Corps officers were allowed to join, the company changed its name to United Services Automobile Association. By the mid-1950s the company had some 200,000 members. During the 1960s the company formed USAA Life Insurance Company (1963) and USAA Casualty Insurance Company (1968).

In 1969 Robert McDermott, a retired US Air Force brigadier general, became president. He cut employment through attrition, established education and training seminars for employees, and invested in computers and telecommunications (drastically cutting claims-processing time). McDermott added new products and services, such as mutual funds, real estate investments, and banking. Under McDermott, USAA's membership grew from 653,000 in 1969 to over 3 million in 1993.

During the 1970s, in an effort to go paperless, USAA became one of the insurance industry's first companies to switch from mail to toll-free (800) numbers. In the early 1980s the company introduced its discount purchasing program, USAA Buying Services. In 1985 it opened the USAA Federal Savings Bank. In the late 1980s USAA began installing an optical storage system to automate some customer service operations.

McDermott retired in 1993 and was succeeded by Robert Herres. The following year USAA Federal Savings Bank began developing a home banking system, offering members information and services over advanced screen telephones provided by IBM.

In the early 1990s USAA's real estate activities increased dramatically. In 1995 USAA restructured its interest in the Fiesta Texas theme park in San Antonio in order to focus on previously developed properties in geographically diverse areas. That year Six Flags Theme Parks (now Premier Parks) assumed operation and management of Fiesta Texas, which it purchased from USAA in 1998. That year, USAA opened the Westin La Cantera Resort in San Antonio.

In 1997 USAA began including enlisted military personnel as members. It also started to experiment with a "plain English" mutual fund prospectus.

The next year USAA began offering Choice Ride in Orlando, Florida. For about $1,100 per quarter and a promise not to drive except in emergencies, the pilot program provided 36 round trips and a 90% discount on car insurance, in hopes of keeping older drivers from unnecessarily getting behind the wheel.

In 1998, as part of its new Financial Planning Network, USAA began offering retirement and estate planning assistance aimed at 25- to 55-year-olds for a yearly $250 fee. In 1999, USAA moved to consolidate its customers' separate accounts (such as mutual fund holdings, stocks and bonds, life insurance products) into one main account to strengthen customer relationships and reduce operational costs.

OFFICERS

OFFICERS

Chairman and CEO: Robert T. Herres
President and COO: Robert G. Davis
Deputy CEO, Property and Casualty Operations, Alliance Services and Corporate Support: Bill Cooney
SVP and Chief Communications Officer: Steven M. Eames
SVP, CFO, and Corporate Treasurer: Joe Robles Jr.
SVP and Chief Planning and Analysis Officer: Duane G. Divich
SVP, Secretary, and General Counsel: Bradford W. Rich
SVP Business Integration: J. Earl King
SVP Human Resources: Elizabeth Conklyn
Chief Information Officer; President and CEO, USAA Information Technology Company: Donald R. Walker
President and CEO, USAA Alliance Services Company: Janice E. Marshall
President and CEO, USAA Federal Savings Bank: Mark H. Wright
President and CEO, USAA Investment Management Company: Michael J. C. Roth
President and CEO, USAA Life Insurance: Edwin L. Rosane
President, USAA Property and Casualty Insurance Group: Henry Viccellio Jr.
President and CEO, USAA Real Estate Company and La Cantera Development Company: Edward B. Kelley
Auditors: KPMG LLP

LOCATIONS

HQ: 9800 Fredericksburg Rd., USAA Bldg., San Antonio, TX 78288
Phone: 210-498-2211   **Fax:** 210-498-9940
Web site: http://www.usaa.com

PRODUCTS/OPERATIONS

1998 Assets

	$ mil.	% of total
Cash & equivalents	776	3
Bonds	11,946	41
Stocks	2,312	8
Net loans	6,352	22
Real estate	681	2
Receivables	842	3
Other assets	5,922	21
Total	**28,831**	**100**

1998 Sales

	$ mil.	% of total
Insurance premiums	5,213	68
Investment income	925	12
Fees, sales & loan income	907	12
Real estate	164	2
Other	478	6
Total	**7,687**	**100**

COMPETITORS

20th Century	Liberty Mutual
AXA Financial	MassMutual
Allstate	MetLife
American Express	Morgan Stanley Dean Witter
American Financial	
American General	Mutual of Omaha
Berkshire Hathaway	Nationwide Insurance
CIGNA	New York Life
CNA Financial	Northwestern Mutual
Charles Schwab	Pacific Mutual
Chubb	Paine Webber
Citigroup	Prudential
FMR	St. Paul Companies
Guardian Life	State Farm
John Hancock	T. Rowe Price
The Hartford	Transamerica
Kemper Insurance	

HISTORICAL FINANCIALS & EMPLOYEES

Mutual company FYE: December	Annual Growth	1989	1990	1991	1992	1993	1994	1995	1996	1997	1998
Assets ($ mil.)	11.3%	10,562	12,258	14,520	16,235	18,494	19,548	22,244	23,622	25,007	28,831
Net income ($ mil.)	15.0%	424	321	413	140	676	564	730	855	1,189	980
Income as % of assets	—	4.0%	2.6%	2.8%	0.9%	3.7%	2.9%	3.3%	3.6%	4.8%	3.4%
Employees	4.7%	12,515	13,884	14,222	14,667	15,905	15,233	15,677	16,571	17,967	20,120

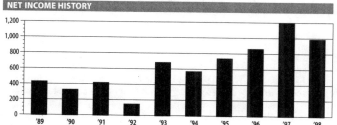

NET INCOME HISTORY

1998 FISCAL YEAR-END

Equity as % of assets: 24.9%
Return on assets: 3.6%
Return on equity: 13.9%
Long-term debt ($ mil.): 2,596
Sales ($ mil.): 7,687

THE VANGUARD GROUP, INC.

OVERVIEW

If you buy low and sell high, don't panic, invest for the long term, and generally disapprove of those whippersnappers at Fidelity, then you may end up in the Vanguard of the financial market.

Based in Malvern, Pennsylvania, The Vanguard Group offers a line of highly sought-after mutual funds and brokerage services; it is the #2 fund manager after Fidelity. Vanguard's fund options include stock, bond, mixed, and international offerings. The company is known as much for its puritanical thriftiness and conservative investing (it actively discourages short-term investing with redemption fees, defining "short-term" as three years) as for its line of index funds, which track the performance of such groups of stock as the S&P 500. In addition to being a low-cost mutual fund provider, Vanguard also offers funds actively managed by outside contractors.

Unlike other funds, Vanguard is set up like a mutual insurance company. The funds (and by extension, their investors) own the company, so fees are low to nonexistent; funds are operated on a tight budget so as not to eat into results. The company spends next to nothing on advertising, relying instead on strong returns and word-of-mouth. As part of the low-cost culture, managers at Vanguard may be switched at a moment's notice to answering telephones when market conditions prompt a flood of concerned investor phone calls.

Largely in response to the popularity of Web-based discount brokerages, Vanguard is quietly touting its previously low-profile brokerage division. Despite its no-broker, no-load background, Vanguard is developing cheap ways to dole out advice, especially through the use of 800 numbers and the Internet. Analysts expect Vanguard to pass Fidelity as the top fund in a few years.

HISTORY

A distant cousin of Daniel Boone, Walter Morgan knew a few things about pioneering. He was the first to offer a fund with a balance of stocks and bonds, serendipitously introduced early in 1929, months before the stock market collapsed. Morgan's balanced Wellington fund (named after Napoleon's vanquisher) emerged effectively unscathed.

In 1951 Morgan hired fellow Princeton alum John Bogle, having been impressed by Bogle's senior thesis on mutual funds. Morgan retired in 1967 and picked Bogle to replace him. That year Bogle engineered a merger with old-school investment firm Thorndike, Doran, Paine and Lewis. After culture clashes and four years of shrinking assets, the Thorndike-dominated board fired Bogle. Bogle appealed to the mutual funds, which had a separate board of directors. The fund directors decided to split up the funds and the advisory business.

Bogle named the new fund company The Vanguard Group, after the flagship of Lord Nelson, another Napoleon foe. Vanguard worked like a cooperative; mutual fund shareholders owned the company, so all services were provided at cost. The Wellington Management Company remained Vanguard's distributor until 1977, when Bogle convinced Vanguard's board to drop the affiliation. Without Wellington as the intermediary, Vanguard sold its funds directly to consumers as no-load funds (without service charges). In 1976 the company launched the Vanguard Index 500, the first index fund. These measures attracted new investors in droves.

Vanguard rode the boom of the 1980s. The Windsor fund grew so large the company closed it, launching Windsor II in 1985. Vanguard weathered the 1987 crash and began the 1990s as the US's #4 mutual fund company. FMR's actively-managed Fidelity funds, most notably its Magellan fund, led the market then. The retirement of legendary Magellan manager Peter Lynch, and the underperformance of the fund under his successors spurred a rush to index funds. Vanguard moved up to #2.

Vanguard played against type in 1995 when it introduced the Vanguard Horizon Capital Growth stock fund, an aggressively-managed fund designed to go head-to-head with Fidelity's funds.

In 1997 Vanguard added brokerage services and began selling its own and other companies' funds on the Internet to allow its clients to consolidate their financial activities. In 1998 Bogle passed the chairmanship to CEO John Brennan, a soft-spoken technology wonk, and Vanguard began selling mutual funds in Europe. Founder Walter Morgan died later that year at age 100.

Investors were ruffled the following year when 70-year-old Bogle announced that corporate bylaws regarding age limits would force him to leave the board of directors at the end of the year.

Senior Chairman: John C. Bogle, age 70
Chairman, President, and CEO: John J. Brennan
SVP and CFO: Ralph K. Packard
SVP Information Technology: Robert A. DiStefano
SVP, Fixed Income Group: Ian A. MacKinnon
SVP, Individual Investor Group: James H. Gately
SVP, Institutional Investor Group: F. William McNabb III
Secretary: Raymond J. Klapinsky
Treasurer: Richard F. Hyland
Controller: Robert Snowden
Managing Director Human Resources: Kathy Gubanich
Director Sales, Institutional Investor Group:
Gerard P. Mullane

LOCATIONS

HQ: 100 Vanguard Blvd., Malvern, PA 19355
Phone: 610-648-6000 **Fax:** 610-669-6605
Web site: http://www.vanguard.com

PRODUCTS/OPERATIONS

Selected Vanguard Funds
Vanguard 500
Vanguard Admiral Treasury Money Market Fund
Vanguard Aggressive Growth Fund
Vanguard Asset Allocation Fund
Vanguard Balanced Index Fund
Vanguard Capital Opportunity Fund
Vanguard Convertible Securities Fund
Vanguard Emerging Markets Stock Index Fund
Vanguard Energy Fund
Vanguard Equity Income Fund
Vanguard Explorer Fund
Vanguard Extended Market Index Fund
Vanguard Federal Money Market Fund
Vanguard Global Asset Allocation Fund
Vanguard GNMA Fund
Vanguard Gold and Precious Metals Fund
Vanguard Growth Index Fund
Vanguard Health Care Fund
Vanguard High-Yield Corporate Fund
Vanguard Insured Long-Term Tax-Exempt Fund
Vanguard International Value Fund
Vanguard LifeStrategy Conservative Growth Fund
Vanguard Mid-Cap Index Fund
Vanguard Morgan Growth Fund
Vanguard Pacific Stock Index Fund
Vanguard Preferred Stock Fund
Vanguard PRIMECAP Fund
Vanguard REIT Index Fund
Vanguard Selected Value Fund
Vanguard STAR Fund
Vanguard Tax-Managed Balanced Fund
Vanguard Total Bond Market Index Fund
Vanguard Total International Stock Index Fund
Vanguard Treasury Money Market Fund
Vanguard Utilities Income Fund
Vanguard Wellesley Income Fund
Vanguard Wellington Fund
Vanguard Windsor Fund

COMPETITORS

Alliance Capital	Mellon Financial
Barclays	Merrill Lynch
Charles Schwab	Prudential
FMR	T. Rowe Price
Franklin Resources	USAA

HISTORICAL FINANCIALS & EMPLOYEES

Private FYE: December	Annual Growth	1989	1990	1991	1992	1993	1994	1995	1996	1997	1998
Estimated sales ($ mil.)	33.3%	—	—	—	—	—	—	—	—	900	1,200
Employees	100.0%	—	—	—	—	—	—	—	—	5,000	10,000

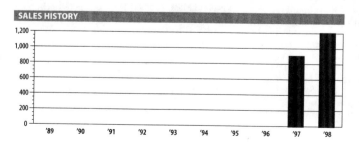

SALES HISTORY

THE**Vanguard**GROUP.

VISA INTERNATIONAL

OVERVIEW

Visa International, the reigning emperor of e-money, is putting its plastic where its mouth is. With a Visa card of any stripe (or microchip), consumers can get service at more than 16 million merchant locations in more than 300 countries. Foster City, California-based Visa operates the world's #1 payment system, with almost half of the market, followed by MasterCard (25%) and American Express (19%). The classic credit card (beloved of Americans) has been joined by smart cards, debit cards, and disposable cash cards (all of which are favored by Europeans). Visa International operates through six autonomous regional groups and is owned by its 21,000 member financial institutions.

Traditionally, Visa acts as brand manager, with members contributing to the overall marketing budget. However, Citigroup's defection to MasterCard (attributed at least partially to Visa's unwillingness to play down its own brand name) has helped convince Visa CEO Malcolm Williamson to be more flexible. On a trial basis, member banks will be allowed to relegate the Visa logo to the back of the card.

Visa is accelerating its push to introduce chip cards over magnetic stripe technology, and it is maneuvering its Open Platform technology into position against the MasterCard-supported Mondex platform and Microsoft's Smart Card for Windows. Winner takes all in this contest, with losers having to adopt the new system or face a shrinking market share.

HISTORY

Although the first charge card was issued by Western Union in 1914, it wasn't until 1958 that Bank of America (BofA) issued its BankAmericard, which combined the convenience of a charge account with credit privileges. When BofA extended its customer base outside California, the interchange system controlling payments began to falter because of design problems and fraud.

In 1968 Dee Hock, manager of the BankAmericard operations of the National Bank of Commerce in Seattle, convinced member banks that a more reliable system was needed. Two years later National BankAmericard Inc. (NBI) was created as an independent corporation (owned by 243 banks) to buy the BankAmericard system from BofA.

With its initial ad slogan, "Think of it as Money," the Hock-led NBI developed BankAmericard into a widely used form of payment in the US. A multinational corporation, IBANCO, was formed in 1974 to carry the operations into other countries. People outside the US resisted BankAmericard's nominal association with BofA, and in 1977 Hock changed the card's name to Visa. NBI became Visa USA, and parent company IBANCO became Visa International.

By 1980 Visa had debuted debit cards, begun issuing traveler's checks, and created an electromagnetic point-of-sale authorization system. Visa developed a global network of ATMs in 1983; it was expanded in 1987 by the purchase of a 33% stake in the Plus System of ATMs, then the US's second-largest system. Hock retired in 1984, with the company well

on its way to realizing his vision of a universal payment system.

The company built the Visa brand image with aggressive advertising, such as sponsorship of the 1988 and 1992 Olympics, and by co-branding (issuing cards through other organizations with strong brand names, such as Blockbuster and Ford Motor Company).

In 1994 Visa teamed up with Microsoft and others to develop home banking services and software. Visa Cash was introduced during the 1996 Olympics. Visa pushed its debit cards in 1996 and 1997 with humorous ads featuring presidential also-ran Bob Dole and showbiz success story Daffy Duck.

Visa expanded its smart card infrastructure in 1997. It published, with MasterCard, encryption and security software for online transactions. The gloves came off the next year as the companies vied to convince the world to rally around their respective e-purse technology standards.

During the 1990s, Visa fought American Express' attempts to introduce a bank credit card of its own by forbidding Visa members in the US from issuing the product; the Justice Department responded with an antitrust suit against Visa and MasterCard (the case is pending).

Citing excessive dues and limited brand promotion, Citigroup (generating some 20% of Visa's bank dues) defected to competitor MasterCard in 1999. To help address marketing concerns and stave off further desertions, Visa split its marketing and card processing operations into separate organizations that year. The company also announced a technology venture capital fund open to member banks.

OFFICERS

Chairman: William P. Boardman
President and CEO: Malcolm Williamson
President, Global Support Services: Daniel R. Eitingon
Group EVP and Chief Administrative Officer:
Raymond Barnes
EVP Global Products Group: Stephen Schapp
EVP Human Resources: Elizabeth Rounds
EVP International Marketing: Rupert Keeley
VP International Corporate Relations: David Demarett
Chairman, Visa USA: Philip G. Heasley
President, Visa USA: Carl Pascarella
EVP Corporate Relations, Visa USA: John C. Onoda
EVP Marketing and Product Management, Visa USA:
Tony McEwen
EVP Member and Integrated Solutions, Visa USA:
Bond R. Isaacson
EVP, Southeast Asia and Greater China:
James G. Murray
President, Visa Asia/Pacific: Dennis M. Goggin
President, Visa Canada: Derek A. Fry
**President, Visa Central and Eastern Europe, Middle
East, and Africa Region:** Anne L. Cobb
President, Visa European Union (EU): Johannes I. van
der Velde
President, Visa Latin America and Caribbean:
Jonathan Sanchez-Jaimes
Auditors: KPMG LLP

LOCATIONS

HQ: 900 Metro Center Blvd., Foster City, CA 94404
Phone: 650-432-3200   **Fax:** 650-432-3087
Web site: http://www.visa.com

PRODUCTS/OPERATIONS

Products and Services
ATMs (530,000 locations)
Electron (debit card outside the US)
Interlink (debit card)
Visa Business card (for small businesses and professionals)
Visa Cash (smart cards)
Visa Classic card (credit/debit card issued by Visa's
21,000 member banks)
Visa Corporate card (for travel and entertainment
expenses)
Visa Debit card (accesses bank account for immediate
settlement of payments)
Visa ePay (electronic bill payment)
Visa Global Customer Assistance Service (emergency
assistance)
Visa Gold card (higher spending limits)
Visa Purchasing card (for corporate purchases)
Visa Travelers Cheques
Visa TravelMoney (prepaid card in any currency)
VisaNet (electronic transaction processing network)
VisaPhone (long-distance telephone payment service)

COMPETITORS

American Express
Citigroup
MasterCard
Morgan Stanley Dean Witter

HISTORICAL FINANCIALS & EMPLOYEES

Private FYE: September	Annual Growth	1990	1991	1992	1993	1994	1995	1996	1997	1998	1999
Estimated sales ($ mil.)	16.3%	720	785	920	1,040	1,260	1,330	1,650	2,050	2,550	2,800
Employees	10.4%	—	—	2,500	3,000	3,500	4,000	4,800	5,000	5,000	5,000

SALES HISTORY

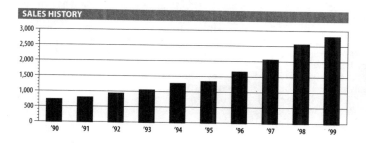

VULCAN NORTHWEST INC

OVERVIEW

Paul Allen is making sci-fi fantasies reality. The US's third-richest man (after Microsoft co-founder Bill Gates and investor Warren Buffett), Allen invests in companies that promote a "wired world."

Based in Bellevue, Washington, Vulcan Northwest is the umbrella organization for Allen's ventures, including his interest in Microsoft (5%, which he uses to fund his acquisitions) and six charities supporting the arts, medical research, land conservation, and other causes. Allen has stakes in dozens of companies offering computer, multimedia, or communications products and services. His Vulcan Ventures finds investment opportunities; think tank Interval Research develops

new technology and business opportunities promoting Allen's vision. His sister Jody Patton oversees both his business and charitable ventures.

"Broadband" is the buzzword *du jour*, and Allen's once scattershot investments are coalescing in a network of service, technology, and content providers that together will create a couch potato's dream: Information, entertainment, communication, and shopping available through the TV. Allen's push into cable has created the #4 provider (his Charter Communications ranks behind AT&T, Time Warner, and Comcast), but before the wired world becomes reality, Allen will be spending more money upgrading the cable networks.

HISTORY

Paul Allen and Bill Gates first worked together on computer projects as schoolmates in Seattle. They developed a computer program to determine traffic patterns and started their first company, Traf-O-Data; the operation failed because the state provided the information for free. When Allen saw an article on the MITS Altair 8800 minicomputer in 1975, the two realized it needed a simplified programming language to make it useful. They offered MITS a modified version of BASIC they had written for Traf-O-Data. The company set them up in an office in Albuquerque, New Mexico. They then began their biggest collaboration of all: Microsoft. While Gates concentrated on the business, Allen focused on technical issues.

They moved to Bellevue, a Seattle suburb, in 1979. The next year IBM asked them to create a programming language for a PC project. Allen bought Q-DOS (quick and dirty operating system) from Seattle Computer; the pair tweaked it and renamed it MS-DOS. Allen and Gates made a key decision to structure their contract with IBM to allow clones. They also helped design many aspects of the original IBM PC.

Allen developed Hodgkin's disease in 1982. Facing his own mortality, he ended his daily involvement in Microsoft (keeping about 13% of the company and a seat on its board) and began to play more (traveling and playing the electric guitar). With his cancer in remission in 1985, Allen founded his own multimedia software company, Asymetrix. The next year he set up Vulcan Northwest to hold his diversified interests and Vulcan Ventures. He also began helping small startups, indulging his personal interests (buying the NBA's Portland Trail Blazers in 1988 and donating some $60 million to

build a museum honoring his musical idol, Jimi Hendrix, and other Pacific Northwest artists), and funding civic improvements in the Seattle area.

In 1990 Allen hired William Savoy to help organize his finances; Savoy later became president of Vulcan Ventures. Seeing a need for more research and development in the US, in 1992 Allen started Interval Research. He also invested in America Online that year (sold 1994). In 1993 Allen bought 80% of Ticketmaster (the US's top ticket agency; sold 1997), and in 1995 he invested in DreamWorks SKG, the multimedia company founded by Steven Spielberg, Jeffrey Katzenberg, and David Geffen.

Allen made a rare acquisition outside the entertainment and high-tech worlds with the 1996 investment in power turbine maker Capstone Turbine. To prevent the Seattle Seahawks from moving to California, Allen bought the team in 1997 and helped build a new stadium for it. That year he consolidated his management operations under Vulcan Northwest and dissolved the Paul Allen Group (founded 1994), keeping Vulcan Ventures.

Allen pushed into cable, buying Marcus Cable in 1998 and folding it into his 1999 purchase of Charter Communications, which became the #4 US cable firm after further acquisitions. In 1999 several Allen investments (Charter Communications, Vulcan Ventures, Internet service providers RCN and High Speed Access, and content provider Go2Net) joined to form wired world venture Broadband Partners.

Chairman: Paul G. Allen
CEO: Jody Patton
Member Presidents Council; President and CEO, Asymetrix: Jim Billmaier
Member Presidents Council: Bert Kolde
Member Presidents Council; President and CEO, Interval Research: David E. Liddle
Member Presidents Council; President, Vulcan Ventures: William D. Savoy
CFO: Joseph Franzi
Director Human Resources: Pam Faber
Director Public Relations: Susan Pierson

HQ: 110 110th Ave. NE, Ste. 550, Bellevue, WA 98004
Phone: 425-453-1940   **Fax:** 425-453-1985
Web site: http://www.paulallen.com

Selected Holdings
800.com (online consumer electronics retailer)
ARI Network Services, Inc. (e-commerce network services)
Avio Digital, Inc. (home networking technology)
Beyond.com Corporation (online software retailer)
Capstone Turbine Corporation (power turbogenerators)
Certicom, Inc. (cryptographic technology)
Charter Communications (cable-TV system)
click2learn.com, inc. (multimedia development software)
CNET (computer information cable-TV channel and online service)
Command Audio (audio-on-demand service)
CyberSource (ecommerce transaction services)
Dick's Clothing & Sporting Goods (online retailer)
DreamWorks SKG (entertainment company)
Drugstore.com (online retailer)
Egghead.com (hardware and software seller)
Fatbrain.com (online information resource retailer)
Go2net, Inc. (online portal)
High Speed Access Corp. (digital subscriber line provider)
InterNAP Network Services (Internet connectivity services)
inviso (display developer)
Liquid Audio (digital music software and delivery service)
Mercata (online retailer)
Metricom, Inc. (wireless data-transmission products)
Net Perceptions, Inc. (Internet information filtering software)
Netpodium Inc. (live Web-based communications)
Nexabit Networks, Inc. (switch/router maker)
NorthPoint Communications (digital subscriber line provider)
Portland Trail Blazers (professional basketball team)
Replay Networks, Inc. (television programming technology provider)
RioPort, Inc. (digital audio provider)
Seattle Seahawks (professional football team)
Sharewave Inc. (digital wireless technology)
Stamps.com (online postage retailer)
Telescan, Inc. (online investor information)
TeraStor Corporation (rewritable mass-storage products)
TiVo (television programming technology provider)
United States Satellite Broadcasting Company, Inc. (digital satellite television)
Value America (online retailer)
Vision Software (business software developer)
Visionary Design Systems (mechanical engineering development software)
Wink Communications (television advertising technology)
Zany Brainy (toy retailer)
ZDTV (Internet-focused cable-TV station)
Ziff-Davis, Inc. (media and marketing services)

AT&T
Accel Partners
Associated Group
Austin Ventures
Benchmark Capital
Boston Ventures
Brentwood Venture
CMGI
Draper Fisher Jurvetson
E2Enet.com
Flatiron Partners
Harris & Harris
Hicks, Muse
Hummer Winblad
idealab
Institutional Venture Partners
Kleiner Perkins
Liberty Digital
Matrix Partners
Mayfield Fund
Menlo Ventures
Microsoft
SOFTBANK
Safeguard Scientifics
Sutter Hill
Trinity Ventures
US Venture Partners
Venrock Associates
Veronis, Suhler

WAKEFERN FOOD CORPORATION

OVERVIEW

At Wakefern Food the little guys are Goliath. The largest supermarket co-op in the US, Elizabeth, New Jersey-based Wakefern is owned by about 40 independent grocers who operate some 190 ShopRite supermarkets in five northeastern states. The company provides members and other customers more than 20,000 name-brand items, including groceries, dairy and meat products, produce, frozen foods, and general merchandise. It also offers more than 3,000 items under the ShopRite label, and it offers members support services,

including advertising, merchandising, and insurance through Kemper.

More than half of the ShopRite stores offer full-service pharmacies, and others offer the specialty services like banks, coffee shops, and photo labs that are quickly becoming the norm in food retailing. Members range from single-store owners to Big V Supermarkets, Wakefern's largest customer, with 32 ShopRite stores. All members are given one vote in the co-op, regardless of size.

HISTORY

Wakefern Food was founded in 1946 by seven New York- and New Jersey-based grocers: Louis Weiss, Sam and Al Aidekman, Abe Kesselman, Dave Fern, Sam Garb, and Albert Goldberg (the company's name is made up of the letters of the first five of those founders). Like many cooperatives in the first half of the 20th century, the men sought to lower costs by increasing their buying power as a group. They each put in $1,000 and began operating a 5,000-sq.-ft. warehouse, often putting in double time to keep both their stores and the warehouse running. The shopkeepers' collective buying power proved valuable, and with time the grocers were able to stock many items at the same prices as their larger competitors.

In 1951 Wakefern members began pooling their resources to buy advertising space. A common store name — ShopRite — was chosen, and each week co-op members met to decide which items would be sale priced. Within a year its membership had grown to over 50. Expansion became a priority, and in the mid-1950s co-op members united in small groups to take over failed supermarkets. One such group, called the Supermarkets Operating Co. (SOC), was formed in 1956. Within 10 years it had acquired a number of failed stores, remodeled them, and given them the ShopRite name.

During the late-1950s sales at ShopRite stores slumped after Wakefern decided to buck the supermarket trend of offering trading stamps (which could then be exchanged for gifts), figuring that offering the stamps would ultimately lead to higher food prices. The move initially drove away customers, but Wakefern cut grocery prices across the board and sales returned. The company also embraced another supermarket trend: stocking stores with nonfood items. In the early 1960s ShopRite stores became the first groceries to remain open nights and Sundays and the first

to feature drugstores, fish counters, and liquor departments.

The co-op was severely shaken in 1966 when SOC merged with General Supermarkets, a similar small group within Wakefern, becoming Supermarkets General Corp. (SGC). SGC was a powerful entity, with 71 supermarkets, 10 drugstores, six gas stations, a wholesale bakery, and a discount department store. Many Wakefern members opposed the merger and attempted to block the action with a court order. By 1968 SGC had beefed up its operations to include department store chains as well as its grocery stores. In a move that threatened to break Wakefern, SGC broke away from the co-op, and its stores were renamed Pathmark.

Wakefern not only weathered the storm, it grew under the direction of chairman and CEO Thomas Infusino, elected shortly after the split. The co-op focused on asserting its position as a seller of low-priced products. Wakefern developed private-label brands, including the ShopRite brand. In the 1980s members began operating larger stores and adding more nonfood items to the ShopRite product mix. With its number of superstores on the rise and facing increased competition from club stores in 1992, Wakefern opened a centralized, nonfood distribution center in New Jersey.

In 1995, 30-year Wakefern veteran Dean Janeway was elected president of the co-op. The company debuted its ShopRite MasterCard, co-branded with New Jersey's Valley National Bank, in 1996. The following year the co-op purchased two of its customer's stores in Pennsylvania, then threatened to close them when contract talks with the local union deteriorated. In 1998 Wakefern settled the dispute, then sold the stores.

Chairman and CEO: Thomas Infusino
President: Dean Janeway
EVP: Joe Sheridan
CFO: Ken Jasinkiewicz
VP Human Resources: Ernie Bell

HQ: 600 York St., Elizabeth, NJ 07207
Phone: 908-527-3300   **Fax:** 908-527-3397
Web site: http://www.shoprite.com

Wakefern Food's approximately 40 members operate about 190 ShopRite supermarkets in Connecticut, Delaware, New Jersey, New York, and Pennsylvania.

1998 Stores

	No.
New Jersey	111
New York	44
Pennsylvania	13
Connecticut	10
Delaware	3
Total	**181**

Major Members
Big V Supermarkets
Foodarama Supermarkets
Inserra Supermarkets
Village Super Market

Selected Merchandise
Baked goods
Cigarettes
Dry goods
Frozen foods
General groceries
General merchandise
Produce
Specialty foods
Store supplies

A&P
C&S Wholesale
Di Giorgio
Fleming Companies
Grand Union
IGA
King Kullen Grocery
Pathmark
Royal Ahold
SUPERVALU
Shurfine International
Stop & Shop
Wal-Mart

Cooperative FYE: September	Annual Growth	1990	1991	1992	1993	1994	1995	1996	1997	1998	1999
Sales ($ mil.)	(1.3%)	—	—	—	—	3,740	3,700	4,304	4,613	5,000	3,500
Employees	0.0%	—	—	—	—	3,000	3,700	3,000	3,200	3,000	3,000

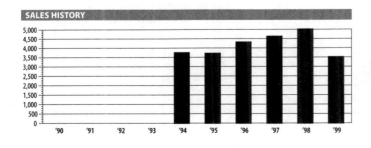

SALES HISTORY

WHITE CASTLE SYSTEM, INC.

OVERVIEW

White Castle System opts for square burgers instead of round tables. The Columbus, Ohio-based company was the country's first fast-food hamburger chain and it still owns all 330 of its restaurants, located primarily in 12 eastern and midwestern states. White Castle steam cooks its square, palm-sized burgers (also known as Slyders) on a bed of onions, the same way it did when the company was founded in 1921. Subsidiary PSB makes stainless-steel fixtures and equipment (including the kitchen equipment used in White Castle restaurants), as well as lawn spreaders under the PrizeLAWN brand.

Little has changed at White Castle over its 75-plus year history, from its Slyders to its castle-shaped buildings. That has helped the chain establish strong loyalty among its customers and its employees. The company's turnover rate for salaried employees is 6%, way below the 60% industry average. But White Castle's reluctance to franchise and its lack of TV advertising, among other things, have allowed burger giants McDonald's and Burger King to dominate the market. Chairman, president, and CEO E. W. Ingram III (grandson of co-founder E. W. Ingram) and his family own the company.

HISTORY

Walter Anderson, a cook in Wichita, Kansas, invented a new way to cook hamburger patties by steam-grilling the meat over a bed of onions. In 1916 he opened his first hamburger stand. Looking to build his string of three stands, Anderson joined real estate broker E. W. "Billy" Ingram in 1921 and opened the first White Castle restaurant in Wichita. At the time, many Americans were skeptical about the sanitary quality of hamburger meat, so Anderson and Ingram chose a name that stood for purity (White) and for strength and permanence (Castle). Whether it was the appellation or the Slyders, White Castle restaurants were a success, and about 100 restaurants opened between 1923 and 1931.

In 1933 Anderson sold his share in the company to Ingram, who moved the company headquarters to Columbus, Ohio, the following year. For the next several decades White Castle distinguished itself with a host of innovative products and ideas. To prove the nutritional value of its food, White Castle once paid a university student to eat nothing but White Castle hamburgers for an entire summer. The student, who ate about 20 to 24 burgers daily, survived, but on the advice of a chemist the company added more flour to its bun to make the meal more nutritious.

The first company in the food industry to use paper cartons, White Castle created its Porcelain Steel Building subsidiary to build its restaurants (some of which were movable) and much of its kitchen equipment. Marketing innovations included the creation of Julia Joyce, a fictional character played by a local housewife. Joyce would give other housewives a tour of White Castle kitchens, showcasing the sanitary conditions while handing out free coupons.

Beef shortages during World War II led to the closure of about a third of the company's restaurants. Those lean times were not helped by Ingram's refusal to hire women or black workers. White Castle yielded on the former by the end of the 1940s but did not hire sizable numbers of black employees until two decades after the war. During the 1950s and 1960s the franchise-oriented operations of Burger King and McDonalds eclipsed White Castle, in part because the company refused to exploit suburban expansion and TV advertising.

After Billy Ingram died in 1966, his son E. W. Ingram Jr. took control of the company. While the fast-food market exploded during the 1970s, White Castle continued its steady but slow growth. In 1977 E. W. Ingram Jr. handed the reins of the company over to his son, E. W. Ingram III. Two years later White Castle opened its first drive-through restaurant.

In 1981 the company started a toll-free number through which US customers could order frozen burgers and have them delivered within 24 hours. The program was so successful that it spawned White Castle Distributing, which debuted in 1986 to market the company's burgers in grocery stores; distribution spread to convenience stores and vending machines by 1995.

The next year the company formed an agreement with Church's Chicken to open co-branded restaurants nationwide. After introducing its first breakfast sandwich in 1998, White Castle launched a Web site in 1999, whatyoucrave.com, featuring tasty tidbits on everything trivial about White Castle.

OFFICERS

Chairman, President, and CEO: E. W. Ingram III
VP Finance and Treasurer: William A. Blake
VP Human Resources: Fred Gunderson
Controller: Russ Meyer

LOCATIONS

HQ: 555 W. Goodale St., Columbus, OH 43215
Phone: 614-228-5781 **Fax:** 614-464-0596
Web site: http://www.whitecastle.com

White Castle System owns restaurants in Illinois, Indiana, Kansas, Kentucky, Michigan, Minnesota, Missouri, New Jersey, New York, Ohio, Pennsylvania, and Tennessee. Subsidiary PSB Company operates plants in Columbus and Dayton, Ohio, and in Rome, Georgia.

1998 Restaurants

	No.
Illinois	50
Ohio	48
New York	46
Indiana	44
Michigan	36
Kentucky	26
Missouri	26
New Jersey	25
Minnesota	15
Tennessee	6
Pennsylvania	4
Kansas	1
Total	**327**

PRODUCTS/OPERATIONS

Selected Menu Items
Breakfast sandwiches
Cheeseburgers
Cheese sticks
Chicken rings
Chicken sandwiches
Chili
Fish sandwiches
French fries
Hamburgers
Onion rings
Shakes

COMPETITORS

Burger King
CKE Restaurants
Checkers Drive-In
McDonald's
Sonic
TRICON
Wendy's
Whataburger

HISTORICAL FINANCIALS & EMPLOYEES

Private FYE: December	Annual Growth	1989	1990	1991	1992	1993	1994	1995	1996	1997	1998
Sales ($ mil.)	5.7%	—	—	—	—	—	—	325	350	360	400
Employees	—	—	—	—	—	—	—	—	—	—	11,000

SALES HISTORY

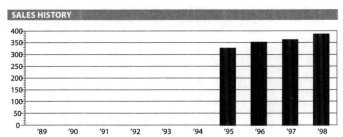

WINGATE PARTNERS

OVERVIEW

It's a win-win situation for Wingate Partners. The Dallas-based equity investment firm acquires controlling interests in manufacturing, distribution, and service businesses and transforms them into moneymakers, which it may operate or sell. Forgoing opportunities in such businesses as banking, media, high technology, insurance, natural resources, and real estate, Wingate generally targets companies that are underperforming or in industries in transition. These companies usually have sales between $100 million and $500 million and may or may not be profitable when purchased. Wingate often makes more expensive purchases in conjunction with other investors.

An active investor, Wingate usually takes seats on the boards of companies it holds, and sometimes manages them. The company's holdings include infant and children's furniture maker Okla Homer Smith and half of Loomis, Fargo & Co., one of the nation's top providers of armored car services. Wingate has launched two investment funds with a combined capitalization of $200 million. Investors include Yale University, The Ford Foundation, BankAmerica Capital, and the Hall family (of Hallmark cards fame).

HISTORY

In 1987 experienced investors Frederick Hegi and James Callier teamed up with Tom Sturgess, a former senior executive with the distribution arm of meatpacker Swift Independent, to form Wingate. Hegi, who began his career as an investment manager at First National Bank of Chicago, was part of an investment group that had acquired Swift. Callier had been a McKinsey & Company management consultant and an investor in his own right.

The trio found 11 prominent individual and institutional investors — including Carl Lindner, Henry Hillman, Hughes Aircraft Pension Fund, the University of Texas endowment fund, and several insurance companies — to establish the $67 million Wingate Partners L.P. fund to support Wingate's acquisition strategy.

The investment fund's initial purchase was manufactured home builder Redman Industries and its aluminum window manufacturing unit Redman Building Products in 1988. To bring the underperforming Redman operations into profitability, Wingate began cutting costs and paring noncore businesses. Wingate also bought children's car seat and crib maker Century Products (an unprofitable subsidiary of Gerber Products) that year.

In 1991 the company bought Loomis Armored; it took three years for Wingate to return the armored-car company to profitability (Loomis Armored had recorded three years of losses prior to its purchase by Wingate). In 1992 Wingate bought Associated Stationers, a network of stationery distribution centers.

By the time Wingate took Redman Industries public in 1993 (earning about $69 million), it had turned the company around. Wingate held on to Redman Building Products (the window unit) until 1997, when it was sold to Robert Bass' Keystone Inc.

When Wingate launched its second investment fund in 1994, it raised $130 million. Investors include BankAmerica Capital Corp., Common Fund, Duke University, The Ford Foundation, the Hall family (Hallmark Cards), Hughes Aircraft Pension Fund, the Kauffman Foundation, The University of Texas, Yale University, and several wealthy families in Dallas, Denver, and Kansas City.

With Wingate Partners II, the firm jumped on the health care bandwagon. Teaming with the former CEO of a hospital chain, Wingate formed rollup company AmeriStat Mobile Medical Services in 1994 to acquire ambulance companies. After making 10 such buys, the business was sold to ambulance operator Laidlaw in 1995.

Wingate bought Associated Stationers' rival United Stationers in 1995 and merged the former competitors under the United Stationers name. Wingate co-founder Sturgess served as United Stationers' chairman, CEO, and president until his resignation in 1996 (he still serves on Wingate's advisory board). Wingate acquired independent tire distributor ITCO Tire that year. In 1997 Wingate merged its Loomis Armored unit with Borg-Warner Security's Wells Fargo Armored Service subsidiary to form Loomis, Fargo & Co.

In 1998 the firm sold Century Products' stroller and car seat operations but kept its Okla Homer Smith unit, which makes cribs. That year Wingate sold ITCO to Heafner Tire Group, a nationwide tire distributor and retailer. In 1999 the company bought 46% of manufactured-housing building products distributor Kevco and acquired three automotive parts distributors to form Pro Parts Xpress.

OFFICERS

Principal; Chairman and CEO, Kevco; Chairman, United Stationers and Loomis, Fargo & Co.:
Frederick B. Hegi Jr., age 55
Principal; Chairman, Pro Parts Xpress:
Jay I. Applebaum, age 37
Principal: Michael B. Decker, age 50
Principal; Chairman, National Spirit Group:
V. Edward Easterling Jr., age 40
Principal; EVP, Kevco: James A. Johnson, age 45
VP: Jason H. Reed, age 31
Controller: Alna Evans

LOCATIONS

HQ: 750 N. St. Paul St., Ste. 1200, Dallas, TX 75201
Phone: 214-720-1313   **Fax:** 214-871-8799
Web site: http://www.wingatepartners.com

PRODUCTS/OPERATIONS

Selected Holdings
Kevco, Inc. (46%, building products)
Loomis, Fargo & Co. (51%, armored cars)
National Spirit Group (student sports and spirits products and services)
Okla Homer Smith (cribs and juvenile furniture)
Pro Parts Xpress (auto parts distributor)
United Stationers (11%, wholesale office products distribution)

COMPETITORS

AEA Investors
Apollo Advisors
Berkshire Hathaway
Blackstone Group
Clayton, Dubilier
Forstmann Little
Haas Wheat
Heico
Hicks, Muse
Interlaken Investment
KKR
Texas Pacific Group
Thomas Lee

W.K. KELLOGG FOUNDATION

OVERVIEW

The W.K. Kellogg Foundation has little trouble with "bran recognition." The Battle Creek, Michigan-based not-for-profit organization, founded by cereal industry pioneer W.K. Kellogg, has equity in the Kellogg Company and is among the top 10 charitable funds in the US. The foundation aims "to help people help themselves through the practical application of knowledge and resources to improve their quality of life and that of future generations."

The foundation and the Kellogg Company have enjoyed a long-standing relationship.

The foundation is controlled by an independent board of trustees, and most of its income comes from the investment of the W.K. Kellogg Trust.

With more than $6 billion in assets, the foundation awards about $220 million in grants to programs involving health, food systems and rural development, education, and volunteerism. The Kellogg Foundation makes its grants primarily in the US, but also in Latin America and Southern Africa.

HISTORY

Born in 1860, W.K. Kellogg's early jobs included those of stock boy and traveling broom salesman. He later went to work as a clerk (and then as bookkeeper and manager) at the Battle Creek Sanitarium, a renowned homeopathic hospital, where his older brother, John Harvey Kellogg, was physician-in-chief. The brothers first made wheat flakes in 1894 as an experiment with grains (for patients' diets). In 1906 W.K. started his own firm to produce corn flakes.

As head of the Battle Creek Toasted Corn Flake Company, W.K. was the first to use full-color magazine ads and widespread consumer sampling. He introduced classic cereals, such as Bran Flakes (1915), All-Bran (1916), and Rice Krispies (1928).

A philanthropist by inclination, W.K. established the Fellowship Corporation in 1925 to build an agricultural school and a bird sanctuary, as well as to set up an experimental farm and a reforestation project. He also gave $3 million to hometown causes, such as the Ann J. Kellogg School for disabled children, and for the construction of an auditorium, a junior high school, and a youth recreation center.

After attending a White House Conference on Child Health and Protection, W.K. established the W.K. Kellogg Child Welfare Foundation in 1930. A few months later he broadened the focus of the charter and renamed the institution the W.K. Kellogg Foundation. That year the foundation began its landmark Michigan Community Health Project (MCHP), which opened public health departments in counties once thought too small and poor to sustain them.

In 1934 W.K. donated more than $66 million in Kellogg Company stock and other investments to establish the W.K. Kellogg Foundation as a major charitable foundation. During WWII the foundation expanded its

programming to Latin America. There the organization funded advanced schooling for dentists, physicians, and other health professionals. After the war, it broadened its programming to include agriculture. To help war-torn Europe, the foundation funded agricultural projects in Germany, Iceland, Ireland, Norway, and the UK.

Following W.K.'s death in 1951, the organization expanded its programming to include support for graduate programs in health and hospital administration, as well as for rural leadership and community colleges.

In the 1970s the foundation lent its support to the growing volunteerism movement and to aiding the disadvantaged, with a special emphasis on programs for minorities. A review of operations in the late 1970s led the Kellogg Foundation to reassert its emphasis on health, education, agriculture, and leadership. The foundation also expanded its programs to Southern Africa.

From 1986 to 1995 the Kellogg Foundation funded the Rural America Initiative — a series of 28 projects meant to develop leadership, train local government officials, and revitalize rural areas. Between 1991 and 1996, through the Community-Based Public Health Initiative, the foundation assisted universities in educating public health professionals by presenting community-based approaches to students and faculty.

In 1998 the organization announced a five-year, $55 million plan to bring health care to the nation's poor and homeless. Also that year it gave Portland State University a $600,000 grant to develop its Institute for Nonprofit Management. In 1999 the Kellogg Foundation started its first geographically based program, pledging $15 million in grants for development of Mississippi River Delta communities in Arkansas, Louisiana, and Mississippi.

Chair: Chris T. Christ
President and CEO: William C. Richardson
SVP and Corporate Secretary: Gregory A. Lyman
SVP Programs: Anne C. Petersen
VP Finance and Treasurer: Paul J. Lawler
VP Programs: Geraldine Kearse Brookins
VP Programs: Richard M. Foster
VP Programs: Gail D. McClure
VP Programs: Dan E. Moore
VP Programs: Gloria R. Smith
Director Human Resources and Administrative Services: Karla Kretzschmer
Director Marketing and Communications: Karen E. Lake
Assistant VP: James E. McHale
Assistant VP Finance and Assistant Treasurer: LaJune Montgomery-Talley
Auditors: PricewaterhouseCoopers LLP

HQ: 1 Michigan Ave. East, Battle Creek, MI 49017
Phone: 616-968-1611   **Fax:** 616-968-0413
Web site: http://www.wkkf.org

Selected Grant Programs
Cross-Cutting Themes
  Capitalizing on Diversity
  Information Systems/Technology
  Leadership
  Social and Economic Community Development
Food Systems and Rural Development
Greater Battle Creek Programs (a regional interest)
Health
Philanthropy and Volunteerism
Special Opportunities
  Devolution
Youth and Education/Higher Education

Foundation FYE: August	Annual Growth	1990	1991	1992	1993	1994	1995	1996	1997	1998	1999
Assets ($ mil.)	2.4%	—	—	—	—	—	—	5,994	7,764	5,549	6,388
Employees	1.7%	—	—	—	—	—	—	276	280	286	290

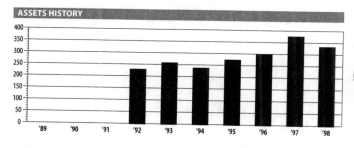

W.K. KELLOGG FOUNDATION

W. L. GORE AND ASSOCIATES, INC.

OVERVIEW

OK, so maybe Al Gore didn't really invent the Internet. But W. L. Gore and Associates certainly did invent Gore-Tex, a waterproof, windproof, lightweight fabric with uses that range from dental floss to space suits. The fabric is particularly popular for hats, jackets, and hiking boots, since it allows perspiration to escape but blocks rain and wind. The Newark, Delaware-based company also produces synthetic blood vessels (the inert material is resistant to infection), electronic cables, filters, and guitar strings.

Besides Gore-Tex, Gore is known for its unusual style of management known as the lattice system. There is no fixed authority, as the company has "sponsors," not bosses, and all employees are considered associates. Company goals and tasks are determined by consensus. To foster this type of reliance and cooperation, each company facility has no more than 200 employees.

Gore is continuously expanding the number of uses for its Gore-Tex material. Newly developed products include the REMEDIA catalytic filter system, which destroys carcinogens produced by industrial combustion. Gore has also developed an abrasion-resistant flouropolymer insulation product for aircraft wiring.

Bob Gore, the founder's son, runs the company which is 75% owned by the Gore family. Gore's associates own the rest.

HISTORY

In 1941 DuPont scientist Bill Gore started developing and researching plastics, polymers, and resins. One of the DuPont projects Gore worked on was for a synthetic substance known as polytetrafluoroethylene, more commonly known as teflon.

Seeing an untapped market for teflon-type products, Gore quit DuPont and in 1958 started his own business. His wife and his son Bob, a chemical engineering student, worked with him. Bob helped his father on the company's first major product line, teflon-insulated electronic wires and cables.

Gore's high-tech cables were a success, and the company was soon able to move out of the family basement and into a facility in Newark, Delaware. By 1965 the company had 200 employees; Bill Gore soon implemented his lattice structure of management, eschewing demands for personal commitments and emphasizing cooperation and teamwork as paramount tenets of the business. A second plant was opened in Flagstaff, Arizona, in 1967.

Two years later Bob, who had by then earned a doctorate in chemistry, hit the synthetic plastic motherlode. While experimenting with teflon, he discovered a way to stretch the material at the microscopic level, creating a fabric with holes large enough for body heat and moisture to pass through, but small enough to deflect raindrops. W. L. Gore and Associates applied for a patent on its Gore-Tex fabric in 1970 and received it six years later. The company experienced an explosive period of growth as Gore-Tex found its way into space suits, sporting apparel, artificial arteries, and filters. Around this time Bob Gore became president of the company. (Since part of the lattice management culture is predicated on a lack of hierarchy, there are only three officers in the entire company.)

By the 1980s Gore-Tex-related products accounted for the majority of sales; W. L. Gore operated around 30 plants worldwide, most of them located in smaller cities (the Gores believed small towns had a better quality of life). Bill Gore died in 1986, but the company continued, finding alternative uses for Gore-Tex. W. L. Gore was involved in various patent lawsuits at the time, and when the company lost a case in 1990 its exclusive patent on Gore-Tex ended, although the company retained patents on certain products and processes.

By 1993 the door was fully open for increased competition, but W. L. Gore still had the advantage of experience and the perception of higher quality and durability. It continued to come out with new uses for Gore-Tex, spooling out dental floss in 1993. Also that year the company moved into the computer market with its purchase of Supercomputer Systems. In 1996 W. L. Gore expanded its US medical product line by marketing a membrane (made from Gore-Tex-related material) used to replace dura mater, the membrane protecting the brain and spinal cord. The company boosted its medical products segment by buying Prograft Medical in 1997.

In 1999 Gore introduced its REMEDIA catalytic filter system which destroys carcinogenic dioxins and furans produced during industrial combustion by converting them into water and harmless chemicals.

President and CEO: Robert W. Gore
Secretary and Treasurer: Genevieve Gore
Human Resources: Sally Gore

HQ: 555 Paper Mill Rd., Newark, DE 19711
Phone: 302-738-4880   **Fax:** 302-738-7710
Web site: http://www.gore.com

Selected Divisions and Products

Consumer Products
ASPEN lighting systems
CleanStream vacuum cleaner filters
ELIXER guitar strings
GLIDE dental floss
ReviveX water and stain repellent
RideOn bicycle cables

Electronics
Cable and assembly products
  Fiber-optic cables
  Flat cables
  High data rate cables
  Hook-up wire
  Microwave products
  Round cables
Electronic packaging and materials
  Chip packaging
  Conductive adhesives
  EMI/RFI shielding - GORE-SHIELD
  PWB materials
  Thermal interfaces

Fabrics
ACTIVENT fabrics
CROSSTECH fabrics
DRYLOFT fabrics
GORE WINDSTOPPER fabrics
GORE-TEX BEST DEFENSE outerwear
GORE-TEX fabrics
GORE-TEX IMMERSION TECHNOLOGY products
GORE-TEX OCEAN TECHNOLOGY outerwear

Medical and Health Care
GLIDE floss
GORE cast liner
GORE surgical barrier fabrics
Implantable medical devices
  GORE RESOLUT XT regenerative material
  GORE subcutaneous augmentation material
  GORE-TEX cardiovascular patches
  GORE-TEX DualMesh biomaterial
  GORE-TEX DualMesh PLUS biomaterial
  GORE-TEX MycroMesh biomaterial
  GORE-TEX MycroMesh PLUS biomaterial
  GORE-TEX surgical membranes
  GORE-TEX suture
  GORE-TEX vascular grafts
  PRECLUDE dura substitute
  PRECLUDE peritoneal membrane
  SEAMGUARD staple line reinforcement material

Membrane Filtration and Separations
Cleanroom garments
CleanStream vacuum cleaner filters
Disk drive filters
Filter bags and cartridges
GORE-SORBER exploration survey
GORE-SORBER screening survey
Liquid filtration tubular filter socks
PRIMEA power assemblies
PRISTYNE UX filter media
RASTEX sewing thread and weaving fiber
REMEDIA catalytic filter system

Sealants and Fibers Technologies
GFO fiber packing
GORE-TEX gasket tape
GORE-TEX joint sealant
ONE-UP pump diaphragms
RASTEX fiber
SEQUEL fiber packing
TENARA sewing thread

Belden	Malden Mills
CardioTech	Milliken
Donaldson	Superior TeleCom
Kellwood	Thoratec Labs
L.L. Bean	Timberland

Private FYE: March	Annual Growth	1990	1991	1992	1993	1994	1995	1996	1997	1998	1999
Sales ($ mil.)	9.3%	—	—	—	750	804	825	958	1,064	1,150	1,280
Employees	6.2%	—	—	—	—	5,170	5,700	5,860	6,100	6,600	7,000

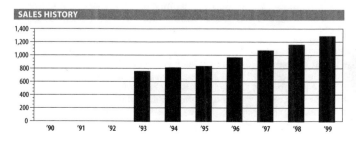

SALES HISTORY

THE YUCAIPA COMPANIES LLC

OVERVIEW

With a hungry eye for bargains, The Yucaipa Companies forged its reputation as the ultimate grocery shopper, executing a series of 16 grocery chain mergers and acquisitions that put the company on the supermarket map. But under the leadership of managing partner Ronald Burkle, the Los Angeles-based investment company is moving away from its past to follow a new path into cyberspace, picking up investments in a variety of Web ventures.

Yucaipa formerly owned 9% of the Fred Meyer grocery chain (whose banners include Ralphs, Smith's, QFC, and Food 4 Less) until Kroger bought Fred Meyer in 1999. Yucaipa owns about 2% of Kroger and is the grocery giant's largest single shareholder. Yucaipa

maintains another link to the food industry through its 70% ownership of Golden State Foods, one of the largest suppliers of food to McDonald's.

Diving into the Internet, Burkle and former Walt Disney president Michael Ovitz have launched the CheckOut.com Web site, where visitors can purchase games, music, and videos. (Retailer Wherehouse Entertainment is buying nearly 50% of CheckOut.com.) Yucaipa's portfolio also includes Alliance Entertainment, a distributor of music, videos, and games; stakes in GameSpy Industries (online games) and Talk City (online chat service); and a 51% interest in Scour.Net (online search and media guide for Internet audio and video).

HISTORY

Ronald Burkle launched his career in the grocery industry as a box boy at his dad's Stater Bros. grocery store. By age 28 Burkle had moved up to SVP of Administration at Stater Bros., but he was fired after botching a buyout of the company in 1981.

Burkle and former Stater Bros. colleagues Mark Resnik and Douglas McKenzie founded Yucaipa (named after Burkle's hometown of Yucaipa, California) as a private investment group in 1986 when they acquired Los Angeles gourmet grocery chain Jurgensen's. In 1987 Yucaipa bought Kansas-based chain Falley's, which had 20 Food 4 Less stores in California.

In 1989 Yucaipa merged with Breco Holding, operator of 70 stores (Boys Markets, Viva, and Cala Foods). It opened three Food 4 Less supermarkets in Southern California that year and also purchased Rhode Island-based Almac's (sold in 1991) and Northern California's Bell Markets.

Yucaipa acquired ABC Markets in Southern California and opened six additional Food 4 Less locations there in 1990. The next year the company purchased the 142-store chain Alpha Beta. Thirty-six Yucaipa stores were damaged in the 1992 Los Angeles riots. Rather than leave the area, Yucaipa rebuilt, working with unions to keep as many workers employed as possible until the stores were operational.

The company acquired the 28-store Smitty's Super Valu chain (now Fred Meyer Marketplace) in 1994. The following year Yucaipa bought the 70-year-old family-owned chain Dominick's Finer Foods. Later in 1995 Food 4 Less merged with Los Angeles competitor Ralphs Grocery (founded in 1873 by George Ralphs), making Yucaipa #1 in Southern California.

Yucaipa sold Smitty's to Utah-based Smith's in 1996, acquiring a minority stake in Smith's (Burkle became Smith's CEO). Dominick's went public in 1996, and Yucaipa retained a minority stake. The next year Fred Meyer bought Smith's for $1.9 billion. Burkle became the acquiring company's chairman, and Yucaipa gained a 9% interest in Fred Meyer.

In 1998 Fred Meyer bought Ralphs and 155-store Quality Food Centers (QFC), which owned Hughes Family Markets in Southern California (since merged with Ralphs). Yucaipa and Wetterau Associates, a management firm, also bought Golden State Foods, giving Yucaipa a 70% stake in the McDonald's food supplier. Yucaipa sold Dominick's to Safeway in 1998.

After Kroger bought Fred Meyer in 1999, Yucaipa turned away from the consolidating grocery industry and began surfing cyberspace. Burkle teamed with Mike Ovitz (former Walt Disney president) to create the CheckOut.com e-commerce Web site (launched in mid-1999). Yucaipa added to its Internet portfolio by taking stakes in GameSpy Industries (online games), Talk City (online chat service), and 51% ownership of Scour.Net (online search and media guide for Internet audio and video). It bought music, video, and games distributor Alliance Entertainment and planned to use the company as the distribution arm for CheckOut.com. Music and video retailer Wherehouse Entertainment agreed to pay $40 million for nearly 50% of CheckOut.com later that year.

Yucaipa hired Richard Wolpert, former president of Disney Online, to oversee its Internet and technology activities.

Managing Partner Yucaipa, Chairman-Alliance:
Ronald W. Burkle, age 45
Partner, Internet Operations: Richard Wolpert
Communications: Robert P. Bermingham
Human Resources: Marla Hunter
Auditors: Arthur Andersen LLP

HQ: 10000 Santa Monica Blvd., 5th Fl.,
Los Angeles, CA 90067
Phone: 310-789-7200 **Fax:** 310-884-2600

Selected Holdings
Alliance Entertainment (music and video distributor)
CheckOut.com (Web site selling games, music,
and videos)
GameSpy Industries (minority interest, online games)
Golden State Foods (70%, McDonald's food supplier)
Kroger (2%)
Scour.Net (51%, online search and media guide)
Talk City (minority interest, online chat service)

Amazon.com
AmeriServe
CDbeat.com
CDnow
HearMe.com
Keystone Foods
Martin-Brower
SYSCO
Tunes.com
U.S. Foodservice
Uproar
Walt Disney
Yahoo!
audiohighway.com
barnesandnoble.com

Hoover's Handbook of Private Companies

KEY PRIVATE COMPANIES

---

84 LUMBER COMPANY

Rte. 519
Eighty Four, PA 15384
Phone: 724-228-8820
Fax: 724-228-4145
Web site: http://www.84lumber.com

CEO: Joseph A. Hardy
CFO: Dan Wallach
HR: Mark Mollico
Type: Private

1998 Sales: $1,625.0 million
1-Yr. Sales Change: 1.6%
Employees: 4,400
FYE: December

With its no-frills stores (most don't have air conditioning or heating), 84 Lumber has built itself to be a low-cost provider of lumber and building materials. Through its about 390 stores, the company sells lumber, siding, drywall, windows, and other supplies, as well as kits to make barns, playsets, decks, and even homes. Professional builders account for three-fourths of sales; other customers include do-it-yourselfers and commercial builders. Its stores are in 30 states, mainly in the eastern US, Southeast, and Midwest; 84 Lumber also sells products internationally. President Maggie Hardy Magerko owns 80% of the company. She's the daughter of CEO Joseph Hardy Sr., who founded 84 Lumber in 1956.

KEY COMPETITORS
Carolina Holdings
Payless Cashways
Sutherland Lumber

See pages 26–27 for a full profile of this company.

AAA

1000 AAA Dr.
Heathrow, FL 32746
Phone: 407-444-7000
Fax: 407-444-7380
Web site: http://www.aaa.com

CEO: Robert L. Darbelnet
CFO: John Schaffer
HR: Carol Droessler
Type: Not-for-profit

1997 Est. Sales: $2,800.0 million
1-Yr. Sales Change: —
Employees: 37,000
FYE: December

This isn't your father's AAA. The not-for-profit organization (formerly the American Automobile Association) still offers its trademark emergency roadside assistance, but it has expanded its offerings in recent years to include various financial services as well. AAA Financial Services Corporation offers credit cards, personal loans, and vehicle financing and leasing. AAA also sells insurance, operates travel agencies, and publishes tour books and maps. A California division has started to repair cars through its Car Care Plus outlets. Founded in 1902 by nine auto clubs, AAA has about 90 clubs and about 1,000 US and Canadian offices. The organization has more than 40 million members.

KEY COMPETITORS
GE Capital
Shell
State Farm

AARP

601 E St. NW
Washington, DC 20049
Phone: 202-434-2277
Fax: 202-434-2525
Web site: http://www.aarp.org

CEO: Joseph S. Perkins
CFO: Jocelyn Davis
HR: J. Robert Carr
Type: Association

1998 Sales: $471.5 million
1-Yr. Sales Change: (10.9%)
Employees: 2,000
FYE: December

AARP is gearing up for the geezer boom. Open to anyone age 50 or older (dues are $8 per year), the not-for-profit organization is changing its image to lure baby boomers reaching the age of eligibility. It is the largest organization of older adults in the US with about 33 million members and is also the largest lobbyist for the elderly (it spends more than $40 million on lobbying and related activities). On a mission to enhance the quality of life for older Americans, AARP is active in four areas: information and education, community service, advocacy, and member services. It also publishes the monthly *AARP Bulletin* and the bimonthly *Modern Maturity* magazine.

KEY COMPETITORS
NCSC
The Seniors Coalition
United Seniors Association

See pages 28–29 for a full profile of this company.

ABBEY CARPET COMPANY, INC.

3471 Bonita Bay Blvd.
Bonita Springs, FL 34134
Phone: 941-948-0900
Fax: 941-948-0999
Web site: http://www.abbeycarpet.com

CEO: Phil Gutierrez
CFO: Herb Gray
HR: —
Type: Private

1998 Sales: $935.0 million
1-Yr. Sales Change: 33.6%
Employees: —
FYE: December

Beating out even McDonald's as the first registered franchise in California, Abbey Carpet Company has become one of the nation's top franchise operations. The company runs a network of more than 750 independently owned and operated stores across the US, the Bahamas, and Puerto Rico, selling brand-name carpet at mill-direct prices, as well as area rugs; hardwood, laminate, and vinyl floorings; ceramic tile; and window coverings. It also offers its own line of carpet and home fashion products. Founded in 1958 by Milton Levinson, Abbey Carpet began as a single floor-covering store in Sacramento, California. Chairman and CEO Phil Gutierrez has owned Abbey Carpet since 1983.

KEY COMPETITORS
Carpet One
Flooring America, Inc.
Home Depot

ABC SUPPLY CO. INC.

1 ABC Pkwy.
Beloit, WI 53511
Phone: 608-362-7777
Fax: 608-362-6529
Web site: http://www.abc-supply.com

CEO: Kenneth F. Hendricks
CFO: Kendra Story
HR: Lisa Indgjer
Type: Private

1999 Sales: $1,162.0 million
1-Yr. Sales Change: 21.0%
Employees: 3,000
FYE: April

ABC Supply has put roofs over millions of heads. The nation's #1 supplier of roofing, siding, insulation, and builder's supplies, ABC Supply has more than 225 outlets in more than 40 states. It carries products from about 100 vendors and distributes via a fleet of 2,200 delivery vehicles. It also operates a building supply catalog and has six subsidiaries: a trucking business, a workers' compensation insurance company (firm businesses only), a real estate leasing and buying arm, a private-label siding sales company, a contracting group, and a roofing and sidewall-coating maker. ABC Supply, one of Wisconsin's largest private companies, was founded in 1982 by CEO Kenneth Hendricks and is still owned by the Hendricks family.

KEY COMPETITORS
Cameron Ashley
Georgia-Pacific Group
North Pacific Group

ACE HARDWARE CORPORATION

2200 Kensington Ct.
Oak Brook, IL 60523
Phone: 630-990-6600
Fax: 630-990-6838
Web site: http://www.acehardware.com

CEO: David F. Hodnik
CFO: Rita D. Kahle
HR: Fred J. Neer
Type: Cooperative

1998 Sales: $3,120.4 million
1-Yr. Sales Change: 7.3%
Employees: 4,672
FYE: December

Ace is the place for thousands of hardware retailers. Owner-dealers of Ace Hardware, the #2 hardware co-op in the US (behind TruServ), operate about 5,100 Ace Hardware stores in the US and more than 60 other countries. The co-op buys products in bulk and distributes them to its retailers from more than 20 warehouses. Ace manufactures its own brand of paints and also supplies other products under the Ace brand. Dealers receive dividends from Ace's profits. Formed in the 1920s, Ace provides a number of services to its members, including advertising, insurance, and training. Faced with competition from such warehouse-style rivals as The Home Depot, Ace has turned to acquisitions to boost its size and buying clout.

KEY COMPETITORS
Home Depot
Lowe's
TruServ

See pages 30–31 for a full profile of this company.

ACF INDUSTRIES, INC.

620 N. 2nd St.
St. Charles, MO 63301
Phone: 636-940-5000
Fax: 636-940-5169

CEO: Jim Unger
CFO: Harry McKinstry
HR: Gary Rager
Type: Private

1998 Sales: $891.0 million
1-Yr. Sales Change: 62.0%
Employees: 2,700
FYE: December

Still on track a century after its founding, ACF Industries makes specialized railroad cars such as tank cars and hoppers. The company also produces railcar components (fans, hitches, and valves) and leases railcars. A subsidiary, American Railcar Industries, offers fleet management, railcar repair, painting, and lining services and makes hoppers and railcar parts. In addition to its railcar manufacturing plants, ACF operates eight repair facilities. Formerly American Car and Foundry, the company was formed by the 1899 merger of 13 railcar makers. ACF has a $1.25 billion multiyear contract to provide nearly 35,500 railcars to GE Capital Rail Services. Billionaire Carl Icahn owns the company.

KEY COMPETITORS
GATX
Greenbrier
Johnstown America

ADVANCE HOLDING CORPORATION

5673 Airport Rd. NW
Roanoke, VA 24012
Phone: 540-362-4911
Fax: 540-561-1448
Web site: http://www.advance-auto.com

CEO: Garnett E. Smith
CFO: J. O'Neil Leftwich
HR: Tammy Finley
Type: Private

1998 Sales: $1,220.8 million
1-Yr. Sales Change: 43.9%
Employees: 24,976
FYE: December

Advance Holding has turned the auto parts retailing business into less of a one-company race. The company pulled behind fast-moving leader AutoZone with its 1998 acquisition of Sears' Western Auto unit. Now the #2 chain, Advance operates more than 1,500 retail stores under the Advance Auto Parts, Parts America, and Western Auto names in 39 states, Puerto Rico, and the Virgin Islands. It also sells merchandise through more than 750 independently owned Western Auto stores in 48 states. Advance's stores offer some 250,000 auto parts and accessories. Formed in 1929, the company was sold to investment firm Freeman Spogli in 1998, which now holds 39%. Sears received 41% of Advance's stock in the Western Auto deal.

KEY COMPETITORS
AutoZone
Pep Boys
Johnstown America

ADVANCE PUBLICATIONS, INC.

950 Fingerboard Rd.
Staten Island, NY 10305
Phone: 718-981-1234
Fax: 718-981-1456
Web site: http://www.advance.net

CEO: Samuel I. Newhouse
CFO: —
HR: —
Type: Private

1998 Sales: $3,859.1 million
1-Yr. Sales Change: 5.2%
Employees: 24,000
FYE: December

Advance Publications is counting on the printed word to always be in *Vogue*, despite the movement to become *Wired*. The company publishes a variety of magazines (*Vogue, Glamour, Vanity Fair, Wired, The New Yorker*) through its Condé Nast unit, owns daily newspapers in 22 cities, and publishes about 40 local business weeklies (American City Business Journals). It also has cable holdings through a joint venture with Time Warner and owns a minority stake in Discovery Communications. In an effort to prevent the Internet from seizing power from its newspapers, Advance has established a new media unit (Condé Net) to build its Web presence. The company is owned by Samuel "Si" Newhouse Jr. and his brother Donald.

KEY COMPETITORS
Gannett
Hearst
Time Warner

See pages 32–33 for a full profile of this company.

ADVANTAGE LOGISTICS MICHIGAN

12701 Middlebelt Rd.	CEO: Larry Savage	1998 Est. Sales: $900.0 million
Livonia, MI 48150	CFO: —	1-Yr. Sales Change: (13.0%)
Phone: 734-523-2100	HR: James Scott	Employees: 660
Fax: 734-523-2108	Type: Joint venture	FYE: March

Advantage Logistics Michigan, formerly a joint venture known as Foodland Distributors, moves munchies throughout Michigan. Now wholly-owned by the nation's #1 supermarket operator, Kroger, the company is a full-line food distributor that warehouses and delivers groceries to Kroger supermarkets only in Michigan. In addition to brand-name groceries, frozen food, meats, and health and beauty products, the company also supplies Kroger with private-label and generic brands. In order to focus its efforts on Kroger, it no longer services small and independent grocers. Advantage Logistics Michigan is managed by former joint venture partner and #1 US food distributor SUPERVALU.

KEY COMPETITORS
C&S Wholesale
GSC Enterprises
Spartan Stores

ADVENTIST HEALTH

2100 Douglas Blvd.	CEO: Donald R. Ammon	1998 Sales: $1,740.4 million
Roseville, CA 95661	CFO: Douglas E. Rebok	1-Yr. Sales Change: 59.7%
Phone: 916-781-2000	HR: Roger Ashley	Employees: 17,129
Fax: 916-783-9909	Type: Not-for-profit	FYE: December
Web site: http://www.adventisthealth.org		

They even stay open on Sundays. Adventist Health is a not-for-profit health care system with strong ties (financially, organizationally, and spiritually) to the Seventh-Day Adventist Church. The West Coast wing of an international organization operating more than 160 Adventist health care operations, Adventist Health runs about 20 Adventist hospitals (with some 2,900 beds), almost 20 home health services facilities, and various other outpatient facilities and hospices in California, Hawaii, Oregon, Utah, and Washington state. The organization also works with its own churches and those of other denominations to offer preventative health care such as physical exams, prenatal care, and health education.

KEY COMPETITORS
Columbia/HCA
Kaiser Foundation
Tenet Healthcare

ADVOCATE HEALTH CARE

2025 Windsor Dr.	CEO: Richard R. Risk	1998 Sales: $1,389.7 million
Oak Brook, IL 60523	CFO: Lawrence J. Majka	1-Yr. Sales Change: (15.0%)
Phone: 630-572-9393	HR: Ben Grigaliunas	Employees: 21,000
Fax: 630-572-9139	Type: Not-for-profit	FYE: December
Web site: http://www.advocatehealth.com		

Advocate Health Care is an integrated health care network with more than 200 sites serving about 220,000 people in the Chicago area. Formed in 1995 by the merger of EHS Health Care and Lutheran General HealthSystem, Advocate's operations include eight hospitals with more than 3,000 beds, as well as one of Illinois' largest private full-service home health care companies. Advocate also has teaching affiliations with area medical schools such as the University of Illinois at Chicago. In addition, Advocate manages a medical ethics center that helps its staff and clients address such issues as cloning and physician-assisted suicide.

KEY COMPETITORS
Columbia/HCA
Northwestern Healthcare
Rush System for Health

AECOM TECHNOLOGY CORPORATION

3250 Wilshire Blvd.	CEO: Richard G. Newman	1999 Sales: $990.0 million
Los Angeles, CA 90010	CFO: Joseph A. Incaudo	1-Yr. Sales Change: 10.0%
Phone: 213-381-3612	HR: Ron Deutsch	Employees: 6,900
Fax: 213-380-2105	Type: Private	FYE: September

AECOM Technology offers a building service for each letter in its name, which stands for architecture, engineering, construction management, operation, and maintenance. Established as a holding company in 1990, AECOM operates through subsidiaries Consoer Townsend Environdyne Engineers; Daniel, Mann, Johnson & Mendenhall; Frederic R. Harris; Holmes & Narver; McClier Corporation; and Turner Collie & Braden. AECOM's projects in the US and abroad have included airports, highways, mass transit systems, ports, prisons, schools, and wastewater plants. AECOM is owned by its employees.

KEY COMPETITORS
Jacobs Engineering
Parsons
Perini

AECTRA REFINING & MARKETING INC.

3 Riverway, Ste. 2000	CEO: Mois Mottale	1998 Est. Sales: $1,000.0 million
Houston, TX 77056	CFO: Anthony J. Voigt	1-Yr. Sales Change: 11.1%
Phone: 713-629-7563	HR: Annie Smith	Employees: 50
Fax: 713-629-4643	Type: Private	FYE: December

It's taken some extra effort, but Aectra Refining & Marketing, a wholesale distributor of petroleum products, has built an extensive system of petroleum terminals and bulk stations. Aectra buys refined products and fuel oil from major refineries along the US's Gulf Coast, Europe, and South America, including Petróleos de Venezuela. The company then stores and distributes these products, which include fuel oil, gasoline, and jet fuel. Aectra also stores naphtha, a light petroleum product. The company sells its products mainly in the southeastern US, but it also does business in northern Europe and South America. Aectra was founded in 1980.

KEY COMPETITORS
Enron
George Warren
Global Petroleum

AEI RESOURCES, INC.

1500 N. Big Run Rd.	CEO: Larry Addington	1998 Sales: $733.4 million
Ashland, KY 41102	CFO: Rick Fasold	1-Yr. Sales Change: 318.5%
Phone: 606-928-3433	HR: Robert Schmidt	Employees: 4,081
Fax: 606-928-9527	Type: Private	FYE: December

You can't buy a vowel from AEI Resources, but you can get some coal from the company, one of the nation's largest producers of steam coal. About 75% of company sales are generated through long-term contracts to supply electric utilities — primarily those on the East Coast — with steam coal. AEI operates 49 mines in Colorado, Illinois, Indiana, Kentucky, Ohio, Tennessee, and West Virginia. The acquisitive company has about 1.1 billion tons of proven and probable coal reserves, and an additional 1.3 billion tons that are available for development. AEI Resources also manufactures Addcar brand highwall mining equipment. Chairman Larry Addington owns the company.

KEY COMPETITORS
Arch Coal
CONSOL Energy
Pittston Minerals

AFFILIATED FOODS INCORPORATED

1401 Farmers	CEO: Benny R. Cooper	1998 Est. Sales: $700.0 million
Amarillo, TX 79118	CFO: Wayne Smith	1-Yr. Sales Change: 9.4%
Phone: 806-372-3851	HR: Merle Voigt	Employees: 1,000
Fax: 806-372-3647	Type: Cooperative	FYE: September

Actually, it's the stores — more than 660 of them — that are affiliated with grocery distributor Affiliated Foods. The cooperative distributes food and nonfood items — including goods under the Shurfine, Shursaving, and Frosty Acres names — to its member-owners' stores in Colorado, Kansas, New Mexico, Oklahoma, and Texas. Founded in 1946 as Panhandle Associated Grocers, Affiliated Foods also distributes ice cream (Blue Bunny and Shurfine brands) and helps retailers implement computer systems and software. The co-op also operates Tri-State Baking (TenderCrust and Always Fresh brands) and owns the Plains Dairy, which produces 60,000 gallons of milk a day and bottles water, juice, and fruit drinks.

KEY COMPETITORS
Associated Wholesale Grocers
Fleming Companies
SUPERVALU

AFL-CIO

815 16th St. NW	CEO: John J. Sweeney	1998 Sales: $56.8 million
Washington, DC 20006	CFO: Richard L. Trumka	1-Yr. Sales Change: (4.2%)
Phone: 202-637-5000	HR: Carl Garland	Employees: —
Fax: 202-637-5058	Type: Labor union	FYE: June
Web site: http://www.aflcio.org		

The American Federation of Labor and Congress of Industrial Organizations (AFL-CIO) is an umbrella organization representing about 13 million workers. An alliance of 68 autonomous national and international unions, the AFL-CIO negotiates with employers and works to improve working and living standards for union members. The organization's membership includes actors and airline pilots, farmworkers and firefighters, and police and postal employees. It also reflects the growth of service and government jobs and the decreasing number of manufacturing and construction workers.

 See pages 34–35 for a full profile of this company.

AG PROCESSING INC

12700 W. Dodge Rd.	CEO: James W. Lindsay	1998 Sales: $2,615.1 million
Omaha, NE 68103	CFO: Kenneth S. Grubbe	1-Yr. Sales Change: (11.3%)
Phone: 402-496-7809	HR: Gordon V. Dorff	Employees: 2,550
Fax: 402-498-5548	Type: Cooperative	FYE: August
Web site: http://www.agp.com		

Soy far, soy good for Ag Processing (AGP), one of the largest soybean processors in the US. AGP's chief soybean products include vegetable oil and commercial animal feeds. The cooperative is also promoting its corn-based ethanol and soybean oil-based bio-fuels, fuel additives, and solvents. AGP processes some 15,000 acres of soybeans a day from its members' farms. Its grain division has the capacity to store over 50 million bushels. The co-op's owners include 300,000 members from 16 states, primarily in the Midwest, represented through more than 300 local co-ops and 12 regional co-ops. AGP and Archer Daniels Midland co-own Consolidated Nutrition, one of the largest US feed manufacturers.

KEY COMPETITORS
ADM
Cargill
ConAgra

See pages 36–37 for a full profile of this company.

A.G. SPANOS COMPANIES

1341 W. Robinhood Dr.
Stockton, CA 95207
Phone: 209-478-7954
Fax: 209-478-3309
Web site: http://www.agspanos.com

CEO: Dean A. Spanos
CFO: Jeremiah Murphy
HR: Charlene Flynn
Type: Private

1999 Sales: $1,440.0 million
1-Yr. Sales Change: 22.6%
Employees: 600
FYE: September

Spanning 15 states, A.G. Spanos Companies bridges many operations: developing land, building master-planned communities, and building, managing, and selling apartment buildings. The firm has built more than 75,000 apartments and developed about 3 million sq. ft. of commercial property since its inception in 1960. Current projects include Spanos Park, a $1 billion master-planned community in founder and chairman Alex G. Spanos' hometown of Stockton, California, that is to include 7,200 dwelling units, six schools, three lakes, retail centers, a marina, and a sports park. Spanos still owns A.G. Spanos Companies; the firm is operated by his four children. Alex Spanos also owns the NFL's San Diego Chargers.

KEY COMPETITORS
Fluor
Perini
Turner Corporation

AGAMERICA, FCB

3636 American River Dr.
Sacramento, CA 95864
Phone: 916-485-6000
Fax: 916-485-6133

CEO: James D. Kirk
CFO: David B. Newlin
HR: John Lovstad
Type: Cooperative

1997 Sales: $660.4 million
1-Yr. Sales Change: (1.2%)
Employees: 100
FYE: December

Part of a national cooperative of banks known as the Farm Credit System, AgAmerica is one of only six Farm Credit Banks in the US. The bank has a joint management agreement with Western Farm Credit Bank. Their combined resources service more than 60,000 borrowers (including aquatic producers, farmers, ranchers, rural homeowners, and timber harvesters) in nine states, primarily in the Northwest. AgAmerica offers operating loans, rural home mortgages, crop insurance, and financial services such as farm record-keeping and financial planning. Its customers own the bank, which wholesales loan funds to local associations with lending capital raised by selling system-wide bonds and notes.

AGFIRST FARM CREDIT BANK

1401 Hampton St.
Columbia, SC 29201
Phone: 803-799-5000
Fax: 803-254-1776
Web site: http://www.agfirst.com

CEO: F. A. Lowrey
CFO: Larry R. Doyle
HR: Steve Francis
Type: Cooperative

1997 Sales: $952.8 million
1-Yr. Sales Change: 3.5%
Employees: 200
FYE: December

AgFirst Farm Credit Bank is a large agricultural lender for the eastern US and Puerto Rico, offering loans to more than 100,000 farmers, ranchers, and rural homeowners through its six regional farm credit banks. Services include real estate, operating, and rural home mortgage loans; crop insurance; and agricultural equipment leasing. Clients also include rural utility businesses, agricultural cooperatives, and agribusinesses. The bank does not accept deposits; it raises money by selling bonds and notes on the capital markets. AgFirst was formed in 1995 when Farm Credit Systems, Farm Credit Bank of Baltimore, and Farm Credit Bank of Columbia merged.

AGRIBANK, FCB

375 Jackson
St. Paul, MN 55164
Phone: 651-282-8800
Fax: 651-282-8666
Web site: http://www.farmcredit.com

CEO: C. T. Fredrickson
CFO: William B. Wolfe
HR: Sandra Schmiesing
Type: Cooperative

1998 Sales: $1,681.2 million
1-Yr. Sales Change: 5.5%
Employees: 3,200
FYE: December

AgriBank, FCB, a cooperative, works with its partner, Farm Credit Services
(FCS), to provide loans and other financial services for farmers and rural
homeowners in 11 midwestern and southern states. AgriBank is a wholesale
bank that provides funding and services to 30 FCS offices. FCS, also a cooperative, provides insurance, credit, record keeping, and other services to
about 120,000 agricultural producers and rural homeowners. Credit is provided to finance purchases of farm machinery, land, seeds, feed, and housing. Insurance includes crop-hail, multiperil, and life-disability products.
The partnership between the two resulted from the merger of St. Louis,
St. Paul, and Louisville Farm Credit Banks.

AGWAY INC.

333 Butternut Dr.
DeWitt, NY 13214
Phone: 315-449-6436
Fax: 315-449-6253
Web site: http://www.agway.com

CEO: Donald P. Cardarelli
CFO: Peter J. O'Neill
HR: Richard Opdyke
Type: Cooperative

1999 Sales: $1,484.4 million
1-Yr. Sales Change: (5.0%)
Employees: 7,200
FYE: June

Agway salutes the tillers of the land. An agricultural co-op with about 80,000
member-owners involved in all types of farming, Agway has operations in 12
northeastern states. Operations include Agway Agricultural Products (making feeds, fertilizers, and other farm-related products), Country Products
Group (processing and selling fresh produce, edible beans and sunflower
seeds, and farm seeds), Agway Retail Services (about 500 Agway stores selling yard and garden supplies, pet food and supplies, and farm-related products), and Agway Energy Products (heating oil, propane, diesel fuel, natural
gas, and electricity). Agway also offers insurance and finances leases for
buildings and equipment.

KEY COMPETITORS
Farmland Industries
Niagara Mohawk
Purina Mills

 See pages 38–39 for a full profile of this company.

AID ASSOCIATION FOR LUTHERANS

4321 N. Ballard Rd.
Appleton, WI 54919
Phone: 920-734-5721
Fax: 920-730-4725
Web site: http://www.aal.org

CEO: John O. Gilbert
CFO: Ronald G. Anderson
HR: Darlene M. Hasselbacher
Type: Not-for-profit

1998 Sales: $3,061.1 million
1-Yr. Sales Change: 1.4%
Employees: 1,751
FYE: December

The fraternal group Aid Association for Lutherans (AAL) isn't directly affiliated with the Lutheran Church, but it offers its 10,000 volunteer groups (1.7
million Lutherans and family members) plenty of service options — both
charitable and financial. AAL, founded in 1902 in Wisconsin, offers insurance, retirement planning, and investment services. Its AAL Capital Management offers mutual fund and brokerage services; affiliate AAL Member
Credit Union offers credit union services. Through subsidiary AAL Trust, the
group offers trust services and estate planning (through its agent network).
Members of the not-for-profit AAL provide some 5 million hours of charity
service each year.

ALCOA FUJIKURA LTD.

105 Westpark Dr., Ste. 200
Brentwood, TN 37027
Phone: 615-370-2100
Fax: 615-370-2176
Web site: http://www.alcoa-fujikura.com

CEO: Robert S. Hughes
CFO: Bill Collier
HR: Joan Luckett
Type: Joint venture

1998 Est. Sales: $1,800.0 million
1-Yr. Sales Change: 104.5%
Employees: 1,600
FYE: December

A joint venture between Alcoa (51%) and Japanese wire and cable maker Fujikura (49%), Alcoa Fujikura makes fiber-optic products for electric utilities and telecommunications, cable television, and data communications markets, as well as electrical distribution systems for the automotive industry. Its fiber-optic products range from splicers, which allow cable providers to add new customers to an existing network, to customized fiber-optic phone and data networks that serve large businesses and universities. The company's automotive customers include DaimlerChrysler, Ford, Audi, PACCAR, and Volkswagen. Alcoa Fujikura has operations in Brazil, Germany, Hungary, Ireland, Mexico, the UK, the US, and Venezuela.

KEY COMPETITORS
Furukawa Electric
Stoneridge
Tyco International

ALEX LEE INC.

120 4th St. SW
Hickory, NC 28602
Phone: 828-323-4424
Fax: 828-323-4435
Web site: http://www.alexlee.com

CEO: Boyd Lee George
CFO: Ronald W. Knedlik
HR: Glenn DeBiasi
Type: Private

1999 Sales: $1,588.0 million
1-Yr. Sales Change: 4.7%
Employees: 7,154
FYE: September

Alex Lee takes pride in providing provisions through its food distribution companies and supermarket chain. The holding company owns Merchants Distributors Inc. (MDI), a wholesale distributor serving independent and chain grocery retailers, and Institution Food House (IFH), a food service supplier to schools, restaurants, and health care providers. MDI and IFH primarily serve North and South Carolina and Virginia, but they provide some services in Georgia, Tennessee, and West Virginia as well. Alex Lee also operates about 100 Lowe's Food Stores located in those six states. The company was founded in 1931 by the George family and remains under their control.

KEY COMPETITORS
Fleming Companies
Food Lion
SUPERVALU

ALLEGHENY HEALTH, EDUCATION AND RESEARCH FOUNDATION

120 5th Ave., 29th Fl.
Pittsburgh, PA 15212
Phone: 412-359-6000
Fax: 412-359-6718
Web site: http://www.auhs.edu

CEO: Anthony M. Sanzo
CFO: David W. McConnell
HR: Dwight Kasperbauer
Type: Foundation

1997 Est. Sales: $1,030.0 million
1-Yr. Sales Change: 3.0%
Employees: 15,000
FYE: June

Not-for-profit Allegheny Health, Education and Research Foundation (AHERF) is a network of hospitals, medical schools, and physician practices throughout Pennsylvania. The health care system operates five hospitals, a hospice, and a nursing center in the Pittsburgh area; and a network of physician practices. The system's center is the MCP Hahnemann University, which has a faculty of more than 3,400 and includes schools of medicine, nursing, public health, and other health professions. The university's flagship is the MCP Hahnemann School of Medicine. AHERF, which is operating under Chapter 11 bankruptcy protection, has sold its Philadelphia hospitals to Tenet Healthcare.

KEY COMPETITORS
Catholic Healthcare Partners
Universal Health Services

ALLIANT FOODSERVICE INC.

1 Parkway North
Deerfield, IL 60015
Phone: 847-405-8500
Fax: 847-405-8980
Web site: http://www.alliantboston.com

CEO: Earl L. Mason
CFO: Joan E. Ryan
HR: Paula Raybould
Type: Private

1998 Sales: $6,100.0 million
1-Yr. Sales Change: 17.3%
Employees: 12,000
FYE: December

Will Alliant Foodservice please report to the cafeteria? One of the nation's top broadline food distributors, Alliant supplies food and other products to hospitals, hotels, restaurants, schools, and other non-retail outlets. The company distributes more than 180,000 products, including cleaning supplies, produce, meats, and prepared foods, all under its Alliant private label. It is the exclusive institutional distributor of Kraft-brand food products such as Miracle Whip salad dressing and Philadelphia Brand cream cheese. Alliant has grown through acquisitions and long-term contracts. Formerly a unit of food and tobacco giant Philip Morris, the company is owned by investment firm Clayton, Dubilier & Rice.

KEY COMPETITORS
AmeriServe
SYSCO
U.S. Foodservice

 See pages 40–41 for a full profile of this company.

ALLINA HEALTH SYSTEM

5601 Smetana Dr.
Minnetonka, MN 55343
Phone: 612-992-2000
Fax: 612-992-2126
Web site: http://www.allina.com

CEO: Gordon M. Sprenger
CFO: Richard Blair
HR: Mike Howe
Type: Not-for-profit

1997 Sales: $2,500.0 million
1-Yr. Sales Change: 4.2%
Employees: 21,200
FYE: December

Allina Health System is a not-for-profit health care system that focuses on prevention and community programs as an alternative means of keeping its members healthy. Allina's health plans, doctors, and hospitals cover Minnesota, North and South Dakota, and Wisconsin. The system's Medica Health Plans, which serves more than 1 million members, offers HMO, PPO, and senior health plans through a network of more than 12,000 health care providers. The Allina Medical Group includes more than 50 clinics. Allina also owns or manages nearly 20 hospitals, seven nursing homes, and a senior housing complex.

KEY COMPETITORS
Columbia/HCA
Mayo Foundation
SSM Health Care

A-MARK FINANCIAL CORPORATION

100 Wilshire Blvd., 3rd Fl.
Santa Monica, CA 90401
Phone: 310-319-0200
Fax: 310-319-0279
Web site: http://www.amark.com

CEO: Steven C. Markoff
CFO: Joseph Ozaki
HR: —
Type: Private

1999 Sales: $2,446.0 million
1-Yr. Sales Change: 144.6%
Employees: 120
FYE: July

Calling all gold bugs: A-Mark Financial trades, markets, and finances rare coins, precious metals, and collectibles. A-Mark Precious Metals trades in gold, silver, platinum, and palladium coins, bars, grain (shot), ingots, and medallions for central banks, corporations, and individuals worldwide. A-Mark distributes coins for government mints, including those of Australia, Canada, Mexico, and the US. Affiliates include Superior Galleries, a collectibles auctioneer; Goldline International, which offers investors rare coins and bullion; and A-M Handling, a melt and assay company. Chairman, president, and owner Steven Markoff — who supports the medical marijuana movement — founded the company in 1965.

KEY COMPETITORS
Anglo American
Dallas Gold and Silver
  Exchange
Degussa-Huls

THE AMERICAN BOTTLING COMPANY

7955 S. Cass Ave., Ste. 201	CEO: Richard A. Beardon	1998 Est. Sales: $1,000.0 million
Darien, IL 60561	CFO: Bill Schumacher	1-Yr. Sales Change: —
Phone: 630-241-3555	HR: Yvonne Hurlbutt	Employees: 5,000
Fax: 630-241-0263	Type: Private	FYE: December

Americans have always loved their cola. American Bottling was formed in 1998 when soft-drink and candy maker Cadbury Schweppes and The Carlyle Group investment firm acquired and combined bottlers Beverage America and Select Beverages. The #1 US 7 UP bottler, American Bottling distributes beverages in 15 mostly midwestern states. Other brands include A&W, Canada Dry, Dr Pepper, Evian, Hawaiian Punch, Royal Crown, Schweppes, and Snapple. It also provides private-label soft drinks and bottles niche-market brands such as Sun Drop. It is merging with Dr Pepper Bottling Company of Texas to become the #1 US independent bottler. The UK's Cadbury runs the firm and owns a 40% stake; US-based Carlyle owns the remainder.

KEY COMPETITORS
Coca-Cola Enterprises
Pepsi Bottling
Whitman

AMERICAN CANCER SOCIETY, INC.

1599 Clifton Rd. NE	CEO: John R. Seffrin	1998 Sales: $677.2 million
Atlanta, GA 30329	CFO: David M. Zacks	1-Yr. Sales Change: 12.5%
Phone: 404-320-3333	HR: Aurelia C. Stanley	Employees: 4,500
Fax: 404-329-5787	Type: Not-for-profit	FYE: August
Web site: http://www.cancer.org		

The American Cancer Society (ACS) works as a firefighter for your lungs. Dedicated to the elimination of cancer, the not-for-profit organization is staffed by professionals and more than 2 million volunteers at some 3,400 local units across the country. ACS is the largest source of private cancer research funds in the US. In addition to research, the ACS supports detection, treatment, and education programs. The organization encourages prevention efforts with programs such as the Great American Smokeout. Patient services include moral support, transportation to and from treatment, and camps for children who have cancer. Programs account for about 71% of expenses; 29% goes to administration and fund-raising.

 See pages 42–43 for a full profile of this company.

AMERICAN CENTURY INVESTMENTS, INC.

4500 Main St., Ste. 1500	CEO: James E. Stowers	1998 Est. Sales: $725.0 million
Kansas City, MO 64111	CFO: Robert T. Jackson	1-Yr. Sales Change: 20.8%
Phone: 816-531-5575	HR: Jerry Bartlett	Employees: 2,800
Fax: 816-340-7270	Type: Private	FYE: December
Web site: http://www.americancentury.com		

American Century Investments, formerly Twentieth Century Mutual Funds, offers about 60 mutual funds ranging from conservative income to aggressive growth. The firm employs direct marketing to sell its three distinct groups of mutual funds: the Benham Group, the American Century Group, and the Twentieth Century Group. It also sells funds through 401(k) retirement plans. The company's predecessor, founded by James Stowers about 40 years ago, specialized in agressive-growth stock funds. It diversified in the 1990s by merging with bond-fund manager Benham Group. J.P. Morgan & Co. owns a 45% stake in American Century Investments, which is still controlled by the founder and his family.

KEY COMPETITORS
FMR
T. Rowe Price
Vanguard Group

AMERICAN CRYSTAL SUGAR COMPANY

101 N. 3rd St.
Moorhead, MN 56560
Phone: 218-236-4400
Fax: 218-236-4422
Web site: http://www.crystalsugar.com

CEO: James J. Horvath
CFO: Joseph J. Talley
HR: David A. Berg
Type: Cooperative

1999 Sales: $844.0 million
1-Yr. Sales Change: 24.7%
Employees: 1,292
FYE: August

Call it saccharine, but for American Crystal Sugar, business is all about sharing. A cooperative, the sugar-beet giant is owned by about 2,800 growers in the Red River Valley of North Dakota and Minnesota. American Crystal, formed in 1899 and converted into a co-op in 1973, divides the 35-mile-wide valley into five districts, each served by a processing plant. During an annual eight-month "campaign," the plants operate continuously, turning beets into sugar, molasses, and beet pulp. The products (under the Crystal brand name and the licensed Pillsbury Best label) are sold through marketing co-ops United Sugars and Midwest Agri-Commodities. The cooperative owns 46% of ProGold, a corn-sweeteners joint venture.

KEY COMPETITORS
Imperial Sugar
Tate & Lyle
U.S. Sugar

AMERICAN FAMILY INSURANCE GROUP

6000 American Pkwy.
Madison, WI 53783
Phone: 608-249-2111
Fax: 608-243-4921
Web site: http://www.amfam.com

CEO: Dale F. Mathwich
CFO: Paul L. King
HR: Vicki L. Chvala
Type: Mutual company

1998 Sales: $3,888.5 million
1-Yr. Sales Change: 8.0%
Employees: 6,940
FYE: December

American Family Insurance Group offers property/casualty, life, and health insurance and investment and retirement planning products. The company cross-sells its other products to buyers of its auto insurance (more than 80% of sales). The company also provides business coverage for apartment owners and garage, restaurant, and contracting businesses. The company's consumer finance division offers home equity and personal loans through its agents as well. American Family operates primarily in the Midwest with outposts in Arizona, Colorado, and Oregon. It is among the five largest mutual auto insurance providers in the US and also offers homeowners policies.

KEY COMPETITORS
Allstate
Nationwide Insurance
St. Paul Companies

 See pages 44–45 for a full profile of this company.

THE AMERICAN RED CROSS

430 17th St. NW
Washington, DC 20006
Phone: 202-737-8300
Fax: 703-248-4256
Web site: http://www.redcross.org

CEO: Bernadine P. Healy
CFO: John D. Campbell
HR: Nancy Breseke
Type: Not-for-profit

1999 Sales: $2,421.5 million
1-Yr. Sales Change: 16.4%
Employees: —
FYE: June

The American Red Cross is a member of the International Red Cross and Red Crescent Movement, a not-for-profit organization committed to helping people, especially after disasters. Though chartered by Congress in 1905 to provide relief services, the American Red Cross isn't a government agency. Its staff is made up largely of volunteers — more than 1.3 million of them. Aside from providing relief to victims of more than 60,000 natural and man-made disasters nationwide each year, the Red Cross teaches CPR, first aid, babysitting, and AIDS awareness courses; provides counseling and emergency message transmission for US military personnel; and maintains the nation's largest blood, plasma, and tissue banks.

KEY COMPETITORS
America's Blood Centers
Ellis & Associates
SeraCare

See pages 46–47 for a full profile of this company.

AMERICAN RETAIL GROUP, INC.

1114 Avenue of the Americas	CEO: Louis Brenninkmeyer	1998 Est. Sales: $1,500.0 million
New York, NY 10036	CFO: Howard Jackson	1-Yr. Sales Change: 8.7%
Phone: 212-704-5300	HR: Elaine Gregg	Employees: 15,000
Fax: 212-704-5095	Type: Private	FYE: January

It's all in the family with retail clothing giant American Retail Group (ARG). ARG is the US piece of the Brenninkmeyer family's $7 billion global retail puzzle. The company sells mid-priced apparel and outdoor clothing through more than 900 stores in 47 states. Its chains include Miller's Outpost, Eastern Mountain Sports, Maurice's, Anchor Blue Clothing, Levi's Outlet by M.O.S.T., Dockers Outlet by M.O.S.T., and Juxtapose; it shuttered its Uptons chain in 1999. The Brenninkmeyers, who entered US retailing in 1948, are a secretive bunch, sometimes sending their children to college under assumed names. The brood runs its empire from a secluded compound in the Netherlands and employs more than 200 family members.

KEY COMPETITORS
J. C. Penney
Sears
TJX

AMERICAN STOCK EXCHANGE, INC.

86 Trinity Place	CEO: Salvatore F. Sodono	1997 Sales: $197.9 million
New York, NY 10006	CFO: Paul R. Shackford	1-Yr. Sales Change: 16.2%
Phone: 212-306-1000	HR: Suzanne Johnson	Employees: 671
Fax: 212-306-1218	Type: Subsidiary	FYE: December
Web site: http://www.amex.com		

The American Stock Exchange (AMEX) is no longer an also-ran among US securities markets — it took itself out of the race when it agreed to be acquired by the National Association of Securities Dealers (NASD). The market now provides a floor-based auction market that complements the NASD's Automated Quotations System (Nasdaq) market. Both are units of NASD's Nasdaq-Amex Market Group subsidiary. AMEX lists about 800 smaller, newer issues and specializes in trading derivatives, foreign issues, ADRs (American depositary receipts), and ADSs (American depositary shares).

KEY COMPETITORS
NYSE
Reuters

See pages 48–49 for a full profile of this company.

AMERICAN UNITED LIFE INSURANCE COMPANY

1 American Sq.	CEO: Jerry D. Semler	1998 Sales: $1,043.0 million
Indianapolis, IN 46206	CFO: James W. Murphy	1-Yr. Sales Change: 7.8%
Phone: 317-263-1609	HR: Jerry L. Plummer	Employees: 1,500
Fax: 317-263-1931	Type: Mutual company	FYE: December
Web site: http://www.aul.com		

Owned by its policyholders, American United Life Insurance Company is licensed in 49 states and the District of Columbia; it also does business in Central and South America. The insurer specializes in pensions and annuities, but also offers such products as individual and group life insurance and disability coverage. The company touts its reinsurance unit (which dates from 1904) as the oldest in continuous operation in North America. American United Life Insurance was formed from the 1936 merger of United Mutual Life Insurance (founded in 1877) and American Central Life Insurance (1899). The company is expanding its business through alliances with other insurers, including Indianapolis Life.

KEY COMPETITORS
CNA Financial
Lincoln National
Principal Financial

AMERISERVE FOOD DISTRIBUTION, INC.

15305 Dallas Pkwy.
Addison, TX 75001
Phone: 972-364-2000
Fax: 972-364-2235
Web site: http://www.ameriserve.com

CEO: John V. Holten
CFO: Diana Moog
HR: Bonnie MacEslin
Type: Subsidiary

1998 Sales: $7,421.0 million
1-Yr. Sales Change: 115.3%
Employees: 8,000
FYE: December

AmeriServe Food Distribution applauds the decline of the home-cooked meal. AmeriServe, one of the top food service distributors in the US, distributes food (meat, produce, beverages), paper products, cleaning supplies, and equipment to over 30 restaurant chains, totaling about 36,000 restaurants in the US, Canada, and Mexico. Its biggest customers include Burger King, KFC, Pizza Hut, Taco Bell, Red Lobster, and Olive Garden. AmeriServe has grown by major acquisitions, including PepsiCo's food service distributor, PFS, and rival ProSource. Holberg Industries owns 93% of AmeriServe. The other 7% is owned by Norwegian consumer goods company Orkla, which also owns 34% of Holberg. John Holten owns the rest of Holberg.

KEY COMPETITORS
Alliant Foodservice
SYSCO
U.S. Foodservice

 See pages 50–51 for a full profile of this company.

AMICA MUTUAL INSURANCE COMPANY

10 Lincoln Center Blvd.
Lincoln, RI 02865
Phone: 401-334-6000
Fax: 401-333-4610
Web site: http://www.amica.com

CEO: Thomas A. Taylor
CFO: Robert A. DiMuccio
HR: Richard S. Glover
Type: Mutual company

1998 Sales: $1,022.0 million
1-Yr. Sales Change: 4.9%
Employees: 3,000
FYE: December

Amica Mutual Insurance Company provides a wide array of personal insurance products, including auto, home, flood, marine, personal liability, and life policies. The company has traditionally relied on referrals from policyholders and independent analysts for business, but it launched its first advertising campaign in 1998. The company has 40 offices across the US. With its roots as an auto insurer going back to 1907, Amica was formed in 1973 through the consolidation of Automobile Mutual Insurance Company of America and Factory Mutual Liability Insurance Company of America.

KEY COMPETITORS
Allstate
CNA Financial
State Farm

AMSTED INDUSTRIES INCORPORATED

205 N. Michigan Ave., Ste. 4400
Chicago, IL 60601
Phone: 312-645-1700
Fax: 312-819-8425
Web site: http://www.griffinpipe.com

CEO: Gordon R. Lohman
CFO: Gary Montgomery
HR: Shirley Whitesell
Type: Private

1999 Sales: $1,370.0 million
1-Yr. Sales Change: 9.5%
Employees: 12,600
FYE: September

Employee-owned AMSTED Industries makes products for general industry, with a focus on the railroads and construction. AMSTED traces its origins to American Steel Foundries, which supplies components for railroad cars and engines, heavy trucks, and construction. Other divisions include Burgess-Norton (piston pins and related parts); Macwhyte (wire-rope products); Griffin Pipe Products (water and wastewater pipes, car recycling); and Baltimore Aircoil (heat-transfer equipment). AMSTED's Diamond Chain, which makes roller-chain products, supplied the chain used to turn the Wright brothers' propeller at Kitty Hawk. The company has 50 plants worldwide following its acqusition of railroad equipment maker Varlen.

KEY COMPETITORS
ABC-NACO
Bethlehem Steel
York International

AMWAY CORPORATION

7575 Fulton St. East	CEO: Steve Van Andel	1999 Est. Sales: $6,000.0 million
Ada, MI 49355	CFO: Lawrence Call	1-Yr. Sales Change: 5.3%
Phone: 616-787-6000	HR: Pamela Linton	Employees: 10,000
Fax: 616-787-6177	Type: Private	FYE: August
Web site: http://www.amway.com		

Most folks who sell Amway don't become billionaires, but founders Richard DeVos and Jay Van Andel did. Amway is the world's largest direct-sales company. The firm and its about 50 affiliates sell over 450 personal care, nutrition, home, and commercial products — plus products of other companies, like long-distance provider MCI WorldCom — in more than 80 countries. Amway employs revival-like techniques to motivate its over 3 million distributors (mostly part-timers) to sell products and find new recruits. Amway has ventured into new territory by creating Quixtar, an Internet consumer products subsidiary, which operates like Amway but does not use the Amway name. The DeVos and Van Andel families own Amway.

KEY COMPETITORS
Avon
Mary Kay
Procter & Gamble

 See pages 52–53 for a full profile of this company.

ANDERSEN CORPORATION

100 4th Ave. North	CEO: Donald Garofalo	1998 Est. Sales: $1,400.0 million
Bayport, MN 55003	CFO: Michael O. Johnson	1-Yr. Sales Change: 7.7%
Phone: 651-439-5150	HR: Jan Grose	Employees: 3,700
Fax: 651-430-5107	Type: Private	FYE: December
Web site: http://www.andersencorp.com		

Windows of opportunity open and shut daily for Andersen, one of the world's largest manufacturers of wood-clad windows and patio doors. Marketed throughout Argentina, Brazil, Canada, Ireland, Israel, Japan, Kuwait, Mexico, Panama, Portugal, South Korea, Spain, the UK, and the US, Andersen windows and doors come in about 50,000 shapes and sizes and are sold in the US through wholesale distributors who supply retail stores. The company also has a retail operation, Renewal by Andersen, that markets window system replacements. Andersen is known for its benefits and incentive programs, and its employees own stock and receive shares of the profits. The Andersen family are major shareholders.

KEY COMPETITORS
JELD-WEN
Pella
Sierra Pacific Industries

 See pages 54–55 for a full profile of this company.

ANDERSEN WORLDWIDE

33 W. Monroe St.	CEO: W. Robert Grafton	1999 Sales: $16,300.0 million
Chicago, IL 60603	CFO: James R. Kackley	1-Yr. Sales Change: 17.3%
Phone: 312-580-0033	HR: Peter Pesce	Employees: 135,000
Fax: 312-507-6748	Type: Partnership	FYE: August
Web site: http://www.arthurandersen.com		

Andersen Worldwide is the second-largest of the Big Five accounting firms, behind PricewaterhouseCoopers. Its Arthur Andersen unit provides traditional outside audit services as well as outsourced internal audit and other accounting services. The firm's Andersen Consulting arm (which accounts for more than half of sales), offers business consulting and re-engineering, customer service system design, Internet sales systems research and design, and securities trading system design. The two divisions have been battling for dominance, and the consulting side's quest for independence is in arbitration. Andersen Worldwide has offices in 78 countries and has correspondent relationships with other firms in 46 others.

KEY COMPETITORS
Ernst & Young
KPMG
PricewaterhouseCoopers

See pages 56–57 for a full profile of this company.

ANTHEM INSURANCE COMPANIES, INC.

120 Monument Circle	CEO: L. Ben Lytle	1998 Sales: $5,878.2 million
Indianapolis, IN 46204	CFO: Michael L. Smith	1-Yr. Sales Change: (6.7%)
Phone: 317-488-6000	HR: Robert C. Heird	Employees: 11,504
Fax: 317-488-6028	Type: Mutual company	FYE: December
Web site: http://www.anthem-inc.com		

Oh, say can you see how Anthem Insurance Companies can compete in the managed care marketplace? The mutual company provides health insurance and services, primarily under the Blue Cross and Blue Shield names, to more than 5 million customers in Connecticut, Indiana, Kentucky, New Hampshire, and Ohio. The company has divested most of its noncore operations to focus on the Blues. Subsidiaries include AdminaStar (Medicare contracting), Anthem Alliance (health insurance for the military), and one non-Blues health plan in New York. Anthem's plans to buy Blues in Colorado, Maine, and Rhode Island are meeting some resistance; critics say the moves would hamstring the not-for-profits' operations.

KEY COMPETITORS
Aetna
CIGNA
Prudential

 See pages 58–59 for a full profile of this company.

ARAMARK CORPORATION

Aramark Tower, 1101 Market St.	CEO: Joseph Neubauer	1999 Sales: $6,718.4 million
Philadelphia, PA 19107	CFO: L. Frederick Sutherland	1-Yr. Sales Change: 5.3%
Phone: 215-238-3000	HR: Brian G. Mulvaney	Employees: 114,000
Fax: 215-238-3333	Type: Private	FYE: September
Web site: http://www.aramark.com		

ARAMARK makes its mark in three lines of business: food and support services, uniforms, and childcare. About two-thirds of the company's sales come from the food, building maintenance, and housekeeping services provided to businesses, prisons, and colleges. A major concessionaire at sports and other recreational facilities, ARAMARK is the world's #3 food service provider (trailing Compass Group and Sodexho Alliance). It also operates before- and after-school programs and employee on-site childcare through Children's World Learning Centers. ARAMARK's uniform rental is the second-largest in the US (behind Cintas). CEO Joseph Neubauer owns about 25% of the firm (total employee ownership accounts for 93%).

KEY COMPETITORS
Cintas
KinderCare
Sodexho Marriott Services

 See pages 60–61 for a full profile of this company.

ARCTIC SLOPE REGIONAL CORPORATION

301 Arctic Slope Ave., Ste. 300	CEO: Jacob Adams	1998 Sales: $888.0 million
Anchorage, AK 99518	CFO: Frank Zirnkilton	1-Yr. Sales Change: —
Phone: 907-852-8633	HR: Karen Burnell	Employees: 3,000
Fax: 907-852-5733	Type: Private	FYE: —
Web site: http://www.asrc.com		

The Inupiat people have survived the Arctic for centuries, and now they're surviving — quite well — in the business world. The Inupiat-owned Arctic Slope Regional Corporation (ASRC) was set up to manage 5 million acres on Alaska's North Slope granted to the Inupiat people after the Alaska Native Claims Settlement Act in 1971. ASRC develops the land and the natural resources in a manner consistent with Inupiat beliefs. Its main subsidiary, Natchiq, is the largest oil field services contractor in Alaska and accounts for 40% of revenues. Other subsidiaries are involved in a wide range of industries, including communications, construction, engineering, finance, manufacturing, tourism, and petroleum refining.

KEY COMPETITORS
Halliburton
Nabors Industries
Noble Drilling

ARMY AND AIR FORCE EXCHANGE SERVICE

3911 S. Walton Walker Blvd.
Dallas, TX 75236
Phone: 214-312-2011
Fax: 214-312-3000
Web site: http://www.aafes.com

CEO: Maj. Gen. Barry D. Bates, USA
CFO: Terry B. Corley
HR: James K. Winters
Type: Government-owned

1999 Sales: $6,782.7 million
1-Yr. Sales Change: 2.5%
Employees: 54,000
FYE: January

Be all that you can be and buy all that you can buy at the PX (Post Exchange). The Army and Air Force Exchange Service (AAFES) runs more than 10,000 facilities — including PXs and BXs (Base Exchanges) — at US military bases around the world. Operations include retail stores, catalog services, fast-food facilities, movie theaters, beauty shops, gas stations, and auto repair shops. AAFES serves active-duty military personnel, reservists, retirees, and their family members. A government agency under the Department of Defense (DoD), it receives no funding from the DoD. More than 70% of profits go into a fund for amenities such as libraries and youth programs. Other profits are used to build or refurbish stores.

KEY COMPETITORS
METRO AG
Sears

 See pages 62–63 for a full profile of this company.

ARTHUR D. LITTLE, INC.

25 Acorn Park
Cambridge, MA 02140
Phone: 617-498-5000
Fax: 617-498-7200
Web site: http://www.arthurdlittle.com

CEO: Lorenzo C. Lamadrid
CFO: Mark A. Brodsky
HR: Michael Eisenbud
Type: Private

1998 Sales: $608.0 million
1-Yr. Sales Change: 3.2%
Employees: 3,500
FYE: December

Being one of the world's oldest consulting firms is no small feat for Arthur D. Little. Founded by a chemist of the same name in 1886, Arthur D. Little (ADL) specializes in environmental, health, and safety consulting, management consulting, and technology and product development. The firm emphasizes scientific research and product development. It operates from more than 50 offices and laboratories in more than 30 countries. Other operations include the Arthur D. Little School of Management (a graduate program in management) and Arthur D. Little Enterprises, which commercializes products developed by the firm's staff. ADL's staff of more than 3,500 owns the company.

KEY COMPETITORS
Andersen Consulting
Booz, Allen
McKinsey & Company

 See pages 64–65 for a full profile of this company.

ASBURY AUTOMOTIVE GROUP

1 Tower Bridge, Ste. 1440
Conshohocken, PA 19428
Phone: 610-260-9800
Fax: 610-260-9804

CEO: Brian E. Kendrick
CFO: Allen Westergard
HR: Marcia Birnbaum
Type: Private

1998 Est. Sales: $3,100.0 million
1-Yr. Sales Change: 287.5%
Employees: 5,100
FYE: December

Asbury Automotive Group has steered its way to megadealer status. Through a rapid series of investments, the company has become the US's #3 auto dealer, behind top consolidator AutoNation and UnitedAuto Group. Asbury controls about 100 car dealership franchises through its stakes in eight major dealership groups: Nalley in Atlanta, Plaza in St. Louis, McDavid in Texas, Coggins and Courtesy in Florida, Thomason in Oregon, Crown in North Carolina, and McLarty in Arkansas. The company's strategy is to buy majority interests in multi-location dealerships with at least $150 million in annual sales, transforming each into a joint venture. Investment firms Ripplewood Holdings and Freeman Spogli & Co. own Asbury.

KEY COMPETITORS
AutoNation
Hendrick Automotive
VT

ASCENSION HEALTH

4600 Edmundson Rd.	CEO: Donald A. Brennan	1999 Est. Sales: $6,400.0 million
St. Louis, MO 63134	CFO: Jerry P. Widman	1-Yr. Sales Change: 3.7%
Phone: 314-253-6700	HR: David A. Smith	Employees: 67,000
Fax: 314-253-6491	Type: Not-for-profit	FYE: June
Web site: http://www.dcnhs.org		

Things are looking up for Ascension Health. Formed by the 1999 merger of Daughters of Charity National Health System and the Sisters of St. Joseph Health System, Ascension is a network of almost 80 Catholic hospitals, nursing homes, psychiatric wards, and other health care facilities in 15 states and the District of Columbia. It is the #1 Catholic hospital system in the US (ahead of Catholic Health Initiatives), and the largest not-for-profit healthcare system. The network is co-sponsored by four US provinces of the Daughters of Charity and the Sisters of St. Joseph religious orders, and is governed by a board made up primarily of sisters of the orders led by a non-clergy CEO.

KEY COMPETITORS
Catholic Health Initiatives
Columbia/HCA
Tenet Healthcare

 See pages 66–67 for a full profile of this company.

THE ASCII GROUP, INC.

7101 Wisconsin Ave., Ste. 1000	CEO: Alan D. Weinberger	1997 Sales: $9,200.0 million
Bethesda, MD 20814	CFO: Jamie Understein	1-Yr. Sales Change: 41.5%
Phone: 301-718-2600	HR: Jill Kerr	Employees: 22
Fax: 301-718-0435	Type: Consortium	FYE: December
Web site: http://www.ascii.com		

Psst, buddy . . . Middle-guy ASCII can help you steal a deal. The ASCII Group is the world's largest buying group for independent, full-service computer resellers, representing more than 1,700 US and Canadian members. Paying a monthly fee entitles members to buy volume products and negotiate better deals with hardware and software distributors. ASCII also offers discounts on credit card processing and leasing rates, access to direct-mail programs, health and business insurance, and other business service program offerings from companies such as Hertz and Airborne Freight. Chairman and CEO Alan Weinberger founded the group in 1984.

KEY COMPETITORS
AmeriQuest
Arrow Electronics
InaCom

ASHLEY FURNITURE INDUSTRIES, INC.

1 Ashley Way	CEO: Ron Wanek	1998 Sales: $650.0 million
Arcadia, WI 54612	CFO: Richard Barclay	1-Yr. Sales Change: 20.4%
Phone: 608-323-3377	HR: Jim Dotta	Employees: 4,567
Fax: 800-678-4492	Type: Private	FYE: December
Web site: http://www.ashleyfurniture.com		

Furniture buyers took a shine to Ashley Furniture Industries when it added a tough, high-gloss polyester finish to its furniture in 1986. Today the company is one of the nation's largest furniture manufacturers. Ashley Furniture makes and imports upholstered, leather, and hardwood furniture, as well as bedding. It has manufacturing plants and distribution centers in California, Florida, Mississippi, New Jersey, Washington state, and Wisconsin. It has also tapped into retail through Ashley Furniture HomeStores, in which independent dealers sell only Ashley Furniture products. Founded by Carlyle Weinberger in 1945, Ashley Furniture is owned by father-and-son duos Ron and Todd Wanek and Chuck and Ben Vogel.

KEY COMPETITORS
Furniture Brands International
LADD Furniture
LifeStyle Furnishings International

ASI CORP.

48289 Fremont Blvd.
Fremont, CA 94538
Phone: 510-226-8000
Fax: 510-226-8858
Web site: http://www.asi2000.com

CEO: Marcel Liang
CFO: Julie Wang
HR: Crystal Yuan
Type: Private

1998 Sales: $730.0 million
1-Yr. Sales Change: 35.2%
Employees: 560
FYE: December

ASI likes being in the middle — of sales. The company, a wholesale distributor of computer software and hardware, sells more than 3,000 products, including CD-ROM drives, modems, monitors, motherboards, networking equipment, and storage devices. It also assembles microcomputers (under the Nspire name) and offers standard and custom configurations, mostly to resellers who are not able to provide such services. ASI offers support services such as marketing, third-party financing, and training. The company sells to mail-order suppliers, OEMs, systems integrators, and VARs. Vendor partners include 3Com, Microsoft, Samsung, and Toshiba. President Christine Liang, who founded ASI in 1987, owns the company.

KEY COMPETITORS
Ingram Micro
MicroAge
Tech Data

ASPLUNDH TREE EXPERT CO.

708 Blair Mill Rd.
Willow Grove, PA 19090
Phone: 215-784-4200
Fax: 215-784-4493
Web site: http://www.asplundh.com

CEO: Christopher B. Asplundh
CFO: Joseph P. Dwyer
HR: Mike Lynch
Type: Private

1998 Sales: $1,026.0 million
1-Yr. Sales Change: 2.6%
Employees: 25,000
FYE: December

Asplundh (Swedish for "aspen grove," not for the sound made when tree experts fall on their aspens) is the leading tree-trimming and line-clearing business in North America. Its tree unit works for utilities and municipalities to clear power lines of limbs, while its rail division trims trees and brush from railroad tracks. Asplundh's subsidiaries offer special utility-related services such as meter reading, storm emergency services, street light maintenance, and pole inspection. Customers include more than 250 utilities, telecommunications companies, pipeline companies, railroads, and municipalities in Australia, Canada, Europe, New Zealand, and the US. Family-owned Asplundh was founded in 1928.

KEY COMPETITORS
Davey Tree
Monroe and Lewis Tree Service
Wright Tree Service

ASSOCIATED FOOD STORES, INC.

1850 W. 21st South
Salt Lake City, UT 84119
Phone: 801-973-4400
Fax: 801-978-8551

CEO: Richard A. Parkinson
CFO: S. Neal Berube
HR: Marla Battles
Type: Cooperative

1999 Est. Sales: $925.0 million
1-Yr. Sales Change: (7.5%)
Employees: 1,500
FYE: March

Associated Food Stores is a regional cooperative wholesaler owned by the more than 600 independent supermarkets and convenience stores it serves. Member stores are sprinkled throughout Arizona, Colorado, Idaho, Montana, Nevada, and Oregon, but the majority of stores are located in Utah. Associated Food Stores also sells to nonmembers. Member services include development assistance for new stores or for improvements to existing stores; subsidiary Market Development assists members with real estate activities. Associated Food Stores owns about 25% of Western Family, a grocery wholesalers' partnership that produces Western Family private-label merchandise. The co-op was formed in 1940.

KEY COMPETITORS
Fleming Companies
SUPERVALU
Unified Western Grocers

ASSOCIATED GROCERS, INCORPORATED

3301 S. Norfolk
Seattle, WA 98118
Phone: 206-762-2100
Fax: 206-764-7731
Web site: http://www.agseattle.com

CEO: Donald W. Benson
CFO: Maureen Murphy
HR: Harold Ravenscraft
Type: Private

1998 Sales: $1,090.0 million
1-Yr. Sales Change: (0.2%)
Employees: 1,300
FYE: September

Associated Grocers (AG) feeds the ability of its members to remain competitive. AG distributes food and nonfood goods and provides support services to about 350 independent grocery retailers in Alaska, Hawaii, Oregon, and Washington state as well as Guam and the Pacific Rim. It distributes more than 12,000 items, including its own private-label brands: Western Family (food and nonfood), Javaworks (coffee), and Ovenworks (baked goods). AG (not to be confused with Associated Grocers in other regions) was formed in 1934 to support 11 Seattle-based neighborhood grocers. The co-op's AG/Fleming Northwest joint venture with Fleming Cos. provides food marketing and distribution to about 75 Washington and Oregon supermarkets.

KEY COMPETITORS
SUPERVALU
Services Group
Unified Western Grocers

ASSOCIATED MILK PRODUCERS INCORPORATED

315 N. Broadway
New Ulm, MN 56073
Phone: 507-354-8295
Fax: 507-359-8651
Web site: http://www.ampi.com

CEO: Wayne Bok
CFO: Ken Spoon
HR: —
Type: Cooperative

1998 Sales: $1,100.0 million
1-Yr. Sales Change: 18.5%
Employees: 1,600
FYE: December

Associated Milk Producers Incorporated's (AMPI) dairy business is solid. Shying away from the liquid stuff, it transforms milk into about 5 billion pounds of butter, cheese, and other solid milk products each year. A regional cooperative of 6,500 member farmers from Iowa, Minnesota, Missouri, Nebraska, North and South Dakota, and Wisconsin, AMPI operates 14 manufacturing plants. The co-op produces 60% of all the instant milk sold in the US and is a large cheddar producer. Aside from its own State brand of cheese and butter, AMPI primarily makes private-label products and is seeking stability in value-added products such as aseptic-packed cheese sauces.

KEY COMPETITORS
Dairy Farmers of America
Foremost Farms
Land O'Lakes

 See pages 68–69 for a full profile of this company.

ASSOCIATED WHOLESALE GROCERS INC.

5000 Kansas Ave.
Kansas City, KS 66106
Phone: 913-288-1000
Fax: 913-288-1508
Web site: http://www.awginc.com

CEO: Doug Carolan
CFO: Gary Phillips
HR: Kathy Black
Type: Cooperative

1998 Est. Sales: $3,180.0 million
1-Yr. Sales Change: 1.6%
Employees: 3,100
FYE: December

Associated Wholesale Grocers (AWG) provides bread to the nation's breadbasket through its 350-plus grocer-owners. The company is one of the nation's largest supermarket cooperatives. AWG's retailers run some 850 grocery stores, primarily in Arkansas, Kansas, Missouri, and Oklahoma, but also in six other midwestern and southern states. The co-op's stores take on a variety of formats and names (known as "banners" in the industry), including conventional supermarket chains Cash Saver, Apple Market, Country Mart, and Thriftway; the upscale Sun Fresh chain; and warehouse chains Price Mart and Price Chopper. AWG is also a food retailer, operating more than 30 Falley's and Food 4 Less stores in Kansas.

KEY COMPETITORS
Fleming Companies
IGA
Nash Finch

See pages 70–71 for a full profile of this company.

ASSOCIATED WHOLESALERS INC.

Route 422
Robesonia, PA 19551
Phone: 610-693-3161
Fax: 610-693-3171
Web site: http://www.awiweb.com

CEO: J. Christopher Michael
CFO: Thomas C. Teeter
HR: Audrey Hausmann
Type: Cooperative

1998 Est. Sales: $730.0 million
1-Yr. Sales Change: (2.9%)
Employees: 1,400
FYE: July

Being associated with Associated Wholesalers means having a supplier of food and nonfood items. The retailer-owned cooperative supplies health and beauty care items, meat, dairy products, produce, baby products, and canned goods to more than 5,000 stores. It supplies independent grocers such as Gerrity's, Sunshine Markets, and Shurfine stores, primarily in Delaware, Maryland, New Jersey, New York, and Pennsylvania. The co-op also provides training and technical services to members. Associated Wholesalers operates two distribution centers in Pennsylvania, one in Robesonia that supplies food and one in York that handles nonfood items.

KEY COMPETITORS
Di Giorgio
Fleming Companies
SUPERVALU

AUSTIN ENERGY

721 Barton Springs Rd.
Austin, TX 78704
Phone: 512-476-7721
Fax: 512-322-6037
Web site: http://www.austinenergy.com

CEO: Charles Manning
CFO: Elaine Kuhlman
HR: Ken Andriessen
Type: Government-owned

1998 Sales: $916.4 million
1-Yr. Sales Change: 12.4%
Employees: 2,195
FYE: September

Despite its laid-back reputation, the capital of Texas has plenty of energy. Austin Energy, formerly the City of Austin Electric Utility Department, is a municipally owned electric utility that serves more than 300,000 residential and commercial customers. The utility generates 2,420 MW from coal, gas, and nuclear sources and is expanding its renewable energy base. In anticipation of deregulation, Austin Energy is adding services such as energy conservation consulting. A portion of the utility's revenue goes to the City of Austin General Fund, which is used for services such as police, fire protection, libraries, and parks.

AUSTIN INDUSTRIES INC.

3535 Travis St., Ste. 300
Dallas, TX 75204
Phone: 214-443-5500
Fax: 214-443-5581
Web site: http://www.austin-ind.com

CEO: William T. Solomon
CFO: Paul W. Hill
HR: Linda Bayless
Type: Private

1998 Sales: $808.0 million
1-Yr. Sales Change: 30.5%
Employees: 6,300
FYE: December

Paving the way for progress, Austin Industries provides civil, commercial, and industrial construction services in the southern US. Its Austin Bridge & Road subsidiary provides road, bridge, and parking lot construction across Texas. Known for its high-rises, the Austin Commercial subsidiary builds corporate headquarters, technology sites, and hospitals throughout the central and southwestern US. The unit is tackling its first major sports arena, American Airlines Center, in Dallas. Austin Industrial focuses on construction, instrumentation, and electrical services for the chemical, refining, power, and manufacturing industries, mostly in the South and Southeast. The employee-owned firm was founded in 1918.

KEY COMPETITORS
Beck Group
Granite Construction
Turner Industries

AVONDALE INCORPORATED

506 S. Broad St.	CEO: G. Stephen Felker	1999 Sales: $880.9 million
Monroe, GA 30655	CFO: Jack R. Altherr	1-Yr. Sales Change: (16.6%)
Phone: 770-267-2226	HR: Sharon L. Rodgers	Employees: 6,800
Fax: 770-267-5196	Type: Private	FYE: August

For vertically integrated Avondale, making textiles must be jean-etic. The company makes apparel fabrics (cotton and cotton blends, indigo-dyed denim, piece-dyed woven cotton), greige fabrics (undyed, unfinished cotton and cotton blends), specialty fabrics (such as coated material for awnings and boat covers), and yarns. Leading apparel makers such as VF Corporation (maker of Lee and Wrangler jeans) buy from Avondale; VF accounts for more than 15% of sales. Avondale operates 26 manufacturing facilities in Alabama, Georgia, North Carolina, and South Carolina. The company was founded in Georgia in 1895; it is still controlled by the founding family and is headed by Stephen Felker, great-grandson of the founder.

KEY COMPETITORS
Cone Mills
Galey & Lord
R. B. Pamplin

BAIN & COMPANY

2 Copley Place	CEO: Orit Gadiesh	1998 Sales: $498.7 million
Boston, MA 02116	CFO: Colin Anderson	1-Yr. Sales Change: 3.9%
Phone: 617-572-2000	HR: Elizabeth Corcoran	Employees: 1,350
Fax: 617-572-2427	Type: Partnership	FYE: December
Web site: http://www.bain.com		

"Bainies" are always at the ready when corporate titans need a little strategic direction. A leader in strategic consulting, Bain & Company is a generalist whose consulting services include business unit, organizational, and corporate strategy; distribution and logistics advice; mergers, acquisition, and privatization consulting; and sales and marketing strategy. Its clients span industries such as media and communications, consumer products and services, financial services, and high tech. Bain has 25 offices in nearly 20 countries. Although founded by the same individuals, Bain & Company and investment firm Bain Capital are separate entities.

KEY COMPETITORS
Booz, Allen
McKinsey & Company
Towers Perrin

 See pages 72–73 for a full profile of this company.

BAKER & MCKENZIE

1 Prudential Plaza, 130 E. Randolph Dr., Ste. 2500	CEO: Christine Lagarde	1999 Sales: $818.0 million
Chicago, IL 60601	CFO: Robert S. Spencer	1-Yr. Sales Change: 4.3%
Phone: 312-861-8800	HR: Wilbert Williams	Employees: 6,900
Fax: 312-861-2899	Type: Partnership	FYE: June
Web site: http://www.bakerinfo.com		

Forget jokes about lawyers changing lightbulbs: Baker & McKenzie is changing attitudes. In 1999 the firm — the world's largest in number of attorneys — became one of the first major practices to appoint a woman as its top partner. Baker & McKenzie has more than 2,500 lawyers serving in 60 offices across 35 different countries. It offers expertise in such practice areas as banking, international trade, securities, and litigation. The firm has conducted legal work for such heavy-duty clients as Chase Manhattan and Ingersoll-Rand. Russell Baker and John McKenzie founded the firm in 1949 with a focus on building an international practice.

KEY COMPETITORS
Clifford Chance
Jones, Day
Mayer, Brown & Platt

See pages 74–75 for a full profile of this company.

BAKER & TAYLOR CORPORATION

2709 Water Ridge Pkwy.
Charlotte, NC 28217
Phone: 704-357-3500
Fax: 704-329-9105
Web site: http://www.baker-taylor.com

CEO: Craig M. Richards
CFO: Edward H. Gross
HR: Claudette Hampton
Type: Private

1999 Sales: $1,021.4 million
1-Yr. Sales Change: 15.6%
Employees: 2,500
FYE: June

The last time you strolled through the public library (when was that?), you probably looked at a lot of books from Baker & Taylor (B&T). The company is the #1 book supplier to libraries and the #2 book distributor overall, behind Ingram Book Group. B&T's institutional division distributes books, tapes, calendars, CD-ROMs, CDs, and videos to 28,000 schools and libraries worldwide. Its retailer division supplies retailers such as Amazon.com, Barnes & Noble, CDNow.com, Virgin Entertainment, and independent booksellers. The Carlyle Group, an investment partnership, owns nearly 85% of B&T. Management, employees, and other private investors own the rest.

KEY COMPETITORS
Handleman
Ingram Entertainment
Ingram Industries

 See pages 76–77 for a full profile of this company.

BAPTIST HEALTH SYSTEMS OF SOUTH FLORIDA

6855 Red Rd.
Coral Gables, FL 33143
Phone: 305-273-2555
Fax: 305-273-2556
Web site: http://www.baptisthealth.net

CEO: Brian E. Keeley
CFO: Ralph Lawson
HR: Carl Gustafson
Type: Not-for-profit

1998 Sales: $1,035.7 million
1-Yr. Sales Change: —
Employees: 7,200
FYE: September

Baptist Health Systems of South Florida is a not-for-profit health care organization composed of five hospitals in the Miami area. A provider for about 30 health plans, Baptist Health offers a wide range of services including a comprehensive cancer program, pediatric services, addiction treatment, outpatient services, and home care. With more than 1,000 hospital beds and about 1,000 physicians, Baptist Health was lined up to merge with Catholic organization Mercy Health System of Miami; the deal was called off in 1998 when Baptist Health refused to stop offering abortions at one of its hospitals.

KEY COMPETITORS
Catholic Health East
Columbia/HCA
HEALTHSOUTH

BARNES & NOBLE COLLEGE BOOKSTORES, INC.

33 E. 17th St.
New York, NY 10003
Phone: 212-539-2000
Fax: 212-780-1866
Web site: http://www.bkstore.com

CEO: Max J. Roberts
CFO: Barry Brover
HR: Gail Gittleson
Type: Private

1999 Est. Sales: $830.0 million
1-Yr. Sales Change: 3.8%
Employees: 6,000
FYE: April

Barnes & Noble College Bookstores is the scholastic sister company of Barnes & Noble, the US's largest bookseller. Started in 1873, the company operates about 350 campus bookstores nationwide, selling textbooks, trade books, school supplies, collegiate clothing, and emblematic merchandise. Universities, medical and law schools, and community colleges hire Barnes & Noble College Bookstores to replace traditional campus cooperatives (the schools get a cut of the sales). The company, which also runs an online textbook retailer, developed a program with Gateway offering students customized computer systems through participating stores. Barnes & Noble's chairman and CEO, Leonard Riggio, owns 80% of the company.

KEY COMPETITORS
Follett
Nebraska Book
Wallace's Bookstores

BARTLETT AND COMPANY

4800 Main St., Ste. 600
Kansas City, MO 64112
Phone: 816-753-6300
Fax: 816-753-0062

CEO: James B. Heberstreit
CFO: Arnie Wheeler
HR: Bill Webster
Type: Private

1998 Est. Sales: $720.0 million
1-Yr. Sales Change: (4.0%)
Employees: 575
FYE: December

When the cows come home, Bartlett and Company will be ready. The company's primary business is grain merchandising, but it also runs cattle feedlots and mills flour. Bartlett operates grain storage facilities in Kansas City, Kansas; St. Joseph and Waverly, Missouri; and Nebraska City, Nebraska. It has terminal elevators in Council Bluffs, Iowa; Kansas City and Wichita, Kansas; and St. Joseph, Missouri, as well as more than 10 country elevators. Bartlett's cattle operations are based in Texas; its flour mills are in Kansas, North Carolina, and South Carolina. Founded in 1907 as Bartlett Agri Enterprises, the company is still owned by its founding family and has been run by Paul Bartlett Jr. since 1961.

KEY COMPETITORS
ADM
Cactus Feeders
Cargill

BARTON MALOW COMPANY

27777 Franklin Rd., Ste. 800
Southfield, MI 48034
Phone: 248-351-4500
Fax: 248-351-4629
Web site: http://www.bmco.com

CEO: Ben C. Maibach
CFO: Edward R. Jarchow
HR: Judy Willard
Type: Private

1999 Sales: $820.7 million
1-Yr. Sales Change: 12.9%
Employees: 1,350
FYE: March

Barton Malow scores by building end zones and home plates. The general contracting and construction management firm's projects include stadiums for the NFL's Detroit Lions, Major League Baseball's Baltimore Orioles, and the 1996 Olympic Games. Barton Malow also provides predesign through close-out services for public schools, hospitals, assembly plants, and offices. Its Barton Malow Rigging subsidiary offers equipment installation services for manufacturers, and subsidiary Argos Group provides architectural design services. Founded in 1924 by C.O. Barton, the company is owned by the Maibach family and has offices in Georgia, Maryland, Michigan, Minnesota, Virginia, and Wisconsin.

KEY COMPETITORS
Clark Enterprises
Gilbane
Huber, Hunt & Nichols

BASHAS' INC.

22402 S. Basha Rd.
Chandler, AZ 85248
Phone: 480-895-9350
Fax: 480-895-1206
Web site: http://www.bashas.com

CEO: Edward N. Basha
CFO: Darl J. Andersen
HR: Michael Gantt
Type: Private

1998 Est. Sales: $1,000.0 million
1-Yr. Sales Change: 14.9%
Employees: 7,600
FYE: December

Bashas' has blossomed in the Arizona desert. Founded in 1932 and owned by the Basha family, the food retailer has grown to about 95 stores, primarily in Arizona, but also in New Mexico and California. Its holdings include warehouse and discount stores, conventional grocery stores, gourmet-style supermarkets, and superstores under the AJ's Fine Foods, Bashas', and Eddie's Country Store banners. About one-third of its stores are located in the Phoenix area. Bashas' also operates Mercado and Food City stores catering to Hispanics and six supermarkets (including its New Mexico store) in the Navajo Nation. Bashas' also offers online grocery shopping through its Groceries On The Go service.

KEY COMPETITORS
Albertson's
Kroger
Safeway

BASIN ELECTRIC POWER COOPERATIVE

1717 E. Interstate Ave.
Bismarck, ND 58501
Phone: 701-223-0441
Fax: 701-224-5336
Web site: http://www.basinelectric.com

CEO: Robert L. McPhail
CFO: Clifton T. Hudgins
HR: Tom Fischer
Type: Cooperative

1998 Sales: $763.2 million
1-Yr. Sales Change: (2.6%)
Employees: 1,684
FYE: December

Ranges at home on the range depend on Basin Electric Power Cooperative, as do light bulbs, heaters, and all the other electric-powered items in eight US states in the West and Midwest. The regional, consumer-owned power generation and transmission co-op has 3,304 MW in generating capacity. It provides power to 119 rural electric member systems, which serve 1.5 million people, and to the Missouri Basin Power Project. Basin Electric's subsidiaries include Granite Peak Energy, its for-profit marketing unit; Dakota Gasification Company (which creates natural gas from coal); Basin Telecommunications Inc., an ISP; and Dakota Coal Company, which purchases coal for resale and to produce lime.

KEY COMPETITORS
Montana Power
Northern States Power
UtiliCorp

BATTELLE MEMORIAL INSTITUTE

505 King Ave.
Columbus, OH 43201
Phone: 614-424-6424
Fax: 614-424-5263
Web site: http://www.battelle.org

CEO: Douglas E. Olesen
CFO: Mark W. Kontos
HR: Bob Lincoln
Type: Not-for-profit

1999 Sales: $901.0 million
1-Yr. Sales Change: 26.9%
Employees: 7,060
FYE: September

When you use a photocopier, hit a golf ball, or listen to a CD, you're using technologies developed by Battelle Memorial Institute. This not-for-profit trust, founded in Gordon Battelle's 1923 will, operates one of the world's largest research firms. Originally formed to promote metallurgy and related industries, the company has diversified into research and development for agriculture, automobiles, chemicals, energy, and medicine in cooperation with corporations and governments in about 30 countries. Primarily a contract research provider, the institute continues to explore next-generation technologies including advanced medical products, alternative fuels, and recycling processes.

KEY COMPETITORS
MIT
MITRE
SAIC

 See pages 78–79 for a full profile of this company.

BAYLOR HEALTH CARE SYSTEM

3500 Gaston Ave.
Dallas, TX 75246
Phone: 214-820-0111
Fax: 214-820-7499
Web site: http://www.baylordallas.edu

CEO: Boone Powell
CFO: John L. Hess
HR: Beverly Bradshaw
Type: Not-for-profit

1998 Sales: $993.2 million
1-Yr. Sales Change: (26.4%)
Employees: 12,900
FYE: June

The Baylor Health Care System (BHCS) offers a bundle of services. Founded in 1981, it was governed by Baylor University until establishing autonomy in 1997. The not-for-profit medical network, which serves eight counties in the Dallas-Ft. Worth metroplex, includes the five-hospital Baylor University Medical Center complex, one of the state's major teaching and referral facilities. Other system members include an acute care rehabilitation facility, a restorative care facility, 13 senior health centers, five family health centers, community hospitals, medical centers, and a cancer center. The system also provides home health care and specialty pediatric services.

KEY COMPETITORS
Columbia/HCA
Texas Health Resources

BDO INTERNATIONAL B.V.

180 N. Stetson Ave., Ste. 4300
Chicago, IL 60601
Phone: 312-240-1236
Fax: 312-240-3311
Web site: http://www.bdo-international.com

CEO: Daniel Pavelich
CFO: J. Terry Manning
HR: Warren Holmes
Type: Private

1999 Sales: $1,610.0 million
1-Yr. Sales Change: 0.6%
Employees: 17,500
FYE: September

BDO International is at the tip-top of the so-called "second tier" of accounting firms worldwide, just below the Big Five (PricewaterhouseCoopers, Andersen Worldwide, Ernst & Young International, KPMG International, Deloitte Touche Tohmatsu). The company offers a broad range of accounting and consulting services, including auditing corporate finance, litigation consulting, appraisals, valuations, and other niche services. Founded in 1963, BDO International has more than 450 offices in more than 80 countries; its US unit, BDO Seidman, has approximately 40 offices that serve primarily family-owned, manager-owned, and private businesses.

KEY COMPETITORS
Deloitte Touche Tohmatsu
Grant Thornton International
KPMG

BE&K INC.

2000 International Park Dr.
Birmingham, AL 35243
Phone: 205-972-6000
Fax: 205-972-6300
Web site: http://www.bek.com

CEO: T. Michael Goodrich
CFO: Clyde M. Smith
HR: Carolyn Morgan
Type: Private

1999 Sales: $960.0 million
1-Yr. Sales Change: (9.5%)
Employees: 8,617
FYE: March

It may not be the be-all and end-all of the construction world, but growing BE&K still keeps busy. BE&K is an industrial design and construction company that provides building, maintenance, engineering, and environmental services to processing industries around the world. The firm designs and upgrades facilities for the pharmaceutical, steel, chemical, pulp and paper, cement, and petrochemical industries. BE&K works throughout the US and has expanded into Eastern Europe, Germany, and Sweden. BE&K has been recognized for its family-friendly work environment. The firm was founded in 1972 by partners Peter Bolvig, William Edmonds, and Ted Kennedy (chairman), who retain ownership.

KEY COMPETITORS
Bechtel
Fluor
Foster Wheeler

BEAULIEU OF AMERICA, LLC

1502 Coronet Dr.
Dalton, GA 30720
Phone: 706-278-6666
Fax: 706-217-1765
Web site: http://www.beaulieu-usa.com

CEO: Carl Bouckaert
CFO: Larry Swanson
HR: Fred Johnson
Type: Private

1998 Sales: $1,130.0 million
1-Yr. Sales Change: 17.6%
Employees: 9,347
FYE: December

Beaulieu Of America creates beautiful places. The company is the third-largest carpet company in the world, after Shaw and Mohawk, and the largest privately held. Originally focused on low-cost, machine-made area rugs sold by major chains and national accounts, Beaulieu has added upscale area rugs for distribution by specialty floor retailers. Improving loom technology and the use of computer-aided design are continuing priorities for the firm. Beaulieu also produces the polypropylene fibers used to make carpets. The company has operations in Australia, Canada, Chile, China, Mexico, and Russia. CEO Carl Bouckaert and his wife, Mieke, whose family made carpets in Europe, founded Beaulieu in 1978.

KEY COMPETITORS
Interface
Mohawk Industries
Shaw Industries

BECHTEL GROUP, INC.

50 Beale St.
San Francisco, CA 94105
Phone: 415-768-1234
Fax: 415-768-9038
Web site: http://www.bechtel.com

CEO: Riley P. Bechtel
CFO: Georganne Proctor
HR: Bob Baxter
Type: Private

1998 Sales: $12,645.0 million
1-Yr. Sales Change: 11.6%
Employees: 30,000
FYE: December

If only the pharoahs could have hired the Bechtel Group. Bechtel, which has made a name for itself on projects as big as the Pyramids, designs and builds facilities for energy generation and transmission, chemical manufacturing, mining and metals, surface transportation, aerospace, telecommunications, and water and waste management. Bechtel has worked on more than 19,000 projects in 140 countries, including the Hoover Dam, San Francisco's Bay Area Rapid Transit system, and the Chernobyl and Three Mile Island nuclear plant cleanups. It built the Saudi Arabian industrial city of Jubail from scratch. The billionaire Bechtel family controls the company, now headed by fourth-generation member Riley Bechtel.

KEY COMPETITORS
Fluor
Halliburton
Peter Kiewit Sons'

 See pages 80–81 for a full profile of this company.

BELK, INC.

2801 W. Tyvola Rd.
Charlotte, NC 28217
Phone: 704-357-1000
Fax: 704-357-1876
Web site: http://www.belk.com

CEO: John M. Belk
CFO: John R. Belk
HR: Carolyn McGinnis
Type: Private

1999 Sales: $2,091.1 million
1-Yr. Sales Change: 5.9%
Employees: 22,000
FYE: January

Department store operator Belk has shed a lot of bulk. Now a relatively svelte 260-store retailer operating in 13 states, the company was a confederation of 112 separate companies before its 1998 reorganization. Belk stores in Alabama, Arkansas, Florida, Georgia, Kentucky, Maryland, Mississippi, North Carolina, South Carolina, Tennessee, Texas, Virginia, and West Virginia offer moderately priced designer fashion lines, cosmetics, and accessories. The Belk family runs the show and owns half of the company, which is the biggest privately held department store chain in the US. Belk grew from a single store (called New York Racket) opened in Monroe, North Carolina, in 1888.

KEY COMPETITORS
Dillard's
Federated
Saks Inc.

 See pages 82–83 for a full profile of this company.

BEN E. KEITH CO.

601 E. 7th St.
Fort Worth, TX 76102
Phone: 817-877-5700
Fax: 817-338-1701
Web site: http://www.benekeithcompany.com

CEO: Robert Hallam
CFO: Mel Cockrell
HR: Carolyn Marshall
Type: Private

1999 Sales: $787.0 million
1-Yr. Sales Change: 15.4%
Employees: 2,000
FYE: June

A leader in food and beverage distribution, Ben E. Keith delivers a full line of foods (produce, dry groceries, frozen food, meat) to more than 12,000 customers in seven southwestern states. One of the world's largest Anheuser-Busch distributors, the company delivers more than 20 million cases of beer annually to customers in 47 Texas counties. With facilities in Arkansas, New Mexico, Oklahoma, and Texas, Ben E. Keith's customers include restaurants (Brinker International), sports stadiums (Texas Stadium), hospitals, and schools. Founded in 1906 as Harkrider & Morrison, the company assumed its current name in 1931 in honor of Ben E. Keith, who served as the company's president until 1959.

KEY COMPETITORS
Alliant Foodservice
SYSCO
U.S. Foodservice

BERWIND GROUP

3000 W. Tower Center Sq., 1500 Market St.
Philadelphia, PA 19102
Phone: 215-563-2800
Fax: 215-563-8347

CEO: C. Graham Berwind
CFO: W. C. Eckenrode
HR: —
Type: Private

1998 Sales: $1,156.0 million
1-Yr. Sales Change: 18.3%
Employees: 4,800
FYE: December

Berwind's multi-industry operations range from manufacturing to real estate and financial services. Founded in 1874 to mine Appalachian coal, the firm began leasing its mining operations in 1962 to fund investments in new ventures. Berwind Industries and SLC Technologies make items such as Supra real estate lock boxes and display screens used in airplanes and cars. Berwind Property Group owns 13 million sq. ft. of commercial, retail, and residential real estate nationwide. Berwind Financial Group provides investment banking services. Berwind Natural Resources and Berwind Pharmaceutical Services round out the group's operations. The Berwind family owns the company.

KEY COMPETITORS
DuPont
FMC
U.S. Foodservice

BIG FLOWER HOLDINGS, INC.

3 E. 54th St.
New York, NY 10022
Phone: 212-521-1600
Fax: 212-223-4074
Web site: http://www.cjds.com/owner.htm

CEO: Edward T. Reilly
CFO: Richard L. Ritchie
HR: Linda Brooks
Type: Private

1998 Sales: $1,739.7 million
1-Yr. Sales Change: 26.4%
Employees: 1,000
FYE: December

Big Flower Holdings helps retailers peddle their wares. Through its operating subsidiary Big Flower Press Holdings, the company prints advertising inserts and circulars, offers direct mail and marketing products, and provides digital printing services. Its Treasure Chest Advertising (more than 60% of sales) is the largest printer of advertising circulars in the US, and also prints Sunday comics and newspaper TV guides for more than 300 newspapers. Subsidiary Webcraft provides direct mail and database marketing services, while the Digital Services unit supplies digital pre-press services to retailers, advertising agencies, and packaging firms. An investor group led by Thomas H. Lee Co. owns the company.

KEY COMPETITORS
Quebecor Printing
R. R. Donnelley
infoUSA

 See pages 84–85 for a full profile of this company.

BIG V SUPERMARKETS, INC.

176 N. Main St.
Florida, NY 10921
Phone: 914-651-4411
Fax: 914-651-7048

CEO: Mark S. Schwartz
CFO: James A. Toopes
HR: Donald J. Trella
Type: Private

1998 Sales: $814.4 million
1-Yr. Sales Change: 6.8%
Employees: 5,200
FYE: December

Nixon flashed the V sign; northeastern shoppers favor the Big V sign. Big V Supermarkets runs some 40 grocery stores, primarily under the ShopRite name, in New Jersey, New York, and Pennsylvania. A member of Wakefern Food, the #1 supermarket cooperative, Big V is a leading chain in the Hudson River Valley. Its stores average nearly 50,000 sq. ft. The grocer is also rolling out its fresh-market format, with expanded produce and meat departments, in most stores. Big V, which began as a single Victory Supermarket in 1942, was publicly held until a management-led LBO in 1987. Thomas H. Lee Company bought the chain in 1990.

KEY COMPETITORS
A&P
Grand Union
Pathmark

BIG Y FOODS INC.

2145 Roosevelt Ave.	CEO: Donald H. D'Amour	1999 Est. Sales: $1,010.0 million
Springfield, MA 01104	CFO: Robert B. Antrasian	1-Yr. Sales Change: 0.1%
Phone: 413-784-0600	HR: Jack Henry	Employees: 7,000
Fax: 413-732-8475	Type: Private	FYE: June
Web site: http://www.bigy.com		

Y not dream big? Big Y Foods, a supermarket chain with more than 40 stores in Massachusetts and Connecticut, has grown from a single 900-sq.-ft. store into a player in the New England grocery market. About half of its stores are Big Y World Class Markets, which offer specialty groceries and one-stop conveniences like banking services. The other half consists of Big Y Supermarkets and one Big Y Wines liquor store. Several Big Y stores provide dry cleaning and photo processing, and their International Cafes offer prepared foods. Big Y is owned by the D'Amour family; Paul D'Amour bought the original store (at a Y intersection in Chicopee, Massachusetts) in 1936 and was quickly joined by teenage brother Gerald.

KEY COMPETITORS
A&P
Shaw's
Stop & Shop

BILL BLASS LTD.

550 7th Ave., 12th Fl.	CEO: Bill Blass	1998 Est. Sales: $800.0 million
New York, NY 10018	CFO: Michael Groveman	1-Yr. Sales Change: —
Phone: 212-221-6660	HR: —	Employees: 40
Fax: 212-302-5166	Type: Private	FYE: December

Bill Blass' signature has marked sophisticated styles for three decades. His namesake company makes tailored men's and women's clothing known to adorn the upper crust from Barbara Bush to Barbra Streisand. Blass started the company in 1970 and made a name for himself with timeless, tailored designs using fine fabrics. Never yielding to the looks of the moment, such as disco or grunge, the Bill Blass name has acquired a loyal fashion following. Bill Blass has issued over 40 licenses for items such as fragrances, furniture, jeans, eyewear, and accessories. Blass, who will retire in 2000, sold the firm in late 1999 to its jeanswear licensee, Resource Club, and CFO Michael Groveman.

KEY COMPETITORS
Chanel
Christian Dior
St. John Knits

BILL HEARD ENTERPRISES

200 Brookstone Center Pkwy., Ste. 205	CEO: William T. Heard	1998 Est. Sales: $1,200.0 million
Columbus, GA 31904	CFO: Ronald A. Feldner	1-Yr. Sales Change: 9.1%
Phone: 706-323-1111	HR: Jim Matthews	Employees: 2,000
Fax: 706-321-9488	Type: Private	FYE: December
Web site: http://www.billheard.com		

The South is alive with the sound of Chevys — music to the ears of Bill Heard Enterprises. The largest Chevrolet dealer in the world (according to Chevrolet Motor Division) has 10 dealerships in Alabama, Florida, Georgia, Tennessee, and Texas. Bill Heard Enterprises (known as "Mr. Big Volume") sells both new and used vehicles and auto supplies and offers repair services; it also owns Oldsmobile and Cadillac franchises in Atlanta and Columbus, Georgia. William Heard Sr. opened his first dealership in 1919. He switched to selling Chevrolets exclusively in 1932, and his son and grandsons, who now run the family-owned business, continue to focus on Chevy sales.

KEY COMPETITORS
AutoNation
Hendrick Automotive
United Auto Group

BJC HEALTH SYSTEM

4444 Forest Park Ave.
St. Louis, MO 63108
Phone: 314-286-2000
Fax: 314-286-2060
Web site: http://www.bjc.org

CEO: Steven H. Lipstein
CFO: Edward Stiften
HR: William M. Behrendt
Type: Not-for-profit

1998 Sales: $1,560.6 million
1-Yr. Sales Change: (1.7%)
Employees: 25,853
FYE: December

BJC Health System is the largest health care provider in the St. Louis area. It operates a network of more than 100 health care facilities in mid-Missouri (including greater St. Louis) and southern Illinois. Affiliated with Washington University School of Medicine through two of its member teaching hospitals, Barnes-Jewish Hospital and St. Louis Children's Hospital, BJC operates 14 hospitals, six nursing homes, its own health plan, and numerous outpatient care centers. With a group of some 2,000 doctors, BJC jointly owns Joint Contracting, a company set up to bargain with managed care plans.

KEY COMPETITORS
SSM Health Care
Sisters of Mercy
Tenet Healthcare

BLACK & VEATCH

8400 Ward Pkwy.
Kansas City, MO 64114
Phone: 913-458-2000
Fax: 913-458-2934
Web site: http://www.bv.com

CEO: Leonard C. Rodman
CFO: Wayne F. Hall
HR: Jim Farr
Type: Private

1998 Sales: $2,100.0 million
1-Yr. Sales Change: 12.9%
Employees: 9,000
FYE: December

From Argentina to Zimbabwe, Black & Veatch provides the ABCs of construction and engineering. The firm handles all phases of projects — from design and engineering, through financing and procurement, to construction. Since 1915 the Kansas City firm has handled projects that run the gamut from the elegant (reconstructing a Renaissance building in Prague) to the industrial (building a coal-fired power plant in Central America). With more than 90 offices worldwide, Black & Veatch mainly caters to the infrastructure, process, and power markets. It also builds facilities for the high-tech, information technology, financial management consulting, telecommunications, and transportation infrastructure fields.

KEY COMPETITORS
Dames & Moore
Harza Engineering
Parsons

BLOOMBERG L.P.

499 Park Ave.
New York, NY 10022
Phone: 212-318-2000
Fax: 212-980-4585
Web site: http://www.bloomberg.com

CEO: Michael R. Bloomberg
CFO: —
HR: Linda Norris
Type: Private

1998 Est. Sales: $1,500.0 million
1-Yr. Sales Change: 15.4%
Employees: 4,900
FYE: December

Bloomberg has its business bases covered. The company's chief financial information product is its Bloomberg proprietary terminals, which provide users with real-time, around-the-clock financial news, market data, and analysis. With about 100,000 terminals installed, Bloomberg ranks behind only #1 Reuters and #2 Bridge Information Systems in the market for such devices. Bloomberg also has a syndicated news service; publishes books and magazines; and disseminates business information via TV, radio, and the Web. The company also offers the Bloomberg Tradebook (an order-matching system). Founder and CEO Michael Bloomberg owns 72% of the company. Merrill Lynch owns 20%, and Bloomberg employees own the remainder.

KEY COMPETITORS
Bridge Information
Dow Jones
Reuters

 See pages 86–87 for a full profile of this company.

BLUE CROSS AND BLUE SHIELD ASSOCIATION

225 N. Michigan Ave.
Chicago, IL 60601
Phone: 312-297-6000
Fax: 312-297-6609
Web site: http://www.blueshield.com

CEO: Patrick G. Hays
CFO: Ralph Rambach
HR: Bill Colbourne
Type: Association

1998 Sales: $94,700.0 million
1-Yr. Sales Change: —
Employees: 150,000
FYE: December

The Blue Cross and Blue Shield Association coordinates 51 chapters that provide health insurance to 72 million Americans through health maintenance organizations, preferred provider organizations, point-of-service plans, and fee-for-service plans. The chapters administer Medicare plans for 38 million people. To compete with managed care companies that can reject poor insurance risks, Blues are merging within the national alliance, creating for-profit units, forming joint ventures with for-profit providers, or dropping their not-for-profit status and going public. Accordingly, the national association is increasingly acting as a brand manager and marketing organization for licensees.

KEY COMPETITORS
Aetna
Foundation Health Systems
Prudential

 See pages 88–89 for a full profile of this company.

BLUE CROSS AND BLUE SHIELD OF MASSACHUSETTS, INC.

100 Summer St.
Boston, MA 02110
Phone: 617-832-5000
Fax: 617-832-4832
Web site: http://www.bcbsma.com

CEO: William C. Van Faasen
CFO: Gary D. St. Hilaire
HR: Arthur E. Banks
Type: Not-for-profit

1998 Sales: $2,040.9 million
1-Yr. Sales Change: (3.9%)
Employees: 2,579
FYE: December

Hobbled by its past, Blue Cross and Blue Shield of Massachusetts (BCBSMA) is working its way back into the race. It offers indemnity insurance, HMOs, preferred provider organizations, Medicare extension, and nongroup and dental programs. It runs HMO Blue, HMO Blue New England, Blue Choice New England, and plans to launch Access Blue (HMO members may see specialists without referrals). For BCBSMA, under pressure in recent years, things are turning around; to refocus on health insurance, it has sold 10 health centers to physician-practice manager MedPartners. As part of its goal to form a New England regional alliance, BCBSMA has announced interest in affiliating with Blue Cross and Blue Shield of Rhode Island.

KEY COMPETITORS
Aetna
Anthem Insurance
Harvard Pilgrim

 See pages 90–91 for a full profile of this company.

BLUE CROSS AND BLUE SHIELD OF MISSOURI

1831 Chesnut St.
St. Louis, MO 63103
Phone: 314-923-4444
Fax: 314-923-5002
Web site: http://www.abcbs.com

CEO: John A. O'Rourke
CFO: Sandra Van Trease
HR: —
Type: Not-for-profit

1998 Sales: $767.5 million
1-Yr. Sales Change: 6.7%
Employees: 1,800
FYE: December

Blue Cross and Blue Shield of Missouri provides HMO, PPO, point-of-service, and medical indemnity coverage to St. Louis and 84 Missouri counties. As a not-for-profit insurer of last resort, the company receives state tax breaks, but it is also vulnerable to competition from for-profit care providers. In response, in 1994 it set up for-profit managed care company RightCHOICE, which serves more than 2 million people. As part of the process of converting to for-profit status, Blue Cross and Blue Shield of Missouri wants to transfer its 80% stake in RightCHOICE into a charitable foundation; RightCHOICE would then absorb the rest of the company and operate as a Blue Cross Blue Shield licensee.

KEY COMPETITORS
Aetna
Humana
UnitedHealth Group

BLUE CROSS BLUE SHIELD OF MICHIGAN

600 E. Lafayette Blvd.
Detroit, MI 48226
Phone: 313-225-9000
Fax: 313-225-5629
Web site: http://www.bcbsm.com

CEO: Richard E. Whitmer
CFO: Mark R. Bartlett
HR: George F. Francis
Type: Not-for-profit

1998 Sales: $8,431.8 million
1-Yr. Sales Change: 9.1%
Employees: —
FYE: December

Blue Cross Blue Shield of Michigan is one of the nation's top Blue Cross Blue Shield health insurance associations, serving more than 4.6 million members, including autoworkers for GM and Ford. The company's insurance plans include traditional indemnity, Blue Preferred (PPO), Blue Care Network (HMO), and Blue MedSave (medical savings plans). Blue Cross Blue Shield of Michigan also offers workers' compensation insurance, health assessment, and health care management services, and owns Preferred Provider Organization of Michigan, a private for-profit health care manager operating in four states.

KEY COMPETITORS
Aetna
Omnicare
UnitedHealth Group

See pages 92–93 for a full profile of this company.

BON SECOURS HEALTH SYSTEM, INC.

1505 Marriottsville Rd.
Marriottsville, MD 21104
Phone: 410-442-5511
Fax: 410-442-1082
Web site: http://www.bshsi.com

CEO: Christopher M. Carney
CFO: Michael W. Cottrell
HR: Virginia Rounsadille
Type: Not-for-profit

1998 Sales: $1,190.0 million
1-Yr. Sales Change: 8.4%
Employees: 20,000
FYE: August

This company succors its clients. Bon Secours Health System is a not-for-profit organization dedicated to providing health care to all, especially the poor and sick. The company was created in 1983 by the Sisters of Bon Secours, an international Catholic group established in 1824 in Paris. Bon Secours Health System is composed of 14 acute care hospitals, seven long-term-care facilities, and a psychiatric hospital. The system also operates clinics, assisted living facilities, hospices, and home health care services. The organization has facilities in Florida, Maryland, Michigan, Pennsylvania, South Carolina, and Virginia.

KEY COMPETITORS
Carilion Health System
Holy Cross
Johns Hopkins Health

BONNEVILLE POWER ADMINISTRATION

905 NE 11th Ave.
Portland, OR 97208
Phone: 503-230-3000
Fax: 503-230-3816
Web site: http://www.bpa.gov

CEO: Judy Johansen
CFO: Jim Curtis
HR: Roy Smithey
Type: Government-owned

1998 Sales: $2,313.3 million
1-Yr. Sales Change: 1.8%
Employees: 2,797
FYE: September

Bonneville Power Administration (BPA) rules as the power-master of the Pacific Northwest, even though it generates no power itself. An agency of the US Department of Energy, BPA owns a 15,000-mile high-voltage transmission grid that carries electricity to about half the people in the region. BPA's power is produced at 29 federally operated Columbia-Snake River Basin hydroelectric plants and one private nuclear facility. The agency sells power wholesale (mostly to public utilities in Idaho, Montana, Utah, and Washington state) and retail to business users. BPA's Energy Services group works to meet conservation responsibilities, including fish and wildlife protection, prescribed by federal law.

BOOZ, ALLEN & HAMILTON INC.

8283 Greensboro Dr.	CEO: Ralph W. Shrader	1999 Sales: $1,600.0 million
McLean, VA 22102	CFO: Martha Clark Goss	1-Yr. Sales Change: 14.3%
Phone: 703-902-5000	HR: Joni Bessler	Employees: 9,000
Fax: 703-902-3333	Type: Private	FYE: March
Web site: http://www.bah.com		

Booz, Allen & Hamilton has been on a big consulting bender for more than 80 years. Founded in 1914, the management and technology consulting firm has a staff of more than 9,000 across the US and more than 30 other countries. Its commercial unit provides a variety of productivity, management, and restructuring consultation services to companies in such industries as communications, energy, engineering, and health care. The technology business unit works primarily with the defense departments and other areas of the US government and other national governments, providing engineering and technology consulting and evaluation services.

KEY COMPETITORS
Andersen Consulting
McKinsey & Company
PricewaterhouseCoopers

See pages 94–95 for a full profile of this company.

BORDEN, INC.

180 E. Broad St.	CEO: C. Robert Kidder	1998 Sales: $1,399.7 million
Columbus, OH 43215	CFO: William H. Carter	1-Yr. Sales Change: (59.8%)
Phone: 614-225-4000	HR: Nancy A. Reardon	Employees: 4,200
Fax: —	Type: Private	FYE: December

No longer in the dairy business, Borden has sent Elsie the cow out to pasture. Borden has been selling several business lines, including dairy, Cracker Jack, and decorative products. Borden also sold Borden Foods and Wise Foods to BW Holdings, an affiliate of Kohlberg Kravis Roberts & Co., Borden's parent company. Borden is focusing on its consumer and industrial adhesives, coatings, and resins (Borden Chemical). Borden still manages Wise Foods and Borden Foods, as well as housewares maker Corning Consumer Products (Pyrex, Corelle, and Corning), which also is owned by BW Holdings.

KEY COMPETITORS
Ashland
ConAgra
Georgia-Pacific Group

See pages 96–97 for a full profile of this company.

BOSCOV'S DEPARTMENT STORES

4500 Perkiomen Ave.	CEO: Albert Boscov	1999 Sales: $1,000.0 million
Reading, PA 19606	CFO: Erwin Rosner	1-Yr. Sales Change: 18.2%
Phone: 610-779-2000	HR: Ed Elko	Employees: —
Fax: 610-370-3495	Type: Private	FYE: January
Web site: http://www.boscovs.com		

Boscov's Department Stores offers merchandise to meet almost any shopper's needs. Its stores sell men's, women's, and children's apparel, shoes, and accessories and also offer jewelry, cosmetics, housewares, appliances, toys, sporting goods, and stationery. Some stores also feature travel agencies, vision and hearing centers, hair salons, and restaurants. Boscov's operates almost 30 general department stores, primarily in malls across Pennsylvania and in Delaware, Maryland, New Jersey, and New York. Its Boscov's Receivable Finance subsidiary handles the store's charge card services. The company was founded in 1911 by Solomon Boscov in Reading, Pennsylvania, and is still owned by the Boscov family.

KEY COMPETITORS
Federated
J. C. Penney
Sears

BOSE CORPORATION

The Mountain	CEO: Amar G. Bose	1999 Est. Sales: $950.0 million
Framingham, MA 01701	CFO: Daniel A. Grady	1-Yr. Sales Change: 11.8%
Phone: 508-879-7330	HR: Stephen Pritchard	Employees: 4,000
Fax: 508-872-6541	Type: Private	FYE: March
Web site: http://www.bose.com		

Bose doesn't subscribe to the theory that bigger is better. The world's #1 speaker maker, with nearly 25% of the market, the company has been concentrating on making its speakers smaller to better blend into home and office decors. Bose makes a variety of audio products, including auto sound systems and speakers, home stereo speakers, music systems, PC sound systems, aviation headsets, and professional loudspeakers. Its critically acclaimed Wave radio (compact in size but not in sound) has been a success despite its $350 price tag. Bose makes its products in North America and Ireland and has nearly 60 stores worldwide. Founder Amar Bose, an MIT professor, owns the company.

KEY COMPETITORS
Bang & Olufsen Holding
Harman International
Matsushita

 See pages 98–99 for a full profile of this company.

THE BOSTON CONSULTING GROUP

Exchange Place, 31st Fl.	CEO: Carl Stern	1998 Sales: $730.0 million
Boston, MA 02109	CFO: David Parkinson	1-Yr. Sales Change: 11.5%
Phone: 617-973-1200	HR: Michael Armano	Employees: 3,000
Fax: 617-973-1399	Type: Private	FYE: December
Web site: http://www.bcg.com		

Perhaps Boston Consulting Group (BCG) could provide Woody Allen with his next movie idea: *Deconstructing Consulting*. The high-end corporate consulting firm provides strategic planning advice based on several of its own innovative ideas, such as "time-based competition" (rapid response to change) and "deconstruction" (an end to vertical integration). Founded in 1963, BCG was one of the first of the consulting firms to specialize in strategic consulting. BCG's clients include corporations in consumer goods, e-commerce, energy, finance, and telecommunications. BCG, an employee-owned company, has nearly 2,000 consultants working in more than 40 offices worldwide.

KEY COMPETITORS
Andersen Consulting
Booz, Allen
McKinsey & Company

 See pages 100–101 for a full profile of this company.

BOSTON UNIVERSITY

121 Bay State Rd.	CEO: Jon Westling	1997 Sales: $960.7 million
Boston, MA 02215	CFO: Kenneth Condon	1-Yr. Sales Change: 13.8%
Phone: 617-353-2000	HR: Manuel Monteiro	Employees: 7,760
Fax: 617-353-0088	Type: School	FYE: June
Web site: http://web.bu.edu		

Dream of reading Einstein's correspondence? You could get your chance at Boston University. Founded as a Methodist seminary in 1839, BU has more than 30,000 students at its campus on the banks of the Charles River. The private university has 15 graduate and undergraduate schools and colleges, including schools of education, law, management, medicine, social work, and theology. It also supports a number of special facilities and research programs, such as the Center for Space Physics, the Einstein Papers Project (which aims to publish 25 volumes of the physicist's writings), and the Center for Human Genetics. Three Nobel laureates — Elie Wiesel, Derek Walcott, and Saul Bellow — are among the faculty of 2,800.

BRIDGE INFORMATION SYSTEMS, INC.

3 World Financial Center, 27th Fl.
New York, NY 10281
Phone: 212-372-7100
Fax: 212-372-7158
Web site: http://www.bridge.com

CEO: Thomas M. Wendel
CFO: Daryl Rhodes
HR: Julie Brown
Type: Private

1998 Sales: $1,330.0 million
1-Yr. Sales Change: 232.5%
Employees: 4,500
FYE: December

Bridge Information Systems spans the gap between Reuters and Bloomberg as the world's #2 provider of financial information (based on number of customer installations). Targeting financial professionals, Bridge provides real-time and historical information from stock exchanges around the world and augments its content with news, transaction services, and workstations. The company's use of standard PCs, rather than proprietary systems, translates to lower costs, which allow Bridge to compete on price and expand beyond the traditional financial services markets. Bridge's owner, Welsh, Carson, Anderson & Stowe, has spent over $1 billion to assemble a new financial information company.

KEY COMPETITORS
Bloomberg
Reuters
Thomson Corporation

 See pages 102–103 for a full profile of this company.

BROOKSHIRE BROTHERS, LTD.

1201 Ellen Trout Dr.
Lufkin, TX 75901
Phone: 409-634-8155
Fax: 409-634-8646

CEO: R. A. Brookshire
CFO: Donny Johnson
HR: Tim Hale
Type: Private

1999 Est. Sales: $675.0 million
1-Yr. Sales Change: (3.6%)
Employees: 5,500
FYE: April

Offering everything from garden-fresh vegetables to gasoline, Brookshire Brothers is a family-owned grocery retailer with about 65 locations, most of which have on-site gas stations bearing the Conoco moniker. Founded in 1928, the company serves East Texas towns under the names Brookshire Brothers, Budget Chopper, and B&B Foods. Brookshire Brothers is not affiliated with the 130-store Brookshire Grocery Company of Tyler, Texas. The companies share a common ancestry, but a split between the founding brothers in the late 1930s resulted in the separate grocery chains.

KEY COMPETITORS
H-E-B
Kroger
Wal-Mart

BROOKSHIRE GROCERY COMPANY

1600 WSW Loop 323
Tyler, TX 75701
Phone: 903-534-3000
Fax: 903-534-2206
Web site: http://www.brookshires.com

CEO: James G. Hardin
CFO: Marvin Massey
HR: Tim Brookshire
Type: Private

1999 Est. Sales: $1,650.0 million
1-Yr. Sales Change: 6.5%
Employees: 10,700
FYE: September

By selling staples, specialties, and Southern hospitality, Brookshire Grocery has grown into a chain of more than 100 Brookshire's supermarkets and two dozen Super 1 Food stores in Texas, Arkansas, and Louisiana. The company also owns two distribution centers, a bakery, a dairy plant, and a large manufacturing facility. Brookshire's stores average about 40,000 sq. ft., while Super 1 Foods are warehouse-style, 60,000-sq.-ft stores. A handful of Brookshire Grocery's stores sell gasoline. Originally part of the Brookshire Brothers grocery chain (founded in 1928), the company separated from it in 1939. The Brookshire family is still among the company's owners.

KEY COMPETITORS
Albertson's
Randall's
Wal-Mart

BROWN AUTOMOTIVE GROUP LTD.

10287 Lee Hwy.	CEO: Charles S. Stringfellow	1997 Est. Sales: $2,200.0 million
Fairfax, VA 22030	CFO: Charles S. Stringfellow	1-Yr. Sales Change: 10.0%
Phone: 703-352-5555	HR: —	Employees: 3,700
Fax: 703-352-5591	Type: Private	FYE: December

Color them diverse. Brown Automotive Group, the largest auto dealer in the mid-Atlantic region, sells about a dozen makes of automobiles from about 20 dealerships in the Washington, DC, and Baltimore areas, as well as in Charlottesville and Richmond, Virginia. The company's new-car makes include Chrysler, General Motors, Honda, Mercedes, Nissan, and Toyota. It also sells used cars and operates five collision centers. Although the company was formed by William Schuiling in 1983, it traces its origins to Schuiling's purchase of one Brown Automotive's Pontiac dealership in Arlington, Virginia, in the early 1970s. The company also develops real estate in Maryland.

KEY COMPETITORS
Jim Koons Automotive
Ourisman Automotive
Rosenthal Automotive

BURT AUTOMOTIVE NETWORK

5200 S. Broadway	CEO: Lloyd G. Chavez	1998 Sales: $837.5 million
Englewood, CO 80110	CFO: John Held	1-Yr. Sales Change: (3.4%)
Phone: 800-535-2878	HR: Vicki Newton	Employees: 1,019
Fax: 303-789-6706	Type: Private	FYE: December
Web site: http://www.burt.com		

John Elway may have retired, but don't think that Burt Automotive Network has stopped trying to sack him. In the Denver area, Burt goes head-to-head with the John Elway AutoNation USA dealerships once owned by (and still named for) the former Broncos star. The state's largest privately held automobile dealer, Burt operates nine dealerships that sell new passenger vehicles from DaimlerChrysler, GM, Toyota, Subaru, Nissan, and Ford. It also sells commercial trucks and used cars and offers parts and repair services. Burt is owned by CEO Lloyd G. Chavez and partner A. J. Guanella and is one of the largest Hispanic-owned businesses in America. A salesman with Burt since 1951, Chavez bought the company in 1987.

KEY COMPETITORS
AutoNation
MNL, Inc.
Phil Long Automotive Group

CALCOT, LTD.

1601 E. Brundage Ln.	CEO: Thomas W. Smith	1998 Sales: $652.0 million
Bakersfield, CA 93307	CFO: Larry Nichols	1-Yr. Sales Change: (4.8%)
Phone: 661-327-5961	HR: Mary Joe Pasek	Employees: 155
Fax: 661-861-9870	Type: Cooperative	FYE: August
Web site: http://www.calcot.com		

With a crop of 2,200 member-owners in California, Arizona, and other western states, Calcot is one of the top cotton marketing cooperatives in the US. Members of the co-op, which started in 1927, grow premium-grade Upland and Pima cottons, among other varieties. More than 80% of Calcot's annual crops are exported to the Far East, particularly Indonesia, Japan, South Korea, and Taiwan. Its warehouses are capable of storing more than 1 million bales at a time. Calcot and three other major US co-ops make up Amcot, a worldwide cotton marketer. To compensate for a continued decrease in California cotton acreage and the effects of El Niño, Calcot has entered the raw almond business, selling them mostly overseas.

KEY COMPETITORS
Cargill
Dunavant Enterprises
Plains Cotton

CALIFORNIA DAIRIES INC.

11709 E. Artesia Blvd.	CEO: Gary Korsmeier	1999 Est. Sales: $1,600.0 million
Artesia, CA 90701	CFO: Joe Heffington	1-Yr. Sales Change: 45.5%
Phone: 562-865-1291	HR: Bette Hunt	Employees: —
Fax: 562-860-8633	Type: Cooperative	FYE: April

Herding dairies to give them greater "ag"-gregate strength has made California Dairies (formerly California Milk Producers) the second largest dairy cooperative in the US, after Dairy Farmers of America. It was formed when California Milk Producers merged with two other California cooperatives, Danish Creamery Association and San Joaquin Valley Dairymen. California Dairies' 700 members account for about 45% of its home state's milk production. It operates five plants that process milk, cheese, and other dairy products, including powdered milk and butter. The coop also markets the milk its members produce and handles tasks such as accounting, lobbying, testing, and transporting for them.

KEY COMPETITORS
Dairy Farmers of America
Dean Foods
Plains Cotton

CALIFORNIA PUBLIC EMPLOYEES' RETIREMENT SYSTEM

Lincoln Plaza, 400 P St.	CEO: James E. Burton	1999 Sales: $27,514.2 million
Sacramento, CA 95814	CFO: Vincent P. Brown	1-Yr. Sales Change: 15.0%
Phone: 916-326-3000	HR: Tom Pettey	Employees: 1,247
Fax: 916-558-4001	Type: Government-owned	FYE: June
Web site: http://www.calpers.ca.gov		

You don't need calipers to measure CalPERS, the California Public Employees' Retirement System. It's the largest public pension system in the US, with about $158 billion in assets. Serving 2,400 government agencies, CalPERS manages retirement and health plans for more than a million California employees and retirees and their beneficiaries. An active investor, CalPERS has become a voice to reckon with in the world of corporate governance; the clout-wielding organization publishes an annual list of the US's worst-performing companies. CalPERS is a recognized trendsetter in negotiating for such services as insurance; rates established by CalPERS serve as benchmarks for other employers.

 See pages 104–105 for a full profile of this company.

CALIFORNIA STATE LOTTERY COMMISSION

600 N. 10th St.	CEO: Melissa Meith	1998 Sales: $2,294.0 million
Sacramento, CA 95814	CFO: Dennis Sequeira	1-Yr. Sales Change: 11.2%
Phone: 916-324-9639	HR: Loretta Stillwell	Employees: 634
Fax: 916-327-0489	Type: Government-owned	FYE: June
Web site: http://www.calottery.com		

At least all the money you lose playing the lottery goes to a good cause. The California State Lottery Commission operates games of chance, including the six-number SuperLotto game, as well as a variety of other number and scratch-off games. Californians also can purchase tickets to win a chance to appear on *Big Spin 2000*, a television show on which contestants spin a wheel and win cash prizes. State law requires that at least 50% of lottery ticket sales must be used to award prizes, at least 34% must go to the California public school system (some $11 billion since 1985), and a maximum of 16% can be used for expenses. The Commission sells its games through more than 19,000 outlets across the state.

KEY COMPETITORS
Multi-State Lottery
Oregon State Lottery
Plains Cotton

THE CALIFORNIA STATE UNIVERSITY

400 Golden Shore, Ste. 330	CEO: Charles B. Reed	1998 Sales: $2,611.9 million
Long Beach, CA 90802	CFO: Richard P. West	1-Yr. Sales Change: 3.6%
Phone: 562-985-2740	HR: Jackie McCalain	Employees: 39,000
Fax: 562-951-4986	Type: School	FYE: June
Web site: http://www.calstate.edu		

The California State University (CSU) is neck and neck with New York as the nation's largest university system. With an enrollment policy that admits California high school graduates who finish in the top third of their classes, CSU's student body has grown to more than 365,000. The system has campuses in 23 cities, including Bakersfield, Los Angeles, San Francisco, and San Jose. CSU emphasizes teacher training and is responsible for 60% of the state's educators. To prepare for a student population expected to nearly double by 2010, CSU is focusing on distance education (via teleconferencing and the World Wide Web) and experimenting with year-round schooling.

 See pages 106–107 for a full profile of this company.

CALTEX CORPORATION

125 E. John Carpenter Fwy.	CEO: Jock McKenzie	1998 Sales: $17,174.0 million
Irving, TX 75062-2794	CFO: Malcolm J. McAuley	1-Yr. Sales Change: (6.4%)
Phone: 972-830-1000	HR: Stephen H. Nichols	Employees: 7,900
Fax: 972-830-1081	Type: Joint venture	FYE: December
Web site: http://www.caltex.com		

When you cross California and Texas, you get a long drive, a culture war, and Caltex, the international petroleum refining and marketing joint venture held equally by US oil giants Chevron and Texaco. Caltex, formerly Caltex Petroleum, operates primarily in Africa, the Asia/Pacific region, and the Middle East. The company has stakes in more than 500 ocean terminals and depots, 13 fuel refineries, 17 lubricant-blending plants, six asphalt plants, and two lubricant refineries; it sells 1.5 million barrels of crude oil and petroleum products per day. Caltex has 8,000 retail outlets, including 425 Star Mart convenience stores. The company was founded in 1936. They recently moved their headquarters to Singapore, but maintain a US presence with offices near Dallas.

KEY COMPETITORS
BP Amoco
Exxon Mobil
Royal Dutch/Shell

 See pages 108–109 for a full profile of this company.

CALVIN KLEIN INC.

205 W. 39th St., 4th Fl.	CEO: Barry Schwartz	1998 Est. Sales: $160.0 million
New York, NY 10018	CFO: Richard Martin	1-Yr. Sales Change: 6.7%
Phone: 212-719-2600	HR: —	Employees: 1,000
Fax: 212-730-4818	Type: Private	FYE: December

Known for its simple (but not inexpensive) styles, Calvin Klein offers clothes — ranging from streetwise to sophisticated — as well as fragrances and accessories. About 90% of its sales come from licensing its well-known name to manufacturers of jeans, underwear, and fragrances, including apparel maker Warnaco. Calvin Klein-branded products make over $5 billion in global retail a year. The company makes its flagship ready-to-wear collection of women's clothing. Calvin Klein also licenses more than 40 retail stores worldwide. VC Calvin Klein and chairman and CEO Barry Schwartz, who founded the company in 1968, are the sole owners, but they are shopping for a partner or buyer.

KEY COMPETITORS
Donna Karan
Polo
Tommy Hilfiger

 See pages 110–111 for a full profile of this company.

C&S WHOLESALE GROCERS INC.

Old Ferry Rd.
Brattleboro, VT 05301
Phone: 802-257-4371
Fax: 802-257-6727

CEO: Richard B. Cohen
CFO: Brenda Edgerton
HR: Mitch Davis
Type: Private

1999 Sales: $6,050.0 million
1-Yr. Sales Change: 18.2%
Employees: 4,000
FYE: September

C&S Wholesale Grocers, one of the US's largest food wholesalers, delivers groceries to more than 4,000 independent supermarkets, major supermarket chains, and mass marketers such as Wal-Mart, military bases, and wholesale clubs, from Maine to Maryland. As a full-line distributor, it delivers everything a supermarket needs; it sells more than 53,000 products, including general groceries, produce, dairy products, deli products, bakery goods, flowers, frozen foods, meats, seafood, beverages, and a variety of nonfood goods. It has facilities in Connecticut, Maryland, Massachusetts, New Jersey, New York, and Vermont. Chairman, president, and CEO Richard Cohen owns the company, which his grandfather started in 1918.

KEY COMPETITORS
Di Giorgio
Fleming Companies
SUPERVALU

See pages 112–113 for a full profile of this company.

CAREGROUP, INC.

375 Longwood Ave., 3rd Fl.
Boston, MA 02215
Phone: 617-975-5000
Fax: 617-975-6065
Web site: http://www.caregroup.org

CEO: James L. Reinertsen
CFO: Eugene C. Wallace
HR: Laura Avakian
Type: Private

1998 Sales: $1,187.9 million
1-Yr. Sales Change: 5.1%
Employees: 13,362
FYE: September

Thanks to CareGroup, there's well-being in Beantown. A 1997 agglomeration of Boston-area health care organizations, CareGroup provides care in more than 30 Massachusetts communities through six Boston-area hospitals. Beth Israel Deaconess, its principal institution, suffered traumatic losses while merging its clinical operations. CareGroup also includes specialty clinics, outpatient facilities, and research facilities. Despite the rejection of a proposed merger with Rhode Island's Care New England, CareGroup continues to look for ways to expand. Through an alliance intended to bolster their power with HMOs, CareGroup Provider Service Network and Lahey Clinic serve more than 400,000 managed-care patients.

KEY COMPETITORS
Baystate Health Systems
Columbia/HCA
Partners HealthCare

CARGILL, INCORPORATED

15407 McGinty Rd. West
Wayzata, MN 55391
Phone: 612-742-7575
Fax: 612-742-7393
Web site: http://www.cargill.com

CEO: Warren R. Staley
CFO: Robert L. Lumpkins
HR: Nancy Siska
Type: Private

1999 Sales: $50,000.0 million
1-Yr. Sales Change: (2.7%)
Employees: 84,000
FYE: May

Private it may be, but when you're Cargill's size it's awfully hard to hide. Cargill is the US's largest private corporation, with diversified operations including commodity trading of grain, coffee, cotton, rubber, sugar, and petroleum; financial trading; food processing; futures brokering; seed, feed, and fertilizer production; and steelmaking. The company is the #1 US grain exporter. Cargill is the #2 US salt company, behind Rohm and Haas (Morton's), and its Excel unit slaughters about one-fifth of US cattle. Descendants of the founders own about 85% of Cargill. The company has operations in about 60 countries, and it trades in about 130 others.

KEY COMPETITORS
ADM
ConAgra
Corn Products International

See pages 114–115 for a full profile of this company.

CARILION HEALTH SYSTEM

1212 3rd St.	CEO: Thomas L. Robertson	1998 Sales: $780.0 million
Roanoke, VA 24016	CFO: Donald E. Lorton	1-Yr. Sales Change: 11.3%
Phone: 540-981-7900	HR: Houston L. Bell	Employees: 8,500
Fax: 540-344-5716	Type: Not-for-profit	FYE: September
Web site: http://www.carilion.com		

As Virginia's largest health care network, Carilion Health System rings true. The system includes 11 hospitals, a nursing home, and a cancer center. Its Medical Center for Children in Roanoke serves as a regional pediatric referral site, and its Carilion Behavioral Health has become western Virginia's largest psychiatric service network. Through its 50%-owned, for-profit Carilion Health Plans subsidiary, the system now markets its own HMO and point-of-service health care plans and also two insurance plans. Carilion also offers hospice and home care services. Affiliated institutions include an athletic club and two wellness centers.

KEY COMPETITORS
Columbia/HCA
Mid Atlantic Medical
Sentara Health

CARLSON COMPANIES, INC.

701 Carlson Pkwy.	CEO: Marilyn Carlson Nelson	1998 Est. Sales: $7,800.0 million
Minnetonka, MN 55459	CFO: Martyn R. Redgrave	1-Yr. Sales Change: 18.2%
Phone: 612-540-5000	HR: Terry M. Butorac	Employees: 147,000
Fax: 612-449-2219	Type: Private	FYE: December
Web site: http://www.carlson.com		

Founded by Curtis Carlson as the Gold Bond Stamp Company in 1938, Carlson Companies is licking the competition. Most sales come from the Carlson Leisure Group, one of the US' largest leisure travel services providers. The Carlson Wagonlit Travel joint venture with France's Accor is the #3 corporate travel agency (after American Express and Japan Travel Bureau) and has more than 3,000 locations worldwide. Carlson Hospitality Worldwide runs or franchises about 550 Radisson Hotels, Regent International Hotels, and Country Inns & Suites. Carlson is spinning off a minority stake in its restaurant operations. Carlson Marketing Group provides marketing consulting and training services.

KEY COMPETITORS
American Express
Brinker
Marriott International

 See pages 116–117 for a full profile of this company.

CARLSON WAGONLIT TRAVEL

701 Carlson Pkwy.	CEO: Jon Madonna	1998 Sales: $11,000.0 million
Minnetonka, MN 55459	CFO: Clive Hole	1-Yr. Sales Change: 3.8%
Phone: 612-212-5000	HR: —	Employees: 20,100
Fax: 612-212-1288	Type: Joint venture	FYE: December
Web site: http://www.carlsonwagonlit.com		

Call it the last emperor of the travel industry. Carlson Wagonlit Travel, descended from both the oldest US travel agency chain and the creator of the Orient Express, manages business travel from about 3,000 travel offices worldwide. The company is the third-largest travel firm in the world behind co-leaders American Express and Japan Travel Bureau (virtually tied for #1). It is co-owned by the US firm Carlson Companies (whose US leisure and franchise operations also fall under the Carlson Wagonlit brand) and France's Accor Group. Carlson Wagonlit has locations in more than 140 countries.

KEY COMPETITORS
American Express
Japan Travel Bureau
WorldTravel

See pages 118–119 for a full profile of this company.

CARONDELET HEALTH SYSTEM

13801 Riverport Dr., Ste. 300
St. Louis, MO 63043
Phone: 314-770-0333
Fax: 314-770-0444
Web site: http://www.chs-stl.com

CEO: Gary Christiansen
CFO: James Green
HR: Nancy Heet
Type: Not-for-profit

1998 Sales: $961.0 million
1-Yr. Sales Change: 9.6%
Employees: 15,500
FYE: June

Through a network of over 20 health care facilities, Carondelet Health System carries on its healing mission in some 10 US states, including Arizona, Missouri, and California. Besides hospitals such as St. Joseph Health System in Kansas City, Missouri, the system also operates skilled nursing care facilities, behavioral treatment centers, hospice care facilities, and home health service provider organizations. The Sisters of St. Joseph Carondelet, a Catholic entity whose members emigrated from France in 1836 and founded St. Mary's Hospital in Arizona in 1880, still sponsors the Carondelet Health System.

KEY COMPETITORS
Catholic Health Initiatives
Columbia/HCA
Tenet Healthcare

CARPENTER CO.

5016 Monument Ave.
Richmond, VA 23220
Phone: 804-359-0800
Fax: 804-353-0694
Web site: http://www.carpenter.com

CEO: Stanley F. Pauley
CFO: Greg Smith
HR: —
Type: Private

1998 Sales: $950.0 million
1-Yr. Sales Change: 8.1%
Employees: 6,500
FYE: December

It's a cushy job for Carpenter Co., making polyurethane foam and polyester fibers used as cushioning by the automotive, bedding, floor covering, and furniture industries, among others. The company started out as a distributor of foam rubber; it now manufactures its raw materials (urethane chemicals) for its own use and for sale to companies that make insulation, packaging material, and tire fill. Carpenter has manufacturing facilities throughout the US, Canada, Mexico, France, Germany, and the UK. The company sells its consumer products, which include comforters, mattress pads, and pillows, through retailers.

KEY COMPETITORS
Foamex
Sealed Air
Trace International Holdings

CARPET CO-OP ASSOCIATION OF AMERICA

1765 The Exchange, Ste. 400
Atlanta, GA 30339
Phone: 770-984-9791
Fax: 770-984-9771
Web site: http://www.carpetone.com

CEO: Alan Greenberg
CFO: Ed Muchnick
HR: —
Type: Cooperative

1998 Sales: $2,450.0 million
1-Yr. Sales Change: 22.5%
Employees: 265
FYE: September

You might say Carpet Co-op Association of America's business is "floor"ishing with more than 1,000 member stores worldwide. The cooperative's members, operating under the Carpet One name, market major name-brand carpets and floor coverings in Australia, Canada, Guam, and the US. Carpet One is the largest retail co-op in North America and the exclusive US marketer of Bigelow-brand carpet. Howard Brodsky and Alan Greenberg, who are co-chairmen and co-CEOs, started the company in 1985 to help independent carpet sellers command more buying power and improve marketing as they battled larger retailers for market share.

KEY COMPETITORS
Abbey Carpet
Flooring America, Inc.
Home Depot

CARQUEST CORP.

12596 W. Bayaud Ave., Ste. 400	CEO: Peter Kornafel	1998 Est. Sales: $1,400.0 million
Lakewood, CO 80228	CFO: —	1-Yr. Sales Change: 7.7%
Phone: 303-984-2000	HR: Louise Veasman	Employees: 35,000
Fax: 303-984-2001	Type: Private	FYE: December
Web site: http://www.carquest.com		

CARQUEST is driven by its mission to get its parts into your car. The replacement auto parts distribution group is owned by its nine member warehouse distributors (the largest is North Carolina-based General Parts). The CARQUEST group includes a network of about 60 distribution centers serving more than 4,000 retail outlets in the US and Canada. Focusing on professional installers, the company sells its own line of auto parts (made by Moog Automotive, Dana, Gabriel, and others). Auto repair shops can join CARQUEST's Tech-Net Professional Service program, which provides members with a marketing plan and other services, as well as a diagnostic telephone hotline.

KEY COMPETITORS
AutoZone
Pep Boys

 See pages 120–121 for a full profile of this company.

CATHOLIC HEALTH EAST

14 Campus Blvd., Ste. 300	CEO: Daniel F. Russell	1998 Sales: $3,800.0 million
Newtown Square, PA 19073	CFO: C. Kent Russell	1-Yr. Sales Change: 26.7%
Phone: 610-355-2000	HR: George Longshore	Employees: 45,000
Fax: 610-355-2050	Type: Not-for-profit	FYE: December
Web site: http://www.chenet.org		

Catholic Health East is the #3 religious health system in the US, behind Ascension Health (formerly Daughters of Charity National Health System) and Catholic Health Initiatives. The network is a product of the consolidation of Eastern Mercy Health System of Pennsylvania, Franciscan Sisters of Allegany Health System of Florida, and Sisters of Providence Health System of Massachusetts. These nuns are on the run to merge as a way of preserving their charitable mission in the face of industry consolidation and declining membership in religious orders. The system offers health care through more than 30 hospitals, about 30 nursing homes, and 20 independent- and assisted-living facilities, primarily on the East Coast.

KEY COMPETITORS
Ascension Health
Columbia/HCA
Foundation Health Systems

 See pages 122–123 for a full profile of this company.

CATHOLIC HEALTH INITIATIVES

1999 Broadway, Ste. 2605	CEO: Patricia A. Cahill	1999 Sales: $5,000.0 million
Denver, CO 80202	CFO: Geraldine M. Hoyler	1-Yr. Sales Change: 11.1%
Phone: 303-298-9100	HR: Michael Fordyce	Employees: —
Fax: 303-298-9690	Type: Not-for-profit	FYE: June

Giant not-for-profit Catholic Health Initiatives is an amalgamation of three Roman Catholic health care systems (Catholic Health Corporation of Omaha, Nebraska; Franciscan Health System of Aston, Pennsylvania; and Sisters of Charity Health Care Systems of Cincinnati). The #2 Catholic health system behind Ascension Health, Catholic Health Initiatives is sponsored by 12 different congregations and serves more than 70 communities in 22 states. Catholic Health Initiatives operates about 70 hospitals and more than 50 long-term-care facilities; it has formed an alliance with the University of Pennsylvania Health System.

KEY COMPETITORS
Beverly Enterprises
Columbia/HCA
Tenet Healthcare

 See pages 124–125 for a full profile of this company.

CATHOLIC HEALTHCARE NETWORK

155 E. 56th St., 2nd Fl.
New York, NY 10022
Phone: 212-752-7300
Fax: 212-752-7547
Web site: http://www.chcn.org

CEO: Mary Healey-Sedutto
CFO: Gerard Vilucci
HR: Exzera Hope
Type: Not-for-profit

1997 Sales: $5,850.5 million
1-Yr. Sales Change: —
Employees: —
FYE: December

While it may not have the high profile of the late Mother Teresa, New York's Catholic Healthcare Network is nonetheless dedicated to providing high-quality health care (rooted in the values of the Catholic Church) to people who need it, regardless of their income or status. The network includes more than 45 hospitals, nursing homes, and affiliated health care providers (such as children's homes and medical centers). Catholic Healthcare Network is co-sponsored by the Archdiocese of New York and the Sisters of Charity of Saint Vincent de Paul of New York.

KEY COMPETITORS
New York City Health and Hospitals
North Shore-Long Island Jewish Health System
Tenet Healthcare

CATHOLIC HEALTHCARE PARTNERS

615 Elsinore Place
Cincinnati, OH 45202
Phone: 513-639-2800
Fax: 513-639-2700
Web site: http://www.health-partners.org

CEO: Michael D. Connelly
CFO: Jay S. Herron
HR: Rick Frederick
Type: Not-for-profit

1998 Sales: $1,820.9 million
1-Yr. Sales Change: 2.4%
Employees: 29,000
FYE: December

Catholic Healthcare Partners offers health care services in Indiana, Kentucky, Michigan, Ohio, Pennsylvania, and Tennessee through the more than 90 corporations that make up the system. Facilities include 23 hospitals, 15 long-term-care facilities, eight residential projects (HUD housing for elderly and retirement communities), and rehabilitation, outpatient, and surgery centers. The system also includes physician practices, a preferred provider organization, and such services as hospice and home health care. The not-for-profit system is co-sponsored by the Sisters of Mercy in Cincinnati and in Dallas, Pennsylvania; The Sisters of the Humility of Mary in Villa Maria, Pennsylvania; and Covenant Health Systems.

KEY COMPETITORS
Columbia/HCA
Franciscan Health Partnership
Universal Health Services

CATHOLIC HEALTHCARE WEST

1700 Montgomery St., Ste. 300
San Francisco, CA 94111
Phone: 415-438-5500
Fax: 415-438-5724
Web site: http://www.chw.edu

CEO: Phyllis Hughes
CFO: Jack Burgis
HR: —
Type: Not-for-profit

1999 Sales: $4,400.0 million
1-Yr. Sales Change: 33.3%
Employees: 38,000
FYE: June

Catholic Healthcare West has found it takes a lot of *nunsense* to be California's #2 hospital network (behind Tenet Healthcare). Catholic Healthcare West's system stretches from Redding to San Diego and into Arizona and Nevada. It includes more than 45 acute care hospitals, seven medical practice groups, two retirement homes, and an alliance with ScrippsHealth, a major San Diego HMO. The organization (formed when the hospital operations of several Roman Catholic women's religious orders consolidated, along with some non-Catholic community hospitals) has discovered that it is not holier than thou: Like for-profit hospitals, it has felt the squeeze of rising health care costs and capped health care spending.

KEY COMPETITORS
Columbia/HCA
Kaiser Foundation
Sutter Health

 See pages 126–127 for a full profile of this company.

CENEX HARVEST STATES COOPERATIVES

5500 Cenex Dr.	CEO: Noel K. Estenson	1999 Sales: $6,434.5 million
Inver Grove Heights, MN 55077	CFO: Thomas F. Baker	1-Yr. Sales Change: 14.7%
Phone: 651-451-5151	HR: Allen J. Anderson	Employees: 2,576
Fax: 651-451-5568	Type: Cooperative	FYE: August
Web site: http://www.cenexharveststates.com		

Cenex Harvest States Cooperatives likes to go with the grain, not against it. Formed by Harvest States' 1998 merger with CENEX, the co-op represents some 300,000 farmers in 17 central and western states. It's the US's #2 agricultural co-op. Grain trading is the co-op's primary business. The co-op also processes soybeans into products such as mayonnaise, margarine, and animal feed. Its wheat-milling operations grind durum and semolina wheat into flour used mainly for pastas. The co-op also offers crop-protection products, plant food, fuel, and insurance; it runs about 160 farm supply stores. A planned merger with Farmland Industries fell through, but Cenex officers vowed to pursue some form of consolidation.

KEY COMPETITORS
ADM
Cargill
ConAgra

 See pages 128–129 for a full profile of this company.

CENTEON L.L.C.

1020 1st Ave.	CEO: Ruedi Waeger	1998 Est. Sales: $1,000.0 million
King of Prussia, PA 19406	CFO: Perry Premdas	1-Yr. Sales Change: 10.6%
Phone: 610-878-4000	HR: Ray Reagan	Employees: 4,700
Fax: 610-878-4009	Type: Joint venture	FYE: December
Web site: http://www.centeon.com		

Take away the red and white blood cells from blood and you get plasma, a protein-rich fluid. Centeon, through its Centeon Bio-Services unit, is among the world's largest fully integrated plasma collection companies. Centeon's plasma protein products are used routinely during surgery, in dialysis, and in the treatment of a range of other disorders, including immune deficiencies, trauma, and burns. Centeon (a US-based joint venture between Rhône-Poulenc Rorer and Germany's Hoechst AG, both of which are part of life sciences group Aventis) has the critical mass to keep rolling while increasing its research.

KEY COMPETITORS
Baxter
Nabi
Serologicals

CENTRA, INC.

12225 Stephen Rd.	CEO: Manuel Moroun	1998 Sales: $725.0 million
Warren, MI 48089	CFO: Norman E. Harned	1-Yr. Sales Change: —
Phone: 810-939-7000	HR: —	Employees: 4,000
Fax: 810-527-0105	Type: Private	FYE: —
Web site: http://www.centraltransportint.com		

At the center of CenTra is the secretive Manuel Moroun, who controls the holding company founded by his father, Tufick, in the 1940s. CenTra's holdings include Central Transport International, a privately held less-than-truckload carrier with 150 terminals. Along with Canadian affiliate Central-McKinlay International, the trucking firm serves major markets in North America. CenTra also owns a minority stake in Chandler Insurance (which US courts have required it to divest) and Ambassador Bridge, a toll bridge linking Detroit and Windsor, Ontario. Moroun has settled a seven-year-old lawsuit with his sisters, who had accused their brother of "shareholder oppression" and shutting them out of the family business.

KEY COMPETITORS
Consolidated Freightways
Roadway Express
Yellow Corporation

CENTRAL NATIONAL-GOTTESMAN INC.

3 Manhattanville Rd.	CEO: Kenneth L. Wallach	1998 Sales: $1,600.0 million
Purchase, NY 10577	CFO: Joshua J. Eisenstein	1-Yr. Sales Change: (20.0%)
Phone: 914-696-9000	HR: Louise Caputo	Employees: 900
Fax: 914-696-1066	Type: Private	FYE: December

Writers put the fiction in pulp fiction, but Central National-Gottesman provides the pulp. One of the world's largest paper agents, the company distributes pulp, paper, lumber, and plywood in about 80 countries worldwide. Central National-Gottesman also engages in joint investments in its core industry with such partners as Beloit and Gaylord Container. Some of the company's activities center around managing investments for its owners, the secretive Gottesman family. Since the mid-1980s Central National-Gottesman has reduced its interests in many companies to below the 5% SEC reporting limit or made its investments in conjunction with other large companies. Central National-Gottesman was founded in 1886.

KEY COMPETITORS
International Paper
Smurfit-Stone Container
Unisource

CERTIFIED GROCERS MIDWEST, INC.

1 Certified Dr.	CEO: James E. Bradley	1998 Sales: $710.0 million
Hodgkins, IL 60525	CFO: —	1-Yr. Sales Change: (0.7%)
Phone: 708-579-2100	HR: Marcy Meister	Employees: 800
Fax: 708-579-9874	Type: Cooperative	FYE: August

If you shop at a Certi-Saver, you can be certain your groceries came from Certified Grocers Midwest (CGM). CGM is a cooperative wholesaler of baked goods, fresh produce, meat products, and health and beauty aids; it distributes both brand-name and private-label goods. The cooperative also provides support services such as advertising, market research, site analysis, and financial assistance to its more than 260 member stores, which operate under the Certi-Saver Supermarket name. In addition, CGM serves approximately 300 nonmember stores. The cooperative was established in 1940 and covers the Upper Midwest-Great Lakes region, including the Chicago area.

KEY COMPETITORS
Central Grocers Cooperative
Nash Finch
Roundy's

CERULEAN COMPANIES, INC.

3350 Peachtree Rd. NE	CEO: Richard D. Shirk	1998 Sales: $1,334.1 million
Atlanta, GA 30326	CFO: John A. Harris	1-Yr. Sales Change: (13.5%)
Phone: 404-842-8423	HR: Eula Austin	Employees: 2,494
Fax: 404-842-8801	Type: Private	FYE: December
Web site: http://www.cerulean-companies.com		

Cerulean Companies has the Blues in Georgia — Blue Cross and Blue Shield. Cerulean, which has agreed to be acquired by WellPoint Health Networks, was formed as the holding company for Georgia Blue when it became a for-profit company in 1996. Through three subsidiaries (HMO Georgia, Greater Georgia Life Insurance, and Group Benefits of Georgia) Georgia Blue offers a variety of insurance plans, including HMOs, preferred provider organizations, point-of-service network plans, and group life, indemnity, accidental death, and disability insurance. It also operates five community health partnership networks. Founded in 1937, Georgia Blue has more than 750,000 insurance contracts with about 1.6 million members.

KEY COMPETITORS
Aetna
Prudential
UnitedHealth Group

CF INDUSTRIES, INC.

1 Salem Lake Dr.
Long Grove, IL 60047
Phone: 847-438-9500
Fax: 847-438-0211
Web site: http://www.cfindustries.com

CEO: Robert C. Liuzzi
CFO: Stephen R. Wilson
HR: William G. Eppel
Type: Cooperative

1998 Sales: $1,200.3 million
1-Yr. Sales Change: (16.2%)
Employees: 1,600
FYE: December

The grass is always greener at CF Industries. Organized in 1946 as Central Farmers Fertilizer Company, CF Industries is an interregional agricultural cooperative that manufactures and markets fertilizers, including nitrogen products (ammonia, granular urea, and UAN solutions), phosphates, and potash (potassium) products to its members in 48 states and two Canadian provinces. The co-op is owned by nine regional agricultural co-ops, including GROWMARK, Land O'Lakes, and CENEX Harvest States Cooperative. CF Industries operates nitrogen and phosphate plants, a phosphate mine, and a network of distribution terminals and storage facilities by which it offers products worldwide.

KEY COMPETITORS
IMC Global
Potash Corporation
Terra Industries

CH2M HILL COMPANIES, LTD.

6060 S. Willow Dr.
Greenwood Village, CO 80111
Phone: 303-771-0900
Fax: 303-846-2231
Web site: http://www.ch2m.com

CEO: Ralph R. Peterson
CFO: Samuel H. Iapalucci
HR: Fred Berry
Type: Private

1998 Sales: $931.9 million
1-Yr. Sales Change: 1.6%
Employees: 7,000
FYE: December

CH2M's name is a company (not a chemical) compound derived from the initials of its founders — Cornell, Howland and Hayes (2 H's), and Merryfield — plus Hill, from its first merger. CH2M Hill Companies offers its clients engineering consulting services related to the environment, industrial facility design, transportation, and water treatment. Specialties include sewer and waste-treatment design, hazardous-waste cleanup, and transportation projects such as highways and bridges. The firm has more than 120 offices on six continents. Subsidiary CH2M Gore & Storrie is Canada's largest water/environmental engineering firm. Employees own CH2M Hill, which was founded in Corvallis, Oregon, in 1946.

KEY COMPETITORS
Bechtel
Dames & Moore
Montgomery Watson

CHARMER INDUSTRIES, INC.

1950 48th St.
Long Island City, NY 11105
Phone: 718-726-2500
Fax: 718-726-3101

CEO: Herman Merinoff
CFO: Steve Meresmen
HR: Annette Perry
Type: Private

1998 Est. Sales: $670.0 million
1-Yr. Sales Change: (0.7%)
Employees: 1,300
FYE: December

Not easily shaken by competition, Charmer Industries has not stirred from its top spot as New York State's #1 wine and liquor wholesaler. It is the state's exclusive distributor for House of Seagram (a Seagram subsidiary), Schieffelin & Sommerset (a joint venture between United Distillers and Moët-Hennessy), and Brown-Forman (maker of Jack Daniel's and Southern Comfort). Charmer also owns Connecticut Distributors and Washington (DC) Wholesale Liquor. The company is owned by CEO Herman Merinoff, who also holds a majority interest in Maryland-based Sunbelt Beverage. He owns 5.5% of beverage maker Todhunter, much of which he acquired through that company's contentious acquisition of Blair Importers.

KEY COMPETITORS
Peerless Importers
Southern Wine & Spirits
Young's Market

CHEMCENTRAL CORPORATION

7050 W. 71st St.	CEO: David W. Courtney	1998 Sales: $880.0 million
Bedford Park, IL 60499	CFO: Lloyd Tarrh	1-Yr. Sales Change: 0.6%
Phone: 708-594-7000	HR: —	Employees: 918
Fax: 708-594-6328	Type: Private	FYE: December
Web site: http://www.chemcentral.com		

A company of substance, CHEMCENTRAL is one of the top three chemical distributors in North America, after Van Waters & Rogers and Ashland Chemicals. Key markets for its wide range of chemicals include the adhesives, coatings, printing, selants, rubber and plastics compounding, and consumer products industries. CHEMCENTRAL emphasizes the local approach to sales and distribution with nearly 60 distribution facilities across North America. One of the largest chemical distributors in Mexico, the company has moved into South America through a joint venture with Holland Chemicals. Founded in 1926 as the William J. Hough Company, the company originally supplied naval stores.

KEY COMPETITORS
Ashland
Cytec Industries
Hercules

CHICK-FIL-A INC.

5200 Buffington Rd.	CEO: S. Truett Cathy	1998 Sales: $798.6 million
Atlanta, GA 30349	CFO: James B. McCabe	1-Yr. Sales Change: 18.8%
Phone: 404-765-8000	HR: Huie H. Woods	Employees: 30,000
Fax: 404-765-8971	Type: Private	FYE: December
Web site: http://www.chick-fil-a.com		

Beloved by bovines, Chick-fil-A is the nation's #3 fast-food chicken restaurant chain (behind TRICON's KFC and AFC's Popeyes/Churchs). It serves chicken entrees, sandwiches, and salads at some 850 stores in nearly 40 US states and in South Africa. Although more than half its restaurants are located in shopping malls, the company is focusing most of its expansion efforts on freestanding outlets. Chick-fil-A also licenses units inside hospitals, schools, airports, and other non-traditional locations. Founder and owner S. Truett Cathy, a devout Baptist, closes his stores on Sundays and boasts of a nearly perfect management retention rate.

KEY COMPETITORS
AFC Enterprises
KFC
McDonald's

THE CITY UNIVERSITY OF NEW YORK

535 E. 80th St.	CEO: —	1998 Sales: $1,784.0 million
New York, NY 10021	CFO: Sherry Brabbam	1-Yr. Sales Change: 3.2%
Phone: 212-794-5555	HR: James Demby	Employees: 28,000
Fax: 212-794-5590	Type: School	FYE: June
Web site: http://www.cuny.edu		

Do students at City University of New York (CUNY) give their teachers bigger apples? The college has 21 campuses in the New York City metropolitan area and is the US's largest urban university system. CUNY's enrollment of undergraduates and graduates exceeds 200,000. The university also teaches some 150,000 students in adult- and continuing-education programs. CUNY has 10 senior colleges, six community colleges, a doctoral-granting graduate school, a four-year technical school, and medical and law schools. Its 900-plus programs range from specialized, career-oriented courses to traditional liberal arts curricula. The school's mission is to serve a broad range of students, especially new immigrants.

See pages 130–131 for a full profile of this company.

CLARK ENTERPRISES, INC.

7500 Old Georgetown Rd.
Bethesda, MD 20814
Phone: 301-657-7100
Fax: 301-657-7263
Web site: http://www.clarkus.com

CEO: A. James Clark
CFO: Lawrence C. Nussdorf
HR: Andrea Danko-Koenig
Type: Private

1998 Est. Sales: $1,500.0 million
1-Yr. Sales Change: 12.8%
Employees: 5,000
FYE: December

Convention does not bind Clark Enterprises. Besides constructing convention centers, Clark Enterprises' Clark Construction unit builds hotels, office buildings, stadiums, and transportation facilities. Clark has built several Maryland projects, including Oriole Park at Camden Yards (home to baseball's Baltimore Orioles), and many other recognizable structures around the country, such as the Los Angeles Convention Center, the US Federal Courthouse in Boston, and the 30th Street Station in Philadelphia. Other subsidiaries provide general contracting and design/build construction including international projects. Clark Enterprises also has interests in radio and real estate. It is owned by CEO James Clark.

KEY COMPETITORS
Bechtel
Bovis Construction
Fluor

CLARK USA, INC.

8182 Maryland Ave.
St. Louis, MO 63105
Phone: 314-854-9696
Fax: 314-854-1580
Web site: http://www.clarkusa.com

CEO: William C. Rusnack
CFO: Maura J. Clark
HR: Juli Sherman
Type: Private

1998 Sales: $4,042.9 million
1-Yr. Sales Change: (6.8%)
Employees: 6,700
FYE: December

Clark USA, all decked out in its refineries, has left its marketing operations behind. One of the largest independent oil refiners in the US, Clark USA produces gasoline, diesel, and aviation fuel. The company owns a refinery in Texas, two in Illinois, and one in Ohio; the four can produce more than 540,000 barrels of crude oil per day. An Apollo Management affiliate has purchased Clark USA's marketing operations — about 700 company-run gas station/convenience stores, 200 franchised sites, and the Clark brand name. Blackstone Group owns 68% of Clark USA (and a 79% voting stake); Occidental Petroleum owns about 31% (and a 20% voting stake).

KEY COMPETITORS
BP Amoco
Tosco
Ultramar Diamond Shamrock

See pages 132–133 for a full profile of this company.

CLUBCORP, INC.

3030 LBJ Fwy., Ste. 700
Dallas, TX 75234
Phone: 972-243-6191
Fax: 972-888-7700
Web site: http://www.clubcorp.com

CEO: Robert H. Dedman
CFO: James P. McCoy
HR: Albert Chew
Type: Private

1998 Sales: $851.3 million
1-Yr. Sales Change: 1.3%
Employees: 21,000
FYE: December

ClubCorp makes its green from the green — the golf green, that is. The world's largest operator of private clubs and resorts, its cadre of roughly 230 resorts, country club and golf facilities, and city clubs spans more than a dozen countries. Its holdings include Mission Hills Country Club near Palm Springs, California, and North Carolina's Pinehurst Resort and Country Club (site of the 1999 US Open). The company also owns 25% of ClubLink, a leading Canadian developer and operator of golf courses, and 30% of PGA European Tour Courses, an operator of tournament golf courses across Europe. Founder and chairman Robert Dedman and his family own 75% of ClubCorp.

KEY COMPETITORS
American Golf
Golf Trust of America
National Golf Properties

See pages 134–135 for a full profile of this company.

COCA-COLA BOTTLING CO. OF CHICAGO

7400 N. Oak Park Ave.	CEO: Marvin J. Herb	1998 Est. Sales: $830.0 million
Niles, IL 60714	CFO: Maura Neuendamke	1-Yr. Sales Change: 5.5%
Phone: 847-647-0200	HR: Robert T. Palo	Employees: 4,300
Fax: 847-647-9306	Type: Private	FYE: December

Quenching big thirsts in "the City of the Big Shoulders" and beyond, the Coca-Cola Bottling Co. of Chicago bottles and distributes soft drinks for The Coca-Cola Company. Its major brands include Coca-Cola classic, diet Coke, Sprite, and Barq's. It also bottles Sunkist and Welch's beverages. Purchased by Marvin Herb in 1981, the company is one of the top bottlers in the US. The Coca-Cola Bottling Co. of Chicago serves Illinois, Indiana, and Wisconsin, as well as parts of Pennsylvania and New York. Its subsidiaries include Coca-Cola Bottling Company of Indianapolis, Coca-Cola Bottling Company of Wisconsin, Keystone Coca-Cola Bottling, and Terre Haute Coca-Cola Bottling.

KEY COMPETITORS
American Bottling
Pepsi Bottling
Whitman

COLSON & COLSON CONSTRUCTION COMPANY

2250 McGilchrist, Ste. 200	CEO: William Colson	1998 Sales: $674.7 million
Salem, OR 97302	CFO: Kristine Wiegel	1-Yr. Sales Change: 12.5%
Phone: 503-370-7070	HR: Kathryn Smedema	Employees: 6,500
Fax: 503-364-5716	Type: Private	FYE: December

Colson & Colson Construction builds homes where the weary can rest their bones. The company develops affordable retirement home properties nationwide for Holiday Retirement Corp. (HRC), the #1 owner and manager of retirement homes in the US and Europe (and #3 in Canada). Colson & Colson has interests in more than 20,000 HRC units. The typical property is a traditional retirement facility of about 115 units and is located in a mid-sized town. The company uses a prefabrication process to speed construction and keep costs down. William Colson is CEO of HRC and managing general partner of Colson & Colson; members of the Colson family are the majority owners of Colson & Colson and own about 40% of HRC.

KEY COMPETITORS
Del Webb
Lennar
U.S. Home

COLUMBIA HOUSE COMPANY

1221 Avenue of the Americas	CEO: Richard C. Wolter	1998 Sales: $1,400.0 million
New York, NY 10020	CFO: —	1-Yr. Sales Change: —
Phone: 212-596-2001	HR: —	Employees: 3,000
Fax: 212-596-2803	Type: Joint venture	FYE: March
Web site: http://www.columbiahouse.com		

If the house is a-rockin', it's probably Columbia House. A 50-50 joint venture between entertainment giants Sony and Time Warner, Columbia House is the top club-based direct marketer of music and videos in North America. The company sells over 15,000 music selections via mail-order, its namesake Web site, and its Total E site. Started in 1955, Columbia House boasts over 16 million members in the US, Canada, and Mexico. Columbia House is buying online retailer CDnow, which offers more than 500,000 CDs, cassettes, videos, DVDs, and related items to 2.3 million customers. Time Warner and Sony will each retain a 37% stake in the resulting publicly traded company; CDnow shareholders will own 26%.

KEY COMPETITORS
Amazon.com
Bertelsmann
Musicland

COLUMBIA UNIVERSITY IN THE CITY OF NEW YORK

2690 Broadway
New York, NY 10027
Phone: 212-854-1754
Fax: 212-749-0397
Web site: http://www.columbia.edu

CEO: George Rupp
CFO: John Masten
HR: Colleen M. Crooker
Type: School

1998 Sales: $1,447.7 million
1-Yr. Sales Change: 8.1%
Employees: 15,300
FYE: June

Predating the American Revolution, Columbia University in the City of New York ranks as the fifth oldest institution of higher learning in the country. With a student population exceeding 22,000 students and a campus spread across 32 acres in Manhattan, the university grants undergraduate degrees in 65 subjects, Master of Arts and professional degrees in 183 subjects, and Master of Philosophy and Doctor of Philosophy degrees in 91 subjects. Columbia also has a strong reputation for research and ranks #1 among universities earning funds through patents and royalties. After struggling through some lean years during the 1970s and 1980s, Columbia University is experiencing an academic and fiscal resurgence.

 See pages 136–137 for a full profile of this company.

COMARK, INC.

444 Scott Dr.
Bloomingdale, IL 60108
Phone: 630-924-6670
Fax: 630-924-6684
Web site: http://www.comark.com

CEO: Chuck Wolande
CFO: Dave Keilman
HR: Eileen Sirrell
Type: Private

1998 Sales: $1,478.0 million
1-Yr. Sales Change: 34.4%
Employees: 1,320
FYE: December

Comark wants to put its mark on your co. Founded in 1977 by fraternity brothers Philip Corcoran and Chuck Wolande, Comark is the leading private reseller of computers, peripherals, and computer supplies in the US. The company sells to large global companies, government agencies, and schools. It has developed partnerships with industry leaders such as IBM, Hewlett-Packard, and Compaq to sell and provide service for their products. Comark also offers its own brand of PCs (Plus Data). The company's services include asset management and network, system, and Internet consulting. Comark's offices are located primarily in the Midwest and the East. Co-CEOs Corcoran and Wolande own the company.

KEY COMPETITORS
CompuCom
Ingram Micro
Tech Data

 See pages 138–139 for a full profile of this company.

COMMUNITY HEALTH SYSTEMS, INC.

155 Franklin Rd., Ste. 400
Brentwood, TN 37027
Phone: 615-373-9600
Fax: 615-371-1068

CEO: Wayne T. Smith
CFO: Larry Cash
HR: Linda K. Parsons
Type: Private

1998 Sales: $840.0 million
1-Yr. Sales Change: 12.6%
Employees: 12,000
FYE: December

Community Health Systems (CHS) owns and operates full-service, acute-care hospitals in nonurban communities where the CHS hospitals typically are the prominent providers of primary health care services. CHS operates about 40 acute-care hospitals in 15 states, primarily in the southeastern and southwestern US, and offers a variety of inpatient and outpatient medical, surgical, and emergency services. Some offer other services, including obstetrics, psychiatric care, and chemical-dependency treatment. CHS's multi-hospital structure provides greater leverage in negotiating purchasing agreements (including one with Tenet Healthcare's BuyPower) and HMO contracts. Investment firm Forstmann Little & Co. owns CHS.

KEY COMPETITORS
Columbia/HCA
HMA
Quorum Health

CONAIR CORPORATION

1 Cummings Point Rd.	CEO: Leandro P. Rizzuto	1998 Est. Sales: $750.0 million
Stamford, CT 06904	CFO: Pat Yannotta	1-Yr. Sales Change: 4.7%
Phone: 203-351-9000	HR: Ann Marie Cioffi	Employees: 3,800
Fax: 203-351-9180	Type: Private	FYE: December
Web site: http://www.conair.com		

Counter intelligence has shown that Conair has a place in many bathrooms and kitchens. A leading manufacturer of personal products and small appliances, Conair home and professional beauty lines include curling irons, brushes, hair dryers, shavers, mirrors, and salon products (Jheri Redding, Rusk). Its Cuisinart unit produces blenders, food processors, and other kitchen appliances and accessories. Conair also sells the Interplak electric toothbrush, telephones and answering machines through its Conairphone division, and private-label appliances and personal products for retailers. President and CEO Leandro Rizzuto, who founded Conair in 1959 with his parents, owns the company.

KEY COMPETITORS

Gillette
Helen of Troy
SEB

CONNECTICUT LOTTERY CORPORATION

270 John Downey Dr.	CEO: George Wandrak	1999 Sales: $805.7 million
New Britain, CT 06051	CFO: James Vance	1-Yr. Sales Change: 4.3%
Phone: 860-348-4001	HR: Karen Mehigen	Employees: 115
Fax: 860-348-4015	Type: Government-owned	FYE: June
Web site: http://www.ctlottery.org		

The Connecticut Lottery Corporation gives residents of the Constitution State a chance to amend their household incomes. The quasi-governmental agency operates a variety of numbers games like Cash 5 and Play 4, as well as dozens of instant win games including Cash in a Flash and Casino Action. Connecticut also participates in the multistate Powerball Lottery. About 30% of the money raised goes to the state and is used to fund initiatives such as Medicaid programs, education, and human services. The lottery pays out about 60% of the money as prizes. Created in 1996, the Connecticut lottery also is working with anti-gaming groups to increase awareness of problem gambling.

KEY COMPETITORS

Massachusetts State Lottery
New York State Lottery
Pennsylvania Lottery

THE CONNELL COMPANY

45 Cardinal Dr.	CEO: Grover Connell	1998 Est. Sales: $1,300.0 million
Westfield, NJ 07090	CFO: Terry Connell	1-Yr. Sales Change: 2.0%
Phone: 908-233-0700	HR: Maureen Waldrum	Employees: 225
Fax: 908-233-1070	Type: Private	FYE: December
Web site: http://www.connellco.com		

The Connell Company, a leading international distributor of sugar and rice, is ready to sweeten the pot. Although Connell's core business of rice distribution is conducted through subsidiary Connell Rice & Sugar, the company has branched out into other interests, such as brokerage and financial services, commercial real estate development, equipment leasing (everything from locomotives to large passenger aircraft), exporting, and food distribution. Connell has remained a family-owned business since it was founded in 1926. President and CEO Grover Connell is a well-connected Democrat.

KEY COMPETITORS

Cargill
Merrill Lynch
Riceland Foods

CONNELL LIMITED PARTNERSHIP

1 International Place, Fort Hill Sq.	CEO: William F. Connell	1998 Sales: $1,110.0 million
Boston, MA 02110	CFO: Kathleen A. Murphy	1-Yr. Sales Change: (6.7%)
Phone: 617-737-2700	HR: Maurice Heller	Employees: 2,836
Fax: 617-737-1617	Type: Private	FYE: December
Web site: http://www.connell-lp.com		

In 1987, six industrial subsidiaries organized, and the die was cast for a new maker of metals-recycling and industrial equipment. Connell Limited Partnership operates through several operating units. Wabash Alloys recycles scrap aluminum for steelmakers and the die- and sand-casting industries. Mayville Metal Products produces electronic enclosures for customers in the high-tech and medical industries. Danly Die Set designs and makes die sets and die makers' supplies. IEM offers bushings and cams. Yuba Heat Transfer provides heat-transfer equipment to the petroleum, chemical, and pulp and paper industries. CEO William Connell owns the company.

KEY COMPETITORS
Commercial Metals
Kennametal
Trinity Industries

CONSOLIDATED ELECTRICAL DISTRIBUTORS INC.

31356 Via Colinas, Ste. 107	CEO: Keith W. Colburn	1998 Est. Sales: $1,950.0 million
Westlake Village, CA 91362	CFO: Stanley Graham	1-Yr. Sales Change: 1.3%
Phone: 818-991-9000	HR: —	Employees: 4,500
Fax: 818-991-6858	Type: Private	FYE: December

With more than 400 locations nationwide, electrical equipment wholesaler Consolidated Electrical Distributors (CED) has its US distribution wired. The company sells wiring supplies and construction material, including electrical fittings, wire and cable, lighting fixtures, industrial controls, and transformers. Its suppliers include such companies as Allen-Bradley, Duracell, General Electric, and Littlefuse. CED serves commercial, residential, and industrial customers, including electrical contractors, utilities, and government agencies such as the US Navy. Started in 1913 under the name Incandescent Supply Co., the firm merged with Phillips & Edwards Corp. in 1958 and adopted its current name in 1964.

KEY COMPETITORS
Hughes Supply
Thomas & Betts
WESCO International

CONSUMERS UNION OF UNITED STATES, INC.

101 Truman Ave.	CEO: Rhoda H. Karpatkin	1998 Sales: $140.3 million
Yonkers, NY 10703	CFO: Conrad Harris	1-Yr. Sales Change: 4.0%
Phone: 914-378-2000	HR: Rick Lustig	Employees: 475
Fax: 914-378-2900	Type: Not-for-profit	FYE: May
Web site: http://www.consumersunion.org		

Consumers Union of United States (CU) inspires both trust and fear. Best known for publishing *Consumer Reports* magazine (4.6 million subscribers), the not-for-profit organization also serves as a consumer watchdog through newsletters, books, TV and radio programming, the Internet, and *Zillions* children's magazine. CU derives revenue from sales of its publications, from car and insurance pricing services, and from contributions, grants, and fees. It tests and rates thousands of products annually. CU also testifies on consumer issues and files lawsuits on behalf of consumers. Its Consumer Policy Institute focuses on research and education in issues such as air pollution.

KEY COMPETITORS
Consumers' Research
Hearst
Underwriters Labs

 See pages 140–141 for a full profile of this company.

CONTIGROUP COMPANIES, INC.

277 Park Ave.
New York, NY 10172
Phone: 212-207-5100
Fax: 212-207-2910
Web site: http://www.contigroup.com

CEO: Paul J. Fribourg
CFO: Michael J. Zimmerman
HR: Teresa McCaslin
Type: Private

1999 Sales: $10,500.0 million
1-Yr. Sales Change: (30.0%)
Employees: 14,000
FYE: March

Need some bacon, real or financial? ContiGroup Companies (CGC, formerly Continental Grain) can provide it. Its ContiAgriIndustries unit is the world's top cattle feeder and one of the US's leading pork and poultry producers; it also has interests in flour milling and animal feed and nutrition. CGC owns 78% of publicly traded ContiFinancial, a leading consumer/commercial loan provider. CGC holds interests in real estate, shipping, fund management, and natural resources through its investment arm, ContiInvestments. Chairman emeritus Michel Fribourg (the founder's great-great-grandson) and his family own CGC, which was the #2 US grain exporter until it sold its commodities marketing unit to Cargill in 1999.

KEY COMPETITORS
Farmland Industries
The Associates
Tyson Foods

 See pages 142–143 for a full profile of this company.

CONTRAN CORPORATION

5430 LBJ Fwy., Ste. 1700
Dallas, TX 75240
Phone: 972-233-1700
Fax: 972-385-0586

CEO: Harold C. Simmons
CFO: Bob O'Brien
HR: Keith A. Johnson
Type: Private

1998 Sales: $1,077.0 million
1-Yr. Sales Change: (3.1%)
Employees: 8,500
FYE: December

Founded by Texas billionaire Harold Simmons, Contran is a holding company that controls more than 90% of publicly traded Valhi, Inc., which operates in North America and Europe, serving more than 100 countries. Valhi's diversified operations include chemicals, computer support systems, precision ball bearing slides and locking systems, titanium metals, and waste management services. Holdings include NL Industries, which makes titanium dioxide pigments for creating whiteness in consumer products, and CompX International, which makes component products for office furniture and computers. Trusts benefiting two of Simmons' four daughters and his grandchildren own Contran.

KEY COMPETITORS
ICI
Steelcase
Titanium Metals

CORE-MARK INTERNATIONAL, INC.

395 Oyster Point Blvd., Ste. 415
South San Francisco, CA 94080
Phone: 650-589-9445
Fax: 650-952-4284
Web site: http://www.coremark.com

CEO: Robert A. Allen
CFO: Leo F. Korman
HR: Henry Hautau
Type: Private

1998 Sales: $2,476.4 million
1-Yr. Sales Change: 3.4%
Employees: 2,389
FYE: December

Got a late-night craving for sweets or a smoke? Core-Mark International distributes cigarettes and candy — plus health and beauty aids, fast food, snacks, groceries, beverages, batteries, and film — to retailers in the western US and Canada. Cigarettes bring in about two-thirds of the company's sales. Core-Mark also offers store services, including help with displays, promotions, and marketing. The company operates 19 distribution centers in the western US (mainly in California) and Canada. Core-Mark's customers range from drugstores and convenience, liquor, and grocery stores to movie theaters and prisons. Investment firm Jupiter Partners owns 75% of Core-Mark; the company's senior management owns 25%.

KEY COMPETITORS
Fleming Companies
SUPERVALU
Wal-Mart

CORNELL UNIVERSITY

Cornell University Campus, 305 Day Hall
Ithaca, NY 14853
Phone: 607-255-2000
Fax: 607-255-5396
Web site: http://www.cornell.edu

CEO: Hunter R. Rawlings
CFO: Frederick A. Rogers
HR: Mary George Opperman
Type: School

1998 Sales: $1,898.8 million
1-Yr. Sales Change: 11.1%
Employees: 11,873
FYE: June

To excel at Cornell you'll need every one of your brain cells. The Ivy League university has been educating young minds since its founding in 1865. Its more than 19,000 students can select from seven undergraduate and four graduate and professional colleges and schools. In addition to its Ithaca, New York campus, the university also offers two medical graduate and professional colleges and schools in New York City and has set up education-outreach centers in every county and borough of New York. Cornell's 2,775-member faculty includes four Nobel laureates, and the university has a robust research component studying everything from animal health to solid-state physics.

CORPORATE SOFTWARE & TECHNOLOGY, INC.

2 Edgewater Dr.
Norwood, MA 02062
Phone: 781-440-1000
Fax: 781-440-7718
Web site: http://www.corpsoft.com

CEO: Howard S. Diamond
CFO: Jackie Barry Hamilton
HR: Ilene McCune
Type: Private

1998 Est. Sales: $1,000.0 million
1-Yr. Sales Change: —
Employees: 1,000
FYE: December

Corporate Software & Technology (CS&T) helps companies do what they love — save money. The company resells software from such industry leaders as Adobe Systems, Computer Associates, and IBM. CS&T also provides software support services including license consulting, license management, order processing, and purchase reporting, plus technology consulting services such as data migration, systems integration, and Web site design. Its auditing services help corporations determine the cost-effectiveness of the software they have licensed. The company sells primarily to *FORTUNE* 500 corporations, but is targeting small and midsized companies. CS&T was spun off from Stream International in 1998.

KEY COMPETITORS
CompuCom
EDS
Merisel

COX ENTERPRISES, INC.

1400 Lake Hearn Dr.
Atlanta, GA 30319
Phone: 404-843-5000
Fax: 404-843-5109
Web site: http://www.coxenterprises.com

CEO: James C. Kennedy
CFO: Robert C. O'Leary
HR: Marybeth H. Leamer
Type: Private

1998 Sales: $5,355.4 million
1-Yr. Sales Change: 8.5%
Employees: 55,500
FYE: December

Family-owned Cox Enterprises, one of the largest media conglomerates in the US, publishes 16 daily newspapers, including its flagship, *The Atlanta Journal-Constitution*. It owns about a dozen TV stations, about 70% of Cox Radio (owner or operator of nearly 60 radio stations), and more than 80% of Cox Communications. With 4.7 million subscribers, Cox Communications is one of the nation's largest cable systems. Cox's Manheim Auctions operates more than 80 automobile auctions in Canada, France, the UK, and the US. The company, which has a reputation for taking advantage of emerging technologies, operates 28 city-specific Internet sites. It also offers digital cable services and high-speed Internet access.

KEY COMPETITORS
News Corp.
Time Warner
Tribune

 See pages 144–145 for a full profile of this company.

CROWLEY MARITIME CORPORATION

155 Grand Ave.	CEO: Thomas B. Crowley	1998 Est. Sales: $1,200.0 million
Oakland, CA 94612	CFO: Richard M. Oster	1-Yr. Sales Change: 9.1%
Phone: 510-251-7500	HR: Susan Rogers	Employees: 5,000
Fax: 510-251-7625	Type: Private	FYE: December
Web site: http://www.crowley.com		

Crowley Maritime has pushed and pulled its way into prominence as one of the largest tug and barge operators in the world. The firm transports freight and petroleum products by ship and, to a lesser extent, engages in trucking services, commuter and passenger service in California, ship assists, towing, and environmental cleanup projects. Clients include agricultural and industrial firms as well as shipping companies, commuters, and government agencies. The firm has a fleet of more than 400 vessels and more than 100 offices in major US, Latin American, and Caribbean ports and cities. CEO Thomas Crowley (grandson of the founder), his family, and employees own about 90% of the firm, which was founded in 1892.

KEY COMPETITORS
APL
CSX
Overseas Shipholding

CROWN EQUIPMENT CORPORATION

44 S. Washington St.	CEO: James F. Dicke	1999 Sales: $968.0 million
New Bremen, OH 45869	CFO: Kent W. Spille	1-Yr. Sales Change: 13.2%
Phone: 419-629-2311	HR: Randy Nikamp	Employees: 6,440
Fax: 419-629-2900	Type: Private	FYE: March
Web site: http://www.crownlift.com		

Save your back — Crown Equipment Corporation is a leading maker of electric heavy-duty lift trucks that are used to maneuver goods in warehouses and distribution centers. Products include narrow-aisle stacking equipment, powered pallet trucks, order-picking equipment, and forklift trucks. Its equipment can move four-ton loads and stack pallets more than 40 feet high. Crown Equipment sells its products through retailers worldwide. The company was founded in 1945 by brothers Carl and Allen Dicke. At first it made temperature controls for coal furnaces, but the company moved into making material-handling equipment in the 1950s. The Dicke family still controls the company.

KEY COMPETITORS
Ingersoll-Rand
Komatsu
NACCO Industries

CUMBERLAND FARMS, INC.

777 Dedham St.	CEO: Lily H. Bentas	1999 Est. Sales: $1,140.0 million
Canton, MA 02021	CFO: Donald Holt	1-Yr. Sales Change: (17.8%)
Phone: 781-828-4900	HR: Foster G. Macrides	Employees: 6,900
Fax: 781-828-5246	Type: Private	FYE: September
Web site: http://www.cumberlandfarms.com		

Tracing its roots to a one-cow dairy, Cumberland Farms owns and operates about 800 convenience stores (three-fourths of which sell gasoline) located in Florida, New England, and the mid-Atlantic states. The company also has bakery operations that supply its stores. (It has sold its dairy business to Dallas-based Suiza Foods.) Cumberland Farms owns a majority of Gulf Oil, a petroleum wholesaler, which gives it the right to use and license Gulf trademarks in Delaware, New Jersey, New York, most of Ohio, Pennsylvania, and the New England states. The company was founded by Vasilios and Aphrodite Haseotes (daughter Lily Bentas is CEO) in 1938 and remains family-owned.

KEY COMPETITORS
7-Eleven
BP Amoco
Exxon Mobil

CUSHMAN & WAKEFIELD INC.

51 W. 52nd St.
New York, NY 10019
Phone: 212-841-7500
Fax: 212-841-7867
Web site: http://www.cushwake.com

CEO: Arthur Mirante
CFO: Thomas Dowd
HR: Carolyn Sessa
Type: Private

1998 Sales: $700.0 million
1-Yr. Sales Change: 75.0%
Employees: 7,700
FYE: December

Cushman & Wakefield (C&W) serves the real estate needs of corporations and financial institutions around the globe and has changed its logo for the first time in almost 30 years to reflect its reach. Cushman & Wakefield Worldwide allows the firm to operate in Africa, Asia, Europe, the Middle East, and North and South America. Landmark projects include the American Express Tower in Manhattan. J. Clydesdale Cushman and Bernard Wakefield founded the firm in 1917. In 1998 C&W bought a longtime affiliate, UK-based Healey & Baker. Together, the firms have about 130 offices in 40 countries, although each will retain its own identity. C&W is controlled by a wholly owned subsidiary of Mitsubishi Estate Co., Ltd.

KEY COMPETITORS
CB Richard Ellis
Grubb & Ellis
Trammell Crow

CZARNIKOW-RIONDA INC.

1 William St.
New York, NY 10004
Phone: 212-806-0700
Fax: 212-968-0825

CEO: Daniel Gutman
CFO: John Gethins
HR: Donna White
Type: Private

1999 Sales: $735.0 million
1-Yr. Sales Change: (8.1%)
Employees: 45
FYE: September

Sugar brokerage Czarnikow-Rionda had its beginnings in the 1870s when founder Manuel Rionda and his siblings left Cuba. Rionda became involved in the sugar trade in New York and in 1909 took over a trading firm, renaming it Czarnikow-Rionda. For decades the firm was a dominant seller of sugar exported from Cuba; it also owned six plantations in Cuba (through Cuban Trading Company) and was involved in all levels of production, from cane growing to refining to sales. When Fidel Castro seized power in 1959, the firm lost its Cuban holdings; Rionda's relatives fled to the US to build new sugar operations, one of which became the Fanjul family's powerful Flo-Sun. CEO Daniel Gutman is Czarnikow-Rionda's majority owner.

KEY COMPETITORS
Cargill
Connell Company
United Sugars

DADE BEHRING INC.

1717 Deerfield Rd.
Deerfield, IL 60015
Phone: 847-267-5300
Fax: 847-267-5408
Web site: http://www.dadebehring.com

CEO: Steven Barnes
CFO: Glenn Richter
HR: Karen Balderman
Type: Private

1998 Sales: $1,285.2 million
1-Yr. Sales Change: 31.4%
Employees: 6,600
FYE: December

As far as Dade Behring is concerned, blood had better be thicker than water — the company's diagnostic instruments test how well blood coagulates. Other products test for infectious diseases, monitor therapeutic drugs, and test for recreational ones. Customers include clinical laboratories and hospitals. Dade Behring is the product of a merger between Dade International and Hoechst division Behring. It operates in 31 countries, and about half its sales come from the US. Hoechst (now Aventis) owns about one-third of the company, and the balance is controlled by investment firms Bain Capital and Goldman Sachs and the former management of Dade International, which was spun off from Baxter International in 1994.

KEY COMPETITORS
Beckman Coulter
Johnson & Johnson
Roche Holding

DAIRY FARMERS OF AMERICA

10220 N. Executive Hills Blvd.
Kansas City, MO 64190
Phone: 816-801-6455
Fax: 816-801-6456
Web site: http://www.dfamilk.com

CEO: Gary E. Hanman
CFO: Jerry Bos
HR: Ray Silver
Type: Cooperative

1998 Sales: $7,325.0 million
1-Yr. Sales Change: 91.9%
Employees: 5,300
FYE: December

Dairy Farmers of America (DFA) are partners in cream and ready to curdle their competitors. Formed by the merger of four separate dairy cooperatives, DFA is now the largest US dairy cooperative, with 25,000 members in 45 states. The co-op produces about a quarter of the US milk supply. It also produces cheese, butter, and other products for wholesale and retail customers worldwide. To better compete with larger food manufacturers, DFA is seeking strength in value-added products and joint ventures to distribute its milk to wider regions. It supplies milk for Suiza Fluid Dairy Group, a 34%-owned joint venture it has with dairy firm Suiza Foods.

KEY COMPETITORS
Danone
Dean Foods
Land O'Lakes

 See pages 146–147 for a full profile of this company.

DAIRYLEA COOPERATIVE INC.

5001 Brittonfield Pkwy.
East Syracuse, NY 13057
Phone: 315-433-0100
Fax: 315-433-2345
Web site: http://www.dairylea.com

CEO: Richard P. Smith
CFO: Craig Buckhout
HR: Ed Bangel
Type: Cooperative

1998 Est. Sales: $750.0 million
1-Yr. Sales Change: 7.3%
Employees: 200
FYE: March

Dairylea Cooperative is a major milk marketing and agricultural service organization owned by a herd of more than 2,800 dairy farmers in the northeastern US. In addition to marketing efforts, the cooperative invests in dairy companies, provides members with financial and farm-management services, and markets livestock. Dairylea subsidiary Agri-Service Agencies, Inc., provides life, health, dental, and workers' compensation insurance for workers in agriculture-related businesses nationwide. In hopes of lowering its members' operational costs, Dairylea is also leading a pilot program for the deregulation of New York State's energy services.

KEY COMPETITORS
AMPI
Foremost Farms
Dairy Farmers of America

DARIGOLD INC.

635 Elliott Ave. West
Seattle, WA 98119
Phone: 206-284-7220
Fax: 206-281-3456
Web site: http://www.darigold.com

CEO: John E. Mueller
CFO: Phil Defliese
HR: —
Type: Cooperative

1999 Sales: $1,000.0 million
1-Yr. Sales Change: 4.7%
Employees: 1,300
FYE: March

Founded in 1918, Darigold is one of the largest dairy cooperatives in the US and is owned by its approximately 900 dairy farmer members in Northern California, Idaho, Oregon, and Washington. With 12 processing plants and 19 distribution facilities, the co-op makes and markets butter; cheese; milk powder; ice cream, yogurt, and novelties; sour cream; and, naturally, pasteurized milk. The Darigold trade name is also used by Darigold Farms, a milk-marketing cooperative representing the Darigold members, and by its subsidiary Dairy Export, which manages seven Darigold Farm Stores in Idaho, Oregon, and Washington. Dairy Export also owns about 80% of Olympic Foods.

KEY COMPETITORS
Dairy Farmers of America
Foremost Farms
Land O'Lakes

DART CONTAINER CORPORATION

500 Hogsback Rd.
Mason, MI 48854
Phone: 517-676-3803
Fax: 517-676-3882
Web site: http://www.dartcontainer.com

CEO: Kenneth B. Dart
CFO: William Myer
HR: Mark Franks
Type: Private

1998 Est. Sales: $1,150.0 million
1-Yr. Sales Change: 15.0%
Employees: 5,000
FYE: December

Dart Container is a world cup winner — maybe not in soccer, but it is the world's top maker of foam cups and containers. The company controls about half the global market. Products include cups, lids, dinnerware, and cutlery, using a secret method of molding expandable polystyrene. To cut costs, Dart Container makes its own feedstocks, builds its own molding machinery, and operates its own distribution trucks. The company runs four polystyrene-recycling plants and more than a dozen facilities in Argentina, Australia, Canada, Mexico, the UK, and the US. It also has an oil and gas exploration business, Dart Energy. Although often embroiled in litigation, the Dart family continues to own the company.

KEY COMPETITORS
Smurfit-Stone Container
Sweetheart Cup
Temple-Inland

 See pages 148–149 for a full profile of this company.

DATEK ONLINE HOLDINGS CORP.

399 Thornall St.
Edison, NJ 08837
Phone: 732-516-8000
Fax: 732-548-7668
Web site: http://www.datek.com

CEO: Edward J. Nicoll
CFO: John Grifonetti
HR: Dana Gershgorn
Type: Private

1998 Est. Sales: $75.0 million
1-Yr. Sales Change: 87.5%
Employees: 377
FYE: December

One of the top five online brokerages by market share (Charles Schwab's is #1), Datek Online Holdings provides investors with market access and up-to-the-second market information through its Datek Online Brokerage Services subsidiary which offers real-time market and balance information and trades of up to 5,000 shares at about $10 per trade. The company also offers direct electronic trading services to brokers through its Island ECN subsidiary as well as trade clearing services through its Datek Online Clearing Corp. subsidiary. The software behind these operations is developed by Datek's in-house software development company, Big Think. Owners include Bernard Arnault, Aaron Elbogen, and Erik Maschler.

KEY COMPETITORS
Charles Schwab
E*TRADE
TD Waterhouse Securities

See pages 150–151 for a full profile of this company.

THE DAVID AND LUCILE PACKARD FOUNDATION

300 2nd St., Ste. 200
Los Altos, CA 94022
Phone: 650-948-7658
Fax: 650-948-5793
Web site: http://www.packfound.org

CEO: Susan P. Orr
CFO: George Vera
HR: Stephanie McAuliffe
Type: Foundation

1998 Sales: $1,017.4 million
1-Yr. Sales Change: 53.5%
Employees: —
FYE: December

One of the wealthiest philanthropic organizations in the US, The David and Lucile Packard Foundation draws on its more than $13 billion in assets to provide grants to not-for-profit entities operating in seven areas: arts; conservation; children, families, and communities; organizational effectiveness; population; philanthropy; and science. The late David Packard (co-founder of Hewlett-Packard) and his wife, the late Lucile Salter Packard, created the foundation in 1964. Now run by their children, the foundation contributed 11% of its assets in 1999 to the Packard Humanities Institute, which the Packards' son David Woodley Packard founded in 1987 to promote greater interest in history, literature, and music.

DAY & ZIMMERMANN, INC.

1818 Market St.
Philadelphia, PA 19103
Phone: 215-299-8000
Fax: 215-299-8208
Web site: http://www.dayzim.com

CEO: Harold L. Yoh
CFO: John P. Follman
HR: Larry Kludt
Type: Private

1998 Sales: $1,080.0 million
1-Yr. Sales Change: 8.5%
Employees: 16,500
FYE: December

Every day, Day & Zimmermann provides technical and engineering consulting and construction services somewhere in the world. The company has some 20 operating units that offer project management, security, property appraisal, and temporary personnel, among other services. Clients include financial, educational, and health care institutions; public utilities; government agencies; and private companies. The company also operates dedicated offices to serve individual clients, such as its Charlotte, North Carolina, location that serves DuPont. Founded in 1901, Day & Zimmermann has completed projects in more than 75 countries and has some 140 locations. The company is owned by the family of chairman Harold Yoh Jr.

KEY COMPETITORS
Bechtel
Fluor
Foster Wheeler

DEBRUCE GRAIN, INC.

4100 N. Mulberry Dr.
Kansas City, MO 64116
Phone: 816-421-8182
Fax: 816-821-2351
Web site: http://www.debruce.com

CEO: Paul DeBruce
CFO: Curt Heinz
HR: —
Type: Private

1999 Sales: $772.0 million
1-Yr. Sales Change: 6.8%
Employees: 250
FYE: March

DeBruce Grain stores, handles, and sells grain and fertilizer for the agribusiness industry. The company runs about 10 grain elevators in Iowa, Kansas, Nebraska, and Texas for the collection, storage, and distribution of grain for area farmers. The company's elevators have a combined storage capacity of more than 47 million bushels. The company also trades fertilizer and brokers truck freight through subsidiary DeBruce Transportation. DeBruce Grain's Wichita, Kansas, facility — the largest grain elevator in the world — exploded in 1998, killing five people. Founder and CEO Paul DeBruce runs the company.

KEY COMPETITORS
ADM
Cargill
ConAgra

DELAWARE NORTH COMPANIES INC.

1 Delaware North Place, 438 Main St.
Buffalo, NY 14202
Phone: 716-858-5000
Fax: 716-858-5479
Web site: http://www.delawarenorth.com

CEO: Jeremy M. Jacobs
CFO: John Fernbach
HR: —
Type: Private

1998 Sales: $1,224.0 million
1-Yr. Sales Change: 2.0%
Employees: 25,000
FYE: December

When it comes to corn dogs and nachos, Delaware North is ready to make a lot of concessions. A giant in the food concession industry, the company has a string of subsidiaries ready to make hungry folks happy. Among the company's holdings are Sportservice (food service at sports stadiums), CA One Services (airport food service), Delaware North Parks Services (visitor services for national parks and tourist attractions), and New Boston Garden (operates Boston's FleetCenter). Delaware North was founded in 1915 by brothers Charles, Louis, and Marvin Jacobs, and the Jacobs' descendants (including chairman and CEO Jeremy Jacobs Sr., owner of the NHL's Boston Bruins) continue to own the company.

KEY COMPETITORS
Compass Group
Host Marriott Services
Ogden

DELOITTE TOUCHE TOHMATSU

1633 Broadway
New York, NY 10019
Phone: 212-492-4000
Fax: 212-492-4154
Web site: http://www.deloitte.com

CEO: James E. Copeland
CFO: William A. Fowler
HR: James H. Wall
Type: Partnership

1999 Sales: $10,600.0 million
1-Yr. Sales Change: 17.8%
Employees: 90,000
FYE: August

Global accounting giant Deloitte Touche Tohmatsu (DTT) is the world's #5 accounting firm (after PricewaterhouseCoopers, Andersen Worldwide, Ernst & Young International, and KPMG International). The company operates in two areas: accounting (which includes auditing and tax services) and consulting (covering financial management, information technology, real estate, and corporate fraud). DTT has offices in more than 130 countries. The consulting business has grown more quickly than auditing, which is increasingly subject to pricing and liability issues. DTT has seen its market position erode because of industry consolidation and has fought back with aggressive marketing.

KEY COMPETITORS
Andersen Worldwide
Ernst & Young
KPMG

 See pages 152–153 for a full profile of this company.

DELTA DENTAL PLAN OF CALIFORNIA

100 1st St.
San Francisco, CA 94105
Phone: 415-972-8300
Fax: 415-972-8366
Web site: http://www.deltadentalca.org

CEO: William T. Ward
CFO: Elizabeth Russell
HR: Teri Forestieri
Type: Not-for-profit

1998 Sales: $2,440.0 million
1-Yr. Sales Change: 5.4%
Employees: 2,400
FYE: December

Delta Dental Plan of California is one of the nation's largest dental insurers, providing coverage through health maintenance organizations, preferred provider plans, and government programs such as California's Denti-Cal. A not-for-profit organization, the company is a member of the Delta Dental Plans Association and has affiliates nationwide. The company serves more than 10 million enrollees in California. Non-government clients account for about half of its California participants. Delta Dental also has more than 1 million members outside California. More than two-thirds of the nation's dentists and more than 90% of California's dentists participate in Delta Dental's programs.

KEY COMPETITORS
PacifiCare
Pacific Mutual
WellPoint Health Networks

DEMOULAS SUPER MARKETS INC.

875 East St.
Tewksbury, MA 01876
Phone: 978-851-8000
Fax: 978-640-8390

CEO: William F. Marsden
CFO: Donald Mulligan
HR: Lucille Lopez
Type: Private

1998 Est. Sales: $1,700.0 million
1-Yr. Sales Change: (8.1%)
Employees: 12,350
FYE: December

Supermarket or soap opera? Demoulas Super Markets operates almost 60 grocery stores under the Market Basket and Demoulas Super Market names in Massachusetts and New Hampshire. The firm also has real estate interests. The company was founded in 1954 when brothers George and Mike Demoulas bought their mom and pop's mom-and-pop grocery store. The men agreed that, upon one brother's death, the other would care for the deceased's family and maintain the firm's 50-50 ownership. In 1990 George's family alleged that Mike had defrauded them of all but 8% of the company's stock; a long-running court battle was decided in favor of George's family and upheld on appeal. Mike resigned as president and CEO in early 1999.

KEY COMPETITORS
Hannaford Bros.
Shaw's
Stop & Shop

DESERET MANAGEMENT CORP.

60 E. South Temple, Ste. 575
Salt Lake City, UT 84111
Phone: 801-538-0651
Fax: 801-538-0655

CEO: Rodney Brady
CFO: Dale Bailey
HR: Roland A. Radack
Type: Private

1998 Est. Sales: $750.0 million
1-Yr. Sales Change: 3.4%
Employees: 3,000
FYE: December

Deseret Management sells religion for the Church of Jesus Christ of Latter-day Saints (LDS). It acts as a holding company for the diverse commercial businesses of the Mormon Church. Deseret's broad portfolio of media businesses includes a Mormon-based radio network broadcast by cable, satellite, and 10 FM subcarrier signals in major markets; TV broadcasting; a 33-store chain of booksellers in eight western states (offering LDS publications); and the *Deseret News* newspaper. The company also has real estate investment holdings and owns three life insurance firms. Founded in 1932, Deseret Management does not accept advertising for alcohol or other goods objectionable to the church.

KEY COMPETITORS

Barnes & Noble
Reader's Digest
Thomas Nelson

DETROIT MEDICAL CENTER

Orchestra Place, 3663 Woodward Ave.
Detroit, MI 48201
Phone: 313-578-2000
Fax: 313-578-3225
Web site: http://www.dmc.org

CEO: Arthur T. Porter
CFO: Nickolas Vitale
HR: Ruthann Voelker
Type: Not-for-profit

1998 Sales: $1,572.6 million
1-Yr. Sales Change: 8.6%
Employees: 16,500
FYE: December

The seeds for the Detroit Medical Center were planted in 1955, when four Detroit hospitals joined efforts to provide coordination between the hospitals and Wayne State University's medical school. Today the medical center (which became a nonprofit corporation in 1985) serves patients throughout southeast Michigan with about 3,000 health care facility beds and 3,300 physicians. The center is made up of eight hospitals, more than 100 outpatient facilities, and two nursing centers. The Detroit Medical Center is the teaching and clinical research site for Wayne State University; it is also allied with the Barbara Ann Karmanos Cancer Institute.

KEY COMPETITORS

Henry Ford Health System
Mercy Health Services
William Beaumont Hospital

DFS GROUP LIMITED

525 Market St., 33rd Fl.
San Francisco, CA 94105
Phone: 415-977-2700
Fax: 415-977-2956
Web site: http://www.dfsgroup.com

CEO: Edward J. Brennan
CFO: Caden Wang
HR: James Wiggett
Type: Private

1998 Sales: $1,574.2 million
1-Yr. Sales Change: (29.7%)
Employees: 8,500
FYE: December

Some travelers prefer seeing sites, but as DFS Group knows, some prefer seeing sales. The world's largest travel retailer, DFS (Duty Free Shoppers) runs 150 stores, located primarily in the Asia/Pacific region and on the US West Coast. DFS airport stores account for less than 30% of sales; it also runs about a dozen Galleria stores in downtown and resort locations. Asian economic woes and a related slowdown in Asian tourism forced the company to trim its organization and shift its focus from duty-free stores to specialty stores. Galleria centers now account for over 60% of sales. DFS also handles the non-European operations of cosmetics chain Sephora. French conglomerate LVMH owns more than 60% of the company.

KEY COMPETITORS

BAA
King Power
Vendome Luxury Group

 See pages 154–155 for a full profile of this company.

DHL WORLDWIDE EXPRESS

333 Twin Dolphin Dr.
Redwood City, CA 94065
Phone: 650-593-7474
Fax: 650-593-1689
Web site: http://www.dhl.com

CEO: Rob Kuijpers
CFO: Simon Clayton
HR: Bob Parker
Type: Private

1998 Est. Sales: $5,000.0 million
1-Yr. Sales Change: 4.2%
Employees: 60,486
FYE: December

DHL Worldwide Express has a split personality — one domestic, one global — but a single air express network. The world's largest international express delivery company provides shipping services in the US through DHL Airways, while its DHL International handles everything everywhere else. DHL's air express services link more than 635,000 cities in more than 225 countries. The privately held company is pushing its global logistics management services by providing Internet tracking and order fulfillment services. DHL owns more than 200 aircraft and 13,500 delivery vehicles. Deutsche Post and Lufthansa each own 25% of DHL International.

KEY COMPETITORS
Air Express
FDX
UPS

📖 See pages 156–157 for a full profile of this company.

DI GIORGIO CORPORATION

380 Middlesex Ave.
Carteret, NJ 07008
Phone: 732-541-5555
Fax: 732-541-3590
Web site: http://www.whiterose.com

CEO: Arthur M. Goldberg
CFO: Richard B. Neff
HR: Jackie Simmons
Type: Private

1998 Sales: $1,196.9 million
1-Yr. Sales Change: 11.7%
Employees: 1,229
FYE: December

Di Giorgio delivers little apples (and other foods) in the Big Apple. Founded in 1920, the firm is a food wholesaler and distributor primarily in New York City, Long Island, and New Jersey. It offers about 17,000 products to more than 1,800 stores ranging from independents and members of cooperatives to regional chains (A&P accounts for more than 30% of sales). Although Di Giorgio distributes national brands, it also supplies frozen and refrigerated products under its White Rose brand, a name known in New York City for well over a century. Chairman and CEO Arthur Goldberg, who also heads gaming firm Park Place Entertainment, owns nearly all of Di Giorgio; he took the company private in a $1 billion LBO in 1990.

KEY COMPETITORS
C&S Wholesale
Fleming Companies
Krasdale Foods

DILLINGHAM CONSTRUCTION CORPORATION

5960 Inglewood Dr.
Pleasanton, CA 94588
Phone: 925-463-3300
Fax: 925-847-7029
Web site: http://www.dillinghamconstruction.com

CEO: D. E. Sundgren
CFO: Larry L. Magelitz
HR: Julien R. Hansen
Type: Private

1999 Sales: $1,189.0 million
1-Yr. Sales Change: 1.2%
Employees: 8,000
FYE: October

Aloha, World! Dillingham Construction provides a range of construction services for the civil, commercial, industrial, and marine markets. Founded in the 1880s by Benjamin Dillingham to build a railroad through the swamps of Hawaii, the firm has reached out internationally to complete projects in Africa, Bolivia, Cuba, Russia, Singapore, and Turkey. It offers design, engineering, purchasing, construction, management, maintenance, and development services globally. Accomplishments include airports, industrial plants, embassies, military sites, educational facilities, water treatment plants, and rapid transit systems. Japan's Shimizu Corporation owns a 45% stake in the firm, and employees own the remaining 55%.

KEY COMPETITORS
Bechtel
Parsons
Peter Kiewit Sons'

DISCOUNT TIRE CO.

14631 N. Scottsdale Rd.	CEO: Bruce T. Halle	1998 Est. Sales: $900.0 million
Scottsdale, AZ 85254	CFO: Bob Holman	1-Yr. Sales Change: 4.2%
Phone: 480-951-1938	HR: Staci Salem	Employees: 6,500
Fax: 480-951-0206	Type: Private	FYE: December
Web site: http://www.tires.com		

Concerned about that upcoming "re-tire-ment?" Discount Tire, one of the largest independent tire dealers in the US, can provide several options. With more than 370 stores in 15 states, the company sells leading brands and its Arizonian (made by Kelly-Springfield Tire) and Phantom (made by Michelin) private-label tires. Discount Tire operates mostly in the Midwest and Southwest and fixes flat tires for free, regardless of where they were bought. The company's 60 West Coast stores operate as America's Tire Co. because of a name conflict. Discount Tire also sells tires online through Discount Tire Direct. Owner and CEO Bruce Halle founded the company in 1960 with six tires — four of them recaps.

KEY COMPETITORS
Sears
TBC
Wal-Mart

DISCOVERY COMMUNICATIONS, INC.

7700 Wisconsin Ave.	CEO: John Hendricks	1998 Sales: $1,100.0 million
Bethesda, MD 20814	CFO: Greg Durig	1-Yr. Sales Change: 27.9%
Phone: 301-986-0444	HR: Pandit Wright	Employees: 1,800
Fax: 301-771-4064	Type: Private	FYE: December
Web site: http://www.discovery.com		

Discovery Communications, Inc. (DCI) brings nature shows and documentaries right into the living room through the Discovery Channel, one of the US's top cable channels. DCI also owns and operates Discovery People, The Learning Channel, Animal Planet, and The Travel Channel. Its programming reaches some 320 million homes in about 145 countries. Its retail chains — Nature Company and Discovery — sell videos, CD-ROMs, computer software, and other merchandise related to natural science. Discovery is owned by AT&T's Liberty Media Group (49%), Cox Communications (about 24%), Advance Publications (24%), and DCI founder, chairman, and CEO John Hendricks.

KEY COMPETITORS
Time Warner
Viacom
Walt Disney

See pages 158–159 for a full profile of this company.

DO IT BEST CORP.

6502 Nelson Rd.	CEO: Michael J. McClelland	1998 Sales: $1,900.0 million
Fort Wayne, IN 46803	CFO: Dave Dietz	1-Yr. Sales Change: 3.8%
Phone: 219-748-5300	HR: Nancy Harris	Employees: 1,250
Fax: 219-493-1245	Type: Association	FYE: June
Web site: http://www.doitbest.com		

If you'll be building a house or fixing one up anyway, you might as well Do it Best — at least, that's the hope of the hardware industry's third-largest cooperative. Trailing TruServ and Ace Hardware, Do it Best has about 4,400 member-owner stores across the US and in more than 30 countries. Its stores stock more than 65,000 products, and their sales are split evenly between hardware and building supplies. The co-op, whose buying power enables members to get their retail products at competitive prices, also offers unifying store-design programs using the names Do it center, Do it Best, and Do it Express. Do it Best (formerly Hardware Wholesalers) began in 1945; it bought the Our Own Hardware co-op in 1998.

KEY COMPETITORS
Ace Hardware
Home Depot
TruServ

DOANE PET CARE ENTERPRISES, INC.

103 Powell Ct., Ste. 200	CEO: Douglas J. Cahill	1998 Sales: $686.7 million
Brentwood, TN 37027	CFO: Thomas R. Heidenthal	1-Yr. Sales Change: 21.6%
Phone: 615-373-7774	HR: Bob Murray	Employees: 2,453
Fax: 615-309-1195	Type: Private	FYE: December

Doane Pet Care Enterprises has no quibble with kibble. The company is the #1 US manufacturer of dry pet food (26% of the market) and the leading maker of private-label dog and cat food. Doane also makes canned, semi-moist, and soft dry foods, as well as soft treats and dog biscuits. It sells these products to more than 350 mass merchandisers, grocery and pet store chains, and farm and feed stores; it also makes products for other pet food companies. Doane makes Ol' Roy and Special Kitty brands for Wal-Mart, its largest customer with more than 36% of sales. The company is owned by a number of investors and investment firms, including affiliates of Chase Manhattan and Donaldson, Lufkin & Jenrette.

KEY COMPETITORS

Heinz
Mars
Ralston Purina

DOMINO'S PIZZA, INC.

30 Frank Lloyd Wright Dr.	CEO: David A. Brandon	1998 Sales: $1,176.8 million
Ann Arbor, MI 48106	CFO: Harry J. Silverman	1-Yr. Sales Change: 12.6%
Phone: 734-930-3030	HR: Robert Clayton	Employees: 14,200
Fax: 734-668-1946	Type: Private	FYE: December
Web site: http://www.dominos.com		

No pawn in the pizza wars, Domino's is scrabbling away to ensure that success is in the cards. The world's #1 pizza delivery company and the #2 pizza chain overall (behind TRICON's Pizza Hut), Domino's Pizza boasts in excess of 6,200 stores (almost 90% are franchised) in more than 60 countries. While the company has bolstered its reputation with speedy delivery (it has no "eat-in" restaurants), it has also begun to emphasize the quality of its fare. Thomas Monaghan, who founded Domino's in 1960, retired from the company in 1998 to concentrate on religious pursuits. He sold 93% of his company to Boston-based investment firm Bain Capital.

KEY COMPETITORS

Little Caesar
Papa John's
Pizza Hut

 See pages 160–161 for a full profile of this company.

DON MASSEY CADILLAC, INC.

40475 Ann Arbor Rd.	CEO: Donald Massey	1998 Sales: $979.9 million
Plymouth, MI 48170	CFO: Mike Carusello	1-Yr. Sales Change: 7.8%
Phone: 734-453-7500	HR: Lowell Peterson	Employees: 1,525
Fax: 734-453-6680	Type: Private	FYE: December
Web site: http://www.donmasseycadillac.com		

The dice on the rearview mirror are sold separately, but high rollers seeking a high-dollar ride can find one at Don Massey Cadillac. One of the nation's leaders in auto retail sales, Don Massey Cadillac has about 20 dealerships located throughout Colorado, Florida, Kentucky, Michigan, North Carolina, and Texas. The company sells new and used cars, primarily General Motors automobiles (Buicks, Cadillacs, Chevrolets, Oldsmobiles), but it also sells Hondas at some dealerships. In addition, its Plymouth, Michigan, location — the #1 Cadillac seller in the world — sells Rolls-Royce and Bentley models. Founded in 1961, Don Massey Cadillac is owned by president and CEO Don Massey.

KEY COMPETITORS

AutoNation
Hendrick Automotive
Jordan Motors

DOT FOODS, INC.

Route 99 South
Mount Sterling, IL 62353
Phone: 217-773-4411
Fax: 217-773-3321
Web site: http://www.dotfoods.com

CEO: Patrick F. Tracy
CFO: William Metzinger
HR: Mike Hulsen
Type: Private

1998 Sales: $814.0 million
1-Yr. Sales Change: —
Employees: 1,307
FYE: December

If Dot Foods needed a theme song, it might choose "We Are Family." Founders Robert and Dorothy Tracy have 12 children, seven of whom work for Dot Foods, and the company's employees have expressed their closeness to the founders by purchasing a 53-ft. trailer and dedicating it in their honor. Dot Foods puts that trailer to use as it receives products from food manufacturers and redistributes them to food processors and food service distributors. The company has facilities in California, Georgia, Illinois, Missouri, and Maryland, and it serves customers in all 50 states. Perks enjoyed by Dot Foods' employees include no-interest home loans and a continuing education center. The Tracys founded the company in 1960.

DOW CORNING CORPORATION

2200 W. Salzburg Rd.
Midland, MI 48686
Phone: 517-496-4000
Fax: 517-496-8240
Web site: http://www.dowcorning.com

CEO: Gary Anderson
CFO: John W. Churchfield
HR: Gifford Brown
Type: Joint venture

1998 Sales: $2,568.0 million
1-Yr. Sales Change: (2.9%)
Employees: 9,000
FYE: December

Cosmetic surgery has caused major health problems at Dow Corning (a 50-50 joint venture of chemical titan Dow Chemical and glass giant Corning). The company is operating under bankruptcy protection as a result of the thousands of claims by women who allege they have been harmed by the company's silicone-gel breast implants. Dow Corning produces more than 10,000 silicone products, including nipples for baby bottles, sealants for the construction industry, capsules for drugs, and needle lubricants for medical use. Because silicone does not conduct electricity, it is used in its hard polycrystalline form (silicon) as the basic chip on which semiconductors are built.

KEY COMPETITORS
GE
3M
Witco Corporation

 See pages 162–163 for a full profile of this company.

DPR CONSTRUCTION INC.

555 Twin Dolphin Dr., Ste. 260
Redwood City, CA 94065
Phone: 650-592-4800
Fax: 650-592-1167
Web site: http://www.dprinc.com

CEO: Peter Nosler
CFO: Ron Davidowski
HR: Lynn Safford
Type: Private

1998 Sales: $1,300.0 million
1-Yr. Sales Change: 46.1%
Employees: 2,500
FYE: December

Building on its past success, DPR Construction caters to high-growth industries, including microelectronics, biotech, pharmaceuticals, and health care. The company was founded in 1990 when Douglas Woods, Peter Nosler, and Ronald Davidowski (the D, P, and R) left rival Rudolph & Sletten and pooled $750,000. DPR Construction's client list includes AT&T and Sun Microsystems. One of Silicon Valley's biggest contractors, the employee-owned company also has offices in five other western states and Virginia. In 1997 DPR Construction and Rudolph & Sletten settled a suit for $6.75 million; the three partners were alleged to have stolen company secrets and recruited workers while still employees of Rudolph & Sletten.

KEY COMPETITORS
Bechtel
Dillingham Construction
Rudolph & Sletten

DR PEPPER BOTTLING COMPANY OF TEXAS

2304 Century Center Blvd.
Irving, TX 75062
Phone: 972-579-1024
Fax: 972-721-8147

CEO: Jim L. Turner
CFO: —
HR: —
Type: Private

1998 Sales: $877.5 million
1-Yr. Sales Change: 23.8%
Employees: 2,700
FYE: December

The Dr Pepper Bottling Company of Texas rings up sweet results for Cadbury Schweppes. It is a leading bottler of soft drinks in the US, distributing over much of Nevada, New Mexico, Southern California, and Texas. UK-based Cadbury Schweppes (the #3 soft-drink company in the world) owns the Dr Pepper and 7 UP brands; Dr Pepper Bottling Company of Texas handles more than 10% of its US volume. It also bottles RC Cola and Snapple for Triarc Companies. Cadbury Schweppes and The Carlyle Group own 93% of the bottler and are merging it with American Bottling to form Dr Pepper/Seven Up Bottling Group. CEO and former owner Jim Turner joined Dr Pepper Bottling Company of Texas in 1982 and built it by acquiring franchises.

KEY COMPETITORS
Coca-Cola Enterprises
Cott
Pepsi Bottling

DREAMWORKS SKG

100 Universal Plaza, Bungalow 477
Universal City, CA 91608
Phone: 818-733-7000
Fax: 818-733-9918
Web site: http://www.dreamworks.com

CEO: Steven Spielberg
CFO: Ronald L. Nelson
HR: Pierre Towns
Type: Private

1998 Est. Sales: $1,000.0 million
1-Yr. Sales Change: —
Employees: 1,600
FYE: December

DreamWorks SKG has moguls times three. Created in 1994 by principal partners Steven Spielberg (famed film director/producer), Jeffrey Katzenberg (former Disney film executive and animation guru), and David Geffen (recording industry heavyweight), DreamWorks quickly established itself in the entertainment industry. The company produces films (*Saving Private Ryan, American Beauty*) and TV shows (*Spin City*) and has record deals with artists including George Michael and Randy Travis. DreamWorks also produces interactive software in a joint venture with Microsoft and co-owns 14 SEGA GameWorks video arcades with SEGA and Universal Studios. Microsoft co-founder Paul Allen is also a major investor in DreamWorks.

KEY COMPETITORS
News Corp.
Sony
Walt Disney

 See pages 164–165 for a full profile of this company.

DRESSER-RAND COMPANY

10077 Grogans Mill Rd., Ste. 500
The Woodlands, TX 77380
Phone: 281-363-7650
Fax: 281-363-7654
Web site: http://www.dresser-rand.com

CEO: David Norton
CFO: Barry E. Cottrell
HR: J. Brian Gallagher
Type: Joint venture

1998 Sales: $1,300.0 million
1-Yr. Sales Change: 7.9%
Employees: 6,300
FYE: December

All dressed up with no place to go? Not Dresser-Rand. This joint venture between Halliburton (51%) and Ingersoll-Rand (49%) makes compressors, drills, generators, turbines, and other industrial equipment. The sale of refurbished products is also in Dresser-Rand's wardrobe. The company has more than 70 regional offices, nearly 30 service facilities, and nine manufacturing sites worldwide. Dresser's products can be found in chemical, gas and oil, mining, steel, and paper plants. More than 85% of the air compressors found on US Navy ships carry the Dresser-Rand label. Ingersoll-Rand is buying Halliburton's stake in the joint venture with an aim toward selling the unit.

KEY COMPETITORS
Cooper Cameron
Emerson
Woodward

DRUMMOND COMPANY, INC.

530 Beacon Pkwy. West
Birmingham, AL 35209
Phone: 205-945-6500
Fax: 205-945-4254
Web site: http://www.drummondco.com

CEO: Garry N. Drummond
CFO: Walter F. Johnsey
HR: Joe Bilich
Type: Private

1998 Sales: $734.0 million
1-Yr. Sales Change: (1.6%)
Employees: 2,900
FYE: December

Getting its business growing from the ground up, Drummond operates three surface coal mines and one underground coal mine in Alabama. Extracting about 6.4 million tons of coal annually, Drummond is the state's largest producer of metallurgical and steam coal. Through an affiliate, it mines in Colombia (producing about 7 million tons annually) and operates a port facility there. Drummond also operates a coke plant in Alabama and a real estate business that builds housing communities and office parks in California and Florida. Heman Drummond began the company in 1935 with one mine staffed by workers with pickaxes and mules. With five sons associated with the firm, the Drummond family still owns the company.

KEY COMPETITORS
CONSOL Energy
Eastern
Zeigler Coal

DUCHOSSOIS INDUSTRIES, INC.

845 Larch Ave.
Elmhurst, IL 60126
Phone: 630-279-3600
Fax: 630-530-6091

CEO: Craig J. Duchossois
CFO: Robert L. Fealy
HR: Diane Krause-Stetson
Type: Private

1998 Est. Sales: $1,250.0 million
1-Yr. Sales Change: —
Employees: 8,000
FYE: December

Duchossois Industries has led a horse to water — and made it drink. Through subsidiaries, the company builds railroad cars (Thrall Car) and makes garage door openers and keyless entry systems (Chamberlain Group). It also manages famed Arlington International Racecourse, which was closed to thoroughbred racing by its owners until winning tax breaks from the Illinois government. Meanwhile, the track has been holding concerts and offering off-track betting, and it houses TV production facilities. (Racing is expected to resume in 2000.) The Chamberlain Group is consolidating plants in California, Illinois, and Mexico. The family of Chairman Richard Duchossois owns Duchossois Industries, which was founded in 1906.

KEY COMPETITORS
GATX
Johnstown America
Stanley Works

DUKE UNIVERSITY

Allen Bldg, Ste. 211
Durham, NC 27708
Phone: 919-684-8111
Fax: 919-684-3200
Web site: http://www.duke.edu

CEO: Nannerl O. Keohane
CFO: Tallman Trask
HR: H. Clint Davidson
Type: School

1998 Sales: $1,633.9 million
1-Yr. Sales Change: 1.6%
Employees: 20,000
FYE: June

The devils at Duke University shouldn't feel blue: *U.S. News & World Report* ranks the school among the top 10 US universities. Venerable Duke is home to almost 12,000 Blue Devils attending classes in its eight schools and colleges, including the Trinity College of Art and Sciences, the Fuqua School of Business, and the Edmund T. Pratt Jr. School of Engineering. Both its law school and medical school are highly regarded nationally. The private institution has an endowment of more than $1.3 billion. Founded in 1838 as Trinity College, Duke adopted its present name in 1924 after American Tobacco Co. magnate James Duke established the Duke Endowment.

DUNAVANT ENTERPRISES INC.

3797 New Getwell Rd.
Memphis, TN 38118
Phone: 901-369-1500
Fax: 901-369-1608
Web site: http://www.dunavant.com

CEO: William B. Dunavant
CFO: Louis Baioni
HR: Cheryl Cooley
Type: Private

1998 Est. Sales: $1,200.0 million
1-Yr. Sales Change: (4.0%)
Employees: 700
FYE: June

King Cotton is alive and well in Memphis, thank you very much. Home-grown Dunavant Enterprises is one of the largest and most influential cotton traders in the world. The company was founded in 1960 by William Dunavant, his son Billy (who is actually allergic to cotton), and Samuel T. Reeves. (The elder Dunavant died shortly after the founding, and Reeves left in 1995 to form international investor Pinnacle Trading.) The company, which grew by selling aggressively to China and the Soviet Union, maintains offices in Asia, Australia, Europe, South America, Mexico, and the southern US. The company's other business interests include real estate, warehousing, and farming. Dunavant is 95% employee-owned.

KEY COMPETITORS
Calcot
Cargill
Plains Cotton

DUNN INDUSTRIES, INC.

929 Holmes
Kansas City, MO 64106
Phone: 816-474-8600
Fax: 816-391-2510

CEO: Terrence P. Dunn
CFO: Gordon Lansford
HR: Dave Foster
Type: Private

1998 Sales: $686.0 million
1-Yr. Sales Change: 5.5%
Employees: 2,000
FYE: December

Although it dates back to 1924, this company is far from done. Family-owned Dunn Industries' construction companies include flagship J. E. Dunn Construction, Drake Construction, Witcher Construction, Dunn Industrial Group, and LTB Ward Contractors. Dunn provides construction and program management; it also designs and builds institutional, commercial, and industrial projects. Dunn operates mostly in the Midwest and is dedicated to improving the Kansas City area, overseeing other contractors' projects as well as its own. Projects include $273 million in public school contracts and a children's hospital. Chairman William Dunn and son Terry (president of the firm) promote civic affairs.

KEY COMPETITORS
Bechtel
Foster Wheeler
Turner Corporation

DYNCORP

2000 Edmund Halley Dr.
Reston, VA 20191
Phone: 703-264-0330
Fax: 703-264-8714
Web site: http://www.dyncorp.com

CEO: Paul V. Lombardi
CFO: Patrick C. FitzPatrick
HR: Roxane P. Kerr
Type: Private

1998 Sales: $1,233.7 million
1-Yr. Sales Change: 7.7%
Employees: 16,000
FYE: December

In terms of technology services, DynCorp is master-of-all-trades, from operating an undersea simulation environment for the US Navy to providing test support for space projects. One of the largest employee-owned high-tech companies in the nation, DynCorp offers technical, managerial, and professional services to government and industry. Its aerospace technology unit accounts for about 40% of sales. DynCorp also provides enterprise management and information and engineering technology. Contracts range from systems integration to maintaining defense department airplanes. The US government, its biggest client, accounts for about 70% of sales. Founded in 1946, the company was taken private in a 1988 buyout.

KEY COMPETITORS
Halliburton
Johnson Controls
Lockheed Martin

THE DYSON-KISSNER-MORAN CORPORATION

565 5th Ave., Room 4
New York, NY 10017
Phone: 212-661-4600
Fax: 212-986-7169

CEO: Robert R. Dyson
CFO: M. J. Zilinskas
HR: —
Type: Private

1999 Sales: $767.0 million
1-Yr. Sales Change: 14.5%
Employees: 4,500
FYE: January

Investment firm Dyson-Kissner-Moran is one of the largest privately held companies in the US. Through takeovers and leveraged buyouts (LBOs) over the years, the firm has diversified its holdings to include businesses from manufacturing to broadcasting. Subsidiary DKM Properties develops real estate, primarily in New Jersey. Founded in the mid-1950s, its acquisitions have included Household Finance and electronic-parts maker Kearney-National. Dyson-Kissner-Moran is controlled by the family of co-founder Charles Dyson (prominent philanthropist, LBO pioneer, and #5 on Richard Nixon's political enemies list), who died in 1997. His son Robert is Dyson-Kissner-Moran's chairman and CEO.

KEY COMPETITORS
Mack-Cali Realty
Medallion Financial
SYSCO

EAGLE-PICHER INDUSTRIES, INC.

250 E. 5th St., Ste. 500
Cincinnati, OH 45202
Phone: 513-721-7010
Fax: 513-721-2341
Web site: http://www.epcorp.com

CEO: Andries Ruijssenaars
CFO: Carroll D. Curless
HR: David Wilson
Type: Private

1998 Sales: $826.1 million
1-Yr. Sales Change: (8.8%)
Employees: 6,600
FYE: November

From earthmoving equipment accessories to spacecraft batteries, Eagle-Picher makes hundreds of products for the automotive, aerospace, construction, and defense markets. The company's products also include filters used in processing food, semiconductor materials, and germanium substrates for the fiber optics industry. Eagle-Picher makes wheel tractor scrapers, sold by Caterpillar, and provides vibration dampers, gaskets, and seals for automobiles. The company has about 60 plants in North America and Europe. Founded in 1843, Eagle-Picher emerged in 1996 from bankruptcy caused by asbestos- and lead-related personal injury claims. Dutch investment firm Granaria Holdings owns Eagle-Picher.

KEY COMPETITORS
Invensys
Johnson Controls
Steiner

E. & J. GALLO WINERY

600 Yosemite Blvd.
Modesto, CA 95354
Phone: 209-341-3111
Fax: 209-341-3569
Web site: http://www.gallo.com

CEO: Ernest Gallo
CFO: Tony Youga
HR: Mike Chase
Type: Private

1998 Est. Sales: $1,500.0 million
1-Yr. Sales Change: 15.4%
Employees: 5,000
FYE: December

Let them drink wine! E. & J. Gallo Winery brings merlot to the masses. The world's largest wine maker controls approximately 25% of the US table-wine market, thanks to its inexpensive jug brands Carlo Rossi and Gallo and the fortified Thunderbird. The company cultivates 4,000-plus acres in Sonoma County, California; makes its own labels and bottles; and is the leading US wine exporter. It imports and sells Italian wine under the Ecco Domani label and is a leading brandy producer. Gallo has traditionally sold wine in the low-to-moderate price range, but it has expanded into premium wines such as Turning Leaf and Gossamer Bay, which don't have the Gallo name on the label. The Gallo family owns the firm.

KEY COMPETITORS
Beringer
Canandaigua Brands
Robert Mondavi

 See pages 166–167 for a full profile of this company.

EARLE M. JORGENSEN COMPANY

3050 E. Birch St.
Brea, CA 92821
Phone: 714-579-8823
Fax: 714-577-3784
Web site: http://www.emjmetals.com

CEO: Maurice S. Nelson
CFO: William S. Johnson
HR: Inger Lane
Type: Private

1999 Sales: $915.8 million
1-Yr. Sales Change: (12.8%)
Employees: 1,900
FYE: March

When you're looking for a good bar, try independent steel distributor Earle M. Jorgensen Company. The holding company sells tubing, pipes, and bar, as well as structural, plate, and sheet metal products made from carbon, alloy steel, stainless steel, and aluminum. The company markets its products to the automotive, agriculture, chemical, medical, oil, defense, food, petrochemical, and machinery-manufacturing industries. The firm's operations include 25 service centers (two in Canada), a cutting center, a tube-honing facility, and four plate-processing centers. Investment banking firm Kelso & Companies owns more than 60% of Earle M. Jorgensen.

KEY COMPETITORS
LTV
Ryerson Tull
USX-U.S. Steel

EARNHARDT AUTO CENTERS

1301 N. Arizona Ave.
Gilbert, AZ 85233
Phone: 480-926-4000
Fax: 480-497-7230
Web site: http://www.earnhardt.com

CEO: Hal J. Earnhardt
CFO: Robbyn McDowell
HR: Sue Camrud
Type: Private

1998 Sales: $800.0 million
1-Yr. Sales Change: 23.1%
Employees: 1,500
FYE: December

Milking the Southwest for all it's worth, self-proclaimed "no bull" Earnhardt Auto Centers sells more than 35,000 new and used vehicles each year. The company's four auto dealerships in Arizona feature Chrysler, Dodge, Ford, Hyundai, Kia, Plymouth, and Suzuki autos. The outlets also operate parts and service departments and offer financing. A fifth Arizona dealership sells new and used RVs. Earnhardt's Web site allows customers to "build" their next car online: Shoppers can select from a complete list of options before submitting it electronically. Founded in 1951 by Tex Earnhardt, the company is family-owned and operated.

KEY COMPETITORS
AutoNation
Larry H. Miller Group
Tuttle-Click

EBSCO INDUSTRIES INC.

5724 Hwy. 280 East
Birmingham, AL 35242
Phone: 205-991-6600
Fax: 205-995-1636
Web site: http://www.ebscoind.com

CEO: James T. Stephens
CFO: Richard L. Bozzelli
HR: John Thompson
Type: Private

1999 Est. Sales: $1,210.0 million
1-Yr. Sales Change: 21.0%
Employees: 4,200
FYE: June

Searching for fulfillment of the nonpersonal variety? EBSCO (short for Elton B. Stephens Company) Industries, primarily a magazine subscription service company, provides fulfillment, sales, telemarketing, and promotional services. The company is also a commercial printer and academic and educational publisher, and it serves the library market with online information resource operations. In addition, EBSCO makes retail point-of-purchase displays, promotional products, fishing lures, rifles, and specialty office and computer furniture. It has 80 subsidiaries in more than 20 countries. The company was founded by Elton Stephens (chairman) and his wife, Alys, in 1944; the Stephens family owns the company.

KEY COMPETITORS
Quebecor
Reed Elsevier
RoweCom

See pages 168–169 for a full profile of this company.

EBY-BROWN CO.

280 W. Shuman Blvd., Ste. 280
Naperville, IL 60566
Phone: 630-778-2800
Fax: 630-778-2830
Web site: http://www.eby-brown.com

CEO: Thomas G. Wake
CFO: Mark Smetana
HR: Steve Bundy
Type: Private

1998 Sales: $1,700.0 million
1-Yr. Sales Change: 3.0%
Employees: 1,550
FYE: December

Eby-Brown makes its money on vices such as munchies and nicotine. The company is a leading supplier of over 10,000 name-brand products, including tobacco, candy, snacks, health and beauty aids, and general merchandise, to convenience stores. The company's nine distribution centers serve more than 25,000 stores in about 22 midwestern and southeastern states, including the Speedway SuperAmerica chain owned by Marathon Ashland Petroleum. Eby-Brown also has a marketing division, which offers its customers advertising and promotion services. Co-CEOs Tom and Dick Wake, the sons of William Wake (who started the company more than 100 years ago), own and operate Eby-Brown.

KEY COMPETITORS
GSC Enterprises
McLane
Spartan Stores

THE EDWARD J. DEBARTOLO CORPORATION

7620 Market St.
Youngstown, OH 44512
Phone: 330-965-2000
Fax: 330-965-2077

CEO: Marie Denise DeBartolo York
CFO: Lynn E. Davenport
HR: Linda Pearce
Type: Private

1998 Est. Sales: $250.0 million
1-Yr. Sales Change: 0.0%
Employees: 4,000
FYE: June

Survey says . . . lawsuit! *Family Feud* is the name of the game at The Edward J. DeBartolo Corporation. The siblings who own the parent company of the San Francisco 49ers, a racetrack, real estate interests, and an 11% stake in Simon Property Group have been fighting over the business for some time. After former CEO Eddie DeBartolo Jr. pleaded guilty in 1998 to felony charges of failing to report wrongdoing, his sister, chairman Denise DeBartolo York, took over the firm and sued her brother (for debt owed to the company). He countersued, and they eventually reached a tentative settlement to divide the firm's assets (she's to get the company name, the 49ers, and the racetrack; he's to get real estate and stock).

KEY COMPETITORS
Atlanta Falcons
Fair Grounds
General Growth Properties

See pages 170–171 for a full profile of this company.

EL CAMINO RESOURCES INTERNATIONAL, INC.

21051 Warner Center Ln.
Woodland Hills, CA 91367
Phone: 818-226-6600
Fax: 818-226-6794
Web site: http://www.elcamino.com

CEO: David Harmon
CFO: Brian Ofria
HR: Jo Glascock
Type: Private

1999 Sales: $668.0 million
1-Yr. Sales Change: (1.5%)
Employees: 900
FYE: April

For its competitors, El Camino Resources International is the lessor of more than just two evils. The reseller and lessor of IBM mainframe and midrange computer equipment also provides software, technical support, and integration services, plus specialties such as disaster recovery, all of which can be combined in a single lease payment. Its REALXpress.com Internet business draws IBM AS/400 users seeking applications and services. The company has exited the midrange wholesale distributing business, conducted by subsidiary REAL Application. Founded in 1979, El Camino operates throughout the Americas and in Germany and the UK. President and CEO David Harmon owns the company.

KEY COMPETITORS
Amplicon
Comdisco
Forsythe Technology

ELECTROLUX

5956 Sherry Ln.	CEO: Joseph Urso	1997 Est. Sales: $680.0 million
Dallas, TX 75225	CFO: John Horigan	1-Yr. Sales Change: 0.7%
Phone: 770-933-1000	HR: Bob McComas	Employees: 230
Fax: 214-378-7561	Type: Private	FYE: December
Web site: http://www.electrolux-usa.com		

A pioneer in the vacuum cleaner business, Electrolux has been steaming shags and butting baseboards since 1924. The floor care equipment manufacturer peddles its Electrolux-brand vacuum cleaners, shampooers/polishers, and accessories from almost 600 Electrolux sales centers in the US and Canada. Salesman Axel Wenner-Gren, instrumental in the 1919 formation of Swedish appliance maker AB Electrolux, started the Electrolux sales companies in North America, South America, and Europe in the 1920s. All were later bought by AB Electrolux, except the US company, which today has no affiliation with the Swedish firm. Formerly owned by Sara Lee, Electrolux was bought by investment group Engles Urso Follmer in 1998.

KEY COMPETITORS
Kirby
Maytag
Royal Appliance

EMORY UNIVERSITY

1380 S. Oxford Rd. SE	CEO: William M. Chace	1998 Sales: $1,738.9 million
Atlanta, GA 30322	CFO: John L. Temple	1-Yr. Sales Change: 23.5%
Phone: 404-727-6123	HR: Alice R. Miller	Employees: 15,491
Fax: 404-727-0646	Type: School	FYE: August
Web site: http://www.emory.edu		

"Have a Coke and a smile" means a little more to Emory University than it does to the rest of us. The school, which boasts more than 11,300 students and 2,500 faculty members, was transformed from Emory College to Emory University in 1915 by a $1 million donation from Coca-Cola Company owner Asa Candler. Today, some 60% of Emory's endowment consists of Coca-Cola stock. The university offers undergraduate, graduate, and professional degrees in a wide range of fields, including medicine, theology, law, nursing, and business. Founded in 1836, the private university also maintains several research centers and operates a joint venture with Columbia/HCA to offer managed health care.

EMPIRE BLUE CROSS AND BLUE SHIELD

1 Rural Trade Center	CEO: Michael A. Stocker	1998 Sales: $3,276.5 million
New York, NY 10048	CFO: John W. Remshard	1-Yr. Sales Change: (1.6%)
Phone: 212-476-1000	HR: S. Tyrone Alexander	Employees: 6,000
Fax: 212-476-1281	Type: Not-for-profit	FYE: December
Web site: http://www.empirehealthcare.com		

Even New Yorkers get the Blues. Empire Blue Cross and Blue Shield serves more than 4 million customers in eastern New York and northern New Jersey, making it the largest health care provider in its market. It offers indemnity coverage and managed care, including HMO, PPO, and EPO (exclusive provider organization offering no out-of-network benefits) plans. Empire operates several for-profit subsidiaries, including accident and health insurance provider Empire Health Choice Assurance and HMO Empire Health Choice. Empire has announced plans to convert to for-profit status but says it will form a charitable foundation to help care for New York's poor and uninsured.

KEY COMPETITORS
Aetna
Health Insurance of New York
Oxford Health Plans

See pages 172–173 for a full profile of this company.

ENCYCLOPAEDIA BRITANNICA, INC.

310 S. Michigan Ave.
Chicago, IL 60604
Phone: 312-347-7000
Fax: 312-347-7399
Web site: http://corporate.britannica.com

CEO: Paul Hoffman
CFO: Richard Anderson
HR: Karl Steinberg
Type: Private

1998 Est. Sales: $300.0 million
1-Yr. Sales Change: (7.7%)
Employees: 400
FYE: September

Encyclopaedia Britannica publishes the 32-volume *Encyclopaedia Britannica,* the oldest and largest English-language encyclopedia. Its other print publications include the *Britannica Book of the Year, Great Books of the Western World, Merriam-Webster's* dictionaries, and the *Britannica Atlas.* Britannica.com, the firm's electronic products subsidiary, provides the nation's oldest online encyclopedia and a multimedia CD-ROM version of its encyclopedia. Britannica.com also offers *Merriam-Webster Online,* a free Internet-based dictionary service, a database of more than 130,000 reviewed and indexed Web sites, and selected articles from about 70 magazines. The company is owned by Swiss financier Jacob Safra.

KEY COMPETITORS
Berkshire Hathaway
Grolier
Microsoft

 See pages 174–175 for a full profile of this company.

ENTERPRISE RENT-A-CAR

600 Corporate Park Dr.
St. Louis, MO 63105
Phone: 314-512-5000
Fax: 314-512-4706
Web site: http://www.enterprise.com

CEO: Andrew C. Taylor
CFO: John T. O'Connell
HR: Ed Adams
Type: Private

1999 Sales: $4,730.0 million
1-Yr. Sales Change: 13.2%
Employees: 40,000
FYE: July

Enterprise Rent-A-Car has a pickup line that gets noticed. The company, which offers to ferry its customers to the rental office, oversees the biggest US car rental fleet — about 370,000 vehicles. Enterprise operates in Canada, Germany, the UK, and the US. Shunning airport travelers, the company targets customers who need cars because of accidents or repairs to their own vehicles or for short trips. Its rates are up to 30% lower than most airport car rental companies. Enterprise subsidiaries lease vehicles, manage fleets for other companies, and sell cars and trucks. Through Enterprise Capital Group, the company owns a host of businesses, including suppliers of goods to hotels and prisons.

KEY COMPETITORS
AutoNation
Budget Group
Hertz

 See pages 176–177 for a full profile of this company.

ENTEX INFORMATION SERVICES, INC.

6 International Dr.
Rye Brook, NY 10573
Phone: 914-935-3600
Fax: 914-935-3650
Web site: http://www.entex.com

CEO: John A. McKenna
CFO: Michael G. Archambault
HR: Kim Nathanson
Type: Private

1999 Sales: $483.6 million
1-Yr. Sales Change: (80.3%)
Employees: 5,800
FYE: June

ENTEX Information Services keeps corporate networks intact. The company, whose PC retailing roots date back to 1982, is now a provider of higher-margin desktop and network systems integration and support services. ENTEX manages about 800,000 desktops worldwide and provides outsourced services including network operation and support, maintenance and repair, and systems management (about 60% of sales). ENTEX also offers consulting and managed staffing services. An investor group led by chairman Dort Cameron owns about 75% of the company, which counts Microsoft and IBM as small-stakes investors.

KEY COMPETITORS
CompuCom
DecisionOne
EDS

See pages 178–179 for a full profile of this company.

EPIX HOLDINGS CORPORATION

3710 Corporex Park Dr.
Tampa, FL 33619
Phone: 813-664-0404
Fax: 813-621-6816
Web site: http://www.pti-info.com

CEO: Thomas S. Taylor
CFO: —
HR: Irv Dupre
Type: Private

1998 Sales: $734.0 million
1-Yr. Sales Change: 87.2%
Employees: 38,300
FYE: December

More and more employers are picking EPIX to handle their human resource concerns. EPIX Holdings (formerly Payroll Transfers) is a leading professional employer organization (PEO) that provides human resources management for its clients' permanent full-time workers. The company's services include insurance, tax administration, employee benefits programs, regulatory compliance, and payroll processing. The company provides administrative services for 30,000 employees from some 1,600 small and mid-sized businesses in 46 states. EPIX, which was founded in 1989, has been included in *Inc.* magazine's list of the 500 fastest-growing companies.

KEY COMPETITORS
Administaff
NovaCare
Staff Leasing

EQUILON ENTERPRISES LLC

1100 Louisiana Dr.
Houston, TX 77210
Phone: 713-277-7000
Fax: 713-277-7560
Web site: http://www.equilonmotivaequiva.com

CEO: James M. Morgan
CFO: David C. Crikelair
HR: Terry Bean
Type: Joint venture

1998 Sales: $22,246.0 million
1-Yr. Sales Change: —
Employees: 14,000
FYE: December

For Equilon Enterprises and its sister company Motiva, East is East and West is West, and never the twain shall meet. Shell Oil (owner of 56% of Equilon) and Texaco (44%) formed Equilon as a joint venture in 1998. Equilon refines and markets gasoline and other petroleum products under the Shell and Texaco brand names in 32 midwestern and western US states, with 9,400 outlets. (Motiva does the same in the Northeast and Southeast as a venture of Shell, Texaco, and Saudi Aramco.) Motiva and Equilon together form the #1 US gasoline retailing business. Equilon owns and has interests in more than 60 crude oil and product terminals. It operates four West Coast refineries and one in Ohio, which it is selling.

KEY COMPETITORS
7-Eleven
BP Amoco
Exxon Mobil

EQUISTAR CHEMICALS, LP

1221 McKinney St., Ste. 700
Houston, TX 77010
Phone: 713-652-7300
Fax: 713-652-4151
Web site: http://www.equistarchem.com

CEO: Dan F. Smith
CFO: Kelvin Collard
HR: Myra Perkinson
Type: Partnership

1998 Sales: $4,363.0 million
1-Yr. Sales Change: 1,095.3%
Employees: 5,000
FYE: December

Credit good chemistry, but Equistar Chemical — a partnership of Lyondell (41%), Millennium, and Occidental (29.5% each) — is one of the world's largest producers of olefins, polymers, and ethylene and its derivatives. Equistar's olefin products are used to make food packaging, adhesives, antifreeze, nylon clothing, and paint. The company also makes oxygenated products such as automobile starting fluid, gunpowder, hair spray, cosmetics, and polishes. Its polymer products include trash bags, grocery bags, milk crates, and disposable cups. Equistar's plants are mostly in the Gulf Coast area; it also has a technology center in Cincinnati.

KEY COMPETITORS
Formosa Plastics
Geon
M. A. Hanna

EQUITY GROUP INVESTMENTS, L.L.C.

2 N. Riverside Plaza, Ste. 600
Chicago, IL 60606
Phone: 312-454-1800
Fax: 312-454-0610

CEO: Sheli Z. Rosenberg
CFO: Greg Stegimen
HR: Dan Harris
Type: Private

Sales: —
1-Yr. Sales Change: —
Employees: —
FYE: December

Billionaire Sam Zell's Equity Group Investments is the privately held parent of affiliates involved in real estate, restaurants, cruise ships, and other ventures. Zell has made his niche — and a lot of money — by purchasing distressed properties and turning them into profitable investments (for which he earned the nickname "Grave Dancer"). Zell's REIT portfolio makes him the US's largest owner of property leased by manufactured homeowners (Manufactured Home Communities), office buildings (Equity Office Properties Trust), and apartments (Equity Residential Properties Trust). As bargains dry up in the US, Zell is heading overseas to buy real estate and companies with his Equity International Properties fund.

KEY COMPETITORS
Blackstone Group
Goldman Sachs
JMB Realty

 See pages 180–181 for a full profile of this company.

ERNST & YOUNG INTERNATIONAL

787 7th Ave.
New York, NY 10019
Phone: 212-773-3000
Fax: 212-773-6350
Web site: http://www.eyi.com

CEO: William L. Kimsey
CFO: Hilton Dean
HR: Lewis A. Ting
Type: Partnership

1999 Est. Sales: $12,510.0 million
1-Yr. Sales Change: 14.8%
Employees: 97,800
FYE: September

Ernst & Young International, the fourth-largest of the Big Five accounting firms (behind PricewaterhouseCoopers, Andersen Worldwide, and KPMG International), offers accounting and consulting services from its more than 660 offices in over 130 countries. In addition to corporate audit services, Ernst & Young provides internal audit and accounting oversight and advice. Its tax practice, one of the world's largest, helps its international clientele cope with the tax laws of many countries. The firm's business consultancy, which has grown through acquisitions, provides information and assistance in fields that include health care, personnel, and information technology.

KEY COMPETITORS
Andersen Worldwide
KPMG
PricewaterhouseCoopers

 See pages 182–183 for a full profile of this company.

FALCON BUILDING PRODUCTS, INC.

Sears Tower, 233 S. Wacker Dr., Ste. 3500
Chicago, IL 60606
Phone: 312-906-9700
Fax: 312-906-9704

CEO: William K. Hall
CFO: Anthony J. Navitsky
HR: Mary Anne Flanagan
Type: Private

1998 Sales: $765.8 million
1-Yr. Sales Change: 11.6%
Employees: 4,900
FYE: December

Falcon Building Products keeps its ducts in a row. The company makes residential and commercial construction and home improvement products and distributes them throughout the US. It produces flexible duct, gas vent, and chimney systems for heating, ventilation, and air conditioning. The company also makes ceramic, enameled steel, and acrylic plumbing fixtures. It is selling its air compressor and pressure washer unit. Falcon markets its products through wholesalers, manufacturers' representatives, and mass merchandisers and retail chains. The company's brand names include Hart & Cooley, Metlvent, Reliable, and Tuttle & Bailey. Bahrain-based investment firm Investcorp owns about 90% of the company.

KEY COMPETITORS
Masco
Nortek
U.S. Industries

FARMLAND INDUSTRIES, INC.

3315 N. Oak Trafficway
Kansas City, MO 64116
Phone: 816-459-6000
Fax: 816-459-6979
Web site: http://www.farmland.com

CEO: H. D. Cleberg
CFO: Terry M. Campbell
HR: Holly D. McCoy
Type: Cooperative

1999 Sales: $10,709.1 million
1-Yr. Sales Change: 22.0%
Employees: 17,700
FYE: August

At the end of the workday for Farmland Industries' members, it's time for a hoedown. Farmland Industries is the #1 agricultural cooperative in the US and is a competitor in agribusiness worldwide, exporting products (primarily grain) to about 90 countries. It is a major beef packer in the US and also a top producer of pork products. Farmland Industries is owned by 1,500 local co-ops which are made up of about 600,000 farmers in the US, Canada, and Mexico. Farmland's operations include crop processing, fertilizer plants, a petroleum refinery, grain elevators, feed mills, and a transportation fleet. A planned merger with Cenex Harvest States fell through in 1999, but officers kept talks open for future attempts.

KEY COMPETITORS
Cargill
Cenex Harvest States
IBP

 See pages 184–185 for a full profile of this company.

THE FAULKNER ORGANIZATION

4437 Street Rd.
Trevose, PA 19053
Phone: 215-364-3980
Fax: 215-364-0706
Web site: http://www.faulknerfamily.com

CEO: Henry Faulkner
CFO: Bill Febold
HR: Walt Huber
Type: Private

1997 Sales: $711.2 million
1-Yr. Sales Change: 12.9%
Employees: 1,000
FYE: December

The sound and the fury of Buicks moving off the lot is coming from The Faulkner Organization, one of Pennsylvania's largest-volume dealers of Pontiacs, Buicks, and GMC trucks. The company operates 21 automobile dealerships in Pennsylvania and Delaware. Its domestic car franchises also include Cadillac, Ford, Oldsmobile, Chevrolet, Mercury, and Saturn; its import franchises sell Toyotas, Hondas, Mitsubishis, and Mazdas. In addition to new and used cars, the company sells auto parts and offers automotive repairs, car financing, a fleet service, and credit life insurance. Founded in 1932 by Henry Faulkner, the company is still owned and operated by the Faulkner family.

KEY COMPETITORS
Brown Automotive
Pacifico
Planet Automotive Group

FEDERAL RESERVE BANK OF NEW YORK

33 Liberty St.
New York, NY 10045
Phone: 212-720-5000
Fax: 212-720-7459
Web site: http://www.ny.frb.org

CEO: William J. McDonough
CFO: Suzanne Cutler
HR: —
Type: Member-owned banking authority

1998 Sales: $10,482.0 million
1-Yr. Sales Change: 20.6%
Employees: 3,600
FYE: December

The Federal Reserve Bank of New York is the largest in the Federal Reserve System, which regulates and examines US banks. One of 12 regional banks, it can issue currency, set discount interest rates (the rate at which member banks borrow), clear money transfers, and buy or sell US government securities to regulate the money supply. In addition, the New York Fed conducts the US's foreign currency transactions and buys or sells on the world market to support the dollar's value. It also stores gold for foreign governments and other international agencies.

See pages 186–187 for a full profile of this company.

FEDERATED INSURANCE COMPANIES

121 E. Park Sq.
Owatonna, MN 55060
Phone: 507-455-5200
Fax: 507-455-5452
Web site: http://www.federatedinsurance.com

CEO: Kirk N. Nelson
CFO: Raymond R. Stawarz
HR: A. Daniel Lewis
Type: Mutual company

1998 Sales: $1,066.3 million
1-Yr. Sales Change: 0.7%
Employees: 2,950
FYE: December

Federated Insurance Companies, founded in 1904, offers group life and health coverage, as well as workers' compensation, automobile, property/casualty, and individual life insurance throughout the US. Since its inception, the company has primarily served businesses — automobile and tire dealers, printers, power equipment dealers, petroleum marketers, and specialty trade contractors. Federated Insurance covers more than 29,000 businesses nationwide; commercial lines and group health account for approximately two-thirds of premiums written.

KEY COMPETITORS
Blue Cross
CNA Financial
State Farm

FELD ENTERTAINMENT, INC.

8607 Westwood Center Dr.
Vienna, VA 22182
Phone: 703-448-4000
Fax: 703-448-4100
Web site: http://www.ringling.com

CEO: Kenneth Feld
CFO: Mike Ruch
HR: Richard Felsenstein
Type: Private

1999 Est. Sales: $645.0 million
1-Yr. Sales Change: 2.4%
Employees: 2,500
FYE: January

For more than 125 years, patrons have known this business as "The Greatest Show on Earth." Feld Entertainment owns the Ringling Bros. and Barnum & Bailey Circus. The circus has three camps: Two perform the traditional circus in local arenas, and the third is an upscale version that performs under the big top. Feld Entertainment also produces nine touring ice shows (including Walt Disney's World on Ice) and Las Vegas illusionists Siegfried & Roy. About 25 million people each year attend the company's shows (which have toured 44 countries), making it one of the largest family entertainment businesses in the world. Kenneth Feld, whose father began managing the circus in 1956 and bought it in 1967, owns the company.

KEY COMPETITORS
Cirque du Soleil
Clyde Beatty-Cole Brothers Circus

 See pages 188–189 for a full profile of this company.

FEROLIE GROUP

2 Van Riper Rd.
Montvale, NJ 07645
Phone: 201-307-9100
Fax: 201-782-0882
Web site: http://www.feroliegroup.com

CEO: Lawrence J. Ferolie
CFO: Cathy Ferolie
HR: Julie Shasteen
Type: Private

1998 Sales: $970.0 million
1-Yr. Sales Change: 21.3%
Employees: 615
FYE: December

A food broker serving New York, New Jersey, and Connecticut, the Ferolie Group broke into the business in 1948. The company provides sales and marketing services for packaged food and other packaged goods companies. Through exclusive regional or area contracts, the group distributes products to warehouse stores, drugstores, supermarkets, and mass merchandisers. Some of Ferolie Group's biggest clients are Gillette's Duracell, Fort James, Kraft Foods, Unilever's Lipton, McCormick & Company, and Schering-Plough. The Ferolie Group is affiliated with Eastern Sales and Marketing, a partnership of food brokerages operating in the eastern US. Founded by A. Joseph Ferolie, the company remains family-owned.

KEY COMPETITORS
Atlantic Mktg
Marketing Specialists
Marketing Specialists Sales

FIESTA MART INC.

5235 Katy Fwy.
Houston, TX 77007
Phone: 713-869-5060
Fax: 713-865-5514
Web site: http://www.fiestamart.com

CEO: Louis Kaptopodis
CFO: Vicki Baum
HR: Mimi Buderus
Type: Private

1999 Est. Sales: $825.0 million
1-Yr. Sales Change: 5.8%
Employees: 8,000
FYE: May

Fiesta Mart's food party happens every day of the year. The company runs about 50 Texas stores that sell ethnic and mainstream groceries, including items popular with Mexican- and Asian-Americans (its target customers). The company also leases outdoor kiosks to vendors who offer such items as vinyl jackets and T-shirts. While mariachi music plays, Fiesta customers browse for such ethnic foods as cactus and fresh tortillas. With stores in the Houston, Dallas, and Austin areas, the chain has found inner-city locations to be more successful than suburban sites. Fiesta Mart also manages almost 20 Beverage Mart liquor stores owned by other companies. Donald Bonham and O. C. Mendenhall founded Fiesta Mart in 1972.

KEY COMPETITORS
H-E-B
Minyard Food Stores
Randall's

FIRSTAMERICA AUTOMOTIVE, INC.

601 Brannan St.
San Francisco, CA 94107
Phone: 415-284-0444
Fax: 415-808-4838
Web site: http://www.pricefactor.com

CEO: Thomas A. Price
CFO: Debra L. Smithart
HR: Cathi DeMacsek
Type: Private

1998 Sales: $783.1 million
1-Yr. Sales Change: 65.2%
Employees: 1,583
FYE: December

The product of Californian collaboration, FirstAmerica Automotive is one of the Golden State's largest auto dealers. Formed when three high-volume San Diego- and San Francisco-area dealers combined in 1997, the acquisitive company has about 20 dealerships, including locations in the Los Angeles and San Jose areas. It sells and leases new and used vehicles, and it also sells replacement parts and provides maintenance, warranty, financing, and insurance services. Nissan, Toyota, Honda, and Dodge are FirstAmerica's best-selling brands, but it also sells Lexus, BMW, Volkswagen, and Isuzu, among others. Sonic Automotive is acquiring the company. President and CEO Thomas Price owns about 38% of the company.

KEY COMPETITORS
AutoNation
Marty Franich
Penske Automotive

FLETCHER JONES MANAGEMENT GROUP

175 E. Reno, Ste. C-6
Las Vegas, NV 89119
Phone: 702-739-9800
Fax: 702-739-0486
Web site: http://www.fjmercedes.com

CEO: Fletcher Jones
CFO: Tom Downer
HR: Vicki Sylvia
Type: Private

1998 Sales: $661.8 million
1-Yr. Sales Change: 13.3%
Employees: 1,047
FYE: June

Image is important at Fletcher Jones Management Group. The company's Newport Beach, California, dealership (Fletcher Jones Motorcars) is one of the nation's top Mercedes-Benz sellers. The company operates seven car dealerships in California and Nevada, selling Chevrolet, Lexus, Mazda, and Toyota models and other imports. Fletcher Jones Motorcars operates a 176,000-sq.-ft. superstore that features a putting green, a manicurist, 140 service stalls, and free Saturday car washes for any Mercedes-Benz. The group is owned by president and CEO Fletcher Jones Jr.; his father started the company in 1954 with one Los Angeles dealership.

KEY COMPETITORS
AutoNation
House of Imports
Lithia Motors

FLINT INK CORPORATION

4600 Arrowhead Dr.	CEO: H. Howard Flint	1998 Sales: $1,216.0 million
Ann Arbor, MI 48105	CFO: Michael J. Gannon	1-Yr. Sales Change: 31.6%
Phone: 734-622-6000	HR: Glenn T. Autry	Employees: 3,500
Fax: 734-622-6060	Type: Private	FYE: December
Web site: http://www.flintink.com		

Flint Ink — a major North American ink producer that sells its products across several other continents — has drawn a bull's-eye on the European market, which it entered with its purchase of Manders Premier, a leading UK ink maker. Flint Ink has plants throughout the Americas, Australasia, and Europe. The company's customers include firms that print magazines, newspapers, catalogs, and packaging materials. Flint Ink also makes specialty inks (for printing lottery tickets) and environment-friendly vegetable oil-based inks. Howard Flint II represents the third generation of the Flint family to head the firm, which was founded in 1920. He is the majority owner.

KEY COMPETITORS
Akzo Nobel
Borden
Engelhard

FLYING J INC.

50 W. 990 South	CEO: J. Phillip Adams	1999 Sales: $1,562.0 million
Brigham City, UT 84302	CFO: Paul F. Brown	1-Yr. Sales Change: (2.4%)
Phone: 435-734-6400	HR: Jerry Beckman	Employees: 9,000
Fax: 435-734-6556	Type: Private	FYE: January
Web site: http://www.flyingj.com		

Flying J founder Jay Call thinks people with dirty cars don't make good employees. Maybe he's right — Call applied his standards when building the nation's largest chain of truck stops from the humble beginnings of four gas stations in the 1960s. Nearly 120 Flying J Travel Plazas (known for their cleanliness) serve truckers and other travelers with fuel, convenience stores, restaurants, lube centers, truck washes, and motels. The #1 diesel fuel retailer in the US, the firm is adding more US plazas and expanding into Canada and Mexico. Flying J also owns a 25,000-barrel-a-day oil refinery in Utah and oil and gas reserves in Utah, Wyoming, and North Dakota. Call and his family own a majority of the company.

KEY COMPETITORS
Petro Stopping Centers
Pilot
TravelCenters of America

FMR CORP.

82 Devonshire St.	CEO: Edward C. Johnson	1998 Sales: $6,770.0 million
Boston, MA 02109	CFO: Stephen P. Jonas	1-Yr. Sales Change: 15.2%
Phone: 617-563-7000	HR: Ilene B. Jacobs	Employees: 28,000
Fax: 617-476-6150	Type: Private	FYE: December
Web site: http://www.fidelity.com		

FMR, aka Fidelity Investments, is a financial services conglomerate with interests in mutual funds, life insurance, banking, and retirement services. Fidelity, the #1 mutual fund company worldwide, manages some 280 funds for 15 million customers. FMR also has investments in telecommunications (COLT Telecom Group plc), real estate (Boston World Trade Center), and a job placement service (J. Robert Scott). Fidelity Management and Research was formed in 1946 by Edward Johnson as the investment adviser to the Fidelity Fund. FMR is still controlled by its executives, including the founder's son Ned (CEO) and granddaughter Abigail (SVP). FMR is launching a savings and loan, Fidelity Personal Trust Company.

KEY COMPETITORS
Charles Schwab
T. Rowe Price
Vanguard Group

 See pages 190–191 for a full profile of this company.

FOLLETT CORPORATION

2233 West St.
River Grove, IL 60171
Phone: 708-583-2000
Fax: 708-452-9347
Web site: http://www.follett.com

CEO: Kenneth Hull
CFO: Kathryn Stanton
HR: Richard Ellspermann
Type: Private

1999 Sales: $1,200.0 million
1-Yr. Sales Change: 11.8%
Employees: 8,000
FYE: March

Not all kids like to read, but (fortunately for Follett) by the time they reach college, they don't have a choice. Follett's retail division, Follett College Stores, is the #1 operator of US college bookstores, with more than 500 campus bookstores in 48 states and Canada. Its campus stores sell other items, including clothing. The company's divisions include Custom Academic Publishing (obtains copyrights and publishes custom academic coursepacks), Follett Library Resources (supplies books to libraries at more than 45,000 US schools), and Follett Software. Follett also provides library management services. The Follett family has owned the company for four generations.

KEY COMPETITORS

Barnes & Noble College
 Bookstores
Ingram Industries
Kinko's

 See pages 192–193 for a full profile of this company.

THE FORD FOUNDATION

320 E. 43rd St.
New York, NY 10017
Phone: 212-573-5000
Fax: 212-599-4584
Web site: http://www.fordfound.org

CEO: Susan V. Berresford
CFO: Nicholas M. Gabriel
HR: Bruce D. Stuckey
Type: Foundation

1998 Sales: $1,087.0 million
1-Yr. Sales Change: 8.2%
Employees: 580
FYE: September

The Ford Foundation provides grants or loans to individuals and institutions that meet its stated goals of strengthening democratic values, reducing poverty and injustice, promoting international cooperation, and advancing human achievement. Grants are made in three program areas: Asset Building and Community Development (human, economic, and resource development and reproductive health programs); Peace and Social Justice (promotion of peace and the rule of law, human rights, and freedom); and Education, Media, Arts, and Culture. Funds are derived from a diversified investment portfolio.

 See pages 194–195 for a full profile of this company.

FOREMOST FARMS USA

E10889A Penny Lane
Baraboo, WI 53913
Phone: 608-356-8316
Fax: 608-356-5458
Web site: http://www.foremostfarms.com

CEO: Donald Storhoff
CFO: Duaine Kamenick
HR: John Murphy
Type: Cooperative

1998 Sales: $1,375.9 million
1-Yr. Sales Change: 15.3%
Employees: 1,800
FYE: December

No jokes about "herd mentality," please. It's just that Foremost Farms USA — owned by roughly 6,000 dairy farmers in seven midwestern states, mainly Wisconsin — is the third-largest dairy co-op in the US. From its nearly 30 plants, the cooperative produces cheese, fluid and powdered milk, whey, butter, and pharmaceutical-grade lactose under brands including Foremost, Golden Guernsey Dairy, and Morning Glory Dairy and private labels. The co-op also licenses the Foremost trademark to other dairy producers in the US and Mexico. Foremost was formed in 1995 when Wisconsin Dairies Cooperative and Golden Guernsey Dairy Cooperative consolidated operations. Cheese accounts for over 50% of its sales.

KEY COMPETITORS

AMPI
Dairy Farmers of America
Land O'Lakes

FOREVER LIVING PRODUCTS INTERNATIONAL, INC.

7501 E. McCormick Pkwy. 135 South
Scottsdale, AZ 85038
Phone: 480-998-8888
Fax: 480-905-8451
Web site: http://www.foreverlivingproducts.com

CEO: Rex Maughan
CFO: David Hall
HR: Glen B. Banks
Type: Private

1998 Est. Sales: $650.0 million
1-Yr. Sales Change: (48.2%)
Employees: 1,700
FYE: December

Although Forever Living Products International might not lead to immortality, its aloe vera-based health care products could improve your overall well-being. Founded in 1978, the firm sells an aloe vera juice drink (its first product), as well as aromatherapy products, cosmetics, dietary and nutritional supplements, deodorant, honey, lotion, and tooth gel products. Owner Rex Maughan also owns aloe vera plantations in the Dominican Republic, Mexico, and Texas; Aloe Vera of America, a processing plant; and Forever Resorts, 17 US resorts/marinas, including Dallas-area South Fork Ranch (of *Dallas* TV show fame). Forever Living Products sells its goods through a global network of independent distributors.

KEY COMPETITORS
Herbalife
Nature's Sunshine
Sunrider

FOSTER POULTRY FARMS

1000 Davis St.
Livingston, CA 95334
Phone: 209-394-7901
Fax: 209-394-6342
Web site: http://www.fosterfarms.com

CEO: Robert A. Fox
CFO: Larry Keillor
HR: Tim Walsh
Type: Private

1998 Sales: $990.0 million
1-Yr. Sales Change: (1.0%)
Employees: 7,000
FYE: December

As the West Coast's top poultry company, Foster Poultry Farms has a secure place in the pecking order. The company's vertically integrated operations see chickens and turkeys from the incubator to grocers' meat cases (under the Foster Farms brand). Foster Poultry Farms also serves the food service industry. In addition to hatching, raising, slaughtering, and processing chickens and turkeys into fresh and frozen products, the company grinds its own feeds and operates a fleet of refrigerated trucks. Already strong in western states, Foster Poultry Farms has cast its gaze eastwards, and it aims to compete nationally. Max and Verda Foster founded the company in 1939; it is still owned by the Foster family.

KEY COMPETITORS
Gold Kist
Perdue
Tyson Foods

FRANCISCAN HEALTH PARTNERSHIP, INC.

8 Airport Park Blvd.
Latham, NY 12110
Phone: 518-783-5257
Fax: 518-783-5548

CEO: James H. Flynn
CFO: Paul N. MacGiffert
HR: Katherine Bazar
Type: Not-for-profit

1997 Sales: $1,420.1 million
1-Yr. Sales Change: 6.3%
Employees: 11,807
FYE: December

The Franciscan Health Partnership, formerly Franciscan Sisters of the Poor Health System, works through a network of 11 hospitals, 13 long-term and continuing-care facilities, nine nursing homes, seven home health agencies, and five community service centers. The name change was designed to open the system to agreements not solely focused on their sponsor order, the Franciscan Sisters of the Poor. Operating in Kentucky, New Jersey, New York, Ohio, Pennsylvania, and South Carolina, the not-for-profit network has followed the national trend of hospital consolidation to reduce costs and joined the Catholic Health Care Network.

KEY COMPETITORS
Catholic Healthcare Partners
Columbia/HCA
Quorum Health

FRANK CONSOLIDATED ENTERPRISES

666 Garland Place
Des Plaines, IL 60016
Phone: 847-699-7000
Fax: 847-699-4047
Web site: http://www.wheels.com

CEO: James S. Frank
CFO: Mary Ann O'Dwyer
HR: Joan Richards
Type: Private

1998 Sales: $1,181.0 million
1-Yr. Sales Change: 15.2%
Employees: 574
FYE: August

Frank Consolidated Enterprises has an old lease on life. Subsidiary Wheels, Inc., which claims to have pioneered the auto leasing concept, provides administrative, management, and financing services to help corporations manage their vehicle fleets. The company manages more than 170,000 vehicles. It operates in the US as Wheels and in other countries through Interleasing, an alliance of about 20 international fleet management and leasing companies. Wheels was founded in 1939 by Zollie Frank. Frank's family still owns the parent company; his widow serves as its chair and his son is its president. Frank Consolidated Enterprises also owns Z Frank Chevrolet, a Chicago-based auto dealership.

KEY COMPETITORS
Enterprise Rent-A-Car
GE Capital
PHH Vehicle Management Services

FREEDOM COMMUNICATIONS, INC.

17666 Fitch Ave.
Irvine, CA 92614
Phone: 949-553-9292
Fax: 949-474-7675
Web site: http://www.freedom.com

CEO: Samuel Wolgemuth
CFO: David Kuykendall
HR: Mark Ernst
Type: Private

1998 Sales: $672.6 million
1-Yr. Sales Change: 4.2%
Employees: 7,000
FYE: December

Southern California is the real cradle of Freedom. Media conglomerate Freedom Communications owns more than two dozen daily newspapers, including its flagship, California's *Orange County Register,* with a circulation of about 360,000. In addition, the company owns 35 weekly papers, eight television stations, and nearly 20 niche magazines (including *P.O.V., Latin Trade,* and *MODE*). Freedom Communications also operates more than 50 Web sites, which range from online versions of its printed properties to regional information guides. The company is owned by the family of R. C. Hoiles.

KEY COMPETITORS
E. W. Scripps
Gannett
Times Mirror

THE FREEMAN COMPANIES

1421 W. Mockingbird
Dallas, TX 75247
Phone: 214-670-9000
Fax: 214-670-9100
Web site: http://www.freemanco.com

CEO: Donald S. Freeman
CFO: Joseph V. Popolo
HR: Dan Camp
Type: Private

1999 Sales: $675.0 million
1-Yr. Sales Change: 8.0%
Employees: 33,296
FYE: June

There's no business like the trade show business. Having staged thousands of conventions, corporate meetings, expositions, and trade shows annually, The Freeman Companies knows that maxim well. Freeman's operations include AVW Audio Visual (presentation technologies), Freeman Air (air freight services), Freeman Decorating (event design and production services), Freeman Exhibit (exhibit production), and Sullivan Transfer (material handling services). The company's projects have ranged from single trade show exhibits to the Republican National Convention. Founded in 1927 by D. S. "Buck" Freeman, the company is owned by the Freeman family (including chairman and CEO Donald Freeman) and company employees.

KEY COMPETITORS
Caribiner International
Reed Elsevier
United News & Media

FRESHPOINT, INC.

15305 Dallas Parkway, Ste. 1010	CEO: Mitt Parker	1999 Sales: $732.0 million
Dallas, TX 75248	CFO: Bernadette Kruk	1-Yr. Sales Change: —
Phone: 972-392-8100	HR: —	Employees: 2,500
Fax: 972-392-8130	Type: Private	FYE: June
Web site: http://www.freshpoint.com		

Eating veggies isn't just good for your body, it's good for FreshPoint, too. The company, the largest food service distributor of fruits and vegetables in the nation, owns over 30 distribution facilities in North America. Its operations involve food service and retail distribution, wholesale supply, procurement, and transportation. To assist customers, FreshPoint provides online ordering, procurement analysis, promotions, and weekly market reports; it also teaches customers the basics on managing and storing produce. Fresh-Point became independent when UK-based Albert Fisher sold its US distribution business to management in 1996. A planned merger with rival Fresh America failed in 1999.

KEY COMPETITORS
Fresh America
Nash Finch
SUPERVALU

FRY'S ELECTRONICS, INC.

600 Brokaw Rd.	CEO: John Fry	1998 Est. Sales: $1,250.0 million
San Jose, CA 95112	CFO: David Fry	1-Yr. Sales Change: 31.6%
Phone: 408-487-4500	HR: Kathryn Kolder	Employees: 4,000
Fax: 408-487-4700	Type: Private	FYE: December

Service may be heavy-handed, but where else can you buy appliances, build a computer, grab some Ho Hos or Maalox, and find the latest *Playboy* or *Byte*? The 16-store Fry's Electronics chain offers all this plus low prices, extensive inventory (including Crock-Pots, vacuums, stereos, TVs, and computer software and hardware), and whimsically themed displays (such as Wild West or UFO motifs). The technogeek's superstore — whose notoriously bad service is chronicled on unaffiliated Web pages — began in 1985 as the brainchild of CEO John Fry (with brothers Randy and David) and VP Kathryn Kolder. The Fry brothers, who got their start at Fry's Food Stores, still own the company.

KEY COMPETITORS
Best Buy
CompUSA
Good Guys

 See pages 196–197 for a full profile of this company.

FURR'S SUPERMARKETS, INC.

1730 Montano Rd. NW	CEO: Jan Friederich	1998 Est. Sales: $950.0 million
Albuquerque, NM 87107	CFO: Andrew Kann	1-Yr. Sales Change: (5.0%)
Phone: 505-998-3877	HR: Delwyn James	Employees: 5,600
Fax: 505-761-0866	Type: Private	FYE: December
Web site: http://www.furrs.com		

Out in the West Texas town of El Paso, folks buy their fajita fixins at Furr's Supermarkets. The company (no longer related to Furr's Cafeterias) operates about 70 grocery stores throughout New Mexico and West Texas, with nearly one-third in the El Paso area. In addition to groceries, various Furr's stores offer video rentals, pharmacies, banks, and post offices. Furr's is also testing online shopping. The company, founded as Furr's Inc. in 1904, became Furr's Supermarkets in 1991 as a result of a management-led LBO of 65 stores from the German parent company of Furr's Inc. Windward Capital Partners is the majority owner of the company; grocery wholesaler Fleming Companies has a 30% stake.

KEY COMPETITORS
Albertson's
Smith's Food & Drug
United Supermarkets

GAF CORPORATION

1361 Alps Rd.
Wayne, NJ 07470
Phone: 973-628-3000
Fax: 973-628-3326
Web site: http://www.gaf.com

CEO: Samuel J. Heyman
CFO: William Lang
HR: John Sinnott
Type: Private

1998 Sales: $1,088.0 million
1-Yr. Sales Change: 15.1%
Employees: 3,300
FYE: December

Working hard to keep a roof over your head? GAF is one of the US's oldest sources of commercial roofing material. Through its subsidiary, GAF Materials, the company manufactures commercial and residential roofing and other building products such as fiber-cement siding and roof insulation. Other products include the Sovereign and Timberline series of residential shingles; GAF CompositeRoof, for commercial asphalt roofing; and GAFWARE, a software program used by construction project managers to select the best roof for a building. GAF Materials, which is employee owned, has more than 25 plants in the US.

KEY COMPETITORS
Dow Chemical
DuPont
Elcor

GENAMERICA CORPORATION

700 Market St.
St. Louis, MO 63101
Phone: 314-231-1700
Fax: 314-525-6444
Web site: http://www.genamerica.com

CEO: Richard A. Liddy
CFO: David L. Herzog
HR: Marcia S. McMillian
Type: Mutual company

1998 Sales: $3,913.9 million
1-Yr. Sales Change: 24.1%
Employees: 4,725
FYE: December

Atten-shun! General American Life Insurance is now GenAmerica Corporation, which may pick up extra stars for its conversion to a mutual/stock ownership structure. General American Mutual Holding is the policyholder-owned mutual holding company for GenAmerica and its subsidiaries, including General American Life Insurance. The firm operates throughout the US and Canada, offering individual life, investment management, and other products. GenAmerica's Reinsurance Group of America operates in Europe, Latin America, North America, and the Pacific Rim. GenAmerica is being acquired by Metropolitan Life Insurance; its group health business is being bought by a US subsidiary of The Great-West Life Assurance Company.

KEY COMPETITORS
Allmerica Financial
MetLife
New York Life

See pages 198–199 for a full profile of this company.

GENERAL PARTS, INC.

2635 Millbrook Rd.
Raleigh, NC 27604
Phone: 919-573-3000
Fax: 919-573-3562

CEO: O. Temple Sloan
CFO: Bill Kuykendall
HR: Deborah Bowers
Type: Private

1998 Sales: $1,248.0 million
1-Yr. Sales Change: 17.7%
Employees: 10,150
FYE: December

Feel free to salute General Parts, a nationwide distributor of replacement automotive parts, supplies, and tools for every make and model of foreign and domestic car, truck, bus, and farm or industrial vehicle. The largest member of the CARQUEST network, employee-owned General Parts distributes its products to more than 2,700 CARQUEST and other auto parts stores across the US and in Canada through nearly 40 distribution centers. The company, which has been growing through acquisitions, sells its parts to do-it-yourself mechanics, professional installers, body shops, farmers, and fleet owners (commercial customers account for about 85% of CARQUEST's sales).

KEY COMPETITORS
AutoZone
Genuine Parts
Pep Boys

GENMAR HOLDINGS, INC.

100 S. 5th St., Ste. 2400	CEO: Grant E. Oppegaard	1999 Sales: $704.7 million
Minneapolis, MN 55402	CFO: Roger R. Cloutier	1-Yr. Sales Change: 20.3%
Phone: 612-339-7900	HR: —	Employees: 4,600
Fax: 612-337-1886	Type: Private	FYE: June
Web site: http://www.genmar.com		

Genmar Holdings cruises the pleasure-boat market with a line of luxury yachts, recreational powerboats, and fishing boats. Sold under brand names including Glastron and Wellcraft, Genmar's boats range from 50-footer yachts (servants not included) to fishing skiffs. It makes the boats at 10 sites in the US and Canada and has agreements with Outboard Marine, Brunswick, and others to supply engines. Genmar's boats are sold through more than 1,000 independent dealers in all 50 states and 30 other countries. CEO Irwin Jacobs formed the company in 1994 by merging the operations of Minstar and Miramar Marine, both of which he controlled. Jacobs owns a majority stake in Genmar.

KEY COMPETITORS
Brunswick
Fountain Powerboat
Outboard Marine

GENUARDI'S FAMILY MARKETS, INC.

301 E. Germantown Pike	CEO: Charles A. Genuardi	1998 Est. Sales: $725.0 million
Norristown, PA 19401	CFO: Tim Kullman	1-Yr. Sales Change: 6.3%
Phone: 610-277-6000	HR: Candace Krier	Employees: 5,000
Fax: 610-277-2908	Type: Private	FYE: December
Web site: http://www.genuardis.com		

Gaspare Genuardi put the horse before the cart in 1920, selling produce from a horse-drawn wagon. The company he founded, Genuardi's Family Markets, today owns about 30 Genuardi's stores in southeastern Pennsylvania and northern Delaware and two Zagara's upscale markets in New Jersey. Genuardi's stores ring up about 10% of the Philadelphia area's food sales. The company's 1997 purchase of Zagara's (a specialty store and bakery) is indicative of its move to serve higher-income markets; some company stores sport sushi bars and lobsters steamed to order. Genuardi's Family Markets has been family-owned and operated for three generations, although management is increasingly being recruited from the outside.

KEY COMPETITORS
A&P
Albertson's
Pathmark

GEOLOGISTICS CORPORATION

13952 Denver West Pkwy., Ste. 150	CEO: Roger E. Payton	1998 Sales: $1,600.0 million
Golden, CO 80401	CFO: Miles Stover	1-Yr. Sales Change: 4.9%
Phone: 303-704-4400	HR: Lou Roden	Employees: 6,300
Fax: 303-704-4411	Type: Private	FYE: December
Web site: http://www.geo-logistics.com		

GeoLogistics gets goods going, globally. With operations in 140 countries, GeoLogistics provides multi-modal freight-forwarding, customs brokerage, warehousing, and distribution services, as well as logistics and supply chain management, executive relocation services, and trade-show logistics. Shipments can be tracked through the company's Internet-based GeoVista system. Clients include Procter & Gamble, Porsche, and hard-disk manufacturer Western Digital. GeoLogistics was founded in 1996 by William E. Simon & Sons (which owns 26%), Oaktree Capital Management (46%), and CEO Roger Payton (with other officers, 25%).

KEY COMPETITORS
APL
CHR
Evergreen Marine

GEORGE E. WARREN CORPORATION

605 17th St.	CEO: Thomas L. Corr	1998 Sales: $1,406.2 million
Vero Beach, FL 32960	CFO: Jonathan W. Taylor	1-Yr. Sales Change: (46.0%)
Phone: 561-778-7100	HR: Martin Paris	Employees: 25
Fax: 561-778-7171	Type: Private	FYE: December

If you need to unload a little liquid natural gas, let George do it. George E. Warren is a refiner and major private wholesale distributor of liquid natural gas and other petroleum products in the southeastern US. It was founded in Boston as a coal and oil distributor by George E. Warren in 1907; it moved to Florida in the early 1990s. The company, which distributes its products by tank trucks and pipeline, has eight refining facilities in Port Everglades and Tampa, Florida; Venice, Louisiana; Greenville and Hattiesburg, Mississippi; Monument, New Mexico; and Galena and Bellville, Texas. Its products include propane, propylene, ethylene, gasoline, and heating oil. President Thomas Corr owns the company.

KEY COMPETITORS
Columbia Energy
Exxon Mobil
Williams Companies

THE GEORGE WASHINGTON UNIVERSITY

2121 I St. NW, 8th Fl.	CEO: Stephen J. Trachtenberg	1997 Sales: $887.6 million
Washington, DC 20052	CFO: Louis H. Katz	1-Yr. Sales Change: (4.9%)
Phone: 202-994-1000	HR: Susan B. Kaplan	Employees: 11,272
Fax: 202-994-0654	Type: School	FYE: June
Web site: http://www.gwu.edu		

With its main campus located just four blocks from the White House, George Washington University stands in the heart of our nation's capital. Chartered by the US Congress in 1821 as The Columbian College in the District of Columbia, the university adopted its present name in 1904. Its more than 16,900 students and 4,300 faculty members (about a third of whom teach full-time) are scattered across the university's primary campus at Foggy Bottom as well as its campuses in Mount Vernon and Ashburn, Virginia. George Washington University also offers several off-campus graduate programs. Its academic programs run the spectrum from business to law to medicine.

GEORGETOWN UNIVERSITY

37th and O Sts. NW	CEO: Leo J. O'Donovan	1999 Sales: $814.4 million
Washington, DC 20057	CFO: Nicole F. Mandeville	1-Yr. Sales Change: 0.9%
Phone: 202-687-5055	HR: Jo-Ann Henry	Employees: —
Fax: 202-687-5595	Type: School	FYE: June
Web site: http://www.georgetown.edu		

Founded in 1789 by John Carroll, the nation's first Catholic bishop, Georgetown University is the oldest Catholic university in the US. Its more than 12,400 students (about half are undergraduates) are instructed by an 1,800-member faculty in eight schools ranging from the university's renowned Law Center to the Edmund A. Walsh School of Foreign Service to Georgetown's School of Medicine. The university is also home to the Georgetown University Medical Center, and has forged numerous ties with its neighbors in the Washington, DC, community. Among its alumni are President Bill Clinton, basketball great Patrick Ewing, and former US Surgeon General Antonia Novello.

GEORGIA CROWN DISTRIBUTING

7 Crown Circle
Columbus, GA 31907
Phone: 706-568-4580
Fax: 706-561-1647

CEO: Donald M. Leebern
CFO: Orlene Boviard
HR: Mary Beth Gibbon
Type: Private

1999 Sales: $700.0 million
1-Yr. Sales Change: 3.7%
Employees: 1,600
FYE: July

Aptly named Fate D. Leebern may have died for Georgia Crown Distributing, a bottler and beverage distributor. He founded Georgia Crown as Columbus Wine Company Distributor in 1938, the same year Georgia prohibition was repealed. After the first rail shipment of legal liquor was received, someone — reportedly the Dixie Mafia — murdered Leebern. Today the family-owned company distributes several varieties of wine, liquor, beer, water, and juices to Georgia, Alabama, and Tennessee. Georgia Crown also distributes its own Melwood Springs brand of bottled water. CEO Donald Leebern Jr. is the grandson of the company's founder.

KEY COMPETITORS
Coca-Cola Enterprises
National Distributing
Southern Wine & Spirits

GEORGIA LOTTERY CORPORATION

250 Williams St., Ste. 3000
Atlanta, GA 30303
Phone: 900-225-8259
Fax: 404-215-8871
Web site: http://www.galottery.com

CEO: Rebecca Paul
CFO: Andy Davis
HR: Margaret Bode
Type: Government-owned

1998 Sales: $1,735.2 million
1-Yr. Sales Change: 0.9%
Employees: 250
FYE: June

The Georgia Lottery's big winners? More than 450,000 students who have attended college on lottery-funded HOPE scholarships. Established in 1993, the Georgia Lottery has contributed nearly $3.5 billion to the state's education coffers. In addition to the HOPE program, the lottery helps finance a pre-kindergarten program and public school capital improvements. More than 6,500 retailers throughout Georgia sell tickets for lottery games, including instant-ticket games, online games, keno-style games, and a Powerball-like game aptly named Big Game. In its first year the Georgia Lottery reached $1.1 billion in sales, and it has been growing ever since.

KEY COMPETITORS
Florida Lottery
Multi-State Lottery
Southern Wine & Spirits

GIANT EAGLE INC.

101 Kappa Dr.
Pittsburgh, PA 15238
Phone: 412-963-6200
Fax: 412-963-0374
Web site: http://www.gianteagle.com

CEO: David S. Shapira
CFO: Mark Minnaugh
HR: Raymond A. Huber
Type: Private

1999 Est. Sales: $4,360.0 million
1-Yr. Sales Change: 7.7%
Employees: 25,600
FYE: June

With its talons firmly around western Pennsylvania, Giant Eagle is eyeing new territory to the West. The #1 food retailer in Pittsburgh, it operates more than 200 company-owned and independent supermarkets (about 50,000 sq. ft. in size) throughout western Pennsylvania, eastern Ohio, and northern West Virginia. It also provides wholesale goods to supermarkets in the region. In addition to food, many Giant Eagle stores feature video rental, banking, photo processing, and ready-to-eat meals. The company's purchase and integration of the 35-store Rini-Rego Stop-n-Shop chain made it the #1 food seller in eastern Ohio. Giant Eagle, owned by five founding families, including CEO David Shapira, was started in 1931.

KEY COMPETITORS
Kroger
Royal Ahold
SUPERVALU

 See pages 200–201 for a full profile of this company.

GILBANE, INC.

7 Jackson Walkway
Providence, RI 02903
Phone: 401-456-5800
Fax: 401-456-5936
Web site: http://www.gilbaneco.com

CEO: Paul J. Choquette
CFO: Ken Alderman
HR: Dan M. Kelly
Type: Private

1998 Sales: $2,200.0 million
1-Yr. Sales Change: 14.4%
Employees: 1,200
FYE: December

For four generations, family-owned Gilbane has tried to be the bane of its rivals. Gilbane, one of the US's oldest builders, has two subsidiaries. Gilbane Building constructs commercial and industrial facilities (including pharmaceutical plants, R&D labs, schools, prisons, and water-treatment plants) and provides construction management services. Projects include the National Air and Space Museum, Lake Placid's 1980 Winter Olympics facilities, and the US Justice Building renovation. Gilbane Properties does real estate development, property management, and finance. CEO Paul Choquette is a descendant of William and Thomas Gilbane, who founded the firm in 1873. Gilbane has offices in 17 US states.

KEY COMPETITORS
McCarthy
Turner Corporation
Whiting-Turner

GLAZER'S WHOLESALE DRUG COMPANY INC.

14860 Landmark Blvd.
Dallas, TX 75240
Phone: 972-702-0900
Fax: 972-702-8508

CEO: Bennett Glazer
CFO: Cary Rossel
HR: Rusty Harmount
Type: Private

1998 Sales: $855.0 million
1-Yr. Sales Change: 12.8%
Employees: 2,700
FYE: December

Glazer's Wholesale Drug took its name during Prohibition, when only drugstores and drug wholesalers could deal in liquor. Owned by chairman and CEO Bennett Glazer, it is a wholesale distributor of alcoholic beverages. The largest distributor of malts, spirits, and wines in Texas and one of the largest US wine and spirits distributors, it also operates in Arizona, Arkansas, Indiana, Iowa, Kansas, Louisiana, and Missouri. Among the lines it distributes are Robert Mondavi, Hiram Walker, and Jim Beam. Glazer's has been acquiring wholesalers and distributors in the Midwest, including Superior Wines & Liquors (Missouri), Premier Wines & Spirits (Kansas), and Messer Distributing (Iowa).

KEY COMPETITORS
Block Distributing
Southern Wine & Spirits
Young's Market

GLOBAL PETROLEUM CORP.

800 South St.
Waltham, MA 02454
Phone: 781-894-8800
Fax: 781-398-4160

CEO: Alfred A. Slifka
CFO: Thomas McManmon
HR: Barbara Rosenblum
Type: Private

1997 Sales: $1,900.0 million
1-Yr. Sales Change: (9.4%)
Employees: 175
FYE: December

With global ambitions and petroleum sources from around the world, Global Petroleum is an independent wholesaler of gasoline, heating oil, natural gas, and residual fuel oil. From its regional roots, it has grown to annual revenues of more than $2 billion. Global Petroleum sells to retail gas chains, utility power plants, and industrial users. The company makes a proprietary low-sulfur diesel fuel, and Global's Casey Petroleum subsidiary distributes a full line of Mobil lubricants. Founded in 1933 by the father of current president and CEO Alfred Slifka, the company is still owned by the Slifka family.

KEY COMPETITORS
Koch
Tauber Oil
Tosco

GOLD KIST INC.

244 Perimeter Center Pkwy. NE
Atlanta, GA 30346
Phone: 770-393-5000
Fax: 770-393-5262
Web site: http://goldkist.com

CEO: Gaylord O. Coan
CFO: Stephen O. West
HR: William A. Epperson
Type: Cooperative

1999 Sales: $1,766.1 million
1-Yr. Sales Change: 7.0%
Employees: 17,500
FYE: June

Gold Kist isn't too chicken to run after Tyson or Perdue. An agricultural co-operative operating in 11 states (mainly in the South), Gold Kist is a top US poultry processor, selling whole chickens and chicken parts to the food service industry and retailers. It also processes pork and breeds catfish and is involved in metal fabrication as well as financing for farmers. The company produces nuts through #1 US pecan processor Young Pecan Company (a partnership with Young Pecan Shelling Company) and Golden Peanut Company (a partnership with Archer-Daniels-Midland and Alimenta). Focusing on food, Gold Kist sold its farm supply assets, including 100 farm stores, to Southern States Cooperative in 1998.

KEY COMPETITORS
ConAgra
Perdue
Tyson Foods

 See pages 202–203 for a full profile of this company.

GOLDEN STATE FOODS CORPORATION

18301 Von Karman Ave., Ste. 1100
Irvine, CA 92612
Phone: 949-252-2000
Fax: 949-252-2080

CEO: Mark S. Wetterau
CFO: Gene L. Olson
HR: Ron Childers
Type: Private

1998 Est. Sales: $1,600.0 million
1-Yr. Sales Change: 6.7%
Employees: 1,800
FYE: December

Did somebody say McDonald's? Food processor and distributor Golden State Foods is listening. The company is one of the fast-food giant's largest suppliers, providing its restaurants with more than 130 products (beef, buns, ketchup, mayonnaise, salad dressing). McDonald's is the company's sole customer. Golden State Foods has 12 plants and distribution centers in Australia, Egypt, and the US. The company was founded in 1947 by the late William Moore. Investment firm Yucaipa owns 70% of Golden State; management company Wetterau Associates owns most of the remainder.

KEY COMPETITORS
JR Simplot
Keystone Foods
Martin-Brower

 See pages 204–205 for a full profile of this company.

THE GOLUB CORPORATION

501 Duanesburg Rd.
Schenectady, NY 12306
Phone: 518-355-5000
Fax: 518-355-0843
Web site: http://www.pricechopper.com

CEO: Lewis Golub
CFO: John Endres
HR: Curt Hopkins
Type: Private

1999 Est. Sales: $1,720.0 million
1-Yr. Sales Change: 6.8%
Employees: 18,000
FYE: April

Hungry to take a bite out of the competition, Golub is offering tasty come-ons such as table-ready meals, gift certificates, automatic discount cards, and a hotline where cooks answer food-related queries. The company operates more than 100 Price Chopper supermarkets in Massachusetts, upstate New York, northeastern Pennsylvania, and Vermont. It also operates Mini Chopper convenience stores. The company recently implemented its second try at home shopping and delivery with its HouseCalls grocery service. Descendants of the Golub brothers (who founded the stores in 1932) run the company. Employees own more than 40% of the company's stock.

KEY COMPETITORS
A&P
Grand Union
Royal Ahold

GOODMAN HOLDING CO.

1501 Seamist Dr.
Houston, TX 77008
Phone: 713-861-2500
Fax: 713-861-2176
Web site: http://www.goodmanmfg.com

CEO: John B. Goodman
CFO: Lewis Fox
HR: Cliff Reily
Type: Private

1998 Est. Sales: $2,055.0 million
1-Yr. Sales Change: 8.2%
Employees: 7,500
FYE: December

Like a good air conditioner or washing machine, Goodman Holding operates
quietly. Through subsidiaries Amana Appliances and Goodman Manufacturing, the low-profile company makes air-conditioning and heating equipment
and large appliances (such as washers, dryers, microwave and range ovens,
and refrigerators) for residential and commercial use. Goodman Holding,
which sells its products through retailers and distributors worldwide, is
among the top US makers of air conditioners (United Technologies' Carrier
unit is #1). Its brand names include Amana, Caloric, Goodman, and Janitrol.
Goodman Holding is owned by the family of the late Harold Goodman, who
founded the company in 1977.

KEY COMPETITORS
American Standard
Fedders
United Technologies

GOODWILL INDUSTRIES INTERNATIONAL, INC.

9200 Rockville Pike
Bethesda, MD 20814
Phone: 301-530-6500
Fax: 301-530-1516
Web site: http://www.goodwill.org

CEO: Fred Grandy
CFO: Samuel W. Cox
HR: Patricia Williams
Type: Not-for-profit

1998 Sales: $1,507.0 million
1-Yr. Sales Change: 10.7%
Employees: 60,000
FYE: December

Founded to give those in need "a hand up, not a handout," Goodwill
Industries International supports the operations of about 230 independent Goodwill chapters worldwide. Though known mainly for its more
than 1,700 thrift stores, Goodwill focuses on providing rehabilitation,
training, placement, and employment services for those with disabilities
and other barriers to employment. Goodwill is one of the world's largest
providers of such services, as well as one of the world's largest employers
of the disabled. Funding comes primarily from the retail stores, contract
services provided to local employers, and grants. More than 80% of revenues go to job training and rehabilitation programs.

KEY COMPETITORS
Salvation Army
Fedders
United Technologies

GORDON BROTHERS GROUP, LLC

40 Broad St.
Boston, MA 02109
Phone: 888-424-1903
Fax: 617-422-6222
Web site: http://www.gordonbrothers.com

CEO: Michael G. Frieze
CFO: Alan R. Goldstein
HR: Karen Meier
Type: Private

1998 Est. Sales: $1,000.0 million
1-Yr. Sales Change: —
Employees: 234
FYE: December

Gordon Brothers Group (GBG) has built its success story on the failures of
others. One of the nation's largest liquidators, the company closes some
2,000 stores encompassing nearly $2 billion worth of inventory each year,
and handles the sale of merchandise, real estate, fixtures, and furniture.
GBG prides itself on discretion and speed (projects generally take two to
three months). The company also provides secured bridge loans through its
Gordon Brothers Capital unit and makes equity investments in various companies through GB Equity Partners. Clients include Laura Ashley, Kay Jewelers, Crown Books, and Discovery Zone. GBG was founded in 1903 by Jacob
Gordon, whose grandson Michael Frieze serves as CEO.

KEY COMPETITORS
Hilco/Great American Group
Schottenstein Stores
The Nassi Group, LLC

GORDON FOOD SERVICE INC.

333 50th St. SW
Grand Rapids, MI 49548
Phone: 616-530-7000
Fax: 616-249-4125
Web site: http://www.gfs.com

CEO: Dan Gordon
CFO: Steve Plakmeyer
HR: David Vickery
Type: Private

1998 Sales: $1,700.0 million
1-Yr. Sales Change: 6.3%
Employees: 3,400
FYE: October

Gordon Food Service (GFS) helps satisfy the appetites of Midwesterners and Canadians. A food distributor serving schools, restaurants, and other institutions, GFS boasts more than 12,000 items ranging from fresh produce to sanitation systems. The company also makes its own line of foods under names such as Triumph Packaging and Ready, Set, Serve. Not merely a food distributor, the company also sells food in bulk through its 70 GFS Marketplace retail stores across four states (think Sam's Club without the membership fee). The late Isaac VanWestenbrugge (an ancestor of the Gordon family) founded the company as a butter and egg distributor in 1897. GFS is still owned by the Gordon family.

KEY COMPETITORS
AmeriServe
SYSCO
U.S. Foodservice

GOULD PAPER CORPORATION

11 Madison Ave., 14th Fl.
New York, NY 10010
Phone: 212-301-0000
Fax: 212-320-4333
Web site: http://www.gouldpaper.com

CEO: Harry E. Gould
CFO: Dan J. Lala
HR: Michelle Meadows
Type: Private

1998 Sales: $815.0 million
1-Yr. Sales Change: 10.1%
Employees: 450
FYE: December

Paper is as good as gold for Gould Paper, one of the largest privately owned distributors of printing and fine writing paper in the US. The company sells papers for multiple markets, including fine arts papers, commercial printing and lithography, book and magazine publishing, direct mail and catalogs, envelopes, and specialty converting papers. Gould Paper also makes agricultural equipment for harvesting and mowing. Harry Gould Sr. (father of chairman, president, and company owner Harry Gould Jr.) formed the company in 1924 as a printing paper merchant primarily for the greeting card industry. The company has expanded over the years by acquiring other paper companies.

KEY COMPETITORS
Clifford Paper
International Paper
WWF Paper

GOYA FOODS, INC.

100 Seaview Dr.
Secaucus, NJ 07096
Phone: 201-348-4900
Fax: 201-348-6609
Web site: http://www.goyafoods.com

CEO: Joseph A. Unanue
CFO: Miguel Lugo
HR: Karmen A. Reccio
Type: Private

1999 Sales: $653.0 million
1-Yr. Sales Change: 5.3%
Employees: 2,200
FYE: May

Featuring black beans and yellow rice, Goya Foods' palette of products, aimed at Hispanic palates, are shipped by the pallet. One of the biggest Hispanic-owned companies in the US, Goya makes more than 850 grocery products, including a variety of canned and dried beans, olives and olive oil, rice mixes, seasonings, fruit nectars, and a line of frozen Caribbean entrees. A growing interest in ethnic foods throughout the US is helping Goya become more recognized outside Hispanic homes. However, the company faces increased competition from food giants, such as Campbell Soup, as well as foods exported from Mexico. The Unanue family, which founded, owns, and runs Goya, is one of the richest Hispanic clans in the US.

KEY COMPETITORS
Authentic Specialty Foods
Bestfoods
Del Monte

See pages 206–207 for a full profile of this company.

GRANT THORNTON INTERNATIONAL

Prudential Plaza, Ste. 800, 130 E. Randolph St.	CEO: Robert A. Kleckner	1998 Sales: $1,506.0 million
Chicago, IL 60601	CFO: Louis A. Fanchi	1-Yr. Sales Change: 7.2%
Phone: 312-856-0001	HR: Debbie Pastor	Employees: 20,160
Fax: 312-861-1340	Type: Partnership	FYE: December
Web site: http://www.gti.org		

Grant Thornton International is a kid brother to the Big Five. The partnership of accounting and management consulting firms operates from about 580 offices in 93 countries, placing it among the top second-tier companies that trail around behind the biggest of the big guys (PricewaterhouseCoopers, Andersen Worldwide, Ernst & Young International, KPMG International, and Deloitte Touche Tohmatsu). In addition to the traditional business of accounting firms, Grant Thornton focuses on such niche areas as information technology and corporate finance. With the lowering of trade barriers in Latin America and Europe, Grant Thornton has moved to help smaller firms develop business in these emerging markets.

KEY COMPETITORS
Andersen Worldwide
Ernst & Young
PricewaterhouseCoopers

 See pages 208–209 for a full profile of this company.

GRAYBAR ELECTRIC COMPANY, INC.

34 N. Meramec Ave.	CEO: Carl L. Hall	1998 Sales: $3,744.1 million
St. Louis, MO 63105	CFO: John W. Wolf	1-Yr. Sales Change: 12.2%
Phone: 314-512-9200	HR: Jack F. Van Pelt	Employees: 7,900
Fax: 314-512-9453	Type: Private	FYE: December
Web site: http://www.graybar.com		

Keeping connected is no problem for Graybar Electric, one of the largest distributors of electrical products in the US. Purchasing from thousands of manufacturers, the company distributes more than 100,000 electrical and communications components, including wire, cable, and lighting products. Its customers include electrical contractors (which account for nearly 40% of sales), industrial plants, power utilities, and telecommunications providers. Subsidiary Graybar Financial Services offers equipment leasing and financing. Employee-owned Graybar Electric has 275 offices and distribution facilities in Canada, Mexico, Puerto Rico, Singapore, and the US.

KEY COMPETITORS
Arrow Electronics
W.W. Grainger
WESCO International

See pages 210–211 for a full profile of this company.

GREAT DANE LIMITED PARTNERSHIP

502 E. Lathrop Ave.	CEO: C. F. Hammond	1998 Est. Sales: $1,000.0 million
Savannah, GA 31415	CFO: Tom Horan	1-Yr. Sales Change: 0.0%
Phone: 912-644-2100	HR: Thor Egede-Nissen	Employees: 4,700
Fax: 912-644-2624	Type: Private	FYE: December
Web site: http://www.greatdanetrailers.com		

Great Dane is a company that's going places. Serving both Canada and the US, it's one of the largest makers of truck trailers in North America, and it plans to expand into Latin America. Great Dane makes refrigerated and freight vans and platform trailers at nine manufacturing plants, which along with its sales and service centers, are located in the US, primarily in the Midwest, East, and South. The company also sells used vans. Great Dane is a unit of Chicago-based investment group CC Industries, which is controlled by the Henry Crown family. The company started in 1900 as a maker of steel products and switched to trailer making in 1931.

KEY COMPETITORS
Dorsey Trailers
Utility Trailer
Wabash National

GREAT LAKES CHEESE COMPANY, INC.

17825 Great Lakes Pkwy.
Hiram, OH 44234
Phone: 440-834-2500
Fax: 440-834-1002
Web site: http://www.greatlakescheese.com

CEO: Hans Epprecht
CFO: Russ Mullins
HR: Beth Wendell
Type: Private

1998 Sales: $700.0 million
1-Yr. Sales Change: 12.0%
Employees: 1,000
FYE: December

Sure, the very name, Great Lakes Cheese Company, tells you what it makes and where it sells it, but it doesn't tell you to whom and to what degree. The firm makes, buys, packages, and distributes natural and process cheeses. Its products include cheddar, Swiss, mozarella, and provolone, primarily for bulk and food service sale. It also sells deli cheese products under its own name and packs chunks, slices, and shredded cheese under private labels for retailers. Great Lakes Cheese also imports cheeses from several countries in Europe. President and CEO Hans Epprecht, a Swiss immigrant, founded the company in 1958 as a bulk-cheese distributor in Cleveland. Epprecht owns the majority of Great Lakes Cheese.

KEY COMPETITORS
ConAgra
Land O'Lakes
Saputo Group

THE GREEN BAY PACKERS, INC.

1265 Lombardi Ave.
Green Bay, WI 54304
Phone: 920-496-5700
Fax: 920-496-5738
Web site: http://www.packers.com

CEO: Robert E. Harlan
CFO: John Jones
HR: Mark Schiefelbein
Type: Not-for-profit

1999 Sales: $102.7 million
1-Yr. Sales Change: 24.9%
Employees: 95
FYE: March

If winning is indeed the only thing, then the Green Bay Packers were making their old coach Vince Lombardi proud in the 1990s. They made the playoffs in six consecutive seasons this past decade, including two Super Bowl appearances and one championship. Playing in historic Lambeau Field, the Green Bay Packers are the only publicly owned team in the NFL. (The Packers are a not-for-profit corporation with more than 100,000 shareholders; shares do not appreciate and pay no dividends.) Green Bay is the league's smallest market, however, and the team is falling badly behind other teams in stadium revenues, prompting discussions of a major renovation or replacement of Lambeau Field, which was built in 1957.

KEY COMPETITORS
Chicago Bears Football Club
Detroit Lions
Minnesota Vikings

 See pages 212–213 for a full profile of this company.

GROCERS SUPPLY CO. INC.

3131 E. Holcombe Blvd.
Houston, TX 77021
Phone: 713-747-5000
Fax: 713-746-5797
Web site: http://www.grocerssupply.com

CEO: Milton Levit
CFO: —
HR: Phil Thompson
Type: Private

1999 Sales: $1,400.0 million
1-Yr. Sales Change: 0.0%
Employees: 1,800
FYE: May

Grocers Supply Co. distributes groceries near and far. The company distributes groceries, health and beauty items, household products, and school and office supplies to convenience stores and supermarkets throughout Texas and Louisiana. Its Grocers Supply International division takes orders by e-mail and ships supplies to commercial customers, US embassies, and oil company operations anywhere in the world. The company is owned by the Levit family of Houston, investors in the Houston-based hot dog company James Original Coney Island Inc.

KEY COMPETITORS
Fleming Companies
GSC Enterprises
SUPERVALU

GROUP HEALTH COOPERATIVE OF PUGET SOUND

521 Wall St.
Seattle, WA 98121
Phone: 206-326-3000
Fax: 206-448-5963
Web site: http://www.ghc.org

CEO: Cheryl M. Scott
CFO: Jim Truess
HR: John Nagelmann
Type: Not-for-profit

1998 Sales: $1,322.7 million
1-Yr. Sales Change: 30.2%
Employees: 9,602
FYE: December

Group Health Cooperative of Puget Sound is a not-for-profit managed health care group serving more than 30 counties in Washington state and five counties in Idaho. Members may participate in HMO, PPO, or point-of-service health plans. The co-op, which is governed by an 11-member board, controls Group Health Northwest. Group Health Cooperative of Puget Sound has allied with Virginia Mason Medical Center to share medical centers and hospitals. Despite strong market share, the cooperative had experienced less-than-stellar financial performance in years past, prompting its 1997 affiliation with Kaiser Permanente, the nation's largest health care delivery system. The organization is owned by its nearly 700,000 members.

KEY COMPETITORS
Adventist Health
Foundation Health Systems
PacifiCare

GROVE WORLDWIDE LLC

1565 Buchanon Trail East
Shady Grove, PA 17256
Phone: 717-597-8121
Fax: 717-593-5039
Web site: http://www.groveworldwide.com

CEO: Salvatore J. Bonanno
CFO: Stephen L. Cripe
HR: Donald Mallo
Type: Private

1999 Sales: $775.0 million
1-Yr. Sales Change: 96.8%
Employees: —
FYE: September

A heavy lifting specialist, Grove Worldwide is North America's leading crane manufacturer. The company makes mobile hydraulic cranes, truck-mounted cranes, and self-propelled aerial work platforms. Marketed under the Grove Crane name, its more than 40 models of mobile hydraulic cranes account for 70% of sales. Its aerial work platforms are sold under the Grove Manlift name, while its telescoping, truck-mounted cranes go by the National Crane brand. Founded in 1947 as Grove Manufacturing, the firm has plants in the US, UK, Europe, the United Arab Emirates, Singapore, and China. It sells to equipment rental companies and end users and is owned by Keystone Inc., the investment arm of Texas financier Robert Bass.

KEY COMPETITORS
Chatwins Group
JLG Industries
Terex

GROWMARK INC.

1701 Towanda Ave.
Bloomington, IL 61701
Phone: 309-557-6000
Fax: 309-829-8532
Web site: http://www.growmark.com

CEO: Bill Davisson
CFO: Vern McGinnis
HR: Stan Nielson
Type: Cooperative

1998 Est. Sales: $1,300.0 million
1-Yr. Sales Change: (17.2%)
Employees: 966
FYE: August

Fuse farming essentials "growing" and "marketing" and the result is GROWMARK, a retail farm-supply and grain-marketing cooperative. Through its member/owner co-ops — more than 120 in retail and 270-plus in grain marketing — GROWMARK serves more than 250,000 farmers in the midwestern US and Ontario, Canada. Under the FS name, the co-op sells farm supplies such as feed and fuel. Corn and soybeans are among the major crops it markets. GROWMARK's partnerships include ADM/GROWMARK, a grain marketing venture with Archer Daniels Midland; fertilizer maker and distributor CF Industries; pet food producer PRO-PET; seed and feed ventures with Land O'Lakes; and an energy alliance with Countrymark Cooperative and Land O'Lakes.

KEY COMPETITORS
Agway
Cenex Harvest States
Farmland Industries

GS INDUSTRIES, INC.

1901 Roxborough Rd., Ste. 200
Charlotte, NC 28211
Phone: 704-366-6901
Fax: 704-365-4340

CEO: Mark Essig
CFO: Luis E. Leon
HR: Richard Luzzi
Type: Private

1998 Sales: $815.9 million
1-Yr. Sales Change: 0.8%
Employees: 2,400
FYE: December

GS Industries (GSI) is one of the US's top makers of wire rod, and is the only producer of wire rod for radial tire cord in North America. GSI produces other wire products and grinding media, such as steel balls and mill liners which are used by the mining industry to process ore. The company has mining-products plants in Australia, and through its ME International subsidiary, it has a joint venture with Elecmetal to build a mill liner foundry in Chile. GSI was established by the merger of Georgetown Steel and GS Technologies, formerly part of steelmaker Armco. Investment firm Bain Capital owns more than 45% of the company, which is selling its Florida Wire & Steel unit that makes pre-stressed concrete strand.

KEY COMPETITORS
Keystone Consolidated
Northwestern Steel & Wire
Olin

GSC ENTERPRISES, INC.

130 Hillcrest Dr.
Sulphur Springs, TX 75482
Phone: 903-885-0829
Fax: 903-885-6928
Web site: http://www.gscenterprises.com

CEO: Michael K. McKenzie
CFO: Kerry Law
HR: Theresa Patterson
Type: Private

1998 Sales: $1,082.4 million
1-Yr. Sales Change: (11.6%)
Employees: 1,650
FYE: December

GSC Enterprises brings the groceries to the grocery store. The wholesale distributor (whose name stands for "Grocery Supply Company," not to be confused with Grocers Supply Co.) supplies independently owned convenience stores, grocers, discounters, and other retailers and wholesalers. It serves a total of some 15,000 stores in about 15 states in the Southwest, Southeast, and Midwest. GSC stocks and distributes tobacco, candy, grocery items, prepared foods (Chicago Style Pizza, Chester Fried Chicken, Deli-Fast Foods), and other items. The firm also owns Fidelity Express, whose Entronics unit sells money orders in stores. GSC is owned by the McKenzie family, descendants of two of the men who founded it in 1947.

KEY COMPETITORS
Eby-Brown
Fleming Companies
SUPERVALU

GUARDIAN INDUSTRIES CORP.

2300 Harmon Rd.
Auburn Hills, MI 48326
Phone: 248-340-1800
Fax: 248-340-2395
Web site: http://www.guardian.com

CEO: William Davidson
CFO: Jeffrey A. Knight
HR: Bruce Cummings
Type: Private

1998 Est. Sales: $2,200.0 million
1-Yr. Sales Change: 10.0%
Employees: 15,000
FYE: December

Giving its customers a break would never occur to Guardian Industries, the world's fourth-largest glassmaker. With facilities in 15 countries on five continents, Guardian primarily produces float glass and fabricated glass products for the automobile and construction markets. It also makes architectural glass, fiberglass insulation, and automotive trim parts. President and CEO William Davidson took Guardian Industries public in 1968 and bought it back for himself in 1985. Davidson also is the owner of the Detroit Pistons basketball team, the Detroit Shock women's basketball team, and the Detroit Vipers hockey team.

KEY COMPETITORS
Asahi Glass
Owens Corning
PPG

See pages 214–215 for a full profile of this company.

THE GUARDIAN LIFE INSURANCE COMPANY OF AMERICA

7 Hanover Sq.
New York, NY 10004
Phone: 212-598-8000
Fax: 212-919-2790
Web site: http://www.theguardian.com

CEO: Joseph D. Sargent
CFO: Peter L. Hutchings
HR: Douglas C. Kramer
Type: Mutual company

1998 Sales: $8,498.7 million
1-Yr. Sales Change: 18.4%
Employees: —
FYE: December

Guardian Life Insurance has chosen to remain part of the old guard — a mutual — when many competitors are going public. The company provides individual and group insurance and investment products. Facing deregulation and industry consolidation, the company is increasing its traditional indemnity group health insurance to a comprehensive line of employee benefits, including HMO, PPO, and dental and vision plans, as well as disability plans. It is growing its retirement and wealth management offerings with the addition of brokerage and trust services. Guardian Life Insurance Company of America has operations in all 50 states, the District of Columbia, and Puerto Rico.

KEY COMPETITORS
Aetna
MetLife
Prudential

See pages 216–217 for a full profile of this company.

GUIDE CORPORATION

121 E. 11th St.
Anderson, IN 46016
Phone: 765-641-5437
Fax: 765-641-6151

CEO: Michael N. Hammes
CFO: Mike Yukich
HR: Dennis Stachelski
Type: Private

1998 Est. Sales: $665.0 million
1-Yr. Sales Change: —
Employees: 4,000
FYE: December

This Guide shows motorists the way through the dark. The company designs and makes auto lighting systems: headlamps, turn signals, tail lamps, and license plate lamps. The company has factories in Indiana, Louisiana, and Mexico and supplies its products to General Motors, Isuzu, Toyota, and other carmakers. Guide is owned by New York-based investment firm Palladium Equity Partners, which purchased the lighting operations of GM's former subsidiary, Delphi Automotive Systems, to create the company in 1998. The company took its name from Guide Motor Lamp Manufacturing, which developed the first electric headlamp before it was acquired by GM in 1928.

KEY COMPETITORS
Federal-Mogul
Robert Bosch
Visteon Automotive Systems

GULF OIL, L.P.

90 Everett Ave.
Chelsea, MA 02150
Phone: 617-889-9000
Fax: 617-884-0637
Web site: http://www.gulfoil.com

CEO: John Kaneb
CFO: Alice Kuhne
HR: Karen Channel
Type: Partnership

1999 Sales: $1,808.0 million
1-Yr. Sales Change: 0.4%
Employees: 185
FYE: September

Gulf Oil bridges the gap between petroleum producers and retail sales outlets. The petroleum wholesaler distributes gasoline and diesel fuel to 2,400 Gulf-branded stations as well as to other operators in 11 northeastern states. The company, which owns and operates 14 storage terminals, also distributes motor oils, lubricants, and heating oil to commercial, industrial, and utility customers. Cumberland Farms, an operator of about 800 convenience stores, owns a majority interest in the company and markets Gulf-branded products. Gulf Oil sponsors a NASCAR racing team and several New England hockey teams.

KEY COMPETITORS
BP Amoco
Exxon Mobil
Tosco

GULF STATES TOYOTA, INC.

7701 Wilshire Place Dr.
Houston, TX 77040
Phone: 713-744-3300
Fax: 713-744-3332

CEO: —
CFO: Frank Gruen
HR: Dominic Gallo
Type: Private

1999 Est. Sales: $2,500.0 million
1-Yr. Sales Change: 8.7%
Employees: 1,600
FYE: December

Even good ol' boys buy foreign cars from Gulf States Toyota. One of only two US Toyota distributors not owned by Toyota Motor Sales (the other is JM Family Enterprises' Southeast Toyota Distributors), the company distributes Toyota cars, trucks, and sport utility vehicles in Arkansas, Louisiana, Mississippi, Oklahoma, and Texas. Founded in 1969 by Thomas Friedkin and still owned by The Friedkin Companies, Gulf States distributes new Toyotas, parts, and accessories to around 140 dealers in its region. Because Toyota has had success converting Internet leads into actual sales, Gulf States offers customizable Web site packages to its entire dealership network, and it conducts Internet sales seminars.

KEY COMPETITORS
Ford
General Motors
Nissan

HALE-HALSELL CO.

9111 E. Pine St.
Tulsa, OK 74158
Phone: 918-835-4484
Fax: 918-641-5471

CEO: Robert D. Hawk
CFO: Michael Owens
HR: Ron Stacey
Type: Private

1998 Sales: $815.0 million
1-Yr. Sales Change: 11.5%
Employees: 4,674
FYE: December

Hale-Halsell Co. doesn't make cattle drives, but the food retailer and wholesaler does round up and move out grocery goods throughout Arkansas, Kansas, Missouri, Oklahoma, and Texas. On the retail side, the company operates more than 130 Git-n-Go convenience stores and 12 SUPER H supermarkets, primarily in small Oklahoma towns. Hale-Halsell also runs a restaurant supply business. Tom Hale and Hugh Halsell started the company in 1901 to supply settlers in the newly opened Native American lands in Oklahoma. Hale-Halsell is owned by Hale's descendant, Elmer Hale Jr.

KEY COMPETITORS
Fleming Companies
Kroger
Wal-Mart

HALLMARK CARDS, INC.

2501 McGee St.
Kansas City, MO 64108
Phone: 816-274-5111
Fax: 816-274-5061
Web site: http://www.hallmark.com

CEO: Irvine O. Hockaday
CFO: Robert J. Druten
HR: Ralph N. Christensen
Type: Private

1998 Sales: $3,900.0 million
1-Yr. Sales Change: 5.4%
Employees: 20,945
FYE: December

As the #1 maker of meaningful missives, Hallmark Cards is the Goliath of greeting cards. The company's cards are sold under brand names such as Hallmark, Shoebox, and Ambassador and can be found in more than 47,000 US retail stores (about 7,500 of these stores bear the Hallmark name; the company owns less than 5% of these stores and the rest are franchised). Hallmark also owns Binney & Smith (makers of Crayola brand crayons) and portrait studio chain Picture People. It offers electronic greeting cards through its Web site, Hallmark.com, and produces television movies through its Hallmark Entertainment unit. Members of the founding Hall family own two-thirds of Hallmark; company employees own the remainder.

KEY COMPETITORS
American Greetings
CSS Industries
Gibson Greetings

See pages 218–219 for a full profile of this company.

HARBOUR GROUP

7701 Forsyth Blvd., Ste. 600
St. Louis, MO 63105
Phone: 314-727-5550
Fax: 314-727-0941
Web site: http://www.harbourgroup.com

CEO: Sam Fox
CFO: Joseph Gutierrez
HR: —
Type: Private

1997 Est. Sales: $1,500.0 million
1-Yr. Sales Change: 15.4%
Employees: 10,000
FYE: December

Troubled manufacturers can seek refuge with Harbour Group, a conglomerate that acquires manufacturing companies through LBOs. Since its founding in 1976, Harbour Group has grown by acquisitions to operate about 115 companies, some of which have been combined with other businesses and taken public. Principal shareholder Sam Fox (also chairman and CEO) and his sons acquire small manufacturers in slow-growth industries such as cutting tools, medical products, plastics, aluminum pumps, robotics, and rubber seals. Taking a hands-on approach, Harbour Group assists its portfolio companies in several areas, including corporate strategy and finances. The Harbour businesses operate about 45 plants.

KEY COMPETITORS
Kennametal
Swagelok
United States Surgical

HARPO, INC.

110 N. Carpenter St.
Chicago, IL 60607
Phone: 312-633-1000
Fax: 312-633-1976
Web site: http://www.oprah.com

CEO: Oprah Winfrey
CFO: Doug Pattison
HR: Bernice Smith
Type: Private

1998 Sales: $162.0 million
1-Yr. Sales Change: 8.0%
Employees: 190
FYE: December

Harpo (unrelated to the silent Marx brother) is built on a foundation of talk. Harpo produces *The Oprah Winfrey Show,* the highest-rated TV talk show in history. The show is seen in more than 200 US markets and about 142 international markets. The company also produces feature films and made-for-TV movies. Winfrey founded Harpo ("Oprah" spelled backward) in 1986, the same year her talk show went into syndication. A group of Texas cattle ranchers claimed that her 1996 show on mad cow disease prompted a drop in beef futures prices; they sued, unsuccessfully, under the "veggie libel" laws. Winfrey will provide original programming for new women's cable station Oxygen, and is launching a magazine with Hearst.

KEY COMPETITORS
Lifetime
Time Warner
USA Networks

 See pages 220–221 for a full profile of this company.

HARTZ GROUP INC.

667 Madison Ave.
New York, NY 10021
Phone: 212-308-3336
Fax: 212-644-5987
Web site: http://www.hartz.com

CEO: Leonard N. Stern
CFO: Curtis B. Schwartz
HR: Frank Gomez
Type: Private

1998 Est. Sales: $935.0 million
1-Yr. Sales Change: 48.4%
Employees: 2,600
FYE: December

Billionaire Leonard Stern's Hartz Group may be the only real estate development firm with a reason to encourage pet ownership. The group, which has developments in New Jersey and New York, also owns Hartz Mountain pet products. Stern's father started Hartz Mountain in 1926 (selling birds, cages, and feed) after immigrating to the US from Germany with 2,100 canaries. The Hartz Group is also into newspapers — Stern Publishing owns several newspapers, including such alternative weekly publications as the *Village Voice.* Many of the group's papers (which have a combined circulation of more than 850,000) are distributed at no cost to readers. Leonard Stern's sons control day-to-day management of the company.

KEY COMPETITORS
Colgate-Palmolive
Lefrak Organization
New York Times

HARVARD PILGRIM HEALTH CARE, INC.

10 Brookline Place West
Brookline, MA 02146
Phone: 617-745-1000
Fax: 617-730-4692
Web site: http://www.harvardpilgrim.org

CEO: Charles D. Baker
CFO: Elly Fant
HR: Charlie Baker
Type: Not-for-profit

1998 Sales: $2,670.0 million
1-Yr. Sales Change: 13.7%
Employees: 5,000
FYE: December

This Harvard bleeds green rather than crimson. Harvard Pilgrim Health Care is Massachusetts's largest provider of managed health care (though Blue Cross and Blue Shield of Massachusetts has more members). The company offers its more than 1 million customers HMO, PPO, point-of-service, and Medicaid/Medicare plans through some 20,000 physicians and about 150 affiliated hospitals throughout New England (though it plans to pull out of Rhode Island). Formed by the 1995 merger of Harvard Community Health Plan and Pilgrim Health Care, the company has financial problems with its Medicare business as well as physician relations. The state of Massachusetts gave it a cash injection and has put the company in receivership.

KEY COMPETITORS
Blue Cross (MA)
CIGNA
Tufts Health Plan

HARVARD UNIVERSITY

Massachusetts Hall
Cambridge, MA 02138
Phone: 617-495-1000
Fax: 617-495-0754
Web site: http://www.harvard.edu

CEO: Neil L. Rudenstine
CFO: Elizabeth Huidekoper
HR: Mary Cronin
Type: School

1999 Sales: $1,787.5 million
1-Yr. Sales Change: 6.4%
Employees: —
FYE: June

Harvard — maybe you've heard of it? The university is one of the world's most prestigious, with alumni that include six US presidents, more than 30 Nobel Prize winners, and renowned authors such as Ralph Waldo Emerson, Gertrude Stein, and T. S. Eliot. It has about 17,600 students and is among the US' most competitive universities. The private, coeducational school consists of Harvard College (undergraduate) and 10 graduate schools. Radcliffe College, primarily women's undergraduate, was closely tied to Harvard but remained legally separate until 1999. At $14 billion, Harvard's endowment is the largest of any US university.

 See pages 222–223 for a full profile of this company.

HAWORTH INC.

1 Haworth Center
Holland, MI 49423
Phone: 616-393-3000
Fax: 616-393-1570
Web site: http://www.haworth.com

CEO: Gerald B. Johanneson
CFO: Calvin W. Kreuze
HR: Nancy Teutsch
Type: Private

1998 Sales: $1,510.0 million
1-Yr. Sales Change: 0.0%
Employees: 10,000
FYE: December

Haworth isn't as square thinking as you might think they'd be. The company is the #3 office furniture manufacturer in the US (behind Steelcase and Herman Miller, #1 and #2, respectively). Haworth — whose invention of pre-wired partitions made today's cubicled workplace possible — has a reputation for being efficient and aggressive and for regularly underpricing competitors. The company, growing through acquisitions, operates in more than 70 countries and offers a full line of office furniture, including desks, storage products, panel systems, tables, and seating. Haworth is owned by the family of Gerrard Haworth, who founded the company in 1948.

KEY COMPETITORS
HON INDUSTRIES
Herman Miller
Steelcase

See pages 224–225 for a full profile of this company.

H. B. ZACHRY COMPANY

527 Logwood
San Antonio, TX 78221
Phone: 210-475-8000
Fax: 210-475-8060
Web site: http://www.zachry.com

CEO: Henry Bartell Zachry
CFO: Joe J. Lozano
HR: Bill Wimberley
Type: Private

1998 Sales: $670.0 million
1-Yr. Sales Change: 1.5%
Employees: 7,500
FYE: December

H. B. Zachry began building power plants in 1924. The family-owned industrial and commercial construction firm's business today includes building and maintaining process/chemical plants, refineries, roads, dams, reservoirs, pipelines, missile sites, and hotels. Operating mostly in the South, H. B. Zachry also works internationally (it is rebuilding the US Embassy in Moscow). US projects include the Alaska Pipeline Project and runways at DFW International Airport. Affiliate H. B. Zachry Realty is managing partner of Sunset Station Group's planned $52 million entertainment and retail complex in San Antonio. Zachry has an interest in the San Antonio Spurs basketball team. CEO Henry Zachry is the founder's son.

KEY COMPETITORS
Bechtel
Fluor
Peter Kiewit Sons'

H. E. BUTT GROCERY COMPANY

646 S. Main Ave.
San Antonio, TX 78204
Phone: 210-938-8000
Fax: 210-938-8169
Web site: http://www.heb.com

CEO: Charles C. Butt
CFO: John C. Brouillard
HR: Diane Peck
Type: Private

1998 Sales: $7,500.0 million
1-Yr. Sales Change: 15.4%
Employees: 45,000
FYE: October

The Muzak bounces between Tejano and country, and the tortillas and ribs are big sellers at H. E. Butt Grocery Company (H-E-B). Texas' largest private company, H-E-B is the #1 food retailer in South and Central Texas, with more than 260 H-E-B supermarkets, including about 90 smaller H-E-B Pantry stores mostly in rural towns. Stores offer a full line of groceries, and some have gas pumps. H-E-B also has facilities for processing meat, dairy products, and bread, and it offers the H-E-B and Hill Country Fare private labels. Already familiar with the tastes of Latinos (who make up about half of its Texas market), it is expanding in Mexico with upscale and discount stores. The founding Butt family owns the company.

KEY COMPETITORS
Albertson's
Randall's
Wal-Mart

 See pages 226–227 for a full profile of this company.

HEALTH CARE SERVICE CORPORATION

300 E. Randolph
Chicago, IL 60601
Phone: 312-653-6000
Fax: 312-819-1220
Web site: http://www.bcbsil.com

CEO: Raymond F. McCaskey
CFO: Sherman M. Wolff
HR: Robert Ernst
Type: Mutual company

1998 Sales: $7,819.0 million
1-Yr. Sales Change: 53.1%
Employees: —
FYE: December

Health Care Service Corporation is made up of Blue Cross Blue Shield of Illinois (that state's oldest and largest health insurer) and Blue Cross and Blue Shield of Texas. Health Care Service Corporation provides a wide range of group and individual insurance and medical plans, including indemnity insurance and managed care programs. The mutual company licenses the Blue Cross Blue Shield name from the Blue Cross and Blue Shield Association, and offers insurance under the brand nationwide. The company also offers life insurance, retirement services, and medical financial services through subsidiaries.

KEY COMPETITORS
Humana
Prudential
UnitedHealth Group

 See pages 228–229 for a full profile of this company.

HEALTH INSURANCE PLAN OF GREATER NEW YORK

7 W. 34th St.
New York, NY 10001
Phone: 212-630-5000
Fax: 212-630-8747
Web site: http://www.hipusa.com

CEO: Anthony L. Watson
CFO: Steven Titan
HR: Fred Blickman
Type: Not-for-profit

1997 Sales: $1,567.6 million
1-Yr. Sales Change: (9.6%)
Employees: 1,483
FYE: December

Founded in 1944 to provide health care services for city workers, Health Insurance Plan of Greater New York (HIP) is a not-for-profit health maintenance organization with close to 1 million members. City, state, and federal workers make up approximately 40% of HIP's enrollment. The organization serves the New York City area through about 50 medical facilities that provide medical care and laboratory and pharmacy services. HIP has sold its affiliate, HIP Health Plan of New Jersey, to PHP Healthcare, a Virginia-based manager of health plan networks.

KEY COMPETITORS
Aetna
Empire Blue Cross
Kaiser Foundation

HEALTH MIDWEST

2304 E. Meyer Blvd.
Kansas City, MO 64132
Phone: 816-276-9297
Fax: 816-276-9222
Web site: http://www.healthmidwest.org

CEO: Richard Brown
CFO: Thomas Langenberg
HR: Sue Heiman
Type: Not-for-profit

1998 Sales: $652.7 million
1-Yr. Sales Change: (2.5%)
Employees: 14,700
FYE: December

Health Midwest operates about 15 hospitals in metropolitan Kansas City, and serves people within a 150-mile radius of the city. With more than 2,000 physicians and about 100 service locations, Health Midwest is not only the largest health care provider in the area, but is also a major employer. Services include primary care, rehabilitation, and home health care. Specialized programs and community outreach services include childbirth classes, health screenings, a program for older adults, physician referral, and a family practice residency program. Despite expansion efforts by health care giant Columbia/HCA, Health Midwest and other local hospitals retain top market shares in the area.

KEY COMPETITORS
Catholic Health Initiatives
Columbia/HCA
Saint Luke's Shawnee Mission

THE HEARST CORPORATION

959 8th Ave.
New York, NY 10019
Phone: 212-649-2000
Fax: 212-765-3528
Web site: http://www.hearstcorp.com

CEO: Frank A. Bennack
CFO: Ronald J. Doerfler
HR: Ruth Diem
Type: Private

1998 Sales: $2,375.0 million
1-Yr. Sales Change: (16.2%)
Employees: 13,555
FYE: December

Family-owned Hearst Corporation is a media giant with interests in newspaper, magazine, and business publishing; TV and radio broadcasting; cable network programming; and online services. The company owns 12 daily newspapers, including the *San Francisco Examiner* (Hearst plans to either sell the *Examiner* or fold it into the *San Francisco Chronicle* once it completes buying the rival paper) and the *Houston Chronicle;* 12 weeklies; about 20 US consumer magazines, including *Cosmopolitan;* stakes in cable TV networks, including A&E and ESPN; TV and radio stations (through Hearst-Argyle Television); and business publishers. Hearst also owns about 48% of Women.com Networks, the Internet's largest site for women.

KEY COMPETITORS
Advance Publications
Chronicle Publishing
Viacom

 See pages 230–231 for a full profile of this company.

HENDRICK AUTOMOTIVE GROUP

6000 Monroe Rd., Ste. 100
Charlotte, NC 28212
Phone: 704-568-5550
Fax: 704-566-3295
Web site: http://www.hendrickauto.com

CEO: Jim C. Perkins
CFO: James F. Huzl
HR: Suzanne Wrenn
Type: Private

1998 Sales: $2,434.0 million
1-Yr. Sales Change: (0.9%)
Employees: 4,300
FYE: December

For megadealer Hendrick Automotive Group, variety is the spice of life. The company sells new and used cars and light trucks from 17 automakers, including makes such as General Motors, Honda, Porsche, and Saturn. Hendrick has a network of about 85 franchises in over 10 states, from the Carolinas to California. The company also offers financing, leasing, and insurance, as well as automobile parts, accessories, service, and body repair. Founder Rick Hendrick pleaded guilty in 1997 to mail fraud relating to alleged bribes of American Honda executives, forcing an ownership rearrangement: Hendrick owns half of the company through a family trust; investment firm Warburg Pincus owns the other half.

KEY COMPETITORS
AutoNation
CarMax
United Auto Group

HENRY FORD HEALTH SYSTEM

1 Ford Place
Detroit, MI 48202
Phone: 313-876-8700
Fax: 313-876-9243
Web site: http://www.henryfordhealth.org

CEO: Gail L. Warden
CFO: David Mazurkiewicz
HR: Robert Rieny
Type: Not-for-profit

1998 Sales: $1,302.9 million
1-Yr. Sales Change: (40.8%)
Employees: 17,000
FYE: December

In 1915 automaker Henry Ford founded the hospital that would be the starting point for the Henry Ford Health System, which today is a southeastern Michigan hospital network that also provides medical research and education. The system includes six hospitals with nearly 2,000 beds, more than 35 other health care facilities, and about 1,800 physicians offering a wide range of specialties. The system's Health Alliance Plan provides managed care and health insurance to more than 500,000 members. The Henry Ford Health Sciences Center Research Institute, Josephine Ford Cancer Center, and other research centers and affiliated hospitals are also part of the health care system.

KEY COMPETITORS
Blue Cross (MI)
Detroit Medical Center
Sisters of St. Joseph

HENSEL PHELPS CONSTRUCTION CO.

420 6th Ave.
Greeley, CO 80632
Phone: 970-352-6565
Fax: 970-352-9311
Web site: http://www.henselphelps.com

CEO: Jerry L. Morgensen
CFO: Stephen J. Carrico
HR: Muriel Reitz
Type: Private

1999 Sales: $1,165.0 million
1-Yr. Sales Change: 24.7%
Employees: 2,151
FYE: May

From the courthouse to the Big House, Hensel Phelps Construction has built it. The company has come a long way since Hensel Phelps started the firm in 1937 as a one-man homebuilder. It now concentrates on the nonresidential market; projects have included courthouses, hospitals, passenger terminals, and prisons. Hensel Phelps Construction is the general contractor for the Denver Pavilions downtown retail/entertainment complex. Affiliate Phelps Program Management manages construction programs and development and offers facilities operation and maintenance. Affiliate HP Environmental Services provides environmental construction and hazardous-waste remediation services. The company is owned by its employees.

KEY COMPETITORS
Centex
Clark Enterprises
MA Mortenson

HEWITT ASSOCIATES LLC

100 Half Day Rd.
Lincolnshire, IL 60069
Phone: 847-295-5000
Fax: 847-295-7634
Web site: http://www.hewitt.com

CEO: Dale L. Gifford
CFO: Dan DeCanniere
HR: David Wille
Type: Private

1999 Sales: $1,075.0 million
1-Yr. Sales Change: 25.3%
Employees: 10,930
FYE: September

Hewitt Associates is one of the nation's largest benefits-consulting services, covering human resources, employee benefits, compensation, financial management, and administration for more than 10 million employees and dependents. The company's Hewitt 401(k) Index keeps track of 401(k) records, encompassing $62 billion in assets and 1.4 million participants. The company serves about 2,800 clients, and has about 70 offices in 31 countries in the Asia/Pacific region, Europe, and North and South America. Hewitt Associates was founded in Illinois by Edwin "Ted" Hewitt in 1940.

KEY COMPETITORS
PricewaterhouseCoopers
Towers Perrin
Watson Wyatt

HICKS, MUSE, TATE & FURST INCORPORATED

200 Crescent Ct., Ste. 1600
Dallas, TX 75201
Phone: 214-740-7300
Fax: 214-720-7888

CEO: Thomas O. Hicks
CFO: Darron Ash
HR: Lynita Jessen
Type: Private

1998 Sales: —
1-Yr. Sales Change: —
Employees: —
FYE: December

Hicks, Muse, Tate & Furst wants to get the word out, so the leveraged buy-out firm is building a media empire. Hicks, Muse assembles limited partnership investment pools and targets companies in specific niches that can form a nucleus for other investments. In addition to its media holdings (its AMFM broadcast group is set to merge with Clear Channel Communications to form the US's largest television, radio, and outdoor advertising firm), the firm owns International Home Foods (makers of Jiffy Pop and Chef Boyardee products), real estate, and other holdings. Hicks, Muse is also moving abroad, accumulating cable, radio, food, and other companies in Latin America and Europe.

KEY COMPETITORS
Clayton, Dubilier
Investcorp
KKR

 See pages 232–233 for a full profile of this company.

HIGHMARK INC.

5th Avenue Place, 120 5th Ave.
Pittsburgh, PA 15222
Phone: 412-544-7000
Fax: 412-544-8368
Web site: http://www.highmark.com

CEO: John S. Brouse
CFO: Robert C. Gray
HR: Thomas C. Sommers
Type: Not-for-profit

1998 Sales: $7,543.5 million
1-Yr. Sales Change: 1.9%
Employees: 12,000
FYE: December

Highmark aims to be at the acme of HMOs. Formed by Pennsylvania Blue Shield's merger with Veritus (formerly Blue Cross of Western Pennsylvania), Highmark provides health-related coverage to nearly 6 million customers. It also processes Medicare claims (Veritus Medicare and Xact Medicare), offers administrative and information services (Alliance Ventures), and sells group life, disability, and employer stop loss insurance through its Highmark Life and Casualty Group subsidiary. The company also provides community service programs, such as the Western Pennsylvania Caring Foundation.

KEY COMPETITORS
Aetna
CIGNA
Guardian Life

See pages 234–235 for a full profile of this company.

HINES INTERESTS L.P.

2800 Post Oak Blvd., Ste. 4800
Houston, TX 77056
Phone: 713-621-8000
Fax: 713-966-2051
Web site: http://www.hines-ww.com

CEO: Jeffery C. Hines
CFO: C. Hastings Johnson
HR: David LeVrier
Type: Private

1998 Est. Sales: $700.0 million
1-Yr. Sales Change: 7.7%
Employees: 2,700
FYE: December

Founded by Gerald Hines in Houston in 1957, Hines Interests is a private commercial real estate development company that handles most aspects of real estate development, including site selection, re-zoning, design, construction bidding and management, and financing. Hines also manages more than 75 million sq. ft. of real estate in the US and 10 international markets. Management services include public relations, security, tenant relations, and vendor contract-negotiation services. The company's commercial portfolio includes more than 160 million sq. ft. of commercial property, including the Gallerias in Houston and Dallas, two of the US's largest shopping complexes. It has put them both up for sale.

KEY COMPETITORS
Lefrak Organization
Lincoln Property
Trammell Crow Residential

HOBBY LOBBY STORES, INC.

7707 SW 44th St.
Oklahoma City, OK 73179
Phone: 405-745-1100
Fax: 405-745-1636
Web site: http://www.hobbylobby.com

CEO: David Green
CFO: Patrick Jones
HR: —
Type: Private

1998 Sales: $664.0 million
1-Yr. Sales Change: 12.5%
Employees: 11,000
FYE: December

Hobby Lobby Stores has something for idle hands. The company operates about 210 stores in 21 states, selling arts and crafts supplies, baskets, silk flowers, frames, and other items. In its statement of purpose, Hobby Lobby says it operates according to biblical principles, and it has closed most of its stores on Sundays in spite of the lost sales. Hobby Lobby runs Basket Market, an Oklahoma City bulk retail store; Worldwood, maker of wood products, T-shirts, and candles; and frame maker Greco Frame & Supply. Sister company Mardel sells Christian materials and office and educational supplies at 11 stores in Oklahoma, Texas, and Arkansas. CEO David Green, who founded the company in 1972, owns Hobby Lobby.

KEY COMPETITORS
Garden Ridge
Hancock Fabrics
Jo-Ann Stores

HOLIDAY COMPANIES

4567 W. 80th St.
Bloomington, MN 55437
Phone: 612-830-8700
Fax: 612-830-8864

CEO: Ronald Erickson
CFO: Arnold D. Mickelson
HR: Bob Nye
Type: Private

1998 Est. Sales: $1,700.0 million
1-Yr. Sales Change: 54.5%
Employees: 6,000
FYE: December

Days off from retailing and wholesaling are few at Holiday Companies, which owns convenience stores, wholesale grocery warehouses, and sporting goods stores in the upper Midwest and the Northwest. It operates about 250 Holiday convenience stores, all of which sell gas supplied by the company's Erickson Petroleum subsidiary. It also owns about 30 sporting goods stores (mostly Gander Mountain stores) in the Midwest; current expansion plans could double that number. Holiday is closing or selling its three Fairway Foods grocery distribution warehouses. The company was founded in 1928 as a general store in a small Wisconsin town by two Erickson brothers, whose descendants own and operate the company.

KEY COMPETITORS
Exxon Mobil
Fleming Companies
SUPERVALU

HOLIDAY RETIREMENT CORP.

2250 McGilchrist St. SE, Ste. 200
Salem, OR 97302
Phone: 503-370-7070
Fax: 503-364-5716
Web site: http://www.holidayretirementcorp.com

CEO: William E. Colson
CFO: Christine Wiegal
HR: Kathryn Smedema
Type: Private

1998 Est. Sales: $680.0 million
1-Yr. Sales Change: 18.3%
Employees: 8,750
FYE: December

With meal and maid services and organized social activities for their enjoy-
ment, residents of Holiday Retirement communities probably feel like
they're on a permanent vacation. The company, with more than 200 facilities in Europe and North America, is the top retirement community operator in Europe and the US and is #3 in Canada. It has its own property
developer (Colson & Colson Construction), architects (Curry-Brandaw), and
builders (Colson & Colson General Contractors). Colson & Colson owns the
properties, and Holiday Retirement manages them, hiring a few couples to
live on-site. Peverel, a joint venture between the company and Westminster
Health Care, is the #1 operator of retirement homes in the UK.

KEY COMPETITORS
Castle & Cooke
Host Marriott
Life Care Centers

HOLMAN ENTERPRISES INC.

7411 Maple Ave.
Pennsauken, NJ 08109
Phone: 856-663-5200
Fax: 856-665-3444
Web site: http://www.holmanauto.com

CEO: Joseph S. Holman
CFO: Ken T. Coppola
HR: Paul Toepel
Type: Private

1998 Sales: $1,870.0 million
1-Yr. Sales Change: (0.0%)
Employees: 2,700
FYE: December

Holman sells a whole lot of cars. Family-owned Holman Enterprises owns
20 car and truck dealerships in southern New Jersey and southern Florida.
Founded in 1924, Holman sells Ford, Lincoln, Mercury, Saturn, BMW,
Infiniti, Jaguar, and Rolls-Royce cars, and Ford, Kenworth, and Sterling
trucks. Holman's RMP engine and parts distributor sells small parts and
powertrains authorized by Ford. Its Automotive Resources International
unit, one of the largest independently owned vehicle fleet leasing management groups in the world, also operates a truck upfitting company. Holman
is expanding with a Jaguar/Infiniti dealership in New Jersey and a Lincoln-
Mercury dealership in Florida.

KEY COMPETITORS
AutoNation
Penske
United Auto Group

HOLY CROSS HEALTH SYSTEM CORPORATION

3575 Moreau Court
South Bend, IN 46628
Phone: 219-233-8558
Fax: 219-233-8891
Web site: http://www.hchs.org

CEO: Sister Patricia Vandenberg
CFO: Stephen A. Felsted
HR: Brent Miller
Type: Not-for-profit

1998 Sales: $1,500.0 million
1-Yr. Sales Change: 7.1%
Employees: 19,135
FYE: May

Holy Hoosiers! Holy Cross Health System Corporation (HCHS) is a not-for-
profit health care system founded in 1979 and sponsored by the Sisters of
the Holy Cross, a Catholic religious order. It has seven hospitals in California, Idaho, Indiana, Maryland, and Ohio; a community services organization
in Utah; an insurance firm, a long-term care organization, a practice management company; home health programs, educational programs, health
care services for the poor, and a nursing school. To help provide for the poor,
HCHS has moved into managed care, building primary care networks.
HCHS plans to merge with the larger Mercy Health Services to create the #3
Catholic health care system in the US.

KEY COMPETITORS
Blue Cross
Columbia/HCA
Tenet Healthcare

HONICKMAN AFFILIATES

8275 Rte. 130	CEO: Jeffrey Honickman	1998 Est. Sales: $1,005.0 million
Pennsauken, NJ 08110	CFO: Walt Wilkinson	1-Yr. Sales Change: —
Phone: 856-665-6200	HR: June Raufer	Employees: 5,200
Fax: 856-661-4684	Type: Private	FYE: December

Honickman Affiliates doesn't mind bottling up its creative juices. The firm is the nation's largest privately owned bottling company, bottling and distributing soft drinks and other beverages primarily in Maryland, New Jersey, New York, and Ohio through 11 facilities. It is a major East Coast bottler of Pepsi and 7 UP, and it also bottles AriZona, Mistic, Nantucket Nectars, and SoBe beverages for select markets. Honickman has been in talks with PepsiCo about becoming an anchor bottler for that company. Honickman also produces its own beverage brands and private-label brands for supermarkets. Chairman and owner Harold Honickman started the company in 1957 when his father-in-law built a bottling plant for him.

KEY COMPETITORS
Coca-Cola Bottling (NY)
Cott
Philadelphia Coca-Cola

HORSEHEAD INDUSTRIES INC.

110 E. 59th St.	CEO: William E. Flaherty	1998 Est. Sales: $770.0 million
New York, NY 10022	CFO: Ronald Statile	1-Yr. Sales Change: 2.7%
Phone: 212-527-3000	HR: —	Employees: 2,900
Fax: 212-527-3008	Type: Private	FYE: December

Horsehead Industries says "Nay" to pollution with its environmental cleanup services; it also produces zinc metal products. Through Horsehead Resources Development, the company recovers and recycles zinc left over from steelmaking operations. It also reclaims soil on damaged lands. Horsehead sells the recycled zinc products through its subsidiary Zinc Corporation of America. Horsehead might have felt like the horse's other end in 1995 when it was hit with a $5.6 million fine by the EPA and an obligation to spend up to $40 million to reduce its cadmium and lead emissions. Horsehead faced a $12 million lawsuit filed by the US government in 1998 to recover cleanup costs for a zinc refining site.

KEY COMPETITORS
Cominco
Noranda
Rio Algom

H.T. HACKNEY COMPANY

502 S. Gay St.	CEO: William B. Sansom	1998 Sales: $1,818.0 million
Knoxville, TN 37902	CFO: Mike Morton	1-Yr. Sales Change: 12.0%
Phone: 423-546-1291	HR: —	Employees: 2,900
Fax: 423-546-1501	Type: Private	FYE: December
Web site: http://www.hthackney.com		

The H.T. Hackney Company hitched up a horse and buggy and began delivering goods to small groceries in 1891; it now supplies independent grocers and convenience stores in more than 20 states, primarily in the Southeast, but also in the Midwest and Texas. H.T. Hackney distributes more than 10,000 name-brand items, including frozen food, coffee, tobacco products, candy, health and beauty items, deli products, and meat. It also offers inventory and accounting software to its customers. In addition, H.T. Hackney owns Eli Witt, another convenience store wholesaler, and it has operations that make furniture (Volunteer Fabricators) and distribute petroleum. Chairman and CEO Bill Sansom owns the company.

KEY COMPETITORS
Alex Lee
Eby-Brown
GSC Enterprises

HUBER, HUNT & NICHOLS INC.

2450 S. Tibbs Ave.	CEO: Michael D. Kerr	1998 Sales: $1,039.0 million
Indianapolis, IN 46241	CFO: Jeffrey J. Lewis	1-Yr. Sales Change: 2.9%
Phone: 317-241-6301	HR: —	Employees: 625
Fax: 317-243-3461	Type: Private	FYE: December
Web site: http://www.huberhuntnichols.com		

Huber, Hunt & Nichols knows that if they build it, you will come. A private company held by The Hunt Corporation, the construction firm is a leading builder of sports arenas. Its projects include more than 45 stadiums and arenas, such as the Alamodome in San Antonio, the Superdome in New Orleans, Riverfront Stadium in Cincinnati, Jacobs Field in Cleveland, and retractable-dome stadiums in Seattle, Phoenix, and Milwaukee. Besides sports projects, the company's portfolio includes office buildings, detention facilities, laboratories, industrial operations, hotels, and hospitals. Huber, Hunt & Nichols is owned by its employees.

KEY COMPETITORS
Barton Malow
Gilbane
Turner Corporation

HUNT CONSOLIDATED INC.

Fountain Place, 1445 Ross at Field	CEO: Ray L. Hunt	1998 Sales: $700.0 million
Dallas, TX 75202	CFO: Don F. Robillard	1-Yr. Sales Change: (30.0%)
Phone: 214-978-8000	HR: Chuck Mills	Employees: 2,600
Fax: 214-978-8888	Type: Private	FYE: December

Hunt Consolidated is a holding company for the oil and real estate businesses of Ray Hunt, son of legendary Texas wildcatter H. L. Hunt. Founded in 1934 (reportedly with H. L.'s poker winnings), Hunt Oil is an independent oil and gas production and exploration company with interests throughout the southern and Rocky Mountain regions of the US, the Gulf of Mexico, the Middle East, and South America. Its high-risk, high-reward exploration strategy led to the discovery of a huge oil field in Yemen. In hopes of a repeat, Hunt has explored for oil in western Ghana and in Newfoundland. Hunt's real estate operations, concentrated in Dallas, include commercial and residential development and third-party property management.

KEY COMPETITORS
BP Amoco
Exxon Mobil
Lincoln Property

HUNTSMAN CORPORATION

500 Huntsman Way	CEO: Jon M. Huntsman	1998 Sales: $5,200.0 million
Salt Lake City, UT 84108	CFO: J. Kimo Esplin	1-Yr. Sales Change: 9.5%
Phone: 801-532-5200	HR: William Chapman	Employees: 10,000
Fax: 801-584-5781	Type: Private	FYE: December
Web site: http://www.huntsman.com		

Missing its favorite "soaps" would be unthinkable for Huntsman, maker of a wide range of industrial and specialty chemicals used in detergents and by the plastics, rubber, and packaging industries. Its units make polypropylene, expandable polystyrenes, protective packaging, and surfactants. The company has sold its polystyrene and styrene monomer businesses and has bought the bulk chemical lines of UK-based Imperial Chemical Industries, nearly doubling its size. Family-owned Huntsman is the US's largest privately held chemical business. Chairman Jon Huntsman has given millions to educational and charitable causes and medical research, including a billion-dollar commitment to Utah's Huntsman Cancer Institute.

KEY COMPETITORS
BASF AG
Dow Chemical
DuPont

📖 See pages 236–237 for a full profile of this company.

HYATT CORPORATION

200 W. Madison St.	CEO: Thomas J. Pritzker	1999 Est. Sales: $3,400.0 million
Chicago, IL 60606	CFO: Frank Borg	1-Yr. Sales Change: 4.6%
Phone: 312-750-1234	HR: Linda Olson	Employees: 80,000
Fax: 312-750-8550	Type: Private	FYE: January
Web site: http://www.hyatt.com		

Hyatt, one of the nation's largest hotel operators, is at your service. The company has more than 110 full-service luxury hotels and resorts in North America and the Caribbean (Hyatt International, a separate company, operates 80 hotels and resorts in about 35 other countries). Hyatt features professionally designed golf courses and Camp Hyatt (supervised activities for children) at a number of its resorts. In addition to hotels, the company offers casinos (resort and riverboat), a time-share resort, and luxury retirement communities. Hyatt caters to business travelers, convention-goers, and upscale vacationers. The Pritzker family owns both the US and international Hyatt operations.

KEY COMPETITORS
Hilton
Marriott International
Starwood Hotels & Resorts Worldwide

 See pages 238–239 for a full profile of this company.

HY-VEE, INC.

5820 Westown Pkwy.	CEO: Ronald D. Pearson	1999 Sales: $3,500.0 million
West Des Moines, IA 50266	CFO: Michael D. Wheeler	1-Yr. Sales Change: 9.4%
Phone: 515-267-2800	HR: Jerry Willis	Employees: 42,900
Fax: 515-267-2817	Type: Private	FYE: September
Web site: http://www.hy-vee.com		

With the slogan "A Helpful Smile in Every Aisle," Hy-Vee Food Stores operates about 180 Hy-Vee supermarkets in Illinois, Iowa, Kansas, Minnesota, Missouri, Nebraska, and South Dakota. About half of its Hy-Vee supermarkets are in Iowa, where the company also operates most of its 26 Drug Town drugstores. Hy-Vee Food Stores distributes products to its stores through several subsidiaries, including Lomar Foods (specialty foods), Perishable Distributors of Iowa (fresh foods), and Florist Distributing (floral supplies). Charles Hyde and David Vredenburg founded the company with a general store in 1930, eventually picking a corporate name by combining their own.

KEY COMPETITORS
Albertson's
Eagle Food
Kroger

ICC INDUSTRIES INC.

460 Park Ave.	CEO: John J. Farber	1998 Est. Sales: $855.0 million
New York, NY 10022	CFO: Linda Pleurites	1-Yr. Sales Change: (17.0%)
Phone: 212-521-1700	HR: Frances Foti	Employees: 2,200
Fax: 212-521-1970	Type: Private	FYE: December
Web site: http://www.iccchem.com		

ICC Industries keeps US pharmaceutical companies supplied with the raw materials used in manufacturing drugs. An international maker and marketer of chemicals, plastics, and pharmaceutical products, ICC also trades and distributes nutritional supplements and food ingredients. Its operates through its main subsidiary, ICC Chemical Corporation, which maintains trading and marketing offices in Asia, Europe, South America, and the US. The company's Prior Energy Corporation has natural gas distribution interests in Alabama, Florida, Mississippi, and Tennessee. ICC Industries also owns 67% of Pharmaceutical Formulations, a manufacturer and distributor of generic over-the-counter drugs.

KEY COMPETITORS
Formosa Plastics
IFF
IVAX

ICON HEALTH & FITNESS, INC.

1500 S. 1000 West
Logan, UT 84321
Phone: 435-750-5000
Fax: 435-750-5238
Web site: http://www.iconfitness.com

CEO: Scott R. Watterson
CFO: S. Fred Beck
HR: Doug Younker
Type: Private

1999 Sales: $749.3 million
1-Yr. Sales Change: (10.4%)
Employees: 4,200
FYE: May

ICON Health & Fitness is showing some muscle as one of the nation's leading home fitness equipment makers, producing treadmills, ellipticals, exercise bikes, stair steppers, rowers, and weight benches. Brands include Proform, HealthRider, Image, NordicTrack, and Weslo. The company also markets recreational sports and sports medicine products, fitness accessories, trampolines, spas, and massage products. ICON Health & Fitness makes 80% of its products at plants in Canada, Colorado, Texas, and Utah. Equipment is sold through specialty dealers, sporting goods chains, department stores (Sears is its top customer), catalog showrooms, and infomercials. Management and Bain Capital control more than 90% of the company.

KEY COMPETITORS
Cybex International
Schwinn/GT
Soloflex

IGA, INC.

8725 W. Higgins Rd.
Chicago, IL 60631
Phone: 773-693-4520
Fax: 773-693-1271
Web site: http://www.igainc.com

CEO: Thomas S. Haggai
CFO: Duane Martin
HR: Juanita Brodkorb
Type: Association

1998 Sales: $18,000.0 million
1-Yr. Sales Change: 0.0%
Employees: 92,000
FYE: December

IGA grocers are independent, but not *that* independent. The world's largest voluntary supermarket network, IGA has more than 3,600 stores, including members in 47 states and in about 30 other countries. Collectively, its members are among North America's leaders in terms of supermarket sales. IGA (for "International Grocers Alliance" or "Independent Grocers Alliance") is owned by 18 worldwide marketing and distribution companies, including Fleming Companies and SUPERVALU. Members can sell IGA Brand private-label products and take advantage of joint operations and services such as advertising and volume buying. IGA is continuing its expansion overseas.

KEY COMPETITORS
Kroger
Safeway
Wakefern Food

 See pages 240–241 for a full profile of this company.

ILITCH VENTURES, INC.

2211 Woodward Ave.
Detroit, MI 48201
Phone: 313-983-6000
Fax: 313-983-6494

CEO: Richard J. Peters
CFO: James Weissenborn
HR: —
Type: Holding company

1998 Sales: $800.0 million
1-Yr. Sales Change: —
Employees: 8,000
FYE: December

How to get to the Big Leagues? Pizza. Ilitch Ventures brought numerous businesses owned by Mike and Marian Ilitch under a single umbrella. Among the subsidiaries of Ilitch Ventures are Little Caesar Enterprises (the pizza chain the Ilitches launched with a single restaurant in 1959), the NHL's Detroit Red Wings, Major League Baseball's Detroit Tigers, and indoor soccer team the Detroit Rockers. Other subsidiaries include Olympia Entertainment (management and concessions at sports stadiums), Olympia Specialty Foods, and Olympia Development (real estate). The company was formed in 1999 to pave the way for growth in the Ilitches' holdings.

KEY COMPETITORS
Cleveland Indians
Pizza Hut
St. Louis Blues

ILLINOIS DEPARTMENT OF THE LOTTERY

201 E. Madison
Springfield, IL 62702
Phone: 217-524-5157
Fax: 217-524-5154
Web site: http://www.illinoislottery.com

CEO: Lori Montana
CFO: Dave Mizeur
HR: Charles Pirrera
Type: Government-owned

1998 Sales: $1,577.0 million
1-Yr. Sales Change: (2.9%)
Employees: 284
FYE: June

The home of the Windy City will sell you a chance to become a millionaire, but the odds of winning might blow you away. Created in 1974, the Illinois Department of the Lottery runs numbers games, including Pick 3 and Pick 4 games, and participates in the seven-state Big Game, in which players can win jackpots starting at $5 million (odds of winning: 1 in 76 million). It also offers instant-win scratch-off games. Of the money collected from ticket sales, 54% is paid in prizes and 36% goes to the state's Common School Fund, which helps finance K-12 public education. The rest covers retailer commissions and expenses. GTECH Holdings operates the lottery's 7,000 online terminals and 2,500 ticket validation machines.

KEY COMPETITORS
Hoosier Lottery
Kentucky Lottery
Multi-State Lottery

IMG

1360 E. 9th St., Ste. 100
Cleveland, OH 44114
Phone: 216-522-1200
Fax: 216-522-1145

CEO: Mark H. McCormack
CFO: Arthur J. LaFave
HR: Dan Lewis
Type: Private

1998 Est. Sales: $1,100.0 million
1-Yr. Sales Change: 0.0%
Employees: 2,125
FYE: December

Led by founder and owner Mark McCormack (aka, the "original Jerry Macguire"), IMG is the world's largest sports talent and marketing agency. In addition to representing a string of sports idols (Wayne Gretzky, Tiger Woods), IMG also counts artists such as Placido Domingo and Itzhak Perlman and model Tyra Banks among its more than 700 clients. Its Trans World International division produces thousands of hours of sports TV programming each year, and the company also promotes more than 1,000 sports events annually. In addition, IMG represents corporate clients and organizations (Rock and Roll Hall of Fame), acts as a literary agent, and is active in sports academies, golf course design, and financial consulting.

KEY COMPETITORS
Interpublic Group
SFX Entertainment
William Morris

 See pages 242–243 for a full profile of this company.

INCARNATE WORD HEALTH SYSTEM

9311 San Pedro Ave., Ste. 1250
San Antonio, TX 78216
Phone: 210-524-4100
Fax: 210-525-8443
Web site: http://www.incarnatewordhealth.org

CEO: Joseph Blasko
CFO: Tony Tomandl
HR: Bill Boles
Type: Not-for-profit

1997 Sales: $663.6 million
1-Yr. Sales Change: 23.4%
Employees: 7,500
FYE: December

Incarnate Word Health System operates primarily in South Texas and includes nine acute-care hospitals, a children's hospital, a rehabilitation hospital, and a psychiatric hospital. The organization also owns 50% of Baptist St. Anthony's Health System in Amarillo, Texas, and has a hospital in St. Louis. Incarnate Word Health System is planning to merge with Sisters of Charity Health Care System, based in Houston, to form Christus Health. In addition to its hospitals, the organization operates a network of clinics, educational centers, hospice services, and physician partnerships.

INDIANA UNIVERSITY

530 E. Kirkwood Ave.	CEO: —	1998 Sales: $1,470.3 million
Bloomington, IN 47408	CFO: Judith G. Palmer	1-Yr. Sales Change: 6.6%
Phone: 812-855-3911	HR: Linda Rasmussen	Employees: 14,458
Fax: 812-855-7002	Type: School	FYE: June
Web site: http://www.indiana.edu		

Chances are good IU has a program for you. The Indiana University system offers more than 180 associate, 390 bachelor's, and 340 advanced-degree programs on eight campuses, including the liberal arts and sciences, journalism, medicine, and law. It also offers teaching exchanges, research partnerships, and study abroad programs on five continents. IU is among the largest universities in the US, with more than 92,000 students. Under the leadership of president Myles Brand and chancellor Gerald Bepko, it has mapped out a strategy involving the creation of the Advanced Research & Technology Institute, Clarian Health Partners, and a push into information technology. IU is considered one of the nation's top "wired" campuses.

INDUCTOTHERM INDUSTRIES, INC.

10 Indel Ave.	CEO: Henry M. Rowan	1999 Sales: $800.0 million
Rancocas, NJ 08073	CFO: Frank Manley	1-Yr. Sales Change: (1.0%)
Phone: 609-267-9000	HR: David L. Braddock	Employees: 5,320
Fax: 609-267-5705	Type: Private	FYE: April
Web site: http://www.inductothermindustries.com		

The heat is on at Inductotherm Industries, the parent company for an international group of more than 50 engineering and technology companies that produce a variety of products, primarily for the metals industry. A leading maker of induction-heating equipment, with more than 10,000 installations, Inductotherm also controls companies that produce welding equipment, electrical components, electronics, engineered products, metal components, plastic products, and silkscreen printing. Inductotherm operates worldwide. Chairman Hank Rowan and Betty Rowan financed the startup of the company in 1953 from the sale of their home.

KEY COMPETITORS
Krauss-Maffei
Milacron
SPX

INGRAM ENTERTAINMENT INC.

2 Ingram Blvd.	CEO: David B. Ingram	1998 Sales: $1,048.0 million
La Vergne, TN 37089	CFO: William D. Daniel	1-Yr. Sales Change: 14.7%
Phone: 615-287-4000	HR: —	Employees: 1,030
Fax: 615-287-4982	Type: Private	FYE: December
Web site: http://www.ingramentertainment.com		

Companies selling books and CDs online might get the star treatment, but Ingram Entertainment doesn't mind its supporting role. The company is the #1 independent video and computer game distributor in the US. It also distributes CD-ROMs, DVDs, and audio books. Ingram distributes through more than 15 facilities, but it has been hurt by the trend among its customers, including Hollywood Entertainment, to source more products directly. It ventured online by acquiring a stake in Speedserve, a fulfillment company serving online book and video sellers, but sold it to Buy.com for a small stake in that company. David Ingram owns 95% of the company, which was spun off from family-owned Ingram Industries in 1997.

KEY COMPETITORS
Baker & Taylor
Handleman
Rentrak

INGRAM INDUSTRIES INC.

1 Belle Meade Place, 4400 Harding Rd.
Nashville, TN 37205
Phone: 615-298-8200
Fax: 615-298-8242
Web site: http://www.ingrambook.com

CEO: Orrin H. Ingram
CFO: Robert W. Mitchell
HR: Dennis Delaney
Type: Private

1998 Est. Sales: $2,000.0 million
1-Yr. Sales Change: 11.4%
Employees: 6,500
FYE: December

Ingram Industries is into books, boats, and bad drivers. Ingram Book Group is the #1 wholesale book distributor in the US; it ships more than 115 million books and audiotapes annually, serving some 32,000 retail outlets and 12,000 publishers. (Its deal to sell the unit to Barnes & Noble is off.) Ingram Marine Group operates Ingram Materials and 2,600 barges through Ingram Barge; Ingram's Permanent General Insurance covers high-risk drivers in about 10 states. The Ingram family, led by chairman Martha Ingram, owns and runs Ingram Industries and controls nearly 85% of the voting shares of top computer products wholesaler Ingram Micro. Ingram's son David owns top video distributor Ingram Entertainment.

KEY COMPETITORS
American Commercial Lines
Baker & Taylor
State Farm

See pages 244–245 for a full profile of this company.

INOVA HEALTH SYSTEM

2990 Telestar Ct.
Falls Church, VA 22042
Phone: 703-289-2000
Fax: 703-289-2070
Web site: http://www.inova.com

CEO: Knox Singleton
CFO: Richard Magenheimer
HR: Ellen Menard
Type: Not-for-profit

1998 Sales: $962.0 million
1-Yr. Sales Change: 6.9%
Employees: 13,000
FYE: December

Inova Health System is Virginia's largest not-for-profit health care provider. It provides acute and subacute care, long-term care, home health care, and mental health, obstetrics, and gynecological services in the Virginia suburbs of Washington, DC. Inova's network includes five hospitals, as well as assisted living centers (for those needing less-constant care than nursing homes provide) and several family practice locations. The system maintains affiliations with about 3,500 physicians. Founded in 1956 as a country hospital in Fairfax, Virginia, the system has grown in sophistication and scope as metropolitan Washington, DC, has expanded into its area.

KEY COMPETITORS
Columbia/HCA
Johns Hopkins Health
MedStar

INSERRA SUPERMARKETS, INC.

20 Ridge Rd.
Mahwah, NJ 07430
Phone: 201-529-5900
Fax: 201-529-1189

CEO: Lawrence R. Inserra
CFO: Theresa Inserra
HR: Marie Larson
Type: Private

1998 Sales: $750.0 million
1-Yr. Sales Change: 41.5%
Employees: 4,000
FYE: December

Tailgating before Giants and Jets games would be less hale and hearty without Inserra Supermarkets. The company owns and operates over 20 ShopRite supermarkets and superstores in northern New Jersey and southeastern New York State (most are in the New York City metro area). Inserra's superstores feature pharmacies, bagel bakeries, cafes, and accoutrements such as toy trains and animated animals to make shopping kid-friendly. The company also offers banking services in selected stores through an agreement with Poughkeepsie Savings Bank. Owned by the Inserra family, the retailer is one of 40-plus members that make up Wakefern Food, the largest US food cooperative and owner of the ShopRite name.

KEY COMPETITORS
A&P
Grand Union
Royal Ahold

INTERMOUNTAIN HEALTH CARE

36 S. State St.
Salt Lake City, UT 84111
Phone: 801-442-2000
Fax: 801-442-3327
Web site: http://www.ihc.com

CEO: William H. Nelson
CFO: Everett Goodwin
HR: Gary Hart
Type: Not-for-profit

1998 Sales: $2,156.1 million
1-Yr. Sales Change: 7.3%
Employees: 23,000
FYE: December

Intermountain Health Care (IHC) is a full-service health care organization serving more than 425,000 members in Utah, Idaho, and Wyoming. It operates more than 20 hospitals and is affiliated with more than 2,500 physicians, including 400 employed by the IHC Physician Group. IHC Health Plans offers health insurance to individuals, families, businesses, and persons covered by Medicaid. The IHC Foundation donates heavily to support health programs in its communities. The company was formed in 1975 when the Mormons (Church of Jesus Christ of Latter day Saints) decided to donate 15 of their hospitals to the communities they served.

KEY COMPETITORS
Columbia/HCA
Holy Cross
Kaiser Foundation

INTERNATIONAL BROTHERHOOD OF TEAMSTERS

25 Louisiana Ave. NW
Washington, DC 20001
Phone: 202-624-6800
Fax: 202-624-6918
Web site: http://www.teamster.org

CEO: James P. Hoffa
CFO: —
HR: Adam Downs
Type: Labor union

1997 Sales: $89.3 million
1-Yr. Sales Change: (0.5%)
Employees: —
FYE: December

The International Brotherhood of Teamsters is the US's largest, most diverse, and arguably most (in)famous labor union. With approximately 1.4 million members, the Teamsters represents truckers, United Parcel Service workers, warehouse employees, cab drivers, airline workers, and factory and hospital employees. The union negotiates with employers for contracts that guarantee its members fair promotion policies, health coverage, job security, paid time off for vacations and holidays, pay levels and pay raises, protection from discrimination and favoritism, and retirement benefits. The Teamsters union has about 650 local chapters in the US, Canada, and Puerto Rico.

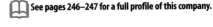 See pages 246–247 for a full profile of this company.

INTERNATIONAL DATA GROUP

1 Exeter Plaza, 15th Fl.
Boston, MA 02116
Phone: 617-534-1200
Fax: 617-659-8642
Web site: http://www.idg.com

CEO: Kelly P. Conlin
CFO: Jim Ghirardi
HR: Tom Mathews
Type: Private

1999 Sales: $2,560.0 million
1-Yr. Sales Change: 24.9%
Employees: 12,000
FYE: September

International Data Group (IDG) is a leading provider of computer information. Its IDG Communications subsidiary is the world's #1 publisher of computer-related periodicals (ahead of Ziff-Davis and CMP Media), with more than 290 magazines (including *Macworld* and *PC World*) and newspapers in 75 countries. It also operates 225 related Web sites. IDG Books Worldwide (75%-owned) prints some 1,000 titles (including the . . . *For Dummies* series) in 36 languages. Subsidiary International Data Corporation leads the industry in computer market research and analysis. IDG also sponsors conferences, trade shows, and other events for the computer industry. Founder and chairman Patrick McGovern owns about 65% of IDG.

KEY COMPETITORS
CMP Media Inc.
Gartner Group
SOFTBANK

See pages 248–249 for a full profile of this company.

INTERNATIONAL TELECOMMUNICATIONS SATELLITE ORGANIZATION

3400 International Dr. NW
Washington, DC 20008
Phone: 202-944-7500
Fax: 202-944-7890
Web site: http://www.intelsat.int

CEO: Conny Kullman
CFO: Joseph Corbett
HR: Benjamin Katcoff
Type: Consortium

1998 Sales: $1,020.4 million
1-Yr. Sales Change: 6.1%
Employees: —
FYE: December

International Telecommunications Satellite Organization (INTELSAT), operator of the world's largest global communications satellite system, launched its first satellite, Early Bird, in 1965. A not-for-profit consortium, INTELSAT is made up of 141 member nations that contribute capital depending on their use of the system, and it provides voice/data and video services to users in more than 200 countries. Customers include major broadcasters (CNN), long-distance telephone services (BT), airlines, and international banks. The sky may be falling for INTELSAT, however, as private satellite operators join the fray because of the January 1998 deregulation of the industry by the World Trade Organization.

KEY COMPETITORS
Hughes Electronics
Loral Space
PanAmSat

INVESTORS MANAGEMENT CORP.

5151 Glenwood Ave.
Raleigh, NC 27612
Phone: 919-781-9310
Fax: 919-881-4686
Web site: http://www.goldencorralrest.com

CEO: James H. Maynard
CFO: Richard Urquhart
HR: Paul Weber
Type: Private

1998 Sales: $864.0 million
1-Yr. Sales Change: 12.2%
Employees: 16,000
FYE: December

Investors Management Corporation hopes you'll join them in an eat-out at the Golden Corral. The holding company has more than 450 Golden Corral family-style restaurants, some franchised and some company-owned, in 38 states and Mexico. The restaurants offer steak, chicken, and fish entrees on the trademark 140-item Golden Choice Buffet, which averages a little more than $6 a plate. Each restaurant also features a Brass Bell Bakery, which rings a bell to notify patrons that fresh pastries and baked goods have come out of the oven. Founded in 1973, Golden Corral is one of the nation's largest family steak house restaurant chains. Founder and CEO James Maynard owns the company.

KEY COMPETITORS
Advantica Restaurant Group
Buffets
Ryan's Family Steak Houses

IRIDIUM LLC

1575 Eye St. NW
Washington, DC 20005
Phone: 202-408-3800
Fax: 202-408-3801
Web site: http://www.iridium.com

CEO: John A. Richardson
CFO: David R. Gibson
HR: Barbara Murkel
Type: Consortium

1998 Sales: $0.2 million
1-Yr. Sales Change: —
Employees: 536
FYE: December

Space-age idea or lead zeppelin? Iridium, the $5 billion global satellite communications system, is having trouble staying aloft. The consortium provides wireless phone service anywhere in the world through its network of 66 low-earth-orbit (LEO) satellites linked to 15 ground stations and through agreements with existing cellular networks. But Iridium has failed to meet subscriber goals (it has 20,000 customers), even after cutting prices for its service and clunky phones. After defaulting on $1.5 billion in loans, Iridium has filed for bankruptcy protection. The 19-member consortium is made up of telecom and industrial companies; Motorola is the primary technology partner and largest stakeholder, with 18%.

KEY COMPETITORS
Globalstar
ICO Global Communications
INTELSAT

📖 See pages 250–251 for a full profile of this company.

THE IRVINE COMPANY INC.

550 Newport Center Dr.
Newport Beach, CA 92660
Phone: 949-720-2000
Fax: 949-720-2501
Web site: http://www.irvineco.com

CEO: Donald L. Bren
CFO: Michael D. McKee
HR: Bruce Endsley
Type: Private

1998 Sales: $1,000.0 million
1-Yr. Sales Change: 22.5%
Employees: 236
FYE: June

The Irvine Company develops residential and commercial real estate in Southern California. With 54,000 acres of prime Orange County real estate, the firm develops hotels, industrial real estate, land, office buildings, and retail and residential real estate. Its holdings come from the 120,000-acre Irvine Ranch, which was formed in the mid-1800s when James Irvine bought out the debts of Mexican and Spanish land-grant holders. Chairman Donald Bren owns the company, which is famous for its master-planned communities stretching for miles throughout Orange County. The Irvine Company has reacquired its former spinoff, real estate investment trust (REIT) Irvine Apartment Communities.

KEY COMPETITORS

Castle & Cooke
Kaufman & Broad
Spieker Properties

 See pages 252–253 for a full profile of this company.

ISLAND LINCOLN-MERCURY INC.

1850 E. Merritt Island Causeway
Merritt Island, FL 32952
Phone: 407-452-9220
Fax: 407-453-3498
Web site: http://www.islandlincolnmercury.com

CEO: R. Bruce Deardoff
CFO: E. Renee Cheney
HR: Fran Parnell
Type: Private

1997 Sales: $753.0 million
1-Yr. Sales Change: 7.6%
Employees: 327
FYE: December

No dealership is an island, entire of itself . . . except maybe Island Lincoln-Mercury. Island is one of the nation's largest private automotive dealers, with four dealerships in Cocoa, Melbourne, Merritt Island, and Orlando, Florida. In addition to the Lincoln and Mercury lines, these dealerships carry such models as Audi, Ford, Jaguar, and Mercedes, as well as commercial vehicles. The company also offers financing and parts and service departments. Island Lincoln-Mercury was established in 1985 by owner R. Bruce Deardoff, who has served as CEO since founding the company.

KEY COMPETITORS

Holman Enterprises
JM Family Enterprises
Morse Operations

J. CREW GROUP INC.

770 Broadway
New York, NY 10003
Phone: 212-209-2500
Fax: 212-209-2666
Web site: http://www.jcrew.com

CEO: Mark Sarvary
CFO: Scott M. Rosen
HR: —
Type: Private

1999 Sales: $824.3 million
1-Yr. Sales Change: (1.2%)
Employees: 8,900
FYE: January

The J. Crew Group made its name on the minimal look, and now it's making itself over in the same fashion. After selling off two catalogs, the company's sales come entirely from its J. Crew brand. J. Crew sells classic-styled jeans, khakis, and other basic (but pricey) items to young professionals through its Web site, catalogs, and about 110 US retail and factory outlets. It also has nearly 70 outlets in Japan through a joint venture with Itochu. The company has been reducing its reliance on mail-order by expanding its retail outlets. Investment concern Texas Pacific Group owns 62% of J. Crew; chair Emily Cinader Woods (daughter of founder Arthur Cinader) owns about 20%.

KEY COMPETITORS

L.L. Bean
Lands' End
The Gap

See pages 254–255 for a full profile of this company.

THE J. PAUL GETTY TRUST

1200 Getty Center Dr.
Los Angeles, CA 90049
Phone: 310-440-7300
Fax: 310-440-7722
Web site: http://www.getty.edu

CEO: Barry Munitz
CFO: Russell S. Gould
HR: Marianne Rusk
Type: Foundation

1998 Sales: $762.9 million
1-Yr. Sales Change: (6.2%)
Employees: 1,200
FYE: June

Oilman J. Paul Getty opened a small antiquities museum in 1953. Today the J. Paul Getty Trust operates the $1 billion Getty Center, a hilltop haven that focuses on art and humanities. It is best known for the J. Paul Getty Museum, which primarily displays pre-20th-century works of art by Rembrandt and van Gogh, among others. The center also houses the Getty Education Institute for the Arts, the Getty Conservation Institute, and institutes dedicated to history and museum management. In addition, the trust has awarded more than $80 million to various art projects. The trust received $1.2 billion from Getty's estate in 1982 and has grown to about $5 billion.

J & R ELECTRONICS

23 Park Row
New York, NY 10038
Phone: 212-238-9000
Fax: 212-238-9195
Web site: http://www.jandr.com

CEO: Joe Friedman
CFO: Zvi Hirsch
HR: Dean Shilenok
Type: Private

1998 Est. Sales: $675.0 million
1-Yr. Sales Change: 12.5%
Employees: 2,000
FYE: June

With several stores in the same New York City block, J & R Electronics is the nation's largest single-location computer and software outlet. The company's stores are all part of one retail megastore (J & R Music and Computer World) which measures about 250,000 sq. ft. and is known for discount prices and good customer service. It also sells through a 200-plus page catalog that reaches more than 1 million people and is published every six weeks. Products include personal computers, software, appliances, televisions, music, and movies. Owners Joe and Rachelle Friedman used wedding gifts to finance the founding of J & R Electronics in 1971.

KEY COMPETITORS
Gateway
Musicland
The WIZ

JEA

21 W. Church St.
Jacksonville, FL 32202
Phone: 904-665-6000
Fax: 904-665-6549
Web site: http://www.jea.com

CEO: Walter P. Bussells
CFO: Mary B. Arditti
HR: Joan Clark
Type: Government-owned

1998 Sales: $898.5 million
1-Yr. Sales Change: 13.7%
Employees: 2,211
FYE: September

The Jacksonville Jaguars aren't the only ones who throw off sparks. JEA (formerly Jacksonville Electric Authority), established in 1895, provides electricity to more than 335,000 customers in Jacksonville and portions of three adjacent counties. The municipally owned utility has a generating capacity of 2,742 MW from its three power plants and joint ownership in two more. Most of JEA's energy is produced from coal and petroleum fuel. In 1997 the utility took over the city's water and wastewater systems. With 98 artesian wells, 28 water plants, and five regional wastewater treatment plants, it serves more than 80% of the water and sewage customers in Duval County and part of another county.

KEY COMPETITORS
FPL
Florida Public Utilities
United Water Resources

JELD-WEN, INC.

3250 Lakeport Blvd.
Klamath Falls, OR 97601
Phone: 541-882-3451
Fax: 541-884-2231
Web site: http://www.jeld-wen.com

CEO: Richard L. Wendt
CFO: Karen Hoggarth
HR: Eileen Harris
Type: Private

1998 Est. Sales: $1,500.0 million
1-Yr. Sales Change: 7.1%
Employees: 11,000
FYE: December

JELD-WEN wants you to kick in the door and break out the windows. The world's largest maker of doors and windows, JELD-WEN owns more than 150 companies in 40 US states and Canada, Latvia, Poland, Spain, and the UK. Subsidiaries of the company develop real estate and build prefabricated houses. JELD-WEN also sells time-shares at several resorts in British Columbia, Mexico, and the US, including the Eagle Crest Resort, the Running Y Ranch Resort, Trend West Resorts, and the Silver Mountain ski resort. Current CEO Richard Wendt and his siblings founded JELD-WEN, which has grown through acquisitions, in 1960.

KEY COMPETITORS
Andersen Corporation
Nortek
Pella

J. F. SHEA CO., INC.

655 Brea Canyon Rd.
Walnut, CA 91789
Phone: 909-594-9500
Fax: 909-594-0935
Web site: http://www.jfshea.com

CEO: John F. Shea
CFO: James G. Shontere
HR: Ron Lakey
Type: Private

1998 Sales: $1,620.7 million
1-Yr. Sales Change: 61.8%
Employees: 2,000
FYE: December

From digging holes in the ground to building bridges in the sky, J. F. Shea's crews have got you covered. The company helped construct the Washington, DC, subway system, Golden Gate Bridge, and Hoover Dam, but it also builds single-family houses, mainly for move-up buyers. J. F. Shea also manages apartments and commercial buildings and produces gravel, asphalt, and concrete. Its major divisions are Heavy Construction, Redding, Shea Homes, and Shea Properties. Shea Homes (with residential developments in Arizona, California, Colorado, and North Carolina) is building the second-largest planned community in the US, in Colorado. Founded as a plumbing company in 1876, the firm is still owned by the Shea family.

KEY COMPETITORS
Kaufman & Broad
Perini
Tutor-Saliba

JITNEY-JUNGLE STORES OF AMERICA, INC.

1770 Ellis Ave., Ste. 200
Jackson, MS 39204
Phone: 601-965-8600
Fax: 601-371-2814
Web site: http://www.jitneyjungle.com

CEO: Ronald E. Johnson
CFO: David R. Black
HR: Jerry L. Jones
Type: Private

1998 Sales: $2,054.1 million
1-Yr. Sales Change: 79.4%
Employees: 17,000
FYE: December

How easy is it to steer a Jitney through the fierce grocery jungle? Not very. Jitney-Jungle Stores of America runs nearly 200 supermarkets in Alabama, Arkansas, Florida, Louisiana, Mississippi, and Tennessee. Its chains include conventional stores (Jitney-Jungle, Delchamps), food-and-drug-combination stores (Jitney Premier, Delchamps Premier), and discount stores (Sack & Save). It operates 10 liquor stores and 55 gas stations at various supermarket locations. Though it has grown by acquisitions, the company has been slammed by larger rivals such as Wal-Mart, forcing it into Chapter 11 bankruptcy protection. Investment firm Bruckmann, Rosser, Sherill & Co. owns 84% of Jitney-Jungle, which was founded in 1919.

KEY COMPETITORS
Kroger
Wal-Mart
Winn-Dixie

JM FAMILY ENTERPRISES, INC.

100 NW 12th Ave.	CEO: Patricia Moran	1998 Sales: $6,200.0 million
Deerfield Beach, FL 33442	CFO: Jim Foster	1-Yr. Sales Change: 14.8%
Phone: 954-429-2000	HR: Gary L. Thomas	Employees: 3,000
Fax: 954-429-2244	Type: Private	FYE: December

Founder and chairman Jim Moran and president and CEO Pat Moran (Jim's daughter) make JM Family Enterprises a family affair. JM is a holding company with about a dozen automotive-related businesses (including the nation's largest-volume Lexus retailer). JM's major subsidiary, Southeast Toyota Distributors, is the world's largest Toyota distribution franchise, delivering the Japanese automaker's cars, trucks, and vans to more than 160 dealers in Alabama, Florida, Georgia, and North and South Carolina. Other JM divisions include JM&A Group and World Omni Financial, which provide consumer auto leasing, warranty services, insurance, dealer financing, and other related financial services to US auto dealers.

KEY COMPETITORS
Gulf States Toyota
Morse Operations
United Auto Group

📖 **See pages 256–257 for a full profile of this company.**

J. M. HUBER CORPORATION

333 Thornall St.	CEO: Peter T. Francis	1998 Est. Sales: $1,500.0 million
Edison, NJ 08837	CFO: Philip Betsch	1-Yr. Sales Change: 0.0%
Phone: 732-549-8600	HR: Pete Tortorello	Employees: 5,000
Fax: 732-549-2239	Type: Private	FYE: December
Web site: http://www.huber.com		

Toothpaste, paint, and tires — J. M. Huber plays a part in the production of each of these everyday items. Family-owned J. M. Huber, founded in 1883, is a diversified company that supplies engineered materials, natural resources and technology-based services to international customers in the energy, paper, rubber, construction, plastics, and other industries. Its engineered materials utilize specialty chemicals to make additives for the rubber and papermaking industries. Wood products include oriented strand board, a plywood substitute. The company supplies natural resources from its timberland and oil, gas, and coal reserves. J. M. Huber sold its AVEX Electronics subsidiary to Benchmark Electronics.

KEY COMPETITORS
Baker Hughes
Georgia-Pacific Group
Minerals Technologies

JMB REALTY CORPORATION

900 N. Michigan Ave., Ste. 1100	CEO: Rigel Barber	1998 Est. Sales: $1,000.0 million
Chicago, IL 60611	CFO: Steve Lovelett	1-Yr. Sales Change: 0.0%
Phone: 312-440-4800	HR: Gail Silver	Employees: 10,700
Fax: 312-915-1768	Type: Private	FYE: December

JMB Realty is a major US commercial real estate investment firm that owns, develops, and manages a variety of large real estate projects throughout North America, including regional malls, hotels, planned communities, and office complexes. JMB owns about 40% of Urban Shopping Centers, a real estate investment trust (REIT) that owns such upscale mall properties as Chicago's Water Tower Place. JMB was founded in 1968 by Robert Judelson, Judd Malkin, and Neil Bluhm using $5,000 they had pooled; Judelson (the "J" of JMB) is no longer involved with JMB, but Malkin remains as chairman and Bluhm is president.

KEY COMPETITORS
Edward J. DeBartolo
Lincoln Property
Trammell Crow

JOHN HANCOCK MUTUAL LIFE INSURANCE COMPANY

200 Clarendon St.
Boston, MA 02117
Phone: 617-572-6000
Fax: 617-572-6451
Web site: http://www.jhancock.com

CEO: Stephen L. Brown
CFO: Thomas E. Moloney
HR: A. Page Palmer
Type: Mutual company

1998 Sales: $13,653.4 million
1-Yr. Sales Change: 18.8%
Employees: 7,959
FYE: December

This company wants your John Hancock on the dotted line. John Hancock Mutual Life Insurance sells life insurance products and annuities as well as long-term-care insurance and a variety of retirement and investment products, including guaranteed investment contracts (which offer a fixed return for the life of the contract) and mutual funds. The company also offers various specialty funds for institutional investors, and is one of the largest managers of investments in timberland and agricultural property. John Hancock operates throughout the US and Canada, as well as in Europe and Asia. The company, currently owned by its policyholders, plans to demutualize.

KEY COMPETITORS
MetLife
Northwestern Mutual
Prudential

See pages 258–259 for a full profile of this company.

THE JOHNS HOPKINS HEALTH SYSTEM CORPORATION

600 N. Wolfe St.
Baltimore, MD 21287
Phone: 410-955-5000
Fax: 410-955-6575
Web site: http://www.jhu.edu/www/medicine/

CEO: Ronald R. Peterson
CFO: Ronald J. Werthman
HR: Joan Williams
Type: Not-for-profit

1998 Sales: $1,661.1 million
1-Yr. Sales Change: —
Employees: 20,987
FYE: June

If you don't eat your apple a day, you may end up in The Johns Hopkins Health System, which operates hospitals and other facilities affiliated with the medical schools of Johns Hopkins University. These include Johns Hopkins Hospital (annually deemed one of the US's best) and Johns Hopkins Bayview Medical Center, both of which are acute-care hospitals. The hospitals, owned by Johns Hopkins Medicine, are staffed by faculty members from the medical school and are the training ground for the medical school. Other divisions include Johns Hopkins Medical Services and Johns Hopkins Employer Health Plans. Johns Hopkins Medicine has contracted with Singapore to build and operate medical and research facilities.

KEY COMPETITORS
Bon Secours Health
Columbia/HCA
Mayo Foundation

THE JOHNS HOPKINS UNIVERSITY

3400 N. Charles St.
Baltimore, MD 21218
Phone: 410-516-8000
Fax: 410-516-6097
Web site: http://www.jhu.edu

CEO: William R. Brody
CFO: James T. McGill
HR: Audrey Smith
Type: School

1998 Sales: $1,664.1 million
1-Yr. Sales Change: 5.8%
Employees: 23,000
FYE: June

Founded in 1876 with a $7 million bequest from its namesake, The Johns Hopkins University established its reputation from the beginning by molding itself in the image of a European research institution. While renowned for its School of Medicine, the private university offers eight academic divisions spanning fields of study including arts and sciences, engineering, and music. Its 16,500 students and 2,375 full-time faculty members are scattered across three Baltimore campuses; one campus in Washington, DC; and international programs in China and Italy.

JOHNSON PUBLISHING COMPANY, INC.

820 S. Michigan Ave.
Chicago, IL 60605
Phone: 312-322-9200
Fax: 312-322-0918
Web site: http://www.ebony.com

CEO: John H. Johnson
CFO: Eunice W. Johnson
HR: LaDoris Foster
Type: Private

1998 Sales: $371.9 million
1-Yr. Sales Change: 3.0%
Employees: 2,647
FYE: December

Johnson Publishing's business is black and white and read all over. Led by its flagship publication, *Ebony* (with a circulation of 1.75 million), the family-owned company is one of the largest minority-owned businesses and the largest black-owned publishing firm in the country. It also prints *Jet* and *Ebony South Africa,* and it has a book division. Besides the printed page, Johnson Publishing markets the Fashion Fair cosmetics line and hosts the Ebony Fashion Fair, a benefit fashion show that visits about 170 cities a year. Chairman and CEO John Johnson owns the firm founded in 1942.

KEY COMPETITORS
BET
Essence Communications
L'Oréal

 See pages 260–261 for a full profile of this company.

THE JONES FINANCIAL COMPANIES, L.P., LLP

12555 Manchester Rd.
St. Louis, MO 63131
Phone: 314-515-2000
Fax: 314-515-2622

CEO: John W. Bachmann
CFO: Steven Novik
HR: Michael R. Holmes
Type: Private

1998 Sales: $1,450.0 million
1-Yr. Sales Change: 27.7%
Employees: 15,795
FYE: December

This is not your father's broker — or, well, maybe it is. The Jones Financial Companies is the parent of Edward D. Jones & Co., an investment brokerage network catering to individual investors. Most of its clients are retired people and small-business owners in rural communities and suburbs. The firm has some 4,600 satellite-linked offices in the US, Canada, and the UK. Brokers offer relatively low-risk investment vehicles such as government bonds, blue-chip stocks, and high-quality mutual funds. Edward D. Jones also provides investment banking for such clients as Wal-Mart. The firm accepts brokers with no experience, provides extensive training, and closely monitors their activities.

KEY COMPETITORS
A.G. Edwards
Merrill Lynch
Raymond James Financial

 See pages 262–263 for a full profile of this company.

JORDAN INDUSTRIES, INC.

ArborLake Center, Ste. 550, 1751 Lake Cook Rd.
Deerfield, IL 60015
Phone: 847-945-5591
Fax: 847-945-5698

CEO: John W. Jordan
CFO: Jonathan F. Boucher
HR: —
Type: Private

1998 Sales: $943.6 million
1-Yr. Sales Change: 33.4%
Employees: 7,092
FYE: December

Biblical-sounding Jordan Industries owns more than 30 companies that make everything from bibles to bicycle reflectors. Its ark-load of operations include fiber-optic cable tubing (Dura-Line), motors for major appliances and vending and business machines (Merkle-Korff), auto transmission products (DACCO), corporate promotional items (Sales Promotion Associates), motors for elevators and floor-care equipment (Imperial), and packaging materials (Seaboard). Through its acquisitions of AirPage and PagingOne, the company claims 95% of the paging market in Austria, although Emerson Electric has agreed to acquire Jordan's telecommunications unit. Chairman and CEO John Jordan owns more than 40% of the company.

KEY COMPETITORS
Aftermarket Technology
Baldor Electric
Raymond James Financial

JORDAN MOTORS INC.

609 E. Jefferson Blvd.
Mishawaka, IN 46544
Phone: 219-259-1981
Fax: 219-255-0984
Web site: http://www.jordanauto.com

CEO: Craig Kapson
CFO: George Merryman
HR: Sandra Eggers
Type: Private

1998 Sales: $2,000.0 million
1-Yr. Sales Change: (3.0%)
Employees: 200
FYE: December

Jordan Motors scores points for being one of the nation's largest Ford dealers and one of the largest fleet dealers. The family-owned company runs two dealerships in Indiana that sell new and used vehicles, including Ford, Toyota, Volvo, Mitsubishi, Lincoln-Mercury, and Kia models. Both sites also offer parts and service departments. Jordan Motors' fleet business includes the sale of flat beds, dump trucks, construction trucks, and other heavy-duty vehicles. Chairman Jordan Kapson founded the company as a single Dodge dealership in 1949; his son Craig is the company's president.

KEY COMPETITORS
Bob Rohrman Auto
Hendrick Automotive
Holman Enterprises

JOURNAL COMMUNICATIONS INC.

333 W. State St.
Milwaukee, WI 53203
Phone: 414-224-2374
Fax: 414-224-2469
Web site: http://www.jc.com

CEO: Steven J. Smith
CFO: Paul M. Bonaiuto
HR: Daniel L. Harmsen
Type: Private

1998 Sales: $732.4 million
1-Yr. Sales Change: 8.6%
Employees: 6,968
FYE: December

Journal Communications has found lots of ways to speak out. The diversified media and communications company generates about 40% of its sales from its newspaper publishing operations. These include the *Milwaukee Journal Sentinel* and a variety of community newspapers, shoppers, and business and specialty publications, primarily in the eastern US. The company's commercial printing operations (which account for 32% of sales) include the printing of computer manuals, trade journals, newspapers, and labels for consumer goods. The company also owns TV and radio stations in seven states, and provides telecommunications and direct marketing services. Journal Communications is 90% employee-owned.

KEY COMPETITORS
Gannett
Hearst
News Corp.

JPI

600 E. Las Colinas Blvd., Ste. 1800
Irving, TX 75039
Phone: 972-556-1700
Fax: 972-556-3784
Web site: http://www.jpi.com

CEO: Frank Miller
CFO: Frank B. Schubert
HR: Joe McSadin
Type: Private

1998 Sales: $1,062.8 million
1-Yr. Sales Change: 57.1%
Employees: 1,500
FYE: December

JPI can walk your dog, rent you a bike, and mail your letters, but what the company does best is build and manage apartments. JPI is one of the largest multifamily housing builders in the nation, operating in more than a dozen states. The company specializes in luxury apartments (it also has some housing for college students). JPI manages more than 20,000 units. Projects include apartment communities complete with theaters, putting greens, mail centers, 24-hour concierge, and other services such as dog-walking. Founded in 1976 as Jefferson Properties, Inc., the company was a subsidiary of Southland Financial until the early 1990s when Ray L. Hunt invested in it. Hunt is still a major shareholder.

KEY COMPETITORS
Castle & Cooke
Gables Residential Trust
Trammell Crow Residential

J.R. SIMPLOT COMPANY

1 Capital Center, 999 Main St., Ste. 1300	CEO: Stephen A. Beebe	1999 Sales: $2,730.0 million
Boise, ID 83702	CFO: Dennis Mogensen	1-Yr. Sales Change: (2.5%)
Phone: 208-336-2110	HR: Ted Roper	Employees: 12,000
Fax: 208-389-7515	Type: Private	FYE: August
Web site: http://www.simplot.com		

J.R. Simplot hopes you'll have fries with that. Potato potentate J. R. "Jack" Simplot simply shook hands with McDonald's pioneer Ray Kroc in the mid-1960s, and his company's french fry sales have sizzled ever since. J.R. Simplot produces 2 billion pounds of spuds annually, making it one of the largest processors of frozen potatoes. Other operations include cattle ranches and feedlots (with feed from potato peels), phosphate mining (for fertilizer), and frozen fruits and vegetables. Retail products include Micro-Magic microwaveable sandwiches and J.R. Simplot-brand frozen fries, nuggets, and hashbrowns. Although officially retired, Simplot, founder of the family-owned firm, is one of the richest Americans.

KEY COMPETITORS
Cargill
IMC Global
McCain Foods

 See pages 264–265 for a full profile of this company.

KAISER FOUNDATION HEALTH PLAN, INC.

1 Kaiser Plaza	CEO: David M. Lawrence	1998 Sales: $15,500.0 million
Oakland, CA 94612	CFO: L. Dale Crandall	1-Yr. Sales Change: 6.9%
Phone: 510-271-5910	HR: James B. Williams	Employees: 100,000
Fax: 510-271-6493	Type: Not-for-profit	FYE: December
Web site: http://www.kaiserpermanente.org		

No longer the master of the HMO universe, Kaiser Foundation Health Plan is still the largest not-for-profit managed health care company in the US, with almost 9 million members in 18 states and the District of Columbia. It sponsors the Permanente Medical Groups, associations of doctors that provide medical care to Kaiser health plan subscribers under the Kaiser Permanente name. The company has some 10,000 group-practice physicians and also runs a network of Kaiser Foundation hospitals. Faced with skyrocketing costs and stiff competition from commercial providers of managed care, Kaiser has sold its Texas operations and is selling its unprofitable operations in North Carolina and the Northeast.

KEY COMPETITORS
Aetna
PacifiCare
WellPoint Health Networks

 See pages 266–267 for a full profile of this company.

THE KEMPER INSURANCE COMPANIES

1 Kemper Dr.	CEO: David B. Mathis	1998 Sales: $3,300.0 million
Long Grove, IL 60049	CFO: Walter L. White	1-Yr. Sales Change: (2.4%)
Phone: 847-320-2000	HR: Frederic C. McCullough	Employees: 9,000
Fax: 847-320-2494	Type: Mutual company	FYE: December
Web site: http://www.kemperinsurance.com		

Customers of all types keep company with The Kemper Insurance Companies. Kemper's insurance, financial, and service units offer an array of personal, risk management, and commercial property/casualty products. Its Lumbermens Life Agency offers personal term life and disability income insurance, wealth accumulation programs, and other services. Kemper Insurance also provides automobile, homeowners, and general liability coverage. The company has realigned its operations to focus on property/casualty coverage and risk management services. Kemper Insurance operates throughout the US, as well as overseas.

KEY COMPETITORS
Liberty Mutual
St. Paul Companies
Travelers

See pages 268–269 for a full profile of this company.

KEYSTONE FOODS CORP.

401 City Ave., Ste. 800
Bala Cynwyd, PA 19004
Phone: 610-667-6700
Fax: 610-667-1460
Web site: http://www.keystonefoods.com

CEO: Herbert Lotman
CFO: Michael Mardy
HR: Jerry Gotro
Type: Private

1998 Sales: $2,342.0 million
1-Yr. Sales Change: 7.2%
Employees: 4,300
FYE: December

Keystone Foods hopes you won't just have the salad. The company is one of the largest makers of hamburger patties and processed poultry. It's a major supplier to McDonald's restaurants; in the 1970s Keystone persuaded the fast-food giant to switch to frozen beef, greatly reducing the health risks associated with fresh beef. The company was also instrumental in developing Chicken McNuggets. Keystone is a joint venture partner with poultry grower Cagle's. In addition to its worldwide meat processing facilities, which crank out millions of burgers daily, Keystone also operates M&M Restaurant Supply. Chairman and CEO Herbert Lotman owns the company, which started in the early 1960s.

KEY COMPETITORS
ConAgra
Golden State Foods
IBP

KFC NATIONAL PURCHASING COOPERATIVE, INC.

950 Breckinridge Ln.
Louisville, KY 40207
Phone: 502-896-5900
Fax: 502-893-4162

CEO: Thomas D. Henrion
CFO: William V. Holden
HR: Carol L. Mudd
Type: Cooperative

1998 Sales: $664.8 million
1-Yr. Sales Change: 10.8%
Employees: 181
FYE: October

KFC National Purchasing Cooperative (which does business as FoodService Purchasing Cooperative) buys some $600 million a year in food, equipment, and supplies for KFC and Taco Bell franchises. In addition, it provides distribution advisory, insurance, and equipment financing services. The cooperative's clients include franchise operators, as well as independent distributors serving those franchises. It has joined with TRICON Global Restaurants (owner of the KFC, Taco Bell, and Pizza Hut brands) to form Unified Food-Service Purchasing Cooperative, which serves all three restaurant chains and has an annual purchasing volume of more than $4 billion.

KING KULLEN GROCERY COMPANY INC.

1194 Prospect Ave.
Westbury, NY 11590
Phone: 516-333-7100
Fax: 516-333-7929
Web site: http://www.kingkullen.com

CEO: John B. Cullen
CFO: J. D. Kennedy
HR: Thomas Nagle
Type: Private

1999 Sales: $714.0 million
1-Yr. Sales Change: (1.5%)
Employees: 4,100
FYE: September

How's this for a crowning achievement: King Kullen Grocery claims to have been the originator of the supermarket format. Heralding itself as "America's first supermarket," the company operates about 50 stores in New York City and on Long Island, mostly standard 35,000-sq.-ft. supermarkets. King Kullen Grocery also runs a Wild By Nature natural foods store, and its newest store format is a 60,000-sq.-ft. upscale market with such features as ethnic fare, catering, and in-house cafes. The food retailer was started in a Queens warehouse in 1930 by Michael Cullen. Today it is owned and operated by Cullen's relatives.

KEY COMPETITORS
A&P
Ahold USA
Grand Union

KING RANCH, INC.

1415 Louisiana St., Ste. 2300
Houston, TX 77002
Phone: 713-752-5700
Fax: 713-752-0088
Web site: http://www.king-ranch.com

CEO: Jack Hunt
CFO: Bill Gardiner
HR: Rickey Blackman
Type: Private

1998 Est. Sales: $300.0 million
1-Yr. Sales Change: —
Employees: 700
FYE: December

Meanwhile, back at the ranch . . . the sprawling King Ranch, that is. Deep in South Texas, King Ranch, founded in 1853, extends beyond the legendary 825,000 acres that are home to about 55,000 cattle and a wide variety of animal species. The family-owned business oversees ranching and farming interests in Texas and Florida, but these days the company also benefits from oil and gas royalties, farming (cotton, citrus, and sugar), and retail operations (designer saddles, leather goods). In addition, King Ranch also beefs up revenues with tourist dollars from hunters and sightseers. It sold its Kentucky horse farm, once a producer of champion thoroughbreds, and is selling its primary oil and gas subsidiary.

KEY COMPETITORS
Cactus Feeders
Koch
Tejon Ranch

 See pages 270–271 for a full profile of this company.

KINGSTON TECHNOLOGY COMPANY

17600 Newhope St.
Fountain Valley, CA 92708
Phone: 714-435-2600
Fax: 714-435-2699
Web site: http://www.kingston.com

CEO: John Tu
CFO: Henri Tchen
HR: Daniel Hsu
Type: Private

1998 Est. Sales: $1,000.0 million
1-Yr. Sales Change: —
Employees: 670
FYE: December

Kingston Technology is memory industry royalty. The company is a leading manufacturer of memory boards for boosting the capacity and speed of computers and printers, storage peripherals such as hard drives, processor upgrades, networking equipment (adapters, hubs, routers), and housings for storage products. Kingston, which sells worldwide through distributors and resellers, also offers contract manufacturing services. The employee-friendly company is securing its market presence with flash memory products for digital devices. In 1999 founders John Tu and David Sun reacquired Kingston from SOFTBANK, paying a fraction of the $1.5 billion 1996 acquisition price.

KEY COMPETITORS
Cisco Systems
Micron Technology
Samsung

 See pages 272–273 for a full profile of this company.

KINKO'S, INC.

255 W. Stanley Ave.
Ventura, CA 93002
Phone: 805-652-4000
Fax: 805-652-4347
Web site: http://www.kinkos.com

CEO: Joseph Hardin
CFO: Bennett Nusbaum
HR: Paul Rostron
Type: Private

1999 Est. Sales: $1,800.0 million
1-Yr. Sales Change: 12.5%
Employees: 25,000
FYE: June

Kinko's has come a long way since its founding as a college town copy shop. It operates more than 1,000 business service centers 24 hours a day in Australia, Canada, China, Japan, the Netherlands, South Korea, the UK, the United Arab Emirates, and the US. Originally providing self-service copying, Kinko's now offers a full range of services, including videoconferencing, binding and finishing services, custom printing, package shipping, oversize copies, and computer rentals. Most of its sales come from small- and home-office customers, but it also provides digital document services to large companies. Founder and chairman Paul Orfalea, who plans to take Kinko's public, owns 32% of the company.

KEY COMPETITORS
Mail Boxes Etc.
Office Depot
Xerox

 See pages 274–275 for a full profile of this company.

KINRAY, INC.

152-35 10th Ave.
Whitestone, NY 11357
Phone: 718-767-1234
Fax: 718-767-4388
Web site: http://www.kinray.com

CEO: Stewart Rahr
CFO: Bill Bodinger
HR: Howard Hershberg
Type: Private

1999 Sales: $1,110.0 million
1-Yr. Sales Change: 23.3%
Employees: 325
FYE: June

Kinray, the US's #3 privately held wholesale drug distributor (behind Neuman and Quality King), is nothing if not independent. It provides drugs, health and beauty products, medical equipment, small electronics, and school supplies and has a 500-item private label program. The company serves nearly 1,500 pharmacies in Connecticut, New Jersey, New York, and Pennsylvania. Kinray spearheaded creation of the Wholesale Alliance Cooperative, a group of about 20 independent regional drug distributors that hopes to aid independent pharmacies in their dealings with such third-party payors as HMOs and PPOs. The company was founded in 1936 by Joseph Rahr. His son, CEO and president Stewart Rahr, owns the company.

KEY COMPETITORS
McKesson HBOC
Neuman Distributors
Quality King

KLAUSSNER FURNITURE INDUSTRIES INC.

405 Lewallen Rd.
Asheboro, NC 27203
Phone: 336-625-6175
Fax: 336-626-0905
Web site: http://www.klaussner.com

CEO: J. B. Davis
CFO: Bob Shaffner
HR: Mark Walker
Type: Private

1998 Est. Sales: $750.0 million
1-Yr. Sales Change: 1.6%
Employees: 6,600
FYE: December

Klaussner Furniture Industries makes furniture for the couch potato in all of us. It is one of the US's largest makers of upholstered furniture. Klaussner sells fabric- and leather-upholstered sofas and recliners, dining furniture, and office furniture under the JDI, Realistic, Revolution Motion, Paoli, Tellus, and Klaussner brand names. It also offers sofas and chairs under the licensed Sealy name. Its 20 plants produce items exported to more than 40 countries. Klaussner also owns 20% of furniture retailer Jennifer Convertibles. Chairman Hans Klaussner has owned the company since 1979; it was founded in 1964 as Stuart Furniture Industries.

KEY COMPETITORS
Furniture Brands International
LifeStyle Furnishings
 International
Steelcase

KNOLL, INC.

1235 Water St.
East Greenville, PA 18041
Phone: 215-679-7991
Fax: 215-679-1755
Web site: http://www.knoll.com

CEO: John H. Lynch
CFO: Douglas J. Purdom
HR: Barbara E. Ellixson
Type: Private

1998 Sales: $948.7 million
1-Yr. Sales Change: 17.0%
Employees: 4,061
FYE: December

Designer cubicles make for happier workers, or so goes the gospel at Knoll. Knoll makes office furniture and accessories, such as rolling chairs, tables, metal and wood desks, file cabinets, lighting, and computer and desk accessories. Its cubicles — or office systems — are distinctively designed and sold under the names Reff, Morrison, Equity, Dividends, and Currents. Many of its products are created by high-profile designers such as Vietnam War Memorial architect Maya Lin. Knoll also sells textiles and leather upholstery. It sells furniture through independent dealers in North and South America, Europe, and Asia. Investment firm Warburg, Pincus and Knoll management own the company.

KEY COMPETITORS
Haworth International
Herman Miller
Steelcase

KNOWLEDGE UNIVERSE, INC.

150 Shoreline
Redwood City, CA 94065
Phone: 650-628-3000
Fax: 650-628-3201
Web site: http://www.knowledgeu.com

CEO: Thomas Kalinske
CFO: —
HR: —
Type: Private

1998 Est. Sales: $1,200.0 million
1-Yr. Sales Change: —
Employees: 8,000
FYE: December

Knowledge Universe ties its earning to your learning. The company, founded in 1996 by former junk-bond kingpin Michael Milken, his brother Lowell, and Oracle CEO Lawrence Ellison (still its three principal owners), is using acquisitions to become a cradle-to-grave education industry services specialist. Among its growing galaxy of interrelated market specializations are computer education (Productivity Point International), vocational training (Spring), management consulting (Nextera Enterprises), educational toys (LeapFrog), childcare centers (Knowledge Beginnings), career development (Teacher Universe), and proficiency exams (Bookman Testing).

KEY COMPETITORS
IBM
Learning Tree
SmartForce

KOCH INDUSTRIES, INC.

4111 E. 37th St. North
Wichita, KS 67220
Phone: 316-828-5500
Fax: 316-828-5739
Web site: http://www.kochind.com

CEO: Charles G. Koch
CFO: F. Lynn Markel
HR: Paul Wheeler
Type: Private

1998 Sales: $35,000.0 million
1-Yr. Sales Change: (3.3%)
Employees: 16,000
FYE: December

This Koch adds businesses. Koch Industries — "Koch" is pronounced "coke" — is the second-largest private US company (after Cargill), with extensive holdings in petroleum, agriculture, and chemicals. The company's two Texas and Minnesota refineries process about 540,000 barrels of crude oil a day, and it owns about 35,000 miles of pipeline between Texas and Canada. Other businesses include Purina Mills, the #1 US commercial animal feed producer, and KoSa, a venture with Mexico's Saba family that is one of the world's top polyester producers. Koch also provides ocean transport for minerals and produces asphalt and equipment for the chemical industry. Brothers Charles and David Koch own the company.

KEY COMPETITORS
Cargill
Enron
Tosco

 See pages 276–277 for a full profile of this company.

KOHLBERG KRAVIS ROBERTS & CO.

9 W. 57th St., Ste. 4200
New York, NY 10019
Phone: 212-750-8300
Fax: 212-750-0003

CEO: Henry R. Kravis
CFO: —
HR: Sandy Cisneros
Type: Partnership

Sales: —
1-Yr. Sales Change: —
Employees: —
FYE: December

The barbarians at the gate are now knocking politely. Kohlberg Kravis Roberts (popularly known as KKR) assembles multibillion-dollar funds to invest in individual companies via leveraged buyouts (mostly friendly, these days). KKR collects fees for its fund- and company-management activities and takes an active role in increasing the value of companies. Holdings include stakes in publishing company PRIMEDIA, diversified manufacturer Borden, and online mortgage lender Nexstar Financial. As targets in the US become scarce and costly, KKR is shopping in Europe, where bloated corporations are shedding noncore operations to streamline. KKR's senior partners are cousins Henry Kravis and George Roberts.

KEY COMPETITORS
Clayton, Dubilier
Forstmann Little
Hicks, Muse

See pages 278–279 for a full profile of this company.

KOHLER CO.

444 Highland Dr.
Kohler, WI 53044
Phone: 920-457-4441
Fax: 920-457-9064
Web site: http://kohlerco.com

CEO: Herbert V. Kohler
CFO: Jeffery P. Cheney
HR: —
Type: Private

1998 Est. Sales: $2,400.0 million
1-Yr. Sales Change: 8.6%
Employees: 18,000
FYE: December

When plumbing powerhouse Kohler says profits are in the toilet, it's not complaining. Kohler is the US's leading bathroom fixture maker, with such brands as Ann Sacks (ceramic tile, marble, stone products), Kallista (bathroom and kitchen fixtures), and Kohler and Sterling (plumbing products). European brands include Jacob Delafon and Neomediam plumbing products and Sanijura bath cabinetry and related products. Kohler also makes small engines, generators, electrical switchgear, and high-end furniture; it owns The American Club resort hotel, golf courses, and other real estate. Chairman Herbert Kohler Jr. and his sister Ruth — both grandchildren of the firm's founder — control more than 70% of Kohler.

KEY COMPETITORS
American Standard
Fortune Brands
Masco

 See pages 280–281 for a full profile of this company.

KOPPERS INDUSTRIES, INC.

436 7th Ave.
Pittsburgh, PA 15219
Phone: 412-227-2001
Fax: 412-227-2333
Web site: http://www.koppers.com

CEO: Walter W. Turner
CFO: Donald E. Davis
HR: Joseph E. Boan
Type: Private

1998 Sales: $670.6 million
1-Yr. Sales Change: 13.1%
Employees: 1,927
FYE: December

Koppers Industries treats wood right. The company makes carbon compounds and treated-wood products for the chemical, railroad, aluminum, and steel markets. Its carbon materials and chemicals segment (more than 50% of sales) makes materials for producing aluminum, polyester resins, plasticizers, and wood pressure-treatments. The railroad and utility segment supplies pressure-treated crossties and utility poles to railroads and utility companies. Koppers bought a 50% interest in KSA Limited Partnership, a concrete crosstie maker, in response to railroad experimentation with alternative products. The company operates in the Australasia region, Europe, and the US. Private investment fund Saratoga owns the firm.

KEY COMPETITORS
Cytec Industries
Kerr-McGee
Stepan

KPMG INTERNATIONAL

345 Park Ave.
New York, NY 10154-0102
Phone: 212-758-9700
Fax: 212-758-9819
Web site: http://www.kpmg.com

CEO: Paul C. Reilly
CFO: Joseph E. Heintz
HR: Timothy P. Flynn
Type: Partnership

1999 Sales: $12,200.0 million
1-Yr. Sales Change: 15.1%
Employees: 102,000
FYE: September

KPMG International is #3 among the Big Five accounting firms after PricewaterhouseCoopers and Andersen Worldwide. KPMG provides accounting and consulting services from some 800 offices in more than 150 nations, from Albania to Zimbabwe, and is the only one of the Big Five larger in Europe than in North America. Traditionally a loose federation of national firms, KPMG is consolidating to offer more complete service. Also, the firm has separated its accounting and consulting businesses in the US and is selling 20% of the latter to networking equipment maker Cisco Systems prior to taking the consulting arm public.

KEY COMPETITORS
Andersen Worldwide
Ernst & Young
PricewaterhouseCoopers

 See pages 282–283 for a full profile of this company.

K-VA-T FOOD STORES, INC.

201 Trigg St.
Abingdon, VA 24210
Phone: 540-628-8173
Fax: 540-628-1592
Web site: http://www.foodcity.com

CEO: Jack C. Smith
CFO: Robert L. Neeley
HR: Mark Millwood
Type: Private

1998 Est. Sales: $760.0 million
1-Yr. Sales Change: 6.7%
Employees: 6,500
FYE: December

What do you call a chain of supermarkets in Kentucky, Virginia, and Tennessee? How about K-VA-T Food Stores? K-VA-T is one of the largest grocery chains in the region, with more than 85 supermarkets primarily under the Food City banner but also the Super Dollar name. Some Food City stores offer salad bars, in-store banking, video sections, pharmacies, and Gas 'N Go gasoline outlets. Founded in 1955, the company has expanded by acquiring stores from other regional food retailers. The founding Smith family owns a majority of K-VA-T; employees own the rest.

KEY COMPETITORS
Kroger
Ruddick
Wal-Mart

LAND O'LAKES, INC.

4001 Lexington Ave. North
Arden Hills, MN 55126
Phone: 651-481-2222
Fax: 651-481-2022
Web site: http://www.landolakesinc.com

CEO: John E. Gherty
CFO: Ronald O. Ostby
HR: Jack Martin
Type: Cooperative

1998 Sales: $5,174.2 million
1-Yr. Sales Change: 23.3%
Employees: 6,500
FYE: December

Land O'Lakes butters up its customers. Its network of more than 1,000 community cooperatives serves 300,000 farmers and ranchers in 29 states. The dairy co-op (#2 in the US, behind Dairy Farmers of America) provides its members with wholesale fertilizer and crop protection products, seed, and animal feed. Its oldest product, Land O'Lakes butter, is the #1 brand in the US. Land O'Lakes also produces packaged milk, margarine, snack dips, sour cream, and cheese. The dairy industry and its markets have been consolidating, and the co-op has responded with acquisitions and joint ventures at home and abroad; it has even entered into hog production to offer its farmer members more choices.

KEY COMPETITORS
AMPI
ConAgra
Dairy Farmers of America

 See pages 284–285 for a full profile of this company.

LANE INDUSTRIES, INC.

1200 Shermer Rd.
Northbrook, IL 60062
Phone: 847-498-6789
Fax: 847-498-2104

CEO: William N. Lane
CFO: Forrest M. Schneider
HR: Linda Datz
Type: Private

1998 Sales: $1,020.0 million
1-Yr. Sales Change: 14.6%
Employees: 8,650
FYE: December

From the seeds of a humble office machine and supplies manufacturer grew the mighty oak of Lane Industries. The diversified holding company's oldest investment is its nearly 63% stake in General Binding, a maker of binding and laminating equipment, marker boards, and paper shredders, founded by William Lane II in 1947. Lane Industries is also active in the lodging industry through Lane Hospitality, which owns or operates more than 50 hotels, resorts, and time-share properties. Through Lane Security, the company owns Protection Services Industries, a security alarm firm in the western US. Members of the Lane family (including Lane Industries chairman William Lane III) own the company.

KEY COMPETITORS
Fellowes Manufacturing
Starwood Hotels & Resorts
  Worldwide
Tyco International

LANOGA CORPORATION

17946 NE 65th St.	CEO: Daryl Nagel	1998 Est. Sales: $1,030.0 million
Redmond, WA 98052	CFO: William P. Brakken	1-Yr. Sales Change: 4.0%
Phone: 425-883-4125	HR: —	Employees: 4,085
Fax: 425-882-2959	Type: Private	FYE: December

Lanoga is a lumbering giant. The company is one of the top 10 US retailers of lumber and building materials, operating about 190 stores in 17 states. Catering to professional contractors as well as consumers, Lanoga favors stores in rural areas to avoid competition with larger chains. It has grown through dozens of small acquisitions. Its divisions include United Building Centers (about 130 stores in the Midwest), Lumbermen's Building Centers (about 50 stores in the Northwest), and Spenard Building Supply (a dozen or so stores in Alaska). Cousins William Laird and Matthew Norton founded the company in the mid-1800s. "Lanoga" comes partially from their names, and their descendants own the company.

KEY COMPETITORS
84 Lumber
Building Materials Holding
Home Depot

LARRY H. MILLER GROUP

5650 S. State St.	CEO: Larry H. Miller	1997 Sales: $1,018.7 million
Murray, UT 84107	CFO: Clark Whitworth	1-Yr. Sales Change: 21.1%
Phone: 801-264-3100	HR: Carolyn Ashburn	Employees: 3,200
Fax: 801-264-3198	Type: Private	FYE: December
Web site: http://www.lhmauto.com		

You wouldn't hire the Larry H. Miller Group for your late night bebop, but the firm does know a little something about all that jazz. Its interests include automobiles, television, and basketball. The company operates almost 40 auto dealerships in Arizona, Colorado, Idaho, New Mexico, Oklahoma, Oregon, and Utah; most are in Utah. Its dealerships sell Toyota, Cadillac, Chevrolet, Honda, Lexus, and other makes of cars. The Utah Jazz professional basketball team, its home (the Delta Center arena), and Salt Lake City TV station KJZZ also fall under the group's umbrella. The group, owned by its CEO with the same name, also operates Larry Miller Advertising and publishes *Spirit* magazine.

KEY COMPETITORS
AutoNation
Burt Automotive
Earnhardt Auto Centers

LDI, LTD.

54 Monument Circle, Ste. 800	CEO: Andre Lacy	1998 Est. Sales: $1,000.0 million
Indianapolis, IN 46204	CFO: Michael P. Hutson	1-Yr. Sales Change: —
Phone: 317-237-2251	HR: Joyce Schooley	Employees: 3,100
Fax: 317-237-2280	Type: Private	FYE: December
Web site: http://www.ldiltd.com		

The "D" is definitely for "diversified" at LDI. The company, whose initials stand for "Lacy Diversified Industries," deals in videotapes, motorcycle and bicycle parts, and auto refinishing products. It owns Major Video Concepts, a wholesale distributor of prerecorded movie videocassettes, and has a 74% stake in automotive paints and coating distributor FinishMaster, which has operations in over 20 states. Its other businesses include Tucker-Rocky, a distributor of aftermarket equipment for the watercraft, motorcycle, and snowmobile markets, and Answer Products, a distributor of Manitou bike parts and apparel. Founded in 1912 as the U.S. Corrugated-Fiber Box Co., LDI is owned by CEO Andre Lacy.

KEY COMPETITORS
Blockbuster
Genuine Parts
Global Motorsport Group

THE LEFRAK ORGANIZATION

97-77 Queens Blvd.	CEO: —	1998 Sales: $2,750.0 million
Rego Park, NY 11374	CFO: Richard S. LeFrak	1-Yr. Sales Change: (19.1%)
Phone: 718-459-9021	HR: Mitchell Ingerman	Employees: 16,000
Fax: 718-897-0688	Type: Private	FYE: November
Web site: http://www.lefrak.com		

"If you build it, they will come" could be the Lefrak Organization's motto. The private firm is one of the largest residential development and management companies in the New York City metropolitan area. In addition to a variety of smaller properties, its major developments include Lefrak City (5,000 units) and Battery Park (2,200 units), both in New York City, and Newport City (about 10,000 units), which is still under construction in Jersey City, New Jersey. Owned by the LeFrak family, the company owns and manages a variety of commercial and retail properties throughout the city. Other interests include Lefrak Oil & Gas Organization and Lefrak Entertainment (a production company).

KEY COMPETITORS
Dyson-Kissner-Moran
Helmsley
Trump

 See pages 286–287 for a full profile of this company.

THE LEO GROUP, INC.

35 W. Wacker Dr.	CEO: Richard B. Fizdale	1998 Sales: $949.8 million
Chicago, IL 60601	CFO: Roger A. Haupt	1-Yr. Sales Change: 8.2%
Phone: 312-220-5959	HR: —	Employees: 9,029
Fax: 312-220-3299	Type: Private	FYE: December
Web site: http://www.leoburnett.com		

The Leo Group (formerly Leo Burnett Company) has created some of the most successful marketing icons in the US, including Tony the Tiger, the Marlboro Man, and the Pillsbury Doughboy. The company provides advertising, marketing, and communications services to such clients as Coca-Cola and General Motors. It also offers specialized services, including interactive advertising, minority targeting, and direct marketing. Its Starcom Worldwide handles media buying and planning for clients such as McDonald's. The employee-owned company has offices in about 70 countries. Leo Group has agreed to merge with MacManus Group to form a new advertising behemoth named BDM (of which Japan's Dentsu will also own a stake).

KEY COMPETITORS
Interpublic Group
Omnicom Group
WPP Group

 See pages 288–289 for a full profile of this company.

LEPRINO FOODS COMPANY

1830 W. 38th Ave.	CEO: James Leprino	1999 Est. Sales: $1,550.0 million
Denver, CO 80211	CFO: Tom Briggs	1-Yr. Sales Change: 24.0%
Phone: 303-480-2600	HR: Dave Swan	Employees: 2,800
Fax: 303-480-2605	Type: Private	FYE: October

To pizza chains Domino's, Pizza Hut, and Little Caesar, Leprino Foods really is the big cheese. The company is the world's largest maker of mozzarella cheese, with seven plants in the US, including a mozzarella plant in New Mexico that is the world's biggest. To make its products, Leprino uses about 5% of the US milk supply, which it receives from the nation's large dairy co-ops, including Dairy Farmers of America. The company also makes sweet whey, whey protein concentrate, and lactose for use in baby formula, ice cream, and baked goods. The company was founded in 1950 by Italian immigrant Michael Leprino Sr. as part of a family-owned grocery store. It is still owned by the Leprino family.

KEY COMPETITORS
Kraft Foods
Saputo Group
Schreiber Foods

LES SCHWAB TIRE CENTERS

646 N. Madras Hwy.
Prineville, OR 97754
Phone: 541-447-4136
Fax: 541-416-5208
Web site: http://www.lesschwab.com

CEO: Les Schwab
CFO: Tom Freedman
HR: Larry Smith
Type: Private

1998 Est. Sales: $750.0 million
1-Yr. Sales Change: (11.8%)
Employees: 5,300
FYE: December

If it be tires that ye seek, Les Schwab Tire Centers looks like the land of milk and honey. Of course, it doesn't hurt that the owner wrote the bible of tire retailing: *Pride in Performance — Keep It Going.* The company sells tires and batteries and does alignment, brake, and shock work at about 300 stores in Alaska, California, Idaho, Montana, Nevada, Oregon, and Washington state. With a story that rivals Moses', founder and owner Les Schwab was raised in a logging camp, went to school in a converted boxcar, and was orphaned as a teenager. In 1952 he bought a tire shop that eventually became Les Schwab Tire Centers. The company's culture is based on treating employees as family: They receive 50% of profits.

KEY COMPETITORS
CSK Auto
Sears
Wal-Mart

LEVI STRAUSS & CO.

1155 Battery St.
San Francisco, CA 94111
Phone: 415-501-6000
Fax: 415-501-3939
Web site: http://www.levistrauss.com

CEO: Philip Marineau
CFO: William B. Chiasson
HR: Donna J. Goya
Type: Private

1998 Sales: $6,000.0 million
1-Yr. Sales Change: (13.0%)
Employees: 30,000
FYE: November

Good ol' trusty Levi's are one thing. Hip, funky, stylish Levi's are another. Blue-jeans maker Levi Strauss & Co. (LS&CO.) wants to be known for both. LS&CO., the world's #1 maker of brand-name clothing, sells jeans and sportswear under the Levi's, Dockers, and Slates names in more than 60 countries. Levi's jeans — department store staples — were once the uniform of American youth, but LS&CO. has lost touch with the trends in recent years, and slow sales have led the company to slash its US workforce. To re-tap the youth market, LS&CO. is exploring a host of nontraditional advertising methods and abandoning its one-style-fits-all design approach. The Haas family (relatives of founder Levi Strauss) owns LS&CO.

KEY COMPETITORS
The Gap
Tommy Hilfiger
VF

 See pages 290–291 for a full profile of this company.

LIBERTY MUTUAL INSURANCE COMPANIES

175 Berkeley St.
Boston, MA 02117
Phone: 617-357-9500
Fax: 617-350-7648
Web site: http://www.libertymutual.com

CEO: Edmund F. Kelly
CFO: J. Paul Condrin
HR: Helen Sayles
Type: Mutual company

1998 Sales: $10,964.0 million
1-Yr. Sales Change: 63.5%
Employees: 37,000
FYE: December

At Liberty Mutual, an ounce of prevention is worth a pound of cure. Injury-prevention services (analyzing work sites and practices to ensure safety and prevent losses) are stressed by the US's #1 workers' compensation insurer. For times when prevention isn't enough, the firm also offers rehabilitation services and has alliances with health care providers to manage disability care. Noncommercial insurance lines include homeowners, auto, and group life. Liberty Mutual's financial services, grouped under the Liberty Financial umbrella, provide investment management and sell annuities and mutual funds. The company has more than 900 offices in 13 countries, including Canada, Japan, Mexico, Singapore, and the UK.

KEY COMPETITORS
Allstate
Prudential
State Farm

 See pages 292–293 for a full profile of this company.

LIBERTY TRAVEL, INC.

69 Spring St.
Ramsey, NJ 07446
Phone: 201-934-3500
Fax: 201-934-3651
Web site: http://www.libertytravel.com

CEO: Gilbert Haroche
CFO: Richard Cowlan
HR: Patt Harmes
Type: Private

1997 Sales: $1,320.0 million
1-Yr. Sales Change: 1.8%
Employees: 1,700
FYE: December

Liberty Travel gives independent travelers the freedom to travel autonomously. The company is one of the US leaders in leisure vacations and owns almost 200 offices in the Northeast and in Florida; it sells directly to the holiday traveler. Liberty's GOGO Worldwide Vacations division is a leading US independent wholesale travel operator that offers travel packages from almost 90 offices located in most major US cities. Efficient in its growth, the company makes its own office furniture. The privately held company was founded in 1951 by owners Gilbert Haroche and Fred Kassner. Kassner died in late 1998.

KEY COMPETITORS
AAA
Carlson Wagonlit
TravelFest Superstores, Inc.

See pages 294–295 for a full profile of this company.

LIFE CARE CENTERS OF AMERICA

3570 Keith St. NW
Cleveland, TN 37120
Phone: 423-472-9585
Fax: 423-339-8337
Web site: http://www.lcca.com

CEO: Lane Bowen
CFO: Steve Ziegler
HR: Mark Gibson
Type: Private

1998 Est. Sales: $1,210.0 million
1-Yr. Sales Change: 10.0%
Employees: 22,000
FYE: December

Life Care Centers of America is the largest privately owned operator of retirement and health care centers in the US. The company manages more than 200 facilities in 28 states — including retirement communities, assisted living facilities, and nursing homes — and provides such specialized services as home health care. Founder and CEO Forrest Preston opened his first center in 1970 and continues to tout a "corporate culture based on Judeo-Christian ethics." However, complaints of poor-quality care have been filed at several locations, a situation that plagues the industry overall. More than 20% of the company's facilities are owned by Meditrust, the #1 US health care real estate investment trust.

KEY COMPETITORS
Beverly Enterprises
Mariner Post-Acute Network
Sun Healthcare

LIFESTYLE FURNISHINGS INTERNATIONAL LTD.

4000 Lifestyle Ct.
High Point, NC 27265
Phone: 336-878-7000
Fax: 336-878-7015

CEO: Wayne B. Lyon
CFO: Ronald J. Hoffman
HR: William J. Frakes
Type: Private

1998 Sales: $2,001.9 million
1-Yr. Sales Change: 1.7%
Employees: 30,000
FYE: December

LifeStyle Furnishings International bets the house on its collection of brand names. The #2 US home furnishings manufacturer (behind Furniture Brands International) sells bedroom, dining room, living room, outdoor, and upholstered furniture under eight principal brands: Benchcraft, Berkline, Drexel Heritage, Henredon, La Barge, Lexington, Maitland-Smith, and Universal. Some collections bear the names of designers and celebrities such as Ralph Lauren and Arnold Palmer. It also makes fabrics (Ametex, Robert Allen). LifeStyle makes its products in North America, Asia, and Europe and sells them through specialty retailers, department stores, showrooms, and independent stores that sell only LifeStyle products.

KEY COMPETITORS
Furniture Brands International
Klaussner Furniture Group
La-Z-Boy

See pages 296–297 for a full profile of this company.

LINCOLN PROPERTY COMPANY

500 N. Akard, Ste. 3300
Dallas, TX 75201
Phone: 214-740-3300
Fax: 214-740-3313
Web site: http://www.lincolnproperty.com

CEO: Mack Pogue
CFO: Nancy Davis
HR: —
Type: Private

1999 Sales: $1,462.1 million
1-Yr. Sales Change: 4.5%
Employees: 4,600
FYE: June

Founded on Lincoln's birthday in 1965, Lincoln Property is the US's largest diversified real estate development and investment company. From building and operating apartment developments in the Dallas area, Lincoln Property branched out into office buildings, warehouses, shopping centers, hotels, and other nonresidential projects. It also offers a variety of management and investment services. The company is joining with Sam Zell's Equity Residential Properties REIT to build 25 multifamily developments in the western US. Lincoln Property has completed projects in 19 US states as well as in Western Europe and the Middle East. Founder Mack Pogue, who still runs the company, bought out co-founder Trammell Crow in 1977.

KEY COMPETITORS
JMB Realty
Tishman Realty
Trammell Crow Residential

LITTLE CAESAR ENTERPRISES, INC.

2211 Woodward Ave.
Detroit, MI 48201
Phone: 313-983-6000
Fax: 313-983-6494
Web site: http://www.littlecaesars.com

CEO: Michael Ilitch
CFO: James Weissenborn
HR: Darrel Snygg
Type: Subsidiary

1998 Sales: $605.0 million
1-Yr. Sales Change: (2.3%)
Employees: 90,000
FYE: December

Not-so-Little Caesar Enterprises is the #3 US pizza chain (after #1 Pizza Hut and #2 Domino's). With 4,500 stores in more than a dozen countries, Little Caesar is best known for its "Pizza! Pizza!" deal, which offers two pies for the price of one. Little Caesar is part of Ilitch Ventures, a company formed by owners Mike and Marian Ilitch in 1999 to oversee their various Detroit-area holdings. Among the other businesses under the Ilitch Ventures umbrella are the NHL's Detroit Red Wings and Major League Baseball's Detroit Tigers. Little Caesar is facing flagging pizza sales and continued bombardment in the pizza wars from upstart Papa John's.

KEY COMPETITORS
Domino's Pizza
Papa John's
Pizza Hut

 See pages 298–299 for a full profile of this company.

L.L. BEAN, INC.

Casco St.
Freeport, ME 04033
Phone: 207-865-4761
Fax: 207-552-6821
Web site: http://www.llbean.com

CEO: Leon A. Gorman
CFO: Lee Surace
HR: Bob Peixotto
Type: Private

1999 Sales: $1,070.0 million
1-Yr. Sales Change: 0.2%
Employees: 4,000
FYE: February

Enjoy the outdoors or just want to look like you do? Outdoor specialty cataloger L.L. Bean publishes 50 catalogs a year and operates a flagship retail store and a children's clothing store in Freeport, Maine (both are open 24 hours a day, year-round). L.L. Bean also has 10 US factory outlets and more than 20 retail stores in Japan, and it sells its merchandise online. Known for customer service (including unlimited returns), it offers more than 16,000 items ranging from outdoor wear and sporting goods to household furnishings. L.L. Bean also conducts classes on topics such as bicycle maintenance, camping, and sea kayaking. The firm was founded in 1912 by Leon Leonwood Bean and is controlled by his descendants.

KEY COMPETITORS
Lands' End
REI
Spiegel

See pages 300–301 for a full profile of this company.

LONG JOHN SILVER'S RESTAURANTS, INC.

Kincaid Towers
Lexington, KY 40508
Phone: 606-388-6000
Fax: 606-388-6363
Web site: http://www.ljsilvers.com

CEO: Sidney J. Feltenstein
CFO: Mark Plummer
HR: Michael Allen
Type: Subsidiary

1999 Est. Sales: $500.0 million
1-Yr. Sales Change: —
Employees: 14,000
FYE: June

Arrh! The pirate king of the quick-service seafood ocean, Long John Silver's was on the verge of walking the corporate plank during the 1990s when the financially troubled company didn't have enough loot to pay its debts. The company was flying the Chapter 11 flag at half-mast when landlubber A&W Restaurants came to its rescue in 1999. A&W bought the chain, created holding company Yorkshire Global Restaurants, and now both Long John Silver's and A&W are Yorkshire subsidiaries. Long John Silver's more than 1,270 franchised or company-owned restaurants serve menu items such as batter-dipped fish, chicken, clams, shrimp, sandwiches, salads, and desserts.

KEY COMPETITORS
Arthur Treacher's
McDonald's
Shoney's

 See pages 302–303 for a full profile of this company.

THE LONGABERGER COMPANY

1500 E. Main St.
Newark, OH 43058
Phone: 740-322-5000
Fax: 740-322-5240
Web site: http://www.longaberger.com

CEO: Tami Longaberger
CFO: Stephanie Imhoff
HR: Dennis Dowdell
Type: Private

1998 Sales: $700.0 million
1-Yr. Sales Change: 14.6%
Employees: 7,000
FYE: December

A tisket, a tasket, a Longaberger basket. Each year The Longaberger Company makes about 9 million handwoven baskets in more than 80 styles. The baskets sell for $25-$227 and are available only in the US through in-home shows conducted by Longaberger's 50,000 independent sales associates. The company also sells pottery, fabrics, window treatments, and wrought-iron home accessories. Longaberger's home office is a seven-story rendition of a basket with two 75-ton handles on top. The company's Longaberger Homestead tourist attraction offers 34 acres of shopping, eating, and entertainment. The family-owned firm is run by the daughters of the late Dave Longaberger, who founded the company in 1972.

KEY COMPETITORS
Euromarket Designs
Pier 1 Imports
Williams-Sonoma

LOS ANGELES COUNTY DEPARTMENT OF HEALTH SERVICES

313 N. Figueroa
Los Angeles, CA 90012
Phone: 213-240-8101
Fax: 213-481-0503
Web site: http://www.dhs.co.la.ca.us

CEO: Mark R. Finucane
CFO: Gary Wells
HR: Alan Knauss
Type: Government-owned

1998 Sales: $3,256.8 million
1-Yr. Sales Change: 11.8%
Employees: 21,694
FYE: June

Los Angeles County Department of Health Services (DHS) is the second-largest publicly supported health system in the nation (behind New York City's Health and Hospitals Corporation). The system operates six hospitals and about 45 community health centers and is the health care provider of last resort for the poor and uninsured. It provides primary care and oversees public health functions such as emergency medical services, addiction treatment, and disease control. DHS is affiliated with several medical schools and provides a training ground for medical and health professionals. It is also responsible for inspecting housing, medical facilities, restaurants, and swimming pools.

KEY COMPETITORS
Catholic Healthcare West
Columbia/HCA
UniHealth

LOS ANGELES DEPARTMENT OF WATER AND POWER

111 N. Hope St.	CEO: S. David Freeman	1998 Sales: $2,588.0 million
Los Angeles, CA 90012	CFO: Phyllis E. Currie	1-Yr. Sales Change: 6.3%
Phone: 213-367-1338	HR: Raman Raj	Employees: 8,290
Fax: 213-367-1438	Type: Government-owned	FYE: June
Web site: http://www.ladwp.com		

The Los Angeles Department of Water and Power keeps the movie cameras running and the swimming pools full. The largest city-owned utility in the US provides electricity and water to 3.5 million residential and commercial customers. Electricity is produced from coal (45%), oil and natural gas (20%), and nuclear (9%) sources. Hydroelectricity (12%) is generated from two aqueduct systems that transport most of the city's water from the eastern Sierra Nevada Mountains; the utility also purchases power. Other water sources include wells in the San Fernando Valley, local groundwater basins, and purchases from the Metropolitan Water District of Southern California. The utility is preparing for deregulation.

LOUISIANA STATE UNIVERSITY SYSTEM

3810 W. Lakeshore Dr.	CEO: William Jenkins	1998 Sales: $1,258.7 million
Baton Rouge, LA 70808	CFO: Jerry J. Baudin	1-Yr. Sales Change: 4.5%
Phone: 225-388-3202	HR: Sharyon Lipscomb	Employees: 19,030
Fax: 225-388-5524	Type: School	FYE: June
Web site: http://www.lsu.edu		

The Louisiana State University (LSU) System oversees a string of higher education institutions across the Bayou State. Flagship institution LSU in Baton Rouge was founded in 1853 and boasts more than 30,000 students. The Baton Rouge campus is home to the Paul M. Hebert Law Center, the LSU Agricultural Center, the LSU Medical Center, and the Pennington Biomedical Research Center (nutritional research). Also within the LSU System are LSU Shreveport (with about 4,000 students) and the University of New Orleans. The LSU System also includes LSU Alexandria and LSU Eunice, both two-year institutions.

LOYOLA UNIVERSITY OF CHICAGO

6525 N. Sheridan Rd.	CEO: John J. Piderit	1998 Sales: $916.2 million
Chicago, IL 60626	CFO: David Meagher	1-Yr. Sales Change: 8.6%
Phone: 773-274-3000	HR: Thomas M. Kelly	Employees: 6,287
Fax: 312-915-6455	Type: School	FYE: June
Web site: http://www.luc.edu		

Loyola University of Chicago is a Jesuit Catholic university whose reach extends beyond the Windy City. In addition to its four Chicago-area campuses, the university also maintains an undergraduate campus in Rome. Loyola's 13,600 students can choose from 46 undergraduate, 59 graduate, 36 doctoral, and three professional programs. Established in 1870, Loyola University is struggling to overcome fiscal difficulties resulting from the 1995 creation of a separate corporation for its health care operations. (Surplus revenue from this unit formerly helped support the entire university, but is presently dedicated exclusively to the medical center.)

LUMBERMENS MERCHANDISING CORPORATION

137 W. Wayne Ave.
Wayne, PA 19087
Phone: 610-293-7000
Fax: 610-293-7134
Web site: http://www.cyberyard.com

CEO: Anthony J. DeCarlo
CFO: David J. Gonze
HR: Patricia Moynihan
Type: Cooperative

1998 Est. Sales: $1,700.0 million
1-Yr. Sales Change: 2.0%
Employees: 200
FYE: September

Membership has its privileges. Through Lumbermens Merchandising Corporation (LMC), lumber retailers in the eastern half of the US pool their buying resources to leverage volume discounts from vendors and increase their own efficiency. Members of the cooperative meet monthly in each state or region, but advertising and promotional plans are handled on a national level. None of the cooperative's more than 300 members is in direct competition with one another. With billion-dollar revenues, LMC is the largest dealer-owned lumber building materials buying group. The cooperative does not release sales figures, and it holds members to strict confidentiality, in part to safeguard vendor contracts.

KEY COMPETITORS
BMA
Cameron Ashley
Do it Best

LUPIENT AUTOMOTIVE GROUP

750 Pennsylvania Ave.
Golden Valley, MN 55426
Phone: 612-544-6666
Fax: 612-513-5517
Web site: http://www.lupient.com

CEO: James Lupient
CFO: Keith Phillips
HR: Barbara Lupient
Type: Private

1997 Sales: $707.6 million
1-Yr. Sales Change: (9.4%)
Employees: 1,000
FYE: December

Auto dealers in Minnesota take a backseat to Lupient Automotive Group. The company, the largest auto dealer in Minnesota, with more than 25 locations, also sells and leases automobiles in Wisconsin. Lupient Automotive sells a variety of models, including those made by General Motors, Isuzu, Nissan, Kia, and Suzuki. Lupient Automotive is also one of the nation's leading dealerships in terms of fleet sales and offers title and license administration and nationwide delivery. Founded in 1969 by President and CEO James Lupient as an Oldsmobile dealership, the company also performs warranty, maintenance, and service work.

KEY COMPETITORS
GE Capital
Jordan Motors
Russ Darrow

LUTHERAN BROTHERHOOD

625 4th Ave. South
Minneapolis, MN 55415
Phone: 612-340-7000
Fax: 612-340-6897
Web site: http://www.luthbro.com

CEO: Robert P. Gandrud
CFO: Jerald E. Sourdiff
HR: Jennifer H. Martin
Type: Not-for-profit

1998 Sales: $1,693.0 million
1-Yr. Sales Change: 5.6%
Employees: 2,648
FYE: December

Founded in 1917 to provide members with life insurance, Lutheran Brotherhood now offers that and other financial services to more than 1.1 million Lutherans across the US. Members can enroll in life, health, and major medical insurance programs. The brotherhood's financial services include mutual funds, fixed annuities, and a range of variable annuity portfolios (from high-yield to blue chip). Members and agents must be Lutherans (account managers do not have to be church members). The brotherhood's tax-exempt status provides savings, which are passed on to Lutheran congregations, church members, and such charitable causes as Habitat for Humanity.

KEY COMPETITORS
Aetna
MetLife
Prudential

M. FABRIKANT & SONS

1 Rockefeller Plaza	CEO: Charles Fortgang	1999 Sales: $820.0 million
New York, NY 10020	CFO: Michael Shaffet	1-Yr. Sales Change: 5.1%
Phone: 212-757-0790	HR: Deborah Gianelli	Employees: 800
Fax: 212-262-9757	Type: Private	FYE: July

A major US diamond wholesaler, family-owned M. Fabrikant & Sons claims to be one of the oldest diamond and jewelry companies in the world. With holdings that include about 20 companies in 10 countries, the company purchases, manufactures, and sells to retailers a full range of loose and polished diamonds; diamond, gold, and silver jewelry; and precious stones, such as rubies, emeralds, sapphires, opals, and pearls. Non-diamond jewelry accounts for about 10% of Fabrikant's business. Leer Tokyo Pearl, Fabrikant's joint venture with a Japanese firm, supplies the US market with Japanese, Tahitian, and Australian pearls. Fabrikant began as a loose diamond wholesaler in New York City in 1895.

KEY COMPETITORS
Atlas Pacific
LJ International
Lazare Kaplan

MA LABORATORIES, INC.

2075 Capitol Ave.	CEO: Abraham Ma	1998 Sales: $700.0 million
San Jose, CA 95132	CFO: —	1-Yr. Sales Change: (5.4%)
Phone: 408-941-0808	HR: Amy Ching	Employees: —
Fax: 408-941-0909	Type: Private	FYE: December
Web site: http://www.malabs.com		

No surprise that a company named MA Laboratories sells motherboards. But MA Laboratories also provides computer resellers and distributors with a mother lode (more than 1,300 products) of high-tech and computer items, such as memory, modems, and monitors. The company sells just about everything commonly found in a computer, including hard drives, CPUs, CD-ROMs, video cards, and its own memory modules (which it manufactures at its Silicon Valley facility). Other products include software, fax modems, network cards, digital cameras, notebooks, and notebook accessories. MA Laboratories, founded in 1983 by owner Abraham Ma, resells products by AMD, IBM, Intel, Iomega, Microsoft, and Toshiba.

KEY COMPETITORS
Kingston Technology
Pioneer-Standard Electronics
Solectron

M. A. MORTENSON COMPANIES, INC.

700 Meadow Lane North	CEO: M. A. Mortenson	1998 Sales: $904.0 million
Minneapolis, MN 55422	CFO: Peter A. Conzemius	1-Yr. Sales Change: 12.6%
Phone: 612-522-2100	HR: Maritza DeJesus	Employees: 1,873
Fax: 612-287-5430	Type: Private	FYE: December
Web site: http://www.mortenson.com		

It's bricks, mortar, and more for M. A. Mortenson Companies, one of the largest US contractors. The company constructs aviation, education, health care, and sports facilities as well as water-treatment and power plants, dams, and other heavy industrial projects. Mortenson conducts most of its operations in the Midwest; it is one of the few major US contractors that keeps its business completely domestic. Among Mortenson's projects are Lincoln Centre and Target Center in Minneapolis, Denver International Airport, Coors Field in Denver, and Iowa's tallest building, the 44-story 801 Grand in Des Moines. The company was founded in 1954 by M. A. Mortenson Sr., whose son M. A. Mortenson Jr. runs the company today.

KEY COMPETITORS
Bechtel
Parsons
Turner Corporation

MACANDREWS & FORBES HOLDINGS INC.

35 E. 62nd St. New York, NY 10021 Phone: 212-688-9000 Fax: 212-572-8400	CEO: Ronald O. Perelman CFO: — HR: — Type: Private	1998 Est. Sales: $4,900.0 million 1-Yr. Sales Change: (19.3%) Employees: 19,500 FYE: December

Lipstick pushers Cindy, Halle, and Ron? Through MacAndrews & Forbes Holdings, financier Ron Perelman has had even stranger bedfellows. The holding company has investments in an array of public and private companies, including Revlon (the #2 cosmetics company in the US), Sunbeam (small appliances and Coleman camping equipment), Golden State Bancorp (the nation's #2 thrift), M&F Worldwide (licorice flavors), and Weddingchannel.com. Perelman focuses on consumer products operations. He made a hefty profit when Consolidated Cigar Holdings (the #1 US cigar maker) was sold to French tobacco maker Seita in early 1999. Perelman once controlled Marvel Entertainment Group (the top US comic book publisher).

KEY COMPETITORS
Cosmair
Esteé Lauder
Procter & Gamble

 See pages 304–305 for a full profile of this company.

THE MACMANUS GROUP

1675 Broadway New York, NY 10019 Phone: 212-468-3622 Fax: 212-468-4385 Web site: http://www.dmbb.com	CEO: Roy J. Bostock CFO: Craig D. Brown HR: Leslie Engel Type: Private	1998 Sales: $890.0 million 1-Yr. Sales Change: 5.6% Employees: 7,619 FYE: December

For The MacManus Group, the pampering never stops. The advertising company is one of the firms consumer giant Procter & Gamble calls on to hawk its household brands, including Pampers diapers and Cheer detergent. D'Arcy Masius Benton & Bowles (which operates under the shortened name D'Arcy) is MacManus' flagship agency with some 130 offices in 75 countries. The company also operates The Kaplan Thaler Group and N. W. Ayer & Partners (the oldest US ad agency), as well as media buying unit MediaVest Worldwide, and public relations firm Manning, Selvage & Lee. Clients include Burger King and General Motors. MacManus has agreed to merge with The Leo Group (formerly Leo Burnett) to form a new ad giant called BDM.

KEY COMPETITORS
Interpublic Group
Omnicom Group
WPP Group

 See pages 306–307 for a full profile of this company.

MAJOR LEAGUE BASEBALL

Office of the Commissioner, 245 Park Ave. New York, NY 10167 Phone: 212-931-7800 Fax: 212-949-8636 Web site: http://www.majorleaguebaseball.com	CEO: Allan H. Selig CFO: Jeffrey White HR: Wendy Lewis Type: Association	1998 Sales: $3,173.6 million 1-Yr. Sales Change: 43.2% Employees: — FYE: October

Play ball! Major League Baseball's (MLB) 30 franchises are divided into the American and National Leagues. The teams are run as separate businesses, but they share some broadcasting revenues, gate receipts, and licensing fees. Bud Selig, owner of the Milwaukee Brewers, is the game's commissioner. The organization's other subsidiaries include Major League Baseball Properties and the Major League Scouting Bureau. Baseball received a much-needed boost in popularity in 1998 from the exciting home run race between St. Louis Cardinal slugger Mark McGwire and Chicago Cubs outfielder Sammy Sosa, both of whom broke Roger Maris' single season home run record.

KEY COMPETITORS
NBA
NFL
NHL

 See pages 308–309 for a full profile of this company.

MANUFACTURERS' SERVICES LTD.

300 Baker Ave.
Concord, MA 01742
Phone: 978-287-5630
Fax: 978-287-5635
Web site: http://www.manserve.com

CEO: Kevin Melia
CFO: Robert Donahue
HR: James Poor
Type: Private

1998 Sales: $838.0 million
1-Yr. Sales Change: 49.1%
Employees: 3,000
FYE: December

Manufacturers' Services puts the "M" in "OEM." The company is among the largest electronics manufacturing service providers in the world, procuring equipment, assembling printed circuit boards, and offering engineering and design services to the computer, communications, medical, and peripherals industries worldwide. Manufacturers' Services oversees every aspect of production, from design and manufacturing to testing, packaging, and delivery. Clients include Ericsson, Hewlett-Packard, IBM, and Unisys. Former Sun Microsystems executive Kevin Melia founded the company in 1994 with equity funding from majority owner Donaldson, Lufkin & Jenrette.

KEY COMPETITORS
Benchmark Electronics
SCI Systems
Solectron

MARATHON ASHLAND PETROLEUM LLC

539 S. Main St.
Findlay, OH 45840
Phone: 419-422-2121
Fax: 419-425-7040
Web site: http://www.mapllc.com

CEO: J. Louis Frank
CFO: Garry L. Peiffer
HR: Randy K. Lohoff
Type: Joint venture

1998 Sales: $19,339.0 million
1-Yr. Sales Change: (13.9%)
Employees: 30,000
FYE: December

It's not hard to find Marathon Ashland Petroleum (MAP) on the map — the company has operations in 20 states and is charting a course to sustain its position as one of US's leading oil refiners. A joint venture between 62%-owner USX-Marathon (a business unit of USX) and 38%-owner Ashland, MAP operates seven refineries in the Midwest and Texas that handle about 935,000 barrels of oil a day. MAP sells refined products through its retail subsidiary, Speedway SuperAmerica, which has about 5,400 outlets. MAP also holds stakes in more than 8,000 miles of pipeline and operates a terminal network in the Midwest and Southeast.

KEY COMPETITORS
BP Amoco
Chevron
Exxon Mobil

MARITZ INC.

1375 N. Highway Dr.
St. Louis, MO 63099
Phone: 636-827-4000
Fax: 636-827-5505
Web site: http://www.maritz.com

CEO: W. Stephen Maritz
CFO: James W. Kienker
HR: Terry L. Goring
Type: Private

1999 Sales: $2,200.0 million
1-Yr. Sales Change: —
Employees: 6,500
FYE: March

Maritz can not only send your employees on business trips; it can make them want to go. With about 240 offices in North America and Europe, Maritz offers travel, employee motivation, and marketing services. Its employee motivation and incentive programs help client companies improve quality and customer satisfaction. The company is also one of the nation's largest custom market research companies. Its Maritz Travel Company is one of the leading travel firms in the US, providing travel services, including event management, to corporations. It also has a majority stake in GTM, a global travel network with more than 1,250 offices. The company is owned by the founding Maritz family.

KEY COMPETITORS
American Express
Carlson Wagonlit
J.D. Power

See pages 310–311 for a full profile of this company.

MARK III INDUSTRIES, INC.

5401 NW 44th Ave.
Ocala, FL 34478
Phone: 352-732-5878
Fax: 352-351-1017
Web site: http://www.markiii.com

CEO: Larry W. Lincoln
CFO: Robert Moore
HR: Ken Lefko
Type: Private

1999 Est. Sales: $825.0 million
1-Yr. Sales Change: (13.2%)
Employees: 800
FYE: June

Mark III Industries can put you in that deluxe land yacht you've always wanted. As one of the leading custom van converters in the US, Mark III re-models vans, sport utility vehicles (SUVs), and trucks from GM, Ford, and other carmakers, and outfits them with upholstery, TVs, video cassette players, window shades, and other amenities. Since its founding in 1978, the company has converted more than 350,000 vehicles, including public transit vehicles and other commercial vans. Mark III sells its converted vans throughout the US and abroad. A planned merger between Mark III and fellow industry player Glaval Corporation has been called off. The company is owned by M III Acquisition Corp.

KEY COMPETITORS
Coachmen Industries
Fleetwood Enterprises
Starcraft

THE MARMON GROUP, INC.

225 W. Washington St.
Chicago, IL 60606
Phone: 312-372-9500
Fax: 312-845-5305
Web site: http://www.marmon.com

CEO: Robert A. Pritzker
CFO: Robert C. Gluth
HR: Larry Rist
Type: Private

1998 Sales: $6,031.8 million
1-Yr. Sales Change: 0.5%
Employees: 35,000
FYE: December

With more monikers than most, The Marmon Group monitors a melange of more than 100 autonomous manufacturing and service companies. Marmon's manufacturing units make medical products, mining equipment, industrial materials and components, consumer products, transportation equipment, building products, and water-treatment products. Services include marketing and distribution and consumer credit information. Overall, Marmon companies operate about 550 facilities in more than 40 countries. Chicago's Pritzker family (owners of the Hyatt hotel chain) owns The Marmon Group.

KEY COMPETITORS
ITT Industries
Mannesmann AG
TRW

 See pages 312–313 for a full profile of this company.

MARS, INC.

6885 Elm St.
McLean, VA 22101
Phone: 703-821-4900
Fax: 703-448-9678
Web site: http://www.mars.com

CEO: Forrest E. Mars
CFO: Vito J. Spitaleri
HR: —
Type: Private

1998 Est. Sales: $15,000.0 million
1-Yr. Sales Change: —
Employees: 30,000
FYE: December

Mars is a private planet orbiting around chocolate, rice, and pet food. The #2 US candy maker (behind Hershey) makes global favorites, including M&M's, Snickers, and the Mars bar. Other products include 3 Musketeers, Dove, Milky Way, Skittles, Twix, and Starburst sweets; Combos and Kudos snacks; Uncle Ben's rice (the US market leader); and pet food under the names Kal Kan, Pedigree, Sheba, and Whiskas. Mars also makes drink vending equipment and electronic automated payment systems. The Mars family (including co-presidents and brothers John Mars and Forrest Mars Jr. and their sister, VP Jacqueline Mars Vogel) own the highly secretive firm — making the Mars family one of the richest in the country.

KEY COMPETITORS
Hershey
Nestlé
Ralston Purina

See pages 314–315 for a full profile of this company.

THE MARTIN-BROWER COMPANY

333 E. Butterfield Rd., #500
Lombard, IL 60148
Phone: 630-271-8300
Fax: 630-271-8680

CEO: Dennis M. Malchow
CFO: John Winton
HR: Dave Jaski
Type: Private

1999 Est. Sales: $2,380.0 million
1-Yr. Sales Change: 3.3%
Employees: 2,200
FYE: June

Ronald McDonald is worth his weight in gold(en arches) to The Martin-Brower Company. Martin-Brower is the largest distributor of food and supplies to McDonald's in the US and Canada, serving some 40% (more than 6,000) of the fast food company's restaurants. The company makes regular deliveries to each store through a network of 21 distribution centers. In addition, the company serves McDonald's through joint ventures in Puerto Rico and Mexico. Martin-Brower changed hands in 1998 when privately owned food and beverage distributor Reyes Holdings purchased the company from UK-based Dalgety (now PIC International).

KEY COMPETITORS
Golden State Foods
JR Simplot
Keystone Foods

MARTY FRANICH AUTO CENTER

550 Auto Center Dr.
Watsonville, CA 95076
Phone: 831-722-4181
Fax: 831-724-1853

CEO: Steven Franich
CFO: —
HR: —
Type: Private

1998 Sales: $946.0 million
1-Yr. Sales Change: —
Employees: 104
FYE: December

Fleet customers find smooth sailing at the Marty Franich Auto Center dealerships. Founded in 1948, the company consists of two full-service dealerships in Watsonville, California, that sell Chrysler, Dodge, Eagle, Ford, Jeep, Lincoln, Mercury, and Plymouth vehicles. Marty Franich also operates parts and service departments. The company receives about 95% of its sales from fleet buyers. It also sell cars to rental outfits nationwide, including Hertz, Budget Rent a Car, and Avis Rent A Car. President and CEO Steven Franich, the son of founder Martin (Marty) Franich, heads the company.

KEY COMPETITORS
AutoNation
FirstAmerica Automotive
Prospect Motors

MARY KAY INC.

16251 Dallas Pkwy.
Dallas, TX 75001
Phone: 972-687-6300
Fax: 972-687-1609
Web site: http://www.marykay.com

CEO: John P. Rochon
CFO: David Holl
HR: Darrell Overcash
Type: Private

1998 Sales: $1,000.0 million
1-Yr. Sales Change: (4.8%)
Employees: 3,500
FYE: December

Mary Kay is in the pink (and in Avon's shadow) as the US's #2 direct seller of beauty products. It sells more than 200 products in eight product categories: facial skin care, cosmetics, fragrances, nutritional supplements, sun protection, nail care, body care, and men's skin care. Some 500,000 direct-sales consultants demonstrate Mary Kay products in the US and 28 other countries. Consultants vie for prizes such as the use of cars (including pink Cadillacs, first given in 1969, and white sport utility vehicles, added in 1998). Mary Kay has a mostly female workforce, although it does employ some men (such as its chairman/CEO and CFO). Founder Mary Kay Ash and her family own most of the company.

KEY COMPETITORS
Amway
Avon
L'Oréal

📖 See pages 316–317 for a full profile of this company.

MARYLAND STATE LOTTERY AGENCY

6776 Reisterstown Rd., Ste. 204
Baltimore, MD 21215
Phone: 410-318-6200
Fax: 410-764-4263
Web site: http://www.msla.state.md.us

CEO: Buddy Roogow
CFO: Sandra Long
HR: Bobby Sinclair
Type: Government-owned

1998 Sales: $1,069.9 million
1-Yr. Sales Change: 2.8%
Employees: 170
FYE: June

The Maryland State Lottery Agency offers players a variety of ways to amass a fortune. Its games of chance include lotto games Pick 3, Keno, and Cash In Hand, as well as scratch-off games bearing titles such as Friday Night Poker and Bushel of Crabs. Nearly 40% of proceeds go into Maryland's General Fund, which supports education, public health, the environment, and public safety. Maryland also participates in the seven-state Big Game lottery, which helps fund (along with designated scratch-off games) the Maryland Stadium Authority. These proceeds helped finance the construction of Baltimore's Camden Yards baseball stadium. The agency has doled out some $8 billion in prizes since its creation in 1973.

KEY COMPETITORS
Multi-State Lottery
New Jersey Lottery
Pennsylvania Lottery

MASHANTUCKET PEQUOT GAMING ENTERPRISE INC.

Rte. 2
Mashantucket, CT 06339
Phone: 860-312-3000
Fax: 860-312-1599
Web site: http://www.foxwoods.com

CEO: Floyd M. Celey
CFO: John O'Brien
HR: Larry Fowler
Type: Private

1998 Est. Sales: $1,000.0 million
1-Yr. Sales Change: —
Employees: 11,500
FYE: September

The wealthiest tribe in the US, the Mashantucket Pequot Tribal Nation has seen its fortunes rise through Mashantucket Pequot Gaming Enterprise, the operator of the Foxwoods Resort Casino in Ledyard, Connecticut. Foxwoods is the world's largest casino, boasting nearly 6,000 slot machines, 350 gaming tables, and several hotels, restaurants, lounges, and retail shops. Estimates of the casino's annual revenues exceed $1 billion; the state of Connecticut receives 25% of the take from all slot machines. The Pequots also own Pequot River Shipworks, Fox Navigation, the Pequot Pharmaceutical Network, and three Connecticut hotels. The tribe established the Mashantucket Pequot Museum and Research Center in 1998.

KEY COMPETITORS
Connecticut Lottery
Sun International Hotels
Trump Hotels & Casinos

 See pages 318–319 for a full profile of this company.

MASSACHUSETTS INSTITUTE OF TECHNOLOGY

77 Massachusetts Ave.
Cambridge, MA 02139
Phone: 617-253-1000
Fax: 617-253-8000
Web site: http://web.mit.edu

CEO: Charles M. Vest
CFO: Glenn P. Strehle
HR: Laura Avakian
Type: School

1998 Sales: $1,479.9 million
1-Yr. Sales Change: 2.3%
Employees: 8,500
FYE: June

It is patently clear that the Massachusetts Institute of Technology (MIT) is one of the nation's leading research universities. The school receives more than 100 patents a year, ranking it above all but the University of California. Founded in 1865, privately endowed MIT is considered one of the world's most prestigious science and engineering institutions. Research accounts for some 60% of the school's revenue and has led to such advances as a magnetic core memory that allowed digital computers to be developed. The US Department of Defense, NASA, and other government agencies sponsor much of its research. MIT is composed of five schools with 21 academic departments and has an enrollment of about 10,000.

MASSACHUSETTS MUTUAL LIFE INSURANCE COMPANY

1295 State St.
Springfield, MA 01111
Phone: 413-788-8411
Fax: 413-744-6005
Web site: http://www.massmutual.com

CEO: Robert J. O'Connell
CFO: Joseph M. Zubretsky
HR: Susan A. Alfano
Type: Mutual company

1998 Sales: $11,728.4 million
1-Yr. Sales Change: 9.4%
Employees: 7,885
FYE: December

Massachusetts Mutual Life Insurance (MassMutual), after considering switching from collective ownership to a stock company, has decided to stay the course. Founded in 1851, MassMutual offers upper-income individuals and small businesses a variety of life insurance and pension products through more than 1,200 office in the US. Its Investment Group offers investment management products (securities and real estate) and includes subsidiaries OppenheimerFunds (mutual fund management), David L. Babson & Company (individual and institutional investor services), and Cornerstone Real Estate (real estate equities management). Massachusetts Mutual Life has opened offices overseas and plans to sell securities in Europe.

KEY COMPETITORS
New York Life
Northwestern Mutual
Prudential

See pages 320–321 for a full profile of this company.

MASSACHUSETTS STATE LOTTERY COMMISSION

60 Columbian St.
Braintree, MA 02184
Phone: 781-849-5555
Fax: 781-849-5509
Web site: http://www.masslottery.com

CEO: Jay Mitchell
CFO: Jeanette Maillet
HR: Deborah Keyes
Type: Government-owned

1999 Sales: $3,381.6 million
1-Yr. Sales Change: 4.9%
Employees: 397
FYE: June

The Massachusetts State Lottery Commission offers residents of the commonwealth an opportunity to Take Home Millions. The lottery offers several numbers games (Mass Cash, Mass Millions, Megabucks) and scratch-off games (Take Home Millions, Lifetime Cash, Sparkling Gold). Massachusetts also participates in the seven-state Big Game lottery. State law requires that at least 45% of lottery proceeds go to pay prizes, a maximum of 15% be used for operating expenses, and the remainder be distributed to individual cities and towns in Massachusetts. Created in 1971, the Massachusetts State Lottery Commission distributed more than $800 million to the state's cities and towns during fiscal 1999.

KEY COMPETITORS
Connecticut Lottery
Multi-State Lottery
New Hampshire Lottery

MASTERCARD INTERNATIONAL INCORPORATED

2000 Purchase St.
Purchase, NY 10577
Phone: 914-249-2000
Fax: 914-249-4206
Web site: http://www.mastercard.com

CEO: Robert W. Selander
CFO: Frank J. Cotroneo
HR: Michael W. Michl
Type: Private

1998 Sales: $1,257.4 million
1-Yr. Sales Change: 15.4%
Employees: 2,400
FYE: December

Surpassing Visa in market share — now that would be priceless. MasterCard International is the US's #2 payment system and is owned by its more than 23,000 financial institution members worldwide. The company provides marketing and approval and transaction processing services for its payment products, including branded MasterCard credit and debit and Maestro debit cards. It is also promoting Mondex chip-based smart cards (it owns 51% of Mondex). MasterCard also operates the Cirrus ATM network. The company has attempted to gain market share from Visa with a variety of promotional programs and has moved into the wireless e-commerce field.

KEY COMPETITORS
American Express
Morgan Stanley Dean Witter
Visa

See pages 322–323 for a full profile of this company.

MAYO FOUNDATION

200 1st St. SW
Rochester, MN 55905
Phone: 507-284-2511
Fax: 507-284-0161
Web site: http://www.mayo.edu

CEO: Robert R. Waller
CFO: David R. Ebel
HR: Marita Heller
Type: Not-for-profit

1998 Sales: $2,370.0 million
1-Yr. Sales Change: (7.6%)
Employees: 32,531
FYE: December

If you're trying to lead a healthy life, don't hold the Mayo. The not-for-profit Mayo Foundation provides health care, most notably for difficult medical conditions, through its renowned Mayo Clinic in Rochester, Minnesota. The foundation also operates major facilities in Scottsdale, Arizona, and Jacksonville, Florida as well as a network of 13 affiliated community hospitals and clinics in Iowa, Minnesota, and Wisconsin. Mayo's reputation attracts high-profile clientele, as well as ordinary people from around the world. The foundation also conducts research and trains physicians, nurses, and other health professionals. It dates back to a frontier practice launched by William Mayo in 1863.

KEY COMPETITORS
Ascension
Columbia/HCA
Tenet Healthcare

See pages 324–325 for a full profile of this company.

MBM CORPORATION

2641 Meadowbrook Rd.
Rocky Mount, NC 27801
Phone: 252-985-7200
Fax: 252-985-7241

CEO: Jerry L. Wordsworth
CFO: Jeff Kowalk
HR: Ed Whirty
Type: Private

1998 Sales: $2,000.0 million
1-Yr. Sales Change: 25.0%
Employees: 1,600
FYE: December

What's on the menu at your favorite restaurant? Just ask MBM Corporation, a heavyweight in the business of food, glorious food. A privately held food distributor, the company specializes in providing food to national restaurant chains. MBM fills its customers' orders through its network of more than a dozen distribution centers across the US. J.R. Wordsworth founded the company nearly 50 years ago as a retail food distributor. MBM made the transition to its present role in restaurant food distribution after Wordsworth's children bought the business in the 1970s.

KEY COMPETITORS
AmeriServe
SYSCO
U.S. Foodservice

MCCARTHY

1341 N. Rock Hill Rd.
St. Louis, MO 63124
Phone: 314-968-3300
Fax: 314-968-0032
Web site: http://www.mccarthy.com

CEO: Michael D. Bolen
CFO: George Scherer
HR: James Faust
Type: Private

1999 Est. Sales: $1,200.0 million
1-Yr. Sales Change: 5.8%
Employees: 2,000
FYE: March

A construction company that began operations before Reconstruction, McCarthy is one of the oldest privately held builders in the US. The company is a leading builder of hospitals and other health care facilities; other projects have included hotels, bridges, parking garages and water treatment plants. McCarthy, which operates out of eight regional offices, has projects in more than 40 US states and several other countries. CEO Michael Bolen is the first non-McCarthy family member to serve in that role at the company, which was founded in Michigan in 1864.

KEY COMPETITORS
Bechtel
Peter Kiewit Sons'
Turner Corporation

MCCRORY CORPORATION

12 W. Market St.	CEO: Meshulam Riklis	1998 Est. Sales: $175.0 million
York, PA 17405	CFO: Paul Weiner	1-Yr. Sales Change: (60.9%)
Phone: 717-757-8181	HR: John Gaunt	Employees: 2,184
Fax: 717-699-4207	Type: Private	FYE: January

Despite operating under bankruptcy for nearly six years (or perhaps because of it), McCrory can claim to have outlived five-and-dime brethren Woolworth and Ben Franklin. The company operates about 175 discount variety stores under the names H. L. Green, McLellan, McCrory, J. J. Newberry, and T.G.& Y. Most of the McCrory stores are in the northeastern US; however, there are stores in Arizona, New Mexico, Oregon, Texas, and Washington. Once 1,300 stores strong, McCrory divested more than 600 stores while in bankruptcy protection. In mid-1997 HGG Acquisition Corp., a company controlled by financier and McCrory chairman and CEO (and primary creditor) Meshulam Riklis, acquired the company.

KEY COMPETITORS
Kmart
Target Stores
Wal-Mart

 See pages 326–327 for a full profile of this company.

MCJUNKIN CORPORATION

835 Hillcrest Dr.	CEO: H. B. Wehrle	1998 Sales: $731.0 million
Charleston, WV 25311	CFO: M. H. W. Wehrle	1-Yr. Sales Change: 4.4%
Phone: 304-348-5211	HR: Kimberly Isaac	Employees: 1,600
Fax: 304-348-4922	Type: Private	FYE: December
Web site: http://www.mcjunkin.com		

McJunkin deals in products that do a lot of clunkin'. The firm is a nationwide distributor of pipe, valves and fittings, oil field tubular goods, and drilling, electrical, and mining supplies. It also provides services such as assembly, systems engineering, valve actuation and servicing, and project management. McJunkin's clients include the power, paper, mining, and automotive industries. It has more than 90 locations in 27 states. Subsidiaries include Precision Pipe Cleaning, McA Target Oil Tools, and McJunkin Process Automation and Controls, Inc. It also operates in Mexico through a joint venture, Trottner-McJunkin, S.A. de C.V. Founded in 1921, the firm is owned by descendants of the McJunkin family.

KEY COMPETITORS
Cooper Cameron
Tyco International
Wal-Mart

MCKEE FOODS CORPORATION

10260 McKee Rd.	CEO: Jack McKee	1999 Sales: $855.0 million
Collegedale, TN 37315	CFO: Barry Patterson	1-Yr. Sales Change: 2.9%
Phone: 423-238-7111	HR: Eva L. Disbro	Employees: 5,393
Fax: 423-238-7127	Type: Private	FYE: June
Web site: http://www.mckeefoods.com		

When Little Debbie smiles up out of your lunch bag, you know you are loved. McKee Foods' Little Debbie is the US's leading brand of snack cake, named for and featuring the smiling face of a granddaughter of the company's founders. The company's treats include Devil Cremes, Oatmeal Creme Pies, and Swiss Cake Rolls. McKee Foods also sells granola bars, fruit snacks, and cereals under its Sunbelt brand. Low prices and family packs of individually wrapped treats — both conducive to quick lunch packing — have driven sales. The company started in 1934 with founder O. D. McKee and his wife, Ruth, selling nickel cakes from the back seat of their car. McKee Foods is still owned and operated by the McKee family.

KEY COMPETITORS
Grist Mill Company
Interstate Bakeries
Lance

MCKINSEY & COMPANY

55 E. 52nd St.
New York, NY 10022
Phone: 212-446-7000
Fax: 212-446-8575
Web site: http://www.mckinsey.com

CEO: Rajat Gupta
CFO: Donna Rosenwasser
HR: Jerome Vascellaro
Type: Private

1998 Sales: $2,500.0 million
1-Yr. Sales Change: 13.6%
Employees: 10,000
FYE: December

McKinsey & Company is a global business consulting firm known for focusing on the big picture. With about 74 offices worldwide, it provides consulting services primarily to private companies, but also to family-owned businesses and foreign governments. Recruiting the top graduates from business schools, it uses Darwinian "move up or get out" policies to weed out all but the best and brightest. McKinsey's reputation comes from a few basic ideals established by Marvin Bower, who led the company after founder James McKinsey's death in 1937: The client's interests come first; be discreet; be honest; don't overextend yourself. Alumni include American Express chairman Harvey Golub and former CBS chief Michael Jordan.

KEY COMPETITORS
Andersen Consulting
Booz, Allen
Boston Consulting

See pages 328–329 for a full profile of this company.

MEDIANEWS GROUP, INC.

1560 Broadway, Ste. 1450
Denver, CO 80202
Phone: 303-837-0886
Fax: 303-894-9340
Web site: http://www.medianewsgroup.com

CEO: William D. Singleton
CFO: Joseph J. Lodovic
HR: E. Michael Fluker
Type: Private

1999 Sales: $1,010.0 million
1-Yr. Sales Change: 18.8%
Employees: 8,997
FYE: June

MediaNews Group makes news of its own as one of the nation's Top 10 newspaper companies. Its 50 daily and more than 120 non-daily publications across 13 states include its flagship *The Denver Post* (80%) and the *Los Angeles Daily News* (through Garden State Newspapers). MediaNews focuses on building newspaper clusters, primarily in California and Pennsylvania. It also operates Web sites for many of its papers. The company is a venture of VC, president, and CEO Dean Singleton and chairman Richard Scudder, who began buying newspapers together in 1983. MediaNews is known for operating frugally and shedding unprofitable papers such as the *Dallas Times Herald* and the *Houston Post* (both of which have folded).

KEY COMPETITORS
E. W. Scripps
Gannett
Times Mirror

MEDLINE INDUSTRIES, INC.

1 Medline Place
Mundelein, IL 60060
Phone: 847-949-5500
Fax: 847-949-2686
Web site: http://www.medline.net

CEO: Charles S. Mills
CFO: Bill Abington
HR: Al Savage
Type: Private

1998 Sales: $755.9 million
1-Yr. Sales Change: 15.4%
Employees: 2,300
FYE: December

Medline Industries, a private medical equipment distributor and manufacturer, goes toe-to-toe with the bigger guns, selling more than 100,000 products — bandages, liquid-proof surgical gowns, wheelchairs, and more. Medline distributes its products to more than 25,000 customers, including hospitals, extended care facilities, hospital laundries, and home care providers. Medline's five plants make about 70% of its products, which are sold through some 500 sales representatives and 19 distribution centers. Medline is owned by the Mills family, which founded the company in 1910 as a manufacturer of nurses' gowns.

KEY COMPETITORS
Allegiance
Kimberly-Clark
Owens & Minor

MEDSTAR HEALTH

9881 Broken Land Pkwy.
Columbia, MD 21046
Phone: 410-290-6800
Fax: 410-290-9958
Web site: http://www.medlantic.mhg.edu

CEO: John P. McDaniel
CFO: Michael P. O'Boyle
HR: Linda Hitchcock
Type: Not-for-profit

1998 Est. Sales: $1,400.0 million
1-Yr. Sales Change: 117.7%
Employees: 21,000
FYE: June

When two not-for-profit health care providers doubled up in 1998, MedStar Health, formerly Helix/Medlantic, was the result. Formed by the merger of Medlantic Healthcare Group and Helix Health, the firm operates seven hospitals, five nursing homes, and other research, outpatient, and home care units in Baltimore and Washington, DC. Its hospitals include Church Hospital, Franklin Square Hospital Center, Good Samaritan Hospital, Harbor Hospital Center, National Rehabilitation Hospital, Union Memorial Hospital, and Washington Hospital Center. The new organization dominates the region. Almost 100,000 patients stay in MedStar's hospitals each year, and it treats more than 1 million more on an outpatient basis.

KEY COMPETITORS
Ascension
Bon Secours Health
Johns Hopkins Health

MEIJER, INC.

2929 Walker Ave. NW
Grand Rapids, MI 49544
Phone: 616-453-6711
Fax: 616-791-2572
Web site: http://www.meijer.com

CEO: Jim McLean
CFO: Jim Walsh
HR: Windy Ray
Type: Private

1999 Est. Sales: $8,300.0 million
1-Yr. Sales Change: 20.3%
Employees: 86,200
FYE: January

Meijer (pronounced "Meyer") is the green giant of retailing in the Midwest. The company operates about 130 combination grocery and general merchandise stores in Illinois, Indiana, Kentucky, Michigan, and Ohio. Its huge stores (which average 200,000 to 250,000 sq. ft. each, or about the size of four regular grocery stores) stock about 130,000 items, including Meijer private-label products. Customers can choose from about 40 departments, including hardware, apparel, toys, and electronics. Most stores also sell gasoline, offer banking services, and have multiple in-store restaurants. Founder Hendrik Meijer opened his first store in 1934; the company is still family-owned.

KEY COMPETITORS
Kroger
SUPERVALU
Wal-Mart

 See pages 330–331 for a full profile of this company.

MEMORIAL HERMANN HEALTHCARE SYSTEM

7737 Southwest Fwy., Ste. 200
Houston, TX 77074
Phone: 713-222-2273
Fax: 713-776-5665
Web site: http://www.mhcs.org

CEO: Dan S. Wilford
CFO: John D. Gay
HR: R. Eugene Ross
Type: Not-for-profit

1998 Sales: $1,003.2 million
1-Yr. Sales Change: (16.4%)
Employees: 12,000
FYE: June

Memorial Hermann Healthcare System is a "munster" of an organization. The largest not-for-profit health care system in the Houston area, it consists of 12 hospitals, including a children's hospital, two long-term nursing facilities, and a retirement community. Its subsidiaries include a home health care company, a managed-care company, and a physician practice company. The company's Hermann Hospital is the teaching hospital for The University of Texas-Houston Medical School. Memorial Regional Healthcare Services provides support for health care needs at 16 affiliated hospitals. Memorial Hermann Healthcare was formed in 1997 from the $1 billion merger of Hermann Hospital and Memorial Healthcare System.

KEY COMPETITORS
Columbia/HCA
Methodist Health Care
Tenet Healthcare

MEMORIAL SLOAN-KETTERING CANCER CENTER

1275 York Ave.
New York, NY 10021
Phone: 212-639-3573
Fax: 212-639-3576
Web site: http://www.mskcc.org

CEO: Paul A. Marks
CFO: Michael P. Gutnick
HR: Michael Browne
Type: Not-for-profit

1998 Sales: $747.3 million
1-Yr. Sales Change: 7.8%
Employees: 6,618
FYE: December

Ranked as one of the nation's top cancer centers, Memorial Sloan-Kettering Cancer Center includes Memorial Hospital for pediatric and adult cancer care and the Sloan-Kettering Institute for cancer research activities. The center specializes in bone-marrow transplants and chemotherapy and offers programs in cancer prevention, treatment, research, and education. More than 500 scientists and physicians staff Memorial Sloan-Kettering, which annually admits almost 20,000 patients and logs nearly 250,000 outpatient visits. Other services include oncology nursing, pain management, and rehabilitation. The center's budget includes close to $60 million in federal and corporate research grants.

KEY COMPETITORS
Columbia University
New York City Health and Hospitals
Partners HealthCare

MEMPHIS LIGHT, GAS AND WATER DIVISION

220 S. Main St.
Memphis, TN 38103
Phone: 901-528-4011
Fax: 901-528-4758
Web site: http://www.mlgw.com

CEO: Herman Morris
CFO: John McCullough
HR: Curtis Dillihunt
Type: Government-owned

1998 Sales: $1,074.8 million
1-Yr. Sales Change: 3.5%
Employees: 2,600
FYE: December

Memphis citizens, like Elvis, say "thank you very much" to Memphis Light, Gas and Water Division, the municipally owned utility system for all of Shelby County, Tennessee, including the city of Memphis. The company provides residential, commercial, and industrial customers with electricity, water, and natural gas services. Memphis Light, Gas and Water buys electricity from the Tennessee Valley Authority and distributes it to more than 380,000 customers. The company purchases natural gas on the spot market and delivers it to more than 280,000 customers through Texas Gas Transmission and Trunkline Gas. Through its artesian water system, the company supplies water to nearly 220,000 customers.

MENARD, INC.

4777 Menard Dr.
Eau Claire, WI 54703
Phone: 715-876-5911
Fax: 715-876-5901

CEO: John R. Menard
CFO: Earl R. Rasmussen
HR: Terri Jain
Type: Private

1999 Est. Sales: $4,000.0 million
1-Yr. Sales Change: 8.1%
Employees: 7,000
FYE: January

Menard knows what it takes to build a solid home and a solid business. The company is the nation's #3 retail home improvement chain (behind The Home Depot and Lowe's) with about 135 stores in nine upper-midwestern states. Its supermarket-style Menards' stores are smaller than those of its rivals, but they offer a similar selection by keeping a smaller quantity of items on store shelves, then quickly restocking them from an adjacent warehouse. Menard's manufacturing facility, which makes doors and picnic tables, among other items, helps keep prices down while fattening profit margins. The company, owned by president and CEO John Menard, also sponsors an Indy race car team.

KEY COMPETITORS
Home Depot
Lowe's
Wickes

See pages 332–333 for a full profile of this company.

MENASHA CORPORATION

1645 Bergstrom Rd.
Neenah, WI 54956
Phone: 920-751-1000
Fax: 920-751-1236
Web site: http://www.menasha.com

CEO: Thomas Prosser
CFO: Richard Finkbeinver
HR: David H. Rust
Type: Private

1998 Sales: $952.0 million
1-Yr. Sales Change: 2.0%
Employees: 6,000
FYE: December

Founded in 1849 as a woodenware business, Menasha now makes packaging, plastics, forest products, materials handling items, and promotional and information graphics. The company's forest products group harvests and sells timber from the northwestern US, and its packaging and graphics units make containers, cardboard, and printed forms, labels, and related products. Menasha's plastics business makes reusable containers, materials handling products, and molded components for original equipment manufacturers. The company has more than 60 facilities in about 20 US states and 10 countries. Descendants of founder Elisha Smith own a majority of Menasha, which is the third-oldest private firm in the US.

KEY COMPETITORS
Boise Cascade
Smurfit-Stone Container
Sonoco Products

MERCY HEALTH SERVICES

34605 W. Twelve Mile Rd.
Farmington Hills, MI 48331
Phone: 248-489-6000
Fax: 248-489-6836
Web site: http://www.mercyhealth.com

CEO: Judith C. Pelham
CFO: James H. Combes
HR: Darryl Robinson
Type: Not-for-profit

1998 Sales: $2,533.7 million
1-Yr. Sales Change: 5.6%
Employees: 26,436
FYE: June

Mercy Health Services keeps hearts beating in the heartland. The US's #4 Catholic health care system (Ascension Health is #1), Mercy Health Services is a not-for-profit company with 39 hospitals and 200 clinics, as well as nursing homes and hospices in Michigan and Iowa. Subsidiaries include Mercy Health Plans, a managed care company offering the HMO and PPO plans; care provider Amicare Home Healthcare; and GNA, which offers occupational, physical, respiratory, and speech therapy to health care facilities. The company joint ventures with Catholic Health Initiatives to provide health care in Iowa through Mercy Health Network. Mercy is planning to merge with Holy Cross Health System.

KEY COMPETITORS
Ascension
Detroit Medical Center
Henry Ford Health System

METHODIST HEALTHCARE

1211 Union Ave., Ste. 700
Memphis, TN 38104
Phone: 901-726-7070
Fax: 901-726-2394
Web site: http://www.methodisthealth.org

CEO: Maurice W. Elliot
CFO: Robert N. Trumpis
HR: Kathy Sullivant
Type: Not-for-profit

1998 Sales: $721.9 million
1-Yr. Sales Change: 6.0%
Employees: 8,000
FYE: December

You don't have to be Methodist, just sick. Methodist Healthcare (formerly Methodist Health Systems) operates hospitals, home health agencies, and clinics in Tennessee and Mississippi. The not-for-profit health care system serves patients of all denominations and includes four hospitals and one pediatric center in the Memphis area, seven hospitals elsewhere in Tennessee, and four in Mississippi. Methodist Healthcare's other offerings — some of which are operated through affiliations and joint ventures — include home care and hospice services, substance abuse recovery programs, sleep disorder centers, and physical therapy. Methodist Healthcare also operates physician practices and a physician referral service.

KEY COMPETITORS
Catholic Healthcare Partners
Columbia/HCA
HMA

METROMEDIA COMPANY

1 Meadowlands Plaza
East Rutherford, NJ 07073
Phone: 201-531-8000
Fax: 201-531-2804
Web site: http://www.metromediarestaurants.com

CEO: John W. Kluge
CFO: Robert A. Maresca
HR: Jamie Smith
Type: Private

1998 Est. Sales: $2,000.0 million
1-Yr. Sales Change: 2.6%
Employees: 63,000
FYE: December

Metromedia is one of the nation's largest private companies. It owns or franchises more than 1,000 Ponderosa, Bennigan's, Bonanza, and Steak and Ale restaurants worldwide. Through Metromedia International Group, it has interests in telecommunications ventures in China, Eastern Europe, and the former Soviet Union. These include wireless cable-TV systems, radio stations, and toll-calling services. Metromedia also controls Metromedia Fiber Network, which operates fiber-optic networks in the Chicago, Philadelphia, and New York City areas. Its Metromedia Energy is an energy broker and provider of long-distance telephone services. Founder and CEO John Kluge and partner Stuart Subotnick run Metromedia.

KEY COMPETITORS
Carlson Restaurants Worldwide
Deutsche Telekom
Outback Steakhouse

See pages 334–335 for a full profile of this company.

METROPOLITAN LIFE INSURANCE COMPANY

1 Madison Ave.
New York, NY 10010
Phone: 212-578-2211
Fax: 212-578-3320
Web site: http://www.metlife.com

CEO: Robert H. Benmosche
CFO: Stewart G. Nagler
HR: Lisa M. Weber
Type: Mutual company

1998 Sales: $27,077.0 million
1-Yr. Sales Change: 10.7%
Employees: 42,300
FYE: December

Metropolitan Life Insurance (MetLife) is the #2 US life insurance company by assets (behind Prudential). MetLife offers a variety of individual life and property/casualty insurance products (including homeowners and auto coverage), as well as savings, retirement, and other financial services for groups and individuals. Its insurance affiliates include Metropolitan Property and Casualty, Metropolitan Tower, and Texas Life; it is also buying fellow insurer GenAmerica. The company's State Street Research subsidiary and 45%-owned Nvest affiliate provide asset management services to institutions and individuals. MetLife has filed to demutualize and sell about 31% of the company to the public.

KEY COMPETITORS
AIG
Prudential
State Farm

See pages 336–337 for a full profile of this company.

METROPOLITAN TRANSPORTATION AUTHORITY

347 Madison Ave.
New York, NY 10017
Phone: 212-878-7174
Fax: 212-878-0186
Web site: http://www.mta.nyc.ny.us

CEO: E. Virgil Conway
CFO: Stephen V. Reitano
HR: Dave Knapp
Type: Government-owned

1998 Sales: $5,706.9 million
1-Yr. Sales Change: 3.6%
Employees: 57,551
FYE: December

You probably won't bump into David Letterman on the subway, but New York City's Metropolitan Transportation Authority (MTA) does move almost 6 million people on an average weekday. The largest public transportation system in the US, the MTA moves 1.7 billion passengers a year. The MTA runs buses in New York City's five boroughs, provides subway service to all but Staten Island, and operates the Staten Island Ferry. It also offers bus and rail service to Connecticut and Long Island and maintains toll bridges and tunnels. The MTA has adopted bus-to-subway transfers and the electronic fare and toll cards MetroCard and E-ZPass.

KEY COMPETITORS
Coach USA
Laidlaw
Port Authority of NY & NJ

See pages 338–339 for a full profile of this company.

MICHIGAN LOTTERY

101 E. Hillsdale
Lansing, MI 48909
Phone: 517-335-5600
Fax: 517-335-5651
Web site: http://www.state.mi.us/milottery

CEO: Don Gilmer
CFO: Scott Matteson
HR: Mark Hoffman
Type: Government-owned

1998 Sales: $1,703.0 million
1-Yr. Sales Change: 4.1%
Employees: 200
FYE: December

Michigan's kids are game for the Michigan Lottery, which has contributed some $8.5 billion to public education in the Great Lakes State since the lottery was started in 1972. The Michigan Lottery runs the Michigan Lotto and Cash 5 jackpot games, as well as daily numbers games and instant-win games such as Wild Time and Break the Bank. About half of ticket sales are awarded in prizes, while more than one-third goes to the state's K-12 education fund. Retailers also get a small commission on ticket sales (about 7%). In addition, Michigan takes part in the multistate lottery, The Big Game, with Georgia, Illinois, Maryland, Massachusetts, and Virginia.

KEY COMPETITORS
Hoosier Lottery
Multi-State Lottery
Ohio Lottery

MICRO ELECTRONICS, INC.

4119 Leap Rd.
Hilliard, OH 43026
Phone: 614-850-3000
Fax: 614-850-3001
Web site: http://www.microelectronics.com

CEO: Dale Brown
CFO: James Koehler
HR: Deanna Lyon
Type: Private

1998 Est. Sales: $1,235.0 million
1-Yr. Sales Change: 11.3%
Employees: 1,950
FYE: December

Micro Electronics is the parent of more than a half dozen technologically gifted children: its divisions. The company operates a chain of about a dozen Micro Center computer retail stores in the US. The stores feature about 36,000 products in 700 different categories, which makes Micro Center the largest of Micro Electronics' divisions. Micro Electronics' WinBook division makes notebook computers and offers Web technical support, and its Power-Spec unit makes desktop PCs. MEI/Micro Center is the company's mail-order operation and its Corporate Sales Micro Center serves businesses. Training is provided through the Micro Center Computer Education unit. Founder and president John Baker owns the company.

KEY COMPETITORS
Best Buy
Circuit City
CompUSA

See pages 340–341 for a full profile of this company.

MILLIKEN & COMPANY INC.

920 Milliken Rd.
Spartanburg, SC 29304
Phone: 864-503-2020
Fax: 864-503-2100
Web site: http://www.milliken.com

CEO: Roger Milliken
CFO: John Lewis
HR: Tommy Hodge
Type: Private

1998 Est. Sales: $3,100.0 million
1-Yr. Sales Change: (3.1%)
Employees: 16,000
FYE: November

Milliken & Company's fabrics and chemicals are used in everything from crayons to spacesuits. One of the US's largest textile companies, it produces finished fabrics for uniforms, spacesuits, rugs, and carpets, as well as textiles for tennis balls, printer ribbons, and sails. The company also makes chemicals that are used in dyes, plastics, and petroleum products. Milliken owns more than 1,500 patents and operates almost 70 plants, including a large textile research center. The company has about 200 shareholders (most from the Milliken family), but Roger Milliken, brother Gerrish, and cousin Minot control Milliken. Roger, a strong supporter of conservative causes, has led the company since 1947.

KEY COMPETITORS
Burlington Industries
DuPont
Shaw Industries

See pages 342–343 for a full profile of this company.

THE MINNESOTA MUTUAL LIFE INSURANCE COMPANY

400 Robert St. North
St. Paul, MN 55101
Phone: 651-665-3500
Fax: 651-665-4488
Web site: http://www.minnesotamutual.com

CEO: Robert L. Senkler
CFO: Gregory S. Strong
HR: Keith M. Campbell
Type: Mutual company

1998 Sales: $1,633.2 million
1-Yr. Sales Change: (2.3%)
Employees: 4,400
FYE: December

With 10,000 lakes in their state, Minnesotans have learned to be careful. Minnesota Mutual Life helps them take that caution a step further. The company's nationwide agency network sells individual and group life and disability insurance, annuities, and investment and pension products. The company also provides mortgage life insurance, homeowners and auto insurance, and provides investment and pension management services, including the Advantus family of mutual funds. Subsidiary Ministers Life Resources provides financial services for church members and religious professionals. Minnesota Mutual Life is examining the possibility of converting to mutual holding company status.

KEY COMPETITORS
New York Life
Northwestern Mutual
Prudential

MINYARD FOOD STORES INC.

777 Freeport Pkwy.
Coppell, TX 75019
Phone: 972-393-8700
Fax: 972-462-9407
Web site: http://www.minyards.com

CEO: Elizabeth Minyard
CFO: Mario J. LaForte
HR: Alan Vaughan
Type: Private

1999 Sales: $1,075.0 million
1-Yr. Sales Change: 7.5%
Employees: 8,000
FYE: June

Everything's bigger in Texas, including regional grocery chains. Minyard Food Stores operates nearly 85 supermarkets located primarily in the Dallas/Fort Worth area. More than half of its stores are conventional supermarkets that operate under the Minyard name. The rest include Sack 'n Save warehouse stores, which offer low-cost grocery shopping (customers bag their own groceries), and Carnival Stores, which stock more ethnic products. Minyard also owns eight On The Go gas stations. The Minyard family started the company in 1932 with one East Dallas neighborhood grocery. It is among the largest private companies in the US owned and run by women — sisters Elizabeth Minyard and Gretchen Minyard Williams.

KEY COMPETITORS
Albertson's
Kroger
Randall's

MODERN CONTINENTAL COMPANIES, INC.

600 Memorial Dr.
Cambridge, MA 02139
Phone: 617-864-6300
Fax: 617-864-8766
Web site: http://www.moderncontinental.com

CEO: Lelio Marino
CFO: Peter Grela
HR: Edward Burns
Type: Private

1999 Sales: $665.0 million
1-Yr. Sales Change: —
Employees: 4,750
FYE: —

It's a modern company with Old World values. Modern Continental Companies was founded in 1967 when Italian immigrant Lelio Marino quit his job at a Boston construction company and teamed up with co-worker Kenneth Anderson to form a new firm. One of the largest general contractors in New England, Modern Continental Construction focuses on highways, mass transit systems, and airports. Notable projects include Boston's Artery/Tunnel Project, known as "The Big Dig." The firm also builds skyscrapers and does infrastructure work. Modern Continental has diversified beyond construction into such industries as tourism and health care. Marino owns 75% of the company; Anderson owns 25%.

KEY COMPETITORS
Bechtel
Granite Construction
Peter Kiewit Sons'

MONTEFIORE MEDICAL CENTER

111 E. 210th St.
Bronx, NY 10467
Phone: 718-920-4321
Fax: 718-920-6321

CEO: Spencer Foreman
CFO: Joel A. Perlman
HR: George Dugan
Type: Not-for-profit

1997 Sales: $958.4 million
1-Yr. Sales Change: 8.0%
Employees: 7,935
FYE: December

As the university hospital for the Albert Einstein College of Medicine, Montefiore Medical Center is a leading teaching and research center. More than a century old, the hospital serves residents of New York City (particularly the Bronx, where it is located) and suburban Westchester County. Specialties include vascular and infectious diseases, asthma and allergies, infertility, and pain management. It also has a geriatric program and a children's medical center. The hospital has a partnership with Bentley Health Care, created by renowned oncologist Bernard Salick, to open three cancer clinics, an AIDS center, and a network of AIDS/HIV facilities in the Bronx, Manhattan, and Westchester County.

KEY COMPETITORS
Catholic Healthcare Network
Franciscan Health Partnership
New York City Health and
 Hospitals

MONTGOMERY WARD HOLDING CORP.

Montgomery Ward Plaza
Chicago, IL 60671
Phone: 312-467-2000
Fax: 312-467-3975
Web site: http://www.mward.com

CEO: Roger V. Goddu
CFO: Thomas J. Paup
HR: Sherry Harris
Type: Private

1998 Sales: $3,634.0 million
1-Yr. Sales Change: (32.5%)
Employees: 49,000
FYE: December

Montgomery Ward Holding is a mouthful, so just say Wards. One of the largest privately owned US retailers, the firm runs about 250 Montgomery Ward department stores in 30-plus states. Its stores typically target middle-income female shoppers with such offerings as apparel, furniture, and jewelry. To boost sales, it is rolling out a new store format (with the "Wards" banner) and upgrading its merchandise. Several years after filing for Chapter 11, and after closing more than 100 money-losing stores, it has emerged from bankruptcy under the auspices of GE Capital (which acquired the half it didn't already own). GE Capital's Financial Assurance unit acquired Montgomery Ward's Signature Group direct marketing arm.

KEY COMPETITORS
J. C. Penney
Sears
Wal-Mart

 See pages 344–345 for a full profile of this company.

MORSE OPERATIONS, INC.

6363 NW 6th Way, Ste. 400
Fort Lauderdale, FL 33309
Phone: 954-351-0055
Fax: 954-771-6493
Web site: http://www.edmorse.com

CEO: Edward J. Morse
CFO: Nancy Cera
HR: Betty Anne Beaver
Type: Private

1997 Sales: $1,761.5 million
1-Yr. Sales Change: (12.0%)
Employees: 2,023
FYE: December

Morse Operations has to calm some people down when it tells them it has a lot of hot models on display. The company owns 20 new-car dealerships in Florida and one in Alabama, making it one of the largest auto megadealers in the nation. Most of the dealerships operate under the Ed Morse name. The company sells new cars by DaimlerChrysler, General Motors, Honda, Kia, Mazda, Suzuki, and Toyota, as well as used cars. Morse has stuck with negotiated prices on its cars, saying it can provide a better deal than one-price shops such as AutoNation's dealerships, owned by fellow Floridian Wayne Huizenga. Owner Ed Morse began his first dealership in 1968.

KEY COMPETITORS
AutoNation
Holman Enterprises
United Auto Group

MOTIVA ENTERPRISES LLC

910 Louisiana St.
Houston, TX 77002
Phone: 713-277-8000
Fax: 713-241-4044

CEO: L. Wilson Berry
CFO: William M. Kaparich
HR: Jerry Bean
Type: Joint venture

1998 Sales: $5,371.0 million
1-Yr. Sales Change: —
Employees: 3,750
FYE: December

Motiva Enterprises mainstreams downstream operations for three oil giants. Motiva was formed in 1998 to combine the eastern and Gulf Coast US refining and marketing businesses of Texaco, Shell Oil, and Saudi Aramco. (Star Enterprise, Texaco and Saudi Aramco's joint venture, was absorbed by the new company.) Motiva, which together with its sister company Equilon forms the #1 US gasoline retailer, operates about 14,200 Shell and Texaco outlets in 26 Northeast and Southeast states. Motiva also owns or has interests in nearly 50 product terminals, and it operates three refineries on the Gulf Coast and one in Delaware. Shell Oil owns 35% of the company, and Texaco and Saudi Aramco's Saudi Refining each own 32.5%.

KEY COMPETITORS
7-Eleven
BP Amoco
Exxon Mobil

See pages 346–347 for a full profile of this company.

MTD PRODUCTS INC.

5965 Grafton Rd
Valley City, OH 44280
Phone: 330-225-2600
Fax: 330-225-0896
Web site: http://www.mtdproducts.com

CEO: Curtis E. Moll
CFO: Ronald C. Houser
HR: Regis A. Dauk
Type: Private

1999 Est. Sales: $725.0 million
1-Yr. Sales Change: 6.6%
Employees: 6,600
FYE: July

MTD Products strives to mow down the competition. The outdoor power equipment manufacturer makes walk-behind and tractor mowers, mulchers, snow-throwers, edgers, and tillers for the residential market under the Cub Cadet, White, Yard-Man and Yard Machines brand. In addition, its mechanical systems division makes transmissions and subassemblies for appliances. MTD has plants and distributors in the US, Canada, and Europe; it also distributes products in Australia. The company owns about 44% of steel processor Shiloh Industries. MTD was formed in 1932 by German immigrants Theo Moll, Emil Jochum, and Erwin Gerhard as the Modern Tool and Die Company. The Moll family owns MTD.

KEY COMPETITORS
Deere
Magna International
Toro

MTS, INCORPORATED

2500 Del Monte St., Bldg. C
West Sacramento, CA 95691
Phone: 916-373-2500
Fax: 916-373-2535
Web site: http://www.towerrecords.com

CEO: Michael T. Solomon
CFO: DeVaughn D. Searson
HR: Shauna Pompei
Type: Private

1999 Sales: $1,026.4 million
1-Yr. Sales Change: 1.8%
Employees: 7,500
FYE: July

It can name that tune in three letters, but it's still not the winner. MTS, the #2 US music retailer (after Musicland), operates about 225 stores in 17 countries. Stores include Tower Records, Tower Books, Tower Video, and WOW! superstores (joint venture with electronics retailer The Good Guys) offering a wide selection of music, books, and videos tailored to local tastes. Facing stiff competition from discounters and online retailers, MTS is continuing overseas expansion (it runs 40 stores in Japan) and broadening its Web presence. Founder and chairman Russell Solomon, a high-school dropout and self-described "aging hippie," is majority owner; son Michael became president and CEO in 1998.

KEY COMPETITORS
Musicland
Trans World Entertainment
Virgin Group

See pages 348–349 for a full profile of this company.

MULTI-STATE LOTTERY ASSOCIATION

1701 48th St., Ste.210
West Des Moines, IA 50266
Phone: 515-453-1400
Fax: 515-453-1420
Web site: http://www.musl.com

CEO: Charles Strutt
CFO: J. Bret Toyne
HR: Doug Orr
Type: Association

1998 Est. Sales: $1,000.0 million
1-Yr. Sales Change: —
Employees: 9
FYE: June

Only the muscle of MUSL can produce the largest jackpots in the world. Made up of 21 member lotteries, the Multi-State Lottery Association (MUSL) operates the Powerball drawing, which has produced the world's biggest jackpot prize ($161 million in cash or $295 million paid over 25 years). Through MUSL, smaller states can combine their buying power to get large jackpots and drive lottery sales. The not-for-profit association also allows the states to share the cost of lottery operation. Half of the money collected is paid out in prizes, while the rest is returned to the states. MUSL was founded in 1988 by six state lotteries. While Powerball is its most popular game, MUSL also offers Cash4Life and Wild Card 2.

KEY COMPETITORS
Illinois Lottery
Massachusetts State Lottery
New York State Lottery

MURPHY FAMILY FARMS

4134 S. US Hwy. 117
Rose Hill, NC 28458
Phone: 910-289-2111
Fax: 910-289-6400

CEO: Wendell H. Murphy
CFO: Russ Collingwood
HR: Jay Dustin
Type: Private

1998 Est. Sales: $650.0 million
1-Yr. Sales Change: (16.1%)
Employees: 1,900
FYE: December

Murphy Family Farms brings home the bacon, pig time. The #2 hog producer in the US (after Smithfield Foods) is owned by pork potentate Wendell Murphy and his family. The company's approximately 325,000 sows produce some 5.5 million piglets at more than 850 farms in North Carolina and the Midwest. (The farms play country music in the nursing rooms to calm piglets.) Piglets are then raised by contract farmers paid to keep them until they reach a slaughtering weight of 250 pounds; they are then delivered to packers. Pending federal approval, Smithfield Foods has agreed to purchase Murphy Family Farms, which will then operate as a separate unit.

KEY COMPETITORS
Premium Standard Farms
Smithfield Foods
Tyson Foods

THE MUTUAL OF OMAHA COMPANIES

Mutual of Omaha Plaza
Omaha, NE 68175
Phone: 402-342-7600
Fax: 402-351-2775
Web site: http://www.mutualofomaha.com

CEO: John W. Weekly
CFO: Tommie D. Thompson
HR: Robert B. Bogart
Type: Mutual company

1998 Sales: $3,486.5 million
1-Yr. Sales Change: (12.9%)
Employees: 7,111
FYE: December

The people at The Mutual of Omaha Companies want to protect human (and wild) life. Known for its *Mutual of Omaha's Wild Kingdom* nature show, the company provides individual health and accident coverage (via subsidiary Mutual of Omaha Insurance); its United of Omaha unit offers individual life insurance and annuities. The company also offers personal property/casualty lines (homeowners, boat, auto, and flood coverage), brokerage services, and mutual funds. Offering products mainly through agent networks, Mutual of Omaha has moved to de-emphasize its traditional indemnity insurance in favor of developing managed care alternatives; it is also working to increase sales of its life insurance and annuities products.

KEY COMPETITORS
Aetna
CIGNA
Guardian Life

 See pages 350–351 for a full profile of this company.

MUZAK LIMITED LIABILITY COMPANY

2901 3rd Ave., Ste. 400
Seattle, WA 98121
Phone: 206-633-3000
Fax: 206-633-6210
Web site: http://www.muzak.com

CEO: William A. Boyd
CFO: Brad D. Bodenman
HR: Geanie Willis
Type: Private

1998 Sales: $99.7 million
1-Yr. Sales Change: 9.4%
Employees: 1,041
FYE: December

If you believe your shopping trip to a trendy store like The Gap puts you worlds away from Muzak, think again. Founded in 1922, Muzak has moved away from its easy-listening background filler and now supplies several national chain stores and restaurants with "foreground" music made up of today's current hits. It supplies some 250,000 business locations with a choice of 60 different channels covering 10 different musical genres, as well as custom-designed programs picked from its library of more than a million titles. In addition, Muzak provides video programming and on-hold phone messages. Investment firm ABRY Partners owns about 70% of the private company; AMFM (formerly Chancellor Media) owns 23%.

 See pages 352–353 for a full profile of this company.

KEY COMPETITORS
AEI Music Network
Liberty Digital
PlayNetwork

NASHVILLE ELECTRIC SERVICE

1214 Church St.
Nashville, TN 37203
Phone: 615-747-3981
Fax: 615-747-3596
Web site: http://www.nespower.com

CEO: Matthew C. Cordaro
CFO: Donald Kohanski
HR: Donald R. Wells
Type: Government-owned

1998 Sales: $710.5 million
1-Yr. Sales Change: 22.5%
Employees: 974
FYE: June

It's a little bit country: The "Nashville Sound" would be hard to hear without Nashville Electric Service, the power distributor to more than 300,000 customers in Middle Tennessee. One of the largest government-owned utilities in the US, the company is required to purchase its power from the Tennessee Valley Authority (TVA). TVA has exclusive rights to the area it serves, and its distribution contract requires 10 years' notice before Nashville Electric can terminate. But Nashville Electric is ready to rock 'n roll: Anticipating deregulation, the company wants to cut its obligations to TVA and be free to pursue other power sources, including purchasing on the open market and self-generation.

NATIONAL AERONAUTICS AND SPACE ADMINISTRATION

300 E St. SW
Washington, DC 20546
Phone: 202-358-0000
Fax: 202-358-3047
Web site: http://www.nasa.gov

CEO: Daniel S. Goldin
CFO: Andrew G. Holz
HR: Vicki A. Novak
Type: Government-owned

1998 Sales: $13,500.0 million
1-Yr. Sales Change: (1.5%)
Employees: 19,559
FYE: September

From the people who developed technology used in everything from pacemakers to footwarmers in ski boots comes the International Space Station (ISS). The National Aeronautics and Space Administration (NASA) was created by Congress in 1958 partly in response to the Soviet Union's launch of Sputnik. The Russian Space Agency now is one of NASA's chief partners in the ISS, which can house astronauts conducting research in outer space. NASA, whose Apollo program put men on the moon, also runs the space shuttle program and launches unmanned satellites and probes to explore the solar system. Strapped for funding, NASA is seeking investors beyond the defense and aerospace industries as partners in the ISS.

NATIONAL AMUSEMENTS INC.

200 Elm St.
Dedham, MA 02026
Phone: 781-461-1600
Fax: 781-461-1412
Web site: http://www.national-amusements.com

CEO: Sumner M. Redstone
CFO: Jerome Magner
HR: Maureen Dixon
Type: Private

1998 Est. Sales: $2,917.5 million
1-Yr. Sales Change: 1,141.5%
Employees: 116,700
FYE: December

Media mogul Sumner Redstone puts the business in show business through National Amusements. What began as a humble operator of drive-in theaters has evolved into a powerhouse that controls about 68% of media giant Viacom. Redstone is chairman and CEO of Viacom, whose holdings span several cable networks, video retailer Blockbuster (80%), and Paramount Pictures, and will expand after its merger with CBS. National Amusements hasn't abandoned its roots — it owns theaters housing about 1,300 screens across the US, the UK, and South America. The company also owns 24% of casino gaming machine maker WMS Industries, and Redstone and National Amusements' combined stake in video game maker Midway Games is about 25%.

KEY COMPETITORS
Regal Cinemas
Time Warner
Walt Disney

NATIONAL ASSOCIATION FOR STOCK CAR AUTO RACING

1801 W. International Speedway Blvd.
Daytona Beach, FL 32115
Phone: 904-253-0611
Fax: 904-252-8804
Web site: http://www.nascar.com

CEO: Bill France
CFO: Doris Rumery
HR: Starr Gsell
Type: Private

1998 Est. Sales: $2,000.0 million
1-Yr. Sales Change: —
Employees: —
FYE: December

The National Association for Stock Car Auto Racing (NASCAR) has come a long way. For the 10 years after the sport's 1947 inception, the cars tried to outpace each other on the packed sand of central Florida beaches. Today NASCAR is one of the fastest-growing US spectator sports, sponsoring dozens of races. It is expanding beyond its original fans (Southern men) and entering new markets such as Los Angeles and Las Vegas; women now make up 40% of its audience. NASCAR's Winston Cup Series draws more than 6 million race fans. Networks including NBC and Fox are taking note, paying $2.4 billion over six years for broadcast rights. NASCAR is owned by the family of president Bill France Jr.

KEY COMPETITORS
Championship Auto Racing
NBA
NFL

NATIONAL ASSOCIATION OF SECURITIES DEALERS, INC.

1735 K St. NW
Washington, DC 20006
Phone: 202-728-8000
Fax: 202-293-6260
Web site: http://www.nasd.com

CEO: Frank G. Zarb
CFO: Salvatore F. Sodano
HR: Diane E. Carter
Type: Not-for-profit

1998 Sales: $739.5 million
1-Yr. Sales Change: 16.6%
Employees: 2,900
FYE: December

The National Association of Securities Dealers (NASD) is parent of the Nasdaq-Amex Market Group, home of the #2 and #3 US stock markets — the NASD Automated Quotations system (Nasdaq) and the American Stock Exchange (AMEX). Nasdaq is an electronic dealer exchange and lacks a physical trading floor; dealers set buy and sell prices, pocketing the difference. About 5,500 companies are listed on Nasdaq. AMEX offers an auction-based exchange of 800 companies. The NASD's other main subsidiary, NASD Regulation, oversees over-the-counter securities trading and disciplines traders. Virtually all US securities dealers are members. NASD is making plans to spin off Nasdaq as a for-profit exchange.

KEY COMPETITORS
Archipelago
Instinet
NYSE

 See pages 354–355 for a full profile of this company.

NATIONAL BASKETBALL ASSOCIATION

Olympic Tower, 645 5th Ave.
New York, NY 10022
Phone: 212-407-8000
Fax: 212-754-6414
Web site: http://www.nba.com

CEO: David J. Stern
CFO: Robert Criqui
HR: Patrica E. Swedin
Type: Association

1999 Sales: $955.5 million
1-Yr. Sales Change: (49.0%)
Employees: —
FYE: August

The NBA is the #3 US sports league, behind the NFL and Major League Baseball. The 29-team league, divided into the Eastern and Western Conferences, includes two Canadian teams, the Vancouver Grizzlies and the Toronto Raptors. The NBA also operates the Women's NBA (WNBA). A six-month lockout by the owners stalled the opening of the 1998-99 NBA season, while the owners and players argued furiously over salary issues. Once the labor dispute was settled, the league played a 50-game season instead of a normal 82-game season. When fully operational, the NBA is a multifaceted business with activities in consumer products, network television, and new media projects. NBA games are broadcast to nearly 200 countries.

KEY COMPETITORS
Major League Baseball
NFL
NHL

 See pages 356–357 for a full profile of this company.

NATIONAL COOPERATIVE REFINERY ASSOCIATION

1391 Iron Horse Rd.
McPherson, KS 67460
Phone: 316-241-2340
Fax: 316-241-5531
Web site: http://www.ncrarefinery.com

CEO: James Loving
CFO: John Buehrle
HR: Ronald Schaumburg
Type: Cooperative

1998 Est. Sales: $700.0 million
1-Yr. Sales Change: (9.5%)
Employees: 560
FYE: August

Cooperation is a refined art and refining a cooperative art for the National Cooperative Refinery Association (NCRA), which provides three farm supply cooperatives (Cenex Harvest States, GROWMARK, and MFA Oil) with fuel through its oil refinery in Kansas. In 1943, five regional farm supply cooperatives, tired of wartime fuel shortages, created the NCRA to buy the Globe oil refinery in McPherson, Kansas. In 1998 the refinery's production capacity was 75,000 barrels per day. Fuel from the refinery is allocated to member-owners on the basis of ownership percentages. In addition to the refinery, NCRA owns Jayhawk Pipeline, minority interests in two other pipeline companies, and an underground oil storage facility.

KEY COMPETITORS
Farmland Industries
Tosco
Valero Energy

NATIONAL DISTRIBUTING COMPANY, INC.

1 National Dr. SW
Atlanta, GA 30336
Phone: 404-696-9440
Fax: 404-691-0364
Web site: http://www.ndcweb.com

CEO: Jay M. Davis
CFO: —
HR: Bruce E. Carter
Type: Private

1998 Est. Sales: $1,300.0 million
1-Yr. Sales Change: 26.8%
Employees: 2,000
FYE: December

Although National Distributing Company tries to be a wallflower, it often is the life of the party, thanks to the beer, liquor, and wine it sells. An intensely private company founded in the 1900s by Chris Carlos (joined by Alfred Davis in 1942), National Distributing is the #2 wholesale vendor of wine, spirits, and beer in the US (after Southern Wine & Spirits). Through subsidiaries such as Forman Bros., Standard Distributing, and Midwest Wine & Spirits, the company distributes brands including Heineken beer, Jim Beam bourbon, Jose Cuervo tequila, Smirnoff and Stolichnaya vodkas, and Korbel wine. The Carlos and Davis families own and operate National Distributing.

KEY COMPETITORS
Georgia Crown Distributing
Southern Wine & Spirits
Sunbelt Beverage

NATIONAL FOOTBALL LEAGUE

280 Park Ave.
New York, NY 10017
Phone: 212-450-2000
Fax: 212-681-7573
Web site: http://www.nfl.com

CEO: Paul J. Tagliabue
CFO: Thomas E. Spock
HR: John Buzzeo
Type: Not-for-profit

1999 Sales: $3,270.7 million
1-Yr. Sales Change: 33.6%
Employees: —
FYE: March

The National Football League (NFL) hopes you're ready for some football. The NFL has been the nation's most popular sports league since football surpassed baseball in the 1970s as America's favorite sport. It has 31 franchised teams (with a 32nd team in Houston on the way) organized into the American and National Football Conferences. The teams are run as separate businesses but share much of the revenue from broadcast rights and gate receipts. The NFL acts as a trade association for the teams' owners to promote the game, license team names and logos, collect dues, and develop new programs. A $2.2 billion-a-year television contract with four networks should foster the league's financial health through 2006.

KEY COMPETITORS
Major League Baseball
NBA
NHL

 See pages 358–359 for a full profile of this company.

NATIONAL GEOGRAPHIC SOCIETY

1145 17th St. NW
Washington, DC 20036
Phone: 202-857-7000
Fax: 202-775-6141
Web site: http://www.nationalgeographic.com

CEO: John M. Fahey
CFO: Christopher A. Liedel
HR: Robert E. Howell
Type: Not-for-profit

1998 Sales: $536.8 million
1-Yr. Sales Change: 9.8%
Employees: 1,410
FYE: December

It's not your father's National Geographic Society anymore. Still publishing its flagship *National Geographic* magazine (with about 9 million member/subscribers), the not-for-profit organization has expanded into an array of venues to enhance our knowledge of the big blue marble. For-profit subsidiary National Geographic Ventures is fortifying the organization's presence on television and the Web and in map-making and retail. The organization owns 25% of the National Geographic Channel, a cable channel it operates jointly with NBC and Fox. It also continues to support geographic expeditions (it has funded some 7,000 treks) and sponsors exhibits, lectures, and education programs.

KEY COMPETITORS
Discovery Communications
Rand McNally
Time Warner

 **See pages 360–361 for a full profile of this company.**

NATIONAL HOCKEY LEAGUE

1251 Avenue of the Americas, 47th Fl.
New York, NY 10020
Phone: 212-789-2000
Fax: 212-789-2020
Web site: http://www.nhl.com

CEO: Gary B. Bettman
CFO: Craig Harnett
HR: Janet A. Meyers
Type: Association

1999 Sales: $1,476.3 million
1-Yr. Sales Change: 10.5%
Employees: —
FYE: June

The National Hockey League (NHL) may be the coolest game on earth, but someone should tell that to professional sports fans. The NHL still ranks fourth among the four major North American professional sports leagues despite steady increases in revenue in the 1990s. Twenty-eight teams in the US and Canada are geographically aligned into the Eastern Conference (Atlantic, Northeast, and Southeast divisions) and Western Conference (Central, Northwest, and Pacific). Two more expansion teams will start play in the 2000-01 season, which also will feature a new $600 million TV deal with ABC and ESPN secured by commissioner Gary Bettman. Founded in 1917, the NHL also oversees seven minor and semi-pro hockey leagues.

KEY COMPETITORS
Major League Baseball
NBA
NFL

See pages 362–363 for a full profile of this company.

NATIONAL LIFE INSURANCE CO.

1 National Life Dr.	CEO: Patrick Welch	1998 Sales: $1,060.5 million
Montpelier, VT 05604	CFO: Bill Smith	1-Yr. Sales Change: 0.2%
Phone: 802-229-3333	HR: Susan S. Chiapetta	Employees: 750
Fax: 802-229-9281	Type: Mutual company	FYE: December
Web site: http://natlifeinsco.com		

Founded in 1850, National Life Insurance is one of the oldest life insurance firms in the US. Through its subsidiaries, the company offers a full range of individual life insurance and annuity products and is shifting its status from that of an insurance outfit to that of a financial services company by increasing its investment services segment. Affiliates include Life Insurance Company of the Southwest (annuities) and the Sentinel Family of Funds (investment products and services). National Life is a mutual company owned by its policyholders, but it is restructuring to become a public stock company.

KEY COMPETITORS
MetLife
New York Life
Prudential

NATIONAL RAILROAD PASSENGER CORPORATION

60 Massachusetts Ave. NE	CEO: George D. Warrington	1998 Sales: $2,285.2 million
Washington, DC 20002	CFO: Alfred S. Altschul	1-Yr. Sales Change: 36.5%
Phone: 202-906-3000	HR: Lorraine A. Green	Employees: 24,000
Fax: 202-906-3306	Type: Government-owned	FYE: September
Web site: http://www.amtrak.com		

Fueled by government dollars, Amtrak keeps on chugging, hoping to operate under its own steam. The National Railroad Passenger Corporation, better known as Amtrak, carries about 21 million passengers a year. It has three operating segments: Northeast Corridor, Intercity, and Amtrak West. A for-profit company that has never been profitable, Amtrak is almost wholly owned by the US Department of Transportation and receives large subsidies (a projected $600 million for 1999) from the federal government, which wants Amtrak to be self-sufficient. To do that by 2002, Amtrak is developing high-speed service for its Boston-Washington, DC, commuter route and is carrying mail and other express cargo to boost revenues.

KEY COMPETITORS
AMR
Delta
Greyhound

 See pages 364–365 for a full profile of this company.

NATIONAL RURAL UTILITIES COOPERATIVE FINANCE CORPORATION

2201 Cooperative Way	CEO: Sheldon C. Petersen	1999 Sales: $790.8 million
Herndon, VA 22071	CFO: Steven L. Lilly	1-Yr. Sales Change: 24.0%
Phone: 703-709-6700	HR: Melanie Smith	Employees: 182
Fax: 703-709-6773	Type: Cooperative	FYE: May
Web site: http://www.nrucfc.org		

Forget *Sesame Street* morals — try Wall Street money. Because cooperation alone only goes so far, the National Rural Utilities Cooperative Finance Corporation (CFC) is the financial arm of the National Rural Electric Cooperative Association, a lobby representing about 1,000 electric co-ops in 46 states. The CFC issues quarter stocks on the NYSE and sells commercial paper, medium-term notes, and collateral trust bonds to its members. The company also offers short-term lines of credit and finances intermediate- and long-term loans. Owned by the cooperative utilities that make up its membership, the CFC was founded in 1969 to supplement the government loans that traditionally fueled rural electric utilities.

NATIONWIDE INSURANCE ENTERPRISE

1 Nationwide Plaza
Columbus, OH 43215
Phone: 614-249-7111
Fax: 614-249-7705
Web site: http://www.nationwide.com

CEO: Dimon R. McFerson
CFO: Robert A. Oakley
HR: Donna A. James
Type: Mutual company

1998 Sales: $25,301.1 million
1-Yr. Sales Change: 10.8%
Employees: 32,815
FYE: December

Nationwide Insurance Enterprise (now called simply Nationwide) is a mutual insurance company that sells property/casualty policies (#6 in the US), life insurance and financial services, managed health care, and commercial insurance. The company sells property/casualty and life insurance throughout the US through affiliates that include Nationwide Life and Farmland Mutual. It also sells policies in Germany (Neckura), Puerto Rico, and the US Virgin Islands. The company owns most of Nationwide Financial Services, which it spun off in 1997. Nationwide sold a group of 17 radio stations to Jacor Communications (later bought by Clear Channel Communications) and bought ALLIED Group in 1998.

KEY COMPETITORS
Allstate
Prudential
State Farm

 See pages 366–367 for a full profile of this company.

NAVY EXCHANGE SYSTEM

3280 Virginia Beach Blvd.
Virginia Beach, VA 23452
Phone: 757-463-6200
Fax: 757-631-3659
Web site: http://www.navy-nex.com

CEO: Richard T. Ginman
CFO: Bob Clark
HR: Craig Sinclair
Type: Government-owned

1999 Sales: $1,696.2 million
1-Yr. Sales Change: 2.1%
Employees: 16,000
FYE: January

The Navy Exchange System (NEX) provides active duty, reservist, and retired members of the US Navy with a wide range of goods and services at "guaranteed best prices." NEX customers can shop at more than 110 NEX retail stores (brand-name merchandise ranging from food to home electronics), about 200 NEX ship stores (basic necessities), and more than 120 NEX uniform stores (the sole source of authorized uniforms). Customers can also stay at over 40 Navy lodges and obtain services such as hair care and auto repair at a network of support service stores. NEX receives tax dollars for its shipboard stores, but is otherwise self-supporting. Profits are funneled into morale, welfare, and recreational programs for sailors.

KEY COMPETITORS
Dayton Hudson
Kmart
Wal-Mart

NAVY FEDERAL CREDIT UNION

820 Follin Ln.
Vienna, VA 22180
Phone: 703-255-8000
Fax: 703-255-8741
Web site: http://www.navyfcu.org

CEO: Brian L. McDonnell
CFO: Brady Cole
HR: Louise Foreman
Type: Cooperative

1998 Sales: $848.0 million
1-Yr. Sales Change: 7.7%
Employees: 3,100
FYE: December

"Once a member always a member" promises Navy Federal Credit Union (NFCU). The policy undoubtedly helped the 1.6 million members of NFCU become the nation's largest credit union. Formed in 1933, Navy Federal Credit Union provides US Navy and Marine Corps personnel and their families with checking and savings accounts, mortgages, IRAs, and a variety of loans (auto loans make up nearly 30% of NFCU's portfolio; mortgage loans add nearly 25%). Members (who can retain their credit union privileges even after discharge from the armed services) get access to Visa's PLUS Network and the Armed Forces Financial Network automated teller machines. In 1998 Navy Federal absorbed the Dallas-based Joint Services Credit Union.

KEY COMPETITORS
Bank of America
BANK ONE
Citigroup

NESCO, INC.

6140 Parkland Blvd.
Mayfield Heights, OH 44124
Phone: 440-461-6000
Fax: 440-449-3111
Web site: http://www.nescoinc.com

CEO: Robert J. Tomsich
CFO: Frank Rzicznek
HR: —
Type: Private

1998 Sales: $1,065.0 million
1-Yr. Sales Change: 6.5%
Employees: 700
FYE: December

To have and to hold is a vow NESCO doesn't take lightly. NESCO is a holding company for several engineering and industrial manufacturing firms that make machine tool equipment, die-casting equipment, office printing equipment, and other products. It also has interests in real estate and operates a professional staffing service. Among its companies are Continental Conveyor & Equipment, a materials-handling company that makes conveyor equipment for the mining industry, and Paragon Corporate Holdings, an investment concern. Other holdings include A.B.Dick Company and Penn Union. NESCO has clients in Europe, the Pacific Rim, and North America. Founder and chairman Robert Tomsich owns the company.

KEY COMPETITORS
Giddings & Lewis
Ingersoll-Rand
Mannesmann AG

NEUMAN DISTRIBUTORS, INC.

250 Moonachie Rd.
Moonachie, NJ 07074
Phone: 201-941-2000
Fax: 201-931-0046
Web site: http://www.neumandistributors.com

CEO: Samuel Toscano
CFO: Philip A. Piscopo
HR: Barbara Toscano
Type: Private

1999 Sales: $2,400.0 million
1-Yr. Sales Change: 22.9%
Employees: 965
FYE: April

When pharmacists need drugs, Neuman Distributors can deliver. The company is the largest regional wholesale pharmaceutical distributor in the US (McKesson HBOC is #1 overall). The primary operating unit of Neuman Health Services, Neuman Distribution also distributes health and beauty aids to retailers and health providers in Connecticut, New Jersey, and New York. The Neuman organization has diversified into other pharmacy-related businesses. These operations include a pharmacy co-op (Legend Pharmaceuticals), a pharmacy benefits manager (NeuCare), a disease management company, and consumer information kiosks. Customers include Duane Reade and Genovese. The company was founded in 1951 as the Silver Rod Supply Co.

KEY COMPETITORS
Bergen Brunswig
Cardinal Health
McKesson HBOC

NEW COLT HOLDING CORP.

545 New Park Ave.
West Hartford, CT 06110
Phone: 860-236-6311
Fax: 860-244-1442
Web site: http://www.colt.com

CEO: William Keys
CFO: Thomas Gilboy
HR: Rae Holmes
Type: Private

1998 Sales: $96.0 million
1-Yr. Sales Change: 4.3%
Employees: 700
FYE: December

New Colt Holding aims to be #1 with a bullet. The company, through its Colt's Manufacturing and Colt Rifles subsidiaries, makes handguns (Cowboy, Defender), semiautomatic rifles, and military assault weapons (M-16, M-4), which are sold to the US and international governments as well as commercial distributors. Founded in 1836 by Samuel Colt, the company is about 83%-owned by investment firm Zilkha & Co., which has been reviving the company since 1994. New Colt also owns military weapons manufacturer Saco Defense. In the face of lawsuits, New Colt is discontinuing a number of cheaper consumer handguns and is focusing on its "smart gun" technology (in which weapons can only be fired by the weapon's owner).

KEY COMPETITORS
Beretta
Sturm, Ruger
Tomkins

See pages 368–369 for a full profile of this company.

NEW JERSEY STATE LOTTERY COMMISSION

1 Lawrence Park Complex, Brunswick Avenue Circle
Lawrenceville, NJ 08648
Phone: 609-599-5800
Fax: 609-599-5935
Web site: http://www.state.nj.us/lottery

CEO: Virginia E. Haines
CFO: William Jourdain
HR: Delores Matos
Type: Government-owned

1998 Sales: $1,630.3 million
1-Yr. Sales Change: 4.8%
Employees: 152
FYE: June

Tollbooths aren't the only state operation to throw your money at in New
Jersey. The New Jersey Lottery Commission operates the state's official lottery, featuring a variety of instant-play scratch tickets and traditional lotto-
type games such as Pick 3 and Pick 6 Lotto. More than $800 million in prize
money is awarded each year. New Jersey is also part of a multistate lottery
called The Big Game. About 40% of the proceeds from the state's various
lottery games supports dozens of state programs for corrections, education,
human services, law and public safety, and military and veterans affairs.

KEY COMPETITORS
Maryland State Lottery
Multi-State Lottery
New York State Lottery

NEW UNITED MOTOR MANUFACTURING, INC.

45500 Fremont Blvd.
Fremont, CA 94538
Phone: 510-498-5500
Fax: 510-770-4010
Web site: http://www.nummi.com

CEO: Kanji Ishii
CFO: Y. Toyoda
HR: Gregg Vervais
Type: Joint venture

1998 Sales: $4,699.0 million
1-Yr. Sales Change: 2.2%
Employees: 4,800
FYE: December

What do you get when Japanese production processes meet California? New
United Motor Manufacturing, Inc. (NUMMI). Begun in 1984, NUMMI — a
50-50 joint venture between General Motors (GM) and Toyota — makes
Tacoma pickup trucks and Corolla sedans for Toyota and Chevrolet Prizms
(similar to Corollas) for GM. Toyota's Tacoma is made exclusively at the
NUMMI plant; it and the Corolla account for about 60% of the plant's out-
put. The last automobile manufacturing plant on the West Coast, NUMMI
has the capacity to make 240,000 cars and 150,000 pickups a year. As emissions requirements grow stricter, GM and Toyota have agreed to a five-year
deal to develop and possibly build alternative-fuel vehicles at NUMMI.

KEY COMPETITORS
DaimlerChrysler
Ford
Nissan

 See pages 370–371 for a full profile of this company.

NEW YORK CITY HEALTH AND HOSPITALS CORPORATION

125 Worth St., Ste. 510
New York, NY 10013
Phone: 212-788-3339
Fax: 212-788-3348
Web site: http://www.ci.nyc.ny.us/html/hhc

CEO: Luis R. Marcos
CFO: Rick Langfelder
HR: Pamela S. Silverblatt
Type: Government-owned

1999 Sales: $4,131.2 million
1-Yr. Sales Change: 7.7%
Employees: 33,403
FYE: June

When Gothamites feel god-awful, there's New York City Health and Hospitals, overseer of NYC's municipal health services, the largest such system in
the US. The organization runs 11 acute care hospitals, as well as community
clinics, diagnostic and treatment centers, long-term-care centers, and emergency medical services. It also operates MetroPlus, an HMO. The publicly
supported corporation has long suffered from the trend toward managed
care (which pulls away paying patients) and the burden of poverty-induced
illnesses among its largely uninsured clientele. New York City Health and
Hospitals is trying to cut costs through home health, preventative care, and
community-based primary care programs.

KEY COMPETITORS
Catholic Healthcare Network
Catholic Medical Center of
  Brooklyn & Queens
Columbia/HCA

 See pages 372–373 for a full profile of this company.

NEW YORK LIFE INSURANCE COMPANY

51 Madison Ave.
New York, NY 10010
Phone: 212-576-7000
Fax: 212-576-8145
Web site: http://www.newyorklife.com

CEO: Seymour Sternberg
CFO: Howard I. Atkins
HR: Richard A. Hansen
Type: Mutual company

1998 Sales: $18,350.0 million
1-Yr. Sales Change: 6.0%
Employees: 13,000
FYE: December

Though not the only New York life insurance company, *the* New York Life Insurance Company is one of the US's top five providers of life insurance policies, annuities, mutual funds, and other investments. It also provides third-party asset management services to institutions and has an agreement with the AARP to provide insurance to its members. Unlike its competitors, the company is not rushing to demutualize, claiming it has a large enough warchest to fund its growth without selling stock. Outside the US, New York Life has operations in Argentina, Bermuda, China, Hong Kong, Indonesia, Mexico, South Korea, Taiwan, and the UK.

KEY COMPETITORS
MetLife
Prudential
TIAA-CREF

 See pages 374–375 for a full profile of this company.

NEW YORK STATE LOTTERY

1 Broadway Center
Schenectady, NY 12301
Phone: 518-388-3300
Fax: 518-388-3368
Web site: http://www.nylottery.org

CEO: Margaret R. DeFrancisco
CFO: Jerry Woitkoski
HR: Charlie Titus
Type: Government-owned

1999 Sales: $3,830.7 million
1-Yr. Sales Change: (8.5%)
Employees: 345
FYE: March

The Empire State's lottery can make you a millionaire in a New York minute. The New York State Lottery is the largest and second-oldest lottery in the US (after New Hampshire), offering both instant-win games as well as the multimillion dollar jackpots of its lotto games like Pick 10 and Take Five. It also operates Quick Draw, a Keno-style game in which numbers are picked every five minutes. The lottery sells tickets through more than 17,000 retailers and some 14,000 online terminals (maintained by GTECH Holdings). About 50% of sales are returned to players as prizes, while nearly 40% goes to the state's education system. Started in 1967, the New York State Lottery has raised about $17 billion for the state.

KEY COMPETITORS
Connecticut Lottery
Massachusetts State Lottery
Multi-State Lottery

 See pages 376–377 for a full profile of this company.

NEW YORK STOCK EXCHANGE, INC.

11 Wall St.
New York, NY 10005
Phone: 212-656-3000
Fax: 212-656-2126
Web site: http://www.nyse.com

CEO: Richard A. Grasso
CFO: Keith R. Helsby
HR: Frank Z. Ashen
Type: Not-for-profit

1998 Sales: $728.7 million
1-Yr. Sales Change: 14.1%
Employees: 1,500
FYE: December

It's not called the Big Board for nothing: The New York Stock Exchange (NYSE) is the world's premier stock market and the US's oldest and largest. The member-owned, not-for-profit group lists more than 3,100 companies, including most of the largest US corporations, and is actively recruiting international companies seeking to trade in the US. The NYSE is an auction exchange, meaning that stock prices are set largely by demand on a central trading floor. The stock exchange's predecessor was founded in 1792, and had become the NYSE by 1863. The NYSE has made plans to go public in 2000.

KEY COMPETITORS
E*TRADE
Instinet
NASD

See pages 378–379 for a full profile of this company.

NEW YORK UNIVERSITY

70 Washington Sq. South
New York, NY 10012
Phone: 212-998-1212
Fax: 212-995-4040
Web site: http://www.nyu.edu

CEO: L. Jay Oliva
CFO: Harold T. Read
HR: Karen Bradley
Type: School

1998 Sales: $1,770.7 million
1-Yr. Sales Change: 6.1%
Employees: 12,937
FYE: August

New York University (NYU), founded in 1831, has 13 schools and colleges at five centers in Manhattan (and branch campus programs in Westchester and Rockland Counties, New York) serving about 35,000 students. The private school offers more than 25 degrees in liberal arts, sciences, education, health professions, medicine, arts, and performing arts. It has strong professional programs in law (it has one of the oldest law schools in the US), medicine and dentistry, and business (the Leonard N. Stern School of Business). NYU also offers a variety of foreign study programs. Its alumni include Federal Reserve Chairman Alan Greenspan and film producer Ismail Merchant (*Howards End, The Remains of the Day*).

THE NEWARK GROUP

20 Jackson Dr.
Cranford, NJ 07016
Phone: 908-276-4000
Fax: 908-276-2888
Web site: http://www.newarkgroup.com

CEO: Fred G. von Zuben
CFO: William D. Harper
HR: Carl R. Crook
Type: Private

1999 Sales: $800.0 million
1-Yr. Sales Change: 11.9%
Employees: 3,900
FYE: April

The Newark Group is one of the leading recyclers of wastepaper in the US. The company, founded in 1912, is highly decentralized. Its recycled fibers division operates paper mills from 16 US locations and converts wastepaper into several grades of paper and fiber products, including envelopes, corrugated cardboard, and newspaper. The paperboard division produces 1.3 million tons of paperboard per year from its 15 US mill sites. Recycled paperboard ends up in books, puzzles, gameboards, packaging, and other products. The Newark Group acquires marginal mills and updates the existing technologies in order to gain economies of scale and fight volatile used-paper prices.

KEY COMPETITORS
International Paper
Smurfit-Stone Container
Weyerhaeuser

NIKKEN GLOBAL INC.

15363 Barranca Pkwy.
Irvine, CA 92618
Phone: 949-789-2000
Fax: 800-669-8856
Web site: http://www.nikken.com

CEO: Tom Watanabe
CFO: Kendall Cho
HR: Joann Kaplan
Type: Private

1998 Est. Sales: $1,500.0 million
1-Yr. Sales Change: —
Employees: 250
FYE: December

Nikken Global wants to attract you — and your friends and relatives — to buy and sell magnetic therapeutic devices through its global distribution network (think Amway). The company, #1 in magnetic therapy, has pulled in over 60,000 independent distributors who sell its "wellness" products, such as pillows, sleep masks, support wraps, shoe inserts, and blankets. Nikken tugs at Fido and Fluffy too, offering pet products such as blankets and vitamins as well as human nutritional supplements, jewelry, and skin care. The company does business in 19 countries in the Asia/Pacific region, Europe, and North America. Nikken is owned by Isamu Masuda, who founded the company in Japan in 1975.

KEY COMPETITORS
BIOflex
Biomagnetics
Magnetherapy

NORTH PACIFIC GROUP, INC.

815 NE Davis
Portland, OR 97208
Phone: 503-231-1166
Fax: 503-238-2641
Web site: http://www.north-pacific.com

CEO: Thomas J. Tomjack
CFO: George R. Thurston
HR: Karen Austin
Type: Private

1998 Sales: $1,126.0 million
1-Yr. Sales Change: —
Employees: 850
FYE: December

Since its home base is famed for its tall trees, it's natural that North Pacific Group (NOR PAC) works with wood. The company is one of North America's largest wholesale distributors of building materials. Employee-owned since the 1986 retirement of its founder, Doug David, NOR PAC distributes wood, steel, electrical, agricultural, and food products. Wood products, which make up the majority of its business, include lumber, millwork, and poles and pilings. NOR PAC operates through 30 sales facilities and over 175 inventory locations, selling its products to furniture makers, retailers, and metal fabricators. Its subsidiaries include Cascade Imperial Sales, Landmark Building Products, and Contact International.

KEY COMPETITORS
Building Materials Holding
Georgia-Pacific Group
Weyerhaeuser

NORTH SHORE-LONG ISLAND JEWISH HEALTH SYSTEM

145 Community Dr.
Great Neck, NY 11021
Phone: 516-465-8000
Fax: 516-482-5024
Web site: http://www.nslij.com

CEO: John S. T. Gallagher
CFO: Rick Annis
HR: Ronald Stone
Type: Not-for-profit

1998 Sales: $2,164.9 million
1-Yr. Sales Change: 1.9%
Employees: 27,000
FYE: December

The result of a merger of two top-tier medical systems, North Shore-Long Island Jewish Health System operates a health care network serving New York City boroughs Brooklyn, Queens, and Staten Island, plus Nassau and Suffolk Counties. Its two anchor hospitals, North Shore University Hospital and Long Island Jewish Hospital, are affiliated with prestigious medical schools (NYU and Albert Einstein College of Medicine, respectively). The outfit, one of the largest hospital groups in the Northeast, has more than 4,000 beds in 10 hospitals, including a rehab center, a biomedical research center, a children's hospital, and an ambulatory surgery center. The company has a tie-up with PhyMatrix to develop care centers.

KEY COMPETITORS
Catholic Healthcare Network
Franciscan Health Partnership
New York City Health and Hospitals

NORTHWESTERN HEALTHCARE

980 N. Michigan Ave., Ste. 1500
Chicago, IL 60601
Phone: 312-335-6000
Fax: 312-335-6020

CEO: Gary A. Mecklenburg
CFO: Tom Chan
HR: Dean Manheimer
Type: Not-for-profit

1998 Sales: $1,700.0 million
1-Yr. Sales Change: (6.7%)
Employees: 16,000
FYE: September

Through its nine member institutions, Northwestern Healthcare provides medical care to some 125,000 people annually. The largest integrated health system in the Chicago area, it boasts a staff of almost 5,000 physicians. The system's managed health care programs cover pediatrics, neonatal care, mental health, cardiac care, and cancer treatment. Other group operations include outpatient and wellness centers, physician practice management units, and hospice and home health care. Like many hospitals around the country, the members of Northwestern Healthcare opted to sacrifice some of their autonomy to join a network whose multitude of services and numerous locations would better attract paying customers.

KEY COMPETITORS
Advocate Health Care
Columbia/HCA
New York City Health and Hospitals

THE NORTHWESTERN MUTUAL LIFE INSURANCE COMPANY

720 E. Wisconsin Ave.
Milwaukee, WI 53202
Phone: 414-271-1444
Fax: 414-299-7022
Web site: http://www.northwesternmutual.com

CEO: James D. Ericson
CFO: Gary E. Long
HR: Susan A. Lueger
Type: Mutual company

1998 Sales: $13,479.0 million
1-Yr. Sales Change: 9.4%
Employees: 4,117
FYE: December

If you listen carefully, you might hear The Quiet Company at work. Northwestern Mutual Life Insurance is an insurance and financial services company and one of the top 10 US life insurers. Owned by its nearly 3 million policyholders, the company sells life insurance (about 80% of its sales), health and retirement products, fixed and variable annuities, and mutual funds. Targeting small businesses and fiscally-fit professionals, Northwestern markets its wares via a network of some 7,500 agents and is renowned for employee training practices. Other operations include Robert W. Baird & Co., a regional investment bank based in Milwaukee, and pension manager Frank Russell Company.

KEY COMPETITORS
New York Life
Prudential
TIAA-CREF

 See pages 380–381 for a full profile of this company.

NORTHWESTERN UNIVERSITY

633 Clark St.
Evanston, IL 60208
Phone: 847-491-3741
Fax: 847-491-8406
Web site: http://www.nwu.edu

CEO: Henry S. Bienen
CFO: Eugene S. Sunshine
HR: Guy E. Miller
Type: School

1998 Sales: $815.7 million
1-Yr. Sales Change: 13.2%
Employees: 5,985
FYE: August

The home of the blues is also home to the purple and white. With its main campus in the Chicago suburb of Evanston, Northwestern University serves its 17,700 students through 12 schools and colleges, including the McCormick School of Engineering and Applied Sciences and the Medill School of Journalism. Its Chicago campus houses the schools of law and medicine, as well as several hospitals of the McGaw Medical Center. Northwestern's J. L. Kellogg Graduate School of Management is among the top-ranked business schools in the US. The university also is home to numerous research centers and 18 intercollegiate athletic teams. Founded in 1851, Northwestern is the only private institution in the Big 10 conference.

 See pages 382–383 for a full profile of this company.

NOVACARE EMPLOYEE SERVICES, INC.

2621 Van Buren Ave.
Norristown, PA 19403
Phone: 610-650-4700
Fax: 610-650-4705
Web site: http://www.nces.com

CEO: Loren J. Hulber
CFO: Thomas D. Schubert
HR: Kathryn P. Kehoe
Type: Private

1999 Sales: $1,544.6 million
1-Yr. Sales Change: 21.4%
Employees: 54,784
FYE: June

NovaCare Employee Services provides human resources outsourcing services to small and medium-sized businesses. Formed in 1996 by medical rehabilitation firm NovaCare, Inc., the company offers services including payroll management, workers' compensation risk management, employee benefits administration, unemployment insurance cost containment, human resources and compliance management, and other value-added services. NovaCare Employee Services, which derived about 60% of its revenues from services provided to its former parent company, intends to continue to grow through geographic expansion, mostly in areas where its parent has a sizable presence. Investment firm Plato Holdings owns the company.

KEY COMPETITORS
Administaff
Employee Solutions
Staff Leasing

NOVANT HEALTH, INC.

3333 Silas Creek Pkwy.	CEO: Paul M. Wiles	1998 Sales: $752.3 million
Winston-Salem, NC 27103	CFO: Peggy Scott	1-Yr. Sales Change: (31.6%)
Phone: 336-718-5000	HR: Mel Asbury	Employees: 12,000
Fax: 336-718-9258	Type: Not-for-profit	FYE: December
Web site: http://www.novanthealth.org		

A not-for-profit health care system with facilities in North and South Carolina and Virginia, Novant Health was formed in 1997 by the merger of Carolina Medicorp and Presbyterian Health Services. The system includes nine inpatient facilities with about 2,150 beds, three long-term-care facilities, a women's health and wellness center, and more than 60 outpatient offices. Novant Health also includes the for-profit PARTNERS National Health Plans of North Carolina, an HMO covering 275,000 members. Affiliates of the system include Community General Health Partners of Thomasville, North Carolina, and Nash Health Care System of Rocky Mount, North Carolina.

KEY COMPETITORS
Bon Secours Health
Mid Atlantic Medical
Sentara Health

NRT INCORPORATED

6 Sylvan Way	CEO: Robert M. Becker	1998 Sales: $2,121.0 million
Parsippany, NJ 07054	CFO: Gregory W. Hunt	1-Yr. Sales Change: 102.3%
Phone: 973-496-5700	HR: Ross Anthony	Employees: 4,000
Fax: 973-496-4966	Type: Private	FYE: December
Web site: http://www.nrtinc.com		

One of the largest real estate brokerages in the US, NRT's fast-growing operations include almost 700 offices that stretch coast to coast. The company operates primarily under the Coldwell Banker brand, with offices under that brand throughout the US. To a lesser extent, NRT operates offices under the ERA brand in the Mid-Atlantic region and the Century 21 brand in northern California. Through 30,000 sales associates, which operate as independent contractors, NRT offers mortgage, escrow, title, warranty, security system, relocation, and other traditional brokerage services. NRT, jointly owned by Cendant and Leon Black's Apollo Management LP, postponed its 1999 IPO.

KEY COMPETITORS
Citigroup
EdperBrascan
New America Network

OCEAN SPRAY CRANBERRIES, INC.

1 Ocean Spray Dr.	CEO: Thomas E. Bullock	1998 Sales: $1,479.6 million
Lakeville-Middleboro, MA 02349	CFO: John P. Henry	1-Yr. Sales Change: 2.9%
Phone: 508-946-1000	HR: Nancy McDermott	Employees: 2,350
Fax: 508-946-7704	Type: Cooperative	FYE: August
Web site: http://www.oceanspray.com		

Ocean Spray Cranberries has transformed cranberries from turkey sidekick to the stuff of everyday beverages, cereal, and mixed drinks. The company controls three-fourths of the cranberry market, and its signature blue-and-white wave logo marks the US's leading line of canned and bottled juices. A marketing cooperative owned by more than 900 cranberry and citrus growers in the US and Canada, Ocean Spray has blended the cranberry with fruits from apples to tangerines in a line of juices. It also makes other cranberry products (sauce, snacks), grapefruit juice, and Ocean Spray Premium (formerly known as Wellfleet Farms) 100% juice drinks. Ocean Spray was started in 1912 as a cranberry sauce marketer and became a co-op in 1930.

KEY COMPETITORS
National Grape Co-op
Northland Cranberries
Tropicana Products

 See pages 384–385 for a full profile of this company.

OGLETHORPE POWER CORPORATION

2100 E. Exchange Place
Tucker, GA 30085
Phone: 770-270-7600
Fax: 770-270-7872
Web site: http://www.opc.com

CEO: Thomas A. Smith
CFO: W. Clayton Robbins
HR: Tina Hartzell
Type: Cooperative

1998 Sales: $1,144.2 million
1-Yr. Sales Change: 9.2%
Employees: 125
FYE: December

It's not easy when your name is Oglethorpe and you've got LG&E Energy Marketing (LEM) after you. Not-for-profit Oglethorpe Power Corporation is the largest electricity distribution cooperative in the US, with contracts to supply 39 member-owners (which make up most of Georgia's retail electric suppliers) until 2025. Along with its generating plants, Oglethorpe has power contracts with other suppliers — one of them LEM. As electricity prices shoot up higher than the fixed-contract prices, and Oglethorpe's power needs go up too, LEM wants to renegotiate. Oglethorpe has restructured into separate transmission, system operations, and generation companies to respond effectively to electric industry deregulation.

KEY COMPETITORS
MEAG Power
Southern Company
TVA

OHIO FARMERS INSURANCE COMPANY

1 Park Circle
Westfield Center, OH 44251
Phone: 330-887-0101
Fax: 330-887-0840
Web site: http://www.westfield-cos.com

CEO: Cary Blair
CFO: Otto Bosshard
HR: Debra Cummings
Type: Private

1998 Sales: $854.0 million
1-Yr. Sales Change: (5.1%)
Employees: 2,037
FYE: December

Ohio Farmers Insurance has plowed beyond the crop and cattle biz. The 150-year-old company is chartered as a stock company without stockholders. Ohio Farmers and its affiliates — Beacon Insurance, Westfield Insurance, Westfield National, and American Select — are known by the umbrella name The Westfield Companies. In addition to standard personal lines like auto and homeowners insurance, the companies offer a variety of niche products, including fidelity and surety bonds and specialty coverage for farmers, auto repair shops, antiques businesses, and religious organizations. Ohio Farmers is licensed nationwide but concentrates its 2,100-person agency force in 15 states with favorable regulatory climates.

KEY COMPETITORS
Allstate
Prudential
State Farm

OHIO LOTTERY COMMISSION

615 W. Superior Ave.
Cleveland, OH 44113
Phone: 216-787-3200
Fax: 216-787-5215
Web site: http://www.ohiolottery.org

CEO: Mitchell J. Brown
CFO: Gale W. Fisk
HR: Theresa DiPietro
Type: Government-owned

1999 Sales: $2,140.0 million
1-Yr. Sales Change: (2.5%)
Employees: 349
FYE: June

The year was 1974 — Nixon resigned, an energy crisis gripped the nation, and Ray Stevens ignited a streaking sensation. But were residents of the Buckeye State paying attention? Maybe not — they had a brand new state lottery to play! Since selling its first lottery ticket that fateful year, the Ohio Lottery Commission has raised more than $9 billion for education in Ohio, the cause to which lottery proceeds are dedicated. Instant tickets generate more than half of lottery revenues, but the commission also offers several numbers-based games for Ohioans' wagering pleasure. Facing declining sales and competition from other lotteries and casinos, the commission is looking for new ways to boost ticket sales.

KEY COMPETITORS
Michigan Lottery
Multi-State Lottery
Park Place Entertainment

OHIO NATIONAL FINANCIAL SERVICES

1 Financial Way
Cincinnati, OH 45242
Phone: 513-794-6100
Fax: 513-794-4504
Web site: http://www.ohionatl.com

CEO: David B. O'Maley
CFO: Ronald Dolan
HR: Anthony Esposito
Type: Mutual company

1998 Sales: $996.0 million
1-Yr. Sales Change: 6.8%
Employees: —
FYE: December

Ohio National Financial Services subsidiary Ohio National Life Insurance sells individual and group life insurance, disability insurance, pension plans, and annuities, among other products. Other company subsidiaries include Ohio National Equities and O.N. Equity Sales, which offer wholesale and retail brokerage services, and Ohio National Investments, an investment advisor to the ONE Fund series mutual fund. The firm's products are sold in 47 states, the District of Columbia, and Puerto Rico through more than 1,000 salespersons and 3,000 brokers. Now a mutual firm, Ohio National Financial Services plans to become a public stock company.

KEY COMPETITORS
American United Life
Minnesota Mutual
StanCorp Financial Group

THE OHIO STATE UNIVERSITY

1800 Cannon Dr.
Columbus, OH 43210
Phone: 614-292-6446
Fax: 614-292-2387
Web site: http://www.osu.edu

CEO: William E. Kirwan
CFO: William Shkurti
HR: Larry M. Lewellen
Type: School

1999 Sales: $1,923.0 million
1-Yr. Sales Change: 9.9%
Employees: 29,502
FYE: June

Home to a forest of Buckeyes, Ohio State University (OSU) boasts the second-largest single-campus enrollment in the US (behind The University of Texas at Austin) with about 48,000 students at its 1,715-acre Columbus campus. About 6,000 more populate its four other campuses in Lima, Mansfield, Marion, and Newark, Ohio. With a faculty of 4,500, OSU offers more than 175 undergraduate majors along with 220 advanced degrees. Its Big 10 athletic teams (the Buckeyes) are often nationally ranked; Ohio's football team has played in the prestigious Rose Bowl 13 times (the last in 1997). OSU is a land-grant institution that was founded as the Ohio Agricultural and Mechanical College in Columbus in 1870.

 See pages 386–387 for a full profile of this company.

OHIOHEALTH

3555 Olentangy River Rd.
Columbus, OH 43214
Phone: 614-566-5424
Fax: 614-447-8244
Web site: http://www.ohiohealth.com

CEO: William W. Wilkins
CFO: Dennis J. Freudeman
HR: John Boswell
Type: Not-for-profit

1998 Sales: $828.0 million
1-Yr. Sales Change: 3.5%
Employees: 13,400
FYE: June

With some 2,500 affiliated physicians in more than half of the state's 88 counties, OhioHealth aims to keep Buckeyes healthy. The system's member hospitals include Grant Medical Center and Riverside Methodist Hospital in Columbus, Southern Ohio Medical Center in Portsmouth, and Hardin Memorial in Kenton. A network including imagery, surgery, and physical therapy and neurological rehabilitation centers supports OhioHealth. The system also manages three community hospitals in Morrow County, Bucyrus, and Galion, and it operates the OhioHealth Group managed care plan, a 50-50 joint venture with an independent physicians' association. OhioHealth is buying Doctors Hospital, which will add three new facilities.

KEY COMPETITORS
Catholic Health Initiatives
Catholic Healthcare Partners
Holy Cross

OMNISOURCE CORPORATION

1610 N. Calhoun St.	CEO: Leonard Rifkin	1999 Est. Sales: $825.0 million
Fort Wayne, IN 46808	CFO: Gary Rohrs	1-Yr. Sales Change: 21.3%
Phone: 219-422-5541	HR: Ben Eisbart	Employees: 1,500
Fax: 219-424-0307	Type: Private	FYE: September

Finding profit in the once-discarded is a specialty of OmniSource, a scrap-metal processing and trading company. Started in 1943 by Irving Rifkin, the private, family-owned company supplied scrap for WWII. It grew slowly into a regional, then multiregional concern. OmniSource was a pioneer in adopting formal quality-control programs and in turning scrap into briquettes for foundry and steel-mill furnace use. Through a network of six trading offices, it tracks national and international scrap prices and activities. OmniSource operates 27 processing facilities, a secondary-aluminum smelting plant, and a heavy-media-separation facility. The founder's son, Leonard Rifkin, is chairman and CEO.

KEY COMPETITORS
Commercial Metals
Metal Management
Tang Industries

ON SEMICONDUCTOR, L.L.C.

5005 E. McDowell	CEO: Steve Hanson	1998 Sales: $1,500.0 million
Phoenix, AZ 85008	CFO: Dario Sacomani	1-Yr. Sales Change: —
Phone: 602-244-6600	HR: James Stoeckmann	Employees: 14,000
Fax: 602-952-3812	Type: Private	FYE: December
Web site: http://www.onsemi.com		

ON Semiconductor is on top of the world. With nearly 9% of the global market, ON Semiconductor (formerly a division of Motorola) is one of the largest manufacturers of low-cost, high-volume analog, logic, and discrete semiconductors — components that perform basic, vital power control and interface functions in nearly all electronic systems, including appliances, cars, cell phones, and computers. ON Semiconductor makes about 17,000 different components. The company has operations and joint ventures in about 10 countries. Investment gadabout Texas Pacific Group acquired ON Semiconductor in 1999; Motorola kept a 10% stake.

KEY COMPETITORS
National Semiconductor
ROHM
STMicroelectronics

O'NEAL STEEL, INC.

744 N. 41st St.	CEO: Max DeJonge	1998 Sales: $930.0 million
Birmingham, AL 35222	CFO: Don Freriks	1-Yr. Sales Change: 23.2%
Phone: 205-599-8000	HR: Shawn Smith	Employees: 2,675
Fax: 205-599-8037	Type: Private	FYE: December
Web site: http://www.onealsteel.com		

O'Neal Steel has an angle on the steel industry. It is a leading private metals services company in the US (Ryerson Tull is #1 overall). The company sells a full range of metal products — including angles, bars, beams, coil, pipe, plate, and sheet — made from aluminum, brass, bronze, and various steels. It also offers such metal-processing services as cutting, punching, forming, bending, and machining. O'Neal Steel operates 40 plants primarily in the southern and eastern regions of the country. The family-owned company was founded in 1922 in Alabama; it has expanded largely by way of mergers and acquisitions. During WWII, O'Neal Steel made bombs used by the US military in the Pacific theater.

KEY COMPETITORS
National Steel
Reliance Steel
Ryerson Tull

OPUS U.S. CORPORATION

9900 Bren Rd. East
Minnetonka, MN 55343
Phone: 612-936-4444
Fax: 612-936-4529

CEO: Keith P. Bednarowski
CFO: Ron Schiferal
HR: Jan Maistrovich
Type: Private

1998 Sales: $900.0 million
1-Yr. Sales Change: 56.5%
Employees: 1,250
FYE: December

What a piece of work is Opus. Founded in 1953 as Rauenhorst Construction Company, the commercial real estate development firm operates via a regional network of independent companies throughout the US that specialize in designing and constructing office buildings, warehouses, malls, and institutions. It offers services encompassing architecture, engineering, development, property management, and financing and leasing. Subsidiaries Opus Architects & Engineers and Opus Properties provide design services and asset management, respectively. Other subsidiaries include Opus National (customer relations, noncore business) and Normandale Properties (property management). The company has about 20 offices across the US.

KEY COMPETITORS
Brookfield Properties
Irvine Company
Lincoln Property

OREGON STATE LOTTERY

500 Airport Rd. SE
Salem, OR 97301
Phone: 503-540-1000
Fax: 503-540-1001
Web site: http://www.oregonlottery.org

CEO: Chris Lyons
CFO: David R. Brown
HR: Sharon Tietsort
Type: Government-owned

1998 Sales: $722.0 million
1-Yr. Sales Change: (0.6%)
Employees: 400
FYE: June

The Beaver State has been busy building a bevy of state-run gaming operations. Created in 1984, the Oregon State Lottery offers a variety of games promising rich payoffs, including instant-win ticket games, a Keno game (winning numbers every five minutes), a traditional lotto game, and a lottery that lets players wager on professional sports. Oregon also takes part in the multistate Powerball drawing. More than 75% of the lottery's money, however, comes from nearly 9,000 video poker machines located around the state. Oregon owns about 2,500 of the machines and leases the rest. Nearly 30% of the money raised helps fund state education and economic development, park improvement, and salmon restoration programs.

KEY COMPETITORS
California State Lottery
Multi-State Lottery
Washington State Lottery

ORMET CORPORATION

1233 Main St., Ste. 4000
Wheeling, WV 26003
Phone: 304-234-3900
Fax: 304-234-3929
Web site: http://www.ormet.com

CEO: R. Emmett Boyle
CFO: Rich Caruso
HR: Debbie Boger
Type: Private

1998 Sales: $780.0 million
1-Yr. Sales Change: (14.3%)
Employees: 3,300
FYE: December

For the unsophisticated, smelt is olfaction in the past tense; for Ormet, it's big business. The fourth-largest producer of aluminum in the US, Ormet Primary Aluminum Corporation smelts aluminum ore, makes sheet aluminum and other aluminum products, and produces SatinPlus and Velvet*flow* aluminum extrusion billets (pressed bars of aluminum). Ormet Aluminum Mill Products Corporation further processes the aluminum into gift wrap, packaging, auto trim, cans, and other products. Ormet is sensitive to commodities prices and cyclic changes in the finished-products market. CEO Emmett Boyle owns the company, which was founded in Hannibal, Ohio, in 1954.

KEY COMPETITORS
Alcan
Alcoa
Reynolds Metals

PACER INTERNATIONAL, INC.

1340 Treat Boulevard
Walnut Creek, CA 94596
Phone: 925-979-4440
Fax: 925-979-4215
Web site: http://www.pacerintl.com

CEO: Donald C. Orris
CFO: Lawrence C. Yarberry
HR: —
Type: Private

1998 Sales: $970.0 million
1-Yr. Sales Change: 863.8%
Employees: 900
FYE: December

Pacer International provides integrated intermodal transportation and freight services for major manufacturers and retailers throughout the US and abroad. The company contracts with independent truckers, urban transport providers, and railroads to offer shipping and related services, including flatbed and heavy-haul trucking, warehousing, and local transport. The firm relies on a network of agents to dovetail the services of national, regional, and local transportation providers. In addition, Pacer International negotiates rates, consolidates billing, and handles damage claims for its clients. Eos Partners will reduce its stake in Pacer International from 60% to about one-third after the planned IPO.

PACIFIC MUTUAL HOLDING COMPANY

700 Newport Center Dr.
Newport Beach, CA 92660
Phone: 949-640-3011
Fax: 949-219-7614
Web site: http://www.pacificlife.com

CEO: Thomas C. Sutton
CFO: Khanh T. Tran
HR: Anthony J. Bonno
Type: Mutual company

1998 Sales: $2,809.2 million
1-Yr. Sales Change: 9.1%
Employees: 2,700
FYE: December

Life insurance is Pacific Mutual Holding's stock-in-trade. The mutual holding company owns Pacific LifeCorp, a stock company whose primary subsidiary, Pacific Life Insurance, is the largest California-based life insurance outfit. Pacific Life offers fixed and variable life insurance policies, annuities, and pension plans; other subsidiaries manage health plans (PM Group Life) and provide real estate advice (PMRealty Advisors). Through Pacific Mutual Distributors, the company markets such investment products as annuities, mutual funds, and index funds. With operations both in the US and the UK, Pacific Mutual also owns almost a third of PIMCO Advisors, a major investment management firm being bought by Allianz.

KEY COMPETITORS
MetLife
Prudential
Transamerica

 See pages 388–389 for a full profile of this company.

PACKAGING CORPORATION OF AMERICA

1900 W. Field Ct.
Lake Forest, IL 60045
Phone: 847-482-2000
Fax: 847-482-4738
Web site: http://www.packagingcorp.com

CEO: Paul T. Stecko
CFO: Richard B. West
HR: Andrea L. Davey
Type: Private

1998 Sales: $1,571.0 million
1-Yr. Sales Change: 11.3%
Employees: 7,700
FYE: December

As Packaging Corporation of America (PCA) can attest, it pays to know how to box. The firm makes corrugated containers used to protect goods during shipment. Through its five graphic design centers PCA also offers its 9,000 customers sophisticated graphics for customized packaging. PCA operates four containerboard mills, 39 corrugator plants, 26 sheet plants, two specialty facilities, three sawmills, and three paper recycling centers in 25 states. To support its operations, PCA owns, leases, and manages about 950,000 acres of timberland in Georgia, Tennessee, and Wisconsin. Madison Dearborn Partners and J.P. Morgan Capital control 53% of the company; Tenneco's former packaging unit, Pactiv, owns the rest.

KEY COMPETITORS
Four M
Georgia-Pacific Group
International Paper

PACKERLAND PACKING COMPANY, INC.

2580 University Ave.
Green Bay, WI 54311
Phone: 920-468-4000
Fax: 920-468-7453
Web site: http://www.packerland.com

CEO: Richard V. Vesta
CFO: Craig Liegel
HR: Marty Plumb
Type: Private

1998 Sales: $1,174.0 million
1-Yr. Sales Change: 11.8%
Employees: 3,000
FYE: December

Packerland sends cattle packing. One of the largest beef processors in the US, Packerland Packing slaughters about 5,200 head of cattle a day and sells its boxed beef in the US and over 40 other countries. The company operates slaughterhouses in Green Bay, Wisconsin; Hospers, Iowa; Gering, Nebraska; and — through its acquisition of Sun Land Beef — Tolleson, Arizona. The company's Packerland Transport division operates about 300 refrigerated tractor trailers. Founded by the Frankenthal family in 1960, the company was sold in 1977 to George Gillett, who declared bankruptcy in 1992. A management-led investor group (including Gillett and backed by insurance company John Hancock Life) bought Packerland in 1994.

KEY COMPETITORS
Farmland Industries
IBP
Rosen's Diversified

PARKDALE MILLS, INC.

1630 W. Garrison Blvd., #1
Gastonia, NC 28052
Phone: 704-864-8761
Fax: 704-867-3753
Web site: http://www.parkdalemills.com

CEO: W. Duke Kimbrell
CFO: Greg Sellers
HR: Reid Baker
Type: Private

1999 Sales: $934.0 million
1-Yr. Sales Change: 9.9%
Employees: 3,600
FYE: September

Like that nice, soft-spun cotton in your undies? Thank Parkdale. Parkdale Mills is the largest independent yarn spinner in the US. It manufactures cotton and cotton-blended yarns at its plants in North Carolina and Virginia. The company specializes in spun yarn that winds up in consumer goods such as sheets, towels, underwear, and hosiery. Parkdale has worldwide customers that include Vanity Fair, Jockey International, Lands' End, and L.L. Bean. Parkdale operates and owns about 65% of Parkdale America, a company formed with polyester and nylon yarn maker Unifi. A 50-50 joint venture with Burlington Industries is in the works to operate mills in Mexico. Chairman and CEO Duke Kimbrell owns about 50% of the company.

KEY COMPETITORS
Avondale Incorporated
Guilford Mills
Nisshinbo Industries

PARSONS & WHITTEMORE, INCORPORATED

4 International Dr.
Rye Brook, NY 10573
Phone: 914-937-9009
Fax: 914-937-2259

CEO: Arthur L. Schwartz
CFO: Robert Masson
HR: Suzanne Henry
Type: Private

1999 Sales: $790.0 million
1-Yr. Sales Change: (4.2%)
Employees: 2,500
FYE: March

Pulp fiction? No, pulp fact. Parsons & Whittemore is the world's fourth-largest producer of market pulp, the raw material used in papermaking. It is also a supplier of bleached kraft pulp, which is used to make paper bags, butcher wrap, newsprint, strong bond and ledger paper, and tissue. It has pulp mills in Alabama (Alabama River and Alabama Pine) and in Canada (St. Anne-Nackawic Pulp). Its Alabama River pine-pulp facility is the US's largest pulpwood consumer. The company jointly owns Alabama River Newsprint with Abitibi-Consolidated. Chairman George Landegger owns the company. His father, Karl, came to the US from Austria in 1938 and bought Parsons & Whittemore, then a small pulp-trading firm founded in 1909.

KEY COMPETITORS
Champion International
Georgia-Pacific Group
Smurfit-Stone Container

PARSONS BRINCKERHOFF, INC.

1 Penn Plaza
New York, NY 10119
Phone: 212-465-5000
Fax: 212-465-5096
Web site: http://www.pbworld.com

CEO: Thomas J. O'Neill
CFO: Richard A. Schrader
HR: John J. Ryan
Type: Private

1999 Est. Sales: $945.0 million
1-Yr. Sales Change: 24.3%
Employees: 7,700
FYE: October

Though the rough construction industry is no quiet parish, Parsons Brinck-erhoff does good works — planning, engineering, construction management, and maintenance for infrastructure projects. Specialties include transit systems, tunnels, bridges, highways, airports, and marine facilities. William Barclay Parsons founded the company in 1885; among its first jobs was designing New York City's first subway. Other projects have included San Francisco's rapid transit system and Boston's Central Artery/Tunnel. Parsons Brinckerhoff, which has more than 200 offices on six continents, is owned by its employees.

KEY COMPETITORS
CH2M Hill
Morrison Knudsen
Parsons

PARSONS CORPORATION

100 W. Walnut St.
Pasadena, CA 91124
Phone: 626-440-2000
Fax: 626-440-2630
Web site: http://www.parsons.com

CEO: James F. McNulty
CFO: Curtis A. Bower
HR: Shirley Gaufin
Type: Private

1998 Sales: $1,600.0 million
1-Yr. Sales Change: 26.7%
Employees: 11,000
FYE: December

Almost evangelically, Parsons carries its message — and its engineering and construction services — worldwide. The company provides design, planning, and construction management services through three operating groups: energy and chemicals, infrastructure and technology, and transportation. Among its many projects, Parsons has designed power plants, built dams, resorts, and shopping centers, and provided environmental services such as the cleanup of hazardous nuclear wastes. Parsons has also added improvements to airports and helped build rail systems, bridges, and highways. The employee-owned company's clientele includes Amtrak, Disney, and the government of Greece.

KEY COMPETITORS
Bechtel
Fluor
Turner Corporation

 See pages 390–391 for a full profile of this company.

PARTNERS HEALTHCARE SYSTEM, INC.

Prudential Tower, 800 Boylston St., Ste. 1150
Boston, MA 02199
Phone: 617-278-1000
Fax: 617-278-1049
Web site: http://www.partners.org

CEO: Samuel O. Thier
CFO: Cathy Robbins
HR: Dennis Colling
Type: Not-for-profit

1998 Sales: $2,434.4 million
1-Yr. Sales Change: 10.2%
Employees: 19,407
FYE: September

Partners HealthCare System runs Massachusetts' biggest hospital group. Formed in 1994 by Brigham and Women's Hospital and Massachusetts General Hospital, the organization works to improve its members' bargaining power with managed care organizations and insurance companies. Institutions affiliated with Partners HealthCare include the North Shore Medical Center; Dana-Farber/Partners CancerCare, a collaboration between the Dana-Farber Cancer Institute and Partners hospitals; and Partners Community HealthCare, a physician network encompassing nearly 900 practitioners. The organization also sponsors research programs and community health outreach programs.

KEY COMPETITORS
Baystate Health Systems
Columbia/HCA
Tenet Healthcare

PATHMARK STORES, INC.

200 Milik St.
Carteret, NJ 07008
Phone: 732-499-3000
Fax: 732-499-3072
Web site: http://www.pathmark.com

CEO: James L. Donald
CFO: Frank Vitrano
HR: Kevin Kane
Type: Private

1999 Sales: $3,655.2 million
1-Yr. Sales Change: (1.1%)
Employees: 26,700
FYE: January

The chain known for its generic No Frills brand hasn't looked too fancy it-self, and things don't look much brighter now that its sale to supermarket giant Royal Ahold fell through. Pathmark Stores operates more than 130 su-permarkets, mainly in the New York and Philadelphia metro areas, as well as in Delaware. Almost all of its stores are Pathmark Super Centers (one-third larger than the average US supermarket), which offer an expanded selection of general merchandise and foods, including 3,000 private-label items under the No Frills, Pathmark, and Pathmark Preferred brand names. Burdened with debt, Pathmark was hoping Royal Ahold could fuel the company with much needed capital. Merrill Lynch controls Pathmark.

KEY COMPETITORS
A&P
Albertson's
Wakefern Food

See pages 392–393 for a full profile of this company.

PEABODY GROUP

701 Market St., Ste. 700
St. Louis, MO 63101
Phone: 314-342-3400
Fax: 314-342-7799
Web site: http://www.peabodygroup.com

CEO: Irl F. Engelhardt
CFO: George J. Holway
HR: Sharon K. Schergen
Type: Private

1999 Sales: $2,386.6 million
1-Yr. Sales Change: 6.3%
Employees: 7,800
FYE: March

With 25 mines in the US and four in Australia, Peabody Group — a spinoff produced by the sale of the Energy Group (now Eastern Group) to TXU — is the world's largest producer and marketer of coal. The group sells to cus-tomers in nearly 20 countries. Its steam and coal fuels more than 9% of US electricity generation. Most of its US production is sold to electric utilities, with the rest going to US industry and export. Peabody Group markets power in the US through its Citizens Power subsidiary. In an effort to streamline its US coal operations, the company has realigned its manage-ment structure. Lehman Merchant Banking Partners, a Lehman Brothers affiliate, owns Peabody Group.

KEY COMPETITORS
Arch Coal
CONSOL Energy
Zeigler Coal

PENN MUTUAL LIFE INSURANCE CO.

600 Dresher Rd.
Horsham, PA 19044
Phone: 215-956-8000
Fax: 215-956-8347
Web site: http://www.pennmutual.com

CEO: Robert E. Chappell
CFO: Nancy S. Brodie
HR: Michael Biondolillo
Type: Mutual company

1998 Sales: $1,082.4 million
1-Yr. Sales Change: 1.2%
Employees: —
FYE: December

Founded in 1847, Penn Mutual Life Insurance is the fourth-oldest US life in-surer. The company has five main subsidiaries, including Penn Insurance and Annuity and brokerages Janney Montgomery Scott and Hornor, Townsend & Kent. Penn tailors its selling to the affluent: business owners, entrepreneurs, executives, and professionals. Products include term, whole life, universal life, variable universal life, and disability income insurance policies, as well as a full range of deferred and immediate annuity products. The company has prospered by focusing on the individual life and individual and group pension markets.

KEY COMPETITORS
MetLife
New York Life
Prudential

THE PENNSYLVANIA LOTTERY

2850 Turnpike Industrial Dr.
Middletown, PA 17057
Phone: 717-986-4699
Fax: 717-986-4767
Web site: http://www.palottery.com

CEO: Al Taylor
CFO: Larry Beard
HR: Sabrina Gheiss
Type: Government-owned

1998 Sales: $1,682.4 million
1-Yr. Sales Change: (2.1%)
Employees: 152
FYE: June

Even if they don't become millionaires, senior citizens in Pennsylvania can still benefit from the state lottery — its proceeds are dedicated to programs geared toward seniors (property-tax relief, rent rebates, reduced-cost transportation, co-pay prescriptions). Lottery proceeds also fund 52 Area Agencies on Aging across Pennsylvania. State law mandates that at least 40% of lottery proceeds must be awarded in prizes, and at least 30% must be used for programs benefiting the elderly. Pennsylvanians can choose from games ranging from traditional lottery game Super 6 Lotto to daily wagering game Big 4. Automated Wagering International operates the lottery's computer systems.

KEY COMPETITORS
New Jersey Lottery
New York State Lottery
Ohio Lottery

THE PENNSYLVANIA STATE UNIVERSITY

408 Old Main
University Park, PA 16802
Phone: 814-865-4700
Fax: 814-865-7145
Web site: http://www.psu.edu

CEO: Graham B. Spanier
CFO: Gary C. Schultz
HR: Billie S. Willits
Type: School

1999 Sales: $1,789.4 million
1-Yr. Sales Change: 3.2%
Employees: —
FYE: June

Chartered in 1855 to apply scientific principles to farming, The Pennsylvania State University system is one of the largest in the nation, with an enrollment of more than 80,000 students. The university includes 24 campuses — the largest (just over half of undergraduates) and oldest of which is at University Park. Its offerings include degrees in communications, business, science, liberal arts, engineering, and agriculture, as well as a wide range of graduate programs. Penn State's president, Graham Spanier, has made the elimination of underage and binge drinking a priority for the school after a 1998 alcohol-induced riot resulted in about two dozen injured police officers and $100,000 worth of damage.

PENSION BENEFIT GUARANTY CORPORATION

1200 K St. NW
Washington, DC 20005
Phone: 202-326-4040
Fax: 202-326-4042
Web site: http://www.pbgc.gov

CEO: David M. Strauss
CFO: N. Anthony Calhoun
HR: Sharon Barbee-Fletcher
Type: Government-owned

1998 Sales: $3,250.0 million
1-Yr. Sales Change: (15.9%)
Employees: 750
FYE: September

Underfunded pension plans give the heebie-jeebies to PBGC, or Pension Benefit Guaranty Corporation. The government corporation was established to promote the growth of defined-benefit pension plans, provide payment of retirement benefits, and keep pension premiums as low as possible. It protects the pensions of more than 42 million workers and monitors employers to ensure that plans are adequately funded. The agency receives no tax funds; its income is generated by insurance premiums paid by employers (about $19 per employee), investments, and assets recovered from terminated plans. Pension Benefit Guaranty is empowered to take over a company's pension plan if the plan is in financial distress.

📖 See pages 394–395 for a full profile of this company.

PENSKE CORPORATION

13400 Outer Dr. West
Detroit, MI 48239
Phone: 313-592-5000
Fax: 313-592-5256
Web site: http://www.penske.com

CEO: Roger S. Penske
CFO: J. Patrick Conroy
HR: Paul F. Walters
Type: Private

1998 Sales: $6,000.0 million
1-Yr. Sales Change: 3.4%
Employees: 28,000
FYE: December

Penske, headed by race-car legend Roger Penske, seems to be on the right track as a diversified transportation firm. Closely held Penske owns or has stakes in Penske Truck Leasing (the US's #2 commercial truck-rental operation, after Ryder), heavy-duty engine maker Detroit Diesel, and car dealerships through Penske Automotive (six dealerships in California) and UnitedAuto Group (US's #2 chain of auto dealers, with more than 60 locations in 16 states). In addition, Penske Auto Centers perform automobile service and repairs in about 650 Kmarts. The company has sold its interests in racetracks in California, Michigan, North Carolina, and Pennsylvania to International Speedway. Roger Penske owns 57% of the firm.

KEY COMPETITORS
Cummins Engine
Discount Tire
Ryder

 See pages 396–397 for a full profile of this company.

PENSKE TRUCK LEASING

Rte. 10 Green Hills
Reading, PA 19603
Phone: 610-775-6000
Fax: 610-775-6432
Web site: http://www.penske.com

CEO: Brian Hard
CFO: Frank Cosuzza
HR: John W. Kaisoglus
Type: Joint venture

1998 Sales: $1,800.0 million
1-Yr. Sales Change: (5.3%)
Employees: 14,200
FYE: December

Customer-friendly Penske Truck Leasing knows that it's not about being truculent, it's about leasing trucks. Penske Truck Leasing, the second-largest commercial truck rental company in the US (behind Ryder), operates some 100,000 heavy-, medium-, and light-duty trucks in the US, Canada, and Mexico through 650 rental locations. Penske Truck Leasing offers logistics services (in Europe as well as in North America), contract maintenance, full-service leasing, and commercial and consumer truck leasing (most of its customers are large companies with long-term leasing needs). The company, which was formed in 1988, is 79%-owned by GE Capital Services. Diversified transportation firm Penske Corp. owns the rest.

KEY COMPETITORS
Rollins Truck Leasing
Ryder
UniGroup

THE PEPPER COMPANIES, INC.

643 N. Orleans St.
Chicago, IL 60610
Phone: 312-266-4703
Fax: 312-266-6010

CEO: J. Stanley Pepper
CFO: Thomas M. O'Leary
HR: John Beasley
Type: Private

1999 Sales: $690.0 million
1-Yr. Sales Change: 10.8%
Employees: 1,257
FYE: September

Cities across the US have been sprinkled with buildings by The Pepper Companies. Operating through construction, environmental, and real estate subsidiaries, Pepper builds homes, hospitals, and industrial and office buildings in more than 40 states. The firm has ventured overseas to build a hotel in Saudi Arabia. Clients have included Sears, Marshall Field's, and Marriott. The firm was founded by Stanley Pepper as Pepper Construction Co. in Chicago in 1927. Pepper family members and employees own the company, which is run by the founder's grandsons.

KEY COMPETITORS
Centex
Sundance Homes
Walsh Group

PERDUE FARMS INCORPORATED

Old Ocean City Rd.
Salisbury, MD 21804
Phone: 410-543-3000
Fax: 410-543-3874
Web site: http://www.perdue.com

CEO: James A. Perdue
CFO: Michael Cooper
HR: Rob Heflin
Type: Private

1999 Sales: $2,515.0 million
1-Yr. Sales Change: 14.3%
Employees: 20,500
FYE: March

James Perdue makes Big Bird nervous. His family's company is one of the largest in the US poultry market, selling 42 million pounds of distinctly yellow chicken products and 3.5 million pounds of turkey products each week. Vertically integrated Perdue Farms hatches the eggs, grows the chickens, then slaughters, packs, and distributes the meat. Perdue is expanding its value-added chicken parts and food service products and has established a plant in China through a joint venture. It also processes grain and makes vegetable oils and pet food ingredients. Founded by Arthur Perdue (James' grandfather) in 1920, the company sells its products in the East, Midwest, and South, and it exports to more than 30 countries.

KEY COMPETITORS
ConAgra
Gold Kist
Tyson Foods

See pages 398–399 for a full profile of this company.

PEREGRINE INCORPORATED

25200 Telegraph Rd.
Southfield, MI 48034
Phone: 248-354-2100
Fax: 248-223-0309
Web site: http://www.pgrine.com

CEO: James J. Bonsall
CFO: David Rawden
HR: Joseph E. Ruffolo
Type: Private

1998 Sales: $940.0 million
1-Yr. Sales Change: (21.7%)
Employees: 3,300
FYE: December

Peregrine almost fell prey to tough competition in the auto supply business. A maker of interior and exterior automotive parts, the company closed two plants and sold a third to avoid bankruptcy after Jay Alix, a turnaround specialist, bought the firm in 1998. After the plant closings, Peregrine continues to operate four plants in Michigan. Some of Peregrine's products include seat assemblies, airbag canisters, door trim panels, and miscellaneous automotive body parts. Although the company once supplied nearly all of its products to General Motors, it now also sells to Ford, DaimlerChrysler, Takata, TRW, and The Budd Company. Peregrine has sold its Canadian seat and door-panel plant to Lear.

KEY COMPETITORS
Johnson Controls
Lear
Magna International

PETER KIEWIT SONS', INC.

1000 Kiewit Plaza
Omaha, NE 68131
Phone: 402-342-2052
Fax: 402-271-2829
Web site: http://www.kiewit.com

CEO: Kenneth E. Stinson
CFO: Kenneth Jantz
HR: Brad Chapman
Type: Private

1998 Sales: $3,403.0 million
1-Yr. Sales Change: 23.1%
Employees: 16,200
FYE: December

After successful forays into telecommunications and technology, employee-owned construction company Peter Kiewit Sons' is back to the building business. The construction firm is one of the largest general contractors in the US, with projects in more than 40 US states and Washington, DC, as well as in Canada and Puerto Rico. Kiewit specializes in heavy construction projects such as highways, commercial buildings, mining infrastructure, and waste-disposal systems. Government contracts account for about half of its jobs. It has spun off its telecommunications and computer services holdings into Level 3 Communications and has been contracted to build a national fiber-optic network for its offspring.

KEY COMPETITORS
Bechtel
Fluor
Granite Construction

See pages 400–401 for a full profile of this company.

PHOENIX HOME LIFE MUTUAL INSURANCE COMPANY

1 American Row	CEO: Robert W. Fiondella	1998 Sales: $3,463.7 million
Hartford, CT 06102	CFO: David W. Searfoss	1-Yr. Sales Change: (5.0%)
Phone: 860-403-5000	HR: Carl T. Chadburn	Employees: 4,011
Fax: 860-403-5855	Type: Mutual company	FYE: December
Web site: http://www.phl.com		

Phoenix Home Life Mutual Insurance helps folks rise from the ashes of a fiscal firestorm. Owned by some 3.3 million policyholders, the firm sells individual and group insurance and annuities, employee benefit programs, reinsurance, and such investment products as mutual funds and variable annuities. Through publicly traded subsidiary Phoenix Investment Partners, the firm offers investment management; other subsidiaries offer trust services, administrative services, and investment products internationally. Property/casualty insurer American Phoenix is being sold to Hilb, Rogal and Hamilton, which will market selected Phoenix Home Life financial products after the purchase is completed.

KEY COMPETITORS
Allstate
MetLife
Prudential

PILOT CORPORATION

5508 Lonas Rd.	CEO: James A. Haslam	1998 Sales: $2,000.0 million
Knoxville, TN 37909	CFO: Jeffrey L. Cornish	1-Yr. Sales Change: 44.1%
Phone: 423-588-7487	HR: Bob Gregorio	Employees: 7,000
Fax: 423-450-2800	Type: Private	FYE: December
Web site: http://www.pilotcorp.com		

White-line fever? Then pull on over into one of Pilot's about 125 travel centers in 37 states or its about 45 convenience stores in Tennessee, Virginia, and West Virginia. The company's Pilot Travel Centers feature one or more national food chains, including Subway, Dairy Queen, Wendy's, Arby's, T.J. Cinnamon, and Taco Bell. Catering to truckers and travelers alike, Pilot features fuel islands large enough to service several 18-wheelers at a time and private showers for its customers. James Haslam II got Pilot off the ground in 1958 as a gas station that sold cigarettes and soft drinks; now his son, CEO James Haslam III, pilots the company. The Haslam family owns the company.

KEY COMPETITORS
Flying J
Petro Stopping Centers
Tosco

PLAINS COTTON COOPERATIVE ASSOCIATION

3301 E. 50th St.	CEO: Van May	1998 Est. Sales: $1,000.0 million
Lubbock, TX 79404	CFO: Billy Morton	1-Yr. Sales Change: 19.6%
Phone: 806-763-8011	HR: Lee Phenix	Employees: 1,350
Fax: 806-762-7333	Type: Cooperative	FYE: June
Web site: http://www.pcca.com		

Plainly speaking, the Plains Cotton Cooperative Association (PCCA) is one of the nation's largest cotton handlers. The farmer-owned marketing cooperative has more than 25,000 members in Oklahoma and Texas. PCCA markets about 3 million bales of cotton each year through TELCOT, its computerized trading system, which continually updates cotton prices, buyer data, and other information. The co-op has cotton warehouses in Texas and Oklahoma and a denim mill in Texas whose primary customer is Levi Strauss. Through its Mission Valley Textiles unit, PCCA makes yarn-dyed woven fabric. The co-op was formed in 1953 to enable cotton farmers to obtain the most competitive price for their cotton.

KEY COMPETITORS
Calcot
Cargill
Dunavant Enterprises

PLANET AUTOMOTIVE GROUP, INC.

2333 Ponce De Leon Blvd.
Coral Gables, FL 10019
Phone: 305-774-7690
Fax: 305-774-7698
Web site: http://www.planetautomotive.com

CEO: Robert Potamkin
CFO: Peter Paris
HR: George Spallina
Type: Private

1997 Sales: $1,200.0 million
1-Yr. Sales Change: (1.5%)
Employees: 2,000
FYE: December

Expect a lot of iron, glass, and rubber on the surface of Planet Automotive Group. Formerly Potamkin Manhattan, the company coalesced from a network of auto dealerships owned by the Potamkin family. The dealerships operate primarily in New York and New Jersey but also in other East Coast states, such as Florida. It has grown through the acquisition of ailing new- and used-car dealerships, more than 50 in all. One of the company's most notable operations is Potamkin Auto Center, a superstore car dealership offering different makes (bought from other dealerships for resale) on the same floor. The late Victor Potamkin founded the business in 1949, and his two sons, Robert and Alan, now run the company.

KEY COMPETITORS
AutoNation
Holman Enterprises
United Auto Group

PLATINUM EQUITY HOLDINGS

2049 Century Park East, Ste. 2710
Los Angeles, CA 90067
Phone: 310-712-1850
Fax: 310-712-1848
Web site: http://www.peh.com

CEO: Tom Gores
CFO: William Foltz
HR: Kathleen A. Wilkinson
Type: Private

1998 Sales: $700.0 million
1-Yr. Sales Change: —
Employees: 10,000
FYE: December

Platinum Equity Holdings buys old information technology (IT) companies so you won't have to. Founded in 1995, the firm invests mainly in underperforming or noncore IT units of *Fortune* 1000 companies, sometimes closing deals in less than a month. Platinum Equity buys units with sales between $20 million and $500 million a year in such sectors as application software, communication, computer systems, hardware, and information management. It acquires companies around the world and usually takes full ownership, supplying niche markets with the products and services that time forgot (many units acquired are more than 20 years old). The firm owns stakes in about 15 companies and has offices in Los Angeles and London.

KEY COMPETITORS
Apollo Advisors
Clayton, Dubilier
KKR

PMC GLOBAL, INC.

12243 Branford St.
Sun Valley, CA 91352
Phone: 818-896-1101
Fax: 818-897-0180
Web site: http://www.pmcglobalinc.com

CEO: Philip E. Kamins
CFO: Thian C. Cheong
HR: Karen Ferguson
Type: Private

1998 Est. Sales: $920.0 million
1-Yr. Sales Change: 11.1%
Employees: 5,100
FYE: December

PMC Global is one of the biggest manufacturers of plastic foam products in the US. This diversified international company produces film, foam, packaging, plastics, plastic-molding equipment, and specialty chemicals. The company operates through 15 specialized divisions, including Cosrich (licensed and branded bath, cosmetics, and toiletry products), General Foam (flexible polyurethane foam and expanded vinyl), PMC Specialties Group (organic, pharmaceuticals, and fine chemicals), and VCF Films (PVS shrink films and acrylic films). CEO Philip Kamins founded PMC (an acronym for "Plastic Management Corp.") in 1971 as an outgrowth of a small plastics scrap yard he founded in 1964.

KEY COMPETITORS
BASF AG
DuPont
Pactiv

THE PORT AUTHORITY OF NEW YORK AND NEW JERSEY

67 West, 1 World Trade Center
New York, NY 10048
Phone: 212-435-7000
Fax: 212-435-4660
Web site: http://www.panynj.gov

CEO: Robert E. Boyle
CFO: Charles F. McClafferty
HR: Paul Segalini
Type: Government-owned

1998 Sales: $2,361.2 million
1-Yr. Sales Change: 7.1%
Employees: 7,200
FYE: December

The true bridge and tunnel crowd — the Port Authority of New York and New Jersey — keeps people and products moving. The agency operates and maintains tunnels, bridges, airports, shipping terminals, and other facilities within the two-state Port District, a 1,500-sq.-mi. region surrounding the Statue of Liberty. A self-supporting public agency, the Port Authority receives no tax money and relies on tolls, fees, and rents. The agency's facilities include the George Washington Bridge, the Holland and Lincoln tunnels, John F. Kennedy International Airport, the New York-New Jersey Port, and the World Trade Center. Its rail subsidiary, the Port Authority Trans-Hudson (PATH), carries about 220,000 passengers daily.

KEY COMPETITORS
Amtrak
MTA
Ogden

See pages 402–403 for a full profile of this company.

POWER AUTHORITY OF THE STATE OF NEW YORK

123 Main St.
White Plains, NY 10601
Phone: 914-681-6200
Fax: 212-468-6360
Web site: http://www.nypa.gov

CEO: Clarence D. Rappleyea
CFO: Michael H. Urbach
HR: Vincent Vesce
Type: Government-owned

1998 Sales: $1,483.9 million
1-Yr. Sales Change: 0.2%
Employees: —
FYE: December

The Power Authority of the State of New York generates and transmits 26% of New York's electricity and is the US's largest nonfederal public power provider. Operating 12 generating facilities, it sells power to government agencies, community and private utilities, companies, and neighboring states. Customers include some of the biggest electricity users in the US, such as the New York City government. The New York Power Authority receives no state funds or tax credits. Instead, it finances new projects through bond and note sales. The utility is emphasizing low costs and customer service in preparation for the shift from operating as a regulated monopoly to competing in an open market.

KEY COMPETITORS
Con Edison
Energy East
KeySpan Energy

PRAIRIE FARMS DAIRY INC.

1100 N. Broadway St.
Carlinville, IL 62626
Phone: 217-854-2547
Fax: 217-854-6426
Web site: http://www.prairiefarms.com

CEO: Leonard J. Southwell
CFO: Paul Benne
HR: Kris Rosentreter
Type: Cooperative

1998 Est. Sales: $900.0 million
1-Yr. Sales Change: 1.7%
Employees: 2,200
FYE: September

The bittersweet torture Prairie Farms Dairy inflicts upon the lactose intolerant! One of the largest dairy cooperatives in the Midwest, with about 800 members, Prairie Farms Dairy produces milk, butter, cottage cheese, sour cream, and juices, primarily under the Prairie Farms label. It also makes goodies like ice cream, yogurt, sherbet, and dips. The company's products are sold in stores, schools, and to institutional clients in about a dozen mostly midwestern states. Members receive dividends based on sales. Subsidiary PFD Supply distributes food and paper products to fast-food restaurants, including Burger King and McDonald's.

KEY COMPETITORS
AMPI
Dairy Farmers of America
Land O'Lakes

PRICEWATERHOUSECOOPERS

1301 Avenue of the Americas
New York, NY 10019
Phone: 212-596-7000
Fax: 212-259-1301
Web site: http://www.pwcglobal.com

CEO: James J. Schiro
CFO: Marcia Cohen
HR: William K. O'Brien
Type: Partnership

1999 Sales: $15,300.0 million
1-Yr. Sales Change: 2.0%
Employees: 155,000
FYE: June

PricewaterhouseCoopers, the world's largest accounting, auditing, and consulting firm, was formed from the 1998 merger of Price Waterhouse and Coopers & Lybrand. The firm operates through more than 850 offices in 150 countries. The company's services include auditing, accounting and tax advice, information technology and human resource consulting, and business process outsourcing. It also offers legal services through a network of affiliated law firms. To lower administration costs, the firm is cutting 1,000 jobs; it is also considering dividing its consulting and auditing operations into separate units to assure auditing objectivity.

KEY COMPETITORS
Andersen Worldwide
Ernst & Young
KPMG

See pages 404–405 for a full profile of this company.

PRIMUS, INC.

3110 Kettering Blvd.
Dayton, OH 45439
Phone: 937-294-6878
Fax: 937-293-9591

CEO: Richard W. Schwartz
CFO: Jack W. Johnston
HR: —
Type: Private

1998 Sales: $780.0 million
1-Yr. Sales Change: —
Employees: 2,175
FYE: January

Primus is a major investor in a collection of nearly 400 small wholesale distributors that sell plumbing, heating, air-conditioning, electrical, and other supplies to contractors and other customers. The companies are easily recognizable by their names, which contain the city of operation and a word beginning with the prefix "Win-," such as Columbia Winnelson (plumbing products), Salt Lake Windustrial (pipes and valves), and Dayton Winfastener (specialty fasteners), among others. Primus supports its associated companies with bulk purchasing, warehousing, and data processing. Primus was founded in 1956 by Robert Kuhns, Chairman Richard Schiewetz, and others.

KEY COMPETITORS
Ferguson Enterprises
Hughes Supply
Kohler

THE PRINCIPAL FINANCIAL GROUP

711 High St.
Des Moines, IA 50392
Phone: 515-247-5111
Fax: 515-246-5475
Web site: http://www.principal.com

CEO: David J. Drury
CFO: Michael H. Gersie
HR: Thomas J. Gaard
Type: Mutual company

1998 Sales: $7,697.0 million
1-Yr. Sales Change: (11.2%)
Employees: 16,837
FYE: December

Insurance is a matter of principle for this company. The Principal Financial Group's operating units offer a variety of insurance and financial services. Its flagship company, Principal Life Insurance (The Principal) offers life and health insurance to individuals, groups, and businesses. The company also offers investment services, annuities, online banking, mortgage originations and servicing, institutional asset management, and mutual funds. Principal Financial operates in more than 250 locations across North and South America, Europe, and Asia. In 1998 Principal Financial converted to a mutual holding company.

KEY COMPETITORS
MassMutual
New York Life
Northwestern Mutual

See pages 406–407 for a full profile of this company.

PRINTPACK, INC.

4335 Wendell Dr. SW	CEO: Dennis M. Love	1999 Sales: $845.6 million
Atlanta, GA 30336	CFO: R. Michael Hembree	1-Yr. Sales Change: 1.7%
Phone: 404-691-5830	HR: Nicklas D. Stucky	Employees: 3,600
Fax: 404-699-7122	Type: Private	FYE: June

Printpack wraps its flexible packaging around salty snacks, confections, baked goods, cookies, crackers, and cereal, as well as tissues and paper towels. Printpack's packaging includes plastic film, aluminum foil, metallized and other films, and paper and specialized coatings. Frito-Lay is the company's top customer, with some 15% of sales. Other customers include General Mills, Hershey, Mars, Nabisco, Nestlé, and Quaker Oats. Printpack sells, markets, and services its products through 18 sales offices in the US and one in Mexico. The packaging is manufactured at plants throughout the Mid-Atlantic, the Midwest, and the South. Director Gay Love is the controlling shareholder; several relatives are officers.

KEY COMPETITORS
AEP Industries
DuPont
Ivex Packaging

PRO-FAC COOPERATIVE, INC.

90 Linden Place	CEO: Bruce R. Fox	1998 Sales: $719.7 million
Rochester, NY 14625	CFO: Earl L. Powers	1-Yr. Sales Change: (1.5%)
Phone: 716-383-1850	HR: Lois J. Warlick-Jarvie	Employees: 3,727
Fax: 716-383-1281	Type: Cooperative	FYE: June

Pro-Fac proves that fruits and veggies really do make you big and strong. The co-op's Agrilink Foods subsidiary provides marketing and processing services to more than 600 fruit- and vegetable-growing member/owners nationwide. Agrilink doubled its size when it purchased Birds Eye, Freshlike, and VegAll vegetable operations in 1998 and the Agripac frozen-vegetable business in 1999. Agrilink's Curtice Burns unit makes fruit fillings, vegetables, canned and frozen fruits, and popcorn. Agrilink also includes Nalley Fine Foods (chili, stew, pickles, dressings, syrup, salsa) and a unit that makes potato chips and salty snacks. Formed in 1960, Pro-Fac produces private-label and brand-name foods.

KEY COMPETITORS
Del Monte
Dole
Tri Valley Growers

PROSPECT MOTORS INC.

645 North Hwy. 49 & 88	CEO: William Halvorson	1998 Est. Sales: $1,200.0 million
Jackson, CA 95642	CFO: Steve McCarty	1-Yr. Sales Change: 21.3%
Phone: 209-223-1740	HR: Linda Hamilton	Employees: 75
Fax: 209-223-0395	Type: Private	FYE: May
Web site: http://www.prospectmotors.com		

Your prospects for finding an American-made car are pretty good at Prospect Motors, one of the largest General Motors dealers in the US. Prospect sells new and used Buick, Cadillac, Chevrolet, Oldsmobile, Pontiac, and Toyota cars and trucks throughout California. The company also operates a body shop and parts and service departments and engages in auto leasing. Founded in 1970, the Halvorson family's Prospect Motors has made its name by selling and leasing in bulk — mostly fleet sales and leases to car rental agencies in California and other western states. Prospect also owns Amador Motors dealerships in the California towns of Sutter Creek (Chrysler-Plymouth, Dodge, Jeep-Eagle) and Jackson (Toyota).

KEY COMPETITORS
AutoNation
Penske Automotive
Tuttle-Click

PROVENA HEALTH

9223 W. St. Francis Rd.
Frankfort, IL 60423
Phone: 815-469-4888
Fax: 815-469-4864

CEO: Gerald P. Pearson
CFO: John Naiden
HR: John Landstrom
Type: Not-for-profit

1998 Sales: $688.4 million
1-Yr. Sales Change: 8.6%
Employees: 11,500
FYE: December

To stay competitive in the era of managed care, Provena Health was created from the merger of Illinois Catholic hospital groups Franciscan Sisters Health Care (Frankfort), ServantCor (Kankakee), and Mercy Center for Health Care Services (Aurora). One of the largest health systems in Illinois, Provena has seven hospitals, 14 nursing homes, more than 40 clinics, six home health agencies, and its PersonalCare HMO (co-owned with Christie Clinic). The organization, formed in 1997, plans to invite other hospitals and health care plans to join Provena Health, either as affiliates or as full partners. The company has joined MED3000 Group to form Central Health Solutions, a regional physician management group.

KEY COMPETITORS
Advocate Health Care
Northwestern Healthcare
Rush System for Health

PROVIDENT MUTUAL LIFE INSURANCE COMPANY

1000 Chesterbrook Blvd.
Berwyn, PA 19312
Phone: 610-889-1717
Fax: 610-407-1322
Web site: http://www.providentmutual.com

CEO: Robert W. Kloss
CFO: Mary Lynn Finelli
HR: Meg Evangelist
Type: Mutual company

1998 Sales: $747.7 million
1-Yr. Sales Change: 5.5%
Employees: —
FYE: December

Tracing some of its roots nearly 300 years into the past, Provident Mutual Life helps provide for the future. Provident and its affiliates offer life insurance, including traditional and variable life, group pensions, fixed and variable annuities, commercial mortgage lending, and real estate sales. The firm markets its products through about 750 career agents and 2,100 personal producing general agents as well as independent agencies nationwide. Although currently a mutual, Provident owns a stock subsidiary, PLACA, which sells most of the company's individual annuities. The firm itself planned to convert to a mutual holding company structure but a policyholder lawsuit prompted the company to withdraw its plans.

KEY COMPETITORS
MetLife
New York Life
Prudential

THE PRUDENTIAL INSURANCE COMPANY OF AMERICA

751 Broad St.
Newark, NJ 07102
Phone: 973-802-6000
Fax: 973-367-8204
Web site: http://www.prudential.com

CEO: Arthur F. Ryan
CFO: Richard J. Carbone
HR: Michele S. Darling
Type: Mutual company

1998 Sales: $27,087.0 million
1-Yr. Sales Change: (26.9%)
Employees: 50,000
FYE: December

With the financial services world getting a little rocky out there, Prudential Life Insurance is demutualizing. The #1 US life insurer ahead of Metropolitan Life (and #4 worldwide), Prudential offers individual and group life, employee benefits services, and annuities. Its property/casualty lines include homeowners and auto coverage. Known for its Rock of Gibraltar logo, Prudential's reputation in the fast-growing field of asset management and investments has been tarnished by sales scandals. As it repairs the damage (to the tune of more than $2 billion, by some accounts still not enough), the company is chipping away at other business lines, most notably selling its managed health care business to Aetna.

KEY COMPETITORS
Aetna
John Hancock
MetLife

See pages 408–409 for a full profile of this company.

PUBLIX SUPER MARKETS, INC.

1936 George Jenkins Blvd.
Lakeland, FL 33815
Phone: 941-688-1188
Fax: 941-284-5532
Web site: http://www.publix.com

CEO: Howard M. Jenkins
CFO: David P. Phillips
HR: James H. Rhodes
Type: Private

1998 Sales: $12,067.1 million
1-Yr. Sales Change: 7.5%
Employees: 117,000
FYE: December

Shoppers at Publix shouldn't have to worry about being checked out — although with its share of gender and race discrimination lawsuits, they might wonder. Publix Super Markets is one of the nation's largest grocers and is the largest employee-owned supermarket chain. Most of its nearly 600 stores are in Florida, but it also operates in Alabama, Georgia, and South Carolina. Publix produces some of its own deli, bakery, and dairy goods, and many stores offer fresh flowers, housewares, photo processing, and pharmaceutical services. Current and former Publix employees own about 85% of the company, while its officers and directors, including the founding Jenkins family, own the rest.

KEY COMPETITORS
Albertson's
Kroger
Winn-Dixie

 See pages 410–411 for a full profile of this company.

PUEBLO XTRA INTERNATIONAL, INC.

1300 NW 22nd St.
Pompano Beach, FL 33069
Phone: 954-977-2500
Fax: 954-979-5770

CEO: William T. Keon
CFO: —
HR: Ron Ochsenwald
Type: Private

1999 Sales: $784.8 million
1-Yr. Sales Change: (16.4%)
Employees: 5,442
FYE: January

Pueblo Xtra is a leading operator of supermarkets and video rental outlets in Puerto Rico and the US Virgin Islands. Its 50 supermarkets (44 of which are located in Puerto Rico) operate under the Xtra and Pueblo names. In addition, the company holds exclusive rights to operate Blockbuster video stores in Puerto Rico and the US Virgin Islands and has more than 40 Blockbuster stores in these markets. About 45% of the company's video stores are located within its grocery stores. The company also provides its own advertising through wholly owned CaribAd Inc. In 1993 Venezuela-based Cisneros Group acquired Pueblo Xtra, which was founded by Harold Toppel in 1955.

KEY COMPETITORS
Kmart
Walgreen
Wal-Mart

PUERTO RICO ELECTRIC POWER AUTHORITY

Ave. Ponce De Leon 1110
San Juan, PR 00936
Phone: 787-289-3434
Fax: 787-289-4690
Web site: http://www.prepa.com

CEO: Miguel Cordero
CFO: Martin Arroyo
HR: Nydia Verge
Type: Government-owned

1998 Sales: $1,688.0 million
1-Yr. Sales Change: 1.1%
Employees: 10,194
FYE: June

No man is an island, but Puerto Rico Electric Power Authority stands alone on one. The government-owned utility, founded in 1941, is the sole provider of electricity for about 1.3 million customers. Puerto Rico Electric's generating capacity of nearly 4,400 MW is produced primarily from fuel oil at four steam plants and a combustion turbines plant. Because the utility is isolated from other providers and often faces weather problems, it maintains a higher-than-average reserve of power. In order to keep up with increasing demand, Puerto Rico Electric is developing projects with private sector cogenerators.

PURITY WHOLESALE GROCERS INC.

5400 Broken Sound Blvd. NW, Ste. 100
Boca Raton, FL 33487
Phone: 561-994-9360
Fax: 561-241-4628
Web site: http://www.pwg-inc.com

CEO: Jeff Levitetz
CFO: Alan Rutner
HR: Karen McGrath
Type: Private

1999 Sales: $1,500.0 million
1-Yr. Sales Change: 25.0%
Employees: 650
FYE: June

You want it cheap? Purity Wholesale Grocers (PWG) wants you to have it cheap. The alternate source supplier buys grocery products and sells them to retailers at competitive prices. Founded in 1982, PWG distributes grocery (including frozen foods and candy), health and beauty care, and pharmaceutical products to grocery and drug retailers and wholesalers across the US. Its operations — located in Arizona, California, Colorado, Florida, Illinois, Indiana, Michigan, and Tennessee — include independently operated Altitude Wholesale, Creative Distribution, American Wholesale Grocers, and Supreme Distributors. Targeting companies like these, founder and owner Jeff Levitetz is expanding PWG through acquisitions.

KEY COMPETITORS
Fleming Companies
Nash Finch
SUPERVALU

QUAD/GRAPHICS, INC.

W224 N3322 DuPlainville Rd.
Pewaukee, WI 53072
Phone: 414-566-6000
Fax: 414-691-7814
Web site: http://www.qg.com

CEO: Harry V. Quadracci
CFO: John C. Fowler
HR: Emmy M. LaBode
Type: Private

1998 Sales: $1,400.0 million
1-Yr. Sales Change: 16.7%
Employees: 11,000
FYE: December

Quad/Graphics doesn't print money, it makes money by printing — catalogs, magazines, books, direct mail, and other items. The company is the largest private printer in the US. It offers a full range of services, including design, photography, desktop production, printing, binding, wrapping, and (through subsidiary Parcel/Direct) distribution and transportation. At some 18 facilities — six of which are in Wisconsin — the company prints catalogs for Lillian Vernon and Hanover Direct, among others, as well as books for publishers such as McGraw-Hill and periodicals including *Time*, *Newsweek*, and *Wired*. Founder and president Harry Quadracci and company employees own Quad/Graphics.

KEY COMPETITORS
Dai Nippon Printing
Quebecor Printing
R. R. Donnelley

 See pages 412–413 for a full profile of this company.

QUALITY KING DISTRIBUTORS INC.

2060 9th Ave.
Ronkonkoma, NY 11779
Phone: 516-737-5555
Fax: 516-439-2222

CEO: Bernard Nussdorf
CFO: Dennis Barkley
HR: David Negron
Type: Private

1999 Est. Sales: $1,200.0 million
1-Yr. Sales Change: (14.3%)
Employees: 1,000
FYE: October

Quality King Distributors rules a gargantuan gray market empire, buying US name-brand products that have been exported to overseas markets, re-importing them, and then selling them at below suggested retail prices. The practice is deeply disliked by US manufacturers, but its legality has been upheld by the Supreme Court. Quality King distributes drugs, cosmetics, fragrances, and groceries to retailers throughout the US. Customers include pharmacy and grocery chains, grocery distributors, wholesale clubs, and discounters. Chief Executive Bernard Nussdorf founded Quality King in 1960 in Queens, New York; the Nussdorf family still owns the company.

KEY COMPETITORS
Bindley Western
Cardinal Health
McKesson HBOC

QUEXCO INCORPORATED

2777 Stemmons Fwy.
Dallas, TX 75207
Phone: 214-631-6070
Fax: 214-631-4013

CEO: Howard M. Meyers
CFO: William Haberberger
HR: —
Type: Private

1997 Sales: $2,000.0 million
1-Yr. Sales Change: 100.0%
Employees: 7,000
FYE: December

Quexco gets the lead out and puts it back in. A leading secondary lead producer, this private holding company recycles scrapped lead acid-batteries into refined lead and lead products. Quexco's RSR unit is one of the largest lead smelters in the US (trailing battery maker Exide, a former maker of Sears' DieHard batteries). Quexco also owns Eco-Bat Technologies, one of Europe's largest lead smelters. Additionally, the company is one of California's two lead-smelting operations. Quexco's attempt to buy industrial and automotive battery maker GNB Technologies from Australia-based Pacific Dunlop has fallen through despite lengthy negotiations.

KEY COMPETITORS
Exide
Johnson Controls
METALEUROP

QUIKTRIP CORPORATION

901 N. Mingo Rd.
Tulsa, OK 74116
Phone: 918-836-8551
Fax: 918-834-4117
Web site: http://www.quiktrip.com

CEO: Chester Cadieux
CFO: Terry Carter
HR: Jim Denny
Type: Private

1999 Sales: $1,804.0 million
1-Yr. Sales Change: (1.4%)
Employees: 4,796
FYE: April

QuikTrip provides a quick fix for people on the go. QuikTrip owns and operates 330 gasoline and convenience stores in Georgia, Illinois, Iowa, Kansas, Missouri, Nebraska, and Oklahoma. The company's Fleetmaster program offers commercial fueling companies detailed weekly or monthly reports showing the type of products used, amounts spent, and odometer readings; it promises savings of as much as 15% on total expenses. QuikTrip supplies its stores with its own Quick 'n Tasty food brands. QuikTrip was founded in 1958 by Chairman and CEO Chester Cadieux and partners. To differentiate his stores from the competition, Cadieux focuses on keeping stores attractive and prices low.

KEY COMPETITORS
Hale-Halsell
Phillips Petroleum
Texaco

RACETRAC PETROLEUM, INC.

300 Technology Ct.
Smyrna, GA 30082
Phone: 770-431-7600
Fax: 770-431-7612
Web site: http://www.racetrac.com

CEO: Carl E. Bolch
CFO: Robert J. Dumbacher
HR: Bob Stier
Type: Private

1998 Est. Sales: $1,500.0 million
1-Yr. Sales Change: 49.2%
Employees: 3,800
FYE: December

RaceTrac Petroleum hopes it is a popular pit stop for gasoline and snacks in the Southeast. The company operates more than 450 company-owned and franchised gas stations and convenience stores in Alabama, Arkansas, Florida, Georgia, Kentucky, Louisiana, Mississippi, North Carolina, South Carolina, Tennessee, Texas, and Virginia. Carl Bolch founded RaceTrac in Missouri in 1934. His son, chairman and CEO Carl Bolch Jr., moved the company into high-volume gas stations with long self-service islands that can serve many vehicles at once. RaceTrac's convenience stores also sell fresh deli food, rent videos, and offer some fast-food fare. The Bolch family owns the company.

KEY COMPETITORS
Exxon Mobil
Motiva Enterprises
Tosco

RALEY'S INC.

500 W. Capitol Ave.
West Sacramento, CA 95605
Phone: 916-373-3333
Fax: 916-444-3733
Web site: http://www.raleys.com

CEO: Michael J. Teel
CFO: William Anderson
HR: Sam McPherson
Type: Private

1999 Sales: $3,000.0 million
1-Yr. Sales Change: 36.8%
Employees: 15,000
FYE: June

Raley's has to stock fresh fruit and great wines — it sells to the people who produce them. The company operates about 150 supermarkets and larger-sized superstores, mostly in Northern California, but also in Nevada and New Mexico. In addition to its flagship Raley's Superstores, the company operates Bel Air Markets, Nob Hill Foods (an upscale Bay Area chain), and a discount warehouse chain, Food Source. The company recently reopened 27 stores purchased from rival Albertson's. Raley's stores typically offer groceries, natural foods, liquor, and pharmacies. Founded during the Depression by Tom Raley, the company is owned by Raley's daughter, Joyce Raley Teel, and run by Raley family members.

KEY COMPETITORS

Albertson's
Safeway
Save Mart Supermarkets

RAND MCNALLY & COMPANY

8255 N. Central Park Ave.
Skokie, IL 60076
Phone: 847-329-8100
Fax: 847-329-6361
Web site: http://www.randmcnally.com

CEO: Richard J. Davis
CFO: Larry Gyenes
HR: Mary Lynn Smedinghoff
Type: Private

1998 Est. Sales: $175.0 million
1-Yr. Sales Change: 0.0%
Employees: 1,000
FYE: December

The art of cartography is alive and well at mapmaker extraordinaire Rand McNally. The largest commercial mapmaker in the world, the company is famous for its flagship *Rand McNally Road Atlas*, but it also produces travel-related software (*TripMaker, StreetFinder*) and educational products for classrooms. The company has 22 retail travel stores across the US, offers custom cartographic services, and makes mileage and routing software for the transportation industry. Rand McNally, founded in 1856, was owned by the McNally family until AEA Investors bought a controlling interest in 1997.

KEY COMPETITORS

AAA
Michelin
National Geographic

 See pages 414–415 for a full profile of this company.

RANDALL'S FOOD MARKETS, INC.

3663 Briarpark
Houston, TX 77042
Phone: 713-268-3500
Fax: 713-268-3602
Web site: http://www.randalls.com

CEO: Frank Lazaran
CFO: —
HR: Judy Ward
Type: Subsidiary

1999 Sales: $2,585.1 million
1-Yr. Sales Change: 6.9%
Employees: 17,650
FYE: June

How do you become one of the largest regional supermarket chains in the US with stores in only a few areas of a single state? Locate them in the big state of Texas, as has Randall's Food Markets. The company, which is a subsidiary of supermarket giant Safeway, operates more than 115 stores under the names Randalls (in Houston and Austin) and Tom Thumb and Simon David (in the Dallas/Fort Worth metro area). Most of its stores are in the more well-off areas of those cities and are combination food stores and drugstores that offer amenities like video rentals and bakeries. Investment firm Kohlberg Kravis Roberts, which owned 62% of the chain, now has a 7% stake in Safeway.

KEY COMPETITORS

Albertson's
H-E-B
Kroger

See pages 416–417 for a full profile of this company.

R. B. PAMPLIN CORPORATION

900 SW 5th Ave., Ste. 1800	CEO: Robert B. Pamplin	1999 Sales: $844.0 million
Portland, OR 97204	CFO: David Hastings	1-Yr. Sales Change: 0.1%
Phone: 503-248-1133	HR: —	Employees: 7,500
Fax: 503-248-1175	Type: Private	FYE: May

Founded by a man of the cloth, the R. B. Pamplin companies have a range of interests, from textiles, gravel, and concrete to Christian multimedia and retail stores that offer foods and handcrafted goods from the Northwest. The company's Mount Vernon Mills is one of the largest denim producers in the US. Its Christian entertainment division produces books, music, and videos; has expanded into radio in Washington and Oregon; and even produces a traveling roadshow called *Bibleman*. The Pamplin family has restored their ancestral antebellum plantation and created the Pamplin Historical Park in Virginia to commemorate soldiers of the Civil War. R. B. Pamplin is owned and run by father and son Robert Pamplin Sr. and Jr.

KEY COMPETITORS
Avondale Incorporated
Cone Mills
Galey & Lord

RED APPLE GROUP, INC.

823 11th Ave.	CEO: John A. Catsimatidis	1999 Est. Sales: $820.0 million
New York, NY 10019	CFO: Stuart Spivak	1-Yr. Sales Change: (3.5%)
Phone: 212-956-5803	HR: John Geidea	Employees: 3,200
Fax: 212-262-4979	Type: Private	FYE: February

Red Apple Group sells apples (and more) in the Big Apple. Most of the Gotham-based company's sales come from subsidiary United Refining, which produces about 100,000 barrels a day of oil and distributes it to its 350 convenience stores in New York, Pennsylvania, and Ohio. The company controls Gristede's Foods, the operator of about 40 supermarkets under the names Sloan's and Gristede's in New York City and the surrounding area. Red Apple Group has real estate operations in New York, Florida, and the Virgin Islands. Chairman, president, and CEO John Catsimatidis owns Red Apple Group; he started the company with one Red Apple grocery in 1971.

KEY COMPETITORS
Grand Union
King Kullen Grocery
Pathmark

REGAL CINEMAS, INC.

7132 Commercial Park Dr.	CEO: Michael L. Campbell	1998 Sales: $707.0 million
Knoxville, TN 37918	CFO: D. Mark Monroe	1-Yr. Sales Change: 47.6%
Phone: 423-922-1123	HR: Randy Smith	Employees: 12,000
Fax: 423-922-6739	Type: Private	FYE: December
Web site: http://www.regalcinemas.com		

Regal Cinemas is the king of the world of movie theater chains. The company has more than 4,100 screens at about 430 theaters in more than 30 states. Regal operates mostly multiplex theaters in midsized urban and suburban locales. The company also operates a handful of IMAX 3D theaters at select multiplexes and several FunScapes entertainment centers, which house movie theaters, miniature golf courses, video games, and other family-oriented entertainment devices under the same roof. Regal Cinemas is owned by investment firms Kohlberg Kravis Roberts (KKR) and Hicks, Muse, Tate & Furst. (KKR's Act III chain merged with Regal in 1998.)

KEY COMPETITORS
AMC Entertainment
Carmike Cinemas
Loews Cineplex Entertainment

RENCO GROUP INC.

30 Rockefeller Plaza	CEO: Ira L. Rennert	1999 Sales: $2,500.0 million
New York, NY 10112	CFO: Roger L. Fay	1-Yr. Sales Change: (2.0%)
Phone: 212-541-6000	HR: —	Employees: 15,000
Fax: 212-541-6197	Type: Private	FYE: October
Web site: http://www.hummer.com		

Renco Group is a holding company for a diverse group of companies. Its AM General subsidiary makes the HUMVEE, an extra-wide, all-terrain vehicle used by the military, and the HUMVEE's civilian counterpart, the HUMMER. Renco Steel and WCI Steel manufacture, fabricate, and distribute steel. Other companies include Doe Run, the #2 smelter of lead in the world; Rencoal, which mines coal; lumber company R. L. Sweet Lumber; and Consolidated Sewing Machine, which makes industrial sewing machines. Renco was established in 1980 and is owned by industrialist Ira Rennert, a former business consultant and a featured subject in a recent film, *The Awful Truth*, by Michael Moore of *Roger and Me* acclaim.

KEY COMPETITORS
Oshkosh Truck
Singer
USX-U.S. Steel

REPUBLIC TECHNOLOGIES INTERNATIONAL, LLC

3770 Embassy Pkwy.	CEO: Thomas N. Tyrrell	1998 Sales: $802.6 million
Akron, OH 44333	CFO: John B. George	1-Yr. Sales Change: 6.5%
Phone: 330-670-3000	HR: Stanley M. Savukas	Employees: 3,868
Fax: 330-670-3106	Type: Private	FYE: June
Web site: http://www.republictech.com		

Republic Technologies International makes high-purity steel bars and wire rods. Its two divisions — hot rolled and cold finished — develop progressively higher quality steel bars used in the manufacture of automobiles, appliances, hand and machine tools, pumps and valves, and many other products. Republic Technologies operates 14 plants in the eastern US and Canada. The company was forged by combining Republic Engineered Steels, Bar Technologies (together owned by investors The Blackstone Group and Veritas Capital Management), and a joint venture of USX-U.S. Steel and Kobe Steel. Investors Blackstone and Veritas own 64% of Republic Technologies, Kobe and USX own 15% each, and other investors own 6%.

KEY COMPETITORS
Birmingham Steel
Nucor
Quanex

RGIS INVENTORY SPECIALISTS

805 Oakwood Dr.	CEO: Raymond J. Nicholson	1998 Est. Sales: $750.0 million
Rochester, MI 48307	CFO: Mark Papak	1-Yr. Sales Change: 7.1%
Phone: 248-651-2511	HR: Susan Kingman	Employees: 35,000
Fax: 248-651-6787	Type: Private	FYE: December
Web site: http://www.rgisinv.com		

With RGIS Inventory Specialists, you can count on a lot of counting. The company is the largest third-party inventory taker in the US, with about 30,000 employees in 300 offices in North America, Brazil, and Puerto Rico. RGIS uses largely part-time employees who work at night to count inventory for its customers, which are primarily large retailers. Using scanners to send information to a sophisticated computer system at RGIS headquarters, the company can take an inventory in the evening and deliver a report to its customer the next morning. The company, whose name stands for "Retail Grocery Inventory Services," was founded in 1958 by Thomas Nicholson, whose family still controls the company.

RICELAND FOODS, INC.

2120 S. Park Ave.
Stuttgart, AR 72160
Phone: 870-673-5500
Fax: 870-673-5530
Web site: http://www.riceland.com

CEO: Richard E. Bell
CFO: Harry E. Loftis
HR: Linda Dobrovich
Type: Cooperative

1998 Sales: $803.9 million
1-Yr. Sales Change: (7.4%)
Employees: 1,850
FYE: July

Riceland Foods is ingrained in the marketing and milling business. Started in 1921, the co-op markets rice, soybeans, wheat, and feed grains grown by its more than 10,000 member-owners in Arkansas, Louisiana, Missouri, Mississippi, and Texas. Riceland Foods is the world's largest miller and marketer of rice. It sells long grain, brown, wild, and flavored rice (under the Riceland name as well as private labels) to consumers and food service customers. The co-op also sells Chef-way oil and shortening products and processes soybeans, edible oils, and lecithin. The co-op markets its products throughout the US and internationally, mainly in the Caribbean, Mexico, the Middle East, South Africa, and Western Europe.

KEY COMPETITORS
American Rice
Mars
Riviana Foods

RICH PRODUCTS CORP.

1150 Niagara St.
Buffalo, NY 14213
Phone: 716-878-8000
Fax: 716-878-8765
Web site: http://www.richs.com

CEO: Robert E. Rich
CFO: James Haddad
HR: Brian Townson
Type: Private

1998 Sales: $1,400.0 million
1-Yr. Sales Change: 7.7%
Employees: 6,000
FYE: December

Starting in 1945 with "the miracle cream from the soya bean," Rich Products has grown from a niche maker of soy-based whipped toppings and frozen desserts to a major US frozen foods manufacturer. Since the 1960s the company has developed new products, such as Coffee Rich (nondairy coffee creamer), and expanded through acquisitions to include frozen bakery and pizza doughs and ingredients for the food service and in-store bakery markets. Rich Products distributes its products in more than 50 countries, with operations in China, South Africa, and Mexico. The company, owned and operated by the founding Rich family, also owns the Wichita Wranglers and Buffalo Bisons minor league baseball teams.

KEY COMPETITORS
ConAgra
Dean Foods
International Multifoods

RITZ CAMERA CENTERS

6711 Ritz Way
Beltsville, MD 20705
Phone: 301-419-0000
Fax: 301-419-2995
Web site: http://www.ritzcamera.com

CEO: David Ritz
CFO: —
HR: Alan MacDonald
Type: Private

1998 Sales: $650.0 million
1-Yr. Sales Change: 4.0%
Employees: 6,500
FYE: December

Picture this: the US's largest photo-specialty chain with more than 1,000 stores in 47 states and the District of Columbia that provide one-hour photofinishing, digital imaging, and other services. Although most of the company's offerings are photo-related (cameras, frames, film, video cameras), Ritz Camera Centers also sells binoculars and cellular phones, among other items. Its stores operate under the Ritz Camera Center and The Camera Shop names; the company also sells online. Subsidiary Boater's World Marine Centers has over 90 stores nationwide that feature lures, rods, reels, electronics, clothing, watersport supplies, and other supplies. President and CEO David Ritz owns Ritz, which was founded in 1918.

KEY COMPETITORS
Walgreen
West Marine
Wolf Camera

RIVERWOOD INTERNATIONAL CORPORATION

3350 Riverwood Pkwy. Ste. 1400
Atlanta, GA 30339
Phone: 770-644-3000
Fax: 770-644-2962
Web site: http://www.riverwood.com

CEO: Stephen M. Humphrey
CFO: Daniel J. Blount
HR: Robert H. Burg
Type: Private

1998 Sales: $1,135.6 million
1-Yr. Sales Change: (0.3%)
Employees: 4,200
FYE: December

Riverwood International is a CUK above the rest. The company is one of only two major producers of coated unbleached kraft (CUK) paperboard for packaged goods (Mead is the other). The company makes CUK board for packaging beverages (carrierboard) and consumer products (folding cartons). Its products are used by PepsiCo, Sara Lee, and others under brands such as Aqua-Kote. Most of the cartonboard is sold to independent packagers, and most of the carrierboard is used in an integrated operation in which the company creates proprietary packaging for use with its proprietary packaging machinery. Riverwood International has 10 CUK board processing plants. The company sells worldwide.

KEY COMPETITORS
Mead
Smurfit-Stone Container
Sonoco Products

THE ROCKEFELLER FOUNDATION

420 5th Ave.
New York, NY 10018
Phone: 212-869-8500
Fax: 212-764-3468
Web site: http://www.rockfound.org

CEO: Gordon Conway
CFO: Sally Ferris
HR: Charlotte N. Church
Type: Foundation

1998 Sales: $388.3 million
1-Yr. Sales Change: (23.9%)
Employees: 150
FYE: December

The Rockefeller Foundation — one of the world's oldest private charitable organizations — supports grants, fellowships, and conferences that focus on activities in the arts and humanities as well as on equal opportunity. Its science-based programs concentrate on reducing poverty, disease, hunger, and illiteracy. Other initiatives include work on population control (family planning, curbing of unwanted pregnancies) and large-scale vaccination programs. Its arts and humanities programs focus on promoting international and intercultural understanding in the US. Programs for equal opportunity provide litigation and advocacy support, activities that sometimes have made the foundation a target of political attacks.

 See pages 418–419 for a full profile of this company.

ROLL INTERNATIONAL CORPORATION

11444 W. Olympic Blvd., 10th Fl.
Los Angeles, CA 90064
Phone: 310-966-5700
Fax: 310-914-4747

CEO: Stewart A. Resnick
CFO: Robert A. Kors
HR: —
Type: Private

1998 Sales: $1,570.0 million
1-Yr. Sales Change: 3.9%
Employees: 7,500
FYE: December

Churning out collectible family heirlooms (or flea market fodder) is the primary business of Stewart and Lynda Resnick's Roll International. The centerpiece of the Resnicks' empire is The Franklin Mint, the world's largest collectibles company, with operations in more than 15 countries. The Franklin Mint sells goods by mail order, through its Web site, and in company-owned and independent retail stores. It also operates The Franklin Mint Museum, which has displayed such authentic items as a Jacqueline Kennedy Onassis necklace and a Princess Diana gown. Other Roll operations include Paramount Farms (pistachios), Paramount Citrus (citrus products), and Teleflora (floral delivery service).

KEY COMPETITORS
Enesco Group
FTD
Sun-Diamond Growers

 See pages 420–421 for a full profile of this company.

ROOMS TO GO

11540 Hwy. 92 East
Seffner, FL 33584
Phone: 813-623-5400
Fax: 813-620-1717
Web site: http://www.roomstogo.com

CEO: Jeffrey Seaman
CFO: Larry Schwartz
HR: Linda Garcia
Type: Private

1998 Est. Sales: $720.0 million
1-Yr. Sales Change: 20.0%
Employees: 3,500
FYE: December

Need that sofa, recliner, table, and lamp in a hurry? Rooms To Go, with more than 70 stores in Florida, Georgia, North Carolina, South Carolina, and Tennessee, markets its limited selection of furniture to brand-conscious, time-pressed customers. It packages low- to moderately priced furniture and accessories and offers discounts for those willing to buy a roomful. Rooms To Go also operates a Rooms to Go Kids chain with about 15 stores in the Southeast. Rooms To Go has opened a store in Japan and plans to open about 10 more by the end of 2000. CEO and owner Jeffrey Seaman and his father, Morty, founded the firm in 1990 after selling Seaman Furniture Company.

KEY COMPETITORS
Heilig-Meyers
Levitz
Sears

ROONEY BROTHERS

111 W. 5th St., Ste. 1000
Tulsa, OK 74103
Phone: 918-583-6900
Fax: 918-592-4334
Web site: http://www.mccbuilds.com

CEO: Timothy P. Rooney
CFO: Kevin Moore
HR: Brenda Johns
Type: Private

1999 Sales: $925.0 million
1-Yr. Sales Change: 20.3%
Employees: 2,400
FYE: September

Film star Mickey isn't the only Rooney to have landed big contracts: Rooney Brothers, through its Manhattan Construction unit, built much of the Texas Medical Center in Houston and the George Bush Presidential Library Center in College Station, Texas. Family-owned Rooney Brothers (no connection to Mickey) was organized in 1984 to acquire Manhattan Construction, which was founded by patriarch L.H. Rooney in 1896. Rooney Brothers has expanded operations beyond construction to cover the electronics, lumber, and building-materials fields. In addition to US operations, the company does business in Mexico, the Bahamas, and the Dominican Republic.

KEY COMPETITORS
Austin Industries
Bechtel
Turner Corporation

ROSEBURG FOREST PRODUCTS CO.

Old Hwy. 99 South
Dillard, OR 97432
Phone: 541-679-3311
Fax: 541-679-9683
Web site: http://www.rfpco.com

CEO: Allyn Ford
CFO: Ron Burgess
HR: —
Type: Private

1998 Est. Sales: $850.0 million
1-Yr. Sales Change: 9.7%
Employees: 4,000
FYE: December

With roots in a Depression-era sawmill, Roseburg Forest Products is now branching out with more wood products than ever. The privately held timber company, one of the largest in the US, produces specialty panels (melamine, particleboard, and vinyl laminates), plywood products (such as hardwood and concrete forming), and standard lumber products. Roseburg has more than 710,000 acres of land in California and Oregon. The Sierra Club and other groups have been trying to prevent the company from harvesting old growth timber. Roseburg is owned by the heirs of philanthropist Kenneth Ford, who established the Ford Family Foundation, worth $200 million when he died in 1997.

KEY COMPETITORS
Georgia-Pacific Group
Louisiana-Pacific
Weyerhaeuser

ROSENBLUTH INTERNATIONAL

2401 Walnut St.
Philadelphia, PA 19103
Phone: 215-977-4000
Fax: 215-977-4028
Web site: http://www.rosenbluth.com

CEO: Hal F. Rosenbluth
CFO: Robert M. Infarinato
HR: Cecily Carel
Type: Private

1998 Sales: $3,500.0 million
1-Yr. Sales Change: (12.5%)
Employees: 4,500
FYE: December

Rosenbluth International is one of the largest producers of frequent fliers in the US. The company is a leader among US travel agencies. Founded by Marcus Rosenbluth in 1892 to arrange passage to the US for European immigrants, today Rosenbluth handles travel arrangements for some of the biggest names in business. It is owned solely by the Rosenbluth family and serves corporate clients through 1,300 offices in more than 25 countries. Rosenbluth is known for using terms such as "happiness barometer" (employee advisory group) and for testing job applicants for niceness by having them compete in sports. The company's mascot is the salmon, exemplifying its philosophy of "swimming against the current."

KEY COMPETITORS
American Express
Carlson Wagonlit
Japan Travel Bureau

 See pages 422–423 for a full profile of this company.

ROSENTHAL AUTOMOTIVE COMPANIES

1100 S. Glebe Rd.
Arlington, VA 22204
Phone: 703-553-4300
Fax: 703-553-8435
Web site: http://www.rosenthalgroup.com

CEO: Richard Patterson
CFO: Donald B. Bavely
HR: Jerry Griffin
Type: Private

1998 Sales: $823.0 million
1-Yr. Sales Change: 4.7%
Employees: 1,600
FYE: December

A dealer of wheels in a city of wheeler-dealers, Rosenthal Automotive operates about 15 auto dealerships in the Washington, DC, area. Rosenthal's dealerships sell more than 20,000 new cars a year, including Acuras, Chevrolets, Hondas, Hyundais, Jaguars, Mazdas, Nissans, Toyotas, Volkswagens, and Volvos. The company also sells used cars and has wholesale and fleet operations. Chairman and owner Robert Rosenthal founded Rosenthal Automotive in 1954 when he opened his first Chevrolet dealership in Arlington, Virginia. In 1997 Rosenthal joined other dealers in the Washington, DC, area to form Capital Automotive REIT, the first automotive-only real estate investment trust in the US.

KEY COMPETITORS
Brown Automotive
Jim Koons Automotive
Ourisman Automotive

ROSENTHAL GROUP

1370 Broadway
New York, NY 10018
Phone: 212-356-1400
Fax: 212-356-0900
Web site: http://www.rosenthalinc.com

CEO: Stephen J. Rosenthal
CFO: Bob Priser
HR: Phyllis Wilson
Type: Private

1999 Sales: $2,700.0 million
1-Yr. Sales Change: 1,250.0%
Employees: 235
FYE: July

Rosenthal Group won't lend you a hand, but it can loan you a buck. The midsized firm's operations include Rosenthal & Rosenthal Inc. (factoring, or lending against receivables), Rosenthal Mortgage Bankers, Ltd. (real estate lending), and Rosenthal BusinessCredit (asset-based lending). Rosenthal BusinessCredit also engages in secured lending using unconventional collateral such as art works and export factoring for companies engaged in international trade. The company is increasingly blending its asset-based lending and factoring services to better serve its customers. Founded in 1938 by Imre Rosenthal, who remained active in the company until his death in 1997, Rosenthal Group is now headed by his son Stephen.

KEY COMPETITORS
Capital Factors
FINOVA
Heller Financial

ROTARY INTERNATIONAL

1 Rotary Center, 1560 Sherman Ave. Evanston, IL 60201 Phone: 847-866-3000 Fax: 847-866-9732 Web site: http://www.rotary.org	CEO: Carlo Ravizza CFO: Laurie Carami HR: C. Engblom Type: Not-for-profit	1998 Sales: $72.6 million 1-Yr. Sales Change: 1.4% Employees: 400 FYE: June

The members of service organization Rotary International strive to put "Service Above Self." The organization addresses issues such as AIDS, hunger, and polio, and includes about 30,000 clubs across 161 countries with a membership of nearly 1.2 million (predominantly men, although women are its fastest-growing segment). Its not-for-profit Rotary Foundation invests $90 million a year in international education and humanitarian programs (funds are raised through voluntary contributions). Rotary International also sponsors Interact clubs for secondary school students, as well as a network of about 6,500 Rotaract clubs for members ages 18-30. It is governed by a 19-member board and maintains offices worldwide.

 See pages 424–425 for a full profile of this company.

ROUNDY'S, INC.

23000 Roundy Dr. Pewaukee, WI 53072 Phone: 414-547-7999 Fax: 414-547-4540 Web site: http://www.roundys.com	CEO: Gerald F. Lestina CFO: Robert D. Ranus HR: Debra A. Lawson Type: Cooperative	1998 Sales: $2,578.7 million 1-Yr. Sales Change: (1.2%) Employees: 5,193 FYE: December

Roundy's rounds up name-brand and private-label goods and distributes them to about 800 supermarkets and warehouse stores in 12 midwestern and southern states. The company is a wholesale cooperative with nearly 60 members who operate about 120 stores in Wisconsin and Illinois. It also services nearly 700 independent stores (accounting for 50% of sales). In addition, Roundy's owns about 20 food outlets under such names as Pick 'n Save, Mor For Less, and Price Less. The Pick 'n Save chain (which also includes independents) is Milwaukee's #1 food retailer. Roundy's offers its members and customers a host of support services. Co-op members own about 72% of the company; employees and other investors own the rest.

KEY COMPETITORS
A&P
Fleming Companies
SUPERVALU

 See pages 426–427 for a full profile of this company.

ROYSTER-CLARK, INC.

409 Main St. Tarboro, NC 27886 Phone: 252-823-2101 Fax: 252-641-9234 Web site: http://www.roysterclark.com	CEO: Francis P. Jenkins CFO: Walter R. Vance HR: Thomas A. Ergish Type: Private	1998 Est. Sales: $1,100.0 million 1-Yr. Sales Change: — Employees: 2,650 FYE: December

To grow a good crop, many farmers rely on a good rain and a lot of help from Royster-Clark, producer of fertilizer, seed, crop nutrients, pesticides, and herbicides. The company also provides crop management, blending, spreading, and delivery services. The crop management services use global positioning satellite systems and software to provide statistics on crop yields, as well as satellite-linked equipment that can apply precise amounts of fertilizer or crop-protection products to a particular site. Royster-Clark's genetically engineered seeds include Roundup Ready soybeans. The company has more than 330 retail supply and service centers in seven states in the southeastern US, and it distributes to 27 states.

KEY COMPETITORS
Agrium
IMC Global
Terra Industries

RTM RESTAURANT GROUP

5995 Barfield Rd.
Atlanta, GA 30328
Phone: 404-256-4900
Fax: 404-256-7277

CEO: Russell V. Umphenour
CFO: Doug Benham
HR: Sharron Barton
Type: Private

1999 Sales: $664.0 million
1-Yr. Sales Change: 24.1%
Employees: 23,000
FYE: May

RTM doesn't do burgers, but it does know where the beef is. RTM Restaurant Group is the largest franchisee of Arby's Roast Beef restaurants, with about 750 units across the US. The company also operates Del Taco and T.J. Cinnamons Classic Bakery locations. Its Winners International unit operates or franchises some 150 Mrs. Winner's Chicken & Biscuits and more than 200 Lee's Famous Recipe Chicken units. RTM, which stands for Results Through Motivation, was founded in 1973 by president and CEO Russ Umphenour, who started his restaurant career as a worker at a Michigan Arby's in 1967. He retains majority ownership in the company.

KEY COMPETITORS
Burger King
Chick-fil-A
Hardee's

RUSH SYSTEM FOR HEALTH

1653 W. Congress Pkwy.
Chicago, IL 60612·
Phone: 312-942-5000
Fax: 312-942-5581
Web site: http://www.rush.edu

CEO: Leo M. Henikoff
CFO: James T. Frankenbach
HR: G. Thomas Ferguson
Type: Not-for-profit

1998 Sales: $1,457.0 million
1-Yr. Sales Change: (2.1%)
Employees: 7,250
FYE: June

Rush System for Health is a Chicago-area comprehensive health care system comprised of eight medical centers and hospitals and four nursing homes. Its cornerstone is the Rush-Presbyterian-St. Luke's Medical Center. The system also operates the 1,500-student Rush University. The company's wholly owned subsidiary, ArcVentures, develops and markets health care products and services throughout the US. In partnership with Loyola University Medical Center and MacNeal Medical Network, Rush System for Health owns RML Specialty Hospital. Rush, which traces its origins back to 1837, has been at its present location since 1875.

KEY COMPETITORS
Advocate Health Care
Covenant Ministries
Northwestern Healthcare

RUSS DARROW GROUP INC.

4524 Dollar Dr.
West Bend, WI 53095
Phone: 414-629-5531
Fax: 414-629-5558
Web site: http://www.russdarrow.com

CEO: Russell Darrow
CFO: Wayne Breitbarth
HR: Deanna Waldera
Type: Private

1997 Sales: $769.0 million
1-Yr. Sales Change: 48.0%
Employees: 800
FYE: December

Russ Darrow Group, Wisconsin's largest car dealer, keeps its customers on the road through 11 new- and used-car dealerships in Wisconsin and Illinois. The company's dealerships sell and lease new cars, minivans, sport utility vehicles, and trucks made by DaimlerChrysler, GM, Honda, Kia, Nissan, and Toyota. The company also performs service and repair work and sells spare parts. Russ Darrow Group gets about 60% of its revenues from its fleet business — one of the highest percentages among US auto dealers. Russ Darrow Jr. was just 25 when he started the company in 1965, using a $50,000 loan from his parents to buy a Chrysler-Plymouth dealership.

KEY COMPETITORS
CarMax
Lupient Automotive
United Auto Group

RUSSELL STOVER CANDIES INC.

4900 Oaks St.
Kansas City, MO 64112
Phone: 816-842-9240
Fax: 816-842-5593

CEO: Thomas S. Ward
CFO: Dick Masinton
HR: Robinn S. Weber
Type: Private

1999 Est. Sales: $620.0 million
1-Yr. Sales Change: 21.6%
Employees: 6,300
FYE: February

For Russell Stover Candies, life is like a . . . chocolate Batman? The largest US maker of boxed chocolates is protecting its sweet position with an army of icons. Facing growing competition as Hershey and Mars enter the boxed-chocolate arena, it is fighting back with the use of licensed images such as Super Heroes, Snoopy, Bugs Bunny, and Barbie. Whitman's Sampler is the firm's #1 product; it also makes Millionaires candies. Boxed treats make up most of its sales, but Russell Stover sells outside the box with bagged Halloween candy. Founded by Russell Stover in 1923, the company is owned by Tom and Scott Ward and their mother and sister. Candies are sold under the Russell Stover, Pangburn's, and Whitman's names.

KEY COMPETITORS
Cadbury Schweppes
Favorite Brands
Hershey

 See pages 428–429 for a full profile of this company.

S. ABRAHAM & SONS, INC.

4001 3 Mile Rd. NW
Walker, MI 49544
Phone: 616-453-6358
Fax: 616-453-9346
Web site: http://www.sasinc.com

CEO: Alan Abraham
CFO: James Leonard
HR: Keith Anderson
Type: Private

1998 Sales: $693.0 million
1-Yr. Sales Change: —
Employees: 1,100
FYE: December

The Internet isn't the only way to expand a business. From a single store, S. Abraham & Sons (SAS) has grown into a regional wholesale food distributor serving 12 midwestern states and some 9,000 locations, including convenience stores and grocers. The company distributes name-brand groceries, health and beauty aids, snacks, store supplies, and tobacco. SAS offers private-label products such as Smart Choice health and beauty aids and Red & White groceries; its fast-food programs include Beantown (coffee), Salubre (pizza), and Subsations (sandwiches). Founded in 1927 by Sleyman Abraham, SAS is now run by two of his grandsons. SAS also provides services such as category management (shelf management).

KEY COMPETITORS
Fleming Companies
McLane
SUPERVALU

SACRAMENTO MUNICIPAL UTILITY DISTRICT

6301 S St.
Sacramento, CA 95817
Phone: 916-452-3211
Fax: 916-732-5835
Web site: http://www.smud.org

CEO: Jan E. Schori
CFO: Gail R. Hullibarger
HR: Shirley Lewis
Type: Government-owned

1998 Sales: $765.7 million
1-Yr. Sales Change: 10.5%
Employees: 2,029
FYE: December

Because it doesn't want its name to be mud, the Sacramento Municipal Utility District (SMUD) is powering up for competition. SMUD, one of largest publicly owned electric utilities in the US, generates power with geothermal energy, natural gas, solar power, water, and wind generation. After the deregulation of California's utilities, SMUD froze its rates through 2001 (with plans to lower them further in 2002), decreased energy delivery time, and allowed other energy providers to sell electricity to its customers. SMUD's "green" programs strive to be more economically and ecologically sound than previous services. It serves residential and industrial customers, including the Sacramento Zoo.

KEY COMPETITORS
Edison International
PG&E

SAFELITE GLASS CORP.

1105 Schrock Rd.
Columbus, OH 43229
Phone: 614-842-3000
Fax: 614-842-3180
Web site: http://www.safelite.com

CEO: John F. Barlow
CFO: Douglas A. Herron
HR: —
Type: Private

1999 Sales: $876.8 million
1-Yr. Sales Change: 310.1%
Employees: 6,300
FYE: March

Safelite AutoGlass repairs shattered dreams — or at least shattered wind-shields. The #1 US auto-glass repair and replacement company has some 75 warehouses that supply a nationwide network of company-owned service centers and independent contractors. Safelite makes windshields at its Kansas and North Carolina facilities. Its aftermarket services include window tinting and sales and installation of sunroofs, windshield wipers, and truck backslider windows. It serves auto dealers, car-rental agencies, and body shops, as well as insurance and fleet companies. Private equity firm Thomas H. Lee Company controls the company, which changed its name from Safelite Glass Corp. following its merger with rival Vistar.

KEY COMPETITORS
Apogee Enterprises
Guardian Industries
PPG

SALT RIVER PROJECT

1521 N. Project Dr.
Tempe, AZ 85281
Phone: 602-236-5900
Fax: 602-236-2170
Web site: http://www.srpnet.com

CEO: William P. Schrader
CFO: Mark B. Bonsall
HR: Kathy Haake
Type: Government-owned

1998 Sales: $1,536.7 million
1-Yr. Sales Change: 5.4%
Employees: 4,098
FYE: April

Salt River Project, the second-largest publicly owned utility in the US (by customers), provides Phoenix with two kinds of currents, electric and water. Electricity comes from the Salt River Agricultural Improvement and Power District, a utility that generates and distributes power to some 650,000 customers. Water comes from the Salt River Valley Water Users' Association, a private corporation founded in 1903 that provides water to Phoenix residents and to agricultural irrigators, dams, canals, and wells in a 240,000-acre service area. The power district, a political subdivision of the State of Arizona, is preparing for competition under a new state law and has established an energy-marketing subsidiary.

KEY COMPETITORS
PacifiCorp
Pinnacle West
UniSource Energy

SALVATION ARMY USA

615 Slaters Ln.
Alexandria, VA 22314
Phone: 703-684-5500
Fax: 703-684-3478
Web site: http://www.salvationarmyusa.org

CEO: Robert A. Watson
CFO: Larry E. Bosh
HR: Myrtle V. Ryder
Type: Not-for-profit

1998 Sales: $2,078.2 million
1-Yr. Sales Change: (17.7%)
Employees: 39,883
FYE: September

The largest civil army in the land, the Salvation Army is some 450,000 strong. Its programs assist alcoholics, drug addicts, battered women, the elderly, the homeless, people with AIDS, prison inmates, teenagers, and the unemployed through a range of services. These include day-care centers, programs for people with disabilities, substance abuse programs, and tutoring for at-risk students. It also provides disaster relief in the US and abroad. The Salvation Army USA is a national unit of the Salvation Army, an international body based in London, which oversees "Army" activities in more than 100 countries.

KEY COMPETITORS
Goodwill

See pages 430–431 for a full profile of this company.

SAMARITAN HEALTH SYSTEM

1441 N. 12th St.
Phoenix, AZ 85006
Phone: 602-495-4000
Fax: 602-495-4728
Web site: http://samaritan.edu

CEO: James C. Crews
CFO: Dave Lantto
HR: Vic Buzachero
Type: Not-for-profit

1998 Sales: $781.9 million
1-Yr. Sales Change: (47.9%)
Employees: 10,000
FYE: December

Samaritan Health System won't desert you. The not-for-profit company operates six Arizona hospitals, including its 714-bed flagship Good Samaritan Regional Medical Center in Phoenix, Desert Samaritan Medical Center in Mesa, and Williams Health Care Center in Williams. The company provides occupational health services, outreach services to homeless youth, and more than $50 million annually in charity care. After merger attempts with other health care operators failed, Samaritan sold two of its hospitals, the Maryvale Samaritan Medical Center in Phoenix and the Havasu Samaritan Regional Hospital in Lake Havasu City, Arizona, to for-profit companies. Samaritan Health System is funded by the Samaritan Foundation.

KEY COMPETITORS
Columbia/HCA
Maricopa Integrated Health
Tenet Healthcare

SAMMONS ENTERPRISES, INC.

5949 Sherry Ln., Ste. 1900
Dallas, TX 75225
Phone: 214-210-5000
Fax: 214-210-5099

CEO: Robert W. Korba
CFO: Joseph A. Ethridge
HR: Carol Cochran
Type: Private

1998 Sales: $1,725.0 million
1-Yr. Sales Change: 9.2%
Employees: 3,250
FYE: December

Sammons Enterprises is still going strong. The diversified holding company's interests include insurance (Midland National Life Insurance and North American Company for Life and Health Insurance), water bottling (Mountain Valley Spring), and distribution of industrial equipment (Briggs Weaver), industrial trucks (Briggs Equipment), and oil field tubular equipment (Vinson Supply). Sammons Enterprises also owns a mortgage company and hotel and tour operations. The company sold its cable television systems in 1995 as the industry moved toward consolidation. The late Charles Sammons, an orphan who became a billionaire philanthropist, founded the company in 1962. His estate still owns the company.

KEY COMPETITORS
McKesson HBOC
MetLife
Prudential

S&P COMPANY

100 Shoreline Hwy., Bldg. B, Ste. 395
Mill Valley, CA 94941
Phone: 415-332-0550
Fax: 415-332-0567

CEO: William M. Bitting
CFO: Barry Harris
HR: —
Type: Private

1999 Sales: $1,200.0 million
1-Yr. Sales Change: 140.0%
Employees: 700
FYE: June

S&P's blue-ribbon days are over. S&P owns Pabst Brewing, whose down-at-the-heels brands include Pabst, Pearl, and Olympia. It added to that bevy of bargain-priced beers with its 1999 purchase of Stroh brands including Schlitz and Old Milwaukee. Pabst has breweries in Pennsylvania, Texas, and Washington state, and in China, but contracts out most production. S&P has been willed to a charitable trust established by the late Paul (founder) and Lydia Kalmanovitz and overseen by William Bitting, former counsel to Howard Hughes. If a challenge to Lydia's will fails and the trust takes ownership of S&P, federal law requires the trust to transfer control of the company within five years.

KEY COMPETITORS
Adolph Coors
Anheuser-Busch
Miller Brewing

See pages 432–433 for a full profile of this company.

SANFORD C. BERNSTEIN & CO., INC.

767 5th Ave.
New York, NY 10153
Phone: 212-486-5800
Fax: 212-756-4455

CEO: Lewis A. Sanders
CFO: Neil Kuttner
HR: Denise Williams
Type: Private

1998 Est. Sales: $820.0 million
1-Yr. Sales Change: —
Employees: 1,200
FYE: December

Read this firm's reports and you may wind up with your toes in the sand and money to burn. Sanford C. Bernstein & Co. is a closely held investment manager and highly regarded research house. With more than $80 billion in assets under management, the company oversees investment portfolios for affluent families, pension funds, and other corporate investors, including such mutual funds as Vanguard Group's Windsor Fund. The company was founded in 1967 by Sanford Bernstein (who died in 1999) to manage discretionary accounts for the wealthy. Its research reports rank alongside those of such powerhouse companies as Goldman Sachs and Salomon Smith Barney. The firm is rumored to be considering an IPO.

KEY COMPETITORS
Goldman Sachs
Merrill Lynch
Salomon Smith Barney Holdings

SARCOM, INC.

8405 Pulsar Place
Columbus, OH 43240
Phone: 614-854-1000
Fax: 614-854-1074
Web site: http://www.sarcom.com

CEO: Randy Wilcox
CFO: Pete Struzzi
HR: Sharon Dunn
Type: Private

1998 Sales: $687.8 million
1-Yr. Sales Change: 72.%
Employees: 2,300
FYE: December

The acronym SITCOM stands for Single Income, Two Children, Oppressive Mortgage. SARCOM stands for information technology services, hoping to satisfy your computer needs. The company offers consulting and engineering services, procures hardware and software, and designs and implements networks. It also supports company Internet/intranet applications, manages projects, provides technology staffing, training and education, licenses software, and rents and leases systems. SARCOM has helped Cincinnati schools switch from a paper-based spreadsheet inventory of textbooks to a computerized system. The company is expanding its technological capabilities through acquisitions in the mid-Atlantic and West Coast regions.

KEY COMPETITORS
En Pointe
Hartford Computer
InaCom

SAS INSTITUTE INC.

SAS Campus Dr.
Cary, NC 27513
Phone: 919-677-8000
Fax: 919-677-4444
Web site: http://www.sas.com

CEO: James H. Goodnight
CFO: David Davis
HR: David Russo
Type: Private

1998 Sales: $871.4 million
1-Yr. Sales Change: 16.2%
Employees: 5,400
FYE: December

SAS Institute, the world's largest privately held software company, has about 3.5 million users in roughly 120 countries. Its statistical analysis system (SAS) software enables users to extract, manage, and analyze large volumes of data. The company also provides software packages for companies in major industries — banking, manufacturing, and government — to ease tasks including financial reporting and consolidation, clinical trials analysis, and information technology service management. Founded in 1976, SAS Institute boasts a 98% license renewal rate among its customers. Its employee turnover is only about 4% (the industry average is 20%) amid perks that include free M&Ms for employees every Wednesday.

KEY COMPETITORS
Oracle
SAP
SPSS

 See pages 434–435 for a full profile of this company.

SAVE MART SUPERMARKETS

1800 Standiford Ave.	CEO: Robert M. Piccinini	1999 Sales: $1,452.0 million
Modesto, CA 95350	CFO: Ron Riesenbeck	1-Yr. Sales Change: 11.7%
Phone: 209-577-1600	HR: Mike Silveira	Employees: 7,200
Fax: 209-577-3857	Type: Private	FYE: March

Save Mart Supermarkets operates more than 100 grocery stores in Northern and Central California. Its stores include supermarkets, superstores, and warehouse stores, operating under the S-Mart, Save Mart, and Food Maxx names. Save Mart Supermarkets also owns SMART Refrigerated Transport and Yosemite Wholesale (a distribution warehouse) and is a partner in Super Store Industries, which operates a dairy and an ice-cream plant. The company also sponsors the NASCAR Save Mart-Kragen 300 run held annually at Point Raceway in Sonoma, California. Chairman, president, and CEO Robert Piccinini owns the company, which was founded in 1952 by his father, Mike Piccinini, and uncle, Nick Tocco.

KEY COMPETITORS
Raley's
Rite Aid
Safeway

S.C. JOHNSON & SON, INC.

1525 Howe St.	CEO: William D. Perez	1999 Sales: $4,200.0 million
Racine, WI 53403	CFO: W. Lee McCollum	1-Yr. Sales Change: (16.0%)
Phone: 414-260-2000	HR: Gayle P. Kosterman	Employees: 9,500
Fax: 414-260-2133	Type: Private	FYE: June
Web site: http://www.scjohnsonwax.com		

S.C. Johnson & Son helped consumers move from the flyswatter to the spray can. One of the world's largest makers of consumer chemical products, it makes products for household cleaning, insect control, and storage. Brands include Drano drain cleaner, Glade air freshener, Johnson floor wax, OFF! insect repellent, Pledge furniture polish, Windex window cleaner, and Ziploc plastic bags. It has sold most of its personal care lines. It was the first to sell a water-based insecticide (Raid, 1956). Family-owned S.C. Johnson operates in more than 50 countries. Chairman Samuel Johnson, great-grandson of the founder, and his immediate family own about 60% of the firm; descendants of the founder's daughter own about 40%.

KEY COMPETITORS
Clorox
Procter & Gamble
Unilever

 See pages 436–437 for a full profile of this company.

SCHNEIDER NATIONAL

3101 S. Packerland Dr.	CEO: Donald J. Schneider	1998 Sales: $2,711.0 million
Green Bay, WI 54313	CFO: Tom Gannon	1-Yr. Sales Change: 8.0%
Phone: 920-592-5100	HR: Tim Fliss	Employees: 17,000
Fax: 920-592-3252	Type: Private	FYE: December
Web site: http://www.schneider.com		

Schneider National is the Big Daddy of trucking firms. With its signature bright-orange fleet of more than 12,000 trucks, the company is the largest truckload carrier in the US. Known for using the latest technologies, the company links all its trucks by satellite to enhance scheduling and loading efficiency. Its Schneider Logistics division provides supply chain analysis that allows its US and European clients to ship products more efficiently. The logistics unit works with 1,000 carriers in all modes of transportation. Donald Schneider, whose father founded the company, owns and runs Schneider National.

KEY COMPETITORS
CSX
J. B. Hunt
Werner

See pages 438–439 for a full profile of this company.

SCHNUCK MARKETS, INC.

11420 Lackland Rd.
St. Louis, MO 63146
Phone: 314-994-9900
Fax: 314-994-4465
Web site: http://www.schnucks.com

CEO: Craig D. Schnuck
CFO: Todd R. Schnuck
HR: William Jones
Type: Private

1999 Est. Sales: $2,010.0 million
1-Yr. Sales Change: 11.7%
Employees: 16,000
FYE: October

As often as the Three Stooges' Curly says nyuk, nyuk, nyuk, food shoppers in the St. Louis area say Schnuck, Schnuck, Schnuck. The area's #1 food chain, Schnuck Markets operates more than 90 stores, mostly in the St. Louis area, but also in other parts of Missouri and in Illinois and Indiana. All stores offer a full line of groceries, and most have pharmacies, video-rental outlets, and florist shops. Although most stores operate under the Schnuck banner, the company also runs three Logli supermarkets. Like home-delivery service Peapod (not offered in St. Louis), Schnuck Markets allows shoppers to purchase groceries via the Internet. Founded in 1939, the company is owned by the Schnuck family.

KEY COMPETITORS
Dierbergs Markets
Eagle Food
Hy-Vee

SCHOTTENSTEIN STORES CORPORATION

1800 Moler Rd.
Columbus, OH 43207
Phone: 614-221-9200
Fax: 614-449-0403

CEO: Jay Schottenstein
CFO: Tom Ketteler
HR: Gayle Walraven
Type: Private

1999 Est. Sales: $1,480.0 million
1-Yr. Sales Change: 64.4%
Employees: 6,820
FYE: July

Schottenstein Stores is where the Schottenstein family stores its retail holdings. The firm itself, family members, and related holding companies and foundations collectively own interests in a host of retail businesses. These include about 60% of Value City Department Stores (about 140 US stores); Value City Furniture (70 stores in the Midwest, Northeast, and Mid-Atlantic regions); 46% of casual-clothing chain American Eagle Outfitters (nearly 400 mall stores); 53% of midwestern department store operator Crowley, Milner and Company; and retail liquidator Schottenstein Bernstein Capital Group. The firm owns 50 shopping centers; its offer to buy Burnham Pacific Properties, a shopping mall REIT, has been rejected.

KEY COMPETITORS
The Gap
Heilig-Meyers
Wal-Mart

SCHREIBER FOODS, INC.

425 Pine St.
Green Bay, WI 54301
Phone: 920-437-7601
Fax: 920-437-1617
Web site: http://www.sficorp.com

CEO: John C. Meng
CFO: Bryan Liddy
HR: Jeff Ottum
Type: Private

1999 Est. Sales: $1,160.0 million
1-Yr. Sales Change: 5.5%
Employees: 2,600
FYE: September

If you order cheese on that burger, it's likely you're going to get a taste of Schreiber Foods. Founded in 1945, the employee-owned company is one of the largest processors of cheese in the US, supplying about 90% of the cheese used by fast-food restaurants on hamburgers. Schreiber Foods also supplies process, natural, and substitute cheese to grocery stores, delicatessens, schools, food distributors, and institutional clients. Brands include American Heritage, Cache Valley, and Clearfield. Subsidiary Green Bay Machinery makes equipment that slices cheese and packages individually wrapped slices. Its Arden International Kitchens unit makes frozen entrees.

KEY COMPETITORS
AMPI
Dairy Farmers of America
Great Lakes Cheese

SCHWAN'S SALES ENTERPRISES, INC.

115 W. College Dr.
Marshall, MN 56258
Phone: 507-532-3274
Fax: 507-537-8226
Web site: http://www.schwans.com

CEO: M. Lenny Pippin
CFO: Dan Herrmann
HR: Dave Jennings
Type: Private

1999 Est. Sales: $2,875.0 million
1-Yr. Sales Change: (0.9%)
Employees: 6,000
FYE: December

Frozen pizza is the lifeblood of Schwan's Sales Enterprises. The company's food division makes Tony's, Red Baron, and Freschetta pizzas; it is the #2 frozen pizza maker in the US, behind Kraft Foods. Schwan's is also a top supplier for the institutional frozen pizza market. Perhaps best identified by its fleet of delivery trucks, Schwan's delivers pizzas and 250 other foods, including ice cream, to homes, hospitals, and schools. Orders, some from the Internet, are sent to the closest Schwan's representative for delivery. Schwan's Lyon Financial Services subsidiary runs a group of companies that lease equipment and provide financial services. The secretive family of late founder Marvin Schwan owns the company.

KEY COMPETITORS
Domino's Pizza
Kraft Foods
Pillsbury

 See pages 440–441 for a full profile of this company.

SCIENCE APPLICATIONS INTERNATIONAL CORPORATION

10260 Campus Point Dr.
San Diego, CA 92121
Phone: 858-546-6000
Fax: 858-546-6800
Web site: http://www.saic.com

CEO: J. Robert Beyster
CFO: W. A. Roper
HR: Bernard Theull
Type: Private

1999 Sales: $4,740.4 million
1-Yr. Sales Change: 53.4%
Employees: 35,200
FYE: January

Science Applications International Corporation (SAIC) specializes in technical and R&D services for government and commercial customers. Although about half of the company's sales come from projects for the government (including NASA and the US Departments of Defense, Energy, and Transportation), SAIC is increasing its dependence on such commercial industries as health care, the environment, telecommunications, and information technology. Its subsidiaries include Telcordia Technologies (formerly Bellcore, research arm of the regional Bells); SAIC also owns a majority stake in Network Solutions, the company that once assigned Internet addresses. Employees own more than 90% of the company.

KEY COMPETITORS
Computer Sciences
EDS
IBM

 See pages 442–443 for a full profile of this company.

THE SCOULAR COMPANY

2027 Dodge St.
Omaha, NE 68102
Phone: 402-342-3500
Fax: 402-342-5568
Web site: http://www.scoular.com

CEO: Duane A. Fischer
CFO: Timothy J. Regan
HR: Georgia Glass
Type: Private

1999 Sales: $1,729.0 million
1-Yr. Sales Change: 7.7%
Employees: 400
FYE: May

Agriculture is at the root of all of Scoular's businesses. The company is best known for grain marketing, trading more than 400 million bushels of grain and about 1.1 million tons of by-products (used for animal feed) annually throughout North America. Other divisions offer commodity marketing, fishmeal products for aquaculture, truck brokering, livestock marketing (Hackney Ag), and grain elevator services across Nebraska, which is how the company began in the 1890s. The employee-owned company has facilities throughout the nation, with operations in 14 states and in Mexico and Canada.

KEY COMPETITORS
Bartlett & Company
Cargill
ConAgra

SCRIPPSHEALTH

4275 Campus Point Ct.
San Diego, CA 92121
Phone: 858-678-7000
Fax: 858-678-6558
Web site: http://www.scrippshealth.org

CEO: Ames Early
CFO: Edson Rood
HR: Claudia Mazanec
Type: Not-for-profit

1998 Sales: $653.3 million
1-Yr. Sales Change: 6.1%
Employees: 8,400
FYE: September

ScrippsHealth has its lines down cold. The not-for-profit hospital group serves the San Diego area with six acute care hospitals, 15 outpatient clinics, and two skilled nursing facilities. ScrippsHealth oversees beds in the Scripps and Mercy Hospitals and has more than 2,000 affiliated physicians. The system also offers home health care and medical products and operates community outreach programs. Its parent, Scripps Institutions of Medicine and Science, also runs The Scripps Research Institute (TSRI), which performs scientific research. TSRI's Scripps Foundation for Medicine and Science acts as a fundraiser for ScrippsHealth.

KEY COMPETITORS
Adventist Health
Columbia/HCA
Tenet Healthcare

SEALY, INC.

1 Office Pkwy.
Trinity, NC 27370
Phone: 336-861-3500
Fax: 336-861-3501
Web site: http://www.sealy.com

CEO: Ronald L. Jones
CFO: Richard F. Sowerby
HR: Jeffrey C. Claypool
Type: Private

1998 Sales: $891.3 million
1-Yr. Sales Change: 10.7%
Employees: 5,193
FYE: November

Sealy can rest easy: It's North America's #1 bedding maker. The company's Sealy and Stearns & Foster mattresses and box springs are sold at more than 7,000 stores. Sealy also licenses its name to makers of sofas, pillows, and other products. Customers include furniture stores, department stores, warehouse clubs, and mass merchandisers. The US is Sealy's main market, but it has licensees in Australia, Israel, Jamaica, Japan, New Zealand, South Africa, Thailand, and the UK, and it also sells its products in Brazil, Mexico, South Korea, and Spain. Sealy's 28 factories are located in Canada, Mexico, Puerto Rico, and the US. Investment firm Bain Capital, along with company management and other investors, owns Sealy.

KEY COMPETITORS
Serta
Simmons
Spring Air

See pages 444–445 for a full profile of this company.

SECURITY BENEFIT GROUP OF COMPANIES

700 SW Harrison St.
Topeka, KS 66636
Phone: 785-431-3000
Fax: 785-431-5177
Web site: http://www.securitybenefit.com

CEO: Howard R. Fricke
CFO: Donald Schepker
HR: Lyn Chmelka
Type: Private

1998 Sales: $1,285.8 million
1-Yr. Sales Change: 27.0%
Employees: —
FYE: December

Security Benefit Group of Companies is the largest life insurer in the Jayhawk State. The group operates through Security Benefit Life Insurance Company, which offers variable life insurance, annuities, mutual funds, and asset management services. After more than 100 years as a mutual company, the company is converting to stock ownership: The new stock holding company, Security Benefit Corp., will own Security Benefit Life Insurance Company. Security Benefit Corp., in turn, is owned by Security Benefit Mutual Holding Company, which is owned by current policyholders. Security Benefit's roots go back to the Knights and Ladies of Security, a benefit society begun in 1892 in Topeka, Kansas.

KEY COMPETITORS
Aetna
American United Life
John Hancock

SEMATECH, INC.

2706 Montopolis Dr.
Austin, TX 78741
Phone: 512-356-3500
Fax: 512-356-3086
Web site: http://www.sematech.org

CEO: Mark Melliar-Smith
CFO: Dan Damon
HR: Susan Sandberg
Type: Consortium

1998 Sales: —
1-Yr. Sales Change: —
Employees: —
FYE: December

SEMATECH isn't trying to build a better mousetrap, just researching better ways to build semiconductors. The not-for-profit research consortium (whose name stands for "semiconductor manufacturing technology") delves into areas such as design, lithography, and interconnect systems to improve semiconductor manufacturing techniques. Members of SEMATECH (including Advanced Micro Devices, IBM, Intel, Lucent, and Texas Instruments) and of subsidiary International SEMATECH send their employees to the group's Texas headquarters to carry out research. Members' dues fund SEMATECH. The consortium, widely credited with restoring the US to global chip dominance, is struggling as members question its purpose.

KEY COMPETITORS
Lucent
MCC
SAIC

 See pages 446–447 for a full profile of this company.

SENTARA HEALTH SYSTEM

6015 Poplar Hall Dr., Ste. 300
Norfolk, VA 23502
Phone: 757-455-7000
Fax: 757-455-7964
Web site: http://www.sentara.com

CEO: David L. Bernd
CFO: Richard D. Hill
HR: Vicki Humphries
Type: Not-for-profit

1998 Sales: $900.9 million
1-Yr. Sales Change: 10.4%
Employees: 8,190
FYE: April

Health care's a beach for Sentara Health System. The not-for-profit organization operates more than 70 facilities throughout southeastern Virginia and northeastern North Carolina. The system has six hospitals, nine assisted living centers, about 40 health care centers, an integrated outpatient health care campus, and a fitness center. Additionally, Sentara offers health coverage (including HMOs) for more than 270,000 people. The company also provides home health services, ground and air medical transport, community health education programs, and mobile diagnostic vans. After merging with rival Tidewater Health Care, Sentara owns Virginia Beach's two hospitals (Virginia Beach General and Sentara Bayside).

KEY COMPETITORS
Bon Secours Health
Carilion Health System
Riverside Health System

SENTRY INSURANCE, A MUTUAL COMPANY

1800 North Point Dr.
Stevens Point, WI 54481
Phone: 715-346-6000
Fax: 715-346-7516
Web site: http://www.sentry-insurance.com

CEO: Dale R. Schuh
CFO: William J. Lohr
HR: Greg Mox
Type: Mutual company

1997 Sales: $1,497.2 million
1-Yr. Sales Change: (5.2%)
Employees: 4,479
FYE: December

Sentry Insurance offers a variety of insurance coverage, including life, group health, auto, and property/casualty insurance. The mutual company, which is owned by its policy holders, offers the coverage through its subsidiaries, including Sentry Life, Dairyland, Patriot General, and Middlesex. The company's Sentry Equity Services offers mutual fund services through its Sentry Fund. In addition to offering individual insurance, the company offers specialized insurance for large businesses. Sentry was founded in 1904 to provide insurance to members of the Wisconsin Retail Hardware Association. Sentry is buying Deere & Company's insurance unit.

KEY COMPETITORS
Allstate
Prudential
State Farm

SERRA INVESTMENT

3118 E. Hill Rd.
Grand Blanc, MI 48439
Phone: 810-694-1720
Fax: 810-694-6405

CEO: Albert M. Serra
CFO: Mathew Daugherty
HR: Michael Bird
Type: Private

1997 Sales: $746.5 million
1-Yr. Sales Change: (3.1%)
Employees: 1,300
FYE: June

Serra Investment is in the driver's seat as parent company of Team Management, which owns and operates about 20 auto dealerships throughout the US. The dealerships, several of which are in the Upper Midwest, sell Buicks, Chevrolets, and Fords, among other makes. The company was formed in 1972 and is ranked as one of the nation's top 15 auto dealership groups. It is owned by CEO Albert Serra and his son Joseph. The pair, along with a handful of other dealership owners, formed Driver's Mart, a 10-location chain of used-vehicle superstores that was absorbed in 1998 by AutoNation.

KEY COMPETITORS
AutoNation
Don Massey Cadillac
Mel Farr Enterprises

SERTA, INC.

325 Spring Lake Dr.
Itasca, IL 60143
Phone: 630-285-9300
Fax: 630-285-9330
Web site: http://www.serta.com

CEO: Edward F. Lilly
CFO: Maury Knowlton
HR: Merle Hutner
Type: Private

1998 Sales: $763.8 million
1-Yr. Sales Change: 14.0%
Employees: 4,800
FYE: December

Serta, the #2 mattress manufacturer in the world (behind Sealy), hopes to keep the competition awake at night. It is the nation's #1 mattress supplier to hotels and motels; its Perfect Sleeper mattress, which it has been selling since the 1930s, is America's best-selling premium mattress. Serta's top-of-the-line mattress collection is sold under the Perfect Night name. The firm manufactures its bedding products at about 30 locations in the US along with around 20 international locations in the Asia/Pacific region, and in Canada, Central America, Europe, and the Middle East. The company, begun in 1931 by 13 independent mattress makers who licensed the Serta name, is still owned by licensees.

KEY COMPETITORS
Sealy
Simmons
Spring Air

SERVICES GROUP OF AMERICA

4025 Delridge Way SW, Ste. 500
Seattle, WA 98106
Phone: 206-933-5225
Fax: 206-933-5247
Web site: http://www.fsaonline.com

CEO: Thomas J. Stewart
CFO: Dennis J. Sprecht
HR: Lynette Draper
Type: Private

1999 Est. Sales: $1,400.0 million
1-Yr. Sales Change: 3.7%
Employees: 2,500
FYE: January

Though it bears a rather vague company name, Services Group of America's operations are pretty specific. Its subsidiary, Food Services of America, is a leading food service distributor, supplying clients including hospitals, schools, and restaurants in 15 western and midwestern states. Services Group also runs Development Services of America, a real estate developer, and Travel Services of America. The company sold Eagle Insurance Group to focus more closely on food services. After being convicted of violating US election laws in 1998, owner and CEO Thomas Stewart paid $5 million in fines and was sentenced to home detention and community service in a shelter for the homeless.

KEY COMPETITORS
Alliant Foodservice
SYSCO
U.S. Foodservice

SHAMROCK FOODS COMPANY

2228 N. Black Canyon Hwy.	CEO: Norman McClelland	1999 Sales: $1,081.0 million
Phoenix, AZ 85009	CFO: Philip Giltner	1-Yr. Sales Change: 8.6%
Phone: 602-272-6721	HR: Charlie Roberts	Employees: 2,337
Fax: 602-233-2791	Type: Private	FYE: September
Web site: http://www.shamrockfoods.com		

Milk does a business good, too. Thanks to that udder delight, Shamrock Foods has fortified itself from a tiny mom-and-pop dairy into a food processor and distributor serving supermarkets, convenience stores, restaurants, and institutional clients, primarily in about 10 southwestern states. Most of the company's business is dedicated to processing dairy products, including milk, ice cream, eggnog, and snack bars. Products are sold under the Shamrock Farms and Sunland brands, as well as under private labels. It also supplies the Arizona Diamondbacks baseball team with co-branded ice cream goodies, including Rattleshakes. Started in 1922, the company is owned and run by the founding McClelland family.

KEY COMPETITORS
Dean Foods
Fleming Companies
SYSCO

SHEETZ, INC.

5700 6th Ave.	CEO: Stanton R. Sheetz	1999 Sales: $1,161.0 million
Altoona, PA 16602	CFO: Joseph S. Sheetz	1-Yr. Sales Change: 22.0%
Phone: 814-946-3611	HR: Charles Sheetz	Employees: 6,200
Fax: 814-946-4375	Type: Private	FYE: September
Web site: http://www.sheetz.com		

You might say Sheetz is to the convenience store business what Wal-Mart is to discount shopping. The company operates more than 200 combination convenience stores and gas stations, mostly in Pennsylvania but also in Maryland, Virginia, West Virginia, and Ohio. Noted for being exceptionally clean and large (nearly twice the size of the average 7-Eleven), Sheetz stores sell groceries, fountain drinks, baked goods, and made-to-order sandwiches and salads, among other sundries. Volume buying has allowed Sheetz to sell gas and cigarettes at much cheaper prices than competitors. Founded in 1952 by Bob Sheetz, the company is owned and run by the Sheetz family.

KEY COMPETITORS
7-Eleven
Kroger
Uni-Marts

SHERWOOD FOOD DISTRIBUTORS

18615 Sherwood	CEO: J. Lawrence Tushman	1999 Sales: $725.0 million
Detroit, MI 48234	CFO: Earl Ishbia	1-Yr. Sales Change: (3.3%)
Phone: 313-366-3100	HR: Carol Stern	Employees: 500
Fax: 313-366-8825	Type: Private	FYE: October

The merry men and women at Sherwood Food Distributors have enough turkey legs to keep even Friar Tuck from getting hungry. The company is the largest privately owned wholesale distributor of meat and poultry in the US. It serves customers in the Northeast and Midwest through 10 distribution facilities that are supported by a Ryder Transportation Service fleet of about 200 refrigerated trucks. Sherwood Food was formed in 1987 by the merger of the food distribution operations of Orleans International and Regal Packaging, each of which owns half of the company.

KEY COMPETITORS
Fleming Companies
Gordon Food Service
Nash Finch

SHORENSTEIN CO. L.P.

555 California St., Ste. 4900
San Francisco, CA 94104
Phone: 415-772-7000
Fax: 415-772-7022

CEO: Douglas W. Shorenstein
CFO: Rich Chaicotel
HR: Christine Billeter
Type: Private

1998 Est. Sales: $750.0 million
1-Yr. Sales Change: 0.0%
Employees: 620
FYE: December

Shorenstein helps businesses find a room of their own. The company is one of the nation's largest and oldest privately owned real estate firms. It owns or manages almost 25 million sq. ft. of office space. The company is the largest office space landlord in Oakland and San Francisco, where about 10 million sq. ft. of its properties are located. In recent years, the company has expanded nationally, managing or owning properties in Boston; Charlotte, North Carolina; Garden City, New York; New York City; and Phoenix. Founded by Walter Shorenstein after WWII, the company is now run by his son, CEO Douglas Shorenstein.

KEY COMPETITORS

CB Richard Ellis
Equity Group Investments
Helmsley

SHURFINE INTERNATIONAL, INC.

2100 N. Mannheim Rd.
Northlake, IL 60164
Phone: 708-681-2000
Fax: 708-681-2160
Web site: http://www.shurfine.com

CEO: James R. Barth
CFO: John Stanhaus
HR: Cyndi Rettig
Type: Cooperative

1998 Est. Sales: $1,700.0 million
1-Yr. Sales Change: 6.3%
Employees: 160
FYE: May

Sure you haven't heard of Shurfine International? The food-buying co-op is more widespread than you might think, with more than 10,000 private-label products sold to 30,000 food stores, drugstores, and convenience stores throughout the US and in 40 other countries. It also provides a full range of services to help its customers sell those products, including helping customers add pharmacies to their businesses, transport products, and design creative packaging. The co-op's extensive product lines include perishable, automotive, and health and beauty care products under the ShurFine, Shurfresh, Price Saver, Shur Tech, Ultimate Choice, and Saver's Choice labels. Subsidiary Viking Bag manufactures grocery sacks.

KEY COMPETITORS

Fleming Companies
Topco Associates
Wakefern Food

SIERRA PACIFIC INDUSTRIES

19794 Riverside Ave.
Anderson, CA 96007
Phone: 530-378-8000
Fax: 530-378-8242
Web site: http://www.spi-ind.com

CEO: Red Emmerson
CFO: Mark Emmerson
HR: Ed Bond
Type: Private

1998 Est. Sales: $1,210.0 million
1-Yr. Sales Change: 21.0%
Employees: 3,200
FYE: December

Sierra Pacific Industries isn't your run-of-the-mill company. One of the largest US lumber companies, it manufactures millwork products and lumber at its 12 planing mills and sawmills. Subsidiary Sierra Pacific Windows makes a variety of patio doors and specialty windows. Protests in the 1980s against logging on public land prompted the company to begin buying its own timberlands, and it now owns 1.4 million acres of Douglas fir timberlands in California. Although Sierra Pacific was founded in 1969, it traces its roots to a company started in the late 1920s by R. H. "Curly" Emmerson, father of current CEO Red Emmerson. The Emmerson family owns Sierra Pacific.

KEY COMPETITORS

Georgia-Pacific Group
Louisiana-Pacific
Weyerhaeuser

SIGMA PLASTICS GROUP

Page & Schuyler Ave., Bldg. #8
Lyndhurst, NJ 07071
Phone: 201-933-6000
Fax: —

CEO: Alfred Teo
CFO: John Reier
HR: —
Type: Private

1998 Est. Sales: $765.0 million
1-Yr. Sales Change: 57.7%
Employees: 3,000
FYE: October

Although plastic film and sheet products by Sigma Plastics both shrink and stretch, the company itself prefers only to expand. Having grown through acquisitions, Sigma Plastics produces shrink and stretch film, converter-grade packaging, and merchandise, garment, grocery, and trash bags. The company manufactures its diverse range of plastic products at its plants in Canada, the UK, and the US. Sigma also owns Delta Plastics and Polystar Films. It holds a majority interest in Essex Plastics and a 50% interest in Aargus Plastics. It has a joint venture with the UK's IPEL to sell shrink film in Europe.

KEY COMPETITORS
Bemis
DuPont
Sealed Air

SIMPLEX TIME RECORDER CO.

Simplex Plaza
Gardner, MA 01441
Phone: 978-632-2500
Fax: 978-630-7867
Web site: http://www.simplexnet.com

CEO: Edward G. Watkins
CFO: Stanley Clark
HR: —
Type: Private

1998 Sales: $736.0 million
1-Yr. Sales Change: 5.9%
Employees: 6,000
FYE: December

"Punch the clock" might have an entirely different meaning if not for Simplex Time Recorder, the founder of which invented the time clock. Today the firm produces, installs, and services security, fire alarm, communications, and time management systems. Flagship products include time tracking and attendance system WinSTAR and NT 3400, an integrated system that manages every facet of building security from one platform. Simplex manufactures products in Massachusetts and markets them through 170 branch offices in 65 countries worldwide. Edward Watkins invented the first device that could clock-in numerous workers while making written records, founding Simplex in 1902. The Watkins family still owns the company.

KEY COMPETITORS
ITI Technologies
Pittway
Tyco International

SIMPSON INVESTMENT CO.

1301 5th Ave., Ste. 2800
Seattle, WA 98101
Phone: 206-224-5000
Fax: 206-224-5060

CEO: Colin Moseley
CFO: Charles Pollnow
HR: —
Type: Private

1998 Est. Sales: $1,500.0 million
1-Yr. Sales Change: 7.1%
Employees: 4,500
FYE: December

Founded in 1890, Simpson Investment is one of the oldest privately owned forest products companies in the Northwest. The holding company manufactures paper, pulp, and lumber products, such as plywood, through its subsidiaries: Simpson Timber, Simpson Paper Company, and Simpson Tacoma Kraft Company. Simpson Timber owns 867,000 acres of timberland in California, Oregon, and Washington state, and operates wood-processing facilities in Washington and California. Simpson Paper and Simpson Tacoma Kraft make linerboard, natural and bleached papers, shipping sacks, specialty kraft papers, and unbleached pulp. The Simpson family has controlled the company since its founding.

KEY COMPETITORS
Georgia-Pacific Group
International Paper
Weyerhaeuser

SINCLAIR OIL CORPORATION

550 E. South Temple
Salt Lake City, UT 84102
Phone: 801-524-2700
Fax: 801-526-3000
Web site: http://www.sinclairoil.com

CEO: Robert E. Holding
CFO: Charles Barlow
HR: Wendel White
Type: Private

1998 Est. Sales: $1,300.0 million
1-Yr. Sales Change: (23.5%)
Employees: 5,600
FYE: December

Way out west, where fossils are found, brontosaur signs litter the ground. They belong to Sinclair Oil's more than 2,500 service stations and convenience stores in 22 western and midwestern US states. The company also operates three oil refineries, two pipelines (one 45%-owned with Conoco), exploration operations, and a trucking fleet, all in the western half of the US. It owns the Grand America Hotel, the Little America hotel chain, and two ski resorts (Sun Valley in Idaho and Snowbasin in Utah). Snowbasin will be used in the 2002 Winter Olympics. The man behind all of this is Earl Holding, whose storied company, founded in 1916 by Harry Sinclair, was a central figure in the infamous Teapot Dome scandal.

KEY COMPETITORS
Exxon Mobil
Ultramar Diamond Shamrock
Vail Resorts

SISTERS OF CHARITY HEALTH CARE SYSTEM

2600 North Loop West
Houston, TX 77092
Phone: 713-681-8877
Fax: 713-680-4896
Web site: http://www.sch.org

CEO: Christina Murphy
CFO: William Kuehn
HR: Mary Lynch
Type: Not-for-profit

1998 Sales: $2,100.0 million
1-Yr. Sales Change: 13.5%
Employees: 16,000
FYE: June

Sisters of Charity Health Care System is a Catholic, not-for-profit firm that operates 15 acute care hospitals, four long-term care centers, and seven long-term acute care facilities in Arkansas, Louisiana, Texas, Utah, and Ireland. The system also offers HealthPrompt, a free healthcare advice and referral telephone service, and Home Health Care, which provides therapy and healthcare for homebound patients. The Sisters of Charity runs an HMO through its partnership with the Memorial Hermann Healthcare System of Houston. The Sisters first organized in France in 1625 and opened their first US facility in 1867. Sisters of Charity is merging with San Antonio's Incarnate Word Health System, forming Christus Health.

KEY COMPETITORS
Columbia/HCA
Harris County Hospital
Memorial Hermann Healthcare

SISTERS OF CHARITY OF LEAVENWORTH HEALTH SERVICES CORPORATION

Cantwell Hall, 4200 S. 4th St.
Leavenworth, KS 66048
Phone: 913-682-1338
Fax: 913-682-1052
Web site: http://www.sclhsc.org

CEO: Bill Murray
CFO: Gary Jankowski
HR: Dennis Groves
Type: Not-for-profit

1998 Sales: $878.6 million
1-Yr. Sales Change: (1.6%)
Employees: 10,000
FYE: May

In 1857 a group of Catholic sisters arrived in Kansas (then Indian territory) and began teaching and tending the sick; a decade later, they incorporated as the Sisters of Charity of Leavenworth Health Services. The not-for-profit regional health care organization operates more than a dozen hospitals, clinics, and medical centers in California, Colorado, Kansas, and Montana. Its facilities provide health services to lower-income and uninsured people. Along with Boulder-based Lutheran Medical Center, it runs Exempla, a not-for-profit hospital system. The organization has agreed to buy Bethany Medical Center in Kansas City, Kansas, from Columbia/HCA.

KEY COMPETITORS
HMA
Province Healthcare
Tenet Healthcare

SISTERS OF MERCY HEALTH SYSTEM-ST. LOUIS

2039 N. Geyer Rd.
St. Louis, MO 63131
Phone: 314-965-6100
Fax: 314-957-0466
Web site: http://www.smhs.com

CEO: Sister Mary R. Rocklage
CFO: Carrol Aulbaugh
HR: Stephen Isenhower
Type: Not-for-profit

1998 Sales: $2,169.2 million
1-Yr. Sales Change: 10.1%
Employees: 26,000
FYE: June

It's a sister act. Sponsored by the Sisters of Mercy of the St. Louis Regional Community, Sisters of Mercy Health System provides a range of health care and social services through its network of facilities in Arkansas, Illinois, Kansas, Louisiana, Mississippi, Missouri, Oklahoma, and Texas. Through nine regional units, the system runs about 25 hospitals, home health programs, a psychiatric hospital, long-term care facilities, physician practices, and outpatient facilities. Sisters of Mercy also runs several charitable foundations and provides charity care to patients unable to pay for services. For-profit subsidiary Mercy Health Plans offers managed care health plans in Arkansas, Kansas, Missouri, and Texas.

KEY COMPETITORS
BJC Health
Columbia/HCA
Tenet Healthcare

SISTERS OF PROVIDENCE HEALTH SYSTEM

520 Pike St.
Seattle, WA 98101
Phone: 206-464-3355
Fax: 206-464-3038
Web site: http://www.providence.org

CEO: Henry G. Walker
CFO: Maurice M. Smith
HR: Sue Byington
Type: Not-for-profit

1998 Sales: $2,708.9 million
1-Yr. Sales Change: 15.5%
Employees: 23,000
FYE: December

Sisterhood is powerful in health care. The order of the Sisters of Providence runs a health care network (the Sisters of Providence Health System) that spans the West Coast from California to Alaska. The system consists of the PeaceHealth PPO and HMO programs, with more than 1 million members; 11 hospitals; two health resource centers; and two physician networks (one, Medalia Health Network, in cosponsorship with the Franciscan Health System) that focus on primary care. In addition to providing medical and related services for the poor, the organization — whose roots go back to the 1840s — also fulfills its charitable mission by operating housing projects for the poor and elderly and a high school.

KEY COMPETITORS
Adventist Health
Columbia/HCA
Tenet Healthcare

SKADDEN, ARPS, SLATE, MEAGHER & FLOM

919 3rd Ave.
New York, NY 10022
Phone: 212-735-3000
Fax: 212-735-2000
Web site: http://www.skadden.com

CEO: Robert C. Sheehan
CFO: Karl Duchek
HR: Carol Lee H. Sprague
Type: Partnership

1998 Sales: $890.0 million
1-Yr. Sales Change: 7.7%
Employees: 3,200
FYE: December

Have you heard about the law firm that sued the business information publisher for a profile that opened with a wickedly clever lawyer joke? Neither have we, and we'd like to keep it that way. Skadden, Arps, Slate, Meagher & Flom, the #1 US law firm and one of the largest in the world, employs some 1,340 lawyers and associates in 31 offices around the world. The firm offers counsel for corporate dealings, litigation, and international concerns, as well as in regulatory and legislative areas. It's best known for mergers and acquisitions; it also advises in corporate restructuring and proxy contests. Founded in 1948, Skadden, Arps has nearly 300 partners and has offices in Asia, Australia, Europe, and North America.

KEY COMPETITORS
Baker & McKenzie
Davis Polk
Jones, Day

See pages 448–449 for a full profile of this company.

SKIDMORE, OWINGS & MERRILL, LLP

224 S. Michigan Ave., Ste. 1000	CEO: John H. Winkler	1997 Sales: $88.0 million
Chicago, IL 60604	CFO: Joseph Dailey	1-Yr. Sales Change: 7.3%
Phone: 312-554-9090	HR: Carol Able	Employees: 850
Fax: 312-360-4545	Type: Partnership	FYE: September
Web site: http://www.som.com		

Some like it tall: Skyscraper builder Skidmore, Owings & Merrill (SOM) is one of the largest architectural firms in the world. The Chicago-based partnership provides architectural and engineering services, in addition to interior design and site and space planning. Though it earned its fame with innovative modernist design and such high-profile projects as the Sears Tower, in recent years SOM has pursued interior design and renovations, other institutional projects (including airport additions), and international commissions, particularly in Asia. But the Asian economic downturn has SOM focusing on opportunities in the buoyant US market.

KEY COMPETITORS
AECOM
Jacobs Engineering
Takenaka

 See pages 450–451 for a full profile of this company.

SLIM-FAST FOODS COMPANY

777 S. Flagler Dr., West Tower, Ste. 1400	CEO: S. Daniel Abraham	1998 Est. Sales: $700.0 million
West Palm Beach, FL 33401	CFO: Carl Tsang	1-Yr. Sales Change: 0.0%
Phone: 561-833-9920	HR: Chris Hilkers	Employees: 75
Fax: 561-822-2876	Type: Private	FYE: November
Web site: http://www.slim-fast.com		

Fitness fanatic Daniel Abraham helped shake up the weight-loss industry with his Slim-Fast meal-replacement drinks. After finding success with Dexatrim and other over-the-counter drugs, he spun off Slim-Fast Foods in 1990 from his Thompson Medical Co. to capitalize on the needs of weight-conscious consumers. Abraham's company sells shakes (milk- or soy-based), drink powders, and snack bars through retailers in the US and Europe under the Slim-Fast and Ultra Slim-Fast names. It markets the products aggressively, hiring celebrity endorsers such as Los Angeles Dodgers manager Tommy Lasorda and entertainer Kathie Lee Gifford to pitch them.

KEY COMPETITORS
Jenny Craig
Nutri/System
Weider Nutrition International

SMITHSONIAN INSTITUTION

1000 Jefferson Dr. SW	CEO: I. Michael Heyman	1998 Sales: $774.5 million
Washington, DC 20560	CFO: Rick R. Johnson	1-Yr. Sales Change: 6.3%
Phone: 202-357-2700	HR: Carolyn E. Jones	Employees: —
Fax: 202-786-2377	Type: Not-for-profit	FYE: September
Web site: http://www.si.edu		

The Smithsonian Institution is the world's largest museum, with some 23 million visitors each year. It has more than 140 million items in 16 museums and galleries, a zoo, and various research facilities. The Smithsonian is home to exhibits on art, music, TV and film, agriculture, and history, among other areas. Most of its facilities charge no admission and are located on the National Mall between the Washington Monument and the Capitol. The Smithsonian gets more than 50% of its revenues from the federal government. It is headed by a board of regents that includes Vice President Al Gore, Chief Justice William Rehnquist, six members of Congress, and eight private citizens.

See pages 452–453 for a full profile of this company.

SOUTH CAROLINA PUBLIC SERVICE AUTHORITY

1 Riverwood Dr.	CEO: T. Graham Edwards	1998 Sales: $775.6 million
Moncks Corner, SC 29461	CFO: Emily S. Brown	1-Yr. Sales Change: 6.6%
Phone: 843-761-8000	HR: Ronald H. Holmes	Employees: 1,637
Fax: 843-761-7060	Type: Government-owned	FYE: December
Web site: http://www.santeecooper.com		

Someone's got to turn on those bright lights in the big city — and in the small cities, too. South Carolina Public Service Authority, known as Santee Cooper, provides electric service to 15 cooperatives with more than 390,000 customers in about 40 South Carolina counties. It directly retails electric service to 110,000 additional customers. One of the largest US state-owned utilities, Santee Cooper owns or has interests in several generating stations that produce hydroelectric, coal-fired, nuclear, and combustion turbine power. It also distributes water through its Regional Water System, drawing about 24 million gallons of water a day from Lake Moultrie and selling it to the Lake Moultrie Water Agency.

SOUTHERN STATES COOPERATIVE, INCORPORATED

6606 W. Broad St.	CEO: Wayne A. Boutwell	1998 Sales: $1,120.0 million
Richmond, VA 23260	CFO: Jonathan A. Hawkins	1-Yr. Sales Change: (7.9%)
Phone: 804-281-1000	HR: Richard G. Sherman	Employees: 3,800
Fax: 804-281-1383	Type: Cooperative	FYE: June
Web site: http://www.southernstates-coop.com		

Founded in 1923 to provide affordable, high-quality seed to Virginia farmers, Southern States Cooperative serves about 380,000 members, mainly in mid-western and southern states. The co-op offers its farmer-owners feed and fertilizer manufacturing, seed processing, grain marketing, and petroleum and propane services, as well as wholesale farm supplies. Its retail operations (about 630 outlets) provide feed, garden products, and fuel. Other services include GrowMaster crop analysis, a specialty catalog, sales financing, and a commercial insurance program. Southern States Cooperative merged with Michigan Livestock Exchange in 1998, making it the country's largest livestock marketing co-op.

KEY COMPETITORS
Cenex Harvest States
Farmland Industries
GROWMARK

SOUTHERN WINE & SPIRITS OF AMERICA

1600 NW 163rd St.	CEO: Harvey Chaplin	1998 Sales: $2,450.0 million
Miami, FL 33169	CFO: Steven Becker	1-Yr. Sales Change: 3.6%
Phone: 305-625-4171	HR: Mark Krauss	Employees: 4,500
Fax: 305-625-4720	Type: Private	FYE: December
Web site: http://www.southernwineca.com		

Fueled by alcohol and nicotine, Southern Wine & Spirits of America delivers market dominance. The company is the #1 US distributor of wine and spirits, with almost 12% of the market. In addition to importing and distributing wine and spirits, it distributes boutique beers, such as Grolsch and Steinlager; cigars, such as Don Diego and Montecristo; and nonalcoholic beverages, including Angostura Bitters and Rose's Lime Juice. Southern Wine & Spirits has successfully lobbied allowing mail-order companies to ship wine to Florida, the #2 wine consuming state after California. Chairman and CEO Harvey Chaplin and his secretive family own the company.

KEY COMPETITORS
National Distributing
Sunbelt Beverage
Young's Market

SOUTHWIRE COMPANY

1 Southwire Dr.
Carrollton, GA 30119
Phone: 770-832-4242
Fax: 770-832-5374
Web site: http://www.southwire.com

CEO: Roy Richards
CFO: Fred Payton
HR: Mike Wiggins
Type: Private

1998 Est. Sales: $1,400.0 million
1-Yr. Sales Change: (17.6%)
Employees: 4,500
FYE: December

Southwire hopes everyone's cable-ready. One of the US's largest cable manufacturers, Southwire makes building wire and cable, utility cable products, industrial power cable, and telecommunications cable. The company also offers aluminum and alloyed casting products, copper and aluminum rods, cord products, and machining and fabrication services. Southwire has offices in Hong Kong, Mexico City, and Paris to support business with customers in the Pacific Rim, Latin America, and Europe. The company is selling its copper assets and some of its aluminum operations to focus on wire and cable manufacturing. Founded in 1950 by Roy Richards Sr. (the CEO's father), Southwire is owned by the Richards family.

KEY COMPETITORS

Alcatel
Marmon Group
Pirelli S.p.A.

SPARTAN STORES, INC.

850 76th St. SW
Grand Rapids, MI 49518
Phone: 616-878-2000
Fax: 616-878-8802
Web site: http://www.spartanstores.com

CEO: James B. Meyer
CFO: Charles Fosnaugh
HR: Richard Deming
Type: Private

1999 Sales: $2,671.7 million
1-Yr. Sales Change: 7.3%
Employees: 3,500
FYE: March

Spartan Stores is trying to shield mom-and-pop grocers from the slings and arrows of big business. The company provides food and general merchandise to more than 470 independent grocery stores and about 9,600 convenience stores, mostly in Michigan, but also in eight other states as far away as Georgia. Spartan distributes more than 40,000 products, including more than 2,000 private-label products under the Spartan, HomeHarvest, and Save Rite names. The company also provides its members with various support services, including advertising, accounting, and insurance. Once a cooperative, Spartan is owned primarily by about 240 customers. Employees and management also own stakes.

KEY COMPETITORS

A&P
Eby-Brown
SUPERVALU

📖 See pages 454–455 for a full profile of this company.

SPEAR, LEEDS & KELLOGG

120 Broadway, 6th Fl.
New York, NY 10271
Phone: 212-433-7000
Fax: 212-433-7490
Web site: http://www.slk.com

CEO: Peter Kellogg
CFO: Steven Moss
HR: Beverly Fiorentino
Type: Private

1998 Est. Sales: $920.0 million
1-Yr. Sales Change: —
Employees: 2,300
FYE: September

Spear, Leeds & Kellogg makes the most out of market making. It lines up buyers and sellers of stock (a process called "making a market"), and is the #1 specialist (or market-maker) on the auction-based NYSE and AMEX exchanges, where, respectively, it deals in more than 440 and 175 listed stocks. Spear, Leeds & Kellogg is also the market maker for some 5,000 Nasdaq and smaller Bulletin Board stocks, as well as options, futures, and asset-backed securities. Spear, Leeds & Kellogg's REDIBook electronic communication network (ECN) provides fast trade execution over the Internet. Harold Spear and Lawrence Leeds founded the company in 1931; they were joined by James Kellogg in 1945.

KEY COMPETITORS

Island ECN
Knight/Trimark Group
Quick & Reilly/Fleet

SPECIALTY FOODS CORPORATION

520 Lake Cook Rd., Ste. 550 Deerfield, IL 60015 Phone: 847-405-5300 Fax: 847-267-0015	CEO: Lawrence S. Benjamin CFO: Robert L. Fishbune HR: John R. Reisenberg Type: Private	1998 Sales: $742.3 million 1-Yr. Sales Change: (19.3%) Employees: 8,300 FYE: December

Have a cookie, dear, after all, Specialty Foods baked them just for you. It's the #3 US cookie maker (after Nabisco and Keebler), with the Mother's and Archway brands. But — before you can have a cookie — consider that its wholesale baking division, Metz Baking (which The Earthgrains Company is buying), markets bread and rolls in the Midwest, and its Andre-Boudin Bakeries operates about 45 bakery cafés in California and Illinois. There might have been more food units from which to choose had it not sold its non-baking divisions (including Stella Cheese and meat processor H&M Food Systems). Investment facilities headed by Texas billionaire Robert Bass and J. Taylor Crandall own about 55% of Specialty Foods.

KEY COMPETITORS
Earthgrains
Interstate Bakeries
Nabisco Holdings

📖 See pages 456–457 for a full profile of this company.

SPITZER MANAGEMENT, INC.

150 E. Bridge St. Elyria, OH 44035 Phone: 440-323-4671 Fax: 440-323-3623 Web site: http://www.spitzer.com	CEO: Alan Spitzer CFO: Steve Miller HR: — Type: Private	1998 Est. Sales: $850.0 million 1-Yr. Sales Change: — Employees: 1,700 FYE: December

Pick a car, any car. Spitzer Management, with about 35 franchises in Ohio, Pennsylvania, and Florida, sells almost every kind of car from A to V (Acura, Buick, Cadillac, Chevy, Chrysler, Dodge, Ford, GMC, Lincoln, Mazda, Mercury, Mitsubishi, Oldsmobile, Plymouth, Pontiac, Toyota, and Volkswagen). The company also has interests in real estate and manages a golf course and marina. Owner and CEO Alan Spitzer's statewide (Ohio) campaign to legalize gambling failed, ruining plans to build a casino on company-owned land. However, he plans to build homes and condos on the site, as well as expand the company's marina there.

KEY COMPETITORS
AutoNation
Morse Operations
Ricart Automotive

SSM HEALTH CARE SYSTEM INC.

477 N. Lindbergh Blvd. St. Louis, MO 63141 Phone: 314-994-7800 Fax: 314-994-7900 Web site: http://www.ssmhc.com	CEO: Sister Mary J. Ryan CFO: Elizabeth Alhand HR: Steven Barney Type: Not-for-profit	1998 Sales: $1,284.8 million 1-Yr. Sales Change: (0.0%) Employees: 20,500 FYE: December

Founded in 1872 by the Franciscan Sisters of Mary, the not-for-profit SSM Health Care System is one of the largest Catholic health systems in the country. SSM owns, operates, and manages some 20 acute care hospitals, rehabilitation clinics, and nursing homes, with a total of almost 5,500 licensed beds. Its health care facilities are located in Illinois, Missouri, Oklahoma, and Wisconsin (SSM divested ventures in South Carolina to focus on its other operations). Its health-related businesses include information systems, home care management, and clinical engineering and other support services.

KEY COMPETITORS
BJC Health
Columbia/HCA
Tenet Healthcare

STANFORD UNIVERSITY

857 Serra St.
Stanford, CA 94305
Phone: 650-723-2300
Fax: 650-725-0247
Web site: http://www.stanford.edu

CEO: Gerhard Casper
CFO: Mariann Byerwalter
HR: Peggy Hiraoka
Type: School

1998 Sales: $1,558.4 million
1-Yr. Sales Change: 5.7%
Employees: 9,535
FYE: August

Stanford University is one of California's educational gold mines. With a student population exceeding 14,000, the private institution offers undergraduate programs in humanities and sciences, earth sciences, and engineering, as well as graduate programs in fields such as business, engineering, law, and medicine. Stanford is also a top research university, boasting 2,300 externally sponsored research projects and a host of research laboratories, centers, and institutes. Its $4.7 billion endowment ranks among the top six university endowments in the US. Stanford's faculty includes 16 Nobel Laureates and 20 Medal of Science winners.

 See pages 458–459 for a full profile of this company.

STAPLE COTTON COOPERATIVE ASSOCIATION

214 W. Market St.
Greenwood, MS 38935
Phone: 662-453-6231
Fax: 662-453-6274
Web site: http://www.staplcotn.com

CEO: Woods E. Eastland
CFO: —
HR: Eugene A. Stansel
Type: Cooperative

1998 Sales: $704.5 million
1-Yr. Sales Change: 7.3%
Employees: 197
FYE: August

Wear underwear? Chances are Staplcotn had a hand in it. Staple Cotton Cooperative Association, the US's oldest cotton-marketing co-op, provides marketing and warehousing services to its nearly 7,500 members in 36 states. Founded in 1921 by Mississippi cotton producer Oscar Bledsoe and 10 Delta growers, the co-op's Staplcotn business now sells almost 2 million bales of cotton annually, produced by more than 6,000 growers. Most of the yield is sold to the US textile industry to make men's knit underwear, T-shirts, sheets, towels, and denim. Customers include Fruit of the Loom and Levi's. The co-op's Stapldiscount subsidiary offers low-interest loans for equipment, buildings, and land to members and non-members alike.

KEY COMPETITORS
Calcot
Dunavant Enterprises
Plains Cotton

STATE FARM MUTUAL AUTOMOBILE INSURANCE COMPANY

1 State Farm Plaza
Bloomington, IL 61710
Phone: 309-766-2311
Fax: 309-766-3621
Web site: http://www1.statefarm.com

CEO: Edward B. Rust
CFO: Roger S. Joslin
HR: Arlene Hogan
Type: Mutual company

1998 Sales: $27,706.0 million
1-Yr. Sales Change: (1.1%)
Employees: 76,257
FYE: December

More cars are in the hands of State Farm Mutual Automobile Insurance (about 20% of US automobiles) than those of its nearest competitor, Allstate. The US's largest personal lines property/casualty company, State Farm provides auto insurance as well as homeowners, nonmedical health, and life insurance. The firm now has a federal thrift charter and provides such banking services as deposit accounts, CDs, mortgages, and other loans in Illinois and Missouri, with plans to eventually expand into Arizona. State Farm operates throughout the US and Canada and has some 16,500 agents. Since its founding, the firm has been run by only two families, the Mecherles (1922-54) and the Rusts (1954-present).

KEY COMPETITORS
AIG
Allstate
Liberty Mutual

See pages 460–461 for a full profile of this company.

STATE OF FLORIDA DEPARTMENT OF THE LOTTERY

250 Marriott Dr.	CEO: David Griffin	1998 Sales: $2,130.8 million
Tallahassee, FL 32301	CFO: Barbara E. Goltz	1-Yr. Sales Change: (1.3%)
Phone: 850-487-7777	HR: Robert Gwaltney	Employees: 730
Fax: 850-487-4541	Type: Government-owned	FYE: June
Web site: http://www.flalottery.com		

People are always up for an elusive quest, whether it's searching for the Fountain of Youth or trying to hit the jackpot in the Florida Lottery. The State of Florida Department of the Lottery runs instant-play scratch tickets and lotto-type games, including Florida Lotto (the big jackpot), Fantasy 5, and Cash 3. Players also become eligible to play on the Lottery's weekly television game show *Flamingo Fortune*. The Lottery gives 38 cents of every dollar generated to Florida's Educational Enhancement Trust Fund, which provides funding for programs from pre-kindergarten up to the state university. Lottery officials switched the lotto drawing from once to twice a week in hopes of reviving sluggish sales.

KEY COMPETITORS
Georgia Lottery
Multi-State Lottery
Liberty Mutual

STATE UNIVERSITY OF NEW YORK

State University Plaza	CEO: Thomas F. Egan	1998 Sales: $4,563.9 million
Albany, NY 12246	CFO: Brian T. Stenson	1-Yr. Sales Change: 7.6%
Phone: 518-443-5555	HR: —	Employees: 65,000
Fax: 518-443-5321	Type: School	FYE: June
Web site: http://www.suny.edu		

Skies may be gray in The Empire State, but there's always a SUNY campus nearby. The State University of New York (SUNY), with about 370,000 students on 64 campuses, is neck and neck with California State University as the largest university system in the country. SUNY enrolls about one-third of New York's college students. SUNY's system includes 13 university colleges and four university centers offering undergraduate, graduate, postgraduate, and research programs, and a network of community and technology colleges (its 30 community colleges account for the majority of SUNY's enrollment). SUNY also operates colleges specializing in forestry, optometry, maritime studies, and technology.

 See pages 462–463 for a full profile of this company.

STATER BROS. HOLDINGS INC.

21700 Barton Rd.	CEO: Jack H. Brown	1999 Sales: $1,850.0 million
Colton, CA 92324	CFO: Dennis N. Beal	1-Yr. Sales Change: 7.2%
Phone: 909-783-5000	HR: Kathy Finazzo	Employees: 13,000
Fax: 909-783-3930	Type: Private	FYE: September

Although supermarket chain Stater Bros. Markets doesn't serve many movie stars (like rival Ralph's) or command national attention (like rivals Albertson's and Safeway), it is a star to the simple folk in Southern California. Stater Bros. Holdings has about 110 full-service supermarkets, mostly in Riverside and San Bernardino Counties. It also has stores in Kern, Los Angeles, and Orange Counties and is converting nearly 45 outlets it bought from Albertson's to the Stater format. The company also has a 50% stake in milk and juice processor Santee Dairies. Stater Bros. is owned by La Cadena Investments, a general partnership consisting of Stater Bros. CEO Jack Brown and other company executives.

KEY COMPETITORS
Albertson's
Fred Meyer
Safeway

 See pages 464–465 for a full profile of this company.

STEINER CORPORATION

505 E. South Temple	CEO: Richard Steiner	1999 Est. Sales: $650.0 million
Salt Lake City, UT 84102	CFO: Kevin Steiner	1-Yr. Sales Change: 4.0%
Phone: 801-328-8831	HR: —	Employees: 9,100
Fax: 801-363-5680	Type: Private	FYE: June

From aprons to air filters, Steiner does its part to keep things clean. Steiner's businesses include American Industrial, a restroom service provider that also rents and sells uniforms, towels, and restroom supplies; American Linen, a bed and table linen supplier; and National Filter Media, which makes a wide range of air pollution-control and liquid-filtration products. The company also owns half of manufacturer American Uniforms. Steiner sells its products to commercial and industrial consumers in Australia, Brazil, Canada, Germany, Italy, Mexico, and the US. It was founded by George A. Steiner in 1889 as a small linen supplier in Lincoln, Nebraska; the Steiner family still owns and runs the company.

KEY COMPETITORS
Cintas
CLARCOR
Swisher

STEVEDORING SERVICES OF AMERICA INC.

1131 SW Klickitat Way	CEO: Frederick D. Smith	1999 Est. Sales: $835.0 million
Seattle, WA 98134	CFO: Charles Sadowski	1-Yr. Sales Change: (1.8%)
Phone: 206-623-0304	HR: —	Employees: 5,000
Fax: 206-623-0179	Type: Private	FYE: January
Web site: http://www.ssofa.com		

Stevedoring is a romantic-sounding word for heavy lifting. As one of the world's largest stevedoring companies, Stevedoring Services of America loads and unloads ships at ports and terminals from Seattle to New Zealand. The company also provides rail yard services, trucking, and warehousing. Through its information services department, the firm processes orders and organizes and tracks shipments. Founded in 1880, Stevedoring Services of America is owned by the Smith and Hemingway families. In a joint venture with erstwhile Lada-importer Motores Internacionales of Panama, the company constructed Manzanillo International Terminal in Panama, reputed to be one of the most efficient ports in the world.

KEY COMPETITORS
Alexander & Baldwin
International Terminal
 Operating
P&O

STONEGATE RESOURCES, LLC

2200 Ross Ave., Ste. 4900	CEO: John D. Roach	1998 Sales: $826.0 million
Dallas, TX 75201	CFO: Kevin P. O'Meara	1-Yr. Sales Change: —
Phone: 214-880-3500	HR: —	Employees: —
Fax: 214-880-3599	Type: Private	FYE: December

A leading consolidator in the building products industry, Stonegate Resources is constructing a sturdy portfolio. The company was created by CEO John Roach and investment firm Joseph Littlejohn & Levy in 1997 to acquire building supply businesses. Stonegate makes its purchases through its BSL Holdings unit, the US's third-largest distributor of building materials to homebuilders and contractors. BSL Holdings operates over 70 distribution centers in about 10 states through four main subsidiaries: Pelican Companies (Florida, Georgia, North and South Carolina, Tennessee), Builders' Supply & Lumber (Florida, Georgia, Maryland, North Carolina, Virginia), Western Building Products (Ohio), and MBS Holdings (Texas).

KEY COMPETITORS
Cameron Ashley
Carolina Holdings
North Pacific Group

THE STRUCTURE TONE ORGANIZATION

15 East 26th St.
New York, NY 10010
Phone: 212-481-6100
Fax: 212-685-9267
Web site: http://www.structuretone.com

CEO: Anthony Carvette
CFO: Ray Froimowitz
HR: Tony Tursy
Type: Private

1999 Est. Sales: $1,520.0 million
1-Yr. Sales Change: —
Employees: 1,000

Structured to set the right tone for its clients, The Structure Tone Organization (STO) operates three construction firms: Structure Tone, Constructors & Associates, and Pavarini Construction. Founded in 1971, Structure Tone provides general contracting services in the US, Asia, and Europe; its clients include MetLife and Donaldson, Lufkin & Jenrette. Constructors & Associates (which was formed in 1977 and joined STO in 1988) operates in the western and southwestern US. Pavarini Construction, which began in 1896 and joined STO in 1996, helped build such New York City projects as the Seagram Building and The Chrysler Building East. John White and Patrick Donaghy, members of STO's founding family, own the firm.

KEY COMPETITORS
AJ Contracting
Devcon Construction
Turner Corporation

SUBWAY

325 Bic Dr.
Milford, CT 06460
Phone: 203-877-4281
Fax: 203-876-6695
Web site: http://www.subway.com

CEO: Frederick A. DeLuca
CFO: Carmela DeLuca
HR: Wendy Kopazna
Type: Private

1998 Sales: $3,100.0 million
1-Yr. Sales Change: (6.1%)
Employees: —
FYE: December

Subway provides a fast track to low-fat fast food. With some 14,000 submarine sandwich restaurants in nearly 75 countries, Subway has more franchises than any other restaurant chain except McDonald's. There are nearly 12,000 franchised Subway shops in the US alone. Locations range from freestanding units to those in shopping centers, airports, school cafeterias, convenience stores, and truck stops. Subway features a variety of hot and cold sandwiches and markets its sandwiches as healthy alternatives to burgers. The company, which charges the highest royalty fee in fast-food franchising, has had some unhappy franchisees. Co-founders Fred DeLuca (president) and Peter Buck (chairman) own the company.

KEY COMPETITORS
Blimpie
McDonald's
TRICON

 See pages 466–467 for a full profile of this company.

SUNBELT BEVERAGE CORPORATION

4601 Hollins Ferry Rd.
Baltimore, MD 21227
Phone: 410-536-5000
Fax: 410-536-5560

CEO: Gene Luciano
CFO: —
HR: Ronald Meliker
Type: Private

1998 Est. Sales: $770.0 million
1-Yr. Sales Change: 10.0%
Employees: 1,700
FYE: December

A formerly flat division of drugs and sundries wholesaler McKesson HBOC, Sunbelt Beverage has become one of the biggest swigs in its business. A leading wine and spirits wholesaler in a rapidly consolidating industry, the company operates through three subsidiaries — Premier Beverage (Florida), Churchill Distributors (Maryland), Ben Arnold-Heritage Beverage (South Carolina) — and owns 50% of Alliance Beverage Distribution (Arizona). Division management bought Sunbelt Beverage from McKesson and took it private in 1988 with the backing of investment firm Weiss, Peck & Greer. Herman Merinoff, owner of New York-based wholesaler Charmer Industries, has a majority stake in Sunbelt Beverage.

KEY COMPETITORS
National Distributing
Southern Wine & Spirits
Young's Market

SUN-DIAMOND GROWERS OF CALIFORNIA

5568 Gibraltar Dr.
Pleasanton, CA 94588
Phone: 925-463-8200
Fax: 925-463-7439
Web site: http://www.sundiamond.com

CEO: Robert A. Beckwith
CFO: William P. Beaton
HR: Bev Rogers
Type: Cooperative

1997 Sales: $744.0 million
1-Yr. Sales Change: 9.7%
Employees: 1,850
FYE: July

Belonging to Sun-Diamond strikes about 5,000 growers as a bright idea. Sun-Diamond Growers of California is a dried fruits and nuts producers cooperative. It sells products worldwide to grocery chains, cereal companies, bakers, and other industrial users under the Diamond, Sun-Maid, Sunsweet, Blue Ribbon, and Hazelnut Growers brands. Formed in 1980, Sun-Diamond provides sales and support services for its members. It consists of five co-ops: Diamond Walnut Growers, Sun-Maid Growers of California, Sunsweet Growers, Valley Fig Growers, and Hazelnut Growers of Oregon. In 1999 an appeals court overturned a 1996 ruling that convicted Sun-Diamond of giving illegal gifts to former Agriculture Secretary Mike Espy.

KEY COMPETITORS
Dole
John Sanfilippo & Son
Nabisco Holdings

SUNKIST GROWERS, INC.

14130 Riverside Dr.
Sherman Oaks, CA 91423
Phone: 818-986-4800
Fax: 818-379-7405
Web site: http://www.sunkist.com

CEO: Vincent Lupinacci
CFO: H. B. Flach
HR: John R. McGovern
Type: Cooperative

1998 Sales: $1,068.7 million
1-Yr. Sales Change: (0.6%)
Employees: 875
FYE: October

Perhaps the US enterprise least susceptible to an outbreak of scurvy, Sunkist Growers is a cooperative owned by 6,500 citrus farmers in California and Arizona. Sunkist markets fresh oranges, lemons, grapefruit, and tangerines in the US and overseas. Fruit that doesn't meet fresh market standards is sent to the co-op's Processed Products division, where it's turned into juices and oils for use in food products. The Sunkist brand is one of the most recognized names in the US; through licensing agreements, the name appears on dozens of beverages and other products, from flowers to fruit rolls, in more than 50 countries. About one-fourth of Sunkist's sales come from outside the US, mainly Japan and Hong Kong.

KEY COMPETITORS
Chiquita Brands
Dole
Nabisco Holdings

 See pages 468–469 for a full profile of this company.

SUNRIDER INTERNATIONAL

1625 Abalone Ave.
Torrance, CA 90501
Phone: 310-781-3808
Fax: 310-222-9273
Web site: http://www.sunrider.com

CEO: Tei Fu Chen
CFO: —
HR: Kim Carney
Type: Private

1997 Est. Sales: $700.0 million
1-Yr. Sales Change: 0.0%
Employees: 200
FYE: December

Sunrider International markets a variety of health and beauty products made from herbs and herbal extracts, including Sunrider nutritional products and SunSmile and Kandesn personal-care products. Sunrider sells its products, which are made in China, Singapore, Taiwan, and the US, through multilevel marketing via some 1 million independent distributors in more than 25 countries. Owners Tei Fu Chen and Oi-Lin Chen (husband and wife: he studied pharmacy; she's a medical doctor) started the company in 1982. The couple has paid more than $93 million to the US government in relation to charges stemming from nonpayment of taxes and failure to declare items brought into the US.

KEY COMPETITORS
Herbalife
Nature's Sunshine
Nabisco Holdings

SUPERCOM, INC.

410 S. Abbott Ave.
Milpitas, CA 95035
Phone: 408-456-8888
Fax: 408-456-9010
Web site: http://www.supercom.com

CEO: James Fang
CFO: Gabrielle Tetreault
HR: B. B. Sato
Type: Private

1998 Est. Sales: $900.0 million
1-Yr. Sales Change: 24.1%
Employees: 600
FYE: October

Look, it's neither bird nor plane. It's Supercom. The wholesaler offers computer components, custom assembly services, and technical support to retailers throughout the US and in Canada. Founded in 1983, the company distributes computer systems, add-on boards, peripherals, storage devices, servers, networking equipment, and other products to the computer reseller market. Supercom also offers technical support, installation, and repairs for resellers without in-house technical services, and it assembles customized computer systems under the Touch, T-Link, and Alacran brands. President Jim Fang owns the company.

KEY COMPETITORS
Merisel
MicroAge
Micro Warehouse

SUTHERLAND LUMBER COMPANY, L.P.

4000 Main St.
Kansas City, MO 64111
Phone: 816-756-3000
Fax: 816-756-3594

CEO: Steve Scott
CFO: Steve Scott
HR: Shanna Wilson
Type: Private

1998 Sales: $780.0 million
1-Yr. Sales Change: 5.4%
Employees: 3,000
FYE: December

Who says lumber can't be high tech? Sutherland Lumber Company operates about 70 lumber and home improvement stores in 15 mostly southern states and sells its products online through its Housemart.com subsidiary. Its stores range in size from 50,000 to 190,000 sq. ft. Sutherland sells lumber, paints, tools, and building packages for houses, sheds, garages, and farm buildings. In addition, the stores sell plumbing supplies, lawn and garden equipment, and materials for hobbies and crafts. The family-owned company is operated by siblings Donna, Herman, John, and Robert Sutherland. The Sutherland family also has holdings in ranching and timber companies, farmland, and manufacturing.

KEY COMPETITORS
Ace Hardware
Hechinger
Home Depot

SUTTER HEALTH

1 Capitol Mall
Sacramento, CA 95816
Phone: 916-733-8800
Fax: 916-554-6611
Web site: http://www.sutterhealth.org

CEO: Van R. Johnson
CFO: Robert Reed
HR: Ken Buback
Type: Not-for-profit

1998 Sales: $2,881.4 million
1-Yr. Sales Change: 8.2%
Employees: 35,000
FYE: December

Sutter Health is one of the nation's largest not-for-profit health care systems. The company provides services to more than 3 million people in more than 100 Northern California communities; services are provided through the firm's approximately 5,000 affiliated doctors, as well as the California care centers (26 acute care hospitals, seven long-term care centers, 18 regional home health/hospice programs) managed by the firm. Sutter Health also has one hospital in Hawaii. The company has a controlling stake in the Omni Healthcare HMO, which it is trying to sell. Sutter Health was organized in 1996 through the merger of Sutter Health and California Healthcare System.

KEY COMPETITORS
Catholic Healthcare West
Kaiser Foundation
Tenet Healthcare

SWAGELOK

29500 Solon Rd.
Solon, OH 44139
Phone: 440-248-4600
Fax: 440-349-5970
Web site: http://www.swagelok.com

CEO: Francis J. Callahan
CFO: Norge Tobbe
HR: Joe Tucker
Type: Private

1998 Est. Sales: $1,030.0 million
1-Yr. Sales Change: (14.2%)
Employees: 5,000
FYE: December

With sales partners worldwide, it's vital for Swagelok to speak many languages fluidly. The company makes fluid system components, which include plug, pinch, and radial diaphragm valves, sanitary fittings, welding systems, and more than 8,200 other products. Its products are used by bioprocessing and pharmaceuticals research companies and in the oil and gas, power, and semiconductor industries. Swagelok has a network of 270 manufacturing, research, sales, and distribution facilities in about 40 countries. Founded in 1947 by Fred Lennon in his kitchen, the company requires all prospective associates and their families to tour company facilities for two months before coming on board.

KEY COMPETITORS
CIRCOR International
ITT Industries
Tyco International

SWEETHEART CUP COMPANY

10100 Reisterstown Rd.
Owings Mills, MD 21117
Phone: 410-363-1111
Fax: 410-998-1828
Web site: http://www.sweetheart.com

CEO: Dennis Mehiel
CFO: Hans H. Heinsen
HR: Jeffery Seidman
Type: Private

1999 Est. Sales: $1,200.0 million
1-Yr. Sales Change: 42.3%
Employees: 8,050
FYE: September

The words "Can I get that to go?" are like money in the bank for Sweetheart Cup. The company produces disposable paper and plastic cups, plates, cutlery, and food packaging, sold under brand names such as Centerpiece, Lily, Preference, Silent Service, and Sweetheart. Customers include McDonald's (about 12% of sales) and Wendy's, as well as hospitals, schools, and full-service restaurants. Sweetheart also makes and leases container-filling equipment for dairies and food companies, including ice-cream makers Ben & Jerry's Homemade and Blue Bell Creameries. CEO Dennis Mehiel owns 90% of Sweetheart Cup through SF Holdings Group, which also owns disposable-tray and -plate maker Fonda Group.

KEY COMPETITORS
Dart Container
Fort James
Huhtamaki Van Leer

SWIFTY SERVE CORPORATION

1824 Hillandale Rd.
Durham, NC 27705
Phone: 919-384-9888
Fax: 919-384-1578

CEO: Wayne M. Rogers
CFO: C. Alan Bentley
HR: Ronnie Paulk
Type: Private

1998 Sales: $867.0 million
1-Yr. Sales Change: —
Employees: 5,675
FYE: December

Swifty Serve can get you fueled up for that next long road trip. The convenience store operator provides gasoline, coffee, and other essentials for drivers passing through the Southeast. It operates more than 500 stores in Alabama, Florida, Georgia, Louisiana, and Mississippi and plans to expand into North and South Carolina. Co-CEOs W. Clay Hamner and Wayne Rogers (who played Trapper John in the TV series *M*A*S*H*) formed Swifty Serve in 1999 by combining the Swifty Mart and E-Z Serve chains. Hamner and Rogers (previously partners in The Pantry, a rival chain) own 29% of the company. Other shareholders include investment firms Halpern, Denny (29%), Electra Fleming (23%), and Bay Harbour (19%).

KEY COMPETITORS
7-Eleven
The Pantry
Racetrac Petroleum

SWINERTON INCORPORATED

580 California St., Ste. 1100
San Francisco, CA 94104
Phone: 415-421-2980
Fax: 415-433-0943
Web site: http://www.swinerton.com

CEO: David H. Grubb
CFO: James R. Gillette
HR: David Ferretti
Type: Private

1998 Sales: $902.0 million
1-Yr. Sales Change: 13.9%
Employees: 1,500
FYE: December

Swinerton Incorporated, founded in the late 19th century, is riding the crest of the late 20th century's construction boom. The company builds high-rises, but it keeps a low profile. Nonetheless, it earned accolades from an industry publication, the *Engineering News-Record,* as the fastest-growing among the top 50 general builders. Swinerton builds a diverse array of facilities: resorts, subsidized housing, public schools, Hollywood soundstages, hospitals, and airport terminals. It has offices in Arizona, California, Colorado, Florida, Oregon, and Texas. In addition to construction services, the employee-owned company offers consulting, general contracting, and property management services.

KEY COMPETITORS
Gilbane
Hathaway Dinwiddie
 Construction
Whiting-Turner

TAC WORLDWIDE COMPANIES

109 Oak St.
Newton, MA 02164
Phone: 617-969-3100
Fax: 617-244-9849
Web site: http://www.1tac.com

CEO: Anthony J. Balsamo
CFO: Jack Joynt
HR: Bob Moritz
Type: Private

1998 Sales: $737.0 million
1-Yr. Sales Change: 13.7%
Employees: 1,075
FYE: December

TAC Worldwide aims to be a permanent force in the temp business. The company offers contract and temporary employees through 125 offices in all 50 states and more than 22 countries in Europe, North America, and Southeast Asia. TAC places personnel in positions that include automotive and engineering work, technical and computer-related jobs, entertainment staffing, and clerical and office positions. Each year the company places some 50,000 employees in more than 6,500 local, national, and international companies. Family-owned TAC was founded by chairman Salvatore Balsamo in 1969.

KEY COMPETITORS
Adecco
Kelly Services
Manpower

TANG INDUSTRIES, INC.

3773 Howard Hughes Pkwy.
Las Vegas, NV 89109
Phone: 702-734-3700
Fax: 702-734-6766

CEO: Cyrus Tang
CFO: Kurt R. Swanson
HR: Vaughn Kuerschner
Type: Private

1998 Sales: $1,200.0 million
1-Yr. Sales Change: 23.1%
Employees: 3,500
FYE: December

Although it's not a good source of Vitamin C, Tang Industries *is* a diversified holding company; its largest holding is National Material, a metal-fabricating and -distributing company that engages in steel stamping and recycles and trades aluminum and scrap metal. In a joint venture with Acme Steel, National Material operates a wide-steel-coil processing plant in Chicago. The firm also has steel operations in China. Tang Industries' holdings include real estate, manufacturer GF Office Furniture, and Curatek Pharmaceuticals, which specializes in niche markets overlooked by large drugmakers. The company was founded in 1964 by Chinese immigrant Cyrus Tang after he bought a small metal-stamping shop in Illinois.

KEY COMPETITORS
Commercial Metals
Ryerson Tull
Steelcase

TAP HOLDINGS INC.

Bannockburn Lake Office Plaza, 2355 Waukegan Rd.
Deerfield, IL 60015
Phone: 847-317-5700
Fax: 847-940-9801
Web site: http://www.tapholdings.com

CEO: H. Thomas Watkins
CFO: Stafford O'Kelly
HR: Denise Kitchen
Type: Joint venture

1998 Sales: $2,062.7 million
1-Yr. Sales Change: 31.7%
Employees: 2,000
FYE: December

TAP Holdings' research may be of interest to Bob Dole. Rising to Pfizer's challenge, the firm is developing apomorphine, an erection-inducing drug that may be quicker on the draw than Viagra (acting in 10-12 minutes, compared to Viagra's potentially mood-killing hour). This use for apomorphine (originally used to induce vomiting) is in trials; the drug is also being tested to treat Parkinson's disease. TAP, which has more drugs in its pipeline, makes such products as Lupron (primarily for prostate cancer) and Prevacid (for ulcers). TAP Holdings is a joint venture of longtime partners Takeda Chemical Industries and Abbott Laboratories; Takeda's desire to penetrate the US market may weaken the relationship.

KEY COMPETITORS
AstraZeneca
Pfizer
Warner-Lambert

TAUBER OIL COMPANY

55 Waugh Dr., Ste. 700
Houston, TX 77210
Phone: 713-869-8700
Fax: 713-869-8069
Web site: http://www.tauberoil.com

CEO: O. J. Tauber
CFO: Stephen E. Hamlin
HR: Debbie Moseley
Type: Private

1998 Sales: $901.0 million
1-Yr. Sales Change: (20.1%)
Employees: 45
FYE: September

No petrochemical product is taboo for oil refiner and marketer Tauber Oil. The company markets refined petroleum products, natural gas, carbon black feedstocks, liquefied petroleum gases, chemicals, and petrochemicals. Subsidiary Tauber Petrochemical was created in 1997 to beef up the company's international petrochemical business. In 1996 Tauber Oil signed a three-year, $100 million deal with South Korea's Samsung General Chemicals to import styrene monomer, the basic ingredient of plastic and synthetic resins used in various electronic devices, auto parts, and accessories. Tauber Oil was founded by O. J. Tauber Sr. in 1953.

KEY COMPETITORS
Exxon Mobil
Global Petroleum
Lyondell Chemical

TAYLOR CORPORATION

1725 Roe Crest Dr.
North Mankato, MN 56003
Phone: 507-625-2828
Fax: 507-625-2988

CEO: Glen Taylor
CFO: Bill Kozitza
HR: —
Type: Private

1998 Est. Sales: $826.5 million
1-Yr. Sales Change: (8.2%)
Employees: 11,000
FYE: December

Taylor Corporation has an invitation to print just about everything but money. One of the largest specialty printers in the US, Taylor is a holding company for about 70 firms in Australia, Europe, and North America. The company's subsidiaries (such as catalog company Current) print business cards, envelopes, graduation announcements, greeting cards, labels, stationery, and wedding invitations. Other subsidiaries offer direct marketing, office supplies, and online sales of printed products. Chairman and CEO Glen Taylor owns the company he founded in 1975. He is also majority owner of the Minnesota Timberwolves and is a former Minnesota state senator.

KEY COMPETITORS
Banta
Hallmark
Quebecor Printing

TEACHERS INSURANCE AND ANNUITY ASSOCIATION-COLLEGE RETIREMENT EQUITIES FUND

730 3rd Ave.
New York, NY 10017
Phone: 212-490-9000
Fax: 212-916-6231
Web site: http://www.tiaa-cref.org

CEO: John H. Biggs
CFO: Richard L. Gibbs
HR: Matina S. Horner
Type: Not-for-profit

1998 Sales: $45,898.5 million
1-Yr. Sales Change: 10.8%
Employees: 5,000
FYE: December

It's punishment enough to write the name *once* on a blackboard. Teachers Insurance and Annuity Association-College Retirement Equities Fund (known as TIAA-CREF) is the world's largest, if not longest-named, private pension system, providing for teachers and other academic staff members. TIAA-CREF is divided into two business divisions: Retirement Services, which offers pension funds, annuities, and IRAs; and TIAA-CREF Enterprises, which offers tuition financing education IRAs. Other products include life, health, and disability insurance, no-load mutual funds, and trust services through TIAA-CREF Trust Company.

KEY COMPETITORS
Charles Schwab
FMR
Vanguard Group

 See pages 470–471 for a full profile of this company.

TENNESSEE VALLEY AUTHORITY

400 W. Summit Hill Dr.
Knoxville, TN 37902
Phone: 423-632-2101
Fax: 423-632-6783
Web site: http://www.tva.gov

CEO: Craven Crowell
CFO: David N. Smith
HR: Wally Tanksley
Type: Government-owned

1998 Sales: $6,729.0 million
1-Yr. Sales Change: 21.2%
Employees: 13,818
FYE: September

A working monument to the New Deal, the Tennessee Valley Authority (TVA) is the largest electric power producer in the US. The federal corporation transmits electricity primarily to 159 local power companies, which sell it to some 7 million retail customers. TVA is the sole power provider in nearly all of Tennessee and parts of Alabama, Georgia, Kentucky, Mississippi, North Carolina, and Virginia. It also manages the Tennessee River system (the US's fifth-largest). TVA does not pay taxes, and it can use its government affiliation to find loans at favorable rates. The agency is preparing for deregulation with a 10-year business plan that includes halving its large debt.

KEY COMPETITORS
Cinergy
Entergy
Southern Company

 See pages 472–473 for a full profile of this company.

THE TEXAS A&M UNIVERSITY SYSTEM

John B. Connally Bldg., 301 Tarrow, 3rd Fl.
College Station, TX 77843
Phone: 409-845-3211
Fax: 409-845-5406
Web site: http://tamusystem.tamu.edu

CEO: Howard D. Graves
CFO: Tom D. Kale
HR: Patti Couger
Type: School

1998 Sales: $1,694.9 million
1-Yr. Sales Change: 9.3%
Employees: 23,300
FYE: August

The Aggies' school-spirit is appropriately Texas-sized. With nine universities, eight state agencies, and a health sciences center, The Texas A&M University System offers instruction to more than 90,000 students. Texas A&M in College Station, the largest institution in the system, was founded in 1876, the first public college in Texas. Also within the system are Prairie View A&M University, Tarleton State University, Texas A&M International University, West Texas A&M University, and Texas A&M Universities in Commerce, Corpus Christi, Kingsville, and Texarkana. The system's state agencies include the Texas Agricultural Extension Service and the Texas Forest Service.

See pages 474–475 for a full profile of this company.

TEXAS HEALTH RESOURCES

600 E. Las Colinas Blvd.
Irving, TX 75039
Phone: 214-818-4500
Fax: 214-818-4652
Web site: http://www.texashealth.org

CEO: Douglas D. Hawthorne
CFO: Ron Bourland
HR: —
Type: Not-for-profit

1998 Sales: $1,286.3 million
1-Yr. Sales Change: 2.9%
Employees: 15,000
FYE: December

The largest hospital system in North Texas, Texas Health Resources is a not-for-profit health care system with 16 hospitals, most of them in the Dallas/Fort Worth area. The system includes mental health centers, a retirement community and senior care centers, consulting and management services, and Harris Methodist Health Plan, an HMO with some 300,000 members. Texas Health Resources' alliance with Baylor Health Care System is on hold until its troubled HMO merges with Blue Cross and Blue Shield of Texas, creating the state's largest health insurance company. Its physician organization, Harris Methodist Select, may disband if neither Texas Health Resources nor Blue Cross (TX) accepts its 6,000 doctor contracts.

KEY COMPETITORS
Baylor Health
Columbia/HCA
Southern Company

TEXAS LOTTERY COMMISSION

611 E. 6th St.
Austin, TX 78701
Phone: 512-344-5000
Fax: 512-344-5490
Web site: http://www.txlottery.org

CEO: Linda Cloud
CFO: Bart Sanchez
HR: Jim Richardson
Type: Government-owned

1998 Sales: $3,106.2 million
1-Yr. Sales Change: (17.4%)
Employees: 335
FYE: August

The eyes of Texas are watching the lotto jackpot. The Texas Lottery Commission oversees the country's third-largest state lottery (behind New York and Massachusetts), which has pumped more than $7 billion into state coffers since it was created in 1991. About 55% of lottery sales are paid out in prize money, while more than 30% goes to the state's Foundation School Fund. The lottery offers four numbers games, including Lotto Texas, Pick 3, Cash 5, and Texas Million, and several instant-win games sold through retailers and vending machines around the state. Retailers like grocery stores, gas stations, and liquor and convenience stores make a small commission on tickets they sell.

KEY COMPETITORS
Multi-State Lottery
Columbia/HCA
Southern Company

See pages 476–477 for a full profile of this company.

TEXAS PACIFIC GROUP

201 Main St., Ste. 2420
Fort Worth, TX 76102
Phone: 817-871-4000
Fax: 817-871-4010

CEO: David Bonderman
CFO: Jim O'Brien
HR: Michelle Reese
Type: Partnership

Sales: —
1-Yr. Sales Change: —
Employees: —
FYE: December

Yee-hah! Let's round us up some LBOs. Investment firm Texas Pacific Group has staked its claim on the buyout frontier with a reputation for scooping up and reforming troubled companies other firms wouldn't dare touch. Its holdings include Oxford Health Plans, Magellan Health Services, Ducati Motor, J. Crew Group, semiconductor maker Zilog, and wineries. With some $3 billion in funds, Texas Pacific Group makes money not only from fund management fees but also from the increased values of holdings. With the US buyout frontier becoming increasingly settled and expensive, the company is heading overseas to invest in Europe. CEO David "Bondo" Bonderman is known for turning around Continental Airlines.

KEY COMPETITORS
Clayton, Dubilier
Hicks, Muse
KKR

See pages 478–479 for a full profile of this company.

TIMEX CORPORATION

Park Rd. Extension
Middlebury, CT 06762
Phone: 203-573-5000
Fax: 203-573-6901
Web site: http://www.timex.com

CEO: C. Michael Jacobi
CFO: W. John Dryfe
HR: M.A. Saleh
Type: Private

1997 Est. Sales: $600.0 million
1-Yr. Sales Change: (7.7%)
Employees: 7,500
FYE: December

Branching out from its original "Takes a licking" designs, Timex is strapping on new faces in order to tap new markets. The company has expanded its lines from simple, low-cost watches to include high-tech tickers capable of paging or downloading computer data. Its sports watches have gone upscale and gadgety with lines like Humvee and Ironman. (The brightness of its Indiglo watch helped a man lead a group of people down 34 flights of dark stairs after the World Trade Center bombing.) Timex watches are sold in over 90 countries via department stores, about a dozen Timex stores in the US, and online. Timex was founded in 1854 as Waterbury Clock and is owned by Fred Olsen, whose father bought the company in 1942.

KEY COMPETITORS
Casio Computer
Seiko
Swatch

TISHMAN REALTY & CONSTRUCTION CO. INC.

666 5th Ave.
New York, NY 10103
Phone: 212-399-3600
Fax: 212-397-1316

CEO: John Tishman
CFO: Larry Schwarzwalder
HR: Christine Smith
Type: Private

1999 Est. Sales: $1,005.0 million
1-Yr. Sales Change: 7.3%
Employees: 800
FYE: June

Tishman Realty & Construction is an immigrant success story writ large. The privately owned company builds and manages office, hospitality, and recreational property for its own account and offers third-party developers a full menu of real estate design, construction, management, and financing services. High profile projects handled by the company (or its publicly owned predecessor) include Disney World's EPCOT Center, the World Trade Center, and its E Walk entertainment and hotel complex in New York City. Chairman and CEO John Tishman and his family, scions of immigrant Julius Tishman, who began building tenements a century ago, own the company.

KEY COMPETITORS
Gilbane
JMB Realty
Reckson Associates Realty

 See pages 480–481 for a full profile of this company.

TOPA EQUITIES, LTD.

1800 Avenue of the Stars, Ste. 1400
Los Angeles, CA 90067
Phone: 310-203-9199
Fax: 310-557-1837

CEO: John E. Anderson
CFO: Brenda Seuthe
HR: Virginia Flores
Type: Private

1998 Est. Sales: $765.0 million
1-Yr. Sales Change: 1.7%
Employees: 1,300
FYE: December

Holding company Topa Equities casts a wide net. Owned by John Anderson, Topa has three dozen or so businesses involved in banking, insurance, beer distribution, real estate, automobile dealerships (Silver Star Automotive), citrus ranches, and more. Subsidiaries rent land, buildings, and furniture from Topa, which owns most long-term assets. Topa's beverage operations — one of the "cash cows" that Anderson says feed his "pigs" — include Ace Beverage, Paradise Beverages, and Mission Beverages; the company has strongholds in the Hawaiian and Caribbean beer markets. Anderson founded the firm in 1956 when he bought the large Topa Topa ranch in Ojai, California. UCLA's Anderson management school is named for him.

KEY COMPETITORS
Citigroup
Penske Automotive
Young's Market

TOPCO ASSOCIATES INC.

7711 Gross Point Rd.	CEO: Steven K. Lauer	1999 Sales: $4,000.0 million
Skokie, IL 60077	CFO: Steven K. Lauer	1-Yr. Sales Change: 2.6%
Phone: 847-676-3030	HR: Ronald Ficks	Employees: 359
Fax: 847-933-9429	Type: Cooperative	FYE: March
Web site: http://www.topcoess.com		

Originally formed to help grocers deal with WWII shortages, Topco Associates is a cooperative-buying organization owned by 27 retailers, two food service companies, and one cooperative. The company uses the combined size of its members to buy products cheaper than members could buy on their own. Topco buys more than 7,000 private-label items, including fresh meat (which accounts for about 25% of sales), dairy and bakery items, produce, and general merchandise, among other items. Topco brands include Food Club, Kingston, and a line of "Top" brands like Top Crest. It also buys members' brand and name-brand items. Most of Topco's members are in the US, although it does serve Israel, Japan, and Puerto Rico.

KEY COMPETITORS
Loblaw
Shurfine International
Unified Western Grocers

 See pages 482–483 for a full profile of this company.

TOWERS PERRIN

335 Madison Ave.	CEO: John T. Lynch	1998 Sales: $1,125.0 million
New York, NY 10017	CFO: Patrick Gonnelli	1-Yr. Sales Change: —
Phone: 212-309-3400	HR: Ken Ranftle	Employees: 6,314
Fax: 212-309-0975	Type: Private	FYE: December
Web site: http://www.towers.com		

Towers Perrin gives out a lot of friendly advice — for a price. It is one of the world's largest management consultants, focusing on human resources and general management services, employee benefit services, and health industry consulting. The company serves about 10,000 clients (including most top US companies) through more than 70 offices in 24 countries. Its Tillinghast-Towers Perrin division provides insurance, finance, and risk management services, and its Towers Perrin Reinsurance unit assists clients with the placement of their reinsurance programs. Towers Perrin, which was founded in 1934, is owned by company executives and other key employees.

KEY COMPETITORS
Boston Consulting
Hewitt Associates
Watson Wyatt

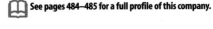 See pages 484–485 for a full profile of this company.

TRACINDA CORPORATION

150 Rodeo Dr., Ste. 250	CEO: Kirk Kerkorian	1997 Est. Sales: $1,500.0 million
Beverly Hills, CA 90212	CFO: Anthony L. Mandekic	1-Yr. Sales Change: 14.1%
Phone: 310-271-0638	HR: Anthony L. Mandekic	Employees: 750
Fax: 310-271-3416	Type: Private	FYE: December

Tracinda owns the MGM Grand hotel in Las Vegas, as well as the majority share of MGM, but its biggest show is billionaire owner Kirk Kerkorian. He has owned all or part of the film and television giant three separate times. Kerkorian bought MGM first in 1969 and sold it to Ted Turner (who kept pre-1986 movie rights), only to buy it back. He then sold MGM to financier Giancarlo Parretti, who defaulted, leaving Credit Lyonnais to auction it off. Again, Kerkorian won the bid, this time over the likes of Rupert Murdoch. Kerkorian also owns a 6% stake in DaimlerChrysler. In 1996 he and Lee Iaccoca failed in a takeover attempt, scoring instead a spot on the carmaker's board for Tracinda executive James Aljian.

KEY COMPETITORS
Mandalay Resort Group
News Corp.
Time Warner

TRADER JOE'S COMPANY

538 Mission St.
South Pasadena, CA 91031
Phone: 626-441-1177
Fax: 626-441-9573
Web site: http://www.traderjoes.com

CEO: John Shields
CFO: Mary Genest
HR: Rosella Moore
Type: Private

1998 Est. Sales: $900.0 million
1-Yr. Sales Change: 9.1%
Employees: 4,500
FYE: June

When it comes to grocery chains, Trader Joe's isn't your average Joe. With about 120 stores in 11 states, the company prides itself in offering low-priced grocery fare with unusual flair, such as unconventional recipes and special nutritional qualities. Its foods, which are sold mostly under the Trader Joe's label, are approved by a tasting panel before reaching the shelves. Started by Joe Coulombe as a Los Angeles convenience store chain in 1958, the company was bought by German billionaires Karl and Theo Albrecht in 1979. Trader Joe's stores are located in Arizona, California, Connecticut, Maryland, Massachusetts, Nevada, New Jersey, New York, Oregon, Virginia, and Washington state.

KEY COMPETITORS
Kroger
Safeway
Whole Foods

TRAMMELL CROW RESIDENTIAL

2859 Paces Ferry Rd.
Atlanta, GA 30339
Phone: 770-801-1600
Fax: 770-801-5395
Web site: http://www.tcrs.com

CEO: J. Ronald Terwilliger
CFO: Michael Collins
HR: Tim Swango
Type: Private

1998 Sales: $1,617.3 million
1-Yr. Sales Change: 22.4%
Employees: 3,500
FYE: December

Trammell Crow Residential is remodeling. One of the top 10 builders and managers of upscale apartment complexes in the country (it concentrates on the coasts where tight zoning laws keep out competition), the firm is selling off many of its properties to competing real estate investment trusts (REITs), including its Florida holdings to Gables Residential Trust, a REIT it spun off in 1994. The moves are to protect itself in the volatile real estate market. The company split off from mammoth Trammell Crow Co. in 1978 but is still associated with the Crow family empire of real estate development firms. In 1994 Trammell Crow Residential spun off its eastern divisions to form REITs Avalon Properties and Gables.

KEY COMPETITORS
Hines Interests
Inland Group
Lincoln Property

TRANSAMMONIA, INC.

350 Park Ave.
New York, NY 10022
Phone: 212-223-3200
Fax: 212-759-1410

CEO: Ronald P. Stanton
CFO: Edward G. Weiner
HR: Marguerite Harrington
Type: Private

1998 Sales: $2,104.0 million
1-Yr. Sales Change: (13.2%)
Employees: 249
FYE: December

Transammonia creates a stink wherever it goes. The company markets and ships some of the earth's smellier things but can clearly see beyond its nose. Transammonia deals in fertilizer, liquefied petroleum gases, and petrochemicals (including the alternative fuel methanol) and controls 25% of the worldwide ammonia market. Transammonia conducts its marketing operations through its Trammochem subsidiary and 20 regional offices, trading with partners in the Caribbean, Central and South America, Eastern and Western Europe, and the US. The company is part of two consortia (which include ammonia producers from Canada, Germany, Spain, and other countries) that are planning to build ammonia plants in Algeria and Trinidad.

KEY COMPETITORS
Agrium
CF Industries
Terra Industries

TRAVELCENTERS OF AMERICA, INC.

24601 Center Ridge Rd., Ste. 200	CEO: Edwin P. Kuhn	1998 Sales: $923.8 million
Westlake, OH 44145	CFO: James W. George	1-Yr. Sales Change: (11.1%)
Phone: 440-808-9100	HR: Ivan Wagner	Employees: 9,800
Fax: 440-808-3306	Type: Private	FYE: December
Web site: http://www.tatravelcenters.com		

TravelCenters of America is in the food, fuel, and relaxation business for the long haul. The company's network of more than 160 interstate highway travel centers in 40 states is the nation's largest. Company-owned and franchised truck stops provide gas, fast-food and sit-down restaurants, convenience stores, laundry and shower facilities, and TV and game rooms. Some outlets offer lodging, Internet kiosks, and truck repair services. Truckers account for about 80% of customers, but to lure more travelers the company is adding decorative enhancements and separate bathrooms (for those uneasy about seeing half-naked truckers shaving). The Clipper Group and management control TravelCenters of America.

KEY COMPETITORS
Flying J
Petro Stopping Centers
Pilot

TRI VALLEY GROWERS

12667 Alcosta Blvd.	CEO: Jeffrey P. Shaw	1998 Sales: $782.0 million
San Ramon, CA 94583	CFO: Dick Gelhaus	1-Yr. Sales Change: (8.4%)
Phone: 925-327-6400	HR: Kathy Borneman	Employees: 11,000
Fax: 925-327-6986	Type: Cooperative	FYE: June
Web site: http://www.trivalleygrowers.com		

Tri Valley Growers hopes it can preserve itself as well as it preserves its perishables. The 500-member fruit and vegetable co-op, one of the nation's largest food processors, produces over half of the US's canned peaches, 20% of its canned olives, and 10% of its canned tomato products. It sells its products under private and brand-name labels (including S&W Fine Foods, Libby, Oberti Olives, and Redpack Tomatoes) to supermarkets, food service companies, and the US government. Started in 1932, the co-op has eight plants in California and one in New Jersey. Tri Valley is trying to recover from sizable losses stemming from a declining canned fruit market and moves made by ousted CEO "Hurricane Joe" Famalette.

KEY COMPETITORS
Del Monte
Dole
Pro-Fac

THE TRUMP ORGANIZATION

725 5th Ave.	CEO: Donald J. Trump	1998 Est. Sales: $6,900.0 million
New York, NY 10022	CFO: Allen Weisselberg	1-Yr. Sales Change: 6.2%
Phone: 212-832-2000	HR: Norma Foerderer	Employees: 22,000
Fax: 212-935-0141	Type: Private	FYE: December

Almost a mythic figure of the Reagan era, real estate developer Donald Trump continues to raise the roof (and rents) in New York City. Through the Trump Organization, The Donald owns and develops several pieces of prime real estate in the Big Apple, including Trump International Hotel and Tower, 40 Wall Street, the General Motors Building, and the Empire State Building (50% interest). Trump also has a 42% stake in publicly traded Trump Hotels & Casino Resort, which operates three Atlantic City casinos (Trump Taj Mahal, Trump Plaza, and Trump Marina) and a riverboat casino in Indiana. Other holdings include a Florida resort and the Miss USA, Miss Teen USA, and Miss Universe beauty pageants.

KEY COMPETITORS
Lefrak Organization
Park Place Entertainment
Port Authority of NY & NJ

 See pages 486–487 for a full profile of this company.

TRUSERV CORPORATION

8600 W. Bryn Mawr Ave.
Chicago, IL 60631
Phone: 773-695-5000
Fax: 773-695-6558
Web site: http://www.truserv.com

CEO: Donald J. Hoye
CFO: Kerry J. Kirby
HR: Rob Ostroy
Type: Cooperative

1998 Sales: $4,328.2 million
1-Yr. Sales Change: 29.9%
Employees: 6,500
FYE: December

TruServ must have played its cards right — it has surpassed rival Ace Hardware as the largest member-owned hardware cooperative in the world. Formed by the merger of Cotter & Company (supplier to the True Value chain) and SERVISTAR COAST TO COAST, the cooperative serves some 10,000 outlets, including hardware chains Coast to Coast, ServiStar, and True Value. (Coast to Coast and ServiStar are being converted to the True Value banner.) Other chains include Grand Rental Station, Taylor Rental Center, Home & Garden Showplace, and V&S. Members are able to take advantage of shared buying power on lumber, hardware, paint, and other home and garden supplies. TruServ also manufactures paint and paint applicators.

KEY COMPETITORS
Ace Hardware
Home Depot
Lowe's

 See pages 488–489 for a full profile of this company.

TRUSTMARK INSURANCE COMPANY

400 Field Dr.
Lake Forest, IL 60045
Phone: 847-615-1500
Fax: 847-615-3910
Web site: http://www.trustmarkinsurance.com

CEO: Edwin R. Fattes
CFO: Richard D. Batten
HR: Robert R. Worobow
Type: Mutual company

1998 Sales: $1,058.2 million
1-Yr. Sales Change: 8.9%
Employees: 3,300
FYE: December

Trustmark Insurance was established in 1913 as the Brotherhood of All Railway Employees to provide disability coverage to railroad workers. A mutual company since 1923, the firm was renamed Trustmark Insurance in 1994. The company, one of the leading mutual insurers in the US, covers more than 2.2 million people. Its operations include group and individual health coverage (medical, dental, and disability benefits and life insurance) and voluntary insurance products (specialty products through voluntary payroll deductions). Trustmark's Star Marketing and Administration subsidiary markets insurance products to small companies through independent agents and through alliances with other providers.

KEY COMPETITORS
Blue Cross
CIGNA
Prudential

TTX COMPANY

101 N. Wacker Dr.
Chicago, IL 60606
Phone: 312-853-3223
Fax: 312-984-3865
Web site: http://www.ttx.com

CEO: R. C. Burton
CFO: Robert E. Zimmerman
HR: Andrew F. Reardon
Type: Private

1998 Sales: $937.0 million
1-Yr. Sales Change: 6.5%
Employees: 2,000
FYE: December

TTX keeps the railroad industry chugging by leasing railcars to railroad companies in the US. Rail companies generally prefer to rent railcars as needed rather than buy them because the cars are often switched and traded along the tracks. With more than 235,000 railcars, TTX's fleet includes cars designed to carry containers, autos, farm and construction equipment, and lumber and steel products. The fleet also accounts for about 80% of the US's intermodal cars. The company has distribution centers in Illinois and Washington state and maintains its fleet through repair centers in 17 US states. TTX is owned by the largest railroads in the US, including #1 Union Pacific and #2 Burlington Northern Santa Fe.

KEY COMPETITORS
GATX
Greenbrier
XTRA

TUFTS ASSOCIATED HEALTH PLANS, INC.

333 Wyman St.
Waltham, MA 02254
Phone: 781-466-9400
Fax: 781-466-8583
Web site: http://www.tufts-healthplan.com

CEO: Harris A. Berman
CFO: Richard Hallworth
HR: Paula LaPalme
Type: Not-for-profit

1998 Sales: $1,600.0 million
1-Yr. Sales Change: 32.2%
Employees: 2,500
FYE: December

Tufts Associated Health Plans provides management, administrative, and marketing services for its affiliates and subsidiaries, including Tufts Associated Health Maintenance Organization (TAHMO), Total Health Plan (THP), and TAHP Brokerage. Its provider network includes about 16,000 physicians and has more than 950,000 members. TAHMO offers HMO and point-of-service plans through its Tufts Health Plan of New England subsidiary. It also offers third-party administration services through its Tufts Benefits Administrators subsidiary. THP provides support to participants in insured and self-insured point-of-service arrangements.

KEY COMPETITORS
CIGNA
Harvard Pilgrim
Oxford Health Plans

TURNER INDUSTRIES, LTD.

8687 United Plaza Blvd., Ste. 500
Baton Rouge, LA 70809
Phone: 225-922-5050
Fax: 225-922-5055
Web site: http://www.turner-industries.com

CEO: Bert S. Turner
CFO: David R. Carpenter
HR: Russell Gauthreaux
Type: Private

1999 Sales: $673.0 million
1-Yr. Sales Change: 12.2%
Employees: 10,000
FYE: October

Turner Industries turns out large-scale construction projects and provides industrial maintenance services for oil refiners, chemical and petrochemical companies, pulp and paper mills, and other operations throughout the US. Turner's services include water treatment, general construction, pipe fabrication and bending, tank cleaning, blasting and coating, plant shutdown and turnaround, and environmental remediation. It also rents heavy equipment and scaffolding and offers project scheduling and control systems. Chairman Bert Turner owns the company, which he founded in 1961.

KEY COMPETITORS
Bechtel
Dames & Moore
Jacobs Engineering

TUTOR-SALIBA CORPORATION

15901 Olden St.
Sylmar, CA 91342
Phone: 818-362-8391
Fax: 213-872-2917
Web site: http://www.tutorsaliba.com

CEO: Ronald N. Tutor
CFO: William Sparks
HR: Gene Zondlo
Type: Private

1998 Sales: $791.0 million
1-Yr. Sales Change: 27.8%
Employees: 2,490
FYE: December

Underneath California's glamour, Tutor-Saliba is making tracks. Among the largest transportation construction firms in the US, the company is the primary builder of the new subway system in Los Angeles and has provided services for San Francisco's BART. Besides transportation projects, Tutor-Saliba works on public buildings such as the Los Angeles Central Library, the San Francisco Main Post Office, and Folsom Prison. Subsidiaries include Black Construction in Guam and E. E. Black in the Philippines. A. G. Tutor founded the construction firm in 1949. His son, Ronald Tutor, is CEO and owner of Tutor-Saliba and also VC of heavy construction firm Perini, which has been a joint venture partner of Tutor-Saliba.

KEY COMPETITORS
Bechtel
Granite Construction
Peter Kiewit Sons'

TUTTLE-CLICK AUTOMOTIVE GROUP

14 Auto Center Dr.
Irvine, CA 92618
Phone: 949-830-7122
Fax: 949-830-0980
Web site: http://www.tuttleclick.com

CEO: James H. Click
CFO: Chris Cotter
HR: Angie Mejia
Type: Private

1998 Sales: $665.0 million
1-Yr. Sales Change: 13.8%
Employees: 1,310
FYE: December

Despite what you might think, Tuttle-Click Automotive Group does sell cars to Democrats. The firm operates over 15 new- and used-car dealerships throughout Orange County, California, and in Tucson, Arizona. The firm's dealerships sell DaimlerChrysler, Ford, GM, Hyundai, Mazda, Mitsubishi, Nissan, and Suzuki cars and trucks. The company was founded by Holmes Tuttle, who sold Ronald Reagan a car in 1946 and ended up a prominent GOP fundraiser; he even persuaded Reagan to run for governor of California in 1966. Tuttle's son, co-CEO Robert Tuttle (a White House aide under Reagan), and Arizona-based co-CEO James Click own the company; both men are majority owners of Arizona Bank, which is based in Tucson.

KEY COMPETITORS
AutoNation
FirstAmerica Automotive
Larry H. Miller Group

TY INC.

280 Chestnut
Westmont, IL 60559
Phone: 630-920-1515
Fax: 630-920-1980
Web site: http://www.ty.com

CEO: H. Ty Warner
CFO: Michael W. Kanzler
HR: Sharon Salcman
Type: Private

1998 Est. Sales: $1,000.0 million
1-Yr. Sales Change: 150.0%
Employees: 1,000
FYE: December

Take some fabric, shape it like an animal, fill it with plastic pellets, and you too could own a Manhattan luxury hotel. That's the lesson taught by Ty Warner, sole owner of the firm behind Beanie Babies and their international cult following. Since 1993 Ty Inc. has produced over 225 different Beanies, with such colorful names as Scat the cat and Pinchers the lobster, as well as Pillow Pals, Attic Treasures, and Beanie Buddies. Beanies debut at about $6, but once "retired" they can fetch hundreds or thousands of dollars among collectors. Ty doesn't advertise, limits production, and sells Beanies only through small, specialty retailers. Beanie bucks enabled Warner to buy the New York City Four Seasons in 1999.

KEY COMPETITORS
Applause Enterprises
Hasbro
Play By Play

 See pages 490–491 for a full profile of this company.

UCSF STANFORD HEALTH CARE

5 Thomas Mellon Circle
San Francisco, CA 94134
Phone: 415-353-4500
Fax: 415-353-4520
Web site: http://www.ucsfstanford.org

CEO: Peter Van Etten
CFO: Lawrence Furnstahl
HR: Felix R. Barthelemy
Type: Private

1998 Sales: $1,300.0 million
1-Yr. Sales Change: 74.8%
Employees: 12,500
FYE: August

With hospitals ranking in the nation's top 10, UCSF Stanford Health Care isn't hurting. The organization was formed by the 1997 merger of the medical operations of the University of California at San Francisco and Stanford University, each of which owns half of the organization. The system consists of UCSF/Mount Zion Medical Center, UCSF Medical Center, Stanford Hospital and Clinics, Lucile Salter Packard Children's Hospital at Stanford, and the schools' combined clinical practices. The schools of medicine are not affiliated with the system. UCSF Stanford and BMJ Publishing have purchased the *Western Journal of Medicine* (renamed *WJM*), the official journal of the California Medical Association.

KEY COMPETITORS
Catholic Healthcare West
Columbia/HCA
Sutter Health

UIS, INC.

15 Exchange Place	CEO: Andrew E. Pietrini	1998 Sales: $1,020.0 million
Jersey City, NJ 07302	CFO: Joseph F. Arrigo	1-Yr. Sales Change: 3.4%
Phone: 201-946-2600	HR: —	Employees: 8,614
Fax: 201-946-9325	Type: Private	FYE: December

The maker of the little candy hearts called Sweethearts that carry tiny Valentine messages, UIS is probably better known for its somewhat tougher products, such as its car parts. UIS also makes iron and steel forgings and millwork products. Its subsidiaries include Champion Laboratories (engine filters), Mid-South Manufacturing (vehicle parts), Neapco (drive line parts), New England Confectionery (Sweethearts, Necco wafers, candy cigarettes), and Wells Manufacturing (ignition and electrical components). Founder Harry Lebensfeld started the company in 1945 with the purchase of an Indiana desk maker. UIS is owned by a trust for Lebensfeld's only child (who is married to EVP Richard Pasculano) and her children.

KEY COMPETITORS
Dana
Federal-Mogul
Hershey

UJC OF NORTH AMERICA

111 8th Ave., Ste. 11E	CEO: Stephen Solender	1998 Est. Sales: $1,500.0 million
New York, NY 10016	CFO: Chaim Chesler	1-Yr. Sales Change: —
Phone: 212-284-6500	HR: Lance Jacobs	Employees: 500
Fax: 212-284-6835	Type: Not-for-profit	FYE: June
Web site: http://www.ujc.org		

From supporting nursing homes in the US to helping èmigrès fleeing the former Soviet Union, UJC Federations of North America works to better Jewish life across the globe. One of the nation's leading not-for-profit organizations, UJC raises more than $1 billion annually. It comprises three philanthropic outfits: the United Jewish Appeal, the Council for Jewish Federations, and the United Israel Appeal. The three operations bring nearly 200 Jewish welfare agencies and organizations together under the auspices of the UJC. The United Jewish Appeal was founded in 1939 as a response to the previous year's infamous *Kristallnacht,* a coordinated attack on Jews in Germany and Austria.

KEY COMPETITORS
Goodwill
Salvation Army
United Way

UNIFIED WESTERN GROCERS

5200 Sheila St.	CEO: Alfred A. Plamann	1999 Sales: $1,893.5 million
Commerce, CA 90040	CFO: —	1-Yr. Sales Change: 3.4%
Phone: 323-264-5200	HR: —	Employees: 3,945
Fax: —	Type: Cooperative	FYE: September
Web site: http://www.certifiedgrocers.com		

Unified Western Grocers guarantees that food and general merchandise reach about 3,700 mostly independent grocery stores in Arizona, California, Hawaii, Nevada, and Oregon. The food wholesaler and cooperative supplies dry groceries, frozen and prepared foods, meats, and deli items, as well as its own bakery and dairy goods. In addition to name-brand items, its offerings include private labels Springfield, Gingham, and Special Value. The co-op also provides member support services, including store remodeling, financing, and insurance. Unified serves about 800 patrons, many of whom own shares in the company. It was formed in 1999 when Certified Grocers of California merged with United Grocers.

KEY COMPETITORS
Associated Food
Fleming Companies
SUPERVALU

 See pages 492–493 for a full profile of this company.

UNIGROUP, INC.

1 Premier Dr.
Fenton, MO 63026
Phone: 636-305-5000
Fax: 636-326-1106
Web site: http://www.unigroupinc.com

CEO: Robert J. Baer
CFO: Donald Ellington
HR: Sherry Fagin
Type: Private

1998 Sales: $1,800.0 million
1-Yr. Sales Change: 2.9%
Employees: 1,600
FYE: December

Moving household goods has made many of UniGroup's companies household names. Several subsidiaries of moving service company UniGroup (United Van Lines, Mayflower Transit, and UniGroup Worldwide) transport household goods and other items globally. UniGroup's other businesses sell and lease trucks and trailers and sell movers' supplies (Total Transportation Services), outsource moving services to corporate clients (Pinnacle Group Associates), and sell property/casualty insurance to the moving and storage industries (Vanliner Group). UniGroup, which operates in more than 100 countries, was founded in 1987. It is owned by agents of United Van Lines and Mayflower Transit and senior management of UniGroup companies.

KEY COMPETITORS
Atlas World
NFC
Penske Truck Leasing

THE UNION CENTRAL LIFE INSURANCE COMPANY

1876 Waycross Rd.
Cincinnati, OH 45240
Phone: 513-595-2200
Fax: 513-595-5418
Web site: http://www.unioncentral.com

CEO: Larry R. Pike
CFO: Stephen R. Hatcher
HR: Stephen K. Johnston
Type: Mutual company

1998 Sales: $1,175.8 million
1-Yr. Sales Change: 16.6%
Employees: 800
FYE: December

Union Central Life Insurance Company is a mutual life insurance company that operates in all 50 states and the District of Columbia. The company offers a range of individual life and disability insurance, investment products, annuities, group retirement plans, and group insurance. Union Central also offers employee and executive benefit planning, estate planning, and retirement planning. One-third of Union Central's investments are in collateralized mortgage obligations, of which mortgage investments accounted for about 18%. Union Central was founded in 1867.

KEY COMPETITORS
MetLife
New York Life
Prudential

UNITED ARTISTS THEATRE CIRCUIT, INC.

9110 E. Nichols Ave., Ste. 200
Englewood, CO 80112
Phone: 303-792-3600
Fax: 303-790-8907
Web site: http://www.uatc.com

CEO: Kurt C. Hall
CFO: Trent J. Carman
HR: Ray Nutt
Type: Private

1998 Sales: $661.3 million
1-Yr. Sales Change: (3.5%)
Employees: 10,000
FYE: December

Be it art or summer blockbuster, United Artists Theatre Circuit (UATC) exhibits them all. One of the largest movie theater chains in the US, the operating subsidiary of United Artists Theatre Company (88%-owned by Merrill Lynch) runs more than 2,000 screens in almost 400 theaters in 23 states. UATC continues to expand its screen presence by renovating its older theaters and building new "smaller" megaplex theaters with 12 to 18 screens each, instead of the popular 20 to 30 screen houses being constructed by other exhibitors. The company's Satellite Theatre Network uses movie theaters during off-hours for activities such as seminars and corporate conferences.

KEY COMPETITORS
AMC Entertainment
Loews Cineplex Entertainment
Regal Cinemas

UNITED DEFENSE INDUSTRIES, INC.

1525 Wilson Blvd., Ste. 700
Arlington, VA 22209
Phone: 703-312-6100
Fax: 703-312-6148
Web site: http://www.uniteddefense.com

CEO: Thomas W. Rabaut
CFO: Francis Raborn
HR: Robert N. Sankovich
Type: Private

1998 Sales: $1,217.6 million
1-Yr. Sales Change: (3.1%)
Employees: 5,425
FYE: December

Before going after Cobra Command, make sure your G.I. Joes are armed to the teeth with the latest military vehicles United Defense has to offer. The company makes defense systems and armored combat vehicles for the US government and its allies. Best known for making the Bradley Fighting Vehicle for the US Army, the company also makes combat and support vehicle systems, weapons delivery systems, fire support, amphibious assault vehicles, and combat support services. The company operates at 26 facilities in 12 states and has managed joint ventures in Saudi Arabia and Turkey. The company is an indirect wholly-owned subsidiary of investment firm (and defense and aerospace industry consolidator) The Carlyle Group.

KEY COMPETITORS
AM General
General Dynamics
Rolls-Royce

UNITED STATES POSTAL SERVICE

475 L'Enfant Plaza
Washington, DC 20260
Phone: 202-268-2000
Fax: 202-268-3488
Web site: http://www.usps.gov

CEO: William J. Henderson
CFO: M. Richard Porras
HR: Yvonne D. Maguire
Type: Government-owned

1998 Sales: $60,072.0 million
1-Yr. Sales Change: 3.2%
Employees: 792,041
FYE: September

The United States Postal Service is grateful that "going postal" still has a positive connotation for most consumers and businesses. It delivers more than 190 billion pieces of mail a year. An independent government agency, it relies on postage and fees for income. The agency has a monopoly on the delivery of nonurgent letters but faces competition for services such as package delivery, in which it has less than 10% of the market. The budget of the United States Postal Service is nearly 1% of the US's gross domestic product. A board of nine governors (appointed by the president) oversees the agency, selects the postmaster general, and establishes policies, objectives, and goals, including postal rates.

KEY COMPETITORS
DHL
FDX
UPS

See pages 494–495 for a full profile of this company.

UNITED WAY OF AMERICA

701 N. Fairfax St.
Alexandria, VA 22314
Phone: 703-836-7100
Fax: 703-683-7840
Web site: http://www.unitedway.org

CEO: Betty S. Beene
CFO: Richard W. Gushman
HR: Dorothy Myles
Type: Not-for-profit

1998 Sales: $3,580.0 million
1-Yr. Sales Change: 5.3%
Employees: 10,000
FYE: December

About 45,000 agencies benefit from the financial support they receive from United Way of America (UWA). A not-for-profit organization, UWA's 1,400 local organizations help to fund a range of endeavors, including the American Cancer Society, the Arthritis Foundation, Catholic Charities, Girl Scouts and Boy Scouts, and Planned Parenthood. During its 1997-98 fund-raising year, UWA raised $3.4 billion (nearly 50% came from employee contributions; corporations contributed another 22%), and its administrative expenses average 13% of all funds raised. Each of the local organizations is an independent entity, and UWA supports them with services such as national advertising and research.

See pages 496–497 for a full profile of this company.

THE UNIVERSITY OF ALABAMA SYSTEM

401 Queen City Ave.	CEO: Thomas C. Meredith	1997 Sales: $1,504.6 million
Tuscaloosa, AL 35401	CFO: JoAnne G. Jackson	1-Yr. Sales Change: 8.6%
Phone: 205-348-5862	HR: John Minor	Employees: 15,468
Fax: 205-348-5915	Type: School	FYE: September
Web site: http://www.ua.edu		

The University of Alabama System oversees three campuses located in Tuscaloosa, Birmingham, and Huntsville. The flagship Tuscaloosa campus offers 275 degree programs to its more than 18,500 students. The University of Alabama at Birmingham offers 140 degree programs and has an enrollment of more than 15,800 students; it is also home to the university's school of medicine and a 900-bed hospital. The University of Alabama at Huntsville has more than 8,200 students enrolled in its five colleges and graduate school. Each campus offers bachelor's, master's, and doctoral degree programs. The University of Alabama was founded in Tuscaloosa in 1831 as the state's first public university.

UNIVERSITY OF CALIFORNIA

1111 Franklin St.	CEO: Richard C. Atkinson	1999 Sales: $13,074.4 million
Oakland, CA 94607	CFO: V. Wayne Kennedy	1-Yr. Sales Change: 39.5%
Phone: 510-987-0700	HR: Lubbe Levin	Employees: 99,890
Fax: 510-987-0894	Type: School	FYE: June
Web site: http://www.ucop.edu		

Along with celebrities and smog, California boasts one of the nation's leading systems of higher education. The University of California (UC) offers areas of study in more than 150 disciplines. It has nearly 175,000 students at its nine undergraduate and graduate campuses (which include three law schools and five medical schools): Berkeley, Davis, Irvine, Los Angeles, Riverside, San Diego, San Francisco, Santa Barbara, and Santa Cruz. The university's 10th campus, UC Merced, is scheduled to open in 2005. In addition, UC operates three research labs in California and New Mexico. While no longer using affirmative action in its admissions process, the university is making efforts to boost minority enrollment.

 See pages 498–499 for a full profile of this company.

THE UNIVERSITY OF CHICAGO

5801 S. Ellis Ave.	CEO: Hugo F. Sonnenschein	1998 Sales: $1,507.1 million
Chicago, IL 60637	CFO: Patricia Woodworth	1-Yr. Sales Change: 9.4%
Phone: 773-702-1234	HR: G. Chris Keeley	Employees: 12,869
Fax: 773-702-0809	Type: School	FYE: June
Web site: http://www.uchicago.edu		

You won't find Bluto or the other members of Animal House among the University of Chicago's 12,000 students. With an emphasis on research in its graduate schools and a common core based on the Great Books in its college, the U of C lists 70 Nobel Prize winners, including economist Milton Friedman and author Saul Bellow, among its past and present faculty, researchers, and alumni. Other notable alumni include journalist David Broder and former US Attorney General Ramsey Clark. Among its five professional schools, *U.S. News & World Report* ranks its law and business schools in the top 10 of US universities. The school was founded in 1891 with an initial gift from John D. Rockefeller.

 See pages 500–501 for a full profile of this company.

UNIVERSITY OF FLORIDA

226 Tigert Hall
Gainesville, FL 32611
Phone: 352-392-3261
Fax: 352-392-6278
Web site: http://www.ufl.edu

CEO: Charles E. Young
CFO: John P. Kruczek
HR: Larry T. Ellis
Type: School

1999 Sales: $1,062.1 million
1-Yr. Sales Change: (1.1%)
Employees: 22,500
FYE: June

UF students know it's great to be a Florida Gator. Founded in 1853, the University of Florida is the state's oldest and largest university. The school is a major land-grant research university located on 2,000 acres 115 miles north of Orlando. It has about 43,000 students, making it one of the nation's largest universities. Its 23 colleges and schools offer more than 100 undergraduate majors and nearly 200 graduate programs, including law, dentistry, pharmacy, medicine, and veterinary medicine. A founding member of the Southeastern Conference, the university fields athletic teams (the Florida Gators) that are typically nationally ranked. UF also rivals Florida State as the nation's top party school.

UNIVERSITY OF ILLINOIS

346 Henry Administration Bldg., 506 S. Wright
Urbana, IL 61801
Phone: 217-333-3070
Fax: 217-337-3070
Web site: http://www.uillinois.edu

CEO: James J. Stukel
CFO: Craig S. Bazzani
HR: Robert K. Todd
Type: School

1998 Sales: $2,445.8 million
1-Yr. Sales Change: 7.0%
Employees: 26,148
FYE: June

The log cabins that used to dot the landscape in the Land of Lincoln have given way to the three campuses of the University of Illinois. Established as a land grant institution in 1867, the university has grown to include campuses in Chicago, Springfield, and Urbana-Champaign. Its more than 65,000 students (more than half of whom study at the Urbana-Champaign campus) can choose from academic fields ranging from business to fine arts to medicine. The Urbana-Champaign campus is the site of the National Center for Supercomputing Applications (which developed Mosaic, the basis for popular Internet browsers such as AOL's Navigator), while the university's Springfield campus houses the Institute for Public Affairs.

THE UNIVERSITY OF IOWA

101 Jessup Hall
Iowa City, IA 52242
Phone: 319-335-3500
Fax: 319-335-0860
Web site: http://www.uiowa.edu

CEO: Mary Sue Coleman
CFO: Douglas K. True
HR: Robert Foldesi
Type: School

1998 Sales: $1,241.3 million
1-Yr. Sales Change: (7.6%)
Employees: 17,129
FYE: June

The University of Iowa Hawkeyes see clearly from their perch as Iowa's largest university. Founded in 1847 (just 59 days after Iowa became a state), the university has nearly 29,000 students (more than 19,500 undergraduate and more than 9,300 postgraduate) on its Iowa City campus. The university houses 10 colleges that host a variety of majors and disciplines, including distinguished programs in audiology, creative writing, dentistry, and physical therapy. The lowest undergraduate tuition in the Big Ten conference got a spike in 1999 when Iowa's board of regents approved a 7% increase in tuition and fees.

THE UNIVERSITY OF KENTUCKY

Administration Bldg., Room 104	CEO: Charles T. Wethington	1999 Sales: $1,053.3 million
Lexington, KY 40506	CFO: Henry Clay Owen	1-Yr. Sales Change: 5.9%
Phone: 606-257-9000	HR: Robert Wilson	Employees: 13,000
Fax: 606-323-1075	Type: School	FYE: June
Web site: http://www.uky.edu		

Bluegrass and basketball. Perennial basketball powerhouse The University of Kentucky serves about 31,000 students on its main campus at Lexington (as well as Lexington Community College) through 10 undergraduate colleges, a college of law, and two graduate schools. It offers nearly 100 certified degree programs, such as agriculture, communications, dentistry, education, engineering, and fine arts. The university also operates the Chandler Medical Center, which works with its nationally ranked College of Medicine and College of Pharmacy. A public university and research institution, the school was founded in 1865 as the Agricultural and Mechanical College of the Kentucky University.

UNIVERSITY OF MASSACHUSETTS

1 Beacon St., 26th Fl.	CEO: William M. Bulger	1997 Sales: $1,403.7 million
Boston, MA 02108	CFO: Stephen W. Lenhardt	1-Yr. Sales Change: (3.8%)
Phone: 617-287-7000	HR: Roy Milbury	Employees: 10,296
Fax: 617-287-7044	Type: School	FYE: June
Web site: http://www.umassp.edu		

The University of Massachusetts (UMass) has been expanding across the commonwealth since its founding in 1863. The university's flagship campus in Amherst offers the whole range of academic programs from associate to doctoral degrees, and has gained recognition in areas of study such as chemical engineering and computer science. UMass established campuses in Boston and Worcester in the 1960s, and added campuses in Lowell and Dartmouth in 1991. It set up another campus, the UMass Center for Professional Education in Westboro, in 1999. More than 57,000 students attend the university.

THE UNIVERSITY OF MICHIGAN

3074 Fleming Administration Bldg.	CEO: Lee C. Bollinger	1998 Sales: $2,881.0 million
Ann Arbor, MI 48109	CFO: Robert A. Kasdin	1-Yr. Sales Change: 9.5%
Phone: 734-764-1817	HR: Jackie R. McClain	Employees: 23,000
Fax: 734-764-4546	Type: School	FYE: June
Web site: http://www.umich.edu		

Michigan — it's shaped like a mitten, and higher education fits the state like a glove. The University of Michigan has been a leader in the state's education effort since its founding in 1817. With more than 51,000 students and 5,600 faculty members scattered across three campuses (Ann Arbor, with about 37,000 students; Dearborn; and Flint), the university's diverse academic units span areas of study including architecture, dentistry, education, law, medicine, music, and social work. The University of Michigan is also home to the Gerald R. Ford Presidental Library.

UNIVERSITY OF MINNESOTA

234 Morrill Hall, 100 Church St. SE	CEO: Mark G. Yudof	1998 Sales: $2,050.9 million
Minneapolis, MN 55455	CFO: Georgina Y. Stephens	1-Yr. Sales Change: 9.5%
Phone: 612-625-5000	HR: Carol Carrier	Employees: 30,708
Fax: —	Type: School	FYE: June
Web site: http://www.umn.edu		

The University of Minnesota — this place is a zoo! Gophers scurry about the university's Minneapolis-St. Paul campus, Bulldogs roam its campus in Duluth, Cougars prowl its Morris campus, and Golden Eagles soar across its campus in Crookston. Feeble mascot jokes aside, the land grant institution has been educating students since 1869. Its more than 58,000 students can choose academic fields ranging from agriculture to medicine to law. In 1999 the university was rocked by an athletics scandal involving allegations of weak oversight and academic fraud. University president Mark Yudof responded by instituting a one-year ban on post-season basketball action.

UNIVERSITY OF MISSOURI SYSTEM

321 University Hall	CEO: Manuel T. Pacheco	1999 Sales: $1,487.0 million
Columbia, MO 65211	CFO: James E. Cofer	1-Yr. Sales Change: 6.5%
Phone: 573-882-0600	HR: R. Kenneth Hutchinson	Employees: —
Fax: 573-882-2721	Type: School	FYE: June
Web site: http://www.system.missouri.edu		

"Show-Me" the education! The University of Missouri was founded in 1839 (it's the first state university established west of the Mississippi) and educates more than 54,000 students each year at four campuses across the Show-Me state. More informally known as "Mizzou," the university's cadre of campuses includes flagship UM-Columbia (home to 17 schools and colleges and the University of Missouri Health Sciences Center), UM-Kansas City (primarily a commuter school), UM-Rolla,.and UM-St. Louis. About 43% of the university's nearly 9,900-member faculty teach full-time in areas of study ranging from agriculture to fine arts to social work.

THE UNIVERSITY OF NEBRASKA

3835 Holdrege St.	CEO: L. Dennis Smith	1998 Sales: $1,248.5 million
Lincoln, NE 68583	CFO: John W. Goebel	1-Yr. Sales Change: (1.7%)
Phone: 402-472-2111	HR: John Russell	Employees: —
Fax: 402-472-2410	Type: School	FYE: June
Web site: http://www.uneb.edu		

The University of Nebraska's campuses are less crowded these days — but that was expected when admission standards were raised. The 130-year-old school (Nebraska's only state university) offers bachelor's, master's, and doctoral programs ranging from art to engineering to snow and ice research. Labeled Cornhuskers, nearly 45,000 students attend its four campuses (including the University of Nebraska Medical Center). The university also manages the College of Technical Agriculture in Curtis, Nebraska. Enrollment in the university system is still recovering from a 1997 drop of several thousand resulting from tighter admissions standards and increased interest in private schools and community colleges.

THE UNIVERSITY OF PENNSYLVANIA

3451 Walnut St.
Philadelphia, PA 19104
Phone: 215-898-5000
Fax: 215-898-9659
Web site: http://www.upenn.edu

CEO: Judith Rodin
CFO: Kathryn Engebretson
HR: John J. Heuer
Type: School

1999 Sales: $2,823.1 million
1-Yr. Sales Change: 8.5%
Employees: 18,331
FYE: June

When he wasn't otherwise engaged in founding our country or experimenting with lightning, Benjamin Franklin took the time to establish the University of Pennsylvania, the first university in the US. Since opening its doors to students in 1751, the Ivy League university has accumulated a notable list of accomplishments, including the creation of the first medical school in the US and the invention of ENIAC, the world's first electronic computer. The university's more than 21,000 students pursue academic fields of study in a dozen schools, such as the renowned Wharton School and the Annenburg School for Communications.

UNIVERSITY OF PITTSBURGH OF THE COMMONWEALTH SYSTEM OF HIGHER EDUCATION

4200 5th Ave.
Pittsburgh, PA 15260
Phone: 412-624-4141
Fax: —
Web site: http://www.pitt.edu

CEO: Mark A. Nordenberg
CFO: Arthur Ramicone
HR: Ron Frisch
Type: School

1998 Sales: $888.2 million
1-Yr. Sales Change: 8.3%
Employees: 9,600
FYE: June

Now this is a school that really needs a nickname. The University of Pittsburgh of the Commonwealth System of Higher Education (whew! Pitt for short) has about 32,000 students spread across its five campuses. Its flagship Pittsburgh campus has more than 25,000 students. The Pitt Panthers pounce on more than 100 majors in 16 schools and colleges, including liberal arts, engineering, and business. Through its schools of health sciences and medicine, Pitt is also affiliated with the UPMC Health System (which operates a network of hospitals and an insurance company), manages physicians' offices, and offers long-term care and in-home services. The university was founded in 1787.

UNIVERSITY OF ROCHESTER

Administration Bldg.
Rochester, NY 14627
Phone: 716-275-2121
Fax: 716-275-0359
Web site: http://www.rochester.edu

CEO: Thomas H. Jackson
CFO: Ronald J. Paprocki
HR: Richard P. Miller
Type: School

1998 Sales: $1,060.7 million
1-Yr. Sales Change: 22.6%
Employees: 12,568
FYE: June

The buzz about the University of Rochester is music to some ears. The private, upstate New York institution is nationally recognized for its programs in medicine, economics, and business, and its Eastman School of Music (founded by George Eastman, founder of Eastman Kodak) is one of the top music schools in the US. The school, with an endowment of more than $1 billion, offers more than 175 bachelor's, master's, and doctoral degrees to its almost 8,000 full- and part-time students. Undergraduate tuition runs more than $22,000. Founded as a Baptist-sponsored institution in 1850, the university is nonsectarian today.

UNIVERSITY OF SOUTHERN CALIFORNIA

University Park
Los Angeles, CA 90089
Phone: 213-740-2311
Fax: 213-740-4749
Web site: http://www.usc.edu

CEO: Steven B. Sample
CFO: William C. Hromadka
HR: Dennis F. Dougherty
Type: School

1999 Sales: $1,142.0 million
1-Yr. Sales Change: (12.6%)
Employees: 17,000
FYE: June

More than 28,000 Trojans entered the University of Southern California (USC) in 1999. Founded in 1880, the private university (home of the Trojans) grew up with the city of Los Angeles. It offers 76 undergraduate majors and 122 postgraduate degrees. Recognized for distinguished programs in business, engineering, film, law, medicine, public administration, and science, USC boasts two Los Angeles campuses and a string of research centers and health care facilities. The university also supports medical staffs at five Los Angeles hospitals. USC is the largest private employer in Los Angeles.

UNIVERSITY OF TENNESSEE

800 Andy Holt Tower
Knoxville, TN 37996
Phone: 423-974-2225
Fax: 423-974-6435
Web site: http://www.utenn.edu

CEO: J. Wade Gilley
CFO: Emerson H. Fly
HR: Alan Chesney
Type: School

1999 Sales: $1,232.1 million
1-Yr. Sales Change: 0.9%
Employees: 14,967
FYE: June

Home sweet home to nearly 43,000 students, the University of Tennessee (UT) has campuses in Chattanooga, Knoxville (its main campus), Martin, and Memphis as well as agriculture, space, and public-service institutes. UT's academic programs include business, engineering, pharmacy, medicine, and veterinary medicine. The school also operates the UT Medical Center in Knoxville. UT is struggling to cope with inadequate state funding by enacting a hiring freeze and putting a cap on freshman enrollment. Founded in 1794 as Blount College, the school became the nation's first coeducational college when it admitted women for a few years in the early 1800s (it began admitting women again in 1892).

THE UNIVERSITY OF TEXAS SYSTEM

601 Colorado St.
Austin, TX 78701
Phone: 512-499-4200
Fax: 512-499-4218
Web site: http://www.utsystem.edu

CEO: William H. Cunningham
CFO: R. D. Burck
HR: Gerald Schroeder
Type: School

1998 Sales: $5,243.7 million
1-Yr. Sales Change: 9.2%
Employees: 77,112
FYE: August

Everything's big in Texas, and The University of Texas (UT) System is no exception. With more than 148,000 students, UT is one of the largest university systems in the nation, and its main campus in Austin is the largest university in the US with more than 49,000 students. UT has nine academic institutions spread across the state that include six health centers, four medical schools, two dental schools, and seven nursing schools. UT spends more than $870 million each year on research, and its $10.2 billion endowment (managed by the University of Texas Investment Management Co.) is the second largest in the country, after Harvard's.

See pages 502–503 for a full profile of this company.

UNIVERSITY OF VIRGINIA

1404 University Ave.	CEO: John T. Casteen	1998 Sales: $1,186.0 million
Charlottesville, VA 22903	CFO: Leonard W. Sandridge	1-Yr. Sales Change: 7.7%
Phone: 804-924-0311	HR: Thomas E. Gausvik	Employees: 10,294
Fax: 804-982-4378	Type: School	FYE: June
Web site: http://www.virginia.edu		

It says a lot that the University of Virginia (UVa) is Thomas Jefferson's proudest achievement. The nation's third president (as well as inventor, philosopher, and author, among other titles) founded the US' first nonreligious public university in 1819. With some 18,500 students enrolled in its graduate and undergraduate schools, UVa is one of the most prestigious public universities in the US. It is also one of the most selective, accepting about a third of its applicants. The school has been noted for its top-rated law program and English department and for its 150-year-old, student-enforced conduct code (the Honor System). *U.S. News & World Report* ranks the school as the nation's #2 public university.

UNIVERSITY OF WASHINGTON

301 Gerberding Hall, Ste. 400	CEO: Richard L. McCormick	1998 Sales: $1,747.9 million
Seattle, WA 98195	CFO: V'Ella Warren	1-Yr. Sales Change: 8.2%
Phone: 206-543-2560	HR: Margot Ray	Employees: 34,757
Fax: 206-543-5651	Type: School	FYE: June
Web site: http://www.washington.edu		

The University of Washington (UW) is Husky indeed, with more than 34,000 students enrolled at its main Seattle campus. Founded in 1861 as the Territorial University of Washington, UW (pronounced "U-dub" by those on campus) also has smaller branches in Tacoma and Bothell. The university maintains 16 schools and colleges for both undergraduate and graduate students (more than 70% of students on the main campus are undergrads). It also operates a health sciences center and an academic medical center, which includes the University of Washington Medical Center and Harborview Medical Center.

THE UNIVERSITY OF WISCONSIN SYSTEM

Van Hise Hall, 1220 Linden Dr.	CEO: Katharine C. Lyall	1998 Sales: $2,543.3 million
Madison, WI 53706	CFO: Deborah A. Duncan	1-Yr. Sales Change: 6.0%
Phone: 608-262-2321	HR: George H. Brooks	Employees: 25,500
Fax: 608-262-3985	Type: School	FYE: June
Web site: http://www.uwsa.edu		

Looking for something to do in Baraboo, Wisconsin? You could always take some classes at UW Baraboo, one of The University of Wisconsin System's 26 campuses. The system, one of the largest in the nation, serves more than 150,000 students through 13 four-year and 13 two-year campuses. Its top school is the University of Wisconsin at Madison, which offers undergraduate, graduate, and doctoral degrees and regularly ranks as one of the US' top public schools. It has more than 40,000 students and a nationally recognized graduate program in sociology. The system's other major campus is the University of Wisconsin at Milwaukee, with nearly 23,000 students.

See pages 504–505 for a full profile of this company.

UNIVERSITY SYSTEM OF MARYLAND

3300 Metzerott Rd.	CEO: Donald N. Langenberg	1998 Sales: $2,032.7 million
Adelphi, MD 20783	CFO: Joseph F. Vivona	1-Yr. Sales Change: 6.5%
Phone: 301-445-2740	HR: Donald Tynes	Employees: 28,115
Fax: 301-445-2761	Type: School	FYE: June
Web site: http://www.usmh.usmd.edu		

Maryland's nickname — "The Free State" — doesn't apply to its system of higher education. The University System of Maryland (USM) has 11 public campuses and two research institutes that serve about 126,000 undergraduate and graduate students. Formed in 1988, the system includes the former University of Maryland's five campuses and six other institutions. It offers more than 600 academic programs, including bachelor's, master's, doctoral, and professional degrees. USM has about 200 sites worldwide. Its flagship campus at College Park was founded in 1856 and became a public land-grant university in 1862.

U.S. CENTRAL CREDIT UNION

7300 College Blvd., Ste. 600	CEO: Dan Kampen	1998 Sales: $1,373.6 million
Overland Park, KS 66210	CFO: Kathy Brick	1-Yr. Sales Change: 19.8%
Phone: 913-661-3800	HR: Linda Pfingsten	Employees: 190
Fax: 913-661-5360	Type: Cooperative	FYE: December
Web site: http://www.uscentral.org		

United credit unions stand in U.S. Central Credit Union. Formed in 1974, this "banker's bank" offers its 36 corporate credit union members a variety of investing, liquidity, settlement, and technology services, including a program which buys auto loans, mortgages, and other loans from member credit unions needing funds. U.S. Central Credit Union also operates MemberNet, an intranet connecting its 36 corporate members and providing them with information. Subsidiary U.S. Central Capital Markets provides brokerage and investment advising services to corporate credit unions, while Corporate Network Brokerage Services provides those same services to thousands of smaller retail credit unions.

KEY COMPETITORS
Charles Schwab
EDS
Merrill Lynch

U.S. SECURITIES AND EXCHANGE COMMISSION

450 5th St. NW	CEO: Arthur Levitt	1997 Sales: $990.4 million
Washington, DC 20549	CFO: Brian J. Lane	1-Yr. Sales Change: —
Phone: 202-942-7040	HR: —	Employees: 2,139
Fax: 202-942-9659	Type: Government-owned	FYE: October
Web site: http://www.sec.gov		

The U.S. Securities and Exchange Commission (SEC) regulates both the sale of securities and also the people and organizations involved in the sale of securities. The five presidentially appointed SEC commissioners are assisted by accountants, economists, examiners, lawyers, and others to protect investors from securities fraud. With five regional and six district offices, the SEC has divisions overseeing inspections and examinations, corporate finance, investment management, law enforcement, and market regulation. A reduced staff and budget, as well as increased pressure from Congress to leave the market alone, are hampering the SEC's attempt to regulate the booming world of online trading.

USAA

9800 Fredericksburg Rd., USAA Bldg.
San Antonio, TX 78288
Phone: 210-498-2211
Fax: 210-498-9940
Web site: http://www.usaa.com

CEO: Robert T. Herres
CFO: Joe Robles
HR: Elizabeth Conklyn
Type: Mutual company

1998 Sales: $7,687.0 million
1-Yr. Sales Change: 3.1%
Employees: 20,120
FYE: December

USAA has a decidedly military bearing. The mutual insurance company serves more than 3 million customers, primarily military personnel and their families. Its products and services include property/casualty and life insurance, banking, discount brokerage, and investment management. USAA is also involved in real estate development. The company sells merchandise (computers, furniture, giftware, jewelry, and home and auto safety items) in seasonal catalogs, and it offers car rental and long-distance telephone services through USAA Buying Services.

KEY COMPETITORS
MetLife
Nationwide Insurance
State Farm

See pages 506–507 for a full profile of this company.

VANDERBILT UNIVERSITY

2201 West End Ave.
Nashville, TN 37235
Phone: 615-322-7311
Fax: 615-343-3930
Web site: http://www.vanderbilt.edu

CEO: Joe B. Wyatt
CFO: Lauren J. Brisky
HR: Darlene Lewis
Type: School

1998 Sales: $1,245.9 million
1-Yr. Sales Change: 10.7%
Employees: 13,993
FYE: June

The house that Cornelius built, private Vanderbilt University was founded in 1873 with a $1 million grant from industrialist Cornelius Vanderbilt. The university's endowment has grown to about $1.8 billion, and the campus today is a haven for more than 10,000 students and 1,800 full-time faculty members. Vanderbilt has 10 schools and colleges offering degrees in subjects such as business, engineering, health sciences, law, music, and religion. Its Owen Graduate School of Management and its medical school have been among the top-ranked in national surveys. A major research university, Vanderbilt receives nearly $200 million a year in sponsored awards to fund its facilities. Chancellor Joe Wyatt plans to retire in July.

THE VANGUARD GROUP, INC.

100 Vanguard Blvd.
Malvern, PA 19355
Phone: 610-648-6000
Fax: 610-669-6605
Web site: http://www.vanguard.com

CEO: John J. Brennan
CFO: Ralph K. Packard
HR: Kathy Gubanich
Type: Private

1998 Est. Sales: $1,200.0 million
1-Yr. Sales Change: 33.3%
Employees: 10,000
FYE: December

Just like its namesake, Lord Nelson's flagship, fund manager The Vanguard Group is in battle — with the world's largest mutual fund company, FMR. Vanguard offers a wide variety of stocks, bonds, and mixed funds of securities of US and foreign companies. Its most popular funds are index funds, which track the market and are generally a safe, long-term investment. Unlike other fund companies, Vanguard keeps costs low; the investor-owned company plows those investments back into its funds, rather than diverting them into fees or advertising. It also reduces costs on its actively managed funds by outsourcing management to other companies.

KEY COMPETITORS
Barclays
FMR
Mellon Financial

See pages 508–509 for a full profile of this company.

VARIETY WHOLESALERS, INC.

3401 Gresham Lake Rd.
Raleigh, NC 27615
Phone: 919-876-6000
Fax: 919-790-9526

CEO: John W. Pope
CFO: Ed Anderson
HR: Frances Burger
Type: Private

1998 Est. Sales: $820.0 million
1-Yr. Sales Change: (18.0%)
Employees: 10,500
FYE: December

Variety is not only the spice of life — it's also a major purveyor of discount retail goods. With over 550 stores in 14 states from Louisiana to Delaware, Variety Wholesalers has survived even Wal-Mart's march through rural America. The company, which has aggressively bought other chains while closing poorly performing stores, tends to set up shop in small towns where the retail giants fear to tread. The company's retail outlets include Bargain Town, Maxway, Rose's, Super 10 (which prices all items at or below $10), Super Dollar, and Value-Mart. Variety Wholesalers was founded in 1932 by James Pope; the Pope family, including chairman and CEO John Pope, owns and leads the company today.

KEY COMPETITORS
Dollar General
Family Dollar Stores
Fred's

VARTEC TELECOM, INC.

3200 W. Pleasant Run Rd.
Lancaster, TX 75146
Phone: 972-230-7200
Fax: 972-230-7339
Web site: http://www.vartec.com

CEO: A. Joe Mitchell
CFO: Gary Egger
HR: Judy Armstrong
Type: Private

1998 Sales: $913.0 million
1-Yr. Sales Change: 7.4%
Employees: 1,460
FYE: December

Actors and comedians employed promoting 10-10 calling plans can thank VarTec Telecom, which helped to popularize that method of calling. VarTec remains a leading provider of "dial-around" long-distance service. The firm's residential and business offerings include the 10-10-811 FiveLine number and other plans such as Small Change (flat-rate plan) and Dime Club (10 cents a minute). VarTec also sells prepaid phone cards, pager service, and 1+ and residential 800-number service. The company, which has extended its offerings from the US into Mexico and the UK, has sold its BizOnThe.Net Web-hosting unit to Prodigy. Telecommunications holding company Telephone Electronics Corp. owns a majority stake in VarTec.

KEY COMPETITORS
AT&T
MCI WorldCom
Sprint

VIASYSTEMS GROUP, INC.

101 S. Hanley Rd., Ste. 400
St. Louis, MO 63105
Phone: 314-727-2087
Fax: 314-746-2233
Web site: http://www.viasystems.com

CEO: James N. Mills
CFO: James G. Powers
HR: Larry S. Bacon
Type: Private

1998 Sales: $1,031.9 million
1-Yr. Sales Change: 14.7%
Employees: 9,300
FYE: December

Viasystems Group is one of the largest printed circuit board (PCB) and backplane assembly manufacturers worldwide. The company's double-sided and multilayer PCBs are used to connect microprocessors and integrated circuits in electronics, and its backplanes connect PCBs and power supplies. Founded in 1996, Viasystems, which also offers custom contract services, sells its products to the telecommunications, computer, automotive, and consumer electronics industries, among others. About 39% of sales come from Lucent Technologies. Owned by investment firm Hicks, Muse, Tate & Furst (nearly 90%) and management company Mills & Partners, Viasystems is focusing on expanding its American and European operations into Asia.

KEY COMPETITORS
Hadco
Molex
Sanmina

VIEWSONIC CORPORATION

381 Brea Canyon Rd.
Walnut, CA 91789
Phone: 909-444-8800
Fax: 909-869-7958
Web site: http://www.viewsonic.com

CEO: James Chu
CFO: Jerry Kanaly
HR: Joanne Thielen
Type: Private

1998 Sales: $941.0 million
1-Yr. Sales Change: 13.9%
Employees: 700
FYE: December

ViewSonic likes to think of itself as colorful. The company makes color computer monitors including the Professional series for such applications as high-end computer-aided design, desktop publishing, and graphic design; the Graphics line (designed for the mainstream market) for graphics applications, home use, and small office automation; the Multimedia Series for 3-D gaming, video editing, and videoconferencing; and the value-priced E2 series for small business and personal use. ViewSonic also makes the ViewPanel family of wall-mountable flat-panel displays, as well as LCD projectors and calibration kits for monitor color matching. CEO James Chu, who founded ViewSonic in 1987, owns the company.

KEY COMPETITORS
ADI Systems
NEC
Tyco International

VIRGINIA STATE LOTTERY

900 E. Main St.
Richmond, VA 23219
Phone: 804-692-7000
Fax: 804-692-7102
Web site: http://www.valottery.com

CEO: Penelope W. Kyle
CFO: Rick Wilkinson
HR: Christopher Goldson
Type: Government-owned

1998 Sales: $912.4 million
1-Yr. Sales Change: (0.9%)
Employees: 286
FYE: June

Virginia might be for lovers, but it's also got a passion for picking numbers. The Virginia State Lottery operates several instant-win scratch-off games, as well as popular number games (Pick 3, Pick 4, and a six-number Lotto game). About half of the money raised from ticket sales is paid out in prizes; about one-third goes to the state's public school districts. Virginia also participates in the seven-state Big Game lottery with Georgia, Illinois, Maryland, Massachusetts, Michigan, and New Jersey. Created in 1987, the Virginia lottery has collected more than $3 billion for the state.

KEY COMPETITORS
Kentucky Lottery
Maryland State Lottery
Multi-State Lottery

VISA INTERNATIONAL

900 Metro Center Blvd.
Foster City, CA 94404
Phone: 650-432-3200
Fax: 650-432-3087
Web site: http://www.visa.com

CEO: Malcolm Williamson
CFO: Raymond Barnes
HR: Elizabeth Rounds
Type: Private

1999 Sales: $2,800.0 million
1-Yr. Sales Change: 9.8%
Employees: 5,000
FYE: September

Paper or plastic? Visa International hopes you'll choose the latter. The firm operates the world's largest consumer payment system, ahead of both American Express and MasterCard, with around 800 million cards in circulation. The corporation is owned by 21,000 banks, each of which issues and markets its own Visa products in competition with the others. They all participate in the VisaNet payment system, which provides authorization, transaction processing, and settlement services for purchases from 16 million merchants worldwide. Visa also provides its customers with debit cards, Internet payment systems, value-storing smart cards, and traveler's checks.

KEY COMPETITORS
American Express
MasterCard
Morgan Stanley Dean Witter

See pages 510–511 for a full profile of this company.

VITALITY BEVERAGES, INC.

400 North Tampa St., 17th Fl.	CEO: Robert A. Peiser	1998 Est. Sales: $825.0 million
Tampa, FL 33602	CFO: —	1-Yr. Sales Change: —
Phone: 813-301-4600	HR: —	Employees: 2,000
Fax: 813-301-4670	Type: Private	FYE: December

Vitality Beverages wants to be the big orange in the beverage industry. The company stocks hospitals and cafeterias with fruit drinks and sells private-label juices to grocery store chains through subsidiaries Vitality Foodservice and Pasco Beverage Group. Vitality also markets juice under the Sunkist and Ocean Spray brands. The company decided it had the juice for the international market when it bought Pride Beverages, a juice processor in Canada. It also bought the food service and citrus-processing assets of Orange-co. in Florida. Vitality was formed when Caxton-Iseman Capital and Engles, Urso, Follmer Capital acquired the juice operations of Lykes Bros. in 1999.

KEY COMPETITORS
Alliant Foodservice
SYSCO
Tropicana Products

VT INC.

8500 Shawnee Mission Pkwy., Ste. 200	CEO: Cecil Van Tuyl	1998 Sales: $2,587.0 million
Merriam, KS 66202	CFO: Robert J. Holcomb	1-Yr. Sales Change: 6.8%
Phone: 913-432-6400	HR: John A. Morford	Employees: 5,000
Fax: 913-789-1039	Type: Private	FYE: December

VT is in pursuit of the pole-position as one of the top five US car dealers. The company operates about 35 dealerships in Arizona, Illinois, Missouri, and Texas. It sells nearly 50 brands of new and used cars made by General Motors, Ford, Honda, Isuzu, and Nissan, among others. VT also engages in fleet sales and receives a significant portion of its revenues from back-shop operations such as parts and service and body shop sales. Founder and co-CEO Cecil Van Tuyl began his automotive empire with United Auto Sales, a used-car dealership he founded in 1947. He owns the company with son and co-CEO Larry Van Tuyl.

KEY COMPETITORS
AutoNation
Hendrick Automotive
Jordan Motors

VULCAN NORTHWEST INC

110 110th Ave. NE, Ste. 550	CEO: Jody Patton	1996 Sales: —
Bellevue, WA 98004	CFO: Joseph Franzi	1-Yr. Sales Change: —
Phone: 425-453-1940	HR: Pam Faber	Employees: —
Fax: 425-453-1985	Type: Private	FYE: December
Web site: http://www.paulallen.com		

Even with all his Vulcan logic, could Spock invest like *this?* Brainy billionaire Paul Allen organizes his business and charitable ventures under Vulcan Northwest. Allen, who co-founded Microsoft with Bill Gates, promotes a "wired world" vision, in which everyone is united through interconnecting communications, entertainment, and information systems. Vulcan Northwest includes Allen's stake in Microsoft (about 5%), as well as holdings in dozens of companies providing computer, multimedia, or communications products and services, and six charitable organizations supporting the arts, medical research, and conservation. Allen also owns the NBA's Portland Trail Blazers and the NFL's Seattle Seahawks.

KEY COMPETITORS
idealab
Kleiner Perkins
Safeguard Scientifics

See pages 512–513 for a full profile of this company.

WAKE FOREST UNIVERSITY BAPTIST MEDICAL CENTER

Medical Center Blvd.
Winston-Salem, NC 27157
Phone: 336-716-2011
Fax: 336-716-6841
Web site: http://www.wfubmc.edu

CEO: Richard H. Dean
CFO: Donny C. Lambeth
HR: Ron Hoth
Type: Not-for-profit

1997 Sales: $959.7 million
1-Yr. Sales Change: 0.3%
Employees: 9,400
FYE: June

The mind-body connection is clear at Wake Forest University Baptist Medical Center. Formerly known as Bowman Gray/Baptist Hospital Medical Center, the non-profit is comprised of Wake Forest University School of Medicine and The North Carolina Baptist Hospitals, including the Sticht Center on Aging and Rehabilitation, the Comprehensive Cancer Center, the Heart Center, Brenner Children's Hospital, CompRehab, the Nursing Center at Oak Summit, and three home care services. The not-for-profit system has also developed QualChoice, a health maintenance organization (HMO) with over 75,000 members and 1,400 physicians, and a practice management service for more than 1,000 physicians.

KEY COMPETITORS
Columbia/HCA
Novant Health
UnitedHealth Group

WAKEFERN FOOD CORPORATION

600 York St.
Elizabeth, NJ 07207
Phone: 908-527-3300
Fax: 908-527-3397
Web site: http://www.shoprite.com

CEO: Thomas Infusino
CFO: Ken Jasinkiewicz
HR: Ernie Bell
Type: Cooperative

1999 Sales: $3,500.0 million
1-Yr. Sales Change: (30.0%)
Employees: 3,000
FYE: September

Started by seven men who invested $1,000 each, Wakefern Food has grown into the largest supermarket cooperative and wholesaler in the US. The co-op is owned by about 40 independent grocers who operate about 190 ShopRite supermarkets in Connecticut, Delaware, New Jersey (where it is a dominant chain), New York, and Pennsylvania. About half of ShopRite stores offer pharmacies. In addition to name-brand and private-label products, Wakefern supports its members with advertising, merchandising, insurance, and other services. Although the holdings of members range in size from one store to 32 (Big V Supermarkets), each member holds an equal voting share.

KEY COMPETITORS
A&P
C&S Wholesale
Pathmark

 See pages 514–515 for a full profile of this company.

THE WALSH GROUP

929 W. Adams St.
Chicago, IL 60607
Phone: 312-563-5400
Fax: 312-563-5466
Web site: http://www.walshgroup.com

CEO: Matthew M. Walsh
CFO: Larry Kibbon
HR: Tracy Reitz
Type: Private

1998 Sales: $1,170.0 million
1-Yr. Sales Change: 17.9%
Employees: 3,500
FYE: December

The Walsh Group has built walls, halls, malls and more since 1898. Walsh provides contracting services for industrial, infrastructure, and commercial projects throughout the US. Its undertakings have ranged from prisons to skyscrapers to shopping malls. The group consists of Walsh Construction Company of Chicago and Archer Western Contractors of Fort Lauderdale, Florida. Operating from 10 regional offices, Walsh provides complete project management services, from planning and pre-construction to general contracting and finance. The Walsh family owns the company.

KEY COMPETITORS
Huber, Hunt & Nichols
MA Mortenson
McCarthy

THE WASHINGTON COMPANIES

101 International Way
Missoula, MT 59807
Phone: 406-523-1300
Fax: 406-523-1398
Web site: http://www.washcorp.com

CEO: Michael Haight
CFO: Greg Stricker
HR: —
Type: Private

1998 Sales: $744.0 million
1-Yr. Sales Change: 6.3%
Employees: 4,400
FYE: December

Crossing the Delaware was the feat of one Washington, but traversing several industries was done by another. Washington Companies is a mining, construction, machinery, and transportation group owned by Dennis Washington. Washington started his empire in 1964 with a highway construction firm that became Montana's largest contractor. He moved into mining with the purchase of the Anaconda copper mine. He took on railroading with the purchase of a Burlington Northern rail line, which he renamed Montana Rail Link. Washington also owns a British Columbia-based tugboat and barge company. The group's Washington Corporation supplies management and other business services to the Washington transportation companies.

KEY COMPETITORS
Granite Construction
Phelps Dodge
McCarthy

WASHINGTON UNIVERSITY

1 Brookings Dr.
St. Louis, MO 63130
Phone: 314-935-5000
Fax: 314-935-4259
Web site: http://www.wustl.edu

CEO: Mark S. Wrighton
CFO: Barbara Feiner
HR: John Loya
Type: School

1998 Sales: $941.8 million
1-Yr. Sales Change: 0.7%
Employees: 8,017
FYE: June

Along with the Cardinals and the Arch, St. Louis is home to Washington University (WU). Founded in 1853, the highly regarded private university is renowned in the fields of medicine, science, and engineering. It is also a leading research university; WU's largest research sponsor, the National Institutes of Health, contributes some $200 million to the school each year. WU offers its 11,600 students more than 80 bachelor's, master's, and doctoral programs in fields such as architecture, law, medicine, engineering, social work, and business. Famed Forest Park separates the university's Hilltop Campus from the 59-acre campus that contains the medical school and associated hospitals.

WATKINS ASSOCIATED INDUSTRIES

1958 Monroe Dr. NE
Atlanta, GA 30324
Phone: 404-872-3841
Fax: 404-872-2812

CEO: William Freeman
CFO: —
HR: Milton Eades
Type: Private

1998 Sales: $796.0 million
1-Yr. Sales Change: 9.8%
Employees: 8,300
FYE: December

A family business involved in trucking, seafood, and concrete may sound fishy, but the highly-diversified Watkins Associated is on the up and up. Its Watkins Motor Lines, which accounts for about 80% of revenues, is a long-haul, less-than-truckload (LTL) carrier serving customers in the US, Canada, Europe, and Mexico. The trucking company operates some 2,500 tractors, 8,000 trailers, and 125 terminals. Watkins Associated's other activities include shrimp processing, real estate development (the company owns about 20 strip shopping centers and 4,500 apartment units), door manufacturing, bridge building, and citrus growing. Bill Watkins founded the family-owned company in 1932 with a $300 pickup truck.

KEY COMPETITORS
CNF Transportation
Roadway Express
Yellow Corporation

WAWA INC.

260 Baltimore Pike
Wawa, PA 19063
Phone: 610-358-8000
Fax: 610-358-8878
Web site: http://www.wawa.com

CEO: Richard D. Wood
CFO: Edward Chambers
HR: Vincent P. Anderson
Type: Private

1998 Est. Sales: $1,000.0 million
1-Yr. Sales Change: (1.0%)
Employees: 12,000
FYE: December

It's not baby talk — when folks say they need to go to the Wawa, they need groceries. Wawa runs more than 500 convenience stores, mostly in Pennsylvania, but also in Delaware, Maryland, New Jersey, and Virginia. The company opened its first store in 1964, but it has roots in a dairy founded by George Wood in 1902 in Wawa, Pennsylvania. Unlike many convenience store chains, Wawa maintains its own dairy, and its stores feature Wawa dairy items. In addition, only a handful of outlets sell gas. Wawa stores are also noted for their salad and deli offerings, including hoagie sandwiches. Its wholesale dairy unit supplies hospitals, schools, and other institutions. Wawa is still owned and operated by the Wood family.

KEY COMPETITORS
7-Eleven
Cumberland Farms
Uni-Marts

WEGMANS FOOD MARKETS, INC.

1500 Brooks Ave.
Rochester, NY 14624
Phone: 716-328-2550
Fax: 716-464-4664
Web site: http://www.wegmans.com

CEO: Robert B. Wegman
CFO: Jim Leo
HR: Gerald Pierce
Type: Private

1998 Est. Sales: $2,450.0 million
1-Yr. Sales Change: 4.7%
Employees: 25,000
FYE: December

Where can you get Flutie Flakes? Wegmans Food Markets. The supermarket chain, which uses Buffalo Bills' quarterback Doug Flutie as its spokesman, runs about 60 stores, primarily in the Rochester and Buffalo areas of New York, but also in New Jersey and Pennsylvania. Wegmans has adopted such concepts as in-store cafes and gourmet cooking classes. In addition, the stores feature Nature's Marketplace, a section of all-natural foods and health items, and its own W-Pet line of pet foods. Wegmans also runs Chase-Pitkin Home & Garden Centers, as well as a commercial bakery, egg farm, and meat processing plant. CEO and owner Robert Wegman is the nephew of founder John Wegman, who started the company in 1916.

KEY COMPETITORS
A&P
Ahold USA
Penn Traffic

WHITE CASTLE SYSTEM, INC.

555 W. Goodale St.
Columbus, OH 43215
Phone: 614-228-5781
Fax: 614-464-0596
Web site: http://www.whitecastle.com

CEO: E. W. Ingram
CFO: William A. Blake
HR: Fred Gunderson
Type: Private

1997 Sales: $384.0 million
1-Yr. Sales Change: 6.7%
Employees: 11,000
FYE: December

White Castle doesn't rook hamburger lovers out of a meal. White Castle System's little square hamburgers, known as Slyders, are steamed over a bed of onions and can be found at roughly 330 restaurants in 12 eastern and midwestern states. White Castle, founded in 1921, was the first fast-food hamburger chain; it still owns all of the White Castle restaurants. White Castle's PSB subsidiary makes metal products and equipment, including fixtures and cooking tools needed at the restaurants. PSB also makes lawn spreaders under the PrizeLAWN brand. Chairman E. W. Ingram III (grandson of co-founder E. W. Ingram) and his family own the company.

KEY COMPETITORS
Burger King
McDonald's
Wendy's

See pages 516–517 for a full profile of this company.

THE WHITING-TURNER CONTRACTING COMPANY

300 E. Joppa Rd.	CEO: Willard Hackerman	1998 Sales: $1,260.0 million
Baltimore, MD 21286	CFO: Charles Irish	1-Yr. Sales Change: 20.0%
Phone: 410-821-1100	HR: Edward Spaulding	Employees: 1,800
Fax: 410-337-5770	Type: Private	FYE: December
Web site: http://www.whiting-turner.com		

Whiting-Turner Contracting is a big fish in an ocean of builders. The employee-owned firm provides construction management, general contracting, and design-build services, primarily for large commercial, institutional, and infrastructure projects in the US. Although the company subcontracts about 85% of its volume, in-house activities include mechanical and electrical work, concrete forming, and foundation services. Projects span a wide range of facilities, including biotech cleanrooms, schools, shopping centers, stadiums, and corporate headquarters for such clients as AT&T, General Motors, and the US Army. Founded in 1909 by G. W. C. Whiting to build sewer lines, the firm has 16 offices, primarily in the East.

KEY COMPETITORS

Clark Enterprises
Gilbane
Turner Corporation

WILBUR-ELLIS COMPANY

345 California St., 27th Fl.	CEO: Brayton Wilbur	1998 Est. Sales: $1,500.0 million
San Francisco, CA 94104	CFO: Herbert B. Tully	1-Yr. Sales Change: 25.0%
Phone: 415-772-4000	HR: Ofelia Lee	Employees: 2,500
Fax: 415-772-4011	Type: Private	FYE: December
Web site: http://www.wilbur-ellis.com		

With respect to the children's song, the farmer spends as much time with the products supplied by Wilbur-Ellis Company as he does farming the dell. The company distributes animal feed, fertilizer, insecticides, seed, and machinery through more than 100 outlets in North America and about 20 international offices, including locations in Asia and Australia. Subsidiary Connell Brothers distribute chemicals and feed throughout the Pacific Rim. Additionally, Wilbur-Eillis provides consulting and other agriculture-related services. Founded in 1921 by Brayton Wilbur Sr. and Floyd Ellis as a fish-oil supplier, the company is now managed by Brayton Wilbur Jr.

KEY COMPETITORS

Agrium
Agway
Purina Mills

WILLIAM BEAUMONT HOSPITAL

3601 W. 13 Mile Rd.	CEO: Ted Wasson	1998 Sales: $839.1 million
Royal Oak, MI 48073	CFO: Dennis R. Herrick	1-Yr. Sales Change: 5.7%
Phone: 248-551-5000	HR: Wesley Kokko	Employees: 11,000
Fax: 248-551-1555	Type: Private	FYE: December
Web site: http://www.beaumont.edu		

William Beaumont Hospital consists of two teaching hospitals, both ranked among the busiest in the US for inpatient admissions. It also includes medical buildings, a rehabilitation center, a primary health care clinic, five nursing homes, a research institute, and a comprehensive home care service, all serving the Detroit area. A number of special programs are available, including the Preventative and Nutritional Medicine Clinic for treatment of obesity and related illnesses, an eating-disorders treatment facility, and InterHealth, a health service for international travelers. The Michigan hospitals, one in Royal Oak and the other in Troy, are affiliated with Wayne State University.

KEY COMPETITORS

Detroit Medical Center
Henry Ford Health System
Mercy Health Services

WILLIAMSON-DICKIE MANUFACTURING CO.

509 W. Vickery Blvd.
Fort Worth, TX 76104
Phone: 817-336-7201
Fax: 817-336-5183
Web site: http://www.dickies.com

CEO: Philip C. Williamson
CFO: Craig Mackey
HR: Estelle Lewis
Type: Private

1998 Sales: $690.0 million
1-Yr. Sales Change: 9.1%
Employees: 6,000
FYE: December

Appreciated by the working class and the sophomore class alike, Williamson-Dickie Manufacturing Co. is the maker of Dickies khaki pants, bib overalls, jeans, and women's and children's apparel. It also makes Workrite safety uniforms. The company's work clothes were originally tailored with the blue-collar set in mind, but these days the clothes are in favor with hip kids, who like to wear their pants and overalls several sizes too big. Dickies T-shirts are made extra long to prevent the display of "plumber's crack" by squatting workmen. Williamson-Dickie's products are sold worldwide through retailers and directly to businesses. The Williamson family, which founded the company in 1922, owns the firm.

KEY COMPETITORS
Carhartt
Levi Strauss
VF

WINCO FOODS, INC.

650 N. Armstrong Pl.
Boise, ID 83704
Phone: 208-377-0110
Fax: 208-377-0474

CEO: William D. Long
CFO: Gary Piva
HR: Roger Cochell
Type: Private

1999 Sales: $940.0 million
1-Yr. Sales Change: —
Employees: 4,900
FYE: March

WinCo Foods isn't just big on self-service — it's giant. Inside the immense 60,000 to 90,000-sq.-ft. stores of this employee-owned supermarket chain, customers are asked to shop for food in bulk and bag their own groceries. The company's 30-plus stores also feature pizza shops and fresh-baked goods. WinCo Foods, formerly known as Waremart Foods, was renamed as a shortened version of "winning company." The name is also an acronym for its states of operation, which include Washington state, Idaho, Nevada, California, and Oregon. The company eschews advertising and is known for discount pricing. WinCo Foods formerly operated stores under the Cub Foods and Waremart names.

KEY COMPETITORS
Albertson's
Raley's
Safeway

WINGATE PARTNERS

750 N. St. Paul St., Ste. 1200
Dallas, TX 75201
Phone: 214-720-1313
Fax: 214-871-8799
Web site: http://www.wingatepartners.com

CEO: Frederick B. Hegi
CFO: Alna Evans
HR: Alna Evans
Type: Private

Sales: —
1-Yr. Sales Change: —
Employees: —
FYE: December

Wingate Partners gets by on more than a wing and a prayer, rescuing lackluster manufacturing, distribution, and service businesses. It avoids banking, media, high-tech, insurance, natural resources, and real estate companies, investing instead in firms that are underperforming or that are in industries in transition. The targets often have revenues between $100 million and $500 million and may or may not be profitable at the time of purchase. Wingate's portfolio includes holdings in Okla Homer Smith (cribs and children's furniture); Loomis, Fargo & Co. (armored car services); publicly traded United Stationers (office products wholesaler); and Kevco (manufactured-housing building products distributor).

KEY COMPETITORS
Clayton, Dubilier
KKR
Texas Pacific Group

See pages 518–519 for a full profile of this company.

WIRTZ CORPORATION

680 N. Lake Shore Dr., 19th Fl.
Chicago, IL 60611
Phone: 312-943-7000
Fax: 312-943-9017

CEO: William W. Wirtz
CFO: Max Mohler
HR: Cindy Krch
Type: Private

1999 Est. Sales: $830.0 million
1-Yr. Sales Change: 18.6%
Employees: 2,100
FYE: June

From sports to liquor to real estate, Wirtz has its wealth in a melting pot of interests. The company owns the Chicago Blackhawks hockey team as well as liquor distributorships operating in Illinois, Minnesota, Nevada, Texas, and Wisconsin. It also owns half of the United Center (home of the Chicago Bulls) and has various Chicago-area real estate holdings. Arthur Wirtz (father of CEO William Wirtz) founded the family-controlled empire in 1922 when he began snagging lakefront real estate in Chicago. He branched out into sports, buying several arenas (including Madison Square Garden) that were later sold.

KEY COMPETITORS
Detroit Red Wings
Johnson Brothers
Southern Wine & Spirits

W.K. KELLOGG FOUNDATION

1 Michigan Ave. East
Battle Creek, MI 49017
Phone: 616-968-1611
Fax: 616-968-0413
Web site: http://www.wkkf.org

CEO: William C. Richardson
CFO: Paul J. Lawler
HR: Karla Kretzschmer
Type: Foundation

1998 Sales: $330.0 million
1-Yr. Sales Change: (11.7%)
Employees: 286
FYE: August

Built on a foundation of corn and oats, the W.K. Kellogg Foundation is one of the 10 largest in the US. Started in 1930 by cereal industry pioneer W.K. Kellogg and granted more than $66 million in Kellogg Company stock in 1934, the foundation promotes "health, happiness, and well-being." It has more than $6 billion in assets, and it annually awards about $220 million in grants to programs involving health, food systems and rural development, education, and volunteerism. It makes grants primarily in the US, but also in Latin America, Africa, and other regions.

 See pages 520–521 for a full profile of this company.

W. L. GORE AND ASSOCIATES, INC.

555 Paper Mill Rd.
Newark, DE 19711
Phone: 302-738-4880
Fax: 302-738-7710
Web site: http://www.gore.com

CEO: Robert W. Gore
CFO: Genevieve Gore
HR: Sally Gore
Type: Private

1999 Sales: $1,280.0 million
1-Yr. Sales Change: 11.3%
Employees: 7,000
FYE: March

What do hernia repair and guitar strings have in common? Gore-Tex. W. L. Gore and Associates makes the breathable, lightweight fabric that lets perspiration out, but won't let in rain or wind. In addition to clothing and shoes popular among hikers and hunters, Gore-Tex is used in hernia repair patches, guitar strings, dental floss, space suits, and sutures. Gore also makes insulated wire and cable and air filters. The company is known for its lattice management style: bosses are "sponsors" and employees are "associates" working under no fixed authority, and consensus determines objectives. Each office has no more than 200 workers. The Gore family owns 75% of the company; Gore associates own the rest.

KEY COMPETITORS
Belden
Malden Mills
Thoratec Labs

See pages 522–523 for a full profile of this company.

WORLDTRAVEL PARTNERS

1055 Lenox Blvd., Ste. 420
Atlanta, GA 30319
Phone: 404-841-6600
Fax: 404-814-2983
Web site: http://www.worldtravel.com

CEO: Jack Alexander
CFO: Lee Turner
HR: —
Type: Private

1998 Est. Sales: $3,300.0 million
1-Yr. Sales Change: 10.0%
Employees: 5,000
FYE: December

Business partners travel the world through WorldTravel Partners, the #3 US travel agency (behind American Express and Carlson Wagonlit). The company generates about 80% of sales from providing corporate travel services to clients such as IBM, Glaxo Wellcome, and Turner Broadcasting System. It has more than 1,700 locations across the US. WorldTravel Partners also develops travel software and provides Internet booking services through affiliated companies. The company's 1998 merger with competitor BTI Americas doubled its sales. Chairman John Fentener van Vlissingen holds a majority stake in the company.

KEY COMPETITORS
American Express
Carlson Wagonlit
Rosenbluth International

WWF PAPER CORPORATION

2 Bala Plaza, 2nd Fl.
Bala Cynwyd, PA 19004
Phone: 610-667-9210
Fax: 610-667-2691
Web site: http://www.wwfpaper.com

CEO: Edward V. Furlong
CFO: George D. Sergio
HR: Gloria Gregg
Type: Private

1999 Sales: $768.0 million
1-Yr. Sales Change: (7.5%)
Employees: 420
FYE: June

In this corner, weighing in at 1 million tons per year, WWF Paper Corporation. WWF produces not big men in tights body-slamming each other, but fine paper for customers in North America and Western Europe. The privately controlled paper distributor represents more than 100 US and international paper mills and buys more than a million tons of fine paper each year from its mill partners. WWF serves the publishing, business communication, commercial printing, direct mail, financial printing, magazine, and packaging industries. The company has warehouses throughout the US, and it operates subsidiaries in Canada, Mexico, and the UK. The firm was founded in 1922 as Wilcox Walter Furlong Paper and remains family-owned.

KEY COMPETITORS
Gould Paper
International Paper
Willamette

YALE UNIVERSITY

451 College St.
New Haven, CT 06520
Phone: 203-432-4771
Fax: 203-432-7891
Web site: http://www.yale.edu

CEO: Richard C. Levin
CFO: Joseph P. Mullinix
HR: Kitty Matzkin
Type: School

1998 Sales: $992.4 million
1-Yr. Sales Change: 6.6%
Employees: 10,000
FYE: June

What do former President George Bush, writer William F. Buckley Jr., and cartoonist Garry Trudeau have in common? They are all Yalies. Yale University is one of the nation's most prestigious private liberal arts institutions, as well as one of its oldest (founded in 1701). The school consists of an undergraduate college, a graduate school, and 10 professional schools. Programs of study include architecture, law, medicine, and drama. Its 12 residential colleges (a system borrowed from Oxford) serve as dormitory, dining hall, and social center. The school has nearly 11,000 students and nearly 3,200 faculty members.

YMCA OF THE USA

101 N. Wacker Dr.
Chicago, IL 60606
Phone: 312-977-0031
Fax: 312-977-9063
Web site: http://www.ymca.net

CEO: David Mercer
CFO: Kate Spencer
HR: C. L. Parham
Type: Not-for-profit

1998 Sales: $3,137.3 million
1-Yr. Sales Change: 15.4%
Employees: 30,000
FYE: December

If the Village People can be believed, it's fun to stay at the YMCA. One of the nation's largest not-for-profit community service organizations, YMCA of the USA assists the more than 2,200 individual YMCAs across the country and represents them on both national and international levels. YMCAs serve nearly 17 million people and can be found in all 50 states. One of the largest child-care providers in the US, YMCAs also provide services such as job training, GED assistance, sports, and mentoring. Individual YMCAs belong to the World Alliance of YMCAs, an organization of independent YMCAs from 120 countries.

YOUNG'S MARKET COMPANY, LLC

2164 N. Batavia St.
Orange, CA 92865
Phone: 714-283-4933
Fax: 714-283-6175
Web site: http://www.youngsmkt.com

CEO: Charles Andrews
CFO: Dennis J. Hamann
HR: Naomi Buenaslor
Type: Private

1999 Sales: $1,090.0 million
1-Yr. Sales Change: 9.0%
Employees: 1,600
FYE: February

Young's Market is the third-largest distributor of beer, wine, and distilled spirits in the US, after Southern Wine & Spirits and National Distributing. It is a major supplier in Los Angeles and the surrounding area, and it also operates in Hawaii through subsidiary Better Brands. The company was founded in 1888 by John Young, who started with a meat concession stand. He incorporated in 1906 with his brothers. Young's was bought by the Underwood family, relatives of the Young family, in 1990. Young's formerly distributed meat and seafood as well, but it now concentrates solely on its beverage business.

KEY COMPETITORS
Liquid Investments
National Distributing
Southern Wine & Spirits

THE YUCAIPA COMPANIES LLC

10000 Santa Monica Blvd., 5th Fl.
Los Angeles, CA 90067
Phone: 310-789-7200
Fax: 310-884-2600

CEO: Ronald W. Burkle
CFO: —
HR: Marla Hunter
Type: Private

1990 Sales: $1,318.0 million
1-Yr. Sales Change: —
Employees: —
FYE: December

Moving away from its past in the grocery store game, Yucaipa is blasting into cyberspace. While Yucaipa still owns 70% of Golden State Foods (one of McDonald's largest food suppliers) and is the largest single shareholder of grocery giant Kroger (it owns about 2%), it has plunged headlong into the Internet. Yucaipa managing partner Ron Burkle has teamed with former Walt Disney president Michael Ovitz to launch the CheckOut.com Web site, an e-commerce venue offering games, music, and videos. Yucaipa also owns Alliance Entertainment (music and video distributor), has minority stakes in GameSpy Industries (online games) and Talk City (online chat service), and owns 51% of Scour.Net (online search and media guide).

KEY COMPETITORS
Amazon.com
CDnow
Martin-Brower

See pages 524–525 for a full profile of this company.

Hoover's Handbook of Private Companies

THE INDEXES

Spartan Stores, Inc. **454–455**, 742
Holland
Haworth Inc. **224–225**, 626
Lansing
Michigan Lottery 678
Livonia
Advantage Logistics Michigan 531
Mason
Dart Container Corporation **148–149**, 585
Midland
Dow Corning Corporation **162–163**, 592
Plymouth
Don Massey Cadillac, Inc. 591
Rochester
RGIS Inventory Specialists 718
Royal Oak
William Beaumont Hospital 780
Southfield
Barton Malow Company 551
Peregrine Incorporated 706
Walker
S. Abraham & Sons, Inc. 725
Warren
CenTra, Inc. 571

MINNESOTA
Arden Hills
Land O'Lakes, Inc. **284–285**, 655
Bayport
Andersen Corporation **54–55**, 542
Bloomington
Holiday Companies 631
Golden Valley
Lupient Automotive Group 663
Inver Grove Heights
Cenex Harvest States Cooperatives **128–129**, 571
Marshall
Schwan's Sales Enterprises, Inc. **440–441**, 731
Minneapolis
Genmar Holdings, Inc. 612
Lutheran Brotherhood 663
M. A. Mortenson Companies, Inc. 664
University of Minnesota 768
Minnetonka
Allina Health System 537
Carlson Companies, Inc. **116–117**, 567
Carlson Wagonlit Travel **118–119**, 567
Opus U.S. Corporation 699

Moorhead
American Crystal Sugar Company 539
New Ulm
Associated Milk Producers Incorporated **68–69**, 547
North Mankato
Taylor Corporation 752
Owatonna
Federated Insurance Companies 604
Rochester
Mayo Foundation **324–325**, 671
St. Paul
AgriBank, FCB 535
The Minnesota Mutual Life Insurance Company 679
Wayzata
Cargill, Incorporated **114–115**, 566

MISSISSIPPI
Greenwood
Staple Cotton Cooperative Association 744
Jackson
Jitney-Jungle Stores of America, Inc. 644

MISSOURI
Columbia
University of Missouri System 768
Fenton
UniGroup, Inc. 763
Kansas City
American Century Investments, Inc. 538
Bartlett and Company 551
Black & Veatch 557
Dairy Farmers of America **146–147**, 584
DeBruce Grain, Inc. 586
Dunn Industries, Inc. 595
Farmland Industries, Inc. **184–185**, 603
Hallmark Cards, Inc. **218–219**, 624
Health Midwest 628
Russell Stover Candies Inc. **428–429**, 725
Sutherland Lumber Company, L.P. 749
St. Charles
ACF Industries, Inc. 530
St. Louis
Ascension Health **66–67**, 545
BJC Health System 557
Blue Cross and Blue Shield of Missouri 558
Carondelet Health System 568
Clark USA, Inc. **132–133**, 575

Enterprise Rent-A-Car **176–177**, 600
GenAmerica Corporation **198–199**, 611
Graybar Electric Company, Inc. **210–211**, 619
Harbour Group 625
The Jones Financial Companies, L.P., LLP **262–263**, 647
Maritz Inc. **310–311**, 666
McCarthy 671
Peabody Group 703
Schnuck Markets, Inc. 730
Sisters of Mercy Health System-St. Louis 739
SSM Health Care System Inc. 743
Viasystems Group, Inc. 774
Washington University 778

MONTANA
Missoula
The Washington Companies 778

NEBRASKA
Lincoln
The University of Nebraska 768
Omaha
Ag Processing Inc **36–37**, 533
The Mutual of Omaha Companies **350–351**, 682
Peter Kiewit Sons', Inc. **400–401**, 706
The Scoular Company 731

NEVADA
Las Vegas
Fletcher Jones Management Group 605
Tang Industries, Inc. 751

NEW JERSEY
Carteret
Di Giorgio Corporation 589
Pathmark Stores, Inc. **392–393**, 703
Cranford
The Newark Group 692
East Rutherford
Metromedia Company **334–335**, 677
Edison
Datek Online Holdings Corp. **150–151**, 585
J. M. Huber Corporation 645
Elizabeth
Wakefern Food Corporation **514–515**, 777
Jersey City
UIS, Inc. 762
Lawrenceville
New Jersey State Lottery Commission 690

HOOVER'S HANDBOOK OF PRIVATE COMPANIES 2000